Great Lives from History

The 18th Century

1701-1800

Great Lives from History

The 18th Century

1701-1800

Volume 2

Mikhail Vasilyevich Lomonosov - Count von Zinzendorf
Indexes

Editor

John Powell

Oklahoma Baptist University

Editor, First Edition

Frank N. Magill

SALEM PRESS

Pasadena, California   Hackensack, New Jersey

Editor in Chief: Dawn P. Dawson

Editorial Director: Christina J. Moose	*Production Editor:* Andrea E. Miller
Acquisitions Editor: Mark Rehn	*Graphics and Design:* James Hutson
Research Supervisor: Jeffry Jensen	*Layout:* Eddie Murillo
Research Assistant: Rebecca Kuzins	*Photo Editor:* Cynthia Breslin Beres
Manuscript Editors: Desiree Dreeuws, Andy Perry	*Editorial Assistant:* Dana Garey

Cover photos: Pictured left to right, top to bottom: Alessandro Volta (The Granger Collection, New York), Toussaint Louverture (The Granger Collection, New York), Fanny Burney (The Granger Collection, New York), Catherine the Great (The Granger Collection, New York), Johann Sebastian Bach (The Granger Collection, New York), Mustafa III (Hulton Archive/Getty Images), Junípero Serra (The Granger Collection, New York), Betsy Ross (Library of Congress), Daniel Boone (The Granger Collection, New York)

Some of the essays in this work originally appeared in the following Salem Press sets: *Dictionary of World Biography* (© 1998-1999, edited by Frank N. Magill) and *Great Lives from History* (© 1987-1995, edited by Frank N. Magill). New material has been added.

Library of Congress Cataloging-in-Publication Data

Great lives from history. The 18th century, 1701-1800 / editor, John Powell ; editor, first edition, Frank N. Magill.
    p. cm.
    Some of the essays in this work were originally published in Dictionary of world biography and the series of works collectively titled, Great lives from history, both edited by Frank N. Magill.
    Includes bibliographical references and index.
    ISBN-13: 978-1-58765-276-9 (set : alk. paper)
    ISBN-10: 1-58765-276-5 (set : alk. paper)
    ISBN-13: 978-1-58765-278-3 (v. 2 : alk. paper)
    ISBN-10: 1-58765-278-1 (v. 2 : alk. paper)
    [etc.]
  1. Biography—18th century. I. Title: 18th century, 1701-1800. II. Title: Eighteenth century, 1701-1800.
III. Powell, John, 1954- IV. Magill, Frank Northen, 1907-1997. V. Dictionary of world biography. VI. Great lives from history.
  D285.G74 2006
  909.7092′2—dc22
                          2006005336

First Printing

CONTENTS

KEY TO PRONUNCIATION

Many of the names of personages covered in *Great Lives from History: The Eighteenth Century, 1701-1800* may be unfamiliar to students and general readers. For these unfamiliar names, guides to pronunciation have been provided upon first mention of the names in the text. These guidelines do not purport to achieve the subtleties of the languages in question but will offer readers a rough equivalent of how English speakers may approximate the proper pronunciation.

Vowel Sounds

Symbol	Spelled (Pronounced)
a	answer (AN-suhr), laugh (laf), sample (SAM-puhl), that (that)
ah	father (FAH-thur), hospital (HAHS-pih-tuhl)
aw	awful (AW-fuhl), caught (kawt)
ay	blaze (blayz), fade (fayd), waiter (WAYT-ur), weigh (way)
eh	bed (behd), head (hehd), said (sehd)
ee	believe (bee-LEEV), cedar (SEE-dur), leader (LEED-ur), liter (LEE-tur)
ew	boot (bewt), lose (lewz)
i	buy (bi), height (hit), lie (li), surprise (sur-PRIZ)
ih	bitter (BIH-tur), pill (pihl)
o	cotton (KO-tuhn), hot (hot)
oh	below (bee-LOH), coat (koht), note (noht), wholesome (HOHL-suhm)
oo	good (good), look (look)
ow	couch (kowch), how (how)
oy	boy (boy), coin (koyn)
uh	about (uh-BOWT), butter (BUH-tuhr), enough (ee-NUHF), other (UH-thur)

Consonant Sounds

Symbol	Spelled (Pronounced)
ch	beach (beech), chimp (chihmp)
g	beg (behg), disguise (dihs-GIZ), get (geht)
j	digit (DIH-juht), edge (ehj), jet (jeht)
k	cat (kat), kitten (KIH-tuhn), hex (hehks)
s	cellar (SEHL-ur), save (sayv), scent (sehnt)
sh	champagne (sham-PAYN), issue (IH-shew), shop (shop)
ur	birth (burth), disturb (dihs-TURB), earth (urth), letter (LEH-tur)
y	useful (YEWS-fuhl), young (yuhng)
z	business (BIHZ-nehs), zest (zehst)
zh	vision (VIH-zhuhn)

COMPLETE LIST OF CONTENTS

VOLUME 1

VOLUME 2

LIST OF MAPS AND SIDEBARS

Volume 1

Volume 2

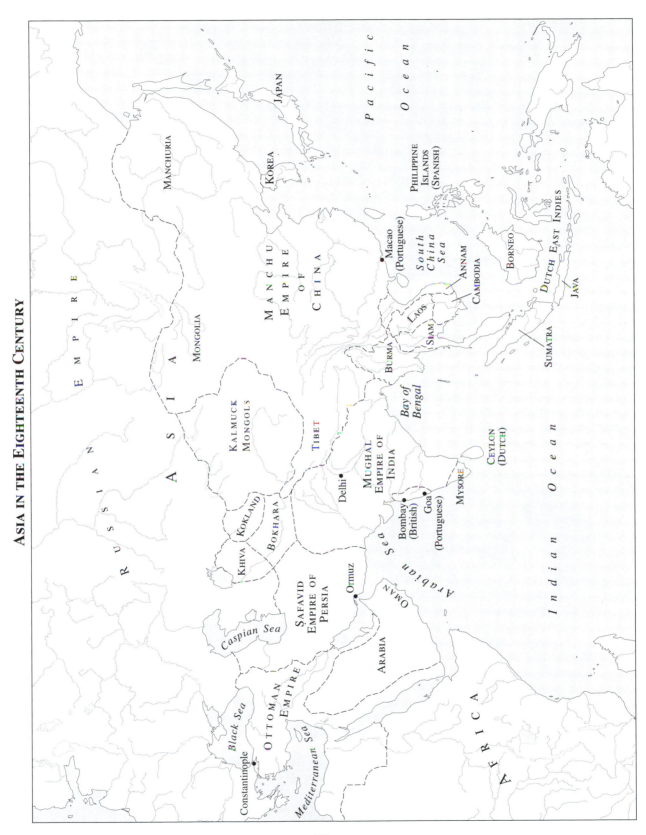

ASIA IN THE EIGHTEENTH CENTURY

RUSSIAN EMPIRE

ASIA

MANCHURIA

KOREA

JAPAN

MONGOLIA

MANCHU EMPIRE OF CHINA

Pacific Ocean

PHILIPPINE ISLANDS (SPANISH)

Macao (Portuguese)

South China Sea

ANNAM

CAMBODIA

BORNEO

DUTCH EAST INDIES

JAVA

SUMATRA

KALMUCK MONGOLS

TIBET

LAOS

SIAM

BURMA

Bay of Bengal

KOKLAND

BOKHARA

KHIVA

Delhi

MUGHAL EMPIRE OF INDIA

Bombay (British)

Goa (Portuguese)

MYSORE

CEYLON (DUTCH)

Indian Ocean

SAFAVID EMPIRE OF PERSIA

Ormuz

Arabian Sea

Caspian Sea

OMAN

ARABIA

Black Sea

OTTOMAN EMPIRE

Constantinople

Mediterranean Sea

AFRICA

AFRICA IN THE EIGHTEENTH CENTURY

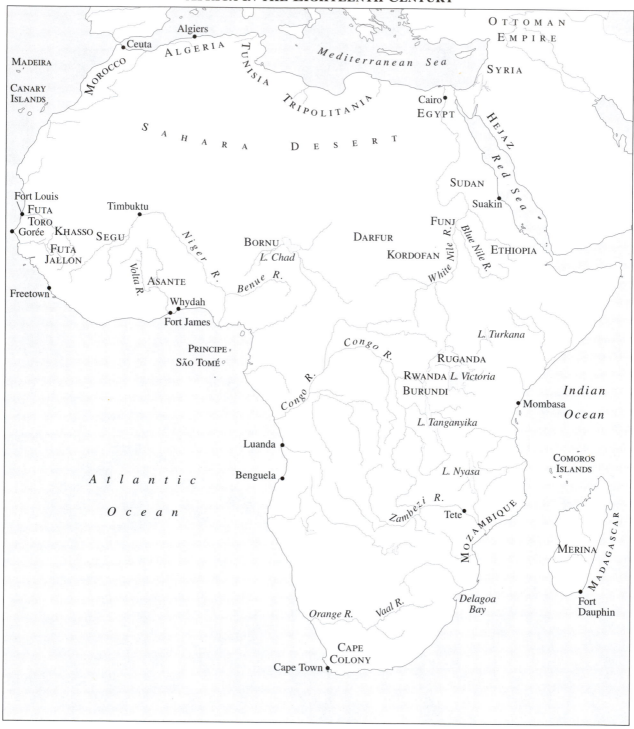

OTTOMAN EMPIRE

MADEIRA

CANARY ISLANDS

MOROCCO
Ceuta
Algiers
ALGERIA
TUNISIA
TRIPOLITANIA
Mediterranean Sea
SYRIA

SAHARA DESERT

Cairo
EGYPT

HEJAZ
Red Sea

Fort Louis
FUTA TORO
Gorée
KHASSO SEGU
Timbuktu
Niger R.
BORNU
L. Chad
DARFUR
SUDAN
Suakin
FUNJ
KORDOFAN
White Nile R.
Blue Nile R.
ETHIOPIA

FUTA JALLON

Freetown

Volta R.
ASANTE
Whydah
Fort James
Benue R.

PRINCIPE
SÃO TOMÉ

Congo R.
L. Turkana

RUGANDA
RWANDA *L. Victoria*
BURUNDI
Mombasa

Congo R.
L. Tanganyika

Indian Ocean

Luanda

Atlantic Ocean

Benguela

L. Nyasa

COMOROS ISLANDS

Zambezi R.
Tete
MOZAMBIQUE

Delagoa Bay

MERINA

MADAGASCAR

Orange R.
Vaal R.

Fort Dauphin

CAPE COLONY
Cape Town

SOUTH AMERICA IN THE EIGHTEENTH CENTURY

= Portuguese South America

= Spanish South America

Porto Bello

Caracas

DUTCH GUIANA

Paramaribo

Cayenne

FRENCH GUIANA

Santa Fé de Bogota

NEW GRANADA

Quito

Japurá R.

Negro R.

Amazon R.

Manaus

A m a z o n   B a s i n

Madeira R.

Purus R.

Lima

Cuzco

A n d e s   M o u n t a i n s

Arequipa

Santa Cruz

P E R U

La Plata

BRAZIL

MINAS GERAIS

Bahia (Salvador)

Minas Novas

Paraná R.

Rio de Janeiro

Asunción

Porto Alegre

Colonia do Sacramento

Santiago

Buenos Aires

Montevideo

P a c i f i c   O c e a n

Negro R.

P a t a g o n i a

A t l a n t i c

O c e a n

Malvinas (Falkland Islands)

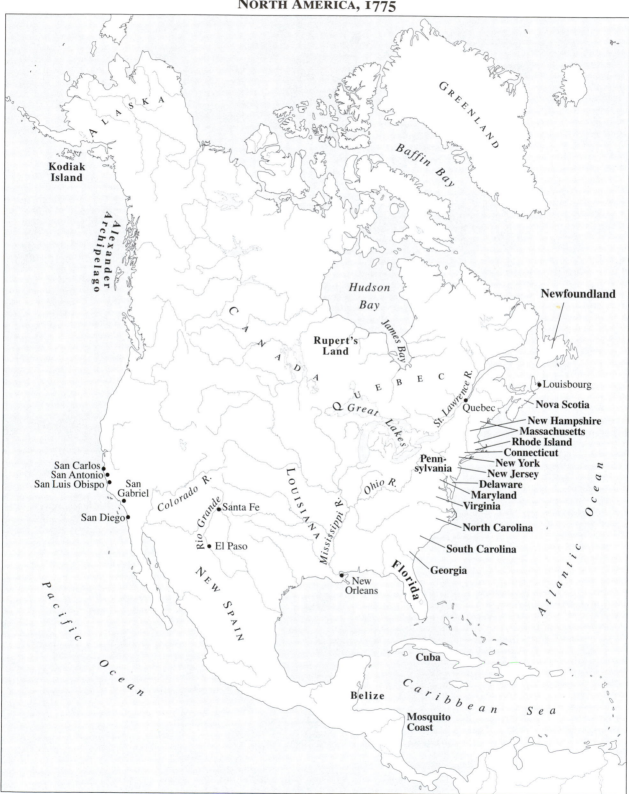

ALASKA

Kodiak
Island

Alexander
Archipelago

GREENLAND

Baffin Bay

Hudson
Bay

CANADA

Rupert's
Land

James Bay

Newfoundland

QUEBEC

St. Lawrence R.

Louisbourg

Quebec

Q Great Lakes

Nova Scotia

New Hampshire
Massachusetts
Rhode Island
Connecticut
New York
New Jersey
Delaware
Maryland
Virginia

Penn-
sylvania

San Carlos
San Antonio
San Luis Obispo

San
Gabriel

Colorado R.

Santa Fe

LOUISIANA

Ohio R.

Mississippi R.

North Carolina

San Diego

Rio Grande

El Paso

NEW SPAIN

New
Orleans

South Carolina

Georgia

Florida

Pacific
Ocean

Cuba

Atlantic Ocean

Belize

Caribbean Sea

Mosquito
Coast

EUROPE IN THE EIGHTEENTH CENTURY

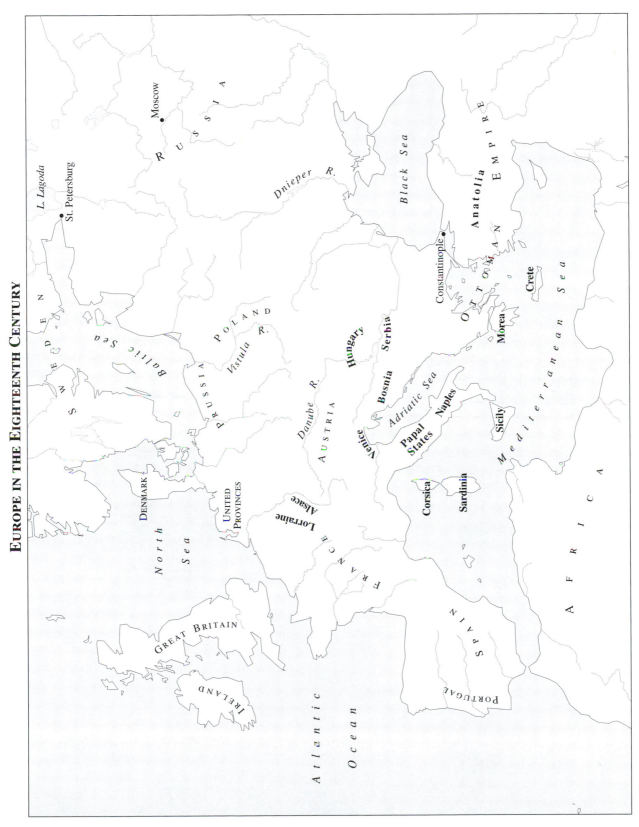

The 18th Century

1701-1800

MIKHAIL VASILYEVICH LOMONOSOV
Russian scientist and scholar

Through his reform of the Russian literary language, his scientific investigations, and his reinterpretation of early Russian history, Lomonosov was at the beginning of modern Russian intellectual history and a founder of Russian nationalism.

Born: November 19, 1711; Denisovka (now Lomonosovo), near Kholmogory, Russia
Died: April 15, 1765; St. Petersburg, Russia
Areas of achievement: Literature, chemistry, physics, historiography, science and technology

EARLY LIFE

Mikhail Vasilyevich Lomonosov (myihkh-uh-EEL vuhs-YEEL-yihv-yihch luh-muh-NAW-suhf) was the son of prosperous peasant parents who lived near Kholmogory, Russia. His father was a fisherman. Lomonosov seems to have been a voracious reader at an early age, and gradually he came to outgrow the small village of his birth. In 1730, he went to Moscow on foot, pretending to be the son of a priest, to enroll in the Slavo-Greco-Latin academy of the Zaikonospassky monastery, where he studied Greek and Latin. From there, he continued to study at the St. Petersburg Imperial Academy of Sciences in 1736, but he soon secured a newly created traveling scholarship to study in Germany.

From 1736 to 1739, Lomonosov studied principally the humanities under the mathematician Christian von Wolff at the University of Marburg. From 1739 to 1741, he changed his program of study to chemistry, mining, and metallurgy at the University of Freiburg in Saxony. He may have married a German woman in 1740, but, apparently to escape from her, as well as from his own drunkenness and debts and the threat of imprisonment they carried, Lomonosov joined the Prussian army later in that same year. In 1741, he returned home to Russia to become a professor of chemistry at the new University of St. Petersburg Imperial Academy of Sciences and a member of the academy.

LIFE'S WORK

In St. Petersburg, Lomonosov became Russia's first great scientist. By 1748, he had founded the first chemistry laboratory in the Russian Empire. He worked on the mechanical nature of heat and developed a kinetic theory of gases. In 1752, his investigations led to the initial discovery of the law of conservation of matter eighteen years before similar work of the French chemist Antoine-Laurent Lavoisier was published, earning for Lavoisier the lion's share of the credit. Lomonosov also had an impact on the development of Russian geography and cartography. For example, he redrew and reconstructed an immense globe of 10 feet (3.1 meters) in diameter that had been a gift from Duke Christian August of Schleswig-Holstein-Gottorf to Peter the Great at the end of the Great Northern War in 1721. Lomonosov and his team took almost seven years (1748-1754) to complete the work.

Under Empress Elizabeth Petrovna, the Russian Empire was still somewhat too far out of the mainstream of Western civilization for achievements such as Lomonosov's to be fully noticed, yet his work could not be denied. He published numerous scientific studies of importance, including *Slovo o proiskhozhdeni sveta* (1756; comments on the origin of light representing a new theory of color). For his accomplishments in the fields of chemistry, optics, metallurgy, geography, natural sciences, physics, and astronomy, Lomonosov was made a member of the Swedish Academy of Sciences in 1760 and the Bologna Academy of Sciences in 1764.

As important a scientist as Lomonosov was, his influence on the development of the arts, especially literature, in Russia, was far greater. He revived the ancient art of mosaics in Russia and was a folklorist, poet, dramatist, historian, and philologist. In 1755, Lomonosov contributed to the founding of the University of Moscow, which is now called Mikhail Lomonosov University.

While his poems and plays were very artificial, mechanical, and typically classicist (many being in honor of Elizabeth), Lomonosov's most important achievement was in the field of philology. In 1757, he published his monumental *Rossiyskaya grammatika* (Russian grammar), which initiated the reform of the Russian literary language. In opposition to the ideas of many of the leading Russian literary figures of the time, including Vasily Trediakovsky, Lomonosov adopted a syllabotonic versification system (one dominated by the number of stressed syllables in a line) between Old Church Slavonic and vernacular Russian for the standard written Russian language. These linguistic changes, fostered by Lomonosov in the middle of the eighteenth century, formed the basis for the literary achievements of the golden age of Russian literature in the first half of the nineteenth century.

Mikhail Vasilyevich Lomonosov. (Library of Congress)

During his study of Old Church Slavonic, Lomonosov came to know the early Russian chronicle literature quite well. He wrote several works critiquing this genre, including *Kratkoy rossiyskoy letopisets* (1759; brief Russian chronicle). Gradually, his examinations of the chronicles led him into the field of historiography to challenge the Normanist interpretation of the founding of the first Russian state, the Kievan Rus', in the ninth and tenth centuries.

The Normanist view was the product of the serious scholarship of several prominent German historians who had been brought into Russia since the reign of Peter the Great to help staff the Russian Academy. Largely based on the evidence provided by the chronicle literature, the Normanist historians, including G. A. Bayer, G. F. Müller, and August Ludwig von Schlözer, attributed the establishment of the first Russian state to outside (primarily Norse and Germanic) influences. This interpretation was an affront to Lomonosov's nascent Russian nationalism, evident in his work in Russian philology and based on his critique of the chronicles. He sought to counter it and to combat the influence of the so-called German Party in the Russian Academy. In so doing, he

became, along with a fellow Russian historian, Vasily Nikitich Tatischev, a founder of the anti-Normanist interpretation of early Russian history and the nationalist or state school of Russian historiography. Lomonosov's final ideas on the subject appeared posthumously in 1766.

As an early Russian nationalist, Lomonosov came to admire Peter the Great for making the Russian Empire great. In part because of his praise for Elizabeth Petrevna and her father and because he shared her anti-German sentiments, Lomonosov was favored by Elizabeth but not by her more Germanic-oriented successors, Peter III and Catherine the Great. Lomonosov died in St. Petersburg in 1765, probably of complications of alcoholism.

SIGNIFICANCE

Mikhail Vasilyevich Lomonosov was the unheralded founder of modern Russian science, literature, and culture. He was a protean intellect and a genius, rightfully compared to Benjamin Franklin, another universal thinker of the eighteenth century. Lomonosov laid the foundation for scientific investigation in Russia, and many times his own discoveries led to or even predated later accredited advancements in the West. He pointed the way to the greatness of Russian literature and historiography in the nineteenth and twentieth centuries.

In his Russian self-consciousness, Lomonosov mirrored and stimulated the early stirrings of nationalism that were beginning to manifest themselves among some of the more progressive members of Russia's elite. He not only felt them and reflected them in his linguistic, literary, and historical works but also began to provide these nationalist feelings with a sound intellectual matrix. In this respect, Lomonosov can be seen as an early advocate of what would become the early nineteenth century conservative Romantic nationalism of Russian Slavophilism. At the same time, his achievements became a source of pride, inspiration, and direction for the Russian nation and helped it to contribute to and to move closer to the mainstream of Western civilization.

—*Dennis Reinhartz*

FURTHER READING

Florinsky, Michael T., ed. *McGraw-Hill Encyclopedia of Russia and the Soviet Union.* New York: McGraw-Hill, 1961. This older standard reference work offers a rather lengthy and balanced listing on Lomonosov. His artistic and scientific achievements are generally treated equally.

Jones, W. Gareth. "Russian Literature in the Eighteenth Century." In *Routledge Companion to Russian Liter-*

ature, edited by Neil Cornwell. New York: Routledge, 2001. This survey of Russian literature includes information on the works of Lomonosov.

Kudryavtsev, B. B. *The Life and Work of Mikhail Vasilyevich Lomonosov*. Moscow: Foreign Languages, 1954. A rare English translation of a Soviet biography. A thorough treatment, stressing Lomonosov's scientific achievements and offering the standard Stalinist-nationalist view of him.

Menshutkin, B. N. *Russia's Lomonosov: Chemist, Courtier, Physicist, Poet*. Princeton, N.J.: Princeton University Press, 1952. An updated and edited translation of the czarist 1912 original. Still one of the best and most readable biographies of Lomonosov.

Mirsky, D. S. *A History of Russian Literature*. Rev. ed. New York: Alfred A. Knopf, 1964. This work goes well beyond placing Lomonosov in perspective with the development of modern Russian literature, lionizing him as the father of modern Russian civilization.

Rice, Tamara Talbot. *Elizabeth, Empress of Russia*. New York: Praeger, 1970. Chapter 8 of this cultural biography of the daughter of, and successor to, Peter the Great and her times is largely about Lomonosov and his literary achievements. Easy reading and well illustrated.

Rogger, Hans. *National Consciousness in Eighteenth Century Russia*. Cambridge, Mass.: Harvard University Press, 1960. Lomonosov is put into perspective with the development of Russian nationalism in the eighteenth century and the eighteenth century Russian intelligentsia. Includes essential background on Lomonosov and his Russia. Scholarly and well written.

Segel, Harold B., ed. *The Literature of Eighteenth Century Russia*. Vol. 1. New York: E. P. Dutton, 1967. This multivolume anthology includes several good examples of Lomonosov's more important literary works, with rather extensive introductions.

Silbajoris, Frank R. "Mikhail Vasilievich Lomonosov." In *Handbook of Russian Literature,* edited by Victor Terras. New Haven, Conn.: Yale University Press, 1985. A capsulization of the more current interpretations of Lomonosov and his literary work. De-emphasizes his scientific contributions.

Stacy, Robert H. *Russian Literary Criticism: A Short History*. Syracuse, N.Y.: Syracuse University Press, 1974. This volume contains an informative chapter on Lomonosov's life and achievements.

See also: Catherine the Great; Elizabeth Petrovna; Benjamin Franklin; Antoine-Laurent Lavoisier; Peter the Great; Peter III.

Related articles in *Great Events from History: The Eighteenth Century, 1701-1800*: 1724: Foundation of the St. Petersburg Academy of Sciences; 1745: Lomonosov Issues the First Catalog of Minerals.

LOUIS XV
King of France (r. 1715-1774)

Louis XV was a respected yet largely ineffectual leader. His reign saw the expansion of France's arts and manufactures and the rise of the Enlightenment. The country also experienced increasing fiscal problems and was embroiled in a number of domestic conflicts and external wars. Louis's policies helped lead to the downfall of the monarchy under his successor, Louis XVI.

Born: February 15, 1710; Versailles, France
Died: May 10, 1774; Versailles, France
Also known as: Louis the Well-Beloved
Area of achievement: Government and politics

EARLY LIFE

Louis (lwee) XV was a great-grandson of his predecessor, Louis XIV. His grandfather, the dauphin, died of smallpox in 1711, and his parents, the duke and duchess de Bourgogne, along with his one living elder brother, all died of measles in February and March, 1712. He thus grew up as an orphan, cared for by his governess, Madame de Ventadour. When Louis XIV died on September 1, 1715, the five-year-old Louis became king.

Louis's first cousin twice removed, Philippe II, Duke d'Orléans, a nephew of Louis XIV, governed France as regent during the king's minority. He moved the court back to Paris until June, 1722, when he returned it to Versailles. During this time, Louis first lived at Vincennes and then in Paris at the Tuileries. He was an intelligent, shy, and curious child who did well in his lessons and took seriously his ceremonial duties. At the age of seven, his care passed from Ventadour to a governor and tutor, André Hercule de Fleury, the bishop of Fréjus. The king's coronation, an affirmation of his rule by divine right, was held in Reims on October 25, 1722; the Regency officially ended and his full rule began on February 16, 1723; the following week, on February 22, this was ceremonially confirmed at the Parlement (royal law court) of Paris.

LIFE'S WORK

In 1725, after a broken engagement to a younger Spanish princess, Louis XV married Marie Leszczyńska, the daughter of Stanisław I Leszczyński, exiled king of Poland. They had eight daughters and two sons; six daughters and one son, Louis the dauphin, survived to maturity. The dauphin, who predeceased his father in 1765, was the father of the next king, Louis XVI. One of Louis's first independent acts after the marriage was to banish the duc de Bourbon, who had assisted him in governing after the Regency, and to take on Fleury as his chief adviser in 1726. Fleury, who was created a cardinal, remained in that influential position, effectively governing France, until his death in 1743.

After Fleury's death, Louis decided to reign alone, without a chief minister to share in the top-level decisions. He was not deeply interested in the intricacies of

Louis XV, king of France. (Library of Congress)

government, however, and left the nuts and bolts of running the country largely to his various ministers. During his reign, France became embroiled in the wars that swept Europe. These included the War of the Polish Succession, in which France supported the queen's father in his unsuccessful attempt to win back his throne; the War of the Austrian Succession, which brought France very few gains but earned Louis his nickname of "the Beloved" when he recovered from a serious illness while fighting with his army in Lorraine in August, 1744; and the Seven Years' War, in which France lost most of its North American colonies. The high costs of these wars ultimately contributed to the fiscal crises that were to lead to the revolution.

Under Louis XIV, who maintained a firm personal grip upon the reins of government, the power of the nobility and the *parlements* had been weakened. Under Louis XV, these groups began to demand more governmental power, and Louis's reign was fraught with internal problems as the parlementarians attempted to assert more control. Their desire for greater autonomy spilled over into a religious conflict pitting the Jansenists, a Catholic sect whom they tended to support, against the Jesuits, who were supported by France's more conservative elements. Much of Louis's reign was marked by persecution of the Jansenists and related unrest: In 1753-1754, Louis banished the entire Parlement of Paris because of their Jansenist leanings. Less than a decade later, in 1762, under parlementarian pressure, the Jesuits were suppressed. Only nine years later, in 1771, the *parlements* were once more exiled. Such reversals of fortune were a hallmark of Louis's reign and point to his and his ministers' lack of a firm policy with regard to legislative and religious matters. France's economy and trade generally flourished, but most of the population lived in rural poverty.

Louis's favorite occupation was hunting, which he pursued at every opportunity in the forests surrounding his numerous palaces. He is widely viewed as a libertine and indeed had a succession of mistresses, although his amorous pursuits were often marked by love and long-standing fidelity. After a long period of faithfulness to his wife succeeded by relationships with four sisters, he took up with Jeanne-Antoinette Poisson, Madame d'Étioles, whom he created the Marquise de Pompadour. From 1745 until her death in 1764, the two were first lovers and then friends, and she exerted a great influence upon him.

Louis then took Jeanne Bécu, comtesse du Barry, as his official mistress from 1768 until his death. Despite this, he was religiously deeply faithful and was known for his modesty, being greatly aware of his sins and shortcomings. He had a true love for his children, and he truly loved his subjects as well, although his reign did little to ease their burdens. In addition to his legitimate offspring, Louis had eight illegitimate children, for all of whom he provided.

Although Louis was the victim of a failed assassination attempt by Robert-François Damiens at Versailles on January 5, 1757, for most of his reign he lived up to his nickname, being "beloved" by his subjects. The attack was found to be not part of a conspiracy but the work of a single individual who was, despite Louis's immediate forgiveness of him, brutally tortured and executed as an example against regicide. Louis XV died of smallpox in 1774.

SIGNIFICANCE

Louis XV's reign, reviled during the revolution and subsequently as the epitome of frivolity and despotism, marked the long, slow transition from the high point of absolutist government under Louis XIV to the downfall of the monarchy under Louis XVI. Under Louis XV, although primarily without his direct interest, France was the intellectual and cultural center of Europe: Literature, the arts, and the sciences flourished. The visual arts of the period were known for the delicacy and grace of the rococo style, also called the "Louis XV style," which rejected the heavy formality of Louis XIV's time and successively swept the other European courts.

Louis was responsible for the creation of the Petits Appartements, his personal, comfortable, and intimate living space at Versailles, and he was the patron of numerous other architectural projects, including the Panthéon, the Trianon, the École Militaire, and what is today the Place de la Concorde. During a time which, in addition to advances in the arts and sciences, saw the writings of Montesquieu, Denis Diderot, Voltaire, and Jean-Jacques Rousseau, Louis XV is probably best remembered as having benignly and benevolently presided over the Enlightenment, a period and movement that was to change the course of history.

—Andria Derstine

FURTHER READING

Antoine, Michel. *Le Conseil du roi sous le règne de Louis XV*. Geneva: Librairie Droz, 1970. A history of the organization of, and the deliberations and decisions undertaken by, the closest advisers of Louis XV during the entirety of his reign. Their competence and their relationship with the king are discussed.

_____. *Louis XV*. Paris: Librairie Arthème Fayard, 1989. A detailed biography of the king by the scholar most responsible for extensive studies into the governmental and administrative aspects of Louis XV's reign. Includes a lengthy bibliography and an index.

Campbell, Peter R. *Power and Politics in Old Regime France, 1720-1745*. New York: Routledge, 1996. A history of the politics of the first half of Louis XV's reign, and the ministries of the duc de Bourbon and Cardinal Fleury. The workings of the court, with its various factions, are illuminated, and the crises of Jansenism and with the Paris Parlement are newly analyzed. Substantial bibliography, appendices, and chronological table of events in the Paris Parlement.

Editors of Time-Life Books. *What Life Was Like During the Age of Reason: France, AD 1660-1800*. Alexandria, Va.: Time-Life Books, 1999. Aimed at the very general reader, but with a good, basic biography of Louis XV, many color illustrations, glossary, pronunciation guide, and bibliography.

Fantin-Desodoards, Antoine. *Louis Quinze*. 3 vols. Paris: F. Buisson, 1797. A three-volume study published during the revolutionary years, and thus a comprehensive near-contemporary account of Louis XV's life. Important early account of how public opinion changed towards the monarchy during the eighteenth century. Includes extensive index.

Garrioch, David. *The Making of Revolutionary Paris*. Berkeley: University of California Press, 2002. A synthetic account of life in eighteenth century Paris, focusing on broad social trends and controversial issues in private and public life, including much information on the impact of the policies of Louis XV's government.

Graham, Lisa Jane. *If the King Only Knew: Seditious Speech in the Reign of Louis XV*. Charlottesville: University Press of Virginia, 2000. Accounts of five authors imprisoned for seditious libel between 1745 and 1771. Discusses the law, conspiracies, the growth of free speech, and the importance of public opinion during Louis's reign.

Rogister, John. *Louis XV and the Parlement of Paris, 1737-1755*. New York: Cambridge University Press, 1995. An account of Louis's stormy relationship with the most important French law court during the middle of his reign.

See also: Denis Diderot; André-Hercule de Fleury; Louis XVI; Marie-Antoinette; Montesquieu; Duc d'Orléans; Madame de Pompadour; Jean-Jacques Rousseau; Voltaire.

Related articles in *Great Events from History: The Eighteenth Century, 1701-1800*: 1718: Geoffroy Issues the *Table of Reactivities*; 1720: Financial Collapse of the John Law System; 1722: Réaumur Discovers Carbon's Role in Hardening Steel; May, 1727-1733: Jansenist "Convulsionnaires" Gather at Saint-Médard; 1733: De Moivre Describes the Bell-Shaped Curve; 1733: Du Fay Discovers Two Kinds of Electric Charge; October 10, 1733-October 3, 1735: War of the Polish Succession; December 16, 1740-November 7, 1748: War of the Austrian Succession; 1743-1744: D'Alembert Develops His Axioms of Motion; August 19, 1745-September 20, 1746: Jacobite Rebellion; 1748: Montesquieu Publishes *The Spirit of the Laws*; 1748: Nollet Discovers Osmosis; 1749-1789: First Comprehensive Examination of the Natural World; 1751: Maupertuis Provides Evidence of "Hereditary Particles"; 1751-1772: Diderot Publishes the *Encyclopedia*; 1754: Condillac Defends Sensationalist Theory; January, 1756-February 15, 1763: Seven Years' War; July 27, 1758: Helvétius Publishes *De l'esprit*; January, 1759: Voltaire Satirizes Optimism in *Candide*; April, 1762: Rousseau Publishes *The Social Contract*; July, 1764: Voltaire Publishes *A Philosophical Dictionary for the Pocket*; October 23, 1769: Cugnot Demonstrates His Steam-Powered Road Carriage; 1770: Publication of Holbach's *The System of Nature*; 1786-1787: Lavoisier Devises the Modern System of Chemical Nomenclature.

LOUIS XVI
King of France (r. 1774-1792)

Louis XVI's encouragement of limited reforms did not prevent the outbreak of the French Revolution. As the revolution became increasingly radical, he demonstrated flexibility in surrendering many of the traditional prerogatives of the French monarchy, but his attempted escape and antirevolutionary attitudes eventually led to his trial, condemnation, and execution.

Born: August 23, 1754; Versailles, France
Died: January 21, 1793; Paris, France
Also known as: Louis-Auguste (birth name); Louis Capet; Duke of Berry
Area of achievement: Government and politics

EARLY LIFE

Born Louis-Auguste in 1754, Louis (lwee) XVI was the grandson of King Louis XV and the third son of the dauphin Louis-Ferdinand and Marie-Joséphe of Saxony. Following the deaths of his two elder brothers and then his father in 1765, Louis-Auguste became the dauphin, or successor to the king. At the age of sixteen, he married Marie-Antoinette, a member of the Austrian Habsburg family. Because of a physical problem, the marriage was not consummated until he had surgery several years later. Their first child, a daughter, was born in 1778, and they eventually would have four children. Louis's love and affection for his wife continued to grow, and in contrast to many monarchs of the period, he never had a mistress.

As a student, Louis-Auguste demonstrated above-average intelligence, and he took a great deal of interest in the subjects of science, geography, and history. At an early age, he became strongly committed to orthodox Catholicism, a belief system he retained throughout his life. His surviving journal records his traditional training in the theory and responsibility of kingship. Naturally timid, he tended to keep his opinions to himself. Beginning in 1766, he kept a diary (actually a combination of engagement diary and hunting record), which gives the impression (probably misleading) of a dull mind and superficial understanding.

In contrast to his father, Louis-Auguste enjoyed a close and friendly relationship with Louis XV, who gave him much advice and allowed him to attend important governmental functions. He inherited the throne after his grandfather died of smallpox on May 10, 1774, and he was formally crowned in a ceremony on June 11, 1775.

LIFE'S WORK

Because his grandfather was almost universally despised, Louis XVI at first was beloved by the people. It soon became apparent, however, that he did not have the personality or strength of will to deal with the antagonistic factions in his court. Although his actions indicated a willingness to undertake moderate political and economic reforms, he lacked the decisiveness and vision needed to deal with the serious problems that he inherited, problems that continued to worsen into the 1780's.

Following a bitter conflict with the *parlements* (powerful courts that registered edicts), Louis XV's chancellor had dissolved the *parlements* and exiled the judges, which greatly angered most of the nobility. Upon his ascension, Louis XVI dismissed the chancellor and restored the *parlements*. His most pressing problem was the government's debt. From 1774 to 1776, his first controller-general of finance, Anne-Robert-Jacques Turgot, tried to deal with the problem by reducing spending and restoring free circulation of grain. After a series of bread riots, the next director of finances, Jacques Necker, regulated grain prices and relied on high-interest loans. The financial situation worsened as the government borrowed large sums to support the cause of American independence.

In 1781, Louis appointed a new controller-general, Charles de Calonne, who proposed several reforms, including a direct land tax and a reduction of the privileges of the nobles. To gain support, Calonne convinced Louis to call an Assembly of Notables, but the assembly rejected the proposed reforms in 1787. After the Parlement of Paris refused to register a land tax the next year, Louis agreed to order elections for a meeting of the Estates-General, a representative assembly of three classes: nobles, clergy, and commoners. He also recalled Necker, whose policies had been quite popular.

When the Estates-General met on May 5, 1789, the commoners, or Third Estate, demanded that the three orders meet together and vote individually. As Louis, indecisive as usual, wavered, the deputies of the Third Estate proclaimed themselves the national assembly on June 17. When Louis appeared ready to oppose their initiatives, they took the Tennis Court Oath, pledging not to adjourn without a constitution. On June 27, the king yielded to the demands of the Third Estate. At the same time, he dismissed Necker. Less than a month later, the Bastille prison-fortress was stormed by Parisian militants. As violence spread, Louis meekly agreed to a reduction of his powers.

On October 5, 1789, a Parisian crowd, aroused by inflationary food costs, forced Louis and his family to move from Versailles to Paris. Held under close supervision, Louis was forced to approve policies he disliked, such as the assembly's anti-Catholic program. In this difficult situation, there is evidence that Louis was suffering from clinical depression, which increased his indecisiveness and dependency on an unpopular queen with poor political judgment.

Louis and the queen attempted a dramatic escape on June 20-21, 1791. Although historians debate Louis's

Louis XVI. (Library of Congress)

exact intentions, he apparently hoped to join the foreign and domestic enemies of the revolution. He left behind a declaration denouncing the persecution of the Church and complaining that his reduced powers made it impossible to govern. Captured at Varennes, the royal family was brought back in great humiliation. In September, Louis had no choice but to approve the new constitution, which established a constitutional monarchy.

With the radical insurrection of October 10, 1792, the royal family became prisoners in the Temple. Under pressure from the Parisian radicals, the assembly suspended Louis and called for elections to a national convention, which met on September 21. The convention, dominated by revolutionaries, quickly abolished the monarchy and established a republic. After incriminating documents involving Louis were discovered, the convention began his trial on December 11. Although Louis was allowed a lawyer, a majority of representatives had already decided that he was guilty of high treason. After a one-vote majority of delegates approved the death penalty, the delegates, by a 380-310 margin, rejected a reprieve on January 20, and the date for the execution was set for the next day. He maintained his dignity as he walked to the guillotine before a cheering crowd.

SIGNIFICANCE

Louis XVI was lacking in charisma, physically unattractive, taciturn, often indecisive, and sometimes seriously depressed—yet he had a number of good qualities. He was hardworking and moderately intelligent, and in contrast to his reactionary brothers, he was willing to make substantial compromises and abandon many of the powers of the absolute monarchy. He gave every indication of desiring reforms designed to bring about greater equality in tax obligations and social status. It is questionable whether another monarch, even if dynamic and decisive, would have more successfully met the great challenges posed by the social and economic tensions of his reign.

Perhaps Louis would have survived if he had not tried to flee from Paris in 1792. It would certainly have been in his interests to give more unqualified support (even if only lip service) to the notion of a constitutional monarchy and to keep a greater distance from conservative individuals who were committed to opposing the revolution. It is unrealistic, however, to expect that he could completely transcend his perceived interests and cultural education.

The execution of Louis XVI was one of the most dramatic moments of the French Revolution. To conservatives, the event became a negative symbol of the dangers of excessive democracy and disorder. To persons of the radical left, the execution became a positive symbol of the need to overthrow and punish oppressors of the people. For liberals and moderates, his execution has often been a symbol of the consequences of failure to make gradual reforms in political and social institutions.

—*Thomas Tandy Lewis*

FURTHER READING

Cronin, Vincent. *Louis and Antoinette*. New York: William Morrow, 1975. Emphasizes the personal lives and personalities of the king and queen.

Fäy, Bernard. *Louis XVI: Or, The End of a World*. Chicago: Henry Regnery, 1968. Although dated, this work is a good historical biography that emphasizes the events and ideas of the revolution.

Hardman, John. *Louis XVI: The Silent King*. New York: Oxford University Press, 2000. Compact but richly detailed political biography that gives a somewhat favorable view of Louis and minimizes his opposition to constitutional reforms. Highly recommended even if difficult reading in places.

Jordan, David. *The King's Trial: The French Revolution vs. Louis XVI*. Berkeley: University of California Press, 1979. A detailed account of the legal issues, procedures, and events of the trial and verdict.

Maceron, Claude. *Twilight of the Old Order, 1774-1778*. New York: Alfred A. Knopf, 1977. A detailed account of the fiscal problems and policies during Louis XVI's early reign.

Mansel, Philip. *The Court of France, 1789-1830*. New York: Cambridge University Press, 1988. A scholarly account of policies, institutions, and leaders of French governments, including Louis XVI's last three years.

Padover, Saul. *The Life and Death of Louis XVI*. New York: Taplinger, 1963. The first notable English-language biography, which is readable and useful, even though it is considered less scholarly than more recent works by Hardman and others.

Price, Munro. *The Road from Versailles: Louis XVI, Marie Antoinette, and the Fall of the French Monarchy*. New York: St. Martin's Press, 2003. Concentrating on the diplomacy and correspondence of the Baron de Breteuil, Price argues, in contrast to Hardman, that Louis refused to compromise with the legislature and fled Paris in hopes of restoring the absolute monarchy.

Stone, Bailey. *The Parlement of Paris, 1774-89*. Chapel Hill: University of North Carolina Press, 1981. A scholarly study of the conflicts between Louis and the High Court of Paris when the royal government attempted to enact reforms in taxation.

Walzer, Michael, ed. *Regicide and Revolution: Speeches at the Trial of Louis XVI*. New York: Cambridge University Press, 1974. A dozen speeches from the trial as well as a stimulating introduction.

See also: Louis XV; Marie-Antoinette; Jacques Necker; Anne-Robert-Jacques Turgot.

CATHERINE MACAULAY
English historian and pamphleteer

Macaulay, the first Englishwoman to write a major multivolume work in history, also was actively involved in politics. As an outspoken republican, Macaulay wrote antimonarchical evaluations of history, a protofeminist work on education, and works on politics, ethics, and philosophy. Her reevaluation and reinterpretation of seventeenth century history proved to be central to the development of radical politics in eighteenth century England, America, and France.

Born: April 2, 1731; Olantigh, Wye, Kent, England
Died: June 22, 1791; Binfield, Berkshire, England
Also known as: Catherine Sawbridge (birth name);
   Catherine Macaulay Graham
Areas of achievement: Historiography, philosophy,
   government and politics, women's rights

EARLY LIFE

Catherine Macaulay, née Sawbridge, was the second daughter and third child of John Sawbridge and his second wife, Elizabeth Sawbridge (née Wanley). She was born into a wealthy mercantile family that held an established Whig position. Not much is known about her earliest years. After her mother's death during childbirth in 1733, when Catherine was only two years old, Catherine and her siblings faced neglect by their father, but Catherine and her only brother, John, did receive educations, at home, by a governess. Very early on, Catherine began to read extensively about Roman history in books from her father's library and seemed to have developed a strong commitment to republican values and to liberty. Since she apparently received a domestic education only, it is not known where she learned Latin and history, which were unusual accomplishments for girls of her time.

In 1760, Catherine married George Macaulay, a Scottish physician, and moved with him from rural Kent to London. Their marriage was a happy one, with her husband giving strong support to her intellectual work. When George died, Catherine was left with one daughter, Catherine Sophia. By that time, Catherine Macaulay had already achieved fame as a historian.

LIFE'S WORK

Catherine Macaulay was a prolific writer. Her major achievement was her eight-volume *The History of England from the Accession of James I to that of the Brunswick Line* (1763-1783). She had instant success with the publication of the first volume in 1763. The work is considered outstanding in part not only because it conveyed a new methodology in history writing but also because it conveyed Macaulay's politics.

Traditionally, historiography rested largely upon previously published sources, Macaulay's *History of England*, however, is based on her extensive research in the collection of the British Museum among unpublished legal and parliamentary documents as well as private letters. The book chronicles English dissent and opposition and was intended to answer David Hume's *History*, which was sympathetic to the Royalist cause in England. Macaulay, in contrast, provided a Whig interpretation of the Glorious Revolution, which had failed to produce the degree of liberty and sovereignty for the people that Macaulay, and other radical Whigs, demanded. Her reinterpretation—as well as reevaluation—of seventeenth century history proved foundational for the development of radical politics in eighteenth century England, America, and France. (Macaulay had visited France several times.) The *History of England* was particularly admired by colonial American politician Benjamin Franklin, and it convinced many other American colonists to reject monarchy.

Macaulay also was known for entering political and public debates through her written pamphlets; these debates, called the "pamphlet wars," traditionally excluded women. *Loose Remarks on Certain Positions to be Found in Mr. Hobbes's "Philosophical Rudiments of Government and Society"* (1767) rejected Hobbes's arguments of contractual politics in favor of liberty. Her other pamphlets—*A Modest Plea for the Property of Copyright* (1774) and *An Address to the People of England, Scotland, and Ireland, on the Present Important Crisis of Affairs* (1775)—were concerned with avoiding war in the American colonies.

Edmund Burke was Macaulay's primary opponent in the pamphlet wars of the eighteenth century. She wrote two replies to Burke: *Observations on a Pamphlet, Entitled, Thoughts on the Cause of the Present Discontents* was published in 1770, and, in 1790, she attacked Burke's conservative agenda in *Observations on the Reflections of the Right Hon. Edmund Burke on the Revolution in France*.

Macaulay moved to Bath in 1774, hoping to improve her frail health. There, she was invited by one of her admirers, Reverend Doctor Thomas Wilson, to share his residence. A seventy-three-year-old widower, he formally adopted Macaulay's daughter in 1775. Rumors spread about this unusual arrangement, particularly given Wilson's age, and the two were considered possible lovers. Unfortunately, Wilson turned out to be an embarrassingly obtrusive admirer. He arranged an extravagant celebration for Macaulay's forty-sixth birthday, complete with the unveiling of a marble statue of her in a church at Wolbrooke. This caused ridicule for them both, and it permanently ruined Macaulay's reputation.

During her time in Bath, however, she was able to write one volume of *The History of England from the Revolution to the Present Time in a Series of Letters to a Friend* (1778). It was rather poorly received, probably because it lacked the meticulous research and good scholarship of her previous volumes. She did not write a sequel, perhaps because of circumstances from her breakup with Wilson, who aggressively circulated scandalous rumors about Macaulay when she married a second time in 1778. Her new husband, William Graham (brother of the quack doctor James Graham, who was called to cure Macaulay of a chronic illness), was twenty-six years younger than Macaulay and from a lower class. The age difference between the two, and their different social-class backgrounds, caused further negative and slanderous reactions from critics as well as friends.

In 1784, Macaulay traveled through parts of America with her husband, visiting prominent Americans, such as George Washington, John and Abigail Adams, and Mercy Otis Warren, discussing history and revolutionary politics. After her philosophical work *Treatise on the Immutability of Moral Truth* (1783), she published her last work, *Letters on Education with Observations on Religious and Metaphysical Subjects*, in 1790. Her ideas on education were very much ahead of her time and covered a wide variety of subjects, such as nursing, the care of infants, and the upbringing and education of children. In the second part of this final text, she linked private and public education by detailing educational approaches in ancient Greece, Sparta, and Rome and by drawing connections among education, philosophy, and religion. As she had become very aware of the vulnerability of her gender, she demanded, particularly in "Letter XXII: No Characteristic Difference in Sex," an equal education for boys and for girls. Macaulay died in 1791, after a long illness.

SIGNIFICANCE

Catherine Macaulay was a rather unconventional eighteenth century intellectual. At a time when the writing of

history was considered to be a masculine domain, her achievements and methodological innovations were unique. While many of her well-known contemporaries, such as Horace Walpole and Thomas Gray, praised her work, her reputation was ultimately marred by rumors about her private life, a common fate faced by women in the public realm. The rumors turned her into the object of satire and were especially harmful because she was accused of violating feminine propriety, an accusation that still affects how her work is received; she has yet to be included in the canon of important historians, and her historical work is not easily accessible, given that there are no modern reprints of her scholarship.

However, Macaulay is acknowledged now as a pioneer of protofeminist thought, and she is known to have inspired Mary Wollstonecraft's equality feminism. Macaulay was praised in Wollstonecraft's *A Vindication of the Rights of Woman* (1792) and by Mary Hays in *Female Biography* (1803).

The change in political climate and the conservative backlash following the French Revolution limited the subsequent reception of her works, but her comprehensive and outstanding work of history is certainly deserving of more scholarly attention.

—Miriam Wallraven

FURTHER READING

Gunther-Canada, Wendy. "The Politics of Sense and Sensibility: Mary Wollstonecraft and Catherine Macaulay Graham on Edmund Burke's *Reflections on the Revolution in France*." In *Women Writers and the Early Modern British Political Tradition*, edited by Hilda L. Smith. New York: Cambridge University Press, 1998. Analyzes the rhetorical and argumentative strategies in response to Edmund Burke's *Reflections on the Revolution in France*.

Hill, Bridget. "The Links Between Mary Wollstonecraft and Catherine Macaulay: New Evidence." *Women's History Review* 4, no. 2 (1995): 177-192. Shows that the two influential English radicals—Macaulay and Wollstonecraft—corresponded with one another, and compares their feminist and political positions.

_____. *The Republican Virago: The Life and Times of Catherine Macaulay, Historian*. Oxford, England: Clarendon Press, 1992. A well-researched and accessible study of Macaulay's life and times, with thorough analyses of her works.

Pocock, J. G. A. "Catherine Macaulay: Patriot Historian." In *Women Writers and the Early Modern British Political Tradition*, edited by Hilda L. Smith. New

York: Cambridge University Press, 1998. Provides historical context and political background on Macaulay's republicanism and patriotism.

Schnorrenberg, Barbara Brandon. "An Opportunity Missed: Catherine Macaulay on the Revolution of 1688." *Studies in Eighteenth-Century Culture* 20 (1990): 231-240. Focuses on Macaulay's criticism of the Glorious Revolution and elucidates her radical Whig principles.

Wiseman, Susan. "Catherine Macaulay: History, Republicanism, and the Public Sphere." In *Women, Writing, and the Public Sphere, 1700-1830*, edited by Elizabeth Eger et al. New York: Cambridge University Press, 2001. Explores the ways in which republicanism and gender shaped Macaulay's career as a historian, with particular attention to the dynamics between private and public spheres.

See also: Abigail Adams; John Adams; Edmund Burke; Georgiana Cavendish; Benjamin Franklin; Edward Gibbon; Johann Gottfried Herder; David Hume; Adam Smith; Mercy Otis Warren; George Washington; Mary Wollstonecraft.

Related articles in *Great Events from History: The Eighteenth Century, 1701-1800:* 1726-1729: Voltaire Advances Enlightenment Thought in Europe; March 9, 1776: Adam Smith Publishes *The Wealth of Nations*; May, 1776-September 3, 1783: France Supports the American Revolution; July 4, 1776: Declaration of Independence; 1784-1791: Herder Publishes His Philosophy of History; 1790: Burke Lays the Foundations of Modern Conservatism; 1792: Wollstonecraft Publishes *A Vindication of the Rights of Woman*; April 20, 1792-October, 1797: Early Wars of the French Revolution.

FLORA MACDONALD
Scottish heroine

MacDonald helped Prince Charles Edward Stuart escape King George II's soldiers in 1745 and flee to France. In 1774, MacDonald and her husband moved their family to America and became involved in the American Revolution, fighting for the British. MacDonald's heroism was noted by several contemporaries, including Scottish writer James Boswell and English writer Samuel Johnson.

Born: 1722; Milton, South Uist, Outer Hebrides, Scotland

Died: March 4, 1790; Kingsburgh House, Skye, Inner Hebrides, Scotland

Also known as: Fionnghal MacDonald; Flory MacDonald

Area of achievement: Government and politics

EARLY LIFE

Flora MacDonald was born on one in a group of islands, the Outer Hebrides, off the coast of Scotland. She was the youngest of three children born to Ranald MacDonald and his second wife, Marion. Ranald was a tackman, which meant he ran two tacks, or farms, on the island. Flora's father died when she was two years old, leaving her mother a young widow with three small children and two farms to manage. Four years later, Marion married Hugh MacDonald, a young man from Skye. Hugh also was a tackman.

The main products of the MacDonalds' farm were cattle and sheep. During the summer months the family drove the cattle up the nearby mountain slopes to pasture, and then slept in little huts away from home. On the farm, the MacDonalds lived in a small, plain, but well-furnished cottage consisting of three rooms and a kitchen.

Life on South Uist was not easy. Flora received no formal education. It was the custom for boys to be sent away to school, but girls were expected to learn from their mothers. Flora learned to speak without a Scottish accent, like other Scots of her class. She also learned how to sing, sew, read, and write. It was once believed that Flora left the island to attend school in Edinburgh, but that is inaccurate. The first time Flora left the islands was in 1744, when, at age twenty-two, she visited cousins on the mainland. When Flora's older brother Angus was old enough to run the tacks himself, Hugh MacDonald moved the rest of the family to Skye.

LIFE'S WORK

In 1745, Prince Charles led one of two major attempts to put his father, James II, on the throne of England. The attempt failed, and Charles found himself on the run from British soldiers with a reward of £30,000 on his head. His boat landed at Eriskay, a small island off South Uist. The first person he met upon landing was Hugh MacDonald, Flora MacDonald's stepfather.

Flora MacDonald. (The Granger Collection, New York)

Around this time, Flora MacDonald was in South Uist visiting Angus. Also on the island was Colonel Felix O'Neil, who was one of several men traveling with Prince Charles. The prince was hiding in a glen on the eastern side of South Uist. O'Neil and the other men took turns scouting the island for information on the whereabouts of the English troops. On Friday, June 20, MacDonald had taken her brother's cattle to the hill pasture behind his farm. That night, she was awakened by a cousin with a "friend" who wanted to speak with MacDonald. Dressing quickly, MacDonald went outside to see Colonel O'Neil standing in the moonlight. O'Neil told her about their plan to get the prince off the island and to safety. He proposed that MacDonald travel back to Skye with Charles dressed as her female servant, "Betty Burke."

At first MacDonald did not want to help. She felt the whole idea too dangerous, for herself as well as the prince. O'Neil tried to assure MacDonald that there would be no trouble, but she was still not convinced. At this point, Charles himself stepped out of the shadows to talk to her. The prince was well known for his charm and, despite his dirty, shabby appearance, Mac-Donald agreed to help. There were no women's clothes large enough for Charles to wear, so they had to wait several days for some to be made.

On June 30, MacDonald, Charles, and Mac-Donald's cousin sailed for Skye, intending on meeting Lady Margaret, wife of the clan's chief, but she had an unexpected visitor, an English lieutenant in search of the prince. Charles was left at the boat, and MacDonald was sent to the house with instructions to keep the lieutenant occupied while the others decided the best way to get the prince to safety. When a plan was devised, MacDonald was relieved of her duties. When they parted, the prince gave her the garters he wore under his maid's costume.

On July 12, MacDonald was arrested and questioned. She told the authorities as much as she could without involving her family and friends, taking most of the blame herself. She was kept prisoner aboard several ships at varying times before being sent to London in November. By the time general amnesty was declared on July 4, 1747, MacDonald had spent a year in prison.

After returning to Scotland, MacDonald renewed a friendship with Allan MacDonald, son of Sir Alexander MacDonald of Kingsburgh. They were married on November 6, 1750, and eventually had six children. By 1774, Flora and Allan were deep in debt because of high rents, bad crops, and the loss of cattle; they decided to emigrate to America.

By 1774 tension had begun to rise between Britain and the American colonies. The Highlanders raised an army on behalf of British king George III. On February 28, 1776, Allan helped lead fifteen hundred men in the Battle of Moore's Creek Bridge against the Americans. The charge was unsuccessful, and many men, including Allan, were taken prisoner. The women left at home had to endure difficulties under the hands of the Americans. Their homes were robbed, and they feared for their lives. Flora managed to get her family to safety in New York and was reunited with Allan. She then followed him to Halifax, Nova Scotia, in 1778. The winter was too harsh for her health, though, and she headed back to Scotland. Allan did not join her until 1784.

Flora's health was never the same. She was in constant pain from an arm broken during the trip to Scotland, a break that had not been set properly, and on March 4, 1790, she died after an illness.

SIGNIFICANCE

Flora MacDonald was known as a quiet, modest, steadfast woman who captured the imaginations and the affections of the Scottish people. Though not a Jacobite herself, MacDonald helped Prince Charles in his escape from the British out of loyalty to her stepfather and the Highland chiefs. Treason against the throne was a punishable offense, and MacDonald was much admired for her bravery. Even during her year of captivity, she managed to keep her dignity. MacDonald's fame and influence followed her to America, where she rallied the Highlanders to the king's side during the American Revolution.

MacDonald's small but important part in history managed to catch the attention of several authors, most notably James Boswell and Samuel Johnson. Both men mentioned meeting her during their trip through the Hebrides. Several years after her death, MacDonald's son John built a monument in her honor, but it disappeared within a few months, chipped away bit by bit by Scottish pilgrims. A second monument, built in 1871, was blown down during a violent gale. A third monument was built, and it still stands.

—Maryanne Barsotti

FURTHER READING

Daiches, David. *The Last Stuart: The Life and Times of Bonnie Prince Charlie*. New York: G. P. Putnam's Sons, 1973. A contemporary account of why Prince Charles, also known as Bonnie Prince Charlie, became one of the great romantic figures in history. Illustrated.

Douglas, Hugh. *Flora MacDonald: The Most Loyal Rebel*. Stroud, England: Sutton, 1999. A biographical and historical examination of MacDonald's role as heroine and rebel in the context of Jacobite Scotland.

Erickson, Carolly Charles. *Bonnie Prince Charlie: A Biography*. New York: William Morrow, 1989. An account of Charles Stuart, the English prince who attempted to overthrow King George III and place his father on the throne. Illustrated.

Fletcher, Inglis. *The Scotswoman*. New York: Bobbs-Merrill, 1954. A historical novel based on MacDonald's life in America and her role in the American Revolution.

Herman, Arthur. *How the Scots Invented the Modern World*. New York: Three Rivers Press, 2001. Examines how eighteenth century and nineteenth century Scotland made crucial contributions in forming the modern world.

Houston, R. A., and W. W. J. Knox. *The New Penguin History of Scotland*. New York: Penguin Books, 2001. This work contains a detailed examination of the history of Scotland, including the Jacobite uprising and MacDonald's part in saving Prince Charles.

MacLeod, Ruairidh H. *Flora MacDonald: The Jacobite Heroine in Scotland and North America*. London: Shepheard-Walwyn, 1995. A historical account of MacDonald's significance to the greater Jacobite struggle in Scotland and in North America.

Magnusson, Magnus. *Scotland: The Story of a Nation*. New York: Grove Press, 2000. An exploration of the events that shaped Scotland as a nation.

Toffey, John J. *A Woman Nobly Planned: Fact and Myth in the Legacy of Flora MacDonald*. Durham, N.C.: Carolina Academic Press, 1997. Examines the rich legacy, including the facts and myths, surrounding MacDonald's life.

Vining, Elizabeth Gray. *Flora, A Biography*. New York: J. B. Lippincott, 1966. One of the more thorough, and factual, accounts of MacDonald's life and her contributions to the Jacobite Rebellion. Illustrated.

See also: James Boswell; George II; George III; Samuel Johnson.

Related articles in *Great Events from History: The Eighteenth Century, 1701-1800:* February, 1706-April 28, 1707: Act of Union Unites England and Scotland; September 6, 1715-February 4, 1716: Jacobite Rising in Scotland; August 19, 1745-September 20, 1746: Jacobite Rebellion; April 19, 1775: Battle of Lexington and Concord.

ALEXANDER MCGILLIVRAY
Creek political and military leader

McGillivray was one of the earliest mixed-blood Creek leaders to use his bicultural abilities to protect both indigenous sovereignty and his own power. He negotiated trade agreements between the British and Spanish in the American South, led indigenous warriors to protect the American interests of the British, and persuaded his people to resist treaties with expansionist colonial Americans.

Born: c. 1759; near present-day Montgomery, Alabama
Died: February 17, 1793; Pensacola, Florida
Areas of achievement: Government and politics, diplomacy, military

EARLY LIFE

Alexander McGillivray was the son of Sehoy Marchand, a Creek-French woman, and Lachlan McGillivray, a Scottish trader from Georgia. McGillivray's mother was a member of the influential Red Stick clan, a connection that would give the young man important influence in tribal politics. His father, on the other hand, was one of many Scots who had come to Georgia seeking fortune.

Tradition has it that the young McGillivray was taken by his father to Savannah, Georgia, where the youngster was to be educated. Unfortunately, there is no verifiable evidence of such schooling. One of his father's fellow traders declared that the young McGillivray "was raised among the whites." One bit of circumstantial evidence is that on the eve of the American Revolution, Alexander McGillivray signed for a cash advance against his father's account at Cowper, Telfair, and Company, an Indian trading firm in Savannah. His signature is the bold rounded hand of a trained penman, the same flowing style found in his numerous letters located in the archives of the United States, Great Britain, and Spain.

When fighting erupted between Great Britain and its North American mainland colonies, Alexander's father, Lachlan, was one of the king's subjects who chose to return to his homeland. The wily trader returned to Scotland, leaving his son behind in Georgia. Once his father fled, Alexander had no safe choice but to return to indigenous life in the Creek towns among his mother's people. Returning to the Upper Creek towns was in effect a return to family, since Creek social and political organization, like that of the other Southeastern tribes, was matrilineal. On his mother's extended family Alexander could draw for political and economic support.

Quickly, McGillivray put his clerical talents to work by securing a position as an assistant commissary, or storekeeper, at the British trading post maintained by David Tait in McGillivray's home village of Little Tallassees. Tait, another Scot who had come to Georgia seeking his fortune, had gained a position in the British Southern Indian Department as commissary to the Upper Creek. It was Tait's responsibility to cultivate harmonious diplomatic relations with the Upper Creek on behalf of the British crown. Tait thus welcomed the young Alexander McGillivray as an ally in his struggle to maintain the British presence in the Creek towns and to keep some order in the often disorderly American Indian trade.

McGillivray's value to Tait was more than political. In the late summer of 1777, as a result of anti-British activities by the Georgians, a band of pro-American Lower Creek plotted the assassination of David Tait. By virtue of his intelligence network in the tribe, McGillivray learned of the conspiracy and warned Tait in time for him to flee. During the fall and winter of 1777, McGillivray was, through Tait's absence, the British agent in charge at the Upper Creek trading post. This was extremely valuable experience for the emerging Creek leader.

In addition to this position as a member of the British Southern Indian Department, McGillivray used the tribal connections he had inherited from his mother to good advantage. Thus he secured his own economic base at the same time that he was building political support both in his own village and in neighboring ones.

LIFE'S WORK

During the years from 1775 to 1783, Alexander McGillivray gained a following as one of the young leaders among the Upper Creek. Nineteenth century accounts, especially those of the French adventurer Louis Milfort, disparage McGillivray and question his courage in time of war. British records reveal, however, that such accusations are untrue.

In January, 1779, McGillivray led a party of Creek warriors to assist the British army then invading Georgia. For several months thereafter, McGillivray and the warriors remained with the British forces as auxiliaries. When the Spanish besieged Pensacola in 1780, McGillivray organized and led seventeen hundred warriors to support the British defenders there. Even the Spanish commander, Bernardo de Gálvez, admitted that the presence of the forest soldiers helped persuade him to withdraw. Repeated cries of "wolf, wolf" by the British commander so disillusioned the Creek in late 1780 that McGillivray could not persuade the warriors to return to Pensacola when the Spanish besieged the town again in 1781.

The surrender of the British garrison at Pensacola forced McGillivray to consider the options open to him as leader of the Upper Creek. If his people were to survive the onslaught of American expansionism, they needed someone to back them in resisting the intrusions of the land-hungry Georgians. The natural choice was Spain, which was ever alert to the possibility that avaricious neighbors might covet their territories. Not only did the Spanish governor in New Orleans recognize McGillivray's position, but he also was willing to consider McGillivray's recommendation that the Southern Indian trade be channeled through the British firm of Panton, Leslie, and Company, which was headquartered in Pensacola. McGillivray would be given a fractional share by the grateful firm. However mercenary this relationship might appear, as "Great Beloved Man" of the Upper Creek, McGillivray knew that trade was fundamental to Native American economic survival. Decades of trading with one or another European power had left the Creek, like all the tribes, totally dependent on the flow of goods arriving from Europe's factories. Scarcity of supplies would depress Creek economic life and shorten McGillivray's political career.

In the spring of 1782 McGillivray was able to take advantage of a political power vacuum. The longtime head warrior of the Upper Creek, Emistisiguo, was killed in a skirmish with American troops in Georgia. When news of this tragedy reached the Creek country, McGillivray turned his experiences and connections to advantage in persuading the Upper Creek to elect him as their head warrior in 1783.

It was then as head warrior that McGillivray approached the Spanish. On New Year's Day, 1784, McGillivray wrote Arturo O'Neill, the Spanish governor at Pensacola, seeking an agreement between the Spanish and the Creek. The shrewd Creek leader warned O'Neill that hordes of Americans soon would descend the Mississippi into Spanish territory. Perhaps the Creek could be of assistance in stopping this invasion. McGillivray further warned the Spanish that the American officials intended to compete with the Spanish for the indigenous trade, so the Spanish would be well-advised to guarantee the trade. Most convenient for the Creek, moreover, would be a trade through Pensacola or Mobile. Indeed, in

his initial overture, McGillivray suggested that he would be happy to be responsible for the trade himself.

As the selected leader of the Upper Creek towns, representing himself at times as head warrior of all the Creek peoples, McGillivray signed the Treaty of Pensacola with the Spanish in 1784. Until his death in 1793, McGillivray continued to cling to that agreement as his guarantee against immediate subjugation by the Americans.

Acting in his capacities as the elected leader of the Upper Creek towns, representative of Spanish interests, and partner in a British Indian trading firm, McGillivray performed a delicate diplomatic juggling act. In his capacity as headman of the Upper Creek he had to placate the many factions within the villages, keeping at bay his rivals for power. His entrepreneurial activities created additional friction for him, as jealous Creek and traders observed his growing personal wealth. On the other side of the Georgia frontier at the same time, active land speculators and state officials sought to bring the Creek into agreement about land cessions, transactions steadily opposed by McGillivray. He sought both to protect his peoples' lands and to further the Spanish policy of keeping the American settlers as far away as possible. Furthermore, as long as he kept the Spanish happy and the Creek towns at peace, he was serving also the interests of Panton, Leslie, and Company, which wanted no disturbance in the flow of trade goods.

Because of such connections, virtually anyone doing business on the frontier of the old Southwest from 1783 to 1793 had to reckon with McGillivray. So extensive was McGillivray's influence that when groups of American land speculators sought control of lands in the territory later to become the state of Mississippi, McGillivray was offered almost 300,000 acres of land for his cooperation. Had this scheme gone through, McGillivray might have been hard-pressed to explain his action to Spain.

In 1790, McGillivray added another ball to his diplomatic juggling act. At the invitation of George Washington, newly installed president of the United States, the head warrior of the Creek, along with several other Creek and Seminole chiefs, undertook the long journey to New York. President Washington hoped to impress McGillivray and his entourage; in turn, perhaps, he could persuade McGillivray that a treaty could be signed with the United States that might protect the Creek from the land speculators on the Southwestern frontier. Fearful lest British and Spanish representatives in New York discourage the Creek leaders from signing, the American diplomats kept McGillivray and his party well protected from outside influences.

Ever the cautious negotiator, McGillivray agreed that certain parts of the articles of the treaty be kept secret. Those could be revealed when and to whom he saw fit. He would, for example, need an extremely creative explanation for the article commissioning him a brigadier general in the American army at an annual salary of $1,200.

In some ways this "grand tour" of the United States was the last great public act of McGillivray's career. For a decade he had dominated Creek politics through his wit and skill. Although still a young man, he was given to bouts of recurrent illness, especially gout, rheumatism, and respiratory infections. While visiting his friend and supporter, William Panton, in Pensacola, McGillivray died of pneumonia and complications of gout on February 17, 1793. For ten years he had fought successfully defending the Creek; they would never see his like again.

SIGNIFICANCE

Alexander McGillivray's contribution to Native American history lies in the model of leadership he established during his decade in control. McGillivray emerged at a particularly critical juncture in the affairs of both his people and the fledgling United States. As of 1783 the established patterns of frontier diplomacy were disrupted. The longtime nemesis of the Creek, the colonial settlers, were now unleashed. Gone was the British Indian Department, which had given lip service to the idea of indigenous rights. In its place stood representatives of a newly victorious government that assumed the triumphant attitude of the victor claiming the spoils of war. In the logic of American thought, the Creek had been the allies of the British in the war, the British had been defeated, and, therefore, the Creek had been defeated. Creek land was the trophy the Americans demanded.

Son of a father who had once held many acres in colonial Georgia, and of a mother whose people once controlled those same lands, McGillivray held the unique perspective of a bicultural leader. Since he knew the appetite for land that drove the Americans, he knew the only answer was to deny them even the smallest morsel. One nibble and they would be even more unrelenting in their demands. Consequently, McGillivray practiced a firm and consistent policy—no land cessions. Whenever the Georgians or others persuaded a handful of chiefs to sign a treaty, McGillivray denounced it, whatever the terms.

By courting the Spanish, backing a trading firm that favored him, and cultivating his Creek power base, McGillivray kept the Americans at bay for almost a decade.

Time and circumstance favored him, but his own diplomatic and intellectual abilities were fundamental to the success he enjoyed. He was the first of the Creek mixed-blood leaders. None of those who followed him equaled him in skills or accomplishments; no one could truly replace him as the "Great Beloved Man" of the Creek.

—*James H. O'Donnell III*

FURTHER READING

Cashin, Edward J. *Laclan McGillivray, Indian Trader: The Shaping of the Southern Colonial Frontier.* Athens: University of Georgia Press, 1992. A biography of McGillivray's father, Lachlan McGillvray, which follows Lachlan's career as an American Indian trader to examine the interaction of European settlers and the indigenous Americans in the colonial south.

Caughey, John W. *McGillivray of the Creeks.* Norman: University of Oklahoma Press, 1938. Caughey's volume remains the classic, basic study for understanding McGillivray's career. The bulk of the volume consists of translations of selected letters from McGillivray to Spanish officials and others, written between 1783 and 1793. The biographical introduction is brief and based primarily on nineteenth century sources.

Coker, William S., and Thomas D. Watson. *Indian Traders of the Southeastern Spanish Borderlands: Panton, Leslie and Company and John Forbes and Company, 1783-1847.* Pensacola: University of West Florida Press, 1986. A volume based on the papers of Panton, Leslie, and Company, now gathered on microfilm or in copies and housed at the University of West Florida. This study aids in understanding the relationship of the trading firm with McGillivray as well as his diplomatic machinations.

Corbitt, D. C., trans. and ed. "Papers Relating to the Georgia-Florida Frontier, 1784-1800." *Georgia Historical Quarterly* 20-25 (1936-1941). Papers fundamental to an understanding of McGillivray's career during this period. Researchers, however, should also consult the John W. Caughey volume.

Ethridge, Robbie. *Creek Country: The Creek Indians and Their World.* Chapel Hill: University of North Carolina Press, 2003. A comprehensive history of the Creek Indians, including information about McGillivray.

Kinnaird, Lawrence. "International Rivalry in the Creek Country, Part I: The Ascendancy of Alexander McGillivray, 1783-1789." *Florida Historical Quarterly* 10 (1931): 59-85. Kinnaird explores the importance of Panton, Leslie's trading activities as fundamental to McGillivray's diplomacy. This is another study that tends to de-emphasize McGillivray's Creek connections and his personal abilities.

O'Donnell, James H., III. "Alexander McGillivray: Training for Leadership, 1777-1783." *Georgia Historical Quarterly* 49 (1965): 172-186. In this article the author chronicles McGillivray's experiences in the British Indian Department and how these prepared him for his later role as tribal leader. This publication represents the beginning of the newer scholarship about McGillivray.

Wright, Amos J., Jr. *The McGillivray and McIntosh Traders on the Old Southwest Frontier, 1716-1815.* Montgomery, Ala.: NewSouth Books, 2001. A history of two Scottish clans that traded in the colonial United States. Includes a chapter entitled "Alexander McGillivray: The Creek Chief" and another chapter on McGillivray's father.

Wright, J. Leitch, Jr. "Creek-American Treaty of 1790: Alexander McGillivray and the Diplomacy of the Old Southwest." *Georgia Historical Quarterly* 51 (1967): 379-400. This well-known student of the old Southwest places McGillivray within the context of the intrigue and negotiation that seemed the constant companion of frontier diplomacy. Wright knows frontier history well and succeeds in giving this account a balanced perspective.

See also: Daniel Boone; Joseph Brant; John Jay; Little Turtle; Pontiac; Thanadelthur; George Washington; Anthony Wayne.

Related articles in *Great Events from History: The Eighteenth Century, 1701-1800:* September 22, 1711-March 23, 1713: Tuscarora War; June 20, 1732: Settlement of Georgia; May 28, 1754-February 10, 1763: French and Indian War; October 5, 1759-November 19, 1761: Cherokee War; May 8, 1763-July 24, 1766: Pontiac's Resistance; May 24 and June 11, 1776: Indian Delegation Meets with Congress; October 18, 1790-July, 1794: Little Turtle's War; 1799: Code of Handsome Lake.

SIR ALEXANDER MACKENZIE
Scottish explorer

By crossing Canada in 1793, Mackenzie became the first nonindigenous person north of Mexico to reach the Pacific Ocean via an overland route.

Born: c. 1764; Stornoway, Scotland
Died: March 12, 1820; Mulnain, near Dunkeld, Scotland
Area of achievement: Exploration

EARLY LIFE

The third of four children, Alexander Mackenzie was born on a farm on the island of Lewis. His mother, Isabella Maciver Mackenzie, died when he was still young. When a depression struck the island of Lewis, Alexander's father, Kenneth, took him to New York in 1774. Hardly had they arrived when the early stages of the American Revolution broke out. Kenneth joined the King's Royal Regiment of New York—he was to die suddenly in 1780—and young Alexander was left in the care of aunts in New York's Mohawk Valley.

By 1778, Tories were so unpopular in the Mohawk area that Alexander was sent to school in Montreal. There he was attracted by the money and adventure afforded by the fur trade. Since Great Britain had acquired

Canada in 1763, opportunities for British nationals abounded. In 1779, still a teenager, Mackenzie entered the employ of the fur-trading firm of Finlay and Gregory, which later became Gregory, MacLeod, and Company.

LIFE'S WORK

Alexander Mackenzie had worked in the Montreal office for five years when Mr. Gregory sent him to the company's trading post at Detroit. Soon Mr. MacLeod, impressed with young Mackenzie's capabilities, offered him a partnership on the condition that he go to posts in the Far West in what would become Alberta and Saskatchewan.

Although the area was rich in furs, competition among the fur-trading companies was keen and often violent. Mackenzie was in charge of the company post at Île-à-la-Crosse (Saskatchewan) from 1785 to 1787. In that latter year, Gregory, MacLeod, and Company amalgamated with the larger North West Company. Mackenzie received one share in the enlarged company, which had a total of twenty shares. He was sent to a post on the Athabasca River as second-in-command to Peter Pond, a trapper who had already killed at least two people.

Pond was the source of much misinformation. He calculated Lake Athabasca to be 700 miles west of its true location. He explored the region and incorrectly believed that the large river flowing from the Great Slave Lake emptied into the Pacific Ocean. Although Pond returned to the East in 1788, Mackenzie was greatly influenced by him, stating that "the practicality of penetrating across the continent" was the "favorite project of my ambition." From this ambition resulted two great expeditions.

Acting on instructions from the North West Company, Mackenzie embarked on his first voyage on June 3, 1789, with four other white men and a small party of American Indians. Upon leaving the Great Slave Lake, he entered the river that was to bear his name. When it became apparent that the river was flowing north to the Arctic Sea and not to the Pacific, Mackenzie decided to continue to its mouth, recording in his log that "it would satisfy people's curiosity, though not their intentions." The journey down the full length of the Mackenzie River (1,075 miles) was completed in only fourteen days. Seeing the tides and the saltwater, Mackenzie was, contrary to some reports, well aware that he had reached the Arctic Sea or some arm of it. Mackenzie's expedition started back up the river, which, according to myth, he called River Disappointment. The men returned safely to Fort Chipewyan on Lake Athabasca on September 12, 1789, having explored one of the greatest rivers on Earth. Although his exploration was of no practical use to the North West Company, Mackenzie's efforts were appreciated; he was awarded another share in the North West Company, giving him a one-tenth interest in the business.

Even before the first expedition was completed, Mackenzie was planning a second, although four years were to pass before he could undertake it. In the interim (in 1791-1792), he went to London to receive instructions on using astronomical apparatus, as the maps he had were useless. Despite the relative lack of equipment, even by the standards of the day, Mackenzie's observations in plotting his position on the next expedition were remarkably accurate. On October 10, 1792, he left Fort Chipewyan with the intention of spending the winter farther west and assembling a crew. At the junction of the Peace and Smoky Rivers he build Fort Fork (later Peace River, West Alberta). Having assembled a modest-sized crew of nine, including two American Indian interpreters, the expedition departed Fort Fork on May 9, 1793, in canoes, each twenty-five feet long and capable of carrying three thousand pounds.

Sir Alexander Mackenzie. (Library of Congress)

Mackenzie headed due west up the Peace River. Its headwaters were shallow and exceedingly rocky, making travel difficult. Many members of the expedition urged turning back and abandoning the mission, but Mackenzie would not yield. After crossing the watershed of the Peace River over the Continental Divide to the Frazer River, he was advised by indigenous peoples to take the shorter overland route instead of following the Frazer to its mouth. The overland route was more difficult, however, for the party was required to use a pass at about 6,000 feet (1,800 meters) above sea level. When they descended into the Bella Coola River valley, the explorers met friendly Indians. From a high point at the Indian village, Mackenzie wrote on July 17, "I could perceive the termination of the river, and its discharge into a narrow arm of the sea." Proceeding farther, they encountered unfriendly Indians whose presence prevented any extensive exploration of the area. Nevertheless, they did canoe into the North Bentinck Arm at the mouth of the Bella Coola. There, on a large rock, Mackenzie wrote, "Alexander Mackenzie, from Canada, by land, the twenty-second of July, one thousand seven hundred and ninety-three." The following day they began the return trip to Fort Chipewyan, which they reached on August 24, having traveled more than 2,300 miles.

Both expeditions are noted not only for their length but for their speed as well. Mackenzie was a man of considerable physical strength and stamina. Given the difficulties involved, he was also not easily discouraged. He expected the same from others, and they met those expectations. It is noteworthy that the wisdom of his leadership brought both expeditions back safely. At twenty-nine years of age, Mackenzie was the first white person to cross English-speaking North America—but these efforts exacted a heavy price. Mackenzie spent the winter of 1793 at Fort Chipewyan on Lake Athabasca, where he experienced a deep depression and nearly had a nervous breakdown.

The rest of his life was almost an anticlimax. Mackenzie left the West in 1794 and unsuccessfully tried to implement a plan for a unified fur trade that would include the North West Company; its longtime rival, the Hudson's Bay Company; and the British East India Company. If the plan had been adopted, it would have unified the collecting and marketing of furs in the British Empire.

Mackenzie's interest in this trade plan was diverted for a time when he was offered a partnership in McTavish, Frobisher, and Company, which controlled a majority of the North West Company stock. Mackenzie and McTavish continually argued about Mackenzie's plans for the fur trade. When the partnership expired in November of 1799, Mackenzie left for England. There he wrote an account of his travels. His book, popularly known as *Voyages*, was published in 1801. This work attracted such immediate attention that he was knighted only two months after its publication.

Voyages also outlined Mackenzie's grand plan for the fur trade. Mackenzie even presented the plan to the British colonial secretary. Returning to Montreal in 1802, Mackenzie tried again to implement his trading plan through his involvement with yet another fur-trading company, but to no avail. Thwarted, Mackenzie briefly entered politics and was elected to the House of Assembly of Lower Canada, serving from 1804 to 1808. He seldom attended sessions and returned to Great Britain several times, making his permanent home there in 1810.

On April 12, 1812, at the age of forty-eight, Sir Alexander Mackenzie married the wealthy fourteen-year-old Geddes Mackenzie (no relation). At their estate at Avoch, Scotland, a daughter and two sons were born. By this time his health began to fail, and he went to Edinburgh for medical attention. On the return trip to Avoch, Mackenzie died suddenly at an inn near Dunkeld, on March 12, 1820.

SIGNIFICANCE

In some ways, Sir Alexander Mackenzie's life could be accounted a failure. He was unable to help the Montreal-based North West Company to outflank its more centrally based rival, the Hudson's Bay Company, by finding a water route to the Pacific Ocean. When he did reach the Pacific, the route was not practical. His dream of uniting the fur trade under one cooperative venture came to nothing.

In other, more significant, ways, however, Mackenzie was a success. He explored to its full extent one of the greatest rivers on Earth. He crossed North America twelve years before Lewis and Clark. Through his expeditions, and through his book, *Voyages*, Mackenzie greatly enlarged knowledge of British North America. These explorations greatly strengthened Great Britain's territorial claims in the area. His efforts not only amassed a personal fortune but also gained for him recognition in the many geographical features named for him, most notably the Mackenzie River and the district of Mackenzie in Canada's Northwest Territories. They remain monuments to this intrepid explorer.

—Joseph F. Rishel

FURTHER READING

Daniells, Roy. *Alexander Mackenzie and the North West.* New York: Barnes and Noble Books, 1969. Although concentrating on his explorations, this book has a chapter treating Mackenzie's later life and a chapter assessing his achievements. Six maps; illustrated.

Gough, Barry M. *First Across the Continent: Sir Alexander Mackenzie.* Norman: University of Oklahoma Press, 1997. Biography of Mackenzie, portraying him as a hardheaded businessman who traveled to Canada to garner profits in the fur trade.

Hayes, Derek. *First Crossing: Alexander Mackenzie, His Expedition Across North America, and the Opening of the Continent.* Vancouver, B.C.: Douglas & McIntyre, 2001. A detailed account of Mackenzie's expedition, placed within the context of the Canadian fur trade. Contains numerous illustrations, maps, and photographs.

Mackenzie, Alexander. *The Journals and Letters of Sir Alexander Mackenzie.* Edited by Kaye Lamb. Toronto, Ont.: Macmillan of Canada, 1970. This book is one of a series published for the Hakluyt Society. It includes Mackenzie's diary for both expeditions and all of his letters. Contains an excellent bibliography.

_____. *Voyages from Montreal, on the River St. Laurence, Through the Continent of North America, to the*

Frozen and Pacific Oceans, in the Years 1789 and 1793: With a Preliminary Account of the Rise, Progress, and Present State of the Fur Trade of That Country. Edited by William Combe. London: T. Cadell, Jr., and W. Davies, 1801. Published in New York and Philadelphia in the same year, this is Mackenzie's original work. About one-fourth of the book is devoted to a discussion of the fur trade, one-fourth to the first expedition, and one-half to the second expedition.

Sheppe, Walter. *First Man West: Alexander Mackenzie's Journal of His Voyage to the Pacific Coast of Canada in 1793.* Berkeley: University of California Press, 1962. This is Mackenzie's diary with Sheppe's intermittent explanations. Contains true maps of Mackenzie's route.

Smith, James K. *Alexander Mackenzie, Explorer: The Hero Who Failed.* New York: McGraw-Hill Ryerson, 1973. Quotes much primary source material. Ap-

praises Mackenzie, taking into account the social and economic setting. Gives some treatment of his later life. Well illustrated.

Vail, Philip. *The Magnificent Adventures of Alexander Mackenzie.* New York: Dodd, Mead, 1964. This book reads easily. It discusses Mackenzie's early life as well as his explorations but devotes only four pages to his life after 1793.

See also: Vitus Jonassen Bering; William Bligh; Louis-Antoine de Bougainville; James Bruce; James Cook; Richard Howe; Arthur Phillip; George Vancouver.

Related articles in *Great Events from History: The Eighteenth Century, 1701-1800:* December 5, 1766-March, 16, 1769: Bougainville Circumnavigates the Globe; August 25, 1768-February 14, 1779: Voyages of Captain Cook; July 22, 1793: Mackenzie Reaches the Arctic Ocean.

COLIN MACLAURIN
Scottish mathematician

Maclaurin, the greatest British mathematician of the eighteenth century, developed and extended Sir Isaac Newton's work in fluxions (calculus) and gravitation and made important new discoveries in geometry and mathematical analysis.

Born: February, 1698; Kilmodan, Argyllshire, Scotland
Died: January 14, 1746; Edinburgh, Scotland
Areas of achievement: Mathematics, physics

EARLY LIFE
Colin Maclaurin was born in the western Scottish county of Argyll. He was the youngest of the three sons of John Maclaurin, a learned minister of Kilmodan parish. John, the eldest son, followed in his father's footsteps and became a minister. Daniel, the second son, manifested signs of extraordinary genius but died young. Colin, too, was a child prodigy, but he never knew his father, who died when Colin was six weeks old. Further tragedy struck when he was nine years old, with the death of his mother. His father's brother, also a minister, became guardian of the children.

In 1709, at the early age of eleven, Colin entered the University of Glasgow, where he studied theology for a year. During this time, he became friendly with Robert Simson, a professor of mathematics, from whom he ac-

quired a passionate interest in Euclid's geometry and in other ancient Greek mathematics. He also became interested in Sir Isaac Newton's work, and this led to his thesis "On the Power of Gravity," which he publicly defended in 1715 and for which he was awarded a master of arts degree. He remained at Glasgow another year to study theology, after which he returned to live with his uncle in their Highland home beside Loch Fyne.

He enjoyed wandering over the hills as well as reading mathematics, philosophy, and the classics. Some of his notebook entries that have survived from this time reveal his sensitivity to the beauties of nature, which he deeply believed manifested God's perfections. He abandoned this Highland life in 1717, when, following a competitive examination, he was appointed to the chair of mathematics at Marischal College, Aberdeen, even though he was only nineteen years old. This first appointment marked the start of his brilliant mathematical career.

LIFE'S WORK
Colin Maclaurin's accomplishments grew out of Newton's. He first met Newton in 1719 on a visit to London. Newton was favorably impressed by the young Scottish mathematician, and they became friends. Maclaurin had already contributed papers to the *Philosophical Transac-*

tions of the Royal Society, and he was soon elected a fellow of this society of which Newton was president.

During this time, Maclaurin was working on a book about geometry, which was published, with Newton's approval, in 1720. The book, whose full title was *Geometria organica: Sive, Descriptio linearum curvarum universalis* (organic geometry, with the description of universal linear curves), contained new and elegant methods for generating conics (circle, ellipse, hyperbola, and parabola). Maclaurin also devised an elaborate treatment of higher plane curves that was superior to Newton's earlier results. Maclaurin proved many important theorems that could be found, without proof, in Newton's work. He also discovered many new theorems; for example, he showed that many curves of the second and higher degrees could be described by the intersection of two movable angles.

In 1722, Maclaurin left Scotland to serve as companion and tutor to the eldest son of Lord Polwarth, British plenipotentiary at Cambrai in northern France. Maclaurin and his young charge visited Paris for a short time and then resided for a much longer period at Lorraine, where Maclaurin wrote a paper on the impact of bodies, for which he was awarded a prize by the Academy of Sciences. The sudden death of his pupil caused him to return to Aberdeen, but, because of problems connected with his three-year absence from the university without leave, he was unable to resume his position. Newton again stepped in to help, and it was largely through his strong recommendation that Maclaurin became, in November, 1724, deputy professor for the elderly James Gregory at Edinburgh University. (This James Gregory was the nephew of the famous Scottish mathematician of the same name, who had been appointed to the first chair of mathematics at Edinburgh in 1674, a year before his tragic death at the age of thirty-six.) Newton even wrote privately to the lord provost of Edinburgh, offering to contribute £20 a year toward Maclaurin's salary.

A short time later, in 1725, the Edinburgh position in mathematics became available, and on the recommendation of Newton, Maclaurin took up the position that he would occupy for the rest of his life. His outstanding success at Edinburgh fully vindicated Newton's trust in him. He lectured on a wide range of topics, including the *Elements* of Euclid, spherical trigonometry, astronomy, and Newton's *Philosophiae naturalis principia mathematica* (1687; *The Mathematical Principles of Natural Philosophy*, 1729; best known as *Principia*). His classes were well attended, and his lectures as well as his writings were models of lucid and logical construction.

Edinburgh provided Maclaurin with the opportunity to develop and share his many talents. He was a skilled experimenter who constructed clever and useful mechanical devices. He made valuable astronomical observations, and he advocated building an observatory in Scotland. He also made actuarial tables for the budding insurance companies of Edinburgh. He took an active part in improving the maps of the Orkney and Shetland Islands, and he was even eager to make a voyage to find a northeast polar passage by way of Greenland to the southern seas.

Maclaurin's growing fame also gave him the opportunity to play an important role in Edinburgh society. For example, he was influential in persuading the members of the newly formed Edinburgh Society for Improving Medical Knowledge to enlarge its scope. The new organization, named the Philosophical Society, reflected this change, and Maclaurin became one of its secretaries. This society later became the Royal Society of Edinburgh.

In 1733, Maclaurin married Anne Stewart, the daughter of the solicitor general for Scotland. They had seven children, of whom two sons and three daughters survived him. An engraving of Maclaurin from the Edinburgh period depicts him as a stocky man with heavy eyebrows, a strong nose, and a weak chin. His mien is determined and serious, as befits a distinguished Scottish professor and disciple of Newton.

Throughout his Edinburgh career Maclaurin sought to silence the criticism of Newton's work on differential calculus (which he and Maclaurin called fluxions). The most influential of these critics was George Berkeley, bishop of Cloyne. In 1734, Berkeley published *The Analyst: Or, A Discourse Addressed to an Infidel Mathematician*, in which he attacked Newton's ideas on fluxions. The infidel mathematician was Edmond Halley, the great astronomer and religious skeptic, who had convinced one of Berkeley's dying friends to refuse the last rites because of the untenability of Christian doctrines. Berkeley denied neither the utility of fluxions nor the validity of their results. He did confess, however, to confusion about the meaning of fluxions. According to their defenders, fluxions were neither finitely large nor infinitely small, and yet they were not nothing. Berkeley concluded acidly that they were the "ghosts of departed quantities."

Berkeley's criticism stung. Maclaurin felt that a reply was necessary. He thought that Berkeley had misrepresented the method of fluxions by depicting it as full of mysteries and based on false reasoning. Since fluxions were opaque to someone of Berkeley's intelligence, Maclaurin believed that Newton's method needed new and more vigorous arguments to support it.

A Treatise of Fluxions, Maclaurin's greatest work, was published in 1742. The book was an attempt to establish fluxions on as sound a basis as Greek geometry. Maclaurin began, like Newton, with the concepts of space, time, and motion, and then he systematically elaborated Newton's version of the calculus. Since his readers were more familiar with velocity than with strictly mathematical variables, Maclaurin approached Berkeley's difficulties by considering motion. Maclaurin agreed with Berkeley that the infinitely small was inconceivable, but he did not see any objection to bringing into geometry the idea of an instantaneous velocity. Indeed, for Maclaurin, mathematics included both the properties of motion and the properties of figures. Using this background analysis of motion, he went on to show how fluxions were measured by the quantities they would generate if they were to continue moving uniformly.

Maclaurin's search for a rigorous foundation for fluxions was commendable but in the end unsuccessful. Nevertheless, his analysis did leave hints that future mathematicians would fruitfully follow. Furthermore, his book was not only a defense of Newton's methods; it was also an investigation into a variety of other problems in geometry and physics. For example, he developed a test for the convergence of an infinite series, and, for the first time, he gave the correct method for deciding between a maximum and a minimum of a function by investigating the sign of a higher derivative.

In *A Treatise of Fluxions*, Maclaurin also built on many of the physical principles enunciated by Newton in the *Principia*. For example, he analyzed the tides as a problem in applied geometry. His interest in this subject had begun in 1740 when he submitted an essay on the cause of the tides for a prize offered by the French Academy of Sciences. He shared the award with Daniel Bernoulli and Leonhard Euler, both of whom also based their work on a proposition in the *Principia*. In his account, Maclaurin showed that a homogeneous fluid revolving uniformly about an axis under the action of gravity assumes at equilibrium the shape of an ellipsoid of revolution.

Maclaurin's concerns were not always centered on mathematics and physics. In 1745, when Charles Edward Stuart, the Young Pretender, landed in Scotland and proclaimed that his father James was rightful king, Maclaurin took an active role in opposing him. When the

Young Pretender and his army of Highlanders marched against Edinburgh, Maclaurin helped prepare trenches and barricades for the defense of the city. Despite these efforts, the Jacobite rebels captured the city, and Maclaurin, to avoid submitting to the pretender, was forced to flee to York. Here he found refuge with Archbishop Thomas Herring. When it became clear that the Jacobites were not going to occupy Edinburgh, Maclaurin returned to Scotland, but the energy he had expended in the trench warfare and in the flight to York sapped his strength and severely undermined his health. He died soon after his return to Edinburgh, in 1746, shortly before his forty-eighth birthday. A few hours before his death, he dictated some passages of a work he had been writing on Newton's philosophy, in which he affirmed his unwavering belief in a future life.

SIGNIFICANCE

Colin Maclaurin was the ablest and most spirited of the defenders and developers of Newton's methods. He was a strong advocate of Newton's geometrical techniques, and his success in using them influenced other, less able British mathematicians to try to follow. He has been best remembered for his defense of Newton against Berkeley, but he also extended Newton's work; for example, he applied Newton's analysis of the gravitation of a sphere to the problem of ellipsoids.

Like Newton, Maclaurin loved geometry. One of the ironies of Maclaurin's work is that, though he emphasized geometry over analysis, his name is commemorated for the discoveries he made in analysis. Continental mathematicians emphasized analysis over geometry, and some of them—Euler, for example—rejected geometry completely as a basis for the calculus and tried to work solely with algebraic (analytic) functions. Maclaurin, on the other hand, adopted a geometric style in his book on fluxions because of certain logical difficulties that seemed to him to be insurmountable unless one were to use geometry.

Newton and Maclaurin showed the power of the geometric approach to solve many mathematical and physical problems, but this success also had harmful consequences, for it led Britons to follow these geometric methods and to neglect the analytic methods that were being pursued so successfully in the rest of Europe. As a result, most British mathematicians came to think that many problems could be solved without using the calculus. This had the effect of retarding the more powerful analytic methods in Great Britain. Thus, after Maclaurin, British mathematics suffered an eclipse because he and

Newton had inadvertently helped steer it into unproductive paths.

Despite the ultimate infertility of Maclaurin's geometric style, he still had admirers, such as Joseph-Louis Lagrange, the great French mathematician. Lagrange was proud that his famous book on analytic mechanics contained not a single geometric diagram. Maclaurin's work, on the other hand, dealt largely in lines and figures, and he saw the great book of the universe written in this geometric language. Lagrange, who pictured the universe in terms of numbers and equations, nevertheless appreciated the insight and integrity of Maclaurin, whose work, Lagrange once said, surpassed that of Archimedes—a compliment that would have deeply pleased Maclaurin.

—*Robert J. Paradowski*

FURTHER READING

Boyer, Carl B. *A History of Mathematics*. New York: John Wiley and Sons, 1968. Written by a historian of mathematics, this book is intended to be a basic textbook for students of mathematics. Also appropriate, however, for general readers.

_____. *The History of the Calculus and Its Conceptual Development*. Mineola, N.Y.: Dover, 1959. An unabridged reprint of the work published in 1949 under the title *The Concepts of the Calculus*. Boyer traces the development of calculus from antiquity to the twentieth century, and offers a good account of Maclaurin's role as defender of Newton's theory of fluxions.

Grabiner, Judith V. "Was Newton's Calculus a Dead End? The Continental Influence of Maclaurin's Treatise of Fluxions." *American Mathematical Monthly* 104, no. 5 (May, 1997): 393. Explains how Maclaurin's treatise helped to further the development of Newtonian calculus.

Guicciardini, Niccoló. *The Development of Newtonian Calculus in Britain, 1700-1800*. New York: Cambridge University Press, 1989. A comprehensive survey of the research and teaching of Newtonian calculus, including information on Maclaurin's ideas about fluxions.

Hedman, Bruce. "Colin Maclaurin's Quaint Word Problems." *College Mathematics Journal* 31, no. 4 (September, 2000): 286. Discusses Maclaurin's solutions to several algebra word problems, including the Ptolemaic riddle and wage, age, and rate problems.

Kline, Morris. *Mathematical Thought from Ancient to Modern Times*. New York: Oxford University Press, 1972. Covers major mathematical developments from ancient times through the first few decades of the twentieth century. Kline aims to present the chief ideas that have shaped the history of mathematics rather than focus on individual mathematicians. Consequently, his treatment of Maclaurin emphasizes the principal themes of his work rather than the events of his life.

Maclaurin, Colin. *An Account of Sir Isaac Newton's Philosophical Discoveries*. Sources of Science 74. Introduction by L. L. Laundan. New York: Johnson Reprint, 1968. A reprint of a 1748 work on Newton by Maclaurin.

_____. *The Collected Letters of Colin Maclaurin*. Edited by Stella Mills. Nantwich, England: Shiva, 1982. Maclaurin's letters provide details of his life and ideas.

Mooney, John, and Ian Stewart. "Colin Maclaurin and Glendaruel." *Mathematical Intelligencer* 16, no. 1 (Winter, 1994): 48. Recounts Maclaurin's life and career by focusing on his hometown, Glendaruel, site of a memorial in his honor.

Turnbull, Herbert Westren. *The Great Mathematicians*. New York: New York University Press, 1961. This brief but excellent book, a biographical history of mathematics, attempts to show how mathematicians use both imagination and reason to make discoveries.

See also: Maria Gaetana Agnesi; Jean le Rond d'Alembert; George Berkeley; Leonhard Euler; William Herschel; Joseph-Louis Lagrange.

Related articles in *Great Events from History: The Eighteenth Century, 1701-1800:* 1704: Newton Publishes *Optics*; 1705: Halley Predicts the Return of a Comet; March 23-26, 1708: Defeat of the "Old Pretender"; 1718: Bernoulli Publishes His Calculus of Variations; 1726-1729: Voltaire Advances Enlightenment Thought in Europe; 1733: De Moivre Describes the Bell-Shaped Curve; 1740: Maclaurin's Gravitational Theory; 1743-1744: D'Alembert Develops His Axioms of Motion; August 19, 1745-September 20, 1746: Jacobite Rebellion; 1748: Agnesi Publishes *Analytical Institutions*; 1748: Euler Develops the Concept of Function; 1763: Bayes Advances Probability Theory.

JAMES MADISON
President of the United States (1809-1817)

Madison was the primary architect of the U.S. Constitution and the fourth U.S. president. His lasting reputation is based less on his conduct as president or as secretary of state than on his contribution to the writing of the Constitution and securing its ratification. He also is remembered for helping to establish the new government and political parties, and for being a superior legislator and nation-builder.

Born: March 16, 1751; Port Conway, Prince George County, Virginia
Died: June 28, 1836; Montpelier, Orange County, Virginia
Area of achievement: Government and politics

EARLY LIFE
James Madison was the son of James Madison, Sr., and Nelly Conway Madison. James, Jr., was the eldest of twelve children. The family was not wealthy but lived in comfortable circumstances. Young Madison was enrolled at the age of eleven in the boarding school of Donald Robertson, and he studied under him for five years. He studied two additional years at home under the tutelage of Thomas Martin, an Anglican minister. In 1769, Madison entered Princeton. Because of his previous training, he was able to complete the four-year course in two years, graduating in September, 1771. This effort took a toll on his health. He appears to have suffered from depression and epileptiform hysteria.

In May, 1776, Madison began his political career as a member of the convention that drew up the Virginia constitution. He was then elected to the Virginia Assembly. There, Madison joined with Thomas Jefferson in an effort to disestablish the Church of England. They eventually became lifelong friends and close political associates. Madison was not reelected, but he was chosen by the legislature in 1778 to the governor's council. Despite his unimposing five-foot, six-inch stature and a slender frame and boyish features, Madison obviously made an impression upon the legislature with his intelligence and diligence. He was never a great orator, but he was an agreeable, persuasive speaker. He possessed great political skill and generally was a dominating figure in legislative bodies throughout his career.

In December, 1779, Madison was chosen a delegate to the Continental Congress. He took his seat in March, 1780, and quickly established himself as one of the most effective and valuable members of that body. For most of the next forty years, he would play an important, and at times major, role in the critical years of the early republic.

LIFE'S WORK
In the Continental Congress, James Madison took a nationalist position. He often collaborated with Alexander Hamilton. He labored hard to strengthen the government and amend the Articles of Confederation to give it the power to levy duties. Madison wrote an earnest address to the states, pleading for national unity, but it was to no avail, and the amendment failed.

In 1784, Madison was elected to the Virginia legislature, where he worked to defend religious freedom. His famous "Memorial and Remonstrance Against Religious Assessments" helped defeat a scheme by Patrick Henry to impose a general assessment for the support of religion. Madison then pushed Jefferson's "Bill for Religious Liberty" to passage, completing the disestablishment of the Anglican Church begun in 1779. Madison's "Memorial and Remonstrance" foreshadowed the clause on religious liberty in the First Amendment to the U.S. Constitution.

Madison was a delegate to the Annapolis Convention of 1786, and he was named to the Virginia delegation to attend the federal convention at Philadelphia in 1787. When the convention opened in May, Madison had prepared an extensive proposal to revise the Articles of Confederation. The Virginia Plan, presented by Edmund Randolph but based on Madison's ideas, became the basis of discussion throughout the summer months. Madison led the movement to grant the federal government greater authority over national affairs. While he did not always carry his point of view, he clearly was the dominating figure in the convention, so that he is often called the "Father of the Constitution." The journal that he kept on the convention is the most complete record of the proceedings available.

Madison also played a prominent role in securing the ratification of the Constitution in Virginia. His influence was crucial in overcoming the opposition of Patrick Henry and George Mason. In retrospect, perhaps his most important work was in cooperating with Alexander Hamilton and John Jay in writing a series of essays for New York newspapers that were later collected and published in 1788 as *The Federalist*, also known as the Federalist papers. Madison wrote nearly thirty of the eighty-five essays, which are justly celebrated today as still the most authoritative commentary on the U.S. Constitution and a major contribution to political science. His most notable contributions were his reflections on the plural society in numbers ten and fifty-one; the dual nature of the new government, federal in extent of powers and national in operation, in number thirty-nine; and the interrelationship of checks and balances in number forty-eight.

Madison was elected to the House of Representatives, and within a week of entering the House in April, 1789, he began the work of establishing a strong and effective central government. He led the movement to establish revenues for the new government by imposing import duties; he presented a motion to create the Departments of State, Treasury, and War and gave the executive broad powers over these offices; and he proposed a set of constitutional amendments that eventually became the Bill of Rights.

Madison served in the first five Congresses. His inherent conservatism manifested itself in his growing opposition to Hamilton's fiscal policies and the government's pro-British tendency. After 1790, Madison organized the congressional alliances that became the basis for the first national political parties. More than Jefferson, Madison deserves to be called the founder of the modern-day Democratic Party.

On September 15, 1794, at the age of forty-three, Madison married a young widow, Dolley Payne Todd. It proved to be a long and happy marriage, and the young wife, Dolley Madison, gained a reputation as a famous hostess during her husband's presidential years.

Madison retired from Congress in 1797. Federalists, taking advantage of the hysteria generated by the XYZ affair and the quasi-war with France, passed the Alien and Sedition Acts to curb foreign- and native-born critics of the administration. Madison and Jefferson drafted resolutions adopted by the Kentucky and Virginia legislatures in 1798. These resolutions not only criticized the Alien and Sedition Acts but also laid down the doctrine of nullification for states' rights. In later years, Madison argued that these statements were protests intended primarily to secure the cooperation of the states, but they also expressed positions dangerous to the unity of the new republic. Nevertheless, these resolutions contributed to the overthrow of the Federalists and secured the election of Jefferson in 1800. Jefferson brought his long-time friend into the government as his secretary of state.

Later, in 1807, Madison became president, primarily a result of support from Jefferson, but his presidency was beset by many problems in the early years of the nineteenth century. In the closing years of his presidency, Madison signed bills establishing a standing army and enlarging the naval establishment, the Bank of the United States, and a protective tariff. He did, however, veto an internal improvement bill as unconstitutional. He left office on March 4, 1817, and except for participation in the Virginia Constitutional Convention in 1829, his political career was over. He lived his remaining years quietly at Montpelier. Occasionally, he offered advice to his successor, James Monroe, and he wrote defending his actions over his long career. He also devoted time to arranging his notes on the Constitutional Convention for publication. They were not published until 1840, four years after his death on June 28, 1836.

President James Madison. (Library of Congress)

SIGNIFICANCE

James Madison was truly a nation-builder. Perhaps the outstanding political theorist and political writer in a generation that produced many first-rate thinkers, Madison often carried his position by sheer brilliance and cool, dispassionate reasoning. He lacked the dramatic style often useful in public life. He advanced because of his abilities and not because of his personality. He was a first-rate legislator, one of the most effective this country has produced. He was, on the other hand, only an average administrator. He failed to provide dynamic leadership during his presidency, especially during the War of 1812.

There are certain consistent themes throughout his career. First, there were his efforts to secure freedom of conscience and other personal rights and liberties. Second, he consistently supported and advanced the republican form of government based broadly on the popular will. Finally, throughout his life his devotion to the union was paramount. One of the last actions of his life was to write a document entitled "Advice to My Country." It concluded with the advice that the union "be cherished and perpetuated."

—*C. Edward Skeen*

FURTHER READING

Brant, Irving. *The Fourth President: A Life of James Madison*. Indianapolis, Ind.: Bobbs-Merrill, 1970. A distillation of Brant's standard six-volume biography of Madison. Valuable especially because of the author's extensive knowledge of his subject. For a complete study of Madison's life, consult Brant's six-volume study.

Cooke, Jacob E., ed. *The Federalist*. Middletown, Conn.: Wesleyan University Press, 1961. There are many editions of the *Federalist* papers, but this collection is especially useful because of Cooke's extensive and valuable notes.

Ketcham, Ralph. *James Madison: A Biography*. New York: Macmillan, 1971. The best one-volume biography. Ketcham's work is well researched, well documented, and well written. Although based heavily on Irving Brant's six-volume study, it is more balanced than Brant's biography.

Koch, Adrienne. *Jefferson and Madison: The Great Collaboration*. New York: Alfred A. Knopf, 1950. An excellent study of the collaboration of the two men, but weighted heavily to the years before Jefferson's presidency. Koch is superb at analyzing political philosophies, describing how Madison was more cautious and often exerted a calming influence on Jefferson.

Matthews, Richard K. *If Men Were Angels: James Madison and the Heartless Empire of Reason*. Lawrence: University Press of Kansas, 1995. A revisionist, negative interpretation of Madison, portraying him as a consistent liberal who highly valued personal liber-

ties. Matthews argues that Madison's views produced a vulgar, materialistic, and anti-intellectual nation.

Meyers, Marvin, ed. *The Mind of the Founder: Sources of the Political Thought of James Madison*. Indianapolis, Ind.: Bobbs-Merrill, 1973. A collection of Madison's letters and writings oriented toward his political thought. Includes an informative introduction by the editor.

Moore, Virginia. *The Madisons: A Biography*. New York: McGraw-Hill, 1979. A combined biography written in a breezy, journalistic style, concentrating on the Madisons' private lives. It is well researched and illuminates early nineteenth century society.

Rutland, Robert Allen. *James Madison: The Founding Father*. Columbia: University of Missouri Press, 1997. A biography by a noted Madison scholar and the editor of Madison's papers. Rutland brings a human dimension to his subject, recounting Madison's goals, frustrations, victories, and defeats.

Stagg, J. C. A. *Mr. Madison's War: Politics, Diplomacy, and Warfare in the Early American Republic, 1783-1830*. Princeton, N.J.: Princeton University Press, 1983. An extremely well researched and well written work. Madison's political and economic views are extensively covered.

Wills, Garry. *James Madison*. New York: Times Books, 2002. One in a series of books providing brief overviews of American presidents' lives and accomplishments. Despite his many achievements before becoming president, Madison, the author argues, lacked executive ability, and his presidency was a near disaster.

See also: John Adams; John Dickinson; Benjamin Franklin; Alexander Hamilton; Patrick Henry; John Jay; Thomas Jefferson; George Mason.

Related articles in *Great Events from History: The Eighteenth Century, 1701-1800:* September 5-October 26, 1774: First Continental Congress; May 10-August 2, 1775: Second Continental Congress; July 4, 1776: Declaration of Independence; March 1, 1781: Ratification of the Articles of Confederation; September 17, 1787: U.S. Constitution Is Adopted; October 27, 1787-May, 1788: Publication of *The Federalist*; 1790's: First U.S. Political Parties; December 15, 1791: U.S. Bill of Rights Is Ratified; October 4, 1797-September 30, 1800: XYZ Affair; June 25-July 14, 1798: Alien and Sedition Acts.

MAHMUD I
Ottoman sultan (r. 1730-1754)

Mahmud I took over a troubled Ottoman Empire following the abdication of his uncle, Ahmed III. He was thwarted in his attempts to rule by unrest within the empire and by skirmishes abroad. He sought to improve the empire by modernizing the army and establishing a military technical school in Uskudar. He is best remembered for brokering the Treaty of Belgrade in 1739.

Born: August 2, 1696; Edirne, Ottoman Empire (now in Turkey)

Died: December 13, 1754; Constantinople, Ottoman Empire (now Istanbul, Turkey)

Areas of achievement: Government and politics, warfare and conquest

EARLY LIFE

Mahmud (mah-MOOD) I was raised in a climate of political stress in the Ottoman Empire. He was secluded for much of his early life and had little direct experience with the outside world. The empire, although led by his uncle, Ahmed III, was essentially controlled by a renegade band of Janissaries.

The reign of Ahmed III is often referred to as the Tulip Age, because Ahmed was caught up in the fever of the brisk trade in tulip bulbs. Finally, angered by the luxurious living and obvious excesses of the sultancy, the Janissaries staged a rebellion that toppled Ahmed III, clearing the way for Mahmud I to become sultan.

The once-elite Janissaries, after they were permitted to marry, became family oriented, making them reluctant to travel to the distant places where they were needed and causing them to practice nepotism, pushing into the Janissary corps their male children, many of whom could not have met the corps' earlier high standards. When he was forced to yield to the Janissaries, Ahmed turned over to them his grand vizier and another important official, both of whom were summarily strangled. Ahmed III went into seclusion, appointing his inexperienced and unworldly thirty-four-year-old nephew, Mahmud, the son of his brother, Mustafa II, to become sultan.

For much of his childhood, Mahmud I was confined in the Cage, a prison, albeit a quite luxurious one. This measure was meant to ensure that he could neither rise up himself nor inspire others to overthrow his uncle Ahmed. Ironically, Ahmed III, after releasing Mahmud I from the Cage and making him sultan, took his place there.

Ahmed remained confined to the Cage for the rest of his life.

LIFE'S WORK

Mahmud I acceded to the sultancy in 1730. Since he had been confined in the Cage during Ahmed III's reign, Mahmud was inexperienced and ill-equipped to assume the duties that were suddenly thrust upon him. Fortunately, he had the aid of the Nubian eunuch, Aga Haji Besir (1653-1746), who, during his long life, served as wise counsel to many sultans and grand viziers.

The new sultan's first act, not unlike the first acts of his Ottoman predecessors, was to execute the leaders of the rebellion that had caused his uncle's sultancy to collapse. Such acts were meant publicly to demonstrate the strength and determination of the new sultan, whose hold on his position was often tenuous at best. The next matter Mahmud faced was the Ottoman-Persian War. Relations with Europe under Ahmed had been quite peaceful, but such was not the case with his eastern neighbors. Forces led by Mahmud experienced some initial victories. Part of western Persia that had been lost during Ahmed's sultancy was recaptured. A treaty in 1732 formally recognized the reclaimed Ottoman territory in Azerbaijan, Daghestan, and Georgia.

These small victories, however, did not continue. By 1733, the flames of war had been rekindled, and Ottoman forces were repulsed as the Persians won back parts of northern Persia near the Ottoman border and portions of the Caucasus. Finally, in 1736, Mahmud was able to broker an agreement, the Treaty of Istanbul, in which his government agreed to recognize the boundaries set by the Treaty of Kasr-I Şirin, which Murad IV had enacted and agreed to in 1639, almost a century earlier. In this treaty, Erivan, Tabriz, and the Zagros Mountains fell on the Iranian side of the Ottoman-Iranian boundary, whereas the Ottomans were given Kars, Van, Kirkuk, Baghdad, and Basra.

Just as this accord was being enacted, a war broke out between the Ottomans and the Russians following a Russian attack on the Crimea in which major Ottoman fortifications were attacked. This conflict was followed in 1737 by an ill-fated Austrian attack on Banja Luka and Niš. The Ottomans subdued the Habsburg forces in Belgrade, forcing the Habsburg army to negotiate a peace with Mahmud's forces and marking a significant victory for the sultan.

This victory for Mahmud had a domino effect, because, even though Russia occupied Khotin, the Austrian defeat brought about Ottoman alliances with Poland, Prussia, and Sweden that placed the Russians in an untenable situation and forced them to negotiate a peace with the Ottomans. The Treaty of Belgrade, brokered by the French and adopted in 1739, called for the withdrawal of Austrian and Russian forces from Ottoman territory. This treaty also ceded Belgrade to the Ottomans.

With French-Ottoman relations at a new high, the Sublime Porte, or council of the grand viziers, granted capitulation to France. Capitulation could be granted to non-Muslims to assure their safety in Muslim countries. Such provisions were first established in the late seventeenth century and were used quite frequently in the following three centuries to protect non-Muslim merchants and others doing business in the Ottoman Empire and to grant them some reduction in the tariffs they faced in their trades.

Peace did not last long. The Iranian ruler, Nādir Shāh, demanded that the Ottomans recognize the Iranian Imamiyya Shia belief as a fifth legitimate school of Islam. In 1743, after Mahmud refused to recognize the Imamiyya Shia as requested, another war, lasting until 1746, erupted between the Ottomans and the Persians. There was no clear victor in this conflict, so, despite considerable loss of life on both sides, the original land borders were preserved.

Early in his sultancy, Mahmud engaged the French strategist Claude Alexandre de Bonneval, also known as Ahmed Pasha, to reorganize the Ottoman grenadiers, a process that began in 1733 and continued for some years. Simultaneously, Mahmud established a military technical school (*Hendesehāne*) in Üsküdar to provide technical training for those who would lead future Ottoman military forces. These initiatives, which, if extended, would greatly have strengthened his nation's armed forces, were strongly resisted by powerful Janissaries, who thwarted any changes that threatened to compromise their authority and position.

SIGNIFICANCE

Mahmud I is one of the least recognized Ottoman sultans. He began his reign under a cloud, because he had little training to be sultan, having suffered confinement during his first thirty-four years. He inherited a nation at odds with its rulers and dominated by a splinter group of dissidents, the Janissaries, who limited the power of the sultancy.

Mahmud continued some of the excesses of the Tulip Age, holding firmly to its social and cultural practices. He attempted to serve his subjects in positive ways, engaging in public works that he hoped might being some honor to a regime that was, at best, viewed with public suspicion and scorn. He was responsible for the building of many mosques, as well as libraries and schools. In a country where a safe water supply was not always assured, he saw to it that water mains were installed where they were most needed to bring that vital substance to the populace.

During Mahmud's reign, İbrahim Müteferrika operated a printing press and, with Mahmud's apparent blessing, employed a contingent of twenty-five translators to bring out Turkish editions of European works of scientific importance in such fields as physics, economics, geography, cartography, medicine, and astronomy. He introduced the Ottomans to the thinking of such giants as Aristotle, René Descartes, and Galileo.

Mahmud served as sultan until the end of his life. On December 13, 1754, on his way home after attending Friday services at a mosque in Istanbul, he fell to the ground and died, the victim of a heart attack that took his life at age fifty-eight. His brother, Osman III, succeeded him.

—R. Baird Shuman

FURTHER READING

Barber, Noel. *The Sultans*. New York: Simon and Schuster, 1973. Barber presents intimate portraits of the lives of the sultans. Although he devotes little time specifically to Mahmud I, he provides compelling background material that helps one understand the Ottoman sultans.

Kinross, John Patrick. *The Ottoman Centuries: The Rise and Fall of the Turkish Empire*. New York: William Morrow, 1977. A detailed resource that covers well the Austrian campaign of Mahmud I and also, although dubbing him an ineffective ruler, shows how he brought new scientific knowledge to his empire.

Mansel, Philip. *Constantinople: City of the World's Desire, 1453-1924*. New York: St. Martin's Press, 1996. This readable book is broad in its coverage of almost half a millennium of Ottoman history.

Somel, Selçuk Aksin. *Historical Dictionary of the Ottoman Empire*. Lanham, Md.: Scarecrow Press, 2003. Although the entries in this excellent reference book are brief, they are direct and include valuable cross-references. An outstanding resource for all aspects of the Ottoman Empire.

See also: Ahmed III; Claude Alexandre de Bonneval; Mustafa III; Nādir Shāh.
Related articles in *Great Events from History: The Eighteenth Century, 1701-1800*: 1702 or 1706: First Arabic Printing Press; November 20, 1710-July 21, 1718: Ottoman Wars with Russia, Venice, and Austria; 1718-1730: Tulip Age; 1736-1739: Russo-Austrian War Against the Ottoman Empire; September 18, 1739: Treaty of Belgrade; 1746: Zāhir al-ʿUmar Creates a Stronghold in Galilee; 1748-1755: Construction of Istanbul's Nur-u Osmaniye Complex; October, 1768-January 9, 1792: Ottoman Wars with Russia.

MARY DE LA RIVIÈRE MANLEY
English political writer

Manley, the first professional female political propagandist in England, supported herself by editing Tory journals and writing novels, plays, poems, and pamphlets. Her politically motivated writings satirized the illicit behavior of major political and court figures, leading to her arrest for libel. Her novel Zarah *is considered one of English literature's first* romans à clef, *a novel that features actual but disguised persons or events.*

Born: c. 1670; Jersey, Channel Islands
Died: July 11, 1724; London, England
Also known as: Delarivière Manley; Delarivier Manley
Areas of achievement: Literature, government and politics

EARLY LIFE

Mary de la Rivière Manley (deh leh reev-yehr man-lee) was the fourth of five children born to Sir Roger Manley and his wife. Some sources cite a birth year of 1663, but documents drafted during Mary's lifetime and the recorded details of her father's life make 1670 a more likely birth date. An older sister named Mary Elizabeth may account for the confusion.

Roger Manley, whose family roots date to William the Conqueror, was knighted by King James I in 1628 and appointed governor of the Channel Islands in 1667. He served in the English navy and honored his commanding officer's wife by giving the uncommon Delarivier name to his own daughter.

Little is known about Mary's mother, other than that she died when the family's two smallest children were quite young. Roger died in 1687, leaving his first cousin, John Manley, guardian of Mary and her younger sister, Cordelia; John boarded them with an elderly aunt. The Glorious Revolution occurred the next year, resulting in the deposition of King James II and spoiling Mary's anticipated rise as lady-in-waiting to the king's wife, Mary of Modena.

In 1688 or 1694, John Manley announced that his wife had died. He then married Mary, who was his cousin, and sequestered her in London. Upon learning Mary was pregnant, he confessed that his first wife was alive and so abandoned Mary less than three years later. Mary's marriage with John, a close relative, left her disgraced and without economic support. She resided with a former mistress of Charles II for about six months and relied possibly on the largesse of a wealthy man until she began supporting herself through writing.

LIFE'S WORK

Mary de la Rivière Manley produced a tremendous number of plays and political writings. During a twenty-one-year period, English theatergoers saw four of her plays performed on the stage. *The Lost Lover: Or, The Jealous Husband* played at London's Theatre Royal in Drury Lane in 1696. The comedy flopped. Soon after, *The Royal Mischief* (1696) ran for six nights at Lincoln's Inn Fields. Although considered a success, the tragedy gained notoriety for its sexually charged subject matter and became the basis for *The Female Wits*, an anonymously authored play ridiculing Manley and two other women playwrights.

About ten years later, in 1706, *Alymna: Or, The Arabian Vow* played at the Queen's Theatre in the Haymarket. The feminist drama closed after only three nights, a victim of strong competition from the opera house and a lavish production that drove up ticket prices. Manley's final play may have been her most successful, but there is some dispute as to whether *Lucius, The First Christian King of Britain: A Tragedy* ran for just three performances or played a profitable fifteen-night run. Shown at Drury Lane in 1717, the drama eschews inflammatory political and feminist subjects in favor of a more "respectable" plot.

The work that propelled Manley to fame, however, was the novel she wrote in 1709 called *Secret Memoirs and Manners of Several Persons of Quality, of Both*

Sexes from the New Atalantis, an Island in the Mediterranean. The political allegory, constructed as a conversation between three female spies, became the best-selling novel of the decade. *Secret Memoirs and Manners* and subsequent volumes in the series pillory notable Whig personalities from Charles II to Queen Anne.

Within two weeks of the release of the second volume, in October of 1709, Manley was arrested for libel, along with her printer and publishers. Four months later, after successfully defending against the charges, the author was set free. She immediately began penning the third volume of the series.

Manley had already proven herself a formidable political propagandist prior to *Secret Memoirs and Manners*. She wrote polemical Tory pamphlets beginning in 1704, and she published *The Secret History of Queen Zarah and the Zarazians* in 1705. The book chronicles Zarah's (Sarah Churchill, duchess of Marlborough) rise to power and vilifies other prominent Whigs along the way. Scholars acknowledge *The Secret History* as one of the first *romans à clef* in English literature.

The Female Tatler was launched in response to the literary periodical the *Tatler* in 1709, and Manley probably edited the first year's issues under the pseudonym Mrs. Crackenthorpe. In 1711, she replaced Jonathan Swift as editor of *The Examiner*, a Tory paper dedicated to abusing the Whig Party and its proponents. She was employed by Swift as a pamphlet writer around the same time. In 1714, Manley publicly retired as a political writer, but her continued prolific output proved the statement disingenuous.

Also in 1714, Manley issued her fictionalized autobiography, *The Adventures of Rivella: Or, The History of the Author of the Atalantis*, under the pen name Sir Charles Lovemore. The book tells the story of Manley's life and is supposedly the posthumous translation into English of a conversation between Lovemore and a young Frenchman. The book barely discusses Manley's writing career and instead focuses on the personal events that shaped her life. Manley's early biographers tended to accept the autobiography as truth, but later scholars have approached it more cautiously.

The Adventures of Rivella recounts Manley's unfortunate marriage to her first cousin, John Manley, as well as numerous other amorous liaisons. Her relationship with John Tilly, the love of her life, fills a considerable number of pages. Although Tilly was married, the pair lived together openly from about 1696 to 1702 and may have had a child together. They engaged in a number of ill-conceived business projects, including alchemy, leaving them in a sorry financial state. When Tilly's wife died in 1702, he married a wealthy widow (reputedly with Manley's blessing), went insane, and died in 1709.

Sometime around 1710 or 1711, Manley moved in with printer John Barber. She wrote *The Adventures of Rivella* during this time and published it with a rival printer. Barber is never mentioned in the book, and he eventually took up with another woman. Manley died soon thereafter, in 1724.

SIGNIFICANCE

Mary de la Rivière Manley is best known for writing scandalous political novels and for flouting social convention. However, this characterization fails to recognize the substantial power she exercised in the English political arena. As one of the first English writers to exploit the press for political ends, Manley figured prominently in the development of scandal reporting as a political weapon. Her works, especially those penned between 1709 and 1711, publicized the vices and illicit behavior of such luminaries as Charles II and Sarah Churchill. Manley's ability to influence public opinion proved such a threat to her political foes, leading to her arrest for libel in 1709.

Being characterized as a writer of the scandalous also overlooks Manley's important place in feminist history. She was able to utilize the press to advance feminist causes, and she openly criticized the social and sexual double standards of her time. She employed her writing as a defense against gender-biased criticism and as a vehicle for promoting her personal interests and the interests of women in general. Her use of a consciously female narrative voice, and in particular the device of female conversation, impacted writers of her time and continues to influence feminist and political writing.

—*Rose Reifsnyder*

FURTHER READING

Anderson, Paul Bunyan. *"Mary Delarivière, a Cavalier's Daughter in Grub Street."* Unpublished Ph.D. dissertation, Harvard University, 1931. A primary source for scholars of Manley, written by her chief biographer.

_____. "Mistress Delarivière Manley's Biography." *Modern Philology* 33 (1936): 261-278. A thoroughly researched and heavily footnoted account of Manley's childhood, family history, and literary career.

Clark, Constance. *Three Augustan Women Playwrights.* New York: Peter Lang, 1986. The introduction to this work provides a social and theatrical context for Manley and other female playwrights. The chapter on

Manley offers biographical details and considers the sources, influences, and critical reception of her plays and political writings. Includes a thorough synopsis of and critical response to her four performed plays.

Herman, Ruth. *The Business of a Woman: The Political Writings of Delarivier Manley*. Newark: University of Delaware Press, 2003. Analyzes Manley's writing techniques and her significance as the first professional woman political journalist. Discusses her writing in its function as Tory propaganda. Includes some biographical information and an extensive bibliography.

McDowell, Paula. *The Women of Grub Street: Press, Politics, and Gender in the London Literary Marketplace, 1678-1730*. New York: Clarendon Press, 1998. Argues that dramatic shifts in English politics and literary production created an unprecedented opportunity for female political involvement, and that Manley's writings and literary strategies exploited this phenomenon for political and personal ends.

Manley, Delarivier. *The Adventures of Rivella*. Edited by Katherine Zelinsky. Orchard Park, N.Y.: Broadview Press, 1999. Manley's fictionalized autobiography of her life. The introduction provides a social and literary context for the novel, and the appendices present texts and excerpts of text written by Manley and her contemporaries.

See also: Joseph Addison; James Boswell; Fanny Burney; Hester Chapone; Sarah Churchill; Hannah Cowley; Samuel Johnson; Mary Wortley Montagu; Hannah More; Samuel Richardson; Anna Seward; Jonathan Swift; Mary Wollstonecraft.

Related articles in *Great Events from History: The Eighteenth Century, 1701-1800:* March 1, 1711: Addison and Steele Establish *The Spectator*; April 25, 1719: Defoe Publishes the First Novel; 1740-1741: Richardson's *Pamela* Establishes the Modern Novel; 1742: Fielding's *Joseph Andrews* Satirizes English Society; March 20, 1750-March 14, 1752: Johnson Issues *The Rambler*; 1792: Wollstonecraft Publishes *A Vindication of the Rights of Woman*.

FIRST EARL OF MANSFIELD
English jurist

As chief justice of the Court of King's Bench, Mansfield made many reforms in procedure and substantive law, virtually initiated the creation of a code of commercial law, and developed an attitude toward judgment consistent with a changing world.

Born: March 2, 1705; Scone, Perthshire, Scotland
Died: March 20, 1793; London, England
Also known as: William Murray (birth name)
Area of achievement: Law

EARLY LIFE

Although William Murray, first earl of Mansfield, modestly ascribed his success to his having been born the son of a nobleman and having the funds to support himself well, he was actually the fourth son of David, the Fifth Viscount Stormont, an impoverished and minor Scottish noble who could give his son little aid in attaining the heights that he eventually achieved, and Margaret, the only daughter of David Scott of Scotsarvet.

Murray received his early education at Perth Grammar School. Leaving Scotland for London in 1718, he studied at Westminster School and Christ Church College, Oxford, and was called to the English bar at Lincoln's Inn in 1730. From the first, he distinguished himself as a fine orator, but, although he won considerable acclaim in several cases, he did not obtain the financial success that marked advocates of the law. Not until his speech before the jury as a junior counsel to Sergeant of the Law Eyre in *Cibber v. Sloper* (1738), in which he appeared for the defendant, did Murray begin to see financial success. Later in life he remarked that as a result of *Cibber v. Sloper*, "Henceforth business poured in upon me from all quarters, and from a few hundred pounds a year, I fortunately found myself in the receipt of thousands." With such financial success assured, he was married to the Lady Elizabeth Finch, daughter of the earl of Winchelsea, with whom, although there were no children, he had a long and happy marriage.

This marriage aided him in embarking into the field of politics as well, without which alliance it would have been difficult for an attorney, no matter how fitted, to advance in the judiciary. On the fall of Robert Walpole from the prime ministry in 1742, the earl of Winchelsea became the first lord of the Admiralty, and through his influence Murray not only gained the friendship of the influential duke of Newcastle but also entered Parliament as a member of the House of Commons from Boroughbridge, while at the same time he became solicitor general on November 27, 1742, a post he retained until 1754, when he became attorney general. During those years as solicitor general, he was not only the major law officer of the Crown but also, as a result of his natural abilities, the leader of the House of Commons.

John C. Campbell, writing in the early nineteenth century, in his *Lives of the Chief Justices of England* (1857), declared the years 1742 to 1754 to be "the longest and most brilliant Solicitor Generalship in the annals of Westminster Hall," a solicitorship marked not only by the brilliance of Murray's speeches but also by a morality and honesty that raised the position far above the venality and corruption of many other offices in the government. For example, although Murray was a Scotsman whose family strongly supported the ambitions of the Stuarts to return to the throne of England, he had cast his allegiance to the Hanover kings. Although it must have been painful for Murray to take an active part in the 1746-1747 prosecutions of the rebels—a number of whom included his own cousins—after their failure in the Battle of Culloden, he did so with firmness and moderation, so much so that he was lauded after trial by several of the rebel chieftains themselves, such as Lord Balmerino and Lord Lovat. Although he was noteworthy in his zeal for justice based on law, he was also equally known for the moderation he exhibited in applying the law with regard to the frailties of human nature and with a definitive kindliness that stood in contrast to the reputation for harshness attributed to his great predecessor, Sir Edward Coke.

While solicitor general, he drafted in 1752 an answer to Frederick the Great of Prussia that was termed a response without equal by Montesquieu and has been accepted by some writers as the foundation of the modern law of neutrality.

In the political arena, Murray was not as successful, for in the House of Commons he was forced to endure the fierce opposition of the finest orator in England, the great Commoner, William Pitt the Elder. Murray was simply not equipped by nature for political life. In the words of one of his biographers, "He lacked the eagerness in attack, the resilience in defeat, the relish for a shrewd blow, offered or received, which are essential factors in a final Parliamentary success." On the death of Henry Pelham in 1754, Murray could have become prime minister, but

First Earl of Mansfield. (Library of Congress)

he refused this position, and the position as speaker of the House of Commons as well.

Therefore, when Sir Dudley Ryder, attorney general, became chief justice of the Court of King's Bench, the highest court in the land with the exception of the Court of Exchequer Chamber and the House of Lords itself, Murray was appointed attorney general in his place. Two years later, when Ryder died, Murray became chief justice of the Court of King's Bench, although still retaining the very difficult duty of being government leader in the House of Commons under the prime ministry of the duke of Newcastle. On May 25, 1756, he was sworn in as chief justice of the Court of King's Bench, was created Baron Mansfield of Mansfield in the County of Nottingham, and presided for the first time in King's Bench on November 11, 1756. On October 31, 1776, he was elevated to the rank of earl of Mansfield.

LIFE'S WORK

As a judge, Mansfield not only had attained his life's ambition but also was able to satisfy his particular type of temperament, which found little pleasure in the management of men that politics required, but which thrived on the quiet research and scholarship into the history and function of law that the judiciary provided. Although Mansfield held the post of first lord of the Admiralty from April to June of 1757, served as a cabinet member from 1757 to 1765, and even after leaving the cabinet addressed the House of Lords on certain occasions (where, for example, he claimed the right of Parliament to tax the American colonies), his efforts were more and more directed toward the judiciary. Jean Baptiste Van Loo's portrait of him at the age of twenty-eight shows him to have been of ruddy complexion, with brown eyes, a high forehead, and a rather aquiline nose. The portrait by David Martin in Christ Church showed him in later years to have a touch of humor about a sensitive mouth. He is reported to have been slightly under middle height.

Mansfield was continually concerned with improvement of procedure. For example, he shortened the time for the hearing of trials by limiting the number of motions that a counsel could make at any one time prior to the trial, restricted repeated rehearings of questions of law that formerly received as many as four to five rehearings, allowed less time for making decisions, eliminated the mass of redundant paperwork that delayed the hearing of cases, passed a general order that even with the consent of the parties no cases could be postponed without the permission of the court (which permission was granted only sparingly), insisted that reasons be given by the court for its decisions, restricted the speech-making of counsel on each side to the jury, and eliminated much of the irregularity prevailing in the examination and cross-examination of witnesses. He also fought, with limited success, for the unification of equity (granting of orders by the court) and common law (granting of money damages) in the same courts.

Yet it was in the principles of the law that Mansfield gained his fame as one of the major chief justices in the history of the realm. In the *Somersett* case (1771), he established the doctrine that the air of England is too pure to be breathed by a slave and freed James Somersett, a black man who had been brought to England by his master from Jamaica, from being transported back to the New World as a slave, stating, "Every man who comes into England is entitled to the protection of English law, whatever oppression he may heretofore have suffered, and whatever may be the colour of his skin. . . ." Although, contrary to what some persons have supposed, this decision did not free the slaves in the British Empire, it helped to pave the way for their emancipation in 1834.

In *Leach v. Three King's Messengers* (1765), Mansfield and the other three judges of the court declared general warrants to be illegal, declaring that "no degree of antiquity could give sanction of an usage bad in itself," a doctrine that, whether so intended by Mansfield, gave support to the American colonies in their struggle against the so-called fishing expeditions that general warrants provided the king's officers in America.

He worked hard for religious toleration, as demonstrated by his acquittal in *Rex v. Webb* (1768) of a defendant who celebrated Mass as a Roman Catholic priest, his use of the mandamus to protect the rights of religious minorities, and his argument before the House of Lords in *Chamberlain of London v. Allen Evans* (1767) that "it is now no crime for a man to say he is a dissenter; nor is it any crime for him not to take the sacrament according to the rites of the Church of England; nay, the crime is, if he does it contrary to the dictates of his conscience." These views on religious toleration, contrary to the tenor of the times, led to the "No Popery" (or Gordon) Riots of 1780, allegedly incited by George, Lord Gordon, which resulted in the sacking of Mansfield's home in Bloomsbury Square and the burning of his library. Yet Mansfield not only refused to accept any compensation from the government but also conducted the trial of *Rex v. Gordon* (1781) with such fairness that Gordon was acquitted of the charges brought against him.

With regard to the law of seditious libel, in the case of *Rex v. Almon* (1770), he declared that it was the province of the judge alone to determine the criminality of a libel, leaving to the jury the determination of the questions whether the defendant printed or published, or both, the writing charged with being libelous, then decided himself that the publication and sale of the writing constituted seditious libel. Naturally, as a result of this doctrine, he was accused not only of trying to subvert the jury system in England but also of weakening the freedom of the press.

Mansfield eliminated in *Bright v. Eynon* (1757) the stigma of attaint that levied punishment on the children and issue of guilty persons in treason cases, stated the now generally accepted rule in *Rex v. Delavel* (1763) that conduct contrary to public morals can constitute a criminal offense, and promulgated rules upon marine insurance, bills of exchange, merchant shipping, inheritance (such as the famous case of *Perrin v. Blake* in 1770, which divided the legal profession into opposing factions for many years and was later reversed), the land law, and the law of commerce that drove the common law, however reluctantly, into modern times. Indeed,

Mansfield found the commercial law so weak that he developed sufficient law on the subject to be called the "Father of English commercial law." Prior to Mansfield's work, no treatises had been published on the subjects of the purchase and sale of goods, promissory notes, the negotiability of bonds, consideration, and quasi-contract, and few cases were to be found giving light to their handling.

When he was done, the English common law had a core of scholarship upon which to build its present-day codes both in Great Britain and in the United States. With regard to the law of property, the following centuries after Mansfield found the courts agreeing with his efforts to reform the medieval concept of reality, and the introduction of simplicity into the act of conveyancing property from seller to buyer. To do this, despite considerable adverse criticism, he drew upon his great fund of knowledge of foreign law and usage. In the matter of his views on consideration, however, he was defeated, so that the commercial law either then or now does not seem to have agreed with his doctrines on that subject.

In line with his refusal to side with the American colonies in their efforts to free themselves from taxation by the British parliament, as presented in his February 3, 1766, speech before the House of Lords ("Proceed, then, my Lords, with spirit and firmness"), he gave a considerable amount of his time to colonial law within the empire. In *Campbell v. Hall*, he laid down six propositions by which Great Britain governed its colonies during the century after him, stating that,

1. A country conquered by British arms becomes subject to the Parliament of Great Britain;
2. The subjects of that conquered territory become subjects of the British king;
3. The articles of capitulation upon which that territory surrendered are inviolable according to their true intent and meaning;
4. Any person who chooses to live in that territory is bound by the law of that territory, and whether English or not, has no privilege distinct from the original natives;
5. The laws of a conquered territory continue in force until altered by the British parliament;
6. No changes in the law, however, can be made contrary to fundamental principles governing the rights of all Englishmen.

He was also responsible for the doctrine that a British subject is under the protection of the English constitution in any place where the British flag is unfurled.

Although for thirty years Mansfield was energetic in his duties, the death of his wife on April 10, 1784, after forty-six years of happy marriage, left him deeply saddened, and in the summer of 1786, his health began to fail. He had hoped that his colleague on the King's Bench, Justice Francis Buller, would replace him, but such was not to be the case. When he resigned on June 4, 1788, his replacement was Sir Lloyd Kenyon, who was his antithesis both in knowledge and in approach to the law.

Retiring to his home Caen Wood, Mansfield died in London on March 20, 1793, in his eighty-ninth year, leaving a vast fortune for those times, the interest alone on the mortgages he held amounting to £26,000 a year.

SIGNIFICANCE

Apart from his reforms in procedure and his reforms and creativity in the principles of the English law, the first earl of Mansfield infused into the judiciary a modern attitude toward the judgment of cases. Although he viewed the law as a science demanding deep scholarship on the part of the judge, he departed from the view that the law was merely an intellectual exercise separate from humankind. Just as Mansfield believed that mercantile disputes were to be determined "upon natural justice and not upon the niceties of law," so also he believed that the law, unlike a mathematical equation, had to be varied in accordance with the circumstances of each case and the demands of the times. Custom and tradition could only go so far, and when it worked an injustice, had to be discarded or amended. As C. H. S. Fifoot states in his biography of Mansfield, "The whole temper of Lord Mansfield's mind was modern. He renounced the scholasticism which had infected Coke and the virulence which had impaired the judgment of Holt, and he set a fresh standard of judicial equanimity." It was Mansfield's good fortune to possess a command not only of the past but also of the present, in an attempt to set the stage for a future modern commercial age. The law of England had arisen out of a feudal society based on the ownership of land, but the new world was to be one of factory workers who owned no land, or businessmen who traded largely in personality, so that common sense in the light of changing times had to apply.

The very factors that made him uncomfortable as a politician, such as the need in politics to bow to forces that turned him against his own conscience, were factors that assisted him as a judge. He was attacked by the anonymous author of the so-called Junius Letters that appeared sporadically between November 21, 1768, and the beginning of the year 1772 in attacks upon the government. Several of these letters were directed especially against Mansfield, for his use of non-English sources for his innovations, his seeming subversion of trial by jury, his apparent arbitrariness, and apparent attempts to extinguish the liberty of the press. Yet history has not substantiated these accusations.

His actions in the John Wilkes case demonstrated Mansfield's efforts at fairness with regard to charges that he opposed liberty of the press. In 1764, two informations (government accusations) for seditious libel were filed against John Wilkes. Wilkes fled to France, allowing judgment by default against him, in which he was outlawed. Four years later, Wilkes returned demanding vindication. It would have been easy for Mansfield to rule in favor of the government, but, finding a flaw in the original proceedings that had escaped the eye of Wilkes himself, Mansfield reversed the judgment of outlawry.

In the entire period of thirty-two years in which Mansfield served as chief justice of the Court of King's Bench, a dissenting opinion was recorded to his judgments not more than twenty times, and he was reversed only six times. If he is to be criticized adversely, it must be more for his aloofness, his lack of emotion (particularly as seen in the prosecution of his relatives in the 1745 Scottish uprising or his failure ever to return to his native Scotland), and his tendency in political matters in Parliament, as one biographer has said, to be prudent perhaps to the point of timidity.

—*Robert M. Spector*

FURTHER READING

Campbell, John. *The Lives of the Chief Justices of England from the Norman Conquest till the Death of Lord Mansfield.* 2 vols. London: John Murray, 1849. Volume 2 discusses the life of Mansfield in a rather admiring way, so that the entire presentation is something of a eulogy. Yet some historians have criticized the work for its errors and misstatements.

Fifoot, C. H. S. *Lord Mansfield.* Oxford, England: Clarendon Press, 1936. This is a very usable biography of Mansfield, beginning with a relatively brief biographical sketch and continuing with a discussion of Mansfield's cases organized by legal topics. The work ends with an epilogue that attempts to sum up Mansfield's work.

Heward, Edmund. *Lord Mansfield.* Chichester, England: Barry Rose, 1979. Discusses Mansfield's life and achievements chronologically rather than topically. Although it does not contain any more material than the Fifoot biography, it is considerably more readable for the general reader and is particularly valuable for its bibliography of primary and secondary sources.

Oldham, James. *English Common Law in the Age of Mansfield.* Chapel Hill: University of North Carolina Press, 2004. An abridgment of Oldham's two-volume 1992 work. Oldham summarizes the fundamental principles of English law in the eighteenth century and describes the operations of the nation's common law courts.

_____. *The Mansfield Manuscripts and the Growth of English Law in the Eighteenth Century.* 2 vols. Chapel Hill: University of North Carolina Press, 1992. Oldham uses Mansfield's voluminous trial notes and other previously unexamined documents to reappraise Mansfield's judicial career and his influence in shaping the modern Anglo-American legal system.

See also: Sir William Blackstone; Frederick the Great; Montesquieu; Henry Pelham; William Pitt the Elder; Granville Sharp; Adam Smith; Robert Walpole; John Wilkes.

Related articles in *Great Events from History: The Eighteenth Century, 1701-1800:* 18th century: Expansion of the Atlantic Slave Trade; Beginning April, 1763: The *North Briton* Controversy; March 9, 1776: Adam Smith Publishes *The Wealth of Nations*; June 2-10, 1780: Gordon Riots; February 22, 1791-February 16, 1792: Thomas Paine Publishes *Rights of Man.*

JEAN-PAUL MARAT
French journalist and revolutionary

Marat was a leader of the Jacobins against the Girondists during the French Revolution. As a journalist and a deputy to the national convention, Marat was notorious for his support of popular violence and his advocacy of dictatorship.

Born: May 24, 1743; Boudry, Switzerland
Died: July 13, 1793; Paris, France
Areas of achievement: Government and politics, literature, social reform

EARLY LIFE

Jean-Paul Marat (zhahn-pawl mah-rah) was born into a Swiss Calvinist family of modest circumstances. Following a home education by his parents, Marat, at the age of sixteen, went to France to study medicine. Settling in London, he obtained a medical degree and established a fairly successful practice. Returning to France in 1777, he served as personal physician to wealthy clients until 1783, after which he worked full-time in scientific research and writing.

A man interested in many fields, Marat was the author of numerous books about the natural sciences, government, and philosophy. His *Chains of Slavery* (1774) attacked despotism and defended the concepts of liberty and popular sovereignty, and his *Plan de législation criminelle* (1780; *Plan of Criminal Legislation*) advocated a more humane criminal code, especially for the benefit of the poor. Although he acquired his liberal and democratic views from a variety of Enlightenment writers, he was especially influenced by the egalitarian ideas of Jean-Jacques Rousseau.

As a writer of scientific works, Marat was a failure. When he attacked the established theories of Sir Isaac Newton and others, he was ridiculed as a charlatan. Marat thought that he should be recognized as an important scientist, and he began to show indications of a growing persecution complex. When he was not admitted to the Academy of Sciences, he blamed a conspiracy of academicians, and he never forgave Voltaire and others who criticized his works. The French Revolution would provide him with an outlet for his frustrations and social resentments.

LIFE'S WORK

At the beginning of the revolution in 1789, Marat appeared extremely optimistic about the possibility of constitutional reform, and he explained his ideas for reform in many pamphlets. Until the violent summer of 1789, he remained more of a moderate reformer than a radical revolutionary. Influenced by Montesquieu, he advocated the establishment of a constitutional monarchy, a system of separation of powers, and a declaration of human rights that would include freedom of the press. Recognizing the idea of popular sovereignty, he wanted the Third Estate, which represented the vast majority of the people, to play the dominant role. Emphasizing the need for equality, Marat advocated an end to the special privileges enjoyed by the nobility, such as their traditional tax exemptions and special hunting rights.

Throughout the dramatic events of 1789, Marat was primarily an observer and commentator, although he later claimed to have played a role in the fall of the Bastille on July 14. During the upheaval of the Great Fear, his views rapidly became more and more extreme, and he soon became dissatisfied with the moderation of the national assembly. He was especially critical of Jean Mounier's constitutional committee, which proposed a system of government similar to that of Great Britain, and he published an alternative model for a new constitution in August. Marat's proposal included a unicameral legislature based on universal male suffrage, and he urged that the king should not have the power to veto laws or dissolve the legislature. In addition, Marat wrote passionately about the need for greater social justice and for less inequality of wealth. He stated that because society owes a means of subsistence to all citizens, the government should confiscate part of the property of the wealthy and use it to benefit the poor and working classes.

On September 12, 1789, Marat began to publish a newspaper, *L'Ami du Peuple* (friend of the people). Early in October, Marat began to fear a counterrevolutionary plot by royalists and monarchists, and in response, he called for direct action by the Parisian sansculottes, members of the lower classes who did not wear the knee breeches of the aristocracy. Marat was a leading voice in inciting the insurrection of October 5-6, when a large angry crowd forced the royal family to move from Versailles to Paris. Because of his outspoken advocacy of sedition, the royalist police court ordered his arrest, and he went into hiding for the first of many times. Early in 1790, he sought refuge in England for three months. By then, Marat was not only denouncing royalists but also bitterly attacking moderates such as the Marquis de Lafayette.

Convinced that only popular justice could prevent counterrevolutionary plots, Marat emerged as the most prominent advocate for mass executions. On January 30, 1791, he wrote in *L'Ami du Peuple* that it was perhaps necessary to cut off 100,000 heads for the freedom of the many, and on May 27, he suggested that even 500,000 executions might be required. On July 17, Marat became outraged when the national assembly ordered the national guard to disperse the republican demonstration on the Field of Mars, resulting in about fifty deaths. When Marat's editorials advocated reprisals for the act, the assembly on August 2 decreed that Marat was guilty of seditious libel. He continued to publish his newspaper in hiding.

Despite his radicalism, Marat was slow to abandon the idea of limited monarchy in favor of republicanism. After King Louis XVI's attempted flight and capture at Varennes on June 21, 1791, Marat demanded his execution and the establishment of a regency. Only later did he gradually accept the necessity of a republic.

In hiding at the time, Marat played only a minor role in the insurrection of August 10, 1792, when a mob forced the assembly to suspend the king and to hold elections for a national convention. Just before this "second revolution," Marat's editorials had called for the taking of the royal family as hostages. Therefore, he defended the insurrection as a model of popular democracy in action. On August 19, Marat appealed to the people to "rise and let the blood of traitors flow again." On September 2, he was appointed a member of the Committee of Public Safety of the Paris Commune, which became notorious for ordering the arrest of suspected traitors. Marat always appeared proud of the encouragement he gave to the massacres of September 2-7, in which frenzied mobs killed approximately fifteen hundred prisoners in Paris jails. Although most politicians and writers repudiated the massacres, Marat enthusiastically endorsed them as the righteous indignation of the oppressed masses.

On September 9, 1792, Marat was elected to the national convention as one of the deputies from Paris. When the convention opened on September 22, he probably voted for the establishment of a republic and, thereafter, defended republicanism. As a radical deputy, he was associated with the Jacobins who were seated on the left, a location called the Mountain because of its elevated seats. Marat quickly became the major object of attacks from the more moderate Girondins, who were seated on the right. He was a strong advocate for the speedy trial and execution of Louis XVI. When several Girondins defended leniency, Marat accused them of counterrevolutionary obstructionism. In turn, the Girondins pointed to Marat as one of the chief instigators of the September massacres as well as the 1793 food riots of Paris. On April 5, 1793, Marat became president of the Jacobin Club, and the next day he signed a declaration accusing the Girondins of counterrevolutionary intrigue. On April 13, the convention voted to send Marat before the Revolutionary Tribunal on charges of preaching pillage and advocating dictatorship. When acquitted by the tribunal, he was cheered as "the people's friend" at demonstrations led by enthusiastic Parisian sansculottes.

Marat obtained revenge on the Girondins in the insurrection of May 31-June 2, 1793. Just before the event, Marat had exhorted revolutionary groups to arm for a final conflict with the Girondins. According to legend, Marat himself rang the tocsin that called out the Parisian sansculottes to surround the convention on June 2. Among the deputies, Marat was the most outspoken in

Jean-Paul Marat. (Library of Congress)

calling for the expulsion and arrest of the leading Girondins. By this time, Marat had come to believe that Parisian supporters of the revolution were more representative of "the people" than were the elected representatives of the convention.

About the time that the Girondins were expelled, Marat's skin and lung diseases forced him to curtail most of his political activities, although the convention failed to accept his offer of resignation. To relieve his pain and irritation, Marat spent several hours each day immersed in a bathtub.

Despite his bad health, Marat continued his vigorous opposition to all enemies of the Mountain, whether on the left or the right. Although having much in common with Jacques Roux and other Enragés of the extreme left, he disagreed with several of this group's economic ideas. Rather than imposing a "maximum" or strictly regulating prices, Marat preferred to use the death penalty against food profiteers and monopolists. On July 4, 1793, he charged that the Enragés, in attacking the Mountain, were guilty of treason to the revolution. Marat's last efforts in the convention were devoted to trying to strengthen the Committee of Public Safety, which he criticized for its timidity and moderation. Apparently, he believed that the committee had the potential to exercise the kind of revolutionary dictatorship that he had long supported.

With civil war raging in many provinces, supporters of the Girondins looked upon Marat as the epitome of evil. In Normandy, Charlotte Corday (Marie-Anne-Charlotte Corday d'Armont), at the age of twenty-four, was so shocked by the persecution of the Girondins that she decided to go to Paris to rid France of the tyrant. Claiming to know of plots against the revolution, she gained an audience with Marat while he was in his bath on the evening of July 13, and she stabbed him to death with a knife. She was quickly captured and was guillotined four days later. In the last edition of Marat's paper, which appeared on July 14, Marat called on the Committee of Public Safety to adopt more vigorous policies.

Contrary to Corday's intentions, the death of Marat hastened the executions of the Girondins, and it promoted the establishment of the Reign of Terror under the direction of the Committee of Public Safety. To his supporters, Marat was a martyr for a just cause, and he was venerated in a popular cult. Although Marat's body remained in the Pantheon for less than a year, Jacques-Louis David's portrait of the deceased Marat remains the most famous symbol of the radical phase of the French Revolution.

SIGNIFICANCE

From the days of the revolution, those on the left and right have strongly disagreed about Marat's ideas and character. Leftists have usually admired him as the "people's friend" and been impressed by his devotion to the revolutionary cause, his militant attacks on economic injustices, and his outspoken defense of popular violence. Conservatives and moderates, in contrast, have usually detested him as a vengeful fanatic partly responsible for the Reign of Terror.

Marat anticipated later socialist thought in at least three ways: his insistence that the wealthy were exploiting the poorer classes, his conviction that government should promote the interests of the poor, and his call for a dictatorship of a revolutionary elite. One of his devoted admirers, Gracchus (François Noël) Babeuf, found inspiration in his legacy when he led the Conspiracy of Equals of 1797. In contrast to Babeuf's communist uprising, however, Marat never advocated the communal ownership of property and never formulated any concrete plans for a group dictatorship.

—*Thomas Tandy Lewis*

FURTHER READING

Bax, Ernest. *Jean-Paul Marat: The People's Friend.* London: Grant Richards, 1900. A dated but interesting work that portrays Marat as a great humanitarian statesman with a clear political philosophy.

Censor, Jack. *Prelude to Power: The Parisian Radical Press, 1789-1791.* Baltimore: Johns Hopkins University Press, 1976. A scholarly study of left-wing journalists and newspapers during the French Revolution, with several interesting pages on Marat.

Conner, Clifford. *Jean-Paul Marat: Scientist and Revolutionary.* Atlantic Highlands, N.J.: Humanities Press, 1997. This study of Marat benefits from materials that previously were unavailable to researchers.

Durant, Will, and Ariel Durant. *The Age of Napoleon.* New York: Simon & Schuster, 1975. A well-written history of the period from 1789 to 1815, with interesting descriptions of significant individuals such as Marat.

Germani, Ian. *Jean-Paul Marat: Hero and Anti-Hero of the French Revolution.* Lewiston, N.Y.: E. Mellen Press, 1992. Examines how Marat's image was manipulated during and after the French Revolution by studying funeral orations, newspapers, song sheets, paintings, historical works, and other items from the nineteenth and twentieth centuries. Describes Marat's symbolic importance to the political struggles of France.

Gottschalk, Louis R. *Jean-Paul Marat: A Study in Radicalism.* 1927. Reprint. New York: Greenberg, 1966. Although excessively pro-Marat, this book is a fascinating and scholarly biography with an excellent analysis of Marat's ideas. Highly recommended for both the scholar and the general reader.

Miller, Stephen. *Three Deaths and Enlightenment Thought: Hume, Johnson, Marat.* Lewisburg, Pa.: Bucknell University Press, 2001. Examines the cult of the deathbed scene in eighteenth century France and England to focus on the philosophies of Marat, David Hume, and Samuel Johnson.

Spearing, Joseph. *The Angel of Assassination: Marie Charlotte de Corday d'Armont.* New York: H. Smith, 1935. Although dated and wordy, this is the best English-language biography about the woman who assassinated Marat.

Thompson, James M. *Leaders of the French Revolution.* 1929. Reprint. New York: D. Appleton, 1988. Includes an excellent twenty-page summary of Marat's ideas and activities from a critical point of view.

See also: David Hume; Samuel Johnson; Louis XVI; Montesquieu; Robespierre; Jean-Jacques Rousseau; Louis de Saint-Just; Voltaire.

Related articles in *Great Events from History: The Eighteenth Century, 1701-1800*: January, 1759: Voltaire Satirizes Optimism in *Candide*; April, 1762: Rousseau Publishes *The Social Contract*; May 5, 1789: Louis XVI Calls the Estates-General; June 20, 1789: Oath of the Tennis Court; July 14, 1789: Fall of the Bastille; October, 1789-April 25, 1792: France Adopts the Guillotine; April 20, 1792-October, 1797: Early Wars of the French Revolution; September 20, 1792: Battle of Valmy; January 21, 1793: Execution of Louis XVI; March 4-December 23, 1793: War in the Vendée; July 27-28, 1794: Fall of Robespierre; November 9-10, 1799: Napoleon Rises to Power in France.

ANDREAS SIGISMUND MARGGRAF
German chemist

A pioneer German analytic chemist, Marggraf is most famous for discovering sugar in the beet, for discovering the element zinc, and for realizing commercially applicable ways of extracting each. By the mid-eighteenth century he was Germany's most famous chemist.

Born: March 3, 1709; Berlin, Prussia (now in Germany)
Died: August 7, 1782; Berlin, Prussia
Areas of achievement: Chemistry, science and technology

EARLY LIFE

Andreas Sigismund Marggraf (ahn-DRAY-ehs SEEG-ihs-muhnd mahg-GRAHF) developed an interest in chemistry because of the influence of his father, Henning Christian Marggraf, who first moved to Berlin as a grocer before acquiring a small pharmacy in 1707 and then a large pharmacy in 1720. Henning engaged in some independent chemical research, corresponding with Prussia's leading chemist and metallurgist, Johann F. Henckel. Andreas received schooling while training as an apprentice in his father's apothecary.

In 1726 the seventeen-year-old Andreas transferred to Berlin's Court Apothecary Shop, where he studied for five years under Caspar Neumann, an influential pharmacist and teacher of pharmaceutical chemistry. From 1733 through 1735 he studied chemistry in Berlin and Strasbourg and medicine at the University of Halle. Having a broad interest in science, he also studied mineralogy and metallurgy in Freiberg under the tutelage of Henckel, his father's famous associate.

After completing his studies at the age of twenty-six, Marggraf visited a wide variety of mines to view the commercial methods used to extract ore. He then returned to Berlin, where he took over as chief administrator of his father's apothecary, a position he held from 1735 until 1753, when the apothecary was sold to his brother.

The depth and breadth of Marggraf's scientific training earned him election in 1738 to the Berlin Academy of Sciences. Membership in the academy provided him the opportunity to work in the academy's chemistry laboratory, which at the time was one of the best in Germany. The appointment also carried a salary and an official residence, allowing him to devote his time to chemical research. The importance of his discoveries would earn him the position of head of the chemical laboratory in 1754 and that of director of the physics class in 1760; he held the latter position until his death in 1782. Marggraf helped make the Berlin Academy of Science's Europe's third leading scientific society, trailing only the royal scientific societies in Paris and London.

Marggraf's early research was with phosphorus, an element widely used in the production of matches. He discovered how to prepare phosphoric acid in 1740, and three years later he developed a commercially cheap method for producing phosphorus by distilling urine, using the commonly available materials sand, coal, and lead chloride (horn lead). He next focused his research on developing methods for readily distinguishing compounds containing sodium from those containing potassium. His most significant research was conducted in 1746, when he discovered that zinc was a distinct element, and in 1747, when he developed a method for producing sugar by extracting it from beets.

LIFE'S WORK

Until Marggraf published the results of his conclusive study, zinc was thought to be a blend of metals. By taking calamine ore from four different sources and heating it with carbon in closed vessels, Marggraf was able to extract pure bluish-white metallic zinc from each vessel. Marggraf was also able to extract pure zinc from sphalerite, a mineral containing heavy concentrations of lead. At the time of his discovery, zinc was used to make bronze and brass, which gave Marggraf's methods for extraction immediate commercial value. The element was later used to make battery plates and to rust-proof iron and steel. Marggraf was unaware that similar experiments with zinc were being conducted in England and Sweden. It was Marggraf's methodical study, however, that provided conclusive proof that zinc was an element and gained him a place in history as the discoverer of zinc.

At the same time he was working with zinc, Marggraf experimented with extracting sugar from a variety of plants by dissolving the pulp in alcohol, which left a crystalline substance after evaporation. At the time of his experiments, sugar cane was the only known source of sugar. However, sugar cane grew in tropical climates only, so the only source of Europe's sugar supply had to be imported at considerable expense. Marggraf had long wondered about the sweet taste of the beet, a common vegetable in Europe, which was used for both its bulb and its leaves. Marggraf had particular success in using alco-

hol to extract sugar from the boiled root pulp of the white beet, which was common to the Mediterranean coastal region. To prove that the sugar extracted was the same chemically as cane sugar, Marggraf used a powerful microscope to compare the crystalline structures of the two. This was the first time the microscope was used as an instrument for chemical analysis, and the results provided conclusive proof that the crystalline structure was the same.

Although it had commercial applications, Marggraf's discovery of beet sugar in 1747 remained purely academic during his lifetime, and he rapidly turned to new ventures in chemistry. His work on beet extraction was later continued by his student, Franz Karl Achard, who experimented with developing beets with higher sugar content and processes that would make sugar production commercially profitable. As a result, the first sugar factory was built in 1801 at Cunern in lower Silesia. Within a few years, interruptions of the overseas sugar trade resulting from the Napoleonic Wars caused the rapid growth of sugar beet factories.

Two years after the discovery of sugar in beets, Marggraf developed a process by which formic acid, used in dyeing textiles and treating leather, could be produced through the distillation of ants. His research also led to improved methods for the purification of silver and tin and the discovery of the chemical nature of alum, used in baking powders and dyes. He devised a method of identifying the oxides of aluminum (alumina) and calcium (lime) found in clay.

Marggraf's last major discovery was made in 1758, when he developed a simple method of distinguishing compounds containing sodium from compounds containing potassium by analyzing the flame coloration these compounds exhibited when burned. Fire was particularly important for Marggraf, as he was a lifelong advocate of the phlogiston theory, which held fire to be an elemental substance released from a substance upon combustion. In 1777 the widespread belief in the phlogiston theory was discredited among chemists by the publication of French chemist Antoine-Laurent Lavoisier's study of oxygen. Nevertheless, Marggraf's fame was strong enough in France to gain his appointment as one of six foreign members of the Royal Academy of Sciences.

SIGNIFICANCE

Marggraf helped establish chemistry as an essential discipline for studies of pharmacy, medicine, mineralogy, and physics. He helped popularize the eighteenth century

Scientific Revolution and its diffusion into everyday life by embodying the connection among science, technology, and industry. His work with minerals and metals contributed to the development of theoretical and methodological natural science, but it also had immediate commercial relevance to mining. Similarly, Marggraf's work with formic acid and sugar beets revealed the potential commercial applications of chemical discoveries. Indeed, one of his private students, Achard, established a sugar industry based upon Marggraf's pioneering work. Other students, such as Jacob R. Spielmann, continued important work in pharmacy and chemistry, while Johann C. F. Meyer used his training in chemistry to establish Prussian alcohol distillation industries to offset the need for foreign imports. Marggraf's most famous student, Martin Heinrich Klaproth, succeeded him as Germany's leading chemist, receiving the first chemistry chair at the newly created University of Berlin.

Marggraf's international esteem raised Prussia's reputation as an Enlightenment-based state that stood with France and Great Britain as a place where science thrived. Marggraf's fame also elevated the prestige of his patron, King Frederick the Great. Chemistry would continue to accelerate in Germany, with the country eventually gaining a position of world leadership in this field by the end of the nineteenth century.

—*Irwin Halfond*

FURTHER READING

Hufbauer, Karl. *The Formation of the German Chemical Community, 1720-1795.* Berkeley: University of California Press, 1982. Provides a good analysis of Marggraf's work and its role in the development of Germany's leadership in chemistry. Contains charts, tables, graphs, biographical profiles, and pictures.

Macinnis, Peter. *Bittersweet: The Story of Sugar.* London: Allen and Unwin, 2003. A history of sugar production that contains a treatment of Marggraf's contribution and the subsequent development of the sugar beet industry. Includes a bibliography and footnotes.

See also: Frederick the Great; Antoine-Laurent Lavoisier; Georg Ernst Stahl.

Related articles in *Great Events from History: The Eighteenth Century, 1701-1800:* 1701: Tull Invents the Seed Drill; 1747: Marggraf Extracts Sugar from Beets; February 14, 1788: Meikle Demonstrates His Drum Thresher; 1793: Whitney Invents the Cotton Gin.

MARIA THERESA
Archduchess of Austria (r. 1740-1780) and queen of Hungary and Bohemia (r. 1740-1780)

Beset by adversity, Maria Theresa proved herself to be the greatest ruler produced by the House of Habsburg. She initiated reforms that transformed her vast holdings into a unified state and created modern Austria.

Born: May 13, 1717; Vienna, Austria
Died: November 29, 1780; Vienna, Austria
Area of achievement: Government and politics

EARLY LIFE

Born to Charles VI, Holy Roman Emperor, and his extraordinarily beautiful wife, Elisabeth Christine of Brunswick-Wolfenbüttel, the beautiful and graceful Archduchess Maria Theresa was considered just another daughter by her father. The emperor was obsessed with the hope of fathering a son who would succeed him and consequently neglected to educate his eldest surviving daughter in the affairs of state. Maria Theresa's only brother died in infancy, as did one of her sisters, but these tragedies did not deter her father in his quest for a male heir. He was convinced that he would outlive his empress, who was in frail health, and then he could marry a princess who would give him many sons. The empress outlived her husband, however, and Charles died unexpectedly on October 20, 1740, of a fever contracted on a hunting expedition. He was the last Habsburg in the direct male line.

Despite really not believing that Maria Theresa would succeed him, Charles had taken elaborate precautions to protect his empire and ensure its continued existence. The device by which he sought to accomplish the preservation of the state was the Pragmatic Sanction. To win the support of the various rulers of Europe for this scrap of paper, he made a number of concessions to friend and foe alike. While each in his turn solemnly swore to recognize Archduchess Maria Theresa as her father's successor, not one of them intended to support the provisions of the Pragmatic Sanction beyond their own interests. The emperor was particularly concerned about the elector of Bavaria, who was married to his niece, Maria Amelia. Charles had become emperor in 1711, after the death of his brother, Joseph I, who left two daughters, one of whom was the wife of Charles Albert of Bavaria. In the event of his death, Charles VI was determined that his daughter must be protected from her cousins and their claims on the Habsburg inheritance. He believed that the Pragmatic Sanction would provide that security.

If he could not produce a son of his own, Charles might at least hope for a grandson to whom he might leave his crown, and so in 1736, Maria Theresa was married to her cousin, Francis Stephen of Lorraine. Unfortunately, Francis arrived in Vienna almost a man without a country. At the insistence of France, the new archduke had to exchange his native Lorraine for Tuscany before the marriage could be sanctioned by the great powers, who seemed bent upon humiliating the emperor and his house. Maria Theresa, for her part, cared little for the jealousies of Austria's neighbors, for she was already hopelessly in love with her bridegroom. She was never blind to Francis's faults, but she adored him and defended him until his death in 1765. She spent the rest of her life mourning him. Unfortunately for her father's peace of mind, the three children born to Maria Theresa and Francis before 1740 were all girls, but the child she was carrying at the time of her father's death was the future Emperor Joseph II.

LIFE'S WORK

Maria Theresa inherited a realm near bankruptcy. There was no one to advise her during the first critical weeks of her reign; Archduke Francis had a head for finance but little else, and her counselors were ancient incompetents inherited from her father. Her army was at half strength, all of the primary sources of her imperial revenues were mortgaged, and there was a crushing national debt. Maria Theresa did not hesitate to face these problems and the other burdens that threatened to crush her spirits, but then Frederick the Great struck.

In the spring of 1740, Frederick William I of Prussia died in Berlin, and his son succeeded him. The old king had always been loyal to the emperor, and it was assumed that his son would be as well. In December, 1740, Frederick the Great invaded Silesia. Austria was not prepared to withstand such a blow, but Maria Theresa would not surrender a scrap of territory without a struggle. Her refusal to follow the advice of her ally Great Britain to accommodate Prussia led to the War of the Austrian Succession, which lasted until 1748. Maria Theresa did not regain Silesia, but she proved her mettle and rallied the diverse peoples of the empire to her cause.

Often Maria Theresa had reason to despair in the years between Frederick's invasion and the signing of the Treaty of Aix-la-Chapelle. In 1742, she had made peace with the Prussians at Berlin, only to have her old enemy reenter the war when he feared that he would not receive his fair share of the spoils. On January 24, 1742, Frederick engineered the election of Charles Albert of Bavaria as Holy Roman Emperor, with the title Charles VII. Maria Theresa was furious that her husband had been denied that honor by treachery, and she was determined that Charles VII would not enjoy his triumph. Harried from his capital of Munich, the Holy Roman Emperor became a mere pawn in the hands of the diplomats. On January 25, 1745, he died, and Maria Theresa

Maria Theresa. (Library of Congress)

immediately secured the election of her husband as Emperor Francis I. Only after his election in 1745 and his coronation in 1746 was Maria Theresa able to bear the title of empress; however, there was never any doubt in anyone's mind, including that of Francis, who really exercised the power.

Having prevented the dismemberment of her kingdom, Maria Theresa began to plan her revenge on Frederick the Great. Great Britain had to be discarded as an ally, because George II and his ministers had proved unreliable: They were more interested in preserving the Kingdom of Hanover than in fulfilling their obligations to the empress. During the eight years that separated the War of the Austrian Succession from the Seven Years' War, Austria and France effected a diplomatic revolution that left the traditional alignment of European nations in disarray. Sworn enemies for generations, Austria and France became allies, while Prussia was forced into an uneasy arrangement with Great Britain, its former adversary. The final seal on Maria Theresa's brilliant diplomatic coup would be the marriage of Marie-Antoinette, her ninth child, to the dauphin of France, the future Louis XVI.

During the brief years of peace, Maria Theresa was also able to devote her energies to reforming the antiquated institutions of her empire, while centralizing its government. Blessed with the rare talent for choosing able subordinates and then placing each in the area best suited to his talents, she slowly rebuilt her cabinet.

The great nobles of the empire had regularly ignored any directives from Vienna and ruled their holdings like independent rulers, while the provincial estates passed laws with little or no concern for the central government. Under Maria Theresa, these abuses ceased. Count Haugwitz had been the governor of a portion of Silesia when Frederick invaded that province, and he had observed at close range the reforms the Prussians imposed on their new subjects. With the support of the empress, he then instituted similar reforms in all parts of the empire except Hungary, which was protected by special privileges.

For the first time, the nobility was forced to pay taxes. Increased revenues permitted Maria Theresa to create a centralized bureaucracy, a permanent standing army serviced by military academies, and a system of secondary education. In 1749, the administrative and judiciary functions of the government were separated, and a complete codification of the law was ordered. Begun in 1752, it was finally finished in 1811 during the reign of Maria Theresa's grandson.

Beginning in the forests of North America, the Seven Years' War soon involved most of the world. When the conflict ended in 1763, France was near bankruptcy, while Great Britain was without question the most powerful nation in the world. Austria did not recapture Silesia, but it did regain much of its lost international prestige. Maria Theresa had the satisfaction of watching her archenemy brought to the brink of destruction. Only the accession of a new ruler in Russia and his own daring saved Frederick from disaster. With the war's completion, Maria Theresa resolved never again to commit her nation to battle save in self-defense.

Two years after the peace was signed, Emperor Francis I died unexpectedly. Despite her loss, Maria Theresa sought to devote herself to the service of the state. Her children continued to bring her great joy and at times disappointment. None of them was as difficult as her heir, Joseph II.

Burning with a zeal to reform Austria, the new emperor lacked both tact and caution. Only his mother's resolve kept his often ill-directed enthusiasm in check. Together, they ruled the empire until Maria Theresa's death, but it was not always a cordial relationship. In 1772, Joseph outraged his mother's sense of decency by engaging in the first partition of Poland. Maria Theresa's prediction that no good would come of this despicable act, which was shared with Prussia and Russia, was ignored by Joseph. Mercifully, the empress did not live to see the final dismemberment of Poland. Maria Theresa died in Vienna on November 29, 1780, after a long and painful illness.

SIGNIFICANCE

Against all odds, Maria Theresa succeeded in saving the ramshackle empire that she inherited from her father. She was the architect of modern Austria, and, thanks to her care, the empire survived into the early twentieth century. She had an uncanny talent for selecting subordinates and then placing them in positions that allowed them to employ their talents to the fullest. Even her own husband, Francis I, was assigned to that area of government he best understood, finance. With her advisers, she centralized the imperial government, putting an end to centuries of inefficiency and mismanagement. Only the Hungarians resisted her reforms, but Maria Theresa charmed the Magyars into submission and contained their fierce longing for independence. By her frugality, she restored the financial integrity of her nation, and with the profits of her labor, she built Schönbrunn Palace, her favorite residence, and perhaps the finest example of the Austrian Baroque style.

When she effected a diplomatic revolution by making her country's ancient enemy, France, her firm ally, Maria Theresa sacrificed her daughter to seal the bargain, but she would not willingly countenance the cynical dismemberment of Poland. Her court was adorned with artists, writers, and musicians, such as Joseph Haydn and Wolfgang Amadeus Mozart, but Maria Theresa never forgot that to the ordinary folk she was like a mother. Seeking to improve their lot, she initiated a number of reforms for which her successors were often given the credit. She was the greatest ruler of the Habsburg Dynasty.

—Clifton W. Potter, Jr.

FURTHER READING

Anderson, M. S. *Europe in the Eighteenth Century, 1713-1783*. 3d ed. London: Longman, 1987. A solid treatment of the period. Well written and very easy to follow; it has an excellent annotated bibliography for further study.

Crankshaw, Edward. *The Habsburgs: Portrait of a Dynasty*. New York: Viking Press, 1971. A good introduction to the rather complicated story of Austria's development under the Habsburgs. The chapters on Maria Theresa are quite useful and contain a good outline of her life and reign. Excellent photographs.

_____. *Maria Theresa*. New York: Viking Press, 1969. Like the Hungarian nobility, Crankshaw has fallen under the spell of the beautiful empress, and therefore this work must be read with care. Yet it is a well-written biography and contains a very useful bibliography.

Gooch, G. P. *Maria Theresa and Other Studies*. Reprint. New York: Archon Books, 1965. The two essays that begin this work, "Maria Theresa and Joseph II" and "Maria Theresa and Marie Antoinette," are based on the correspondence between the empress and her children. The humanity of Maria Theresa, as well as her deep feelings for her son and daughter, are easily discernible in these two chapters.

Ingrao, Charles W. *The Habsburg Monarchy, 1618-1815*. 2d ed. New York: Cambridge University Press, 2000. Describes how the Habsburg state emerged as a military and cultural power of enormous influence. Includes information on the reign of Maria Theresa.

Pick, Robert. *Empress Maria Theresa: The Earlier Years, 1717-1757*. New York: Harper & Row, 1966. A remarkably well-written work, meant for the scholar. Balanced, sensitive, and illuminating, it is perhaps the best biography of Maria Theresa in English.

Roider, Karl A., Jr., ed. *Maria Theresa*. Englewood Cliffs, N.J.: Prentice-Hall, 1973. This slender volume is a treasury of materials dealing with Maria Theresa. Part 1 contains the empress's letters and papers on a number of subjects. Part 2 contains views of Maria Theresa by her contemporaries. Part 3 contains eight brief statements by historians.

Wandruszka, Adam. *The House of Habsburg: Six Hundred Years of a European Dynasty*. Translated by Cathleen Epstein and Hans Epstein. Garden City, N.Y.: Doubleday, 1964. The portions of this work concerned with Maria Theresa are valuable, because they briefly analyze her approach to governing and to reform. The influence of the empress on the two sons who succeeded her is carefully considered. Good bibliography.

Wheatcroft, Andrew. *The Habsburgs: Embodying Empire*. New York: Viking Press, 1995. Wheatcroft focuses on the values, concerns, and other personal qualities of the Habsburg rulers, including Maria Theresa.

See also: Charles VI; Frederick the Great; Frederick William I; George II; Joseph Haydn; Joseph II; Louis XVI; Marie-Antoinette; Wolfgang Amadeus Mozart.

Related articles in *Great Events from History: The Eighteenth Century, 1701-1800*: November 18, 1738: Treaty of Vienna; May 31, 1740: Accession of Frederick the Great; October 20, 1740: Maria Theresa Succeeds to the Austrian Throne; December 16, 1740-November 7, 1748: War of the Austrian Succession; October 18, 1748: Treaty of Aix-la-Chapelle; January, 1756-February 15, 1763: Seven Years' War; August 5, 1772-October 24, 1795: Partitioning of Poland; 1775-1790: Joseph II's Reforms.

MARIE-ANTOINETTE
Queen of France (r. 1774-1793)

Marie-Antoinette, through her exaggerated public image as a frivolous and extravagant woman, did much to undermine popular respect for the French monarchy. As queen of France, she opposed the revolutionary movement at every turn.

Born: November 2, 1755; Vienna, Austria
Died: October 16, 1793; Paris, France
Also known as: Maria Antonia Josepha Joanna von Österreich-Lothringen (birth name); Marie-Antoinette-Josèphe-Jeanne d'Autriche-Lorraine
Area of achievement: Government and politics

EARLY LIFE

Marie-Antoinette (mah-ree ahn-twah-neht) was born in Vienna to Empress Maria Theresa and Holy Roman Emperor Francis I. She was the eleventh child in a family of three boys and eight girls; the last child in the family, Maximilian, would be born a year later. Her mother, the intelligent, strong ruler of the widespread Habsburg possessions since 1740, combined statecraft and childbearing with great efficiency. Her father, Emperor Francis of the House of Lorraine, was a pleasant, easygoing man, successful in business ventures. He was an adored though profligate husband and a kind father to his numerous children. His imperial title conferred no power.

Like her siblings, Marie-Antoinette enjoyed a lively musical environment. She played the harp and formed small musical groups with her brothers and sisters to entertain the family. Her education, entrusted to tutors, was mediocre. She learned fluent French but, to the end of her life, spoke it with a German accent. A dainty, pretty child, with blond hair and blue eyes, she was spontaneous and charming. Her mother sheltered her from corrupting influences and schooled her in good manners and morals.

From her tenth year, Marie-Antoinette intended to marry the heir apparent to the French throne in order to seal the Habsburg monarchy's alliance with France. At thirteen, she was grooming for her future role, adding graciousness and polish to her charm. On May 16, 1770, at Versailles, she married the dauphin Louis, a clumsy, shy young man of sixteen. It was assumed that Marie-Antoinette would control her soon-to-be-king husband, so, unwittingly, she became part of a world of intrigue, a threat to the old king's mistress, Madame du Barry, and the other enemies of Étienne François de Choiseul, the chief architect of the French alliance with Austria.

The duc de Choiseul was dismissed a few months after Marie-Antoinette's arrival in Paris, placing her in a somewhat precarious situation. She found a mentor in Graf Florimund Mercy d'Argenteau, Austria's ambassador to the French court, who maintained a constant line of communication between her and her mother. Marie-Antoinette's position also improved as she won the affection of her husband.

LIFE'S WORK

On the death of Louis XV, on May 10, 1774, Marie-Antoinette's husband became King Louis XVI, and she became his queen. Initially popular, she soon attracted the enmity of the anti-Austrian faction at court, angered by her failed attempt to gain the recall of the duc de Choiseul. Her most serious problem was her husband, the king, who failed to consummate their marriage. By 1774, she had become the target of scurrilous pamphlets. She reacted to her predicament by throwing herself into a life of expensive diversion and pleasure. Her closest friends, the princesse de Lamballe and the comtesse Jules de Polignac, sought and received extravagant gifts and offices. She also frequented salons devoted to high-stakes gambling, horse races, and masked balls without the king. Her enemies professed to be scandalized.

In 1777, her eldest brother, Emperor Joseph II, paid her a visit in Paris. He warned her of the dangers of her conduct, then told her husband how to consummate the marriage. Louis accepted the emperor's advice. A few months later, Marie-Antoinette became pregnant, and in December, 1778, she gave birth to a daughter. In October, 1781, a son was born; in March, 1785, another son; and in July, 1786, another daughter. For a time, she reduced her social engagements and proved to be a wise and caring mother.

Although Louis succeeded in performing his marital duties, he failed to satisfy Marie-Antoinette's need for affection and intimacy. After a brief period of self-restraint, she once again threw herself into a hectic social life with the Polignac family and other favorites, heedless of her brother's advice.

In 1785-1786, she became embroiled in the affair of the diamond necklace. Consisting of some five hundred large, perfect diamonds, the necklace was commissioned by the jeweler Boehmer and offered to Louis XV as a present for Madame du Barry. The king had declined the purchase. In 1785, Louis-René-Édouard, prince de

Marie-Antoinette. (Library of Congress)

Rohan, a worldly cardinal, was persuaded by his mistress, Jeanne, comtesse de la Motte, to contract for the necklace on behalf of Queen Marie-Antoinette. His mistress was to arrange for delivery of the necklace, but she passed it to her husband, who fled to England and sold it stone by stone. When the fraud was discovered, Cardinal Rohan was arrested and tried. Because of her reputation for extravagance and scandal, the queen was widely assumed to be involved in the affair, and many believed that the cardinal may have intended to buy sexual favors from her. Rohan's conviction on a reduced charge failed to clear the queen's name in the public eye.

In the following years, as the monarchy reeled in debt and edged ever closer to bankruptcy, the queen, who symbolized frivolous, decadent luxury to the common people, drew much of the blame upon herself. Addicted to pleasure, she was heedless of the calumnies swirling about her, incapable of grasping the point of serious political discussion, and inclined to intrude into affairs of state for personal reasons, such as to advance the cause of her favorites.

In 1789, the monarchy was shaken to its foundations, and the queen's position undermined. On May 4, the Estates-General met at Versailles. A month later, her eldest son died. On July 14, the Bastille fell. In October,

the royal family was forcibly removed from Versailles to the Palace of the Tuileries in Paris. As her husband sank in apathy and indecision, Marie-Antoinette grasped at straws. In vain, she negotiated with the moderate, pragmatic Honoré-Gabriel Riqueti, comte de Mirabeau, a plan to flee Paris and rally the provinces to the king's cause.

After the death of Mirabeau in April, 1791, Marie relied chiefly on the Swedish count Hans Axel von Fersen, who had entered French military service as a young man. She had known the tall, handsome, unmarried aristocrat since 1774. Their relationship had grown intimate over the years, attracting scurrilous comment. How physical their love became is a matter of conjecture; however, certainly, they loved each other deeply. Fersen organized the flight of the royal family from Paris on June 21, 1791, in an attempt to prepare a base in Lorraine from which the king could lead loyal forces to the recovery of his authority. Revolutionaries stopped the royal coach in Varennes and forced it to return to Paris.

The plan's failure, for which Marie-Antoinette shares the blame with her husband, profoundly compromised the royal cause. In September, 1791, Louis was forced to accept a new constitution, leaving him a weak executive under the control of a legislative assembly that distrusted him. Guided by Fersen, the queen came to believe that the monarchy could be saved only by the intervention of Austria and other major powers. This conviction was strengthened in April, 1792, when France declared war on Austria. Marie-Antoinette relayed to Fersen and the Austrians the plans of the French generals and welcomed the advance of the enemy into her country. She endorsed the July manifesto of the duke of Brunswick, commander of the Austro-Prussian army, that threatened dire reprisals on Paris if the royal family were harmed. That declaration was counterproductive. On August 10, a mob stormed the Tuileries. The royal family was imprisoned in the Temple Tower and France was declared a republic.

Initially, the royal family's situation remained comfortable; they were subjected to merely minor indignities. The queen mended the king's clothes while he instructed his surviving son and heir in the Latin classics and the new geography of France. In December, the king was taken from the family and put on trial before the national convention, a revolutionary body lacking legal authority. Accused of conspiring against the safety of the state, Louis defended himself well. It was a political trial, however, and ended in his condemnation. On January 21, 1793, he was guillotined before an immense crowd.

Marie-Antoinette faced a similar fate. She continued to live in the Temple Tower, growing thinner, dressed in the black of mourning. Her only hope of staying alive was that the revolutionary forces might find her useful as a hostage. The allied armies might reach Paris and liberate her and her children before the national convention decided they must all die. Meanwhile, her son, whom she regarded as Louis XVII, took ill. He was taken from her and entrusted to an elderly cobbler who neglected him.

Marie-Antoinette's hope for rescue was dashed. Under pressure from advancing allied armies and growing counterrevolution among peasants in the western region and in several cities in the provinces, the revolutionary government instituted a Reign of Terror, the systematic liquidation of internal dissent. On August 2, 1793, the police arrested Marie-Antoinette, separated her from the rest of her family, and imprisoned her in the Conciergerie to await trial before the Revolutionary Tribunal.

Under close, harsh confinement, her health deteriorated rapidly. Nonetheless, she was alert and cogent when brought before the judges in October. Accused of an absurd variety of crimes, including incest and counterfeiting, she maintained a regal bearing and dismissed the charges with contempt. On October 16, 1793, she was carried in a cart for common criminals to the place of execution, hair white and lank, hands bound behind her back, a scene immortalized in a sketch by the revolutionary artist Jacques-Louis David. She died to the loud applause of the mob.

SIGNIFICANCE

Marie-Antoinette was by nature and training a decent, modest woman, attractive and charming. However, she showed poor judgment in the company she kept, in her choice of favorites, and in the favors she gave them, faults that were exaggerated by her enemies to the detriment of the failing French monarchy. If she had had her mother's political sense as well as her courage, French history might have taken a different course during the reign of Louis XVI. The king needed someone at his side who could compensate for his inability to make decisions or forcefully express himself. Marie-Antoinette could show him affection, but unfortunately, she was poorly equipped to help him rule.

—*Charles H. O'Brien*

FURTHER READING

Barton, H. Arnold. *Count Hans Axel von Fersen: Aristocrat in an Age of Revolution*. Boston: Twayne, 1975. The author presents a detailed, judicious interpretation of the queen's relationship with the Swedish aristocrat, concluding that they loved one another deeply, sincerely, and honestly. Whether they were physically intimate is a secondary issue and, in any case, cannot be resolved for lack of evidence.

Beales, Derek E. D. *Joseph II: In the Shadow of Maria Theresa, 1741-1780*. New York: Cambridge University Press, 1987. The marital difficulty between Marie-Antoinette and her husband has been the subject of scholarly as well as scurrilous discussion. Beales relates Emperor Joseph's frank advice to his brother-in-law in 1777 that led to the successful consummation of the royal marriage.

Crankshaw, Edward. *Maria Theresa*. London: Longmans, 1969. Offers useful insight into Maria Theresa's continuing influence upon her daughter Marie-Antoinette.

Doyle, William. *The Oxford History of the French Revolution*. Oxford, England: Clarendon Press, 1989. The author gives a standard account of the political and social background of the most significant period of Marie-Antoinette's life.

Erickson, Carolly. *To the Scaffold: The Life of Marie-Antoinette*. New York: William Morrow, 1991. The queen's humanity emerges in this well-balanced narrative. According to the author, the intimacy between the queen and Fersen almost certainly became physical in the 1780's.

Fraser, Antonia. *Marie Antoinette: The Journey*. New York: N. A. Talese/Doubleday, 2001. Fraser portrays Marie-Antoinette as good-hearted, badly educated, and totally unprepared to confront the political turmoil of late eighteenth century France.

Hardman, John. *Louis XVI*. New Haven, Conn.: Yale University Press, 1993. The author describes at length how the queen swayed her husband's judgment in political matters on many occasions.

Howarth, T. E. B. *Citizen-King: The Life of Louis-Philippe, King of the French*. London: Eyre and Spottiswoods, 1761. Marie-Antoinette figures prominently in the first nine chapters of this biography of the son of the prince, who was one of the queen's most dangerous enemies.

Mossiker, Frances. *The Queen's Necklace*. New York: Simon & Schuster, 1961. The author reconstructs the affair that proved so damaging to the queen's reputation, quoting extensively from memoirs, letters, and legal documents.

Price, Munro. *The Fall of the French Monarchy: Louis XVI, Marie Antoinette, and the Baron de Breteuil*. London: Macmillan, 2002. Recounts the clandestine campaign to restore the French monarchy to power between 1789 and 1793. Focuses on Breteuil's efforts to win financial and military support from other European monarchs. The book was subsequently published in the United States and retitled *The Road from Versailles: Louis XVI, Marie Antoinette, and the Fall of the French Monarchy.*

See also: Étienne François de Choiseul; Joseph II; Louis XV; Louis XVI; Andreas Sigismund Marggraf; Comte de Mirabeau.

Related articles in *Great Events from History: The Eighteenth Century, 1701-1800*: May 5, 1789: Louis XVI Calls the Estates-General; June 20, 1789: Oath of the Tennis Court; July 14, 1789: Fall of the Bastille; October, 1789-April 25, 1792: France Adopts the Guillotine; April 20, 1792-October, 1797: Early Wars of the French Revolution; September 20, 1792: Battle of Valmy; January 21, 1793: Execution of Louis XVI; March 4-December 23, 1793: War in the Vendée; July 27-28, 1794: Fall of Robespierre; November 9-10, 1799: Napoleon Rises to Power in France.

FIRST DUKE OF MARLBOROUGH
English general

Marlborough was a skillful diplomat and a brilliant general whose stunning victories over France in the War of the Spanish Succession established Great Britain as a major power and ended King Louis XIV's dreams of French hegemony over Europe.

Born: May 26, 1650; Ashe, Devonshire, England
Died: June 16, 1722; Windsor Lodge, Windsor, England
Also known as: John Churchill (birth name)
Areas of achievement: Diplomacy, military, warfare and conquest

EARLY LIFE

John Churchill was the son of Sir Winston Churchill, a member of the lower gentry and a committed supporter of the Stuart monarchy, and Elizabeth Churchill (née Drake). Parliament's victory in the English Civil War left Sir Winston destitute, and he and his growing family (there were twelve children, five of whom survived infancy) were forced to live with his mother-in-law, a Puritan and a staunch Parliamentarian. The poverty and likely family tension of John Churchill's early years were ended only by the restoration of Charles II in 1660. His father stood relatively high in favor with the new regime, and John prospered as well. In late 1665, he left St. Paul's School to become a page of honor to James, duke of York, and two years later, he began his military career as an ensign in the foot guards.

Intelligent, superbly handsome, charming, and doubtless aided by his sister Arabella's position as James's mistress, Churchill continued to prosper at court in the 1670's. He also gained valuable experience abroad. He was for a time at Tangier and served with distinction under the duke of Monmouth, Charles II's illegitimate son, in the Dutch War.

It was in this same period that Churchill fell in love with Sarah Jennings, an attendant upon Princess Anne. The courtship was prolonged and obstructed, first by his own lack of wealth and second by his parents' desire for a richer marriage. Contrary to his later reputation for greed and an overwhelming desire for wealth, however, Churchill rejected his parents' wishes and secretly married Sarah in 1678.

LIFE'S WORK

Despite his rising stature at court, Churchill became a figure of national significance only following the accession of James II in 1685. In May, he was created Baron Churchill of Sandridge, a reward for his loyalty during the Exclusion Crisis, and in June and July he played an important role in crushing Monmouth's ill-fated invasion and rebellion. Churchill soon grew disenchanted, however, with the new king's policies. He refused royal pressure to convert to Roman Catholicism, and in January, 1688, he openly remonstrated with James about the likely consequences of his religious and political program. At the same time, he informed William III and of Orange of his unshakable loyalty to the Protestant religion and pledged his support to the Dutch prince. Action followed words. On November 24, he deserted his command and the Royal Army at Salisbury to join William's invading force. Although he was only one of many in the political nation to desert James's service, Churchill's decision was critical in ensuring the disintegration of the Royal Army and thus in determining that the Glorious

Revolution would not degenerate into a bloody and disastrous civil war.

Churchill initially prospered under the new regime. In 1689, he was appointed to the Privy Council, created earl of Marlborough, and given command of English troops in the Netherlands for the Battle of Walcourt. One year later, he conceived and led a short, brilliant campaign that captured Cork and Kinsdale and brought southeastern Ireland under English control. His relationship with William III and Mary II, however, then deteriorated. In part, the problem lay with his Jacobite contacts. Along with many other prominent Englishmen, Marlborough was in communication with the exiled Stuart court at St. Germain, offering vague promises of support as a sort of insurance policy against an uncertain future. William generally chose to overlook these contacts, recognizing their innocuous character. Marlborough's case proved different, however, largely because of his influence within the English army and with Princess Anne. The earl was a spokesman for many English officers who resented the preferential treatment William appeared to give to foreign officers and to Englishmen and Scotsmen who had entered his service before 1688. In late 1691, he was urging a parliamentary address from the House of Commons, calling on William to deny command of English troops to foreign or naturalized officers. At the same time, William and Mary believed that he was responsible for the growing estrangement between the queen and her sister Anne. In January, 1692, the royal couple responded by removing Marlborough from all offices and places of trust.

Marlborough's reconciliation with William came slowly. His military talents, though, could not be ignored. By 1698, Marlborough had been restored to his former offices and military rank and was a trusted adviser to William. In 1701, he was named commander in chief of the Anglo-Dutch forces in the Netherlands and a plenipotentiary to negotiations at The Hague that were designed to re-create the Grand Alliance against King Louis XIV and France. When William died and was succeeded by Queen Anne in March, 1702, Marlborough assumed the former's role as the effective leader of the Grand Alliance in the new war against France.

Marlborough's first two campaigns in 1702 and 1703 proved to be extremely frustrating. The duke—created the duke of Marlborough in December, 1702—realized that the War of the Spanish Succession could be won and the balance of power in Europe restored only by the defeat of the French armies in the field. He wished to wage an unconventional war of movement and ruthless, deci-

---

MONTAGU'S TRIBUTE TO MARLBOROUGH

In response to the first duke of Marlborough's great victories in the War of the Spanish Succession, especially at the Battle of Blenheim, Mary Wortley Montagu composed a poem in the duke's honor, reproduced here.

When the proud Frenchman's strong rapacious hand
Spread o'er Europe ruin and command,
Our sinking temples and expiring law
With trembling dread the rolling tempest saw;
Destin'd a province to insulting Gaul,
This genius rose, and stopp'd the ponderous fall.
His temperate valour form'd no giddy scheme,
No victory ras'd him to a rage of fame;
The happy temper of his even mind
No danger e'er could shock, or conquest blind.
Fashion'd alike by Nature and by Art,
To please, engage, and int'rest ev'ry heart.
In public life by all who saw approv'd,
In private hours by all who knew him lov'd.

Source: Mary Wortley Montagu, "John Duke of Marlborough," in *The Letters and Works of Mary Wortley Montagu.* 3d ed. (London: Henry G. Bohn, 1861).

---

sive battles; his Dutch allies, however, who retained a veto over his freedom of action over a mixed force of English, Dutch, and German troops, preferred to continue the traditional strategy of sieges, maneuvers, and countermaneuvers around the fortresses on the Meuse and the lower Rhine.

The stalemate was broken in 1704. The French threatened to join forces with the elector of Bavaria, march down the Danube to Vienna, and drive Austria out of the war. Marlborough responded with a daring maneuver that startled all of Europe. Without informing his Dutch allies of his final destination, he marched forty thousand men 250 miles up the Rhine and over to the Danube. There he joined forces with Eugene of Savoy, the imperial general, and on August 12, their combined forces surprised and utterly crushed a numerically superior Franco-Bavarian army at the Battle of Blenheim. For the first time since the 1630's, a French army had been destroyed in combat.

Although Blenheim remained the most dramatic of Marlborough's victories, other stunning triumphs soon followed. He returned to the Low Countries and destroyed another French army at Ramillies on May 12,

1706. Demoralized and panic-stricken, French garrisons readily surrendered a vast belt of fortresses across the Spanish Netherlands. When, in 1708, King Louis XIV attempted to regain his lost provinces, the French army was caught by Marlborough and Eugène at Oudenarde on July 11 and badly beaten.

Marlborough's victories had seemingly won the war, but he failed to win the peace. A French king willing to make generous concessions would not accept the humiliating demand that he use force to expel his grandson, Philip V, from the Spanish throne. Marlborough sincerely desired peace and agreed that the allied demands were too severe. Nevertheless, perhaps because he believed that the collapse of France was imminent, he did not press his government to moderate the proposed peace terms.

The failure to achieve peace was poorly received in England. There was a growing belief that English money and men were being poured into a needless war, a sentiment further strengthened by news of the Battle of Malplaquet. On September 11, 1709, Marlborough and Eugène again defeated the French, but at a frightful cost. The unprecedented carnage of twenty thousand allied casualties stunned public opinion. In this atmosphere, there were revived fears of the threat a standing army offered to English liberties and rumors that Marlborough aspired to be a second Oliver Cromwell. Moreover, the duke no longer possessed the confidence of the queen. Her once-passionate friendship with Sarah Churchill had ended in total estrangement. By 1710, Anne was convinced that Marlborough and the Whig ministers she had been pressured to accept into the government were only prolonging the war for their own selfish interests. In August, she turned to Sir Robert Harley to form a new government. He replaced the old ministers with Tories but retained Marlborough, whose presence was deemed necessary to compel the French to negotiate a favorable peace. By December, 1711, however, the preliminaries were completed. Marlborough was dismissed and censured in Parliament for alleged financial corruption. The charges were palpably false; their sole intent was to silence Marlborough and to blacken his reputation. In November, 1712, he chose voluntary exile abroad rather than endure further humiliations at home. During the next two years, he worked with the electoral court of Hanover to ensure a Protestant succession in England. He did not return to England until August 1, 1714, the day of Queen Anne's death.

Marlborough again enjoyed royal favor following the accession of King George I, but the duke was now an old man. Once remarkable for his intellectual and physical vigor, he had been worn out by his labors and responsibilities. In May and November, 1716, he suffered two paralytic strokes. He recovered, but his remaining years were saddened by bitter quarrels between his wife and surviving children. In June, 1722, he suffered another stroke and died on June 16. He was buried in Westminster Abbey, but his body was later removed to Blenheim Palace, an elaborate residence begun by Queen Anne in happier times as a monument to his victory over the French.

SIGNIFICANCE

The first duke of Marlborough was not without flaws. He was inordinately ambitious for wealth, titles, and fame. These blemishes on his character, however, merely humanize a man who was also an astute diplomat and a brilliant general. William III's death in 1702 left Marlborough with the task of maintaining the unity of the Grand Alliance and leading its forces to victory over France. Yet his powers and influence were much less than those of William. He was neither a prince of Orange nor a stadtholder of the Netherlands nor a king of England, and thus he could not impose his views as his predecessor had done. Nevertheless, he successfully dissuaded the enigmatic Charles XII of Sweden from attacking the Habsburgs, and he achieved a remarkable degree of harmony and cooperation among the allies in the Low Countries. His one great failure was his inability to use his victories on the battlefield to impose a peace that would satisfy all the principal allies. Marlborough's was not the sole or even the preeminent voice at the negotiating table. While he might have used his influence more aggressively, there is no certainty that he could have persuaded the Whig junto to moderate the demands made on Louis XIV.

Whatever Marlborough's failings as a diplomat, there is no doubt that he was the foremost commander of his age. Warfare in the early eighteenth century had evolved into a predictable pattern of long sieges and evasive marches. Marlborough recognized the futility of a strategy of siege warfare in the Low Countries, which could only lead to a lengthy war of attrition and stalemate. Instead, he was determined to force open-field battles which might yield decisive victories. Blenheim, Ramillies, and Oudenarde all rewarded his skill and daring to the fullest. These victories established the prestige of English arms in Europe at a level unmatched since Agincourt in the early fifteenth century. More important, Marlborough's triumphs defeated Louis XIV's final bid for hegemony and restored the balance of power in Europe; not until Napoleon would France again threaten to dominate the Continent.

—*William R. Stacy*

FURTHER READING

Churchill, Winston S. *Marlborough: His Life and Times*. 6 vols. New York: Charles Scribner's Sons, 1933-1938. Perhaps overwritten and certainly sympathetic toward its subject, but still the best biography of Marlborough.

Hibbert, Christopher. *The Marlboroughs: John and Sarah Churchill, 1650-1744*. New York: Viking Press, 2001. Dual biography focusing on the personal lives and political careers of this eighteenth century "power couple."

Holmes, Geoffrey. *British Politics in the Age of Queen Anne*. New York: St. Martin's Press, 1967. An indispensable analysis of the structure of politics during Queen Anne's reign.

Horwitz, Henry. *Parliament, Policy, and Politics in the Reign of William III*. Newark: University of Delaware Press, 1977. A detailed narrative of English politics in the reign of William III. Another indispensable work, but difficult to read.

Jones, J. R. *Marlborough*. New York: Cambridge University Press, 1993. Jones, who wrote about Marlborough's role in the Glorious Revolution, later wrote this biography of Marlborough.

_____. *The Revolution of 1688 in England*. New York: W. W. Norton, 1972. The best study of the Glorious Revolution. Offers a sympathetic analysis of James II's policies.

Macaulay, Thomas B. *The History of England, from the Accession of James II*. Edited by C. H. Firth. 2 vols. 1849. Reprint. Cincinnati, Ohio: E. D. Trunan, 1913-1915. Although dated and marred by the author's Whig bias, this remains a classic survey of the period. Often harsh in its judgments of Marlborough.

Scouller, R. E. *The Armies of Queen Anne*. Oxford, England: Clarendon Press, 1966. Scouller's focus is narrowly confined to the administration, organization, recruitment, and finance of Anne's armies.

Snyder, H. L., ed. *The Marlborough-Godolphin Correspondence*. Oxford, England: Clarendon Press, 1975. Makes available the voluminous written correspondence between the two men from 1702 to 1710.

Trevelyan, George Macaulay. *England Under Queen Anne*. 3 vols. London: Longmans, Green, 1931-1934. Whiggish in its interpretation of events but factually sound and gracefully written. A classic work.

Webb, Stephen Saunders. *Lord Churchill's Coup: The Anglo-American Empire and the Glorious Revolution Reconsidered*. New York: Knopf, 1995. Focuses on the military's role in the Glorious Revolution. Webb argues that the revolution was actually a military coup led by Churchill.

See also: Queen Anne; Second Duke of Argyll; First Viscount Bolingbroke; Lancelot Brown; Charles XII; Sarah Churchill; Eugene of Savoy; George I; First Earl of Godolphin; Philip V; Robert Walpole.

Related articles in *Great Events from History: The Eighteenth Century, 1701-1800:* May 26, 1701-September 7, 1714: War of the Spanish Succession; June 12, 1701: Act of Settlement; May 15, 1702-April 11, 1713: Queen Anne's War; April 13, 1704: Battle of Blenheim; February, 1706-April 28, 1707: Act of Union Unites England and Scotland; March 23-26, 1708: Defeat of the "Old Pretender"; September 11, 1709: Battle of Malplaquet; December, 1711: Occasional Conformity Bill; 1712: Stamp Act; April 11, 1713: Treaty of Utrecht; September 6, 1715-February 4, 1716: Jacobite Rising in Scotland; 1721-1742: Development of Great Britain's Office of Prime Minister.

GEORGE MASON
American politician

Author of the Virginia Declaration of Rights, Mason also had a major role in shaping the Virginia constitution of 1776 and the U.S. Constitution. He was a model proponent of individual and states' rights, and of a limited federal government.

Born: December 11, 1725; Fairfax County, Virginia
Died: October 7, 1792; Gunston Hall, Virginia
Area of achievement: Government and politics

EARLY LIFE

George Mason was born on the family's plantation along the Potomac River in Virginia. His father, the third George Mason, drowned in a ferry accident when Mason was ten years old. His mother, Ann Thomson Mason, then took the family to her dower plantation, Chopawamsic, south of the Occoquan River. Along with his mother, Mason's uncle-in-law, lawyer John Mercer of Marlborough, became his coguardian. The small clergymen's schools of the time afforded what formal education Mason received. Unlike many of the gentry's sons, Mason never attended the College of William and Mary or studied in England. Making use of his uncle's extensive library, however, Mason became learned in the law.

Mason married Ann Eilbeck on April 4, 1750. In the 1750's, Gunston Hall, which still stands in Fairfax County, Virginia, was completed, with architect William Buckland responsible for the distinctive quality of the interior decoration.

Throughout his life, Mason was reluctant to enter into the limelight. Nevertheless, on occasion he accepted public office and exercised leadership in the community. Although losing in a race for a seat in the House of Burgesses in 1748, Mason was successful ten years later, serving as a burgess from 1758 to 1761. Like other gentry, he had long served as a justice of the peace and a vestryman. From 1749 to 1779, Mason was an active partner in the Ohio Company, although the efforts of the company to retain vast land holdings in the Ohio Valley came to naught. He also championed internal improvements and, along with George Washington, had a major role in founding a company for improvement of Potomac River navigation.

Mason became involved with the revolutionary movement, although staying mainly behind the scenes. His first published document was *Scheme for Replevying Goods and Distress for Rent* (1765), which carried a denunciation of slavery. During the Stamp Act crisis (1765-1766), he helped to prepare the text of an agreement adopted by an association formed in the colony to boycott trade with Great Britain. In 1766, he published in the London *Public Ledger* a long letter, signed "A Virginia Planter," which was a reply to a memorial of London merchants, in which Mason made a distinction between legislation and taxation in reference to parliamentary authority. Mason also helped write the Virginia Resolutions of 1769, denouncing the Townshend duties, and he had a leading role at that time in the reforming of the colony's nonimportation association. In 1773, Mason wrote *Extracts from the Virginia Charters*, in defense of Western land claims, which was used in defining boundaries in the Treaty of Paris of 1783.

Mason's first wife died on March 9, 1773, and seven years later he married Sarah Brent. His reluctance to enter public life was owing in part to ill health; he suffered from gout and erysipelas. Nevertheless, Mason assumed leadership in his county with the coming of the resistance movement in 1774, in response to Parliament's Coercive Acts. He wrote the celebrated Fairfax Resolves, which was accepted by both the Virginia Convention and the Continental Congress. He was also the author of the nonimportation resolves, endorsed by the Virginia House of Burgesses and which also formed the basis for the Continental Association established by the Continental Congress. Mason served in the Virginia Conventions of 1775-1776 and was a member of the colony's Committee of Safety, which operated as an executive board to run the colony. Although adopting his father's title of colonel, Mason eschewed any military participation. He did, however, help organize the Fairfax County independent company at the start of the war.

LIFE'S WORK

George Mason's early claim to fame rests on his drafting the Virginia Declaration of Rights, passed by the Virginia Convention in the summer of 1776, and preparing a draft document, which, along with that of Thomas Jefferson, provided the content for the Virginia constitution. As a member of the House of Delegates (1777-1781), Mason had a key role in the assembly's creation of a land office for the disposal of Western lands, and his plans formed the basis of the new United States policies governing the public domain. Also as a delegate, Mason was one of a committee of five who worked on a bill to disestablish religion in Virginia, becoming a legislative enactment in 1786. In 1785, Mason, at the Mount Vernon Conference, helped negotiate the agreement between Maryland and Virginia on the navigation of the Potomac.

Although preferring private to public happiness, Mason was persuaded, after several other appointees bowed out, to be a member of the Virginia delegation to the Constitutional Convention in 1787. During the debates over the writing of the U.S. Constitution, Mason exercised an influence matched by few others. He delivered 139 speeches and left his mark, though not entirely to his liking, on every major issue that came before the convention. He had also been a major contributor to the Virginia Plan, whose general principles were adopted by the convention. Mason denounced slavery. A particular objection that he had to the Constitution was that the three-fifths compromise, regarding counting slaves for the purpose of representation, did not weigh equally with conferring on Congress strong powers in the regulation of commerce, which was part of the compromise and which gave an advantage to Northern economic interests.

Although Mason got much of what he wanted in the Constitution, such as an independent executive, he was disappointed in its overall tone. He feared that the new government would be a cross between a monarchy and a "tyrannical aristocracy." Mason also objected to the authority bestowed on the Senate at the expense of the lower house (namely the Senate having a veto power over appropriations and in singly consenting to treaties, which became the law of the land), and he also feared that, without restrictions, the federal judiciary would encroach on the legal rights of the states. Most of all, Mason disparaged the absence of a bill of rights. Like many other anti-Federalists, however, Mason believed that the Constitution's inadequacies could be remedied by a second convention. He was one of three of those present at the end of the convention who refused to sign the document. Shortly after the adjournment of the convention, Mason published, in broadside form, *The Objections of the Hon. George Mason to the Proposed Federal Constitution* (1787).

At the Virginia ratifying convention in Richmond, during June, 1788, Mason, along with Patrick Henry, James Monroe, and others, led the fight to deny ratification. They almost succeeded, but because of news of ratification by the ninth state, George Washington's strong support of the Constitution, and other factors, the Constitution was narrowly approved, eighty-nine to seventy-nine.

With the ratification of the Bill of Rights, Mason became almost totally reconciled with the Constitution. He was especially pleased with the adoption of the Tenth Amendment, which guaranteed the residual powers of the states. If there were only two or three further amendments, Mason commented, he "could cheerfully put" his "Hand and Heart to the New Government."

In the last years of his life, Mason was content to enjoy solitude and the domestic pleasures of a Virginia gentleman. On the public side, he showed more interest in the locating of the county courthouse than in Congress's decision to place the national capital along the banks of the Potomac, whereby his lands in the area would greatly rise in value. Mason had no concern in serving in the new government. When Senator William Grayson died in 1790, Mason turned down an appointment proffered by Governor Edmund Randolph to fill the vacancy in the Senate, even though he would have as his colleague in the Senate his friend and staunch political ally Richard Henry Lee. Mason followed closely the course of the French Revolution, which he likely inspired, especially since his fourth son, John, a member of the commercial house of Fenwich and Mason in Bordeaux, was in that country from 1788 to 1791. George Mason died quietly at Gunston Hall on Sunday, October 7, 1792.

George Mason. (Library of Congress)

SIGNIFICANCE

As a thinker rather than a publicist or politician, George Mason left a profound imprint upon the creation of constitutional government in America, and his views on the necessity of restricting governmental power so as not to infringe upon individual liberty have afforded a guide by which to interpret the meaning of the U.S. Constitution. Mason is representative of the American Enlightenment because of his emphasis upon balance in government and the right of the individual to pursue private and public happiness. Following the role he had charted for himself, he advised his sons to prefer "the happiness and independence" of a "private station to the troubles and vexations of Public Business."

Making his most important contributions when he was more than fifty years old, Mason was like a Cincinnatus, regarded for his wisdom and devotion to a virtuous republic. Next to James Madison, he had the clearest grasp among the Founding Fathers of the lessons of history and the need to create balanced government, with the assurance that power ultimately resided with the people. His Virginia Declaration of Rights served as a model for other states' bills of rights and inspired the famous French Declaration of the Rights of Man and of the Citizen in 1789 and the later United Nations Declaration of Rights. Finally, Mason's views on American federalism would have influence on the later states' rights philosophy and, with some distortion, upon the doctrines of nullification and secession.

—Harry M. Ward

FURTHER READING

Copeland, Pamela C., and Richard K. MacMaster. *The Five George Masons: Patriots and Planters of Virginia and Maryland*. Charlottesville: University Press of Virginia, 1975. This book was intended to provide the board of regents of Gunston Hall with information on the material culture of Mason's home as well as various facets of his life. Offers extensive genealogical discussion and provides information on plantation economy, civic and parish affairs, and family.

Elliot, Jonathan, comp. *The Debates in the Several State Conventions on the Adoption of the Federal Constitution . . . Together with the Journal of the Federal Convention*. Rev. ed. 5 vols. Philadelphia: J. B. Lippincott, 1836-1845. Reprint. New York: Burt Franklin, 1965. Volume 3 presents the proceedings and debates of the Virginia Ratifying Convention held in Richmond on June 3-27, 1787. Includes reprints of Mason's speeches.

Farrand, Max, ed. *The Records of the Federal Convention of 1787*. 1911. Reprint. 4 vols. New Haven, Conn.: Yale University Press, 1937. Reproduces the notes on the debates and proceedings of the Constitutional Convention from all known sources. Mason's role is clearly defined.

Johnson, George R., Jr., ed. *The Will of the People: The Legacy of George Mason*. Fairfax, Va.: George Mason University Press, 1991. Several essayists examine the American ideal of popular sovereignty from its colonial and revolutionary origins to the present day.

Mason, John. *The Recollections of John Mason: George Mason's Son Remembers His Father and Life at Gunston Hall*. Edited by Terry K. Dunn. Marshall, Va.: EPM, 2004. John Mason (1766-1849), one of George Mason's eight children, wrote this memoir about his childhood.

Miller, Helen H. *George Mason: Constitutionalist*. Gloucester, Mass.: Peter Smith, 1938. Reprint. Cambridge, Mass.: Harvard University Press, 1966. A well-written general biography with emphasis both on Mason's constitutional writing and on his family.

_____. *George Mason: Gentleman Revolutionary*. Chapel Hill: University of North Carolina Press, 1975. A full modern biography of special value because of the book's interpretative quality. Provides an expansive history of the events and movements with which Mason was associated.

Rowland, Kate M. *The Life of George Mason, 1725-1790, Including His Speeches, Public Papers, and Correspondence*. Introduction by General Fitzhugh Lee. 2 vols. New York: G. P. Putnam's Sons, 1892. Reprint. New York: Russell and Russell, 1964. A thorough biography of Mason, interlaced profusely with selections from his writings and correspondence. A good perspective on the times; solid scholarship and readable. The author had access to family papers, many of which have since disappeared.

Rutland, Robert A. *George Mason: Reluctant Statesman*. Foreword by Dumas Malone. Williamsburg, Va.: Colonial Williamsburg, 1961. A brief survey by an authority on George Mason that serves as an introduction to a fuller study.

_____, ed. *The Papers of George Mason, 1752-1790*. 3 vols. Chapel Hill: University of North Carolina Press, 1970. The complete extant writings and letters of Mason and correspondence from others. Also includes a ninety-page biographical and geographical glossary, an introduction, and a Mason chronology for each volume. Excellent annotations.

COTTON MATHER
American religious leader and scholar

Devoted to God and to learning, Mather provided a distinctively American perspective to European thought and sought to reconcile New England Puritanism with the intellectual trends of his day.

Born: February 12, 1663; Boston, Massachusetts
Died: February 13, 1728; Boston, Massachusetts
Areas of achievement: Religion and theology, scholarship

EARLY LIFE

Cotton Mather was the eldest son of Increase Mather, a rising Boston preacher, and the grandson of Richard Mather and John Cotton, generally regarded as the spiritual fathers of Massachusetts Bay Colony. Destined to follow his father and grandfathers into the ministry, Cotton was a child prodigy. He was patiently but rigorously tutored by his father, attended Boston Grammar School, and entered Harvard College at age eleven (the youngest student ever to matriculate there). He received his bachelor's degree in 1678 and master's degree in 1681. After assisting his father for five years as a ministerial candidate, Cotton was ordained and became the second pastor at the Old North Church in 1685.

By both parentage and education, Cotton Mather was thoroughly prepared for the Puritan ministry. The precocious lad did, however, encounter special trials and tribulations. The Puritan tradition weighed heavily upon him, and the expectations of his overly protective father were at best a mixed blessing. In fact, Increase Mather, though a loving father in many ways, was a melancholy man whose aloof behavior may have increased the anxiety of his conscientious son. As a young boy, Cotton developed a serious stammer that threatened his potential as a cleric. After much prayer and practice, he learned to control the stuttering, but it would return periodically throughout his life, abruptly reminding him of his own fallibility. Hardly more than a child as a Harvard freshman, he was at times viciously teased by the older students; his famous name and obvious stammer made him a likely target for bullies. He nevertheless loved Harvard, becoming a fellow of the college in 1690, and he yearned to serve as its president, as his father had done for a few years. His hopes were to be dashed, though, for both Harvard and Massachusetts were moving away from the conservative theology of the Mathers.

By the time of his ordination, Mather had largely overcome his stuttering and was widely known as an eloquent and scholarly young preacher. He was also following in his father's footsteps as counselor to the government and prophet to the people. Father and son made common cause against Governor Edmund Andros and the Dominion of New England over which he governed. In 1689, while Increase carried the protest to London, Cotton remained in Boston and joined with other provincial leaders who took advantage of the Glorious Revolution in England to jail Andros and overturn the Dominion. Three years later, Mather became embroiled in the witchcraft trials at Salem. He believed in the existence of witches and wrote several pamphlets defending the introduction of such spectral evidence as dreams and visions in the judicial proceedings. Although he was more of an observer than an instigator, his defense of the prosecutions was criticized at the time and vigorously denounced by historians ever since. After all, more than 150 persons were jailed and mistreated as accused witches and, at minimum, 19 persons were executed. Indeed, the negative historical image of Mather as the learned but bigoted and superstitious Puritan preacher is based squarely upon his inglorious involvement in the pathetic witchcraft controversy.

While establishing himself as a preacher, Mather was eager to begin his own family. He was reportedly a handsome young man, and the portraits painted of him in later life suggest the bright eyes, the pleasant and expressive face, and the genial personality of the young parson who dressed in style and elegance and pointedly defended the wearing of perukes. For a clergyman with limited income, marrying was especially important. He married at age twenty-three, finding a good and loving wife in Abigail Phillips and a measure of economic security in her prosperous father. Mather took great joy and satisfaction in his family, but he also experienced the heartbreak that only a loving father and husband could know. Five of the nine children Abigail bore died very young, and Abigail herself died of consumption in 1702. Only thirty-nine years old, Mather married again, marrying a young widow, Elizabeth Clark, who gave birth to six more children. By 1713, Elizabeth was dead, and so were four of her children. Mather was a warm and affectionate man who loved his wives and his children dearly and found consolation and fulfillment in his family.

LIFE'S WORK

Cotton Mather was first and foremost a preacher calling his generation back to the religious traditions of the Puritan fathers. Yet, for all of his essential conservatism, Mather was not nearly as inflexible as his critics have claimed. In fact, he recognized that if Puritanism were to be revived in the minds and hearts of the people, it would have to reach an accommodation with the increasingly secular trends of his own day. He saw himself as a peace-

maker, and time and time again, he tried to reconcile antagonistic views, usually finding himself blamed by all sides. In fact, his involvement in the witchcraft trials was an effort to define more precisely the legal status of controversial spectral evidence. A few years later, he sought to unite Congregationalists and Presbyterians against Anglican pretensions and found himself bitterly denounced by other Congregationalists for his ecumenical endeavors. Similarly, he first tried to moderate before outrightly opposing the Presbyterian ideas of Solomon Stoddard in the Connecticut Valley and Benjamin Colman at Boston's Brattle Street Church.

Mather was a prolific writer who felt compelled to address a multitude of issues. He gained a reputation throughout the colonies as the most learned man in America; his library of several thousand volumes indicated the breadth of his interest. He wrote more than four hundred works that were published and left scores of unpublished manuscripts. Much of what he produced was sermonic or homiletic, instructing others on the way to the godly life. He also wrote philosophical discourses, however, as well as historical and biographical essays, medical and scientific treatises, and hymns. His intellectual curiosity knew no bounds.

He corresponded widely with learned men in Europe and America on astronomy, zoology, geology, and meteorology. He was constantly sending specimens of plants and animals to his friends abroad. Undoubtedly, his best work was *Magnalia Christi Americana: Or, The Ecclesiastical History of New-England* (1702), which told the story of New England, its people, and its landscape from the early English migrations to his own time. Mather gained an international reputation for his scholarly endeavors. In 1710, the University of Glasgow awarded him a doctor of divinity degree. Three years later, he was made a fellow of the prestigious Royal Society of London.

Mather wrote so broadly because he wanted to explain God's grand design both in the natural world and in human relationships. He also found release and comfort in his writing as he tried to cope with mounting problems. There were the deaths of his two wives, his father, and thirteen children; only two of his children survived him. His third wife, Lydia Lee George, whom he married in 1715, was neurotic and brought him much despair. His political influence, which had been considerable under Governors William Phips and William Stoughton, almost disappeared as he found it difficult to get along with Governor Joseph Dudley, who held power from 1702 to 1715. His relations with Harvard College also declined during the presidency of John Leverett, whom Mather re-

Cotton Mather. (Library of Congress)

SERMONS AND PRAYERS FOR THE SICK AND DYING

Cotton Mather documented the fatal effects the measles had on his family, and his flock, when the disease reached epidemic proportions in Boston in 1713. Mather lost his wife, three of his children, and the family's maid to measles that year.

October 18, 1713. The Measles coming into the Town, it is likely to be a Time of Sickness, and much Trouble in the Families of the Neighbourhood. I would by my public Sermons and Prayers, endeavour to prepare the Neighbours for the Trouble which their Families are likely to meet withal.

The Apprehension of a very deep Share, that my Family may expect in the common Calamity of the spreading Measles, will oblige me to be much in pleading the great Family-Sacrifice, that so the wrath of heaven may inflict no sad Thing on my Family; and to quicken and augment the Expressions of Piety, in the daily Sacrifices of my Family; and to lay hold on the Occasion to awaken Piety, and Preparation for Death, in the Souls of the children.

November 4, 1713. In my poor Family, now, first, [my] Wife has the Measles appearing on her; we know not yet how she will be handled [treated].

My Daughter Nancy is also full of them; not in such uneasy Circumstances as her predecessors.

My Daughter Lizzy is likewise full of them; yet somewhat easily circumstanced. . . .

November 15, 1713. Tis a Time of much calamity in my Neighbourhood, and a time of much Mortality seems coming on. My Public Prayers and Sermons must be exceedingly adapted for such a Time.

Source: Cotton Mather, "Help Lord" (1713), in *Living History America*, edited by Erik Bruun and Jay Crosby (New York: Tess Press, 1999), pp. 75-77.

latter work signaled Mather's shift intellectually and religiously away "from the supernatural to the civic, from New England to the World, from regeneration to progress." Doing good also meant writing the *Christian Philosopher* (1721), the first book in general science written in colonial America. It meant defying public opinion and advocating inoculation against smallpox during the terrible epidemic of 1721-1722. Indeed, whether sending "Curiosa Americanna" to the Royal Society or writing manuals for young preachers, Mather was driven by his desire to do good in all things. He was thus driven in deed and scholarship until his death on February 13, 1728.

SIGNIFICANCE

Following the example of his father, Cotton Mather was both a preacher and a scholar, with preaching always coming first. In Puritan life, the preacher was counselor as well as prophet, charged with guarding the sacred past, interpreting the troubled present, and obtaining divine guidance for the uncertain future. Increase Mather had filled all these roles, and his son was bound and determined to do the same. It was harder for the son because Massachusetts was growing more secular and less dependent on its ministers. Indeed, Cotton Mather himself was a complex mixture of faith and reason. He bridged the considerable gap that separated the religious seventeenth century from the rationalistic eighteenth. His triumphs and tribulations were directly related to the precarious position he occupied between the Puritan past and the secular future. He wittingly and unwittingly played a significant role in the transition from one era to the next.

Lurking behind the rise and decline of Cotton Mather were economic and intellectual forces that transformed the world he had known as a child. The Puritan vision of society, that City upon a Hill, was gone; even Mather recognized that as he embraced a limited ecumenism. Indeed, many of his problems sprang from the latent resentment against the Puritan ministry that was coming to the fore during his adult years. It played a subtle role in the antics of children thought to be possessed by demons, the disruption of congregations, and the further fraction-

garded as more Anglican than Puritan. He played an important role in establishing Yale in 1716, even serving for a time as its rector, but he expected to be named Leverett's successor at Harvard in 1723 and was bitterly disappointed when the presidency was offered to others instead, including his rival, Benjamin Colman. To make matters worse, Mather faced maddening economic problems involving the estate of his second wife's deceased husband, and he had to deal with numerous petty quarrels and divisions within his own congregation.

Mather responded to adversity by resolving to return good deeds for the evil done him. He was influenced to do so by the writings of European pietists, particularly John Arndt and August Hermann Francke. His resolution to do good inspired numerous essays and books, including *Bonifacious: An Essay upon the Good* (1710). According to Kenneth Silverman, his best biographer, the alizing of politics. Mather intuitively grasped the shift to the secular, even if he did not approve of or fully understand it. Through his prolific writing, he sought to reconcile the Puritan past with the coming Age of Reason. He ultimately failed but enjoyed considerable recognition for his efforts, especially in Europe. He wanted others to carry on and had great hope for his younger son Samuel, who shared his father's love for learning and joined him in the ministry. During his last three years of life, despite failing health, he threw himself into his work, publishing thirty-nine titles on every major aspect of the ministry. He wanted desperately to leave a lasting legacy to instruct his son and other young pastors in the New England way.

Historians have not dealt kindly with Cotton Mather. Indeed, his historical image has ebbed and flowed with that of Puritanism generally. Until the mid-twentieth century, historians tended to perpetuate a caricature that took on mythic proportions. The Mather of legendary fame became a symbol of all that democratic, tolerant, reasonable, and individualistic Americans did not want to become. A complex man was transformed into a national gargoyle, threatening vaguely from the unenlightened past. Yet in reality, Mather was the very essence of the America of his times and place. He strove mightily—and with considerable success—to interject his New England perspective into the major intellectual movements of Europe. As Kenneth Silverman put it, "no other person born in America between the time of Columbus and of Franklin strove to make himself so conspicuous—strove, more accurately, to become conspicuous as an American." Unlike his father, he never had any desire to live anywhere but Boston. He was "the first unmistakably American figure in the nation's history." That judicious assessment of Cotton Mather, when everything else is said and done, is the one that tells most about the man and his mission.

—*Ronald Howard*

FURTHER READING

Beall, Otho T., Jr., and Richard Shryock. *Cotton Mather: First Significant Figure in American Medicine*. Baltimore: Johns Hopkins University Press, 1954. Important in the rehabilitation of Mather's historical image, this work makes it clear that Mather contributed significantly to medical investigations. It demonstrates his advanced thinking on the germ theory and inoculation and contains twelve chapters from his manuscript, *The Angel of Bethesda*, a much-neglected classic.

Boas, Ralph Philip, and Louis Boas. *Cotton Mather, Keeper of the Puritan Conscience*. New York: Harper and Brothers, 1928. An interesting account filled with quotations from Mather's diary and correspondence, illuminating his life and times. Draws upon Freudian psychology to explain Mather's so-called neurotic character, reaching conclusions unwarranted by the facts. Still makes for fascinating reading.

Erwin, John S. *The Millennialism of Cotton Mather: An Historical and Theological Analysis*. Lewiston, N.Y.: E. Mellen Press, 1990. A study of Mather's ardent belief in the millennium, including the millennialism expressed in his unpublished treatise *Triparadisus*.

Levy, Babette M. *Cotton Mather*. Boston: Twayne, 1979. Written for college students, this small book is a fine introduction to Mather. It presents the many sides of his active intellect, focusing on his most prominent writings. Mather's accomplishments are given their just due, but his driving ambition and occasional pettiness are also recognized.

Middlekauff, Robert. *The Mathers: Three Generations of Puritan Intellectuals, 1596-1728*. New York: Oxford University Press, 1971. A superb intellectual biography of Richard, Increase, and Cotton Mather. It goes a long way toward correcting the conventional view of Cotton Mather as a learned bigot, emphasizing both his flexible intellect and his understanding of theological and scientific thought. Especially good in demonstrating the evolution of Puritan thought in one intellectual New England family over a century.

Parrington, Vernon L. *The Colonial Mind, 1620-1800*. Vol. 1 in *Main Currents in American Thought*. New York: Harcourt, Brace & World, 1927-1930. A classic in American intellectual history written by a Progressive historian who considers the Puritans repressive conservatives. Parrington portrays Cotton Mather as a small-minded bigot, the personification of decayed Puritanism. No other historian has done more to confirm the popular view of Mather and New England Puritans.

Silverman, Kenneth. *The Life and Times of Cotton Mather*. New York: Harper & Row, 1984. Regarded as the definitive biography of Cotton Mather, this work combines intellectual and social history to provide the fullest explanation of Mather's life. Thoroughly documented and beautifully written, it is basically sympathetic to Mather, though it does not ignore his vanity or his self-righteousness. Silverman sees Mather as a transitional figure, mediating between the religious seventeenth century and the more secular eighteenth, whose intellectual endeavors made him the first truly conspicuous American figure.

Wendell, Barrett. *Cotton Mather: The Puritan Priest.* New York: Dodd, Mead, 1891. Reprint. New York: Harcourt, Brace & World, 1963. An early scholarly defense of Cotton Mather, this biography seeks to explain his role in the witchcraft hysteria and emphasizes his generally ignored intellectual and religious contributions. Criticized at the time as a defense of New England Puritanism by a New England scholar, Wendell's work foreshadows later scholarly interpretations of the much-maligned Mather.

Winship, Michael P. *Seers of God: Puritan Providentialism in the Restoration and Early Enlightenment.* Baltimore: Johns Hopkins University Press, 1996. Focuses on Mather to examine how the Puritans dealt with the tension between their logic and their belief that the workings of God were evident in events as wide-ranging as storms, fainting, and depression.

See also: Charles Carroll; Jonathan Edwards; Ann Lee; Increase Mather; Samuel Sewall.

Related articles in *Great Events from History: The Eighteenth Century, 1701-1800:* 1739-1742: First Great Awakening; March 22, 1765-March 18, 1766: Stamp Act Crisis; October 30, 1768: Methodist Church Is Established in Colonial America; 1773-1788: African American Baptist Church Is Founded; January 16, 1786: Virginia Statute of Religious Liberty; July 28-October 16, 1789: Episcopal Church Is Established; 1790's-1830's: Second Great Awakening.

INCREASE MATHER
American religious leader, diplomat, and educator

Maintaining Puritan beliefs in seventeenth century Massachusetts, Mather led the Congregational churches of Boston to continue the status quo and sought to retain American independence from British political control. As president of Harvard College and a renowned writer, he aided in the development of higher education and culture in New England.

Born: June 21, 1639; Dorchester, Massachusetts
Died: August 23, 1723; Boston, Massachusetts
Areas of achievement: Religion and theology, diplomacy, education

EARLY LIFE
Increase Mather was born in the parsonage of his father, Richard Mather. His mother, née Katharine Hoult, was a "godly and prudent maid" whose family was not Puritan. Richard Mather, a prominent Puritan minister, was much involved in the life of the new colony and chose the name "Increase" for his son to indicate God's favor and prosperity on the new land. Increase was to be a living reflection of the New Testament scripture that describes fruitfulness: Although one person planted and another waters, "God gave the increase."

As with most colonial boys of that period, Increase received his elementary education from his mother, in his home. To supplement her efforts, Increase's father tutored him in Latin and Greek grammar and later enrolled him in a nearby small schoolhouse. At age twelve, Increase entered Harvard College, from which he was graduated in 1656, planning to enter the ministry. Great Britain was then ruled by the Puritans under Oliver Cromwell, and Increase soon joined two of his brothers in Ireland for further theological studies at Trinity College in Dublin.

With the death of Cromwell in 1658, the movement to return to royal rule gained enough additional support that the Puritans lost power and Charles II ascended the throne in 1660. A staunch Puritan, Increase Mather opposed the Restoration and refused to "drink the king's health." Since ministers at that time were paid their salaries by the government, Mather lost his position and was even threatened with arrest. He decided to return to New England in 1661, and he became teacher of the (Congregational) Second Church in Boston.

LIFE'S WORK
Increase Mather thus embarked upon his life's work, that of an influential minister in colonial New England. His work consisted primarily of spiritual ministration to, and biblical teaching of, his congregation. His position, however, gave him great influence among many of the political and business leaders of the colony. He did, in fact, play a key role in Massachusetts' struggle for freedom within the British Empire and for four years served as a diplomatic representative of the colony to the British crown.

Mather's mother had died when he was fifteen, and, in 1656, his father married the widow of his close friend John Cotton, another distinguished minister of New England. Therefore, John and Sarah Cotton's daughter, Maria, became Increase Mather's stepsister. After his return from Ireland, she also became his wife. Increase and Maria apparently had an excellent marriage. She managed their household well, and his "heart did safely trust in her," as Increase expressed it, quoting from the Book of Proverbs in the Old Testament. He was kind to her and loved her dearly, calling her a "great blessing" from the Lord and the "dear companion" of his "pilgrimage on earth." For her part, she considered Increase "the best husband and the best man in the whole world." With words such as these in their diaries it does not take much imagination to see a happy, romantic love in their relationship.

Increase and Maria had ten children, only one of whom died as an infant. All of them had a substantial role to play in the life of the colonies or of England. The oldest, Cotton Mather, became particularly famous, following a career similar to that of his father and grandfather.

Although Mather served his church throughout his lifetime and considered the ministry his principal calling in life, he was also elected president of Harvard College in 1681. Devoting what time he could to college administration, Mather provided a dignity and quiet stability to Harvard during many of its early and difficult years. The prestige of his new position added to Mather's already considerable influence in the colony. It is not surprising that Mather soon found himself in the midst of a political controversy with England.

In 1678, King Charles II appointed a leading Anglican politician, Edward Randolph, collector of the king's revenue in Massachusetts. A struggle for power ensued between the representatives of the Crown and American officials in Massachusetts. Finally, in 1683, Charles II sent to Boston a declaration that stated that unless there was "full submission, and entire resignation . . . to his pleasure, a quo warranto" would be prosecuted against the original Massachusetts charter, that is, the constitutional authority enabling Massachusetts to have its own self-government. A quo warranto proceeding was a legal investigation to determine "by what authority" an official governed or acted. Such an inquiry would have led to a revocation of the colonial charter, and Massachusetts would have lost its right of self-government.

Mather refused to yield to a tyrannical king. In January, 1684, he spoke the following words at a town meeting:

If we make a submissive and entire resignation, we fall into the hands of men immediately. But if we do it not, we keep ourselves still in the hands of God, and trust ourselves with his providence. And who knows what God may do for us? . . . And we hear from London, that when it came to, the loyal citizens would not make a full submission and entire resignation to pleasure, lest, haply, their posterity should curse them. And shall we do it then? I hope there is not one freeman in Boston that will dare to be guilty of so great a sin.

There was great excitement among the crowd in the hall, and the vote supporting Mather's position carried without a single dissenting vote. Boston led the way for Massachusetts and Massachusetts for New England.

The king did indeed declare the Massachusetts charter void, but within a year he was dead and his brother, James II, ascended the throne. King James was more conciliatory toward Massachusetts than his brother had been, but he sought to control the New England colonies by placing them all in a single administrative unit under the authority of Sir Edmund Andros. Much of popular government was to be revoked in New England. In its place appeared arbitrary government under the authority of the king and the royal governor. Several of the churches in the Boston area urged Mather to act as an informal colonial emissary to discuss the matter with James II.

Randolph, with his power as representative of the Crown, secured a warrant for Mather's arrest in December, 1687. Mather was tried for subversion on the basis of a forged letter, which he had allegedly written, criticizing the king. At a jury trial, however, the charges were disproved and Randolph was ordered to pay court costs. Not deterred, Randolph sought to arrest Mather again, on a different charge. The minister, however, disguised himself and walked past Randolph's agent guarding his house. He was taken by a small boat to meet the ship that he had been prevented from boarding in Boston. Mather thus became a representative of the Massachusetts colonists in England for the next four years.

In May, 1688, after visiting with several Congregational ministers in London, Mather secured an audience with the king himself. In the course of their conversation, Mather requested that the king recall Governor Andros and sought to explain why he should. In several interviews with the king, Mather received assurances of goodwill but no promise of self-government for New England.

The Glorious Revolution of 1688-1689 now intervened in a bloodless coup to depose James II and to

Increase Mather. (Library of Congress)

try the accused and in August, 1692, a group of seven ministers met with Mather at Cambridge to discuss the witchcraft trials. In an attempt to persuade the court to rule out "spectral evidence" because it was unverifiable and could be falsified by a second witness, Mather wrote a pamphlet called *Cases of Conscience Concerning Evil Spirits* (1693). The pamphlet was endorsed by fourteen ministers and sent to Governor Phipps. The governor then dissolved the special court handling the cases and ordered that spectral evidence be ruled out by Massachusetts courts in the future. There were no more condemnations, although by September, 1692, twenty people, mostly girls and women, had been executed in the hysteria. The governor eventually pardoned the few remaining prisoners and never again were people tried as witches in New England. Mather must be given his share of the credit for stopping the practice.

Mather was also an important literary figure in New England. He wrote more than two hundred books and shorter works. His biography of his father, Richard Mather, published in 1670, was one of the earliest examples of that genre produced in the colonies. Mather owned one of the two largest libraries in Boston and was broadly educated and well-read. Most of his writings were theological and philosophical. Influential in his own day, one work at least made an important contribution in the eighteenth century and continues to be read. *An Essay for the Recording of Illustrious Providences* (1684) was an attempt to record systematically any unusual events in the lives of the colonists that Mather interpreted as examples of divine intervention. They are important for later generations as eyewitness accounts of historical events that reflect and reveal life as it was actually lived in the seventeenth century.

Mather sought to deal honestly with the historical record: He recorded "tragical" as well as joyful endings, writing that "the Lord's faithful servants have sometimes been the subject of very dismal dispensations." Against the objection that God the Creator had established inexorable and immutable natural laws that He could not "violate," Mather claimed that God was merely controlling what He had created and was outside creation and not bound by what He himself had made. It was not miracles that the colonists sought to prove, but merely that God was directly behind the events of their lives. Mather's writings contributed to the debate that raged over Enlightenment ideas in the next century. Mather certainly

replace him with William III, prince of Orange, and Mary II, both related to the Stuart kings. Both houses of Parliament approved of the change and welcomed the Dutch armada and the new monarchs. James fled to France.

King William signed the English Bill of Rights of 1689 and showed himself a lover of constitutional government, with its stress on limited and shared powers and civil and political liberties for all English subjects (including those living in the American colonies). Mather hoped for a return to the original Massachusetts charter. In this he was disappointed. He did, however, manage to return to Massachusetts with a new charter, which restored many of the rights and privileges of the earlier charter. Unable to persuade the king to allow the colony to elect its own governor, Mather did secure the appointment as governor of Massachusetts his son Cotton's close friend and church member, Sir William Phipps.

Mather and the new governor returned together on the same ship and arrived in Boston on May 14, 1692, just as the notorious Salem witch trials were in progress. Governor Phipps appointed a special court to meet in Salem to agreed with the application of rationality and systematic logic to any subject. His writings and sermons clearly demonstrated that quality.

SIGNIFICANCE

Minister, teacher, and statesman, Increase Mather was a key leader of seventeenth and early eighteenth century America. His influence was great because, to a large degree, he reflected and represented the dominant attitudes and beliefs of his time. The study of history deals particularly with both continuity and change. "Change" receives much more attention from historians because it stands out from the status quo and is often dramatic and clearly discernible amid the monotony of routine daily life. "Continuity" is usually described as historical setting or analyzed as part of the existing culture. Most of lived history, however, follows tradition and the routine ritual of everyday life. Sometimes the human value of change for the sake of intended improvement or "progress" (if such it be) conflicts with the equally human need for stability and the security of the familiar. Most people like to know what is expected of them from their society and peers and then like to fulfill those expectations. It was in this area of stability and in the perpetuation of a civilization that Mather made his greatest contribution. He was not afraid of change, but he believed in the shared values of his generation and wanted to pass those cultural values on to the next generation.

In his weekly labors within his parish, as he went about the routine duties of his position, he believed that he was fulfilling the purposes of life. In his leadership at Harvard, he sought to pass on traditional values to the next generation. In the many books he wrote, he sought to present evidence that the Puritans of Massachusetts Bay were on the right pathway and that they should "stay the course."

One of the values he sought to preserve was that of self-government for Massachusetts within the greater British Empire. For that reason, he spent four years as a diplomat and for many other years involved himself in the political issues of the colony. Above all, he sought to perpetuate the Judeo-Christian ethic on which the colony was founded. He set a high moral tone among his own congregation but also often counseled condemned criminals and others whom he thought had gone "astray." Through their words of wisdom, moderation, and reason, Mather and his fellow Puritan ministers and political leaders preserved the culture handed to them throughout their lifetimes.

—*William H. Burnside*

FURTHER READING

Burg, Barry R. *Richard Mather of Dorchester.* Lexington: University Press of Kentucky, 1976. The best single-volume history of Increase Mather's father. Includes important background material on Increase Mather.

Hall, David D. *The Faithful Shepherd: A History of the New England Ministry in the Seventeenth Century.* Chapel Hill: University of North Carolina Press, 1972. Describes Mather's cultural milieu and explains the popular expectations for Puritan ministers of the seventeenth and eighteenth centuries.

Hall, Michael G. *The Last American Puritan: The Life of Increase Mather, 1639-1723.* Middletown, Conn.: Wesleyan University Press, 1988. A scholarly biography, drawing on Mather's diaries to recount his personal life and public career.

Mather, Increase. *An Essay for the Recording of Illustrious Providences.* 1684. Reprint. *Remarkable Providences Illustrative of the Earlier Days of American Colonisation.* 1856. Reprint. Portland, Oreg.: Back Home Industries, 1997. This reprint series gives a sample of Mather's thinking on religion and spirituality in colonial New England.

Middlekauff, Robert. *The Mathers: Three Generations of Puritan Intellectuals, 1596-1728.* New York: Oxford University Press, 1971. Presents the perspective of three generations of the Mathers. Middlekauff is not as sympathetic as most other historians who study the Mathers and their time period.

Miller, Perry. *The New England Mind: The Seventeenth Century.* Cambridge, Mass.: Harvard University Press, 1954. A standard intellectual history of the time and place.

Morison, Samuel Eliot. *The Intellectual Life of Colonial New England.* 2d ed. New York: New York University Press, 1956. Although a brief treatment of Increase Mather, this work includes an excellent history of the New England Puritans.

Munk, Linda. *The Devil's Mousetrap: Redemption and Colonial American Literature.* New York: Oxford University Press, 1997. A literary analysis of the sermons of three colonial New England preachers: Mather, Jonathan Edwards, and Edward Taylor. Examines the sources of their religious thought and the language they used to express their respective theologies.

Murdock, Kenneth B. *Increase Mather: The Foremost American Puritan.* Cambridge, Mass.: Harvard University Press, 1925. A classic study, indispensable for a thorough understanding of the life and times of Increase Mather.

Silverman, Kenneth. *The Life and Times of Cotton Mather*. New York: Harper & Row, 1984. A thorough and scholarly study of Increase Mather's son. Useful also for a broader understanding of Increase Mather's place in American history.

See also: Charles Carroll; Jonathan Edwards; Ann Lee; Cotton Mather; Samuel Sewall; Charles Wesley; John Wesley.

Related articles in *Great Events from History: The Eighteenth Century, 1701-1800:* 1739-1742: First Great Awakening; October 30, 1768: Methodist Church Is Established in Colonial America; 1773-1788: African American Baptist Church Is Founded; January 16, 1786: Virginia Statute of Religious Liberty; July 28-October 16, 1789: Episcopal Church Is Established; 1790's-1830's: Second Great Awakening.

MOSES MENDELSSOHN
German philosopher and Jewish reformer

A scholar both of Talmudic Hebrew literature and of Enlightenment philosophy, Mendelssohn demonstrated a middle ground for eighteenth century European Jews, leading to their integration into modern German society.

Born: September 6, 1729; Dessau, Anhalt (now in Germany)
Died: January 4, 1786; Berlin, Prussia (now in Germany)
Areas of achievement: Philosophy, religion and theology

EARLY LIFE

Moses Mendelssohn (MOH-zehs MEHN-duhl-zohn) was the son of Menachem Mendelssohn, a poor Torah scribe who ensured that Moses received a traditional Jewish education. His teacher David Frankel instructed him in Talmud and gave him a thorough introduction to the writings of the Jewish philosopher Moses Maimonides. In 1743, when Frankel received an appointment in Berlin, Mendelssohn followed him. There his study was expanded to include Latin, Greek, French, and English, as well as mathematics and science.

It was Mendelssohn's good fortune at the age of twenty-one to be hired as a tutor for the family of the successful businessman Isaac Bernhard. Soon, he took on responsibilities as bookkeeper and became a partner in the family's silk manufacturing firm. As a result, Mendelssohn achieved the economic independence necessary to engage in his scholarly pursuits.

LIFE'S WORK

Already, in his early twenties, Mendelssohn had developed a close association with the German dramatist Gotthold Ephraim Lessing. It was Lessing who recognized the gifts of his talented young friend and who encouraged him to publish several essays in 1754, as well as a translation of Jean-Jacques Rousseau's *Discours sur l'inégalité* (1754; *A Discourse on Inequality*, 1756). When, in 1763, Mendelssohn was awarded first prize, ahead of Immanuel Kant, from the Prussian Royal Academy of Sciences for a treatise on metaphysics, it was clear that he had arrived as a respected philosopher.

In 1762, Mendelssohn married Fromet Guggenheim of Hamburg, with whom he would have six children. As a Jew, his situation was always precarious. However, in 1763, he was granted the "right of residence" in Berlin by royal edict. This also exempted him from paying taxes for the rest of his life. He was accepted into Berlin's prominent social circles, and his house became a popular gathering place for the academic elite. In 1771, he was elected by his peers into the Royal Academy, but Frederick the Great refused to ratify the election.

Mendelssohn's most important philosophical work was *Phädon: Oder, Uber die Unsterblichkeit der Seele* (1767; *Phaedon: Or, The Death of Socrates*, 1789). As is evident from the title, this was an attempt to imitate Plato's dialogue concerning the immortality of the soul. Influenced by the philosopher Gottfried Wilhelm Leibniz (1646-1716), Mendelssohn argued for an infinite number of souls (called monads) that make up the basic substance of the universe. When individuals die, he asserted, their souls do not cease to be but dissolve into their original substance. It is the belief in the goodness of God that guarantees continued consciousness of the soul after death.

Mendelssohn's popularity as a philosopher led to religious challenges that diverted him from his theoretical philosophic work. In 1769, a Lutheran Swiss pastor, Johann Kasper Lavater, publicly challenged him to explain why, as an enlightened man, he did not convert to Christianity. The assumption, of course, was that Christianity had been proven by the Enlightenment to be the most rational of all religions.

Mendelssohn's response was to oppose any such pressure for Jewish conversion. He often said that he would prefer to rebut derogatory attitudes about Judaism by righteous living. However, he felt compelled to respond, arguing in detail that Judaism was indeed compatible with rationalism. Knowledge of God was something that all humans possessed through rational thought. However, he said, it is the unique revelation of God at Mount Sinai that provides Jews with the laws for righteous living. This belief had been the essence of his upbringing and his years of study; it was not to be deserted or rejected even in the modern era. A year later, Lavater apologized.

Mendelssohn took an active role in supporting Jewish rights in Europe. When another pastor proposed a Jewish homeland in Palestine, Mendelssohn rejected the idea, arguing instead for full integration of Jews into European society. When the Jews of Dresden were threatened with expulsion, he appealed to his Christian friends for support. When new decrees were proposed against the Jews of Switzerland, it was Lavater to whom he turned. Eventually, Mendelssohn himself appealed directly to the Prussian government at the request of the chief rabbi of Berlin. In such endeavors, Mendelssohn was influential.

In 1783, he wrote *Jerusalem: Oder, Über religiöse Macht und Judentum* (1783; *Jerusalem: A Treatise on Ecclesiastical Authority and Judaism*, 1838), again in response to another challenge from the Christian community. In *Jerusalem*, Mendelssohn argued for a separation of church and state similar to that which was emerging in the American experiment (Mendelssohn had even corresponded with George Washington). Church and state both seek the happiness of individuals, Mendelssohn argued, but they go about it in different ways. While the state has the power of coercion, religious institutions have the power of persuasion. Many Jewish rabbis did not respond well to this work, since excommunication was still part of their authority as community leaders.

Mendelssohn also contributed his learning to the Jewish community, translating the Torah and the Psalms into German. Interestingly, when translating these works, he wrote the German in Hebrew characters, since the Gothic German script was still foreign to many German Jews. Likewise, he wrote commentaries on the biblical books Ecclesiastes and the Song of Solomon. While some ac-

cused him of abandoning traditional Judaism, he was dedicated to preserving Jewish culture. He was a coeditor of the Jewish periodical *Kohelet Musar*, which was published in immaculate Hebrew. It was the Yiddish language that he disdained. Jews, in his view, should be fluent in both Hebrew and German. These were the marks of a Torah-true Jew in modern Germany.

Finally, Mendelssohn was able to turn to philosophy again in his *Morgenstunden* (1785; morning hours). There, he argues that people of all religions can have knowledge of God through their own rational thought processes. In many ways, this is the age-old ontological argument that the idea of God within human consciousness is itself proof of God's existence. Mendelssohn died in Berlin on January 4, 1786.

SIGNIFICANCE

Within two years of Moses Mendelssohn's death, Isaac Euchel had written the first biography of Mendelssohn. Such was the legendary character of the philosopher's life. Within fifty-five years of his death, seven volumes of his collected writings had been gathered and published. For later generations, however, Mendelssohn's exemplary character has been preserved in the tolerant and enlightened protagonist of Lessing's well-known play *Nathan der Weise* (pb. 1779, pr. 1783; *Nathan the Wise*, 1781).

As a product of the Enlightenment, Mendelssohn played a central role in assisting European Jews to wrestle with their identity. On one hand, he was a staunch defender of Judaism, yet on the other hand, many saw him as undermining it. His position was certainly complex. He was concerned about Jews who had totally assimilated, and he opposed all attempts by Christians to pressure conversion of Jews, yet he was uncomfortable with the separation among European Jews, especially in eastern Europe. He disdained the artificial Yiddish language, but he held biblical Hebrew in high regard and encouraged Jewish integration into modern society through German and other modern languages. Reform Judaism is indebted to him.

For Mendelssohn, the paradox of religion accessible through knowledge and the acceptance of divine law revealed at Sinai was possible. Even his own family, however, did not hold on to that distinction: Many of them converted to Christianity, including his grandson Felix, the well-known composer. It is interesting that moderns have dubbed him both "the Jewish Socrates" and "the Jewish Luther."

—Fred Strickert

FURTHER READING

Altmann, Alexander. *Moses Mendelssohn: A Biographical Study*. Oxford, England: Littman Library of Jewish Civilization, 1998. This is a republication of a 1973 work published by the University of Alabama Press. The author sets the life of Mendelssohn against the background of eighteenth century Europe, describing the development of German philosophy and the status of European Judaism.

_____, ed. *Moses Mendelssohn—Jerusalem: Or, On Religious Power and Judaism*. Translated by Allan Arkush. Boston: Brandeis University Press, 1983. An English translation and commentary of Mendelssohn's important theological work.

Arkush, Allan. *Moses Mendelssohn and the Enlightenment*. Albany: State University of New York Press, 1994. The author focuses on the rationalist philosophy of Mendelssohn in relationship to his continued adherence to Judaism.

Dahlstrom, Daniel O., ed. *Moses Mendelssohn: Philosophical Writings*. New York: Cambridge University Press, 1997. An updated translation of Mendelssohn's metaphysics.

Hess, Jonathan. *Germans, Jews, and the Claims of Modernity*. New Haven, Conn.: Yale University Press, 2002. This is an analysis of the debate in Germany over the role of Jews in modern society.

Nordhaus, Jean. *The Porcelain Apes of Moses Mendelssohn*. Minneapolis, Minn.: Milkweed Editions, 2002. This is a biography in poems voiced through individuals who encountered Mendelssohn. The title refers to a mandate under Frederick the Great that Prussian Jews were required to purchase a certain amount of porcelain in order to marry.

See also: Ba‘al Shem Tov; Elijah ben Solomon; Immanuel Kant; Gotthold Ephraim Lessing.

Related articles in *Great Events from History: The Eighteenth Century, 1701-1800*: 1739-1740: Hume Publishes *A Treatise of Human Nature*; April, 1762: Rousseau Publishes *The Social Contract*; 1781: Kant Publishes *Critique of Pure Reason*; 1784-1791: Herder Publishes His Philosophy of History; January 16, 1786: Virginia Statute of Religious Liberty; 1792-1793: Fichte Advocates Free Speech.

MENTEWAB
Empress of Ethiopia (r. 1730-1770)

Mentewab's reign represented the last effective central authority before Ethiopia drifted into decentralization and regional turmoil in the second half of the eighteenth century. Mentewab is also remembered for her patronage of the Church and of the arts and architecture. Many of the splendid religious artworks and palaces she commissioned still exist.

Born: c. 1700; Qwara, Ethiopia
Died: 1772; Gondar, Ethiopia
Also known as: Berhan Mogassa; Walatta Giyorgis
Areas of achievement: Government and politics, patronage of the arts

EARLY LIFE

Mentewab, the dowager empress who dominated Ethiopian politics for nearly half a century, was born at the turn of the eighteenth century in the district of Qwara, in northwest Ethiopia. Popular tradition attributes the beginning of her palace career to a chance encounter with the Emperor Bakaffa, who was said to have fallen ill during one of his trips in disguise in a remote part of his empire and was nursed to life by the beautiful Mentewab. This legend notwithstanding, Mentewab's kin from Qwara were already represented in Bakaffa's court, and it is likely that she owed her introduction to the emperor to the influence of her kinsmen rather than to the romantic encounter of the tradition.

Once she arrived in the capital in 1721 as the emperor's consort, Mentewab quickly established herself as a key political player in the imperial court. The fact that Bakaffa was himself a powerful emperor who jealously guarded monarchical authority did not hinder Mentewab from building her own independent base of power in the palace. The illness of the emperor in 1728 afforded Mentewab an opportunity to emerge as the most powerful political actor in the Ethiopian empire.

Mentewab fortified her position in the palace by placing her close relatives from Qwara in key military and administrative posts. These relatives included her brother Wolde Leul, whom she elevated to the rank of *ras* (the highest rank below emperor), her uncles Dajazmach Arkeledis and Ras Niqoliyos, and her cousin Dajazmach

Eshete. When Emperor Bakaffa died on September 19, 1730, Mentewab, who had carefully planned for this eventuality, moved swiftly to ensure the succession of her infant son, Iyasu II. She made herself his regent, thereby becoming the real power behind the Ethiopian throne. A few months later, she had herself crowned as coruler of the Ethiopian empire.

LIFE'S WORK

The extensive political work she had done during the last years of Bakaffa's reign enabled Mentewab to step in immediately to seize the reins of imperial power. She set out to strengthen her personal hold over the provinces through the appointment of a coterie of trusted governors and generals, most of whom came from her own district of Qwara. Mentewab's ambitious centralization of power and the rapid ascendancy of her Qwara clique threatened to erode the authority of the provincial lords, however. In 1732, a coalition of regional lords mounted a rebellion and briefly besieged the capital city of Gondar, threatening to unseat the empress. The rebels sought to turn the predominantly Orthodox Christian public against the empress by accusing her of secretly adhering to Catholicism.

Ironically, the rebellion further enhanced Mentewab's image by providing her with an opportunity to dispel the bias against her gender and to prove to her subjects that she was as capable of decisive leadership as any in her position. She personally led the war council and was instrumental in the suppression of the rebellion. When the crisis was over, despite lingering resistance from disgruntled members of the nobility, Mentewab's position was firmly established throughout the empire.

In later years, especially after the death of some of her trusted lieutenants from Qwara, Mentewab began to look for allies from among the outlying regions of the empire. She married her son Iyasu II to the daughter of a prominent Oromo chief from Wollo, thereby inaugurating a new era of Oromo ascendancy in palace politics. She also married one of her daughters to the son of Mikael Sehul, a rising star in the province of Tigray. Mentewab elevated Mikael to the title of *ras* and after helping him vanquish rival lords in Tigray, she appointed him governor of the entire region of the north. In subsequent years, Mikael married Mentewab's other daughter, enhancing his power further and making himself indispensable both to Mentewab and to Emperor Iyasu II.

Her alliance with Mikael Sehul proved Mentewab's undoing. Posing as a trusted lieutenant, Mikael skillfully cut the ground from under Mentewab's feet by destroying one palace faction after another, eventually leaving only himself as the most powerful figure in the empire. His control of the areas close to the Red Sea coast allowed him to monopolize the import of firearms into the country. Mikael's army was the best equipped in the empire.

The death of Emperor Iyasu II in 1755 and the passing away of many of Mentewab's old guards from Qwara left a political void that was quickly filled by Mikael Sehul. When the new king, Iyoas, attempted to resist Mikael's usurpation of imperial authority, Mikael had the king strangled in 1769 and installed his own puppet on the throne. The old and isolated Mentewab mounted one last effort to eject Mikael from her capital, but she lost and faded into political obscurity until her death in 1772. Although Mikael Sehul himself was defeated and chased out of the capital city by a coalition of rival lords, the precedent he set continued for several decades to come. In this period, popularly referred to as the Era of Princes, the great lords of the country became the kingmakers.

SIGNIFICANCE

Few women in Ethiopia's long history have had roles in public life to rival Mentewab. A young girl from an obscure district, Mentewab quickly carved her own political career in Emperor Bakaffa's palace. By the time that Bakaffa died, Mentewab, who was barely thirty years old, had established herself as the most formidable political figure in the empire. She engineered the succession of two kings, made herself regent to both, and crowned herself as coruler. Mentewab was the last of the illustrious rulers from Gondar who exercised effective centralized power before authority slipped away from the hands of the monarchy and the country was thrown into an era of feudal disorder and political abyss.

Mentewab is also remembered as one of the greatest benefactors of the Ethiopian Orthodox Church. She built magnificent churches and lavished the clergy with generous land grants. She was a great patron of the arts, architecture, and literature. Gondar, the capital city, flourished under Mentewab's care as the center of a refined court life.

—*Shumet Sishagne*

FURTHER READING

Abir, Mordecai. *Ethiopia: The Era of Princes, the Challenge of Islam, and the Reunification of the Christian Empire, 1769-1855.* London: Longmans Green, 1968. One of the most important works on the political history of Ethiopia that traces the rise of the great lords and the usurpation of imperial authority in the second half of the eighteenth century.

Blondel, Weld H., ed. *Royal Chronicles of Abyssinia*. Cambridge, England: Cambridge University Press, 1922. A collection of chronicles of selected Ethiopian kings, indispensable for students interested in the lives and times of eighteenth century Ethiopian emperors.

Bruce, James. *Travels to Discover the Sources of the Nile*. Selected and edited by C. F. Press. New York: Horizon Press, 1964. A fascinating account of eighteenth century Ethiopian politics and court life in the city of Gondar, the capital of Ethiopia, by the Scottish traveler who arrived in Ethiopia in 1770 and was intimately acquainted with the political elite in the Ethiopian kingdom, including the empress dowager, Mentewab.

Crummey, Donald. *Land and Society in the Christian Kingdom of Ethiopia: From the Thirteenth to the Twentieth Century*. Urbana-Champaign: University of Illinois Press, 2000. A social and political history of Ethiopia, with detailed accounts of Mentewab's political career and her patronage of the church.

Doresse, Jean. *Ethiopia*. London: Elek Books, 1959. A survey of the cultural history of Ethiopia with useful description of the art and architecture that flourished in Gondar during the time of Mentewab.

Henze, Paul B. *Layers of Time: A History of Ethiopia*. New York: Palgrave, 2000. A readable general work that is especially useful in tracing the process of the expansion and shrinking of the Christian kingdom of Ethiopia under the leadership of the Solomonic rulers of Ethiopia. It also includes interesting information on daily life, art, architecture, and religion.

Marcus, Harold. *History of Ethiopia*. Berkeley: University of California Press, 1994. A general survey of Ethiopian history from ancient times to the present by a distinguished scholar of Ethiopian studies.

Pankhurst, Richard, ed. *The Ethiopian Chronicles*. Oxford, England: Oxford University Press, 1967. A collection of contemporary writings that chronicle the lives and careers of eighteenth century Solomonid kings.

See also: James Bruce; Sīdī al-Mukhtār al-Kuntī.

Related article in *Great Events from History: The Eighteenth Century, 1701-1800*: December, 1768-January 10, 1773: Bruce Explores Ethiopia.

COMTE DE MIRABEAU
French politician

Mirabeau was a bridge between the aristocracy and the people, as well as between the variously named legislatures and the king. He led the fight to establish the national assembly out of the Estates-General and to save the monarchy as one of the two agents of the people in the French government.

Born: March 9, 1749; estate of Mirabeau, Bignon, near Nemours, France
Died: April 2, 1791; Paris, France
Also known as: Honoré-Gabriel Riqueti (birth name)
Area of achievement: Government and politics

EARLY LIFE

Honoré-Gabriel Riqueti, comte de Mirabeau (kohnt duh mee-rah-boh), was christened Gabriel-Honoré and called Gabriel in the family. Many of his works were first published anonymously, and he seldom used his title. In the legislature, he was mostly referred to as Mirabeau and sometimes as "the Tribune of the People."

The Riquetis have been traced to the small town of Digne, near Marseilles. Family members accumulated wealth in Marseilles through commerce. Mirabeau's father, Victor Riqueti, Marquis de Mirabeau, eager to increase the family estate and to ensure a long and distinguished family line, sought and finally found an heiress with great financial potential, Marie-Geneviève de Vassan, who was sixteen years old at their marriage in 1743. In six years, she produced two daughters and a son who died in an accident. The marquis was overjoyed when his son and heir, the comte de Mirabeau, was born, but he was immediately appalled to see the child's huge head, two teeth, misshapen foot, and malformed tongue. That harsh blow was intensified three years later, when the child was struck by smallpox.

As the young count grew, he seemed more and more to resemble the Vassan side of the family, which his father came more and more to detest. The birth of two normal children, who resembled the Mirabeau side of the family, worsened the situation. Nevertheless, the marquis, who bravely pursued his wife's fortune, devoted himself to saving his son and heir. The marquis gave his son an excellent tutor and three years of study with the famed Abbé Choquard in Paris and found for him a position in the regiment of the Marquis de Lambert in 1768.

When the young Mirabeau quarreled with Lambert and fled, his father saved his son with the first of many personal orders of the king. These orders, or *lettres de cachet*, permitted imprisonment without a (possibly humiliating) public trial. He was released to join an expedition to Corsica, which France had purchased from Genoa and which, under the famed Pasquale Paoli, was in revolt. Mirabeau served with distinction. Returning home in 1770, he spent time occupied with various projects on family estates. He married Marie-Marguerite-Émilie de Covet de Marignane on June 23, 1772.

LIFE'S WORK

Mirabeau's career began with bankruptcy, for which he was jailed under another *lettre de cachet*. While in prison, he met and fell in love with Marie-Thérèse-Richard de Ruffey, the Marquise de Monnier, a married woman. Mirabeau escaped from prison, and the couple fled the country; Mirabeau was eventually arrested in the Netherlands and imprisoned under yet another *lettre de cachet*.

During this period of about ten years, Mirabeau wrote his most important works. His *Essai sur le despotisme* (1775; essay on despotism) eloquently advocated representative government and a strong executive through the monarchy, but opposed an upper chamber of aristocrats. The essay revealed a knowledge of history and contributed to the later view of Mirabeau as an authority on government and an advocate of the people. *Des lettres de cachet et des prisons d'état* (wr. 1777, pb. 1780; of *lettres de cachet* and of state prisons) was a more technical work, ranging over French constitutional history and developing the theme that personal liberty is the liberty essential to all other liberties. Thus, not even the national interest should be invoked to violate it. This work, with impressive citations, considering Mirabeau's confinement, came to be admired in England and contributed to the growing conviction in France that the monarchy needed restraint.

Mirabeau managed to write many other works and letters while in prison, although he complained that his paper was rationed. He wrote a French grammar and a work on mythology for the Marquise de Monnier (who gave birth to his only child, Sophie-Gabrielle, while he was in prison), a study on inoculation, and several translations. He was passionate and ambitious and, like the philosophes, confident of reason, law, and virtue. He supported the American colonists and detested the Church.

If prison served as a graduate school for Mirabeau, it was in court cases in 1782 and 1783 that Mirabeau realized his vocation, or at least his greatest talent—moving people through the spoken word. Two cases received wide public attention. In 1782, he won cases of the government against him. In 1783, he defended himself against suits brought by his wife's wealthy family in Aix-en-Provence. He lost the judgments and the acceptance of his own class, but he won the hearts of the people with his oratory. Six years later, the people would remember and elect him overwhelmingly as a deputy of the Third Estate (Commons).

During the next several years, Mirabeau had a mistress (Henrietta-Amélie de Nehra, who had a good influence on him), traveled to England, and adopted a son, Lucas de Montigny. Mirabeau was not successful in England. Returning to France in March, 1785, Mirabeau fought off his debts by writing pamphlets for speculators on the Paris Bourse, including famous persons such as Étienne Clavière, who was later minister of finance; Pierre-Samuel du Pont de Nemours, who was later chairman of the finance committee of the national assembly; and Talleyrand, then Abbé Périgord, who was later to serve every revolutionary government. Mirabeau also antagonized other famous persons such as Jacques

Comte de Mirabeau. (Library of Congress)

Necker, who was a three-time finance minister, and Pierre-Augustin Caron de Beaumarchais, a playwright.

Mirabeau's attempts at employment as secretary of the Assembly of Notables, a blue-ribbon panel called by the king at the request of his finance minister to endorse his package of fiscal reforms, failed. The 144 notables refused to endorse any reforms, and the minister was dismissed and replaced by a minister who prepared a similar reform package. This reform package was signed by the king and placed before the law courts, which refused it on the grounds that, by taxing privileged classes, the reforms violated the constitution and so could be approved only by the Estates-General representing the three social classes. The Estates-General, however, had three votes, and the two privileged classes expected to defend their interests by a two-to-one vote. The issue from May 4 through July 15 was the revolution of the three-vote Estates-General into the one-man-one-vote national assembly. Mirabeau led this struggle, although he was absent when the Bastille was captured on July 14, because of his father's funeral. When the deputies had been ordered to disperse on June 23, Mirabeau had responded, "go tell the king that we are here by the will of the people and we will leave only by the points of bayonets."

After the king canceled troop movements and accepted the national assembly, the problem was to control the assembly. Mirabeau sought to do that with a responsible ministry. The assembly, however, would not go along with him, even though he proposed that he himself be excluded from that ministry. Next, Mirabeau attempted an alliance with the Crown, and there were tortuous negotiations through the summer of 1790. Mirabeau was rejected by the court and attempted personal control of the assembly. He became president of the Jacobin Club on November 30 and president of the national assembly on January 29, 1791, and he was widely praised for his leadership. Then his health failed. His last speech, on March 27, was as fierce as ever. He then took to his bed and died on April 2, 1791.

SIGNIFICANCE

After the comte de Mirabeau's death, a leading centrist (liberal monarchist) of the assembly, Pierre-Victor Malouet, said of Mirabeau, "his death, like his life, was public misfortune." Generally regarded as scandalous, his past may have been a handicap in relationships with others, but Mirabeau showed no regrets. He devoted the last week of his life to the preparation of his papers. All Paris and the government showed affection for him at his death. His personal life, including the prison time, the court cases, and the voluminous writings, justified his claim to being "the Tribune of the People" and caused him to appear as a lonely combatant standing against the establishment. He could intimidate both the Left and the Right and was correct in perceiving more threat to his objectives from the Left than from the Right. Jean-Sylvain Bailly said, "it cannot be denied that Mirabeau was the moving force in the National Assembly. . . . Whatever may have been his moral character, when he was aroused by some eventuality, his mind became ennobled and refined, and his genius then rose to the heights of courage and virtue."

The history of the national assembly through March 28, 1791, can be traced in Mirabeau's speeches. Called a politician without a party, he was also a minister without a king, an officer without an army, and a teacher without a class. Experience has since confirmed the value of his emphasis on personal liberty and on balance between the executive and the legislature. Yet, after Mirabeau, there were still the Marquis de Lafayette, Talleyrand, and Emmanuel-Joseph Sieyès; the constitution was completed; and the legislative assembly (1791-1792) did function and was terminated only in war panic. Whether constitutional monarchy was a necessary failure in the construction of a responsible and stable government or a tragic failure augmenting the bloodshed, no one saw better than Mirabeau the potential advantages and the dangers of the executive and the legislature. Scholars disagree on Mirabeau's personal ambition and venality, although his motion to exclude himself from the ministry seems sincere; few had more faith than did Mirabeau in nation, law, and king.

—*Frederic M. Crawford*

FURTHER READING

Aulard, Alphonse. *The Revolution Under the Monarchy, 1789-1792.* Vol. 1 in *The French Revolution: A Political History, 1789-1804.* Translated with a preface by Bernard Miall. New York: Russell & Russell, 1965. Aulard was biased toward democracy and republicanism but recoiled from the excesses of both. Contains a full chronology.

Connelly, Owen. *French Revolution: Napoleonic Era.* New York: Holt, Rinehart and Winston, 1979. Chapters 2 and 3 describe Mirabeau's period in the revolution, while later chapters recount succeeding events. Connelly is a Napoleonic scholar, and in this book politicians do not loom as large as in more political surveys. The treatment of Mirabeau and other politicians is clear and reasonable.

Hibbert, Christopher. *The Days of the French Revolution*. New York: Viking Penguin, 1989. Mirabeau's life and political career are prominently featured in this historical narrative aimed at readers unfamiliar with French history.

Higgins, Earl L., ed. and trans. *The French Revolution as Told by Contemporaries*. Boston: Houghton Mifflin, 1938. Contains extracts of Mirabeau's speeches on the veto and the exclusion of ministers, as well as several contemporary views of Mirabeau.

Luttrell, Barbara. *Mirabeau*. Carbondale: Southern Illinois University Press, 1990. An updated biography recounting Mirabeau's life and political career.

Nezelof, Pierre. *Mirabeau: Lover and Statesman*. Translated by Warre Bradley Wells. London: Robert Hale, 1937. One of the best of many older works on Mirabeau, this book reads like a novel, with much conversation and drama. An easy introduction to Mirabeau.

Schama, Simon. *Citizens: A Chronicle of the French Revolution*. New York: Knopf, 1989. Mirabeau's political career is included in this lengthy chronicle of the French Revolution. Schama argues that the revolution did not produce a "culture of citizenship" and that the regime of Louis XVI was a more vital and inventive time for France than the period succeeding it.

Welch, Oliver J. *Mirabeau: A Study of a Democratic Monarchist*. Reprint. Port Washington, N.Y.: Kennikat Press, 1968. The best biography in English. Based on original sources, this study handles the sensationalism prudently and struggles through Mirabeau's controversial career to craft a sympathetic and reasonable judgment.

See also: Jean-Sylvain Bailly; Pierre-Augustin Caron de Beaumarchais; Louis XVI; Jacques Necker; Emmanuel-Joseph Sieyès.

Related articles in *Great Events from History: The Eighteenth Century, 1701-1800*: May 5, 1789: Louis XVI Calls the Estates-General; June 20, 1789: Oath of the Tennis Court; July 14, 1789: Fall of the Bastille; October, 1789-April 25, 1792: France Adopts the Guillotine; April 20, 1792-October, 1797: Early Wars of the French Revolution; September 20, 1792: Battle of Valmy; January 21, 1793: Execution of Louis XVI; March 4-December 23, 1793: War in the Vendée; July 27-28, 1794: Fall of Robespierre; November 9-10, 1799: Napoleon Rises to Power in France.

GASPARD MONGE
French mathematician

Monge founded modern descriptive geometry and revitalized analytic geometry. An enthusiastic supporter of the French Revolution, he helped establish the metric system and the École Polytechnique, an important engineering school.

Born: May 10, 1746; Beaune, France
Died: July 28, 1818; Paris, France
Areas of achievement: Mathematics, chemistry, physics, engineering, science and technology

EARLY LIFE

Gaspard Monge (gah-spahr mohnzh) was born on May 10, 1746, in Beaune, a small town 166 miles southeast of Paris. He was the eldest son of Jacques Monge, an itinerant peddler and knife-grinder, and Jeanne Rousseaux, a woman of humble Burgundian origin. Jacques deeply respected education and sent his three sons to the local school run by the Oratorian religious order and to their Collège de la Trinité in Lyons. Although all three brothers eventually made successful careers in mathematics, Gaspard was clearly the genius. He was the golden boy of the Oratorians, and he regularly won academic prizes and became, at the age of sixteen, a physics teacher at Lyons.

In the summer of 1764, during a vacation to Beaune, Monge used surveying instruments of his own invention and construction to make a detailed map of the town. A military officer who later saw the map was so impressed by the boy's ability that he recommended Monge to the commandant of the military school at Mézières. Created in 1748, the École Royale du Génie had become a prestigious institution for the training of officers, who derived mostly from the nobility. Upon his arrival at Mézières in 1765, Monge learned that he would not study with the officers but would be trained as a draftsman to do the routine work of military surveying. Within a year, however, he had an opportunity to show that his mathematical skills were vastly superior to those of the officers. He was assigned the problem of computing the best places to locate guns in a proposed fortress at Metz. At the time, the calculation of positions shielded from enemy firepower in intricate fortifications was a long and arduous arithmetic procedure, but Monge developed a geometric method that obtained results so quickly that the commandant was initially skeptical. Upon detailed inspection by skilled officers, the advantages of Monge's invention, which formed the basis of what later came to be known as descriptive geometry, became evident. In fact, Monge's method was so highly valued that it was preserved as a military secret for twenty-five years.

LIFE'S WORK

Monge spent the first fifteen years of his career at the military academy of Mézières, where he was *répétiteur* (assistant) to the professor of mathematics, then a teacher of mathematics, and finally a royal professor of mathematics and physics. Through his excellent teaching, he was able to improve the French engineering corps and influence several students who went on to brilliant military careers. His lectures on descriptive geometry (then called stereotomy) allowed him to develop his ideas about perspective, the properties of surfaces, and the theory of machines. Descriptive geometry is basically a way to represent three-dimensional figures on a plane. Albrecht Dürer, the German painter and engraver, had used the idea of orthogonal projection of the human figure on mutually perpendicular planes in the early sixteenth century, and in 1738, A. F. Frézier had suggested a method of representing solid objects on plane diagrams, but Monge developed descriptive geometry into a special branch of mathematics. He systematized its principles, developed its basic theorems, and applied this knowledge to problems of military engineering, mechanical drawing, and architecture.

Documents from his Mézières period reveal that Monge did extensive research in several areas of mathematics. He wrote memoirs on various curves and studied their radii of curvature. He analyzed evolutes (the loci of centers of curvature for a given curve) and systematically applied the calculus, in particular partial differential equations, to his investigations of the curvature of surfaces. In 1775, he presented to the French Academy of Sciences in Paris a paper on a developable surface, that is, a surface that can be flattened on a plane without distortion, a subject of great interest to mapmakers.

During the middle 1770's, Monge's interests began to switch from mathematics to physics and chemistry. In physics, he helped develop the material theory of heat (he called the heat substance "caloric"). This theory was useful to physicists and chemists in the eighteenth cen-

tury (it was replaced by the kinetic theory of heat in the nineteenth century). Working alone at Mézières and with Antoine-Laurent Lavoisier on his trips to Paris, Monge carried out experiments on the expansion, solution, and reaction of various gases. To enable him to better carry out his research in chemistry and physics, Monge established a well-equipped laboratory in the late 1770's at the École Royale du Génie.

In 1777, Monge married a twenty-year-old widow, Catherine (Huart) Horbon, for whose honor he had earlier tried to fight a duel with one of her rejected suitors. The couple had three daughters. Since she owned a forge, Catherine had an indirect influence on her husband's interest in metallurgy. Supervising its operation led Monge to study the smelting and properties of metals. His outstanding work in mathematics and the physical sciences led to his election to the Academy of Sciences in 1780. This honor forced him to divide his time between Paris and Mézières. During his stays in Paris, he taught hydraulics (the science and technology of fluids) at the Louvre, and during his time at Mézières he taught engineering to the military officers and prepared memoirs on physics, chemistry, and mathematics for presentation at the Academy of Sciences.

Monge's researches in chemistry consumed so much of his time that he arranged for a substitute to deliver many of his lectures at Mézières. In the summer of 1783, he carried out his famous experiments on the synthesis of water from its component elements. Monge mixed hydrogen and oxygen gases (then called inflammable air and dephlogisticated air) in a closed glass vessel and ignited the explosive reaction between the gases by an electric spark from a voltaic battery. He found that the weight of the pure water he obtained was very nearly equal to the weights of the two gases. These studies became part of the so-called water controversy over the first discoverer of the compound nature of water. Monge deserves credit for showing quantitatively that water is composed of two elemental gases, but he did not formally publish until 1786. Henry Cavendish, the English physicist who published his results in 1784, showed that water is produced when inflammable air is burned in dephlogisticated air, but he interpreted his experiments in terms of the confusing phlogiston theory. Lavoisier correctly interpreted the reaction as the oxidation of hydrogen.

In the fall of 1783, Monge accepted yet another responsibility in Paris—the examiner of naval candidates. For a while, he tried to continue his professorship at Mézières along with this new position, but this proved impossible; in December, 1784, he resigned from the school where he had spent nearly twenty years of his life. His post as examiner also required him to make tours of inspection of naval schools outside Paris, and this enabled him to reform the teaching of science and technology in the provinces. His time in Paris was spent participating in the activities of the academy and conducting research in chemistry, physics, and mathematics. During the 1780's, he did important work on the composition of nitrous acid, the liquefaction of sulfur dioxide, the nature of different types of iron and steel, and the action of electricity on carbon dioxide gas. In these chemical researches, he interpreted his results through Lavoisier's new oxygen theory rather than the outdated phlogiston theory. In physics, he did research on the double refraction of Iceland spar (a transparent calcite); he also studied capillary action. In mathematics, he continued his work on curved surfaces and partial differential equations.

When the French Revolution began in 1789, Monge was one of its most ardent supporters. His humble birth and his negative experiences with aristocrats gave him firsthand knowledge of the poverty of the masses and the corruption of the *ancien régime*. In 1791, he served on the committee that established the metric system. In 1792, he became minister of the navy and played a significant role in organizing the defense of France against the counterrevolutionary armies. In 1793, he voted in favor of the death of King Louis XVI. After all this, he was still bitterly attacked for not being revolutionary enough. These attacks forced him to resign from his ministerial post. Nevertheless, he continued to support the republic, and as a member of the committee on arms and munitions he worked hard to improve the extraction and purification of saltpeter and the construction and operation of powder-works in Paris and in the provinces. He also became involved in establishing a new system of scientific and technical education. It was during his teaching at the short-lived École Normale that his work on descriptive geometry was finally published.

Monge was very much concerned about preserving the nation's cultural and intellectual heritage during this time of revolutionary turmoil. He was convinced of the value of a national school for training civil and military engineers. As an influential member of the commission of public works, he helped institute the École Polytechnique in 1794. Monge became an important administrator and popular teacher at this school. His textbook on analytic geometry, which appeared in 1795, was used in the course he taught on the application of algebra to ge-

ometry. In pursuing the correspondence between algebraic analysis and geometry, Monge recognized that families of surfaces could be described both geometrically and analytically. He founded a school of geometers at the École Polytechnique, who would exert a powerful influence on the development of mathematics in the nineteenth century.

The last stage of Monge's career began in 1796 and was dominated by his fascination with—some have called it his mesmerization by—Napoleon I. Monge had actually met Napoleon earlier, when he cordially welcomed the young artillery officer from Corsica to the military school at Mézières. Though Monge had forgotten this meeting, Napoleon remembered and called Monge to Italy as a member of the committee supervising the selection of the paintings, sculptures, and other valuables that the victorious army was to bring back to France. Although this looting disturbed Monge's conscience, he accepted it as a way to finance Napoleon's military campaigns. Monge's duties took him to many cities throughout Italy and gave him the opportunity to become Napoleon's confidant and friend.

In the fall of 1797, Monge returned to Paris to begin his new post as director of the École Polytechnique, but his stay was brief, for Napoleon called him back to Rome to conduct a political inquiry. Monge also participated in the creation of the Republic of Rome and in the preparations for Napoleon's Egyptian adventure. Monge arrived in Cairo on July 21, 1798, the day after Napoleon's victory at the Battle of the Pyramids. Napoleon made Monge president of the Institut d'Égypte (Egyptian Institute), modeled on the Institut de France, the revolutionary organization intended to replace the royal academies. Monge was heavily involved in many of the projects of the Institut d'Égypte. He was also a companion of Napoleon on a trip to the Suez region, on his disastrous Syrian expedition, and on his secret voyage back to France in 1799.

Upon his return to Paris, Napoleon rewarded Monge for his services. These favors continued throughout the period of the consulate as well as during Napoleon's reign as emperor. Monge was given more powerful administrative responsibilities along with extensive land grants. Napoleon created Monge count of Péluse, an honor he accepted gratefully, although he had once voted to abolish all titles. Napoleon also named Monge a senator, and by accepting the position Monge became publicly and irrevocably tied to Napoleon. A representation of Monge at this time depicts him in a powdered wig, looking slightly uncomfortable in the trappings of nobil-

Gaspard Monge. (Library of Congress)

ity. His strong and stocky build seems awkwardly confined by the expensive clothes, but his piercing eyes radiate intelligence and confidence, showing him to be a man ready to meet any challenge.

During these Napoleonic years, Monge divided his time among his duties in the senate, at the École Polytechnique, and in the Academy of Sciences. At the École Polytechnique, Monge influenced many young French mathematicians in various kinds of geometry—synthetic, analytic, and infinitesimal. Monge's great contribution to synthetic geometry was his *Géométrie descriptive* (1798; *An Elementary Treatise on Descriptive Geometry*, 1851), a summation of his life's work in descriptive geometry and a book that proved useful not only to mathematicians but also to artists, architects, military engineers, carpenters, and stonecutters. In 1801, Monge published a book on analytic geometry that revealed how useful geometry could be for algebra, and vice versa. In the same year, he published an expanded version of his lectures on infinitesimal geometry, his favorite subject, in which he used ordinary and partial differential equations to study complex surfaces and solids.

Monge's health began to decline in 1809, when he stopped teaching at the École Polytechnique. His health worsened during the autumn of 1812, when Napoleon's army suffered great losses on its retreat from Moscow. Monge deliberately fled Paris and did not participate in the senate session of 1814 that dethroned Napoleon. Seeing Napoleon as the standard-bearer of the revolutionary ideals of liberty, equality, and fraternity, Monge refused to condemn him, and during the so-called Hundred Days in 1815, when Napoleon tried to recover his throne, Monge pledged his allegiance to the emperor, remaining loyal even after Napoleon's defeat at Waterloo and his abdication. When the Bourbons were restored to the French monarchy in 1815, Monge, who refused to modify his anti-Royalism, was deprived of all of his honors and positions, even his membership in the Academy of Sciences. The last years of his life were filled with further humiliations and greater physical sufferings. Following a stroke, he died on July 28, 1818. Many students at the École Polytechnique asked to attend his funeral, but the king refused permission. Although they observed the king's refusal, the next day the students marched en masse to the cemetery and laid a wreath on the grave of their beloved teacher.

SIGNIFICANCE

Gaspard Monge's reputation derives from his work in geometry, and there is no doubt that he was responsible for the revival of interest in geometry that occurred in the late eighteenth and early nineteenth centuries. As a result of his inspiration, a golden age of modern geometry began, and his methods flourished first in France and later throughout Europe, blazing the way for such nineteenth century mathematicians as Carl Friedrich Gauss and Georg Friedrich Bernhard Riemann. Though Monge was not strictly the inventor of descriptive geometry, he was the first to elaborate its principles and methods and to detail its applications in mathematics and technology. He also made valuable contributions to analytic and infinitesimal (or differential) geometry.

Despite his reputation as a geometer, Monge's accomplishments were actually much broader. Besides his exceptional sense of spatial relations, he was also an insightful analyst who could transform geometric problems into algebraic relations. For Monge, geometry and analysis supported each other, and in every problem he emphasized the close connection between the mathematical and practical aspects. His treatment of partial differential equations has a geometrical flavor, and he believed that problems involving differential equations could be solved more readily when visualized geometrically. On the other hand, some problems involving complex surfaces led to interesting differential equations. Many historians of mathematics ascribe to Monge the revival of the alliance between algebra and geometry. René Descartes may have created analytic geometry, but it was Monge and his students who made it a vital field.

Monge was a Renaissance man in the Age of the Enlightenment. He possessed a broad combination of talents: He was a creative mathematician, an excellent chemist, and a talented physicist and engineer. Furthermore, he was an adroit politician, a capable administrator, and an inspiring teacher. His skill as a teacher can be seen in his distinguished pupils, some who continued on paths he had opened and others who created new paths. Charles Dupin applied Monge's methods to the theory of surfaces. Victor Poncelet, the most original of Monge's students, became the founder of projective geometry. Jean Hachette and Jean Baptiste Biot developed the analytic geometry of conics and quadrics.

Throughout his career, Monge was interested in the practical consequences of his work in science and mathematics. At Mézières and at the École Polytechnique, he was interested in the structure and functioning of machines. He took his work on such practical problems as windmill vane design as seriously as the highly abstract problems of differential geometry. He believed that technical progress helped to augment human happiness, and, since technical progress depended on the development of science and mathematics, he supported France's efforts to improve education in these basic fields. In his unified view, science freed the intellect with the truth about the world, and this was the only valid way to social progress.

—Robert J. Paradowski

FURTHER READING

Bell, Eric T. *Men of Mathematics*. New York: Simon & Schuster, 1937. Bell, who spent most of his teaching career at the California Institute of Technology, was skilled in unraveling the mysteries of mathematics for the general reader. In this book, he uses the lives of the men who created modern mathematics to explain some of the most important ideas animating mathematics today. Monge and Joseph Fourier are treated together in the chapter "Friends of an Emperor."

Boyer, Carl B. *History of Analytic Geometry*. New York: Scripta Mathematica, 1956. Reprint. Princeton Junction, N.J.: Scholar's Bookshelf, 1988. An important study of the development of analytic geometry from ancient times to the nineteenth century. Boyer's approach is conceptual rather than biographical, but Monge's work on analytic geometry is extensively

analyzed. Boyer's emphasis is on the history of mathmatical ideas, and some knowledge of algebra and geometry is assumed.

_____. *A History of Mathematics*. New York: John Wiley & Sons, 1968. A textbook for college students at the junior or senior level. Though he assumes an understanding of calculus and analytic geometry, much of the material is accessible to readers with weaker mathematical backgrounds. Boyer analyzes both Monge's contributions to mathematics and his involvement in politics. Extensive chapter bibliographies and a good general bibliography.

Crabbs, Robert Alan. "Gaspard Monge and the Monge Point of the Tetrahedron." *Mathematics Magazine* 76, no. 3 (June, 2003): 193. Explains the Monge Point of the Tetrahedron and discusses some of Monge's other geometric concepts. Includes a biographical profile of Monge, summarizing his career and his contributions to the development of applied and higher mathematics.

Kemp, Martin. "Monge's Maths, Hummel's Highlights." *Nature* 395, no. 6703 (October 15, 1998): 649. A brief, scientific discussion of the isometric perspective and how Monge developed its geometric properties.

Kline, Morris. *Mathematical Thought from Ancient to Modern Times*. New York: Oxford University Press, 1972. Monge's contributions to descriptive geometry and partial differential equations are extensively discussed. Kline's book is aimed at professional and prospective mathematicians, and a knowledge of advanced mathematics is necessary to understand his analysis of Monge's contributions.

Partington, J. R. *A History of Chemistry*. Vol. 3. London: Macmillan, 1962. This volume, dealing with the seventeenth, eighteenth, and early nineteenth centuries, contains an excellent analysis of chemistry in France during the time of Monge's career. Discusses Monge's contributions to chemistry in depth, with extensive references to original documents, some of which are translated into English. Accessible to the general reader.

Taton, René, ed. *The Beginnings of Modern Science*. Translated by A. J. Pomerans. New York: Basic Books, 1964. This work, the third volume in Taton's History of Science series, covers the period from 1450 to 1800. Monge's contributions to geometry and chemistry are discussed in their historical contexts, but this book is best used as a reference rather than for narrative reading.

See also: Henry Cavendish; Jean-Baptiste Vaquette de Gribeauval; Antoine-Laurent Lavoisier; Louis XVI.

Related articles in *Great Events from History: The Eighteenth Century, 1701-1800*: 1704: Newton Publishes *Optics*; 1705-1712: Newcomen Develops the Steam Engine; 1718: Bernoulli Publishes His Calculus of Variations; 1733: De Moivre Describes the Bell-Shaped Curve; 1740: Maclaurin's Gravitational Theory; 1743-1744: D'Alembert Develops His Axioms of Motion; 1748: Agnesi Publishes *Analytical Institutions*; 1748: Euler Develops the Concept of Function; 1763: Bayes Advances Probability Theory; 1781-1784: Cavendish Discovers the Composition of Water; 1784: Legendre Introduces Polynomials; 1786-1787: Lavoisier Devises the Modern System of Chemical Nomenclature; 1796: Laplace Articulates His Nebular Hypothesis.

MARY WORTLEY MONTAGU
English writer

Montagu is best remembered for her epistolary literature—the letter as literature—and for her bold campaign to introduce the practice of smallpox inoculation into Europe.

Born: May 26, 1689 (baptized); London, England
Died: August 21, 1762; London, England
Also known as: Mary Pierrepont (birth name); Lady Mary Montagu
Areas of achievement: Literature, medicine, women's rights

EARLY LIFE

Mary Wortley Montagu was the eldest daughter of Evelyn Pierrepont, the fifth earl and first duke of Kingston, and Lady Mary Fielding (a cousin of the novelist Henry Fielding), who died when her daughter was about four years old. From childhood, Mary exhibited high intelligence and a strong will. Primarily self-educated, as a young teen she taught herself Latin in her father's library and wrote poetry under male and female pseudonyms, both practices strongly forbidden a proper young lady of her day. Her childhood included the attentions of such literary personages as Joseph Addison, Richard Steele, and William Congreve.

In 1712, she rejected a marriage arranged by her father, eloping instead with Edward Wortley Montagu, a Whig member of Parliament, after a two-year secret correspondence. They had two children, a daughter who was to become Lady Bute as the wife of John Stuart (prime minister under George III), and a son. While her husband remained at court, Mary wrote letters and poetry and cultivated friendships with such literary luminaries as Alexander Pope and John Gay. During this period, in 1715, she survived the dreaded smallpox; her face, however, was permanently disfigured and scarred. This experience influenced her decision later in life to take action to help eradicate the disease.

After the Whigs came to power in 1714, Montagu's husband was appointed British ambassador to Turkey. In 1716, she journeyed across Europe with his embassy to Constantinople (now Istanbul), where she took up residence for two years. During this formidable journey she learned the Turkish language and customs, gave birth to a daughter, observed the practice of inoculation against smallpox, and—something absolutely forbidden male travelers—visited a Turkish harem.

LIFE'S WORK

Mary Wortley Montagu's earlier literary efforts included a set of six satirical "Town Eclogues" (1716) written in the style of the Roman poet Vergil, but it was the series of letters she wrote to friends and family during her Turkish adventure that established her literary reputation. They provided the primary source material for the fifty-two immensely popular *Turkish Embassy Letters*, written upon her return to England in 1718. The *Turkish Embassy Letters*, however, were not published until 1763, the year after her death. Mary Astell, a friend and popular feminist writer of the time, wrote the preface, and subsequent volumes featured Montagu's poetry.

Dressed in the Turkish fashion, completely covered from head to foot, Montagu explored Constantinople's markets, streets, and baths to see at first hand everyday life in the eighteenth century Turkish Empire. Instead of feeling restrained by Turkish dress, Montagu found that it invoked feelings of freedom because women could in effect experience more privacy and walk around with "entire liberty . . . without danger of discovery." Montagu's letters echo dissatisfaction at the constrained social role eighteenth century upper-class British women

---

A GRANDDAUGHTER'S LEARNING

Mary Wortley Montagu's literary brilliance comes through in her letters, including the following, which was written to her daughter in 1753. Montagu shows her delight in hearing that her granddaughter is good with numbers and encourages her—through her mother—to keep learning, for learning brings contentment, pleasure, and happiness.

Dear Child,

You have given me a great deal of satisfaction by your account of your eldest daughter. I am particularly pleased to hear she is a good arithmetician; it is the best proof of understanding: the knowledge of numbers is one of the chief distinctions between us and the brutes [beasts]. If there is anything in blood, you may reasonably expect your children should be endowed with an uncommon share of good sense. . . .

I will therefore speak to you as supposing Lady Mary [Montagu's granddaughter] not only capable, but desirous of learning: in that case by all means let her be indulged in it. You will tell me I did not make it a part of your education: your prospect was very different from hers. As you had not defect either in mind or person to hinder, and much in your circumstances to attract, the highest offers it seemed your business to learn how to live in the world, as it is hers to know how to be easy [contented] but of it. It is the common error of builders and parents to follow some plan they think beautiful (and perhaps it is so), without considering that nothing is beautiful that is misplaced. . . . Learning, if she has a real taste for it, will not only make her contented, but happy in it. No entertainment is so cheap as reading, nor any pleasure so lasting.

Source: Mary Wortley Montagu, "To the Countess of Bute, Lady Montagu's Daughter," in *The Norton Anthology of Literature by Women: The Tradition in English*, edited by Sandra M. Gilbert and Susan Gubar (New York: W. W. Norton, 1985), pp. 118-119.

---

were expected to play: "Upon the whole, I look upon the Turkish women as the only free people in the empire," she wrote in a letter to a female friend. The *Turkish Embassy Letters* provide a playful, tongue-in-cheek account of her experiences, but on another level they were written to counteract much of the travel writing of contemporary men, many of whom tended to denigrate and exaggerate the differences between people. Montagu, herself in Turkish costume, tended to admire and identify with others and encourage tolerance.

Montagu also returned from Turkey deeply motivated to spread the concept of inoculation, the now-obsolete method of immunizing patients against smallpox by infecting them with a small amount of the virus. In one of the *Turkish Embassy Letters* written in 1717 to friend Sarah Chiswell, Montagu wrote, "I am patriot enough to take pains to bring this useful invention into fashion in England." She described in the same letter how smallpox was in Turkey "entirely harmless" because of the process

of ingrafting, the term used by the Turks for inoculation. Montagu emphasized that thousands underwent this procedure yearly but that no deaths were ever reported to have been caused by it.

Against the vehement British medical community's advice, Montagu had her own two children inoculated. Sarcastically, she maintains that the British doctors refused to listen to information concerning this Eastern procedure because they might lose money. She wrote, "I should not fail to write to some of our doctors very particularly about it, if I knew any one of them that I thought had virtue enough to destroy such a considerable branch of their revenue for the good of mankind." Between 1721 and 1722, Montagu publicly campaigned to make this Eastern knowledge available to the European public. Indeed, her efforts constitute the first step toward smallpox eradication. The next step was taken by Edward Jenner, who used cowpox as an immunizing agent, in 1796.

Although she never considered herself a professional writer, in the 1720's during her campaign against smallpox, Montagu composed satirical commentaries on marriage, divorce, and British social life in epistolary (letter) form. Her literary quarrels with her close friend Pope (who nicknamed her "Sappho," after the Greek classic author of lyric verse, and who viciously attacked her in his 1728 *The Dunciad*) and Jonathan Swift are famous. The reasons for her falling out with Pope remain unclear, but she incensed the poet by collaborating with his enemy John Hervey in *Verses Addressed to the Imitator of Horace* (1733). In 1735, she translated the play *Simplicity* from the French of Marivaux. During 1737 and 1738, Montagu anonymously penned her own political journal, *The Nonsense of Common Sense*, in response to a series of attacks by the Tory journal *Common Sense* against Prime Minister Robert Walpole's Whig government. In "Number Six," her feminist voice is particularly vocal: "Amongst the most universal errors I reckon that of treating the weaker sex with contempt which has a very bad influence on their conduct." In later life, she continued to write letters to her daughter, Lady Bute, in which she detailed the simplicity of her life on the Continent: "Perhaps I shall succeed better in describing my manner of life, which is as regular as that of any monastery."

Although scholars still debate the reasons for the breakdown in the relationship between Montagu and her husband, it is clear that by the late 1730's the marriage was merely one of convenience. In 1736, well into middle age, she fell deeply in love with the handsome bisexual Francesco Algarotti, an Italian writer much her junior. Pretending illness to her husband and friends, in 1739 she traveled to Italy to live with him. He, however, failed to join her. In 1742, she settled in Avignon, France, where she lived until 1746. She spent the next ten years in Italy and returned home to England only upon the death of her husband in 1761; she died there of cancer shortly thereafter.

SIGNIFICANCE

Clearly, Mary Wortley Montagu followed her own counsel. Indeed, one scholar has referred to her as "the most colourful Englishwoman of her time and a brilliant and versatile writer." A leading member of British society in a letter-writing century that also saw the works of Thomas Gray, Horace Walpole, and William Cowper, she stood out for her eloquent epistolary style. "What fire, what ease, what knowledge of Europe and Asia!" historian Edward Gibbon remarked upon the publication of her Turkish letters. Voltaire praised her letters above those of Madame de Sévigné, the popular French seventeenth century letter writer.

Montagu's poetry, published first by Walpole in 1747 and deeply admired in the London of her day, has continued to rise in popularity. Two of her most popular poems are "The Lover: A Ballad," written during the 1720's, and "The Reasons That Induced Dr. S to Write a Poem Called 'The Lady's Dressing-Room,'" which she penned in retaliation for Swift's satire on women's vanity. As an author, Montagu is remembered chiefly for her letters, but she is also well regarded as an essayist, traveler, feminist, and historian. Yet despite her broad range of literary accomplishments, her pioneering efforts on behalf of smallpox inoculation in Europe may stand as her most important contribution.

—*M. Casey Diana*

FURTHER READING

Bohls, Elizabeth. *Women Travel Writers and the Language of Aesthetics, 1716-1818.* New York: Cambridge University Press, 1995. Scholarly work that traces the experiences of eighteenth and early nineteenth century women travelers. In addition to Montagu's works, the journals, letters, travelogues, position papers, and novels of Mary Wollstonecraft, Dorothy Wordsworth, Ann Radcliffe, and Mary Shelley are explored to show how women actively participated in travel and exploration.

Carrell, Jennifer Lee. *The Speckled Monster: A Historical Tale of Battling Smallpox.* New York: Dutton, 2003. Describes the efforts of Montagu and Zabdiel Boylston, a Boston physician, to promote inoculation as a means of preventing smallpox. The two met and became friends when Boylston visited London in 1725.

Cove, Joseph Walter. *The Admirable Lady Mary: The Life and Times of Lady Mary Wortley Montagu (1689-1792).* London: J. M. Dent, 1949. Covers the biographical background that invoked Montagu's letters. Also discusses the historical, cultural, and social milieu to permit a deeper understanding and appreciation of her work. Bibliographical appendix included.

Grundy, Isobel. *Lady Mary Wortley Montagu.* New York: Clarendon Press, 1999. A detailed, 680-page account of Montagu's life, with analysis of her poems, fiction, correspondence, and other writings.

Halsband, Robert. *The Life of Lady Mary Wortley Montagu.* London: Oxford University Press, 1956. Highly readable biography. Provides background information on her life and on the historical, social, and literary context of her work. Illustrated. Makes mention of Montagu's bold campaign against smallpox.

Lowenthal, Cynthia. *Lady Mary Wortley Montagu and the Eighteenth-Century Familiar Letter.* Athens: University of Georgia Press, 1994. Examines Montagu's letters to friends and relatives to show how the familiar letter acted as a method for women to express themselves, critically and aesthetically, during an era when female authors were dismissed. Includes bibliographical references and index.

MacMillan, Duncan. "Sex, Smallpox, and Seraglios: A Monument to Lady Mary Wortley Montagu." In *Femininity and Masculinity in Eighteenth-Century Art and Culture.* Manchester, England: Manchester University Press, 1994. Discusses the *Turkish Embassy Letters* and includes medical and historical references to smallpox and Montagu's visit to the Turkish seraglio. Includes bibliographical references and index.

Montagu, Lady Mary Wortley. *The Complete Letters of Lady Mary Wortley Montagu.* Edited by Robert Halsband. 3 vols. New York: Oxford University

Press, 1965-1967. The authoritative first full edition of Montagu's letters, including the *Turkish Embassy Letters* and the later letters written to her daughter, Lady Bute.

_____. *The Letters and Works of Lady Mary Wortley Montagu.* Edited by W. Thomas Moy. London: Henry G. Bohn, 1861. Reprint. New York: AMS Press, 1970. Contains additions and corrections derived from the original manuscripts published by Lord Wharncliffe in 1837, including introductory anecdotes contributed by Lady Louisa Stuart, illustrative notes, and a memoir by the editor. Includes Montagu's poem "The Lover."

_____. *Selected Letters.* New York: Penguin Books, 1997. An assortment of Montagu's letters that date from before her marriage; contains the Turkish letters, including the letter dealing with smallpox inoculation. Bibliographical references and an index.

See also: Abigail Adams; Joseph Addison; Anna Barbauld; Fanny Burney; Hester Chapone; Aagje Deken; Daniel Gabriel Fahrenheit; Henry Fielding; Edward Jenner; Sophie von La Roche; Alexander Pope; Ann Radcliffe; Benjamin Rush; Richard Steele; Jonathan Swift; Mary Wollstonecraft.

Related articles in *Great Events from History: The Eighteenth Century, 1701-1800:* 1714: Fahrenheit Develops the Mercury Thermometer; 1718-1730: Tulip Age; 1792: Wollstonecraft Publishes *A Vindication of the Rights of Woman*; 1796-1798: Jenner Develops Smallpox Vaccination.

MARQUIS DE MONTALEMBERT
French soldier, engineer, and statesman

Montalembert was a military realist who recognized that proper fortifications and adequate supply were more important than personal daring in the winning of wars. Though unpopular with the flamboyant traditionalists of his time, his ideas about the potential of strong defensive works anticipated the transformations in warfare in the following century.

Born: July 16, 1714; Angoulême, France
Died: March 28, 1800; Paris, France
Also known as: Marc-René de Montalembert (full name)
Areas of achievement: Warfare and conquest, military

EARLY LIFE

Marc-René, the Marquis de Montalembert (mahr-kee duh moh-tah-lahn-behr), was the son of a noble father and common mother. His father, Jacob, was a captain in the French navy, following a military tradition in their family that extended back into the thirteenth century. Montalemberts had served as soldiers for François I, Louis XII, and Henri II, and Marc-René's father participated in the wars of Louis XIV. It was, therefore, no surprise that Marc-René continued the family tradition, serving Louis XV and Louis XVI.

Very little is known of Montalembert's childhood and education. He attended the Jesuit college of Saint Louis at Angoulême, where it appears that he showed an interest and aptitude for the sciences and mathematics. In 1732, when he was eighteen, he entered the French army, enrolling in the Conty-cavalry regiment. His introduction to the profession of arms was immediate: His regiment was sent to Poland in 1733, serving in the War of the Polish Succession until its end in 1735.

Montalembert's baptism into the life of a soldier was sufficiently impressive that he was promoted to the rank of captain in 1734. When the War of the Austrian Succession broke out in 1740, he was once again on the front line, serving in Bavaria, Egra, Duhendorff, and Italy. In 1745, he was elevated to the rank of *maître-de-camp* in the cavalry. However, his attention was drawn from the operations of the cavalry on the battlefield toward the intriguing mathematical and mechanical problems involved in designing and building successful fortifications. Foreign campaigns had given him the opportunity to study the fortifications of opposing armies, while service on French soil (fighting at Montalhan, Villefranche, Nice, Château-Dauphin, Demont, and Coni) gave him insights into the strengths and weaknesses of his own army's efforts.

LIFE'S WORK

When the war ended in 1748, Montalembert returned to France, where King Louis XV recognized his service by making him a knight of Saint Louis. Several of his essays on mathematics and the design of fortresses had previously been noticed by French scientists, who elected him to the Academy of Sciences, where he remained until its dissolution during the French Revolution in 1793. Honored by his king and recognized by the intellectual community, Montalembert tried to settle into a comfortable civilian life.

Much of the artillery used by the French was produced in Angoumois, the region surrounding Angoulême, where Montalembert had been born. Certain that the French military would have a continuous need for iron cannon and cannonballs, he hoped to expand his presence in the business. Already the owner of the forges of Forgeneuve in the parish of Javerlhac, he endeavored to rent the forges of Montizon, Jomiliere, Bonrecueil, and La Chapelle. Discovering that a paper mill and a piece of land on the River Touvre, near Angoulême, were for sale, Montalembert decided that he had found the perfect location for a new cannon factory.

Unfortunately, when Montalembert acquired the property in 1750, an unexpected problem arose: The township of Angoulême refused to grant permission to build the new factory, arguing that it would decrease work in the vineyards, cause an increase in the local price of firewood, and pollute the river from which many took both water and fish. Montalembert responded systematically, purchasing the water and fishing rights on the river and obtaining permission to procure his wood from the Royal Forest of Braconne. Bypassing the township, he sought and received royal permission to build and operate his forge.

Optimistically, Montalembert inaugurated his enterprise with a mammoth contract to provide the navy with 1,400 cannon. Though he was paid an advance of 1,230,000 livres, he could manage to send the navy only 149 cannon. The problem was not one of casting; more than 1,000 barrels had been cast. The problem lay in the total insufficiency of his machinery for boring. Frustrated by Montalembert's delinquency, in October, 1755, the minister of the navy sent M. Maritz, who had invented a new drilling machine, to requisition the forges and complete the cannon. The situation, already tense, became critical two months later, when an intentional fire was set in the forge's supply of charcoal. Ultimately, Montalembert sued the king for the return of his property, a legal action that lasted sixteen years and ended unsatisfactorily for all. The government was required to return the property and pay damages, but it was allowed to force Montalembert to rent his forges to the king for a nominal sum.

Happily for Montalembert, the trials of operating a heavy industry were soon replaced by a return to government service. Sent to Sweden in April, 1758, on a diplomatic and military mission, he was promoted to the rank of brigadier of the cavalry, then ordered east to aid Russia in its war with Prussia. In 1760, Montalembert was promoted to the rank of *marechal de camp*, the second lieutenant of the Royal Guards.

With his interest in fortifications reinvigorated by a new round of military service, Montalembert was intrigued by Sébastien le Prestre de Vauban's *De l'attaque et de la defense des places* (1737; on attacking and defending places). Disagreeing with some of Vauban's views on fortification, Montalembert produced a work that he expected would revolutionize military engineering, *La Fortification perpendiculaire* (1776-1784; perpendicular fortification). When he advertised imminent publication in 1761, Étienne François de Choiseul, minister of war, requested the manuscript for Louis XV. It took Montalembert fifteen years to get his manuscript back. Thus, it was not until 1776 that the first volume was published (four more followed through 1784). Though his ideas and his open criticism of the shortcomings of Vauban's theories were uncongenial to the more conservative military leaders of his time, Montalembert gained a significant following, prompting many to conclude that while Vauban was useful in planning the attack of fortifications, Montalembert was equally valuable in planning their defense.

The French Revolution complicated Montalembert's life, requiring him to demonstrate allegiance to a new government that was suspicious of those of even partially noble descent. His desire to study fortification under the direction of the English mathematician Charles Hutton required him to invent excuses for trips across the English Channel. Luckily, as an old man, he could claim infirmity and the need to take the waters at Bath. When, in 1792, his first wife chose to remain in England upon his return to France, the separation allowed him to end a marriage that had produced two children who died in infancy. Two years later, on December 24, 1794, at the age of eighty, he married his second wife, Rosalie-Louise Cadet, the twenty-four-year-old daughter of a pharmacist. Three years later, their only daughter, Rosalie-Gasparrine, was born.

Montalembert retained the respect of the revolutionary government, finally attaining the rank of general of division. His last years were spent writing; when Montalembert died in 1800, at the age of eighty-five, he had published eleven volumes under the title *L'Art défensif supérieur à l'offensif* (defensive arts superior to offensive ones), as well as several novels, songs, and comedies.

SIGNIFICANCE

The Marquis de Montalembert was part of the generation in Europe that moved from the flamboyance and personality-driven heroics of seventeenth century warfare into the Enlightenment's vision of rationality and science applied to all things. Though a cavalryman, he recognized that wars could be won or lost through the skill of military engineers who applied the art of mathematics to the construction of ideal fortifications, and by the manufacturers at home who could supply the numbers of weapons sufficient to support the growing scale of modern warfare. Living his life at the intersection of two worldviews, he saw no contradiction in being a man of letters, of war, of science, and of commerce; though his efforts were not evenly blessed with success, he continued through his life to engage in the enterprises by which his century introduced the seeds of change into the Western world, setting the stage for the industrial, political, social, and military transformations of the century to follow.

—*Denyse Lemaire and David Kasserman*

FURTHER READING

Brice, Martin. *Forts and Fortresses: From the Hillforts of Prehistory to Modern Times—The Definitive Visual Account of the Science of Fortification.* New York: Facts On File, 1990. A comprehensive description and study of fortification containing many illustrations.

Jones, Colin. *The Great Nation: France from Louis XV to Napoleon.* New York: Penguin Books, 2003. Exhaustive account of the history of eighteenth century France.

Merriman, John. *A History of Modern Europe from the French Revolution to the Present.* New York: W. W. Norton, 1996. The essential reference book explaining in detail the evolution of France in the eighteenth century and the onslaught of the French Revolution.

Pierron, Yvon. *Marc René, marquis de Montalembert, 1714-1800: Les Illusions perdues.* Paris: Arléa, 2003. A biography of Montalembert describing his peregrinations in the late eighteenth century from metallurgist to military man. In French.

See also: Étienne François de Choiseul; Jean-Baptiste Vaquette de Gribeauval; Louis XV; Louis XVI.

Related articles in *Great Events from History: The Eighteenth Century, 1701-1800*: October 10, 1733-October 3, 1735: War of the Polish Succession; December 16, 1740-November 7, 1748: War of the Austrian Succession; January, 1756-February 15, 1763: Seven Years' War; July 14, 1789: Fall of the Bastille; April 20, 1792-October, 1797: Early Wars of the French Revolution.

LOUIS-JOSEPH DE MONTCALM
French general

Montcalm assumed command of the French forces in North America in 1756. With the 1756 entrance of the English into the ongoing French and Indian War, the Seven Years' War began. Montcalm won important battles against the English at Oswego, Fort William Henry, and Fort Ticonderoga, but he lost his last battle and his life on the Plains of Abraham in Quebec City. This final defeat led to the demise of New France.

Born: February 28, 1712; Candiac, France
Died: September 14, 1759; Quebec City (now in Quebec, Canada)
Also known as: Louis-Joseph de Montcalm-Gozon (full name); Marquis de Montcalm de Saint-Véran; Marquis de Montcalm
Areas of achievement: Warfare and conquest, military

EARLY LIFE

The eldest son of a noble military family, Louis-Joseph de Montcalm (mohn-kahlm) was also a scholar. He was not quite a child prodigy like his younger brother, who unfortunately died at the age of seven. The older Montcalm was accused by his own tutor of being opinionated and stubborn, but he applied himself dutifully to his Greek, Latin, and history and enjoyed such pursuits his whole life. He began his active military career in 1732, serving in the Rhineland during the War of the Polish Succession with armies commanded by Maurice, comte de Saxe, and the marechal duke of Berwick.

In 1736 he married Angelique-Louise Talon de Boulay, whose family also belonged to the French nobility of the robe. The couple had ten children, but only five of them survived to adulthood. Montcalm appears to have been devoted to his family, made especially clear by the letters he sent home during his service in New France at the end of his life.

In his early military career, he also fought in the War of the Austrian Succession (1740-1748), where he was wounded in the Siege of Prague. He became a colonel in 1743 and was made a knight of Saint-Louis the following year. He was wounded and taken prisoner in the crushing Italian victory at Piacenza in June of 1746. Released in a prisoner of war exchange, he returned to the front and was again wounded in the Battle of Assiette in the Italian Alps. By this time, Montcalm had participated in eleven campaigns and had been wounded five times. He was awarded a pension in 1753.

LIFE'S WORK

France had been at peace and Louis-Joseph de Montcalm enjoyed the life of a provincial nobleman for a number of years, but he was called to active duty again when war with England started in 1756. The commander of the regular French army in America, baron de Dieskau, had been wounded and captured in a battle near Fort

Ticonderoga in upstate New York. Montcalm was asked to assume this command, and his place in history is based on his performance for the next three years in this role.

Arriving in Canada in the spring of 1756, he immediately began consultations with the governor general, the Marquis de Vaudreuil, about an assault on the English fort at Oswego on Lake Ontario. Because of a personality clash and the competitive nature of their virtually equal status in the French hierarchy, the relationship between these two men was strained from the beginning. Still, New France did very well in the war during the first two years of Montcalm's leadership.

The victory at Oswego secured French control of Lake Ontario. That area of English influence had been the missing link in a chain of French military emplacements, which encircled the British colonies in the New World. Roughly, the chain traced the St. Lawrence River and the Great Lakes west; then it followed the Mississippi River south to the Gulf of Mexico. The British presence in North America at this time was confined to a

Montcalm attempts to stop an Indian attack on settlers at Fort William Henry. (Library of Congress)

narrow strip of settlements along the east coast. Unfortunately for the French and Montcalm, the population of the British colonies outnumbered the French on the Continent by more than fourteen to one.

The British colonies, though, were fragmented and quarrelsome. At first, they could not react together in a timely fashion to military pressure exerted by the French and their indigenous allies. However, after the surrender of Fort William Henry in August of 1757, there was a massacre of more than five hundred prisoners, despite the best efforts of Montcalm and others to prevent it. This tragedy motivated the beginning of a sense of urgency among British colonists, which was effectively organized and supported by the new secretary of state in England, William Pitt the Elder. Victories by the British at Louisbourg in the Gulf of St. Lawrence and at Fort Duquesne, where the city of Pittsburgh is now located, began to turn the tide against New France.

The critical confrontation took place in the summer of 1759 at Quebec City. By this time, Montcalm commanded all forces in America, Canadian and indigenous as well as French regular troops. Assisted by captured French-Canadian pilots, the British Royal Navy negotiated the hazardous passage up the St. Lawrence River with eighty-five hundred well-trained British regular troops and arrived at Quebec City in June. Altogether, Montcalm had almost twice as many men under his command, but most of them were poorly organized militia and indigenous troops. The ensuing standoff lasted all summer.

Montcalm's forces occupied the high ground overlooking the river where the Chateau Frontenac Hotel now stands, a seemingly impregnable position. Major-General James Wolfe, the British commander, considered the natural strength of the terrain to be his most formidable enemy. Finally, on September 13, a desperate gamble by Wolfe paid off. A sizable force was able to land at Anse au Foulon and ascend the steep cliff there undetected. In the morning, forty-five hundred British regulars confronted Montcalm's forces on the Plains of Abraham.

Montcalm's troops were weary, inexperienced, and nervous. In addition, Montcalm was unsure of support from his rival, the Marquis de Vaudreuil, who controlled needed reinforcements. Therefore, Montcalm decided to gamble and attack the British without delay. He has often been criticized for this move because his troops were routed, the battle was decisively lost, and Montcalm was fatally wounded.

SIGNIFICANCE

James Wolfe also was killed on the Plains of Abraham, but because of the British victory, his place in history is much less ambiguous than that of Louis-Joseph de Montcalm. The ongoing rivalry between Vaudreuil and Montcalm still attracts partisans on both sides. In France, Montcalm has been awarded the honors of a fallen hero, but historians in Canada tend to favor Vaudreuil. On balance, the corruption in the French court of King Louis XV at the time, which also reached into the ruling elite of New France, was probably impossible for either man to rise above.

The French and Indian War, known as the Seven Years' War beginning in 1756, was a relatively minor part of the major conflict in Europe at the time, involving France and England. The war was not going well for the side to which France rallied. Sufficient resources could not be spared for the North American theater.

New France survived another year after Montcalm's death, until Vaudreuil signed the Capitulation of Montreal on September 8, 1760, and Canada became part of the British Empire. The battle on the Plains of Abraham had been the decisive turning point, and that defeat is still memorialized in Quebecer folklore. The inscription on automobile license plates in Quebec reads, *je me souviens*, meaning "I remember," and refers indirectly to Montcalm's last battle. In fact, Quebec's desire for independence from English domination remains a major factor in Canadian politics into the twenty-first century.

—*Steven Lehman*

FURTHER READING

Casgrain, H. R. *Wolfe and Montcalm*. Toronto, Ont.: University of Toronto Press, 1964. First published in 1905, this account presents a traditional clerical view of Montcalm and his period.

Dorn, W. L. *Competition for Empire, 1740-1763*. New York: Harper & Brothers, 1940. An excellent treatment of the European aspects of the conflict.

Fregault, Guy. *Canada: The War of the Conquest*. Toronto, Ont.: Oxford University Press, 1969. The military history of this period from a French Canadian perspective.

Kennet, Lee. *The French Armies in the Seven Years' War: A Study in Military Organization and Administration*. Durham, N.C.: Duke University Press, 1967. A sound and concise examination of the logistics of this conflict.

Leckie, Robert. *A Few Acres of Snow*. New York: John Wiley and Sons, 1999. Chronicles the struggle between England and France for domination in North

America from 1689 to 1759, without taking a political position.

MacLeod, Peter. *The Canadian Iroquois and the Seven Years' War*. Toronto, Ont.: Dundurn Press, 1996. Details the Iroquois alliance with Montcalm and the French.

Parkman, Francis. *Montcalm and Wolfe: The Decline and Fall of the French Empire in North America*. Toronto, Ont.: Collier-Macmillan, 1962. This dramatic account of the French and Indian War from the point of view of the English colonies was originally published in 1884.

Stacey, C. P. *Quebec, 1759: The Siege and the Battle*. Toronto, Ont.: Macmillan, 1959. An excellent study of the Battle of the Plains of Abraham, which resulted in the death of Montcalm and led to the demise of New France.

See also: Lord Amherst; Sir Guy Carleton; Louis XV; William Pitt the Elder; Pontiac; Comte de Saxe; John Graves Simcoe; James Wolfe.

Related articles in *Great Events from History: The Eighteenth Century, 1701-1800:* 1713: Founding of Louisbourg; December 16, 1740-November 7, 1748: War of the Austrian Succession; May 28, 1754-February 10, 1763: French and Indian War; January, 1756-February 15, 1763: Seven Years' War; June 8-July 27, 1758: Siege of Louisbourg; May 8, 1763-July 24, 1766: Pontiac's Resistance; May 20, 1774: Quebec Act; 1791: Canada's Constitutional Act.

Montesquieu
French political philosopher

Montesquieu defended and developed the theory behind separation of powers in government, significantly influencing the framers of the U.S. Constitution. Philosophically, he is best known for positing history as the basis for normative judgment. Before Montesquieu, normative judgment had generally been based on nature.

Born: January 18, 1689; La Brède, near Bordeaux, France
Died: February 10, 1755; Paris, France
Also known as: Charles-Louis de Secondat (birth name); Baron de La Brède et de Montesquieu
Area of achievement: Philosophy

Early Life

In his youth, Montesquieu (mohn-tehs-kyew) experienced a strange mixture of luxury and scarcity. His family was of noble heritage, yet his parents wanted him to be sensitive to the needs of the poor. His godfather was a beggar, and his first three years were spent nursing with a peasant family. His mother died when he was seven, which contributed to his shy and withdrawn manner.

At age eleven, Montesquieu was sent to school at Tuilly, where he spent the next five years. The school, which was maintained by the Congregation of the Oratory, provided him with a solid classical education. He was a good student who took a special interest in language. Drawn especially to Latin, Montesquieu acquired a special interest in Stoic philosophy. In 1705, Montesquieu, fulfilling the wish of his uncle, began to study law. Three years later, he received his license and became a legal apprentice in Paris. In 1713, he returned to Bordeaux, in the same year his father died, which forced him to settle down and assume the responsibilities of head of the family.

In 1716, when his uncle died, Montesquieu inherited wealth, land, and office. The office was the presidency of the Parliament of Bordeaux, a chief judgeship in the local court. He worked hard at his legal duties but did not enjoy them. After ten years, he sold his position to pursue his true interests in science, literature, and the more theoretical aspects of law.

Life's Work

Once he was freed from his judicial responsibilities, Montesquieu moved back to Paris to enjoy the literary fame acquired by publication of his *Lettres Persanes* (1721; *Persian Letters*, 1722). The *Persian Letters* were initially published anonymously and were a fictitious account of two Persians touring Europe. The book focused on the corruption of humanity. The accounts cited in the letters were critical of both French and Parisian society. For this reason, they proved to be a mixed blessing when Montesquieu was identified as the author. The instant fame he received was accompanied by the French court's displeasure. While Montesquieu considered his comments a reflection on European society at large, the court blocked his initial proposal to the French Academy.

Montesquieu spent the years from 1728 to 1731 traveling in Europe. The last two years of his travels were spent in England; this period greatly influenced his later works. His admiration for the English government made him a favorite at the court of Queen Caroline, which led to his election to the Royal Society. It is believed that this is where he first recognized the virtues of separation of powers. Many commentators on his work note the curiosity of his basing so much on a misreading of the British system of government.

When Montesquieu returned to France, he spent considerably more time at his family estate in La Brède. At this point in his life, he settled into more scholarly pursuits. His next major work was his *Considérations sur les causes de la grandeur des Romains et de leur décadence* (*Reflections on the Causes of the Grandeur and Declension of the Romans*, 1734). Published in 1734, this work developed his notion of historical causation. This book also set the groundwork for his more famous political writing, *De l'éspirit des loix: Ou, Du rapport que les loix doivent avoir avec la constitution de chaque gouvernement, les mouers, le climat, la religion, le commerce . . .* (1748; *The Spirit of the Laws*, 1750). Montesquieu's examination of the history of Rome led him to conclude that the strength of the Roman republic could not be sustained by the larger and more authoritarian Roman Empire. At the heart of his argument was his commitment to a free society. Much like Niccolò Machiavelli and William Shakespeare, Montesquieu believed that the tensions and conflicts that characterize free societies are the key to their political stability and strength. According to Montesquieu, tranquil republics are not as free as turbulent and divided ones.

The Spirit of the Laws is Montesquieu's best-known work. Montesquieu had spent some twenty years on this book. In his preface to *The Spirit of the Laws*, Montesquieu indicates that this is at least his most and possibly his only mature work. This book is often criticized for its lack of organization, yet Montesquieu claimed that there was a method to the work and that he chose to keep the method obscure so that he could present unorthodox views without being punished by church or state. After Montesquieu's death, Jean le Rond d'Alembert supported this thesis, claiming that the book was designed with two audiences in mind and that the structure of the book allowed Montesquieu to address both audiences at once.

The Spirit of the Laws is certainly one of the most detailed and sweeping examinations of law ever attempted. Montesquieu's historical approach permitted him to make vast generalizations about human nature and its consequences on society, generalizations that were unheard of in previous works on law. For him, law was the application of human reason, and, therefore, the range of law must parallel the range of human reason. All things are governed by laws, and human laws must be understood in the light of this fact.

Montesquieu's goal was to establish a social science that would rival the natural sciences; this aim led to his abandonment of spirituality as a basis for human activity. In spirituality's place, he put history: All human activity was assessed in the light of historical studies. According to Montesquieu, history was the only key that could unlock the mysteries of causation; it was history that would make sense of the relationship between theory and practice.

The hallmark of Montesquieu's teachings was his conviction that laws can be understood only in relationship to the form of government that produced them. This assertion led to his detailed examination of the different types of political structures. Montesquieu identified three species of government: republican, monarchical, and despotic. He believed that a republican government can be either democratic or aristocratic and that types of government are distinguished by the passions and prejudices that are permitted to guide the political institutions.

Montesquieu. (Library of Congress)

He also considered moderation to be one of the most important civic virtues. According to Montesquieu, the principles of a government are what shape and direct the actions of the government.

Montesquieu believed that republics place power in the hands of many of its citizens or in only a few and that this distinction determines whether a republic is a democratic-republic or an aristocratic-republic. In either case, for Montesquieu, virtue is the guiding principle of republics. It is important to remember that his was not a Christian understanding of virtue but a political one. Montesquieu understood virtue as a kind of patriotism that is derived from love of one's republic and the laws that are produced by the republic. He believed that the main strength of republics is their ability to maintain the devotion of their citizens and that such devotion is best maintained in a political society wherein there is not great wealth. Montesquieu understood republican virtue to be strongest when a fair degree of equality exists among the citizens. For this reason, he argued that the natural place for a republic is a small society. He considered the history and development of Rome a good example of a small, healthy republic that outgrew its basic principle. In contrast, Montesquieu believed that the principle behind monarchy is honor and that the principle behind despotism is fear. Thus honor and fear are the respective principles that integrate these types of societies as virtue integrates republics. While Montesquieu did not consider any particular political system the best purely and simply, he did harbor a decided preference for republican government.

Montesquieu's political and social trademark was his unswerving commitment to liberty. Liberty, as he described it, is the right to do whatever the law permits. For Montesquieu, the key element to liberty is that it helps produce a stable, well-ordered society. His devotion to the separation of powers derives from these ideas, for only a restrained government could guarantee the liberty he so strongly desired.

Montesquieu's adult life was largely consumed by his writings, so much so that some biographers have complained that even his appearance remained a mystery to many outside his immediate circle of friends. Yet it is known that he had blue eyes, a long pointed chin, and a prominent nose—features that were rumored to make him appear much older than he really was.

SIGNIFICANCE

Although some have criticized Montesquieu for placing greater faith in history than in nature, his approach to so-cial and political matters is now commonplace. He may not have been an inventor in the purest sense, but there is little question about his intellectual independence. It would probably be an exaggeration to call him one of the great political thinkers of the Western world, yet his impact on practical politics—especially in the United States—is without question. Despite the confusion over the organization of *The Spirit of the Laws*, few works of political theory have had such a lasting impact on political practice.

Montesquieu's thoughts on commerce may help illustrate this point. He was the first theorist to consider commerce a topic deserving of serious consideration in a major political treatise. He believed that commerce is an important form of communication for modern societies and that it not only draws people together but also forges links between nations. Like separation of powers, commerce is another device that complicates social systems, which, to Montesquieu, is one of commerce's great virtues. Montesquieu further argued that commerce is one of the main social forces that encourage the arts and sciences. Montesquieu believed that the industry created by commerce serves every aspect of life, mental as well as physical. This broad perspective is characteristic of Montesquieu's prescient political thought.

—*Donald V. Weatherman*

FURTHER READING

Berlin, Isaiah. "Montesquieu." In *Against the Current: Essays in the History of Ideas*, edited by Henry Hardy. Princeton, N.J.: Princeton University Press, 2001. Collection of essays by the late Berlin, a noted twentieth century philosopher. The essays explore the historical importance of dissenters, such as Montesquieu, whose ideas challenged conventional wisdom.

Carrithers, David W., Michael A. Mosher, and Paul A. Rahe, eds. *Montesquieu's Science of Politics: Essays on "The Spirit of the Laws."* Lanham, Md.: Rowman & Littlefield, 2001. Collection of essays analyzing Montesquieu's best-known work and his contributions to the field of political science.

Jones, W. T. "Charles Louis de Secondat, Baron de Montesquieu." In *Masters of Political Thought: Machiavelli to Bentham*. Boston: Houghton Mifflin, 1947. After a short biography, this essay mixes selections from Montesquieu's writings with commentary. Though limited in scope, it highlights Montesquieu's key political teachings.

Lowenthal, David. "Montesquieu." In *History of Political Philosophy*, edited by Leo Strauss and Joseph

Cropsey. Chicago: Rand McNally, 1963. A concise but thorough topical breakdown of Montesquieu's political teachings covering topics such as nature, commerce, religion, and political liberty.

McDonald, Lee Cameron. "Montesquieu." In *Western Political Theory: The Modern Age*. New York: Harcourt, Brace & World, 1962. A standard short essay that mixes biographical information with some analysis. The analysis is presented in a topical format with an especially long section on separation of powers. Not as probing or complete as the Lowenthal essay.

Montesquieu, Baron de. *The Spirit of the Laws*. Translated by Thomas Nugent. New York: Hafner Press, 1949. A complete volume of Montesquieu's most important work. This edition includes a useful introductory essay by Franz Neumann.

Pangle, Thomas L. *Montesquieu's Philosophy of Liberalism*. Chicago: University of Chicago Press, 1973. A commentary on *The Spirit of the Laws*, this work examines Montesquieu's thought in a complete and objective manner. Pangle is especially strong on Montesquieu's understanding of nature and normative reasoning.

Schaub, Diana. *Erotic Liberalism: Women and Revolution in Montesquieu's "Persian Letters."* Lanham, Md.: Rowman & Littlefield, 1995. An analysis of Montesquieu's novel, which Schaub maintains is a critique of all forms of despotism—political, religious, and sexual.

Shackleton, Robert. *Montesquieu: A Critical Biography*. Oxford, England: Oxford University Press, 1961. The most complete biography on Montesquieu available in English. Presented in chronological order, this book is a mix of biographical data and analysis. A wonderful resource work on every aspect of Montesquieu's life and writings. Includes a complete bibliography of Montesquieu's works.

See also: Jean le Rond d'Alembert; Benedict XIV; Edmund Burke; Caroline; Denis Diderot; First Baron Erskine; Claude-Adrien Helvétius; Jean-Jacques Rousseau; Voltaire.

Related articles in *Great Events from History: The Eighteenth Century, 1701-1800*: 1721-1750: Early Enlightenment in France; October, 1725: Vico Publishes *The New Science*; 1739-1740: Hume Publishes *A Treatise of Human Nature*; 1748: Montesquieu Publishes *The Spirit of the Laws*; 1751-1772: Diderot Publishes the *Encyclopedia*; July 27, 1758: Helvétius Publishes *De l'esprit*; April, 1762: Rousseau Publishes *The Social Contract*; August 10, 1767: Catherine the Great's Instruction; 1770: Publication of Holbach's *The System of Nature*; January 10, 1776: Paine Publishes *Common Sense*; 1784-1791: Herder Publishes His Philosophy of History; 1790: Burke Lays the Foundations of Modern Conservatism; February 22, 1791-February 16, 1792: Thomas Paine Publishes *Rights of Man*; 1792: Wollstonecraft Publishes *A Vindication of the Rights of Woman*.

JACQUES-ÉTIENNE AND JOSEPH-MICHEL MONTGOLFIER
French inventors

The Montgolfier brothers contributed to the invention, improvement, and flying of lighter-than-air craft. Their greatest achievement was successfully coordinating the invention and flying of the first balloon.

JACQUES-ÉTIENNE MONTGOLFIER

Born: January 6, 1745; Vidalon-les-Annonay, France
Died: August 2, 1799; Serrières, France

JOSEPH-MICHEL MONTGOLFIER

Born: August 26, 1740; Vidalon-les-Annonay
Died: June 26, 1810; Balaruc-les-Bains, France
Areas of achievement: Engineering, science and technology

EARLY LIVES

Jacques-Étienne Montgolfier (zhahk-ay-tyehn mohn-gawl-fyay) and Joseph-Michel (zhoh-zehf-mee-shehl) Montgolfier were born at Vidalon-les-Annonay to Pierre Montgolfier, a paper manufacturer, and Anne Duret. Joseph-Michel, the elder of the two brothers, showed an early inclination toward creativity and inventiveness when, at the age of twelve, he glided from the second floor of the family residence to the ground, supported by umbrellas, which he held in his hands. He was sent to the College of Touron in the Rhone Valley, from which he twice ran away. The second time he fled to Saint-Étienne, where he developed a new process for making Prussian blue dye, which was used in his father's paper-making industry. Joseph-Michel returned to Vidalon to work with his father in the family paper mill but then joined another brother, Augustine, at Rives to aid in the development of another Montgolfier plant.

Jacques-Étienne was sent at a very early age to the College of Saint Barbe in Paris. From 1755 to 1763, he studied science, since he had a particular taste and aptitude for precision and exactitude. Upon completion of his secondary studies, he became a student of architecture and had as his professor the famous Jacques-Germain Soufflot. He succeeded remarkably in his chosen field.

From 1763 to 1772, Jacques-Étienne studied and practiced architecture in Paris and its suburbs. His father, however, asked Jacques-Étienne to return to Vidalon to aid him in the management of the family business. Although he had been happy and successful in Paris, he conceded to his father's desires. From the moment of his return to Vidalon until his death, he strove to become very competent in his new profession. Initially he was named as technical adviser to his father. By 1777, Jacques-Étienne was recognized by the French authorities as the inventor of vellum paper.

In about 1780, Joseph-Michel went to Avignon under the pretext of acquiring a degree in law. By 1782, he received his degree, but during this time his dominant interest remained in science and invention. Following the discovery of hydrogen by Henry Cavendish in 1766 and the publication of Joseph Priestley's book on the different types of air, Joseph-Michel and his brother Jacques-Étienne had toyed unsuccessfully at Vidalon with small paper bags that they filled with hydrogen. Although these experiments had proved quite unfruitful, they were the beginnings of the Montgolfiers' invention.

LIVES' WORK

On November 15, 1782, while still at Avignon, Joseph-Michel pondered several of his scientific readings and considered the discoveries of Cavendish and Priestley. One day, he buttoned his shirt and proceeded to hold it over the fire in his fireplace. The shirt filled with the heated air and rose toward the ceiling. Returning to Vidalon, Joseph-Michel and his brother constructed a taffeta vessel and filled it with warm air from a fire of paper mixed with wool and damp straw. This lighter-than-air craft rose to a height of thirty meters. Believing

Brothers Jacques-Étienne and Joseph-Michel Montgolfier. (Library of Congress)

in the outstanding importance of their adventure, the Montgolfier brothers contacted the Academy of Sciences in Paris.

A vessel three times as large ascended on December 14, 1782. It subsequently fell unharmed on the nearby hills of Grattet. This experience was repeated successfully several times and provided Joseph-Michel and his brother occasion to calculate the characteristics of a "globe" considerably greater in size.

The new balloon was about 40 feet (12 meters) in diameter and made of sections of thin paper of several layers. It was fortunate that the Montgolfier family owned a paper mill. The different parts were held together and strengthened with ropes and metal wires. The base was held open by a wooden form 8 feet (2.5 meters) wide, to which was attached a metallic stove, in which straw and pieces of vine were burned to produce the necessary heat. The whole machine weighed more than 490 pounds (225 kilograms).

After several experiments, June 4 was chosen by the Montgolfier brothers as the official date for the public presentation of their new invention. The event was to occur in the center of Annonay, in the place des Cordeliers. The whole experience was to be witnessed by the general council of the Vivarais region, whose meeting coincided with this auspicious aerial adventure.

On June 4, 1783, at about five o'clock in the afternoon, the spectators, almost suffocated by the smoke, could see a strange contraption begin to take shape and start to rise from the earth. On the command of Joseph-Michel and his brother, the restraining ropes were released and the balloon was freed. It rose without any difficulty over the heads of the admiring spectators and attained an estimated altitude of more than half a mile (1,000 meters). The south wind carried it more than a mile (2 kilometers) from the center of Annonay. Upon the request of the inventors, the senators of the Vivarais who had witnessed the event signed a succinct report of all that had occurred.

Jacques-Étienne had written to the Academy of Sciences in Paris in December, 1782. He confided the discovery of the balloon to the geologist Nicolas Desmarest. Yet Desmarest did not bring it to the attention of the academy, whose members learned of it by the official version describing the event at Annonay on June 4, 1783.

A commission of the academy was formed to invite Jacques-Étienne to Paris in order to demonstrate the new finding to the Parisians. It was normal that Jacques-Étienne be chosen rather than Joseph-Michel, since the former had studied and worked previously in the French capital. Socially and professionally he was a well-known personage in the Parisian world of that time. The decision was taken to allocate academy funds to the Montgolfiers' project. The king also decided to give a small sum of money to the scientists. Jacques-Étienne undertook in his Paris demonstration to have a lamb, a chicken, and a duck as passengers in the ascent of the newest balloon. This larger craft was made by Jacques-Étienne at the factory of a good friend. On September 19, 1783, the latest version of the Montgolfier craft was shown to King Louis XVI, the representatives of the academy, and the court at Versailles. Jacques-Étienne directed the whole operation with great success, and all the royal assistants witnessed the ascension of the new balloon to an estimated altitude of more than 3 miles (5,000 meters). After eight minutes of flight, the craft descended about 2 miles (3.5 kilometers) from Versailles. Its passengers were slightly shaken, but only the chicken suffered an injury: a broken beak.

Joseph-Michel and Jacques-Étienne communicated faithfully all during these new experiences. They now decided that it was time to have one of their balloons transport two human beings. The two men chosen were Marquis François d'Arlandes and Jean-François Pilâtre de Rozier. Yet it is certain that on October 12, prior to the ascent of the two chosen airmen, Jacques-Étienne received his aerial baptism during a ten-minute ascent. This would be his first and last flight.

During this time, Joseph-Michel had brought his aerial experience to Lyons. After several improvements in technique, he completed, on November 18, a flight of 15 kilometers from Lyons. The Lyonnais no longer were envious of the flights directed by Jacques-Étienne near Paris.

With its new basket large enough for two passengers, Pilâtre de Rozier and Arlandes ascended in the attached container on November 21, 1783. Jacques-Étienne had improved, for this memorable event, the method of heating the air within the balloon.

Jacques-Étienne next established his new point of departure for the first free balloon flight of Pilâtre de Rozier and Arlandes. It was to take place from the grounds of the Château de la Muette, in Paris. After a few unsuccessful attempts, Jacques-Étienne made a final inspection and permitted this historic departure. The two valiant airmen rose majestically above Paris, floated over the Seine, Saint Sulpice, and the Luxembourg Gardens. Finally, the landing took place at the Butte aux Cailles, more than 6 miles (10 kilometers) from the Château de la Muette. The Montgolfiers had succeeded in their dream. Two days later, Jacques-Étienne was invited by another aeronautical engineer to christen the latter's hydrogen-fueled balloon. Within two days the first human flights in lighter-than-air craft had taken place.

On December 10, 1783, the Montgolfier brothers were named to the French Academy of Sciences. Jacques-Étienne received the Order of Saint Marcel; Joseph-Michel received a royal pension as well as gifts conferred by the king and Marie-Antoinette. Other gifts and honors also were proffered to these successful inventor brothers.

Joseph-Michel then proceeded in his typically impetuous fashion to launch the largest balloon in the world from Lyons on January 19, 1784. Joseph-Michel himself ascended in this balloon, which was more than 100 feet (31 meters) in diameter and nearly 125 feet (38 meters) in height. The so-called Fleselles did not successfully complete the trip from Lyons to Paris as planned. Jacques-Étienne returned to the paper mill at Vidalon and continued to produce inventions in that industry. Joseph-Michel returned to the responsibility of the paper mill at Rives.

SIGNIFICANCE

The Montgolfier brothers worked successfully at the invention of hydraulic machines for use in the paper-making industry and at other innovations in this field. Yet their most outstanding achievement was the invention of the lighter-than-air balloon.

While Jacques-Étienne was at home assisting his father in the family paper mill, Joseph-Michel returned to Vidalon to seek the partnership of his brother. The two young men, though very different from each other, had from very early childhood a marked, fraternal affection that made them most compatible in their future invention endeavors. A distracted though remarkably scientific genius, Joseph-Michel was responsible for many other types of inventions in papermaking, hydraulics, and chemistry. Yet his invention of lighter-than-air craft remains his outstanding contribution to the advancement of science. He was successfully seconded by his younger brother, Jacques-Étienne, who was educated formally earlier than Joseph-Michel. The stabilizing effect of Jacques-Étienne on the more impetuous genius of Joseph-Michel produced a very well-balanced inventive team.

The Montgolfier brothers had been the original inventors and the primary moving force in the development of lighter-than-air craft. Later inventors, in turn, would build on the Montgolfiers' elementary findings, perfect their balloons, and advance into the new forms of lighter-than-air craft called dirigibles.

—*William C. Marceau*

FURTHER READING

Christopher, John, and Brian Jones. *Riding the Jetstream: The Story of Ballooning from Montgolfier to Brietling*. London: John Murray, 2002. A history of ballooning. Contains information on the Montgolfier brothers but focuses on twentieth century balloonists.

Dwiggins, Don. *Riders of the Wind: The Story of Ballooning*. New York: Hawthorn Books, 1973. A history of ballooning, featuring narration by balloonists who participated in the invention and development of this activity. Includes pictures, diagrams, and outlined maps of flights in various parts of the world. Rather elementary and narrative in style, it is intended for younger readers.

Gillispie, Charles Coulston. *The Montgolfier Brothers and the Invention of Aviation, 1783-1784*. Princeton, N.J.: Princeton University Press, 1983. The most comprehensive book in English on the family history of the Montgolfiers and the inventions of Joseph-Michel and Jacques-Étienne. Sources are all in French. Each subject is treated very thoroughly. Includes copious notes and illustrations, some in color. The details of the Montgolfiers' other inventions are very well integrated.

Jackson, Donald Dale. *The Aeronauts*. Alexandria, Va.: Time-Life Books, 1980. A fine presentation of aeronautical history, including events, inventions, and persons from the early nineteenth century through the use of aerostats. Includes a good section on the use of balloons and dirigibles in war. Contains excellent illustrations and pictures, black-and-white as well as color, a bibliography, and an index.

Marevalas, Paul. "Joseph Montgolfier: The Ballooning Pioneer." *Ballooning* (September/October, 1981): 59-63.

_____. "The Montgolfiers' Moment in History." *Ballooning* (May/June, 1981): 59-63. Two good articles by a twentieth century balloonist who writes briefly on the invention of lighter-than-air craft. The author makes interesting contrasts with modern methods and frank statements regarding the limitation of practical uses of balloons and dirigibles. Provides a modern point of view on the state of the art of ballooning.

Rosenband, Leonard N. *Papermaking in Eighteenth-Century France: Management, Labor, and Revolution at the Montgolfier Mill, 1761-1805*. Baltimore: Johns Hopkins University Press, 2000. A detailed description of labor-management relations at the Montgolfier family's paper mill, the site of a bitter strike and lockout in 1879. The book describes the conditions that led to the labor dispute and how the family ultimately benefited by training a new type of worker and altering factory procedures.

See also: Henry Cavendish; Louis XVI; Marie-Antoinette; Joseph Priestley.

Related articles in *Great Events from History: The Eighteenth Century, 1701-1800*: August 1, 1774: Priestley Discovers Oxygen; 1781-1784: Cavendish Discovers the Composition of Water; November 21, 1783: First Manned Balloon Flight; January 7, 1785: First Cross-Channel Flight.

HANNAH MORE
English writer and philanthropist

More, often credited with leading the ideological change from the permissiveness of eighteenth century English literature to the moralism of the Victorian age, was an influential literary advocate of Evangelical Christianity and practical charity during a time that saw the English react to French revolutionary ideology. She wrote imaginative literature advocating morals, religious faith, and civil obedience as a counter to the radical, revolutionary street literature that was circulating at the time.

Born: February 2, 1745; Stapleton, Gloucestershire, England

Died: September 7, 1833; Clifton, Bristol, Gloucestershire

Areas of achievement: Literature, religion and theology, education, social reform, women's rights

EARLY LIFE

Hannah More was born near Bristol to Mary Grace, a farmer's daughter, and Jacob More, a schoolmaster. The fourth of five sisters, Hannah was a delicate child who showed intellectual promise. She was educated in classics and mathematics by her father and by tutors in Bristol. However, when Hannah's father realized his daughter was better than his male pupils in mathematics, he discontinued her mathematics lessons, believing them inappropriate for a girl. She studied history, literature, and romance languages instead, keeping hidden notebooks of essays, stories, and poetry.

As a young teacher in the girls' school set up by her sister Mary, she used her literary talents for the benefit of her students. In 1761, the school performed her pastoral play *The Search After Happiness*, with its moral message. Published in Bristol in 1773 and reissued in London by Thomas Cadell in 1800, it was ubiquitously performed in girls' schools. This play, in essence, set the tone for her life's work: Her career as a teacher and moral reformer had begun.

LIFE'S WORK

The ironies of Hannah More's life and works are many. While she advocated feminine modesty, her work thrust her into the public arena. She wrote poems, a novel, plays for the stage, and essays and tracts for the poor as well as for the upper classes (and for a princess). She fostered the growth of charity schools and religious foundations. She was at once the stereotype of the ultra-proper Evangeli-cal schoolmarm of Bristol and the creative artist, the London Bluestocking.

More never married. Neither did her longtime suitor, William Turner, who postponed marriage three times in six years, but established for her an annuity of £200 and a bequest of £1,000, which gave her the freedom to write. In 1776, John Langhorne reviewed her poems in the *Monthly Review*, giving her visibility in London's literary circles. David Garrick helped produce her first play, *The Inflexible Captive*, at Bath's Theatre Royal (1775) and wrote its epilogue; he also wrote the prologue and epilogue for her enormously popular *Percy*, which played in London's Covent Garden in 1777. Translated into French, and performed in Vienna, *Percy* secured her place in the literary establishment.

In 1774, she began annual visits to London, where she met Samuel Johnson and, among others, Samuel Richardson, Sir Joshua Reynolds, Frances Boscawen, Richard Brinsley Sheridan, Edmund Burke and Richard Burke, and Elizabeth Montagu, through whom she became part of the illustrious Bluestocking circle. When More was writing *Fatal Falsehood* in 1779, for which Sheridan wrote the epilogue, Garrick died. More abandoned playwriting, but she did not withdraw from literary production. In 1782, her poem *Bas Bleu*, about the Bluestockings, earned Johnson's praise as "the most powerful versificatrix" in English.

In her earlier life, More had been part of the witty and sparkling London literary scene, but in her later years, she became devoted to religious philanthropy and to the publication of religious tracts for the moral edification of the upper classes and for the education and improvement of the lower, earning from Horace Walpole the nickname "Holy Hannah."

In 1784, More and her sisters built a cottage in Wrington Vale, Somerset, as a retreat from the bustle of the city. There she gardened daily, worked for religious and charitable organizations, and received numerous visitors, including London Bluestockings and William Wilberforce, with whom she worked in the Abolitionist and charity school movements in the Mendips. In the 1790's, Wilberforce introduced her to the Clapham sect, a group of Evangelicals living in and around Clapham Common outside London. The Clapham "Saints," as they were called, eschewed activities such as theater-going and novel-reading and founded the British and Foreign Bible Society, the Church Missionary Society, and the Society for Bettering the Condition and Improving the Comforts of the Poor.

The elitist Clapham Saints initially addressed their reforming zeal to the upper classes, for whom More wrote *Thoughts on the Importance of the Manners of the Great to General Society* (1788), which drew a devoted readership. A later work, *An Estimate of the Religion of the Fashionable World* (1790), received a less-than-enthusiastic reception, which undermined her confidence in the reform of "quality" people. Finally, her *Strictures on the Modern System of Female Education: With a View to the Principles and Conduct Prevalent Among Women of Rank and Fortune* (1799) advocated religion and education as the means by which upper-class women could be the stanchion of the nation's spirit in troubled times.

In 1790, the More sisters retired to Bath. Controversy over Edmund Burke's *Reflections on the Revolution in France* (1790) and Thomas Paine's *Rights of Man* (1791-1792) was now raging, and the establishment feared the spread of Jacobin sentiment among the lower classes. More was asked to counter radical inflammatory street literature with imaginative literature inculcating religion, morals, and civic obedience. She gained approval

Mrs. Hannah More. (Library of Congress)

for her pamphlet series "Cheap Repository Tracts" from the bishop of London, Beilby Porteus, selling more than two million copies by 1796.

Although her schools were flourishing, the Blagdon Controversy plagued her from 1799 to 1802. The curate of Blagdon had accused the schools of being "methodistic," because a teacher named Younge conducted extemporaneous prayers. For refusing to fire him, More was accused of heresy. Although she was supported by the bishop of Bath and Wells, the school nonetheless closed, Younge was transferred, and More fell ill.

Seeking respite from the world, but not from charity work, the More sisters left Bath for Barley Wood in Wrington parish in 1801. Despite ill health and accusations of "enthusiasm," More responded to many requests to publish, earning more than £30,000. Though she had little ideological sympathy with the efflorescent Romantic movement, she admired the poems of Sir Walter Scott and William Wordsworth's *The Excursion*, and she was visited at Barley Wood by Wordsworth, Samuel Taylor Coleridge, and Thomas de Quincey.

More's reputation, which had suffered from the Blagdon Controversy, was restored with the enormously popular *Hints Towards Forming the Character of a Young Princess* (1805), written at the request of Queen Charlotte to provide educational guidelines for the neglected Charlotte Augusta, daughter of the prince regent and Caroline of Brunswick.

More, who had expatiated on the immorality of writing and reading modern novels, now published, anonymously, *Coelebs in Search of a Wife* (1808), which, by the time of her death, had run through thirty editions in England and America. Part quest narrative, part conduct literature, part devotional manual, *Coelebs in Search of a Wife* also constructs a stereotype of the "lady" recognizable to the Victorians in Coventry Patmore's *The Angel in the House* (1854-1861): "Charity is the calling of a lady; the care of the poor is her profession." More was mortified when the Evangelical press commented that *Coelebs in Search of a Wife* was "apt to be vulgar," and refused to write another novel.

However, further best-selling works of moral instruction followed: *Practical Piety: Or, The Influence of the Religion of the Heart on the Conduct of Life* (1811); *Christian Morals* (1812), advocating the responsibilities of the upper classes; and the *An Essay on the Character and Practical Writings of Saint Paul* (1815). In 1813, she had participated with Wilberforce in his successful drive to amend the charter of the British East India Company to allow Christian missionary work among Indians, as well as advocating the abolition of suttee (the ritual burning of Hindu widows).

Because of the French wars and because of economic changes, the lower classes were living in extreme poverty and desperation, yet resultant manifestations of social unrest were little understood. When, in 1817, the government suspended the Habeas Corpus Act and called for the arrest of authors and distributors of seditious or blasphemous material, More produced, at official request, a work countering the writings of radical politician William Cobbett, author of the *Weekly Political Register*. More's work advocated religion as a palliative and was enormously popular. As always, she continued to contribute her time, money, and energies to alleviate suffering. In 1817, when calamine miners at Shipham lost their jobs, with fifteen hundred people at risk of starvation, she provided food and clothing and, with others, purchased all the ore.

Between 1813 and 1819, More's sisters had died. Her own health was declining, and, ill from 1818 to 1825, she was barely able to leave her rooms. Cheated by her staff, she was persuaded by Zachary Macaulay to close the house at Barley Wood and move to Clifton, where she lived in the care of friends from 1828 until her death in 1833. Her memorial at All Saints Church, Wrington, eulogizes her for devoting "her time and talents to the cause of pure religion, sound morality and wide culture."

SIGNIFICANCE

Hannah More's life and writings exemplify the transformation from Enlightenment culture—via the Romantic era—to Victorian values, from the age of David Garrick and Horace Walpole—by way of the Clapham sect—to nineteenth century English evangelism and Pietism. In her "Cheap Repository Tracts" she adapted the format of contemporary chapbooks and broadsides to serve Evangelical goals.

Her *Strictures* contributed to the debate on women's education, both amplifying aspects of Mary Wollstonecraft's *A Vindication of the Rights of Woman* while paradoxically advocating positions that anticipated Victorian stereotypes. Her only novel, *Coelebs in Search of a Wife*, embodied propriety as the most desirable quality of a good woman and helped popularize Evangelical tenets. Her life focused on bringing practical relief to suffering humanity while employing her literary talents to what she deemed the public good, and for Evangelical Christianity.

—*Donna Berliner*

FURTHER READING

Demers, Patricia. *The World of Hannah More*. Lexington: University Press of Kentucky, 1996. Demers contextualizes More's work in her life and times.

Jones, M. G. *Hannah More*. Cambridge, England: Cambridge University Press, 1952. Jones presents the standard biography of More.

More, Hannah. *Strictures on Female Education*. New York: Woodstock Books, 1995. A modern reprint of More's book advocating both religious education and general education for girls and women.

Stott, Anne. *Hannah More: The First Victorian*. New York: Oxford University Press, 2003. A reevaluation that argues More was a pioneer of Victorian mores.

See also: Anna Barbauld; Edmund Burke; Queen Charlotte; Hannah Cowley; David Garrick; Samuel Johnson; Sophie von La Roche; Mary de la Rivière Manley; Thomas Paine; Sir Joshua Reynolds; Samuel Richardson; Anna Seward; Richard Brinsley Sheridan; William Wilberforce; Mary Wollstonecraft.

Related articles in *Great Events from History: The Eighteenth Century, 1701-1800:* August, 1763-April, 1765: David Garrick's European Tour; 1790: Burke Lays the Foundations of Modern Conservatism; February 22, 1791-February 16, 1792: Thomas Paine Publishes *Rights of Man*; 1792: Wollstonecraft Publishes *A Vindication of the Rights of Woman*.

GOUVERNEUR MORRIS
American politician and diplomat

Morris played major roles in writing not only the New York State constitution but also the U.S. Constitution, including its preamble. Also, the creation of the American presidency during the Constitutional Convention owes more to Morris than to any other Founding Father.

Born: January 31, 1752; Morrisania, New York, New York

Died: November 6, 1816; Morrisania, New York, New York

Areas of achievement: Government and politics, law, diplomacy

EARLY LIFE

Gouverneur (guhv-ehr-NEER or guhv-ehr-NOHR) Morris was the youngest son of Lewis Morris, Jr., second lord of the manor of Morrisania, which occupied nineteen hundred acres of what became the New York City borough of the Bronx. His mother, Sarah Gouverneur, was of French Huguenot descent and enrolled her son in a French language elementary school. In 1766 he upset a kettle of boiling water, scalding his right arm and destroying much of the muscle. Morris graduated from King's College (later Columbia University) at sixteen years of age, apprenticed himself to a leading New York lawyer for three years, and was admitted to the bar in October 1771 before his twentieth birthday.

Morris was well on his way to becoming a highly successful attorney when he became involved in revolutionary politics. Proud to consider himself a member of the landed aristocracy and contemptuous of the lower orders—he expressed shock upon learning that ordinary people were receiving officer commissions in the revolutionary army—Morris nevertheless vigorously joined the patriot cause after the outbreak of violence at Lexington.

LIFE'S WORK

In May of 1775, Gouverneur Morris was elected to the New York Provincial Congress. His oldest brother, the last lord of the manor, went to the Continental Congress, where he signed the Declaration of Independence; his second oldest brother sided with Britain, becoming a general in the British army and a member of Parliament. Morris played a significant role in debates on the state constitution, successfully arguing for property qualifications for voting but failing to convince delegates to establish a strong governor with veto power.

Morris defeated attempts to limit the religious freedom of Catholics, but his arguments in favor of abolishing slavery in the state were ignored. During the rest of his life Morris maintained the positions he articulated in the 1770's, advocating a strong government to control the common people while defending personal and religious freedom.

The New York congress elected Morris to the Continental Congress in October, 1777. There he proved a staunch nationalist, urging expansion of congressional power over the states and rejecting peace proposals from Britain that did not recognize the complete independence of the United States. Morris admired and strongly supported General George Washington in his dealings with Congress. Recognizing his literary skills, Congress appointed Morris to draw up letters of instruction for American diplomats.

Defeated in his campaign for reelection in 1779, Morris moved to Philadelphia and resumed his legal career. He was soon notorious for squiring (escorting) married women around the city. On May 14, 1780, setting out to visit a lady friend, Morris was thrown from his carriage. His left leg caught in a wheel, and the badly broken limb was amputated below the knee. The replacement wooden peg leg thereafter defined his image. In 1781, U.S. supervisor of finance Robert Morris (no relation), appointed Gouverneur Morris assistant supervisor. The two struggled to raise funds for Washington's army and to protect the credit of the United States. After the peace, he joined Robert Morris as a junior partner, investing in upstate New York land that ultimately made him very wealthy.

The Pennsylvania legislature chose Morris to represent the state at the 1787 Constitutional Convention. At first unwilling to attend, once the convention opened Morris spoke more frequently than any other delegate. He forcefully advocated his long-held conservative beliefs, but then helped craft compromises that produced a document most members supported. Morris desired a strong executive branch. He proposed a president elected for life by popular vote of property holders, unimpeachable, with a veto over legislation and the power to appoint senators to life terms. However, he accepted a president chosen indirectly by a college of electors for a four-year term, impeachable for treason and corruption, with a veto subject to a two-thirds override by Congress. Morris reluctantly agreed to the formation of a federal-level senate in which each state had equal representation as a necessary compromise to keep the support of smaller states. He strongly objected to any concessions to slavery in the Constitution, unsuccessfully opposing clauses keeping the slave trade open for twenty years and awarding southern states seats in the House of Representatives based on their slave population.

Congress appointed a "committee on style" to turn the agreements reached during the discussions into a single consistent document. The committee, impressed with Morris's literary talent, asked him to compose the text. Morris took the rambling set of twenty-three articles recording the decisions of the convention and condensed them into seven coherent and rationally ordered articles. In addition, he added the preamble, with its powerful invocation of his nationalist beliefs.

In December of 1788, Morris left for France to pursue his partners' interest in land sales and the tobacco trade with Europe. Morris's aristocratic manners and command of French earned him entrée into the upper levels of French society, where he enjoyed their relaxed sexual attitudes. His diary records a long-running affair with the mistress of Charles Maurice de Talleyrand-Périgord, the bishop of Autun and later the foreign minister in the revolutionary, Napoleonic, and monarchical governments. The diary, which Morris kept until early 1793, when he decided continuing it had become too dangerous, provides a firsthand view of the French Revolution by a privileged observer. Morris was shocked by mob violence. Recording the scene as Parisians paraded with heads of victims impaled on pikes, Morris noted how mild American people are in comparison. He instinctively sided with the monarchy, insisting the French needed a strong leader, predicting that the republic would inevitably degenerate into a dictatorship.

In January, 1790, President Washington asked Morris to undertake an informal mission to London to see whether Britain was ready to settle differences between the two countries. After months of waiting, without receiving satisfactory answers to his queries, Morris informed Washington that Britain showed no interest in addressing American complaints.

Washington named Morris the American minister plenipotentiary to France in January, 1792. Morris promised to maintain neutrality in French politics, but he found his pledge impossible to keep. He advised the king on how to conduct himself as a constitutional monarch, a role Louis XVI could not perform, and he helped arrange

an unsuccessful attempt by the king to flee France. He was the only foreign representative to remain in Paris throughout the Reign of Terror and opened his house to endangered royalists, helping smuggle them out of France. In 1794 the Jacobin government, the French Revolution's most famous radicals, requested Morris's recall.

Morris spent the next four years traveling through war-torn Europe attending to business matters before returning to New York on December 23, 1798. In April, 1800, the Federalist New York legislature elected him to fill the last three years of an unexpired U.S. Senate term. Morris proved an ardent partisan, breaking rank with the Federalists only once—supporting Thomas Jefferson's Louisiana Purchase. Morris's travels in upstate New York convinced him of the need for a canal from the Hudson River to the Great Lakes, so he joined Governor De Witt Clinton in urging construction of the Erie Canal. Morris bitterly opposed the War of 1812, calling it a conspiracy by slave states to annex Canada. Deviating in his old age from the nationalism he had espoused since 1775, Morris not only endorsed the 1814 Hartford Convention but also advocated New York's and New England's immediate secession from the Union.

On Christmas Day, 1809, Morris married Anne Cary Randolph, twenty-two years younger than Morris, ignoring rumors of incest, adultery, and murder of a newborn child that had driven her out of Virginia. They had one son.

SIGNIFICANCE

Gouverneur Morris played a critical role in the development of the United States in its formative years. Despite his aristocratic and conservative beliefs, Morris wholeheartedly enlisted in the cause of American independence. He was critical to the success of the revolution and the writing of the Constitution. Personally, he would have preferred a nation in which birth and wealth were the predominant determinants of political participation and leadership, one in which the executive branch was in effect an elective kingship. His political pragmatism, however, led him to compromise and join in establishing a democratic republic.

Morris's lasting gift to the new nation was the clarity and simplicity of the language he provided for the text of the Constitution and the inspiring prose of his preamble, with its promise to "form a more perfect Union, . . . and secure the Blessings of Liberty to ourselves and our Posterity."

—Milton Berman

FURTHER READING

Adams, William Howard. *Gouverneur Morris: An Independent Life*. New Haven, Conn.: Yale University Press, 2003. A thorough, scholarly biography that exaggerates Morris's significance, while denigrating the significance of most revolutionary leaders.

Brookhiser, Richard. *Gentleman Revolutionary: Gouverneur Morris, the Rake Who Wrote the Constitution*. New York: Free Press, 2003. Brookhiser's work stresses Morris's colorful life.

Crawford, Alan Pell. *Unwise Passions: A True Story of a Remarkable Woman, and the First Great Scandal of Eighteenth Century America*. New York: Simon & Schuster, 2000. An entertaining biography of Morris's wife that is not always accurate in its depiction of Virginia history and culture.

See also: Georges Danton; Thomas Jefferson; Louis XVI; Robert Morris; George Washington.

Related articles in *Great Events from History: The Eighteenth Century, 1701-1800:* September 5-October 26, 1774: First Continental Congress; April 19, 1775: Battle of Lexington and Concord; May 10-August 2, 1775: Second Continental Congress; July 4, 1776: Declaration of Independence; September 17, 1787: U.S. Constitution Is Adopted; April 20, 1792-October, 1797: Early Wars of the French Revolution.

ROBERT MORRIS
English-born American businessman and politician

Combining an intimate knowledge of the political workings of the early revolutionary and Confederation periods with his experience as America's leading merchant, Morris saved the young United States from financial collapse and the consequent danger of losing its war for independence from Great Britain.

Born: January 31, 1734; Liverpool, England
Died: May 8, 1806; Philadelphia, Pennsylvania
Areas of achievement: Economics, government and politics

EARLY LIFE

Few details are known of the early life of Robert Morris. The name of his mother is unknown. His father, also named Robert Morris, was a tobacco agent at Oxford in Maryland, on the Chesapeake. At some time, the younger Robert was brought to Maryland, and at age thirteen, he briefly attended a school in Philadelphia. Following this, he was placed with a prominent shipping family, the Willings.

By 1754, armed with a substantial inheritance from his father and his own considerable talents, he was made a partner in the new firm of Willings, Morris and Company. Remarkably, in a period when business arrangements were much less formal and durable than those made in the twenty-first century, the firm survived and thrived for twenty years. Morris actively directed it for a large part of that time. The company expanded over the years, concentrating on the importation of British and colonial manufactures and the exportation of American goods and on owning ships, a general exchange, and banking business. Morris, along with the firm, came to hold a leading position in the trade of Philadelphia and in America generally by the time of the first crisis with Great Britain over the question of taxation in 1765: the Stamp Act crisis.

LIFE'S WORK

Robert Morris first became prominent in public affairs in 1765, during the resistance to the Stamp Act, as one of the signers of the nonimportation agreement. Later in the year, he served on the citizens' committee appointed to force the collector of the stamp tax in Philadelphia to desist from carrying out the duties of his office. The following year, Morris was named warden of the Port of Philadelphia. Although not immediately committed to the patriot cause when the First Continental Congress met in Philadelphia in 1774, a few months later, he was among its leading representatives. It is said that his mind was made up upon hearing the news of the Battle of Lexington and Concord. In October, 1775, he was elected to the Pennsylvania Assembly, the last to meet under the colonial charter. From there, he was sent the following month as delegate to the Continental Congress.

Morris quickly emerged as one of the leading members of the Congress, the driving force in many of its committees between 1775 and 1778. He was a member of both the Committee of Correspondence and the Committee of Commerce, and he played a leading part in managing the purchase of goods and ships on a scale unprecedented in the American experience. It was a period of confusion, the mixing of personal and public affairs, the problems of a fluctuating currency, a long lapse between the placing of orders and their fulfillment, and a hopelessly overtaxed accounting and bookkeeping system.

Criticisms and charges were made against Morris as against several others. John Adams for one, however, was quite clear in his opinion. Writing to Horatio Gates, Adams said,

> You ask me what you are to think of Robert Morris?... I think he has a masterly Understanding, an open Temper and an honest Heart.... He has vast designs in the mercantile way. And no doubt possesses mercantile ends, which are always gain; but he is an excellent Member of our Body.

In March, 1778, Morris signed the Articles of Confederation on behalf of Pennsylvania. When his term in Congress expired in November of the same year, he was ineligible for reappointment under the terms of his state's democratic constitution. During his period out of national office, Morris concentrated on his business affairs. The Willing and Morris partnership was terminated in 1777, but between 1778 and 1781, Morris formed nine major partnerships and took part in a large number of lesser concerns. He derived great profit from the West India trade and from privateering and attempted to corner the tobacco market. By 1781, Morris was acknowledged as the leading merchant in the United States and its richest citizen.

In 1781, Morris was a big man in every sense. He stood six feet tall, with blue eyes and graying sandy hair. He had the assurance of the self-made man and was outgoing, warm, and generous. He was a most lavish host, and his wife, Mary, was a dazzling hostess. He lived a princely life, and wherever he went, he was the center of a social whirl. Primarily he was a man of action rather than reflection; he displayed zeal, great ability, an amazing grasp of detail, and tremendous executive ability.

Therefore, it was no surprise that Congress turned to Morris that same year when the country was on the verge of financial collapse and public credit was all but destroyed. His wealth and political experience as well as his personal abilities made him the obvious choice for the new post of superintendent of finance or, as he was soon

Robert Morris. (Library of Congress)

known, "financier of the revolution." Morris assumed office at a time when depreciation of paper currency made money more expensive to print than its face value and when the armies of the republic were, as a result of apathy and mismanagement, lacking in pay, clothing, and supplies. Outside the public realm, however, the economy was sound. Morris was well aware that drastic and fundamental measures were needed. His program aimed at restoring public credit by establishing a national bank and mint to bind people to the national government through economic self-interest, to reorganize the treasury in order to cut out extravagance and waste, to issue notes based on his private credit—known as Morris notes—to bolster that of the government, and to fund the Confederation's debts by raising revenues from the states.

In addition to these long-term objectives, Morris faced the immediate problem of the plight of the armies. It was largely because of his efforts that a successful contracting system was established to supply and provision

General George Washington's forces and that transport was secured to place the army in a physical position to lay siege to the British at Yorktown. The American victory at Yorktown was significant but did not immediately promise an end to war. Through Morris's reforms, the Continental army went into winter quarters in 1782 better supplied than at any time previously, and well equipped to fight.

The efforts Morris made to restore public credit were intimately connected with political battles raging in the country. His major problem lay in raising revenue from the reluctant states. The financier headed a powerful group in Congress that advocated an effective central government, and he developed the detailed policies and groundwork for the later successful challenge to the Articles of Confederation and their replacement by the U.S. Constitution as well as the triumph of the Federalists led by Alexander Hamilton. At this time, however—1783—Morris and his friends were unable to overcome the fears of central authority held by many in the states. Morris personally was subjected to much abuse and, after a protracted battle in Congress, the financier resigned.

He left office in 1784 with the accounts in detailed order and a surplus of $22,000, a remarkable achievement. James Madison, no ally of Morris, said,

> My charity, I own, cannot invent an excuse for the . . . malice with which the character and services of this gentleman are murdered. I am persuaded that he accepted his offices from motives which were honorable and patriotic. I have seen no proof of misfeasance. I have heard of many charges which were palpably erroneous. Every member in Congress must be sensible of the benefit which has accrued to the public from his administration; no intelligent man out of Congress can be altogether insensible.

Morris never completely left politics. He remained in Pennsylvania politics, heading the state's delegation to the Constitutional Convention in 1786. Throughout the remainder of his life, he was an intimate friend of Washington and was even seriously considered by Thomas Jefferson for the post of secretary of the Navy in 1800. In the optimistic postwar atmosphere in the United States, however, Morris became ever more deeply entangled in speculation in land, and his affairs became ever more precarious owing to the protracted credit squeeze brought on first by postwar depression in the American economy, then by the failure of the Bank of England in 1793, and, finally, by the French Revolution and its sub-

sequent invasion of Holland and the resulting British naval blockade. Many important debts owed to Morris were tied up in these countries, and he was unable to collect. After several years of juggling his accounts, Morris's affairs collapsed, and he was jailed as a debtor in 1798. Despite the efforts of his friends, Morris's debts were so large and so complex that he was released only in 1801, when a federal law was passed allowing bankrupted individuals to live outside prison. From that time until his death in 1806, Morris lived quietly on the charity of family and friends.

SIGNIFICANCE

Robert Morris was a controversial figure in his time. His wealth, ostentatious lifestyle, and high-handed and sometimes crude mode of political behavior made him the target of much popular suspicion in a period of revolutionary ferment and antiaristocratic and antimonarchical feelings. Added to this, Morris was a centralizer in an age when the American colonies had for years declared against the control of a distant, centralized empire, and the states remained committed to the promotion of their own local interests.

Finally, Morris was unequivocally identified with the Middle States and appointed his cronies and business associates to government positions at a time when sectional antagonism was already a factor in American life. Morris remains controversial: His political defeat in 1783, his rather ignominious decline after 1793, enmeshed in what is now considered quite unethical business practices, and his death in poverty serve to diminish his importance in the eyes of posterity.

Nevertheless, Morris must rank as one of the more important founders of the United States. Through his actions rather than his words, he was involved at almost every critical stage in the birth of the young republic. He played a most significant part in pulling his country through a crisis that might well have spelled the end of its independence. For four years, he was the most powerful figure in government. In March, 1783, Joseph Reed wrote to General Nathanael Greene,

> Mr. Morris has been for a long time the *dominus factotum*, whose dictates none dare oppose, and from whose decisions lay no appeal; he has, in fact, exercised the power really of the three great departments, and Congress have only had to give their fiat to his mandates.

Moreover, Morris laid the foundations and the detailed policies of the group soon to be called Federalists.

Through his financial policies, Morris established an economic interest in altering the Articles of Confederation to make for an effective national government by establishing national responsibility for paying Revolutionary War debts at a time when Congress had no power of direct taxation and requisitioning from the states was ineffective. Morris also went some way toward reestablishing public credit by a combination of foreign loans, domestic loans from the Bank of the United States, and the issuance of Morris notes, which circulated at or near par and were backed by his own private credit. He established order in a chaotic government and rationalized requisition and procurement systems, relying heavily and, on the whole, successfully on the issuance of secret competitive bidding for government contracts. Morris established efficiency in government at a time notorious for waste and extravagance.

Morris's achievements were both political and financial. Upon his policies was erected the sound financial and constitutional structure, completed by the Federalists under more favorable circumstances, which has been so important to the long-term stability of the United States.

—*Stephen Burwood*

FURTHER READING

Buel, Richard, Jr. *In Irons: Britain's Naval Supremacy and the American Revolutionary Economy.* New Haven, Conn.: Yale University Press, 1998. Examines the economic damage Great Britain inflicted upon its American colonies by denying Americans access to overseas markets and seizing major colonial centers. Includes information about Morris's role in the early American economy.

Carp, E. Wayne. *To Starve the Army at Pleasure: Continental Army Administration and American Political Culture, 1775-1783.* Chapel Hill: University of North Carolina Press, 1984. Not as much of a cure for insomnia as its title suggests, this book ably shows the severe problems facing the Continental armies. Chapters 7 and 8 in particular show the tremendous difference made by Morris as financier and his role in the victory at Yorktown. Carp casts doubt about the outcome of Yorktown had Morris not been a factor.

Dos Passos, John. *The Men Who Made the Nation.* Garden City, N.Y.: Doubleday, 1957. Dos Passos perceives Morris as a threat to democracy and questions the financier's political and financial morality. However, chapter 4 provides a sense of the speculative atmosphere of the 1780's and 1790's and illus-

trates that Morris was certainly not alone in going to ruin.

Ferguson, E. James. *The Power of the Purse: A History of American Public Finance, 1776-1790.* Chapel Hill: University of North Carolina Press, 1961. This is an enlightening book that shows the ideological aspects of financial policies and explains the economics of the time in easy-to-understand terms. The role of Morris figures very prominently.

Ferguson, E. James, et al., eds. *The Papers of Robert Morris, 1781-1784.* 9 vols. Pittsburgh, Pa.: University of Pittsburgh Press, 1973-1998. A collection of Morris's papers from his days as financier, a time when he was at the height of his power and influence. The papers show the range of his interests and provide insights into his thinking. Ferguson's introductory essay is a model of clarity and perception.

Oberholtzer, E. P. *Robert Morris: Patriot and Financier.* New York: Macmillan, 1903. This was the first work to draw on the Morris papers, which had been acquired by the Library of Congress after their rescue from a rubbish heap in France. It is very favorable to its subject.

Sumner, William Graham. *The Financier and the Finances of the American Revolution.* 2 vols. New York: Dodd, Mead, 1891. Reprint. New York: Augustus M. Kelley, 1968. Despite the lack of access to Morris's papers as financier, this is a more perceptive work than E. P. Oberholtzer's book.

Swiggett, Howard. *The Forgotten Leaders of the Revolution.* Garden City, N.Y.: Doubleday, 1955. The author injects personal and familial information into this public and political account of revolutionary leaders in attempt to discredit Morris. Chapters 6 and 8 focus on Morris's lack of financial judgment and common sense, while slighting his activities as a public servant.

Ver Steeg, Clarence L. *Robert Morris: Revolutionary Financier.* Philadelphia: University of Pennsylvania Press, 1954. This is recognized as the one of the best studies of Morris. It concentrates on Morris as financier, though his early career is briefly but adequately covered. It is short, well written, and highly recommended.

See also: John Adams; Alexander Hamilton; Thomas Jefferson; John Paul Jones; Betsy Ross; Adam Smith; George Washington; James Wilson.

Related articles in *Great Events from History: The Eighteenth Century, 1701-1800:* March 22, 1765-March

18, 1766: Stamp Act Crisis; September 5-October 26, 1774: First Continental Congress; April 19, 1775: Battle of Lexington and Concord; May 10-August 2, 1775: Second Continental Congress; March 9, 1776: Adam Smith Publishes *The Wealth of Nations*; July 4, 1776: Declaration of Independence; March 1, 1781: Ratification of the Articles of Confederation; October 19, 1781: Cornwallis Surrenders at Yorktown; September 17, 1787: U.S. Constitution Is Adopted; January, 1790: Hamilton's *Report on Public Credit*; April 20, 1792-October, 1797: Early Wars of the French Revolution.

WOLFGANG AMADEUS MOZART
Austrian composer

Along with Joseph Haydn and Ludwig van Beethoven, Mozart represents the fullest achievement of the Viennese classical style. Prolific and precocious, Mozart worked in a wide range of musical forms, from court dances and chamber music to symphonies and operas, producing some of the most enduring and masterful compositions in each.

Born: January 27, 1756; Salzburg, Austria
Died: December 5, 1791; Vienna, Austria
Also known as: Johan Crysostom Wolfgang Amadeus Mozart (full name)
Area of achievement: Music

EARLY LIFE

Wolfgang Amadeus Mozart (VAWLF-gahng ah-mah-DAY-oos MOHT-sahrt) was the second of the seven children born to Leopold Mozart and Anna Maria Mozart to survive infancy. He and his older sister, Maria Anna (Nannerl), received the full benefit of the musical education bestowed on them by their father, himself a composer. Although both children proved to be musically precocious, greater attention was lavished on young Mozart. By 1762, both he and Nannerl were attracting much attention, both in their native Salzburg and in the musically more prestigious capital city of Vienna. In 1763, the family set off for Paris and London, with the young Mozart giving performances along the way, both to extend his reputation and to help defray the family's expenses.

Mozart's early European travels were especially important to his development. He was able to display his talent and skills and thereby dispel any doubts held by those who had not heard him. More important, he was exposed to a wide variety of styles, which he would master and synthesize into a personal style at once imitative and distinctive. Still more important was the trip father and son took seven years later to Italy, then a hotbed of musical experiments. Already a precocious and prodigious composer of a wide variety of musical forms, Mozart now added opera to his growing list of accomplishments, as well as five new symphonies in a newly adopted Italian style. Exactly how much of the work attributed to this child prodigy was actually and solely composed by him is impossible to determine. Many of the manuscripts survive only in Leopold's hand or in texts heavily corrected by him.

Nevertheless, it is clear that Mozart's talent was far in excess of the opportunities available to him in Salzburg, whose archbishop considered the young musician little more than a servant. Realizing that his son's prospects would be brighter elsewhere, Leopold traveled with him to Vienna. Mozart came under the influence of the Viennese classical style, which characterizes the symphonies he wrote during this period. The works he wrote during his stay in Vienna also mark his leap from precocity to mastery, even genius.

By 1777, the situation in Salzburg had deteriorated so much that Leopold asked for his son's release from service, which, after some initial reluctance, the archbishop granted. Whether that release was the consequence or the cause of Mozart's growing independence is difficult to determine. While traveling with his mother to Mannheim, he fell in love with Aloysia Weber (whose sister, Constanze, he would later marry), much to his father's displeasure. When his mother died on July 3, 1777, Mozart was suddenly on his own, and when his father summarily ordered him home, he made the return trip slowly and reluctantly. Still under his father's influence and once again in the archbishop's service, Mozart, on temporary leave from the latter, traveled to Munich to write the opera *Idomeneo, rè di creta* (1781; *Idomeno, King of Crete*, 1951); when he returned to Vienna, he made his decisive break both from home and from the archbishop.

Thus began Mozart's Vienna period, which lasted from 1781 until his death a decade later. It was to be a period of triumph and frustration, of independence and decline. It began with the success of the opera *Die*

Entführung aus dem Serail (1782; *The Abduction from the Seraglio*, 1827), written in German rather than the more conventionally accepted Italian, and this was soon followed by his marriage to Constanze, which Leopold opposed and which may well have been orchestrated by the bride's conniving mother. For better or worse, Mozart had in a sense come of age.

LIFE'S WORK

One may say that Mozart matured either very early or very late, depending on whether one defines maturity along musical or psychological lines. Short, slightly built, and pallid, perhaps sickly, yet energetic and prodigiously talented, Mozart had to face a host of difficulties during his Vienna period, including a strained relationship with a father who has alternately been described as a tyrant and as a selfless, tireless promoter of his son's career, financial problems exacerbated by marital responsibilities that Mozart may have been poorly prepared to handle, a love of artistic independence that put him at odds with the very people upon whom his success and financial well-being depended, and, corollary to this last, his failure ever to obtain positions and pay commensurate with his talent. Clearly, the picture of Mozart ruined by an uneducated spendthrift wife who was herself the cause of the rift that occurred between father and son is far too simplistic, particularly in the way it absolves Mozart of all responsibility and elevates the greatest of all the composers of the classical period into a caricature of legendary Romantic genius.

The sheer variety of forms in which Mozart was able to compose so many works of incomparable distinction during this period proves not to be surprising when one considers the breadth of his early training and exposure. More surprising is the fact that Mozart seemed never to tire of experimenting, borrowing from others yet transforming their works and styles into something new and entirely his own. One detects in the six string quartets he composed from 1781 to 1784, modeled on the works of Joseph Haydn (and dedicated to him), a new sense of strength and discipline. Mozart simultaneously sought to make his music—his piano concertos in particular—able to please both musical connoisseurs and less sophisticated listeners.

Although Mozart wrote only four symphonies during the 1781-1784 period—and one of these, *Haffner* (1782), originated as a serenade—the piano concertos of the mid-1780's differ from the earlier ones chiefly in their being decidedly symphonic in structure and effect. The experiments in style and structure that he undertook at

Wolfgang Amadeus Mozart. (Library of Congress)

this time indicate that Mozart was reaching a turning point. He was done with that desire to synthesize existing forms and styles that had characterized his earlier work. In the works composed from 1785 to 1788, the change becomes especially noticeable. The style is freer, the texture deeper and more sensuous, yet even this change would not be Mozart's last. By 1789, his style had changed again, becoming, as one critic noted, "more austere and refined, more motivic and contrapuntal, more economical in its use of materials and harmonically and texturally less rich."

The second half of the decade witnessed the growth not only of Mozart's reputation throughout Europe but of his financial difficulties as well. Even as he sought ways to supplement his income, he managed to produce many of his greatest works. He wrote two of his three DaPonte operas in quick succession, *Le nozze di Figaro* (1786; the marriage of Figaro) and *Don Giovanni* (1787), written the year of his father's death. His three final symphonies were arguably the greatest of the forty-one he produced. They included *Die Zauberflöte* (1791; *The Magic Flute*, 1911), in which he successfully combined serious music and subject matter with the popular form of the German singspiel, all for production on the stage of Emanuel Schikaneder's theater, located in a working-class suburb. Despite its popular success, *The Magic Flute* had one especially unfortunate result. Interpreted by some as a betrayal of the secret rituals of the Order of Freemasons, which Mozart had joined in 1784, the opera led to his estrangement from one of his few remaining sources of income, his fellow Masons in general and baron von Swieten in particular, who had long served as one of Mozart's most ardent champions and most consistent patrons.

Not surprisingly, Mozart's remarkable achievements, as well as his untimely death at age thirty-five, have given rise to a number of equally remarkable legends, many of which focus on his final year. In was in that year, 1791, that he received from Count Walsegg-Stuppach a commission to write in secret a requiem mass, which the count planned to have performed as his own composition. While working on the requiem (a work he would not live to complete), Mozart had premonitions of his own death, or so goes the legend retrospectively concocted by certain imaginative biographers. The facts are that Mozart died on December 5, 1791, of rheumatic fever, not, as some have speculated, of uremia brought on by years of alcoholic (as well as sexual) excess or of poison administered by his "rival," Antonio Salieri, whose generosity toward many of his contemporaries is a matter of record.

However odd by modern standards, the circumstances of Mozart's burial conform to the Viennese practice of the time: The corpse went unaccompanied to the cemetery and was buried in a mass grave. Yet that did not prevent others from seeing in it further evidence of Mozart's having been a romantic outcast whose genius went unrecognized and unrewarded in his own time. Similarly, although Mozart's precocity is a fact, the claim that he could effortlessly compose first and only drafts of some of the most brilliant music ever written is less true. Mozart, it seems, did revise on occasion, and although he did often compose rapidly (often out of financial necessity), he generally did so less rapidly than his adulators have claimed. Available evidence suggests, for example, that he did not write *La Clemenza di Tito* (1791; *The Clemency of Titus*, 1930) in eighteen days—some of it in a carriage—though he may have composed all of its arias in so short a span.

Finally, dramatic as it may be for a biographer (as recently as Wolfgang Hildesheimer in 1982) to claim a significant Oedipal relation between the death of Leopold and the composition of *Ein musikalischer Spass* (1787; a musical joke) a short time after, scholarly research makes clear that Mozart could not have conceived it as a joke aimed at his dead father, because most of it was written before Leopold died. This is not to say that certain of the conclusions drawn by Mozart's most responsible Freudian critics do not have a certain validity. Brigid Brophy, for example, is surely right in seeing Mozart as a deeply divided figure in revolt against, as well as paradoxically obedient to, not only his father but also all figures and forms of authority, including the archbishop, emperor, Church, and Masons, as well as other, more established and older composers and the musical traditions Mozart absorbed, mastered, and transformed.

SIGNIFICANCE

Wolfgang Amadeus Mozart's reputation is rivaled by only a handful of composers and surpassed by none. His work is as renowned for its melodic beauty, rich texture, innovativeness, and formal perfection as Mozart is for his virtuosity, improvisation, and ability to imitate and combine popular and serious forms. Above all, one must be impressed by the sheer variety of Mozart's compositions, as well as by the excellence of the music he created in each of the many forms in which he worked: sacred, chamber, orchestral, keyboard, and both serious and comic opera. Even in the composition of works in an admittedly minor form, such as the dances he wrote in his capacity as court *Kammermusicus* (to which he was appointed in 1787 at less than half the salary of his predecessor, Christoph Gluck), he displays the same variety and craftsmanship evident in his quartets, concertos, symphonies, and operas.

Although his reputation has grown immensely in the twentieth century, his genius did not go unrecognized during his own lifetime. Genius, however, did not necessarily translate into either financial security or popular acclaim, especially in the case of a composer who was often believed to put too many demands on his listeners and who tended toward innovation rather than predictability and conventionality. Although his preeminence among composers is universally accepted and his operas generally recognized as having changed the very nature of that form, both the man and his art remain at least partly shrouded in legend. The popularity of Peter Shaffer's brilliant play *Amadeus* (1979) and the 1984 film version by Miloš Forman will, when balanced by the meticulous scholarship of researchers such as Alan Tyson, ensure greater understanding of Mozart and his art.

—*Robert A. Morace*

FURTHER READING

Blom, Eric. *Mozart*. London: J. M. Dent and Sons, 1935. Rev. eds. 1962, 1974. The most authoritative, balanced, and accessible study of Mozart's life and works. Designed for all who are interested in the composer, from the general listener to the music scholar. Blom devotes half of his book to Mozart's life and half to discussion (rather than detailed technical analysis) of the music.

Brophy, Brigid. *Mozart the Dramatist: The Value of His Operas to Him, to His Age, and to Us*. London: Libris, 1988. An unabashedly psychoanalytical reading of Mozart and his operas, but one that sheds surprising light on Mozart and on works such as *The Marriage of Figaro*, *Don Giovanni*, and *The Magic Flute* (the latter's internal contradictions, in particular).

Deutsch, Otto Erich. *Mozart: A Documentary Biography*. Translated by Eric Blom, Peter Branscombe, and Jeremy Noble. Stanford, Calif.: Stanford University Press, 1965. This treasure trove of Mozart-related materials is chronologically arranged and annotated where necessary but without intrusive interpretation. Includes petitions, church records, death certificates, diary entries, title pages from Mozart's published works, newspaper items (including reviews), and letters from the Mozart family circle. (For letters from the composer himself, see *The Letters of Mozart and His Family*. London: Macmillan, 1938, 2d ed. 1966, edited by Emily Anderson.)

Einstein, Alfred. *Mozart: His Character, His Work*. Translated by Arthur Mendel and Nathan Broder. 2d ed. New York: Oxford University Press, 1945. Einstein makes no attempt to retell Mozart's life in detail; he chooses instead to define Mozart's character in terms of the events and people that exerted the greatest influence on him. In the book's latter half, he discusses Mozart's music according to general type (orchestral, vocal, operatic). The emphasis throughout this enthusiastic study is on Mozart's development.

Eisen, Cliff, and Stanley Sadie, eds. *The New Grove Mozart*. New York: Grove Press, 2002. The editors have adapted the information originally published in *The New Grove Dictionary of Music and Musicans* to create a shorter introduction to Mozart's life and work. About one-third of the book lists Mozart's compositions by the type of work and date. A good starting place for research.

Gutman, Robert W. *Mozart: A Cultural Biography*. New York: Harcourt, Brace, 1999. Gutman's comprehensive biography describes Mozart's artistic evolution and personal maturity, placing his life and compositions within the context of intellectual, political, and artistic developments in eighteenth century Europe. His explanations of Mozart's musical compositions can be easily understood by the general reader.

Hildesheimer, Wolfgang. *Mozart*. Translated by Marion Faber. New York: Farrar, Straus & Giroux, 1982. The most readable and perhaps the most compelling, but certainly the most unreliable biography of Mozart. The author, a German novelist, views Mozart psychoanalytically. He chips away at the musical mask Mozart chose to hide behind in order to expose the doomed figure Mozart actually was. Mozart emerges as a man totally frustrated in his attempts to win the favor of a public incapable of understanding his music.

Jahn, Otto. *Life of Mozart*. Translated by Pauline D. Townsend. 3 vols. London: Novello, Ewer, 1891. Although now dated, Jahn's work remains an indispensable source for the facts of Mozart's life. Later biographers have not so much supplanted Jahn's work as supplemented it, adding new facts or reading them in a different light.

Keefe, Simon, ed. *The Cambridge Companion to Mozart*. New York: Cambridge University Press, 2003. Collection of essays about numerous topics, including Mozart's life, compositional methods, compositions, and his reception in the nineteenth and twentieth centuries.

Landon, H. C. Robbins. *1791: Mozart's Last Year*. New York: Macmillan, 1988. Landon does not so much offer new material as bring together material unearthed by previous scholars. In doing so he manages to demystify Mozart's final year, which has been the subject of so many legends. Landon is particularly interested in correcting what he believes are the errors popularized by Hildesheimer and Peter Shaffer.

Landon, H. C. Robbins, and Donald Mitchell, eds. *The Mozart Companion*. 1956. Reprint. Westport, Conn.: Greenwood Press, 1981. An excellent and comprehensive selection of essays on a wide variety of topics: Mozart's style and influence, keyboard music, concertos, operas, concert arias, church music, and even Mozart portraits.

Shaffer, Peter. *Amadeus*. New York: Harper & Row, 1980. Shaffer's popular and controversial play was first performed in London and later made into a film directed by Miloš Forman. The play closely follows

Hildesheimer's psychoanalytical reading of Mozart's character, but Shaffer presents his story in a more theatrical, or even fictional, manner, from the point of view of Mozart's "rival," Antonio Salieri. The play is not biography (nor does it claim to be); it is, rather, a brilliant meditation on genius.

Tyson, Alan. *Mozart: Studies of the Autograph Scores.* Cambridge, Mass.: Harvard University Press, 1987. A detailed and fascinating study of Mozart's manuscripts, which enables Tyson to redate a number of works. He proves that Mozart did not always compose his works completely before he set them down on paper. Many of the works, especially the later ones, were composed in distinct stages over time. Scholarly yet readable, Tyson's essays will have a profound impact on Mozart studies.

See also: Johann Sebastian Bach; Christoph Gluck; George Frideric Handel; Joseph Haydn.

Related articles in *Great Events from History: The Eighteenth Century, 1701-1800*: c. 1701-1750: Bach Pioneers Modern Music; April 13, 1742: First Performance of Handel's *Messiah*; January, 1762-November, 1766: Mozart Tours Europe as a Child Prodigy; October 5, 1762: First Performance of Gluck's *Orfeo and Euridice*; April 27, 1784: First Performance of *The Marriage of Figaro*; 1795-1797: Paganini's Early Violin Performances.

WILLIAM MURDOCK
Scottish inventor

Through his experimentation, Murdock helped to establish gas lighting in England and made improvements in the steam engine.

Born: August 21, 1754; Bellow Mill, near Old Cumnock, Ayrshire, Scotland
Died: November 15, 1839; Birmingham, England
Area of achievement: Science and technology

EARLY LIFE

William Murdock came from a family of millers and millwrights. His father, John Murdoch, was responsible for having cast the first iron-toothed gear in Scotland. While the young Murdock seems to have received little formal schooling, he was trained in the family crafts. In 1777, he left Scotland to seek employment with the partnership of Boulton & Watt in Birmingham.

The company was formed by Matthew Boulton and James Watt in 1775 to purvey Watt's new, more efficient steam engines. Watt had patented his engine in 1769, with a parliamentary extension granted in 1775. A popular story is often cited of Murdock appearing before Boulton as a diffident and awkward young Scot, a younger, less polished version of the later portraits showing a massive, craggy Scot of considerable physical presence. Murdock nervously fingered an oddly painted wooden hat, while Boulton, fascinated, recognized that milling such a hat on a personally built lathe spoke volumes about Murdock's mechanical ability. He hired Murdock on the spot. The decision to hire Murdock was wise and fruitful for the firm, and for the next two years he served in a variety of mechanical capacities in the firm's Soho factory. He also changed the spelling of his name to conform to English pronunciation and spelling.

In 1779, Murdock was sent by the firm to Cornwall to assist in the erection of the Watt steam engines to operate pumps in the mines and to supervise the company's business. Watt engines—the first was installed in 1776—were rapidly replacing the older engines of Thomas Newcomen because of their greatly increased efficiency, from the use of a separate condenser, establishing a virtual monopoly of engines in Cornwall. British industrialization was placing heavy demands on Cornish mines, leading them to develop greater depths, in turn creating increased demand for pumps to empty the mines and steam engines to operate the pumps. Lacking local coal supplies, Cornish miners were forced to import coal, so the nearly two-thirds increase in efficiency offered by the Watt engines was a major incentive for their adoption. Boulton & Watt did not actually fabricate the engines; rather, it supervised construction by the owner, in a licensing operation, charging a royalty for the use of the company's patented process. Therefore, the company needed a reliable engine erector and supervisor on the scene in Cornwall, the role that Murdock filled successfully for the next fifteen years. In this position, Murdock clearly showed qualities of initiative and innovation, traits that did not always please the conservative Watt but impressed Boulton.

LIFE'S WORK

In Cornwall, William Murdock established his home at Redruth in the heart of the mining district, marrying the daughter of a local mine captain and rearing two sons, William and John. His wife died in 1790 at the age of twenty-four and he never remarried. He fit easily into the rough-and-tumble mining community, assisted by his reputed willingness to take on the local miners in physical combat if necessary. His reputation for hard work made him indispensable to the Cornish industry.

At Redruth, Murdock displayed an urge to invent and tinker, making continual improvements to the steam engines he was charged with supervising. The most dramatic evidence of this appeared sometime between 1784 and 1786, when he became fascinated with the idea of putting a steam engine on wheels, creating a steam carriage. By August, 1786, Murdock had constructed a small steam engine and applied it to a three-wheel carriage that attained speeds up to 7 miles per hour. A month later, apparently by accident, Boulton, on an inspection tour in Cornwall, met Murdock near Exeter making his way to London to patent his steam carriage. "However I prevaild upon him readily to return to Cornwall by the next days diligence," Boulton wrote to Watt. "I think it

William Murdock. (Library of Congress)

fortunate that I met him as I am persuaded I can either cure him of the disorder or turn the evil to good—at least I shall prevent a Mischief that would have been the consequence of his journey to London," he added.

Murdock was not completely dissuaded, for he seems to have built at least three versions of his carriage, one of which frightened the Redruth vicar late one evening as it charged along the main street belching fire and smoke. His employers, however, discouraged his experimentation, for as Watt wrote, "I am extremely sorry that W. M. still busies himself with the steam carriages. . . . I wish W. could be brought to do as we do, to mind the business in hand and let such as Symington and Sadler throw away their time and money hunting shadows." It is interesting that Watt's version of minding the business was to attain a steam carriage patent for himself, simply to cover future eventualities.

Steam carriage experiments were not Murdock's only interests at this time, for he applied his practical knowledge and mechanical aptitude to every phase of steam engine operation. He is reputed to have played a role in the sun and planet motion for imparting rotary motion from the reciprocating motion of a steam engine, a process patented by Watt in 1781. He also constructed a wooden model of an oscillating engine in 1784. The range of Murdock's innovative ideas is amply illustrated by a patent issued to him in 1799. Specifying a broad range of interests, the patent included a new machine for boring cylinders, an improved method for casting jacketed cylinders, and a new valve that later became a widely adopted industry standard known as the long D slide valve.

The 1790's marked an important transition for Boulton & Watt, as well as Murdock. Direct responsibility for the factory and foundry businesses was passed to the partners' sons, James and Gregory Watt and Matthew Boulton, and the new partnership of Boulton, Watt & Sons was formed in 1794. By 1800, the Watt steam engine patent had expired, opening the firm to increasing competition; Boulton and Watt's formal partnership ended, and both partners substantially retired from active direction of the business. To ease the transition and to maintain some level of continuity at Soho, in the late 1790's Murdock was recalled to Birmingham. Authorities differ on dates between 1794 and 1798 for the recall, but certainly he was permanently there in 1798. In this period of change to new management, Murdock was the stable link into the new management who kept the mechanical operation functioning smoothly. He had been a useful handyman in Cornwall, at a salary of one guinea per week. In 1800, he was named engineer and superintendent of the Soho works, with one percent of the partnership and a yearly salary of £300. In 1810, in lieu of a full partnership, he was granted a salary of £1,000 per year.

Murdock remained a key figure at Soho until his retirement in 1830. At that time he stepped forward in his own right as an innovator. As early as 1792 he had begun experimenting with the use of coal gas for lighting his home in Redruth; the exact date is open to some argument. Certainly no later than 1795, he had devised a method of heating coal and using the resulting gases to light at least a portion of his house, although at least one commentator believes that the extent of Murdock's experiments has been exaggerated. Once returned to Soho, Murdock's coal gas experiments caught the passing interest of the elder Watt, then in the process of marketing retorts for the production of oxygen and hydrogen as medicinal cures. No patent was applied for, however, and the whole gas project was allowed to molder.

Then, in 1801, Gregory Watt returned from Paris with news that Phillipe Lebon had just presented his first public demonstration of the production of coal gas and its utility for lighting and heating. Work at Soho then progressed rapidly, and in 1802 the factory was illuminated by the new gas lights, as part of Birmingham's citywide illumination to celebrate the Treaty of Amiens. The following year, a portion of the factory was permanently lit by gas, and in 1805 the company received its first commercial order for a gas plant from George Augustus Lee of Phillips & Lee, cotton spinners of Manchester. The problem of lighting factories was a critical one, especially as the steam engine made extended working hours an economic reality and candle lighting was expensive, inefficient, and dangerous. By January, 1806, Murdock reported that the Phillips & Lee installation was working well as "we have lighted 50 lamps of the different kinds this night which have given the greatest satisfaction to Mr. Lee & the spinners." He also noted that "there is no Soho stink," and that "Mrs and the Misses Lee have visited it this night & their delicate noses have not been offended." In February, 1808, Murdock read a paper on the "Economical Uses of Gas from Coal" to the Royal Society; subsequently, he received the society's Rumford Gold Medal, which had been established in 1800 specifically to recognize discovery in the area of heat and light.

The production of gas for illumination from individual plants was soon challenged by companies offering to manufacture gas at a central location and distribute it to customers. By 1809, the National Heat and Light Company of Frederick Albert Winsor was applying to Parliament for incorporation. Gregory Watt and Murdock were among those appearing before Parliament to oppose the incorporation, and Murdock issued "A Letter to a Member of Parliament . . . in Vindication of his Character and Claims" to defend his prior rights. A mechanic rather than a scholar, this "Letter" and the Royal Society paper constitute his entire literary effort. In 1812, the London and Westminster Chartered Gas Light and Coke Company was incorporated, and gas lighting quickly became a function of centralized distribution and manufacturing, rather than the individual Boulton, Watt & Sons model. Greater efficiency of scale, ability to purify the gas, and the subsequent sale of the resulting coke all made the company model more practical. Soon after 1810, the Boulton, Watt & Sons gas business had substantially disappeared.

Murdock continued to be active inventing through this period. His fellow engineer John Southern expressed it as "the torrent of ingenuity which Murdock's genius pours forth." In 1802, with Southern, he made the first freestanding steam engine, the bell-crank engine, requiring no separate engine building. Valves worked by eccentrics, special paint for ship bottoms, machines for cutting stone water pipes, a steam gun and iron cement made of sal-ammoniac and iron filings provide only a small indication of his creativity.

SIGNIFICANCE

William Murdock was the type of British workingman without whom the Industrial Revolution could never have progressed as rapidly as it did and who was fundamental to its success. Lacking formal schooling yet gifted with precise, capable hands and fertile mechanical imaginations, individuals such as Murdock were able to maintain the newly introduced machinery simply on the basis of experience and in many cases intuition. Never satisfied with any mechanical solution, always searching for the simplest and easiest way of doing anything, these men tinkered their way into a new world.

Murdock's master, employer, and fellow Scot, James Watt, serves as a primary example of the inventive tinkerer in spurring the Industrial Revolution. His membership in the Royal Society aside, Watt was essentially craft trained and bereft of formal education. He created his inventions through pragmatic experimentation, rather than through the formal application of science. Watt was frequently unwilling to present his inventions to the public, lacked a clear sense of how to market them, and was always more concerned with perfecting inventions than placing them in operation. Only the entrepreneurial skills of Matthew Boulton made Watt a business success. Murdock lacked only the fortuitous partnership with an entrepreneurial genius such as Boulton to have made his own fortune, and to the end he remained a hired hand rather than an independent businessman. While Watt often seems to have worried about Murdock, possibly sensing an inventive rival, the two men remained close until Watt's death in 1819, with Murdock even assisting Watt in building a sculpture-duplicating machine in the last years.

—*William E. Eagan*

FURTHER READING

Dickinson, Henry W. *James Watt and the Industrial Revolution.* Oxford, England: Clarendon Press, 1927. Provides a thorough technical background and context.

_____. *James Watt, Craftsman and Engineer.* New York: Cambridge University Press, 1935. Rev. ed. New York: A. M. Kelley, 1967. The standard scholarly biography. As in all biographies of Watt, there are passing mentions of Murdock's role and personality.

Falkus, M. E. "The Early Development of the British Gas Industry, 1790-1815." *Economic History Review* 35 (May, 1982): 217-234. A general survey of Murdock competing to get his model of individual generators in each home or factory and the eventually more successful distribution company model. Also good on the industrial need for gas lighting. While technical, still readable and accessible.

Griffiths, John. *The Third Man: The Life and Times of William Murdock, 1754-1839, the Inventor of Gas Lighting.* London: A. Deutsch, 1992. The only biography of Murdock, recounting his life, inventions, and role in the Industrial Revolution.

Rolt, L. T. C. *James Watt.* London: B. T. Batsford, 1962. This short biography is one of the best. Clearly written, with good detail while maintaining an interesting narrative.

Schivelbusch, Wolfgang. *Disenchanted Night: The Industrialization of Lighting in the Nineteenth Century.* Translated by Angela Davies. Berkeley: University of California Press, 1995. A paperback edition of an already classic work on the mass development of street lighting. Although it focuses on the nineteenth century, this work offers necessary historical background. Originally published in 1983 in German.

Smiles, Samuel. *Lives of the Engineers: Boulton and Watt.* London: John Murray, 1904. A popular biography in the Victorian tradition of lauding the virtues of hard work and upright honesty. A didactic look at Watt, although Murdock may come across as the better model. Widely available in innumerable editions.

Williams, Trevor I. *A History of the British Gas Industry.* New York: Oxford University Press, 1981. Includes information about gas lighting.

See also: Matthew Boulton; James Brindley; Henry Cavendish; Abraham Darby; John Fitch; John Kay; Thomas Newcomen; John Roebuck; James Watt; Eli Whitney; John Wilkinson.

Related articles in *Great Events from History: The Eighteenth Century, 1701-1800:* 1705-1712: Newcomen Develops the Steam Engine; 1723: Stahl Postulates the Phlogiston Theory; 1765-1769: Watt Develops a More Effective Steam Engine; 1767-1771: Invention of the Water Frame; October 23, 1769: Cugnot Demonstrates His Steam-Powered Road Carriage; 1781-1784: Cavendish Discovers the Composition of Water; April, 1785: Cartwright Patents the Steam-Powered Loom.

MUSTAFA III
Ottoman sultan (r. 1757-1774)

Mustafa III, who became sultan of the Ottoman Empire when it was declining precipitously, attempted to strengthen the empire, whose treasury was drained and whose administration was virtually out of control. A long war with Russia, however, thwarted his attempts. The Ottoman Empire finally disintegrated following his death.

Born: January 28, 1717; Constantinople, Ottoman Empire (now Istanbul, Turkey)
Died: January 21, 1774; Constantinople, Ottoman Empire
Also known as: Mustapha III; Djikhangir (pseudonym)
Area of achievement: Government and politics

EARLY LIFE

Mustafa (moos-tah-FAH) III, son of Sultan Ahmed III and Mikharimah Sultana, was a true intellectual and a visionary. He dreamed of massive projects such as building a canal across the Isthmus of Suez to link the Red Sea to the Mediterranean, so that ships could sail between the Middle East and Europe without making the arduous trip around the southern tip of Africa. Although he was unable to bring this project to fruition, the fact that he considered it suggests the scope of his imagination.

Mustafa was physically strong, of medium height but with a substantial body and an impressive face whose most notable feature was its large nose. His eyes were bright and expressive. His native curiosity made him an excellent student, quite receptive to the outstanding education available to him in his early years. Well trained in mathematics and science, he also studied literature, medicine, and astronomy, which fascinated him.

Devoutly religious, Mustafa studied Islamic and Ottoman history extensively and had a comprehensive knowledge of the Qurʾān, the holy book of Islam. A persevering scholar, he systematically studied the broad range of subjects that intrigued him. Despite the breadth of his interests, he was not a dilettante. Prior to becoming sultan, Mustafa led a reclusive life, a life that encouraged contemplation and introspection.

Writing under the pseudonym Djikhangir, Mustafa produced a body of poetry. He used poetry as a vehicle for expressing his deepest concerns about his country and its future. In one oft-quoted poem, commenting on how badly the sultanate had been run, he called everyone in the Imperial Palace false and base. He sought Allah's help to resolve the desperate situation of the Ottoman Empire.

Mustafa's reputation for being kindly and merciful both as sultan and in his early youth can be verified by numerous examples. On one occasion, when an earthquake devastated Constantinople, Mustafa drew heavily upon his personal resources to help those who had lost everything in the disaster and contributed generously to rebuilding Constantinople. He clearly had a love for his country and a genuine concern for his subjects.

LIFE'S WORK

On October 30, 1757, the day on which his cousin, Sultan Osman III died, Mustafa replaced him as sultan. Mustafa was ten months beyond his fortieth birthday, and he served for seventeen years, until his death on January 21, 1774. The empire Mustafa inherited was plagued with a panoply of looming problems. Earlier administrations had drained the Ottoman treasury. The provincial leaders (*āyāns*), who were supposed to turn over to the central government much of the money they received through taxation, repeatedly reneged on that responsibility and became difficult to control.

Moreover, the ultraconservative views of the empire's religious leaders (imams) and the Janissaries held considerable sway and made progressive leadership extremely difficult. The imams, staunch fundamentalists who insisted on literal interpretations of the Qurʾān, imposed their repressive views upon the community at large and were resistant to change. The Janissaries, formed in the fourteenth century as an elite palace guard, had originally been a celibate corps. During the reign of Murad III (r. 1574-1595), the relaxation of the rule that forbade Janissaries to marry resulted in several problems. As married men with children, the Janissaries undertook greater financial responsibilities, causing most of them to take part-time jobs in their communities to support their families.

The Janissaries became increasingly reluctant to leave their families to serve in the distant parts of the empire, where they were frequently needed. Numerous Janissary revolts weakened the sultancy, as did the spread of nepotism within the ranks as Janissary fathers used their influence to have their often unqualified sons admitted to the corps. The financially strained empire found it difficult to support the Janissary corps.

For the first six years of Mustafa's sultancy, much of the sultan's decision making fell to the grand vizier, Koca Rāgib Pasha, who realized that the empire's most pressing needs were to enact reforms that would help rebuild the treasury and to maintain peace with the empire's neighbors, with which the financially strained government could not afford to engage in armed conflict. Mustafa strongly supported Koca Rāgib Pasha's efforts for reform and his pacifist policies. Upon the grand vizier's death in 1763, his successor, Muhsinzāde Mehmed Pasha, essentially continued to pursue the same protocols his predecessor had initiated, but now Mustafa became more directly involved in administering the government.

Realizing the need to strengthen his armed forces, Mustafa turned to Baron François de Tott, a renowned French artillery officer, to help him implement reforms within his own military corps. With Tott's assistance, the Ottoman artillery was totally reorganized. An engineering school in Constantinople that had been closed by the Janissaries in 1747 was reopened. In 1773, shortly before his death, Mustafa established a school of mathematics for naval personnel.

In 1739, before Mustafa's sultancy, the Treaty of Belgrade was enacted as a means of maintaining peace among the Ottomans and their neighbors. Even though the French and the Prussians tried to convince Mustafa to abrogate the treaty and enter into alliances with them, the sultan, keenly aware of the immediate benefits to be gained through neutrality, refused. He needed to buy time to replenish the Ottoman treasury and strengthen the military.

Finally, however, in 1768, Mustafa was forced to abandon his neutral stand, as Russia began to make significant incursions into both the Crimea and Poland. This aggression convinced Mustafa that he had to declare war on Russia. He felt confident that his armed forces, now reorganized and strengthened, could meet the demands this declaration entailed.

In the early phases of the war, the Ottomans scored some notable victories, but these successes were soon eclipsed by Russian victories in battles along the Danube River and in the Crimea. Mustafa's forces suffered a devastating blow in 1770, when the Russians destroyed the Ottoman naval fleet during a battle in the Aegean Sea. The first phase of the Ottoman-Russian Wars continued until shortly after Mustafa succumbed to a heart attack on January 21, 1774.

Mustafa III. (Hulton Archive/Getty Images)

SIGNIFICANCE

When Mustafa III took titular command of the Ottoman Empire in 1757, it had already declined to such an extent that, despite his strenuous efforts, it could not be revived or returned to its past glory. Mustafa cannot be faulted for failing to prevail in what clearly was an impossible situation. It is remarkable that he was able to make as many beneficial changes as he did during his seventeen-year rule. Notable among his accomplishments were his reopening of the engineering school the Janissaries had closed and his founding of a school of mathematics for the Ottoman navy. He valued education and strove to encourage it. He insisted that those serving in his military forces continue to pursue their formal education even as they served.

Mustafa made strides toward reversing the economic plight of the empire, enacting reforms that made the provincial leaders more accountable to the central government than they had been. He encouraged the building of several new mosques in the empire, employing Mehmed Tāhir Aga as architect for these projects. Mehmed designed the Ayazma Mosque, begun in 1760, and the Iskele Mosque, built between 1759 and 1763. These mosques, still standing, are outstanding examples of Ottoman architecture.

On a practical level, Mustafa implemented the fixing of bayonets on the rifles of his artillery forces. He established maritime and artillery academies to train military personnel. Noted for both his energy and his superior intelligence, Mustafa worked assiduously to stem the decline of the empire over which he ruled, but the damage already done to it was so great that a successful outcome for this task was unachievable.

—R. Baird Shuman

FURTHER READING

Barber, Noel. *Subjects of the Sultan: Culture and Daily Life in the Ottoman Empire*. New York: I. B. Tauris, 2000. An inside glimpse into the personal lives of the human beings who ruled the Ottoman Empire.

_____. *The Sultans*. New York: Simon and Schuster, 1973. A detailed and intimate account of the lives of the Ottoman sultans. Well written and easily accessible to general readers.

Goodwin, Godfrey. *The Janissaries*. London: Saqi, 1997. Goodwin traces in detail the decline of the Janissaries and the effects of their conservatism on Ottoman politics, focusing particularly on the problem of nepotism after Janissaries were permitted to marry.

_____. *Ottoman Turkey*. London: Scorpion, 1977. Among the best investigative accounts of politics in Ottoman Turkey.

Somel, Selcuk Aksin. *Historical Dictionary of the Ottoman Empire*. Lanham, Md.: Scarecrow Press, 2003. Somel offers a brief but useful overview of Mustafa III and his rule.

See also: Ahmed III; Mahmud I.

Related articles in *Great Events from History: The Eighteenth Century, 1701-1800*: November 20, 1710-July 21, 1718: Ottoman Wars with Russia, Venice, and Austria; 1718-1730: Tulip Age; 1736-1739: Russo-Austrian War Against the Ottoman Empire; October, 1768-January 9, 1792: Ottoman Wars with Russia; July 21, 1774: Treaty of Kuchuk Kainarji.

Nādir Shāh
Shāh of Persia (r. 1736-1747)

As the Ṣafavid Dynasty fell into decline, Nādir Shāh assembled an army in northern Persia and reconsolidated the country under his control. He expelled the Afghan rulers from Persia, reconquered the northwestern provinces from the Ottomans, and invaded Afghanistan, India, and Uzbekistan, annexing their territory.

Born: October 22, 1688; Dastgird, Persia (now in Iran)
Died: June, 1747; Khabushan, Persia (now in Iran)
Also known as: Nādir Qolī Beg (birth name); Ṭahmāsp Qolī Khan; Nādir Shāh Afshar; Nādir Khan Afshar; Nāder Shāh
Areas of achievement: Warfare and conquest, government and politics

Early Life

Nādir Shāh (NAH-duhr shah), born Nādir Qolī Beg, was born in 1688 to a family of the Kirklu clan of the Turkoman Afshar tribe. His mother gave birth to him at Dastgird, in northern Khorāsān, during the clan's seasonal migration to winter pastures. In his youth, Nādir joined the retinue of a local governor, Bābā ʿAlī Beg Kūsā-Ahmadlu, who eventually gave him two daughters in marriage and, upon his death in 1723, passed on his own property to the young man.

During the anarchy caused by the Afghan invasion of Persia, Nādir joined the service of Malik Maḥmūd of Sistan, who had occupied Mashhad. After some time, Nādir formed his own band of raiders and, in alliance with a Kurdish group, contested control of the city. This brought him to the notice of the Ṣafavid heir-apparent, Ṭahmāsp Mirzā, who recruited Nādir and his small army as protectors along with Fatḥ ʿAlī Khān Qājār and his troops. In 1727, as Persia was in the process of being dismembered by the Ottomans and Russians, Ṭahmāsp designated Nādir his military commander.

In 1729, Nādir initiated his career by stopping the Ghilzai army in Khorāsān. He then defeated the Ottoman forces in Western Persia in 1730 and recovered Herāt from the ʿAbdali Afghans in 1732. During this period, Ṭahmāsp had been obliged to sign unfavorable treaties with the Ottomans and the Russians. As a result, Nādir was able to persuade the Kizilbash leaders to depose Ṭahmāsp and place his son, ʿAbbās III, on the throne with Nādir as his regent. In this position, Nādir defeated the Ottomans in a second series of battles between 1733 and 1735, in response to which the Russians withdrew their

forces from Persia. In 1735, they signed the Treaty of Ganjeh, which established boundaries between the two countries and formed a defensive alliance.

Life's Work

Early in 1736, following his significant successes, Nādir called an assembly of notables near his hunting encampment on the Mughan Plain. There, army commanders, governors, nobles, and the learned class of ulama (religious scholars and jurists) were brought together from all over his realm. During this staged event, Nādir informed the gathered dignitaries that he planned to retire to Khorāsān and asked the assembly to elect a new Ṣafavid ruler. His cunning tactic worked, and all insisted that he become shāh himself. After a few days, Nādir accepted, on the condition that the Sunni faith be adopted in place of the Shiism formerly sponsored by the Ṣafavid state.

Under Nādir's plan, Shiism could still be practiced but only in a form deemed acceptable by the shāh. This version, which he called Jafari Shiism, was stripped of practices offensive to Sunni Muslims, such as cursing the first three caliphs (successors to the Prophet Muḥammad). This abrupt shift in religious policy had multiple causes. It served to diffuse the religious prestige of the Ṣafavid house. It also sought to remove a source of much bloodshed between Persia and Ottoman Turkey. Immediately, Nādir drafted a peace treaty with the Ottomans that stipulated the status of the Jafari faith within Sunni Islam. Soon after the settlement of the treaty, on March 8, 1736, Nādir was crowned shāh.

Having secured peace on his western borders, Nādir Shāh turned his attention eastward. The following spring, he led an army against Qandahār, where Hussein Sultan Ghilzai, brother of the invader Maḥmūd, was seated as a last reminder of Afghan victory over Persia. In 1738, after a long siege, Nādir's troops finally captured Qandahār. They then set out for India by way of Kabul and Peshawar. The army captured Lahore and defeated the Mughal army at Karnal. By March of 1739, it stormed the city of Delhi. After amassing large amounts of booty, including the famous Koh-i-Noor diamond and jewel-encrusted Peacock Throne, Nādir left the Mughal emperor Muḥammad Shāh in power. After Muḥammad Shāh had ceded all territories west of the Indus River to Persia, Nādir returned to Herāt. Next, he defeated the Uzbeks, making the Oxus River the northeastern boundary of his kingdom. Meanwhile, he attempted to build a fleet in the Persian Gulf to prepare for an impending invasion of Oman.

Though he was successful as a military commander, problems began to mount for Nādir Shāh after 1741. Suspended hostilities with the Ottoman Empire were soon resumed. Though his army forced Kirkuk into submission in 1743, the renewal of hostilities was costly. To pay for the resumption of campaigns in the west, Nādir rescinded the tax amnesty he had declared while in India and increased his tax extractions from the Persian populace. Around this time, pretenders to the Ṣafavid throne began to revolt in several areas, including Azerbaijan, Dagestan, Khwārizm, and the Ottoman frontier. After quelling these rebellions, Nādir returned to Eṣfahān in December of 1745 to extort funds and punish his officials.

After a short time, in 1746, he instituted these punishments with renewed vigor. Then, after signing another treaty with Turkey that essentially restored the frontiers of 1639, Nādir behaved with arbitrary ferocity against his nobles and his populace. Reports of European visitors to his court judged him to be deranged. Contemporary sources report that as he left Eṣfahān for Kermān and Khorāsān, he erected towers of heads wherever he stopped. On June 20, 1747, while putting down a rebellion against the Kurds in Khabushan, a group of Nādir's Persian, Afshar, and Qājār officers assassinated him at the encampment. Nādir's army then disbanded, his treasure was plundered, and his progeny were killed. On July 6, 1747, his nephew ʿAli Qolī Khan ascended the throne as ʿAdil Shāh.

SIGNIFICANCE

Nādir Shāh is credited with rescuing Persia from partition and foreign domination. He excelled as a commander and military strategist, and the scope of his achievements may be compared with those of the fourteenth century ruler Tamerlane, whose exploits he consciously emulated. Nādir's military endeavors had a significant impact upon broader political dynamics in the eighteenth century, initiating a shift of power from the two dynasties on Persia's eastern and western borders. His campaigns against Turkey weakened the Ottoman state and ultimately swayed the balance of power in favor of Russia, while his humiliation of the Mughal emperor hastened the empire's eventual fall under the British.

Nādir Shāh succeeded in reversing Ṣafavid policies of the previous century: He confiscated properties secured in pious endowments, threatened to abolish state sponsorship of Shiism, and favored Sunni Afghans and Uzbeks over Shīʿite Persian and Turkoman Kizilbash officers.

Nonetheless, by the end of his life, Nādir's military endeavors had begun to turn sour, and through his irrational behavior he fully alienated all of his former political supporters.

—*Anna Sloan*

FURTHER READING

Avery, Peter. *Nadir Shah and the Afsharid Legacy*. Vol. 7 in *The Cambridge History of Iran*. New York: Cambridge University Press, 1991. The most comprehensive source on political developments in Persia during the fall of the Ṣafavid Dynasty and the reign of Nādir Shāh. Contains plates, maps, and genealogical tables.

Daniel, Elton L. *The History of Iran*. Westport, Conn.: Greenwood Press, 2001. A general survey, which locates Nādir Shāh's rule in the larger scope of Persia's history. Contains maps, a glossary of terms, and a bibliographical essay.

Lockhart, Laurence. *The Fall of the Safavid Dynasty and the Afghan Occupation of Persia*. Cambridge, England: Cambridge University Press, 1958. The study that laid out the historical framework of the late Ṣafavid period and that still offers unsurpassed information on the end of Ṣafavid rule and the rise of Nādir Shāh. Contains illustrations, maps, a genealogical table of the Ṣafavid Dynasty, and a bibliography listing primary sources, including European travelers' accounts.

_____. *Nadir Shah: A Critical Study Based Mainly upon Contemporary Sources*. London: Luzac, 1938. The principal monograph on Nādir Shāh's life and achievements. This study, which contains material from difficult-to-access primary sources, is yet to be surpassed. Contains a genealogical table, maps, and a bibliography of primary sources.

Perry, John R. "The Last Ṣafavids, 1722-1793." *Iran* 9 (1971): 59-69. A scholarly article that investigates the relationship between the Ṣafavids and Nādir Shāh Afshar in the early eighteenth century.

_____. "Nadir Shah Afshar." In *The Encyclopedia of Islam*, edited by H. A. R. Gibb. Rev. ed. Vol. 7. Leiden, the Netherlands: E. J. Brill, 1960-2004. A comprehensive synopsis of scholarship on Nādir Shāh's life and accomplishments. Includes a thorough bibliography complete with sources published in Persian, Russian, and Turkish.

See also: Karīm Khān Zand; Vaḥīd Bihbahānī; Muḥammad ibn ʿAbd al-Wahhāb.

Related articles in *Great Events from History: The Eighteenth Century, 1701-1800*: 1709-1747: Persian-Afghan Wars; 1725-November, 1794: Persian Civil Wars; June 10, 1749: Saʿīd Becomes Ruler of Oman.

NANNY
Jamaican rebel leader

Nanny inspired generations of black Jamaicans to seek and secure freedom and equality, which began with the First Maroon War in the early eighteenth century. Her legendary actions and clever tactics against British troops won limited territory and some rights for many fugitive slaves and initiated what would be the emancipation of all enslaved Jamaicans. Also, Nanny ensured that African traditions and lore would continue to influence Jamaican culture.

Born: Unknown; probably Africa
Died: 1750's; Jamaica
Also known as: Granny Nanny; Right Excellent Nanny of the Maroons
Areas of achievement: Social reform, warfare and conquest

EARLY LIFE

Scholars have sought clues about the enigmatic Nanny for decades, and many have pondered whether she existed or was only a mythical creation to motivate rebels and intimidate soldiers. Few Jamaican histories note her role in rebellions or accurately portray her significance, if she is mentioned at all. Documents, including a land grant and peace treaty, indicate that a black woman named Nanny lived in Jamaica in the 1730's. Oral sources, including songs, emphasize that Nanny affected Jamaican culture by contributing her insights, ingenuity, and fortitude to liberate Jamaican slaves. A conglomeration of these resources, in addition to geographical namesakes and a grave-site memorial, have increased the likelihood that Nanny existed and therefore had a profound influence on Jamaican history.

Precise information about Nanny is elusive. Many biographical details about her have been distorted or misrepresented by interpreters' agendas. Most scholars accept that Nanny was probably born in the 1680's in the Gold Coast region of what is now Ghana in Africa, based on a description of her in a 1740 land grant indicating that she was middle aged. Some researchers hypothesize she belonged to a royal family in the Asanti band or Akan ethnic group because followers used the title "queen" to refer to her. Her parents' names were not recorded, and "Nanny" might not have been her birth name. Many Jamaican women were called "Nanny," which was a name probably derived from African terms that affectionately describe wise women who acted as caretakers of their people and preserved and transferred ancestral traditions

and stories between generations. Nanny's mother or female kin may have taught her African techniques and traditions that helped her appear powerful in Jamaica.

Several accounts tell how Nanny and her sister, who was identified by many names, including Sekesu, arrived in Jamaica (the date not specified), where Nanny chose to rebel against slavery. Sekesu remained enslaved (captured possibly during an escape when her crying baby revealed their location). The sisters became the symbolic mothers of eighteenth century Jamaican blacks. Some stories refer to Nanny's brothers—Cudjoe, Cuffee, Quaco, Accompong, and Johnny—who also were associated with black rebellions in Jamaica, and sources consistently name Nanny's husband Adou. The couple had no known offspring.

LIFE'S WORK

Whether African royalty or a slave, Nanny rallied black Jamaicans to defy and seek independence from British slave owners and officials. Slavery had existed in Jamaica since sixteenth century Spaniards gained control and imported Africans. Several slave revolts occurred during the seventeenth century. English troops conquered the Spanish in the mid-seventeenth century, and many slaves escaped into the Jamaican rain forest and hills.

English officials had encouraged settlers to establish sugarcane plantations and utilize slave labor, importing more Africans. Many slaves resisted and sought ways to impede agricultural production. Some escaped, eluding captors in Jamaica's mountainous terrain. These fugitive slaves, known as Maroons, formed communities to help each other. Both the Windward Maroons, living in the northeast, and the Leeward Maroons, living in the west, strived to free slaves. Nanny, also called Granny Nanny, lived on eastern Jamaica's Blue Mountain in a settlement called Nanny Town in her honor. Maroons revered her because she guided fugitives to sanctuaries, helped them survive, and urged them to seek freedom. Nanny demanded autonomy for all Maroons.

The Maroons gathered information about the British from allied slaves on plantations. Tensions intensified as more settlers arrived, blocking Maroon access to land. The Maroons soon raided plantations. By the 1720's, enraged British officials mobilized troops and militias to capture the Maroons. Although Nanny never served as a combatant, she achieved acclaim as a military leader, sometimes being referred to as a general, sharing strategies on how best to fight and eliminate the British. She emboldened Maroon guerrillas to fight even though their forces numbered several hundred men compared to several thousand men fighting for the British.

Nanny's reputation as a masterful leader grew as tales of her daring and cunning circulated. She seemed invincible to most people, and she provoked fear in the British. Among her alleged feats was her ability to snatch fired bullets and shoot them back at enemies. Although this seems impossible, some Africans reported bullet catching as a war tactic. Legend describes how Nanny's kettle could boil water without a fire and how she used the kettle to trap British soldiers or startle them, causing them to fall into gorges. Nanny may have used herbs to sedate enemies as well. These tales led many of the colonists to believe that Nanny was supernatural and had magical powers. The Maroons believed her powers reinforced her role as an *obeah*, or spiritual director, who retained African ways within Maroon communities. Spiritual guidance included respect for forebears. When Nanny despaired of defeating the British, ancestors told her to plant the pumpkin seeds she found in her clothes and to persist. Those seeds quickly produced food that strengthened the Maroon fighters.

Furthermore, the resilient Nanny offered Maroons practical advice, often based on African military customs and an awareness of nature. Cleverness often defeated technology. She told fighters how to use *abeng* (cow horns) to alert Maroons when British troops approached and to designate where to attack. She taught Maroons how to use jungle leaves, ferns, and bark to disguise themselves as trees, then to control breathing muscles and to stand silently before ambushing enemy soldiers.

British forces attacked and occupied Nanny Town in 1734, but Nanny and her followers regrouped in the jungle and soon formed Moore Town. Fighting continued until the Windward Maroons signed a peace treaty with the British in 1739. Nanny, probably distrusting the British and resenting the use of the word "surrender" in the treaty, did not sign it. The government issued Nanny a land grant in 1740, giving 500 acres to the Windward Maroons.

Although a slave seeking reward money lied to authorities, telling them that Nanny had been killed in 1733, the 1740 land grant indicates she was alive in 1740. Historians believe she lived until the 1750's. A monument was placed by her grave by Maroons in Moore Town.

SIGNIFICANCE

Nanny had an impact on Maroons even after her death. Seeking independence, Maroons pressed for emancipation from British rule, which was finally achieved in 1834. Nanny and the legends she inspired have retained credibility in modern Jamaica. Her spirit prevails in Maroon communities, where people believe she is often present. They credit her for uniting and strengthening Maroons, past and present. An annual Nanny Day celebrates her achievements on behalf of her people and her determination to protect and maintain African traditions in Maroon cultures. Some of the festivities, however, are closed to non-Maroons out of respect to her, because it is believed that Nanny observes the festivities.

Furthermore, Nanny has many namesakes, and she is pictured on local currency and praised in poetry and song. She was featured in Phyllis Cousins's *Queen of the Mountain* (1967), a fictionalized biography for children that was approved by the Jamaican ministry of education. In 1976, Nanny was named a Jamaican national hero, the only woman—and the only Maroon—to receive such recognition.

Nanny, the touchstone for a significant Caribbean community, merits further study. Unfortunately, many older histories have relied on biased accounts that were based on hearsay from British sources, which often were racist; some were distorted to detract from Nanny's military successes against British troops. The secrecy of Nanny's identity and an indigenous reliance on oral history obscure some facts. Modern Maroons protect Nanny's legacy, warning that non-Maroons who travel to the site of the original Nanny Town risk curses and illness. Such superstitions guard Nanny and the African-Maroon culture she struggled to perpetuate while resisting opponents who would have assimilated Maroons and destroyed their ethnic traditions and culture.

—Elizabeth D. Schafer

FURTHER READING

Campbell, Mavis C. *Maroons of Jamaica, 1655-1796: A History of Resistance, Collaboration, and Betrayal.* South Hadley, Mass.: Bergin & Garvey, 1988. Campbell, a historian who has lived with Maroons, claims to have proof that Nanny existed. The author also explores the rebel activities based on archival records and Maroon lore and cultural practices.

Gottlieb, Karla Lewis. *The Mother of Us All: A History of Queen Nanny, Leader of the Windward Jamaican Maroons.* Trenton, N.J.: Africa World Press, 2000. The most thorough source of information about

Nanny, including legal documents, the author's interpretation of the 1739 treaty, and a poem. Illustrations, bibliography.

Hochschild, Adam. *Bury the Chains: Prophets and Rebels in the Fight to Free an Empire's Slaves.* Boston: Houghton Mifflin, 2005. A history of the British abolition movement, including the role of Granville Sharp and others in founding the Society for the Abolition of Slavery.

Monteith, Kathleen E. A., and Glen Richards, eds. *Jamaica in Slavery and Freedom: History, Heritage, and Culture.* Kingston, Jamaica: University of the West Indies, 2002. A scholarly collection of essays that includes suggestions for primary resources useful for placing Nanny in context with other Jamaican rebels.

Sherlock, Philip, and Hazel Bennett. *Story of the Jamaican People.* Princeton, N.J.: Markus Wiener, 1998. A chapter features Africans in Jamaica, including Nanny, fighting for independence. Maps, bibliography, index, and an illustration of the 1740 land grant.

Zips, Werner. *Black Rebels: African-Caribbean Freedom Fighters in Jamaica.* Translated by Shelley L. Frisch. Foreword by Franklin Knight. Princeton, N.J.: Markus Wiener, 1999. Originally published in German, this text was written by an anthropologist and director of the documentary "Accompong: Black Rebels in Jamaica," which presents events from a Maroon perspective.

See also: Joseph Boulogne; Guillaume-Thomas Raynal; Granville Sharp; Toussaint Louverture; Tupac Amaru II.

Related articles in *Great Events from History: The Eighteenth Century, 1701-1800:* 18th century: Expansion of the Atlantic Slave Trade; April 6, 1712: New York City Slave Revolt; 1730-1739: First Maroon War; November 23, 1733: Slaves Capture St. John's Island; 1760-1776: Caribbean Slave Rebellions; 1780-1781: Rebellion of Tupac Amaru II; August 22, 1791-January 1, 1804: Haitian Independence; July, 1795-March, 1796: Second Maroon War.

JACQUES NECKER
Swiss financier and politician

Necker was the best-known and perhaps most successful financier, financial writer, and reform minister during the reign of King Louis XVI—at a time when all three fields were in their pioneer stage. Controversies about his abilities and policies have continued to the present, and he is a major figure in the continuing debates over mercantilism and Physiocracy.

Born: September 30, 1732; Geneva, Switzerland
Died: April 9, 1804; Coppet, Switzerland
Areas of achievement: Business, economics, government and politics

EARLY LIFE

The early life of Jacques Necker (zhahk nay-kehr) was short and sweet—short in the telling and sweet to him. His father, Karl Friedrich Necker, born in Kostrzyn, Pomerania, in 1686, was serious and hardworking, as probably were generations of north German Neckers, many of them Lutheran pastors. Of considerable intellect, Jacques's father was trained in law, gained political

appointments, published on international law, and was elected professor of public law in 1726 at the Genevan Academy, where he flourished in a serious and respectful environment. He became a Genevan citizen and married Jeanne-Marie Gautier of a prominent Genevan family. Their first son, Louis, later known as Louis of Germany for the estate he purchased, was serious and bright.

Jacques was a precocious student. He completed his secondary curriculum when he was fourteen, and although he wished to pursue literature, he followed his father's wishes and went to work in the banking firm of Isaac Vernet, brother of a colleague of Jacques's father. Jacques pleased his employer and in 1750 was transferred to the Paris branch. There he served a long apprenticeship. Vernet retired in 1756, and a new company, Thelluson and Necker, was formed. Apparently, George-Tobie de Thelluson, the son of a Genevan banker, supplied most of the capital, and Necker supplied most of the hard work and banking skills. The apprenticeship continued; modest profits and valuable experience were gained in making government loans during the Seven Years' War (1756-1763).

LIFE'S WORK

Necker turned thirty-one in 1763, began dating (then called courting), and began establishing his fortune. He made money in speculation in grain, Canadian notes, and the Company of the Indies, as many did, although few retained their fortunes. Famines, the loss of Canada in the Treaty of Paris (1763), and the reorganization of war debts made these three areas lucrative. Critics tried to prove shady dealings on Necker's part, but at worst it could be said that he exploited the practices and standards of the times. His activities left him with the lifelong conviction that "business enterprise should be left to businessmen," a belief contrary to the dictates of mercantilism, to which Necker was believed to adhere, because he opposed the allegedly Physiocratic (laissez-faire) reform minister Anne-Robert-Jacques Turgot.

In 1763, Necker began to court Germaine de Vermenoux, a well-to-do widow; her sister was married to Necker's partner, Thelluson. Probably concerned about their different social statuses, Germaine resisted Necker's attention. Escaping to a health spa near Geneva with her young son, she met Suzanne Curchold, a governess of unusual wit and charm, and took her back to Paris in 1764 as companion-governess. Suzanne and Necker fell in love and married at the end of the year. Germaine forgave her former suitor and her employee, and remained a friend of the Neckers until her death in 1785. Necker acknowledged the great help he had received from "the companion of his life." Suzanne rapidly became a fashionable hostess in Paris; her "Fridays," by 1768, were well frequented by *lumières* (bright, famous, and promising persons). The unfriendly accused her of entertaining (and living) only to advance her husband's career; the generous, including Voltaire, Denis Diderot, and Jean-Jacques Rousseau, found her to be a genuine *lumière*.

Necker retired from Thelluson and Necker in 1772. He then devoted most of his time to writing and to his political appointments and showed little interest in increasing his personal fortune. He had enough to live comfortably all of his life. Necker won the prize of the French Academy in 1773 for his *Éloge de Jean-Baptiste Colbert* (eulogy of Colbert). In 1775, Necker published an essay on legislation and the grain trade, which attacked Finance Minister Turgot's free-trade policy and fixed the view of Necker as a mercantilist and anti-Physiocrat and therefore antiphilosophe. Actually, Necker was more of a pragmatist than a theorist, as is fitting to a finance minister, which is what he was to

Jacques Necker. (Library of Congress)

become. He was first placed in complete control of France's finances when he was named director of the Royal Treasury in 1776. The following year, he was made finance minister.

Necker faced enormous difficulties in his first administration. Turgot had commenced reform, but the main result had been to awaken the opposition of the special interests and to establish the inconsistency of the king. Five months of inattention increased the disorder, and Necker had to struggle to meet current obligations. He managed enough loans to finance participation in the American Revolution and institute reforms to lessen the cost of those long-term obligations. Special interest groups mounted a pamphlet offensive against him; his appeals to the king for support were ignored. He issued his famous *Compte rendu au roi* (1781; *State of the Finances of France*, 1781) and resigned amid consternation in the financial community.

Finances worsened. Even conservative ministers such as Charles-Alexandre de Calonne and Étienne-Charles de Loménie de Brienne were forced to recommend reforms. Facing the refusal of the Assembly of Notables to endorse reforms and the Law Court of Paris to enregister reform edicts, and lacking the resolve to call out troops, Louis XVI, in August, 1788, recalled Necker to head finances, quibbling over his title, and announced a meeting of the Estates-General for May, 1789. The market value of government securities surged.

Contrary to public belief, Necker was not in command; in fact, the king, the ministers, and the court paid little attention to him. The Estates-General nearly ignored him when it met on May 5. Leaders of the clergy and leaders of the nobility were intent on the protection of their privileges; leaders of the Third Estate (Commons) were equally intent on changing the composition of the Estates-General and on clarifying the constitution, or on writing one (they disagreed on whether there was one), so few deputies were able to concentrate on Necker's three-hour presentation. While he received some praise and support, mostly he was blamed for not being able to communicate. The king expected Necker to control the Commons, but neither king nor Commons listened to Necker. At court, Necker's party, looking toward a British type of constitution, pressed Louis to meet major demands, and the queen's party pressed the king to bring in troops to disperse the legislature. The queen won. Necker was dismissed and left Paris on July 11. By July 13, Paris was not only "in a fury but roaring drunk." On July 14, the Bastille fell, and on July 15 a letter of reappointment was sent to Necker at Basel.

Necker's concern in his third ministry was to restore to the public mind the moral authority of the king. The national assembly did not respond to his numerous financial reports and recommendations, and was not moved by his eloquence. He concluded that the deputies wanted to enjoy all the power and prestige as representatives of the nation but none of the responsibility for government. The greatest problem was the disposal of the property that had been confiscated from the Church during the revolution. The national assembly issued *assignats*, or interest-bearing bonds; Necker urged that nothing be spent until land was sold, lest speculation, inflation, and depreciation of the *assignats* mushroom. Again, the assembly did not listen. Necker resigned in September, 1790.

Necker's retirement is usually forgotten, but it is instructive. He lived at Coppet for fourteen years. He cared for his ailing wife and, after her death, arranged and published her writings in five volumes. He published a study of the executive power in large states in 1792 and a three-volume history of the revolution in 1796. A fifteen-volume edition of his works assembled by his grandson was published in 1820-1821.

SIGNIFICANCE

A patient, line-by-line analysis of Jacques Necker's personal and professional financial dealings substantiates the claim that Necker was the most experienced and knowledgeable financier of the late eighteenth century. One of the reasons he has not had more acclaim is that so few then (or later) understood finances well enough to judge. Many, such as the comte de Mirabeau, believed Necker to be "full of wind." His presentation on the opening day of the Estates-General was long and frustratingly detailed, and the reaction to his speech was not positive. He did, however, advise the assembly well when he concluded, "You will not be envious of what time can achieve and will leave something for it to do. For if you attempt to reform everything that seems imperfect, your work itself will be so."

Necker offered advice to many friends. He urged the émigrés to make peace with the revolution. He deplored the absence of executive power of the king and recoiled in horror at the evidence of violence against persons and property. He likened himself to the sixteenth century chancellor of Queen Regent Catherine de Médicis, Michel de l'Hospital, who had tried to mediate between Catholics and Protestants; forty years of violence followed.

—*Frederic M. Crawford*

FURTHER READING

Bosher, J. F. *French Finances 1770-1795: From Business to Bureaucracy.* New York: Cambridge University Press, 1970. Convincingly contradicts the older view that bankruptcy was a terminal illness of the Old Regime and that the royal administration was beyond reform. Includes a helpful table of French terms, five organization charts, five tables of expenses and revenues, a list of treasurers, treasurers general, and receivers general, and a bibliography.

Doyle, William. *Origins of the French Revolution.* New York: Oxford University Press, 1980. Part 1 describes writings on revolutionary origins since 1939, with page 39 clearly contrasting the old and new judgments of Necker. Part 2 is a thirteen-chapter topical study of the breakdown of the Old Regime and a good supplement to Jean Egret's narrative.

Egret, Jean. *The French Prerevolution, 1787-1788.* Translated by Wesley D. Camp. Introduction by J. F. Bosher. Chicago: University of Chicago Press, 1977. The best study of the period. This work reaps the financial effects of the reaction to Necker's first ministry and sets the stage for his second.

Gershoy, Leo. *The French Revolution and Napoleon.* New York: F. S. Crofts, 1933. The best-organized and most clearly written of the many older surveys. Presents the older view of Necker in chapter 4, "The Reform Movement During the Old Regime," and chapter 5, "The Destruction of the Old Regime."

Harris, Robert D. *Necker: Reform Statesman of the Ancien Régime.* Berkeley: University of California Press, 1979. The first four chapters describe Necker's early life and professional career up to his first appointment as finance minister. Contains a bibliography and a list of terms.

_____. *Necker and the Revolution of 1789.* Lanham, Md.: University Press of America, 1986. A continuation of Harris's study of Necker's political career. Analyzes royal administration in the 1780's, finance ministries between Necker's first and second terms, and Necker's second and third terms. Contains a complete twenty-page bibliography.

Herold, J. Christopher. *Mistress to an Age: A Life of Madame de Staël.* Indianapolis, Ind.: Bobbs-Merrill, 1958. As close to a biography of Necker as is available in English. Part 1, "The Neckers," is most germane to Necker, but he is an important figure throughout the book because Madame de Staël, Necker's daughter, was unusually devoted to her father and unusually influenced by him.

Hibbert, Christopher. *The Days of the French Revolution.* New York: Viking Penguin, 1989. Originally published in 1980 under the title *The French Revolution*, Hibbert's book provides detailed descriptions of events from 1789 until the rise of Napoleon. The book includes information on Necker. Well written and understandable to readers with little or no knowledge of the period.

Schama, Simon. *Citizens: A Chronicle of the French Revolution.* New York: Knopf, 1989. Schama's history of the period includes information on Necker. Schama argues the revolution did not create a "patriotic culture of citizenship," but was preceded by a more vital, inventive culture.

See also: Denis Diderot; Louis XVI; Comte de Mirabeau; Jean-Jacques Rousseau; Madame de Staël; Anne-Robert-Jacques Turgot; Voltaire.

Related articles in *Great Events from History: The Eighteenth Century, 1701-1800*: 1720: Financial Collapse of the John Law System; 1751-1772: Diderot Publishes the *Encyclopedia*; April, 1762: Rousseau Publishes *The Social Contract*; April 27-May, 1775: Flour War; March 9, 1776: Adam Smith Publishes *The Wealth of Nations*; May 5, 1789: Louis XVI Calls the Estates-General; June 20, 1789: Oath of the Tennis Court; July 14, 1789: Fall of the Bastille; October, 1789-April 25, 1792: France Adopts the Guillotine; April 20, 1792-October, 1797: Early Wars of the French Revolution; September 20, 1792: Battle of Valmy; January 21, 1793: Execution of Louis XVI; March 4-December 23, 1793: War in the Vendée; July 27-28, 1794: Fall of Robespierre; 1798: Malthus Arouses Controversy with His Population Theory; November 9-10, 1799: Napoleon Rises to Power in France.

JOHN NEWBERY
English publisher and businessman

Newbery was the first to make the writing and sale of books especially targeted to children an important branch of the book trade.

Born: July 19, 1713 (baptized); Waltham St.
   Lawrence, Berkshire, England
Died: December 22, 1767; London, England
Areas of achievement: Literature, business

EARLY LIFE

As is the case with many eighteenth century individuals, John Newbery's date of birth is not known; his baptism, however, was registered in the records of his native parish. The Newberys were a publishing family, although John's father, Robert Newbery, was a small farmer in Waltham St. Lawrence, Berkshire. The future publisher spent his childhood in his home district, receiving his early education there, an education befitting a farmer's son. The boy did, however, read widely and thus developed an early appreciation for books.

In 1729, at the age of sixteen, Newbery left home, moving to nearby Reading (about nine miles distant), where he became apprenticed and later assistant to the printer William Carnan, publisher of the *Reading Mercury*. Carnan died in 1737, leaving his business jointly to his brother and to Newbery, who consolidated his position soon afterward by marrying Carnan's widow, by whom he was eventually to have three children.

Under Newbery's direction, the *Reading Mercury* became one of the leading provincial newspapers of the time, sold in almost fifty markets by 1743. This success might well have been in part the consequence of a tour through parts of England that Newbery had taken in 1740. His diary from this excursion suggests that while he was representing the firm and seeking to promote its business, he was also seeking to learn more about commercial conditions and opportunities. This same journal for the six-week tour indicates the nature of Newbery's mind, ever alert to new ways to further the firm's business. He mentions, for example, the idea of issuing two fortnightly items, the *Reading Mercury* and the *Reading Courant*, to avoid having to pay the tax on more frequent publications. There is no evidence that this scheme was ever put into operation, but the expansion of the paper's distribution area within three years of his trip shows how he utilized some of his experiences.

The first book to bear Newbery's own imprint appeared in 1740, but running a publishing house was not his only occupation. In 1743, Newbery entered into partnership with John Hooper of Reading to sell "female pills." This later operation suggests the restless nature of Newbery's mind, one perpetually alert to new money-making possibilities. In fact, throughout his lifetime, he sold Dr. James' Fever Powders, advertisements and references to which appeared in many of his publications. Indeed, although bookselling remained at all times Newbery's main interest, a considerable portion of his fortune came from the sale of some thirty patent medicines.

Some contemporary sketches of Newbery have survived, but they are so imprecise that it is impossible to gain a good impression of his physical appearance. More important are the portraits in words left by Samuel Johnson and the poet-historian Oliver Goldsmith. Newbery emerges as a simple, jolly, resourceful, and ever-busy individual without time to pay attention to his somewhat shabby and mud-spattered clothing, a portly man nearly overwhelmed with increasing business commitments but always eager to have still more of them. It was this eagerness that led him to move to London in 1744.

LIFE'S WORK

John Newbery moved to London in 1744, initially running a warehouse before moving to the Bible and Sun publishers at St. Paul's Churchyard in 1745. He was to have twenty-three years of hard-earned prosperity in the nation's capital. Newbery was now managing a prosperous, many-faceted company; publishing was joined with the selling of various patent medicines, especially the aforementioned fever powder, in which Newbery held a half interest. Already, however, the major thrust of his talents was in the writing and publication of books for children's amusement and instruction, for which there was an increasing demand in eighteenth century England, especially at Christmastime.

Although Newbery was best known and remembered as the publisher of children's books, that was not his only literary undertaking. After the move to London, he continued his association with newspapers of both London and the provinces, employing many eminent authors. By the end of the 1740's, Newbery was associated with many of the leading literary figures of the day. Johnson borrowed money from Newbery, Goldsmith was also in the publisher's debt financially and otherwise, and Christopher Smart married one of his stepdaughters in 1753, a year after a volume of the poet's works had been published. In 1758, he started *The Universal Chronicle or Weekly Gazette*, in which Johnson's *The Idler* (1758-1760) first appeared; later, he issued Johnson's *The Rambler* (1750-1752) and *Lives of the Poets* (1779-1781). In 1760, Newbery issued the inaugural edition of the *Public Ledger*, in which Goldsmith's *The Citizen of the World* first appeared, maintaining a publishing association established as early as 1757 and continued into the future, for Newbery was the first publisher of Goldsmith's *The Vicar of Wakefield* (1766), in which a flattering portrait of the printer appears.

Newbery was the first English publisher to profit from the publication and sale of books written especially for children. His first testing of this market came in 1744 with the publication of *A Little Pretty Pocket-Book*. In this work can be seen the characteristics of Newbery's approach to business. He rejected the cheap and drab appearance of earlier chapbooks, setting a high standard for appearance and quality. At all times he was concerned about details. He went to the expense of copperplate engravings to illustrate the books; the title pages had charm even if they were not spectacular in terms of typography. Binding also received careful attention; *A Little Pretty Pocket-Book* was covered in gilt and embossed papers that were to be a mark of Newbery's taste for the remainder of his life. These same publications indicate Newbery's business acumen. In one of his advertisements he states, "The books are given away, only the binding is to be paid for," and the cost was only sixpence. *A Little Pretty Pocket-Book* suggests another of the approaches meant to increase purchases. For an additional two pence, the purchaser of the book could acquire a pincushion for a daughter or a ball for a son.

This initial venture into children's literature enjoyed tremendous success and was followed by many additional titles. Some were meant to amuse; others, such as *Circle of the Sciences: Writing* (1746), and *Circle of the Sciences: Arithmetic* (1746) were to teach. Newbery tried a children's magazine, *The Lilliputian*, but that was one of his rare failures. Other works from the Newbery press offered the young (adolescent) mind exposure to contemporary ideas. *The Newtonian System of Philosophy Adapted to the Capacities of Young Gentlemen, and Ladies . . . by Tom Telescope* (1761; better known as *Tom Telescope*) made available to the young reader the scientific ideas of Sir Isaac Newton. The authorship of this work, as in the case of many of the children's books, is in doubt; some suggest that Goldsmith wrote *Tom Telescope*—the same suggestion is made for *The History of Little Goody Two-Shoes* (1766)—while others believe that Newbery himself penned the book.

Tom Telescope was a book for children, but it provides the modern historian with novel insight into how the ideas of the Enlightenment were disseminated throughout society. In its publication history, *Tom Telescope* also reveals other aspects of Newbery's usual approach to business. The initial printing of 1761 was a small one, merely enough to test the market. The book's immediate success mandated a new and much larger edition this same year; a third edition emerged in 1766, a fourth in 1770, and at least ten by 1800. There is almost no way to ascertain the size of individual printings or to identify the number of copies sold. J. H. Plumb estimates conservatively that between twenty-five thousand and thirty thousand copies of *Tom Telescope* were sold between 1760 and the end of the century and that an edition of ten thousand was issued of the ever-popular *A Little Pretty Pocket-Book*. As a result of Newbery's methods of operation, there are very few first editions of his works extant; frequently, the earliest surviving copies are from second or third printings.

Newbery's peak as a publisher lasted from the time of the opening of his shop in St. Paul's Churchyard in 1744 until the year of his death, 1767. He died at the age of fifty-four and was buried in the town of his birth. The business was continued at first by his son and a nephew, both named Francis Newbery, and then by the nephew's widow until 1801. None of these publishers, however, was the equal of his forebear, John Newbery.

SIGNIFICANCE

The career and achievement of John Newbery may be analyzed from several perspectives. The most obvious is his role as the first successful seller of books especially aimed at the children's market. It is therefore appropriate that the American Library Association since 1922 has bestowed annually the Newbery Award to the author of the outstanding book published in the area of children's literature.

On a related level, Newbery is worthy of study as an illustration of the increasing entrepreneurial ingenuity that was necessary to survive in the commercialized market of England. The land had become increasingly wealthy, and there was more leisure time for relatively well-to-do members of the middle class—Newbery's market. The middle class was now in a position to spend not only more money on its children but also more time with them. Newbery was shrewd enough to realize that and to enter the business on the ground floor. England's wealth was merely a single facet of the greater sophistication of the publishing industry at large, a market made possible by the growing literacy of the population.

There is yet another path to follow in connection with Newbery's place in history, the implementation of the educational theories of John Locke in his *Some Thoughts Concerning Education* (1693). In these informal letters, Locke speaks almost for the first time in modern history about children as children rather than miniature adults, suggesting new ways for parents to act toward their children. Rather than considering children as wild animals to be tamed, Locke tells his readers that children are humans who should be treated as rational creatures and allowed their freedom and liberty, a freedom and liberty appropriate to their age. Locke urged his readers to allow them to be children, allow them to play games, and accept that they have short attention spans and that variety and change delight and occupy their young minds; encourage their curiosity, he argued, but do not seek to satisfy it by pouring into their heads the accumulated wisdom of the elder generation. Perhaps consciously and perhaps unconsciously, what Newbery did was to provide materials, the books for children, that put Locke's advice into operation. His materials amused, entertained, and challenged, but more than that, they taught to the young of the land, especially those between the ages of twelve and fourteen, the knowledge of the times.

—*Ronald O. Moore*

FURTHER READING

Darton, F. J. Harvey. *Children's Books in England: Five Centuries of Social Life.* 3d ed. Revised by Brian Alderson. London: British Library. Devotes one chapter to Newbery, relating him and his works to the social milieu of the eighteenth century.

McKendrick, Neil, John Brewer, and J. H. Plumb. *The Birth of Consumer Society.* Bloomington: Indiana University Press, 1982. Plumb's two chapters, "Commercialization of Leisure" and "The New World of Children," while discussing Newbery the publisher, are much more concerned with placing him and his achievements within the context of commercial and attitudinal changes in eighteenth century England.

Meigs, Cornelia, et al. *A Critical History of Children's Literature.* 1953. Rev. ed. London: Macmillan, 1969. Meigs, who wrote the chapter concerned with Newbery, suggests the significance of the Lockean revolution in changing attitudes toward children.

Muir, Percy. *English Children's Books, 1600 to 1900.* New York: Praeger, 1954. Muir challenges Newbery's claim to discovering and satisfying the children's literature market.

Noblett, William. "John Newbery: Publisher Extraordinary." *History Today* 22 (April, 1972): 265-271. A brief but comprehensive article on Newbery's career, emphasizing the publishing side.

Townsend, John Rowe, ed. *John Newbery and His Books: Trade and Plumb-Cake Forever, Huzza!* Metuchen, N.J.: Scarecrow Press, 1994. Essays summarizing Newbery's life and achievements as a publisher and bookseller.

Welsh, Charles. *A Bookseller of the Last Century, Being Some Account of the Life of John Newbery.* London: Griffith, Farran, Okeden and Welsh, 1885. Reprint. London: Augustus M. Keeley, 1972. Welsh was essentially Newbery's literary executor, being a partner in the firm that succeeded in the nineteenth century to John Newbery's operation. This biography is primarily responsible for establishing Newbery's claim to primacy in discovering the children's market. Useful, also, for a listing of books published by Newbery.

See also: Joseph Addison; John Baskerville; Oliver Goldsmith; Samuel Johnson; Samuel Richardson; Richard Steele.

Related articles in *Great Events from History: The Eighteenth Century, 1701-1800:* January 7, 1714: Mill Patents the Typewriter; 1741: Leadhills Reading Society Promotes Literacy; 1746-1755: Johnson Creates the First Modern English Dictionary; March 20, 1750-March 14, 1752: Johnson Issues *The Rambler;* 1751-1772: Diderot Publishes the *Encyclopedia;* 1782-1798: Publication of Rousseau's *Confessions.*

THOMAS NEWCOMEN
English inventor

Newcomen invented and developed the first commercially practical steam engine for pumping water out of British coal and tin mines. His work inaugurated the age of steam power, which made possible the rapid development of the Industrial Revolution.

Born: January or February, 1663; Dartmouth, Devonshire, England
Died: August 5, 1729; London, England
Areas of achievement: Science and technology, engineering

EARLY LIFE

Thomas Newcomen was born shortly after the end of Lord Cromwell's protectorate and the restoration of King Charles II. The noble lineage of his family has been traced back to Hugo le Newcomen, lord of the manor of Saltfleetby in Lincolnshire, who joined the crusade of King Richard I, known as Richard the Lion-Hearted, to the Holy Land in the twelfth century. After four hundred years of unbroken succession, the Newcomens lost their manor when King Henry VIII confiscated their lands as a result of the Lincolnshire Rising of 1536; the family fled to London and thence to Ireland and Devonshire.

Thomas's grandfather, Thomas Newcomen, was the son of the famous scholarly rector of Stoke Fleming Church near Dartmouth, the Reverend Elias Newcomen. That grandfather became a merchant adventurer, an owner of several sailing ships, a freeholder of Dartmouth, and treasurer of the town during the English Civil War. Thomas's father, Elias, also a freeholder and merchant, continued the seafaring trade with the ship *Nonsuch,* which he inherited from his father. He married Sarah about 1660. The union produced two sons, John Newcomen of Chard, who became an apothecary, and Thomas.

Little is documented about the education of Thomas. One writer of Devon history claims that he was apprenticed to an ironmonger in Exeter. Most likely, he learned to read and write early and probably entered his father's business. In the 1680's, he opened his own shop, or took over his father's business, as a merchant and ironmonger in Dartmouth, dealing in hardware goods and heavy metal products, some made in his own shop.

At the age of forty-two, Thomas married Hannah Waymouth, a farmer's daughter from Marlborough, near Kingsbridge; they had two sons, Thomas and Elias, and one daughter, Hannah. Two years after his marriage, Newcomen leased a large house that extended between Higher and Lower Streets in Dartmouth, part of which he used for Baptist services for the local congregation, for which he also served as preacher and teacher. Apparently, his religious convictions and leadership ability made Newcomen a respected Baptist preacher among out-of-town congregations of Nonconformists (Protestants who did not attend the established Church of England), for he often preached in churches when away on business trips. In an era when Scripture was the sole source of authority for Protestants and ministers' sermons were long and detailed, Newcomen's self-education was remarkable. He was no ordinary blacksmith, nor was he a common lay churchman.

LIFE'S WORK

Biographical data about the first twenty years of Thomas Newcomen's business career remain very sketchy, and much that has been written must be discarded as undocumented myth or derogatory without fact. The young tradesman kept no diary or journal, left no collection of correspondence, and won no awards during his lifetime—hence the paucity of historical information about the man who invented and improved the first commercially practical steam engine by 1712.

He called himself an "ironmonger," a British term describing one who operates a shop making or selling iron products or hardware. Town records of Dartmouth list items purchased from him after 1688, including locks, latches, and nails. The treasurer later paid him for repairs on the town clock and for serving as Overseer of the Poor. Yet the scope of his business was far larger than that of a village shop. Conceivably, he served as a wholesale merchant in his port town, buying large tonnages of tin and iron from Devon and the Midlands and reselling smaller lots to other ironmongers or shipping overseas.

Newcomen engaged a fellow Baptist named John Calley (often spelled Caley or Cawley), who was trained as a plumber and glazier, to be his associate in his business and in the development and construction of his steam engines. Calley spent his life working with Newcomen on the atmospheric "fire engines," the early name for the steam engine. As a plumber, his experience in making metal and wooden pipes provided practical knowledge for making parts for the engines and the long wooden pipes used in the pumps in the mines. Early reports of the Dartmouth steam engines often gave credit to the inventors "Newcomen and Calley."

The steam engine invented by Newcomen was a significant and different design of the first British steam pump invented by Thomas Savery, who was granted a historic patent on July 25, 1698, for "raising water by the impellent force of fire," a fourteen-year patent later extended by an Act of Parliament in 1699 until 1733. In contrast to Newcomen's engine, Savery's had no heavy mechanical moving parts, but it was dangerous since it lacked any steam safety valves and boilers were not yet capable of containing great steam pressures safely.

Evidence indicates that Newcomen and Calley worked from ten to fourteen years with small-scale models of steam engines before erecting the first known successful atmospheric steam engine in 1712 at the Coneygree Coalworks, Tipton, in southeastern England. Somehow, Newcomen and Calley had been able to devote part of their business time to experimenting with steam power as a means of forcing air out of a piston cylinder in order that atmospheric pressure would press it down again and thereby raise and lower a beam to pump water out of mines. Savery had given up his efforts to make his steam pumps work in mines in 1705.

Because Savery had obtained a master patent in 1698, Newcomen could not patent his engine. No evidence establishes when Newcomen and Savery agreed that Newcomen would build his own engines under the Savery patent, but sometime between 1705 and 1715, when Savery died, such an agreement was made; all early Newcomen engines were protected by the Savery patent of 1698. Savery's widow turned over her rights to the patent, in return for an annuity, to a joint-stock company known as the Proprietors of the Invention for Raising Water by Fire, one of whom was Newcomen. These proprietors raised £21,600 and began large-scale building of engines for mines and town water-pumping stations. More than one hundred Newcomen engines were built in England and Europe in the next seventy-five years.

One feature that led to the success of the Dartmouth engine allegedly came about by accident, or as a contemporary Swedish visitor, Marten Triewald, wrote, "a special ordering of Providence." While working on the prototype in their shop, cold water in the leaden jacket that surrounded the cylinder wall suddenly leaked into the steam-filled vessel through a faulty tin-soldered hole and created such a strong vacuum that the piston crashed through the bottom of the cylinder and the chain on the little beam was broken. The astonished inventors had accidentally discovered that injecting cold water directly into the steam-filled piston would bring about quicker condensing of the steam and a resulting greater force of atmospheric pressure to push the piston. When full-size engines were erected at mines, with pistons ranging from 21 inches to 87 inches in diameter by 1733, the tremendous lifting power of Newcomen's atmospheric steam engines became one of their great selling points.

Success with the first Newcomen engine at the Tipton mine rapidly led to the erection of other engines at coal and tin mines in England. An advertisement in the *London Gazette* in 1716 referred to "diverse Engines of this Invention new at work in the several Counties of Stafford, Warwick, Cornwall and Flint." Sometime before 1725, an engine was at work at a mine at Elphingstone in Scotland. Another engine built that year at Edmonstone Colliery, Midlothian, cost more than £1,000; the brass cylinder was worth one-fourth of that total price, and a royalty of £80 per year went to the proprietors in London, who granted the license for eight years. Word soon spread to the Continent, and in 1722 the first Newcomen steam engine was erected at Königsberg in the mining district of Upper Hungary (now Czechoslovakia). In 1726, an engine was built to raise water from the Seine River at Passy outside Paris to supply the city with water; it is possible that Newcomen was present at its dedication.

Newcomen died of a fever in London, where he had gone, probably on business, in August, 1729. He was buried in Bunhill Fields; the exact spot is now unknown. Only one document in Newcomen's handwriting remains and no portrait of him exists. Little is known of his private life. It is doubtful that he benefited much materially from his invention.

At least three Newcomen engines have been preserved as museum pieces: One is in the Science Museum in South Kensington, England; another was re-erected at Dartmouth to celebrate the three hundredth anniversary of his birth; and in the United States, Henry Ford in 1930 restored an engine from a mine at Bardsley at his Dearborn Museum in Michigan.

SIGNIFICANCE

Thomas Newcomen's practical atmospheric steam engine found immediate success in Britain and other European countries for the pumping of water out of mines and for raising water for towns. While payment of royalties may have restricted the construction of Newcomen engines before the expiration of the Savery patent in 1733, at least 110 were erected by that date and no less than 1,454 atmospheric engines, including the rotary type, were built in England before 1800. Many Newcomen engines raised water that then turned water wheels to create a rotary power for mills and factories.

Although modern scholarship credits earlier scientists for development of the original ideas of the "heat engine," or "fire engine," including Salomon de Caus, David Ramsay, the marquess of Worcester, Samuel Morland, and Denys Papin—who published his paper on his discovery of the idea for a steam engine in 1690—Newcomen was the first to put these borrowed ideas into industrial practice. L. T. C. Rolt called the first Newcomen engine,

> with its combination of boiler, cylinder, piston and automatic valve gear . . . the undoubted sire of the steam engine of modern times. Like Watt's refinements, the introduction of high-pressure steam was accomplished without making any fundamental change in those major components which the genius of Newcomen first successfully combined.

Rolt also called Newcomen the "first great mechanical engineer." Thus, although his design involved no new components, Newcomen's genius was in combining known parts to produce a design that made steam power, and therefore the rapid rise of industry.

—*Paul F. Erwin*

FURTHER READING

Dickinson, H. W. *A Short History of the Steam Engine.* 2d ed. London: Frank Cass, 1963. Written by an engineering historian, this book contains A. E. Musson's introduction, which evaluates the claims of other writers and of Dickinson's conclusions in his 1938 edition. Chapter 3 covers Newcomen's vacuum engine.

_____. *Thomas Newcomen, Engineer, 1663-1729.* Rev. ed. Hanover, N.H.: Dartmouth Newcomen Association, 1975. A readable biography of the inventor, written with an engineer's concern for strict attention to detail.

Marsden, Ben. *Watt's Perfect Engine: Steam and the Age of Invention.* New York: Columbia University Press, 2002. Despite the book's title, Marsden emphasizes that Watt did not single-handedly invent the first steam engine. He explains how Newcomen invented a steam engine and how Watt redesigned that engine to make it more efficient.

Petroski, Henry. "Harnessing Steam." *American Scientist* 84, no. 1 (January/February, 1996): 15. Petroski

recounts how the steam engine was invented, including a description of Newcomen's engine and its application in the eighteenth century.

"Puffed Up." *Economist* 353, no. 8151 (December 31, 1999): 99. A history of the steam engine, describing Newcomen's invention and how it was used before it was redesigned by Watt. The article also analyzes the impact of the steam engine on the Industrial Revolution and on the millennium ending in 1999.

Rolt, L. T. C., and J. S. Allen. *The Steam Engine of Thomas Newcomen.* New York: Science History, 1977. The best story of both the life of Newcomen and the particular steam engine he invented. A fine introduction for amateur or engineer. Includes numerous engravings, drawings, charts, and photographs of steam power equipment as well as a list of all the known engines built by Newcomen and later builders before the Savery patent expired in 1733. Good bibliography.

Thirring, Hans. *Energy for Man: Windmills to Nuclear Power.* Bloomington: Indiana University Press, 1958. An introductory text on energy sources, with a full chapter devoted to the rise of steam power. The author argues that Watt was a creative genius who was not the inventor, but rather the most important improver of the steam engine.

Von Tunzelmann, G. N. *Steam Power and British Industrialization to 1860.* Oxford, England: Clarendon Press, 1978. Provides an in-depth economic and social analysis of the role of the steam engine in the Industrial Revolution, suggesting that it was not the major factor but instead played a "shadowy supporting role." Graphically depicts the relationship of the steam engine to the textile and mining industries, and analyzes the reasons various kinds of steam engines were purchased by manufacturers and mine operators.

See also: Matthew Boulton; James Brindley; Henry Cavendish; Abraham Darby; John Fitch; William Murdock; John Roebuck; James Watt; John Wilkinson.

Related articles in *Great Events from History: The Eighteenth Century, 1701-1800:* 1705-1712: Newcomen Develops the Steam Engine; 1723: 1765-1769: Watt Develops a More Effective Steam Engine; 1767-1771: Invention of the Water Frame; October 23, 1769: Cugnot Demonstrates His Steam-Powered Road Carriage; April, 1785: Cartwright Patents the Steam-Powered Loom; 1790: First Steam Rolling Mill.

NGUYEN HUE
Emperor of Vietnam (r. 1788-1792)

Together with his two brothers, Nguyen Hue successfully fought the two feudal dynasties that divided Vietnam, annihilating a Thai army supporting his southern Vietnamese adversary and conquering northern Vietnam. His greatest triumph was his defeat of an invading Chinese army during the Tet Festival of 1789, which turned him into a national hero. Recognized as emperor and ruling nearly all of Vietnam, he died before his reforms took root.

Born: c. 1752; Tay Son village, Vietnam
Died: 1792; Phu Xuan (now Hue), Vietnam
Also known as: Quang Trung; Nguyen Van Hue
Areas of achievement: Warfare and conquest, government and politics

EARLY LIFE

Nguyen Hue (ehn-gi-EHN HWAY) was born in the central Vietnamese village of Tay Son, about twenty-five miles inland from the coast and on the road to the highland city of Play Cu (Pleiku). His father, Ho (later Nguyen) Phi Phuc, was a descendant of Chinese immigrants to northern Vietnam. During civil warfare in the previous century (in 1655), the family was captured by a Nguyen army and sent south to settle in Tay Son. Nyugen's father was headman of the village, and the family was prosperous by local standards. His mother, Nguyen Thi Dong, was Vietnamese. Some historians believe that she was a Cham, from the original inhabitants of the land conquered by the Vietnamese.

While growing up, Nyugen Hue got involved in the family business of trading with coastal Vietnamese. He dealt in natural goods, such as areca nuts and betel leaves. He also traded in eaglewood, collected by Chams chosen in a religious rite. He was informally educated by a dissident teacher named Hien, who opposed the feudal system of the Nguyen lords ruling southern Vietnam. A contemporary description of the young-adult Nyugen Hue calls him remarkably tall, thin, with curly black hair and a pockmarked face, dark complexion, a full beard, and brightly shining eyes. Historians view these features as indicators of his mixed ethnic heritage.

LIFE'S WORK

When Nyugen Hue was about nineteen years old, he joined his oldest brother Nhac, followed by their brother Lu, in taking to the hills of their village and starting an uprising. They chose the popular last name of their mother, Nguyen, even though they were not related to the ruling Nguyen lords. Taking its name from their village, the Tay Son rebellion quickly gathered strength. Nyugen Hue supported Nhac, who utilized local resentment against heavy taxation. In 1773, they celebrated their first triumph when Nhac captured Qui Nhon, which would serve as the brothers' headquarters.

Nyugen Hue distinguished himself when the Trinh, the northern enemies of the Nguyen, invaded the south in 1774 to take advantage of the Tay Son rebellion. In 1775, he stormed the Phu Yen headquarters of the Nguyen lords. For this, his older brother promoted him to general. When Nhac allied himself with the Trinh to fight the Nguyen, Nyugen Hue participated in the 1777 Tay Son raid on Gia Dinh (next to modern Saigon). The raid led to the killing of all but one young noble survivor, Nguyen Phuc Anh, who would become the mortal enemy of the Tay Son brothers.

Back in Qui Nhon in 1778, Nyugen Hue was promoted by Nhac, who proclaimed himself Emperor Thai Duc of central Vietnam. In March, 1782, Nyugen Hue participated in another raid on Gia Dinh during which ten thousand Chinese residents were murdered. When Nguyen Anh retook the city in October, 1782, Nyugen Hue and his brother Lu returned en force in early 1783. They reconquered the place using seaborne elephant regiments and incendiary rockets, but Nguyen Anh escaped to Thailand.

Nyugen Hue's first victory of national importance came on January 19, 1785. He ambushed and defeated an army of twenty thousand Thai soldiers supported by up to three hundred warships that Rama I, king of Thailand, loaned to Nguyen Anh to reestablish his rule. Only two or three thousand Thai soldiers survived to flee home, and Nguyen Anh escaped again.

In 1786, famine struck the realm of the Trinh lords. Nguyen Hue was ordered by his brother Nhac to invade the north. In June, 1786, Nyugen Hue conquered Phu Xuan (modern Hue). Instead of stopping as ordered, Nyugen Hue was persuaded by one of his generals to strike at the northern capital. Encountering very little resistance, and with the captured lord Trinh Khai committing suicide, Nyugen Hue entered Vietnam's capital of Thang Long (modern Hanoi) on July 21, 1786.

Nyugen Hue then visited Emperor Le Hien Tong on July 26 and professed his loyalty. In return, the nearly seventy-year-old emperor made Nyugen Hue a duke and gave him as his wife his twenty-first daughter, the well-educated, intelligent, and beautiful poet Ngoc Han. A few days later, the emperor died and was succeeded by his grandson Le Man De, who resented Nyugen Hue.

In August, Nhac arrived and ordered Nyugen Hue to move south and make his capital at Phu Xuan. Nyugen Hue obeyed, but as soon as the Tay Son brothers left, another Trinh lord took control of Thang Long. Early in 1787, Nyugen Hue and Nyugen Nhac fought over war booty. Nyugen Hue besieged Nhac's capital of Qui Nhon, and Lu sent relief troops from the south that weakened the Tay Son there. Finally, Nyugen Hue agreed to a division of rule: Nhac would control central Vietnam as emperor, Nyugen Hue would be the north pacification king, and Lu would rule the south.

After this division of power, Nyugen Hue used one general to depose the final Trinh lord, and then another to have this general torn apart by four elephants before using a third general to stab to death the second, indicating great instability at Thang Long. In 1788, emperor Le Man De fled to China. Under the influence of the ambitious border general Sun Shiyi, the Qianlong emperor sent 200,000 Chinese troops to invade Vietnam in November, 1788.

This led to Nyugen Hue's finest hour. Declaring himself Emperor Quang Trung on November 22, 1788, he called his 100,000 Vietnamese Tay Son troops to a war of national liberation on November 26. After the Chinese occupied Thang Long on December 17, Quang Trung sent out false reports of submission while force-marching his army north. Deciding to strike during the Tet holidays, Quang Trung overran the first enemy garrison on January 25, 1789, and conquered the first Chinese fort on January 28. The next morning, Quang Trung launched his assault on the forts that guarded Thang Long. Personally commanding his troops from atop an elephant, Quang Trung defeated the Chinese in fierce combat. General Sun fled at night to China, where he was joined by the fugitive Le Man De.

In the afternoon of January 30, 1789, on the seventh day of Tet, Quang Trung entered the capital in armor that was black with soot from gunpowder. He quickly concluded peace negotiations. In exchange for nominal tribute, China recognized Quang Trung as emperor of Vietnam. Yet Quang Trung soon left to rule from Phu Xuan and secretly sent a double to his official coronation at Thang Long in July of 1789; he did the same for his state visit to China in 1790.

However great his victory over the Chinese, Quang Trung ruled Vietnam only up to the domain of Nhac. In

the south, Nguyen Anh recaptured Gia Dinh on September 7, 1788, ejecting Lu, who died at Qui Nhon. As Quang Trung set about to reform Vietnamese society in the north, Nguyen Anh continued his raids.

Four years later, on September 16, 1792, Quang Trung died of a stroke. He was succeeded by his ten-year-old son, Nguyen Quang Toan, who became Emperor Canh Thinh. His widow, Ngoc Han, lamented his death in a beautiful elegy.

SIGNIFICANCE

Nguyen Hue, later Emperor Quang Trung, is most celebrated for his crushing defeat of the invading Chinese army in 1789, which ensured Vietnamese independence. His strategy of attacking a dormant enemy during the holidays enabled him to destroy a numerically superior army. Similarly, Vietnamese historians celebrate his 1785 defeat of his Vietnamese rival's Thai army as national victory.

Nyugen Hue's social program favoring a distribution of land and economic justice has endeared him to contemporary Marxist Vietnamese historians. There is scholarly debate concerning the extent to which the Tay Son rebellion was a local, minority, and anti-Vietnamese uprising. The rebels' use of red banners, for example, is believed to be linked to the worship of a Western Cham deity linked to the sinking mountain sun.

Finally, for all his military triumphs, Nyugen Hue never succeeded in eliminating his fierce southern rival, Nguyen Anh. Ten years after Nyugen Hue's death, when internal dissent weakened the surviving Tay Son, Nguyen Anh ultimately defeated the Tay Son. While Nguyen Hue shook up the centuries' long feudal division of Vietnam, complete reunification would be accomplished by his great rival, who became Emperor Gia Long in 1802. Under Gia Long's dynasty Vietnam remained united and free until the French conquest of the late nineteenth century.

—*R. C. Lutz*

FURTHER READING

Chapuis, Oscar. *A History of Vietnam*. Westport, Conn.: Greenwood Press, 1995. Discusses Nyugen Hue's life in great detail, but with occasional jumps back and forth in time. Devotes chapter 6 to "The Nguyen Hue Epic." Maps, bibliography, index.

Hall, Daniel George. *A History of Southeast Asia*. 4th ed. London: Macmillan, 1981. Still a standard work on the period. Chapter 24 thoroughly covers Nyugen Hue's life. Illustrations, maps, bibliography, and index.

Karnow, Stanley. *Vietnam: A History.* 2d ed. New York: Viking Press, 1997. Still the most widely available source in English. Places Nyugen Hue's rebellion in the context of rising European influence in Vietnam but does not mention his defeat of the Chinese. Photographs, chronology, index.

Li, Tana. *Nguyen Cochinchina.* Ithaca, N.Y.: Cornell University Press, 1998. Places Nyugen Hue in the context of the heterogeneous society of southern Vietnam of his time. The final chapter strongly argues that the Tay Son rebellion was a local rather than social uprising. Also emphasizes Nyugen Hue's mixed ethnic heritage. Maps, notes.

See also: Alaungpaya; Taksin.

Related articles in *Great Events from History: The Eighteenth Century, 1701-1800:* 1752-1760: Alaungpaya Unites Burma; September, 1769-1778: Siamese-Vietnamese War; 1771-1802: Vietnamese Civil Wars.

LORD NORTH
English prime minister (1770-1782)

As prime minister of England, North endeavored to keep the Crown and Parliament working together by adopting policies of moderation and consensus. The American Revolution made it impossible for him to achieve this objective, and in 1782, when the House of Commons turned against the war, North resigned. In so doing, he helped establish the convention that the prime minister and cabinet can continue in office only with the support of a majority of the House of Commons.

Born: April 13, 1732; London, England
Died: August 5, 1792; London, England
Also known as: Frederick North (full name); Second Earl of Guilford; Baron Guilford
Areas of achievement: Government and politics, diplomacy

EARLY LIFE

Frederick North was the eldest son of Francis North, earl of Guilford. His father was associated with Frederick, prince of Wales, heir to the throne and father of King George III. As a child, North was frequently in the company of the future king, whom he would later serve as prime minister.

North received the classical education usual for a young man of his social class and political expectations. He attended Eton College and Trinity College, Oxford, where he was a good student. Throughout his life, he was able to express himself clearly and argue effectively, qualities that such an education fostered. In 1750, after receiving his master of arts degree from Oxford, he began a three-year Grand Tour of the Continent.

Although North served most of his political career in the House of Commons, he was called Lord North, a courtesy title given to the son and heir of a peer. He was twenty-two years of age when he entered the House of Commons in 1754, representing the borough of Banbury, which was controlled by the North family. He continued to represent Banbury as long as he remained in the House of Commons. In appearance, North was rotund and awkward, with large rolling eyes, a full mouth, a quick smile, and a ready wit. He was well liked, even by those who disagreed with him.

North's close political and personal connections with King George III opened the doors to political office, but his ability and diligence enabled him to move steadily up the ladder of political preferment. In 1759, he was appointed a junior lord of the treasury, an office commonly used to initiate potential leaders into the inner workings of government. When George III took the throne in 1760, the young king and his adviser, Lord Bute, began building a body of political supporters who would be loyal to the king instead of to parliamentary leaders, chief of whom were Thomas Pelham-Holles, duke of Newcastle, and William Pitt. The policies of George III and Bute provoked the resignation of Pitt in 1761 and Newcastle in 1762. Bute became prime minister in 1762, but he resigned a year later because of poor health. The young George III had to fend for himself and learn how to govern in a parliamentary system.

The next seven years were marked by a series of unstable ministries, as the king floundered, ambitious politicians quarreled among themselves, respect for government declined, and difficult issues arose in the North American colonies, Ireland, and India. By 1766, a group of politicians and administrators had emerged who called themselves "The King's Friends." They advocated stronger authority in the Crown, and each new ministry brought recruits who remained in office when the ministry fell. It was natural that North would gravitate to support of King George III and the royal authority. In 1767, North accepted the post of first lord of the Admiralty in the Chatham ministry. In 1770, he became first lord of the treasury and nominal prime minister. Lord North had served his political apprenticeship and had emerged as a major figure in British politics.

LIFE'S WORK

Lord North accepted the conventional view of British government in the eighteenth century: a "mixed and balanced" constitution in which the king, House of Lords, and House of Commons worked together to provide strong government while preventing any one element from becoming too powerful. In the 1760's, it seemed to many that the royal authority had become too weak, both at home and in the colonies. George III actively encouraged this view, and North enlisted willingly in the ranks of those who served the king, both in office and in the House of Commons. His extensive correspondence with George III shows that the king trusted North and was willing to give him extensive responsibility, while North never lost sight of the importance of staying in step with the king on major issues.

At the same time, North was loyal to the powers and practices of the House of Commons, where he was an effective speaker and respected leader. He was an advocate of moderation and economy, seeking to build a consensus that would keep Crown and Parliament working together. In his first four years as first lord of the treasury, North was successful in reducing expenditure and bringing good order into public finance, always a major concern of Parliament. He championed the passage of legislation to establish public control over the British East India Company, which had become corrupted by its swollen territories and revenues in India. He removed some of the taxes that had caused conflict with the American colonists, keeping only the tax on tea. Persons who were politically ambitious found it prudent to fall in line behind the king and his ministers, and the independent members of the House of Commons trusted North's moderation and common sense. The major opposition lead-

ers, Charles Watson-Wentworth, marquess of Rockingham, and William Pitt the Elder, earl of Chatham, were unable to generate significant support in Parliament or the country. By 1774, North seemed to have brought a decade of political turbulence to a close.

The American Revolution led to the downfall of North and his politics of consensus. The king, the Parliament, and a majority of the nation agreed that the power and prosperity of Great Britain depended on its empire and that the empire required a controlling center and subordinate parts. The Boston Tea Party in 1773 appeared to George III and most of the political nation as a violation of law and order that could not be tolerated. When Great Britain responded by punishing Massachusetts, the colonists called the Continental Congresses and began raising troops, a challenge the king and most of the political nation decided must be met by the use of force. The Whig statesman Edmund Burke, a follower of Lord Rockingham, called for conciliation, but the North ministry, with strong political and popular support, prepared for war. The Declaration of Independence in 1776 set-

Lord North. (Library of Congress)

tled the matter and the War of the American Revolution began.

North was not a vigorous or effective war minister, but perhaps he faced an impossible task. Despite Great Britain's overwhelming financial, military, and naval resources, the British redcoats could make little headway against the Continental army under George Washington, backed by militiamen who formed for battle and then disappeared into their towns and farms. Prospects became worse when France entered the war in 1778 and Spain followed in 1779. In November, 1781, news arrived of the surrender of General Charles Cornwallis at Yorktown. The Spanish captured Florida and launched a great siege of Gibraltar, which came within an eyelash of success. Ireland was in arms demanding greater self-government, and the forces of the British East India Company were fighting with their backs to the wall against Indian princes instigated by the French. In 1780, the opposition, led by Rockingham and Burke, attacked North at his most vulnerable spot—the financial administration of the war—and nearly forced his resignation.

The British scored victories in 1782, but by that time it was too late. The nation was tired of the war, although George III was determined to continue the struggle. In March, 1782, the independent members of the House of Commons turned against the North ministry and its policies. Despite the wrath of George III, North resigned and a ministry led by Rockingham, who was pledged to American independence, took office. George III had to accept the loss of his American colonies and a bitter political defeat at home. He never forgave North for abandoning him in his time of troubles.

The remainder of North's political career was an anticlimax. George III resented the Rockingham ministry, which had been imposed on him by Parliament against his will. From the beginning of his reign, the king had resisted domination by parliamentary politicians, insisting on the right to appoint his own ministers. Shortly after taking office, Rockingham died. George III tried to retrieve his power by appointing Lord Shelburne to lead a ministry, although Shelburne had little support in Parliament and was personally unpopular with most political leaders. At this point, North and his following held the balance of parliamentary power between Shelburne and Charles James Fox, who had assumed leadership of the former followers of Rockingham. Forced to choose between support for the king and Shelburne or the majority of the House of Commons, North chose the latter. Shelburne resigned when he found a majority in the House of Commons against him, and once again George III was compelled to accept a ministry that was not of his own choosing. Fox and North formed a coalition ministry that had the overwhelming support of the House of Commons.

In December, 1783, George III turned the tables. He dismissed the coalition, forming a ministry led by William Pitt the Younger that won a decisive victory in the election of 1784. North never held office again. In 1790, when his father died, North entered the House of Lords as earl of Guilford. He died two years later.

SIGNIFICANCE

Lord North was an intelligent, hardworking, good-natured, and practical politician who attempted to apply the conventional ideas of his time when they were challenged by new forces. He served a strong-willed, stubborn king whose policies eventually led to disaster in the American Revolution. North worked with the king and other political leaders to develop a group of court supporters in Parliament, who gave him comfortable majorities until failure in war led to a reaction among the independent members. He was a capable minister of the finances in time of peace, but the administrative institutions of Great Britain could not cope with the enormous expenses of war. When North resigned in 1782, his financial policies lay in shambles. As a war leader, he had no clear strategic concepts, and he left the military aspects of the war to others. North was well liked as a person, even by those who opposed his politics and policies, but he lacked the leadership and imagination to cope effectively with the crisis brought on by the American Revolution.

North left a permanent mark on the British constitution when he decided to resign in 1782, despite the determination of King George III that ministries should not depend upon parliamentary majorities. Like Robert Walpole in 1742, North resigned when he lost the support of the House of Commons. Although the resignations of Walpole and North by no means established the principle that the prime minister should be responsible to the House of Commons, these two resignations helped destroy the principle that the king must be able to appoint ministers of his own choosing without regard to the wishes of Parliament. In the course of time, the modern British system of cabinet government emerged, with the monarch as a nonpolitical head of state and the executive power vested in the prime minister and cabinet supported by a majority in the House of Commons.

—Earl A. Reitan

FURTHER READING

Christie, Ian R. *The End of North's Ministry, 1780-1782*. London: Macmillan, 1958. A detailed study of the politics predominating at the time of North.

_____. *Wars and Revolutions: Britain, 1760-1815*. Cambridge, Mass.: Harvard University Press, 1982. A historical survey by a leading scholar of the period.

George III. *The Correspondence of King George the Third with Lord North from 1768 to 1783*. Edited by W. Bodham Donne. 2 vols. London: J. Murray, 1867. Reprint. New York: Da Capo Press, 1971. Although this reprint has some textual deficiencies, it is a convenient primary source for the relationship of the king and his prime minister.

Pares, Richard. *King George III and the Politicians*. Oxford, England: Clarendon Press, 1953. Still the best general study of the role of the king in politics.

Reitan, E. A. *George III: Tyrant or Constitutional Monarch?* Lexington, Mass.: D. C. Heath, 1964. Selections illustrating scholarly controversy concerning the political role of George III.

Thomas, Peter D. G. *Lord North*. London: Allen Lane, 1976. A brief scholarly biography that emphasizes North's role in the House of Commons.

Watson, J. Steven. *The Reign of George III: 1760-1815*. Oxford, England: Clarendon Press, 1960. A well-balanced overview of the period that emphasizes North's role as the minister of moderation and consensus.

Weintraub, Stanley. *Iron Tears: America's Battle for Freedom, Britain's Quagmire, 1775-1783*. New York: Free Press, 2005. Weintraub argues that colonial America was Britain's Vietnam—a guerrilla war fought in a faraway location that eventually led to protests and lack of support by British politicians and citizens.

Whiteley, Peter. *Lord North: The Prime Minister Who Lost America*. London: Hambledon, 1996. Scholarly account of North's life and political career. Whiteley explains how North and other British officials underestimated the determination of the American rebels and overestimated Britain's ability to maintain its colony.

See also: Lord Amherst; Edmund Burke; First Marquess Cornwallis; Charles James Fox; George III; William Pitt the Elder; William Pitt the Younger; Robert Walpole; George Washington.

Related articles in *Great Events from History: The Eighteenth Century, 1701-1800:* 1721-1742: Development of Great Britain's Office of Prime Minister; January, 1756-February 15, 1763: Seven Years' War; June 8-July 27, 1758: Siege of Louisbourg; June 29, 1767-April 12, 1770: Townshend Crisis; December 16, 1773: Boston Tea Party; May 20, 1774: Quebec Act; April 19, 1775: Battle of Lexington and Concord; July 4, 1776: Declaration of Independence; June 21, 1779-February 7, 1783: Siege of Gibraltar; June 2-10, 1780: Gordon Riots; October 19, 1781: Cornwallis Surrenders at Yorktown; September 3, 1783: Treaty of Paris.

JAMES EDWARD OGLETHORPE
English administrator and military leader

With his social vision, promotional genius, military ability, and personal guidance, Oglethorpe established the colony of Georgia. His repulsion of the Spanish from southeastern North America in 1742 effectively ended Spanish incursions in the southern mainland colonies and secured Great Britain's southern frontier.

Born: December 22, 1696; London, England
Died: June 30, 1785; Cranham Hall, Essex, England
Areas of achievement: Military, government and politics

EARLY LIFE

James Edward Oglethorpe was the seventh and last child of Sir Theophilus and Lady Eleanor Wall Oglethorpe, two Jacobites who surrounded young Oglethorpe with intrigue and endowed him with the family's strong moral courage, conviction, loyalty to the Crown, and military and parliamentary tradition. Oglethorpe received the education of an English gentleman, first at Eton and then at Corpus Christi College, Oxford, where Jacobite sentiment was strong.

Oglethorpe then held a commission in the British army but resigned to join Eugene of Savoy in fighting the Ottoman Turks. He gained a reputation for military prowess at the Battle of Belgrade (1717). After a brief Jacobite flirtation at Saint Germain, France, where his widowed mother and sisters attended the pretender James III (also known as James the Old Pretender), Oglethorpe returned to the family estate of Westbrook at Godalming in Surrey. The move ended his Jacobite interest.

In 1722, Oglethorpe was elected to Parliament, succeeding his father and two elder brothers as representative for Haslemere, a seat he would hold for thirty-two years. In Parliament, Oglethorpe shook off suspicions about his Jacobitism. He won respect for integrity and hard work. More important, for his ambitions and interests, he cultivated several powerful friends. In Parliament, Oglethorpe opposed royal extravagance and the machinations of Robert Walpole and advocated naval preparedness, mercantile and colonial expansion, relief for the oppressed, and, later, the Industrial Revolution. Oglethorpe's humanitarianism, probably a product of his family's high-mindedness, first appeared in *The Sailor's Advocate* (1728), an anonymously published pamphlet attacking the Royal Navy's practice of impressment. The pamphlet went through eight editions.

Throughout his life, Oglethorpe also professed antislavery beliefs. It was Oglethorpe's interest in penal conditions, however, that led him to his life's work.

LIFE'S WORK

In 1729, James Edward Oglethorpe was named chairman of a committee to inquire into the state of England's jails. In three reports issued in 1730, the committee cataloged the abuses of debtors' prisons. The reports electrified the public, in part because of their lurid detail and in part because such exposés were rare in an indifferent age. Oglethorpe's investigation convinced him that the nation and the debtors would be better served by settling the debtors in British colonies. There they could render service to the Crown by colonizing and defending new territory and producing crops and other goods needed in the mother country, while remaking their own lives.

Such an argument was hardly new to England in the eighteenth century, for since the Elizabethan age colonizers had promised similar benefits. What gave Oglethorpe's appeal energy was the renewed public interest generated by his reports on penal conditions and his friendship with such influential men at court and in Parliament as John Lord (later the first earl of Egmont) and Thomas Bray (founder of several religious and philanthropic societies), who shared his interest in reform and in America.

Oglethorpe, Egmont, and eighteen other associates received a charter in June, 1732, creating the "Trustees for Establishing the Colony of Georgia in America." The proprietary grant was for a period of twenty-one years, after which the colony would revert to the Crown. The associates benefited from the British government's interest in placing a buffer colony on Carolina's southern frontier to protect against French, Spanish, and American Indian attacks and also from its desire to increase imperial trade and navigation. Relief for domestic unemployment was a third consideration, but it lagged behind the former two. Indeed, the interest of defense and the production of exotic crops and naval stores for the mother country so outweighed the humanitarian objective that few debtors were actually recruited for the colony.

Oglethorpe quickly proved himself an energetic promoter for a project that would evoke the most vigorous and extravagant promotional literature in the British North American experience. In 1732, at his own expense, he published *A New and Accurate Account of the Provinces of South Carolina and Georgia*, stressing the commercial and agricultural advantages of the colony. Georgia's strategic position, combined with Oglethorpe's and the appeals of the trustees, helped secure regular financial support from Parliament. When his mother died in 1732, leaving Oglethorpe free of domestic responsibilities, he decided to accompany the first group of settlers to the colony—a move that fundamentally influenced the colony's development.

In November, 1732, Oglethorpe and 116 emigrants set sail for Georgia on the *Anne*. Arriving in America in January, 1733, after a successful voyage, Oglethorpe directed the settlers to the Savannah River. There he chose the site for the principal city. Oglethorpe conciliated the indigenous peoples of the area, securing from them both a grant for the land and an agreement whereby they would cut their ties to the French and Spanish. He laid out Savannah's distinctive pattern of squares and grids, which dominates the city even today, and then parceled out the land according to the trustees' system of entailed grants designed to hold the settler to the soil. The cumbersome land system—which prohibited the holder from selling his property or bequeathing it to any but a male heir—would cause much trouble soon enough, but Oglethorpe imposed military discipline on the first settlers. He made a treaty with the Lower Creeks and fortified the southern reaches of the colony.

In 1734, Oglethorpe set out for England to answer charges that he was overspending and being uncommunicative. Accompanied by several American Indians, Oglethorpe received an ecstatic public welcome. The press revived interest in the colony. Strengthened by the public showing, Oglethorpe gained additional support from the trustees, including new restrictions on the colony that prohibited the sale of rum and black slavery and regulated the American Indian trade through a licensing system. Meanwhile, Oglethorpe's policy of religious toleration encouraged other emigrants to join the experiment, a policy that, in 1734, led a group of Salzburger Lutherans to seek asylum in Georgia. Other German groups followed, including subsequent contingents of Salzburgers and Swiss Moravians, and Scotch Highlander Presbyterians came as well. The British government was cool toward Oglethorpe's efforts to attract non-British emigrants, but Oglethorpe persisted. The colony needed people.

It also needed Oglethorpe's attention. Rumors of insurrection drew Oglethorpe back to Georgia in 1735. He brought John and Charles Wesley and a new batch of settlers with him. The Wesleys soon fell into disputes with Oglethorpe and the settlers and returned to England. Oglethorpe did better with George Whitefield, who came later and established an orphanage that Oglethorpe supported. Oglethorpe found the Georgia government in disarray. Lines of authority were blurred and the trustees retained essential power in their hands, but Oglethorpe's unwillingness to delegate authority hardly helped matters. Oglethorpe further fanned the colony's troubles by his own intransigence. Vain and unbending, he insisted on enforcing the new restrictions he brought from London and honoring the trustees' unpopular land policy. Traders from South Carolina resented the licensing system for the American Indian trade, farmers chafed at re-

A statue of James Edward Oglethorpe, founder of the Georgia colony. (Library of Congress)

strictions on establishing a plantation-style agriculture, and the Spanish complained about Oglethorpe's southward movement, which included a new settlement at Frederica in 1736 and a fort on Cumberland Island soon after. In London, malcontents from Georgia told tales of incompetence and venality in Oglethorpe's administration. Oglethorpe responded by going to London, where he pacified the trustees and answered all charges. He returned to Georgia in 1738 with a regiment of soldiers that he had raised at his own expense.

Military matters thereafter preoccupied Oglethorpe in Georgia. With war between Spain and England imminent, Oglethorpe repaired relations with the American Indians. He persuaded the Chickasaw and Lower Creeks not to join Britain's enemies should war occur and even settled differences between the Creeks and Choctaw. He also put down a mutiny among his own men, personally grabbing the ringleaders as they shot at him. When Parliament declared war on Spain in 1739 (the War of Jenkins's Ear), which eventually became part of the larger War of the Austrian Succession, Oglethorpe moved rapidly. He led a futile attack on St. Augustine in 1740, which failed partly from Oglethorpe's indecision. Although personally brave, Oglethorpe had little experience commanding a military expedition. His inability to distinguish between the trivial and the significant—a trait that afflicted his civil administration as well—further embarrassed his campaign. Oglethorpe redeemed his military reputation in 1742 when, in a series of skirmishes known collectively as the Battle of Bloody Marsh, he and his men rebuffed a superior Spanish force invading St. Simon's Island. The Spanish withdrew their army from Georgia, never again to threaten seriously the British presence in North America. In 1743, Oglethorpe made another unsuccessful feint against St. Augustine, but by then Georgia was safe and Oglethorpe's American career was ending.

Civil discontent in the colony had distracted Oglethorpe while he fought to save the empire. Colonists ignored the trustees' regulations, malcontents launched new campaigns against Oglethorpe and the trustees in England, and the Moravians left for Pennsylvania rather than bear arms in Georgia's defense. Questions of finance especially nagged Oglethorpe. His own expenses became entangled with those of the colony, for he had borrowed against his English property to pay for Georgia's defense—money for which he would be only partially reimbursed. To add to Oglethorpe's problems, the colony storekeeper had kept poor accounts and made unwarranted expenditures. In 1740, the trustees limited Oglethorpe's civil responsibilities so that he could concentrate on military matters.

In 1743, Oglethorpe went to England to respond to criticism and to answer charges brought by a subordinate to a court-martial. He was exonerated, but his colonizing days were over. He never returned to America. Georgia was going its own way already. Indicative of Oglethorpe's declining influence in Georgia's future was the trustees' decision in 1750 to remove the restrictions on rum and slavery and to accept Georgia's development along the lines of South Carolina as a slave-based plantation society.

Oglethorpe married Elizabeth Wright, heiress of Cranham Hall, Essex, in 1744. The match gave him a fortune and the country estate where he lived for the rest of his life. He fought against the Jacobites in 1745, but rumors of his family's Jacobite associations trailed after him and led to charges of misconduct in not pursuing the retreating Jacobites vigorously enough at Lancashire. Oglethorpe was acquitted, but his military career was over. Using an assumed name, however, he did fight on the Continent against the French during the Seven Years' War, and he did earn the friendship of William Pitt the Elder for his endeavors and promotions to general in 1765.

In Parliament, Oglethorpe became something of a liberal Whig freelance, distrusting the Hanoverian ministers, supporting civil rights for religious dissenters in the colonies, attacking arbitrary power, and associating with the antislavery movement in England. After he lost his seat in 1754, he retired from public life. He devoted attention to his estate and to literary and artistic circles, where he became friends with Samuel Johnson, James Boswell, David Garrick, Sir Joshua Reynolds, Hannah More, and Edmund Burke, among others. He died in 1785.

SIGNIFICANCE

From his earliest colonizing promotionals, James Edward Oglethorpe had recognized the place of Georgia in the larger British North American schema. Indeed, imperial considerations of defense and commerce, more than humanitarianism, made Georgia possible. Oglethorpe's negotiations with powerful American Indian tribes marked the growing recognition among British administrators and settlers that European rivalries in southeastern North America dictated accommodations with the American Indian population that held the balance of power. However clumsy, Oglethorpe's military moves underscored that in the eighteenth century England would have to fight for territory in North America. Parliament's willingness to underwrite Georgia bespoke the growing strategic importance of the North American colonies in Great Britain's imperial design. In the age of imperial rivalries, visionaries needed also to be soldiers. Oglethorpe's legacy included frustrating the Spanish effort to push the British out of southeastern North America.

Oglethorpe was the last of the great proprietary colonizers in British North America. Like William Penn, he was a visionary imbued with a strong sense of mission. Oglethorpe's promotion of Georgia captured anew the prospect of America's destiny, and like Penn's plan, it included recruitment of non-British settlers to promise a New World Elysium out of religious and cultural diversity. Unlike Penn, Oglethorpe did not temper his social vision sufficiently with practicality. Although a gentle and even generous man, Oglethorpe bridled at criticism and was egotistic and self-righteous. He never fully adapted to the democratizing tendencies of colonial life, preferring to impose rules on his charges rather than take them into his confidence. Where Penn acceded to local demands for greater self-governance, Oglethorpe insisted on compliance with all regulations. A country Whig in temperament and politics in England, Oglethorpe unwittingly played the autocrat in America. His life in Georgia demonstrated how much the British colonial establishment in the late seventeenth through the early eighteenth centuries rested on the energy and enthusiasm of powerful individuals. It also served to show the limits of Old World authority in the New World.

Oglethorpe had founded Georgia, protected it, and given it purpose, but he could not control the social, economic, and political impulses of diverse peoples in a setting that demanded popular participation and promised individual wealth. To have done so would have defeated the idea of America that inspired Oglethorpe to believe in the Georgia experiment and the people to risk it.

Removed from the hurly burly of Georgia, Oglethorpe seems to have understood that fact himself. He championed America's Sons of Liberty during the American Revolution, and before his death in 1785 he called on John Adams, the United States minister to England, acknowledging America's promise as England's, indeed Europe's, own redemption. By his continued hope for America, the old soldier did not die.

—Randall M. Miller

FURTHER READING

Baine, Rodney M., ed. *The Publications of James Edward Oglethorpe*. Athens: University of Georgia Press, 1994. A collection of tracts, committee reports, letters to the press, and other documents that Oglethorpe wrote or edited for publication. Includes introductions to each document as well as textual and explanatory notes.

Boorstin, Daniel J. *The Americans: The Colonial Experience*. New York: Random House, 1958. Boorstin's influential treatment of Oglethorpe and colonial Georgia criticizes the Georgia trustees for their inability to adapt to the American environment. Boorstin finds in Oglethorpe's and the trustees' failed vision of Georgia a clue to the success of other forms of community in America. By comparing the Georgia experiment with those of Massachusetts and Pennsylvania, Boorstin places Oglethorpe's thought and actions in the context of American utopianism.

Church, Leslie Frederic. *Oglethorpe: A Study of Philanthropy in England and Georgia*. London: Epworth Press, 1932. This study remains valuable for its detail on Oglethorpe's philanthropic interests, his ties to religious figures, especially the Wesleys, and his social and political connections in England.

Coleman, Kenneth. *Colonial Georgia: A History*. New York: Charles Scribner's Sons, 1976. A valuable synthesis of Georgia history. Coleman's account offers an excellent brief introduction to Oglethorpe's ideas and actions and explains how a multiethnic, multireligious colony developed from his policies.

Ettinger, Amos Aschbach. *James Edward Oglethorpe: Imperial Idealist*. Oxford, England: Clarendon Press, 1936. Ettinger's lively and sympathetic account is the fullest and best biography of Oglethorpe. Ettinger approached Oglethorpe in the tradition of George Macauley Trevelyan, who believed the eighteenth century was the age of the individual. As such, Ettinger found Oglethorpe's personality and interest formed from his family traditions of loyalty to the Crown, military service, and parliamentary responsibility.

Inscoe, John C., ed. *James Oglethorpe: New Perspectives on His Life and Legacy*. Savannah: Georgia Historical Society, 1997. A reexamination of Oglethorpe's life and multifaceted career.

Lane, Mills, ed. *General Oglethorpe's Georgia*. Savannah, Ga.: Beehive Press, 1975. Lane includes in this collection a good sampling of Oglethorpe's letters relating to the Georgia years and provides a useful introduction to Oglethorpe and Georgia, including accounts of colonial discontent.

Spalding, Phinizy. *Oglethorpe in America*. Chicago: University of Chicago Press, 1977. Spalding reassesses Oglethorpe's life in the light of the many new materials available since Ettinger completed his research. In a balanced account, Spalding weighs Oglethorpe's ideas against his actions. He argues that Oglethorpe was not blind to American realities and that his ideas regarding a yeoman society were not necessarily doomed by the American environment.

Spalding, Phinizy, and Harvey H. Jackson, eds. *Oglethorpe in Perspective: Georgia's Founder After Two Hundred Years*. Tuscaloosa: University of Alabama Press, 1989. A collection of essays, including discussions of Oglethorpe's role in the Anglican Church in Georgia, his attitudes about race, and his experiences in Europe.

Ver Steeg, Clarence L. *Origins of a Southern Mosaic: Studies of Early Carolina and Georgia*. Athens: University of Georgia Press, 1975. In his important and provocative examination of the origins of Georgia, Ver Steeg discards most previous interpretations and argues that, although strategic considerations loomed largest in shaping policies toward Georgia, each

trustee had his own motives regarding the colony's settlement and development. In the absence of any grand design, Oglethorpe had to contend with the contradictions among both trustees and settlers about Georgia's purpose.

See also: John Adams; James Boswell; Edmund Burke; Eugene of Savoy; David Garrick; Samuel Johnson; Hannah More; William Pitt the Elder; Sir Joshua Reynolds; Granville Sharp; Robert Walpole; Charles Wesley; John Wesley; George Whitefield.

Related articles in *Great Events from History: The Eighteenth Century, 1701-1800:* September 6, 1715-February 4, 1716: Jacobite Rising in Scotland; June 20, 1732: Settlement of Georgia; 1739-1741: War of Jenkins's Ear; September 9, 1739: Stono Rebellion; December 16, 1740-November 7, 1748: War of the Austrian Succession; August 19, 1745-September 20, 1746: Jacobite Rebellion; January, 1756-February 15, 1763: Seven Years' War.

OGYŪ SORAI
Japanese scholar and philologist

Ogyū Sorai helped create a Japanese form of Neo-Confucianism that was pragmatic in application but emphasized the importance of government-imposed order and social control. Though his social ideas were not implemented during his own lifetime, his students continued the development and advocacy of his ideas. His social and educational views formed part of the ideological basis for the increasingly authoritarian regime that developed in the Meiji era and continued until 1945.

Born: February 16, 1666; Edo (now Tokyo), Japan
Died: January 19, 1728; Edo, Japan
Also known as: Ogyū Shigenori; Ogyū Mokei
Areas of achievement: Philosophy, scholarship, government and politics

EARLY LIFE

Ogyū Sorai (ohg-yew soh-ri), whose father was a resident physician serving Tokugawa Tsunayoshi (r. 1680-1709) for some years before Tsunayoshi became shogun, attended the same lectures given by eminent scholars to the children of the highest Edo aristocrats. This gave Sorai a considerable educational advantage at an early

age. In 1679, however, Sorai's father offended Tsunayoshi, and Sorai's family was banished to Kazusa, a town north of Edo, where they remained until 1690, when they were allowed to return to Edo.

Sorai continued his studies on his own in Kazusa and was particularly attracted by Chinese neoclassicism, a movement led by the late Ming scholars Wang Shizhen (1526-1590) and Li Panlong (1514-1570), who advocated the return to classical literary models that were prevalent centuries earlier. The growing popularity of this neoclassicism led to a general respect for Ming literary models, which endured in Japan for several centuries after they were replaced by Qing models in China itself. This affected models for literary Japanese as well as Chinese writers, since Chinese classics with Japanese notations were used in schools in both Tokugawa and Meiji Japan.

LIFE'S WORK

After his family's return to Edo in 1690, Ogyū Sorai established himself as a teacher in Edo, giving private lessons and lectures. He also reinforced his advocacy of using Ming classical Chinese models through his *Yakubun sentei*, a 1692 guide to written Chinese composition and style designed for use by the Tokugawa gentry. Ogyū Sorai's mastery of classical Chinese rhetoric, grammar, and philology came to be admired by the Edo literary establishment in the same way that the British Victorian establishment admired Latin and Greek classical erudition.

In 1696, his scholarly abilities were recognized by Yanagisawa Yoshiyasu (1658-1714), a patron of scholarship and the arts, who was also Tsunayoshi's closest adviser. Yanagisawa became Sorai's patron, recommending him to the shogun. Sorai began as a scholar in residence for Tsunayoshi and Yanagisawa, serving with a regular government stipend and on occasion advising Tsunayoshi and Yanagisawa on the Confucian principles of good government as well. Ironically, Tsunayoshi was popularly regarded as an arbitrary tyrant, and many also viewed Yanagisawa as a sycophant interested only in his own advancement. It is unlikely that Sorai ever directly criticized either of his patrons, since they were known for punishing their critics. Sorai continued to enjoy their favor, as long as they were alive.

Sorai began his residency by giving lectures on classical literature and philosophy attended by Yanagisawa and Tsunayoshi. Sorai persuaded Yanagisawa and Tsunayoshi to give official sanction to his views on neoclassicism among the Japanese literary establishment, and he eventually shared his views on Confucian social teachings with the shogun and Yanagisawa as well.

Sorai's own version of Confucianism was based on a pragmatic interpretation of political and social concepts. He respected the social applications of traditional Confucian virtues, grounded on the main priority of study and self-improvement, leading in turn to harmonious family life. Collective harmonious family life would promote good government, and the country would become peaceful and orderly. While such virtuous modes of behavior were supposed to result in good government and a peaceful country, Sorai viewed good governance and political economy as of equal or greater importance, becoming part of the means to save society rather than the possible end result of behavior according to the traditional Confucian ethic.

In Sorai's view, there are two main determinants of the nature of society: One was the way the social structure was organized and the other was the way people operated within that structure. In keeping with a society in which Tsunayoshi and his shogunate's bureaucracy held most of the real power and in which the samurai and the old military feudal lords had become redundant, Sorai recommended that the warriors should return to the land,

merging once again with the countryside populace from whom they had originated.

Sorai also recommended that country people should, quite literally, be kept in their places by enforcing a system in which people registered their permanent place of residence. To travel would require permission from the government. This sort of system, with limits on mobility, was attempted to a greater or lesser degree before and throughout the Tokugawa era. Yet in peaceful times the system was often circumvented through loopholes, since itinerant clergy, traveling merchants, pilgrims, and others could get exemptions. In times of disorder, such as the recurring periods of famine that afflicted the Tokugawa era, there were so many masses of desperate people roaming the country that it was practically impossible for the government to control their movements.

After Tsunayoshi died in 1709, Yanagisawa quickly retired from public life, but he continued to be Sorai's patron. Finally, after Yanagisawa died in 1714, Sorai opened a private school in Kayabacho, a locale in an area that is now part of Tokyo's financial district. He remained a prominent Confucian intellectual, and even though he was on good terms with the shoguns succeeding Tsunayoshi, he did not receive significant patronage from them. Sorai had begun life as a favored child, then lived in exile, then managed to regain governmental support. In the end, however, he lost that support once more.

At this point in his life, on his own and approaching fifty years old, Sorai focused exclusively on teaching. He had many students from prominent Edo families and made a good income from his school. In the last dozen years of his life, as a private scholar, Sorai finally began to achieve the full scholarly eminence for which he is known in Japanese history, and he did this by training students who continued to promote his teachings and social views long after his death.

SIGNIFICANCE

Ogyū Sorai's leading disciple in the application of his social, economic, and political concepts was Dazai Shundai (1680-1747), the offspring of feudal nobility who ultimately rejected his heritage to spend his life as a scholar. After making several abortive attempts to become a feudal functionary, and also developing a sporadic practice in herbal medicine, Dazai became Sorai's student around 1715, at the age of thirty-five. Dazai later taught and wrote about classical studies and political economy, but he is remembered mainly for his 1729 economic treatise *Keizairoku shūi* (English translation, 1998), which expounded Sorai's ideas on political economy, adding a few extra points, such as the importance of trade and currency transactions. Sorai's ideas were transmitted to posterity through Dazai's work.

Sorai's leading student in traditional classical studies and philology was Hattori Nankaku (1683-1759). Hattori began his career as a young man in the service of Yanagisawa Yoshiyasu, but after Yanagisawa's death in 1714, Hattori became Ogyū Sorai's attendant and student. He became an expert in classical literature and philology and wrote many books about Chinese and Japanese classics. Hattori was extremely successful as a teacher and writer, producing scholarly studies that were used for several generations.

—*Michael McCaskey*

FURTHER READING

Lidin, Olof G. *The Life of Ogyu Sorai: A Tokugawa Confucian Philosopher.* Scandinavian Institute of Asian Studies monograph series. Lund, Sweden: University of Lund, 1973. The only biography of Ogyū Sorai in English, by a foremost Western expert on his life and thought.

_____. *Ogyu Sorai, Distinguishing the Way: Ogyu Sorai's "Bendo."* Tokyo: Monumenta Nipponica Monographs, Sophia University, 1970. An authoritative study of Ogyū Sorai's Confucian masterwork.

_____. *Ogyu Sorai's "Discourse on Government" ("Seidan"): An Annotated Translation.* Wiesbaden, Germany: Harrassowitz, 1999. The culmination of a lifetime of work on Ogyū Sorai by Lidin.

McEwan, J. R. *The Political Writings of Ogyu Sorai.* Cambridge, England: Cambridge University Press, 1962. A work that presents an alternative perspective on Ogyū Sorai's political writings.

Maruyama, Masao. *Studies in the Intellectual History of Tokugawa Japan.* Tokyo: University of Tokyo Press, 1974. A historical analysis of Tokugawa intellectual currents by an authority on Japanese intellectual history.

Najita, Tetsuo, trans. and ed. *Readings in Tokugawa Thought.* Chicago: Center for East Asian Studies, University of Chicago, 1993. A standard source book of writings by Tokugawa scholars, compiled from original sources by a Japanese authority on Tokugawa intellectual life.

_____, ed. *Tokugawa Political Writings.* New York: Cambridge University Press, 1998. Contains translations of work by Ogyū Sorai and by Dazai Shundai.

Yamashita, Samuel Hideo. *Master Sorai's "Responsals": An Annotated Translation of Sorai Sensei's "Tūmonsho."* Honolulu: University of Hawaii Press, 1994. An authoritative study of a work by Ogyū Sorai that is usually overlooked by Westerners.

Yoshikawa, Kojiro. *Jinsai, Sorai, Norinaga: Three Classical Philologists of Mid-Tokugawa Japan.* Tokyo: Toho Gakkai, 1983. Parallel studies of the literary and linguistic scholarship of Ogyū Sorai, his Confucian predecessor Ito Jinsai, and his Japanese studies successor Moto'ori Norinaga, by a noted Japanese authority on Confucian thought.

See also: Hakuin; Honda Toshiaki; Tokugawa Yoshimune.

Related articles in *Great Events from History: The Eighteenth Century, 1701-1800:* February 4, 1701-February 4, 1703: Revenge of the Forty-Seven Ronin; December, 1720: Japan Lifts Ban on Foreign Books.

ANNE OLDFIELD
English actor

A legendary beauty, Oldfield was possibly the best actress, and certainly the most famous, on the London stage of her time. She performed more than one hundred roles, acting in both comedy and tragedy and performing popular epilogues.

Born: 1683; London, England
Died: October 30, 1730; London, England
Also known as: Nance Oldfield
Area of achievement: Theater

EARLY LIFE

The exact date of Anne Oldfield's birth is unknown, and there is no baptismal record. Her parents were Anne Gourlaw and William Oldfield, who married on November 7, 1681, in St. Mary le Bone parish church. They lived on Pall Mall in the St. James district. Her father, a soldier or guardsman, died when Anne was a young child. Her paternal uncle then helped with her care and education, but Anne's formal education was brief, and she hoped for a theatrical career.

In the spring of 1699, sixteen-year-old Oldfield was accepted at Theatre Royal Drury Lane, which was one of the two main theater companies in London. The young playwright George Farquhar had heard her reading a play at the Mitre tavern and was deeply impressed with her speech, beauty, and wit. He introduced her to the eminent playwright Sir John Vanbrugh, who arranged for her to meet Christopher Rich, the manager and proprietor of Drury Lane. Rich hired her at 15 shillings per week, and Oldfield's mother became employed as a seamstress for the actors.

A year later, in the spring of 1700, Oldfield had her first minor role. She played Alinda, the heroine of *The Pilgrim* (pr. 1621), a romantic comedy by John Fletcher and adapted by her patron Vanbrugh. Soon after, on July 6, 1700, she had her first newspaper advertisement in the *Post Boy*, an announcement of a benefit performance of *The Pilgrim* for Oldfield. (It was a common practice for actors to sell special theater tickets to supplement their incomes, especially in times of financial hardship.) Through the spring of 1703, she performed in a variety of roles, with some successful performances. During this period of apprenticeship, she met Colley Cibber, a principal company actor and a playwright who would become her lifelong colleague and friend.

LIFE'S WORK

In the summer of 1703, Anne Oldfield became a virtual overnight success in the role of Leonora in John Crowne's *Sir Courtly Nice* (pr., pb. 1685), performed for Queen Anne in Bath. This role had belonged to the company's principal comic actress, Susannah Verbruggen, who, luckily for Oldfield, had fallen ill and stayed behind in London. Less than a year later, on March 20, 1704, Oldfield became the most highly paid actress in the Drury Lane company, entering a five-year contract for 50 shillings per week. She became unrivaled in comedy and established her position firmly in the competitive company hierarchy.

On December 7, 1704, Cibber's comedy *The Careless Husband* premiered, and was an immediate success. Oldfield brilliantly performed the new role of the coquette, Lady Betty Modish, which became her most famous portrayal and the character with which she is most identified. Oldfield originated the character of Lady Modish and was the only actress to play the role during her lifetime. *The Careless Husband* was so successful that it ran every season until 1730.

Fierce competition existed between the two theater companies Drury Lane and the Lincoln's Inn Fields during the early eighteenth century. On April 8, 1706, Drury Lane presented Farquhar's new comedy, *The Recruiting Officer*, which was an instant success. Oldfield played the role of Sylvia, opposite one of her favorite leading actors, Robert Wilks. Later, from 1710 to 1734, Wilks, Cibber, and the character actor Thomas Doggett would form the celebrated actor-manager triumvirate that administered Drury Lane during one of its most glorious periods.

From 1706 until her early death in 1730, Oldfield was principally a comic actor, but she was also known as an exceptional tragic actor, and she was constantly originating roles. Oldfield performed in plays written by Susannah Centlivre, Cibber, James Carlisle, Thomas Betterton, Nicholas Rowe, Francis Beaumont, Fletcher, John Dryden, John Banks, Thomas Killigrew, and many others.

Socially, Oldfield was quite unconventional. She always earned her own living and was twice a mistress, living openly with two men, one after the other. She also had two children out of wedlock. The first of these two relationships began in 1700, when she met Arthur

Maynwaring, a member of the landed gentry and an auditor in the customs office. Born in 1668, Maynwaring was about fifteen years older than Oldfield. Though never married, they lived together and had a son, also named Arthur. Maynwaring protected Oldfield from the unsolicited and often violent behavior of men that was a common threat to actresses at that time. Maynwaring also was Oldfield's mentor, using his literary skills and wit to compose outstanding prologues and epilogues for her. As short performances separate from the main play, epilogues enabled individual performers to step outside their character and directly address the audience. Maynwaring also coached Oldfield, and she eventually became a popular epilogue performer. They remained together until his death in 1712.

In 1714, Oldfield met Charles Churchill, the illegitimate son of General Charles Churchill, younger brother of the duke of Marlborough. General Churchill had recognized the younger Charles as his legitimate heir, so Charles had received an inheritance when his father died in 1714. Oldfield, who had her own substantial salary of about £400 per year, would live with Churchill, and the two had a son, also named Charles. Churchill helped establish Oldfield in his society of nobility, and she finally had many aristocratic friends, including the earl and countess of Bristol. Churchill and Oldfield remained together until her death in 1730.

On April 28, 1730, Oldfield made her last stage appearance in *The Provok'd Wife* (pr., pb. 1697), by Vanbrugh and Cibber, and then retired because of illness. In constant pain and with a negative prognosis from her physicians, she drafted her will on June 27, 1730. She died from what was most likely cancer of the reproductive system on October 30, 1730, at the age of forty-seven. Instead of a burial at Covent Garden at St. Paul's Church, where actors usually were interred, Churchill arranged for Oldfield to be buried with great ceremony and gentlemen pallbearers at Westminster Abbey. However, his request for a monument in her honor was denied.

SIGNIFICANCE

Anne Oldfield was one of the earliest stage stars, whose talent, glamour, and personal life aroused immense public reaction, both favorable and critical. On one hand, she originated or created about seventy new roles, ranging from tragic heroines or martyrs to idealized aristocratic female characters. On the other hand, her private life was unconventional and controversial because of her success and independence and because she had two children but was never married.

Oldfield was the first theatrical personality whose death elicited widespread public notice. Within a week of her death in 1730, *Authentic Memoirs*, a biography of Oldfield, was published by an anonymous author. Daily newspapers printed eulogies and poetry. In 1731, William Egerton published *Faithful Memoirs of the Life, Amours, and Performances of That Justly Celebrated, and Most Eminent Actress of Her Time, Mrs. Anne Oldfield*. Her legend and the fascination with her life continued. Mildred Aldrich's *Nance Oldfield*, a stage adaptation of a fictional story by Charles Reade, appeared in 1894. The anecdotal *The Palmy Days of Nance Oldfield*, by Edward Robins, was published in 1898. *The Player Queen*, a romantic novel by Constance Fecher, was published in 1968 and then reissued in 1977 in paperback as *The Lovely Wanton*.

—*Alice Myers*

FURTHER READING

Brockett, Oscar G., and Franklin J. Hildy. *History of the Theatre*. 9th ed. Boston: Allyn & Bacon, 2002. This standard, indispensable work on the history of theater provides a section on the English theater up to 1800 and explores the development of theater during Oldfield's lifetime as well. Includes maps, more than 530 illustrations and photos, an index, and a bibliography.

Cibber, Colley. *An Apology for the Life of Colley Cibber: With an Historical View of the Stage During His Own Time*. Edited by Byrne R. S. Fone. Mineola, N.Y.: Dover, 2000. A close friend of Oldfield, Cibber provides the most complete account of her career in his significant autobiography, first published in 1740. Notes, with bibliographic references.

_____. *The Plays of Colley Cibber*. Edited by Timothy J. Viator and William J. Burling. Vol. 1. Madison, N.J.: Fairleigh Dickinson University Press, 2001. As Cibber's favorite actress, Oldfield performed in many of his plays. This book includes two of those plays: *Love's Last Shift* and *Love Makes a Man*. Includes an index.

Fyvie, John. *Tragedy Queens of the Georgian Era*. New York: Benjamin Bloom, 1972. The third chapter of this work provides contemporary descriptions of Oldfield. Includes illustrations and an index.

Gore-Browne, Robert. *Gay Was the Pit: The Life and Times of Anne Oldfield, Actress, 1683-1730*. London: Max Reinhardt, 1957. This early biography covers Oldfield's personal life and acting career, with quotations from many plays. Includes one of her portraits and an index.

Lafler, Joanne. *The Celebrated Mrs. Oldfield: The Life and Art of an Augustan Actress*. Carbondale: Southern Illinois University Press, 1989. A thoroughly researched biography covering Oldfield's early life, apprenticeship, successful stage career, personal life, and legend. Illustrated, including several portraits of the actor. Appendices list her roles (in order of performance), complete repertory, and prologues and epilogues. Includes an index and extensive footnotes.

See also: Fanny Abington; Queen Anne; Fanny Burney; Hannah Cowley; David Garrick; Sarah Siddons; Sir John Vanbrugh; Peg Woffington.

Related articles in *Great Events from History: The Eighteenth Century, 1701-1800:* December 7, 1732: Covent Garden Theatre Opens in London; 1742: Fielding's *Joseph Andrews* Satirizes English Society.

DUC D'ORLÉANS
French noble

Although a Bourbon prince, the duc d'Orléans encouraged opposition to royal absolutism and supported the French Revolution of 1789.

Born: April 13, 1747; Saint-Cloud, France
Died: November 6, 1793; Paris, France
Also known as: Louis-Philippe-Joseph (birth name); Philippe Égalité; Duc de Montpensier; Duc de Chartres
Area of achievement: Government and politics

EARLY LIFE

Louis-Philippe-Joseph, the duc d'Orléans (dewk dawr-lay-ah), was the cousin of King Louis XVI and the son of Louis-Philippe and Louise-Henriette de Conti. He was born in 1747 into the junior branch of the royal family, the one closest to the throne and historically the principal rival. The lineage of Louis-Philippe-Joseph (hereafter, simply Philippe) was distinguished by a tradition of patronage of science and art and an interest in new ideas.

Indolent by temperament but gifted with a quick intelligence, Philippe received a superficial education from his tutors. Following family custom, he became duc de Chartres in 1752. He was formally presented to King Louis XV on October 6, 1759, and baptized November 18 the same year, with the king and queen acting as godparents. In 1761, he attended his first session of the Parlement of Paris, foremost in power and honor among the high courts of France. Within four years, he had become the colonel of a regiment of infantry and two regiments of cavalry.

He was a brave, handsome, amiable man and an accomplished libertine. His marriage in April, 1770, to Louise-Marie-Adélaïde Bourbon-Penthièvre was a match of convenience, uniting the princely rank of the House of Orléans with the greatest family fortune in France.

Philippe's position, fourth in line of succession to Louis XV after the king's three sons, made him suspect in the king's eyes of rivaling the royal family. The lack of any hope of meaningful public employment had the unfortunate effect of encouraging irresponsibility in the newly married prince. At the same time, it made him the preferred alternative heir to the throne for those discontented with the ruling family. Philippe's Paris residence, the Palais Royal, became the center of subversive discussion and writing.

LIFE'S WORK

Together with his father, Philippe took part in the aristocratic movement of protest against the royal suppression of the *parlements* in 1771 for their opposition to arbitrary government by the king. The princes' reconciliation with the king the next year was temporary and superficial. From this episode developed the hostility between Philippe and Marie-Antoinette that would grow more virulent in the following years.

In June, 1771, Philippe became grand master of the Freemasons, a position that brought him into contact with the most enlightened, well-connected men of the day. In 1772, he fell in love with Madame de Genlis, a very beautiful, learned, and ambitious woman, who became his mistress and the tutor of his children, including his son, Louis-Philippe, the future king of the French, born in October, 1773.

Family tensions continued with Louis XVI, who succeeded his father in 1774. Nonetheless, when France joined the American colonies at war with England, Philippe sought the opportunity to serve at sea, hoping to succeed his father-in-law as grand admiral of France. In

The duc d'Orléans. (Hulton Archive/Getty Images)

garden behind the palace. At ground level, he provided space for shops, restaurants, and theaters. The upper levels were occupied by residences and meeting halls. The new buildings, together with the garden and the palace, immediately became the social center of the city.

The complex also served Philippe as a secure base from which he could dispense patronage from his fortune to a loose coterie of like-minded enemies of Louis XVI's government. Some were aristocrats opposed to reforms that threatened their privileges. Most were middle-class journalists and lawyers, who, together with a few reform-minded aristocrats, demanded greater freedom and equality and an end to arbitrary government and privilege. Many of these men—Georges Danton, Jacques-Pierre Brissot, Camille Desmoulins, Antoine-Pierre Barnave, the comte de Mirabeau, Jérôme Pétion, Emmanuel-Joseph Sieyès, and Charles-Maurice de Talleyrand—distinguished themselves in the revolution that grew out of their intrigues at the Palais Royal.

Upon the death of his father in 1785, Philippe inherited the titles duc d'Orléans and first prince of the blood. The sons and grandsons of kings of France were known as Children of France, members of the royal family. Great-grandsons and their descendants, like Philippe, who was descended from Louis XIII, were called princes of the blood. Because of his strained relations with the royal family, Philippe avoided the royal court of Versailles, residing instead in his apartments in the Palais Royal.

During the conflicts that arose in 1787 between Louis XVI and the nobles over the government's attempts to increase its revenues, Philippe assumed the leadership of the opposition. As an honorary member of the Parlement of Paris, he declared the king's forced registration of an edict to be illegal. For this challenge to his authority, the king exiled Philippe for five months to his estates outside Paris and forbade him to receive any visitors other than members of his family.

This experience of arbitrary arrest only strengthened Philippe's detestation of his cousin's regime. Subsequently, Philippe came under the influence of Pierre Choderlos de Laclos, an army officer and author notorious for his scandalous novel, *Les Liaisons dangereuses* (1782; *Dangerous Acquaintances*, 1784; also known as

July, 1778, Philippe commanded a squadron against the English in the Battle of Ouessant, in which the French had the advantage. His performance was less than stellar: He became strangely inactive at a critical point in the conflict. His enemies at court unfairly criticized him, and his naval career came to an end. He returned to the pursuit of pleasure, making frequent expensive visits to England, where the prince of Wales was among his best friends.

In 1781, Philippe had received from his father the Palais Royal, a large Baroque palace built in the seventeenth century by Armand-Jean du Plessis, cardinal de Richelieu, in the heart of Paris. In the 1780's, as a commercial venture, Philippe undertook to build a vast rectangular complex of uniform buildings that enclosed the

Dangerous Liaisons), who served as the duke's secretary at the Palais Royal. Using the duke's name and wealth, Laclos exposed the follies of the royal court and campaigned for greater personal liberty, fairness in taxation, and an end to privilege.

Philippe was elected a representative for the nobles to the Estates-General, which convened on May 5, 1789, in a heightened atmosphere of crisis. The royal government was virtually bankrupt. Nobles and commoners alike demanded sweeping reforms as the condition for supplying any remedy.

Philippe supported the unprivileged Third Estate (bourgeoisie, or commoners) against the two privileged orders (nobles and clergy). On June 25, he and a small group of nobles joined the Third Estate, which had on June 17 proclaimed itself a national assembly. Philippe's Paris residence, the Palais Royal, became a center of popular agitation, and he was viewed as a hero by the crowd that stormed the Bastille on July 14. Feeling threatened by the adulation bestowed on his rival, the king sent him off to England on a spurious diplomatic mission, a disguised if pleasant exile.

On returning from England in July, 1790, Philippe won a seat in the National Assembly. His wife, Marie-Adélaïde, from whom he had been estranged for many years and who had remained devoted to the royal family, deeply resented the revolutionary attitudes being inculcated in her children by Madame de Genlis. When her son, Louis-Philippe, was admitted to the politically radical Jacobin Club, she protested in the strongest terms. Consequently, Philippe expelled her from the Palais Royal early in 1791. He followed his son into the club that same year.

In June, 1791, Louis XVI attempted to escape from Paris, where he could no longer function like the divine-right monarch he believed he was. Having badly bungled his flight, he was captured at Varennes and brought back discredited to Paris. A republican regime was not yet a serious alternative to the constitutional monarchy Louis had betrayed. This opened an opportunity for Philippe to assume the royal executive power as regent, the head of a popularly based monarchy, shunting his royal cousin into oblivion. To seize such an opportunity, however, called for greater strength of character and a stronger sense of purpose than Philippe could muster. On June 29, he rejected the idea of a regency, declaring he preferred to remain a simple citizen.

As France drifted into war with Austria and Prussia early in 1792, Philippe attempted unsuccessfully to receive a military commission. The war went badly for the French, whose armies were poorly disciplined and led. Soon, Paris and the revolution seemed threatened by enemies advancing from the east and others subverting it from within. Philippe was living idle in Paris, August 10, 1792, when radicals seized the Tuilleries Palace, imprisoned the royal family, and went on to declare France a republic. In September, Parisian mobs massacred thousands of prisoners in the city's jails. From a balcony of the Palais Royal, Philippe saw the mob parading the mutilated corpse of his former mistress, the princesse de Lamballe, through the streets.

Though sobered by the carnage, Philippe thought he had no choice but to go with the revolutionary tide. A curious lassitude afflicted his spirit. He renounced his title of nobility and accepted the name Philippe Égalité from the Paris Commune, the municipal government dominated by radicals. His son Louis-Philippe urged him to emigrate to the United States. With characteristic nonchalance, Philippe granted that politics in Paris had become unbearable but added that in the end there was always the opera. Elected to the National Convention, the third successive revolutionary legislature, which convened in September, 1792, Philippe fatalistically supported the radical democratic policies of the Montagnards against their Girondin opponents, who condemned his princely origins.

In December, during the trial of Louis XVI by the Convention, the Girondins attempted to confuse the issue of the deposed king's fate by accusing the Montagnards of conspiring to put Philippe on the throne. Though he could have absented himself, in January, in a state of extreme emotional distress, Philippe voted for the execution of his cousin Louis.

Shortly afterward, Philippe himself fell under suspicion when his son Louis-Philippe, duc de Chartres, defected to the Austrians with the French commander Charles-François du Périer Dumouriez on April 5, 1793. Accused of being an accomplice of Dumouriez, Philippe was arrested on April 6 and confined for months in a dark prison cell in the south of France. Brought back to Paris for a travesty of a trial, he was sent to the guillotine November 6. Throughout this ordeal, he behaved with exemplary courage.

SIGNIFICANCE

Philippe, the duc d'Orléans, was a significant player in revolutionary France not so much because of what he did but because of the support he lent to others. He was an indolent man, devoted to the pursuit of pleasure, who shirked onerous responsibilities and retreated from serious challenges, but with his great wealth and rank, he could make things happen. Superficially enlightened and moved by complex feelings of envy and resentment toward the royal family, Philippe gave crucial support to writers and politicians advocating reform of the autocratic but bankrupt Bourbon monarchy and contributed to its fall.

—*Charles H. O'Brien*

FURTHER READING

Doyle, William. *The Oxford History of the French Revolution.* 2d ed. New York: Oxford University Press, 2002. The author gives a standard account of the political and social background to the most tragic part of Philippe's life.

Erickson, Carolly. *To the Scaffold: The Life of Marie Antoinette.* New York: William Morrow, 1991. In this narrative, which is sympathetic to the queen, Philippe appears frequently as the royal family's nemesis.

Hardman, John. *Louis XVI.* New Haven, Conn.: Yale University Press, 1993. The author describes at length how the king resented and feared his cousin and took steps to thwart his ambitions.

Hibbert, Christopher. *The Days of the French Revolution.* New York: Viking Penguin, 1989. Originally published in 1980 under the title *The French Revolution*, Hibbert's book provides detailed descriptions of events from 1789 until the rise of Napoleon. The book includes information on Philippe. Well written and understandable to readers with little or no knowledge of the period.

Howarth, T. E. B. *Citizen-King: The Life of Louis-Philippe, King of the French.* London: Eyre and Spottiswoode, 1761. Philippe figures significantly in the first nine chapters of this biography of the prince's son, who ruled France from 1830 to 1848.

Louis-Philippe. *Memoires, 1773-1793.* Translated and introduced by John Hardman. Foreword by Henri, comte de Paris. New York: Harcourt Brace Jovanovich, 1977. The future king of the French refers with affection and respect to his father, Philippe, and throws light on the main events of his life.

Schama, Simon. *Citizens: A Chronicle of the French Revolution.* New York: Knopf, 1989. Schama's history of the period includes information on Philippe. Schama argues the revolution did not create a "patriotic culture of citizenship" but was preceded by a more vital, inventive culture.

Scudder, Evarts S. *Prince of the Blood.* London: Collins, 1937. The first full-length study of the prince in English.

Warnick, R. "Radical and Chic: A Duke Who Courted Revolt and Doom." *Smithsonian* 20, no. 4 (July, 1989): 66. A profile of Philippe.

See also: Georges Danton; Louis XVI; Marie-Antoinette; Comte de Mirabeau; Emmanuel-Joseph Sieyès.

Related articles in *Great Events from History: The Eighteenth Century, 1701-1800*: September 8, 1783: Papal Bill *Unigenitus*; 1720: Financial Collapse of the John Law System; 1789: Leblanc Develops Soda Production; May 5, 1789: Louis XVI Calls the Estates-General; June 20, 1789: Oath of the Tennis Court; July 14, 1789: Fall of the Bastille; October, 1789-April 25, 1792: France Adopts the Guillotine; April 20, 1792-October, 1797: Early Wars of the French Revolution; September 20, 1792: Battle of Valmy; January 21, 1793: Execution of Louis XVI; March 4-December 23, 1793: War in the Vendée; July 27-28, 1794: Fall of Robespierre; November 9-10, 1799: Napoleon Rises to Power in France.

ALEKSEY GRIGORYEVICH ORLOV
Russian military leader

Orlov participated in the coup d'état that made Catherine the Great the ruling empress of Russia. The brother of Catherine's lover, Orlov helped protect Catherine from her husband, Czar Peter III, and helped engineer the czar's murder.

Born: October 5, 1737; Lyutkino, Tver Province, Russia
Died: January 5, 1808; Moscow, Russia
Also known as: Count Orlov
Area of achievement: Government and politics

EARLY LIFE

Aleksey Grigorievich Orlov (uhl-yihk-SYAY gryih-GAWR-yihv-yich uhr-LAWF) was born on the Orlov family estate, the third of five sons of a military officer. His grandfather had been a colorful figure, one of the *streltsy*, special sharpshooters who had engaged in a rebellion against Peter the Great and his attempts to re-form Russia in 1698, because his reforms threatened their special status and privileges. Upon receiving word of the revolt, the czar had cut short his European tour, leaving Vienna and hurrying back to Moscow to crush the rebellion. He then ordered the rebellious soldiers executed, some by hanging, some by burning at the stake, and some by beheading in Moscow's Red Square. Peter himself wielded the headsman's ax, and he was quite impressed with one condemned rebel, who coolly approached the block, kicking aside the head of a fellow insurgent and saying, "Make room for me." After asking the man's name, he pardoned Ivan Orlov on the spot and reenlisted him in the army.

Ivan's son Grigori Ivanovich Orlov married late and fathered nine children, five of whom lived to adulthood. These five sons remained close throughout their lives, with little sibling rivalry, and it was said that they shared everything except women. They soon sold their family's estate and used the money to buy a house in St. Petersburg, then the imperial capital. They also bought themselves memberships in St. Petersburg's elite guards unit and amused themselves with boisterous living, whereby they soon amassed enormous debts. However, they were always able to extract themselves from their problems by their skill and luck at cards. Aleksey was said to be the cleverest but the least principled of the brothers.

LIFE'S WORK

Aleksey was drawn into Grand Duchess Catherine's orbit with the ascension of his elder brother Grigori Grigoryevich Orlov to the position of her favorite. Her marriage to Grand Duke Peter, heir apparent to Empress Elizabeth Petrovna, was loveless and unconsummated, and she saw in the handsome Grigori Grigoryevich Orlov the possibility of assuaging her sexual desires.

When Empress Elizabeth died on January 5, 1762 (Christmas Day, 1761, Old Style), Peter ascended the throne as Peter III. However, his sudden attainment of grave responsibility did not mature him. Rather, he remained perpetually childish and stupid, conducting himself with an astonishing lack of decorum during his aunt's funeral, to the point that visiting foreign dignitaries commented upon his behavior and what it might mean for Russia's future. He made no attempt to hide his contempt for the traditions of Russia and its Orthodox Church, instead preferring the Lutheran rites of his childhood and the tight uniforms of Prussia's Frederick the Great. He had soon alienated many of the nationalistic young officers of the elite guards regiments, who were all the more willing to align themselves with his neglected wife.

Peter hated Catherine, and now that Elizabeth was no longer there to protect her, he determined to rid himself of her permanently, whether by forcing her to enter a convent or by outright execution. However, he could not move too quickly, which gave Catherine time to plan.

At the same time, Catherine was prevented from moving too quickly against her husband by her own advanced state of pregnancy: She was carrying Grigori Orlov's baby. Only when she was safely delivered of the boy could she actually move against Peter. By June of 1762, things had become critical: Peter launched into a tirade of abuse at Catherine for failing to rise for a toast to his royal person. When she responded that as a member of the royal family it was not appropriate for her to rise, he ordered her arrested.

Aleksey Orlov and his brothers helped Catherine flee to the safety of an outlying estate, where she hid for the next several weeks, until their plans could be completed. For safety, she left her young son Paul, heir to the throne, in St. Petersburg, but with the caveat that the younger Orlov brothers would keep watch over him. On June 28, the preparations were complete, and the Orlov brothers rallied the guards regiments in the coup d'état that unseated Peter III and placed Catherine the Great on the throne.

Aleksey personally arrested Peter and his clique of Germans. He took Peter into temporary exile on the estate of Ropsha, some distance from St. Petersburg. There he remained for some time, officially until his final place of exile could be determined. However, his continued existence posed an unacceptable threat to Catherine's admittedly precarious position on the throne. Thus, it was necessary to engineer the deposed czar's death, but in a way that would keep Catherine's hands free of his blood.

The end finally came in a rather awkward confrontation between Peter and Prince Fyodor Baryatinski, one of the inner circle of plotters and a longtime friend of the Orlovs. The quarrel quickly decayed into a fistfight, and before the guards could separate the two, the weak and sickly Peter was strangled to death. Aleksey Orlov was present at the fight and may well have helped to instigate it or have even participated in it. In any case, he wrote to Catherine a hasty and rather confused account of the incident, then rode to St. Petersburg to deliver the letter to her.

In reward for having placed her on the throne and ridding her of an inconvenient dynastic obstacle, Catherine richly rewarded Aleksey Orlov and his brothers. They were each given the title of count, substantial sums of money, and responsible positions in the imperial government. Even after Grigori ceased to be her lover, all five of the brothers continued to hold these imperial positions.

Aleksey had the misfortune of outliving his imperial mistress and as a result suffered the indignities of her successor's wrath. Emperor Paul never had any great love for his mother and over the years had developed a fascination with his father, the unlamented Peter III, to the point that his mental instability led historians to question Catherine's claims that her marriage was unconsummated. One of Paul's first orders upon his accession was to have Peter III's bones exhumed and reinterred beside Catherine's in an elaborate ceremony. Aleksey Orlov was given the particular indignity of being "honored" with the privilege of carrying Peter's crown upon a velvet cushion, and two of his fellow surviving conspirators were forced to become pallbearers for the casket in which the deposed czar's bones were carried.

SIGNIFICANCE

The coup against Peter III was a critical turning point in the history of Russia. Peter III was a Lutheran and a Germanophile and was on the verge of implementing "reforms" that would have destroyed the Russian Orthodox Church and transformed it into a parody of the Lutheran Church. Had he continued on the throne, he probably would have triggered a religious civil war that would have made the reaction to the reforms of Patriarch Nikon in the sixteenth century look like a minor disagreement. Although Catherine was by birth a German princess, she

had embraced her adopted motherland so thoroughly that she could be regarded as a proper Russian, in spite of her strong accent and poor Russian grammar, and was able to continue the introduction of Western ideas and reforms while retaining the essential Russianness of the culture.

By taking the initiative to kill Peter III, Aleksey Orlov also spared Catherine any but the most peripheral guilt in her husband's demise, while at the same time securing her claim to the throne by ensuring that Peter's supporters could not free him and restore him to power. However, suspicion continued to linger throughout Catherine's reign about her exact role in Peter III's death, and only the discovery of a letter by her son, Emperor Paul, exonerated her, finally erasing all doubt.

—Leigh Husband Kimmel

FURTHER READING

Alexander, John T. *Catherine the Great: Life and Legend.* New York: Oxford University Press, 1989. Remains one of the best biographies of Catherine the Great, including a final chapter dealing with her place in history and popular culture, including her many loves.

De Madariaga, Isabel. *Russia in the Age of Catherine the Great.* New York: Phoenix Press, 2002. A study of Catherine's effect upon Russia, stripping away some of the lurid folklore that has come to surround her and examining the actuality of her reign, including the coup d'état that brought her into power.

Dixon, Simon. *Catherine the Great.* New York: Longman, 2001. Studies the developing concept of rulership across Catherine's rule, from her ascension in the coup against her husband to her death.

Nikolaev, Vsevolod A., and Albert Parry. *The Loves of Catherine the Great.* New York: Coward, McCann and Geoghegan, 1982. Examines Catherine's relationships with the first three of her lovers, including Grigori Orlov, and discusses the role of Aleksey Orlov in the death of Peter III.

Troyat, Henri. *Catherine the Great.* Reprint. New York: Plume, 1994. Includes a discussion of the significance of the coup led by the Orlov brothers.

See also: Catherine the Great; Elizabeth Petrovna; Frederick the Great; Grigori Grigoryevich Orlov; Peter the Great; Peter III.

Related articles in *Great Events from History: The Eighteenth Century, 1701-1800*: August 10, 1767: Catherine the Great's Instruction; October, 1768-January 9, 1792: Ottoman Wars with Russia; September, 1773-September, 1774: Pugachev's Revolt; July 21, 1774: Treaty of Kuchuk Kainarji.

GRIGORI GRIGORYEVICH ORLOV
Russian military leader

Orlov was the favorite of Catherine the Great as well as the principal conspirator in the coup d'état that made her the ruling empress of Russia. He remained loyal to Catherine and her government long after their romantic affair—which produced a child—came to an end, and he worked to improve Russia's armed forces.

Born: October 17, 1734; Lyutkino, Tver Province, Russia
Died: April 24, 1783; Neskuchnoyne, near Moscow, Russia
Also known as: Count Orlov
Areas of achievement: Government and politics, military

EARLY LIFE

Grigori Grigorievich Orlov (gryih-GAWR-yuhih gryih-GAWR-yihv-yich uhr-LAWF) was the second of five sons of a military officer. His grandfather had been a colorful figure, one of the *streltsy*, or sharpshooters, who had engaged in a rebellion against Peter the Great when he attempted a program of reform in 1698. When the czar returned from his European tour and crushed the revolt, he ordered the rebellious soldiers executed. Peter himself wielded the headsman's ax in Moscow's principal square. He was quite impressed with one condemned rebel, who coolly approached the block, kicking aside the head of a fellow insurgent and saying, "Make room for me." After asking the man's name, he pardoned Ivan Orlov on the spot and reenlisted him in the army.

Ivan's son Grigori Ivanovich Orlov married late and fathered nine children, five of whom lived to adulthood. These five sons remained close throughout their lives, with little of the sibling rivalry that often marks relationships between brothers. They soon sold their family's estate and used the money to buy a house in St. Petersburg, then the imperial capital, as well as memberships in the capital's elite guards unit. The brothers lived boisterously and amassed enormous debts. However, they were always able to extract themselves from these debts by their skill and luck at cards. Grigori was said to be the best looking and most charming of the brothers, but rather slow-witted.

LIFE'S WORK

Grigori Grigoryevich Orlov came to the attention of the young Grand Duchess Catherine sometime in 1759, shortly after she had a particularly unpleasant argument with her husband, the ugly and hopelessly incompetent heir apparent, Grand Duke Peter. According to a common story, she was coming out of the room where the fight had occurred and noticed a gallant-looking young officer escorting a high-born Prussian prisoner who had been taken in one of the battles of the Seven Years' War. Another story claims instead that she saw him while looking out a window and ordered him upstairs to present himself.

Tradition has it that Peter was either physically or psychologically incapable of consummating his marriage, and Catherine had grown increasingly frustrated with her inability to produce an heir, as the Empress Elizabeth Petrovna had sternly instructed her. At length, she had taken other lovers, but her latest beau had been sent to the front to get him away from her. Taken by Orlov's physique and daredevil reputation, she soon invited him into her bedchamber, and their romantic relationship began. Shortly thereafter, she installed him in a room directly beside her bedchamber, where he could come and go without difficulty.

January 5, 1762 (December 25, 1761, Old Style), Empress Elizabeth breathed her last breath, and Grand Duke Peter ascended the throne as Czar Peter III. Immediately, he began planning a way to dispose of his hated wife, even as he behaved with an astonishing lack of decorum during the funeral of his late aunt. However, political necessity meant that he had to move carefully to get rid of the woman he had just acknowledged as his consort, which gave Catherine time to make her own plans. Such plans would inevitably involve her lover and his four brothers, all of whom felt an intense loyalty to this beautiful and intelligent woman and nothing but disgust for the czar.

Catherine, too, had to wait until she safely delivered Grigori Orlov's son, whom she was then carrying. Only then could the plan move ahead. The boy, given the name Aleksey Grigoryevich Bobrinsky, would later become the father of a line of Russian nobility who would enjoy distinguished careers through the remaining century and a half of the Romanovs' rule.

On Sunday, June 9, 1762, matters came to a head. During a formal state dinner, Peter became outraged when Catherine did not rise for the ceremonial toast to the czar. She responded that, as a member of the royal family, it was not appropriate for her to rise for the toast. Peter responded with the most horrific abuse and ordered her placed under arrest. Catherine could wait no longer, and she retreated to the safety of a palace in one of the outlying towns while the guards regiments, loyal to her rather than Peter, made the final preparations.

On June 28, Grigori and his brothers rallied the guards to take Peter prisoner and make Catherine empress in his place. Grigori secured a handsome carriage with which Catherine was able to make her triumphant entry into the city after Peter was deposed. In St. Petersburg, Grigori led the guards officers in making their declarations of loyalty to her.

Grigori Orlov remained Empress Catherine the Great's lover for another twelve years, until 1774. During that time, he and his brother Aleksey delivered a savage beating to a handsome young upstart by the name of Grigori Aleksandrovich Potemkin, intending to remind him of his place. Although they badly disfigured him, and he withdrew from society for a time, Potemkin would ultimately replace Grigori as Catherine's favorite. Virile as Grigori Orlov might be, he was no match for Catherine in intellect, and she was growing hungry for a man with whom she could converse about philosophy and literature. However, Grigori Orlov and his brothers were not banished altogether from Catherine's court. All five of the brothers would continue to hold responsible positions throughout their lives.

SIGNIFICANCE

By helping to depose Peter III and install Catherine the Great on the throne, Grigori Grigoryevich Orlov and his brothers changed the course of Russian history. Peter III was at heart a German Lutheran who saw Frederick the Great of Prussia as his natural ally and wished to impose German Lutheran cultural and religious observances on the Russian people, even over their violent opposition. Although Catherine, too, was a German princess by birth, she had so thoroughly embraced her adopted homeland that she was effectively accepted as a Russian leader by the people and continued the process of incorporating Western ideas and concepts into Russian culture in a manner acceptable to Russian traditionalists.

Catherine's relationship with Grigori Orlov and his successors to her bedchamber fired the salacious imagination, and even during her own lifetime stories were circulated about her supposed sexual antics. For a century and a half after her death, the Russian imperial censors

were kept busy keeping foreign accounts of her alleged sexual dissoluteness from entering Russia and corrupting the imaginations of the czar's subjects. This was, in fact, little more than a symbolic effort, since domestic gossip often produced far more lurid tales than any foreign pen. In the twentieth century, with the development of cinema, Catherine's torrid affair with Grigori Orlov would be featured in several films.

—Leigh Husband Kimmel

FURTHER READING

Alexander, John T. *Catherine the Great: Life and Legend.* New York: Oxford University Press, 1989. A useful examination of the relationship between Catherine's reign and her posthumous reputation.

De Madariaga, Isabel. *Russia in the Age of Catherine the Great.* New York: Phoenix Press, 2002. An attempt to separate fact from fiction in understanding Catherine, her reign, and her lasting impact on Russian history.

Dixon, Simon. *Catherine the Great.* New York: Longman, 2001. A readable biography that studies the developing concept of rulership across Catherine's rule, from her ascension in the coup against her husband to her death.

Nikolaev, Vsevolod A., and Albert Parry. *The Loves of Catherine the Great.* New York: Coward, McCann and Geoghegan, 1982. A frank account of the empress's relationships with her first three lovers, including Grigori Orlov. Discusses Aleksey's role in the death of Peter III.

Troyat, Henri. *Catherine the Great.* New York: Plume, 1994. A reprint of a classic biography, including discussion of the significance of the coup led by the Orlov brothers.

See also: Catherine the Great; Elizabeth Petrovna; Frederick the Great; Aleksey Grigoryevich Orlov; Peter the Great; Peter III; Grigori Aleksandrovich Potemkin.

Related articles in *Great Events from History: The Eighteenth Century, 1701-1800*: January, 1756-February 15, 1763: Seven Years' War; August 10, 1767: Catherine the Great's Instruction; October, 1768-January 9, 1792: Ottoman Wars with Russia; September, 1773-September, 1774: Pugachev's Revolt; July 21, 1774: Treaty of Kuchuk Kainarji.

THOMAS PAINE
English-born American political philosopher

Paine was a participant in both the American and French Revolutions, and, through his writings, he attempted to foment revolution in England as well. He was interested in the new scientific ideas of his age, spent considerable energy on the design of an iron-arch bridge, and tried to resolve the age-old conflicts between science and religion by espousing Deism.

Born: January 29, 1737; Thetford, Norfolk, England
Died: June 8, 1809; New York, New York
Also known as: Thomas Pain (birth name)
Areas of achievement: Philosophy, government and politics, literature, science and technology, religion and theology

EARLY LIFE

Thomas Paine's father, Joseph Pain (Thomas later added an "e" to his name), was a Quaker stay maker. Working as a craftsman, he provided whalebone corsets for local women. Paine's mother, Frances Cocke, the daughter of a local attorney, was an Anglican who was older than her husband and of difficult disposition. Because a daughter died in infancy, the Pains then concentrated all of their efforts on their son.

Thomas was taught by a local schoolmaster from the age of seven to thirteen and then apprenticed to his father to learn the trade of a stay maker. This was clearly not entirely to his liking, as he managed at one point to run away and spend some time at sea. Upon his return, he practiced his craft in various places in England. In 1759, Paine married Mary Lambert, but his wife died a year later. Dissatisfied with his occupation, he tried others, including a brief stint at schoolteaching and perhaps also preaching. Still seeking his niche in the world, Paine returned home for a time to study for the competitive examination to become an excise collector. He passed the exam and obtained positions collecting customs revenues from 1764 to 1765 and from 1768 to 1774. He was twice dismissed from his posts for what higher authorities saw as laxity in the performance of his duties. The second dismissal came after Paine participated in efforts to obtain higher wages for excisemen, during the course of which he wrote a pamphlet, *The Case of the Officers of the Excise* (1772).

The time he spent on these endeavors, as well as his arguments, contributed to the loss of his position. Paine was married to Elizabeth Ollive in 1767, and, while continuing as an exciseman, he also helped her widowed mother and siblings run the family store. By 1774, the business was in bankruptcy, Paine and his wife had separated, and he was without a government position, with little prospect of regaining one. It was at this point in his life that Paine, so far a failure at everything he had tried to do, obtained a letter of introduction from Benjamin Franklin and moved to America.

LIFE'S WORK

Thomas Paine arrived in the colonies at an auspicious moment. A dispute over "taxation without representation," simmering between England and its colonists since the passage of the Stamp Act in 1765, had led to the Boston Tea Party and then to the passage of the Coercive (or Intolerable) Acts (1774). Paine obtained a position as editor for the new *Pennsylvania Magazine*, published in Philadelphia. Meanwhile, American feelings had boiled over, and the Revolutionary War had begun. As an author, Paine had finally found where his true talents lay. In January of 1776, he wrote *Common Sense*, a pamphlet attacking the king, advocating independence, and outlining the form of government that should be adopted. The work was a tremendous success, a consequence of its timely arguments as well as its clear, forceful language. Reprinted in numerous editions, passed from hand to hand, it reached an audience of unprecedented size. At age thirty-nine, Paine had at last achieved a measure of success. He went on to become the leading propagandist of the American Revolution.

During the war, Paine served as secretary to a commission on American Indian affairs and as secretary to the Committee for Foreign Affairs of the Second Continental Congress. He resigned under pressure from the second position during a bitter political debate over the actions of Silas Deane. He later served as a clerk for the Pennsylvania Assembly and participated in a diplomatic venture to France, seeking additional help for the fledgling nation. He is best known, however, for his continued efforts to promote the American cause. By 1783, he had written a total of sixteen *Crisis* papers as well as other pamphlets. In the *Crisis* papers, with ringing language meant to stir the soul and bolster the war effort, he appealed to patriotic Americans to rally to the cause.

As the war came to a conclusion, Paine turned his efforts to providing some measure of financial security for himself. He appealed to the national Congress and a number of state legislatures for compensation for his pre-

Thomas Paine. (Library of Congress)

vious literary efforts on behalf of the American cause. He was ultimately granted a small pension by Congress, land by the New York legislature, and money by the Pennsylvania government. The Virginia legislature refused to come to his aid after he wrote a pamphlet, *The Public Good* (1780), arguing that all the states should cede their Western land claims to the national government. In this work and others, Paine's talents were utilized by those who wanted to bolster the powers of the central government. In 1786, he wrote a pamphlet, *Dissertations on Government, the Affairs of the Bank, and Paper Money*, in which he defended the Bank of America, chartered by Congress and the state of Pennsylvania as an instrument to raise money for the government and to aid commerce. In the course of this work, he condemned paper money, maintaining that anything but gold or silver was a dangerous fraud.

Always interested in science and new technology, he also busied himself with designing an iron-arch bridge that would be able to span greater distances than was possible with existing methods. Unable to obtain sufficient money or interest for his project in the United States, he left for France in 1787 and from there made several trips to England, primarily to raise support for a workable model.

Paine arrived in France just as the French Revolution began to unfold, although this drama did not at first engage his attention. With the publication of Edmund Burke's *Reflections on the Revolution in France* (1790), Paine again took up his pen for a radical cause, producing, in two parts, *The Rights of Man* (1791, 1792). Whereas the conservative Burke emphasized the value of traditions and claimed that all change should come about gradually, Paine argued for government based on consent, defended revolution as a corrective remedy for unjust government, suggested ways to bring revolution to England, and proposed an early form of social welfare. The second part of *The Rights of Man* led to his being tried and convicted in absentia in England for seditious libel. Paine barely escaped arrest by the English authorities and took passage to France, where he became intimately involved in the course of the French Revolution.

When Paine returned to France in 1792, it was as an elected delegate to the French assembly. There he was caught up, and ultimately overcome, by the tide of the revolution. Paine associated with the political representatives of the middle and upper classes, with literary figures, and with those who spoke English, never having mastered French sufficiently to converse without a translator. Despite his attacks on monarchy in his previous writings, the depths of French radicalism, the swiftness of change, and the quick trial and execution of the king all went beyond what he could support.

Associated with the Girondist faction of French politics and an object of increasing antiforeign sentiment, Paine was arrested after the Jacobins achieved power; he subsequently spent ten agonizing months in jail while prisoners around him were carted off to the guillotine. Once the virulence of the revolution ran its course, Paine seemed less of a threat to those in power. As a result, a new American minister to France, James Monroe, was able to appeal for his release from prison, arguing that Paine was an American, rather than English, citizen.

While in prison, Paine began the last work for which he achieved fame, or, in this case, infamy: *The Age of Reason* (1794). The first part of this book was an attack on religion and a defense of Deism, while the second part was specifically aimed at Christianity and included numerous pointed refutations of biblical passages. It was a work that sparked in rebuttal many pamphlets in England and the United States and was also the source of much of the hostility directed against Paine in later years.

Paine's spell in prison had undermined his health and warped his judgment, although he had never been astute in practical politics. Remaining in France, even though after 1795 he was no longer a member of the French assembly, he wrote a pamphlet attacking George Washington and meddled in American foreign policy. In 1802, after an absence of fifteen years, he returned to the United States, taking up residence in, among other places, Washington, D.C., and New York City. He wrote letters and a few pamphlets, but he was anathema to the Federalists and a political liability to the Republicans. He died on June 8, 1809, in New York City, and his body was taken to the farm in New Rochelle, which the New York government had given him years before, and buried. Some

time after his death, his bones were clandestinely dug up by an Englishman who took them off to England hoping to exhibit them; they ultimately disappeared.

SIGNIFICANCE

Thomas Paine said that his country was the world, and his life illustrates the truth of this statement. His numerous pamphlets and books zeroed in on the main issues of his time, while the clarity and strength of his language have given his works an enduring appeal. He wrote in support of freedom from arbitrary government and against what he saw as outdated religious superstitions. In addition, he was an active participant in two major revolutions, as well as a friend and acquaintance of major figures in three countries. He was also the center of some controversy, at times difficult to tolerate, exhibiting a disinclination to bathe, a lack of care about his apparel, a propensity to drink, and a tendency to impose on the hospitality of friends for months, and even years, at a time. He was a complex and interesting individual who sparked debate in England, America, and elsewhere among his contemporaries—debate that has continued among historians since his death.

Paine's interest for Americans, though, stems primarily from his authorship of *Common Sense* and the *Crisis* papers. He has frequently been described as the right person in the right place at the right time. The first pamphlet sold 120,000 copies in three months and went through twenty-five editions in 1776 alone. It met the needs of the moment and substantially helped push Americans toward independence. In it, Paine attacked monarchy as being "ridiculous" and George III for being the "Royal Brute of Great Britain." He thought it absurd for England, an island, to continue to rule America, a continent. Paine maintained not only that it was "time to part" but also that it was America's obligation to prepare a refuge for liberty, "an asylum for

---

ON A SENSIBLE AND RIGHT GOVERNMENT

Political philosopher Thomas Paine wrote in his work Common Sense *(1776) that a representative government, a government of consent, was the only right form of government.* Common Sense *was written to challenge the English king, to advocate American independence, and to present Paine's ideas on an American government.*

Some writers have so confounded society with government as to leave little or no distinction between them; whereas they are not only different, but have different origins. Society is produced by our wants and government by our wickedness; the former promotes our happiness positively by uniting our affections, the latter negatively by restraining our vices. The one encourages intercourse, the other creates distinctions. The first is a patron, the last is a punisher.

In order to gain a clear and just idea of the design and end of government [however], let us suppose a small number of persons settled in some sequestered part of the earth, unconnected with the rest. . . . In this state of natural liberty, society will be their first thought. . . .

[B]ut as nothing but heaven is impregnable to vice, it will unavoidably happen that in proportion as they surmount the first difficulties of emigration, which bound them together in a common cause, they will begin to relax in their duty and attachment to each other; and this remissness will point out the necessity of establishing some form of government to supply the defect of moral virtue.

[A] select number chosen from the whole body, who are supposed to have the same concerns at stake which those who have appointed them, . . . will act in the same manner as the whole body would act were they present. . . . And as this frequent interchange [between represented and representatives] will establish a common interest with every part of the community, they will mutually and naturally support each other, and on this (not on the unmeaning name of king) depends the *strength of government and the happiness of the governed.*

Here then is the origin and rise of government; namely, a mode rendered necessary by the inability of moral virtue to govern the world; here too is the design and end of government, viz., freedom and security.

Source: Thomas Paine, *Common Sense* (1776), excerpted in *The Enlightenment: The Culture of the Eighteenth Century*, edited by Isidor Schneider (New York: George Braziller, 1965), pp. 82-84.

mankind." After independence was declared, Paine, in the first of his numerous *Crisis* papers, noted that in "times that try men's souls," the "summer soldier" or the "sunshine patriot" might "shrink from the service of his country," but the true patriot will stand firm, conquer tyranny, and obtain the precious prize of freedom.

These stirring words, more than anything else he did or wrote in his long and controversial life, assured Paine's place in history. Simply put, he was the most important propagandist of the American Revolution. As such, his later sojourns in England, France, and ultimately back in the United States constitute merely an interesting postscript to his real contribution to American history.

—*Maxine N. Lurie*

FURTHER READING

Aldridge, Alfred Owen. *Man of Reason: The Life of Thomas Paine*. Philadelphia: J. B. Lippincott, 1959. This scholarly work, based on research in England and France, attempts to give a fair assessment of a complex man. Although the book at times is laudatory, Aldridge basically sees Paine's life as a tragedy.

Conway, Moncure Daniel. *The Life of Thomas Paine*. 2 vols. New York: G. P. Putnam's Sons, 1892. The best nineteenth century biography, written by the first scholar to do extensive research on Paine. This is still a useful work. Conway also published a collection of Paine's writings.

Dorfman, Joseph. "The Economic Philosophy of Thomas Paine." *Political Science Quarterly* 53 (September, 1938): 372-386. Examines the economic ideas expressed in Paine's major pamphlets and his other ideas that had economic implications, downplaying their radicalism.

Edwards, Samuel. *Rebel! A Biography of Tom Paine*. New York: Praeger, 1974. This is a popular biography that covers all of Paine's life. It defends the achievements of Paine's early years, emphasizing his radicalism, but is more critical of the older Paine, noting his eccentric behavior. Edwards accepts as fact some scandalous stories about Paine.

Foner, Eric. *Tom Paine and Revolutionary America*. 1976. Rev. ed. New York: Oxford University Press, 2005. This scholarly biography of Paine concentrates on his American years and on his radicalism. Foner analyzes Paine's political and economic thought and emphasizes the degree to which he was consistent throughout his life.

Fruchtman, Jack, Jr. *Thomas Paine: Apostle of Freedom*. New York: Four Walls Eight Windows, 1994. An in-sightful biography. Fruchtman maintains that Paine was a pantheist who saw God's handiwork in nature and in humanity's struggles to improve the common good.

Hawke, David Freeman. *Paine*. New York: Harper & Row, 1974. One of the most complete biographies of Paine. Hawke downplays Paine's radicalism, noting that he frequently was only reflecting the ideas of his times, and emphasizes the degree to which he wrote pamphlets for pay. This is a scholarly work that portrays Paine with all of his faults.

Jordan, Wintrop D. "Familial Politics: Thomas Paine and the Killing of the King, 1776." *Journal of American History* 60 (1973): 294-308. This article discusses the appeal of *Common Sense* and its significance in preparing the way for a republic by attacking the idea of monarchy in general and the "brute" King George III in particular.

Keane, John. *Tom Paine: A Political Life*. London: Bloomsbury, 1995. A comprehensive biography of Paine, who is depicted as a generous, farsighted enemy of hypocrisy and injustice, who also could be conceited and dogmatic.

Paine, Thomas. *The Complete Writings of Thomas Paine*. Edited by Philip S. Foner. New York: Citadel Press, 1945. An accessible and well-prepared edition of Paine's works. Foner also edited a paperback edition of Paine's major pieces.

See also: John Adams; William Blake; Edmund Burke; First Baron Erskine; Benjamin Franklin; George III; William Godwin; Guillaume-Thomas Raynal; George Washington.

Related articles in *Great Events from History: The Eighteenth Century, 1701-1800:* March 22, 1765-March 18, 1766: Stamp Act Crisis; December 16, 1773: Boston Tea Party; September 5-October 26, 1774: First Continental Congress; April 19, 1775: Battle of Lexington and Concord; May 10-August 2, 1775: Second Continental Congress; January 10, 1776: Paine Publishes *Common Sense*; May, 1776-September 3, 1783: France Supports the American Revolution; July 4, 1776: Declaration of Independence; February 6, 1778: Franco-American Treaties; 1790: Burke lays the Foundations of Modern Conservatism; February 22, 1791-February 16, 1792: Thomas Paine Publishes *Rights of Man*; April 20, 1792-October, 1797: Early Wars of the French Revolution.

WILLIAM PALEY
English theologian and philosopher

Paley was the most cogent eighteenth century proponent for the argument that the universe resulted from the intelligent design of a purposeful creator. Several of his books remained standard university texts some fifty years after his death, and his works were a formative influence on the religious faith of early Victorians. The disturbing intellectual challenge later posed by Charles Darwin's theory of evolution was strong evidence of how deeply most of the English had accepted Paley's argument.

Born: July, 1743; Peterborough, England
Died: May 25, 1805; Lincoln, England
Areas of achievement: Religion and theology, philosophy

EARLY LIFE

William Paley was born in Peterborough and baptized August 30, 1743, in the cathedral there, where his father was a minor canon. He attended Giggleswick grammar school (of which his father was also headmaster) and excelled at his studies. He entered Christ's College, Cambridge, in 1759, and two years later he won the prestigious Bunting Prize in mathematics. He graduated in 1763, having also distinguished himself in debating. After teaching school for several years, he was elected a fellow of Christ's College in 1766. He began work on his master of arts degree and spent a decade of successful teaching there.

After his ordination to the Anglican priesthood in 1767, he occupied a series of increasingly remunerative church posts, including chaplain to the bishop of Carlisle (1769) and preacher at the Royal Chapel (1771). In 1776 he married Jane Hewitt. The couple had four sons and four daughters. Hewitt died in 1791, and Paley remarried four years later. In 1782, Paley became archdeacon of Carlisle and then chancellor of the diocese, a well-paid position that established him financially. He also became a justice of the peace in Lincoln and a vocal opponent of slavery. His social views were otherwise generally conservative, as in his printed sermon on *Reasons for Contentment, Addressed to the Labouring Part of the British Public* (1790), which argued that common laborers were happier than their wealthier landowners.

LIFE'S WORK

William Paley's success as a theological writer resulted more from the clarity and persuasive power of his writing than from his sheer originality of thought. Paley published his lectures, *The Principles of Moral and Political Philosophy*, in 1785, and it quickly became a Cambridge textbook. The volume, which codified the thinking on natural law then available from a variety of contemporary thinkers, such as John Locke and David Hartley, presented a moral utilitarianism rooted in theological principles. The book caught the interest of Jeremy Bentham, who four years later issued his famous treatise on utilitarianism (*An Introduction to the Principles of Morals and Legislation*) while avoiding Paley's Christian framework. Paley roots moral behavior in each person's awareness of those actions that will most "promote or diminish the general happiness." In doing so, humans fulfill God's will that all persons be happy.

Paley's first religious work was *Horae Paulinae: Or, The Truth of the Scripture History of St. Paul . . .* (1790), a defense of the reliability of Saint Paul's New Testament letters and of the Acts of the Apostles. Like it, his next major publication, *A View of the Evidences of Christianity* (1794), was a work of apologetics (a defense of the faith). Paley defended the truthfulness of the earliest Christian documents, especially regarding miracles, by arguing for the integrity of the Christian authors themselves. Challenging David Hume's skeptical view of miracles, Paley argued that early Christians would not have been willing to suffer and die for their faith if the miracles had been false. The volume was so popular that it contributed to Paley receiving the doctor of divinity degree in 1795 as well as the post of rector at Bishop-Wearmouth, a position worth £1,200 per year.

The work for which Paley is best known is *Natural Theology: Or, Evidences of the Existence and Attributes of the Deity* (1802). With textbook clarity, Paley presents a case for the existence of God based upon the argument from design. His most famous illustration of this principle is that of a watch supposedly found on a heath (the use of the watch as a metaphor for the precision of creation was not original with Paley, but he became its greatest popularizer). Unlike a mere stone, the intricate parts of the watch signify that it was created for a purpose. Thus, "the inference we think is inevitable, that the watch must have had a maker . . . an artificer or artificers who formed it for the purpose which we find it actually to answer, who comprehended its construction and designed its use."

Paley presented numerous examples of human and animal organs and bone structures to support his claim. Prominent among them was the human eye, whose intricacy he believed demonstrated "the intending mind, the adapting hand, the intelligence by which that hand was directed." Probably influenced by his interest in legal proceedings, Paley listed and answered numerous objections to this governing principle, including the assumption that such design resulted solely from a natural law: "It is a perversion of language to assign any law as the efficient, operative cause of any thing. A law presupposes an agent, for it is only the mode according to which an agent proceeds. . . ." This was to be the very issue Charles Darwin later challenged by suggesting that evolution operated according to a biological principle (the survival of the fittest through the process of natural selection) that was sufficient to produce the intricacy of creation Paley admired but without benefit of a directing intelligence.

Paley had been afflicted for many years with a painful intestinal illness that began to worsen in 1800, probably as a result of a kidney stone. He died a comfortably wealthy man on May 25, 1805, and was buried next to his first wife in Carlisle Cathedral.

SIGNIFICANCE

For at least the first half of the nineteenth century, until Darwin's ideas began to influence mid-Victorian England, William Paley's defense of the intelligent design of the universe was a foundation stone of English religious belief. His textbook on moral philosophy was used at Cambridge University until 1857, and *A View of the Evidences of Christianity* was not removed from the university's reading list until 1920. In his autobiography, Darwin recorded that his reading of Paley at Cambridge gave him

as much delight as did Euclid. The careful study of these works . . . was the only part of the Academical Course which, as I have felt and still believe, was of the least use to me in the education of my mind. . . . I was charmed and convinced by the long line of argumentation.

Challenges to Paley's views, however, had begun well before the spread of the theory of evolution. Romantic authors such as Samuel Taylor Coleridge, Percy Bysshe Shelley, William Hazlitt, and Thomas de Quincey criticized Paley's political conservatism, assertive optimism, and exclusively rational approach to the divine, as opposed to their own more intuitive and imagi-

native inclinations. While his position against slavery would have earned him their respect, they rejected his defense of the social status quo. However, Paley's clarity of argument and consistent faith in a rationally apprehended God make him one of the most influential voices of eighteenth century English philosophical theology.

—*Christopher Baker*

FURTHER READING

Clarke, M. L. *Paley: Evidences for the Man.* Toronto, Ont.: University of Toronto Press, 1974. A concise, readable introduction to Paley's life and work. Contains appendices with his portraits and a list of descendants, and includes notes and an index.

Fyfe, Aileen. "Publishing and the Classics: Paley's Natural Theology and the Nineteenth-Century Scientific Canon." *Studies in History and Philosophy of Science* 33 (December, 2002): 729-751. The long publication history of Paley's *Natural Theology* (at least fifty-seven editions over the course of a century) offers a test case for understanding what makes a text classic. In Paley's case, *Natural Theology* became classic because it appealed to scientific and religious as well as "gentlemen" and middle-class readers.

_____. "The Reception of William Paley's *Natural Theology* in the University of Cambridge." *British Journal for the History of Science* 30, no. 3 (1997): 215-223. Paley's *Natural Theology* (unlike many of his other works) was not a common text at Cambridge in the early nineteenth century, where natural theology was given less emphasis than revealed theology.

Gardner-Thorpe, Christopher. "William Paley (1743-1805): Neuroanatomist?" *Journal of Medical Biography* 10, no. 4 (2002): 215-223. Argues that Paley "wrote about neuroanatomy although he was not what we could call a neuroanatomist." Includes comments on modern critiques of Paley by Daniel C. Dennett and Richard Dawkins.

Gillespie, Neal C. "Divine Design and the Industrial Revolution: William Paley's Abortive Reform of Natural Theology." *Isis* 81, no. 2 (June, 1990): 214-219. Rather than merely comparing living beings by analogy to machines, Paley strengthened his natural theology by asserting that living beings were in fact mechanical creations. In this way he hoped to appeal to the "emerging industrial population of England."

Gould, Stephen Jay. "Darwin and Paley Meet the Invisible Hand." *Natural History* 11 (1990): 8-16. Contrasts Paley's and Darwin's explanations for the origin of biological diversity.

Lightman, Bernard. "The Visual Theology of Victorian Popularizers of Science: From Reverent Eye to Chemical Retina." *Isis* 91, no. 4 (December, 2000): 651-680. Paley's use of the human eye as evidence of a designing creator was adapted by Victorian popularizers of science, who employed inventions such as the camera and spectroscope to reveal God's handiwork.

Nuovo, Victor. "Rethinking Paley." *Synthese* 91 (April/May, 1992): 29-51. Defends Paley against the charge that he was advocating a theological argument already disproved by Immanuel Kant and David Hume. Paley's argument from design is "one of the great the-istic arguments comparable in its sophistication and scope to Anselm's so-called ontological argument."

See also: Jeremy Bentham; David Hume; Immanuel Kant.

Related articles in *Great Events from History: The Eighteenth Century, 1701-1800:* 1739-1740: Hume Publishes *A Treatise of Human Nature*; 1770: Publication of Holbach's *The System of Nature*; 1781: Kant Publishes *Critique of Pure Reason*; 1784-1791: Herder Publishes His Philosophy of History.

MUNGO PARK
Scottish explorer

Combining great ambition with tremendous courage and stamina, Park explored the Niger River in Western Africa, ultimately dying in his efforts to traverse the great river.

Born: September 10, 1771; Foulshiels, near Selkirk, Selkirkshire, Scotland
Died: c. January, 1806; Bussa Rapids on the Niger River (now under the Kainji Reservoir, Nigeria)
Area of achievement: Exploration

EARLY LIFE

Mungo Park was born on the estate of the duke of Buccleuch near Selkirk, Scotland. He was the seventh child of a well-to-do farmer, also called Mungo. Park received his early education at home and in the Selkirk grammar school. In 1786, he was placed as an apprentice to the Selkirk surgeon Dr. Thomas Anderson. This was a disappointment to his father, who wanted him to enter the ministry. With the help of Anderson, Park entered the medical school at Edinburgh University. He passed three sessions of medical studies and earned distinction in botanical studies. In 1791, after completing his medical studies, Park moved to London to seek employment.

Park's brother-in-law, James Dickson, a London botanist, introduced him to Sir Joseph Banks, president of the Royal Society, who secured for him an appointment as assistant medical officer on the British East India Company ship *Worcester*. He sailed to the island of Sumatra in February, 1792, where he collected rare plants. Park's relationship with Banks continued to develop when he returned in 1793 with his specimens and data.

After presenting several papers, Park, acting on the advice of Banks, offered his services to the African Association, an organization formed in 1788 to further geographical studies of Africa.

Banks was the most influential member of the association, and he favored Park as the successor to Major Daniel Houghton, who had disappeared on an association expedition in 1790 trying to locate the course of the Niger River. The association was impressed by Park's medical, botanical, and geographic skills, as well as his physical condition for such a demanding journey. Tall and handsome in a well-chiseled way, Park possessed remarkable stamina that permitted him to perform feats of physical endurance and survive illnesses that would prove fatal to most others. Women found him very attractive, which proved to be important because their kindness helped him several times on his expeditions. Park's reserved personality, religious fatalism, and driving desire for eminence made him the perfect explorer, capable of pursuing success with a single-minded ambition and a certain cold-bloodedness. Park's instructions from the association were to explore the Niger River and to gather information about the nations that inhabited its banks. He received fifteen shillings for each day he spent in Africa and £200 for expenses.

LIFE'S WORK

Park sailed from Portsmouth on May 22, 1795, aboard the *Endeavor*, a brig bound for the Gambia River looking for ivory. He arrived at the British factory of Pisania on the Gambia River on July 5 and resided at the home of Dr. John Laidley for five months, while he studied the

Mandingo language and recovered from his first bout with fever. Unable to travel with a caravan, Park set out on December 2 with an English-speaking Mandingo former slave, a young servant, and his equipment. He followed Houghton's earlier route and was forced to trade off most of his trafficable goods to gain the friendship of the petty chiefs.

Danger arose when Park entered the Islamic African kingdoms. He reached Jarra in the Moorish kingdom of Ludamar before Christmas and discovered that it was the village where Major Houghton had been murdered. As he crossed Ludamar, Park was constantly abused by the people he encountered, until he was seized by Moors and taken to the residence of King Ali of Ludamar. He was held prisoner for three months while suffering the humiliating treatment of his captors. In July, 1796, Park escaped through the assistance of some Ludamar women who befriended him. With only his pocket compass and a horse, he endured incredible hardships before reaching Ségou on the Niger River on July 20. He described the Niger as being as broad as the Thames River at Westminster. From Ségou, he journeyed downriver to Silla, thus proving that the Niger flowed eastward; he was forced to turn back, though, because he could no longer obtain food.

Park started back from Silla on August 3 by another route farther south, where he was again ostracized or mistreated by the Africans he encountered until, nearly dead, he reached Kamalia on foot on September 16. He spent seven months during the rainy season with a Kamali slave-trader who took him on to Pisania in June, 1797. Park sailed from Gambia on June 15 as ship surgeon on the *Charleston*, an American slave ship bound for the Carolinas. Switching ships at Antigua, Park arrived at Falmouth, England, on December 22.

Unannounced, Park arrived in London on Christmas morning and was warmly welcomed by Banks and the Africa Association. He had been gone for more than three years and was believed dead. His return was sensational in itself, but the news of his journey to the Niger created national excitement. Supported by a salary extension from the association, Park wrote *Travels in the Interior of Africa* (1799), which rapidly sold out several editions. The book was written in a dramatic and excellent literary style that made Park's name a household word and produced royalties in excess of £1,000. He returned home to the Scottish countryside and soon married Alice Anderson, daughter of his old master, Dr. Anderson of Selkirk. After living at Foulshiels for nearly two years, Park established a medical practice in the vil-

Mungo Park. (Library of Congress)

lage of Peebles in 1801. He refused an offer from Banks to lead an expedition to Australia because the salary was too small. In the end, however, Park's restlessness at Peebles, as well as Banks's persistence, led him to consider a new offer to return to Africa to lead an officially sponsored government expedition.

This new expedition was originally part of a larger plan by the British government to expel the French from Senegambia and to establish a permanent British presence in that area. There were to be three wings to the operation—commercial, military, and naval—for the purpose of destroying French factories in Senegambia and replacing them with British factories at Wulli and Bondu. Park, as leader of the commercial wing, was to establish the new factories and negotiate trade agreements with the tribes he encountered during his exploration of the Niger. The plan was drastically altered by a change in the British government in 1804. Lord Hobart, who had approved the original plan, was replaced by Lord Camden as colonial secretary. The expeditionary force, including Park's command, was whittled down by Lord Camden.

When Park left for Africa aboard the *Crescent* on January 30, 1805, he held the rank and pay of captain and the privileges of a British envoy. He was to make treaties establishing British trading stations along the Niger while trying to discover the course of the Niger and ascertain if it were navigable from the sea. Park was accompanied by his brother-in-law, Alexander Anderson, as second-in-command, and George Scott, a Selkirk friend, as draftsman. In addition, £5,000 was placed at his disposal by the treasury, and his wife and four children were guaranteed £100 a year if he failed to return.

Park's entourage, which included four carpenters and two sailors, arrived at Gorée on March 28, 1805, where they were joined by Lieutenant John Martyn and thirty-five volunteers from the Royal Africa Corps. The carpenters were to build a 40-foot (12-meter) boat for the expedition when they reached the Niger. This expedition seemed to be efficiently organized, but it had been Park's single-minded determination and endurance that made his previous expedition a success. His second expedition would become a hindrance and could not maintain the grueling pace that Park set.

So began Park's second and fatal expedition. He became impatient and against all advice led his columns into the West African bush during the rainy season. Sailing up the Gambia, Park reached Kayee, where he engaged a Mandingo guide named Isaaco. The overland march to Pisania taught Park that an expedition produced many different problems from those encountered while traveling alone. The first rain fell on June 10, and the soldiers began to contract fevers. When possible, Park left them in villages, but occasionally they were abandoned where they fell. On August 19, when the expedition arrived at Bamako on the Niger, only eleven British members remained.

Park and the remnants of his expedition hired canoes, which took them downstream to Sansanding, a little eastward of Ségou, where they remained for two months in preparation for the passage downriver. Scott had died during the march, and Anderson died on October 28. The expedition's survivors constructed a flat-bottomed boat from two native canoes that Park named HMS *Joliba*, the indigenous name for the Niger River. Only five of the British remained alive: Park, Lieutenant Martyn, and three soldiers. Isaaco was sent back with Park's final dispatches while the rest of the expedition sailed down the Niger with many muskets and ample supplies.

In 1806, rumors about Park's death began to reach the coast. Isaaco was dispatched to the interior to find the truth, but all he produced was Park's belt and a questionable account from Amadi Fatouma, who had guided Park downriver from Sansanding. Isaaco reported that Park had uncharacteristically shunned contact with the local peoples, offended the chiefs by refusing to pay their river customs, and fired upon anyone approaching the *Joliba*. Park sailed down the Niger past Timbuktu to the village of Bussa (located in what would become Nigeria), where the indigenous attempted to stop his progress. During efforts to escape, the *Joliba* had capsized in the narrow Bussa Rapids, and Park and his companions had drowned. Although doubts about Park's death remained, later expeditions confirmed that he did die at the Bussa Rapids, but the manner of his death has always been subject to debate.

SIGNIFICANCE

Mungo Park's second expedition was a tragic failure. Every European in his expedition perished, and despite the loss of life and the distance traversed, no new light had been cast on the termination of the Niger River. Because of the uncertainty of distances, neither the coastward direction of the Niger River nor the magnitude of Park's journey was immediately recognized. Park had commenced his last expedition erroneously believing that the Niger River was the Congo River, and it is possible that he died holding that belief, despite having traveled more than three-fourths of the 2,600-mile (4,200-kilometer) length of the river.

The supreme tragedy in the history of early African exploration was the death of Park, one of the most respected explorers, in an expedition that added very little to geographical knowledge. His death was basically a result of two tragic errors in judgment, first, the decision to enter the bush country during the rainy season, and second, his avoidance of contact with local peoples and his policy of firing on them. Park felt comfortable with the black Africans, but, by contrast, he feared the Moors. It must be remembered that Park left Sansanding a sick, desperate man who possibly lacked his normal clarity of judgment. Park created his own fame, and his achievements are remembered for the manner of his survival and for the death that made him and the Niger River a single historical entity and inspired another generation of explorers.

—*Phillip E. Koerper*

FURTHER READING

Boahen, A. Adu. *Britain, the Sahara, and the Western Sudan, 1788-1861*. Oxford, England: Clarendon Press, 1964. General work on British exploration and trade in Africa. Boahen discusses Park's explorations in the context of British policy in Africa.

Brent, Peter. *Black Nile: Mungo Park and the Search for the Niger*. London: Gordon and Cremonesi, 1977. An excellent biography, well researched and handsomely illustrated.

Burns, Alan. *History of Nigeria*. London: Allen & Unwin, 1964. An excellent history of Nigeria with an emphasis on British influence. Includes a brief but valuable account of Park's explorations.

Duffill, Mark. *Mungo Park*. Edinburgh: National Museums of Scotland, 1999. A brief overview of Park's life, including his experiences as a surgeon in Scotland and his explorations in Africa.

Gramont, Sandre de. *The Strong Brown God: The Story of the Niger River*. Boston: Houghton Mifflin, 1976. The best book on the European expeditions to the Niger River. Park's role and adventures are covered extensively and accurately.

Gwynn, Stephen L. *Mungo Park*. New York: G. P. Putnam's Sons, 1935. This is perhaps the best biography of Park, but it is somewhat dated.

Langley, Michael. "The Last Journey of Mungo Park." *History Today* 21 (June, 1971): 426-432. A popular, well-written article on Park's fatal expedition of 1805-1806. Excellent illustrations and evaluation of Park's accomplishments.

Park, Mungo. *Travels in the Interior Districts of Africa*. Reprint. Edited with an introduction by Kate Ferguson Marsters. Durham, N.C.: Duke University Press, 2000. A reprint of Park's account of his first expedition to the Niger River and Timbuktu. Originally published in 1799.

Severin, Timothy. *The African Adventure*. New York: E. P. Dutton, 1973. A brilliant survey of precolonial expeditions in Africa. Contains new material and excellent illustrations. Good coverage of Park's life.

See also: Sir Joseph Banks; Daniel Boone; James Bruce; James Cook; Sir Alexander Mackenzie; George Vancouver.

Related articles in *Great Events from History: The Eighteenth Century, 1701-1800*: December, 1768-January 10, 1773: Bruce Explores Ethiopia; 1779-1803: Frontier Wars in South Africa.

CHARLES WILLSON PEALE
American painter and arts patron

Peale combined a sense of patriotism in his portraits of revolutionary and early national leaders such as George Washington with a faith in democracy by establishing the Philadelphia Museum, the first public museum of art and science in America. He also helped found the Pennsylvania Academy of the Fine Arts.

Born: April 15, 1741; Queen Anne's County, Maryland
Died: February 22, 1827; Philadelphia, Pennsylvania
Areas of achievement: Art, education, patronage of the arts

EARLY LIFE

Charles Willson Peale's mother was Margaret Triggs of Annapolis, Maryland; his father, Charles Peale, Jr., a convicted forger, had been banished to the colonies in 1735. Peale had five children, of which Charles Willson was the eldest. In 1750, when Charles was only nine years old, his father died, leaving Margaret with five small children. Margaret took the family back to Annapolis and worked as a seamstress there.

Young Charles received whatever education was available, and in 1754, when he was thirteen, his mother apprenticed him to a saddle maker. During the next seven years he learned that craft. At age twenty, the young man completed his apprenticeship and borrowed the money he needed to begin his own business. In February, 1762, he married Rachel Brewer, the first of his three wives. Although successful as a saddle maker, Peale gradually diversified, adding clock making, watch repair, harness making, carriage repair, and sign painting to his skills.

By age twenty-one, Peale, slender and light-complexioned with brown hair and eyes, seemed well started on a career. Yet he longed for something more: He wanted to become a painter. Soon he began painting, using himself, his wife, and friends as subjects. When a neighbor offered him a fee of £10 to paint his and his wife's portraits, Charles decided that he needed instruction. He traveled to Philadelphia, bought an art book and what supplies he could afford, and returned home. In 1763, he visited the painter John Hesselius, who lived at a nearby plantation. Peale offered Hesselius an expensive saddle in return for some instruction and for a chance to watch him paint.

The next year his carriage-making partner absconded with most of the funds from their business. Deeply in debt, Peale sold most of his leather goods and supplies but failed to pay all of his bills. Then he joined the country party in a hotly contested election. His group won, but his creditors belonged to the losing side and they sued for the repayment of his debts. With the sheriff bearing warrants searching for him, Peale sailed to New England, beyond the reach of his creditors. He later recalled this incident as the turning point in his life: Having lost his business, he turned his attention to art as a full-time occupation. Peale returned to Maryland in 1766 after friends arranged a settlement of his affairs that would keep him out of debtors' prison. Shortly after his return, Peale's association with the local merchants and planters led them to gather funds to send him to England for formal training as a painter.

LIFE'S WORK

With his neighbors paying his way, Charles Willson Peale sailed for England in December, 1766. In London, early the next year, he began working in the studio of Benjamin West. While there, Peale tried many types of artistic endeavors, including oil portraits, miniatures, busts in plaster of Paris, and mezzotints. While in London he showed a painting and several miniatures at the exhibit of the Society of Artists of Great Britain. In early 1769, he became homesick for Maryland and his wife and child, so he returned home.

Back in the colonies, Peale turned his energies to painting full-length portraits of the Maryland gentry. In 1772, he visited Mount Vernon, where he did a portrait of George Washington in his Virginia militia uniform, the only painting of Washington done before the American Revolution. Despite Peale's success at doing portraits for the scattered planters, he hoped to move to Philadelphia so that the family could live together. Before that happened, however, the strain between England and the colonies broke into open revolt.

In 1776, the Peales moved to Philadelphia because Charles thought that an urban center offered more opportunity. A man of strong patriotic feelings, he enlisted in the city militia and was soon elected a first lieutenant. Peale's unit participated in the Battles of Trenton and Princeton, and, by June, 1777, he received an appointment as a captain of infantry. Early the next year, the British occupied Philadelphia and Peale was out of the army, serving instead on several civil and military committees as well as being elected as a representative to the Pennsylvania legislature. In late 1780, his bid for reelection to the legislature failed, and he retired from local politics.

Throughout the disruptions caused by the war and his political activities, Peale continued to paint. In fact, the executive council of Pennsylvania commissioned him to do a portrait of Washington in the middle of the war. He bought a home in Philadelphia during 1780 and during the next several years added a studio and an exhibition room. He continued to paint portraits and miniatures of leading military and political figures throughout the revolutionary era. At the same time, Peale strove to gain some economic security for his family. He opened a portrait gallery to show his work in 1782 and several years later offered the public an exhibition of "moving pictures."

In 1786, Peale opened the Philadelphia Museum. At the time, there were no museums in America, and the few museums that existed in Europe were open only for the privileged classes. Peale saw his museum as a logical part of the American Revolution. In addition to making the government open to the citizens, he would make art and science available too. Also, by charging a modest fee he hoped for a satisfactory family income. His museum was the first such venture in the United States, and it put Peale at the head of a group of American scientists, artists, and intellectuals then living in or around Philadelphia.

In 1790, Rachel Brewer Peale, Peale's first wife, died, and a year later he married Elizabeth DePeyster. As the museum collections grew, Peale moved his operations twice. In 1802, the Pennsylvania government allowed him to relocate in the vacant state house (Independence Hall). Between moves, Peale found time to buy some mastodon bones, and in 1801 he organized an expedition to Newburgh, New York, to excavate the rest of the animal's remains. While digging, the searchers unearthed a second mastodon, and from these bones Peale and his associates assembled one complete skeleton for display. By this time the museum contained hundreds of birds, mammals, and insects, in addition to Peale's paintings. To display them he introduced the practice of using their natural habitat as background, a distinct change from the then-current practice of using single-color or neutral backgrounds.

Peale retained his broad range of interests throughout his adult life. He developed a type of fireplace, experimented with plows and types of seeds, and introduced the physiognotrace for making profiles, then so popular. Continuing to paint, he also met or corresponded with the most prominent artists, scientists, and intellectuals of the day. In 1804, his wife Elizabeth died, and the next year he married Hannah More (not the British writer). He remained active in artistic and scientific activities in Philadelphia, helping to found the Pennsylvania Academy of the Fine Arts that same year. In 1810, he retired, deeding the museum to his son, Rubens Peale.

Although he claimed to be retired, Peale's curiosity and drive continued. He corresponded frequently with Thomas Jefferson, wrote essays, gave public addresses, and continued his active interest in American scientific and artistic activities, painting portraits of President James Monroe and also of John Quincy Adams and Henry Clay. He also did portraits of the officers and scientists of Stephen H. Long's 1819 Scientific Expedition being sent west to explore the Missouri Valley. In 1822, Peale reassumed management of the museum and remained active in Philadelphia until his death in 1827.

SIGNIFICANCE

Charles Willson Peale's paintings provide an unmatched view of late colonial American society. By no means a brilliant artist, he was nevertheless a keen observer and a highly competent craftsman. His early portraits show the elegance of plantation society along the Chesapeake Bay. He participated in both military and political aspects of the American Revolution, and through long acquaintance with many leading figures in early American history he had repeated chances to depict them. For example, Peale painted many portraits of George Washington, who is known to have sat for him at least seven different times. Local and regional leaders, too, sat for his work as he painted individuals from presidents and statesmen to his neighbors and family during the first half century of national independence.

Peale was also an inventor, natural scientist, and museum curator. His Philadelphia Museum began as a sort of hall of fame for early national heroes but soon evolved into the nation's first repository for scientific and natural specimens. Here Peale's contributions were varied. Offering such displays to the public was new and daring. Yet his skills in preserving and displaying specimens were impressive, too. He used habitat settings for the displays, varied the museum holdings, and used the lighting and surroundings to depict his material in a natural manner. Peale depicted his own view of his contributions to American society in a self-portrait painted when he was eighty-one years old. There he appears smiling and urging the public to enter while he lifts a curtain showing the museum display room. To him, American democracy was not simply about making politics available to the cit-

izenry; it also was about making art, science, and knowledge available to all.

—Roger L. Nichols

FURTHER READING

Briggs, Berta N. *Charles Willson Peale, Artist and Patriot.* New York: McGraw-Hill, 1952. A popular account of Peale's life. Although the author included no sources, the work is based on solid scholarship.

Brigham, David R. *Public Culture in the Early Republic: Peale's Museum and Its Audience.* Washington, D.C.: Smithsonian Institution Press, 1995. A history of Peale's Philadelphia Museum, outlining its development as an educational resource, a business, and even a form of entertainment. Brigham describes how the museum helped define the terms of public participation in early American cultural institutions.

Miller, Lillian B., ed. *Charles Willson Peale: Artist in Revolutionary America, 1735-1791.* Vol. 1 in *The Selected Papers of Charles Willson Peale and His Family.* New Haven, Conn.: Yale University Press, 1983. A detailed, scholarly collection of Peale family papers, including letters, diaries, and legal notices. Likely of more interest to scholars than to the general reader, it offers an intimate glance into life in colonial America.

Richardson, Edgar P., Brooke Hindle, and Lillian B. Miller. *Charles Willson Peale and His World.* New York: Harry N. Abrams, 1982. This book grew out of an exhibition of Peale's art at the Metropolitan Museum of Art in New York City. Each contributor provides a thoughtful essay focusing on a particular aspect of Peale's career or character.

Sellers, Charles Coleman. *Charles Willson Peale.* 2 vols. Philadelphia: American Philosophical Society, 1947. A biography that includes generous excerpts from Peale's diary, letters, and autobiography. This is the first of Sellers's several books on Peale.

_____. *Charles Willson Peale.* New York: Charles Scribner's Sons, 1969. This lavishly illustrated full-length biography is based on Sellers's 1947 two-volume study but includes new material and corrections of minor errors in the earlier version. The narrative is clear and interesting, and the conclusions are well presented.

_____. *Mr. Peale's Museum: Charles Willson Peale and the First Popular Museum of Natural Science and Art.* New York: W. W. Norton, 1980. Sellers focuses on Peale and his family to discuss their role in early museum operations and the growth of American art and natural science. Places Peale within the broad context of American intellectual and artistic development during the first half century of independence.

_____. *Portraits and Miniatures of Charles Willson Peale*. Philadelphia: American Philosophical Society, 1952. Meant for the serious student of early American portrait art, this volume includes an assessment of Peale's skills and techniques. It provides an alphabetical listing and discussion of 1,046 of his works and reproductions of 471 of his paintings.

Ward, David C. *Charles Willson Peale: Art and Selfhood in the Early Republic*. Berkeley: University of Cali-

fornia Press, 2004. A comprehensive, insightful biography. Ward portrays Peale as a self-made polymath, who carefully created and controlled his image through his autobiography, self-portraits, and other means.

See also: Benjamin Banneker; Thomas Jefferson; Gilbert Stuart; George Washington; Benjamin West.
Related articles in *Great Events from History: The Eighteenth Century, 1701-1800:* April 19, 1775: Battle of Lexington and Concord; July 4, 1776: Declaration of Independence.

HENRY PELHAM
English politician

Pelham helped forge the British parliamentary system of government into one in which the cabinet is answerable to the House of Commons and not to the monarch.

Born: September 24, 1694; Laughton, Sussex, England
Died: March 6, 1754; London, England
Area of achievement: Government and politics

EARLY LIFE

Henry Pelham was the younger son of Thomas, First Baron Pelham, and Lady Grace Holles, the youngest daughter of Gilbert, earl of Clare, and sister of John Holles, duke of Newcastle. Pelham attended Westminster School and in 1710 matriculated at Hart Hill, Oxford (from which he was never graduated). In 1715, he was commissioned a captain in the army and fought with distinction at Preston (November, 1715), where a minor rebellion was crushed.

Following the suppression of the rebellion, Pelham toured the Continent. While touring, he learned of his election to Parliament. He had been returned for Seaford at a by-election in February, 1717. Once in Parliament, he immediately became a supporter of the Whig Party, then led by Robert Walpole and Charles, Lord Townshend. (Pelham was related to both through marriage.) He rose rapidly in Parliament. In 1720, he was appointed treasurer for the House of Commons and on April 3, 1721, became one of the lords of the treasury. In 1722, Pelham was returned to the House of Commons for Sussex. He would represent Sussex for the remainder of his

tenure in the Commons. (In 1734, both Aldborough and Sussex elected him; he chose to represent Sussex.) On April 1, 1724, he was appointed secretary at war and was therefore required to resign as a lord of the treasury. In June, 1725, he was sworn as a member of the Privy Council. There his talents as a mediator and peacemaker were identified and put to good use. He was frequently needed to still the troubled waters between Walpole and his brother, Sir Thomas Pelham-Holles, duke of Newcastle. These two men manifested a mutual jealousy which flared into frequent, if petty, disputes.

In 1730, Pelham was promoted to the very lucrative position of Paymaster of the Forces. Shortly thereafter, Pelham became involved in a disagreement with William Pulteney, earl of Bath. So serious was this dispute that a duel was requested. Only the intervention of the speaker of the House prevented it from occurring. This conflict with Pulteney would continue to be a cause of friction affecting the careers of both men for the next twenty years. On one other occasion, Pelham had a dispute that would affect his career. He intervened to prevent a mob from physically attacking Walpole on the steps of the House of Commons. From then until Walpole's fall from power in February, 1742, Pelham served with distinction, if not great notice, near the center of power in England.

Pelham's brother, Thomas, assigned him half of his property. To this, Pelham added some major holdings. He purchased Esher Place in Surrey, which he greatly improved. (Alexander Pope makes reference to Esher in his *Epilogue to the Satires,* 1738.)

Pelham married Lady Katherine Manners, the eldest daughter of John, duke of Rutland, by whom he had two sons and six daughters. Both of the sons died in 1739 of ulcerated sore throats, a condition that came to be called Pelham's Fever. Four of his daughters survived infancy. Catherine, who was born July 24, 1727, married Henry Fynes Clinton, earl of Lincoln and later duke of Newcastle. Pelham's second daughter, Frances (born August 18, 1728), and Mary, his fourth (born in September, 1739), never married. Grace (born in January of 1735) married Lewis Watson, Baron Sondes.

LIFE'S WORK

The collapse of Walpole's government in February, 1742, following the loss of back-bench support in the Commons over the conduct of the War of the Austrian Succession (1740-1748), was the turning point in Pelham's career. At that time, the Commons was divided into several groups, the Old Corps Whigs and the New Whigs being the two major divisions. The Tories were another, though lesser, group. A power struggle developed. The Old Corps Whigs, who had supported Walpole, did not automatically lose position with the collapse. In the new administration, several members of the opposition had to be included, John, Lord Carteret (later the earl of Granville), and Pulteney being the two most important. King George II preferred the New Whigs and the Tories and used his influence in an attempt to prevent

Henry Pelham. (Library of Congress)

Pelham from assuming a major position in the newly reorganized government. In the restructured cabinet, Spencer Compton, earl of Wilmington, became the first lord of the treasury, the position desired by Pelham. Though Compton then offered him the chancellorship of the exchequer, Pelham refused it, choosing to remain as paymaster. (In April, 1743, Pelham was appointed a lord justice of Great Britain.)

The sudden death of the earl of Wilmington forced major cabinet changes. In spite of the opposition of Carteret, and perhaps because of the continuing influence of Walpole, Pelham stepped closer to the center of power. He became the first lord of the treasury and the chancellor of the exchequer in August, 1743. In this position, as the leader of the government, Pelham was a force between the supporters of the king, who lavished aid upon Great Britain's continental allies during the War of the Austrian Succession, and the Old Corps Whigs, who dominated in the House of Commons and favored an end to the hostilities in Europe. Old Corps Whigs preferred to see taxes kept down. Pelham favored an early end to the war, but neither he nor his brother was able to challenge the power of the New Whigs, who curried favor with George II by supporting Hanover and the continental alliances. That support and those alliances required substantial monetary outlays from the treasury.

In some interesting parliamentary maneuverings, in which William Pitt the Elder played a major role, Carteret and several of the New Whigs were ousted. The issue on which the crisis turned involved new taxes on imported sugars and upon a memorial from Pelham and the cabinet addressed to the king. The memorial urged that efforts be launched immediately to bring about a general pacification. Pelham proceeded to reorganize the government. The new cabinet was termed the "Broad Bottom" cabinet as it was an effort to balance the power among the Tories, the Old Corps Whigs, the New Whigs, and the backbenchers supporting the rising power of Pitt.

The Broad Bottom cabinet gave Pelham, who was at least nominally prime minister, the ability to meet several immediate goals. First, a closer alliance with the Dutch on the Continent was achieved and second, George II (elector of Hanover as well as king of Great Britain) was forced to join the war not only as a supporter of Hanover but also as a principal. Assisting Pelham at this particular stage in history was a Jacobite Rebellion, the Forty-five, which lasted from June of 1745 until September of 1746. While his policies in the handling of that rebellion have very little to commend themselves, they strengthened Pelham's power base in the House of Commons, although they cost him the support of his monarch. George II labeled the cabinet members "pitifull fellows" and called for their resignations. George proposed to recall both Carteret and Pulteney to power.

George's decision led to a major confrontation, which has had a lasting impact on British parliamentary government. Pelham, on learning of the king's plan, which he considered intolerable interference by the monarch, immediately resigned (on February 11, 1746) all of his offices. Subsequently, the cabinet collapsed as mass resignations (forty-five in number) followed. King George discovered that he had virtually no support in the Commons. Neither Carteret nor Pulteney could organize a government. As a result, George recalled Pelham on February 14 and asked him to form an administration.

In the new cabinet, Pelham found a place for Pitt (as joint vice treasurer for Ireland). From this crisis until his death, Pelham maintained political peace—even more disciplined than that achieved by Walpole. Examples of his exercise of control include permitting publication of the debates in both the Lords and the Commons and accepting a French proposal for peace that eventually led to the Treaty of Aix-la-Chapelle (1748). Pelham had forced peace in spite of the king's opposition. Pelham argued, in defense of that treaty, that while it did not bring Great Britain great advantage, it was much more satisfactory than continuing an unsuccessful war (Austrian Succession).

During the period of peace that followed the war and that endured until his death in 1754, Pelham pursued policies that resulted in a reduction of national expenditures and in a rearrangement of governmental finances. In 1749, he implemented an extensive plan to reduce the interest rates on the national debt. (This action led to a violent, if temporary, break with his brother, the duke of Newcastle.) In 1751, he sponsored the Chesterfield Act to reform the calendar by adopting the new, or Gregorian, style that Europe had been using since 1582. The Chesterfield Act set January 1, 1752, as the beginning of the new year instead of March 25, 1752, and provided that the eleven days between the second and fourteenth of September would be omitted. Pelham also supported the measure to maintain, in certain situations, a standing army. He supported the law that allowed for naturalization of foreign-born Protestants. He supported, but later endorsed repeal of, a law to naturalize Jews. So loud was the public outcry against this latter law that the government backed down and revoked the Jewish Naturalization Bill. Other legislative achievements of Pelham's administration include a law (Gin Act of 1751) to supervise

more closely the distillation and sale of alcohol; a law to permit local magistrates greater authority in the suppression of crime and vice; and a law to prevent the clandestine marriages of young females (the Hardewick Marriage Act, 1753) by providing for greater governmental supervision.

Pelham died on March 6, 1754, from an attack of erysipelas believed to have been caused by immoderate eating and failure to engage in proper exercise.

SIGNIFICANCE

Henry Pelham was a peace-loving man with neither outstanding abilities nor much strength of character. He has been described as a "good man of business" and as an able and economical financier. He had a temper, was an able debater, and possessed much common sense. He was in a position of power in England at the time when control of the ministers of government passed from the monarch to the House of Commons.

Scholars disagree as to whether Pelham's role was that of a catalyst or of a beneficiary of changes outside his control. Some historians argue that the events of 1744-1746 are less similar to the workings of a modern cabinet than they appear to be. Those historians argue that Pelham did not come to the king as the leader of a majority in the Commons and demand changes. Rather, they argue, Pelham emerges as the compromise choice between those in the Commons who rejected Carteret and Pulteney (or any suggestion of the king) and the king, who detested Pelham less than he detested other opposition leaders. In any event, the foundations for the modern cabinet system were laid at this time and Pelham played the leading role in those developments.

—Richard J. Amundson

FURTHER READING

Black, Jeremy, ed. *British Politics and Society from Walpole to Pitt, 1742-1789*. Basingstoke, Hampshire, England: Macmillan, 1990. Collection of essays about eighteenth century Britain, including one on the changing nature of parliamentary politics.

Gipson, Lawrence Henry. *The British Isles and the American Colonies: Great Britain and Ireland, 1748-1754*. New York: Alfred A. Knopf, 1958. Deals with the years of relative international peace while Pelham served as prime minister. The chapter "Under the Shadow of the Pelhams" deserves careful attention by those wishing to judge Pelham's use of power.

Kulisheck, P. J. *The Duke of Newcastle, 1693-1768, and Henry Pelham, 1694-1754: A Bibliography*. Westport, Conn.: Greenwood Press, 1997. Comprehensive list of material about the Pelham brothers, including personal papers, manuscript collections, memoirs, dairies, articles, and books.

Owen, John B. *The Rise of the Pelhams.* London: Methuen, 1957. Rev. ed. New York: Barnes and Noble Books, 1971. Contains detailed information on the long political careers of Henry and Thomas Pelham. Owen's work is among the best sources for understanding Pelham's private life and his family history.

Plumb, J. H. *The First Four Georges.* London: B. T. Batsford, 1956. A colorful account of the Hanoverians, containing much political detail. Pelham's role in the crises of 1744 and 1746 is seen from the perspective of the monarch and receives special attention.

Williams, Basil. *The Whig Supremacy, 1714-1760.* Oxford, England: Clarendon Press, 1936. A major source dealing with the entire Whig Party and detailing the role of Henry and Thomas Pelham. The years in which Henry served as the first minister to the king are given careful examination.

Willson, David Harris. *A History of England.* Hinsdale, Ill.: Dryden Press, 1972. One of the many standard histories of England. Willson offers a balanced account of the developments of the office of the modern prime minister.

See also: Georgiana Cavendish; George II; William Pitt the Elder; Richard Brinsley Sheridan; Robert Walpole.

Related articles in *Great Events from History: The Eighteenth Century, 1701-1800:* 1721-1742: Development of Great Britain's Office of Prime Minister; 1736: *Gentleman's Magazine* Initiates Parliamentary Reporting; December 16, 1740-November 7, 1748: War of the Austrian Succession; October 18, 1748: Treaty of Aix-la-Chapelle; January, 1756-February 15, 1763: Seven Years' War.

PETER THE GREAT
Czar of Russia (r. 1682-1725)

Borrowing both ideas and technology from the West, Peter the Great modernized Russian society, introduced significant military reforms, and built a navy almost from scratch. He won important territories on the Baltic coast from Sweden and transformed Russia into a great European power.

Born: June 9, 1672; Moscow, Russia
Died: February 8, 1725; St. Petersburg, Russia
Also known as: Pyotr Alekseyevich (birth name); Czar Peter I
Areas of achievement: Government and politics, social reform

EARLY LIFE

Peter the Great was born on June 9, 1672, the first child of Czar Alexis's second wife, Natalia Naryshkin. From his first wife, Maria Miloslavskaya, Alexis had several daughters, the eldest of whom was Sophia, and two sons, Fyodor and Ivan. Inevitably, even while Peter's father was still alive, the court factions centering on the Miloslavsky and Naryshkin families contended for power and influence. On Alexis's death in 1676, the eldest son Fyodor, though physically weak, became the czar. He died in 1682 without leaving an heir.

Thus, Peter was only ten years old when the Kremlin saw an open and violent struggle of power between the Naryshkins and Miloslavskys, who were now supported by the *streltsy*, the special regiments created in the sixteenth century by Ivan the Terrible. Peter witnessed the brutal killings of several members of the Naryshkin faction, including his mother's former guardian, Artamon Matveyev. Although the struggle ended by making Peter and his mentally disabled half brother Ivan co-czars, these unnecessary and savage killings created a deep hatred in Peter for the *streltsy* and a permanent revulsion against the Kremlin and its politics.

During the next seven years, when Sophia acted as a regent, Peter spent most of his time in the nearby village of Preobrazhenskoe. Because of neglect, he had failed to get a good education even before the 1682 events; this continued to be the case. Peter used his own devices, however, to acquaint himself with military matters and Western technology. While in Preobrazhenskoe, he amused himself with live "toy" soldiers and later organized them in two well-trained battalions. He learned, at least on a rudimentary basis, about Western science, military technology, and shipbuilding from foreigners, mainly German and Dutch, who lived in a nearby German settlement.

In 1689, a number of events affected Peter. In January, his mother married him to Eudoxia Lopukhin, a court official's daughter, by whom he had a son, Czarevitch Alexis, a year later. In August, 1689, as he lay asleep at Preobrazhenskoe, he was awakened and told that the *streltsy*, at the orders of Sophia, were on their way to kill him. He ran to take shelter at the Monastery of the Trinity in the northeast, where he was joined by his "toy" regiments and his mother and the patriarch. Sophia quickly lost support and was imprisoned in the Novodevichy Convent in Moscow. Peter's mother now served as a regent. Her death in 1694, and that of Ivan in 1696, left Peter as the sole ruler of Russia.

Eager to acquire Western knowledge and to seek European allies against Turkey, Peter undertook a long journey to the West in 1697-1698. Traveling with a large Russian delegation as an ordinary member, he spent several months in the Netherlands, learning how to make ships. He also visited England, Austria, and Prussia, and was about to go to Italy when he learned of the revolt by the *streltsy*. Although the revolt had already been crushed, he hurried home to destroy the force forever. Beside executing thousands of the *streltsy* savagely and publicly so that no one would dare oppose him in the future, Peter forced Sophia to become a nun. Peter now enjoyed unchallenged power.

Peter the Great. (Library of Congress)

LIFE'S WORK

A very important part of Peter's work consisted of acquiring territories on the Black Sea in the south and on the Baltic in the north in order to establish direct links with Central and Western Europe. Just before he left for his European journey in 1697, he had captured Azov on the Black Sea from the Turks. This acquisition was now formalized in a treaty that the two countries signed in July, 1700.

Although Peter had failed to acquire allies against Turkey during his stay in Europe, he did enter into an alliance with Poland-Saxony and Denmark, against the youthful Swedish ruler, Charles XII. While Poland-Saxony and Denmark entered the Great Northern War in early 1701, however, Peter waited until after the signing of his treaty with Turkey to join the fray. Charles XII proved a tough adversary. He forced Denmark out of the war and then inflicted a humiliating defeat on the Rus-

sian army at Narva. It would be very hard to predict what the outcome would have been had he decided to continue his march toward Moscow, but he suddenly turned toward Poland first.

For Peter, Charles XII's decision to turn first against Poland became a blessing, which he exploited to the fullest with great determination, inexhaustible energy, and imagination. From melting church bells (to replace lost artillery) to making it necessary for individuals of noble background to rise in the military ranks only after the proper training (as well as enabling commoners to become officers), Peter soon succeeded in recruiting and training a large and efficient army.

As Charles XII remained entrenched in his struggle against Augustus II of Poland, Peter used his new army skillfully and effectively in making inroads into Livonia and Estonia and inflicted defeat on the Swedes at many points, thus firmly establishing his predominance over the Gulf of Finland. In 1703, he founded the city of St. Petersburg on the Neva River as his future capital, and, in order to protect it, he ordered the construction of a fortress on Kronstadt Island. He also rapidly built a navy in the Baltic Sea.

Having defeated Poland in 1706, Charles was now free to turn toward Moscow. Rather than attack from the north, he decided to go southward into the Ukraine, hoping to secure the support of the Cossacks and the Ukrainians. The Russians succeeded, however, in interrupting and destroying some of his supplies at Lesnaia in September, 1708. Though the Cossack leader Ivan Stepanovich Mazepa did support him, the majority of the Ukrainians still remained loyal to Peter. The two armies finally faced each other at Poltava in the Ukraine in July, 1709. At this historic battle, a depleted Swedish army met Peter's larger force and was defeated. Both Charles and Mazepa had to escape into Turkey.

Peter's great victory at Poltava was complicated by Turkey's entry into the war. Rather than making peace with the Turks, at a time when he was still at war with Sweden, Peter, in an overconfident mood, entered the Balkans hoping to incite Turkey's Christians against their masters. He soon decided to extricate himself by returning the hard-won Azov to Turkey in the Treaty of Pruth of 1711.

Peter could now concentrate on the north, where his army was already active in acquiring new territories on the Baltic. War with Sweden finally ended in 1721. In the Treaty of Nystadt, Peter obtained more than what he had hoped for when he first went to war against Sweden in 1700. In addition to the territories now known as Latvia, Lithuania, and Estonia, Russia annexed Ingria and part of Karelia with the strategic Viborg.

Peter's success in foreign affairs was not confined to his acquisitions from Sweden. His efforts to establish links with China would result in the Treaty of Kiakhta in 1727, establishing important trade links with Beijing. He encouraged further exploration of Siberia and obtained, from Persia, territory along the Caspian Sea, including the important Port of Baku.

His efforts to modernize Russia, which initially appeared haphazard and were often undertaken more to facilitate his war efforts than with a clear vision to change Russian society, finally began to take shape toward the latter part of his reign. While his efforts to force the Russians to surrender their beards and traditional long dresses had only a limited impact, steps taken to develop industry and simplify the Russian language (making it possible to translate a large number of European scientific works into Russian) had lasting positive results.

One of Peter's most interesting and effective innovations was the creation of a table of ranks. Providing for fourteen categories in a hierarchical order for all officials, including officers in the military, this device enabled Peter to reward individuals of non-noble background, even allowing them to become nobles. In this manner, without abolishing the institution of serfdom, he was able to secure for the empire the services of all its talented subjects, regardless of their social status.

A very important administrative reform, undertaken in 1711 when he was away fighting Turkey, also proved lasting: So the work of the government could continue in his absence, Peter created a senate to supervise all judicial and administrative functions. Its head, the ober-procurator, served as the direct agent of the czar, a kind of modern prime minister. In 1717, Peter created colleges for such governmental functions and branches as foreign affairs, finance, and the navy. Again, Peter's reform resembled a modern institution, this time the modern ministries of parliamentary governments. He also made significant but less successful attempts to restructure local government.

Although the church in Russia had gradually come under the control of Muscovite rulers since the days of the Mongolian rule, it was still led by a patriarch who could attempt to undermine the czar's wishes. Peter wanted to abolish that anomaly, and in line with the model of state-church relations existing in the German Lutheran states, he wanted the state's absolute primacy over the church. When Patriarch Adrian died in 1700, Peter decided not to appoint a replacement. After intense personal interest and painstaking work over a number of years, he decided in 1721 to create a synod of members of the Orthodox clergy to replace the office of the patriarch and to be headed by a lay official: The church administration almost became a function of the government.

SIGNIFICANCE

A man of inexhaustible energy and determination, Peter the Great succeeded, in a span of only a quarter of a century, in fulfilling all of his ambitions on the Baltic. Russia now came to replace Sweden as a great European power. Flopan Prokopavich, Peter's adviser on church affairs, in his funeral oration was not amiss when he said that Peter had "found but little strength" in Russia but succeeded in making its "power strong like a rock and diamond." On the territory he won from Sweden, he built his new capital as a living symbol of his orientation toward the West, and even today it stands as one of the most beautiful cities of Europe.

While there is hardly any dispute regarding the significance of his accomplishment in creating a modern army and navy and his remarkable military victories made possible by them, the nature and impact of his reforms aroused much controversy in his own time. Even in the later period, when the problems of change and modernization still concerned the Russians, Peter aroused both deep hatred and admiration, as, for example, in the bitter debate between the Slavophiles and the Westernizers in the nineteenth century. Peter's policies raised a fundamental question: Which path should Russia take in order to modernize itself and create a better society and political system?

In one respect, though, Peter followed the old Russian tradition. He did not hesitate to use maximum force, as was the case in his treatment of the rebellious *streltsy*, in order to suppress the opposition. He remains the only Russian ruler who did not even hesitate in torturing and eventually causing the death of his only son, Czarevitch Alexis. In his total dedication to the welfare of his country, he also remains one of the earliest examples of an enlightened despot. Russia, in a fundamental way, was a country transformed when Peter died in 1725.

—Surendra K. Gupta

FURTHER READING

Anderson, M. S. *Peter the Great*. 2d ed. Harlow, Essex, England: Longman, 2000. A standard biography, pointing both to Peter's failures and to his successes. Written by a British historian, it makes liberal use of the observations of foreign visitors to Russia and of the dispatches sent by foreign diplomats in the Russian capital. Includes an annotated bibliography of both Russian and Western works.

Bushkovitch, Paul. *Peter the Great: The Struggle for Power, 1671-1725*. New York: Cambridge University Press, 2001. Examines the politics of the Russian court during Peter's reign, describing how Peter compromised and worked with the powerful aristocracy to implement his reforms and create a European-style monarchy.

Cracraft, James. *The Revolution of Peter the Great*. Cambridge, Mass.: Harvard University Press, 2003. Describes Peter's many reforms and how they changed Russian language, architecture, dress, and other aspects of the nation's life and culture.

De Jonge, Alex. *Fire and Water: A Life of Peter the Great*. New York: Coward, McCann & Geoghegan, 1979. Attempts to place Peter and his work in the context of Russian historical traditions. The author has no hesitation in linking the nature of Petrine Russia to the subsequent periods in Russian history, including the Soviet era. Includes a short bibliography.

Hughes, Lindsey. *Peter the Great: A Biography*. New Haven, Conn.: Yale University Press, 2003. A scholarly yet accessible biography providing an overview of Peter's life and accomplishments.

Massie, Robert K. *Peter the Great: His Life and World*. New York: Alfred A. Knopf, 1980. Popular biography, presenting an admiring and somewhat uncritical portrait of Peter. What distinguishes this biography from others is its attempt to give readers a picture of the European world so Peter's accomplishments can be seen in a larger context. Contains an excellent but unannotated bibliography.

Oliva, L. Jay. *Russia in the Era of Peter the Great*. Englewood Cliffs, N.J.: Prentice-Hall, 1969. Avoids the temptation of linking Petrine Russia to later periods, including the Soviet era. The emphasis is on the heritage of Peter's Russia and on the eighteenth century environment in which Peter tried to shape his work. Includes a good, briefly annotated bibliography.

Riasanovsky, Nicholas V. *The Image of Peter the Great in Russian History and Thought*. New York: Oxford University Press, 1985. Starting with the image of Peter in the Russian Englightenment during the period from 1700 to 1826, the author covers the nineteenth century as well as the Soviet period. Contains a long and very useful bibliography.

See also: Catherine the Great; Charles XII; Elizabeth Petrovna; Peter III.

Related articles in *Great Events from History: The Eighteenth Century, 1701-1800*: 1701: Plumier Publishes *L'Art de tourner*; c. 1701-1721: Great Northern War; May 27, 1703: Founding of St. Petersburg; June 27, 1709: Battle of Poltava; November 20, 1710-July 21, 1718: Ottoman Wars with Russia, Venice, and Austria; 1724: Foundation of the St. Petersburg Academy of Sciences; October 21, 1727: Treaty of Kiakhta; 1745: Lomonosov Issues the First Catalog of Minerals.

PETER III
Czar of Russia (r. 1762)

Czar of Russia for only 186 days, Peter III nevertheless influenced both Russia and the rest of Europe. He emancipated the Russian nobility from compulsory state service, secularized the property of the Russian Orthodox Church, and reversed Russia's traditional pro-Austrian foreign policy in favor of Prussia.

Born: February 21, 1728; Kiel, Holstein (now in Germany)
Died: July 18, 1762; Ropsha, Russia
Also known as: Pyotr Fyodorovich; Karl Peter Ulrich (birth name); Grand Duke Peter Fedorovich
Area of achievement: Government and politics

EARLY LIFE

Christened Karl Peter Ulrich, the future Czar Peter III was born in the capital of the small German duchy of Holstein. He was the only son of Karl Friedrich, duke of Holstein-Gottorp, and Anna Petrovna, eldest daughter of Russia's Peter the Great. Through his father, a nephew of Sweden's Charles XII, Karl Peter had claims to the Swedish throne; through his mother, he stood in line for the Russian throne. Accordingly, his early education focused on preparing him to rule.

Until 1741, Karl Peter's prospects of ruling Russia looked dim, because the Russian throne seemed firmly entrenched in the family of Peter the Great's half brother, Ivan V, who died in 1696. In November of that year, however, Karl Peter's maternal aunt, Elizabeth Petrovna, overthrew the infant ruler Ivan VI and established herself as Empress Elizabeth I. Unmarried and without an heir, and thus looking for a way to consolidate her position, Elizabeth brought her by then orphaned nephew to Russia in January, 1742. Following his formal conversion to the Orthodox faith, Karl Peter was proclaimed Grand Duke Peter Fedorovich, heir to the throne of the Russian Empire, on November 18, 1742.

In the years immediately following his designation as Elizabeth's heir, Peter completed his formal education. From 1742 to 1747, Jacob von Staehlin, a member of the Russian Academy of Sciences, tutored the young grand duke in a variety of subjects. Although historians have traditionally depicted Peter as a dull-witted student interested in military affairs exclusively, Staehlin's memoirs paint a different picture. According to the tutor, the grand duke possessed an excellent memory, was logical and thoughtful, and came away from their association with a solid grounding in geography, Russian history, and the achievements of Peter the Great. Other sources provide evidence that under Staehlin's tutelage, Peter developed an interest in the arts, music becoming a particular passion.

While completing his education, Peter also married. In September, 1745, he married sixteen-year-old Grand Duchess Catherine Alekseyevna. Formerly Princess Sophie Friederike Auguste von Anhalt-Zerbst, Catherine was brought to Russia for the express purpose of providing Peter a wife. Unfortunately for both Peter and Catherine, the marriage proved unhappy from the beginning, and subsequently, both took lovers. According to Catherine, the blame belonged to Peter, who she claimed neglected her and showed a greater interest in toy soldiers than in his husbandly duties. Although officially the marriage produced a child, questions remain about the paternity of Grand Duke Paul Petrovich, later Paul I (1796-1801), born in October, 1754.

As Peter's marriage deteriorated, his relationship with Empress Elizabeth grew increasingly strained. Disagreements over Russia's pro-Austrian and anti-Prussian foreign policy, especially after the outbreak of the Seven Years' War in 1756, led to the grand duke's virtual exclusion from governmental affairs and prompted some discussion in court circles about Peter being bypassed in favor of Paul Petrovich. As events turned out, the discussions of Peter's exclusion from the succession remained just that, and when Elizabeth died on January 5, 1762, the thirty-three-year-old Peter Fedorovich ascended the Russian throne as Czar Peter III.

LIFE'S WORK

Peter's most celebrated and arguably most significant accomplishment was his emancipation of the Russian nobility from compulsory state service. Beginning in the reign of Peter the Great, nobles became obliged to serve the state—either in the military, in the government, or at court—on a full-time, lifelong basis. In fact, Peter the Great made nobility and the privileges associated with it dependent upon performance of service. Any noble who refused to fulfill service obligations forfeited both title and privileges, including the right to own land and serfs. Although Empress Anna I had ameliorated the service requirement somewhat, reducing its length to twenty-five years, the Russian noble's obligation to perform service remained in place.

By a manifesto of March 1, 1762, Peter III granted "freedom and liberty to the entire Russian nobility," stipulating that those then in state service—and who had achieved officer's rank in the armed forces or equivalent rank in the government or at court—could retire in time of peace. Peter's manifesto further proclaimed that this privilege was to be regarded as "a perpetual and fundamental principle" binding on subsequent Russian rulers. Although the manifesto emphasized that nobles who had yet to achieve officer's rank had to serve twelve years before retiring, that nobles had to continue to educate their children in preparation for state service, and that nobles remained subject to recall in wartime, the days when nobles had no choice but to serve had disappeared forever, a development leading one eminent historian of eighteenth century Russia to characterize Peter's act as "one of the most important milestones in the modernization of Russia."

While Russia's nobles certainly welcomed their liberation from compulsory service—although the evidence suggests that most chose to remain in service—this was not enough to offset other decisions by which Peter rapidly alienated members of the country's military, governmental, and religious elite. Among Peter's most personally damaging decisions, four stand out: his withdrawal of Russia from the Seven Years' War; his secularization of property belonging to the Russian Orthodox Church; his efforts to "Prussianize" the Russian army; and his decision to go to war against Denmark.

Peter's decision to withdraw from the Seven Years' War came when Russia and its allies, Austria and France, verged on a decisive victory over Prussia. On February 23, 1762, the Russian court announced that it intended to seek peace with Prussia. Peter then proceeded to negotiate a settlement without consulting his allies and without regard for the advice of his foreign minister, Mikhail Vorontsov. The result was a peace treaty actually drafted by the Prussian envoy and without real benefit to Russia. Signed on May 5, 1762, the treaty provided that Russia return all territorial conquests to Prussia. Russia's allies, not surprisingly, felt betrayed. More important, Russia's generals felt as if the new czar had thrown away all they had won since 1756 simply because of his well-known admiration of Prussia's king Frederick the Great.

Peter's secularization of the property belonging to the Russian Orthodox Church, enacted April 1, 1762, transferred all church lands and peasants to the Russian state. While welcomed by the affected peasants, who greatly preferred the state as a direct overlord, secularization proved the last straw for the Orthodox hierarchy, already

disenchanted by what it perceived as Peter's Lutheran proclivities and his toleration of religious dissenters. In regard to the latter, the Orthodox leadership was especially disconcerted by Peter's lifting of sanctions on Old Believers (dissenters who had broken with the Church in the second half of the seventeenth century and who had been persecuted by both Church and state since that time) and his inviting those who had fled to Poland and other neighboring countries to return to Russia without fear of persecution.

Peter's "Prussianization" of the Russian army began from the moment he ascended the throne. The new czar established a military commission and entrusted it with introducing Prussian-style uniforms and drill in the army. This, along with Peter's disbanding of the imperial bodyguard created by Elizabeth I in favor of a corps from his native Holstein, caused tremendous consternation among soldiers of Russia's imperial guards regiments, who were quite attached to the uniforms introduced by Peter the Great. Quite possibly, Peter's alienation of the imperial guards represented his most critical error, since, as one prominent historian has pointed out, the imperial guards were a "body that no eighteenth century Russian monarch could afford to alienate."

Peter's decision to go to war against Denmark was driven not by concern for Russian interests but by a desire to win Schleswig for his native Holstein (of which he had become duke in 1745). Military and diplomatic preparations for this conflict began shortly after Peter declared his intention to make peace with Prussia and continued throughout the spring of 1762. Senior government officials attempted to slow Peter's drift toward war, while Prussia's Frederick the Great counseled the czar against going on campaign before he had consolidated his power. Peter, however, remained committed to the acquisition of Schleswig. On June 23, he departed St. Petersburg for his estate at Oranienbaum, from where he intended to leave for the campaign. Shortly thereafter, the imperial guards received orders to join with the regular army in preparation for an assault on Denmark. This further inflamed the already discontented guards regiments.

Peter's absence from St. Petersburg and the tremendous dissatisfaction engendered by his decisions provided his ambitious wife an opportunity to seize power. On July 9, 1762, Catherine—with the assistance of her lover, Captain Grigori Grigoryevich Orlov—staged a coup d'état, announcing Peter's deposition and her accession as Empress Catherine the Great. Having alienated Russia's generals, the Orthodox hierarchy, senior government officials, and the imperial guards, Peter found himself isolated and unable to counter his wife's seizure of power. On July 10, he meekly surrendered and renounced the throne, issuing a manifesto in which he acknowledged his inability to rule.

Following his abdication, Peter was moved to Ropsha. There, on July 18, he died in rather mysterious circumstances. A manifesto explained that Peter had died of colic following an acute hemorrhoidal attack. Many historians, however, believe that Peter was killed in a drunken brawl with Aleksey Grigoryevich Orlov, brother of Catherine's lover. Initially buried at the Alexander Nevskii Monastery in St. Petersburg, Peter's body was, in November, 1796, following Catherine's death, transferred to the Cathedral of the Peter and Paul Fortress, the final resting place of Russia's czars and empresses since the days of Peter the Great.

SIGNIFICANCE

Despite ruling only 186 days, Peter III had a major impact on both Russia and Europe. His liberation of the Russian nobility from compulsory state service inaugurated a new era in the history of the Russian nobility and in the relationship between the Russian government and the country's leading socioeconomic class. Peter's secularization of the property of the Orthodox Church deprived the Church of much of its economic power and thereby left it almost completely dependent financially on the Russian state. This completed a process begun by Peter the Great, who in the early eighteenth century subordinated the Church politically to the state by placing a lay official in charge of the Church.

Finally, Peter reversed Russia's traditional pro-Austrian foreign policy in favor of a pro-Prussian foreign policy. This entailed Russia's abrupt withdrawal from the Seven Years' War, a critical development that allowed Frederick the Great and Prussia to avoid a decisive defeat, perhaps even annihilation. Peter's reorientation of Russia's foreign policy also ushered in an era, lasting more than a century, during which Russia and Prussia stood together to combat the forces of revolution in Europe.

—Bruce J. DeHart

FURTHER READING

Bain, R. Nisbet. *Peter III, Emperor of Russia.* New York: Dutton, 1902. The first biography of Peter in English. Bain paints a somewhat sympathetic portrait.

De Madariaga, Isabel. *Russia in the Age of Catherine the Great.* 2d ed. New Haven, Conn.: Yale University Press, 2002. Chapter 1 describes in some detail Peter's alienation of Russia's elite and the events of his overthrow.

Erickson, Carolly. *Great Catherine: The Life of Catherine the Great, Empress of Russia.* New York: Crown, 1994. Comprehensive popular biography. Includes information about Peter's life and reign, his relationship with Catherine, and his abdication.

Jones, Robert E. *The Emancipation of the Russian Nobility, 1762-1785.* Princeton, N.J.: Princeton University Press, 1973. Attempts to explain Peter's motivation in liberating nobles from compulsory state service and shows how Catherine the Great built on the decision.

Leonard, Carol S. *Reform and Regicide: The Reign of Peter III of Russia.* Bloomington: Indiana University Press, 1993. An updated political biography of Peter that questions the accepted negative view of Peter and paints him as an energetic ruler who attempted to reform Russia in accordance with Enlightenment principles.

Lincoln, Bruce W. *The Romanovs: Autocrats of All the Russias.* Garden City, N.Y.: Anchor Press/Doubleday, 1981. Lincoln chronicles the achievements and significance of the Romanov Dynasty, including Peter III.

Raeff, Marc. "The Domestic Policies of Peter III and His Overthrow." *American Historical Review* 75 (June, 1970): 1289-1310. Explains Peter's deposition primarily in terms of the unpopularity of his domestic policies.

Raleigh, Donald J., ed. *The Emperors and Empresses of Russia: Rediscovering the Romanovs.* Armonk, N.Y.: M. E. Sharpe, 1996. Authored by Soviet historian Aleksandr Sergeevich Mylnikov, the chapter on Peter closely resembles Carol Leonard's challenge to the accepted views of the czar, his character, and his abilities.

See also: Catherine the Great; Charles XII; Elizabeth Petrovna; Frederick the Great; Aleksey Grigoryevich Orlov; Grigori Grigoryevich Orlov; Peter the Great.

Related articles in *Great Events from History: The Eighteenth Century, 1701-1800*: November 20, 1710-July 21, 1718: Ottoman Wars with Russia, Venice, and Austria; 1736-1739: Russo-Austrian War Against the Ottoman Empire; May 31, 1740: Accession of Frederick the Great; January, 1756-February 15, 1763: Seven Years' War; August 10, 1767: Catherine the Great's Instruction.

PHILIP V
King of Spain (r. 1700-1746)

Philip V established the Bourbon Dynasty in Spain and, by putting into force needed reforms in government and economics devised by his French and Italian advisers as well as his queen consort, Isabella, helped Spain recapture some of its diminished international prestige.

Born: December 19, 1683; Versailles, France
Died: July 9, 1746; Madrid, Spain
Also known as: Philippe, duc d'Anjou
Area of achievement: Government and politics

EARLY LIFE

Born in France, Philip V was called Philippe, duc d'Anjou, for his first sixteen years. His father, the dauphin Louis, was the son of Louis XIV of France and the grandson of Philip IV, king of Spain. His mother, Marie Anne, was the daughter of Ferdinand of Bavaria. Philip retained his title, duke of Anjou, until 1700, but when Philip's uncle, Charles II, the childless king of Spain, Naples, and Sicily, died on November 1, 1700, he left to Philip his holdings in Spain, the Spanish Netherlands, Spanish America, and parts of Italy.

Charles II, who was born in 1661, had been king since 1665, with his mother, Mariana of Austria, serving as his regent. Even when Charles reached his majority, his mother continued as regent because Charles was physically and mentally disabled. As he neared death, Charles signed a document dated October 2, 1700, that named the duke of Anjou as his successor. Charles had executed two similar documents previously, each naming a different successor.

Following Charles's death, Philip's grandfather, Louis XIV, declined to exclude Philip from the French line of succession, an act that led to the War of the Spanish Succession (1701-1714). Meanwhile, the young Philip, who was installed as king of Spain a few months short of his seventeenth birthday, loathed Spain and longed to return to France. Early in 1701, Philip, who was basically weak and, suffering from an acute bipolar disorder, at times deranged, entered into an arranged marriage with María Luisa of Savoy, who served essentially as Philip's regent.

During her lifetime, María Luisa saw to it that France maintained a strong influence in the Spanish court. Realizing that the Spanish government was in serious need of reform, María Luisa arranged for a French economist, Jean Orry, to become a de facto first minister to help bring to the Spanish court economic reforms that Orry, in league with María Luisa, deemed necessary. It was at her urging that the French ambassador to Spain held a prominent position in Spain's council of state.

LIFE'S WORK

The War of the Spanish Succession ended first with the signing of the Treaty of Utrecht in 1713 and then with the Treaties of Rastatt and Baden in 1714. Under the terms of these treaties, Philip lost the Spanish Netherlands and the Italian possessions held by the Spanish Habsburgs, but he retained the Spanish throne and his extensive holdings in Spanish America, bequeathed to him by Charles II.

In the early years of Philip's reign, Spain was threatened by many external forces. In 1705, Archduke Charles seized command of Barcelona. The Portuguese occupied Castile and the Austrians invaded Naples, which at that time was part of Philip's kingdom. Philip faced the possibility of losing Spain to a host of invaders. Louis XIV was on the brink of refusing to support Philip's efforts, but the besieged king rallied and held on to Spain, gaining support from the Castilians and retaking Barcelona in 1714. Louis XIV was said to have been a forceful and fearless leader in the conflicts that led to Spain's military victories.

Within a few months of the signing of the Treaty of Utrecht, Philip lost his wife. María Luisa, who had given birth to Ferdinand (the future King Ferdinand VI) on September 23, 1713, succumbed to tuberculosis on February 14, 1714. The official search for a new wife began immediately and was narrowed to a choice between two: the daughter of the king of Poland or Isabella Farnese, the niece of the duke of Parma.

A union between Philip and Isabella Farnese was considered the most politically advantageous, and on September 16, 1714, proxy marriage ceremonies took place simultaneously in Italy and in Spain. Isabella came to Spain in December of the same year, and on December 24, a service confirming the earlier proxy ceremony was held in Guadalajara.

Most historians have concluded that Philip had a compelling need to be closely associated with strong women. Certainly María Luisa had been a dominant and, according to many accounts, a domineering force in his life. If she dominated Philip, the twenty-two-year-old Isabella far outdid María Luisa in that regard. Isabella was bright and determined. Philip's marriage to her heralded a change in emphasis in the Spanish court. Isabella immediately set about eradicating many of the French influences imposed by her predecessor. She saw to it that the princess des Ursins, who had brokered Philip's first marriage and had also arranged Isabella's marriage to him, was exiled after she engaged in a heated exchange with Isabella upon her arrival in Guadalajara. Isabella was instrumental in replacing Philip's French advisers with Italians, the most influential of whom was Giulio Alberoni, a prelate who was made a cardinal in 1717, presumably as repayment for his services to Philip and the Spanish court. Isabella made strenuous efforts to regain for the benefit of her two sons, Luis and Fernando, the Italian holdings Philip had ceded to Austria in the Treaty of Utrecht and the Treaties of Rastatt and Baden.

Scholarly opinion is sharply divided regarding who brought about the significant changes in Spanish government that became the basis for the Spanish state as it currently exists. Philip, whether acting independently or acquiescing to Isabella's initiatives, was officially responsible for bringing about drastic changes in Spain's foreign policy and international relations. During his reign, the Spanish economy was reformed and Spain's armed forces were substantially strengthened. Under his forty-six-year rule, Spain emerged as a dominant force in Europe.

In 1724, Philip abdicated in favor of his son, Luis, who became king of Spain on January 15, 1724. Historians generally concede that the major reason for Philip's abdication was that he hoped to succeed the ailing Louis XIV as king of France. On August 31, 1724, however, just seven months after assuming the throne, Luis died, a victim of smallpox, and Philip was forced to reign a second time. Philip suffered throughout his life from a severe bipolar disorder. At times he was clearly demented and unable to discharge his official responsibilities. During such periods, particularly in the last decade of his life, Isabella undoubtedly assumed many of his official duties.

SIGNIFICANCE

During the long reign of Philip V, dramatic changes took place in Spain. Philip established the Bourbons as the nation's official rulers and, except for the usurpation of the throne by Francisco Franco for four decades until 1975, the Bourbons have ruled Spain since.

Under Philip, with Isabella's help, a new Spanish state took shape, the early organization of which has persisted to the present day. There is considerable uncer-

tainty about the extent to which Philip was personally involved in the changes that occurred, but because they took place during his official reign, they are generally attributed to him.

In addition to reform in Spain's economy, foreign policy, and military forces, the country under Philip entered a period during which the official encouragement of literature, art, and music led to a revival of culture throughout the country. This revival helped Spain regain recognition throughout Europe as a significant cultural force.

Although many historical accounts of Philip's reign are inconclusive, revisionist historians are exploring extensive archival materials to present a more accurate account of his time on the throne. Philip's life was convoluted and, in many ways, puzzling, but historians such as Henry Kamen are beginning to put it into a new, more accurate perspective.

—*R. Baird Shuman*

FURTHER READING

Hamilton, Earl J. *War and Prices in Spain, 1651-1800.* New York: Russell and Russell, 1969. This carefully presented study offers valuable information about Spain's economic state during the rule of Philip V and also provides details about the abortive reign of Charles II.

Kamen, Henry. *Philip V of Spain: The King Who Reigned Twice.* New Haven, Conn.: Yale University Press, 2001. By far the best researched and most appealingly written book about the life and reign of Philip V. The book is fascinating and is a model of excellence in analytical biographical writing.

_____. *The War of Succession in Spain, 1700-1715.* Bloomington: Indiana University Press, 1969. A thorough presentation of the conflict that arose when Louis XIV refused to exclude Philip V from the line of succession in France after he became king of Spain.

Lynch, John. *Bourbon Spain, 1700-1808.* Oxford, England: Basil Blackwell, 1989. A detailed presentation of the politics of Bourbon rule in Spain, including the reign of Philip V.

McLachlan, Jean. *Trade and Peace with Old Spain, 1667-1750.* Cambridge, England: Cambridge University Press, 1940. McLachlan investigates the economy of Spain during the reign of Philip V. The book is somewhat dated, but contains useful insights into Philip's rule.

See also: Charles III; Charles VI; José de Gálvez; First Duke of Marlborough.

ARTHUR PHILLIP
English admiral and administrator

An officer in the British navy, Phillip served as the first governor of Australia from 1788 to 1792. To this prudent and judicious head of the struggling convict colony, the modern nation of Australia owes its existence.

Born: October 11, 1738; London, England
Died: August 31, 1814; Bath, Somerset, England
Areas of achievement: Military, government and politics

EARLY LIFE

Arthur Phillip was the son of a language teacher, Jakob Phillip, who had emigrated to England from Frankfurt, Germany, and married an Englishwoman, Elizabeth Breach. After attending school in London, Phillip went to sea at age sixteen and completed his mercantile marine apprenticeship a year later. In 1755, he joined the Royal Navy, starting as a midshipman and retiring as an admiral.

On active duty during the Seven Years' War against France, Phillip was promoted to lieutenant. In 1763, the war over, he retired on half pay and for eleven years was a farmer. During this period he was married, not happily, however, for in 1769 he and his wife were formally separated; they had no children. Tired of country life at Lyndhurst, Phillip obtained permission from the British Admiralty in 1774 to join the Portuguese navy. Four years later, the British and French again at war, he returned to the Royal Navy and attained the rank of captain in 1781. Retired once more on half pay, he went back to his farm and probably would have spent the remaining years in obscurity had it not been for his appointment in 1786 as the governor of the proposed penal settlement in Australia.

Portraits of Phillip show him to have been slightly built and far from handsome—all too ordinary looking for the founder of a nation. Little in his outwardly lackluster career had indicated that he would at almost fifty years of age undertake so formidable a venture or meet it with such daring and enterprise. Although Phillip recorded in official correspondence and journals detailed accounts of his public life, he revealed little about his personal side. The diaries of others who shared the Australian experience with him provide scant evidence of their leader's personality; they do suggest that he was a solitary man devoted to duty, sometimes in their eyes stubbornly so.

The reason Lord Thomas Townshend Sydney, the home secretary, decided to choose Phillip first as captain of the First Fleet of convicts and then as their governor is not known. Yet during Phillip's tenure with the Portuguese navy, he had served as captain of a ship that transported four hundred Portuguese convicts safely across the Atlantic to Brazil; not to lose even one person on such a dangerous voyage was impressive for that time. Phillip's superiors must have considered this ordinary officer to be a reliable and competent leader, a man firm yet equitable in his actions.

Phillip had spent the first forty or so years of his life as a prelude to the morning of May 13, 1787, when he took the First Fleet out of Portsmouth, the flagship *Sirius* leading the eleven vessels bound for a perilous 16,000-mile journey to an unknown land.

LIFE'S WORK

Once appointed as the captain general of the First Fleet, Phillip proved his efficiency, attending to every possible detail, especially in regard to supplies. His years of experience at sea had taught him that survival might well hang on the humblest of items; he soon discovered, however, that his superiors, anxious to be rid of the convicts, failed to share his concern for the safety and health of this human cargo. After endless confrontations—some lost, others won—the fleet departed, holding in its cramped quarters 736 male and female convicts, along with about 300 marines and their dependents, a few servants, and a handful of civil officials.

Captain Phillip, as he is generally known in Australian history, had plotted what appears at first sight to have been an indirect course but which was actually one along which sailing ships could take advantage of prevailing winds and currents. En route to its antipodean destination, the fleet stopped at the Canary Islands, Rio de Janeiro, and Cape Town, each time adding to depleted supplies. Finally, on January 20, 1788, during the Southern Hemisphere's summer, the ragged assembly landed at Botany Bay on the eastern coast of Australia. Although recommended by Captain James Cook after his earlier explorations there, this location soon proved to be dismal, its anchorage exposed, its water undrinkable, and its soil poor. Phillip and his close associates explored the nearby coast, sailing before long into a harbor that Phillip described in his journal as "the finest in the world." Along the shore of one of the numerous coves, christened Sydney in honor of the home secretary, Phillip established the settlement.

Under his expert direction, the 252-day voyage may well be one of the most remarkable in history: every ship safe; convict rebellions prevented and discipline maintained among the marines; only forty-eight people dead in spite of overcrowding, inadequate medical care, and unhealthful diet; and an almost mythical destination reached. Still, Phillip, now governor, faced an even greater challenge once his motley crew had moved from sea to land. On February 7, with all the convicts finally ashore and assembled before him with the marines on guard, Phillip read the official proclamations giving him unlimited power to govern this penal colony as he saw fit to ensure its survival.

At times that survival seemed doomed. Although more promising than Botany Bay, the land around the harbor proved unyielding, the weather unpredictable, the unfamiliar animals and landscape frightening. The convicts, most city-bred and long debauched—"reluctant pioneers" as they have been called—showed a lack of enthusiasm for constructing their own prison settlement, determined instead to pursue the shiftless and degenerate ways they had always known. Quarrelsome, homesick, frequently jealous and uncooperative, sometimes ill, the marine guards and other officials contributed to the chaos. The indigenous Australians, aborigines who had

lived on the continent for centuries, at first expressed curiosity but later hostility when they realized that the visitors intended to stay and appeared set on disturbing the natural environment.

At times, Phillip, faced with such a multitude of problems, must have despaired. To combat the near starvation that plagued the settlement, he rationed food and put his own portion into the common store, insisted on continuing agricultural development in spite of repeated failures, and sent ships to Cape Town for supplies. To ensure discipline among the convicts as well as the marines, he dispensed punishment with a severity tempered by his well-defined sense of justice. To learn something of the land beyond the fringes of the coast and to secure it for the Crown, he dispatched exploration parties into the interior and established a settlement on Norfolk Island, 1,000 miles to the east. To form friendly relations with the aborigines, he ordered that they not be harmed and attempted to befriend them, although he understood neither their culture nor the crippling effect of European civilization on it.

Through the force of his leadership, the colony maintained itself for two years. In June of 1790, the Second Fleet arrived, bringing many convicts but few supplies. The subsequent ships, with their pathetic cargoes, compounded a situation that often verged on the hopeless. When Phillip, by then in ill health, sailed for England at the end of 1792, however, the worst days had passed. Sydney Cove, still a shabby outpost, was destined to become a great city, the land beyond a nation.

SIGNIFICANCE

Arthur Phillip was never to see Australia again, even though he lived for another twenty years, during which he continued to serve in the navy, married again, and received the rank of admiral shortly before his death. After retiring in 1805, he campaigned tirelessly on behalf of the colony he had founded, to the extent, in fact, that his pleas annoyed the authorities, who thought of Australia as a convenient dumping ground for England's undesirables.

Even as he supervised the creation of the rude penal colony, he foresaw a time when this land would be a home to free settlers. He encouraged the convicts who worked and reformed to take their place in the democratic society he envisioned. For those who did not, he had little sympathy. He believed, too, that the aborigines should have a place in this new state, giving up what he saw as their primitive ways and adopting the mores of white civilization. Above all, though, he looked toward the day when free English immigrants would come, not to exploit and leave, but to stay and build.

When Phillip died in 1814, his role in the new colony had been largely forgotten, even belittled by his detractors, and few took notice of his death. As the years passed, he remained a shadowy figure in Australian history. Now that Australia has begun to claim its history, recognition—so long deserved—has come to Captain Phillip: Australia's first governor, indeed its first patriot.

—*Robert Ross*

FURTHER READING

Barnard, Marjorie. *A History of Australia*. New York: Praeger, 1963. A general history that covers in detail and with clarity the events leading up to the formation of the First Fleet, its voyage, and the early settlement, stressing Phillip's important role. By giving the complete history of Australia, the book offers a look at the course taken by the nation Phillip envisioned.

Clark, C. M. H. *A History of Australia: From the Earliest Times to the Age of Macquarie*. Vol. 1. Melbourne, Vic.: Melbourne University Press, 1962. A scholarly work that provides excellent background on not only the founding of the penal colony but also the continent's history prior to European settlement. The chapter devoted to Phillip gives a detailed account of his background and his important role in the colony, along with an evaluation of his contribution. Subsequent chapters trace the colony's development.

Dark, Eleanor. *The Timeless Land*. New York: Macmillan, 1941. Although a novel, this work follows the historical events faithfully. The partially imaginative approach to Phillip's character succeeds in drawing a picture of what he may have been like in his day-to-day life. Treatment of the aborigines and Phillip's relations with them is especially revealing.

Eldershaw, M. Barnard. *Phillip of Australia: An Account of the Settlement at Sydney Cove, 1788-92*. Sydney: Angus and Robertson, 1972. As the title indicates, this study tells little of Phillip's life before or after his time in Australia, but it covers those years in minute detail. A well-researched book that relies on many unpublished diaries and official records; shows Phillip's interactions with the civil and military officials involved in the founding of Sydney Cove.

Frost, Alan. *Arthur Phillip, 1738-1814: His Voyaging*. Melbourne, Vic.: Oxford University Press, 1987. Frost has written several books about early Australian history and has collected and edited documents pertaining to the First Fleet and the colonization of New South Wales. His biography of Phillip goes into great detail about his life before he founded the Australian colony as well as describing Phillip's best known achievement.

Hughes, Robert. *The Fatal Shore: The Epic of Australia's Founding*. New York: Alfred A. Knopf, 1987. May well be the most readable of any book on Australia's founding. Although it does not concentrate on Phillip, the text surveys his career and attempts to define the nature and extent of his contribution. Covers the events that follow Phillip's tenure up to the time the penal colony was disbanded in the mid-nineteenth century and Phillip's idea of a free colony started to be realized fully.

Moorhouse, Geoffrey. *Sydney: The Story of a City*. New York: Harcourt, 1999. This history of Sydney includes information about Phillip's discovery of the site and founding a colony at Sydney Cove.

Taylor, Peter. *Australia: The First Twelve Years*. Winchester, Mass.: Allen & Unwin, 1982. Aimed at the general reader rather than the historian, this lively account depends heavily on primary sources written by those in the colony with Phillip. Unfortunately, these sources are not documented. Reproduces paintings and sketches from the period and includes photographs of historical places.

Tennant, Kylie. *Australia: Her Story*. New York: St. Martin's Press, 1959. A general history of Australia from its beginnings to the mid-1950's. The chapter "The Reluctant Pioneers" offers a succinct rendering of Sydney Cove's pioneer days under the guidance of Phillip. Excellent source for a quick overview of the period.

See also: William Bligh; James Cook; Richard Howe; Sir Alexander Mackenzie; George Rodney; George Vancouver.

Related articles in *Great Events from History: The Eighteenth Century, 1701-1800:* December 5, 1766-March, 16, 1769: Bougainville Circumnavigates the Globe; August 25, 1768-February 14, 1779: Voyages of Captain Cook; January 26, 1788: Britain Establishes Penal Colony in Australia; December 5, 1766-March 16, 1769: Bougainville Circumnavigates the Globe; July 22, 1793: Mackenzie Reaches the Arctic Ocean.

WILLIAM PITT THE ELDER
English prime minister (1757-1761, 1766-1768)

With his brilliant administrative skill and his magnificent oratory, Pitt was the architect of Great Britain's success in the Seven Years' War against France, making Great Britain the foremost maritime and commercial nation in the world.

Born: November 15, 1708; London, England
Died: May 11, 1778; Hayes, Kent, England
Also known as: Viscount Pitt of Burton-Pynsent; First Earl of Chatham; the Great Commoner
Areas of achievement: Government and politics, diplomacy, economics

EARLY LIFE

William Pitt's mother, Lady Harriet Villiers, was a member of the Anglo-Irish nobility, and his father, Robert Pitt, was a member of Parliament. At the age of ten, Pitt was sent to school at Eton, but he hated its brutality so much that he would later refuse to send his own children to school. He then went to Trinity College, Oxford, where he studied history, philosophy, and classics, but he left after one year without having taken a degree. For a brief period he considered entering the Church. As a younger son he needed a profession, particularly since his family was squandering the wealth that had been accumulated by Pitt's grandfather through trade with India.

In January, 1731, family influence secured for Pitt a commission in the King's Own Regiment of Horse. At this time the tall, lean young man with the Roman nose and large, intense gray eyes showed little ambition or sense of vocation. This state of affairs was to change in 1735. Pitt was selected as candidate for the parliamentary seat of Old Sarum, which was controlled by the political faction supported by his family. At the age of twenty-six, Pitt was duly elected to Parliament.

Before taking up his seat he spent the summer at the palatial home of Viscount Cobham, at Stowe in Buckinghamshire. Cobham was one of the leaders of the growing opposition to the fifteen-year tenure of Prime Minister Robert Walpole, and many of his supporters congregated at Stowe. Coming under the influence of these powerful men proved to be a crucial event in Pitt's life. His explosive, manic-depressive personality thrived on conflict, and he relished the presence of an enemy. Now he had found one. Filled with the grievances of the opposition, Pitt denounced Walpole's policies in his first speeches in the House of Commons. He spoke with extraordinary intensity, eloquence, and passion, quickly winning for himself a reputation as a fiery orator and dangerous opponent.

LIFE'S WORK

For nine years, Pitt thundered against Walpole in the House of Commons, arguing that Great Britain's commercial interests were being fatally damaged by a weak policy toward France and Spain. Pitt advocated war in the colonies and on the seas, and his dramatic and passionate speeches made him the most popular politician of the day.

After the fall of Walpole, however, Pitt failed to secure any important office. Instead, he accepted in 1746 a profitable although politically powerless position as paymaster of the forces. Some peaceful and productive years followed, but when Prime Minister Henry Pelham died in March, 1754, Pitt was unable to gain a more senior appointment in the new ministry. At the age of forty-five and in poor health (he suffered from gout in addition to his unstable mental condition), his prospects seemed bleak. An unlikely event helped him through this dark period: He fell in love with Hester Grenville, a friend from his childhood, and they were married in November, 1754. She was to have four children, and it was with his family that Pitt was to enjoy the happiest and most secure interludes in his life.

Pitt now turned to ferocious attacks on the government and was dismissed from office in 1755. The political and military situation was becoming rapidly worse. France captured Minorca, the British base in the Mediterranean, and amassed an army ready to invade England. In 1756, Pitt, who enjoyed overwhelming public esteem, was appointed by the king as secretary of state. He had finally attained the power he had sought for so long, and he came to office with an acute sense of mission, believing that he, and he alone, had the ability to save his country. In the five momentous years that followed, Great Britain was to become established as the foremost maritime and commercial power in the world.

Pitt's strategy was to fight a worldwide war, in the colonies and at sea, rather than becoming involved in a major European war. To this end he planned a successful blockade of French naval bases, which was to prove a major factor in Great Britain's success. He also strengthened the militia to resist a French invasion, subsidized Great Britain's ally, Frederick the Great of Prussia, and launched attacks against the French coast.

Pitt had ambitious plans for seizing Canada from French rule. It was an immensely difficult operation, involving the close cooperation of army and navy, as well as local Indian tribes. Pitt worked with unremitting dedication and energy, paying close attention to the smallest details of materials and supplies. He chose his generals and admirals well and inspired them with the breadth and daring of his vision. In July, 1758, came the first great victory, the fall of Louisbourg. Then Fort Duquesne was captured and renamed Fort Pitt (and eventually Pittsburgh). The following year, Quebec fell, and in 1760 the French surrendered Canada. A series of British victories, in the West Indies, on the west coast of Africa, in India, and on the Continent at Minden, completed the defeat of the French. It was a tremendous personal triumph for Pitt, and he found himself worshiped as a national hero. Pitt's acclaim, however, did not last. He was opposed to peace negotiations with France, and he wanted to extend the war to include Spain. When in 1761 he found that his policies were no longer supported, he resigned. This was a turning point in his life; never again would he enjoy such authority and success.

The peace treaty signed with France in 1763 angered Pitt; he believed that all the gains he had won had been frittered away. Three more years spent in vigorous opposition culminated in his campaign against the controversial Stamp Act, which had imposed a tax on the American colonies. Following the repeal of the act, Pitt's standing was as high as it had ever been, and he was swept back into office in July, 1766, accepting the title of earl of Chatham. His ministry proved to be a disaster. Not only did he lose public esteem by accepting a title, but also as a member of the House of Lords, he was no longer able to master the House of Commons with his oratory. He had also become arrogant and autocratic, treating his colleagues as subordinate clerks. The strain incurred by the frantic activity of the first few months resulted in mental collapse. For the remaining two years of his ministry, he was sunk in profound melancholia, incapable of taking charge of events. In the fall of 1768, he resigned.

In the following years he slowly recovered, and again became the spearhead of the opposition. It was a characteristic shift in mood. After long periods of despair and inaction he would become elated and once more possess the compelling power of the prophet and visionary. Now he argued vehemently, in the celebrated case of John Wilkes, for liberty and democracy against the arbitrary power of the House of Commons. (Wilkes was a member of Parliament who had been imprisoned for libel and had later been expelled from the House.) Pitt also advocated parliamentary reform. Yet his vigor was fading, and from 1771 onward he was able to play only an intermittent part in national affairs. In 1775, he turned once more to the alarming situation in America, and after consultations with Benjamin Franklin he drafted a moderate and liberal bill aimed at reconciliation. Had it been passed by Parliament it might have been an acceptable solution to the crisis.

Pitt made his final speech in the House of Lords in April, 1778. He opposed granting independence to America, a step he thought would ruin England. This final effort of an old and sick man was too much. He was carried from the House, and he died on May 11 at his home in Hayes, Kent.

SIGNIFICANCE

William Pitt the Elder was the greatest English statesman of the eighteenth century, the architect of some of the most important victories in Great Britain's long history. Indeed, it is sometimes said that the biography of Pitt during the years 1757-1761 is the biography of England itself, so completely was he in charge of shaping the des-

William Pitt, the Elder. (Library of Congress)

tiny of the nation. Pitt possessed the uncanny ability to project his gigantic personality abroad, to inspire a campaign that extended to all corners of the globe. He had the gift of selecting men in his own image, bold and wholehearted adventurers who shared his belief in the unquenchable spirit of the English people. The fruits of his endeavors long outlived him, because the Seven Years' War had long-term effects on the history of the world. It dislodged France from its preeminent position in Europe and laid the basis for the huge expansion of the British Empire, which reached its height a century after Pitt's death.

To the British public, Pitt was the "Great Commoner," the man who was above the sordid dealings of political factions and who did not court royal favor. Indeed, Pitt was the first minister whose success was a result as much of the esteem in which he was held by the public as of any personal following, or alliance with any political faction, in the House of Commons. He always prided himself on his independence. To a certain extent this was forced on him by his own personality. The personal qualities that made his foreign policy so overwhelmingly successful did not serve him well in domestic political maneuvering, which he never mastered. Egocentric and proud, he found it difficult to work with others on an equal footing.

Pitt was also a stern defender of constitutional liberty, not only in the Wilkes affair but also in the conflict between Great Britain and the American colonies. He believed that the colonists should enjoy the same rights as all British subjects, which included the right not to be taxed without consent. When the Stamp Act was repealed, his popularity in America was almost as great as it was in England, and it is probable that only a man of his standing could have spoken out so boldly for the colonists' cause.

Pitt's greatness thus consists not only in his mighty achievements in war but also in his defense of the liberties and rights of the individual; as he created a commercial empire for his country, he extended and reinforced a tradition of freedom that was to play such an important role in British history in the two following centuries.

—*Bryan Aubrey*

FURTHER READING

Ayling, Stanley. *The Elder Pitt, Earl of Chatham.* New York: David McKay, 1976. Excellent, comprehensive biography, full of insight and written in a lively style. Gives an accurate and sympathetic portrait of both the public and the private man.

Black, Jeremy. *Pitt the Elder: The Great Commoner.* New ed. New York: Cambridge University Press, 1999. Black explains how Pitt, a political outsider, rose to office during the Seven Years' War, and how England became a world power during his administration.

Brown, Peter D. *William Pitt, Earl of Chatham: The Great Commoner.* Winchester, Mass.: Allen & Unwin, 1978. Competent and objective biography. Brown admires Pitt's role in the Seven Years' War and also argues that the Pitt family strengthened parliamentary democracy.

Middleton, Richard. *The Bells of Victory: The Pitt-Newcastle Ministry and the Conduct of the Seven Years' War, 1757-1762.* New York: Cambridge University Press, 1985. Reprint. 2002. Argues controversially, and with the help of a large amount of original research, that Pitt's contribution to the war has been overestimated at the expense of the duke of Newcastle.

Peters, Marie. *The Elder Pitt.* New York: Longman, 1998. Part of the Profiles in Power series. Peters reassesses Pitt's career, raising doubts about some of his achievements, while acknowledging and explaining his heroic status among his contemporaries.

Pitt, William. *Correspondence of William Pitt.* Edited by Gertrude Selwyn Kimball. 2 vols. London: Macmillan, 1906. Pitt's correspondence, when secretary of state, with colonial governors and military and naval commissioners in America and the West Indies, 1756-1761. Gives a clear picture of Pitt's skill as a practical administrator.

_____. *The Love Letters of William Pitt, First Lord Chatham.* Edited by Ethel Aston Edwards. London: Chapman and Hall, 1926. Pitt's letters written to Hester Grenville during October, 1754, a month before their marriage. Although they have sometimes been dismissed as superficial and insincere, the letters reveal, underneath the ornate and artificial style, a genuine depth of feeling.

Plumb, John H. *Chatham.* Hamden, Conn.: Archon Books, 1965. Concise and lively account that traces Pitt's fluctuating personal and political fortunes against a background of eighteenth century politics.

See also: Frederick the Great; George II; George III; First Earl of Mansfield; Lord North; Henry Pelham; William Pitt the Younger; Robert Walpole; John Wilkes.

Related articles in *Great Events from History: The Eighteenth Century, 1701-1800:* 1713: Founding of

Louisbourg; 1721-1742: Development of Great Britain's Office of Prime Minister; 1739-1741: War of Jenkins's Ear; 1746-1754: Carnatic Wars; October 18, 1748: Treaty of Aix-la-Chapelle; May 28, 1754-February 10, 1763: French and Indian War; January, 1756-February 15, 1763: Seven Years' War; June 8-July 27, 1758: Siege of Louisbourg; February 10, 1763: Peace of Paris; Beginning April, 1763: The *North Briton* Controversy; June 29, 1767-April 12, 1770: Townshend Crisis.

WILLIAM PITT THE YOUNGER
English prime minister (1783-1801)

One of the longest-serving prime ministers in British history, Pitt did much to restore stability to British politics in the aftermath of the American Revolution. He also strengthened the office of prime minister, led the international opposition to revolutionary and Napoleonic France, and changed the constitutional relationship between Great Britain and Ireland.

Born: May 28, 1759; Hayes, Kent, England
Died: January 23, 1806; Putney Heath, London, England
Areas of achievement: Government and politics, diplomacy

EARLY LIFE

William Pitt the Younger grew up in an intensely political environment. His father, William Pitt the Elder (created earl of Chatham in 1766), was one of the preeminent politicians of the mid-eighteenth century and, in 1759, was at the peak of his career thanks to his association with Great Britain's greatest victories in the Seven Years' War. Pitt the Younger's mother, Lady Hester Grenville, was the sister of the Second Earl Temple and George Grenville, both important politicians themselves. Pitt the Elder fostered his son's interest in politics, and this became the younger Pitt's preoccupation.

Suffering from frail health, he was tutored at home before going to Cambridge University at the early age of fourteen. A younger son, Pitt trained for a legal career, but he retained a keen interest in politics and was present in the House of Lords in April, 1778, when his father collapsed in the course of his final speech. Pitt announced his intention of seeking election to Parliament before he attained the minimum age of twenty-one. He stood unsuccessfully for Cambridge University in 1780 but was elected early the following year for Sir James Lowther's pocket borough of Appleby.

Pitt thus entered the House of Commons at twenty-one and soon attracted favorable attention with his measured criticisms of the American policy of Lord North's administration, his advocacy of reform, and his calm and self-assured manner. After North was driven from office in 1782, Pitt was offered a junior position in the administration formed by the marquess of Rockingham. Pitt respectfully declined, letting it be known that he would have a major office or none at all. When Rockingham died in July, 1782, the second earl of Shelburne was asked to form a new government. The new prime minister had been a close ally of Pitt's father, and the young man accepted the position of first lord of the Admiralty.

Tall and lanky, Pitt had a thin, pointed nose that delighted caricaturists. Although he had a small circle of close friends, he was reserved in manner and was more often the object of admiration than affection. He was a lifelong bachelor with few interests outside politics or affairs of state.

LIFE'S WORK

Pitt rose to prominence during the greatest crisis in late eighteenth century British politics. The ministry to which he belonged faced the difficult task of negotiating a peace settlement to the American Revolutionary War. When finally negotiated, the draft treaty faced strong opposition from the unlikely combination of Lord North, who had been prime minister during most of the war, and Charles James Fox, who had been one of North's greatest critics and who now led most of Rockingham's former followers. Though many were shocked by such an unholy alliance, Fox and North between them controlled a majority of the House of Commons. In February, 1782, they defeated the treaty. Shelburne's government resigned, and George III was forced to call in Fox and North.

The king hated the Fox-North coalition, as the new ministry was known, but was forced to tolerate it. He played a waiting game, giving the coalition minimal support and looking for an opportunity to rid himself of it. His chance came in late 1783, when the coalition introduced its India Act. The controversial measure passed the Commons with a comfortable majority. When it reached the lords, George III permitted Pitt's cousin,

Third Earl Temple, to say that the king would regard any lord supporting the bill as a personal enemy. The upper house threw out the bill, and the king dismissed the coalition. It was a move of questionable constitutionality and one that the king would not have chanced without the prospect of an alternative administration. This he had, thanks to Pitt, who had secretly agreed to participate in the formation of a new ministry.

Named first lord of the treasury, Pitt was, in effect, prime minister at the tender age of twenty-four, the youngest in British history. He faced a hostile House of Commons controlled by his enemies. Nevertheless, with the king's support, he stood his ground, and, though suffering defeat after defeat in early 1784, he refused to resign. Eventually, he secured the minimum of legislation necessary to keep government going, and, in March, 1784, the king, at Pitt's request, called new elections. Pitt and his supporters won handily. While no eighteenth century government ever lost a general election, the degree of Pitt's victory was increased by a public opinion still offended at the union of Fox and North.

After the election of 1784, Pitt was secure in Parliament. During the next nine years, he did much to restore stability to British politics and enjoyed considerable legislative success in the process. The first major statesman to acknowledge the ideas of Adam Smith, Pitt gained a reputation as a master of government finance. He continued the reorganization of the treasury, overhauled the existing system of customs and excise taxes, established a "sinking fund" for the gradual reduction of the national debt (which had grown enormously as a result of the war with America), and had a commercial treaty negotiated with France.

Like his father, Pitt was a convinced imperialist, and his administration oversaw a number of important developments overseas that showed that the loss of the American colonies did not mean the end of the British Empire. In 1785, Pitt secured his own East India Act, which gave the British government much more control over the political activities of the British East India Company. Great Britain also became more active in the Pacific. Trade was expanded with China, and the settlement of Australia (as a penal colony) began. In North America, the old colony of Quebec was reorganized by the Canada (or Constitutional) Act of 1791. This established separate colonies of Upper and Lower Canada, each with an elected assembly as part of its government.

Pitt, however, was not always successful, especially as a reformer. In 1785, he introduced a bill calling for a modest measure of parliamentary reform. The Com-

mons defeated it, 248 to 171. Other initiatives for freer trade with Ireland and for an end to the slave trade also failed. Pitt took the reverses in stride. His calm outward appearance was little ruffled by such personal disappointments.

By the late 1780's, Pitt was the dominant personality in British politics. His position, like that of all successful eighteenth century prime ministers, was based on the simultaneous support of the king and Parliament. The former owed much to Pitt's rescue of George III from the despised coalition, and the king made available to Pitt all the personal support and powers of patronage that he had denied to the coalition. Fox's best hope of returning to power became the possibility that the king would die. This seemed a distinct possibility in 1788, when the king became dangerously ill. Pitt remained calm, outmaneuvered Fox yet again, and came through the Regency Crisis, as this political episode became known, unscathed. Pitt's sway over Parliament was based on his dominant position in the House of Commons. This dominance was based not on a party but on a combination of Pitt's personal followers, a sizable group of officeholders, and a large number of independent members who had confidence in Pitt's abilities.

Pitt's success at home was matched by an effective foreign policy, as he often took the dominant role in foreign affairs. His administration did much to restore British prestige in the aftermath of the American war. His greatest diplomatic triumph came, perhaps, in the Nootka Sound crisis, when Spain was forced to recognize a British presence on the northwest coast of North America. In the early 1790's, however, the French Revolution began to change the political landscape. Like most of his contemporaries, Pitt was slow to appreciate the significance of the French Revolution, and he initially welcomed it as something that promised to weaken Great Britain's traditional enemy. It was only after the revolution began to display aggressive tendencies and disturb the balance of power in Europe that Pitt became alarmed. Events flowing from the French Revolution dominated the rest of Pitt's political career.

In February, 1793, France declared war, adding Great Britain to its list of external enemies. By this time the revolution was entering its most radical phase, thoroughly frightening supporters of the established order throughout Europe. Pitt devoted himself to the war effort, but he proved to be less successful in war than he had been in peace. His task was similar to his father's in the Seven Years' War, and Pitt adopted a maritime, peripheral strategy with alliances that was roughly similar. Though there were naval victories and successes overseas (some of which expanded the empire), the French were increasingly victorious on the Continent and shattered the first two coalitions that Pitt helped to organize against them. By the end of the century, Great Britain was largely fighting alone against an expanding France led by Napoleon Bonaparte.

At home, the war was having a powerful impact on Pitt, the government, and the people. The financial demands imposed by the war threatened Pitt's earlier reforms and resulted in the introduction of the first income tax in modern British history. The war took on the trappings of a counterrevolutionary crusade to many and short-circuited any hopes that the 1790's would be an age of reform. Instead, with Pitt's participation, it became one of the most repressive periods in British history as the middle and upper classes increasingly viewed reformist activities as revolutionary agitation. The right of habeas corpus was suspended (from 1794 to 1801), while other measures effectively cracked down on political dissent by restricting the freedom of the press, broadening the definition of treason, limiting political meetings, and outlawing unions of workers.

The wars against France also caused Pitt to play a major role in altering the relationship of Ireland to Great Britain. Ireland erupted in rebellion in 1798; though order was eventually restored, all of the old fears about Ireland as a backdoor through which the French might pass were revived. Pitt was not alone in concluding that a semi-independent Ireland was a luxury that Great Britain could not afford. His solution was a union with Ireland along the lines of the Union of 1707 between England and Scotland. It required all of Pitt's political ability, as well as some outright bribery, to persuade the Irish parliament to vote itself out of existence. The union went into effect in 1801, creating the United Kingdom of Great Britain and Ireland and establishing the constitutional framework within which later controversies over Ireland's status would develop.

Pitt had hoped to make the union palatable to the Catholic majority in Ireland by following it with a general measure of Catholic emancipation (removing the remaining political and civil restrictions on Catholics), and advocates of the union had made liberal use of his sentiments. Pitt, however, was unable to deliver Catholic emancipation. The obstacle was George III, who believed that to sanction such a policy would be to violate his coronation oath. Faced with such royal intransigence—and a war that was not going well—Pitt resigned. He was succeeded as prime minister by Henry Addington. Pitt refused to go into opposition, though some of his followers did. Addington did succeed in obtaining the Treaty of Amiens, which lasted about fourteen months. With the return of war in 1803, however, there was a growing demand for Pitt's recall. In 1804, he returned to the prime ministership, making a promise in deference to the king's health that he would not raise the question of Catholic emancipation.

Pitt's second ministry was short, unhappy, and dominated by the struggle with Napoleon. Great Britain established its dominance at sea, but French victories on land destroyed Pitt's Third Coalition. Great Britain continued to fight, but Pitt would not live to see the end of the fight. The man whom Napoleon now regarded as the most implacable of his foes died on January 23, 1806. The war continued for almost another decade.

SIGNIFICANCE

William Pitt the Younger was the dominant political figure of the last quarter of the eighteenth century. He was integral to the restoration of political stability after the political chaos that accompanied the end of the American Revolution, and British politics was largely realigned into supporters of Pitt and his opponents, the Foxite Whigs. Pitt's first ministry was a tenure of power surpassed in length only by that of Robert Walpole. The son and nephew of prime ministers, Pitt had an important impact on the office. He did much to institutionalize the position of prime minister and demonstrated, when he ousted Lord Chancellor Edward Thurlow in 1792, that the prime minister could control the composition of the cabinet. (The major attribute of a modern prime minister that Pitt lacked was that of resting his claim to the office on the support of a party controlling the House of Commons.)

Pitt also left an imprint on his country through his administrative and financial reforms, his influence on the empire, and his refusal to admit French dominance in Europe. Other aspects of Pitt's legacy are more debatable. The repression of the 1790's provided a precedent for the even more repressive period after 1815. Also questionable was Pitt's Irish policy: Not only did it raise, in Catholic emancipation, an issue that would bedevil the next generation of British politicians, but also the creation of the United Kingdom provided the context within which the contentious Irish Question of the nineteenth century would arise.

—William C. Lowe

FURTHER READING

Bolton, G. C. *The Passing of the Irish Act of Union: A Study in Parliamentary Politics.* London: Oxford University Press, 1966. Best and fullest account of the creation of the United Kingdom. Deals with the act's origins and consequences, as well as its passage. Useful for putting Pitt's role into context.

Cannon, John. *The Fox-North Coalition: Crisis of the Constitution, 1782-1784.* Cambridge, England: Cambridge University Press, 1969. The best account of the circumstances that surrounded Pitt's rise to power, written from a neo-Whiggish point of view. Cannon shows that Pitt was more actively involved in the intrigues that led to the coalition's fall than was previously thought.

Derry, John W. *Politics in the Age of Fox, Pitt, and Liverpool: Continuity and Transformation.* 1990. Rev. ed. New York: Palgrave, 2001. This examination of late eighteenth century British politics describes how the government was resilient enough to withstand the disruptions of war, the French Revolution, and dramatic social and economic changes.

Ehrman, John. *The Younger Pitt: The Years of Acclaim.* New York: E. P. Dutton, 1969. Takes Pitt's career through the Regency Crisis, giving due attention to Pitt's political success during the 1780's.

_____. *The Younger Pitt: The Reluctant Transition.* Stanford, Calif.: Stanford University Press, 1983. This sequel to the above volume covers Pitt's life and times from 1789 through 1796. The emphasis is on Pitt's transition to war minister and opponent of the French Revolution. The product of immense research.

Jarrett, Derek. *Pitt the Younger.* London: Weidenfeld and Nicolson, 1974. Brief, well-illustrated volume in the British Prime Ministers series. A good introduction to Pitt and the major issues of his political career.

Mackesy, Piers. *War Without Victory: The Downfall of Pitt, 1799-1802.* Oxford, England: Clarendon Press, 1984. Study, by an eminent military historian, of one of the least successful phases of the war with France. Concentrates on war policy at the highest levels and sees Pitt's frustration with the war (and his cabinet colleagues' disagreements over it) as a more important factor in Pitt's resignation than the king's position on Catholic emancipation.

Pares, Richard. *King George III and the Politicians.* Oxford, England: Clarendon Press, 1953. The classic study of George III's involvement in politics, especially strong in its treatment of his dealings with his ministers. A useful supplement to Barnes in assessing Pitt's relationship with the king.

Reilly, Robin. *William Pitt the Younger, 1759-1806.* New York: G. P. Putnam's Sons, 1979. A solid biography that provides a generally well-balanced treatment of Pitt's life and career. Makes some interesting suggestions as to why Pitt never married.

Rose, J. Holland. *The Life of William Pitt.* 2 vols. London: G. Bell and Sons, 1923. Long the standard biography of Pitt, generally favorable in its assessment. Still useful, especially for its coverage of his later years. Gives a higher appraisal of Pitt as a war leader than most subsequent historians.

Turner, Michael J. *Pitt the Younger: A Life.* London: Hambledon and London, 2003. Focuses on Pitt's political career, describing how Pitt gained and used power. Turner defends charges that Pitt unconstitutionally suppressed radical activities during the French Revolution, arguing that Pitt's security measures were constitutional and limited.

See also: Edmund Burke; Charles James Fox; George III; Henry Grattan; Thomas Hutchinson; Lord North; William Pitt the Elder; Wolfe Tone; Robert Walpole.

Related articles in *Great Events from History: The Eighteenth Century, 1701-1800:* April 19, 1775: Battle of Lexington and Concord; March 9, 1776: Adam Smith Publishes *The Wealth of Nations*; July 14, 1789: Fall of the Bastille; 1791: Canada's Constitutional Act; March 16, 1792: Denmark Abolishes the Slave Trades; April 20, 1792-October, 1797: Early Wars of the French Revolution; November 19, 1794: Jay's Treaty; May 6, 1795: Speenhamland System; May-November, 1798: Irish Rebellion; November 9-10, 1799: Napoleon Rises to Power in France; July 2-August 1, 1800: Act of Union Forms the United Kingdom.

PIUS VI
Roman Catholic pope (1775-1799)

In an era when popes were secular rulers and often imitated worldly princes in their lifestyles, the adversity forced upon Pius VI by world events made him a respected spiritual leader by the end of his life. Thought by some to be the last pope, his example in suffering and humiliation strengthened the Papacy, giving it renewed vigor and setting a new direction for his successors.

Born: December 27, 1717; Cesena, Papal States (now in Italy)
Died: August 29, 1799; Valence, France
Also known as: Giovanni Angelo Braschi (birth name); Giannangelo Braschi
Areas of achievement: Religion and theology, government and politics, patronage of the arts

EARLY LIFE

The future Pius VI, Giovanni Angelo Braschi, was born in Cesena, about 60 miles northeast of Florence. He was the eldest of the eight children of Count Marcantonio Braschi and Anna Teresa Bandi. The family was noble but not rich. His early schooling was by the Jesuits at Cesena, and at the age of seventeen he received a law degree from the university at Ferrara.

Engaged to be married, he changed his mind and decided on the priesthood. Whether the breaking of the engagement was entirely his decision or was by mutual agreement is not clear, but in any event, he entered the priesthood and his former fiancée became a nun. He was ordained in 1758, when he was forty years of age.

Braschi's contemporaries describe him as having an imposing presence and great charisma. He was tall and handsome, vain, and not a man of great spirituality. He became the private secretary of Cardinal Fabrizio Ruffo and after a diplomatic mission to Naples was appointed papal secretary.

LIFE'S WORK

On July 21, 1773, Clement XIV published his famous brief *Dominus ac Redemptor*, suppressing the Society of Jesus (Jesuits). This was done in response to intense political pressure on the part of Catholic monarchs, who resented the power, wealth, and influence of the Jesuits in their lands. While the suppression was supposed to bring healing to the Church, it in effect was a victory for the forces that sought supremacy and control of the Church by the state in each of these Catholic countries. The pope

therefore deprived himself of a powerful arm in fighting state control of religion.

In the following year, 1774, Clement XIV died. The conclave to elect a new pope lasted more than four months. At issue was the ban on the Jesuit order. Some cardinals were concerned that the ban would be softened by a new pope; others were hoping for a reversal. The conclave finally chose Braschi, who had been the late pope's treasurer at the time of his death. Braschi took the name Pius VI. While he was well disposed toward the Jesuits, he overcame the opposition of the monarchs by letting it be known that he would not lift the ban on the order.

Since he was not a bishop when he was elected pope, Braschi could not immediately assume the Papacy: He had to be consecrated as a bishop before he could become bishop of Rome. The consecration ceremony took place on February 22, 1774, a week after his election. At the beginning of his pontificate, Pius VI was quite popular because of his programs of public works and beautification of the city of Rome. His popularity waned, however, when a nephew, Luigi Braschi, became a duke through papal money and influence and another nephew was made a cardinal. Allegations of financial irregularities were also made against the former treasurer.

In 1780, Emperor Joseph II became sole ruler fo the Habsburg monarchy. He pursued a policy toward the Church that became known as Josephism. It put the state in almost total control of the Church in Austria. More than six thousand edicts were issued regulating religious practices. All bishops were to be chosen by the state. All religious bodies, monasteries, and seminaries were placed under governmental supervision. Pius VI, thinking that the emperor, a devout Catholic, could be persuaded to soften his policy toward the Church, made a rare journey outside Italy to visit him in Vienna. This was the first trip out of Italy made by a pope since Clement VII traveled to France in 1533. In Vienna, the pope was received cordially by the emperor, but there was no resolution of their differences despite a month of talks.

In 1789, the French Revolution began. It soon produced legislation and decrees aimed at the Church. The Church was deprived of tithes, which amounted to 40 percent of its income. Church lands were nationalized and sold, and religious orders were suppressed. In July of 1790, the Civil Constitution of the Clergy was enacted.

This legislation reorganized the Church structure in France and provided that bishops were to be elected by the laity. The pope was merely to be notified of their election. The clergy were to become state employees. The obvious intent of this legislation was to nationalize the Church in France and to diminish papal authority to such an extent that the pope would be nothing more than a figurehead. The French clergy were required to take an oath supporting the Civil Constitution. About one-third took the oath, and they were suspended by the pope. Many of the priests who refused the oath emigrated to other countries.

In 1796, Napoleon I, who was then a young officer in the revolutionary army, was dispatched to northern Italy. After Milan was occupied by Napoleon, he announced that he would install a republic in the Papal States. The pope attempted to resist, but his forces were easily defeated. By the Treaty of Tolentino, the Papacy was required to pay a huge indemnity and deliver priceless works of art and valuable manuscripts to the French. Substantial portions of the Papal States' territory were also ceded. Shortly thereafter, a French general was killed in Rome during a riot in December, 1797. This gave the French a pretext to invade and occupy Rome, depose the pope as head of state, and proclaim a republic.

When the French arrived in Rome, the pope was told that he had three days to prepare for his departure from the city. Before dawn on February 20, 1797, the half-paralyzed octogenarian was hurried into a carriage and sent to Sienna. After a short stay in Sienna, he was removed to Florence.

The French government, concerned that a rescue attempt might be made and that his continued presence in Italy would rally anti-French forces, ordered that Pius be brought to France. Semiconscious, he was carried by bearers through the snow over the Alps. He eventually arrived at Valence in France, and being too ill to be moved further, died there on August 29, 1799.

SIGNIFICANCE

The pontificate of Pius VI was quite eventful, but there were few achievements attributable to papal leadership. For the most part, Pius was indecisive. His few initiatives, such as the journey to Vienna to resolve differences with the emperor, met with little success. Pius VI, however, was a good administrator, having risen through the

An etching depicting Pope Pius VI being reprimanded by God, in the form of a bird. (Library of Congress)

ranks of the bureaucracy. Artistic activities flourished in Rome during his papacy, obelisks were erected, and an opulent sacristy was built at St. Peter's. The Vatican museum was completed, and work started on draining the Pontine marshes.

Following the independence of the United States, it was appropriate that an American diocese be established. Pius VI named John Carroll as bishop of the new diocese of Baltimore. This appointment was quite popular in America, as members of the Carroll family were patriots who advanced the cause of American independence. Carroll's bishopric laid the foundation for a flourishing Catholic Church in the United States in years to come.

Pius's enemies gave him his greatest triumph. The treatment accorded to the pope by the French made him a martyr to his faith. Henceforth, the perception of the popes as monarchs was diminished and their spiritual leadership advanced.

—Gilbert T. Cave

FURTHER READING

Dully, Eamon. *Saints and Sinners: A History of the Popes*. New Haven, Conn.: Yale University Press, 1997. A beautifully illustrated book with a critical account of the Papacy.

Goodwin, Sister Mary Clare. *The Papal Conflict with Josephinism*. New York: Fordham University Press, 1938. A detailed and definitive account of the controversy between Pius VI and Emperor Joseph II.

Hales, E. E. Y. *Revolution and Papacy, 1769-1846*. New York: Hanover House, 1960. An excellent source for matter regarding the relationship between Pius VI and Napoleon.

Von Pastor, Ludwig Freihan. *The History of the Popes: From the Close of the Middle Ages*, translated by E. F. Peeler. Vols. 39-40. London: Routledge and Kegan Paul, 1952. The classic, standard reference for papal history translated from the original German work.

Wright, A. D. *The Early Modern Papacy: From the Council of Trent to the French Revolution, 1564-1789*. Essex, England: Pearson Education, 2000. An excellent source on the pontificate from the Renaissance through the French Revolution.

See also: Charles Carroll; Joseph II.

Related articles in *Great Events from History: The Eighteenth Century, 1701-1800*: January 19, 1759-August 16, 1773: Suppression of the Jesuits; 1775-1790: Joseph II's Reforms; July 14, 1789: Fall of the Bastille; April 20, 1792-October, 1797: Early Wars of the French Revolution; January 21, 1793: Execution of Louis XVI; March, 1796-October 17, 1797: Napoleon's Italian Campaigns.

MARQUÊS DE POMBAL
Portuguese statesman

The most influential statesman in modern Portuguese history, Pombal was an effective though despotic leader. He reorganized the economy, government, and society of Portugal in accord with the rational, secular principles of the Enlightenment.

Born: May 13, 1699; Lisbon, Portugal
Died: May 8, 1782; Pombal, Portugal
Also known as: Sebastião José de Carvalho e Mello (birth name); Count of Oeiras
Area of achievement: Government and politics

EARLY LIFE

The marquês de Pombal (muhr-KAYSH thuh puhm-BAHL) was the son of Manuel de Carvalho e Ataíde, a military officer and member of the landed gentry, and Teresa Luiza de Mendonça e Mello. Thus, in Portuguese tradition, he was christened Sebastião José de Carvalho e Mello. He studied law at the University of Coimbra and eloped with the aristocratic Teresa de Noronha e Bourbon Mendonça e Almada. The marriage was childless and had been opposed by her family. Teresa died in 1737. Carvalho e Mello was appointed the following year as ambassador to Great Britain and then, in 1745, to Austria. In 1746, he married the Austrian countess Maria Leonor Ernestina Daun, daughter of a renowned military leader, with whom he had five children.

Carvalho e Mello was recalled to Portugal in 1749 and, with the ascension a year later of King Joseph I, was appointed secretary of state for foreign affairs. Growing in the esteem of the new monarch, he was appointed in 1755 as secretary of state for the *reino* (kingdom), the equivalent of prime minister. He executed that office with a direction and force unprecedented in Portuguese history. Joseph confided to him virtually all aspects of government, honoring him with the title of count of Oeiras in 1759 and marquês of Pombal in 1769. It is by the latter title that Pombal has become most widely known in history.

Influenced by the Enlightenment, which he had observed and admired throughout Europe, Pombal resolved to apply rational administration to Portuguese national affairs. In the fifteenth century, Portugal had been at the forefront of the advance of Western Europe around the world, but its empire had been progressively checked and reduced by Spain, the Netherlands, France, and Great Britain. A second life had been given the Portuguese empire with the discovery of gold and diamonds in Brazil at the beginning of the eighteenth century, but over the latter half of the century, that wealth steadily diminished. It was to achieve a sustained and enduring development of Portugal's economy and society that Pombal resolved to reform the country in accord with rational, Enlightenment principles.

LIFE'S WORK

From the point of view of history, Pombal's career as chief minister has become synonymous with sweeping reform. In accord with mercantilist theories of the time, he considered Portugal's most serious economic problem to be its chronic trade deficits. The wealth of gold and diamonds that Portugal received from Brazil became a conduit to Great Britain. Portugal imported the bulk of its high-value manufactured products and trade services from Britain, exporting to that country in return lower-value agricultural products, especially wine.

During the first years of his government, Pombal established a series of trade monopolies to keep the prices of Portuguese agricultural products stable and relatively high. These state monopolies controlled products such as cacao, sugar, and tobacco from Brazil and wine from Portugal. Pombal also aided the development of Portuguese manufacturing to substitute domestic products for imported ones. His economic measures favored the rise of large businesses, disadvantaging smaller ones. Such measures also gave new political and social power to the bourgeoisie, weakening the traditional aristocracy.

Pombal's authority was greatly enhanced in the wake of one of the worst disasters in modern European history, the massive earthquake that struck Lisbon on November 1, 1755. Calculated as possibly having measured near a catastrophic 9.0 on the Richter scale (a twentieth century invention), the earthquake and consequent tsunamis

and fires leveled one-third of the capital. Acting swiftly, effectively, and imaginatively, Pombal and his team of architects and military engineers rebuilt Lisbon in a few years, making it one of the most modern and efficient ports in Europe. His administrative effectiveness empowered him to pursue his autocratic reform policies.

In 1758, a group of traditional landed nobility, led by the duke of Aveiro, attempted to assassinate King Joseph. The attempt failed, and Pombal had the conspirators killed or banished. The following year, he had the Jesuit religious order dissolved and banished from the country. He considered this group of clergy a "state within the state" that manipulated elites and controlled a stagnant educational system.

With the Jesuits dissolved, Pombal began a massive campaign to reform the Portuguese educational system. The curriculum and physical structure of the traditional University of Coimbra was changed beginning in 1772 to incorporate scientific and more modern philosophical subjects. A school for the children of the aristocracy had earlier been established in Lisbon with a curriculum emphasizing scientific and entrepreneurial values. The Indian mission schools of the Jesuits in Brazil were taken over by the state. One of Pombal's brothers was a chief administrator in Brazil. The capital of that colony was moved from Salvador to Rio de Janeiro in 1763 to keep government vigilance closer to the sources of gold and diamonds in the interior.

In 1769, Pombal reformed the Inquisition in Portugal. From a religious tribunal that prosecuted religious deviation and with the authority to burn heretics, he transformed the tribunal into a secular court for the prosecution of political opponents of the state. The new, secular Inquisition was headed by another of Pombal's brothers. Pombal had abolished slavery earlier in the decade but only in the Portuguese homeland, not in Brazil, where it was the crucial form of labor.

Pombal radically changed the Portuguese economy and state in many respects. In doing so, he accumulated numerous aristocratic, commercial, and clerical enemies, filling numerous jail cells with his critics. However, he was always protected by the support of the monarch, for whom Pombal had become the prime architect of royal absolutism, until Joseph died in 1777. When Joseph's daughter, Maria I, became queen, she forced Pombal from office. Earlier Pombal had attempted to block her from succeeding, because she was a woman. Pombal was tried for abuses of power and corruption, but the tribunal of judges was divided in its conclusions. Queen Maria urged exemplary punishment but tolerated the decision to banish Pombal to his estates because of his advanced age and fragility after a series of strokes. The marquês died just before he would have turned eighty-three.

SIGNIFICANCE

On the one hand, the marquês de Pombal left a legacy of considerable improvements in Portugal: He made the agricultural sector more productive, invigorated manufacturing, and redressed the country's trade deficit. He set standards for a scientific educational system, commercial values, and a service-oriented government bureaucracy. However, he effected these changes within a context of increasingly authoritarian practices that were ultimately prejudicial to his core objectives. Despotism ultimately repressed the core of small businesses and farms, the spirit of intellectual inquiry, and constructive challenges to the government made by its critics. Pombal maintained Portugal as a fundamentally corporatist state. What he effected was a shift in its corporate nature, from one dominated by a traditional aristocracy to a government in which power was shared by the landed aristocracy and a bourgeois oligarchy.

—*Edward A. Riedinger*

FURTHER READING

Boxer, Charles R. "Brazilian Gold and British Traders in the First Half of the Eighteenth Century." *Hispanic American Historical Review* 49, no. 3 (1969): 454-472. Traces the crucial role of Brazilian gold in the Portuguese economy and its export to Great Britain, transforming Britain into leading banking center of Europe.

Duncan, Thomas Bentley. *Pombal and the Suppression of the Portuguese Jesuits: An Inquiry into Causes and Motives.* Unpublished master's thesis. University of Chicago, 1961. Reviews scholarly literature regarding the motives, methods, and consequences of Pombal's hostility toward the Jesuits.

Galvão-Telles, João Bernardo, and Miguel B. A. Metelo de Seixas. *Sebastião José de Carvalho e Melo, 1º Conde de Oeiras, 1º Marquês de Pombal: Memória genealógica e heráldica nos trezentos anos do seu nascimento, 13 de Maio de 1699-13 de Maio de 1999.* Oeiras, Portugal: Universidade Lusíada, Câmara Municipal de Oeiras, 1999. A record of Pombal's genealogy, presented on the tercentenary of his birth. In Portuguese.

Maxwell, Kenneth. "Pombal and the Nationalization of the Portuguese Economy." *Hispanic American Historical Review* 48, no. 4 (1968): 608-631. Reviews Pombal's measures to make Portugal less dependent on Great Britain by strengthening Brazil within the Atlantic economy of Portugal and enhancing Portuguese entrepreneurial values.

_____. *Pombal: Paradox of the Enlightenment.* New York: Cambridge University Press, 1995. An updated and complete account in English of the life and work of Pombal by a noted scholar of Portuguese history. Richly illustrated.

Schneider, Susan. *The General Company of the Cultivation of the Vine of the Upper Douro: A Case Study of the Marquis of Pombal's Economic Reform Program, 1756-1777.* Unpublished doctoral dissertation, University of Texas at Austin, 1970. Traces the development of the port-wine industry under Pombal.

Theileman, Werner. *Século XVIII: Século das luzes, século de Pombal.* Frankfurt, Germany: TFM, 2001. Papers from a European conference on Pombal and the Enlightenment.

See also: Charles III; Frederick the Great; Joseph II; Peter the Great.

Related articles in *Great Events from History: The Eighteenth Century, 1701-1800*: 1750: Treaty of Madrid; November 1, 1755: Great Lisbon Earthquake; January 19, 1759-August 16, 1773: Suppression of the Jesuits; 1769: Pombal Reforms the Inquisition.

MADAME DE POMPADOUR
French noblewoman

As the powerful official mistress and confidante of Louis XV, Madame de Pompadour influenced French governmental affairs, both domestic and international. She was a dedicated patron of the arts and literature, and she promoted the planning and building of splendid palaces and pavilions.

Born: December 29, 1721; Paris, France
Died: April 15, 1764; Versailles, France
Also known as: Jeanne-Antoinette Poisson (birth name); Marquise de Pompadour; Jeanne-Antoinette Le Normant d'Étioles
Areas of achievement: Government and politics, patronage of the arts

EARLY LIFE

Jeanne-Antoinette Poisson, later known as Madame de Pompadour (pohm-pah-dewr), was born into a bourgeois family, the first child of Louise-Madeleine de La Motte and François Poisson, a military purchasing agent. Poisson was employed by the powerful Paris brothers, Paris-Duverney and Paris de Montmartel, who were government bankers. Paris de Montmartel was also Jeanne-Antoinette's godfather. In 1726, when Jeanne-Antoinette was five, her father was accused of black market wheat speculation, contributing to a famine in Paris, and had to flee the country. He remained in exile for the next ten years.

While her father was in exile, Poisson's mother received financial advice and support from Le Normant de Tournehem, a wealthy widower, financier, and tax farmer. Many believed that he was Jeanne-Antoinette's biological father, and he acted as her protector and guardian. From 1726 to 1729, she attended the Convent of the Ursuline Order. In 1730, the famous fortune-teller, Madame LeBon, predicted that the nine-year-old Jeanne-Antoinette would someday be the mistress of King Louis XV.

In 1725, at the age of fifteen, the king had married the twenty-two-year-old Polish princess Marie Leszczyński. By all accounts, the king remained faithful to the queen for ten years, and they had ten children. However, Jeanne-Antoinette and her mother believed the fortune-teller's prophecy. From 1731 to 1741, with financial help from Le Normant de Tournehem, Jeanne-Antoinette received the best education and prepared for life in high society. She studied singing, acting, dancing, the harpsi-

chord, embroidery, the art of conversation, and literature. Visiting the estates of her guardian and wealthy friends, Jeanne-Antoinette became known for her remarkable intelligence, wit, and beauty. She met Voltaire, who became her friend and admirer.

LIFE'S WORK

Le Normant de Tournehem arranged for Poisson to marry his nephew, Charles-Guillaume Le Normant d'Étioles, on March 9, 1741. She became Madame d'Étioles, and on December 26, their first son was born, but he only lived a few months. A daughter, Alessandrina, was born in 1744. From 1741 to 1744, Madame d'Étioles befriended many aristocrats, who introduced her to the leading scientists and artists of the time.

By this time, Louis XV and the queen had agreed upon a nonintimate relationship, and he had had numerous mistresses. In 1744, the king's then-current mistress, the duchess de Chateauroux, died suddenly. In February, 1745, Madame d'Étioles met the king at a masked ball celebrating his son's wedding. By June, the king had decided that she would become his declared mistress. However, she was a member of the bourgeoisie and had no title, making it impossible for her to be presented at court. Louis purchased the estate of the marquisate of Pompadour and Madame d'Étioles became the newly created marquise de Pompadour, or Madame de Pompadour. She obtained a legal separation from her husband. In September, she was introduced to the court at Versailles and became the official mistress of Louis XV, which she remained from 1745 to 1750, when the king tired of her and found other mistresses. However, Madame de Pompadour remained powerful and was the king's friend and confidante until her death in 1764.

At Versailles, Madame de Pompadour organized private theater performances and parties for the king, who preferred small, informal gatherings to pageantry in his apartments. During these two decades, she was adept at political manipulation, providing favors and promotions for trusted friends, and removing her enemies from positions of power. She had the authority to appoint and dismiss generals and ministers, and she supported the appointment of Étienne François de Choiseul, duc de Choiseul, as the ambassador to Vienna in 1757 and then as foreign minister from 1758-1770. Choiseul, however, helped maintain France's alliance with Austria, which kept France in the costly Seven Years' War (1756-1763), resulting in Britain acquiring most of France's overseas possessions, including Canada.

Madame de Pompadour also encouraged the king to construct new buildings and gardens and to renovate existing structures. In 1751, she selected Ange-Jacques Gabriel (1698-1782) to design a military school, the École Militaire, Paris. Gabriel became the principal royal architect, and over the course of forty years, his designs included the Château de Compiègne and the Louis XV Square (later called the Place de la Concorde). He also directed the regular remodeling of the interiors of the Petit Trianon, Versailles, and the Royal Opera. His long career followed the transition from the floral rococo or "Pompadour" style to neoclassicism.

Madame de Pompadour was a generous patron of the arts. A competent engraver and etcher herself, she sponsored the best painters, including François Boucher, Charles Vanloo, Jean-Baptiste Oudray, Maurice Quentin de la Tour, and Joseph Vernet. She also supported sculptors, such as Jean-Marie Falconet, Guillaume Coustou,

Adam Lambert, and Jean-Baptiste Pigalle. She commissioned portraits and sculptures of herself to create her desired public persona. For instance, in 1752, Jean-Marc Nattier painted a portrait of her as the goddess Diana. In 1756, Madame de Pompadour's favorite painter, Boucher, portrayed her as an elegant intellectual, with a book in her hand, a writing table nearby, and a bookcase in the background.

Although her public image was carefully constructed, Madame de Pompadour actually was an enthusiastic advocate of literature and writers. She promoted her friend, the celebrated Voltaire, who became historiographer to the king in 1745. She associated with numerous intellectuals, including Bernard Fontenelle, secretary of the Academy of Letters; the mathematician and philosopher Denis Diderot; and the historian Charles Duclos. Madame de Pompadour also defended the 1751 publication of the *Encyclopédie: Ou, Dictionnaire raisonné des sciences, des arts, et des métiers* (1751-1772; *Encyclopedia*, 1965) by Diderot and Jean le Rond d'Alembert.

She also supported French furniture makers such as Pierre Migeon, the cabinet maker who was also a dealer for other craftsmen. In 1754, Jean François Oeben came under the protection of Madame de Pompadour and was appointed the royal cabinet maker. In 1756, she helped establish the pottery factory at Sèvres, which became the Royal Manufactures in 1760.

On April 15, 1764, Madame Pompadour died, and on April 17 she was buried in the Chapel of the Capuchin Friars in Place Vendôme. Ten years later, on May 10, 1774, Louis XV died.

SIGNIFICANCE

Madame de Pompadour was the first French royal mistress to come from the bourgeois class, and she became one of the most famous and powerful women in French history. Her influence on politics and the arts extended well beyond her own era. Many blamed her for France's participation in the Seven Years' War, which greatly reduced France's colonial empire and the royal treasury. The expenses of war and the court extravagances encouraged by Madame de Pompadour depleted the government's financial resources. These economic problems were a major

Madame de Pompadour. (Library of Congress)

cause of the French Revolution during the reign of Louis XVI.

However, many of the splendid works or buildings promoted by Madame de Pompadour survive into the twenty-first century. Her Paris mansion, the Elysée, became France's presidential palace. The Petit Trianon, Place de la Concorde (formerly Louis XV square and home of the infamous guillotine), and the École Militaire are popular tourist attractions.

Madame de Pompadour's patronage of the fine arts, literature, the decorative arts, and furniture design resulted in some of the most notable accomplishments and masterpieces in those areas. Her "pompadour" hairstyle, in which hair is rolled or brushed back away from the forehead, was a popular style for both women and men in the early twentieth century.

—*Alice Myers*

FURTHER READING

Algrant, Christine Pevitt. *Madame de Pompadour: Mistress of France*. New York: Grove Press, 2002. This comprehensive biography describes Madame de Pompadour's role as a patron of the arts and emphasizes her political power and schemes. Large sections examine her ambition, Louis XV's dependence on her advice, and her role as prime minister. Extensive bibliography, color plates, and index.

Goodman, Elise. *The Portraits of Madame de Pompadour: Celebrating the Femme Savante*. Berkeley: University of California Press, 2000. This innovative study concludes that many of her portraits represent feminine intellect as well as beauty. Illustrations, bibliography, notes, and index.

Hunter-Stiebel, Penelope. *Louis XV and Madame de Pompadour: A Love Affair with Style*. New York: Rosenberg & Stiebel, 1990. Catalog of exhibitions held in Memphis, Tennessee (1990), and in New York (1990). The exhibits included objects and artwork of the decorative rocaille or rococo style that was favored by Madame de Pompadour and the king. Illustrations and bibliography.

Jones, Colin. *Madame de Pompadour: Images of a Mistress*. London: National Gallery, 2002. This beautifully illustrated biography was published to accompany an exhibition at the National Gallery. The book examines how Madame de Pompadour commissioned the best artists to promote and diversify her image. Color plates, chronology, extensive chapter notes, and bibliography.

Lever, Evelyne. *Madame de Pompadour: A Life*. New York: Farrar, Straus and Giroux, 2002. This general portrait covers her rise to power, personality, art patronage, political scheming, and relationship with the king and others. Illustrations, bibliography, and index.

Mitford, Nancy. *Madame de Pompadour*. New York: New York Review of Books, 2001. This entertaining biography provides detailed historical context, including fashion, customs, the nobility, manners, and genealogy. Illustrated. Bibliography.

See also: Jean le Rond d'Alembert; Étienne François de Choiseul; Denis Diderot; Louis XV; Louis XVI; Voltaire.

Related articles in *Great Events from History: The Eighteenth Century, 1701-1800*: 1721-1750: Early Enlightenment in France; 1737: Revival of the Paris Salon; 1743-1744: D'Alembert Develops His Axioms of Motion; August 19, 1745-September 20, 1746: Jacobite Rebellion; 1751-1772: Diderot Publishes the *Encyclopedia*; January, 1756-February 15, 1763: Seven Years' War; January, 1762-November, 1766: Mozart Tours Europe as a Child Prodigy; July 14, 1789: Fall of the Bastille; April 20, 1792-October, 1797: Early Wars of the French Revolution; January 21, 1793: Execution of Louis XVI.

PONTIAC
Ottawa nation chief and military leader

Pontiac was one of a series of great North American Indian leaders, including Joseph Brant, Little Turtle, Tecumseh, Black Hawk, Crazy Horse, and Alexander McGillivray, who sought to maintain independence for indigenous peoples of North America.

Born: c. 1720; along the Maumee River (now in northern Ohio)

Died: April 20, 1769; present-day Cahokia, Illinois

Also known as: Obwandiyag

Areas of achievement: Government and politics, diplomacy, military

EARLY LIFE

There is next to no documentation of Pontiac's early life, and many reports are conflicting. He belonged to the Ottawa nation by birth but was not full-blooded; one of his parents was either Chippewa or Miami. This was not unusual, as the Ottawas, Miamis, and Chippewa were friendly neighbors, and intermarriage was common. It is likely that Pontiac was born in the Ottawa village that in 1718 was still on the north side of the Detroit River but by 1732 was located on the other side of the river at the site of modern Walkerville, Ontario.

No accounts of his childhood or early adulthood have been preserved. Probably his youth was passed in typical Ottawa fashion. One of the first ceremonies in which he likely took part was that in which he received his name. An Ottawa tradition of the nineteenth century referred to him as "Obwandiyag" (the prefix "O" being a pronoun in Ottawa), and it is said that the name was pronounced *Bwon-diac.* "Bon" or "bwon" means "stopping"; thus, "obwon" means "his stopping," "stopping it," or "stopping him." No meaning, however, has been discovered for "diyag" or "diac." Pontiac was married, and he had at least three sons.

The Ottawa political and social organization was loose and rather fluid. The Ottawas had no single chief; instead, each village had its chiefs, both civil and military. The village would break up as winter approached, and family hunting parties would go in any direction. They would regroup in the spring, either near a French fort, where they would trade their winter's catch of furs, or in their village, where they planted crops. The Ottawa nation, like many other American Indian nations, was actually a confederation. There were at least four groups that made up the Ottawas: the Kiskakons, Sinagoes, Sables, and Nassauaketons.

It is impossible to describe the Ottawas of the 1740's, when Pontiac came to maturity, without also describing the influence of European culture upon them. By 1720, American Indians were already largely dependent upon French trade, which would become a large part of their culture. They relied on goods imported from France, such as steel knives and axes (formerly the American Indians had used stone), brass kettles (they had fashioned kettles from clay), steel needles (in place of bone), and fabrics. There were also novelties: guns, liquor, horses, and several new communicable diseases. Relations among indigenous nations had been altered drastically by the presence of Europeans and their forts or trading posts for more than a century.

As early as 1645, the Iroquois had attempted to replace the Hurons as principal middlemen in the lucrative fur trade, launching a series of devastating attacks that displaced almost every American Indian nation east of the Mississippi River and north of the Ohio River. The Iroquois annihilated several nations and pushed the Ottawas to the Mississippi Valley, where they encountered the hostile Sioux; the Ottawas were forced to retreat to the south shore of Lake Superior and eventually to the Straits of Mackinac. It is hard to conceive of the Ottawas in Pontiac's time in isolation from the French and other Europeans; the French had a string of forts in the Great Lakes dependent on Montreal and others to the south on the Maumee, Wabash, Allegheny, and Mississippi Rivers. Pontiac lived near the post at Detroit called Fort Pontchartrain.

Pontiac's life was indelibly marked by the outbreak of war between England and France in 1744, when he was approximately twenty-four years old. In the United States, this is known as King George's War, while in Europe it is called the War of the Austrian Succession (1740-1748). In origin it was a European quarrel, but once England and France were on opposite sides, fighting broke out between their colonies in North America for supremacy on the continent.

At the beginning of the war, the Great Lakes were so deep within French territory that the war barely touched the American Indians living in that region; the English, however, had already made contact with the French-dominated indigenous peoples at Sandusky Bay and on the Wabash River. There was sporadic fighting between the French and English throughout the next decade, with Pontiac consistently siding with the French. This warfare

Ottawa chief Pontiac. (Library of Congress)

culminated in the French and Indian War (1754-1763) and was absorbed into the conflict called the Seven Years' War (1756-1763) between the French and the British. French general Louis-Joseph de Montcalm had been defeated by James Wolfe on the Plains of Abraham outside Quebec in late 1759, giving the British nominal control of the eastern half of the North American continent.

LIFE'S WORK
The causes of Pontiac's War (also known as Pontiac's Resistance), which started in 1763, lay in the replacement of the French by the British in the region. In 1760-1761, each of the French forts on the Great Lakes had been taken over by a British commander. Most important, a totally new policy toward the American Indians was put in force. This was the real cause of the war, although Francis Parkman and other American historians following him have focused on different causes. Far from being a European war, it was largely American, beginning only when the European powers made formal peace with one another. The war continued until 1766; although it is identified with Pontiac and bears his name, the attribution is misleading, because Pontiac was able to

express the aspirations of many American Indians from a broad variety of nations.

Although Pontiac is known above all as a warrior, his major accomplishment was as a diplomat. Given the multiplicity of American Indian leaders, indigenous diplomacy was extremely complex. Diplomacy's fluidity and constantly changing nature has made it one of the most difficult domains for the historian or reader to grasp. In addition to the intricate, shifting quality of indigenous confederations and agreements, there was the constant interference of Europeans. If European traders found a village hostile to their advance, they often attempted to entice a few villagers to friendship and decorated them with medals, declaring them to be chiefs in the eyes of the "great white father" across the Atlantic Ocean; the proud, newly decorated "puppets" would return to their town and attempt to supplant the other chiefs or divide the town. This king-making was a standard feature of British "diplomacy" and, after 1779, of U.S. "diplomacy."

The great feat of Pontiac was that, despite the complicated fabric of relationships within and among American Indian groups, he was able to forge a strong alliance among disparate nations. By European standards, this alliance was perhaps weak, beset by constant defections, quarrels, and changes of allegiance, but by the standards of the peoples who were within the alliance—realistic standards—it was a remarkable achievement. Pontiac had many exceptional qualities: He was eloquent and persuasive, resourceful, loyal, stubborn, and intelligent.

The prime grievance of the American Indians of the Great Lakes and farther south was the new British policy concerning indigenous peoples. This appeared in a particularly stark light because of the suddenness of the change from French to British rule. For generations, American Indians had lived with the French, growing dependent on their material culture and accustomed to their habits. It would not be mistaken to see an analogy between the indigenous revolt against the British in 1763-1766 and the later colonial American revolt against the British in 1776.

French policy and practice were to mix with the indigenous far more intimately than the British Americans were willing to mix with them. The French colonists put a high value on peaceful relations with the American Indians; French officials gave them gifts during both peace and war, three or four times a year, and also provided them with a constant supply of ammunition. This became a key issue during Pontiac's War, because the ammunition enabled the indigenous to kill enough game to support their families. Not only did the French colonists live among the indigenous; they frequently intermarried with them. Many American Indians were biracial.

Perhaps the most important difference between French and British rule related to the concept of "land and title" of the two European countries. The French colonists considered themselves tenants in the New World, maintaining themselves in peaceful occupancy by making frequent presents. The British government, however, did not regard the American Indians as members of "the family of nations"; in consequence, the indigenous, in the eyes of the British, had no rights at the bar of international justice. The indigenous "tribes" were not sovereign nations and their people had no more rights than the wild animals that wandered over the land.

In 1760, British policy toward the American Indians was devised by General Jeffrey Amherst, and it is difficult to imagine a policy more likely to provoke war. (A respected American college bears his name.) Amherst ordered his officers and agents at the newly acquired forts to stop giving gifts to the local peoples and to deny them ammunition. For Amherst, the American Indians were conquered subjects. Even his own indigenous agent, William Johnson, was afraid to admit openly to the local peoples the nature of Amherst's new policy. Amherst refused to employ American Indians in the British armies, and shortly afterward, when the war began, his rage and inhumanity increased with each new victory of American Indians allied with Pontiac. He took no prisoners, ordering any indigenous person falling into British hands to be immediately put to death, "their extirpation being the only security for our future safety."

It was Amherst who first used smallpox as a weapon against American Indians, spreading epidemics among them by means of "gifts" of infected blankets. As a result, entire Shawnee and Delaware villages were liquidated. Amherst frequently referred to indigenous peoples as "vermin."

Pontiac's successes filled Amherst with rage, and he offered a reward for Pontiac's head; later, he doubled the reward. Such was the nature of the war between Pontiac and his major adversary. It was during the decade of the 1760's that the belief started to take hold among the indigenous of the Great Lakes region that the British wanted to annihilate them. Pontiac's message to the other American Indian nations was built upon the rejection of the British trade practices, British law, and the

concept of "private property"—in stark contrast to the American Indian notion of shared property—and, above all, British policy toward the indigenous.

There were other elements in Pontiac's appeal to the different American Indian nations that he skillfully played upon in speeches and appeals for help. A Delaware "prophet" called Neolin became prominent in the Ohio Valley around 1760; sometimes called "the Impostor," he was a visionary who exhorted the American Indians to purify themselves and live in their original state before the Europeans came to their country. By following his instructions, they could drive the white people from indigenous lands in a few years—there would be a generalized war followed by victory for the American Indians and a state of bliss resembling the Christian heaven. Pontiac shared many features of this vision and translated it for other indigenous nations in more practical terms. His relationship to the Delaware prophet could be roughly described as resembling that of Paul to Jesus.

Furthermore, important initiatives to revolt had already been made by the Senecas, the Iroquois tribe farthest to the west, who were accustomed to freedom of action in the area that is now western Pennsylvania; they soon became Pontiac's most powerful allies. A final element in Pontiac's message was the continuing alliance with the recently defeated French. He had warm feelings for the French traders, *habitants*, and officials who remained on what was now legally British territory. Although the French, in contrast, had an ambiguous attitude toward Pontiac, and officials tried to discourage his grandiose plans, they secretly sympathized with him—he was attempting what they had recently tried to do and failed—and many *habitants* and traders openly aided him.

The results of Pontiac's diplomacy were electrifying. British forts in the Great Lakes area and farther south fell one after the other. Pontiac laid siege to Detroit; Fort Sandusky fell, as did Presqu'Île, Le Boeuf, Venango, Miamis, St. Joseph, Ouitenons, and La Baye. The indigenous also laid siege to Fort Pitt (formerly Duquesne), but Detroit and Fort Pitt held out. Many British-American settlers were killed. Although none of Pontiac's larger objectives was realized, there were greater losses of soldiers on the British side than on that of the American Indians; at least 450 British regulars and provincials lost their lives in the war, while the British major Gladwin estimated that the American Indians lost one hundred warriors. It is impossible to calculate the number of civilians slaughtered on the frontiers, but a British official, George

Croghan, estimated that no fewer than two thousand British subjects lost their lives. On the other hand, a vast number of American Indians died in the epidemics created by General Amherst.

The forts at Detroit and Fort Pitt (Pittsburgh) were reinforced, and, slowly but surely, the British demonstrated their superior force of arms. Recognizing the reality of the situation, Pontiac finally capitulated. He never liked the British, but he advocated peace in 1766, even though many other American Indians continued to fight. Pontiac was virtually exiled by his own Ottawa village because his attempt to find a durable peace was not popular. Pontiac was assassinated in 1769, struck from behind by a Peoria Indian in Cahokia, Illinois, near the modern city of St. Louis.

SIGNIFICANCE

Pontiac's War marks a watershed in the fortunes of American Indians. Pontiac fought to restore the relative independence enjoyed by the indigenous under the French; he tried to force the British to change their policy, and he failed. His aims were largely ethical and conservative; he wanted the tribes to be sovereign nations, but he did not seek isolation. In essence, Pontiac fought for many of the values of the Enlightenment.

Some indigenous methods of warfare may strike modern readers as barbaric—torture, dismemberment, boiling, eating of the hearts of prisoners, and so on—but these must be carefully weighed against the violent methods employed by the Europeans. The indigenous war practices may seem picturesque, but their reasons are transparent: They were intended to increase the motivation of warriors. Furthermore, the American Indian practices seem quaint in comparison with the bacteriological warfare waged by General Amherst and his wholesale destruction of civilian populations, which ominously foreshadow twentieth century practices during World War II.

In Pontiac's War it was, above all, American Indian independence that was defeated. Ironically, the British Indian policy was inherited by the British-American colonists when they declared their own independence in 1776. One of the first acts of the United States was to nullify the old treaty boundary with the American Indians, and the new Americans inflicted a wound not only on the indigenous peoples—the "old" Americans—but also on themselves, denying some of the most basic principles of their own freshly written Declaration of Independence.

—*John Carpenter*

FURTHER READING

Blackbird, Andrew J. *History of the Ottawa and Chippewa Indians of Michigan.* Ypsilanti, Mich.: Ypsilantian Job Printing House, 1887. An American Indian account of the history of the two nations and the traditions that had been passed down to the 1880's.

Dowd, Gregory Evans. *War Under Heaven: Pontiac, the Indian Nations, and the British Empire.* Baltimore: Johns Hopkins University Press, 2002. Dowd reinterprets the causes and consequences of Pontiac's War. He maintains the issue of status was the root of the conflict: The British held the American Indians in low regard, and American Indian leaders believed the British failed to treat them with appropriate respect.

Franklin, Benjamin. *Narrative of the Late Massacres in Lancaster County.* Philadelphia: Anthony Armbruster, 1764. A subjective account—by an engaging writer—of one aspect of Pontiac's War.

Kinietz, W. Vernon. *The Indians of the Western Great Lakes, 1615-1760.* Ann Arbor: University of Michigan Press, 1940. An excellent source book that includes observations of American Indian life of the period. Many of the works are translated into English for the first time in this collection.

Nester, William R. *"Haughty Conquerors": Amherst and the Great Indian Uprising of 1763.* Westport, Conn.: Praeger, 2000. In this history of Pontiac's War, Nester describes the causes and battles of the war and the victory by American Indians. He also explains how, within a generation after this victory, another group of settlers and another war would eliminate much of what the American Indians had won.

Parkman, Francis. *History of the Conspiracy of Pontiac and the Indian War After the Conquest of Canada.* Boston: Little, Brown, 1857. The best-known account of Pontiac's War, written in a fine literary style and utilizing abundant sources. Parkman believed Pontiac was the initiator and strategist of the whole war. Subsequent information, however, opens this conspiracy theory to doubt. Pontiac's diplomatic achievement, and difficulties encountered, were greater than Parkman claims.

Peckham, Howard H. *Pontiac and the Indian Uprising.* Chicago: University of Chicago Press, 1947. An erudite, modern biography of Pontiac.

See also: Lord Amherst; Joseph Brant; Thomas Gage; George III; William Howe; Little Turtle; Alexander McGillivray; Louis-Joseph de Montcalm; Lord North; Thanadelthur; James Wolfe.

Related articles in *Great Events from History: The Eighteenth Century, 1701-1800:* December 16, 1740-November 7, 1748: War of the Austrian Succession; May 28, 1754-February 10, 1763: French and Indian War; October 5, 1759-November 19, 1761: Cherokee War; May 8, 1763-July 24, 1766: Pontiac's Resistance; May 24 and June 11, 1776: Indian Delegation Meets with Congress; July 4, 1776: Declaration of Independence; October 18, 1790-July, 1794: Little Turtle's War; 1799: Code of Handsome Lake.

ALEXANDER POPE
English poet and scholar

The major English poet in the neoclassical tradition, Pope also wrote critical introductions to his edition of the works of William Shakespeare and his translation of Homer's Iliad *and took up important critical concepts in* An Essay on Criticism *and other works in both verse and prose.*

Born: May 21, 1688; London, England
Died: May 30, 1744; Twickenham, England
Areas of achievement: Literature, scholarship

EARLY LIFE

Alexander Pope was born to Roman Catholic parents, his father being a well-to-do merchant. When he was small, the family moved, apparently first to Hammersmith and then, in 1698, to a small house on a large property at Binfield in Windsor Forest. The move from London was partly or wholly to avoid what had become a law forbidding Roman Catholics to live within 10 miles of Hyde Park Corner in London. Pope attended two Catholic schools, one near the home in Binfield, the other, oddly, at Hyde Park Corner. His regular schooling ended at age twelve. At about that age he became afflicted with Pott's disease, a lifelong problem both because of frequent serious pain and because it left him humpbacked and of very short stature.

Pope turned to writing verse in early adolescence, having read widely in classical, French, English, and some Italian literature. An early poem, which he sent to Henry Cromwell in 1709, made him known to a number of established writers; they encouraged him to seek a publisher for his *Pastorals*, written when he was sixteen years old and published in 1709. The resultant friendships caused him thereafter to spend much time in London. He never married, and while he had close woman friends, particularly Martha Blount, he almost surely had no sexual relationships.

LIFE'S WORK

Other poems quickly followed the *Pastorals: An Essay on Criticism* (1711). These included "The Messiah" (1712; published in Joseph Addison and Richard Steele's the *Spectator*, although Pope and Addison later became enemies), *The Rape of the Lock* (1712, and, in longer form, 1714), *Windsor Forest* (1713), the first portion of his translation of the *Iliad* (1715), and, in 1717, a volume collecting his works to date and adding two new poems, "Verses to the Memory of an Unfortunate Lady" and *Eloisa to Abelard*. All of these poems and all of his later important poems are in heroic couplets (iambic pentameter couplets, rhymed), the popular verse form of the neoclassical period and the form of which he was the outstanding master. ("Neoclassicism" is a term referring to the admiration of, and patterning after, the work of the ancient writers of Greece and Rome, especially Rome. Pope, for example, patterned some of his work after the Roman poets Horace, Ovid, and Lucretius, and he used some of the literary types that the Romans used, such as epic, satire, and epistle.)

Regarding the more important of the poems through 1717, *An Essay on Criticism* was the last and best of a long series of poems on literary theory and practice in Italy, France, and England during the Renaissance and the seventeenth and early eighteenth centuries, the more or less distant origin of which was Horace's *Ars poetica* (c. 17 B.C.E.; *The Art of Poetry*), although Pope's differed from all the earlier ones in being addressed to critics rather than poets.

The Rape of the Lock is the most delightful and important of English mock-epics, a popular neoclassical genre. It is a kind of mockery of the idle, fashionable, upper-class life of Pope's day, with the major characters, under fictitious names, recognizable to most contemporary readers as living persons. Its climactic point is an event that had actually occurred, a young man's "rape" (that is, the cutting off as a souvenir) of a lock of hair of a greatly admired belle—a trivial act but by no means regarded as such by the belle. The poem's later form includes, as actual epics do, some—in this case trivial though interesting—supernatural beings.

"Verses to the Memory of an Unfortunate Lady" and *Eloisa to Abelard* show Pope succeeding in writing emotional poems involving love and death, a type of poem of which he might not otherwise have been thought capable. *Eloisa to Abelard*, the more important of the two, is a dramatic monologue by a nun torn between her love for her former lover, who is now a monk, and her love for God and the Church.

During this period, Pope became a member of the well-known Scriblerus Club, with such other writers as Jonathan Swift, who became his closest friend, and John Gay. The membership itself and Swift's status as an An-

glican clergyman are evidence that Pope's Catholicism had relatively little effect on his social and literary life. The London literary world (which included some noblemen who were not necessarily writers) indeed became divided between his many, mostly well-known, friends and his fewer, mostly also well-known, enemies, some of whom he was to attack in his later works. Loyal and hospitable as a friend, he could be an acidulous enemy.

Pope bought a home on the Thames at Twickenham in 1719 and spent the rest of his life there, visited frequently by his London friends and also visiting his friends in London and many other places. His mother lived with him at Twickenham until her death in 1733. Besides his translation of the *Odyssey* (in which he shared the work with two assistants), his edition of the works of William Shakespeare, and his important philosophical poem *An Essay on Man* (1733-1734), his later work was almost entirely verse satire, the form for which he is most admired and of which he is the outstanding master in English literature. Opinions differ about the value of *An Essay on Man*, a long poem about humankind's place on Earth and in the universe, the purpose of which is "to vindicate the ways of God to man," but it contains many splendid passages and remains among his best-known poems.

Pope's satires include, among others, several based on specific epistles and satires of Horace, with the locales and the phenomena changed to contemporary England; *An Epistle to Dr. Arbuthnot* (1735), addressed to one of his closest friends, which includes his famous attack on Joseph Addison, the portrait of "Atticus"; and another mock-epic, *The Dunciad*, of which his enemy Lewis Theobald was the "hero," published in 1728, followed by an enlarged edition in 1729 and a new edition in 1743, with the "hero" changed to Colley Cibber, the new poet laureate, whose appointment enraged many of the important writers of the day. Pope's

---

THE APOTHEOSIS OF THE LOCK

In Alexander Pope's most famous and distinctive work, The Rape of the Lock, *the poet constructs a mock epic around a minor event, the theft of a lock of hair. In the climax of the final canto, excerpted below, the lock of hair finally, ridiculously ascends to the heavens, becoming a constellation in the night sky.*

> Restore the Lock! she cries; and all around
> *Restore the Lock!* the Vaulted Roofs rebound.
> Not fierce *Othello* in so loud a Strain
> Roar'd for the Handkerchief that caus'd his Pain.
> But see how oft Ambitious Aims are cross'd,
> And Chiefs contend 'till all the Prize is lost!
> The Lock, obtain'd with Guilt, and kept with Pain,
> In ev'ry place is sought, but sought in vain:
> With such a Prize no Mortal must be blest,
> So Heav'n decrees! with Heav'n who can contest?
> Some thought it mounted to the Lunar Sphere,
> Since all things lost on Earth, are treasur'd there.
> There Heroe's Wits are kept in pond'rous Vases,
> And Beau's in *Snuff-boxes* and *Tweezer-cases*.
> There broken Vows, and Death-bed Alms are found,
> And Lovers' Hearts with Ends of Riband bound;
> The Courtier's Promises, and the Sick Man's Pray'rs,
> The Smiles of Harlots, and the Tears of Heirs,
> Cages for Gnats, and Chains to Yoak a Flea;
> Dried Butterflies, and Tomes of Casuistry.
> But trust the Muse-she saw it upward rise,
> Tho' marked by none but quick Poetic eyes:
> (So *Rome's* great Founder to the Heav'ns withdrew,
> To *Proculus* alone confess'd in view.)
> A sudden Star, it shot through liquid Air,
> And drew behind a radiant *Trail of Hair*.
> Not *Berenice's* Locks first rose so bright,
> The Skies bespangling with dishevel'd Light.
> The *Sylphs* behold it kindling as it flies,
> And pleas'd pursue its Progress through the Skies.

Source: Alexander Pope, *The Rape of the Lock*, canto 5, lines 103-132, in *The Works of Mr. Alexander Pope* (London: W. Bowyer, 1717).

later work also includes a prose satire, *Peri Bathos: Or, The Art of Sinking in Poetry* (1727), and a series of verse "moral essays," parts of which also involve satire.

Among other skills, Pope was a master of the epigram. He has more entries in *Bartlett's Familiar Quotations* than almost anyone else except Shakespeare, many of which have become traditional proverbs. His epigrams include the following:

> A little learning is a dangerous thing
> For fools rush in where angels fear to tread
> Hope springs eternal in the human breast
> One truth is clear, whatever is, is right
> An honest man's the noblest work of God
> Damn with faint praise, assent with civil leer
> Who breaks a butterfly upon a wheel?

Pope died in 1744, a victim of his worsening bone ailment and of a disease of the kidney. He was buried in Twickenham (an Anglican) Church.

SIGNIFICANCE

Like that of most important writers of his day, Alexander Pope's life centered on the literary world of London and his broad circle of friends within that world. His important works run from *An Essay on Criticism*, published when he was twenty-three years old, to his final version of *The Dunciad*, published a year before his death.

Other major poets of the heroic couplet in the neoclassical period were John Dryden (1631-1700) and Samuel Johnson (1709-1784). Pope certainly learned from Dryden, and Johnson from Pope, but each has his own distinctive and effective style. Individual poems of Pope remain far better known to the world in general than those of Dryden, and Johnson's output as a poet was small.

With the advent of the Romantic period near the end of the eighteenth century, the work of the neoclassical period—especially the poetry and criticism—became unpopular and remained so throughout the nineteenth century. In the twentieth century, recognition of the quality and value of the neoclassical poets—and again especially Pope—was restored. The heroic couplet as a form, however, has never again approached the popularity of blank verse and other verse forms, and Pope's translations of Homer will almost surely never be as popular as the best blank verse translations. Nevertheless, Pope is now firmly established as one of the truly great poets of English literature.

—Jacob H. Adler

FURTHER READING

Baines, Paul. *The Complete Critical Guide to Alexander Pope*. New York: Routledge, 2000. Designed for general readers, this book provides basic information on Pope's life and writing, and places him within the context of his time. The book also outlines major critical issues in the interpretation of Pope's work and offers suggestions for further reading.

Barnard, John. *Pope: The Critical Heritage*. London: Routledge and Kegan Paul, 1973. Comments by eighteenth century writers and critics on Pope's individual poems and his work in general, ranging from a letter written by William Walsh in 1705 commenting on the *Pastorals,* to comments on Pope's definition of wit by Samuel Johnson in 1782, in a conversation reported by Fanny Burney. An astonishingly varied and useful work.

Guerinot, J. V., ed. *Pope: A Collection of Critical Essays*. Englewood Cliffs, N.J.: Prentice-Hall, 1972. An important early collection, including essays by Maynard Mack, W. H. Auden, Geoffrey Tillotson, and Allen Tate.

Mack, Maynard. *Alexander Pope*. New Haven, Conn.: Yale University Press, 1985. This lengthy and authoritative volume by a major Pope scholar of the twentieth century casts new light on Pope's life and should remain the standard biography of Pope for many years to come.

Mack, Maynard, and James A. Winn, eds. *Pope: Recent Essays by Several Hands*. Hamden, Conn.: Archon Books, 1980. A collection of essays by major scholars such as Ronald Paulson, Hugh Kenner, Patricia Meyer Spacks, Louis Landa, William K. Wimsatt, Paul Hunter, and Irvin Ehrenpreis.

Rosslyn, Felicity. *Alexander Pope: A Literary Life*. New York: St. Martin's Press, 1990. Concise, comprehensive biography about the life Pope described as "warfare upon earth." Rosslyn paints a sympathetic portrait of Pope, who overcame humble origins and physical disability to become the greatest—and richest—poet of his age.

Russo, John Paul. *Alexander Pope: Tradition and Identity*. Cambridge, Mass.: Harvard University Press, 1972. An important contribution to Pope scholarship, this book does an admirable job of interpreting Pope's life through his poetry and his poetry through his life. A major example is Pope's translation of Homer, involving his childhood knowledge of, and love for, the *Iliad* and *Odyssey*, his gradually developed decision to attempt the arduous task of translating the *Iliad* while still a young man, his problem of translating in a style suitable to both Homer and contemporary taste, and his extensive comment on the task in his correspondence and in his preface to the translation.

Winn, James Anderson. *A Window in the Bosom: The Letters of Alexander Pope.* Hamden, Conn.: Archon Books, 1977. An enlightening study of Pope's correspondence, covering such topics as his attitudes toward letter writing; his different styles for different people, such as noblemen, ladies, and adversaries; his adopting of various personas; and his successful efforts in getting carefully chosen parts of his correspondence published.

See also: Joseph Addison; William Blake; Fanny Burney; Robert Burns; Hester Chapone; Daniel Defoe; Oliver Goldsmith; Samuel Johnson; Mary Wortley Montagu; Samuel Richardson; Anna Seward; Jonathan Swift; John Wilkes.

Related articles in *Great Events from History: The Eighteenth Century, 1701-1800:* March 1, 1711: Addison and Steele Establish *The Spectator*; April 25, 1719: Defoe Publishes the First Novel; January 29, 1728: Gay Produces the First Ballad Opera; 1740-1741: Richardson's *Pamela* Establishes the Modern Novel; January, 1759: Voltaire Satirizes Optimism in *Candide.*

GRIGORI ALEKSANDROVICH POTEMKIN
Russian military and political leader

One of the most famous lovers of Empress Catherine the Great, Potemkin was also one of her principal advisers and military leaders. He was largely responsible for Russia's annexation and development of the Crimea.

Born: September 24, 1739; Chizovo, Russia
Died: October 16, 1791; Jassy, Moldavia (now Iaş, Romania)
Also known as: Prince Tavrichesky
Areas of achievement: Government and politics, warfare and conquest

EARLY LIFE

Grigori Aleksandrovich Potemkin (gryih-GAWR-yuhih uhl-yihk-SAHN-druhv-yich puh-TYAWM-kyihn) was born the son of a minor nobleman and army officer who had retired to his estate in the Russian hinterland. The family into which he was born was not overly promising, for his father had married a beautiful young widow while still married to another woman. Even after his first wife retired to a convent to make way for the new one, Aleksandr Potemkin was no ideal husband, proving violent and jealous and even accusing his wife of adultery and threatening divorce.

Grigori was a brilliant but mercurial boy. Consigned to the care of the deacon in charge of the estate's chapel, he played no end of mischievous tricks. However, the threat of being deprived of music quickly brought the boy to heel, and he applied himself to his studies with a fervor that alarmed his family. After his father's death, he moved to Moscow to live with his uncle and godfa-

ther. There he was able to study at Moscow University, Russia's oldest institution of higher learning. He also embarked upon a military career, rising rapidly in the Horse Guards and deciding to visit the glittering courts of St. Petersburg, the imperial capital. Although he was not overly wealthy, he was unwilling to appear poor in front of his well-heeled friends and quickly amassed substantial debts. This habit of overspending in the pursuit of high living would remain with him throughout his flamboyant life.

LIFE'S WORK

Potemkin's rise to power began with his role in the coup d'état that overthrew the incompetent Czar Peter III and installed his wife, Catherine the Great, as empress of Russia. He was instrumental in rallying support in the guards barracks, although his role in the coup itself is more murky. In an often-told story, Catherine was disguised in masculine garb that night, and when it was discovered that she had no sword-knot on her sword, Potemkin gallantly offered her his own. However, the earliest written account of this event has a number of notable discrepancies with known facts about Potemkin's life.

In any case, Potemkin came to Catherine's attention and she began giving him responsible positions and lavishing him with rewards. When she admitted him to court, he amused her with his talent for mimicry, even mocking her own strong German accent. Such boldness could easily have led him into grave trouble, but Catherine found Potemkin amusing and enjoyed the fascination she held for him. Her favor sparked anger, however, in her current favorite, Grigori Grigoryevich Orlov, and with his gigantic brother Aleksey, Orlov brutally beat Potemkin, leaving him disfigured.

Devastated, Potemkin shut himself away, even considering becoming a monk. Catherine herself took measures to bring him back to court, giving him various posts that would force him out of his self-imposed seclusion. He acquitted himself well in the First Turkish War in 1769, being promoted to the rank of major general, and was summoned back to St. Petersburg.

Having grown bored with Orlov by 1774, Catherine was looking for a new lover. After a brief interlude with another young officer, the empress summoned Potemkin to her bedchamber, beginning a liaison that would make him one of the most powerful men in all Russia. He shared her wide-ranging intellectual interests, and they made a formidable partnership, which some have claimed to have extended to a secret marriage. He proved a formidable adviser during the crisis of the revolt led by Yemelyan Ivanovich Pugachev, a disaffected Cossack who claimed to be Peter III.

Even after Potemkin no longer shared Catherine's bed, he continued to select potential new lovers for her. Throughout and after his relationship with the empress, moreover, he continued his own amorous adventures, seducing a wide variety of ladies of the court, and even his own five nieces. Although disfigured and no longer possessing a slender figure, he remained extraordinarily attractive to women, in part as a result of his positions of power, but largely because of his wit and intelligence.

Once his intimate association with the empress was over, Potemkin threw his energies more thoroughly into the work of building her empire. He might not share her bed, but his adoration for her grew all the deeper, and as a result he determined that she should have the most brilliant and glorious empire he could secure for her. As his military rank grew, he involved himself in far-reaching military reforms. In these, he showed himself a humane figure, calling upon officers to take care of their men in a spirit of paternal benevolence, rather than regarding them as little more than two-footed beasts to be flogged into submission.

In 1782, Potemkin began the project that produced the most lasting fame of his name, the annexation and mod-

Grigori Aleksandrovich Potemkin. (Library of Congress)

ernization of the Crimean Peninsula. At the time, the Crimea was an independent Tatar Khanate, Muslim and to a degree friendly with Turkey but not entirely in accord with the sultan. So long as the Crimea Khanate remained independent, it could threaten the open steppe of the Ukraine, long a source of instability because of its strong Cossack nationalism. Although Potemkin himself was afflicted with persistent ill health throughout the Crimean campaign, by 1783 he had broken down the last resistance among the Tatar tribes there, and formal annexation of the peninsula soon followed.

Potemkin then set about a program of building, creating the city of Sebastopol from the ground up as a major harbor and naval base and greatly improving a number of existing cities. He also constructed a number of ships to become the nucleus of a new Black Sea Fleet, although Catherine rebuked him when he proposed to name the flagship in her honor, warning him that it was better to be, than to appear to be but not be. However, he did not take that warning to heart, for he then set about creating a magnificent new city, Yekaterinoslav, on the banks of the Dnieper, when funds and materials were still woefully inadequate for the realization of his plans.

Potemkin was such a consummate showman that he could sweep visitors up in his visions for his new cities, to the point that they could imagine that they saw beautiful avenues and stately buildings where only muddy tracks and wooden hovels stood. When Catherine herself made a tour of inspection in 1787, Potemkin paid particular attention to beautifying the route she would follow, even at the expense of areas she would not see. However, modern scholars have questioned the extent to which he actually produced a false front of beauty over actual squalor, as the common expression "Potemkin village" implies.

In gratitude for his work in the Crimea, Catherine granted Potemkin the title of prince of Taurida (an old name for the region) and authorized the construction of the Tauride Palace in St. Petersburg. Potemkin continued his work of building and diplomacy in Russia's southern lands, and in 1791, while on his way to peace talks in Jassy, he contracted typhoid and died.

SIGNIFICANCE

Potemkin's name has been immortalized in the expression "Potemkin village," which originally referred to his beautification of the Crimea for his empress's visit but has since been expanded to refer to any sham set up for the benefit of a visiting observer. However, there appears to be little evidence that he actually went so far as to strip entire areas of their population in order to line them up in front of false facades while the empress passed, then disassemble them like so many Hollywood sets and relocate them a few miles farther along the road, just in time for the empress's arrival at the next village. These stories first appeared in the journals of a courtier known to hold considerable animosity for Potemkin and show evidence of being deliberately fabricated to damage Potemkin's reputation.

More lastingly, Potemkin's name was given to a battleship that became the site of a famous mutiny during the 1905 revolution, which was often called a dress rehearsal for the 1917 revolution that ultimately toppled the Romanov Dynasty and opened the way for the Bolshevik takeover later that year. The event was immortalized in 1925 by Sergei Eisenstein in a silent movie, and as a result the name "Potemkin" has become more closely associated with the battleship and its mutiny, eclipsing the original owner of the name.

—Leigh Husband Kimmel

FURTHER READING

Alexander, John T. *Catherine the Great: Life and Legend.* New York: Oxford University Press, 1989. Biography includes considerable discussion of Potemkin's role in Catherine's life.

Catherine II et al. *Love and Conquest: Personal Correspondence of Catherine the Great and Prince Grigory Potemkin.* DeKalb: Northern Illinois University Press, 2004. Excellent collection of primary source material sheds light on their intimate relationship.

Montefiore, Simon Sebag. *Potemkin: Catherine the Great's Imperial Partner.* New York: Vintage, 2005. Looks at primary sources with a modern sensibility untainted by the prudery of intervening ages.

Soloveytchik, George. *Potemkin: Soldier, Statesman, Lover, and Consort of Catherine of Russia.* New York: Norton, 1947. Classic source, still good for basic overview of Potemkin's life, useful also for an understanding of how earlier generations viewed the libertine side of his life.

See also: Catherine the Great; Elizabeth Petrovna; Mikhail Illarionovich Kutuzov; Aleksey Grigoryevich Orlov; Grigori Grigoryevich Orlov; Peter the Great; Peter III; Yemelyan Ivanovich Pugachev; Aleksandr Vasilyevich Suvorov.

Related articles in *Great Events from History: The Eighteenth Century, 1701-1800*: August 10, 1767: Catherine the Great's Instruction; October, 1768-January 9, 1792: Ottoman Wars with Russia; September, 1773-September, 1774: Pugachev's Revolt.

JOSEPH PRIESTLEY
English scientist and scholar

One of the eighteenth century's significant experimental scientists, Priestley was a supporter of civic and religious liberty who wrote extensively in a variety of scientific, educational, religious, and philosophical areas.

Born: March 13, 1733; Birstall Fieldhead, Yorkshire (now West Yorkshire), England
Died: February 6, 1804; Northumberland, Pennsylvania
Areas of achievement: Religion and theology, science and technology, philosophy, scholarship

EARLY LIFE

Joseph Priestley's father, Jonas Priestley, was a weaver and cloth dresser, while his mother, née Mary Swift, was the only daughter of a Yorkshire farmer. The eldest of six children, young Joseph, after the death of his mother in 1739, was adopted by Sarah Keighley, his father's sister. Reared in a Dissenting atmosphere, Priestley was brought into contact with a variety of religious and philosophical ideas that challenged conventional norms. Perhaps because of recurring illnesses during this period, Priestley became an avid reader interested in a diverse range of topics.

Priestley's schooling was a combination of classroom activity, independent study, and work with tutors. At an early age, he became proficient in philosophy, mathematics, and a number of ancient and modern languages. In 1752, he entered the newly established Daventry Academy, an institution that fixed his independent thought. In addition to the required curriculum, he pursued his own interests in history, science, and philosophy. Priestley acknowledged that David Hartley's *Observations on Man, His Frame, His Duty, and His Expectations* had an especially important influence, as did Caleb Ashworth, the director of the academy, and Samuel Clark, one of the tutors. It was during this period that Priestley was convinced of the potential for the perfectibility of humankind through proper education and development.

In 1755, Priestley became minister for the small Dissenting congregation of Needham Market in Suffolk. He was not altogether happy, however, as members of his flock opposed his Arian ideas. This opposition led him, in 1758, to move to another congregation at Nantwich in Cheshire. There he operated a small school and pursued a variety of scientific experiments dealing with air and static electricity. Increasingly, he saw science as a tool to improve human life. Several years later, Priestley was appointed tutor in languages and literature at Warrington Academy in Lancashire, a famous and innovative Dissenting academy, and in 1762, he married Mary Wilkinson. They had a happy marriage, rearing three sons and a daughter, until Mary's death in 1796.

LIFE'S WORK

Joseph Priestley firmly believed that humanity could be improved through education and through a proper understanding of the physical and spiritual worlds. During his tenure at Warrington, from 1761 to 1767, he published speculative and scientific works in a variety of fields in which he was to maintain interest throughout his life. In the realm of education, Priestley argued that schools should be designed to serve the needs of contemporary society rather than follow slavishly the classical models of the past. In *The Rudiments of English Grammar* (1761), he stressed contemporary usage rather than an imitation of classical style. In *An Essay on a Course of Liberal Education for Civil and Active Life* (1765), he argued that contemporary subjects such as modern history and languages, public administration, and science were better suited to Dissenters than the classics. The University of Edinburgh awarded him the doctor of laws degree for his popular *A Chart of Biography* (1765), a work that portrayed the succession of eminent men throughout the ages.

His work in a number of areas in science during this period and his experiments and progress with electricity won for him election to the Royal Society in 1766. In *The History and Present State of Electricity* (1767), Priestley described many of his own experiments as well as those of others in an effort to show the development of humanity in discovering and directing the forces of nature.

In 1767, Priestley accepted a position as minister in Leeds, which gave him far more time for experimenting and for writing in areas as diverse as theology, science, and politics. His religious writings included a number of works on rational religion as well as attacks on traditional dogma; the latter incurred the ire of many of his contemporaries. Most notable among these writings was the three-volume *Institutes of Natural and Revealed Religions* (1772-1774), which he had begun during his student days at Daventry. He also founded the *Theological Repository*, a journal of biblical criticism.

Priestley's work in science continued unabated. As the first part of a projected history of experimental philosophy, he published *The History and Present State of Discoveries Relating to Vision, Light, and Colours* (1772). After this first work, the project was never continued. His numerous and significant studies of the properties of gases laid the foundations for modern chemistry. In August, 1774, he discovered oxygen, although because of his persistent belief in the phlogiston theory, he never fully understood the implications of the discovery.

Priestley also published a series of political writings that stressed themes similar to those of his theological works: civil liberty, social responsibility, and the potential for human perfectibility. In *An Essay on the First Principles of Government and on the Nature of Political, Civil, and Religious Liberty* (1768), he argued that both freedom of conscience and civic liberty were fundamental to the welfare of society. At the same time, he contended that political liberty should be extended only to those who would support the welfare of society as a whole. His support of John Wilkes in an anonymous

Joseph Priestley. (Library of Congress)

pamphlet of 1769 and his criticism of the government for attempting to deprive Americans of their rights as Englishmen made him suspect to the authorities.

From 1773 to 1780, Priestley served the earl of Shelburne as librarian and supervised the education of Shelburne's two sons. This post gave him considerable free time for study and writing and brought him into contact with a variety of important persons. During this period of estrangement and then war with the Americans, he generally avoided political topics, instead concentrating on his scientific work as well as on metaphysics and theology. He defended theories of materialism, while rejecting atheism; God's existence could be seen through design, though not necessarily through revelation.

The decade of the 1780's was a crucial one for Priestley. He was recognized as one of Great Britain's important men of science. He also was frequently in the public eye because of his attacks on revealed religion and his challenges to the established order. In 1780, he terminated his relationship with Shelburne and settled in Birmingham, near his brother-in-law, John Wilkinson. While there, he became close to a circle of distinguished men in the Lunar Society, a group of individuals who actively promoted the application of science to society, and continued his investigations into the nature of gases, electricity, and acids.

During this period, Priestley increasingly became identified as a disruptive force in society. His frequent defenses of Unitarianism and attacks on scriptural inspiration, the Trinity, and the nature of Jesus Christ brought him into conflict with clerics. Some of his comments in opposition to the Test and Corporation Acts seemed to suggest that he was a threat to the established political order, although he stressed that he advocated change through persuasion rather than through force. The rising disorder of the late 1780's, coupled with the outbreak of the French Revolution in 1789, reinforced societal suspicions of voices of dissent.

In a strong attack on Edmund Burke, Priestley expressed his support of the French Revolution; he suggested that the revolution would lead to the triumph of reason and thus bring "the extinction of all national prejudices and enmity, and the establishment of universal peace and good-will among all nationals." In *A Political Dialogue on the General Principles of Government* (1791), he called for a reform of the House of Commons that would allow that body to serve as the popular voice of the people.

It was doubtless Priestley's association in the popular mind with the events in France as well as his championing of unorthodox religious ideas that caused him to be singled out by the Birmingham rioters in July, 1791. Priestley's home and laboratory were destroyed, as were most of his scientific equipment, papers, and books.

Although Priestley had hoped to return to Birmingham after the riots, continued hostility made this impossible. He settled at Hackney, near London, and taught history and science at the New College (Hackney College). Although he sought to retain a low profile, the growing estrangement between Great Britain and France and the execution of Louis XVI made his position untenable. In the spring of 1794, Priestley and his wife emigrated to America, where their sons already lived, hoping to find greater freedom for his intellectual pursuits.

Yet Priestley's life in the United States, where he spent his last years, was filled with some of the same tensions that he had left behind. Clergymen attacked his ideas, and the intolerance of the Alien and Sedition Acts alarmed him. His defense of his political and religious ideas in *Letters to the Inhabitants of Northumberland and Its Neighbourhood* (1799) was in many ways a recapitulation of ideas he had long held. Although he wrote a large number of scientific papers during this period, they were generally of little substance. He died on February 6, 1804, in Northumberland, Pennsylvania, and was interred in the local Quaker burial ground.

SIGNIFICANCE

In many ways Joseph Priestley embodied the spirit of the eighteenth century. A man of broad interests and an effective writer, Priestley published extensively on the subjects of education, metaphysics, theology, history, physics, chemistry, and politics. He was convinced that science and its applications could improve humankind and that creating a synthesis of revealed religion and natural science would further contribute to social and material progress. A supporter of religious and civil liberties, he wrote important essays on those topics and became a prominent victim of the intolerance of the late eighteenth century. An active experimenter and contributor to the development of the new science of chemistry, he was unwilling to abandon some of his theories and thus become part of that new science.

—Robert D. Fiala

FURTHER READING

Davis, Kenneth S. *The Cautionary Scientists: Priestley, Lavoisier, and the Founding of Modern Chemistry.* New York: G. P. Putnam's Sons, 1966. A popularly written and useful account of these two important fig-

ures of eighteenth century science. Successfully portrays the intellectual and social milieu of the British and French societies in which they lived and describes their contributions to the scientific tradition.

Gibbs, F. W. *Joseph Priestley: Revolutions of the Eighteenth Century.* Garden City, N.Y.: Doubleday, 1965. The most accurate and readable of the biographies of Priestley, although it lacks an analysis of Priestley and his ideas. Contains many excerpts from contemporary documents.

Graham, Jenny. *Revolutionary in Exile: The Emigration of Joseph Priestley to America, 1794-1804.* Philadelphia: American Philosophical Society, 1995. Examines Priestley's career before and after he emigrated to the United States. Graham explains why he left England, his involvement in American politics, and his influence on Thomas Jefferson. The appendix includes correspondence between Priestley and American statesmen.

Kieft, Lester, ed. *Joseph Priestley: Scientist, Theologian, and Metaphysician.* Lewisburg, Pa.: Bucknell University Press, 1980. The most valuable analytical studies of three major facets of Priestley's career by three leading scholars of science: Erwin N. Hiebert, Aaron J. Ihde, and Robert E. Schofield.

Priestley, Joseph. *Autobiography of Joseph Priestley.* Edited by Jack Lindsay. Rutherford, N.J.: Fairleigh Dickinson University Press, 1970. With a very useful introduction by Lindsay, this book contains the *Memoirs of Dr. Joseph Priestley*, 1806.

_____. *A Scientific Autobiography of Joseph Priestley, 1733-1804: Selected Scientific Correspondence, with Commentary.* Edited by Robert E. Schofield. Cambridge, Mass.: MIT Press, 1966. A virtually complete collection of Priestley's scientific statements. Invaluable for a study of this aspect of his career.

Schofield, Robert E. *The Enlightenment of Joseph Priestley: A Study of His Life and Work from 1733 to 1773.* University Park: Pennsylvania State University Press, 1997.

_____. *The Enlightened Joseph Priestley: A Study of His Life and Work from 1773 to 1804.* University Park: Pennsylvania State University Press, 2004. A comprehensive two-volume biography written by a leading Priestley authority. The first volume recounts Priestley's early years in England; the second volume describes the final forty years of his life, with discussions of his discovery of oxygen, his activism in the Unitarian Church, and his life in the United States.

Uglow, Jenny. *The Lunar Men: Five Friends Whose Curiosity Changed the World.* New York: Farrar, Straus, and Giroux, 2002. Describes how Priestley and other inventors and scientists formed the Lunar Society of Birmingham in the late 1700's. The group's members shared ideas for creating technological and scientific innovations and helped usher in the Industrial Revolution in Great Britain.

See also: Anna Barbauld; Matthew Boulton; Edmund Burke; Henry Cavendish; Benjamin Franklin; Thomas Jefferson; Nicolas Leblanc; Louis XVI; Alessandro Volta; James Watt.

Related articles in *Great Events from History: The Eighteenth Century, 1701-1800:* 1718: Geoffroy Issues the *Table of Reactivities*; 1723: Stahl Postulates the Phlogiston Theory; 1729: Gray Discovers Principles of Electric Conductivity; 1733: Du Fay Discovers Two Kinds of Electric Charge; 1738: Bernoulli Proposes the Kinetic Theory of Gases; June, 1752: Franklin Demonstrates the Electrical Nature of Lightning; June 5, 1755: Black Identifies Carbon Dioxide; 1757: Monro Distinguishes Between Lymphatic and Blood Systems; 1765-1769: Watt Develops a More Effective Steam Engine; 1771: Woulfe Discovers Picric Acid; August 1, 1774: Priestley Discovers Oxygen; 1779: Ingenhousz Discovers Photosynthesis; 1781-1784: Cavendish Discovers the Composition of Water; 1786-1787: Lavoisier Devises the Modern System of Chemical Nomenclature; 1789: Leblanc Develops Soda Production; 1800: Volta Invents the Battery.

YEMELYAN IVANOVICH PUGACHEV
Russian rebel leader

Pugachev led one of the greatest Cossack rebellions against the Russian monarchy, threatening but ultimately strengthening the reign of Catherine the Great, who tightened her control over Russia in the aftermath of the failed revolt.

Born: c. 1742; Zimoveiskaya, Don River Basin, Russia
Died: January 21, 1775; Moscow, Russia
Also known as: Yemelyn Ivanovich Pugachov
Areas of achievement: Government and politics, warfare and conquest

EARLY LIFE

Yemelyan Ivanovich Pugachev (yihm-yihl-YAHN ih-VAHN-uhv-yihch pew-guh-CHAWF) was born in a village in the Don basin sometime in 1742, the exact date being uncertain due to the loss of records in that oft-contested region. He remained illiterate throughout his brief life and probably received only the usual rough-and-ready Cossack education in the handling of horses and of weapons. Certainly, he would have become a proficient rider almost as soon as he could walk, beginning on a small pony and moving up to full-sized horses as he grew. He would have learned how to ford rivers with horses, to plan raids and other mounted military operations, to set up a camp, and to break it down rapidly—all the various skills that were necessary in those semi-military villages on the wild steppe of Russia's southern marches. Like all Cossacks of his time, he was subject to mandatory military service, in which he proved intractably resistant to discipline. After being granted a brief leave of absence for illness, he refused to return to his unit and fled as a deserter.

LIFE'S WORK

Unable to find success in any legitimate pursuit, Pugachev decided to capitalize on the political unrest in the Cossack regions and raise a rebellion against Catherine the Great, whose claim to the throne was shaky at best, because she had come to power as the result of a coup d'état against her weak-willed and incompetent husband, Peter III. Although Peter's death had been engineered by Aleksey Grigoryevich Orlov shortly after being deposed, rumors persisted that he had been spared his fate by divine intervention and now wandered the Russian countryside incognito, awaiting the proper time to reclaim his throne. Several minor rebels had bolstered their positions by claiming to be Peter, but all had been quickly defeated and executed or exiled to Siberia.

In November, 1772, Pugachev entered Yaitsk, capital of the Yaik Cossack Host, disguised as an itinerant merchant and a member of the schismatic Old Believer sect. The latter credential would help gain him sympathy among these people, who had rejected the reforms of Patriarch Nikon more than a century earlier and clung to the old formulas of worship such as making the sign of the cross with two fingers instead of three. Old Believers were treated as heretics by the official Russian Orthodox Church and often treated little better than "nonbelievers" such as Muslims and Buddhists.

In Yaitsk, Pugachev made connections with a number of Cossack dissidents and showed them scars upon his chest, actually from an old illness, which he claimed were "czar marks," stigmata identifying him as God's own anointed czar, Peter III. The folk belief that the legitimate czar would bear special identifying marks upon his body was common in a time before photography, when the average peasant never saw an image (such as a painting or drawing) of the ruler and thus had only a vague and formalized idea of what the monarch might look like. Almost every previous pretender to the throne in that period claimed to possess such "czar marks," and Pugachev was probably just following an established pattern, using a convenient minor disfiguration to further his own program of rebellion.

Eager as the unhappy Cossacks might have been to reclaim their lost autonomy by force of arms, they had to break off their plans when Pugachev was denounced to the government and captured. Taken to Kazan in irons, he was sentenced to be beaten with the knout, a Russian version of the cat-o-nine-tails into which metal and glass were woven, and exiled to Siberia. However, Pugachev contrived to escape his imprisonment, since czarist exile arrangements were comparatively light, a far cry from the Soviet gulag of a later century. By August of 1773, he was back in the Yaitsk region, conspiring once again to raise the banner of rebellion. When czarist officials got wind of the planned uprising and decided to crush it quickly, however, Pugachev moved up his plans and openly declared his rebellion in September, before all his preparations were completed.

With his promises of freedom from Empress Catherine's oppressive policies, Pugachev was able to rally large numbers of unhappy peasants and Cossacks to his cause. Although he was never able to capture Yaitsk, by October his army was able to take several small outposts

An etching of Yemelyan Ivanovich Pugachev imprisoned. (The Granger Collection, New York)

along the Yaik River. Emboldened by their success, they set siege to the czarist outpost of Orenburg and sent emissaries to all the minority nationalities throughout the Ural region. Soon, their numbers were increased by an influx of Muslim Bashkirs and Kazakh tribesmen.

By the middle of October, word of the rebellion reached Catherine in St. Petersburg, Russia's imperial capital. So little did she think of it that she sent a single general at the head of a small punitive expedition, thinking that this disorder could be dealt with as casually as previous years' Cossack revolts. Thus, it was to her surprise that the next news she received was of her general's defeat and flight to Moscow.

Realizing that she had a serious problem on her hands, Catherine dispatched a much larger force under two proven commanders. She also issued proclamations comparing Pugachev to the various False Dmitris, pretenders who had taken advantage of the confused succession following the death of Czar Ivan the Terrible to raise havoc and turn that period into a Time of Troubles. Catherine warned of the consequences of following a pretender's call, including civil disorder and foreign invasion.

Catherine's hopes for a quick resolution of the rebellion were soon dashed, and in spite of mass captures of rebellious peasants, Pugachev was able to elude his pursuers and maintain his movement. Most alarming to Catherine and her advisers was the discovery that Pugachev even had disaffected young men of the upper class among his followers, as demonstrated by the sudden appearance of a manifesto written in German, which was traced to a young officer captured by the rebels when they defeated the original punitive expedition.

In June, Pugachev's fortunes turned with the capture and sack of Kazan. Subsequently, Catherine's forces enjoyed three victories in four days. However, Pugachev was able to escape with a handful of followers and flee down the Volga River to Tsaritsyn (modern Volgograd). There he was finally cornered and captured by Catherine's forces, who brought him to Moscow for trial and punishment. Given that he had escaped custody once before, they took no chances, confining him in an iron cage like an exhibit in a zoo.

Empress Catherine, who wanted to be perceived as an enlightened monarch, deliberately distanced herself from Pugachev's trial and execution by delegating the task to the senate (in imperial Russia, the foremost law court rather than a legislative body). Although Pugachev pled guilty to all his crimes and threw himself on the mercy of the court, they sentenced him to the traditional punishment for traitors, to be quartered alive and then beheaded, with his severed limbs displayed in the various parts of Moscow before his corpse was to be burned, denying his spirit eternal rest. However, the judges of the senate also knew that Catherine would never countenance such a medieval punishment and decided to have the executioner "accidentally" behead Pugachev first, and only then remove his hands and feet. The sentence was carried out without incident on January 21, 1775.

SIGNIFICANCE

Pugachev's unsuccessful rebellion hardened Catherine the Great's resolve to maintain power by any cost, resulting in worsened conditions for the peasantry and delaying actual reforms. To make sure the Cossacks would raise no further rebellions against the throne, she removed the remainder of their autonomy, completing the transformation of these proudly independent people into a military caste who served as the monarchy's special en-

forcers against dissidents and rebels. Thus, the Cossacks would be remembered primarily as the brutal horsemen who rode against peaceful demonstrations and who carried out brutal pogroms against Jewish settlements in the western frontier of Russia.

Catherine also determined to erase the memory of the Yaik Cossacks and of Pugachev himself. She ordered the Yaik Host renamed the Ural Host, the Yaik River the Ural River, and Yaitsk, Ural'sk, names they have since retained. She also ordered Pugachev's brother Dementi, who took no part in the rebellion, to adopt a new surname. This pattern of renaming places and people to erase politically inconvenient memory would find its fullest flower in the Soviet era, particularly under the rule of Joseph Stalin, when various entities might go through three and four renamings in the span of a few years as subsequent honorees were discredited and purged.

—*Leigh Husband Kimmel*

FURTHER READING

Alexander, John T. *Catherine the Great: Life and Legend.* New York: Oxford University Press, 1989. Biography includes a lengthy description of Pugachev's Revolt.

Pushkin, Aleksandr Sergeevich. *The History of Pugachev.* Reprint. New York: Sterling, 2001. This narrative poem by Russia's national poet bears witness of the hold Pugachev had on the Russian literary imagination.

Seaton, Albert. *The Horsemen of the Steppes: The Story of the Cossacks.* New York: Hippocrene Books, 1985. Study of the rise of the Cossacks, from their origins in the cultural collision between Tatar and Russian through the great rebellions of Stenka Razin and of Pugachev.

Ure, John. *The Cossacks: An Illustrated History.* New York: Penguin Books, 2002. Accessible history of the Cossacks, their explorations and their rebellions, particularly of interest since it includes material available only since the fall of the Soviet Union opened various previously secret archives to study by Western scholars.

See also: Catherine the Great; Aleksey Grigoryevich Orlov; Grigori Grigoryevich Orlov; Peter III.

Related articles in *Great Events from History: The Eighteenth Century, 1701-1800*: August 10, 1767: Catherine the Great's Instruction; October, 1768-January 9, 1792: Ottoman Wars with Russia; September, 1773-September, 1774: Pugachev's Revolt.

QIANLONG
Emperor of China (r. 1735-1796)

Qianlong presided over an empire unprecedented in size and power. Under his rule, China reached its apex and enjoyed a long span of peace, order, and prosperity.

Born: September 25, 1711; Beijing, China
Died: February 7, 1799; Beijing, China
Also known as: Ch'ien-lung (Wade-Giles); Ch'ing Kao-tsung (Wade-Giles); Qing Gaozong (Pinyin)
Area of achievement: Government and politics

EARLY LIFE

The Manchus, a vassal tribe of China situated on its northeast border, rose against China as early as 1616, seizing control of all Manchuria by 1621. Between 1610 and 1640, there was much unrest in China itself, with various factions (the gentry, the literati, the eunuchs, and the military) competing for power. Some rebellious generals defected to the Manchus, and, in April, 1644, the beleaguered Ming Dynasty emperor killed himself. The new emperor failed to gain sufficient support for defense of China, and in June, 1644, Manchu troops captured Beijing. It took them another forty-plus years to bring the entire country under their rule, but by the 1680's the Qing Dynasty was in complete control of all China.

The Qing Dynasty (1644-1912) was nearly a century old when Qianlong took the throne. Grandson of Kangxi, considered the greatest of the Qing rulers, Qianlong modeled himself upon this vigorous ruler, successfully blending Chinese and Manchu traditions. As a youth, Qianlong studied Confucian ethics and Manchu military arts, his teachers being a mixture of Chinese and Manchu scholars. The required curriculum included the classics, history, literature, philosophy, and ritual performances.

Under the Qing Dynasty, all important decisions came from the emperor. This centralization of power placed a great burden on the emperors to keep abreast of events in their vast empire. Succeeding his father, Yung-cheng, a harsh but able ruler, Qianlong depended upon a smooth-running administrative machine to help him in decision making.

The chief government organ in Qing times was a grand (later, privy) council, whose members met with the emperor daily to advise him on overall policies; the grand secretariat handled routine business. Below these organs were the six ministries, each having a Manchu and a Chinese minister, along with two Manchu and two Chinese deputy ministers. At all levels of government, Chinese officials were present in large numbers. This was a major factor in the success and long rule of the Qing Dynasty. Conscientious and responsible, Qianlong was assisted by competent statesmen in the first half of his reign. He made several inspection tours of the country, acquainting himself with many areas while satisfying his taste for grandeur.

LIFE'S WORK

Militarily, Qianlong's armies pacified Chinese Turkestan (Xinjiang) between 1745 and 1749. Burma was subjugated between 1766 and 1770. Outer Mongolia, long considered a security threat, was also subdued so that, by 1759, the Qing Empire extended from Outer Mongolia in the north to Guangdong in the south to Central Asia in the west. Taiwan, too, acknowledged Qing overlordship, and neighboring counties sent tribute missions regularly to Beijing, recognizing their dependence on China's goodwill.

Economically, Qing China outstripped any previous dynasty with growth in three particular areas: commerce, agriculture, and manufacturing. Internal trade provided much revenue, with foreign trade gaining fast by the late eighteenth century. China traded worldwide, and the maritime provinces benefited in particular. Western traders were tightly controlled during the Qing Dynasty—until the nineteenth century. Even before Qianlong's reign, they were confined to southern China, and, by government decree in 1757, all foreign trade was conducted in the port of Guangzhou (Canton). Here, all foreigners were treated alike, as inferiors, bearing tribute to China.

Great Britain was the greatest seapower and trading nation of the world by the eighteenth century, and it continually pressured China for more trade rights. Yet the Chinese had little knowledge of England's power or of international law as it was developing in Western Europe. Qianlong exemplified this ignorance in his decree (1793) addressed to King George III, in which he informs the king that "as to your entreaty to send one of your nationals to be accredited to my Celestial Court and to be in control of your country's trade with China, this request is contrary to all usage of my dynasty and cannot possibly be entertained." He goes on to state that "we possess all things . . . and have no use for your country's manufactures."

As in previous dynasties, China was a Confucian state, following strict Confucian principles. Among

817

these was stratification of peoples by class and by nation. Within China, there was a huge gap between superiors and inferiors (upper and lower classes). In foreign relations, this same stratification showed itself in the Chinese term for foreigners, which meant "barbarians." Some forty years after Qianlong's death, England and other European nations would no longer tolerate what they saw as Chinese arrogance and would open Chinese ports all along the coast by military force.

Agriculture provided the greatest share of Qing revenue, reaching highest development during Qianlong's reign. Traditionally, Chinese farming was a precarious occupation. It was labor-intensive (dependent on human power), applied to small plots of land. Recurring problems were those of absentee landlords and high taxation. Yet conditions improved considerably by the eighteenth century. New crops were introduced (such as sweet potatoes, sorghum, and maize) that could be grown even on poor land. Diet improved and, with the widespread practice of irrigation and the use of better fertilizers, many peasants were prospering. Until the last twenty years of Qianlong's rule, peasants were only moderately taxed. Manufacturing reached a peak, also, in the eighteenth century with the textile industry, the largest, most productive of them all. The cotton-goods industry, tea plantations, and porcelain factories filled orders for the court and for wealthy families as well as for exports worldwide. The decorative arts were especially prized in foreign markets, exemplified by a European craze for chinoiserie.

As a patron of the arts, Qianlong collected paintings and porcelains, and himself produced many poems and much calligraphy (not held in high repute). He sponsored a mammoth work entitled *Siguquanshu* (1782-1787; complete library of the four treasuries), containing more than thirty-six thousand volumes, with four main categories of literature: classics, history, philosophy, and belles lettres. Scholarship flourished with contributions on statecraft and philosophy. The function and evaluation of literature were debated, and original writings came under careful scrutiny, their historicity being challenged. Qing writers produced many works—poetry, essays, short stories, and novels. There is a dark side to Qianlong's interest in and sponsorship of learning. Imperial control was strong, and so-called heretical, subversive authors were punished. Unacceptable books were burned; records list 13,862 works being destroyed between 1774 and 1782.

The last twenty or so years of Qianlong's reign were years of dynastic decline. Ironically, part of this was the result of agricultural growth and overall peace and prosperity: China underwent a population explosion. From 1741 to 1796, the population nearly doubled. Production failed to keep pace, and new strains developed on the economy, state, and society. Distant wars in Central Asia, Nepal, Burma (Myanmar), and Western Sichuan, as well as the upkeep of a luxurious court, further drained the state's resources. Administrative laxity and corruption made the government less effective and increasingly costly. As a taste for wealth spread through the upper classes, myriad new taxes burdened the lower classes, the peasants in particular.

In his later years, Qianlong became increasingly autocratic. During the mid-1770's, he bestowed his favor on a young general of the imperial body guard, Heshen, who exerted an all-powerful influence in government. Heshen appointed relatives and henchmen to high positions and amassed for himself a large fortune. Organized resistance to government inefficiency and corruption flourished in secret societies, among them the White Lotus Sect, which led an open rebellion in 1793. Another, more extensive revolt erupted in 1796, taking nine years to suppress. Qianlong abdicated in 1796, while continuing to rule behind the scenes. Upon his death in 1799, his protégé Heshen was arrested by the new emperor, Jiaqing, and was allowed to commit suicide that same year. Yet the dynastic decline was well in motion, and Jiaqing was unable to restore the former glory.

SIGNIFICANCE

There is much to admire in Qianlong's long reign. Certainly, in the first forty years, he strove to be an enlightened ruler, well grounded in the arts of emperorship. Qing China prospered, not unfit to be mentioned with the Han and Tang Dynasties as a golden era. Highly centralized, the Qing Dynasty of the eighteenth century thrived through a combination of military, economic, political, and social adaptations, and, under a benevolent despot such as Qianlong had been in his early years, China reached its apex of power and prestige.

In his old age, Qianlong failed to keep the reins of government firmly in hand, and he must bear the blame for much of China's subsequent weakness as it faced the onslaught of a new enemy, the encroaching Western nations. A major cause of the Qing decline by the late eighteenth century was the lack of competent officials at all levels of government. Many were ignorant of the country outside the state and provincial capitals; many were underpaid and, therefore, were caught up in the struggle for wealth to achieve security for themselves and their families. Worse, Qianlong, like his predecessors and successors, failed to reform an antiquated civil service examination system. The examination system stressed Confucian values, rewarding humanistic achievements rather than science, technology, and industry. Its narrow scope and impractical nature did not help develop administrative ability. Free expression was stifled while orthodox thought was encouraged. Not until the late nineteenth century was the system challenged, and only in 1901 was reform actually implemented. By then it was too late, and the dynasty fell in 1912.

—*S. Carol Berg*

FURTHER READING

Fairbank, John K., Edwin O. Reischauer, and Albert M. Craig. *East Asia: Tradition and Transformation.* Boston: Houghton Mifflin, 1973. Chapter 9, "Traditional China at Its Height Under the Ch'ing," is very helpful. Covers the rise of the dynasty, its administrative structures, military expansion, culture, and population growth. Includes fine pictures, maps, and a detailed index.

Gernet, Jacques. *A History of Chinese Civilization.* New York: Cambridge University Press, 1982. There are three chapters on the Qing Dynasty. Chapter 23, "The Enlightened Despots," is most valuable. Includes maps and charts, a chronological table, and a helpful index and bibliography.

Ho, Chuimei, and Bennet Bronson. *Splendors of China's Forbidden City: The Glorious Reign of Emperor Qianlong.* London: Merrell, 2004. Published to accompany an exhibition with the same name at the Field Museum in Chicago. This beautifully illustrated book describes the art and artifacts created during Qianlong's reign, a great flowering of Chinese imperial culture. Focuses on the emperor's personal life as well as his public life at court, discussing how he met the challenges inherent in administering a large and diverse empire and how he appreciated and patronized the arts. Paintings, calligraphy, ceramics, bronzes, and bamboo and jade carvings are among the artworks featured.

Hsü, Immanuel C. Y. *The Rise of Modern China.* New York: Oxford University Press, 1970. Chapters 2 and 3 are on the Qing Dynasty with five pages on Qianlong's reign. Special concern is taken with political, intellectual, social, and economic history. Includes helpful tables and charts of statistics, and extensive bibliographies after each chapter.

Latourette, Kenneth S. *China.* Englewood Cliffs, N.J.: Prentice-Hall, 1964. Includes one brief chapter on the Qing Dynasty but covers the great emperors up to 1800 with particular emphasis on military campaigns, economics, and foreign relations. Contains a bibliography after each chapter, an appendix of proper names and Chinese words used in the text, and an index.

Millward, James A., et al., eds. *New Qing Imperial History: The Making of the Inner Asian Empire at Qing Chengde.* New York: Routledge, 2004. The authors describe how the Qing Dynasty ruled over a large empire and was involved militarily, culturally, and politically in the affairs of Inner Asia and Tibet. The book focuses on Qianlong's reign to illustrate the nature of Qing rule in the Chinese empire.

Rodzinski, Witold. *The Walled Kingdom: A History of China from Antiquity to the Present.* New York: Free Press, 1984. Contains brief but concise chapters covering all the dynasties and into the post-Mao era. Chapter 7, "China Under Manchu Rule," is most pertinent. Covers foundation, culture, and decline of the dynasty, and is critical of the Manchu emperors. Includes excellent maps, suggested readings, and an index.

Schirokauer, Conrad. *Modern China and Japan.* New York: Harcourt Brace Jovanovich, 1982. Chapter 1, "China Under the Manchus," is brief but thorough. Covers geography, the reign of Qianlong, politics, economics, and the arts. Includes a fine map and illustrations, brief chapter notes, an annotated bibliography, and an index.

See also: Cao Xueqin; Dai Zhen; Yongzheng.

Related articles in *Great Events from History: The Eighteenth Century, 1701-1800:* October 21, 1727: Treaty of Kiakhta; 1750-1792: China Consolidates Control over Tibet; 1771-1802: Vietnamese Civil Wars; 1793-January, 1794: Macartney Mission to China.

FRANÇOIS QUESNAY
French economist and physician

In addition to being an eminent physician, Quesnay was the founder and leading theorist of Physiocratic, or laissez-faire, economics. Often considered the first modern school of economics, those following his theory came to be called the Physiocrats.

Born: June 4, 1694; Méré, France
Died: December 16, 1774; Versailles, France
Areas of achievement: Economics, medicine

EARLY LIFE

Information about the early life of François Quesnay (fran-zwah kay-nay) is rather limited and not always dependable. The son of a modest farmer, he was orphaned at about the age of thirteen. Too poor to attend a school, he apparently learned to read with the limited assistance of either a gardener or a local priest. Soon he developed a voracious appetite for reading and acquiring knowledge, eventually becoming proficient in Greek and Latin. At about the age of seventeen, he entered into training as a Parisian engraver and worked as an apprentice for about five years. Sometime during this period, he married the daughter of a middle-class grocer, which significantly elevated his social status.

During the last years of his apprenticeship, Quesnay became interested in surgery and began to take courses at the surgeon's college and the University of Paris. After completing his training, he was accepted as a member of the community of surgeons in Paris in 1718, and he then earned his living as a barber-surgeon at Mantes, where he acquired a reputation as an outstanding practitioner. While in Mantes, his wife and two of his children died. In 1734, he entered into the service of the duke of Villeroy, who introduced him to many prominent people. Meanwhile, by devoting his spare time to reading, studying, and writing, he developed a broad knowledge of philosophy and the natural sciences.

LIFE'S WORK

In the 1730's, François Quesnay wrote several tracts on surgery that enhanced his reputation. He was a leading voice in the movement to elevate the status of surgery as a medical science. He influenced the issuing of a royal edict in 1743 that separated surgeons from barbers. Awarded the rank of doctor of medicine in 1744, Quesnay subsequently became the physician of Madame de Pompadour, the powerful mistress of King Louis XV. Living at Versailles, he acquired firsthand knowledge of the serious political and financial difficulties of the monarchical government.

Quesnay was elected a member of the Academy of Sciences in 1751. Because of his success in curing the dauphin of smallpox, he was made a noble in 1752, and that year he was also named a member of the Royal Society. Holding these prestigious positions, he established friendships with many of the intellectual leaders of the French Enlightenment.

He began his specialized research in economics in the mid-1750's, when Denis Diderot, editor of the famous *Encyclopédie: Ou, Dictionnaire raisonne des sciences, des arts, et des métiers* (1751-1772; *Encyclopedia*, 1965), asked him to contribute several articles about agriculture and farmers. (Quesnay had a rural background.) In preparation for writing the entries, Quesnay read the works of Sébastien Le Prestre de Vauban, Richard Cantillon, and others. By combining their ideas with his own observations, he gradually developed his own eclectic theory. His first article, "Fermiers" (farmers), appeared in volume 6 (1756), and the following year, volume 7 included his article on grains. He wrote other articles that were never published, probably because the king withdrew permission to continue publishing the *Encyclopedia*.

By the time his encyclopedic articles appeared, Quesnay had developed the major components of his economic theory, called Physiocracy (from two Greek words, *phusis*, meaning nature, and *kratos*, meaning power or rule). As the term implies, he believed that he had discovered "natural laws" of economics that are universally valid. According to the theory, a prosperous agricultural sector provided the only foundation for a healthy economy. It was therefore necessary to maintain low taxes on agriculture and to promote agricultural profits through free trade. Although such a policy might mean high prices for consumers in the short term, farmers would reinvest their profits, which would eventually result in lower prices. Influenced by Jean-Claude-Marie-Vincent de Gournay's writings, Quesney advocated minimal governmental intervention in the economy, an approach that both Gournay and Quesnay called *laissez-faire* (meaning "let it do" or "let it alone").

Quesnay's most famous work, *Tableau économique* (1758; *The Economical Table*, 1766), presented a circular flow diagram, outlining economic activities of production and distribution. According to *The Economical*

Table, society was divided into three main classes: farmers, landowners, and others, who included manufacturers, skilled craftsmen, and merchants. Members of the third class were said to be "sterile" because they consumed everything they produced and left no surplus for future growth. Quesnay was highly critical of the French government's regulations of the economy, which he referred to as Colbertisme (named after Louis XIV's finance minister, Jean-Baptiste Colbert). He argued that protecting French manufacturers from foreign competition had raised the cost of machinery for farmers, and that regulations of grain prices were harmful because they decreased the incentive of farmers to increase production.

By the late 1750's, a group of like-minded associates were holding regular meetings with Quesnay and looking to him as their intellectual leader. His most loyal and outspoken collaborator was the comte de Mirabeau, a writer who later became a major revolutionary leader. Other significant disciples included Pierre-Paul Le Mercier de La Rivière, Pierre-Samuel du Pont de Nemours, and Anne-Robert-Jacques Turgot. Within a few years, Quesney and his followers became known as *économistes* and Physiocrats.

Quesnay and Mirabeau collaborated in writing several works. In 1758, they drafted *Traité de la monarchie, 1757-1759* (treatise on monarchy), which was not published until much later because of its strong criticisms of the French monarchy. In 1764, they published *La Philosophie rurale* (rural philosophy), which summarized Quesnay's mature vision of political economics. In addition to the emphasis on laissez-faire economics, the book advocated a "single tax" on land and a "despotism of the laws." By this date, Quesnay's remarkable followers were widely disseminating, debating, and modifying his ideas with books, articles, and even a journal.

Quesnay continued to write newspaper essays into the late 1760's. In addition to economic issues, he wrote about human rights, despotism, and foreign governments. His last book, *Physiocratie* (1767-1768; Physiocracy), was a two-volume selection of his essays edited and sometimes revised by du Pont de Nemours. In old age he suffered from incessant attacks of gout, and he died at the age of eighty at Versailles in 1774.

SIGNIFICANCE

For historians of economic theory, François Quesnay ranks as one of the greatest economists of all time. He was the acknowledged leader and founder of the Physiocrat school, which usually is said to have produced the first comprehensive approach to economics. Quesnay's

work helped prepare the way for the classical economists, particularly Adam Smith, who frequently acknowledged his influence. As capitalism continued to grow and develop in the next centuries, numerous admirers of the free market and minimal governmental regulations have looked to Quesnay as almost a prophet. Socialists and proponents of activist governmental intervention, in contrast, typically view him as an apologist for the exploitation of the working classes by a wealthy elite.

Economists of the twenty-first century continue to debate the validity of Quesnay's theories. Almost all economists reject his views about the economic "sterility" of manufacturing, commerce, and the service sector. His notions of laissez-faire economics, on the other hand, continue to attract many enthusiastic supporters. When these ideas have been tried, sometimes the results have been remarkably successful, while at other times the results have been almost disastrous. In the eighteenth century, Quesnay's proposals were usually considered "liberal," but in the twenty-first century, at least in the United States, they are classified as "conservative."

—*Thomas Tandy Lewis*

FURTHER READING

Blaug, Mark. *Great Economists Before Keynes: An Introduction to the Lives and Works of One Hundred Great Economists of the Past*. Lyme, N.H.: Edward Elgar, 1997. One of the best sources for the reader wanting relatively short introductions to Quesnay and other major economists.

Fox-Genovese, Elizabeth. *The Origins of Physiocracy: Economic Revolution and Social Order in Eighteenth-Century France*. Ithaca, N.Y.: Cornell University Press, 1976. A left-leaning but fair-minded account of the Physiocrats within the context of the Enlightenment, the problems of the Old Regime, and the nature of capitalism.

Groenewegen, Peter. *Eighteenth-Century Economics: Turgot, Beccaria, and Smith and Their Contemporaries*. New York: Routledge, 2002. A collection of essays by a scholar specializing in eighteenth century economic history. Among other topics, the essays discuss the economic theories of Quesnay, Turgot, Cesare Beccaria, and Adam Smith.

Higgs, Henry. *The Physiocrats: Six Lectures on the French Economics of the Eighteenth Century*. Hamden, Conn.: Archon Books, 1963. A good introduction to the thought of Quesnay and the other Physiocrats.

Kuczynski, Marguerite, and Ronald Meek, ed. *Quesnay's "Tableau économique," with New Materials, Translations, and Notes*. London: Macmillan, 1972. A translation of Quesnay's major work, with helpful notes and explanations.

Landreth, Harry, and David Colander. *History of Economic Thought*. Boston: Houghton Mifflin, 1994. Includes a readable summary of Quesnay's economic theory and his influence.

McCulloch, John. *Treatises and Essays on Subjects Connected with Economical Policy, with Biographical Sketches of Quesnay, Adam Smith, and Ricardo*. New York: Augustus Kelley, 1967. Originally published 1853, this work includes a useful biographical sketch of twelve pages.

Niehans, Jurg. *A History of Economic Theory: Classic Contributions, 1720-1980*. Baltimore: Johns Hopkins University Press, 1995. Provides a good historical introduction into the influences on Quesnay as well as his theories and their influence during his own age and later.

Vaggi, Gianni. *Economics of François Quesnay*. Durham, N.C.: Duke University Press, 1987. The only substantial book devoted to Quesnay's economic theories.

See also: Cesare Beccaria; Edmund Burke; Denis Diderot; Louis XV; Comte de Mirabeau; Madame de Pompadour; Adam Smith; Jethro Tull; Anne-Robert-Jacques Turgot.

Related articles in *Great Events from History: The Eighteenth Century, 1701-1800:* 1720: Financial Collapse of the John Law System; April 27-May, 1775: Flour War; March 9, 1776: Adam Smith Publishes *The Wealth of Nations*; 1790: Burke Lays the Foundations of Modern Conservatism; January, 1790: Hamilton's *Report on Public Credit*.

ANN RADCLIFFE
English novelist and poet

The most popular and imitated novelist in England at the end of the eighteenth century, Radcliffe almost single-handedly created the style of the female gothic, which explores the problems and anxieties resulting from women's dependence and isolation. Not only did the female gothic achieve mythical status as a metaphor for female experience but Radcliffe's works also contributed to the rise of the gothic novel's popularity.

Born: July 9, 1764; London, England
Died: February 7, 1823; London, England
Also known as: Ann Ward (birth name)
Area of achievement: Literature

EARLY LIFE

Ann Radcliffe, a mother of the English novel, was the only child of William and Ann Ward, who was thirty-eight years old at the time of her daughter's birth. Although William Ward, some eleven years younger than his wife, was a tradesman, the family was well connected. When Ann was age seven or eight, the Wards moved to Bath, where William Ward managed a branch of Wedgwood and Bentley.

Ann, who received a good, though not classical, education, was brought up in the Established Church. In 1787, Ann married William Radcliffe, an Oxford graduate, who trained as a lawyer at the Inner Temple. After several terms at one of the inns of court, he became editor and proprietor of a newspaper, *The English Chronicle*. The young couple, who would remain childless, moved to London, where William had been born and raised. In London, Ann led an uneventful, retired life, insisting on seclusion and privacy.

It was not until after her marriage at the age of twenty-three that Radcliffe began writing. Even as her popularity soared and she became a cultural icon, Radcliffe withdrew from society. Formal, reserved, and shy, the Garboesque writer became increasingly reticent about authorship.

LIFE'S WORK

Six of Ann Radcliffe's works appeared in her lifetime, with amazing speed in the eight years from 1789 to 1797. A seventh novel, *Gaston de Blondeville*, was published posthumously in 1826. Starting when she was just twenty-five years old, Radcliffe published her first three novels in three years. Criticized for childishness and his-

torical inaccuracies, Radcliffe's anonymous first work, *The Castles of Athlin and Dunbayne* (1789), received little notice. Her second novel, *A Sicilian Romance*, which was published the following year, was also practically ignored.

Radcliffe's next novel, *The Romance of the Forest* (1791), was so widely praised that it established her reputation, but *The Mysteries of Udolpho* (1794) and *The Italian: Or, The Confessional of the Black Penitents* (1797) made her wildly famous. In these works Radcliffe developed the female gothic by explaining the supernatural and providing it with banal causality. Unlike classic gothic novelists, who explain little in an attempt to make the reader believe that the mysteries are real, Radcliffe dramatizes the struggle between irrationality and reason. Over and over, she demonstrates that apparently supernatural mysteries are caused by human agency. Radcliffe's mundane explanations of mysteries have the effect of convincing the reader to guard against indulging in the imagination. In this way Radcliffe's female gothic is critical of classic gothic exaggerations.

Radcliffe transformed the emotional extravagances of the classic (male) gothic novel, which is usually set in haunted castles, graveyards, ruins, or wild landscapes that create brooding, eerie atmospheres. This form inspires fear by emphasizing the supernatural and the macabre. Although Radcliffe's exuberant novels are replete with similar fantastic details, she uses them to create a female gothic in which her heroines demonstrate their inner strength in the face of persecution when they separate from home, confront conflicts in confinement, thwart male domination, and resolve ambivalent feelings about their mothers.

Another hallmark of Radcliffe's female gothic is her innovative, highly poetical descriptions of landscapes, which have spiritual dimensions. Detailed in prose that approaches poetry, Radcliffe's striking scenery not only reflects and enhances the plot but also defines and summarizes character, evoking elevated emotions. Picturesque scenes are related to characters' emotional and moral awareness: Only sensitive, virtuous characters experience heightened, transcendent reactions to nature. It is, however, this same extreme sensibility that can exaggerate the terror of their situations.

Remarkably, Radcliffe's novels set in Italy (*A Sicilian Romance*, *The Mysteries of Udolpho*, and *The Italian*) depict places she had never visited. If the Radcliffes fre-

---

THE GOTHIC MOMENT

In The Mysteries of Udolpho *and other works, Ann Radcliffe developed the female gothic, using the banalities of daily life to explain the seemingly supernatural and inexplicably mysterious. In the female gothic, mysteries begin and end through the imagination, and Radcliffe makes these mysteries obvious. In this excerpt, Radcliffe describes a scene set in Italy at "Udolpho Castle," a scene horrifying to the protagonist Emily, yet not what first imagined.*

[I]n a chamber of Udolpho, hung a black veil, whose singular situation had excited Emily's curiosity, and which afterwards disclosed an object, that had overwhelmed her with horror; for, on lifting it, there appeared, instead of the picture she had expected, within a recess of the wall, a human figure of ghastly paleness, stretched at its length, and dressed in the habiliments of the grave. What added to the horror of the spectacle, was, that the face appeared partly decayed and disfigured by worms, which were visible on the features and hands. On such an object, it will be readily believed, that no person could endure to look twice. Emily, it may be recollected, had, after the first glance, let the veil drop, and her terror had prevented her from ever after provoking a renewal of such suffering, as she had then experienced. Had she dared to look again, her delusion and her fears would have vanished together, and she would have perceived, that the figure before her was not human, but formed of wax. The history of it is somewhat extraordinary, though not without example in the records of that fierce severity, which monkish superstition has sometimes inflicted on mankind. A member of the house of Udolpho, having committed some offence against the prerogative of the church, had been condemned to the penance of contemplating, during certain hours of the day, a waxen image, made to resemble a human body in the state, to which it is reduced after death.

Source: Ann Radcliffe, *The Mysteries of Udolpho* (1794). Project Gutenberg. http://www.gutenberg.org/dirs/etext02/udolf10.txt. Accessed June, 2005.

---

ant Schedoni in *The Italian*, is magnificent in his mysterious solitude.

With virtue that is beyond reproach, Radcliffe's female victims are conventionally beautiful, prone to tears, and sensitive to landscape. Yet they are unlike the heroines of Samuel Richardson, Frances Burney, or Jane Austen, who all seek moral guidance from male figures. Instead, Radcliffe's female gothic requires her heroines to maintain their independence in romantic relationships. In the end, most are not rescued by their heroes.

The female gothic not only reflects the patriarchal violence of the classic gothic but also stresses female kinship relations. In fact, so important is the mother-daughter bond in her work that is has been described as "matrophobic" gothic, which focuses on the mother's threat to engulf her child and the daughter's issues of identification and separation. At the dramatic heart of the Radcliffean female or matrophobic gothic is the daughter's conflict with maternal figures from whom she cannot totally separate because of her own femaleness and because the figures symbolize the daughter's own fate.

quently traveled around England, a single trip to Holland, western Germany, and the Rhine (recorded in Radcliffe's *Journey Made in the Summer of 1794*) represents the only time she ever went abroad. The vivid descriptions in her Italian novels were influenced by travel literature and by paintings. Her romantic landscapes dramatize Edmund Burke's concept of the sublime, which is inspired by such sources as obscurity, privation, vastness, infinity, difficulty, and magnificence. In this aesthetic model of dominance and submission, the soul experiences transcendence by feeling its own power confronting the unimaginable.

Radcliffe's extreme focus on the energy of the sublime scene and atmosphere to excite fear leaves her characters indiscriminate and one-dimensional. Full of sensibility, Radcliffe's feminized heroes are weak and ineffectual. Her villains, however, are arresting. Her most fully elaborated character, the satanically flamboy-

After achieving her greatest success with *The Italian* at the age of thirty-four, Radcliffe stopped writing for publication. Mysteriously, she published no new novels in the twenty-six years that remained of her life. She spent most of this time secluded at home or traveling around England. A trip to Kenilworth Castle in 1802 inspired the posthumously published *Gaston de Blondeville*, which may have been written collaboratively with her husband in 1802 or 1803. Although *The Italian* had received great acclaim, Radcliffe declined to publish *Gaston de Blondeville* (her only classic gothic) during her lifetime. Many assumed that Radcliffe had died or gone insane. Even though she had wide access to the press, so self-effacing was Radcliffe that she never corrected such rumors.

If not because of madness, why did she stop publishing? For one thing, she probably did not need the money. By 1800, after the death of her parents, her inheritance, together with the considerable profits from her novels, left her in comfortable circumstances. Another reason may have been that she was deeply offended by the criticism, along with parodies and inferior imitations, of her work—even though she must have derived pleasure from appreciations of her work by some of her most famous contemporaries. In addition, she may have been too debilitated to write, at least during her last twelve years, when she suffered from the respiratory and digestive problems that would finally lead to her death in 1823.

SIGNIFICANCE

Ann Radcliffe's works ushered in a gothic craze, most evident from 1789 to 1815, when she emerged as the most popular novelist in Great Britain. Her electrifying female gothic helped to found and sustain a vogue for the picturesque, sentimental, and sublime thriller. She is commonly praised for her use of the unconscious, her evocation of fear and suspense, and her innovative poetic descriptions of architecture and landscape. Her work inspired not only plays, operas, and imitations but also influenced, profoundly, Romantic and Victorian literature; detective, psychological, and horror genres; and a whole host of individual authors including Jane Austen, Charles Robert Maturin, Matthew Gregory Lewis, William Hazlitt, Sir Walter Scott, Lord Byron, the Shelleys, William Wordsworth, John Keats, Samuel Taylor Coleridge, the Brontës, William Thackeray, Charles Dickens, Nathaniel Hawthorne, and Edgar Allan Poe.

Highly praised in her own day—but devalued and mocked as she came to be virtually excluded from the canon—Radcliffe is being approached with new seriousness because of the efforts of feminist revisionist literary critics, who are reclaiming the female tradition in literature. Deservingly, Radcliffe is also at the center of renewed interest in the gothic genre, after establishing the major characteristics of the female gothic novel.

—*Deborah D. Rogers*

FURTHER READING

Bohls, Elizabeth. *Women Travel Writers and the Language of Aesthetics, 1716-1818*. New York: Cambridge University Press, 1995. A scholarly work that traces the experiences of eighteenth and early nineteenth century women travelers. The journals, letters, travelogues, position papers, and novels of Radcliffe, Mary Wollstonecraft, Dorothy Wordsworth, Mary Wortley Montagu, and Mary Shelley are explored to show how women actively participated in travel and exploration and in documenting their experiences.

Norton, Rictor. *Mistress of Udolpho: The Life of Ann Radcliffe*. New York: Leicester University Press, 1999. Despite Norton's flamboyant tendency to equate Radcliffe with her characters, this biography focuses on cultural history to introduce important new ideas.

_____, ed. *Gothic Readings: The First Wave, 1764-1840*. New York: Leicester University Press, 2000. Norton presents selections of gothic literature in the period that includes Radcliffe, along with contemporary criticism and reader responses. A good text for readers new to gothic literature.

Rogers, Deborah D. *Ann Radcliffe: A Bio-Bibliography*. Westport, Conn.: Greenwood Press, 1996. Uses updated manuscript material to construct Radcliffe's life. The comprehensive annotated bibliography includes editions, translations, and criticism from 1789 to 1995.

_____, ed. *The Critical Response to Ann Radcliffe*. Westport, Conn.: Greenwood Press, 1994. Includes almost one hundred critiques of Radcliffe's work, from the last quarter of the eighteenth century to the end of the twentieth century.

See also: Edmund Burke; Daniel Defoe; Henry Fielding; Mary Wortley Montagu; Samuel Richardson; Mary Wollstonecraft.

Related articles in *Great Events from History: The Eighteenth Century, 1701-1800:* April 25, 1719: Defoe Publishes the First Novel; 1740-1741: Richardson's *Pamela* Establishes the Modern Novel; 1792: Wollstonecraft Publishes *A Vindication of the Rights of Woman*.

JEAN-PHILIPPE RAMEAU
French composer

Rameau was the outstanding French composer of his time. His music for the stage was of particular importance, as were his contributions to music theory. Rameau established the modern concept of harmonic practice.

Born: September 25, 1683 (baptized); Dijon, France
Died: September 12, 1764; Paris, France
Area of achievement: Music

EARLY LIFE

Jean-Philippe Rameau (zhahn-fee-leep rah-moh) was the seventh of eleven children born to Jean Rameau and his wife, Claudine (née Demartinecourt). His father was an organist of the collegiate Church of St. Étienne, as well as of the Abbey of St. Bénigne, and his mother was a member of the lesser nobility. His younger brother, Claude, also became a professional musician, serving as organist for various churches in Dijon and Autun. Jean-Philippe was intended for the law and to that end was sent to the Jesuit Collège des Godrans, where he apparently spent more time singing and writing music than studying and was asked to leave. At the age of eighteen, he was sent by his father to Italy to study music, but he traveled only as far as Milan, where he spent a few months before returning to Dijon.

In January, 1702, Rameau was appointed temporary organist at Avignon Cathedral, and in May of that year he signed a contract to serve for six years as organist of the cathedral in Clermont, seemingly prepared to embark on an unexceptional career as a provincial church musician. By 1706, however, he was in Paris, where he published his first collection of harpsichord music, *Premier Livre de pièces de clavecin*, consisting of a single large suite in a markedly conservative style. In March, 1709, he succeeded his father as organist at the Church of Notre Dame in Dijon. In July, 1713, he was at Lyons, where he directed the music in celebration of the Treaty of Utrecht and where he was also employed as organist by the Jacobins. In April, 1715, he returned to Clermont as cathedral organist, signing a contract to serve for twenty-nine years; he remained for only eight.

Nothing is known of Rameau's time in Clermont, but either there or at Lyons he is thought to have written his five surviving motets and a similar number of cantatas. He also undertook the research and writing of his first book, *Traité de l'harmonie* (1722; *Treatise on Harmony*, 1971), which was published in Paris shortly before he re-

located there permanently. He was then in his fortieth year and virtually unknown in the French music world.

LIFE'S WORK

During his first years in Paris, Rameau was considered primarily a theorist and teacher, largely because of the success of the *Treatise on Harmony* and of his next work, *Nouveau Système de musique théorique* (1726; *New System of Music Theory*, 1974). He continued to compose, contributing music to productions of the Fair theaters (Théâtres de la Foire) and publishing his second and third collections of harpsichord music, *Pièces de clavecin avec une méthode pour la mécanique des doights*, in 1724, and *Nouvelles Suites de pièces de clavecin*, probably in 1728. Both contain a mixture of dances and genre pieces, organized by keys but not forming suites.

On February 25, 1726, Rameau married Marie-Louise Mangot, the daughter of a musician from Lyons in the service of the French court and herself an accomplished singer and harpsichordist. They had four children, two of whom survived Rameau. In 1727, he competed for the position of organist of the Church of St. Paul, but Louis-Claude Daquin was selected instead. In the same year, he wrote to Houdar de la Motte, a writer, and obliquely requested a libretto for an opera, but nothing came of the request.

Around this time, Rameau was introduced to the financier Le Riche de la Pouplinière, an avid patron of music and the arts, who from about 1731 maintained a private orchestra under Rameau's direction that gave performances at his house in the rue Neuve des Petits-Champs. The meeting with la Pouplinière was to be the most significant event in Rameau's career. Although from at least 1732 to 1738 he was organist of the Church of Ste. Croix-de-la-Bretonnerie and from 1736 to 1738 also organist at the Jesuit Novitiate, most of the remainder of Rameau's life was spent under the patronage of la Pouplinière both as a theorist and as a composer of music for the stage.

Rameau's first opera, a *tragédie en musique* (or *tragédie lyrique*) titled *Hippolyte et Aricie* (1733), was written to a libretto by Abbé Pellegrin based on Euripides' and Jean Racine's treatments of the Phaedra myth. In the tradition of Jean-Baptiste Lully's operas, it consisted of a prologue and five acts, each interweaving *divertissements* of dance and singing into the dramatic narrative. *Hippolyte et Aricie* was premiered privately at la Pouplinière's in July, 1733, and presented at the Paris Opera on October 1, 1733, shortly after Rameau's fiftieth birthday, and was an immediate and overwhelming success.

Hippolyte et Aricie was virtually the first *tragédie en musique* to succeed at the opera since the death of Lully some forty-five years earlier. Although it was condemned by the conservative *lullistes* as being too Italianate, too contrapuntal, and too modern, the *ramistes*—who included most of the younger musicians—praised it extravagantly. The elderly composer André Campra remarked that "there is enough music in this opera to make ten of them; this man will eclipse us all." Following upon the success of *Hippolyte et Aricie*, Rameau began composing a sacred opera to a libretto written for him by Voltaire. The work, entitled *Samson*, was largely completed by October, 1734, when a concert performance was given, but it never reached the stage and Rameau never again set such a distinguished librettro. Some of the music was apparently reused in *Les Fêtes d'Hébé* (1739), *Castor et Pollux* (1737), and *Zoroastre* (1749).

Rameau then began a remarkable period of activity in which he completed nearly twenty operas or ballets over the course of the next twenty years. Rameau also continued his theoretical studies, which he considered at least

Jean-Philippe Rameau. (Library of Congress)

as important as his efforts at composition. Among his many works of theory, the clearest and most readable is *Démonstration du principe de l'harmonie* (1750; *Demonstration of the Principle of Harmony*, 1976), on which he may have received help from Denis Diderot. As he approached his sixty-fifth birthday, Rameau was at the height of his fame. He had been granted a pension and the title of Compositeur du Cabinet du Roi in May, 1745, and would be granted a further pension in 1750. Objections to his music from the conservative *lullistes* had begun to recede, and some Frenchmen, including Diderot, could admit to recognizing strengths in both composers.

Rameau's tall, thin figure and angular features were familiar to visitors to the gardens of the Tuileries and the Palais Royal, where he often walked alone. His physical resemblance to Voltaire was noted by his contemporaries and became more pronounced as both men grew older. Never a sociable man and always noted for his short temper, Rameau became even more acerbic in his later years. Despite accusations of avarice, however, he seems to have remained generous to his family and as openhearted to his few friends as he was implacable to his more numerous enemies in the field of music theory.

In 1752, an event occurred in Paris that had a startling effect on musical life in that city: a traveling troupe of Italian musicians performed Giovanni Pergolesi's comic intermezzo *La serva padrona* and ignited the so-called War of the Buffoons over the relative merits of French and Italian music. Rameau, although he took no active part in the quarrel, was naturally cast in the role of representative of French music—and a particularly conservative representative at that. Shortly after this event, la Pouplinière, who had separated from his wife, an ardent Rameau supporter, in 1748 took a new mistress, who rapidly dismissed many of the old faces, including Rameau. La Pouplinière, whose tastes ran to the lighter Italian style, acquiesced in the dismissal, and Rameau left in 1752, soon to be replaced as music director by Johann Stamitz.

Rameau was now seventy, and for the remaining twelve years of his life he continued producing operas and ballets, though at a slower rate. His last completed work was a five-act *tragédie lyrique* entitled *Abaris: Ou, Les Boréades*, a remarkable achievement for one who was eighty years old. It was in rehearsal at the opera when Rameau died on September 12, 1764. It was replaced by a revival of an earlier work by André Campra and had to wait more than two hundred years for its premiere performance.

SIGNIFICANCE

Jean-Philippe Rameau's works for the theater form the culmination of the tradition of French Baroque opera begun by Lully. They also contain much of his greatest music. His first opera, *Hippolyte et Aricie*, is also his masterpiece, as it successfully combines a truly dramatic plot with the traditional French love of spectacle and dance, and incorporating the chorus as a participant in the action. He also created authentically dramatic characters in Theseus and, to a lesser extent, Phaedra. *Castor et Pollux* also succeeds dramatically, even though the plot may not be said to be truly tragic, and again the *divertissements* are integrated into the action. The overall effect is gentler and more nostalgic than that of the earlier work.

In many ways, the most remarkable aspect of Rameau's stage works is the astonishing variety of the instrumental music. He was an adept orchestrator, and this is shown most clearly in the descriptive symphonies such as those accompanying the appearance of the monster in *Hippolyte et Aricie* or the summoning of the winds in *Abaris*. His most appealing music is found in his *symphonies de danse*, which include examples ranging from courtly dances such as the gavotte to the newly popular *contredanse* and *tambourin*. In his overtures, he soon broke with the traditional Lullian slow-fast formula and composed programmatic overtures that presaged those of the nineteenth century.

Both Rameau's harpsichord works and his *Pièces de clavecin en concerts* (1741) have remained in the repertoire, and he is especially remembered for his descriptive pieces such as *Le Rappel des oiseaux* and *Les Cyclopes* and his portraits of friends such as *La Forqueray* and *La Cupis*. Many of his keyboard dances reappeared for orchestra in his stage works. His sacred works and cantatas are less important, although they contain much fine music.

Rameau was perhaps more important in his own time as a theorist, and his works made a lasting impression on musical thought. He derived from a study of acoustics the principle of the fundamental bass, whereby each chord possessed a fundamental tone or root whose function was not determined by the lowest sounding pitch. This led to the concept of harmonic inversions, which could be applied either to intervals or to chords, and to the idea of chord progressions, which led in turn to the concept of functional harmony involving tonic, dominant, and subdominant chords and their substitutes. He also had much to say concerning the construction of the seventh chord and the liberal use of dissonance; the presence of both is what gives his own music much of its character. In his later years, he became increasingly fractious and pedantic, but his theories served as the basis for modern views of harmony in Western music.

Rameau seems to have been a man both of his age and apart from it. His theories are clearly the product of the Age of Reason, yet he continued to refer to the earlier concept of "good taste" (*bon goût*). His stage works embody Baroque grandeur dressed in less substantial rococo garb. Throughout his music, there is a sense of detachment, even disillusion, which probably reflects his own philosophy; yet there are moments of deep passion in nearly all of his major works. He was the dominant French musician of the High Baroque and is worthy to stand with Johann Sebastian Bach and George Frideric Handel as the greatest composers of that era.

—*Graydon Beeks*

FURTHER READING

Anthony, James R. *French Baroque Music from Beaujoyeulx to Rameau.* Rev. ed. New York: W. W. Norton, 1978. A good introduction to the subject. The book ends with the rise of Rameau but includes brief discussions of some of his works.

Christensen, Thomas. *Rameau and Musical Thought in the Enlightenment.* New York: Cambridge University Press, 1993. Examines Rameau's musical theories, describing their relationship to the musical and scientific ideas of René Descartes, Sir Isaac Newton, John Locke, and other Enlightenment thinkers. Discusses Rameau's relationship with the Encyclopedists, including Jean-Jacques Rousseau and Diderot.

Dill, Charles. *Monstrous Opera: Rameau and the Tragic Tradition.* Princeton, N.J.: Princeton University Press, 1998. Depicts Rameau as a complicated man, obsessed with musical tradition and theory, his creative instincts, and the public's often negative response to his dramatic style of opera.

Rameau, Jean-Philippe. *Jean-Philippe Rameau: Complete Theoretical Writings.* Edited by Erwin Jacobi. Rome: American Institute of Musicology, 1967-1972. A facsimile edition of Rameau's theoretical works in six volumes, with extensive prefatory material in English.

Rice, Paul F. *Fontainebleau Operas for the Court of Louis XV of France by Jean-Philippe Rameau (1683-1764).* Lewiston, N.Y.: Edwin Mellen Press, 2004. Examines Rameau's operas, including information on Rousseau's criticism of these works, audience response, and Rameau's innovations in using the ariette, or short aria form.

Sadler, Graham, and Thomas Christensen. "Jean-Philippe Rameau." In *The New Grove Dictionary of Music and Musicians*, edited by S. Sadie and J. Tyrrell. London: Macmillan, 2001. The standard music reference article on Rameau, including a complete list of works and an extensive bibliography as well as a detailed biography.

See also: Jean le Rond d'Alembert; Johann Sebastian Bach; François Couperin; Denis Diderot; George Frideric Handel; Louis XV; Jean-Jacques Rousseau; Voltaire.

Related articles in *Great Events from History: The Eighteenth Century, 1701-1800*: c. 1701-1750: Bach Pioneers Modern Music; c. 1709: Invention of the Piano; April 13, 1742: First Performance of Handel's *Messiah*; January, 1762-November, 1766: Mozart Tours Europe as a Child Prodigy; 1795-1797: Paganini's Early Violin Performances.

GUILLAUME-THOMAS RAYNAL
French historian and philosopher

As the animating force behind one of the most influential works of scholarship of the eighteenth century, Raynal helped to define Enlightenment-era critiques of political, economic, and social institutions. His history of European settlements, trade, and commerce in the East and West Indies was encyclopedic in its discussion of European establishments in Asia, Africa, and the Americas, as well as their consequences.

Born: April 12, 1713; Saint-Geniez, France
Died: March 6, 1796; Passay, France
Also known as: Abbé Raynal; Abbé de Raynal
Areas of achievement: Historiography, philosophy, government and politics, literature

EARLY LIFE
The early life of Guillaume-Thomas Raynal (gee-yohm-toh-mah ray-nahl) is not well documented beyond the identities of his parents, Guillaume Raynal, a merchant, and Catherine de Girels, whose father was a government official. Educated in the Jesuit order, he taught humanities and theology at Jesuit centers in Toulouse and was on the verge of taking his final vows when he left the order and ventured to Paris in 1747. His brief association there with the parish of Saint-Sulpice ended because of his questionable ecclesiastical practices, so Raynal made political contacts and pursued his career in letters.

Several popular historical works, including histories of the Dutch stadtholders and the English parliament, brought him attention and financial reward, and in 1750 he became editor of the influential journal *Mercure de France*. Raynal's emerging reputation made him popular in Parisian social circles, won him the support of Voltaire and other intellectuals, and earned him membership in Berlin's Academy of Sciences and Letters and in the Royal Society of London.

LIFE'S WORK
Guillaume-Thomas Raynal was the primary author of *Histoire philosophique et politique, des établissemens et du commerce des Européens dans les deux Indes* (1772-1774; *Philosophical and Political History of the Settlements and Trade of the europeans in the East and West Indies*, 1777), a multivolume exploration of European expansion and imperialism in the East Indies and the West Indies, as Asia and the Americas, respectively, were known at the time. One of the several most popular and influential works of the eighteenth century, this collaborative venture appeared in three major editions and countless printings between 1770 and 1781. Like *Denis Diderot's Encyclopédie: Ou, Dictionnaire raisonné des sciences, des arts, et des métiers* (1751-1772; *Encyclopedia*, 1965), many of whose contributors also collaborated on the *Histoire*, the *Histoire* was a laboratory of Enlightenment ideas and concerns, with an agenda of opposing tyranny and ignorance. The *Histoire*, however, was more thematic in comparing the experiences of European nations in the pursuit of global commerce both in Asia and the New World. Raynal focused on the methods by which colonies and trading stations were established, the impact of colonialism on indigenous cultures, and the effects of imperialism on European countries. He championed eighteenth century ethnocentric perspectives that celebrated Europe's ascendancy and the benefits of European culture for indigenous societies. Although he gave considerable hearing to the debate about the virtues of "primitive" culture versus civilization and he ex-

pressed humanitarian concerns about various societies, the perspective of the *Histoire* was clearly Eurocentric.

The Jesuit-trained Raynal embraced progressive Enlightenment ideals, even though the various editions of the *Histoire* and several of his minor works betrayed many shifts and inconsistencies in his positions. He shared the popular ideology of the French economists known as the Physiocrats in advocating free trade, the elimination of commercial monopolies, and the advantages of free labor over slavery. Indeed, while Raynal came to represent a gradual approach to emancipation, the *Histoire* was viewed by contemporaries as an oracle of the antislavery movement. Raynal championed cultivation in Africa as a way of eliminating slavery in the Caribbean. After Montesquieu's *De l'ésprit des loix* (1748; *The Spirit of the Laws*, 1750), Raynal's *Histoire* was considered by many the most relevant discussion of slavery and abolition.

Raynal warned that the alternative to amelioration of the condition of blacks in the colonies would be a slave uprising that would lead to reprisals and destruction. Yet Raynal's increasingly radical solution to slavery did not continue long past his third edition. By 1785, the voices of Denis Diderot and others were no longer speaking in the pages of the *Histoire*; Raynal had submitted to the

Guillaume-Thomas Raynal. (Library of Congress)

influence of Victor-Pierre Malouet, an associate and colonial official. In an essay he wrote about the administration of Saint-Domingue, Raynal's program better reflected his own attitude toward blacks, whom he had come to believe were happier as slave laborers than as victims of their own barbaric and hostile society in Africa. Caribbean agricultural products could be cultivated only by blacks, and until they could produce among themselves an intellectual such as Montesquieu, blacks were closer to humanity as slaves than as inhabitants in their own lands.

While he was generally sympathetic to the Jesuits, some of Raynal's harshest criticisms were leveled at the claims of religious systems, such as the Catholic Church's doctrine of papal infallibility, which he felt had led to intolerance and fanaticism. A foe of the extremes of political absolutism and popular government, he seemed to have preferred some form of constitutional monarchy. As much as any single literary production, Raynal's *Histoire* influenced the advocates of reform and even revolution on both sides of the Atlantic, but the work was not without criticism. Thomas Paine questioned Raynal's understanding of conditions in colonial North America and suggested that some of Raynal's words were drawn from Paine's *Common Sense* (1776). Also, in *Notes on the State of Virginia* (1785), Thomas Jefferson took issue with Raynal's claim that America had yet to produce a notable poet, mathematician, artist, or scientist.

The monarchy's reaction to the publication of the *Histoire* was increasingly severe. The second edition was condemned by the King's Council, and the edition of 1780, with its challenges to monarchy much influenced by Diderot, was burned by the public executioner. Forced to flee, Raynal spent his exile from 1781 to 1784 in Prussia and Switzerland. Still forbidden to return to Paris, he spent the next years in Rouergue, Montpellier, Toulon, and Marseille, where he was elected to the Estates-General in 1789. Refusing this honor, he ended his exile from Paris in 1791, using the opportunity to criticize the French Revolution's excesses and popular tyranny and offer, in vain, a plea for moderation. In 1795, shortly before his death, he was elected to the Institute of France.

SIGNIFICANCE

Through his literary roles, Guillaume-Thomas Raynal was a magnetic fixture in the Enlightenment world of letters and political maneuvering, but it was through his *Histoire* that he became one of the most influential figures of the eighteenth century. In its own day the *Histoire* was as important a critique of the Old Regime as

IMPERIALISM AND GLOBAL TRADE

In this excerpt from an essay in his multivolume history of European imperialism and trade around the globe, Guillaume-Thomas Raynal discusses the Western world's desire to expand its horizons and conquer and colonize other lands in the name of commerce.

If the art of navigation arose from fishing, as that of war did from the chace [chase]; the navy then owes its existence to commerce. The desire of gain first induced us to make voyages; and one world hath been conquered to enrich another. This object of conquest has been the foundation of commerce; in order to support commerce, naval forces have become necessary, which are themselves produced by the trading navigation. . . .

The Crusades exhausted in Asia all the rage of zeal and ambition, of war and fanaticism, with which the Europeans were possessed: but they were the cause of introducing into Europe a taste for Asiatic luxury; and redeemed by giving rise to some degree of traffic and industry, the blood and the lives they had cost. Three centuries taken up in wars and voyages to the east, gave to the restless spirit of Europe a recruit it stood in need of; that it might not perish by a kind of internal consumption: they prepared the way for that exertion of genius and activity, which since arose, and displayed itself in the conquest and trade of the West-Indies, and of America.

Source: Guillaume-Thomas Raynal, from book 19 of *Philosophical and Political History of the Settlements and Trade of the Europeans in the East and West Indies* (1777), excerpted in *Commerce, Culture, and Liberty: Readings on Capitalism Before Adam Smith*, edited by Henry C. Clark (Indianapolis, Ind.: Liberty Fund, 2003), pp. 611, 612. http://oll.libertyfund.org. Accessed July, 2005.

Montesquieu's *The Spirit of the Laws* or Jean-Jacques Rousseau's *Du contrat social: Ou, Principes du droit politique* (1762; *A Treatise on the Social Contract: Or, The Principles of Politic Law*, 1764; better known as *The Social Contract*). Raynal's work was timely because it crystallized the debates about Europe's imperial activity and promulgated an ideology that was in step with contemporary economic notions. Contemporaries praised Raynal as a leading antislavery advocate, and the *Histoire* was indeed a key treatise in the abolitionist movement in spite of Raynal's later ruminations about blacks. All in all, Raynal gave his age a mirror with which to see its progress and its contradictions.

— *William H. Alexander*

FURTHER READING

Canizares-Esquerra, Jorge. *How to Write the History of the New World: Histories, Epistemologies, and Identities in the Eighteenth-Century Atlantic World*. Stanford, Calif.: Stanford University Press, 2001. This study enlists Raynal in the transatlantic cultural exchange that attempted to interpret the New World and shows how the *Histoire* contributed to this dialogue.

Duchet, Michele. *Anthropology and History in the Century of Enlightenment*. Paris: François Maspero, 1971. An important work that discusses Raynal's role in the development of a colonial ideology that undercut European imperialism and slavery.

Pagden, Anthony. *Lords of All the World: Ideologies of Empire in Spain, Britain, and France, c. 1500-c. 1800*. New Haven, Conn.: Yale University Press, 1998. This comparative study considers Raynal's *Histoire* one of the last major works to develop a theory of empire.

Seeber, Edward. *Anti-Slavery Opinion in France During the Second Half of the Eighteenth Century*. Baltimore: Johns Hopkins University Press, 1937. Although dated, this is still a worthy survey of Raynal's position in the antislavery debate of the eighteenth century.

Wolpe, Hans. *Raynal and His War Machine*. Stanford, Calif.: Stanford University Press, 1957. One of the few analytical monographs on Raynal, this study also traces changes in the several major editions of the *Histoire*.

See also: Benjamin Banneker; Denis Diderot; Thomas Jefferson; Montesquieu; Nanny; James Edward Oglethorpe; Thomas Paine; François Quesnay; Jean-Jacques Rousseau; Samuel Sewall; Granville Sharp; Madame de Staël; Toussaint Louverture.

Related articles in *Great Events from History: The Eighteenth Century, 1701-1800:* 18th century: Expansion of the Atlantic Slave Trade; August, 1712: Maya Rebellion in Chiapas; 1730-1739: First Maroon War; November 23, 1733: Slaves Capture St. John's Island; January 24, 1744-August 31, 1829: Dagohoy Rebellion in the Philippines; 1760-1776: Caribbean Slave Rebellions; April, 1762: Rousseau Publishes *The Social Contract*; 1780-1781: Rebellion of Tupac Amaru II; August 22, 1791-January 1, 1804: Haitian Independence; July, 1795-March, 1796: Second Maroon War.

PAUL REVERE
American industrialist and propagandist

An American revolutionary patriot, Revere also was a prominent silversmith, engraver, and industrialist. He is remembered especially for his service as a civilian messenger, for warning the military of British troop positions and movements, and as a propagandist, producing satirical engravings that criticized British authority.

Born: January 1, 1735; Boston, Massachusetts
Died: May 10, 1818; Boston, Massachusetts
Areas of achievement: Business, government and politics, literature, science and technology, military

EARLY LIFE

Paul Revere was the third of twelve children born to Paul Revere and Deborah Hichborn Revere. Revere's father, a French Protestant Huguenot who at an early age had gone to live with an uncle on the Isle of Guernsey in the English Channel, anglicized his name from Apollos De Revoire. After arriving in Boston in 1715, the thirteen-year-old Revere was apprenticed as a silversmith; he eventually opened his own shop and taught the craft to his son.

From age seven to thirteen, the younger Revere attended the North End Writing School in Boston, then devoted himself to learning silversmithing from his father. Even as a boy, Revere exhibited a strong sense of individual responsibility and dedication to community service, both Calvinist traits. He and several other boys formed a bell-ringers' association dedicated to the principle that no member should beg money from any person. Revere, though he would become a wealthy craftsman, would always be regarded as a member of the "mechanicks" class, a social status ranked below Boston's elite. Of middling height, strong, and stocky, Revere displayed great energy and willingness to assume risks. Upon his death, a Boston newspaper described him as always "cool in thought, ardent in action" and "well adapted to form plans and carry them into successful execution—both for the benefit of himself and the service of others."

At age twenty-one, Revere served as a second lieutenant in a Massachusetts militia expedition against the French in western New York. He did not see any action, however, and after being stationed at Fort William Henry on Lake George from May through November, 1756, he returned to Boston. On August 17, 1757, Revere married Sarah Orne; five months after her death on May 3, 1773, he married Rachal Walker. Each marriage produced eight children; of the sixteen, five died as infants and five in childhood.

Revere, who took over his father's shop upon his father's death in 1754, ran a prodigious business as a silversmith, drawing clientele from his father's network of customers and from organizations to which he belonged. Revere, who like most silversmiths worked in both gold and silver, has been described as the foremost master craftsman of his time. Before the Revolutionary War, his shop produced ninety kinds of silver and gold pieces, all reflecting creative design and skilled craftsmanship, and repaired various items. Although the shop specialized in silver tableware such as tea sets, cups, trays, casters, and candlesticks, it also produced pieces ranging from small items such as thimbles, rings, buttons, and buckles to surgeon's instruments. Revere never sacrificed simplicity of design for elaboration; however, many of his pieces before 1785 carried some rococo-style ornamentation, usually in the form of scrolls and shells.

Always versatile, Revere practiced dentistry, chiefly in the wiring in of false teeth (he never made dentures) and cleaning teeth, and he sold goods imported from England. He also became an accomplished engraver, using copper plates to produce trade cards, book plates, mastheads, and illustrations for broadsides, newspapers, and magazines.

Revere participated in the emerging protest movement against Great Britain from the mid-1760's to the mid-1770's. An active member of Boston's North End Caucus, the Long Room Club, and the Sons of Liberty Whig Club, he was in the thick of every protest. Apparently content simply to make a contribution, he never rose to a high rank of leadership in the revolutionary movement and never ran for public office.

Revere served as an influential propagandist for the revolutionary cause from the passage of the Stamp Act in 1765 to the beginning of the war, publishing satirical engravings that ridiculed British authority. The best-known copper-plate engraving reads "The BLOODY MASSACRE perpetuated in King Street, BOSTON, on March 5th 1770, by a party of the 29th REGT." Though inaccurately depicting the event and appropriating a drawing of the scene by British artist Henry Pelham without giving Pelham credit, the engraving, by placing blame for shedding first blood upon British troops, stirred hearts of patriots everywhere.

In Boston Harbor on December 16, 1773, Revere joined other patriots barely disguised as American Indians and dumped overboard casks of tea belonging to the British East India Company. He then carried the news of the Boston Tea Party to New York City, becoming the official courier of the Massachusetts Provincial Assembly and the Boston Committee of Correspondence. In May, 1774, he rode to New York City and Philadelphia, bringing word of the parliamentary law that closed the port of Boston. In September, 1774, he carried the radical Suffolk Resolves, drawn up by delegates from Boston and other towns in Suffolk County, to the Continental Congress in Philadelphia; Congress quickly committed all the colonies to the document, which called for the colonies to cease trade with Great Britain and to prepare for armed defense. In December, 1774, Revere relayed news to patriots in New Hampshire that the Massachusetts governor and general, Thomas Gage, was planning to reinforce the small British garrison at Fort William and Mary at Portsmouth; this information led patriots to seize the garrison and its munitions, which were later used by the Americans at the Battle of Bunker Hill (1775).

Paul Revere's famous ride. (Library of Congress)

LIFE'S WORK

Paul Revere was almost unknown in the annals of American history until the publication of Henry Wadsworth Longfellow's narrative poem "Paul Revere's Ride" in *The Atlantic* in January, 1861. The poem's publication gave Revere an esteemed place in the pantheon of American heroes. On that fateful night of April 18-19, 1775, Revere rowed across the Charles River, with his oars muffled by petticoats wrapped around them, then galloped by horseback toward Concord to warn of the approach of the British. William Dawes and Samuel Prescott joined him; only Prescott made it to Concord. A less-well-known fact is that two days earlier, Revere had ridden to Concord to warn John Hancock, Samuel Adams, and others of the British troops' plan to march out of Boston, enabling the removal of much of the munitions from Concord before the British arrived.

Involvement in the war effort distracted Revere from his business enterprises from 1775 to 1779. In 1775, Revere manufactured paper money for the Massachusetts government and the Continental Congress, engraving the plates and building a printing press for the task. He also designed coins, medals, and the first seal of the United States and the state of Massachusetts (the latter remains in use).

Commissioned a major in April, 1776, and lieutenant colonel six months later, Revere was in charge of three artillery companies in the Massachusetts militia. During 1778-1779, he commanded the patriot garrison at Castle William in Boston Harbor. Revere served in the expedition of July-August, 1778, commanded by General John Sullivan, which was unsuccessful in ousting British forces from Newport, Rhode Island. His military career came to an end with the Penobscot expedition of July 19-August 15, 1779. A Massachusetts land and naval force was to attack a British base at Castine, Maine, at the mouth of the Penobscot River. When an unexpected and large British reinforcement arrived, the Americans abandoned their ships and fled. Revere was accused of disobedience of orders, unsoldierlike conduct, and cowardice and was relieved of his command at Castle William. Revere insisted upon a court martial, and in February, 1782, he was acquitted on all charges.

After the revolution, Revere's silversmith shop increased production, creating pieces in the neoclassic style, more restrained than before, and incorporating some classical designs, such as fluted teapots. More table items were produced, especially flatware, and fourteen types of spoons were cast. In 1783, Revere opened a hardware store.

The Revere enterprises expanded in 1788 with the establishment in Boston of an iron and brass foundry that cast cannon for the state and the federal government and produced a variety of other items such as nails and bolts. When the bell of the Second Congregational Church in Boston cracked in 1792, Revere offered to cast a new one himself rather than have the church order a replacement from England. His offer led to the creation of the first large-scale bell manufactory in America. From 1792 to 1828, the foundry (the bell operation was moved to Canton, Massachusetts, in 1804) produced 950 bells of all sizes and functions, weighing from a few pounds to about 3,000, and cast with 75 percent copper and 25 percent tin. Revere bells can still be found at many New England churches, including King's Chapel, Boston.

Revere also discovered a process for rolling sheet copper. In 1801, he built a mill at Canton for copper rolling and brass casting. The copper works eventually became one of the largest industries in the United States.

While Revere was in charge, the Revere Copper and Brass Company made copper boilers for steamships and the copper sheeting for the dome of the Massachusetts State House and for the bottom of the USS *Constitution* (Old Ironsides). In 1811, Revere turned over management of his businesses to his son, Joseph Warren Revere. The Revere Copper Company was chartered in 1828 under his son's direction. The company went through major reorganizations and mergers in the twentieth century and is now known as Revere Copper Products. Over the years, Revere copper has been used in the making of warships, shells, torpedoes, tanks, telephones, radios, plumbing, and many other items.

An avid joiner, Revere belonged to many community groups. He joined the Masonic order in 1760 and was a founder of the Massachusetts Grand Lodge and served as its grand master (1795-1797). He helped establish the Massachusetts Fire Insurance Company and presided over the Massachusetts Charitable Mechanic Association from 1795 to 1799. He served as Suffolk County coroner (1794-1800) and assisted in setting up the Boston Board of Health, acting as its president (1799-1800).

In early 1788, when it appeared that Massachusetts might fail to ratify the U.S. Constitution, Boston me-

---

PAUL REVERE'S RIDE

American poet Henry Wadsworth Longfellow in 1860 penned a tribute to the legendary Paul Revere in a poem called "Paul Revere's Ride," first published in 1863, and excerpted here.

> Listen my children and you shall hear
> Of the midnight ride of Paul Revere,
> On the eighteenth of April, in Seventy-five;
> Hardly a man is now alive
> Who remembers that famous day and year.
> He said to his friend, "If the British march
> By land or sea from the town to-night,
> Hang a lantern aloft in the belfry arch
> of the North Church tower as a signal light;—
> One if by land, and two if by sea;
> And I on the opposite shore will be,
> Ready to ride and spread the alarm
> Through every Middlesex village and farm,
> For the country folk to be up and to arm."
> . . . .
> So through the night rode Paul Revere;
> And so through the night went his cry of alarm
> To every Middlesex village and farm,—
> A cry of defiance, and not of fear,
> A voice in the darkness, a knock at the door,
> And a word that shall echo for evermore!
> For, borne on the night-wind of the Past,
> Through all our history, to the last,
> In the hour of darkness and peril and need,
> The people will waken and listen to hear
> The hurrying hoof-beats of that steed,
> And the midnight message of Paul Revere.

Source: Henry Wadsworth Longfellow, "Paul Revere's Ride." Eserver Collective at Iowa State University. http://eserver.org/poetry/paul-revere.html. Accessed June, 2005.

chanics held a mass meeting, unanimously adopting resolutions in favor of ratification. Revere led a delegation from the group to the home of Samuel Adams, a member of the ratifying convention whose support of the Constitution had been wavering. Adams, impressed by the show of support, voted in favor of the Constitution. The action taken by Revere and his associates may well have been the deciding factor for the acceptance of the Constitution in Massachusetts.

After the Constitution went into effect, Revere expected to be appointed director of the mint or a customs house official, but his ambitions were denied, probably because he was a Federalist, opposed to the Jeffersonian Republicans. He thought of himself as a conservative who believed in the liberal principles of the American Revolution, chiefly liberty and opportunity within the confines of law and order. In an 1804 letter to a friend, Revere called himself a "warm Republican," saying "I always deprecated Democracy as much as I did Aristocracy." Revere may be regarded as "one of the last of the Cocked Hats." His conservatism was evident in his persistence in publicly wearing clothes of the revolutionary era—cocked hats, ruffled shirts, knee breeches, long stockings, large shoe buckles, and the like—long after such dress had fallen from fashion.

SIGNIFICANCE

Paul Revere was a true patriot hero. He was willing to serve in any capacity—courier, agitator, soldier, propagandist, or artisan—to further the revolutionary cause. When patriot leaders wanted something done, they could depend on Revere. Longfellow's stirring poem brought Revere a fame that he never sought to achieve.

A master silversmith, Revere operated a shop that produced an astounding amount and variety of silver pieces, setting a high standard of quality for the craft. He was a pioneer in copper-plate engraving and metallurgy and one of America's earliest large-scale industrialists, running iron and brass foundries and a copper-sheeting mill. Revere, one of the first to inaugurate a factory system in America, put investment capital to use for production, employed new technology, organized and managed a large labor force, made arrangements for acquisition of raw materials needed for production, and provided for transportation of goods to market. Revere founded an enduring, major segment of the copper industry. Daring, persistent, and hardworking, he exemplified what could be attained in a land of opportunity.

—*Harry M. Ward*

FURTHER READING

Buker, George E. *The Penobscot Expedition: Commodore Saltanstall and the Massachusetts Conspiracy of 1779*. Annapolis, Md.: Naval Institute Press, 2002. A reexamination of the expedition, including the roles of Revere and Commodore Dudley Saltanstall.

Fischer, David H. *Paul Revere's Ride*. New York: Oxford University Press, 1994. A lively, well-researched narrative focusing on the events of the spring of 1775. Includes copious annotation and a definitive bibliography.

Forbes, Esther. *Paul Revere and the World He Lived In*. Boston: Houghton Mifflin, 1942. This Pulitzer Prize-winning book presents a full biography and a description of the Boston community during Revere's life. Contains a short section of expository footnotes and a bibliography.

Gettemy, Charles F. *The True Story of Paul Revere: His Midnight Ride; His Arrest and Court-Martial; His Useful Public Services*. Boston: Little, Brown, 1905. Mainly a general survey, this volume contains some family letters and quotations from documents. No bibliography.

Goss, Elbridge H. *The Life of Colonel Paul Revere*. 2 vols. Boston: Joseph Cupples, 1891. This work contains a large section on the Penobscot expedition. The Revere family correspondence reproduced in this book is of great value.

Leehey, Patrick M., et al. *Paul Revere—Artisan, Businessman, and Patriot: The Man Behind the Myth*. Boston: Paul Revere Memorial Association, 1988. Essays and illustrations relating primarily to Revere's business and industrial life in the context of an exhibition at the Museum of Our National Heritage at Lexington, Massachusetts, 1988-1989.

Triber, Jayne E. *A True Republican: The Life of Paul Revere*. Amherst: University of Massachusetts Press, 1998. A biography describing Revere's role in the American Revolution, the evolution of his political thought, and his transformation from artisan to entrepreneur. Triber uses Revere's life to illustrate the attraction of republicanism for artisans, social life in colonial and postrevolutionary United States, the importance of Free Masonry, and the development of political parties in the new nation.

See also: Samuel Adams; Hester Bateman; Matthew Boulton; Abraham Darby; Thomas Gage; John Hancock; Granville Sharp; Daniel Shays.

Related articles in *Great Events from History: The Eighteenth Century, 1701-1800:* 1701: Plumier Publishes *L'Art de tourner*; 1759: Wedgwood Founds a Ceramics Firm; March 22, 1765-March 18, 1766: Stamp Act Crisis; December 16, 1773: Boston Tea Party; September 5-October 26, 1774: First Continental Congress; April 19, 1775: Battle of Lexington and Concord; May 10-August 2, 1775: Second Continental Congress.

SIR JOSHUA REYNOLDS
English painter and writer

Founder of the English School of painting, Reynolds served for more than two decades as the first president of the Royal Academy of Arts. His Discourses *express the fundamental tenets of neoclassical art, while his paintings anticipated the Romantic movement.*

Born: July 16, 1723; Plympton, Devonshire, England
Died: February 23, 1792; London, England
Area of achievement: Art

EARLY LIFE
Joshua Reynolds's father, Samuel Reynolds, was a clergyman and headmaster of the local school, where Reynolds received his only formal education. Like his father, his mother, the former Theophila Potter, came from a family of university-trained clerics, but young Reynolds showed little interest in study: One of his surviving Latin exercises is more remarkable for its doodles than its prose.

Even as a child Reynolds showed artistic ability. A sketch of Plympton School impressed his father, and in the family library Reynolds pored over such works as Charles-Alphonse Dufresnoy's *De arte graphica* as translated by John Dryden (1695) and Jonathan Richardson's *The Theory of Painting* (1715). He also copied engravings accompanying texts such as Plutarch's *Lives*. At the age of twelve, Reynolds produced his first portrait, that of the Reverend Thomas Smart. Consequently, when he was seventeen he was apprenticed to Thomas Hudson, a Devonshire native who had gone to London and become England's leading portrait painter.

Reynolds remained with Hudson approximately three years (1740-1743). He then returned home, and for the next six years he traveled between London, Plymouth, and Plymouth Dock, painting portraits of the local gentry.

LIFE'S WORK
Despite his youth and a relatively brief apprenticeship, Joshua Reynolds demonstrated remarkable technical ability, as exemplified by the fancy-dress portrait of Captain John Hamilton (1746). Late in life, Reynolds remarked on how little progress he had made in the decades since he had painted that piece. In this early period one can detect, too, some of the lifelong influences on Reynolds. His self-portrait dating from about 1746 is reminiscent of Rembrandt, as is a posthumous portrait of his father from the same time. The influence of Sir Anthony Van Dyck is apparent in *The Eliot Family* (c. 1746), that of Titian in *First Lieutenant Paul Henry Ourry* (c. 1747). Already, then, Reynolds was beginning to make English art international rather than insular by adopting Flemish chiaroscuro and Venetian coloring.

In 1749, Richard, First Baron Edgcumbe, provided a major stimulus to this tendency. Edgcumbe had been an early patron to Reynolds and had sat for his portrait. Now he introduced Reynolds to Commodore Augustus Keppel, who had stopped in Plymouth on his way to the Mediterranean. Keppel offered to take Reynolds with him, thereby giving the painter a chance to study at firsthand the works of the Italian masters. Keppel's ship, the *Centurion*, left England in May and reached Minorca on August 23, 1749. For the rest of the year, Reynolds toured the island and painted the members of the British garrison. Early the next year he moved on to Italy, where he remained until the middle of 1752.

While there he undertook some caricatures, but chiefly he studied and sketched the masters. In essence, Reynolds was completing his apprenticeship; by the time he returned to England, in October, 1752, he had become a more accomplished artist who was soon able to outdistance all rivals. The sojourn on the Continent marked his physiognomy as well as his work. On Minorca, a fall from a horse permanently injured his upper lip, and a cold he caught while devoting three months to sketching the works of Raphael in the unheated Sistine Chapel left him deaf. For the rest of his life, he carried a large hearing trumpet, evident in a 1775 self-portrait. Less apparent in this and other pictures that Reynolds painted of himself are his florid complexion and his relatively short stature, somewhat under five feet, six inches in height.

Having set up his studio at 104 St. Martin's Lane, London (in 1753), Reynolds was once more aided by Keppel. To thank the commodore for his kindness, Reynolds painted a full-length portrait of him. Reynolds worked diligently on the piece, redoing the head after it was nearly finished and altering the hands and clothing. Everywhere in this work Reynolds's trip to Italy is evident: The pose derives from the Apollo Belvedere, the lighting from Tintoretto. Yet the picture also reveals Reynolds's confidence in his ability to break with tradition. The background, a storm-tossed ocean bearing the wreckage of a ship, anticipates the Romantic fascination with the power of nature. Instead of emphasizing the blue naval coat, Reynolds relies on green-gray, an uncommon color for this kind of picture, and he takes liberties with Keppel's outfit, which suggests the gentleman more than the sailor. Most significant, Reynolds here introduces a new kind of portraiture. For the eighteenth century, the highest form of painting was historical because it was most "general and intellectual," the qualities Reynolds stressed in his ninth *Discourse* (1780). Portraits, and to an even greater extent landscapes, were less highly regarded because they treated the specific person or place. Reynolds's portrait of Keppel seeks to elevate this genre to the historical. The picture itself alludes to a historical event, the wreck of Keppel's ship, the *Maidstone*, in 1747. Beyond this specific episode, though, is the generalized attitude of command and dignity, of calm in the face of danger. Reynolds thus paints the idea as well as the individual.

Before presenting the painting to Keppel, Reynolds exhibited it for a time in his studio to show prospective sitters what he could achieve. It is not clear whether viewers at the time recognized the traditional references or the revolutionary concept of the picture, but it is clear that they were impressed. In 1755, he had 120 sitters; three years later, he had 150, even though his prices were the highest in London. The strength of his reputation is evident from an anecdote concerning his portrait of Jane Bowles (c. 1775). When her parents wanted her picture, they resolved to ask George Romney because Reynolds's work had a reputation for fading. Sir George Beaumont changed their minds, telling them, "No matter . . . ; even a faded picture from Reynolds will be the finest thing you can have." The painting has cracked and faded in the more than two centuries since it was executed, but its overall condition remains good.

That some of Reynolds's pictures have not fared so well is the result of his experimentation. M. Kirby Talley, Jr., has said that Reynolds was more innovative in his techniques than even Leonardo da Vinci, whose experiments also were not always successful. Fascinated by the glowing colors of the Venetian masters, Reynolds sought through various means to duplicate their effects. He was so captivated by technique that he would sometimes rub a picture back to the bare canvas to determine what the artist had done. An example of his experimentation is a portrait of Mrs. Kirkman done in 1772. The piece was waxed, egged, and varnished, then painted, each successive layer applied before the previous one could dry. The original luster must have been impressive, but, not surprisingly, the painting has cracked. Reynolds tried various vegetable pigments, some of which have faded with time, and he used Venetian turpentine and asphaltum that made for rich tones but had unfortunate long-term consequences. Sir Walter Blackett, who was painted by Reynolds in the 1760's and lived to see his portrait fade away, quipped,

Painting of old was surely well designed
To keep the features of the dead in mind,
But this great rascal has reversed the plan,
And made his picture die before the man.

As Beaumont's recommendation indicates, though, sitters were undeterred. By 1760, Reynolds was earning between £6,000 and £10,000 a year and was busy seven days a week, eight hours a day. Between 1753 and 1760, he painted three members of the royal family—the duke of Cumberland and Prince Edward in 1758 and the prince of Wales in 1759—one dozen dukes, and numerous members of the gentry. His paintings thus provide a record of upper-class England in the mid-eighteenth century. In 1760, Reynolds bought the house at 47 Leicester Fields (later Leicester Square) for £1,650 and made an additional £1,500 of improvements, including the construction of a large octagonal studio.

This was also the year of the first London exhibit by British artists. Over the next decade, various societies sought to provide more publicity for native talent; their efforts culminated in the establishment of the Royal Academy on December 10, 1768. Although Reynolds was friendly with both Whigs and Tories—Samuel Johnson once complained to him, "You hate no one living"— he was more closely identified with the former party. Hence, in 1762, King George III named Alan Ramsay as his Painter in Ordinary (a post that Reynolds received in

1784, after Ramsay's death). The king could not, however, overlook England's greatest painter in choosing the first president of the academy. On December 14, 1768, Reynolds was chosen for this post, and on April 21, 1769, he was knighted as a consequence of that election.

Already he had begun to paint fewer portraits than he had earlier in his career; now he reduced the number from about 150 a year to about 50. In part the decline resulted from his presidential duties, which included delivering an address on the anniversary of the Royal Academy's establishment. Those speeches, which were presented annually until 1772 and biennially thereafter, allowed Reynolds to express his artistic theories. Published under the title *Discourses*, they repeatedly elicited the highest praise. The *Gentleman's Magazine* for April, 1772, called the fifth *Discourse* "the best work upon the practice and theory of painting that has yet appeared in the world." Writer Hannah More described the sixth *Discourse* (1774) as "a masterpiece for matter as well as style," and the bishop of London pronounced the last one (1790) "the work of a *Great Master*, whose name will be as much and as justly revered by this country, as that of Michael Angelo is by his." The fifteen discourses not only offered advice to the academy's students but also articulated the principles of neoclassicism. Thus, in the seventh *Discourse* (1776), Reynolds criticized "exact representations of individual objects with all their imperfections" and urged instead the portrayal of "general ideas." In the thirteenth *Discourse* (1786), he states, "Reason . . . must ultimately determine every thing" and goes on to say that the aim of art is not to record what is but "to supply the natural imperfection of things."

Another distraction for Reynolds was his socializing. In Samuel Johnson's terms, Reynolds was a clubbable man. In 1764, he founded The Club, in part to give Johnson a forum for his conversation, in part to provide himself with literary discussions that he regarded as essential for the artist. He was to credit Johnson's talk with having "formed my mind and . . . brushed off from it a deal of

IDEAL BEAUTY

Sir Joshua Reynolds believed that "ideal beauty" is obtainable through an artist's ability to perfect the "original" natural world. He argued that artistic geniuses do not copy *nature as they sense it but* re-form *nature as an abstraction and then make that abstraction tangible—and better—through their art.*

I will now add that Nature herself is not to be too closely copied. There are excellencies in the art of painting beyond what is commonly called the imitation of nature: . . .

The wish of the genuine painter must be more extensive: instead of endeavouring to amuse mankind with the minute neatness of his imitations, he must endeavour to improve them by the grandeur of his ideas. . . .

All the objects which are exhibited to our view by nature, upon close examination will be found to have their blemishes and defects. The most beautiful forms have something about them like weakness, minuteness, or imperfection. But it is not every eye that perceives these blemishes. It must be an eye long used to the contemplation and comparison of these forms. . . . His [the artist's] eye being enabled to distinguish the accidental deficiencies, excrescences, and deformities of things, from their general figures, he makes out an abstract idea of their forms more perfect than any one original; and what may seem a paradox, he learns to design naturally by drawing his figures unlike to any one object. This idea of the perfect state of nature, which the Artist calls the Ideal Beauty, is the great leading principle by which works of genius are conducted.

Source: Sir Joshua Reynolds, third *Discourse* (1770), in *A Documentary History of Art: Michelangelo and the Mannerists, the Baroque & the Eighteenth Century*, vol. 2, edited by Elizabeth G. Holt (Garden City, N.Y.: Anchor Books, 1958), pp. 274, 276.

rubbish." This club met on Mondays; during the rest of the week, Reynolds made the rounds of the Thursday Night Club, the Shilling Rubber Club (for whist, a card game), the Devonshire Club, and the Society of the Dilettanti (which met for Sunday dinner). In addition, he frequently attended and gave private parties.

The paintings that he did produce after 1768 remain of high quality and reveal his psychological penetration as well as his technical virtuosity. Some of his best paintings are of his literary friends, such as the five portraits of Johnson that alternately reflect Johnson's social side and his introspective nature. He could be equally discerning of those whom he knew less well, too. *Lady Worsley* (c. 1776) suggests a boldness and sensuality that led to uncontested charges of adultery a few years after she sat for her picture.

From about the same time as *Lady Worsley* is his monumental *The Marlborough Family*, applying the grand style of historical painting to a family group. The work is full of studied allusions, such as the comic mask held by one of the children and probably borrowed from a work by Nicolas Poussin. Yet it is original in its groupings, so that eight people and three dogs fit nicely onto the canvas, and the formality of the adult world contrasts with the playfulness of the children.

In 1781, Reynolds went to the Netherlands to examine Flemish paintings, and he made a second trip there four years later. The pictures from this decade show a new vitality. The prince of Wales's portrait depicts him preparing to mount his gray stallion and ride into battle (1784); Lieutenant-Colonel Bannistre Tarleton adjusts his uniform as a battle rages behind him (c. 1782). There is an informality about *Colonel George Coussmaker* (c. 1782), with the subject's crossed legs in front of a delicately sketched tree, that is lacking in earlier works. Paintings such as *Miss Gideon and Her Brother, William* (c. 1786), *Master Hare* (1788), and *Penelope Boothby* (1788) move away from the bright colors of the Venetian school to emphasize contrasts of light and dark. The delicate brushstrokes suggest Peter Paul Rubens, the shadows, Rembrandt; the play of light and dark reminds the viewer of Reynolds's younger contemporary Francisco de Goya.

On July 13, 1789, Reynolds abruptly ceased painting, "prevented by my eye beginning to be obscured," he wrote. By the end of the year, he was blind in one eye. His formerly complacent personality suffered as a result. When the academy rejected Reynolds's candidate, Giuseppe Bonomi, for the post of professor of perspective, Reynolds temporarily resigned. Although this quarrel was resolved, others ensued. Nothing, however, could obscure Reynolds's achievements, recorded in some four thousand paintings.

After his death from liver cancer on February 23, 1792, he lay in state at Somerset House, the home of the Royal Academy. His pallbearers included three dukes and two earls; his casket was followed to St. Paul's Cathedral by ninety-one coaches. Reynolds was buried in the crypt near Sir Christopher Wren. England's greatest portrait painter thus lies beside England's greatest architect.

SIGNIFICANCE

When Joshua Reynolds was considering his life's work, he debated between becoming an apothecary and a painter. In many ways, the former seemed the better choice in 1740. William Hogarth had claimed that England could not hope to compete with the Continent in the field of artistic achievement, and he went on to say that the prospects for portrait painters were bleak: "the

majority . . . must either shift how they can among their acquaintances, or live by travelling from town to town like gipsies." There was no school of English art; the country's greatest painters had all come from the Continent: Hans Holbein in the sixteenth century and Sir Anthony Van Dyck, Sir Peter Lely, and Sir Godfrey Kneller in the seventeenth. Nor was there a national academy to train and exhibit English talent.

Reynolds changed all that. When he traveled, he did so as a gentleman, riding in his own gilded coach, and he amply demonstrated that English art could rival, even surpass, the work being done elsewhere in Europe. Symbolic of this changed state of affairs was Reynolds's election to the Academy of Florence in 1775. Ten years later, Catherine the Great asked Reynolds for a historical picture, trusting every detail, including size and subject, to him. Under his direction the Royal Academy gained a reputation that no other artist in England could have given it, and the exhibitions there equaled the salons being held during the same period in Paris.

Much of Reynolds's work consciously relies on the European tradition. Sketches that he made during his visit to Italy find their way into such pieces as Elizabeth Anne Linley Sheridan in the guise of St. Cecilia (1775). *Master Crewe as Henry VIII* (1776) is a mock-heroic rendition of Holbein's famous picture of the Tudor monarch. *Mrs. Lloyd* (1776) takes its pose from Raphael's *Adam Tempted;* Sarah Siddons as the muse of Tragedy is also Siddons as Michelangelo's Isaiah in the Sistine Chapel. Similarly, Reynolds's *Discourses* cling to the traditional. On the title page of the 1798 edition of Reynolds's *Works*, William Blake, the arch-Romantic, wrote, "This man was hired to Deprave Art."

Yet, as the eminent Victorian art and cultural critic John Ruskin noted, Reynolds "exhorted his pupils to attend only to the invariable, while he himself was occupied in distinguishing every variation of womanly temper." Reynolds provided a record of eighteenth century aristocracy, but he also painted a beggar who made cabbage nets for a living (*The Schoolboy*, 1777). Within a single year, 1764, he painted England's two archbishops and the country's two leading courtesans. As Thomas Gainsborough declared, "How various the fellow is."

Despite his devotion to neoclassical modes and doctrines, he looked ahead in some ways to the Romantic revolution to follow. His men are heroic, his women refined, but his children are children, not small adults. He drew his subjects not only from Greek and Roman mythology but also from Dante and Shakespeare. Such sources would be commonplace in the next century but were unusual at the time—the first complete translation of *The Divine Comedy* into English did not appear until 1802. Reynolds was devoted to color, and Ruskin ranked him with Titian and Joseph Turner as a great colorist. At the same time, his use of light and shadow is impressive, and a late picture such as *Georgiana, Duchess of Devonshire, with Her Daughter, Lady Georgiana Cavendish* (1784) is largely a study of white on white.

In his fourteenth *Discourse* (1788), devoted to the recently deceased Gainsborough, Reynolds observed,

> If ever this nation should produce genius sufficient to acquire to us the honourable distinction of an English school, the name of Gainsborough will be transmitted to posterity, in the history of the art among the very first of that rising name.

As Reynolds knew well, the speaker of those words might with greater justice have substituted his own name for that of his distinguished rival.

—Joseph Rosenblum

FURTHER READING

Hilles, Frederick Whiley. *The Literary Career of Sir Joshua Reynolds*. Cambridge, England: Cambridge University Press, 1936. Concentrates on Reynolds's other career, that of a writer. Reveals much about his friendships with those of literary London and the sources of his ideas.

Hudson, Derek. *Sir Joshua Reynolds: A Personal Study*. London: G. Bles, 1958. A sympathetic treatment of a person who rarely evoked sympathy, even from his friends. Concentrates on Reynolds's personal relationships but also offers a good general introduction to his art.

Leslie, Charles Robert, and Tom Taylor. *Life and Times of Sir Joshua Reynolds*. London: John Murray, 1865. Despite its age, this two-volume work remains the most detailed biography of Reynolds. It includes much original material drawn from the artist and his contemporaries.

McIntyre, Ian. *Joshua Reynolds: The Life and Times of the First President of the Royal Academy*. London: Allen Lane, 2003. A comprehensive biography, with a discussion of Reynolds's involvement with the Royal Academy, his rivalry with Gainsborough, his life in Rome, and his activities as an art collector and dealer. McIntyre analyzes Reynolds's subject paintings and sexual "fancy paintings" in addition to his portraits.

Mayoux, Jean Jacques. *English Painting*. New York: St. Martin's Press, 1975. A survey of a century of British art from the mid-1700's to the mid-1800's. Includes a good, though sometimes harsh, discussion of Reynolds and his influence.

Penny, Nicholas, ed. *Reynolds*. New York: Harry N. Abrams, 1986. A catalog of an exhibition of Reynolds's works. In addition to the marvelous reproductions, many of them in color, the volume includes important essays on Reynolds's life and work.

Redgrave, Richard, and Samuel Redgrave. *A Century of British Painters*. Ithaca, N.Y.: Cornell University Press, 1981. Covers the same period as Mayoux's book, but treats Reynolds more kindly. Offers a fine discussion of Reynolds's technique.

Reynolds, Sir Joshua. *The Letters of Sir Joshua Reynolds*. Edited by John Ingamells and John Edgcumbe. New Haven, Conn.: Yale University Press, 2000. The first collection of Reynolds's letters to be published since 1929, this updated collection features additional letters, for a total of 308. Reynolds wrote these letters—which contain detailed notes to help readers understand their contents—to friends, family, and patrons.

Waterhouse, Ellis. *Reynolds*. New York: Phaidon, 1973. Another good source for reproductions (139, with 16 in color). Includes an elegant essay on the artist and his art and a useful bibliography.

Wendorf, Richard. *Sir Joshua Reynolds: The Painter in Society*. Cambridge, Mass.: Harvard University Press, 1996. Wendorf contends that Reynolds became the most famous painter of his time not only because he was talented and lucky but also because he knew how to please his clients. Wendorf situates Reynolds's art within the context of eighteenth century British society.

See also: William Blake; Catherine the Great; Georgiana Cavendish; John Singleton Copley; Thomas Gainsborough; Francisco de Goya; William Hogarth; Samuel Johnson; Thomas Lawrence; Hannah More; George Romney; Sarah Siddons; Benjamin West.

Related articles in *Great Events from History: The Eighteenth Century, 1701-1800:* c. 1732: Society of Dilettanti Is Established; December 10, 1768: Britain's Royal Academy of Arts Is Founded.

SAMUEL RICHARDSON
English novelist

Richardson, a successful London printer, wrote one of the earliest English novels, Pamela. *Its successor,* Clarissa, *is often regarded as the first work of psychological fiction in English. Through these works Richardson influenced the development of the psychologically focused novel throughout Europe.*

Born: August 19, 1689 (baptized); Mackworth, Derbyshire, England
Died: July 4, 1761; London, England
Area of achievement: Literature

EARLY LIFE

Samuel Richardson was one of eight surviving children, born to a father whose support of the Jacobites may have been the reason for the family's flight from London shortly before Samuel was born. The family returned to live in London before the end of the century, settling in a working-class neighborhood. Richardson's father was a tradesman, and although Samuel wished to enter the ministry, limited family funds kept him from pursuing that career. Instead, partly because he was a voracious reader in his youth, he found the printing trade amenable to his interests.

In 1706, he was apprenticed to Jonathan Wilde, a printer and member of the Stationer's Company. By 1715, Richardson had risen to become a freeman in the company. Early evidence of his skill as a writer can be seen in the work he took on during the little time he had for himself while living and working at Wilde's establishment. By age thirteen he was already assisting young women by writing love letters on their behalf. By 1721 he was able to leave Wilde's business to establish his own printing shop, and in the same year he married Martha Wilde, his employer's daughter.

LIFE'S WORK

Unlike many writers of his day, Samuel Richardson worked his entire life at a trade. Long before he thought up the scheme that led to the production of his first novel, he was establishing himself as a printer of some note, and some notoriety. He was a favorite printer of Tory political writers, and he had a hand in producing a number of political pamphlets and newspapers, including the *True Briton* and *Mist's Weekly Journal*. Writers of both publications were eventually pursued by the Whig government for various charges of slander and sedition, and Richardson himself was often under a cloud of suspicion for his activities.

At home Richardson suffered the disappointments common in so many eighteenth century households. None of the children of his marriage to Martha Wilde survived infancy, and Martha died in 1731. Two years later Richardson married Elizabeth Leake, with whom he had four daughters who outlived him. His printing business allowed him to provide for his family while building a circle of influential and noted acquaintances, a group that expanded exponentially after the publication of the first English novel, *Pamela: Or, Virtue Rewarded* (1740-1741). In his early years in the trade, however, he could count among his acquaintances few literary figures, with the exception of the poet Aaron Hill, whose lifelong friendship he cherished.

During the 1720's and 1730's, Richardson was busy at his print shop assisting writers such as Daniel Defoe in bringing their work before the public. In 1730 he issued a work of his own, *The Apprentice's Vade Mecum: Or, Young Man's Pocket Companion,* a conduct book offering advice to young men entering a trade. Its moralizing tone suggests the direction Richardson's later work would take. He also issued a version of *Aesop's Fables* in 1739, revising the morals of several tales to be more suitable for English readers. In 1733 he received an important commission from the House of Commons to handle its printing needs. While he frequently had trouble collecting on his bills, he was then in a position of prominence in his trade, and it was not surprising that he rose through various offices in the Stationer's Company, eventually becoming master of the company in 1754.

Sometime before 1740, Richardson was asked to produce a book of letters that could be used as samples for those who needed assistance in corresponding about social and family matters. His penchant for storytelling soon led him to produce quite another work from this germ of an idea: the tale of a servant girl who resists her master's sexual advances until he agrees to marry her. Issued in four volumes, *Pamela* questioned the separation of social classes and highlighted the moral rectitude that, in Richardson's view at least, was expected of people of all classes. The work caused a sensation in London; within months it was the talk of literary circles in Europe as well.

Pamela went through multiple editions, and suddenly Richardson was sought by ladies of social distinction for his advice, or simply for his friendship. French and German translations appeared and several adaptations were produced, including plays by Voltaire in France and Carlo Goldoni in Italy. Not all were pleased with Richardson's work, however. Henry Fielding, a successful playwright and political writer, savaged the work in a burlesque called *An Apology for the Life of Mrs. Shamela Andrews* (1741) and produced his own version of the proper relationship between conduct and morality in the novel *The History of the Adventures of Joseph Andrews, and of His Friend Mr. Abraham Adams* (1742), a story in which characters from *Pamela* play a prominent role.

Richardson became a sensation at home and abroad. Urged by his new, larger circle of friends, he began writing a new novel in letters, what was to become one of the longest novels in the English language. This time, the novel had a tragic ending. Published in seven volumes in 1747-1748, *Clarissa: Or, The History of a Young Lady* is a story that parallels the events of *Pamela*, but the heroine's virtuous conduct and her decision to die rather than submit to her master leads to an inevitable tragic conclusion. The psychological realism Richardson achieves in his portraits of Clarissa and her seducer, Lovelace, appealed to readers who became emotionally involved in this tale of rape and abandonment.

Buoyed by the encouragement and advice of a group of admirers such as Lady Bradshaigh (Dorothy Bellingham), Sarah Wescomb, the writer Elizabeth Carter, Hester Chapone, and Fielding's sister Sarah, Richardson attempted to capitalize on his success in writing about virtuous women by composing a story about a good man. *Sir Charles Grandison*, a multivolume tale that parallels the story of *Clarissa* by exposing the many temptations faced by a man of character, was published in 1753-1754. The novel was not as well received by the general public, but still it added to Richardson's stature as a literary figure.

In 1752, even before he published his third novel, Richardson was able to use the profits from his literary ventures to build a new printing establishment at White Lyon Court off Fleet Street in London. After the publication of *Sir Charles Grandison*, Richardson spent most of his time revising his works and extracting from them moral sentiments that he published in pamphlets for readers avid to learn the life lessons his fictional characters had to offer them. He died in July, 1761, and was buried beside his wife at St. Bride's Church in London.

SIGNIFICANCE

Had he merely remained a printer, Samuel Richardson might still have been remembered for his activity in bringing out political pamphlets, supporting other writers, and issuing materials for the House of Commons. His decision to turn a series of model letters into a story celebrating conventional virtues, however, assured him a place of prominence in literary annals. *Pamela*, regarded by many as the first novel in English (although

---

THE VIRTUES OF PAMELA

Samuel Richardson's Pamela *is a didactic novel, meant to school its readers in Richardson's idea of the proper moral values. To make sure a reader takes from the novel what its author intended, the text's final words, excerpted below, are devoted to a list of the title character's virtues and an exhortation that readers strive to emulate Pamela in their own lives.*

Her obliging behaviour to her equals, before her exaltation; her kindness to them afterwards; her forgiving spirit, and her generosity;

Her meekness, in every circumstance where her virtue was not concerned;

Her charitable allowances for others, as in the case of Miss Godfrey, for faults she would not have forgiven in herself;

Her kindness and prudence to the offspring of that melancholy adventure;

Her maiden and bridal purity, which extended as well to her thoughts as to her words and actions;

Her signal affiance in God;

Her thankful spirit;

Her grateful heart;

Her diffusive charity to the poor, which made her blessed by them whenever she appeared abroad;

The cheerful ease and freedom of her deportment;

Her parental, conjugal, and maternal duty;

Her social virtues;

Are all so many signal instances of the excellency of her mind, which may make her character worthy of the imitation of her sex. And the Editor of these sheets will have his end, if it inspires a laudable emulation in the minds of any worthy persons, who may thereby entitle themselves to the rewards, the praises, and the blessings, by which PAMELA was so deservedly distinguished.

Source: Samuel Richardson, *Pamela: Or, Virtue Rewarded.* Project Gutenberg. p. 567. http://manybooks.net/pages/richardsonsametext04pam1w10/566.html. Accessed July, 2005.

Daniel Defoe's 1719 *Robinson Crusoe* contends for the honor), and *Clarissa*, considered by many the first work to exploit the psychological dimensions of character, became models for a generation of novelists who shaped the genre in England and throughout Europe.

Furthermore, the high-minded moral tone of Richardson's three novels led to a reaction by writers such as Henry Fielding, Tobias Smollett, and Laurence Sterne, early exponents of a more naturalistic view of human nature. Although the epistolary form did not remain popular beyond the eighteenth century, the immediacy with which readers came to know characters through this technique demonstrated how a skilled writer might use fiction to accomplish what Samuel Johnson, Richardson's contemporary and friend, called the function of great literature: to teach by delighting. Richardson's greatest accomplishment, however, may lie in his ability to shift readers' interest away from action and plot to a more "sophisticated" interest in characterization—a hallmark of the modern novel since the publication of *Pamela* in 1740-1741.

—Laurence W. Mazzeno

FURTHER READING

Blewett, David, ed. *Passion and Virtue: Essays on the Novels of Samuel Richardson*. Toronto, Ont.: University of Toronto Press, 2001. Blewett, editor of *Eighteenth-Century Fiction*, brings together the work of thirteen scholars who provide fresh insights into Richardson's achievement as a novelist by applying techniques of late twentieth century critical theory to an examination of *Pamela*, *Clarissa*, and *Sir Charles Grandison*.

Brophy, Elizabeth Bergen. *Samuel Richardson*. Boston: Twayne, 1987. Brophy's brief overview of Richardson's life and career offers an analysis of the influence of his three novels on the British reading public and examines his reputation among his contemporaries and succeeding generations.

Carroll, John, ed. *Samuel Richardson: A Collection of Critical Essays*. Englewood Cliffs, N.J.: Prentice-Hall, 1969. This collection reprints some of the best criticism written during the first half of the twentieth century. The critics explain the complexities of psychological realism that characterize Richardson's novels and examine his appeal to his contemporaries.

Eaves, T. C. Duncan, and Ben Kimpel. *Samuel Richardson: A Biography*. Oxford, England: Clarendon Press, 1971. In this standard twentieth century critical biography of the novelist, Eaves and Kimpel make extensive use of manuscript sources, memoirs, newspapers, periodicals, and other printed sources to develop a comprehensive portrait of the influential printer and novelist.

Hannaford, Richard Gordon. *Samuel Richardson: An Annotated Bibliography of Critical Studies*. New York: Garland, 1980. A comprehensive, though somewhat dated, annotated bibliography of works exploring Richardson's novels and other writings.

Rivero, Albert J. *New Essays on Samuel Richardson*. New York: St. Martin's Press, 1996. The thirteen essays in this volume provide a critical examination of Richardson's novels through the multiple lenses of modern critical theories. The essay on the novelist's correspondence with his Dutch translator Johannes Stinstra is especially valuable for its insight into the way Richardson's morality influenced his depiction of character in his work.

See also: Hester Chapone; Daniel Defoe; Henry Fielding; Oliver Goldsmith; Samuel Johnson; Sophie von La Roche; Charlotte Lennox; Mary de la Rivière Manley; John Newbery; Voltaire.

Related articles in *Great Events from History: The Eighteenth Century, 1701-1800:* April 25, 1719: Defoe Publishes the First Novel; 1740-1741: Richardson's *Pamela* Establishes the Modern Novel; 1742: Fielding's *Joseph Andrews* Satirizes English Society; March 20, 1750-March 14, 1752: Johnson Issues *The Rambler*.

ROBESPIERRE
French revolutionary leader

Alone among the leaders of the French Revolution, Robespierre was identified with every stage of the revolution. He most clearly enunciated the leftist ideals upon which the revolution was to be based and fought most vigorously for its success.

Born: May 6, 1758; Arras, France
Died: July 28, 1794; Paris, France
Also known as: Maximilien-François-Marie-Isidore de Robespierre (full name)
Areas of achievement: Government and politics, social reform

EARLY LIFE

Robespierre (raw-behs-pyehr) was born at Arras, in the province of Artois, on May 6, 1758. He was the eldest of four surviving children of Maximilien-Barthélemy, a third-generation lawyer, and Jacqueline-Marguerite, née Carraut, de Robespierre. Maximilien was only five years old when his mother died in childbirth, and, soon after, his father abandoned his children and left them to the care of first their maternal grandfather and later their aunts. These events undoubtedly had a profound impact on the young boy. From an early age, he was forced to assume adult responsibilities and to suffer privation. His childhood instilled in him certain distinctive features of his personality, including serious-mindedness, studiousness, and an appreciation of what it meant to be poor.

Robespierre's education was provided by charitable foundations. Following four years at a church-sponsored school in Arras, he won a church scholarship to the prestigious College of Louis-le-Grand of the University of Paris, where for twelve years he studied classics and law and was first exposed to the writings of his later philosophical idol, Jean-Jacques Rousseau. Robespierre excelled as a classical scholar and was chosen, in 1775, to deliver a Latin address of welcome to the newly crowned king, Louis XVI, and his queen, Marie-Antoinette, on their return trip from Reims to Versailles.

In 1780, Robespierre was awarded a law degree and, in 1781, was admitted to practice before the nation's premier court, the Parlement of Paris. After winning a monetary prize from Louis-le-Grand and being allowed to pass on his scholarship to his only brother, Augustin, Robespierre returned to Arras to care for his only surviving sister and to practice law. For the next eight years, he enjoyed the life of a middle-class provincial lawyer who

was inclined, because of his commitment to altruistic principles, to champion the causes of the poor and humble against their social superiors.

Robespierre's life as a country lawyer moved toward its end in 1788, when Louis XVI, under pressure from the nobility, called for a meeting of the Estates-General to address the problem of taxation, which had brought the kingdom to the brink of bankruptcy. The nobility, which comprised the First Estate, intended to join forces with the clergy, the Second Estate, to outvote the rest of the people, the Third Estate, who agreed with the Crown regarding the necessity of taxing the nobility. Election of representatives was authorized, and an outburst of pamphleteering and the drafting of *cahiers de doléances* (lists of grievances) reflected popular enthusiasm and anticipation. Robespierre wrote a *cahier* for the local cobblers' guild, authored a pamphlet in which he called for equal representation, and won election as one of the eight deputies to represent Artois in the Third Estate of the Estates-General. On May 5, 1789, he appeared at Versailles with his fellow deputies to begin work on an anticipated regeneration of France.

LIFE'S WORK

On June 20, in the face of obstructionism by the first two estates and vacillation by the king, the Third Estate, with the adherence of a few nobles and clergymen, took the revolutionary step of proclaiming themselves the national assembly and taking an oath not to disband until they had drafted a constitution for France. During the tumultuous summer of 1789, Robespierre played only a modest role. The fall of the Bastille, the peasant uprisings and the resulting August Decrees that abolished feudalism, and the danger of royalist counterrevolution that forced the removal of the royal family to Paris in October were all events that momentarily made the deliberations of the assembly secondary. Robespierre delivered several speeches, including addresses favoring freedom of the press and limitations on the king's veto power, but his main activities came after the assembly followed the king to Paris. Robespierre was politically astute to court the support of the people of Paris by opposing the imposition of martial law.

During the next two years of relative tranquillity, Robespierre emerged as one of the leaders of the leftist faction of liberal democrats and fought for a democratic franchise and for the granting of civil rights to Jews, Protestants, and actors. Robespierre also became increasingly active in the Jacobin Club, which was to become a major base of his support in Paris and the provinces. During 1790 and 1791, he was in constant attendance in the assembly, delivering 125 recorded speeches in 1790 and 328 in the first nine months of 1791.

Here and at the Jacobin Club, he emerged as the apostle of Rousseau. He envisioned a nation whose laws and institutions would be founded on ethical and spiritual ideals that represented the sovereign will of the people, who were by nature instilled with the virtues of patriotism and selflessness. In conformity with his philosophy, Robespierre opposed the death penalty, censorship, and the distinction between active and passive citizens in establishing property qualifications for voting. Although favoring a constitutional monarchy at this time, he demanded severe limitations on the king's veto power and on his power to declare war. He also demanded that all male citizens be allowed admittance to the national guard without property qualifications. It was also Robespierre who, in May, 1791, introduced the "self-denying" ordinance by which members of the national assembly disqualified themselves for election to the Legislature Assembly provided in the constitution of 1791.

Robespierre. (Library of Congress)

By September, 1791, when the national assembly disbanded, Robespierre had emerged as the revolution's popular hero. He was garlanded and carried in triumph through the streets. Already known as "the Incorruptible" because of his high principles, modest lifestyle, and refusal to accept financial rewards, Robespierre strengthened his ties to the people by moving to the home of a carpenter, in the rue Saint-Honoré, where he could be close to the legislative assembly and the Jacobin Club. Following a brief return to Arras in October, he was to remain there under the doting protection of the carpenter's family, who idolized him, for the remainder of his life.

The new constitutional monarchy with its one-house legislative assembly was to survive from only October, 1791, to August, 1792. The king had already signified his lack of commitment to the constitution when he attempted to flee France to join the émigrés and the Austrian army in June, 1791. In the assembly, a leftist faction developed under the leadership of Jacques Brissot, known as the Brissotins, and later, in the convention, as the Girondins. This faction called for war against the crowned heads of Europe to extend the benefits of the revolution beyond France's frontiers, to force compliance from the king, to divert the lower classes in Paris from the preoccupation with food prices, and to open new markets for the commercial middle class. Robespierre, through the local Jacobin Club, took a great political risk by almost alone opposing the war.

The war went badly for France, and Austrian and Prussian troops crossed the frontier in early August, 1792, dooming the Crown and the constitution of 1791. In the insurrection of August 10, 1792, the king was toppled from the throne and removed, with the royal family, from the Tuileries to the Temple prison. Robespierre, in the Jacobin Club, had played a role in this insurrection and was elected to the general council of the Paris Commune, which had been created on August 9. He now called for the election, by universal male suffrage, of a constitutional convention to draft a new republican constitution. He does not, however, appear to have played a direct role in the gruesome September massacres of Parisian prisoners precipitated by the Austro-Prussian invasion.

Robespierre was elected a delegate from Paris to the national convention, which began its deliberations in September. He emerged as the leader of the leftist faction of Jacobins known as the Mountain, who primarily espoused the interests of Parisians. They were opposed by the Girondins, who had their political base in the provinces. The two factions differed heatedly over a variety of issues. Robespierre and the Mountain called for the trial of the former king, to which the Girondins acceded. They differed, however, over the imposition of the death penalty. Robespierre prevailed, and Louis was guillotined in January, 1793. Girondin ascendancy prevailed, however, so long as the war went well, as it had done again after August, 1792. In April, 1793, however, the tide turned again. England had now joined the coalition that, after driving the French from Belgium, threatened to invade France. Working-class fears, exacerbated by rising prices and food shortages, resulted in the expulsion of the Girondins, the arrests of their leaders, and the flight of those remaining to the provinces to raise the banner of federalist counterrevolution. The Mountain was now in control of the convention.

The convention and the revolution were in grave danger. Foreign armies and their émigré royalist allies were at the gate. In the west, especially in the Vendée, peasants who detested the revolution's religious policy and who remained loyal to the monarchy were in violent revolt. Thus, the convention was faced with the unenviable task of repressing civil strife and counterrevolution, mobilizing the nation's people and resources to win the war against the allies, and giving France a new constitution. To assist in the tasks, the convention established the Committee of Public Safety, including among its most influential members Robespierre and his close associates Louis de Saint-Just and Georges Couthon and the "organizer of victory" Lazare Carnot.

Robespierre soon emerged as the leading spokesman of the committee before the convention. It was he who justified the establishment of the instruments of the Reign of Terror. Defining terror as prompt, severe, and inflexible justice, he argued that a combination of virtue (patriotism) and terror was necessary in a time of revolution. On June 10, 1794, under Robespierre's sponsorship, the convention passed the notorious Law of Twenty-Two Prairial, which expanded the Revolutionary Tribunal, provided for the imposition of the death penalty for all those convicted, expanded the number of kinds of condemned conduct and the types of evidence that could be used, and disposed of the necessity of calling witnesses. As a result, the number of executions increased. Robespierre overextended himself in his support of this law, and the fear that this generated among fellow terrorists contributed to his fall. Robespierre had also frightened his colleagues by his elimination of the leftist Hébertistes in March and by his role in the condemnation of Georges Danton, a popular fellow Jacobin who favored a moderation of the Terror, and his associ-

ates in April. Robespierre and the committee also succeeded on the war front. By the summer of 1794, the allied armies were in retreat and the French Republican army was on the offensive and pushing into the Low Countries.

At the height of his power in June, 1794, Robespierre attempted to institute a civic religion. In the farcical Festival of the Supreme Being over which Robespierre officiated on June 8, he naïvely hoped to reconcile devout Catholics and freethinkers to the new order. Having succeeded in his basic goals and outgrown his usefulness, and having frightened several terrorists whose excesses he intended to punish, Robespierre was outlawed and arrested by the convention on July 27, 1794; he mounted the scaffold the following day with several of his associates, including his brother, Saint-Just, and Couthon.

SIGNIFICANCE

With Robespierre died the popular hope for a truly democratic revolution. The reaction that followed was a betrayal of most of the principles for which the revolution's most indefatigable leader had fought. The shelved 1793 democratic and republican constitution Robespierre had helped to draft was never tried. Robespierre emerged unjustly as the bloodthirsty ogre of the revolution—the vain man with catlike features and a cold and morbidly suspicious nature, who attempted to eliminate all who stood in the way of his ambition for popular adulation.

With time has come increased objectivity. Although Robespierre cannot be relieved of any responsibility for violent excesses during his tenure on the Committee of Public Safety, it must be remembered that he was simultaneously attempting to rule a nation, fight a foreign war and a civil war, control leftist extremism, and draft a constitution. In a less tumultuous time, he might well have realized, at least partially, his dream of a society and nation based on ethical and spiritual principles.

—*J. Stewart Alverson*

FURTHER READING

Cobban, Alfred. *Aspects of the French Revolution*. New York: George Braziller, 1968. In two outstanding essays in this compilation, the author delineates Robespierre's fundamental ideas and traces the changes that took place in the subject's attitudes as the revolution moved into its most critical and violent stages.

Hardman, John. *Robespierre*. New York: Longman, 1999. Part of the Profiles in Power series. This is not a biography, but is instead a study of how Robespierre came to power and how he used the extraordinary power he acquired. Describes the faction of French society who supported Robespierre and the circumstances that led to his downfall.

Haydon, Colin, and William Doyle, eds. *Robespierre.* New York: Cambridge University Press, 1999. A collection of essays examining various aspects of Robespierre's life, political career, and influence from the vantage point of two hundred years after his death. Includes discussions of Robespierre's ideology and vision for the French Revolution, his religious beliefs, his role in revolutionary politics, and the representation of Robespierre in French fiction and European drama.

Korngold, Ralph. *Robespierre and the Fourth Estate.* New York: Modern Age Books, 1941. This is a sympathetic treatment of the subject, in which the author argues that a major factor in Robespierre's overthrow and execution was his championing of the proletariat, the Fourth Estate. Korngold's sympathy for Robespierre was partially caused by the collapse of the Third Republic in 1940, which suggested the problems of the First Republic that Robespierre worked assiduously to save.

Palmer, R. R. *Twelve Who Ruled: The Year of the Terror in the French Revolution.* Princeton, N.J.: Princeton University Press, 1941. This is the first scholarly treatment of the Committee of Public Safety in English. It is most useful in understanding the motivations of Robespierre during the last and most important year of his life.

Rudé, George. *Robespierre: Portrait of a Revolutionary Democrat.* New York: Viking Press, 1976. Although the author provides a useful biography of Robespierre, his main contribution is to trace the changing attitudes of historians toward the subject, from the revolution to the present. Contains a helpful bibliographical note, a useful glossary, and a concurrent chronology of the main events in the revolution and in Robespierre's life.

Thompson, J. M. *Robespierre.* 2 vols. 1935. Rev. ed. New York: Basil Blackwell, 1939. This biography is generally regarded as the best in English and perhaps in any language. As such it is indispensable to the serious student.

_____. *Robespierre and the French Revolution.* New York: Collier Books, 1952. An important contribution to the Teach Yourself History series, this book is especially useful to the beginning student because it treats Robespierre within the broader context of the revolution.

See also: Lazare Carnot; Georges Danton; Louis XV; Louis XVI; Marie-Antoinette; Jean-Jacques Rousseau; Louis de Saint-Just.

Related articles in *Great Events from History: The Eighteenth Century, 1701-1800*: May 5, 1789: Louis XVI Calls the Estates-General; June 20, 1789: Oath of the Tennis Court; July 14, 1789: Fall of the Bastille; October, 1789-April 25, 1792: France Adopts the Guillotine; April 20, 1792-October, 1797: Early Wars of the French Revolution; September 20, 1792: Battle of Valmy; January 21, 1793: Execution of Louis XVI; March 4-December 23, 1793: War in the Vendée; July 27-28, 1794: Fall of Robespierre; November 9-10, 1799: Napoleon Rises to Power in France.

MARY ROBINSON
English writer and actor

Robinson was an actor, poet, writer, and editor who won respect and acclaim among her colleagues, including Mary Wollstonecraft, and had a literary reputation that surpassed that of both William Wordsworth and Samuel Taylor Coleridge. Her written work was gothic, satirical, feminist, sentimental, realist, and politically radical.

Born: November 27, 1758?; Bristol, England
Died: December 26, 1800; Englefield Green, England
Also known as: Mary Darby (birth name)
Areas of achievement: Literature, theater, women's rights

EARLY LIFE

Mary Robinson was born to Nicholas Darby, a successful merchant, and Hester Vanacott. From a very early age she exhibited melancholia, reading funereal inscriptions and elegies by the age of seven. In Bristol, Robinson was educated at the school of Hannah More, who introduced her to the theater in 1764 when More took the entire school to a performance of William Shakespeare's *King Lear* at Bristol's Theatre Royal. It is likely that Robinson acted in More's play for girls, *The Search After Happiness* (pr. 1762, pb. 1763).

Robinson's young life was secure until her father's business interests in Newfoundland and Labrador claimed his attention. In 1768, after her father took a mistress abroad, her parents separated and Robinson's world collapsed. Nicholas Darby ordered his wife to live in the home of a local clergyman and his children to go to boarding schools. It was the eighteenth century, and Hester Darby had no legal right to dispute her husband's orders.

Robinson attended the Chelsea school of Meribah Lorrington, receiving a classical education; Robinson attributed her love of literature and learning to Lorrington. Robinson's mother established her own school, where Robinson taught English and religion. Nicholas Darby, however, demanded the school be closed after only one year. Attending Oxford House school in Marylebone, Robinson was taught dancing by the ballet teacher at Covent Garden and met David Garrick, playwright and manager of the Drury Lane Theatre. She was fourteen when she was received at the Garrick home, and Garrick himself prepared her to play Cordelia to his Lear.

LIFE'S WORK

Through the theater Mary met Thomas Robinson, who would become her husband. Thomas nursed her through illness, winning the loyalty of her mother. They were married in 1773, when she was fifteen years old. Thomas required that the marriage remain secret until he attained his majority. Mary's mother discovered that Thomas was not, as he had claimed, the soon-to-be-financially-secure heir of a Welsh uncle but was, on the contrary, already of age, in debt, and an illegitimate son.

In the early years of their marriage, though in debt, the Robinsons lived well and were introduced into high levels of London society. However, Thomas began gambling and carousing; Mary was pregnant and home alone. Deeper debt and Thomas's increased dissipation ensued, and when Mary was near her delivery date, debtors foreclosed on their home and the couple traveled to Wales, where their daughter, Maria Elizabeth, was born on October 18, 1774.

Thomas feared he would be arrested for debt, so the couple and their infant daughter fled to Mary's grandmother's home in Monmouth. However, Thomas eventually was arrested. He settled his debt but was apprehended again on May 3, 1775, and put in debtors' prison at the Fleet, where Mary and Maria Elizabeth stayed with him until his release on August 3, 1776.

One of their friends brought an old school chum of Thomas to visit—playwright Richard Brinsley Sheridan, who, with Garrick, trained Mary to play Juliet. Her first stage performance was on December 10, 1776, at Drury Lane, initiating her successful stage career and providing income for the couple. She played in plays by Shakespeare, in light comedies, and most famously in so-called breeches roles, playing male characters and wearing men's clothing.

During December, 1779, the prince of Wales, heir to the British throne, saw her and became enamored, and it was said that during a performance of *The Winter's Tale* she played Perdita not to the Florizel on stage but to the prince in his box. The affair became the subject of gossip columns and cartoons about "Perdita" Robinson, as she became known, and "Florizel," the prince. He soon offered her a bond for £20,000, payable upon his majority, if she would quit the stage to become his mistress, an offer she accepted but bitterly regretted all her life. Her last performance was on May 31, 1780. She was acclaimed as one of the most beautiful women in London, "the greatest and most perfect beauty," according to the prince. She embarked upon a life in the grand style, only to be forsaken the next year for another woman. Robinson pressed her claims, eventually receiving £5,000 and an annuity from the prince.

The now notorious Robinson traveled to Paris, where she received a warm reception and was often in the company of Marie-Antoinette, queen of France. When she returned to England—where she was already famous for her fashion sense and innovations—she brought French fashion trends with her, including *la chemise de la reine*, styled after Marie-Antoinette's fashionable clothing. Robinson would engage in many affairs with prominent French and English noblemen and military officers.

This beautiful, talented, and much feted former actor fell seriously ill and became paralyzed in her legs when only in her mid-twenties. Hearing that her lover, Colonel Banastre Tarleton, was to escape debtors' prison by fleeing to the Continent, she paid his debts and took off in the middle of the night to meet him before he embarked, but she was too late. She caught a chill during the night ride, which settled into rheumatic fever and thereafter chronic rheumatism; she suffered a miscarriage and, at some point, possibly a stroke. For a while she maintained her aura of public panache but her financial situation continually worsened.

Robinson, however, had always been adept at reinventing herself, and this time was no different for the former Mary Darby, who had become the young bride, then the illustrious Perdita, and then the notorious Mrs. Robinson. She now became Mary Robinson, an eminent member of the British literary world.

Robinson's early poetry shows the stylistic influence of the Della Cruscans, a group of late eighteenth century English writers of pretentious and rhetorically ornate verse. However, she soon found her own voice: satiric, incisive, realistic. In addition to writing *Poems by Mrs. Robinson* (1791), *Poems by Mrs. M. Robinson: Volume the Second* (1794), a collec-

tion of sonnets titled *Sappho and Phaon* (1796), and incisive social satires such as *Modern Manners* (1793), she regularly contributed poetry to the *Oracle* and the *Morning Post*, often publishing her work under numerous pseudonyms. She was poetry coeditor of the *Morning Post* with poet and critic Samuel Taylor Coleridge, and she succeeded poet Robert Southey as poetry editor of the *Morning Post* in 1799.

Robinson received mixed reviews for her various novels, which include the following: *Vacenza: Or, The Dangers of Credulity* (1792), a Gothic *roman à clef*; *The Widow: Or, A Picture of Modern Times* (1794), a social satire in epistolary form; *Angelina* (1796), a sentimental tale with sociopolitical undercurrents and feminist satire; *Hubert de Sevrac: A Romance of the Eighteenth Century* (1796), a Gothic morality tale of the French Revolution;

"THOUGHTS ON THE CONDITION OF WOMEN"

Bluestocking writer Mary Robinson argues that "universal knowledge"—that is, a truer, inclusive knowledge—can only come about if women, contrary to tradition and custom, are permitted by society to fully exercise their inherent curiosities and intellectual abilities.

Custom, from the earliest periods of antiquity, has endeavoured to place the female mind in the subordinate ranks of intellectual sociability. Woman has ever been considered as a lovely and fascinating part of the creation, but her claims to mental equality have not only been questioned, by envious and interested sceptics; but, by a barbarous policy in the other sex, considerably depressed, for want of liberal and classical cultivation. I will not expatiate largely on the doctrines of certain philosophical sensualists, who have aided in this destructive oppression, because an illustrious British female [Mary Wollstonecraft] (whose death has not been sufficiently lamented, but to whose genius posterity will render justice) has already written volumes in vindication of "The Rights of Woman." But I shall endeavour to prove that, under the present state of mental subordination, universal knowledge is not only benumbed and blighted, but true happiness, originating in enlightened manners, retarded in its progress. Let woman once assert her proper sphere, unshackled by prejudice, and unsophisticated by vanity; and pride (the noblest species of pride) will establish her claims to the participation of power, both mentally and corporeally.

In order that this letter may be clearly understood, I shall proceed to prove my assertion in the strongest, but most undecorated language. I shall remind my enlightened country-women that they are not the mere appendages of domestic life, but the partners, the equal associates of man: and, where they excel in intellectual powers, they are no less capable of all that prejudice and custom have united in attributing, exclusively, to the thinking faculties of man. I argue thus, and my assertions are incontrovertible.

Source: Mary Robinson, "Thoughts on the Condition of Women, and on the Injustice of Mental Subordination" (1799). Bluestocking Archive. http://www.faculty.umb.edu/

Walsingham: Or, The Pupil of Nature (1797), a politically radical and satirical *roman à clef* with a gender-bending protagonist; *The False Friend* (1799), a feminist romance; and *The Natural Daughter* (1799), an implicitly autobiographical novel in which the female protagonist, deserted by her husband, earns her living as a writer and actor. Her feminist essay, first published under the pseudonym Anne Frances Randall, advocated many feminist positions, including university education for women, reflecting her association with feminist author Mary Wollstonecraft.

Poets Coleridge and William Wordsworth published *Lyrical Ballads* in 1798, and Mary Robinson published *Lyrical Tales* in 1800. Her collection enhanced the standing of the experimental *Lyrical Ballads* prior to its 1802 edition. She was acclaimed by her literary colleagues although denounced by conservative critics.

Robinson had financial problems throughout her life and battled illness since that night ride to meet Tarleton at Dover. Despite poor health, in her last years she maintained her position with the *Morning Post* and continued to write and translate. She and daughter Maria Elizabeth lived at Englefield Cottage near Windsor Great Park and had a wide circle of literary friends, including Coleridge and Wollstonecraft. She died of "dropsy of the chest"—possibly congestive heart failure—on December 26, 1800, and is buried at Old Windsor.

SIGNIFICANCE

Mary Robinson was known by the title given her in the *Monthly Review:* Our English Sappho. Coleridge praised her as a "woman of genius," noting her ear for the music of poetry and for innovations in prosody. Her poems are included in the Romantic canon for their metrical brilliance and penetrating realism. Her feminist treatise is read alongside Wollstonecraft's *A Vindication of the Rights of Woman* (1790). Her *Memoirs* (1801) take their place in the tradition of Romantic introspection. *Sappho and Phaon*, Petrarchan in form and classical in subject, has come to be recognized, along with the sonnets of poet Charlotte Smith, as reestablishing the sonnet form in English letters.

Many of Robinson's works represent the spirit of her age, looking forward to a time of sociopolitical and personal regeneration. Hers was a larger-than-life personality. She prevailed over a disastrous marriage, social ambiguity, penury, and paralysis, leaving a substantial contribution to eighteenth century Romantic literature.

—*Donna Berliner*

FURTHER READING

Byrne, Paula. *Perdita: The Literary, Theatrical, Scandalous Life of Mary Robinson*. New York: Random House, 2004. An authoritative biography with an extensive bibliography.

Cross, Ashley J. "From 'Lyrical Ballads' to 'Lyrical Tales': Mary Robinson's Reputation and the Problem of Literary Debt." *Studies in Romanticism* 40 (2001): 571-605. Reviews Robinson's poetry and its relation to the work of her contemporaries.

Curran, Stuart. "Mary Robinson's 'Lyrical Tales' in Context." In *Re-visioning Romanticism: British Women Writers, 1776-1837*, edited by Carol Shiner Wilson and Joel Haefner. Philadelphia: University of Pennsylvania Press, 1994. An in-depth reevaluation of Robinson's work.

Pascoe, Judith. "Mary Robinson and the Literary Marketplace." In *Romantic Women Writers: Voices and Countervoices*, edited by Paula R. Feldman and Theresa M. Kelley. Hanover, N.H.: University Press of New England, 1995. Places Robinson in the context of newspaper publishing and other new commercial venues for writers.

See also: Fanny Abington; Fanny Burney; David Garrick; Marie-Antoinette; Hannah More; Peg Woffington; Mary Wollstonecraft.

Related articles in *Great Events from History: The Eighteenth Century, 1701-1800:* December 7, 1732: Covent Garden Theatre Opens in London; 1740-1741: Richardson's *Pamela* Establishes the Modern Novel; 1792: Wollstonecraft Publishes *A Vindication of the Rights of Woman.*

COMTE DE ROCHAMBEAU
French military leader

Placed in command of the French troops who came to assist the colonists in the American Revolutionary War, Rochambeau helped General George Washington plan the Battle of Yorktown and defeat the British under the command of Cornwallis in 1781.

Born: July 1, 1725; Vendôme, France
Died: May 10, 1807; Vendôme, France
Also known as: Jean-Baptiste Donatien de Vimeur (birth name)
Areas of achievement: Military, warfare and conquest

EARLY LIFE

Born into a well-established French noble family with a military heritage, Jean-Baptiste Donatien de Vimeur, comte de Rochambeau (kohnt duh roh-shahm-boh), was the third son of Joseph Charles de Vimeur, comte de Rochambeau, and Marie Claire Thérèse Bérgon. At age five, he was sent by his parents to school at the Collège de Vendôme, run by the Oratian Fathers, an order of clergy in the Roman Catholic church. There he began to receive excellent training in history, literature, mathematics, and the physical sciences.

Though Rochambeau grew up with heroic stories about the prowess of his ancestors, his family designated him for the priesthood because he was both the youngest son and not very robust. The Oratians, however, were suspected of heresy. A friend of the family, the bishop of Blois, persuaded young Rochambeau's father to transfer his son to a Jesuit school in Blois, where his teachers were more likely to prepare him to receive a bishopric one day.

The event that changed the course of Rochambeau's life was the sudden death of his only surviving brother. He was about to be tonsured, a preparatory step toward receiving the priesthood, when he was informed that he must, from that point on, serve his country with the same vigor he would have devoted to his God. Back at Vendôme, his father began encouraging Rochambeau to follow in the footsteps of his war-loving forefathers. At age fifteen, he set out for Paris and enrolled in the academy for officers.

Having already been influenced by military histories and memoirs read at home, once in Paris, Rochambeau came in contact with some of the most advanced military and political thinking in Europe. He had scarcely begun his studies in earnest when war broke out between Prussia and Austria, a conflict destined to engulf all of Eu-

rope. Young Rochambeau left school and joined the Army of the Rhine, thus beginning fifty years of active military service.

Rochambeau rose rapidly through the ranks of the French army. Early in the War of the Austrian Succession (1740-1748), he obtained a commission as a junior officer of cavalry. In July, 1743, he was promoted to captain and given command of a cavalry unit. In 1746, he became aide-de-camp to a royal prince, the duc d' Orléans, and in 1747 was appointed colonel of an infantry regiment. By the time the war ended, Rochambeau had been severely wounded and had distinguished himself in battle. His gallantry was recognized by King Louis XV, who admitted him to that select circle allowed to dine with the monarch in private and permitted to ride with him in his royal coach. In December, 1749, Rochambeau married the daughter of a wealthy merchant and devoted himself to peacetime training. This did not last long, as France was soon plunged into one of the most disastrous conflicts of its history—the Seven Years' War (1756-1763).

LIFE'S WORK

During the Seven Years' War, Rochambeau honed those skills and qualities that marked the rest of his brilliant career. He again achieved distinction on the battlefields of Germany and was promoted to the rank of brigadier general in 1761. He was appointed to the post of inspector of cavalry and introduced a number of reforms that aided the efficiency of the French army. He came to be known for his emphasis on discipline but also for his concern for the welfare of the common soldier. In 1776, the king of France again rewarded Rochambeau's meritorious service by appointing him governor of Villefranche-en-Roussillon, a post that came with a significant annual stipend of eight thousand francs.

In 1779, after thirty-seven years of military service, including another promotion to the rank of lieutenant-general (a fitting climax to a distinguished career), Rochambeau looked forward to retirement. Ever since the humiliating treaty that had ended the Seven Years' War in 1763, however, France had been looking for a way to reclaim its former position in the world. In 1778, France's political leaders had formed an alliance with the American revolutionaries fighting against England. By February, 1780, the French were persuaded, chiefly by the lobbying of the marquis de Lafayette, to send military

Comte de Rochambeau. (Library of Congress)

forces to the American colonies. Much to the disappointment of Lafayette, the French government called upon Rochambeau, then age fifty-five, to command the expeditionary force. Elaborate preparations were made, and Rochambeau's administrative skill in organizing the expedition benefited the French war department immeasurably.

After several delays, the French fleet carrying Rochambeau's 5,500 troops set sail on May 1, 1780. They anchored off Newport, Rhode Island, on July 11, 1780. The next day, Rochambeau wrote to George Washington, placing himself and his army at the disposal of the colonial leader. Rochambeau's emphasis on discipline again paid off as the good conduct of French troops and officers paved the way for effective cooperation in fighting a common foe—the British. The greatest complicating factor in Rochambeau's command of the French expeditionary force was the interference of the younger and somewhat impetuous Lafayette. At one point, he urged Rochambeau to cast off his lethargy and attack New York without waiting for control of the seas. Yet the older and wiser Rochambeau prevailed, and Washington, who was inclined to favor a New York attack, ended

up putting his trust in the knowledge and experience of his older associate for the rest of the war.

In the fall of 1780, Rochambeau and Washington sent a request to the French government for additional French forces and more money to assist the war effort. Though they waited in vain for extra ground troops, in May, 1781, Rochambeau's son, the vicomte de Rochambeau, arrived with news that the French king had consented to supply an extra six million livres and that another French fleet under the command of Admiral François-Joseph-Paul, comte de Grasse, had been dispatched to the West Indies and would cooperate with Rochambeau and Washington. On May 21, 1781, Rochambeau and Washington met and agreed that together their combined forces could overwhelm British forces under Sir Henry Clinton at New York or defeat the army of the First Marquess Cornwallis in Virginia, but not both. With Rochambeau's urging, they opted to avoid Clinton and strike Cornwallis, and they asked Admiral de Grasse to bring his fleet to Chesapeake Bay to cut off British communications and prevent Cornwallis from being reinforced by Clinton.

On June 10, 1781, Rochambeau's army, which had been wintering in Rhode Island, broke camp and joined with Washington's troops at White Plains, New York, on July 5. Though the combined French-American army now numbered some ten thousand soldiers, Rochambeau did not wish to fully engage a large British force, preferring instead to met the enemy in several small skirmishes.

The strategy of the French-American alliance depended on de Grasse. If the British lost control of the seas and Clinton could be prevented from joining with other British troops, the fate of Cornwallis would be sealed. On August 14, Rochambeau and Washington received word that de Grasse had set sail from the West Indies. On August 19, they began their long march south, feinting an attack on New York as they went. The speed with which the combined armies traveled, and the union they formed, were extraordinary and owed much to the leadership of Rochambeau.

In late August, de Grasse anchored off Chesapeake Bay and deposited an additional four thousand soldiers to join the army of Lafayette, who was busy harassing British troops in Virginia. On September 14, Rochambeau and Washington reached Lafayette at Williamsburg, Virginia, and immediately held a conference to draw up plans for the Siege of Yorktown.

On October 2, 1781, the allies attacked Lord Cornwallis, whose forces were bottled up on the Yorktown peninsula. Seventeen days later, Cornwallis asked for terms of surrender, effectively ending the fighting of the revolution. After brief tours of Virginia and Rhode Island, Rochambeau embarked for France on January 11, 1783.

Back home, Rochambeau's contributions to two nations were recognized by his appointments as commander of the Calais military district in early 1784 and the Alsace district in 1789. Though he retired later that year because of poor health, he was brought back into active service in September, 1790, during France's revolutionary period, and placed in command of the Army of the North. He was declared a marshal of France in 1791. The following year, he became so disenchanted with governmental policy as well as the performance of the poorly trained troops being sent him that he resigned his command for good and was succeeded by Lafayette. During the Reign of Terror, Rochambeau was arrested for treason, and he was awaiting execution at the guillotine when Robespierre's own death in 1794 finally put an end to the carnage in France.

In 1804, Napoleon Bonaparte made Rochambeau a member and grand officer of the Legion of Honor. He died at his château at Thoré on May 10, 1807. His two volumes of memoirs were published in 1809.

SIGNIFICANCE

When Rochambeau traveled to Versailles in 1779 to receive new orders from King Louis XVI, his dreams of a comfortable old age evaporated. Though he had already served his country with distinction, he was to embark on a series of events that changed the world, leading to the independence of the thirteen American colonies and the creation of the United States of America. Few individuals have had so momentous an impact and yet remained so unassuming.

A striking figure, Rochambeau was simple in his tastes and remained dignified in his behavior—qualities he fostered in his soldiers. He disliked ostentation and airs of self importance. He willingly placed himself under the authority of a foreign commander and yet became the pivotal figure in ensuring the victory of that foreign land. Not only was his strategic planning and military execution indispensable, but also at one point he even lent Washington $20,000 in hard currency so that colonial troops could be paid a month's salary despite the depleted American treasury. Yet when the British tried to surrender to him directly, Rochambeau directed them to the Americans, revealing his strict sense of propriety and modesty.

Upon Rochambeau's return to France in 1783, there was no great public celebration for him, in large part because of Lafayette, who monopolized public attention. Among those who knew the truth, however, Rochambeau was esteemed a hero. King Louis XVI declared that France owed the peace to Rochambeau.

—*Andrew C. Skinner*

FURTHER READING

Davis, Burke. *The Campaign That Won America: The Story of Yorktown*. New York: Dial Press, 1970. Places Rochambeau's critical contributions to American independence in the context of the seminal battle that he helped plan and carry out and that effectively ended the Revolutionary War.

Ketchum, Richard M. *Victory at Yorktown: The Campaign That Won the Revolution*. New York: Henry Holt, 2004. Chronicles the final battles of the revolution, including the victory at Yorktown. Includes a great deal of information about Rochambeau's role in the battle and in other aspects of the American Revolution.

Rice, Howard C., and Anne S. K. Brown, eds. *The American Campaigns of Rochambeau's Army*. 2 vols. Princeton, N.J.: Princeton University Press, 1972. This massive work is a collection of documents and maps that present a comprehensive story of the French army in America (encampments, marches, daily life) under Rochambeau from 1780 to 1783.

Rochambeau, Marshal Comte de. *Memoirs of the Marshal Count de Rochambeau Relative to the War of Independence of the United States*. Translated by M. W. E. Wright. New York: Arno Press, 1971. A reprint of an 1838 English translation of extracts from the memoirs of Rochambeau, who describes conditions in colonial America at the time of his arrival on July 12, 1780, and his involvement in the American Revolution, including his command of French forces and association with Washington at Yorktown. Of modest length (113 pages), it is an invaluable resource.

Weelen, Jean-Edmond. *Rochambeau, Father and Son: A Life of the Maréchal de Rochambeau and the Journal of the Vicomte de Rochambeau*. Translated by Lawrence Lee. New York: Henry Holt, 1936. A biography by a French historian who researched family and local archives as well as official French records.

Whitridge, Arnold. *Rochambeau*. New York: Macmillan, 1965. The most complete, readable biography of the great commander available in English. Details unavailable elsewhere help the reader to see Rochambeau as a real person against the backdrop of the monumental events of the eighteenth century. Includes several pages of photographs and illustrations.

See also: Sir Henry Clinton; First Marquess Cornwallis; Louis XV; Duc d'Orléans; Robespierre; George Washington.

Related articles in *Great Events from History: The Eighteenth Century, 1701-1800*: January, 1756-February 15, 1763: Seven Years' War; February 10, 1763: Peace of Paris; December 16, 1773: Boston Tea Party; April 27-October 10, 1774: Lord Dunmore's War; April 19, 1775: Battle of Lexington and Concord; May, 1776-September 3, 1783: France Supports the American Revolution; July 4, 1776: Declaration of Independence; August 6, 1777: Battle of Oriskany Creek; September 19-October 17, 1777: Battles of Saratoga; February 6, 1778: Franco-American Treaties; October 19, 1781: Cornwallis Surrenders at Yorktown; May 5, 1789: Louis XVI Calls the Estates-General; June 20, 1789: Oath of the Tennis Court; July 14, 1789: Fall of the Bastille; October, 1789-April 25, 1792: France Adopts the Guillotine; April 20, 1792-October, 1797: Early Wars of the French Revolution; September 20, 1792: Battle of Valmy; January 21, 1793: Execution of Louis XVI; March 4-December 23, 1793: War in the Vendée; July 27-28, 1794: Fall of Robespierre; November 9-10, 1799: Napoleon Rises to Power in France.

GEORGE RODNEY
English admiral

Utilizing both family connections and his own ability, Rodney advanced to the post of admiral while leading England to naval victories during the Seven Years' War and the American Revolution.

Born: February 13, 1718 (baptized); Middlesex, England
Died: May 24, 1792; Hanover Square, London, England
Also known as: George Brydges Rodney (full name)
Areas of achievement: Military, warfare and conquest, government and politics

EARLY LIFE
George Rodney was baptized in the church of St. Giles-in-the-Fields in Middlesex. His father, Harry Rodney, a retired army captain from an old landed family, settled at Walton-on-Thames after 1715. He married Mary Newton, the daughter of Sir Henry Newton, a diplomat and judge of the High Court of Admiralty. By 1720, Harry Rodney was seriously in debt, and he lost the Walton property when the South Sea Bubble burst. George was reared by his godfather at Avington and was sent to Harrow between 1725 and 1732.

Rodney entered the navy on the *Sunderland* in 1732, as one of the last of the "King's Letter Boys." He next appeared on the *Dreadnaught* as an able seaman on May 1, 1733. When Henry Medley became its captain late in 1734, Rodney advanced to midshipman. He later joined the *Romney*, on May 2, 1738, bound for the Newfoundland station to protect the cod fisheries. Rodney then sailed on the flagship of Rear Admiral Nicholas Haddock, to join the *Dolphin* in the Mediterranean. He was an acting officer and thus received no pay.

He advanced to lieutenant in February of 1740, serving on the *Dolphin*, the *Essex*, and the *Namur*. He became captain of the *Plymouth* on November 9, 1742, and was confirmed by the Admiralty on April 23, 1743. In December, 1745, he received the command of the *Eagle*.

Rodney took part in the June, 1747, capture of part of the French convoy, thus establishing his fortune. In October, Admiral Edward Hawke's fleet defeated the French off La Rochelle, and Rodney added to his growing fame and fortune. In 1748, he was in the squadron that captured part of a Spanish convoy before he returned to Plymouth.

Rodney next commanded the *Rainbow* and received a royal commission as governor of Newfoundland, which was approved by an order in council on May 2, 1749. In December, Rodney resigned as governor to try for Parliament, but no seats were available, so he returned to Newfoundland. Later, in 1751, he gained his first seat in Parliament, for the borough of Saltash, a safe Admiralty seat. Rodney proved a more active and better-informed governor than many others. Upon returning to Portsmouth in March, 1752, he suffered an attack of gout and nervous exhaustion, problems that were to trouble him intermittently for the next forty years.

On January 16, 1753, Rodney was commissioned to the guard ship *Kent*, stationed at Portsmouth, allowing long periods of leave. He married the eldest Compton daughter, Jane (known as Jenny) on January 31 at Oxford Chapel, St. Marylebone Parish in London. Their first child, George, was born on Christmas Day, 1753. Appointments to two more guard ships, the *Fouguex* and the *Prince George*, followed. A second son, James, was born in the autumn of 1754. Rodney sailed late in July, 1755, with Hawke's squadron off the coast of Spain in the *Prince George*. Rodney was then granted an extensive leave to work for a seat in Parliament from Northampton in November.

Late in May, 1755, he was assigned to the *Monarch* at Plymouth. As senior officer, he was also in charge of the dockyards. In the autumn, a daughter, Jane, was born, but Jenny's health declined. Rodney was ill in London and did not participate in Admiral John Byng's court-martial in December. Jenny died at Alresford on January 29, 1757, and little Jane died in 1758.

Rodney next was commissioned on the *Dublin*, in April, 1757. This vessel was probably the first medium-sized two-decker, a ship that formed the main part of the British naval battle line in the remaining days of sail. It took part in the failed attempt to attack Rochefort in the fall of 1757 and carried Major General Jeffrey Amherst to Halifax the next year. The ship also took part in the Siege of Louisbourg in the summer of 1758 and convoyed the prisoners back to Great Britain. Rodney was forty, a good fighter who captured prizes, and a popular captain.

George Rodney. (Library of Congress)

LIFE'S WORK

Rodney was made rear admiral of the Blue Squadron on May 19, 1759. The French prepared to invade Great Britain, and Rodney, in the *Achilles*, led a squadron to destroy boats, workshops, stores, and timber at Le Havre. The attack was successful. On July 19, he sat for Sir Joshua Reynolds, the painter. The portrait shows a graceful, aristocratic man with dark hair, blue eyes, and a generous mouth.

A second campaign against Le Havre failed, resulting in a tedious blockade by the *Deptford* and the *Norwich*. In November, Rodney was elected to another safe seat in Parliament, for Okehampton. He went to sea in the *Deptford* in May patrolling the English Channel. By October, the *Deptford* was replaced by the *Nottingham*, and by the end of January, 1761, Rodney asked for sick leave. Late in February, Parliament was to be dissolved and Rodney wanted a seat, this time for Penryn, Cornwall. The seat, however, was contested and cost Rodney £2,000.

His order as commander in chief in the Leeward Islands came on October 5, 1761. He arrived in Barbados late in November on the *Marlborough*. He and Major General Robert Monckton worked well together in coordinating plans for the invasion of Martinique, which surrendered on February 4, 1762. Rodney went on to seize St. Lucia, Grenada, and St. Vincent, receiving promotion to vice admiral of the Blue Squadron on October 21, 1762. When Admiral Sir George Pocock arrived the following April for the attack on Cuba, Rodney was left at Martinique in the *Rochester*, and lost out on the prize money. With the war over, he returned to Great Britain, striking his flag on August 15, 1763.

Rodney received a deputy lieutenancy for Southampton in November and a baronetcy on January 21, 1764. He was granted the governorship of Greenwich Hospital but had to wait for its vacancy before assuming the position. He also married Henrietta Clies, daughter of the woman who had cared for his children since 1757. A son, John, was born to them on May 10, 1765, and in December, Rodney finally became governor of Greenwich Hospital, living there for the next five years. Another child, Jane, was born on December 24, 1766. Rodney's life settled into visits to Northampton and Bath; attendance at the Commons, the Admiralty, and Greenwich; and gambling on horse races and cards at White's Club and other fashionable spots in London.

Rodney ran for Parliament again, in the Northampton election of 1768, which cost him approximately £30,000. He did win a seat but was ruined financially in the process. By 1769, there were already four lawsuits pending against him for debt. Rodney became vice admiral of the White Squadron in 1770 and hoped that a sea command would restore his finances.

In January, 1771, Lord Sandwich became the first lord of the Admiralty. Rodney could have the Jamaica command but only at the expense of the Greenwich Hospital post. His commission as commander in chief was signed late in January. This command restored some of Rodney's credit, but he lost the income and the protection of the hospital and became plagued by his creditors. To cover his debts, he signed a deed on January 25, 1771, with Sir James Lowther and Robert Mackreth, one of the most notorious usurers in London. Rodney left for Jamaica from a lonely beach at Southampton on the *Princess Amelia*, on May 13. The family, except for young George, would spend the next three years in Jamaica.

Rodney advanced to vice admiral of the Red Squadron in August of 1771, but his half pay was delayed. He was also nominated rear admiral of England, a ceremonial post.

When the governor of Jamaica died in December, 1772, Rodney tried for the post, but Sir Basil Keith was appointed. On May 3, 1773, the *Portland* arrived to become his new flagship and his transport back to Great Britain. When Parliament dissolved in 1774, Rodney had to face his creditors. He fled to France with his family to avoid arrest.

When war broke out with the American colonies and their allies, Rodney could not be employed until his navy office account was cleared. He advanced to admiral

of the White Squadron in January, 1778, but could not leave France, where he had lived for several years, until Marshal de Biron loaned him money to pay his French debts.

Living opposite St. James's Palace in London provided safety and access to the court and ministers. A truce was reached with his creditors in December, 1778, and on October 1, 1779, Rodney became commander in chief of Barbados, the Leeward Islands, and adjoining seas. He was sixty-one, with gout in both hands and feet, recurrent malarial fevers, and urinary difficulties. When he sailed in the *Sandwich* on December 29, Dr. Gilbert Blane accompanied him. Blane later went on to become one of the great reformers and innovators in sea medicine.

After capturing a rich Spanish convoy, Rodney defeated a Spanish squadron in the Moonlight Battle of January 16-17, 1780, off the coast of Portugal. Relieving Gibraltar, he headed for the West Indies, arriving at Barbados in March, and met a French fleet under comte de Guichen off Martinique on April 17. Rodney tried new tactics of breaking the enemy line, but he was not supported properly, and the French fleet escaped destruction. Rodney temporarily commanded from the *Terrible*. Two encounters between the fleets in May were indecisive, but Rodney held a difficult position with an inferior force for four months. Thanks from Parliament and the freedom of several cities resulted.

To avoid the hurricane season, Rodney sailed to New York but was back in the West Indies in December, having received the Order of the Bath in November. With Great Britain at war with Holland, he was ordered to attack the Dutch West Indies. On February 3, 1781, the British fleet captured St. Eustatius with almost no shots fired. Here was the promise of great wealth in prizes for Rodney; unfortunately, the confiscation of British merchants' goods led to prolonged legal action. The French sent reinforcements to the West Indies in July, under comte de Grasse, and gained the advantage of the British fleet. Rodney, in the *Gibraltar*, sailed with a convoy, reaching England on September 19.

After General Cornwallis's surrender to the Americans in October, 1781, the British government decided to send Rodney back to the West Indies. He was made vice admiral of England in November, and his flag was first on the *Arrogant* and then on the *Formidable*. Rodney reached Barbados in February and met de Grasse north of Dominica on April 12, 1782. Rodney broke through the French line and won a great victory in that encounter. Later, arguments arose between Rodney and Samuel Hood, his second in command, over whose idea it was to break the line and the reason the British fleet failed to follow the retreating French.

When Lord North's government was replaced by Lord Rockingham's in 1782, the new first lord of the Admiralty, Augustus Keppel, was forced to replace Rodney with Admiral Pigot before news of Rodney's last great victory arrived. Letters addressed to "My Lord" helped reassure Rodney, for on June 19 he became Baron Rodney of Stoke-Rodney. He arrived in Bristol on the *Montagu*, on September 15, 1782, striking his flag on October 21 for the last time.

Rodney lived for a time in a small house at Kensington Gore. His last child was born in 1783, and the retired admiral traveled for a time on the Continent in 1784 and 1785. He lost the legal actions with the merchants on St. Eustatius in 1786, but thanks to his son George, he could still live out his life in comfort. He died on May 24, 1792, at George's house in Hanover Square, and was buried on June 1 in Old Alresford Church, with monuments in Jamaica and St. Paul's Cathedral in London.

SIGNIFICANCE

George Rodney had a reputation as a humane and considerate captain. Paintings by Reynolds, Thomas Gainsborough, Tilly Kettle, and J. L. Mosnier portray him and his triumphs from 1759 to 1789. His varying position reflected the interests needed in the eighteenth century to advance, political struggles between the Whigs and the Tories, his seats in Parliament, and his great financial troubles. Rodney thought his first battle with Guichen in 1780 was his best, while the action of April 12, 1782, which broke the enemy's line and resulted in a great victory, is regarded by historians as the height of naval achievement.

—*Mary-Emily Miller*

FURTHER READING

Hannay, David. *Rodney*. New York: Macmillan, 1891. Provides some of the anecdotes of Rodney's life and of his financial problems while detailing his victory against the French fleet in the West Indies. Presents the negative, nineteenth century judgment of Rodney. Several reprinted versions.

Hurst, Ronald. *The Golden Rock: An Episode of the American War of Independence, 1775-1783*. London: Leo Cooper, 1996. Chronicles the seizure of St. Eustatius by Rodney and Major-General John Vaughan. Hurst is extremely critical of the two men's actions, charging them with "raping" St. Eustatius and stripping the island of its assets. Hurst provides information on events subsequent to the seizure, including the British administration of St. Eustatius and Britain's eventual loss of the island to France.

Kennedy, Paul M. *The Rise and Fall of British Naval Mastery*. New York: Charles Scribner's Sons, 1976. Kennedy clearly shows the impact of Rodney's reduction of Martinique in the Seven Years' War and points out the superiority of British gunnery at the Battle of the Saints in 1782. Provides excellent political and economic material on the founding of the Second British Empire.

Lewis, Michael. *The Navy of Britain: A Historical Portrait*. London: Allen & Unwin, 1948. Deals with Rodney as the last of the old school of experimenters with the line-of-battle system. Extensive comments on Rodney's greatest naval achievements—the Moonlight Battle of 1780, the battle off Martinique in 1780, and the Battle of the Saints in 1782.

Macintyre, Captain Donald, R.N. *Admiral Rodney*. London: Peter Davies, 1962. A most readable, balanced account of Rodney's life. Provides good descriptions of a ship-of-the-line, battle plans, and naval gunnery in the eighteenth century, a glossary of naval terms, and a valuable index. Also deals with the political situations in England under which the navy had to fight the French.

Mahan, Alfred Thayer. *The Influence of Sea Power upon History, 1660-1783*. Boston: Little, Brown, 1890. The classic reference for naval matters. Mahan deals with the bulk of Rodney's active naval life from the reduction of Martinique in 1761 to his victory over the French in 1782, upholding the then-contemporary criticism of Rodney for not following up his advantage and the role luck played in his engagements.

Mundy, Godfrey Basil. *The Life and Correspondence of the Late Admiral Lord Rodney*. 2 vols. London: John Murray, 1830. This is a nineteenth century account of Rodney by his son-in-law, interspersed with many letters. Presents some interesting stories about different actions and the general details of Rodney's. Contains appendices and a good table of contents for the letters but no index.

Rodney, First Baron. *Letter-Books and Order-Book of George, Lord Rodney, Admiral of the White Squadron, 1780-1782*. 2 vols. New York: New York Historical Society, 1932. Printed for the Naval History Society, these letters and orders from July 6, 1780, to September 21, 1782, deal with the range of activities of a British naval commander in chief. Details of these two years cover conflict in the West Indies, manpower, ships, stores, prisoners, weather, and personalities. The introduction has a brief biography and a bibliography.

Spinney, David. *Rodney*. London: Allen & Unwin, 1969. Definitive, carefully researched, documented account of Rodney's life. Includes eighteenth century attitudes, politics, and social life, with photographs, maps, battle plans, and genealogical tables of Rodney's English and American connections. Shows Rodney's victories and his aristocratic attitude as a naval officer with which earlier writers have not dealt justly.

See also: Lord Amherst; William Bligh; Richard Howe; Sir Alexander Mackenzie; Lord North; Arthur Phillip.

Related articles in *Great Events from History: The Eighteenth Century, 1701-1800:* January, 1756-February 15, 1763: Seven Years' War; June 29, 1767-April 12, 1770: Townshend Crisis; April 27-October 10, 1774: Lord Dunmore's War; April 19, 1775: Battle of Lexington and Concord; June 21, 1779-February 7, 1783: Siege of Gibraltar.

JOHN ROEBUCK
English chemist and industrialist

After learning chemistry as a medical student, Roebuck introduced a new method for manufacturing sulfuric acid on a large scale and a new method of smelting iron.

Born: September 17, 1718 (baptized); Sheffield, Yorkshire, England
Died: July 17, 1794; Kenneil House, Scotland
Areas of achievement: Chemistry, science and technology, medicine

EARLY LIFE

John Roebuck was the third son of John Roebuck, a prosperous local cutler, and the former Sarah Roe. After receiving his early education at the Sheffield Grammar School, Roebuck attended Dr. Doddridge's Academy in Northampton. He became a good classical scholar and retained an interest in the classics throughout his life.

Although his father wanted him to carry on the family business, Roebuck was more interested in becoming a physician. Thus, with his father's assent, he studied medicine at the University of Edinburgh. There, Roebuck made the acquaintance of the prominent chemists William Cullen and Joseph Black and the philosophical circle of David Hume.

Roebuck completed his medical education at Leiden, where the most renowned chemistry professor on the Continent, Hermann Boerhaave, taught. Obtaining a medical degree on March 5, 1742, Roebuck seized upon a promising opening in Birmingham, settled there, and set up a practice, which soon prospered. Roebuck, however, had developed a love for chemistry during his university days at Edinburgh and Leiden. He was especially interested in finding ways to apply chemistry to the improvement of Birmingham's many industries.

Among his inventions for industry was a better method of stripping gold and silver from copper plate and collecting the precious metals. Birmingham had a number of companies that coated copper objects with silver and gold. The coating usually wore thin, however, and the object lost its value. Roebuck's process enabled manufacturers to recover and reuse the costly plating metals and thereby save money. He utilized a mixture of nitric and sulfuric acids. The copper was recovered by dropping in pieces of iron.

In 1746, Roebuck established a plant employing his process on Steelhouse Lane, Birmingham. His partner was Samuel Garbett, a local merchant. The Steelhouse Lane works continued to operate for more than a century, becoming the sole property of Garbett in 1773. Stimulated by his early successes, Roebuck built a large chemical laboratory alongside the plant. Local manufacturers asked him for scientific advice to help improve their industrial operations, and Roebuck carried out experiments for them. He had become, in fact, what eventually would be called a consulting chemist.

LIFE'S WORK

Of the many improvements in chemical manufacturing processes in the eighteenth century, the most important was in the production of sulfuric acid. There were several methods for making it which were centuries old. Earlier in the eighteenth century, Joshua Ward began manufacturing sulfuric acid by burning niter and sulfur over water and condensing the gas that formed in large glass globes. He chose glass because it was immune to the corrosive acid. These glass globes were very expensive, however, and their size (and the amount of sulfuric acid produced) was limited by glassblowing technology.

Roebuck was already familiar with chemical reactions from his medical training. He also had an interest in bringing down the cost of sulfuric acid because his Steelhouse Lane plant consumed large quantities of it. At Leiden, while attending the lectures of Hermann Boerhaave, Roebuck learned that lead and sulfuric acid do not react and replaced Ward's glass globes with lead chambers. In 1746, Roebuck and Garbett built their first lead chambers in Birmingham.

Roebuck's process reduced manufacturing costs and increased the amount of each production run. The result was no less than a revolution in the manufacture of sulfuric acid, which was reduced to a fourth of its former cost. Inexpensive sulfuric acid affected all those industries using it. For example, hatters, paper makers, japanners, and gilders used it for cleaning metal. Linen had been bleached by soaking it in an alkali, then in sour milk, and then exposing it to the sun, repeating the process until the desired degree of whiteness was obtained. Cheaper sulfuric acid meant that the stench of sour milk would be gone from the countryside and that the land used for bleaching cloth could be cultivated.

It was for this last purpose that Roebuck and Garbett established a sulfuric acid works at Prestonpans, East Lothian, 8 miles east of Edinburgh, in 1749. There, salt, pottery, and glass manufacturing already existed. The partners hoped to sell their sulfuric acid locally for bleaching linen, but the lead chamber process produced quantities too large for only the local linen industry. They therefore exported most of their production to the Low Countries. The Prestonpans operation was highly profitable.

Roebuck and Garbett hoped to protect the lead chamber process by keeping it secret and neglected to patent it in either England or Scotland. Rivals tried to bribe employees away and get the secret. Samuel Falconbridge, an employee hired in 1749, returned to his hometown after his dismissal from the works. Unable to find work, he was confined in the bridewell at Warwick, where a Mr. Rhodes paid for his liberty. About 1756, with the help of Falconbridge, Rhodes began making sulfuric acid using the Roebuck process. Later, Falconbridge introduced the process to another rival firm and the method spread.

In 1771, Roebuck applied for a Scottish patent to stave off competition. The patent office rejected the application because the process was already in use in England. Roebuck and Garbett then petitioned against the

decision, but the House of Lords rejected it because the substitution of lead for glass was not a discovery, only a variation; the variation itself was not new, since Roebuck already had used the process for twenty years; and the lead chamber process was known to various people in England and Scotland.

Meanwhile, Roebuck had begun to diversify his business interests and turned his attention to the manufacture of iron. The extraction of iron from its ore consumed considerable amounts of charcoal and so required handy timberlands. Timber, however, was in short supply. The smelting of iron ore by coke made from coal was probably rediscovered by Abraham Darby at Colebrookdale in about 1734. In 1759, Roebuck decided to establish an ironworks in Scotland using coal instead of charcoal.

Iron smelting in Scotland was carried out in very small establishments scattered about the countryside. Roebuck's was the first to operate on any sizable scale. The amount of capital required for such an enormous undertaking was more than Roebuck and Garbett alone could furnish, so a company was formed early in 1760 with seven partners. Roebuck and Garbett each owned a quarter of the shares. Roebuck's three brothers, Benjamin, Thomas, and Ebenezer, equally divided another quarter. The last quarter was owned by William Cadell, Sr., and William Cadell, Jr., Scottish shipowners and traders in timber and iron who already had tried unsuccessfully to produce iron in Scotland on a large scale.

The establishment and organization of the company's works were largely under Roebuck's direction. He chose as the site a place on the banks of the Carron River near Falkirk, Stirling, 3 miles above the river's juncture with the Firth of Forth. The Carron River provided waterpower, the Forth a water transportation route, and the surrounding land held abundant supplies of coal, iron ore, and limestone (used as the flux in iron smelting). The first furnace was blown at Carron on January 1, 1760. During that same year, the Carron works turned out fifteen hundred tons of iron, at that time the entire annual production of Scotland. The site's main business became casting cannon, for which there was a large demand during the war-filled 1760's and 1770's.

At first, the Carron works used large quantities of charcoal, but Roebuck soon switched to coal, a much cheaper fuel. In 1762, he obtained a patent, number 780, for converting cast iron into malleable iron by means of a coal fire. Roebuck's plan to burn coal on a large scale nevertheless required a far more powerful blast than that used with a charcoal fire. Roebuck therefore consulted John Smeaton, a famous engineer familiar with iron-working, who erected the first blowing cylinders of any substantial size for working iron at Carron.

Once the Carron works was solidly established and prosperous, Roebuck began a new enterprise. He leased some large coal mines and saltworks at Borrowstounness (Bo'ness) in Linlithgowshire from the duke of Hamilton. About 1764, he moved his family to Kenneil House, a ducal mansion which came with the lease and overlooked the Firth of Forth.

Although the coal mines and saltworks had yielded little or no profit, Roebuck was determined to make them pay. He hoped to supply his own coal to the Carron ironworks, thereby selling both coal and iron. The slag from the Carron smelting operation could then be used to make sulfuric acid at Prestonpans. Finally, he hoped to manufacture alkali from the Bo'ness saltworks. Joseph Black, Roebuck's acquaintance from the University of Edinburgh, had suggested to him the possibility of making alkali by decomposing salt. Alkalies were important in eighteenth century industry: in making glass and soap, bleaching, manufacturing alum and saltpeter, and for fertilizing in agriculture. As natural resources became scarce and the use of alkalies increased, the need for a manufactured substitute grew more acute.

Roebuck invested all of his own capital in the venture and borrowed from Garbett, who refused to join the enterprise. Roebuck also drew on the capital of the Prestonpans and Carron operations. By 1765, he and Black were experimenting on the decomposition of salt. They soon enlisted the aid of a mutual acquaintance, James Watt, who made mathematical instruments.

It was then that water began flooding Roebuck's coal pits at Bo'ness. A Newcomen steam engine failed to keep pace with the water. Black told Roebuck about Watt's new engine. Roebuck invited Watt to Kenneil House, where Watt assembled a working model of his engine. Roebuck did not appreciate the difficulties of turning a working model into a large-scale machine; hoping that Watt's engine might keep his coal mines dry enough to work, Roebuck began providing Watt with substantial financial backing.

Roebuck agreed to carry the cost of developing Watt's engine, repay Black's loan of £1,200 to Watt, purchase the patent, and handle the business of manufacturing and selling the engine. For this, Roebuck would receive two-thirds of the profits. Watt, however, had a family to support and, in the summer of 1766, he opened an office in Glasgow as a surveyor.

While this enterprise left little time for experimenting on the new engine, with Roebuck's encouragement Watt managed to advance his invention to the point at which it was patentable. The inventor later admitted that he would have given up if he had not been supported by Roebuck. In 1769, Watt obtained his first steam engine patent.

New investors became interested in Watt's invention. On November 28, 1769, Roebuck, Matthew Boulton, and William Small agreed to the purchase of a third of the patent rights. Boulton was an old friend of Garbett; Small was a former professor of natural philosophy at the College of William and Mary, Williamsburg, Virginia, and had a medical practice in Birmingham.

Despite Roebuck's financial support and Watt's ingenuity, the steam engine was not capable of keeping the water out of Roebuck's mines. The attempt to manufacture alkali from salt also failed. As a result, Roebuck incurred heavier and heavier losses. He lost his own money, his wife's fortune, the profits from his other enterprises, and large sums borrowed from friends. Roebuck withdrew his capital from the Carron ironworks, from the Steelhouse Lane works in Birmingham, and the sulfuric acid plant at Prestonpans to satisfy his creditors. By 1773, he was bankrupt.

On March 29, 1773, Roebuck's creditors called a meeting to review the management of his affairs. Boulton appointed Watt as his representative at the meeting. Among Roebuck's debts was £1,200 owed to Boulton. Rather than asking for a monetary settlement, Boulton offered to cancel the debt in return for Roebuck's remaining two-thirds share in Watt's steam engine patent. This was the beginning of the well-known and successful firm of Boulton and Watt.

Roebuck's creditors retained him as manager of the Bo'ness coal and saltworks and paid him an annual allowance sufficient for the support of himself and his family. Meanwhile, Roebuck began farming at Kenneil House on a large scale. He carried out agricultural experiments and was a successful farmer. When he died on July 17, 1794, however, he left his wife without provision.

Roebuck was a member of the Royal Society of Arts in London, the Royal societies of London and Edinburgh, and the Lunar Society of Birmingham, so called because it met during the full moon. He contributed two articles to the *Philosophical Transactions* of the London Royal Society. The first appeared in 1775 and dealt with the temperature of London versus that of Edinburgh. Appearing the following year, the second discussed the nature of heat in bodies and was based upon a series of experiments he carried out in Birmingham with the assistance of Boulton. Roebuck tested whether an iron ball weighed more when heated than when cold and found no indication that heating an object caused an increase in weight, which was contrary to the commonly held scientific theory that heat had weight.

SIGNIFICANCE

The invention and eventual spread of John Roebuck's lead chamber process sparked a revolution in the chemical industry, which the discovery of Nicolas Leblanc's method of manufacturing alkali continued. That chemical revolution, however, was but one of several interrelated revolutions that took place at approximately the same time in Great Britain and which have been named the Industrial Revolution. In addition to the lead chamber process, Roebuck contributed to the larger Industrial Revolution through his establishment of the Carron ironworks, his attempt (though failed) to manufacture alkali, and his support of Watt in the improvement of the steam engine. Iron and coal, sulfuric acid and alkali, and the steam engine were important ingredients of the Industrial Revolution.

One of the salient features of the industrialized societies that have grown out of the British Industrial Revolution is the integration of industries. The purchase of coal mines and railroads by American steel magnates in the late nineteenth century is well known, and both the vertical and the horizontal integration of industries have become common practices. In the eighteenth century, Roebuck pioneered in industrial integration.

Starting with a chemical process that utilized sulfuric acid, he devised the lead chamber method and established a plant for making sulfuric acid on a large scale, the surplus of which he sold. Transferring his business operations to Scotland, Roebuck started manufacturing sulfuric acid at Prestonpans and opened an ironworks at Carron. He then leased the Bo'ness coal and salt works to supply coal for the Carron iron-smelting operation. In turn, he used the slag from the Carron works to manufacture sulfuric acid at Prestonpans. He tried to manufacture alkali from the salt and coal of Bo'ness. Roebuck failed; his coal mines flooded faster than contemporary steam engines could remove the water. Nevertheless, he was a pioneer in industrial integration in an age when the concept did not yet exist; in the process, he helped create the very Industrial Revolution that would put his ideas into practice a century later.

—*Andrew J. Butrica*

FURTHER READING

Cadell, Henry M. *The Story of the Forth.* Glasgow, Scotland: J. Maclehose and Sons, 1913. An old, but still useful history of the area Roebuck chose for his Scottish enterprises.

Clow, Archibald, and Nan L. Clow. *The Chemical Revolution.* London: Batchworth Press, 1952. Detailed history of Roebuck's sulfuric acid and ironworks in the industrialization of Scotland.

Hamilton, Henry. *An Economic History of Scotland.* Oxford, England: Clarendon Press, 1963. Portions relate the role of Roebuck's sulfuric acid and ironworks in the industrialization of Scotland.

Muirhead, James Patrick. *The Origins and Progress of the Mechanical Inventions of James Watt.* 3 vols. London: John Murray, 1854. Still the most complete work on Watt and the steam engine. Relates the contribution of Roebuck at some length.

Roebuck, Arthur W. *The Roebuck Story.* Don Mills, Ont.: T. H. Best, 1963. A family history. Information on John Roebuck is found on pages 6-18.

Roebuck, John. "A Comparison of the Heat of London and Edinburgh." *Philosophical Transactions of the Royal Society* 65 (1775): 459-462. Roebuck's first publication, which is a comparison of city temperatures.

_____. "Experiments on Ignited Bodies." *Philosophical Transactions of the Royal Society* 66 (1776): 509-510. In his second and last scientific publication, Roebuck investigated the nature of heat to determine whether it had weight, as contemporary scientists believed. Eventually, heat was understood no longer as a substance but as a form of energy. An important, if forgotten study.

Schofield, Robert E. *The Lunar Society of Birmingham: A Social History of Provincial Science and Industry in Eighteenth-Century England.* Oxford, England: Clarendon Press, 1963. An excellent study of an informal scientific society in provincial England. Describes Roebuck's sulfuric acid, iron, alkali, and steam engine ventures.

Uglow, Jenny. *The Lunar Men: Five Friends Whose Curiosity Changed the World.* New York: Farrar, Straus, and Giroux, 2002. An updated history of the Lunar Society of Birmingham. Roebuck's Carron ironworks and his experiments with thermometers, the steam engine, and alkalis are included in this book about the scientific and technological innovations that were created by society members.

See also: Joseph Black; Matthew Boulton; Abraham Darby; David Hume; Nicolas Leblanc; William Murdock; Thomas Newcomen; Georg Ernst Stahl; James Watt; John Wilkinson.

Related articles in *Great Events from History: The Eighteenth Century, 1701-1800:* 1705-1712: Newcomen Develops the Steam Engine; 1709: Darby Invents Coke-Smelting; 1714: Fahrenheit Develops the Mercury Thermometer; 1746: Roebuck Develops the Lead-Chamber Process; 1765-1769: Watt Develops a More Effective Steam Engine; 1783-1784: Cort Improves Iron Processing; 1797: Wollaston Begins His Work on Metallurgy.

GEORGE ROMNEY
English painter

Romney was one of the three leading portrait painters, along with Sir Joshua Reynolds and Thomas Gainsborough, in eighteenth century England. At the height of his career Romney's popularity was the equal of his main rival, Reynolds.

Born: December 26, 1734; Dalton-in-Furness, Lancashire, England
Died: November 15, 1802; Kendal, Cumbria, England
Area of achievement: Art

EARLY LIFE

George Romney was born in a small village in northwest England. He was the third child of Ann Romney and John Romney, a carpenter, joiner, and cabinet maker. Romney was sent to the local village school until he was eleven, after which he stayed at home to learn the family business. He worked in the family business for the following nine years, although few details of this period of his life survive. It is known that his early interest in drawing was encouraged by a friend of the family, Mrs. Gardner, and a likeness of her was one of Romney's first attempts at portraiture. Also while young he is known to have studied a translation of Leonardo da Vinci's *Trattato della pintura* (1651; *A Treatise on Painting*, 1721), which he discovered in his father's library. Romney's name is inscribed inside this volume and is dated 1754.

By 1755 it was clear in which direction his talents lay, and he was apprenticed to a traveling portrait painter, Christopher Steele, with whom he remained for two years. Steele's portraits do not survive, and it is therefore difficult to judge how much Romney may have learned from him, but certainly Romney soon became an expert in the grinding and mixing of colors, which was to serve him well throughout his career. His apprenticeship was the only practical instruction he ever received. During this time he married Mary Abbot, the daughter of his landlady, although he had no means of supporting her.

After prematurely breaking off his apprenticeship, he set up his own practice in nearby Kendal. Although he never lacked employment, he was forced to charge low fees, and in consequence had to struggle to make an adequate income. The financial straits of this period did, however, teach him to work quickly, a habit that he was to continue throughout his life and one that enabled him at the peak of his career to take more sitters than his two great rivals, Thomas Gainsborough and Sir Joshua Reynolds.

Highly ambitious and caring little for anything other than his art, Romney was determined to travel to London to further his career. By March of 1762, Romney had accumulated enough money to make the trip, leaving his wife and their infant son behind in Kendal. In London, he became an immediate success.

LIFE'S WORK

In 1762, George Romney painted *The Death of General Wolfe*, which the following year won an award of 25 guineas from the Society of Arts for historical painting. It was the first picture he exhibited. Also in 1763, he was one of the hundred signatories of the Deed of the Free Society of Artists, and he exhibited with them until 1769.

In September, 1764, anxious to improve his knowledge of the old masters, he traveled to Paris with his lifelong friend, the lawyer Thomas Greene. He paid particular attention to the work of Peter Paul Rubens. He met the noted French painter Joseph Vernet and visited Versailles, Marly, and St. Cloud before returning to London after six weeks. In 1765 his painting *The Death of King Edmund* was awarded the second premium of 50 guineas by the Society of Arts, and for the first time one of his paintings attracted the attention of a newspaper critic. During these years he frequently changed lodgings in London and made occasional trips back to Kendal. In 1770, he first exhibited with the Society of Artists. A prolific year of painting followed, and in 1772 he was made a director, and then a fellow, of the Society of Artists. This was the last year he sent works for public exhibition, and in spite of his success he was never to apply for membership in the Royal Academy.

In March, 1773, now on the threshold of recognition and financial security, Romney fulfilled his ambition to travel to Italy, visiting Genoa and Rome. In Rome he devoted himself to studying the works of Raphael and Michelangelo in the Vatican and to making sketches of famous buildings. He also found time to make the acquaintance of other English painters, although his reserved and sensitive nature ensured that he was never the most sociable of men. Romney returned home via Florence, Bologna, where he was offered, but declined, the presidency of the Academy of Painting; Venice, where he studied Titian; and Parma, where he was entranced by the work of Correggio.

He arrived home in July, 1775, and by Christmas he had moved into a large house at Cavendish Square. His best work dates from this period. Sitters were soon arriving in large numbers, including such notable figures as the duke of Richmond, but they came from all classes. Romney would often have up to five sitters a day, and occasionally six. It took three or four sittings to do a three-quarters portrait, making an equivalent of almost one portrait a day. During this most successful period of the painter's life, he gained more commissions than Reynolds and Gainsborough, and by 1778 his reputation was established as one of the finest portrait painters of the day.

He had also been cultivating a few literary and artistic friends, such as the sculptor John Flaxman and the poet William Cowper. His chief friend was William Hayley, an undistinguished poet who enjoyed a brief period of popular esteem but whose verses are now forgotten. Each year Romney would stay with Hayley at his Sussex home. Hayley, providing the only contemporary account of Romney's personal appearance, wrote, "He was rather tall, his features were broad and strong, his hair was dark, his eyes indicated much vigour, and still more acuteness of mind." Although Hayley was kind and well-meaning, anxious to support his friends, his influence on Romney was not entirely beneficial. He persuaded him not to apply for membership in the Royal Academy, for example, convinced that it would only be a trouble to Romney's excessively timid and irritable nature.

In 1782 came a major event in Romney's life: his first meeting with the beautiful young Emma Hart, the future Lady Hamilton. She had been brought to him by his friend Charles Greville to sit for a portrait, and for nearly four years she was a frequent visitor to his studio. He became deeply attached to her and regarded her as a source of inspiration for his art. She was the model for more than forty of his paintings, appearing as a Bacchante, Ariadne, Joan of Arc, Contemplation, Comedy, and many other

mythic figures and personifications. He referred to her as "the divine lady."

During the 1790's, Romney's health began to fail rapidly, and he was frequently depressed. The number of his unfinished paintings, which was always high, increased alarmingly, and they accumulated in heaps in every corner of his house. Although Romney always worked prodigiously hard, he was easily discouraged by any setback or obstacle, such as the loss of a model. Furthermore, he preferred the excitement of a new task to that of finishing an old one. He frequently complained about the drudgery of portrait painting, which he regarded as an inferior genre. He wanted to do more imaginative work, but his efforts in that direction were often restricted to the time between sitters. He did not have the strength of will to strike out completely in a new direction.

From 1796 onward, his attention was taken up with the building of a house and studio at Hampstead. He moved in at Christmas, 1798, before the house was finished. His paintings were stored inadequately, so that they were exposed to the elements; many were destroyed during the course of the winter, and others were stolen.

In his final years, Romney's health and his mental powers broke down completely. In 1798 he returned to the north for the first time in thirty years, and the follow-

George Romney. (Library of Congress)

ing year he retired to Kendal, to be nursed by the patient and forgiving wife whom he had deserted nearly forty years before. He died on November 15, 1802.

SIGNIFICANCE

Since his death, George Romney's reputation has fluctuated between extremes. For fifty years his name sank into obscurity, but then the pendulum began to swing back, until by the first half of the twentieth century his paintings were fetching exaggerated prices in salerooms. There is now general agreement that he was the third most important portrait painter in late eighteenth century England, surpassed only by Gainsborough and Reynolds.

Despite that distinction (or perhaps in accordance with it), Romney remains an unusual figure in art history. He owed little to the direct teaching of others, and he was always hampered by his lack of early training. His own influence on later art was minimal, although three of his pupils at the end of his career, Isaac Pocock, James Lonsdale, and Thomas Stewardson, became distinguished painters.

As a portrait painter, Romney lacked the range and psychological depth of Reynolds and Gainsborough, and he painted much that was of inferior quality. His best portraits, however, especially those of women and children, convey considerable charm. Excellent examples of these are *Mrs. Cawardine and Son*, and the *Duchess of Gordon and Her Son*. His series of portraits of the Stafford family, painted between 1776 and 1782, as well as his *Sir Christopher Sykes and Lady Sykes*, display his work at its finest, particularly in the simplicity, dignity, and clarity of design for which he always strove.

He failed, however, in his ambition to become a major imaginative and historical painter. Although he was easily stimulated to imagine grand designs, many of them for subjects from works by William Shakespeare or John Milton, he lacked the staying power necessary to complete the task. He left only a few such portraits, the chief of which is an illustration of the shipwreck scene from Shakespeare's *The Tempest*, which occupied him for several years during middle age. What remains of his work in this area, however, suggests some of the imaginative power of Henry Fuseli or William Blake.

Fuseli's own comment on Romney, written eight years after Romney's death, remains a fair assessment of his achievement. Fuseli wrote, "If he had not genius to lead, he had too much originality to follow. . . . Romney, as artist and as man, is entitled to commendation and esteem."

—*Bryan Aubrey*

FURTHER READING

Cross, David. *A Striking Likeness: The Life of George Romney*. Brookfield, Vt.: Ashgate, 2000. Biography and critical analysis of Romney's work. The book describes Romney's career, relations with peers and family, and desire to become a history painter. Includes a Romney family tree, a bibliography, and an index.

Hagstrum, Jean H. "Romney and Blake: Gifts of Grace and Terror." In *Blake in His Time*, edited by Robert N. Essick and Donald Pearce. Bloomington: Indiana University Press, 1978. William Blake and Romney knew and admired each other's work, and this article traces with subtlety and insight some of the points of contact between them.

Kidson, Alex. *George Romney, 1734-1802*. Princeton, N.J.: Princeton University Press, 2002. In 2002, several museums in the United States and England exhibited Romney's works to commemorate the bicentennial of his death. This catalog accompanied the exhibition and features reproductions of more than two hundred of Romney's paintings and drawings. Kidson provides an essay featuring biographical material and a critical analysis of Romney's work.

_____, ed. *Those Delightful Regions of Imagination: Essays on George Romney*. New Haven, Conn.: Yale University Press, 2002. A collection of essays about Romney's life and work. The essays examine the artist's personality, his artistic practice and technique, the relation of his work to the theater, central themes in his work, and his rivalry with Sir Joshua Reynolds.

Mayoux, Jean Jacques. *English Painting: From Hogarth to the Pre-Raphaelites*. New York: St. Martin's Press, 1975. A former professor of English literature at the Sorbonne in Paris gives an illuminating, challenging, and idiosyncratic view of English painting, with a section on Romney.

Pointon, Marcia. "Portrait-Painting as a Business Enterprise in London in the 1780's." *Art History* 7 (1984): 187-205. A well-researched article that examines the social and economic conditions under which painters such as Romney, Reynolds, and James Northcote had to work.

Ward, Humphrey, and W. Roberts. *Romney: A Biographical and Critical Essay, with a Catalogue Raisonné of His Works*. 2 vols. London: Thomas Agnew and Sons, 1904. This valuable monograph contains much information unavailable elsewhere, including detailed discussion of many of Romney's paintings. It remains the only catalogue raisonné of his work.

Watson, Jennifer C. *George Romney in Canada*. Waterloo, Ont.: Wilfred Laurier University Press, 1985. A highly informative and well-annotated catalog of an exhibition of Romney's works owned in Canada, held at the Kitchener-Waterloo Art Gallery, and other locations in Canada, in 1985 and 1986.

See also: William Blake; John Singleton Copley; Thomas Gainsborough; William Hogarth; Sir Joshua Reynolds; Gilbert Stuart; James Wolfe.

Related article in *Great Events from History: The Eighteenth Century, 1701-1800:* December 10, 1768: Britain's Royal Academy of Arts Is Founded.

BETSY ROSS
American tradeswoman

Using an original idea presented to her by George Washington, Betsy Ross is reputed to have designed and sewn the first official American flag. She was a lifelong seamstress and upholsterer, and she conducted her own upholstery business until she died at age eighty-four.

Born: January 1, 1752; Philadelphia, Pennsylvania
Died: January 30, 1836; Philadelphia, Pennsylvania
Also known as: Elizabeth Griscom (birth name); Betsy Ashburn; Betsy Claypoole
Areas of achievement: Art, business

EARLY LIFE
Betsy Ross was born Elizabeth "Betsy" Griscom, the eighth of seventeen children of Samuel and Rebecca Griscom and part of the fourth generation of Griscoms in America. The Griscoms lived on Mulberry Street (now Arch Street), near Fourth Street, and Samuel was a well-known carpenter.

Little is known of Betsy Griscom's early life or appearance. She is sometimes described as having blue eyes and auburn hair, but the accuracy of these accounts cannot be confirmed. She attended a Quaker school run by Rebecca Jones and later studied at the Friends Public School on Fourth Street, chartered by William Penn as a public institution but run by Quakers. Her parents, members of the Philadelphia Society of Friends, preferred that she receive a Quaker education.

After her basic education, in keeping with the custom of the time, Griscom was apprenticed to learn a trade. Although many young women learned housekeeping, she studied upholstery in the shop of William Webster, where she applied her seamstress skills to making furniture. It was at Webster's shop that Griscom met John Ross, a fellow apprentice and a native Philadelphian. They fell in love and wished to marry but could not do so because John's father, Eneas Ross, was a minister of the Episcopal Church, and Quakers strongly discouraged

marrying outside the faith. However, the young couple determined to marry despite the lack of parental approval, and on November 4, 1773, they took a boat across the Delaware to Hugg's Tavern, in Gloucester, New Jersey, where they were married by a justice of the peace; Betsy was twenty-one years of age, John was twenty-two.

Because Ross would not apologize for the marriage and repent, as Quaker doctrine required, the monthly meeting of Friends for the Northern District of Philadelphia declared that she was considered disunited from religious fellowship with the Quakers. The Rosses began to worship in the Anglican faith, at Christ Church, where John's father was rector. The couple's pew, number twelve, was immediately adjacent to the one occupied by George and Martha Washington when they were in Philadelphia.

LIFE'S WORK
In 1775, John and Betsy Ross left Webster's shop to start their own upholstery business on Arch Street, near where Betsy was raised. Their business prospered, and the Rosses developed reputations as excellent practitioners of their craft. Apparently, both Rosses were patriots, and John joined the Philadelphia militia to fight in the struggle against the British. He was fatally injured in a gunpowder explosion while guarding a munitions warehouse on the docks. He was buried at Christ Church on January 21, 1776, and Betsy, a widow at the age of twenty-four, was left to manage the shop on her own, which she did with some success.

According to the longstanding legends regarding Ross and the American flag, in late May or early June of 1776, General George Washington, Colonel George Ross (the uncle of Betsy's late husband), and Robert Morris called on Ross at her upholstery shop and requested that she make a flag based on a rough sketch by Washington. The flag was originally designed with six-pointed stars, but Ross proposed that they use five-pointed stars, as these were easier and quicker to make. The legend also states that she changed the flag shape from square to rectangular so that the flag would produce a better rippling effect when seen at a distance.

The specifics of this story cannot be confirmed, as no contemporary accounts provide a definitive description of how the stars and stripes version of the American flag was designed or altered by Ross or any other individual. The first recorded appearance of the Ross legend occurred in 1870, when one of Ross's grandsons, William J. Canby, published a story about his grandmother telling him, when he was eleven years old, about her work on the flag.

For many years, the legend was accepted and became part of American history, but since at least the early twentieth century, the story has been the subject of much debate among historians. The debate was renewed in 1952, when the U.S. Post Office issued a three-cent stamp honoring the one-hundredth anniversary of Ross's birth. Since the 1970's, some feminists have scorned the Ross story as a typical effort to marginalize women's many achievements in the revolution into one narrow, traditionally female field: sewing. The historical accuracy of the account will probably never be conclusively confirmed, but several key facts about the flag are known.

For example, on June 14, 1777, the Continental Congress adopted a resolution that the "flag of the United States be thirteen stripes alternate red and white, that the Union be thirteen stars white in a blue field representing a new constellation." Nothing more is mentioned about the origination of the design or any person involved with the design or manufacture, but this design conforms to that described in the Ross legend. Because of the ongoing war, the announcement met with little fanfare, and it was not until August and September that the press began reporting on the resolution.

The official design remained a matter of some confusion for a long time, and even America's own ambassadors in foreign countries were often not aware of the newly adopted format. Also, individual units of the armed forces frequently created their own distinctive banners, which varied widely from state to state and even from city to city, so that nothing like a uniform adoption and display of the American flag was seen for the duration of the Revolutionary War. However, the stars and stripes design attributed to Washington and Ross is seen in various paintings contemporary to the period, especially those of Charles Willson Peale and Colonel John

Betsy Ross. (Library of Congress)

Trumbull, the latter a painter known for the accuracy of his images of uniforms and insignia. It should also be noted that no other person contemporary with the events ever claimed to have made the first American flag, and there are numerous sworn affidavits by Ross's grandchildren and nieces individually confirming the accuracy of the original story.

Ross remarried on June 15, 1777, at the Gloria Dei Church in Philadelphia. Her husband, Joseph Ashburn, was a sea captain and privateer against the British and someone Ross had known since before her first marriage. Some accounts hold that she was engaged to Ashburn and broke the engagement to marry John Ross, but this remains unconfirmed. She continued to operate her upholstery shop and manufacture flags for the United States government and the Pennsylvania navy. Also, she gave birth to her first two children, both daughters, before Ashburn was captured by the British and sent to Old Mill Prison in Plymouth, England. He died there on March 3, 1782.

In August of 1782, John Claypoole, an American marine lieutenant, was released from Old Mill Prison, where he had befriended Ashburn. He returned to Philadelphia and informed Betsy of the death of her husband, which had long been suspected, as he had not been heard from in more than a year. On May 8, 1783, at the age of thirty-one, Betsy Ross Ashburn married Claypoole; her husband was seven months younger than she. She continued to operate her upholstery shop with Claypoole as her new partner and bore five children with him, all daughters. During this time she joined the Society of Free Quakers, a more liberal sect of the Society of Friends than that which had excommunicated her years earlier.

John Claypoole died on August 3, 1817, and Betsy (Ross) Claypoole continued to run the upholstery shop until her death on January 30, 1836, at the age of eighty-four. Her daughters and granddaughters ran the family upholstery shop until 1857. Her grave is located next to the reputed location of her original shop at 239 Arch Street in Philadelphia.

SIGNIFICANCE

Though widely accepted for many years as a matter of historical fact, it is impossible to state with precision whether the legend involving Betsy Ross and the first American flag is true. Some historians note that the legend very well could be true, based on its conformance to known information, while others ascribe it to sheer self-promotion on the part of Ross's descendants.

In either case, it is easy to see why such a legend was so attractive to late nineteenth century U.S. society: It provided an excellent example of what was called "Republican motherhood." The legendary Ross contributed to the quest for American independence but did so by using her skills as a seamstress, skills traditionally considered appropriate for young women. By originating an impressive flag that symbolized the United States, she demonstrated one way women could contribute to the nation's democratic process without overstepping the time period's bounds of propriety or becoming directly involved in governmental affairs.

Conspicuously absent from the legend are the details of her three marriages, her owning and operating a business throughout her life, and other nontraditional facts.

In many ways, these hidden aspects of her life, and how her story has been manipulated through time to serve the agendas of various generations of historians, may be Ross's most important contribution to the history of the United States as a nation and as an ideal.

—*Vicki A. Sanders*

FURTHER READING

"Betsy Ross Stamp Causes Controversy." *Life* (February 18, 1952): 57-58. A good overview of the 1952 stamp controversy. This fairly short article includes an illustration of the stamp and a capsule history of Ross, as well as examples of how the legend had been questioned by various writers and historians.

Corcoran, Mike. *For Which It Stands: An Anecdotal Biography of the American Flag.* New York: Simon & Schuster, 2002. A pocket-size book of facts about the American flag. Corcoran debunks the Betsy Ross legend, explaining that she neither designed nor sewed the first flag.

Mayer, Jane. *Betsy Ross and the Flag.* New York: Random House, 1952. One of several children's books about Ross, this brief volume is typical of the mainstream treatment the legend received in the United States during the mid-twentieth century. The writer gives a very conventional view of Ross, her first marriage, and her role in the flag design and manufacture process, all meant to appeal to young female readers.

Morris, Robert. *The Truth About the Betsy Ross Story.* Beach Haven, N.J.: Wynnehaven, 1982. The definitive rendering of the legend and its relation to historical fact. Morris gives ample information about Ross, the flag and its various predecessors, and contemporary historical events. He rebuts point by point various Ross detractors and provides numerous illustrations and appendices to support his belief that the flag legend is no legend but true.

Selby, Earl. "They Never Told Me *This* About Betsy Ross." *Collier's* (July 8, 1950): 34. One of the first articles to mention some of the more nontraditional elements of Ross's personal life, this article was published at a time when the legend was still widely accepted as true.

See also: Robert Morris; Charles Willson Peale; John Trumbull; George Washington.

Related articles in *Great Events from History: The Eighteenth Century, 1701-1800:* September 5-October 26, 1774: First Continental Congress; May 10-August 2, 1775: Second Continental Congress.

JEAN-JACQUES ROUSSEAU
French philosopher

Rousseau helped transform the Western world from a rigidly stratified, frequently despotic civilization into a predominantly democratic civilization dedicated to assuring the dignity and fulfillment of the individual.

Born: June 28, 1712; Geneva (now in Switzerland)
Died: July 2, 1778; Ermenonville, France
Areas of achievement: Philosophy, education, literature

EARLY LIFE

Jean-Jacques Rousseau (zhahn-zhahk rew-soh) was born of middle-class parents in the fiercely independent Protestant municipality of Geneva. His mother, the former Suzanne Bernard, died within days of his birth, and he was reared until age ten by his watchmaker father, Isaac Rousseau, with whom the precocious boy shared a passion for romantic novels, a passion that helped to shape Jean-Jacques's emotional and highly imaginative nature. Young Rousseau and the irresponsible Isaac often neglected sleep as they devoured their beloved romances, an escapist reading regimen that Rousseau supplemented with more substantial works by writers such as Plutarch and Michel Eyquem de Montaigne.

This earliest phase of Rousseau's life came to an abrupt end when his father was forced to flee from Geneva to escape imprisonment for wounding a former military officer during a quarrel in the autumn of 1722. Left in the care of a maternal uncle, Rousseau was soon placed, along with his cousin Abraham Bernard, in the home of the Lambercier family, a Protestant minister and his sister, in the village of Bossey, a few miles outside Geneva.

The essentially carefree two years spent with the Lamberciers were followed by a short period of distasteful employment with the district registrar and a longer apprenticeship to an engraver. Petty thefts and other breaches of discipline earned for Rousseau, now in his teens, a series of beatings that in no way altered his recalcitrant behavior but that augmented his hatred of authority. After nearly three years of these confrontations, in March of 1728 he abandoned his apprenticeship and, with it, his native city.

Rousseau was introduced to twenty-nine-year-old Madame de Warens, eventually to be one of the great loves of his life, who sent the destitute and still directionless teenager to Turin's monastery of the Spirito Santo, where, within a few days of his arrival, he found it expedient to embrace the Catholic faith. Released into the streets of Turin with little money, Rousseau held several jobs but eventually returned, probably by mid-1729, to Madame de Warens.

Rousseau's duties as record keeper to Madame de Warens were light enough to allow him ample time for wide reading, but his genius had still not manifested itself, and after his patron had left on a journey to Paris, the aimless youth took the opportunity to add to his store of life adventures. At Lausanne, he attempted, despite insufficient knowledge of music, to conduct an orchestral work of his own composition; the performance was a fiasco.

Succeeding months saw Madame de Warens establish herself as Rousseau's mistress and Rousseau busy himself with the study and teaching of music. Over the next several years, Rousseau also undertook the intensive study of most other branches of human knowledge in an eminently successful effort to overcome the handicap of his earlier haphazard education.

LIFE'S WORK

By 1740, Rousseau had begun serious attempts to write, but he remained essentially unknown. His first minor recognition came in 1742, during his second visit to Paris, when he suggested a new method of musical notation to the Academy of Science. Although the method was judged inadequate, Rousseau's presentation earned for him the respect of and eventual introduction to several figures of importance in the French intelligentsia, most notably Denis Diderot. In 1743, at the salon of Madame Dupin, Rousseau widened his circle of influential acquaintances, and eventually he became Madame Dupin's secretary.

Then, while traveling to Vincennes to visit Diderot, who had been imprisoned in 1749, Rousseau happened across an essay competition that would assure his lasting fame. Had the advancement of science and art, the Academy of Dijon wished to know, improved the moral state of humankind? Rousseau argued in the negative, and his essay *Discours sur les sciences et les arts* (1750; *A Discourse on the Arts and Sciences*, 1751) was awarded first prize on July 10, 1750. Rousseau's central contention, that modern advances in the arts and sciences had produced an abandonment of primitive sincerity and simple virtue, inspired a plethora of attacks and defenses and

Jean-Jacques Rousseau. (Library of Congress)

helped prepare the way for the Romantic reaction against Enlightenment rationalism.

Rousseau's next success was the composition of an operetta, *Le Devin du village* (1752; *Cunning-Man*, 1766), which gained for him some financial security and was honored with a command performance before the French court on October 18, 1752. By refusing an audience with the king and then entangling himself in a dispute over the relative merits of French and Italian music, however, Rousseau almost immediately lost the regal favor he had just gained.

Following this unpleasant interlude, Rousseau achieved another of his great intellectual triumphs with the publication of *Discours sur l'origine et les fondements de l'inégalité* (1755; *A Discourse upon the Origin and Foundation of the Inequality Among Mankind*, 1761), again written in response to a topic proposed by the Academy of Dijon. An analysis of the beginnings of human inequality, this work continues Rousseau's theme of the relative superiority of primitive to civilized humanity. Distinguishing the irremediable inequality produced by natural circumstance from the imposed in-

equality encouraged by artificial social convention, Rousseau attacks many of the assumptions underlying the political and social order of mid-eighteenth century Europe.

With the publication of *Julie: Ou, La Nouvelle Héloïse* (1761; *Eloise: Or, A Series of Original Letters*, 1761; also as *Julie: Or, The New Eloise*, 1968; better known as *The New Héloïse*), Rousseau's career took a new turn. An epistolary novel of sentimental love, *The New Héloïse* focuses on the passionate relationship of the aristocratic Julie d'Étange and her tutor Saint-Preux, a relationship doomed by the disapproval of Julie's intolerant father. The novel's emotional intensity, its portrayal of the corrupting influence of the city, and its association of sublime sentiment with the beauty and grandeur of nature engendered tremendous popularity and established a model for emulation by Romantic writers of the ensuing one hundred years.

More in keeping with his previous publications, *Du contrat social: Ou, Principes du droit politique* (1762; *A Treatise on the Social Contract: Or, The Principles of Politic Law*, 1764; better known as *The Social Contract*) is Rousseau's fullest statement on the proper relationship between a nation's government and its people. *The Social Contract* admits that, in practice, any of the range of governmental structures, from pure democracy through aristocracy to monarchy, may be the most appropriate for a particular state, but Rousseau insists that the source of sovereignty is always the people and that the people may not legitimately relinquish sovereignty to despots who would subvert the general will. If a government acts contrary to the will of the people, the people have a right to replace it.

Published in the same year as *The Social Contract*, *Émile: Ou, De l'éducation* (*Emilius and Sophia: Or, A New System of Education*, 1762-1763) contains his most influential statements on education and religion. The book insists that the developing child be allowed adequate physical activity and that the pace of the child's education be determined by the gradual emergence of the child's own capacities and interests. A slow and deliberate individualized education is infinitely preferable to an education that rushes the child toward an identity that subverts his (or her) natural inclinations. Furthermore, the purpose of education should not simply be the acquisition of knowledge but the formation of the whole human being, whenever possible through life experiences rather than through heavy reliance on books.

From the beginning of his career as a writer and thinker, Rousseau had been the center of perpetual controversy. With his publications of the early 1760's banned in some areas of Europe and burned in others, he found himself again becoming an exile. He left Paris in June of 1762 to avoid imminent arrest and spent the next eight years living for varying periods in Switzerland, England, and France, sometimes driven by actual persecution and sometimes by a growing paranoia. Much of his literary effort during this period went into the composition of the posthumously published *Les*

ROUSSEAU'S SOCIAL CONTRACT

Jean-Jacques Rousseau was one of the founders of social contract theory. In the following excerpt from his seminal work The Social Contract, *he explains the basis and terms of the contract entered into by all members of a particular political body. He begins by explaining that people come together to form a collective association once they notice that it is impossible to survive as individuals at the mercy of nature. The collective association is defined by an implicit contract.*

The clauses of this contract are so determined by the nature of the act that the slightest modification would make them vain and ineffective; so that, although they have perhaps never been formally set forth, they are everywhere the same and everywhere tacitly admitted and recognised, until, on the violation of the social compact, each regains his original rights and resumes his natural liberty, while losing the conventional liberty in favour of which he renounced it.

These clauses, properly understood, may be reduced to one—the total alienation of each associate, together with all his rights, to the whole community; for, in the first place, as each gives himself absolutely, the conditions are the same for all; and, this being so, no one has any interest in making them burdensome to others.

Moreover, the alienation being without reserve, the union is as perfect as it can be, and no associate has anything more to demand: for, if the individuals retained certain rights, as there would be no common superior to decide between them and the public, each, being on one point his own judge, would ask to be so on all; the state of nature would thus continue, and the association would necessarily become inoperative or tyrannical.

Finally, each man, in giving himself to all, gives himself to nobody; and as there is no associate over whom he does not acquire the same right as he yields others over himself, he gains an equivalent for everything he loses, and an increase of force for the preservation of what he has.

If then we discard from the social compact what is not of its essence, we shall find that it reduces itself to the following terms:

"Each of us puts his person and all his power in common under the supreme direction of the general will, and, in our corporate capacity, we receive each member as an indivisible part of the whole."

Source: Jean-Jacques Rousseau, *The Social Contract: Or, Principles of Political Right* (New York: Dutton, 1913), book 1, section 6. http://www .constitution.org/jjr/socon.htm.

Confessions de J.-J. Rousseau (1782, 1789; *The Confessions of J.-J. Rousseau*, 1783-1790), among the most intimately detailed and influential of all autobiographies. A remarkable experiment in self-revelation, his confessions helped to establish the vital relationship between childhood experience and the development of the adult psyche. The work also inspired countless self-analytic memoirs emphasizing their various authors' growth toward a unique individuality, despite Rousseau's belief that he would find no imitators.

By 1770, Rousseau was able to return to Paris, where he supported himself largely as a music copyist and wrote two further experiments in self-revelation, the defensive *Les Dialogues: Ou, Rousseau juge de Jean-Jacques* (1780, 1782) and the more serene *Les Reveries du promeneur solitaire* (1782; *The Reveries of the Solitary Walker*, 1967), both published posthumously. On July 2, 1778, Rousseau died at Ermenonville, just outside the French capital. In 1794, his remains were transferred to the Panthéon in Paris in honor of the influence of his ideas on the French Revolution.

SIGNIFICANCE

Jean-Jacques Rousseau is one of those rare individuals whose life and career epitomize the transition from one historical epoch to another. He was a man perpetually at odds with the world around him, a world dominated by ancient privilege and entrenched power. Through the eloquence of his words, he helped to transform that world. Whatever he might have thought of the various revolutions that swept away the old social order, those revolutions would not have occurred so readily without his ideas to justify them. Nor would the constitutions of the new nations that replaced the old have been framed exactly as they were if he had not written on government and popular sovereignty. His hatred of despotism and of a conformity enforced by authoritarian rule shaped a world in which equality and individuality, if not universally to be encountered, were at least more frequently possible than they once had been. Furthermore, his emphasis on allowing the individual to develop according to his or her own nature rather than according to some externally imposed standard had a profound effect on how modern societies educate their children.

—*Robert H. O'Connor*

FURTHER READING

Copleston, Frederick C. "Rousseau." In *Wolff to Kant.* Vol. 6 in *A History of Philosophy.* Westminster, Md.: Newman Press, 1961. A detailed explication of Rousseau's philosophy by a prominent Jesuit scholar. Copleston places Rousseau against the backdrop of the Enlightenment, suggesting both his affinities and his points of disagreement with his philosophical contemporaries.

Crocker, Lester G. *Jean-Jacques Rousseau: The Quest, 1712-1758.* New York: Macmillan, 1968. A thoroughly researched biography which places heavy emphasis on Rousseau's eccentric psychological development. A necessary corrective to the distortions and omissions of the confessions.

_____. *Jean-Jacques Rousseau: The Prophetic Voice, 1758-1778.* New York: Macmillan, 1973. This companion volume to Crocker's earlier study further supplements the confessions, narrating the years of Rousseau's deepest psychological disturbance, as well as covering the thirteen-year period omitted from the autobiography.

Garrard, Graeme. *Rousseau's Counter-Enlightenment: A Republican Critique of the Philosophes.* Albany: State University New York Press, 2003. Garrard maintains Rousseau was a critical post-Enlightenment thinker, who rejected the philosophes' belief in innate reason and human sociability. Rousseau countered these arguments, maintaining that the social order was artificially constructed so individuals would identify with the common good instead of their own selfish interests.

Grimsley, Ronald. "Jean-Jacques Rousseau." In *The Encyclopedia of Philosophy,* edited by Paul Edwards. Vol. 7. New York: Macmillan, 1967. An overview of Rousseau's life and thought, emphasizing the interrelatedness of his educational, political, and religious theories. Grimsley sees Rousseau's belief in the need to free humankind's natural goodness from

corrupting restraint as his central philosophical assumption.

Havens, George R. *Jean-Jacques Rousseau.* Boston: Twayne, 1978. A concise account of Rousseau's life and career, with analyses of the major works. Like the other volumes in Twayne's World Authors series, this book contains the essential facts about its subject without attempting exhaustive detail.

Riley, Patrick, ed. *The Cambridge Companion to Rousseau.* New York: Cambridge University Press, 2001. Collection of essays providing an introduction to Rousseau's life and works, examinations of his political and religious thought, a discussion of his relationship to Voltaire and Pascal, and analyses of *Émile* and other writings.

Rousseau, Jean-Jacques. *The Confessions.* Translated and introduced by J. M. Cohen. Baltimore: Penguin Books, 1953. A standard translation. Despite its distortions and incompleteness, ending as it does with the year 1765, Rousseau's autobiography is indispensable to any understanding of his life and achievement.

_____. *Jean Jacques Rousseau: His Educational Theories Selected from "Émile," "Julie," and Other Writings.* Edited by R. L. Archer with a biographical note by S. E. Frost, Jr. Great Neck, N.Y.: Barron's Educational Series, 1964. A convenient compendium of Rousseau's statements on education. The introductory material gives a summary of Rousseau's educational theory, and the concluding subject index and general index provide ready access to the book's contents.

Scholz, Sally. *On Rousseau.* Belmont, Calif.: Wadsworth/Thomson Learning, 2001. Covers the classroom essentials.

Strathern, Paul. *Rousseau in Ninety Minutes.* Chicago: Ivan R. Dee, 2002. Provides a brief overview of Rousseau's work to introduce readers to his philosophy.

Wolker, Robert. *Rousseau: A Very Short Introduction.* New York: Oxford University Press, 2001. A concise overview.

See also: Denis Diderot; Immanuel Kant; Voltaire.

Related articles in *Great Events from History: The Eighteenth Century, 1701-1800*: October, 1725: Vico Publishes *The New Science*; 1739-1740: Hume Publishes *A Treatise of Human Nature*; 1748: Montesquieu Publishes *The Spirit of the Laws*; 1751-1772: Diderot Publishes the *Encyclopedia*; July 27, 1758: Helvétius Publishes *De l'esprit*; April, 1762: Rousseau Publishes *The Social Contract*; July, 1764: Voltaire Publishes *A Philosophical Dictionary for the Pocket*; 1770: Publication of Holbach's *The System of Nature*; January 10, 1776: Paine Publishes *Common Sense*; 1781: Kant Publishes *Critique of Pure Reason*; 1784-1791: Herder Publishes His Philosophy of History; 1790: Burke Lays the Foundations of Modern Conservatism; February 22, 1791-February 16, 1792: Thomas Paine Publishes *Rights of Man*; 1792: Wollstonecraft Publishes *A Vindication of the Rights of Woman*.

BENJAMIN RUSH
American physician and educator

Although he is more likely to be remembered as a signer of the Declaration of Independence and an enthusiastic supporter of the U.S. Constitution, Rush also was a physician, the first professor of chemistry in North America, the first American to write a book on psychiatry, a tireless worker against slavery, and an advocate for modernized education, temperance, and prison reform.

Born: January 4, 1746; Byberry, Pennsylvania
Died: April 19, 1813; Philadelphia, Pennsylvania
Areas of achievement: Medicine, chemistry, social reform

EARLY LIFE

Benjamin Rush was the fourth child in a family of seven children. His father, John, a farmer and a gunsmith, died when Benjamin was five years old. As a result, his mother, Susanna (Hall) Harvey Rush, had to open a grocery store to support her family.

When Benjamin was eight years old, he entered a school operated by his uncle, the Reverend Mr. Samuel Finley, and it was there that the boy came into contact with the tenets of the Great Awakening, a movement that was stirring the inert religious energies of the colonies. Rush, who remained devoutly religious throughout his life, went to the College of New Jersey (founded the same year he was born, later to become Princeton University) fully expecting to emerge a minister like his uncle. Acting on the advice of others, he began to consider other career possibilities, however, and finally chose medicine.

After receiving his degree in 1760, Rush studied medicine as an apprentice under John Redman in Philadelphia, where he also attended medical lectures at the College of Philadelphia. In 1766, he enrolled in the University of Edinburgh, in Scotland, where many other Americans had studied medicine. He received his medical degree in 1768, having concentrated on the study of chemistry. His dissertation, on the human digestive system, was the product of much experimentation on his own digestive system.

Following graduation, Rush spent some time visiting England and then returned to Philadelphia, where he began his own practice in 1769. In that same year he was appointed professor of chemistry at the College of Philadelphia, which today is the Medical College of the University of Pennsylvania. He was the first professor of chemistry in North America.

LIFE'S WORK

Although the impact of the Great Awakening was always a part of his thinking, Benjamin Rush was also a man of the Enlightenment. Along with his friend Benjamin Franklin and other enlightened Americans, he was humanistic and optimistic, believing that natural philosophy was the key to expanding knowledge.

Unlike Franklin, Thomas Jefferson, John Adams, and others, however, Rush exhibited little in the way of brilliant or original thinking. He wrote the first chemistry text by an American-born individual (*Syllabus of a Course of Lectures on Chemistry*) in the second year of his teaching career, yet it contained no genuinely original work. He taught the importance of hypotheses in medical and scientific inquiry, but, strangely for a man of the Enlightenment (and very unlike Franklin or Jefferson), Rush eschewed experimentation that would test hypotheses. Finally, Rush became more and more convinced that all fevers were the result of arterial tension, and thus the only way to cure a fever was to relieve that tension through bloodletting. In his enthusiasm for the method, Rush was led to insist that in cases of severe fever, as much as four-fifths of a patient's blood should be drained away. He was certainly not the only one to believe this erroneous view—indeed, for a long period bloodletting had been a universally accepted practice. Unhappily, as the most famous physician in the United States, Rush was in a position to influence, rightly or (in this instance) wrongly, countless other physicians of his own generation and of generations to come.

The year 1776 was an important year for Rush. In that year he married Julia Stockton, with whom he would have thirteen children (including James, who would follow in his father's footsteps as a physician and medical educator). Also, he joined the Continental Congress and signed the Declaration of Independence. During the revolution, he served briefly as surgeon general to the Armies of the Middle Department, and he also served on a governmental committee that encouraged the local production of gunpowder. In this latter endeavor, his knowledge of chemistry came in handy, and his instructions for the manufacturing of saltpeter were widely circulated. Rush was also an early and enthusiastic supporter of the Constitution, a member of the convention that framed it, and a member of the Pennsylvania Convention that ratified it.

After the war, Rush resumed his teaching and his medical practice—a practice that originally had been mostly among the poor but now grew to encompass many of the most prominent of Philadelphia's citizenry. In 1787, Rush took charge of the branch of the Pennsylvania Hospital that housed and treated the insane, and in this new position he showed a deep understanding of the problems of the mind—an understanding that resulted in his study *Medical Inquiries and Observations upon the Diseases of the Mind* (1812), the first book on psychiatry written by an American.

In 1789, Rush surrendered his teaching post in chemistry to accept the position of professor of theory and practice of medicine at the College of Philadelphia. There, Rush began to refine his theories on bloodletting, which he put into vigorous practice during Philadelphia's great yellow-fever epidemic of 1793. His example would, unfortunately, be followed by many physicians during yellow-fever epidemics for almost a century.

In 1791, Rush was appointed professor of institutes of medicine and clinical practice, and in 1796 he became professor of the theory and practice of medicine. He was at the height of his career, the most famous physician in the United States, and the inspiration of a whole generation of medical students, whom he served as both teacher and friend. In addition to his teaching and his medical

Benjamin Rush. (Library of Congress)

practice, Rush was also very active in social and humanitarian work, opposing slavery and capital punishment while supporting improvements in education (especially for women), temperance, and prison reform.

In 1797, Rush accepted the position of treasurer at the U.S. Mint, an office he still held at the time of his death on April 19, 1813. He was sixty-seven years of age.

SIGNIFICANCE

As an enlightened American, Benjamin Rush was a man of wide-ranging interests throughout his life. He was an ardent patriot, a signer of the Declaration of Independence, a strong supporter of the Constitution, and influential among his revolutionary contemporaries. In addition, he took part in a movement to give his home state of Pennsylvania a new constitution in 1788.

His support of numerous social causes was always strong, and many of his views on the insane, slavery, and education were in advance of their time. As a teacher, Rush inspired and nurtured many hundreds of students throughout his long teaching career. As a physician, the most famous of his time, Rush unfortunately fell under the sway of theories that were often prejudicial to the health of his patients—theories that have been thoroughly discredited as medical knowledge has expanded.

—*Kenneth F. Kiple*

FURTHER READING

Brodsky, Alyn. *Benjamin Rush: Patriot and Physician*. New York: Truman Talley Books, 2004. A sympathetic biography, describing Rush's medical practice, political career, relationship with Benjamin Franklin and John Adams, and other aspects of his personal life and multifaceted career. Brodsky credits Rush with writing an essay that instigated the Boston Tea Party and with encouraging Thomas Paine to write *Common Sense*.

Goodman, Nathan G. *Benjamin Rush: Physician and Citizen*. Philadelphia: University of Pennsylvania Press, 1934. The first biography of Rush, portraying him in his many and varied roles as professor, practitioner, politician, and crusader for reform. Perhaps its most important contribution, however, is to reveal Rush as a pioneer practitioner in the field of psychiatry.

Hawke, David. *Benjamin Rush: Revolutionary Gadfly*. Indianapolis, Ind.: Bobbs-Merrill, 1971. An excellent biography of Rush, this study takes the story of his life up to 1790, at which time the author claims that Rush became politically inactive. Prior to that date, however, Rush was almost compulsively active in politics as well as social causes, medicine, and a score of other pursuits. The work reveals Rush in all of his frenetic activities and shows the numerous and baffling contradictions and paradoxes in his behavior. The amount of detail supplied is enormous, as Rush's opinions on myriad subjects are carefully presented.

Powell, John H. *Bring Out Your Dead: The Great Plague of Yellow Fever in Philadelphia of 1793*. Philadelphia: University of Pennsylvania Press, 1949. A popular, well-researched account of the 1793 yellow fever epidemic in Philadelphia, which depicts Rush as a courageous and well-meaning worker among the sick. The book is useful, too, for its account of the debate Rush conducted with other physicians of the city over the question of the contagiousness of yellow fever.

Rush, Benjamin. *The Autobiography of Benjamin Rush*. Edited by George W. Corner. Princeton, N.J.: Princeton University Press, 1948. A collection of notebooks kept by Rush throughout his lifetime. The collection clearly reveals his personality and character as well as his views on the times in which he lived. The war between England and the American colonies, the medical practices of American Indians, the character of the French, and Philadelphia's great yellow fever epidemic of 1793 are among the subjects discussed.

_____. *Letters of Benjamin Rush*. Edited by Lyman H. Butterfield. 2 vols. Princeton, N.J.: Princeton University Press, 1951. These volumes contain a wealth of information on Rush as a teacher and practitioner of medicine, as an essayist, as a political activist, and as a tireless worker for the abolition of slavery, the modernization of education, temperance, and prison reform.

Shryock, Richard Harrison. "The Medical Reputation of Benjamin Rush: Contrasted Over Two Centuries." *Bulletin of the History of Medicine* 45 (1971): 507-552. Considers the changing reputation of Rush as a physician. He was eulogized upon his death, but over time, however, physicians and historians came to realize the consequences of the "heroic" methods of bloodletting and purging practiced by Rush.

Weisberger, Bernard A. "The Paradoxical Doctor Benjamin Rush." *American Heritage* 27 (1975): 40-47, 98-99. Presents Rush as a man of enormous contradictions in medicine and politics, who was often quarrelsome in the latter instance and usually wrongheaded in the former.

See also: Benjamin Franklin; Edward Jenner; John Witherspoon.

Related articles in *Great Events from History: The Eighteenth Century, 1701-1800:* April 14, 1775: Pennsylvania Society for the Abolition of Slavery Is Founded; April 12, 1787: Free African Society Is Founded.

MARQUIS DE SADE
French writer

Sade wrote erotic fiction and drama that some readers consider brilliant expressions of personal freedom and others call pornography. His name has become synonymous with cruelty and with pleasure in the suffering of others.

Born: June 2, 1740; Paris, France
Died: December 2, 1814; Charenton, near Paris
Also known as: Donatien-Alphonse-François de Sade (birth name); Comte de Sade
Area of achievement: Literature

EARLY LIFE

Born into an aristocratic family, the marquis de Sade (mahr-kee duh sahd) spent his first four years in the opulent Palace de Condé in Paris, where his mother, Marie-Eléonore, attended Princess de Condé as a lady-in-waiting. His father, Jean-Baptiste-Françoise-Joseph, was away serving as a diplomat to the court of Cologne, in Germany. After the princess died, Sade's mother took over the rearing of the young prince. Marie Eléonore's intentions to make her son the prince's playmate went awry when, at age four, Sade picked a fight with his eight-year-old companion. As a consequence, Sade was sent to Avignon to live with his paternal grandfather. A year later he was dispatched to his uncle's estate near Saumane.

In 1750, Sade returned to Paris, where he attended the noted Jesuit school Louis-le-Grand. Reportedly an undistinguished student, Sade did not live with his mother but shared an apartment with his mentor and tutor. At age fourteen, he enrolled in the academy at Versailles to train for the elite King's Light Cavalry. At the start of the Seven Years' War (1756), he received a commission as a second lieutenant in the King's Foot Guard. Although he served valiantly in battle, he complained in letters to his father that he disliked the military, found it difficult to respect the officers in charge, and lacked friends. The war's end in 1763 brought about Sade's demobilization and his return to Paris.

Sade's early life was marked by upheaval. Prior to the departure from his mother at age four, he undoubtedly resented her attention to the Prince de Condé and felt that he was being overshadowed. Passed from household to household, he confronted a variety of women, including an unpleasant grandmother and his uncle's mistresses. Sade's mother, noted for her melancholy nature, entered a convent after separating from her husband. Long absent, the elder Sade exerted little influence on his son's development into manhood.

LIFE'S WORK

Sade's obsession with sexual pleasure in varied forms shaped his tempestuous life, which was marked by debauchery, arrests, escapes, money problems, and troubled personal relationships. At the same time, he produced an impressive body of literature that remains highly regarded. Considered a libertine and a pornographer by the authorities of his time, he spent years in prison and died in an asylum. Sade's problems did not stem from his sexual excess, for the French aristocracy was generally decadent. What turned Sade into a criminal were his lack of discretion and, even worse, his determination to write about his sexual exploits and fantasies.

After leaving the military, Sade reveled in the delights of Paris—the theater, dances, and the attention of actresses and prostitutes. The elder Sade disapproved of his son's dissolute ways and hurriedly arranged a marriage with Renée-Pélagie de Montreuil, which took place on May 17, 1763, just two days after the couple met for the first time. Because the Sade family faced financial difficulties, the bride's dowry played an important role in the marriage.

Marriage failed to tame Sade's desire for prostitutes, and a few months later, his angry mother-in-law arranged for his arrest through a *lettre de cachet*. This document, signed by the king, countersigned by a minister in the court, and bearing an official *cachet* or seal, could be obtained easily for a fee. The person named in the letter was sentenced to prison or sent into exile indefinitely without a trial. The *lettre de cachet* in one form or another would haunt Sade for many years to come.

Spending less than a year in exile, Sade returned to Paris in 1764. His father died three years later and left immense debts for his son to pay. After a brief period of exile as punishment for whipping a prostitute, Sade found himself in debtors' prison. He was released in 1771 and moved with his wife to the family château at La Costé. There, he staged plays and initiated an affair with his wife's younger sister, Anne-Prospère. A year later Sade's irate mother-in-law produced another *lettre de cachet*, which sent Sade to prison again. He escaped and settled at La Costé with five servant girls and a male secretary. When the servants' relatives complained of sexual misconduct at the château, Sade fled to Italy, then returned to La Costé a year later.

In 1777, Sade received news that his mother was fatally ill. He rushed to the convent in Paris to see her, only to learn that she had already died. The trip turned out to be unfortunate in more ways than one. Sade was immediately arrested under his mother-in-law's earlier *lettre de cachet* and spent the next thirteen years in prison, first in a château, then in the Bastille. Settled in prison, Sade wrote plays, stories, and novels—all with an erotic bent. He also wrote hundreds of letters, many of which have been preserved. During this period he completed the novel considered his masterpiece, *Les 120 journées de Sodome* (wr. 1785, pb. 1904; *The 120 Days of Sodom*, 1954).

When the French Revolution got under way in 1789, many of the prisoners in the Bastille were freed, but Sade was moved to an insane asylum at Charenton. A year later, the national assembly abolished the *lettre de cachet*, and Sade at last was free. Calling himself Citizen Louis Sade, he joined a radical group and wrote political pamphlets. He also saw his sado-sexual play *Oxtiern: Ou, Les Malheurs du libertinage* (pr. 1791; *Oxtiern: Or, The Misfortunes of Libertinage*, 1966) performed in a Paris theater. For the next ten years, Sade was caught up in the country's political chaos and fell in and out of favor. At one point, he barely escaped the guillotine. Facing poverty, he even resorted to working as a prompter in a theater. He continued to write, producing some of his best-known novels, *Les Crimes de l'amour* (wr. 1788, pb. 1800; partial translation as *The Crimes of Love*, 1964), *Justine* (1791; English translation, 1889), and *Juliette* (1798; English translation, 1958-1960).

Sade's freedom ended in 1801, when authorities arrested him at his publisher's office in Paris after controversy had erupted concerning his erotic novels. Although no formal charges were brought, he was sent to prison. After being accused of attempting to molest young prisoners, Sade was transferred to the asylum at Charenton. His estranged wife, daughter, and two sons agreed to pay for his care. Forming a friendship with the asylum's director, Sade persuaded him to test his theory that participating in plays would be therapeutic for patients. The project proved successful until dubious authorities intervened. Often indulged and at other times mistreated during his lengthy tenure in the asylum, he continued to pursue sexual relations and to write until his death at age seventy-four.

SIGNIFICANCE

In some respects, the marquis de Sade emerges as a legendary figure—condemned as a sex addict, labeled a pornographer, identified as the archetype of evil, and considered totally mad. The German neurologist Richard von Krafft-Ebing (1840-1902), in his groundbreaking book, *Psychopathia sexualis* (1886; English translation, 1892), helped to perpetuate the conventional view of Sade by borrowing his name to signify sexual pleasure through the infliction of pain and subjection.

In the nineteenth century, French writer Charles Baudelaire (1821-1867) acknowledged the importance of Sade's writing, which Baudelaire interpreted as an elucidation of the nature of evil. Another century passed, however, before Sade came into his own as a significant literary figure. Not until the 1960's was his work published, except in clandestine editions, even in France. The books have now been translated into numerous languages and are generally available. French writers and critics Albert Camus (1913-1960), Simone de Beauvoir (1908-1986), and Roland Barthes (1915-1980) defended Sade's long-suppressed work and championed it as a precursor to modernism. Although this assessment of the marquis and his writing is widely accepted, the controversy Sade generated during his life has not altogether disappeared. The questions remain: Is he a pervert or a prophet? Is he a charlatan or a genius? Is he a pornographer or a writer who brilliantly captures the erotic imagination? Is he a lunatic or a man far ahead of his time?

—*Robert Ross*

FURTHER READING

Bloch, Iwan. *Marquis de Sade*. Amsterdam: Fredonia Books, 2002. Reprint of the 1931 detailed and seminal study that initiated the resuscitation of Sade's reputation and stressed his contemporary significance. Written by a distinguished German physician who specialized in sexology.

Bongie, Laurence L. *Sade: A Biographical Essay*. Chicago: University of Chicago Press, 1998. Considers Sade an obnoxious, opportunistic, egotistical, self-absorbed, hollow man whose writing does not deserve recognition.

Crowley, Graham, Richard Appignanesi, and Stuart Hood. *Introducing Marquis de Sade*. London: Totem Books, 1999. Places Sade's work in the mainstream of contemporary thinking and discusses its influence on subsequent writers.

Gray, Francine du Plessix. *At Home with the Marquis de Sade: A Life*. New York: Simon & Schuster, 1999. Focuses on Sade's relationship with his wife and mother-in-law.

Laws, Robert Antony. *The Marquis de Sade: Madman or Martyr?* London: Pauper's Press, 2002. Examines and questions the contradictory views that dominate past and current attitudes toward Sade.

Sawhney, Deepak Marang, ed. *Must We Burn Sade?* Amherst, N.Y.: Humanity Books, 1999. Collection of essays that examine the literary, political, philosophical, theatrical, and social aspects of Sade's writing.

Schaeffer, Neil. *The Marquis de Sade: A Life.* New York: Alfred A. Knopf, 1999. Depicts the unsadistic side of Sade by focusing on his charm and ability to love. Argues that Sade is one of the great writers of the eighteenth century.

See also: Pierre-Augustin Caron de Beaumarchais; Casanova; Alain-René Lesage; Jean-Paul Marat; Jean-Jacques Rousseau; Madame de Staël; Voltaire.

Related articles in *Great Events from History: The Eighteenth Century, 1701-1800*: January, 1756-February 15, 1763: Seven Years' War; 1782-1798: Publication of Rousseau's *Confessions*.

LOUIS DE SAINT-JUST
French revolutionary leader

An acute political theorist and insightful orator, Saint-Just dominated the executive councils of the national convention at a time when internal anarchy and military invasions threatened social order in France.

Born: August 25, 1767; Decize, France
Died: July 28, 1794; Paris, France
Also known as: Louis Antoine Léon de Saint-Just (full name)
Areas of achievement: Government and politics, social reform, military

EARLY LIFE

Louis de Saint-Just (lwee duh sa-zhewst) was born in Decize, a town along the Loire River, but he grew up in southern Picardy, the native province of his father, a retired military officer who had purchased property at Blérancourt. The mother of Saint-Just, Jeanne-Marie Robinot, was the daughter of an established notary. She advocated egalitarian principles; after her son completed his education at the Collège of Saint-Nicolas under the direction of the Oratorian Fathers, she used her influence to obtain a position for him as a clerk in the office of the public prosecutor of Soissons. As a student, Saint-Just was self-indulgent and often impudent. At the age of nineteen, he ran away with some of the family silver, which he sold in Paris. He was arrested and placed in a reformatory for six months; after this episode, he entered the University of Reims, where he studied law, receiving a degree in 1788.

Saint-Just began to frequent the political clubs of Soissons; soon he gained a reputation as an enthusiastic orator, and he was elected lieutenant colonel of the national guard in Blérancourt. In July of 1790, he led the federates from Blérancourt to Paris for "La Fête de la Fédération." When he returned home, he learned that some of his constituents were planning to seize the open markets of Blérancourt; he then wrote an impassioned letter to Robespierre, a lawyer and deputy to the legislative assembly from Arras, in which he encouraged economic equality as a step toward improving the living conditions of the working class. This letter, which greatly impressed Robespierre, marks the beginning of a political relationship that transformed the destiny of France. Both men were obstinately serious, ambitious, and austere, but Saint-Just—with Machiavellian hauteur and tireless energy—was more impetuous and self-righteous.

LIFE'S WORK

In 1791, Saint-Just hoped to run for election as deputy to the national assembly. His rivals, however, succeeded in removing his name from the list of candidates. In preparation for this campaign, Saint-Just had written *Esprit de la révolution et de la constitution de France* (1791; spirit of the revolution). This work is composed primarily of provocative epigrams that follow the ideas of Jean-Jacques Rousseau. To better serve the poor and the peasants, Saint-Just recommended that the French Revolution move beyond benevolent and patriotic activity toward the construction of a new society. According to Saint-Just, the French were not yet free because sovereignty of the people was not possible until everyone was just and rational. In his visionary ardor, he misrepresented Rousseau's intentions and blurred the contours of his philosophy. As the political career of Saint-Just advanced, it became increasingly difficult for him to distinguish between prescriptive theories and irrevocable laws.

On September 22, 1792, France declared itself a republic. The fall of Louis XVI provoked the invasion of the country by the Prussian and Austrian armies. The national assembly called for new elections of deputies from the newly formed *départments*, and Saint-Just was chosen to represent Aisne. By January of 1793, the king had been indicted; the Girondins, or moderates of the national assembly, expressed the view that he should be given a trial, whereas the Jacobins, or extremists, demanded an immediate execution. In this debate, Saint-Just emerged as the most forceful and challenging prosecutor against the king. His cold, implacable logic was an indicator of the rigor he expected from others.

Saint-Just argued against the inviolability of the king according to the ideas of Rousseau's *Du contrat social: Ou, Principes du droit politique* (1762; *A Treatise on the Social Contract: Or, The Principles of Political Law,* 1764). He postulated that a king is a usurper who has stolen the absolute sovereignty that belongs only to the people. Law is an expression of the people's common will. Therefore, the king, as a criminal guilty of tyranny, is an outsider and not a citizen. For this reason, he has no access to the law. Saint-Just concluded that the king must die in order to safeguard the republic. In demanding the death of Louis XVI, Saint-Just relied on the rhetoric of revolution as apocalypse; despite the utopian zeal of his formulations, he was promoting a new order of absolutism, with its own assortment of ingenious and exalted crimes.

After the execution of Louis XVI, Saint-Just rose to prominence as an advocate of national patriotism in the service of a strong, centralized government. He proposed a constitution that would subordinate military affairs to civil power, and he opposed the creation of municipalities favored by the Girondins. In May of 1793, he was asked to join the Committee of Public Safety in order to prepare new constitutional laws. Within two months, he became a definitive member of this heterogeneous and powerful Group of Twelve.

Because of a drastic drop in the volume of foreign trade, the needs of war, inflation, and exploitation by profiteers, the Committee of Public Safety, under Robespierre's direction, began to push for exclusive regulatory privileges. The committee persuaded the national assembly, by means of Saint-Just's compelling arguments, that the provisional government of France

remain revolutionary until peace with France's enemies was unilaterally acclaimed. This proclamation of October 10, 1793, superseded the constitution of June and announced the creation of exceptional measures to force merchants to adhere to the Law of the Maximum, an economic expedient approved by the convention in September of 1793. The result was an intensification of fear. In order to prepare the way for unprecedented coercion, the Revolutionary Tribunal carried out a spectacular series of trials that virtually eliminated the Girondins; at this time, Marie-Antoinette was condemned and executed.

In November of 1793, Saint-Just embarked on a series of military enterprises that led to the high point of his career. He was sent to Alsace as supervisor of the Army of the Rhine, which had suffered numerous setbacks, leaving the officers and soldiers demoralized and inefficient. Saint-Just and his friend and colleague Philippe Le Bas ignored the other nine representatives from the convention already active in Alsace and proceeded to intimidate local authorities in Strasbourg in order to obtain supplies and to check the advances of aristocratic agitators. Saint-Just insisted on unswerving discipline among the troops and galvanized them with imperious commands. In December, the armies of the Rhine and Moselle were united, and Saint-Just led a victorious assault against the Austrian forces, lifting the siege of Landau. The following month, in much the same manner, he reorganized the Army of the North on the Belgian front.

When Saint-Just returned to Paris, he initiated a series of purges, with Robespierre's compliance, designed to eliminate traitors among the ultra-Montagnards, an anarchist group responsible for the "dechristianization" of France. Saint-Just emerged as a ruthless enemy of those who either provoked agitation or favored moderation. He was responsible for the execution of Georges Danton and Camille Desmoulins, heroes of the earlier phase of the revolution. Saint-Just insisted that the elimination of Danton and his followers would pave the way for a pure republic composed of single-minded patriots.

With Danton's death, the revolution entered the period known as the Reign of Terror. In June of 1794, Robespierre drafted the Law of Twenty-Two Prairial, which defined in conveniently vague terms the enemies of the people and denied them right to counsel. Saint-Just disapproved of this measure because the sansculottes, or proletariat, were deprived of power; he declared: "The revolution is frozen, every principle has been attenuated."

Saint-Just returned to the Army of the North and was instrumental in forcing the Prussians to surrender their garrison at Charleroi. That led to the confrontation between the French and the Austrians near the village of Fleurus in Belgium. Despite heavy losses, the French were victorious; refusing accolades, Saint-Just left immediately for Paris. He had been informed by Robespierre that the Committee of Public Safety was hopelessly divided.

In such matters, Saint-Just generally favored reconciliation. Robespierre made a speech before the convention, however, condemning his opponents as a league of conspirators. Out of loyalty to Robespierre, Saint-Just prepared a report that would incriminate Robespierre's rivals on the committee. At the same time, moderates, known as "Thermidorians," who were uncomfortable with Robespierre's attempt at hegemony, united to overthrow him. On July 27, Saint-Just, Robespierre, and about twenty of their supporters were denounced as tyrants and proscribed; they were executed the following day.

SIGNIFICANCE

In March of 1794, Louis de Saint-Just was chosen president of the convention for a fortnight. At this time, he composed notes and observations published posthumously as *Fragments sur les institutions républicaines* (1800; fragments on republican institutions), a work that laid the foundation for a communal society. The "immortal, impassive Republic of Virtue," energized by permanent revolution and sheltered from human temerity, would provide education for all. Saint-Just classified and sharpened Robespierre's theories. In a democratic republic, civic virtue made legalistic bureaucracies obsolete; institutions were the social means for producing responsible republicans. Censorship was condoned as an administrative control over unreliable elements.

At the height of his power, Saint-Just proposed the Laws of Ventôse, by which the convention voted in favor of confiscating the property of counterrevolutionaries in order to assign it to "indigent patriots" (these laws were never put into effect). In addition, the Cadet School of Mars, which emulated Spartan standards, was inaugurated to educate three thousand youths as disciplined patriots who would increase the collective efficiency of the state. As a follower of Rousseau, Saint-Just was consistent in activating Enlightenment ideals, but in order to purify the republic and to execute the Laws of Ventôse, he created a General Police Bureau, whose existence inverted democratic liberties.

The personality of Saint-Just offers a wide range of contradictions. The swiftness with which he consigned authority to himself is impressive, but his collusion with Robespierre added to the apprehension created by his virulent, doctrinaire speeches. Known as the "Panther" or "Angel of Death," Saint-Just often revealed chinks in his armor. In Strasbourg, while addressing a Jacobin Club, he broke down in tears when referring to the vandalism of churches and desecration of the Blessed Sacrament. His impeccable habits and stoical demeanor suggest a puritan strain that was not pursued in private. His Blérancourt mistress visited him regularly in Paris, and his fiancée, the sister of Le Bas, accompanied him on one of his missions to Strasbourg. He once stated that a man who struck a woman should receive the death penalty. He was given to peremptory and sententious speech but displayed a genuine solicitude for soldiers in the lower ranks and for the poor and needy. He was not autocratic; he accepted the sovereign will of the people implicitly. For this reason, when he was indicted, he did not appeal to the sansculottes to challenge the convention.

The rhetoric of Saint-Just anticipates twentieth century forms of totalitarianism; however, his confidence in democratic institutions was pristine. As commissioner of the armies, Saint-Just successfully mobilized the resources of France in order to defend the revolutionary government against an allied front directed by the monarchs of Europe. Military victories were preliminary steps toward the complete regeneration of society. Saint-Just sought to create a nation made up of communities with a common interest that would safeguard the principles of the French Revolution.

—*Robert J. Frail*

FURTHER READING

Béraud, Henri. *Twelve Portraits of the French Revolution*. Translated by Madeleine Boyd. Boston: Little, Brown, 1928. The thirty-page chapter on Saint-Just contains information excluded from subsequent biographies. The presentation of Saint-Just is occasionally melodramatic and there are some factual inconsistencies, but the overall portrait is illuminating.

Bouloiseau, Marc. *The Jacobin Republic, 1792-1794*. Translated by Jonathan Mandelbaum. New York: Cambridge University Press, 1984. The second of a three-volume series designed to provide a synthesis of twentieth century attitudes toward the French Revolution. Bouloiseau studies the economic and social history of the Jacobin organizations to the detriment of political developments. The contribution of women's societies is also explored.

Bruun, Geoffrey. *Saint-Just: Apostle of Terror*. Reprint. Hamden, Conn.: Shoe String Press, 1966. This short but perceptive study appraises the contributions of Saint-Just to policies enacted by the Committee of Public Safety. Bruun analyzes the images of Saint-Just as a fanatic, a designation given him by French Royalist émigrés throughout Europe.

Curtis, Eugene. *Saint-Just: Colleague of Robespierre*. Reprint. New York: Octagon Books, 1973. This exhaustive study uses original documents and manuscripts, including Saint-Just's correspondence, to examine the missions to Alsace, dominated by Saint-Just, to counteract Royalist insurgents. An objective and far-reaching study of the reasons behind the Reign of Terror.

Fisher, John. *Six Summers in Paris, 1789-1794*. New York: Harper & Row, 1966. Richly detailed and wide in scope and investigation, this work chronicles the factionalism that developed among the splinter groups that sustained the momentum of the revolution. Brilliantly conceived but unnecessarily cynical.

Gough, Hugh. *The Terror in the French Revolution*. New York: St. Martin's Press, 1998. A concise overview describing the evolution and consequences of the Terror. Describes Saint-Just's military work in Alsace, his role on the Committee of Public Safety, his proposed Laws of Ventôse, and his execution.

Hampson, Norman. *Saint-Just*. Cambridge, Mass.: Blackwell, 1991. Comprehensive biography written by a noted historian who specialized in the French Revolution and wrote biographies of Danton and Robespierre.

Lefebvre, Georges. *The French Revolution from 1793 to 1799*. Translated by John Hall Stewart and James Friguglietti. London: Routledge & Kegan Paul, 1964. The second part of Lefebvre's comprehensive history, originally published in 1951. An informative, valuable study that clearly outlines Saint-Just's efforts to offset the economic crisis and to mold a national platform of systematic reconstruction.

Loomis, Stanley. *Paris in the Terror: June, 1793-July, 1794*. New York: J. B. Lippincott, 1964. A colorful account of the domestic and foreign intrigue that created a climate of suspicion and panic during the Great Terror. The biographical sketches of Saint-Just place him above and beyond the fray of partisan politics.

Palmer, R. R. *Twelve Who Ruled: The Year of Terror in the French Revolution*. Rev. ed. Princeton, N.J.: Princeton University Press, 1969. A revised edition of the 1941 text by a distinguished translator and authority on France during the revolution. Although occasionally impressionistic, this is a vivid study of the conflicts within the Committee of Public Safety.

See also: Georges Danton; Louis XV; Louis XVI; Jean-Paul Marat; Marie-Antoinette; Robespierre; Jean-Jacques Rousseau.

Related articles in *Great Events from History: The Eighteenth Century, 1701-1800*: May 5, 1789: Louis XVI Calls the Estates-General; June 20, 1789: Oath of the Tennis Court; July 14, 1789: Fall of the Bastille; October, 1789-April 25, 1792: France Adopts the Guillotine; April 20, 1792-October, 1797: Early Wars of the French Revolution; September 20, 1792: Battle of Valmy; January 21, 1793: Execution of Louis XVI; March 4-December 23, 1793: War in the Vendée; July 27-28, 1794: Fall of Robespierre; November 9-10, 1799: Napoleon Rises to Power in France.

Comte de Saxe
German-born French general

An innovative general adept at both attack and siege operations, the comte de Saxe is considered one of the greatest generals of the eighteenth century. He won impressive victories in the War of the Austrian Succession, but he was the only French general to do so, and France did not benefit from the war, despite his accomplishments.

Born: October 28, 1696; Goslar, Saxony (now in Germany)
Died: November 30, 1750; Chambord, France
Also known as: Graf von Sachsen; Hermann Moritz (birth name); Herman-Maurice; Maurice of Saxony; Maurice de Saxe; Maurice
Areas of achievement: Warfare and conquest, military

Early Life

Maurice, the comte de Saxe (kohnt duh sahks), began life inauspiciously. He was one of the more than three hundred illegitimate children recognized by Augustus II, also known as Augustus the Strong, the elector of Saxony (r. 1694-1733) and later king of Poland (r. 1697-1704, 1709-1733). His mother was the Countess Maria Aurora von Königsmark, a strong, intelligent, and well-connected woman in the courts of Europe (Voltaire called her "the most famous woman of two centuries"). The countess maneuvered her son out of the mass of Augustus II's offspring into a more prominent position, where he could make his own way in European society, mainly by preparing her son for a military career. As a young man, Saxe studied the art of war as an aide-de-camp to Prince Eugene of Savoy. Later, Saxe purchased the command of a German regiment serving in the French army.

At the age of thirty, Saxe stepped out of his mother's shadow by asserting his claim to the duchy of Courland, in modern-day Latvia. Rivals backed by the Russians and Poles forced Saxe to cede his claim in 1727, however, and Saxe instead became a professional soldier. He served as a staff officer under the duke of Berwick, the son of England's James II, then employed as a general in the service of France during the War of Polish Succession (1733-1735). That war ended with Saxe's legitimate half brother, Augustus III, retaining the throne of Poland. Saxe distinguished himself at the Battles of Philippsburg and Ettingen, earning him the rank of lieutenant general. When the war ended, Saxe remained in the French army, a foreigner in a foreign army, just like his mentor the duke of Berwick.

Life's Work

Peace in Europe did not last long. In 1740, Charles VI of Austria died, leaving his daughter Maria Theresa as empress and marking the start of the War of the Austrian Succession (1740-1748). Seeking to exploit the change in leadership, Frederick the Great of Prussia seized the province of Silesia, in modern-day Poland. Seeking their own advantages, Spain, France, Bavaria, and Saxony sided with the Prussians. Only England sided with Austria. Louis XV of France granted Saxe a field command and sent him to cooperate with France's Bavarian ally.

In 1741, Saxe marched his joint French-Bavarian force into Bohemia, where he captured the Austrian stronghold at Prague. His offensive, however, soon came to an ignominious end. Defeated in Silesia and Bohemia, Maria Theresa ceded Silesia to the Prussians and signed a peace treaty with Frederick the Great. Free to deal with the overstretched French, the Austrians retook Prague, routed the combined French and Bavarian army, and swept into Bavaria itself. Saxe halted the Austrian offensive and reestablished equilibrium along the French border. This success earned Saxe a promotion to marshal.

Louis XV sent Saxe to northeastern France, where the war was not going well. Prussia was no longer in the war. Bavaria could offer little help. Austria had negotiated an alliance with Sardinia that kept Spain from supporting its ally. Even worse, Saxony had switched its allegiance to the Austrians. France had to deal with Austria and England by itself. An English army, led by George II, king of England and elector of Hanover, had landed on the coast of Europe to participate in the war. British armies had pushed the French across the Rhine, threatening France itself. Saxe's job was to halt the British and Austrian offensive by threatening the Netherlands, an Austrian possession.

In early 1745, Saxe moved a fifty-thousand-man army toward the Dutch city of Tournai. Austria had placed the defense of the Netherlands in the hands of its allies. Prussia had reentered the war in 1744, and Austria was once again dealing with Prussian armies on its northern frontier. Facing Saxe in the Austrian Netherlands was a combined English, Dutch, and Hanoverian army under the command of William, duke of Cumberland.

William II had returned to England to deal with an uprising in Scotland led by the Stuart claimant to the En-

Comte de Saxe. (Library of Congress)

glish throne. Saxe prepared to meet the English at the village of Fontenoy, southeast of Tournai, in May, 1745. Saxe prepared for the English army, equal in number to his, by constructing a fortified line featuring four reinforced redoubts, with its flanks anchored by the Schelde River and the Gavrain Forest. The position forced Cumberland to make frontal assaults into a crossfire generated from the reinforced redoubts. After several futile assaults, Cumberland assembled fourteen thousand men into a wedge formation that stormed into the center of the French line and began to press the French center. Saxe then committed his Irish Brigade, who, with their own particular hatred of Britain, fought ferociously and managed to halt the British advance. With half of his attacking troops dead, Cumberland broke off his assault. Tournai fell to the French, followed by Brussels soon afterward.

Events elsewhere further aided Saxe in his northern campaign. The Stuart uprising in Scotland evolved into a full-scale revolt, and the duke of Cumberland withdrew his army to deal with the Scottish clans, eventually defeating them at the Battle of Culloden in 1746. The Austrians hurried an army under the command of Prince Charles of Lorraine to the Netherlands to replace the En-

glish. Seeking to take advantage of the confusion, Saxe pressed his army northward, toward the city of Rocourt to strike the Austrians before they could establish themselves. On October 11, 1746, in the open fields north of Rocourt, Saxe easily outmaneuvered the inexperienced Prince Charles and sent the Austrians reeling off the battlefield with a loss of more than five thousand men.

The situation in the Netherlands changed again in the spring of 1747. Having suppressed the Scottish, the duke of Cumberland returned to the Netherlands with a new English army with the intent of halting Saxe's advance. Cumberland's plan was to erode Saxe's strength rather than engage the wily general in open battle. With this in mind, Cumberland marched his combined British and Dutch army against a portion of Saxe's army holding the Dutch city of Lauffeld, in modern-day Belgium. Cumberland surrounded and besieged the French force at Lauffeld, believing his plan had worked. Saxe, however, hastily organized his army, marched his men fifty miles in two days, and struck Cumberland from the rear. The British army collapsed, leaving six thousand dead on the battlefield.

The next target was the fortified city of Maastricht, the last Dutch stronghold between the French and the Dutch heartland. In another masterfully orchestrated siege, Saxe outmaneuvered and wore down the battered allied forces, taking the city on May 7, 1748. Maastricht turned out to be Saxe's final battle. After eight years of war, all of Europe was exhausted, and the combatants agreed to a peace in October, 1748. France emerged from the war with little to show for its efforts, as Saxe's victories in the north could not offset French losses elsewhere, such as Italy and North America.

Although a hero when the war ended, bearing the rank of marshal general, Saxe soon became the target of palace jealousies and intrigues, and he retired from the army in disgust. His memoirs, *Mes rêveries* (1757), published posthumously, contained many simple yet complex statements on the nature of warfare, perhaps the most famous being "It is not big armies that win battles, it is the good ones." Maurice, comte de Saxe, died in Chambord, France, on November 30, 1750.

SIGNIFICANCE

While some critics believe that Saxe achieved fame only because he was the sole successful French general in the War of the Austrian Secession, most military historians consider Saxe a brilliant strategist, capable of undertaking all aspects of military operations. He successfully conducted storm assaults, prolonged sieges, and defensive struggles, often while outnumbered by his adversaries. His memoirs, which became standard reading for ambitious military officers throughout Europe, influenced the way Europeans fought wars for decades thereafter.

—*Steven J. Ramold*

FURTHER READING
Bois, Jean-Pierre. *Maurice de Saxe*. Paris: Fayard, 1992. Fully researched and well documented; the best biography of Saxe available.
Hulot, Frédéric. *Le Marechal de Saxe*. Paris: Pygmalion, 1989. A very good biography of Saxe, available only in French.
Liddell-Hart, Basil H. *Great Captains Unveiled*. New York: Da Capo, 1996. An interesting volume that compares great military leaders of different eras. Saxe is compared, for example, to the British general James Wolfe, the Swedish military genius Gustavus Adolphus, and Genghis Khan, leader of the Mongol horde.
Trowbridge, W. R. H. *A Beau Sabreur, Maurice de Saxe, Marshal of France: His Loves, His Laurels, and His Times, 1696-1750*. New York: Brentano, 1910. A flowery account of Saxe's life, concentrating on his scandalous relationship with Adrianne Lecouvreur, the noted French actress.
White, Jon E. *Marshal of France: The Life and Times of Maurice, Comte de Saxe, 1696-1750*. Chicago: Rand McNally, 1962. A lengthy academic account of Saxe's life and campaigns.

See also: Charles VI; Eugene of Savoy; Frederick the Great; George II; Louis XV; Maria Theresa; Voltaire.
Related articles in *Great Events from History: The Eighteenth Century, 1701-1800*: October 10, 1733-October 3, 1735: War of the Polish Succession; 1736-1739: Russo-Austrian War Against the Ottoman Empire; December 16, 1740-November 7, 1748: War of the Austrian Succession; August 19, 1745-September 20, 1746: Jacobite Rebellion.

ALESSANDRO SCARLATTI
Italian composer

Scarlatti was the outstanding Italian composer of operas and cantatas active in the late seventeenth and early eighteenth centuries. His work brought fame to Naples as a center for operatic composition and performance and provided the foundation for the Neapolitan school of composers.

Born: May 2, 1660; Palermo, Kingdom of the Two Sicilies (now in Italy)
Died: October 22, 1725; Naples (now in Italy)
Also known as: Pietro Alessandro Gaspare Scarlatti (full name)
Area of achievement: Music

EARLY LIFE

Alessandro Scarlatti (ah-lays-SAHN-droh skahr-LAHT-tee) was the second of eight children of Pietro Scarlata (or Sgarlata) and his wife, Eleanora d'Amato, and the eldest to survive infancy. Nothing is known of his childhood, although he may have studied music with the chapel master of Palermo Cathedral, Don Vincenzo Amato, a presumed relative of his mother. In June, 1672, at the age of twelve, he was sent to Rome with his two young sisters, Anna Maria and Melchiorra Brigida, presumably to live with relatives. Again, nothing is known of his education at Rome, although he may well have attended a choir school connected with one of the large churches or seminaries. Presumably he would have performed and heard the music of the older composers active or recently active in Rome, including Giacomo Carissimi (with whom he is traditionally held to have studied), Antonio Cesti, Alessandro Stradella, and Bernardo Pasquini.

Scarlatti seems to have acquired patrons among the Roman nobility at an early age, and by 1677 was composing a short opera, as yet unidentified, for an evening gathering in a private home. By this time, he must have been earning a living, for he was married on April 12, 1678, to Antonia Anzalone, a native of Rome whose family may also have come from Sicily. Scarlatti was then just short of his eighteenth birthday and prepared to launch his career as a composer. A portrait of Scarlatti painted by Lorenzo Vaccaro and probably dating from the 1680's shows a young man very much of the seventeenth century, dressed in court finery, with a serious mien, an elongated face, a prominent nose, and penetrating eyes. When he was painted again by an unknown artist near the end of his life, in sober attire and wearing a cross, his face had rounded and his features softened, but the penetrating eyes remained. He seems to have been essentially a serious man, concerned equally with his own music and with the welfare of the large Scarlatti clan of which he had become head after the death of his father.

LIFE'S WORK

The year 1679 marked the beginning of Scarlatti's public career as a composer, although he had undoubtedly composed a number of cantatas and other smaller works as a student. Early in the year, the Arciconfraternita del San Crocifisso commissioned him to compose an oratorio, which was probably the one performed for them on February 24, 1679, but remains otherwise unidentified. His earliest known opera is the *commedia in musica* entitled *Gli equivoci nel sembiante* (1679; *Equivocal Appearances: Or, Love Will Not Suffer Deceptions*, 1975), which privately premiered in early 1679 because of the severe restrictions imposed upon public performances by the reform-minded Pope Innocent XI. The opera, which requires a cast of only four and limited staging, was an immediate success and was performed a number of times at Rome in 1679 and subsequently at Bologna, Naples, Monte Filottrano, Vienna, Ravenna, and Palermo.

Perhaps more important to Scarlatti, his first opera earned for him the patronage of Queen Christina of Sweden, living in Rome after her abdication from the Swedish throne and acting as one of the city's major patrons of the arts. Scarlatti immediately became her chapel master and dedicated to her his next opera, *L'honestà negli amori* (1680). He also acquired other influential Roman patrons, foremost among them being Cardinals Benedetto Pamphili and Pietro Ottoboni, with whom he maintained contact even during his two separate stays at Naples from 1683 to 1702 and from 1709 to 1718. Between 1680 and 1683, Scarlatti wrote at least three more operas, six oratorios, and a number of cantatas for performance in Rome. He may also have been employed at one or more churches, including San Gerolamo della Carità. By 1681, the Scarlatti household consisted of the composer, his wife, two infant children, his sister-in-law, a nurse, and his younger brother Giuseppe.

Scarlatti was a successful young composer in the Rome of the early 1680's, but he had already irritated papal authorities by participating in the annual attempts to bypass the pope's regulations concerning operatic performances. It must have seemed both a political move and a good opportunity when in 1683 the marquis del Carpio, formerly Spanish ambassador to the Vatican and newly installed Spanish viceroy of Naples, invited

Scarlatti to become his chapel master. Since Naples was then the most populous city in Italy and Sicily was also under Spanish control, Scarlatti may have believed that the new position would provide better opportunities both for himself as an opera composer and for the entire Scarlatti family, and he promptly accepted the offer.

In the event, Scarlatti's tenure in Naples was marked by further controversy. Nevertheless, he remained in charge of the viceroy's chapel until 1702 and during that time was the dominant composer in the city. As at Rome, Scarlatti made his principal impact at Naples as a composer of operas. Over a twenty-year period, he composed more than half of the new operas performed at Naples and adapted and supplemented the majority of the operas by a variety of composers that were imported from Venice and elsewhere. For Naples he composed the first of his serenatas—large-scale works for soloists, instruments, and occasionally chorus generally written to celebrate specific occasions—and continued his output of cantatas, at least sixty-five of which date from these years. He was also responsible for the composition and performance of music for the Viceregal Chapel.

Opera at Naples was under the direct patronage of the viceroy, and new works were generally premiered in the theater at the Viceregal Palace before being transferred to the public theater of San Bartolomeo. Scarlatti may have had a hand in the composition and performance of as many as eighty of these, the most successful of which were *Il Pirro e Demetrio* (1694) and *La caduta de' Decemviri* (1697). These works and others carried Scarlatti's fame as a composer and Naples's renown as a center of operatic activity throughout Italy and as far abroad as Germany and England. As with the Roman operas, the subject matter was generally based very loosely on historical figures and events, history being freely altered to provide suitable opportunities for dramatic encounters between characters (generally conveyed in the form of recitative) and reactions by one and occasionally two of the characters to these encounters (generally conveyed in the form of arias or duets).

By the end of the 1690's, Scarlatti apparently felt overworked by the viceroy and underappreciated by the Neapolitan public. He was certainly worried about his financial situation, because his salary was being paid irregularly and the onset of the War of the Spanish Succession in 1701 promised hard times and possibly extensive warfare for the city of Naples. In addition, he was concerned with the future of his son Domenico, the sixth of his ten children and an exceptionally talented keyboard player and composer. In June, 1702, father and son left

Composer Alessandro Scarlatti. (Hulton Archive/Getty Images)

Naples for an approved absence of four months, which stretched to six years for Scarlatti.

Scarlatti and his son went first to Florence in the hope of obtaining an appointment in the service of Prince Ferdinand de' Medici, a great patron of music. No appointment was forthcoming, and father and son returned to Naples before Scarlatti moved to Rome. Over the next six years, Scarlatti sent Ferdinand oratorios, church music, and at least four new operas, the latter completely lost, apparently hoping that the Florentine prince would be interested in more serious fare than was acceptable at Naples. Meanwhile, at the end of 1703 Scarlatti became assistant chapel master of the Church of Santa Maria Maggiore in Rome and probably entered the service of his earlier patron Cardinal Ottoboni, already a patron of Arcangelo Corelli and soon to be the same for George Frideric Handel.

The years 1704-1707 were not banner ones for Scarlatti. The Roman public theaters had been closed since 1700, so operas were seldom performed. Aside from the lost operas sent to Florence, he wrote only two five-act *tragedie per musica* for performance at Venice in 1707. Of these, *Il Mitridate Eupatore* (1707), based on

the Orestes legend, is generally considered one of his greatest works. Instead of operas, Scarlatti produced during this period a stream of cantatas, serenatas, and oratorios written for old and new Roman patrons. He was elected to the Arcadian Academy in 1706 together with Pasquini and Corelli. In 1707, he was promoted to chapel master of Santa Maria Maggiore, but his financial worries continued and Domenico's career was apparently not flourishing at Venice. Naples, which did not suffer extensively during the War of the Spanish Succession, was ceded to the Austrians in 1707, and in 1709, Scarlatti accepted an invitation from Cardinal Grimani, the first Austrian viceroy, to return as viceregal chapel master.

For the next decade, Scarlatti remained at Naples while retaining his Roman contacts. He wrote at least eleven operas for the viceroy, the most famous being *Il Tigrane* (1715) and one of the most interesting being *Il trionfo dell' onore* (1718), his only late opera to be designated *commedia in musica.* He also began to compose purely instrumental music, most notably his twelve *Sinfonie di concerto grosso,* begun in 1715.

Scarlatti had attained the status of a famous and revered composer, even receiving a patent of nobility from Pope Clement XI in 1716 that allowed him to employ the title "Cavaliere." His music, however, was rapidly falling from favor, and his essentially serious operas could not compete with the simpler, livelier style of the younger composers such as Domenico Sarri, Francesco Mancini, or Leonardo Vinci. Even his most famous operas were seldom revived.

In 1718, Scarlatti once more obtained leave from Naples and returned to Rome. He may have anticipated supervising the career of his son Domenico, then serving as chapel master of the Cappella Giulia at St. Peter's Basilica, but the younger Scarlatti had apparently had enough of his father's interference and succeeded in securing an order of legal independence in early 1717. In August, 1719, Domenico gave up his appointments in Rome and left, arriving by September, 1720, in Lisbon. He spent the rest of his life in Portugal and Spain, returning to Italy only three times and visiting his aging father only on the second of those visits in 1725.

Alessandro was in Rome by Carnival, 1718, to direct his new opera *Telemaco.* He also produced the operas *Macro Attilio Regolo* (1719), *La Griselda* (1721), and two more whose music did not survive. He composed an oratorio, several cantatas, and some large-scale sacred works, including his *Mass for S Cecilia* (1708) and several related vespers psalms and motets written in 1720. Several of these later works employ larger orchestras and display more interesting use of instrumentation than his earlier compositions. Even in those scored for soloists with string orchestra alone, the vocal line is independent from that of the first violins, producing a thicker and more complicated texture.

Scarlatti returned to Naples in 1722, where he spent his last years writing some music, entertaining guests, including the younger composers Johann Adolph Hasse and Johann Joachim Quantz, and gradually passing from public memory. He died on October 22, 1725, and is buried in the Santa Cecilia Chapel at the Church of Santa Maria di Montesanto.

SIGNIFICANCE

By his own count, Alessandro Scarlatti composed 114 operas between 1679 and 1721, but this may include his additions to operas by others. He also composed more than six hundred cantatas, most for a single voice accompanied only by a basso continuo, and was the most prolific composer of this genre and the last to make a significant contribution to it. He also wrote at least thirty-five serenatas, forty oratorios, and a substantial body of church music. Only in the area of instrumental music did he fail to make a significant contribution, despite a flurry of interest in his last years, which produced some eighteen concerti and a variety of chamber sonatas and keyboard pieces.

Scarlatti was easily the most prolific vocal composer of his generation and probably the most famous. His greatest success came at Naples in the 1680's and 1690's. As he grew older, his fame remained, but his post-1700 operas, though admired, were seldom popular successes. Although he brought fame to Naples, his own essentially conservative and contrapuntal style had little direct influence on the famous Neapolitan composers of the eighteenth century. His operas and cantatas illustrate the development of musical forms and styles in the late seventeenth century, but his own influence was not substantial. His last operas were clearly underwritten by his loyal Roman patrons and received scant critical or popular acclaim, being too old-fashioned even for so conservative a city. By the time of his death, he was largely forgotten.

Scarlatti's posthumous reputation has suffered much from hearsay and legend. Very little of his music was actually known by succeeding generations. The music to more than half of his operas is completely lost, and more than half of the remainder survive only in fragmentary form. Only since 1974 have a handful of his operas been available in reliable modern editions, and even fewer

have been performed. The cantatas survive in profusion, but only a very few are available in modern editions and only one, *Su le sponde del Tebro*—an atypical work for soprano, trumpet, strings, and continuo—is at all well known. The same holds true for the serenatas. Perversely, several of the less important genres have fared somewhat better, and ten of the oratorios have appeared in reliable modern editions since 1953, as have all the madrigals and a small number of the instrumental and sacred works.

In the late eighteenth and the nineteenth centuries, Scarlatti was mistakenly seen as the founder of the Neapolitan school of opera composers and the teacher of many of its earliest members. In fact, he should more appropriately be seen as a composer of the seventeenth century, whose works mark the culmination of the Italian traditions of opera and cantata composition of that century. His main contributions were to the expansion of the dimensions of arias, the standardization of the use of the *da capo* form, and the more active participation of the orchestra in vocal accompaniments. It was his misfortune to have written some of his greatest works in the eighteenth century, when a newer, lighter style prevailed.

—*Graydon Beeks*

FURTHER READING

Buelow, George J. *A History of Baroque Music.* Bloomington: Indiana University Press, 2004. Chapter 5 focuses on Arcangelo Corelli and Scarlatti, with a portion of the chapter describing Scarlatti's vocal chamber music.

Dent, Edward J. *Alessandro Scarlatti: His Life and Works.* 2d rev. ed. London: Edward Arnold, 1960. The pioneering biography of Scarlatti and, although brief, still the best single-volume work in English. Dent and Frank Walker, who revised this work, were both perceptive students of Scarlatti's life and works, and the former's comments on the music are particularly useful.

Grout, Donald J. *Alessandro Scarlatti: An Introduction to His Operas.* Berkeley: University of California Press, 1979. A brief but very clear introduction to the subject drawn from the Ernst Bloch lectures Grout delivered at Berkeley in 1975-1976. Includes several extended musical examples but no bibliography.

Robinson, Michael F. *Naples and Neapolitan Opera.* New York: Oxford University Press, 1972. Although primarily concerned with events of the later eighteenth century, this book places Scarlatti in context and is a valuable study of the tradition he was long held to have established.

Schulenberg, David. *Music of the Baroque*. New York: Oxford University Press, 2001. Chapter 6 describes secular vocal music in the late seventeenth century, including an eleven-page discussion of Scarlatti and the later cantata.

Smither, Howard E. *The Oratorio in the Baroque Era: Italy, Vienna, Paris*. Vol. 1 in *A History of the Oratorio*. Chapel Hill: University of North Carolina Press, 1977. An exhaustive treatment of the subject, especially valuable for the discussion of the social context. Pages 335-342 are especially relevant. Contains an extensive bibliography.

Westrup, Jack A. "Alessandro Scarlatti's *Il Mitridate* (1707)." In *New Looks at Italian Opera: Essays in Honor of Donald J. Grout*, edited by William W.

Austin. Ithaca, N.Y.: Cornell University Press, 1968. A brief introduction to Scarlatti's serious opera of 1707, which retells the Orestes myth under different names. Regarded as one of Scarlatti's greatest works, *Il Mitridate Eupatore* was long championed by Westrup.

See also: Christoph Gluck; George Frideric Handel; Wolfgang Amadeus Mozart.

Related articles in *Great Events from History: The Eighteenth Century, 1701-1800*: May 26, 1701-September 7, 1714: War of the Spanish Succession; January 29, 1728: Gay Produces the First Ballad Opera; April 13, 1742: First Performance of Handel's *Messiah*; October 5, 1762: First Performance of Gluck's *Orfeo and Euridice*.

FRIEDRICH SCHILLER
German playwright and philosopher

Belonging to the school of German classicism, Schiller was one of the leading contributors to German Idealism in literature, particularly drama and historical drama, and in philosophy, particularly ethics and aesthetics.

Born: November 10, 1759; Marbach, Württemberg (now in Germany)

Died: May 9, 1805; Weimar, Saxe-Weimar (now in Germany)

Also known as: Johann Christoph Friedrich von Schiller (full name)

Areas of achievement: Literature, theater, historiography, philosophy

EARLY LIFE

Born at Marbach in Württemberg, the son of an army surgeon, Friedrich Schiller (FREE-drihkh SHIHL-uhr) went to school in Ludwigsburg, the residence of the dukes of Württemberg. Though Schiller wanted to become a Protestant minister, his father was ordered by Duke Karl Eugen of Württemberg to send his son to the Hohe Karlsschule, the newly established military academy, located near Ludwigsburg. At this academy, young men at an early age were prepared for the civil and military service of the state of Württemberg. Schiller studied first law and then medicine from 1773 until 1780. He was

graduated with a degree in medicine and became regimental surgeon of a regiment stationed in Stuttgart.

During his time at the academy, Schiller wrote poetry and his first drama, *Die Räuber* (*The Robbers*, 1792), written between 1777 and 1780 and published in 1781. This play is rightly regarded as the most representative drama of his Sturm und Drang (storm and stress) period. When Schiller attended the first performance of his play at the Mannheim National Theater in 1782 without leave of absence from his regiment in Stuttgart, he was reprimanded by Karl Eugen, his commander in chief, and forbidden to engage in any further writing with the exception of medical treatises.

Rebelling against this punishment and the strict discipline of military life, Schiller deserted in 1782 and fled to Mannheim, where his first drama had been performed with great success, in order to pursue a career as a dramatist. For almost a year, the fugitive stayed in hiding in the small village of Bauerbach in Thuringia. In 1783, Schiller was appointed *Theaterdichter* (stage dramatist) of the Mannheim National Theater. During his stay in Mannheim, both his dramas *Die Verschwörung des Fiesko zu Genua* (1783; *Fiesco: Or, The Genoese Conspiracy*, 1796) and *Kabale und Liebe* (1784; *Cabal and Love*, 1795) were performed on the Mannheim stage. His drama *Don Carlos, Infant von Spanien* (1787; *Don Carlos, Infante of Spain*, 1798) remained a fragment during those years. In 1784, however, his contract in Mannheim was not renewed, so Schiller followed an invitation from his friend Christian Gottfried Körner to come to Leipzig and later to Dresden.

In 1787, Schiller went to Weimar, which had become the intellectual center of Germany, where he met Johann Gottfried Herder and Christoph Martin Wieland, while Johann Wolfgang von Goethe was in Italy. During the next year, Schiller stayed in the towns of Volksstädt and Rudolstadt, where he met Charlotte von Lengefeld, his future wife. During this time, he began his career as a historian and philosopher, concentrating in his philosophical studies on the major works of Immanuel Kant. These philosophical and historical preoccupations mark Schiller's transition from his Sturm und Drang subjectivity to the objective idealism of his classical period. His dramatic production came almost to a standstill during this time.

LIFE'S WORK

On the basis of his *Geschichte des Abfalls der vereinigten Niederlande von der spanischen Regierung* (1788; *The History of the Defection of the United Netherlands from the Spanish Empire*, 1844), Schiller was appointed professor of history at the University of Jena in 1789 upon the recommendation of Goethe. He was married to Charlotte von Lengefeld in 1790. After a serious illness in 1791, from which he never completely recovered and which led to his early death in 1805, Schiller visited Körner in Dresden and his homeland, Württemberg, in 1793. His friendship with Goethe, which began in 1794, led to a working relationship that became the basis of German classicism. Although their relationship was not without tensions, it proved to be stimulating and rewarding for both writers and gave direction to the course and development of German literature for the next ten years.

Schiller continued to live in Jena until 1799. His correspondence with Goethe records their literary activities and their opinions and projections for the future of German and European culture. From 1795 to 1797, Schiller edited *Die Horen*, a literary journal, to which Goethe contributed a number of his writings. During his stay in Jena, Schiller returned to creative writing with his dramatic Wallenstein trilogy.

In December, 1799, Schiller moved to Weimar, where he wrote the dramas *Maria Stuart* (1800; English translation, 1801), *Die Jungfrau von Orleans* (1801; *The Maid of Orleans*, 1835), *Die Braut von Messina: Oder, Die feindlichen Brüder* (1803; *The Bride of Messina*, 1837), and *Wilhelm Tell* (1804; *William Tell*, 1841). The work

Friedrich Schiller. (Library of Congress)

of this most productive period of his life, from 1794 to 1804, during which Schiller wrote his best dramas and poems, was largely a result of the stimulus of his relationship with Goethe. In 1802, Schiller was raised to the nobility, adding "von" to his last name.

During these years, most of Schiller's creative energies were devoted to the field of drama, especially historical drama. He succeeded in becoming the most important German dramatist second to Goethe at the end of the eighteenth century, and one of the most important of all European dramatists. All of his dramas deal with the concept of freedom. While in his early dramas of the Sturm und Drang period freedom is perceived mostly in terms of physical freedom, his dramas of the classical period center on ethical freedom. For his later plays, Schiller selected mostly historical plots, because he considered world history an ideal proving ground for the conflict between individual freedom and political necessity. His protagonists usually decide in favor of physical annihilation in order to preserve their moral freedom and integrity.

Schiller's principal contributions to lyric poetry consisted of philosophical poems and of historical ballads, which demonstrate his talent for dramatic action and his awareness of philosophical problems. His poems include the philosophical poem "An die Freude" ("Ode to Joy," well known in its musical setting by Ludwig van Beethoven in his ninth symphony), "Die Götter Griechenlands," and the elegy "Der Spaziergang"; among his most famous ballads are "Der Ring des Polykrates," "Die Kraniche des Ibykus," and "Die Bürgschaft."

Schiller was not only a dramatist and poet but also a historian. *The History of the Defection of the United Netherlands from the Spanish Empire* and *Geschichte des dreissigjährigen Krieges* (1791-1793; *History of the Thirty Years' War*, 1799) are examples of his work in this area. Schiller's historical research influenced his dramatic works, supplying him with plots and background material for his dramas.

Schiller's philosophical essays fall mainly under the headings of ethics and aesthetics. His essays on dramatic theory deal with the function of tragic emotions and the use of the pathetic as well as the sublime in dramatic art. In his aesthetics as well as his ethics, Schiller was strongly influenced by Kant, whose moral rigidity Schiller tried to counterbalance by his concept of the *schöne Seele* (beautiful soul), in which duty and inclination are in harmony. In his poetics, Schiller established the so-called naïve attitude and sentimental, or reflective, attitude as two legitimate approaches to literature, while in his philosophical anthropology he projected a dialectic development beyond Enlightenment philosophy.

SIGNIFICANCE

Together with Goethe, Friedrich Schiller is regarded as one of the representative national dramatists and poets of Germany. Historical drama, as he fashioned it at the end of the eighteenth century, became the dominant model for this genre during the nineteenth century. History was conceived in terms of Schillerian drama. Schiller's plays furnished the librettos for many of the operas from Gioacchino Rossini to Giuseppe Verdi. Only with the advent of naturalist drama did the predominance of Schiller's model of the historical drama come to an end.

In the nineteenth century, Schiller was celebrated in Germany as a liberal idealist until 1848, and, after the revolution had failed, as a German nationalist and a representative of German Idealism. This idealism became suspect after World War I and World War II, especially because of its lack of practical experience and its disregard of the realities of political life. Expressionist drama and the non-Aristotelian drama of Bertolt Brecht finally replaced the Schillerian model. Yet even in the 1960's, Rolf Hochhuth's controversial historical drama *Der Stellvertreter* (1963; *The Deputy*, 1963) followed the

Schillerian model and became one of the outstanding works of the postwar years. Schiller's idealism is now considered as more complex and problematical than nineteenth century German ideology would admit. After William Shakespeare, Schiller is still one of the most widely performed dramatists on the German stage.

In the relationship of Jews and Germans, Schiller played an important role. Many Jews considered Schiller to be the speaker of pure humanitarianism and the representative of the highest ideals of humankind. Before the Holocaust of World War II, Schiller personified to the Jews what they considered to be German. For many Austrian, German, Polish, and Russian Jews, the encounter with Schiller was much more real than with the actual Germany. Although Schiller had never addressed himself to the Jews or to Jewish problems, this fact did not affect the Jewish passion for his dramas and poetry. An example of this passion was the adoption of Schiller's name by many Russian Jews, among them famous Zionist leaders.

In Great Britain and the United States, Schiller was received as a representative of German Romanticism. While Thomas Carlyle, who wrote *The Life of Schiller* (1825), and the American Transcendentalists Ralph Waldo Emerson, Margaret Fuller, and Henry David Thoreau were highly appreciative of Schiller's achievements, George Bernard Shaw was negative in his criticism of Schiller's Romanticism in the preface to *Saint Joan*, his own Joan of Arc drama of 1923.

—Ehrhard Bahr

FURTHER READING

Beiser, Frederick C. *Schiller as Philosopher: A Re-Examination*. New York: Oxford University Press, 2005. One of the leading scholars of German Romantic philosophy argues that Schiller's philosophical work is more worthy of attention and respect than has been thought.

Garland, H. G. *Schiller, the Dramatic Writer: A Study of Style in the Plays*. Oxford, England: Clarendon Press, 1969. A study of individual dramas. Includes a two-page bibliography.

Goethe, Johann Wolfgang von. *Correspondence Between Goethe and Schiller, 1794-1805*. Translated by Liselotte Dieckmann. New York: P. Lang, 1994. Contains more than one thousand letters between the two authors. The writers critique each other's work and suggest changes, discuss the works of other contemporary writers, and exchange thoughts on the philosophical and aesthetic ideas of the period.

Graham, Ilse. *Schiller's Drama: Talent and Integrity.* London: Methuen, 1974. Includes individual readings of Schiller's dramas as well as some chapters on special issues raised by the plays as a whole. Includes extensive notes, a bibliography, and an index.

Kooy, Michael John. *Coleridge, Schiller, and Aesthetic Education.* New York: Palgrave, 2002. Argues that Schiller had a decisive effect upon Samuel Taylor Coleridge's development, especially through his idea of an "aesthetic education."

Kostka, Edmund. *Schiller in Italy: Schiller's Reception in Italy, Nineteenth and Twentieth Centuries.* New York: Peter Lang, 1997. Study not only of Schiller's reception in Italy but also of his influence upon Italian culture. Illuminates both Italian history and Schiller's place in the history of ideas.

Martinson, Steven D., ed. *A Companion to the Works of Friedrich Schiller.* Rochester, N.Y.: Camden House, 2005. Includes essays on a wide range of topics, from Schiller's relation to classical antiquity to his reception in the twentieth century.

Miller, R. D. *Schiller and the Ideal of Freedom: A Study of Schiller's Philosophical Works with Chapters on Kant.* Oxford, England: Clarendon Press, 1970. A study of Kant's concepts of moral and aesthetic freedom and Schiller's concept of freedom through harmony. Includes an index.

Pugh, David. *Schiller's Early Dramas: A Critical History.* Rochester, N.Y.: Camden House, 2000. An analysis of the history of Schiller criticism within Germany; discusses each major school of German criticism from the eighteenth through the twentieth centuries and examines Schiller's influence upon, place within, and reception by each of those schools.

Sharpe, Lesley. *Friedrich Schiller: Drama, Thought, and Politics.* New York: Cambridge University Press, 1991. Sharpe examines Schiller's development as a dramatist, poet, and thinker, placing his work within the context of late eighteenth century social, political, and literary events. Includes detailed discussions of his major works.

Simons, John D. *Friedrich Schiller.* Boston: Twayne, 1981. A later study of Schiller's life and work. Includes notes and references, a selected bibliography, and an index.

Stahl, Ernst L. *Friedrich Schiller's Dramas: Theory and Practice.* Oxford, England: Clarendon Press, 1954. A discussion of Schiller's dramas as well as his aesthetic doctrine and theory of tragedy. Includes a chronological table, a selected bibliography, and an index.

Thomas, Calvin. *The Life and Works of Friedrich Schiller.* New York: Henry Holt, 1901. Reprint. New York: AMS Press, 1970. A traditional but reliable biography that includes a brief summary of secondary literature, a general index, and an index of writings.

Witte, William. *Schiller.* Oxford, England: Basil Blackwell, 1949. A study of Schiller as letter writer, poet, and playwright. Includes a bibliography and an index.

See also: Johann Wolfgang von Goethe; Johann Gottfried Herder; Immanuel Kant.

Related articles in *Great Events from History: The Eighteenth Century, 1701-1800*: October, 1725: Vico Publishes *The New Science*; 1739-1740: Hume Publishes *A Treatise of Human Nature*; April, 1762: Rousseau Publishes *The Social Contract*; October 5, 1762: First Performance of Gluck's *Orfeo and Euridice*; July, 1764: Voltaire Publishes *A Philosophical Dictionary for the Pocket*; 1770: Publication of Holbach's *The System of Nature*; 1781: Kant Publishes *Critique of Pure Reason*; 1784-1791: Herder Publishes His Philosophy of History; 1792-1793: Fichte Advocates Free Speech.

JUNÍPERO SERRA
Spanish priest

A highly respected Catholic missionary, Serra supervised the founding of the first nine missions in California. His involvement in the conquest and cruel treatment of American Indians, however, has led to great controversy concerning his suitability for sainthood.

Born: November 24, 1713; Petra, Mallorca, Spain
Died: August 28, 1784; Carmel, Alta California (now California), New Spain
Also known as: Miguel José Serra (full name); Blessed Junípero Serra
Area of achievement: Religion and theology

EARLY LIFE

Junípero Serra (hoo-NEE-pay-roh SEHR-rah) was born on the Spanish island of Mallorca in 1713, the son of Antonio Serra and Margarita Serra, poor farmers without formal education. Some of his ancestors were *conversos*, or Jews who had been forcibly converted to Christianity. He attended the local elementary school taught by Franciscan friars, where he decided at a young age to join their religious order. His baptismal name was Miguel José, but when he joined the Franciscan order at the age of sixteen he took the name Junípero in honor of Saint Francis of Assissi's companion, known for humility and compassion. While studying for the priesthood in Palma de Mallorca, Serra earned a reputation for oratorical excellence and personal piety.

Following ordination in 1738, Serra earned a doctorate in theology at Lullian University in Palma, where he was appointed to the John Duns Scotus chair of philosophy in 1744. Five years later, at the age of thirty-five, he decided to give up his secure and prestigious position to devote his life to missionary activities in the New World. Like other committed clerics of the century, he firmly believed that converting pagans to Christianity was the noblest of endeavors and was influenced by the tradition of Franciscan mysticism, which valued suffering as the path to spiritual enlightenment.

LIFE'S WORK

After receiving permission to become a missionary, Serra sailed to Mexico in 1749. En route, he preached his first sermon as a missionary at San Juan, Puerto Rico. Arriving in Mexico City, he spent several months at the Franciscan College of San Fernando. Beginning in 1750 he worked for eight years as a missionary among the Palmés Indians in the Sierra Gorda region north of Mexico City. He learned to speak the local language and helped to build a large stone church in the town of Jalpán. In 1758 he was assigned to the Mexican capital, where he served as administrator of the College of San Fernando while also assuming the duties of a traveling missionary priest.

In 1767, when King Charles III of Spain expelled the Jesuits from Spain and its colonies, the Spanish government requested the Franciscan friars take over the missions in Baja (lower) California. Hoping to stop Russian expansion southward along the Pacific coast, the government also charged the Franciscans with the task of founding missions in Alta (upper) California. Serra was selected to serve as *presidente* (or chief administrator) of both projects, with his headquarters located at Loreto.

In 1769, when General José de Gálvez, inspector general of New Spain (now Mexico), ordered the military invasion of Alta California, Serra personally accompanied the troops of Don Gaspar de Portolá, the governor of California who commanded the so-called Sacred Expedition to establish Franciscan missions in Alta California. Serra was fifty-five years old and in very poor health, having long suffered from an ulcerated leg and foot. Some historians think his health had been damaged by his practice of self-mortification, which consisted of flogging his back with a whip, beating his breast with a stone, and burning his flesh with candles. Whatever the reasons, Serra had to be lifted onto the saddle of his horse. His friend and biographer, Francisco Pálou, observed Serra's frail condition and tried to discourage him from making the arduous journey, but Serra rebuked his friend for a lack of faith in divine providence.

Serra founded the first mission in Alta California, located in what is now the city of San Diego, on July 16, 1769. In June, 1770, he established a second mission at Carmel, San Carlos Borromeo, which henceforth served as his permanent headquarters. Of the twenty-one missions that the Franciscans founded in California, Serra was directly responsible for nine, including San Antonio de Padua (1771), San Gabriel Arcángel (1771), San Luis Obispo de Tolosa (1772), San Francisco de Asís (1776), San Juan Capistrano (1776), Santa Clara de Asís (1777), and San Buenaventura (1782). By the time of his death the mission system comprised about five thousand American Indians from at least six linguistic stocks, more than thirty-five friars, and approximately five hundred settlers and soldiers.

The missions were separated from each other by about a day's trip on horseback. Serra personally visited each mission several times, often performing baptisms and confirmations. He walked thousands of miles, although at times he traveled by mule, carriage, or packet boat. He usually traveled with a page, sometimes accompanied by military escort. While his main objective was to "prepare souls for heaven," he understood that conversion would not be permanent unless Indians acquired the means to earn their livelihood. In addition to religious instruction, therefore, the Franciscan friars did their best to teach methods of European agriculture and construction as well as other practical skills. The missions operated as miniature empires with farming as the principal industry. American Indian families within the compound were assigned small apartments, and the friars supervised their work schedules.

Serra's critics usually concede that he desired the well-being of the American Indians under his jurisdiction. He frequently came into conflict with political and military officials over issues of rightful payment for labor and proper punishment. He particularly denounced Spanish soldiers for raping indigenous women. In 1773 he presented Viceroy Antonio María de Bucareli de Ursúa, the highest Spanish official in Mexico, with a *representación* containing thirty-two points for increasing the protection of Indians. Bucareli accepted most of the suggestions and incorporated them into California's regulatory code. Serra, however, shared the typical biases of the time, looking upon the Indians as childlike and in need of strict discipline. In several of his letters he instructed his friars about the necessity of using corporal punishment when confronted with disobedience or rebellion.

Despite his deteriorating health, Serra continued to work until his death at the age of seventy in his headquarters on the Carmel River.

SIGNIFICANCE

In 1931, a statue of Father Serra, representing the state of California, was placed in the Capitol Building in Washington, D.C. Still, Serra is a controversial figure. His admirers look upon him as a holy man worthy of canonization, and Franciscan leaders in California recommended him as a candidate for sainthood. In 1985, the first hurdle in the three-stage process of canonization was passed when the pope named Serra "venerable," meaning that his life met the Catholic standards of "heroic virtue." Proponents of his sainthood maintain that he converted many American Indians to Christianity and, with his fellow Franciscans, educated and improved the life conditions of indigenous peoples. Detractors, on the other hand, denounce Serra for his active involvement in a brutal conquest that decimated the American Indian population and destroyed much of American Indian culture.

One of the major issues in this debate is whether Serra should be judged by eighteenth century standards or by modern conceptions of human rights. Despite strong protests by American Indians and others, he was beatified in 1988, but years later, in the early twenty-first century, it remains unclear whether he would ever be proclaimed a saint.

Regardless of one's conclusions, it is impossible to deny that Serra played an important role in the early history of California. He will always be remembered as the founder of the first mission in California, San Diego de Alcalá, which became the basis for the development of the first permanent European settlement in the province. It is impossible to understand the Spanish Empire in the New World without considering the work and ideas of missionaries such as Serra.

—*Thomas Tandy Lewis*

Father Junípero Serra. (The Granger Collection, New York)

FURTHER READING

Cook, Sherburne. *The Conflict Between the California Indian and White Civilization.* Berkeley: University of California Press, 1976. Polemical but scholarly essays emphasizing the thesis of biological conquest, while also criticizing Serra and other missionaries for using excessive cruelty in punishing American Indians.

Costo, Rupert, and Jeanneatte Costo, eds. *The Missions of California: A Legacy of Genocide.* San Francisco, Calif.: Indian History Press, 1987. Collection of passionately written articles opposing Serra's canonization, edited by California Indian activists.

DeNevi, Don, and Noel Moholy. *Junípero Serra.* San Francisco, Calif.: Harper & Row, 1987. Scholarly biography that is highly favorable to both Serra and his religious beliefs.

Fogel, Daniel. *Junípero Serra, the Vatican, and Enslavement Theology.* New York: Ism Press, 1996. Fogel's criticisms of Serra reflect a strong animus against traditional Catholic beliefs and practices.

Geiger, Maynard. *The Life and Times of Junípero Serra.* 2 vols. Monterrey, Mexico: Siempre Adelante, 1959. Detailed biography written by an admiring Franciscan scholar who devoted many years to the subject.

Morgado, Martin. *Junípero Serra: A Pictorial Biography.* Monterrey, Mexico: Siempre Adelante, 1991. A short account with many beautiful illustrations of buildings and artifacts.

Pálou, Francisco. *Life of Fray Junípero Serra.* Translated by Maynard Geiger. Washington, D.C.: Academy of American Franciscan History, 1955. Hagiographic biography written by Serra's good friend and fellow Franciscan missionary.

Sandos, James. "Junípero Serra's Canonization and the Historical Record." *American Historical Review* 93 (1988): 1253-1269. Analyzing the historical evidence, Sandos concludes that despite Serra's sincere love for the American Indians, he probably was responsible for excessive punishment and other abuses.

Tibesar, Antonine, ed. *Writings of Junípero Serra.* 4 vols. Washington, D.C.: Academy of American Franciscan History, 1955-1966. Dealing almost exclusively with mission affairs, these factual reports, instructions, and commentaries provide much insight into his character.

Tinker, George. *Missionary Conquest: The Gospel and Native Americas Cultural Genocide.* Minneapolis, Minn.: Fortress Press, 1993. Written by a Cherokee Lutheran theologian, the book examines Serra and three other respected missionaries, arguing that they inadvertently did great harm to American Indians and their cultures.

See also: Charles III; José de Gálvez; Philip V; Guillaume-Thomas Raynal.

Related articles in *Great Events from History: The Eighteenth Century, 1701-1800:* January 19, 1759-August 16, 1773: Suppression of the Jesuits; July 17, 1769-1824: Rise of the California Missions; 1776: Foundation of the Viceroyalty of La Plata.

SAMUEL SEWALL
English-born American jurist and theologian

Author of one of the first antislavery tracts in America and the only judge at the infamous Salem witchcraft trials to speak out against the proceedings, Sewall became a voice of social conscience in Puritan New England.

Born: March 28, 1652; Bishopstoke, Hampshire, England
Died: January 1, 1730; Boston, Massachusetts
Areas of achievement: Law, social reform, religion and theology, church reform, literature

EARLY LIFE

Although Samuel Sewall was born in England, his father had begun a plantation in Newbury, Massachusetts, in 1635. The family had enjoyed a fair degree of middle-class wealth for several generations. In the 1640's and 1650's, many New England Puritans returned to England because the Puritans were then in power; the Sewalls were one such family. Entering Baddesley "petty school" at about the age of five, young Samuel soon learned to read English, and he was then sent to nearby Rumsey grammar school to study Latin.

With the restoration of a Stuart (and non-Puritan) monarch in 1660, Puritans lost virtually all their political power in England, and a year later the Sewalls sailed for their New England estate on the *Prudent Mary*. Unlike the harsh voyages of the Plymouth pilgrims, that of the Sewalls was made in the comfort of the captain's cabin and with the ministrations of servants. Arriving in the New World, nine-year-old Samuel continued his education at Newbury with the renowned scholar and minister Thomas Parker, who encouraged him in the writing of Latin verse, a pastime Sewall continued throughout his life. In 1667, at the age of fifteen, Sewall entered Harvard College, receiving an A.B. degree in 1671. The training was largely theological, preparing young men for the ministry, but when Sewall was offered a church in New Jersey upon graduation, he declined. Staying on as a tutor and the college librarian, Sewall completed his master's degree in 1674. The following year, he married Hannah Hull, the only child of the treasurer of the Massachusetts colony. In an era when marriages were often like business mergers, this alliance made Sewall one of the most influential and wealthy men in New England. His real-estate and import-export business increased his wealth and importance over the next half century.

In 1681, the city of Boston named him manager of its printing press. Sewall thus took a personal hand in the production of all the books published in Boston until he stepped down in 1684, when he became a member of the city council. It was a crucial year for New England, for the Crown had revoked the Massachusetts charter, which meant that Sewall's vast land holdings might be in jeopardy. Late in 1688, he sailed to England to aid the negotiations for a new charter; the work kept him nearly a full year, and he returned to Boston at the close of 1689. Two years later, a new charter was approved.

LIFE'S WORK

The new charter of 1691 named Sewall a member of the city council, a position he already held, but now strengthened by royal approval. With the charter came a new governor, Sir William Phips, who chose Sewall as one of the judges to preside over the infamous Salem witchcraft trials in 1692 and 1693. Though it is clear that Sewall believed in witchcraft, and though he was the only one of the nine judges to denounce the trial later, there is no way to tell how Sewall felt about the trials at the time they took place. His diary, which was kept in great detail from 1673 to 1729, is virtually without comment on the trials, though it contains many details.

It could not have been easy, however, for a man of Sewall's tender conscience to condemn several neighbors to death. Over the course of the summer of 1692,

Samuel Sewall. (Library of Congress)

Sewall's court ordered a dozen men and women executed; eleven by hanging and one by "pressing," or being crushed by heavy stones. When the court recessed in October, Sewall visited with its most outspoken opponent, Thomas Danforth, and "discoursed . . . about witchcraft," an indication that he was at least open to the criticism of the trials.

After several years, Sewall's own minister, Samuel Willard of Old South Church, began preaching against the witchcraft trials, and many New Englanders began to consider them a mistake. Yet none of the judges said so until January 14, 1697, when Sewall stood up in his pew while the Reverend Willard read Sewall's public recantation of his role in the trials. Sewall's recantation was sweeping: He asked forgiveness of the community, as well as of God, and took the entire "blame and shame of it," since he was "more concerned than any that he knows of" (that is, he believed that he was more to blame).

In November of that same year, Sewall published his first book, *Phaenomena quondam Apolcalyptica* (1697), a reading of the Book of Revelation that attempted to present the New England colonies as the fulfillment of the New Jerusalem promised in scripture. In addition to learned theological language, this short work also contains some of the most moving lyrical prose describing the natural beauty of New England, specifically Plum Island, the praises of which Sewall sings in the closing paragraph of the book.

Sewall's second book, *The Selling of Joseph* (1700), is the first antislavery work in American literature. Already controversial for his recantation of his role in the witchcraft trials, Sewall wrote in his diary that he received "frowns and hard words" for his stand against slavery. The title refers to the events of Genesis 37, in which Joseph's older brothers sell him into slavery in Egypt. This, argues Sewall, was a violation of God's covenant with Adam and Eve: Since all men and women are the heirs of the first parents, they receive liberty as God's deed of gift. No human law can take away this God-given liberty. Slavers in Sewall's time and after attempted to find scriptural justification to counter this basic principle of human liberty and pointed to Noah's curse of his son Ham in Genesis 9:25, "The lowest of slaves shall he be to his brothers." Ham was interpreted as the ancestor of all African races. Sewall countered this notion with the prohibition in Exodus 21:16 against kidnaping, since the ultimate source of all black slaves in America was capture by force.

Part of the "hard words" Sewall encountered for *The Selling of Joseph* were in print; one of his fellow judges, a slaveholder named John Saffin, published *A Brief and Candid Answer* to Sewall's book in 1701. Saffin argued that bringing African slaves into Christian communities improved their lot. Sewall did not respond to this criticism, but he continued to write against slavery in the Boston *News-Letter* (June 12, 1706).

In 1707, the charter of Harvard College was renewed, and as a prominent judge of the day, Sewall became an overseer of his alma mater. A few years later, Sewall published his third book, *Talitha Cumi: Or, An Invitation to Women to Look After Their Inheritance in the Heavenly Mansion* (1711). Though no copy of this book survives, Sewall's records show that he had it printed, and a surviving manuscript copy allowed the Massachusetts Historical Society to reprint it in the *Proceedings* for 1873. His next publication, *Proposals Touching the Accomplishment of Prophecies* (1713), continued the work of his first book in presenting New England as the fulfillment of biblical prophecies. His last book was a 1721 treatise on the Kennebeck Indians.

In 1717, Sewall's wife Hannah died. Fourteen children had been born to them. Two years later, he married Abigail Tilley, who had outlived two previous husbands,

but she died seven months after their Thanksgiving Day marriage. Sewall's diary records a touchingly unsuccessful courtship of Katherine Winthrop in 1720. Less than eighteen months after Winthrop's final "no," however, Sewall was married to another widow, Mary Gibbs. This merger was just as much a business deal as the others; it was contracted by letter, and much of the negotiations with Gibbs's children involved their taking on her debt before Sewall would close the deal.

In 1728, Sewall retired from the superior court, thinking, at seventy-six, that his useful service to Boston was at an end. In June of the following year, just six months before his death, he sat for the portrait that still hangs in the Boston Museum of Fine Arts. It shows a portly man with large placid eyes aimed steadily at the viewer; the shock of shoulder-length white hair does not look like a wig, as his censure of the vanity of wigs in his diary (June 10, 1701) confirms. His prominent nose is straight, and his mouth, while not smiling, is relaxed. In December, 1729, he took to his bed and never arose from it. Early New Year's Day morning, 1730, he died.

SIGNIFICANCE

Even if he had never gained prominence as the only judge to repent the Salem witchcraft trials or as an opponent of the slave trade, Samuel Sewall would have received posthumous note as one of the best diarists of colonial New England. Sewall's diary, kept without a break (except for the disappearance of one volume, 1677-1684) from 1673 to 1729, is the most complete contemporary portrait of late seventeenth century New England. Because Sewall's interests ranged wide, his observations of the life around him were equally various. In addition, his pen recorded the human element of events, not merely names and dates (though some entries are just that).

Moreover, business and the court took him throughout Massachusetts, so his scope was not limited to Boston. Events tend to be recorded as they affected Sewall, but are in no way self-aggrandizing. In recording the death of Dr. Samuel Alcock, for example (March 16, 1677), Sewall confesses to stopping in the kitchen for leisurely conversation when he had been sent for medical aid for Alcock.

As a writer, Sewall represents the manifold literary interests of New England Puritans. A "chum and bedfellow" of Edward Taylor at Harvard, Sewall shared with that best-known of American Puritan poets a passion for verse-making in Latin and English. Some sixty poems by Sewall survive. Though his poetry does not rival Taylor's and is rarely anthologized, Sewall's prose is as lyrical and engaging as any prose of his century. In the history of American jurisprudence, theology, and social thought, Samuel Sewall deserves a permanent place.

—*John R. Holmes*

FURTHER READING

Graham, Judith S. *Puritan Family Life: The Diary of Samuel Sewall*. Boston: Northeastern University Press, 2000. Graham analyzes Sewall's diary to refute the traditional opinion that Puritan family life was joyless and repressive. She finds warmth, sympathy, and love in Sewall's relationships with his wife and children.

Kagle, Steven E. *American Diary Literature, 1620-1799*. Boston: G. K. Hall, 1979. This general introduction to the genre of diary writing in America includes a brief but insightful analysis of Sewall's diary (pp. 147-153) that disputes earlier assertions of Sewall's preeminence as a colonial American diarist, faulting his work's style but accepting it as "still a fine diary."

Kaplan, Sidney, ed. *The Selling of Joseph: A Memorial*. Amherst: University of Massachusetts Press, 1969. The introduction to this edition of Sewall's antislavery tract includes an essay on his role in the history of abolition (pp. 27-63). Kaplan refutes the charge of hypocrisy in Sewall's attack on slavery.

Niebuhr, Gustav. "A Puritan Judge's Antislavery Voice." *The New York Times*, June 24, 2000, p. A-12. An analysis of the literary and historical value of Samuel's writings, focusing on *The Selling of Joseph*. Includes information on Sewall's diaries and assessments of his life and legacy by two contemporary clergymen.

Parrington, Vernon L. *Main Currents in American Thought*. New York: Harcourt, Brace, 1927. A standard reference work in American studies that, though dated in many areas, is still reliable for studying the Puritans. The section on Sewall is a good general assessment of his place in American thought.

"1696." *American Heritage* 47, no. 8 (December, 1996): 104. Focuses on the many tragedies Sewall experienced in 1696, several years after the Salem witchcraft trials. In this year, Sewall's family suffered from sickness, deaths, and accidents, including the birth of a stillborn son. Describes how the Massachusetts state legislature declared a day of fasting and repentance to atone for the witchcraft trials, and how Sewall recanted for his role in the proceedings.

Strandness, T. B. *Samuel Sewall: A Puritan Portrait*. East Lansing: Michigan State University Press, 1967. A thorough treatment of Sewall's life, mostly based on the diary, though marshaling other primary sources detailed in the exhaustive bibliography. Strandness quotes liberally not only from the diary but also from letters and other primary sources.

Thomas, M. Halsey, ed. *The Diary of Samuel Sewall, 1674-1729, Newly Edited from the Manuscript at the Massachusetts Historical Society*. 2 vols. New York: Farrar, Straus & Giroux, 1973. A scrupulous edition of the primary source of information about Sewall and his culture, well indexed and with an excellent preface by Thomas that places Sewall in the context of his era.

See also: Benjamin Banneker; Jonathan Edwards; Ann Lee; Cotton Mather; Increase Mather; James Edward Oglethorpe; Charles Willson Peale; Guillaume-Thomas Raynal; Granville Sharp; William Wilberforce.

Related articles in *Great Events from History: The Eighteenth Century, 1701-1800:* 18th century: Expansion of the Atlantic Slave Trade; April 6, 1712: New York City Slave Revolt; 1739-1742: First Great Awakening; January 16, 1786: Virginia Statute of Religious Liberty; April 12, 1787: Free African Society Is Founded; 1790's-1830's: Second Great Awakening.

ANNA SEWARD
English poet

Seward, a major contributor to the eighteenth century's revival of the sonnet, also wrote the poetical novel Louisa, *which could be viewed as a successful experiment that anticipated themes and modes of Romantic expression.*

Born: December 12, 1742; Eyam, Derbyshire, England
Died: March 25, 1809; Lichfield, Staffordshire, England
Also known as: Swan of Lichfield
Area of achievement: Literature

EARLY LIFE

Anna Seward was the daughter of Thomas Seward, rector of Eyam, Derbyshire, prebendary of Salisbury and canon residentiary of Lichfield, and Elizabeth Hunter, daughter of John Hunter, headmaster of Lichfield grammar school, where writer Samuel Johnson studied. One sister, Sarah, was born in 1744; none of the three siblings born thereafter survived.

When Anna was seven years old, her family moved into Bishop's Palace in Lichfield, the town where Anna remained until her death. She spent her adolescence with her sister Sarah until Sarah's death in 1764. The five-year-old Honora Sneyd, who had been adopted by the Sewards and lived with them from 1754 to 1768, became Anna's companion and pupil.

Anna's father, poet and author of "The Female Right to Literature" (1748), taught Anna to read William Shakespeare, John Milton, and Alexander Pope when she was just three years old. At age nine, she was reciting *Paradise Lost,* and soon she was also reading John Dryden, among others.

Bishop's Palace was a provincial salon, a place of cultural engagement, attended by literary, scientific, and clerical thinkers, including Erasmus Darwin, grandfather of Charles Darwin, and Richard Lovell Edgeworth, father of Maria Edgeworth. Darwin became Anna Seward's mentor, but his advocacy of her as a poet interfered with her parents' progressive attitudes toward her education. Thereafter, she was restrained from writing poetry, although she continued to do so secretly. It may be that without Darwin's mentorship, she would have been a far superior poet. After his death, she wrote *Memoirs of the Life of Dr. Darwin* (1804).

None of Seward's courtships led to marriage, some because of a lack of fortune and some because her suitors were not good prospective husbands—grist for her literary treatment of the "marriage market."

LIFE'S WORK

Anna Seward's life, seemingly idyllic and carefree, did not remain so. The care of ailing parents fell to her, with her mother dying in 1780 and her father, suffering from failing mental and physical faculties, dying ten years later. After her father's death, she remained in the palace for the rest of her life, becoming the provincial *salonnière* of Lichfield. Seward was noted for her fine reading voice and for presentations of Shakespeare and other dramatic works as well as for her impressive presence.

In 1769, Seward had met John André, later Major André, who fell in love with Honora. Seward's description of their romance in her *Monody on the Death of Major André* (1781) led to her establishing several lifelong correspondences. When Richard Lovell Edgeworth returned to Lichfield with Thomas Day in 1770 (both were interested in physical science and drawn to Lichfield by Darwin's work), they were attracted to Honora. Although of these three, Seward favored André for Honora, it was not to be, and Honora married Edgeworth in 1773; by opposing the marriage, Seward painfully estranged herself from Honora. Honora's death from consumption (tuberculosis) in 1780 grieved Seward, who mourned her in poetry for years. As Edgeworth's second wife, Honora had been the beloved stepmother of Maria Edgeworth.

In 1778, Seward was invited by Lady Anna "Laura" Miller to her salon at Bath-Easton, where Seward was awarded first prize for her poem "Invocation of the Comic Muse," the first of many prizes awarded her at the Bath-Easton poetry contests, and where Seward found encouragement for her writing. After Miller's death, Seward wrote Miller's epitaph inscribed on her monument in Bath Abbey as well as in her "Poem to the Memory of Lady Miller" (1782).

Known as "the Swan of Lichfield," Seward was highly praised by many during her lifetime. Her *Elegy on Captain Cook* was reviewed favorably by Samuel Johnson and in the *Monthly Review* (1780), attracting the attention of literary circles. One of her admirers, William Hayley, among the most popular poets in Britain in his day, considered her a "female genius." He began their correspondence by sending his own verses to her, commending her *Elegy on Captain Cook.* Hayley was known for his enormously popular *The Triumphs of Temper* and for the *Poetic Epistle on Epic Poetry*, called by Robert Southey one of the most influential scholarly books of its day.

Seward's *Louisa: A Poetical Novel, in Four Epistles* (1782), which explores cross-genre aesthetics similar to those of Romantic-era verse-romances, contributed to the evolution of the novel by examining the growth of the passions rather than emphasizing plot as its aesthetic device. Praised by Hayley, James Boswell, and others, it had appeared in five editions by 1792.

One of Seward's well-known associations was with Samuel Johnson, whom she refused to idolize. She took personally his devaluation of the cultural life of Lichfield, disagreed with his denigration of pre-Romanticism, and abhorred his misanthropy. After Johnson's death in 1784, Boswell, with whom Seward had enjoyed a brief friendship, even after she repelled an unwanted advance from him, wrote to Seward requesting information concerning Johnson for his famous work *The Life of Samuel Johnson, LL.D.* (1791). To Boswell, she wrote of the forthcoming biography, "If faithful, brilliant will be its lights, but deep its shades." She was concerned that Boswell and Hester Lynch Piozzi (also known as Mrs. Thrale) were creating a Johnson legacy that distorted the truth. So in *Gentleman's Magazine*, she published letters signed "Benvolio" that disputed what she regarded as Boswell's and Piozzi's unwarranted adulation of Johnson's qualities, ignoring his intolerance, irritability, and insolence. Johnson himself had asked for Seward when he was dying. She was deeply sympathetic to the sufferings of his last days and often attended him.

In May, 1786, she made one of her rare visits to London, this time for the appearance of her *Horatian Odes* in the *Gentleman's Magazine*. Although she knew neither Greek nor Latin, but worked from prose translations, she sought to bring forth the poetic spirit of the originals into her translations. In her collection *Original Sonnets on Various Subjects, and Odes Paraphrased from Horace* (1799), Seward included a preface reestablishing the sonnet's place in English letters. Further literary criticism may be found in her essays and correspondence.

Among the acquaintances she made in the 1780's and 1790's, in Lichfield, were General Eliott, the "Hero of Gibraltar," who was the subject of her *Ode on General Eliott's Return from Gibraltar*; Piozzi and her second husband, whom Seward found engaging, in contrast to Johnson's loathing; and Hannah More, whom she met in 1791 at the home of Thomas Sedgewick Whalley in the Mendips, Somerset. With More, Seward had little affinity, Seward being a latitudinarian in her Anglicanism, with small patience for Evangelicalism.

John Saville was, as she said, her "soul's dearest friend." The vicar-choral of Lichfield Cathedral, Saville and Seward shared a mutual though impossible devotion because he was already married. Given that there was no talk of scandal in the cathedral town, their relationship must have been overtly platonic.

In 1792, Seward began fearing for her own health and that of Saville, leading to depression followed by bouts of illness and searches for palliation through medical practices such as bleeding and hydrotherapy. For the last decade of the century, she traveled for medical as well as social reasons, suffering from mixed rheumatic illnesses, perhaps environmental allergies, and possibly asthma.

In 1795, Seward met Lady Eleanor Butler and Sarah Ponsonby, the so-called Ladies of Llangollen, during the first of many visits to Dinbren in Wales, after which Seward published *Llangollen Vale, with Other Poems* (1796). The collection treats the topic of female friendship. Seward would correspond with them for more than a decade.

In December, 1801, Saville suffered a paralytic seizure and was placed in Bishop's Palace for more than one month, nursed back to health, temporarily, by Seward and by his daughter; he died two years later, on August 2, 1803, at the age of sixty-eight. Seward paid his debts, provided for his family, and built a memorial to him. She lived on, grief-stricken and ill, for five more years, less and less able to complete her works. She traveled as long as her health allowed, visiting Whalley and his second wife in the Mendips, and again visited Hannah More. In Bristol, she visited Emmeline and Maria Edgeworth, Honora's stepdaughters.

Seward was considered a "very staunch friend" by Robert Southey, who initiated their correspondence by asking for suggestions for his work *Madoc*. Along with Samuel Taylor Coleridge, Seward considered Southey one of the great new voices in poetry. In 1799, her correspondence with Sir Walter Scott began. Inspired by his *Minstrelsy of the Scottish Border*, Seward wrote *Auld Willie's Farewell*, included by Scott in the third volume of his *Minstrelsy*. He was to serve as Seward's literary executor, editing her poetry. Her letters were brought out by Constable.

In her last lonely years, she had a companion in Miss Fern, a woman in straitened circumstances, in whom Seward found comfort and solace. Seward died of scorbutic fever on March 25, 1809, and is buried in Lichfield Cathedral.

SIGNIFICANCE

Anna Seward, acclaimed as a poet in her day—the *European Magazine* published her biography in 1782—slipped into obscurity as the nineteenth century progressed and the taste for aesthetics waned. Her poetical novel *Louisa* anticipated Romanticism. Along with Charlotte Smith and others, Seward has been recognized as instrumental in the eighteenth century's revival of the sonnet. Comparatively little has been written about Seward, and her legacy awaits reevaluation.

—Donna Berliner

FURTHER READING

Ashmun, Margaret. *The Singing Swan*. 1931. Reprint. New York: Greenwood Press, 1968. Ashmun's work remains the only complete biography of Seward.

Fay, Elizabeth. "Anna Seward, the Swan of Lichfield: Reading *Louisa*." In *Approaches to Teaching British Women Poets of the Romantic Period*, edited by Stephen C. Behrendt and Harriet Kramer Linkin. New York: Modern Language Association, 1997. Evaluates Seward's poetical novel.

Kelly, Jennifer, ed. *Bluestocking Feminism: Writings of the Bluestocking Circle, 1738-1785*. London: Pickering & Chatto, 1999. The fourth volume of this multivolume series includes Seward's writings.

Monk, Samuel. "Anna Seward and the Romantic Poets: A Study in Taste." In *Wordsworth and Coleridge: Studies in Honor of George McLean Harper*, edited by Earl Leslie Griggs. New York: Russell & Russell, 1962. Monk discusses Seward as a transitional figure.

See also: John André; William Blake; James Boswell; Robert Burns; Hester Chapone; Samuel Johnson; Mary de la Rivière Manley; Mary Wortley Montagu; Hannah More; Alexander Pope; Mary Wollstonecraft.

Related articles in *Great Events from History: The Eighteenth Century, 1701-1800:* March 20, 1750-March 14, 1752: Johnson Issues *The Rambler*; 1792: Wollstonecraft Publishes *A Vindication of the Rights of Woman*.

GRANVILLE SHARP
English social reformer

A Radical pamphleteer who championed several humanitarian causes, Sharp had his greatest success in securing the abolition of the slave trade.

Born: November 10, 1735; Durham, England
Died: July 6, 1813; Fulham, England
Areas of achievement: Social reform, law, religion and theology

EARLY LIFE

Granville Sharp's father was Thomas Sharp, archdeacon of Northumberland; his grandfather was John Sharp, archbishop of York. There were fourteen children in the family. Granville was the youngest of nine sons. His older brothers went to Cambridge and entered the professions; Granville's formal education was slim by comparison. He did attend Durham Grammar School but began work at age fifteen when he was apprenticed to a linen draper in London, where two of his older brothers worked at the time. Here, he continued his education by teaching himself Greek and Hebrew.

Sharp was always more interested in religion than business. He obtained a clerical post in the ordinance department in 1758 and in 1764 moved to the minuting branch as a clerk in ordinary. With more time to write, he now began his long career as a pamphleteer. His first pamphlet dealt with an interpretation of the Old Testament as presented by Benjamin Kennicott. Sharp took issue with Kennicott, who had stated that names and numbers in the text were unreliable. Sharp was an Evangelical Christian, a fundamentalist who objected to the claims of the rationalists on the one hand and the Roman Catholics on the other. He was one of the founders of the British and Foreign Bible Society in 1804 and the Society for the Conversion of the Jews in 1808. In spite of his great interest in religion, Sharp never took orders, although he was offered a living in Nottinghamshire in 1767.

LIFE'S WORK

Sharp's main claim to fame grew out of his involvement in the movement to abolish slavery, another humanitarian interest of the British Evangelicals. Jonathan Strong, a black teenager found in the London streets by Sharp, brought national attention to the issue of slavery. Strong had been beaten by his master, David Lisle, a lawyer and planter who had brought him from Barbados as a slave. Sharp and his brothers provided for Strong while he recovered his health, but they were then charged with depriving the owner of his property. This forced Sharp to begin a study of law and to write one of the seminal pamphlets of the abolitionist movement, *A Representation of the Injustice and Dangerous Tendency of Tolerating Slavery* (1769). It was a brilliant legal and moral argument that applied to many cases similar to that of Strong, who never fully recovered from the beating Lisle had given him and died a few years later. Sharp was obsessed with the need to get a decisive ruling, and this came with the case of James Somersett, a runaway slave who was recaptured and was about to be taken from England to Jamaica. The case was tried by William Murray, the first earl of Mansfield, and the famous June, 1772, decision was that Somersett, although legally a slave in the colonies, could not be taken by force from England.

The decision in the Somersett case was a great victory for Sharp but not the end of slavery in Great Britain. The courts were still not in sympathy with the abolitionists. Much more work needed to be done, and Sharp remained part of the effort as chairman of the Society for the Abolition of Slavery, founded in 1787. Sharp was also involved with the Sierra Leone scheme to resettle some of London's poor blacks in West Africa. One of the towns in Sierra Leone was to be named Granvilletown, but the project ended in disaster. Of several hundred blacks who left England in 1787, only one-fourth were still alive a year later. These survivors were saved by provisions sent out by Sharp in 1788, but the colony, even under Governor Clarkson, brother of the abolitionist Thomas Clarkson, was not to prosper.

Fears engendered by the French Revolution and the revolt of the Haitian blacks in the 1790's delayed the reform movement at all levels. Success came gradually on the slavery issue. In 1792, the House of Commons voted overwhelmingly for the eventual abolition of the slave trade, and in 1807 victory was realized when the slave trade was abolished. Sharp was not directly involved in the parliamentary maneuvering that brought this about, but he was clearly part of the moral crusade that prepared the groundwork for this legislation.

In addition to his role in ending the slave trade, Sharp was active in the cause of parliamentary reform and sided with the American colonists in their struggle for independence. He was a backward-looking Radical in the sense that he found medieval precedents, the Anglo-Saxon frankpledge and tithings, for parliamentary reform and the American position in their dispute with England. To

promote his ideas and disengage himself from the government of George III, he resigned his position in the ordinance department and joined the Society for Constitutional Information. His pamphlet *A Declaration of the People's Natural Right to a Share in the Legislature* (1774) was an argument for colonial representation, and his *Address to the People* (1778) denounced the Lord North ministry and asked for political reform in England, especially annual parliaments. The latter idea was carried further in his *A Defense of the Right of the People to Elect Representatives for Every Session of Parliament* (1780). Sharp's interest in reform was clear, but he did not work well with others. Christopher Wyvill and the Yorkshire Association, for example, had declared themselves in favor of triennial parliaments, but Sharp refused any bids for unity on this issue. He also opposed some of the points such as universal manhood suffrage, which had been adopted by many of the leading Radicals. Sharp did support equal electoral districts modeled on the Anglo-Saxon divisions but could find no historical precedents for universal suffrage.

The Gordon Riots of 1780 shocked London, and within the decade came the violence of the French Revolution. These events turned many in England away from political reform. Sharp, however, was not deterred by

Granville Sharp. (Library of Congress)

these events and continued to write for the cause of parliamentary reform, but with little success. Unlike the members of the London Corresponding Society, Sharp was not persecuted by the Pitt government, perhaps because the government knew that he, unlike Thomas Paine, had a very limited audience.

Sharp's interest in reform was wide-ranging, but his turgid style made his pamphlets nearly unreadable. His greatest success was as an abolitionist. In addition to his efforts against the slave trade, he was active in General James Edward Oglethorpe's crusade against press gangs and the efforts to abolish the impressment of seamen. His pamphlet *On Duelling* (1790) called for the end of this practice of settling disputes or avenging honor. These were matters for the courts and the law.

At times, Sharp seems more the conservative than the radical. This is particularly true in the area of religion, where he remained throughout his reforming years a devout and orthodox member of the Church of England. He was also the first chairman of the Protestant Union and consistent in opposing Catholic emancipation. At the close of the American Revolution, he corresponded with Benjamin Franklin and John Jay and worked with Thomas Secker, the archbishop of Canterbury, to bring about the introduction of episcopacy in America.

Sharp's interest in biblical scholarship continued throughout his adult life. His most important contribution was to the study of the New Testament. The pamphlet *Remarks on the Uses of the Definitive Article in the Greek Text of the New Testament* (1798) established what is known as Granville Sharp's canon and was an important reference in the debate about the theological position of the Unitarians. The rule in translation, as put by Sharp, was that in references to "our God and Lord Jesus Christ," "God" and "Jesus" are one and the same. Sharp was a rigid Trinitarian and regarded the Unitarians as heretics. He also put a great emphasis on the prophecies of the Bible, especially those in the books of Daniel and Revelations.

Sharp never married but lived in his last years at the home of his sister-in-law in Fulham. He died there on July 6, 1813, and was buried in the family vault.

SIGNIFICANCE

The American Revolution and English reform ran together in the reign of George III. Granville Sharp was one of the English Radicals who saw the two causes as one. The solution in both cases rested with the historic English constitutional system and the common law. The English constitution in turn rested on religious foundations. The frankpledge structure, for example, was, according to Sharp, derived from the teachings of Moses and was introduced into England in the time of King Alfred. Slavery was abhorrent to both Christian principles and was, according to Sharp, an institution unknown in English law. Sharp worked for and lived to see the end of England's participation in the slave trade but not the end of slavery, which was abolished by the 1833 Act of Parliament, twenty years after his death.

He witnessed the success of the Americans in the Revolutionary War but would have preferred concessions to the American colonists to avoid the conflict. Parliamentary reform was not yet a major political movement in his lifetime, and his call for annual parliaments was never to be realized. Sharp expended his energies on too many causes and lacked the temperament of a fiery Radical, but his sense of justice was profound. A memorial placed by the African Institution in Poets' Corner, Westminster Abbey, has an inscription noting that "he was incessant in his labours to improve the condition of mankind."

—*Norbert Gossman*

FURTHER READING

Armstrong, Anthony. *The Church of England, the Methodists, and Society, 1700-1850*. London: University of London Press, 1973. An excellent introduction to the religious revival in the Church of England at the end of the eighteenth century. A good background for the humanitarian reforms of Sharp and the other Evangelical leaders.

Bonwick, Colin C. *English Radicals and the American Revolution*. Chapel Hill: University of North Carolina Press, 1977. A well-integrated discussion of English Radicalism and the movement for parliamentary reform during the revolutionary era. Sharp receives major attention with his interest in abolition and his correspondence with Benjamin Franklin and Benjamin Rush before and after the American War of Independence.

Fryer, Peter. *Staying Power: The History of Black People in Britain*. London: Pluto Press, 1984. Provides excellent background material on slavery in Great Britain and includes a good summary of Sharp's role in the Somersett case, which led to the abolition of the slave trade and finally to the abolition of slavery in the British Empire.

Gerzina, Gretchen. *Black England: Life Before Emancipation*. London: J. Murray, 1995. Gerzina offers a different perspective of the abolition movement by viewing it through the eyes of black people living in eighteenth century England. She questions the motives and commitment of some of the white abolitionists, arguing, for example, that Sharp probably did not believe in racial equality.

Hochschild, Adam. *Bury the Chains: Prophets and Rebels in the Fight to Free an Empire's Slaves.* Boston: Houghton Mifflin, 2005. A history of the British abolition movement, including the role of Sharp and others in founding the Society for the Abolition of Slavery. Sharp's participation in the abolition movement is prominently featured; there is information about his personality, eccentricity, legal career, and his dream of founding a colony of free blacks in Africa.

Lascelles, Edward. *Granville Sharp and the Freedom of Slaves in England.* London: Oxford University Press, 1928. A well-written, brief account of Sharp's many interests in philanthropy and reform, with an emphasis on the issue of slavery.

Stuart, Charles. *A Memoir of Granville Sharp.* New York: American Anti-Slavery Society, 1836. A tribute to Sharp written by an American abolitionist. This is more of an antislavery tract for the movement in America than a biography, but it does provide some insights into Sharp's moral objections to slavery.

Wise, Steven M. *Though the Heavens May Fall: The Landmark Trial That Led to the End of Human Slavery.* Cambridge, Mass.: Da Capo Press, 2005. Recounts the trial of James Somersett. Includes information about Sharp's role in the trial, his legal arguments to challenge slavery, and his legal career.

See also: Benjamin Banneker; First Baron Erskine; Benjamin Franklin; George III; John Jay; First Earl of Mansfield; Nanny; James Edward Oglethorpe; Guillaume-Thomas Raynal; Paul Revere; Benjamin Rush; Samuel Sewall; Toussaint Louverture; Phillis Wheatley.

Related articles in *Great Events from History: The Eighteenth Century, 1701-1800:* 18th century: Expansion of the Atlantic Slave Trade; April 6, 1712: New York City Slave Revolt; April 14, 1775: Pennsylvania Society for the Abolition of Slavery Is Founded; July 2, 1777-1804: Northeast States Abolish Slavery; June 2-10, 1780: Gordon Riots; April 12, 1787: Free African Society Is Founded.

DANIEL SHAYS
American farmer and rebel leader

In 1786-1787, Shays led farmers in a rebellion against the state government of Massachusetts, protesting unfair debtor laws and inequitable taxation. The rebellion raised fears of anarchy among political leaders throughout the United States, motivating them to meet in Philadelphia, where they would draft the U.S. Constitution.

Born: c. 1747; probably in Hopkinton, Massachusetts
Died: September 29, 1825; Sparta, New York
Areas of achievement: Social reform, business, military, government and politics

EARLY LIFE
Daniel Shays began life in obscurity, born to Patrick and Margaret Shays. For the first thirty years of his life, he remained relatively anonymous; like his father before him, he eked out an existence as a farmer in the Massachusetts countryside. However, in April, 1775, when Paul Revere rode from Boston to warn fellow patriots that the British were on the march, Shays grabbed his musket and stepped from the shadows of anonymity. He fought in the Battle of Lexington and Concord and then joined fifteen thousand militiamen in Boston, where he participated in the Battle of Bunker Hill.

Having survived these two encounters with the British army, a point when many returned to their farms, Shays once again shouldered his musket. This time he headed north, where he served at Fort Ticonderoga, witnessed the surrender of British general John Burgoyne's army at Saratoga, and joined in George Washington's night raid on the redcoats at Stony Point, New York, in July of 1779. Shays was not one to back away from a fight.

After five years of service in the war for independence, Shays resigned from the army with an honorable record. He had attained the rank of captain in the Massachusetts militia and earned a reputation for bravery and leadership. The Massachusetts farmer had even caught the attention of the marquis de Lafayette, who presented Shays with an honorary sword before his return to civilian life in 1780. Shays remained a fervent patriot until the end of the war in 1783. He made a significant contribution to American independence through his service in battle, his leadership, and his political activism, and in the process, he became a hero among neighbors and friends.

LIFE'S WORK

The Revolutionary War record of Daniel Shays was admirable, but he remains best known for his role in a rebellion that precipitated the 1787 Constitutional Convention, where representatives drafted the U.S. Constitution. The rebellion began in the western reaches of Massachusetts, where Shays had returned to farm and family after the war. A slumping postwar economy devastated New England and created a credit shortage as European merchants demanded payment in specie, or coin money, from American wholesalers and importers. This stipulation initiated a chain reaction throughout the Massachusetts economy, forcing merchants in Boston and other seaports to call in debts from shopkeepers, who themselves were strapped for hard-to-come-by gold and silver. For relief, the shop owners turned to their customers, men such as Shays who bought much on credit, paid debts in kind—a bushel of potatoes or a jug of corn liquor—and rarely saw a piece of gold.

The Massachusetts government rubbed salt in the region's economic wounds by enacting high land taxes that fell most heavily on the agrarian west. Like merchants and shopkeepers, tax collectors required payment in specie. Unable to satisfy their creditors, hard-pressed farmers in the west increasingly found themselves in front of a judge's bench, where many lost their farms or endured the humiliation of debtors' prison. By 1786, Shays had seen too many of his neighbors and friends suffer at the hands of the courts. No longer could he sit idly by as inequitable laws destroyed all they had fought for in the revolution and the lives they had built since.

As early as 1784, farmers in western Massachusetts challenged the state government by drawing upon their prewar experience of protesting against a tyrannical British monarchy. They organized county committees to present a united front and to forward petitions to Governor James Bowdoin and the legislature in Boston. In 1786, when their energies produced nothing but contempt from their wealthier eastern neighbors, Shays decided the time for petitions had passed. Early that year, he began to organize and train like-minded men in the use of arms. By June, the movement had grown, with Shays and others leading bands of disgruntled farmers to

county courthouses with the intent of shutting them down to prevent further judgments against their neighbors. Surprisingly, no blood was shed that year even though the governor had organized an army of 4,400 men with Revolutionary War general Benjamin Lincoln in command. Soon after the first of the year, however, the crackle of musket fire broke the cold silence of more than one wintry Massachusetts day.

Shays realized that without adequate weapons the rebellion had little chance of success; he therefore decided, along with other rebel leaders, to attack and seize the federal arsenal at Springfield. Their strategy was complex, requiring three companies of insurgents to attack the well-guarded arsenal simultaneously from different directions. For the untrained and undisciplined farmers, the plan proved too difficult. On January 25, 1787, one company failed to attack on time, allowing the government's army to concentrate its entire firepower on Shays and his fifteen hundred men. The rebel attack rapidly disintegrated in the face of two cannon firing grapeshot. Fleeing from Springfield with General Lincoln in hot pursuit, the insurgents made their way to Petersham, where they were overtaken by Lincoln's men. On February 2, shots again rang out, and Shays's men, able to offer only meager resistance, continued their retreat. The beleaguered rebels headed for Sheffield and set up camp in a heavy snowstorm; they hoped they were at least temporarily beyond the reach of the governor's army.

General Lincoln, however, a tough old warrior, proved to be a tenacious adversary. He drove his troops through the blizzard and at dawn on February 27 surprised Shays and the remainder of his men. A brief but intense skirmish ensued. When the sun finally burned off the haze of fog and smoke, thirty rebels lay dead or injured and the rest were on the run. Three of Lincoln's men were dead; the wounds of others stained the snow. Shays's Rebellion was over.

Following their defeat at Sheffield, the insurgents scattered across western Massachusetts, Vermont, and New York. Most of the rebels, with the exception of a handful of their leaders, including Shays, received a general pardon from Governor Bowdoin and returned to the quiet of their farms. An improving economy alleviated the most severe economic pressures on the westerners, but they continued to battle the easterners in the courts and by joining the anti-Federalist fight against the ratification of the new Constitution. Shays fled to Vermont after the skirmish at Sheffield. The Massachusetts Supreme Court condemned him to death for his part in the rebellion but later granted him a pardon in 1788. He eventually settled in Sparta, New York, where in 1818 he was granted a pension for his service in the Revolutionary War. Shays died September 25, 1825, still averring that the rebellion he helped lead some three decades earlier was motivated not by a wish to overthrow legitimate authority but by a desire to regain the rights and liberties he and others had fought to preserve in the American Revolution.

SIGNIFICANCE

Whether Daniel Shays was a patriotic hero fighting to defend revolutionary ideals or a rebellious subversive plotting to overthrow a legitimately elected government, the significance of the rebellion that bears his name became evident even as some combatants were still nursing their wounds. The rebellion caught the attention of political leaders throughout the nation and contributed to their increasing uneasiness over the future of the United States.

These leaders were already suffering a crisis of confidence in the new government. The Articles of Confederation had failed to provide the nation sufficient power and authority to oversee even the most basic necessities of governing—the authority to regulate commerce, the power to tax, and the ability to maintain civil order. Although state representatives had already agreed to meet in Philadelphia to address these inadequacies, the uprising by farmers such as Shays galvanized proponents of a stronger central government. The Massachusetts rebellion demonstrated the inability of individual states to enforce legally adopted statutes and revealed the impotence of the national government to confront and control outbreaks of civil unrest.

Delegates to the Constitutional Convention arrived in Philadelphia with fresh fears of a Shays-like individual leading a mob against legal authority and order on their own frontiers. Consequently, they took steps to ensure that the new federal government would be prepared to deal with future rebellions. The convention granted Congress the power to call forth the militia to suppress civil disorder and to raise and maintain a regular army. Once the convention adjourned and representatives returned to their home states, Shays's Rebellion became a significant issue in the ratification debates. Proponents of the Constitution pointed to the rebellion as a harbinger of future disorders if Americans turned their backs on the work of the Philadelphia Convention and opted to continue under the ineffective Articles of Confederation. Fears of another Shays leading an insurrection became a

contributing factor in the ratification of the Constitution in 1789. Although Shays and his fellow insurgents did not single-handedly cause delegates to discard the Articles of Confederation, they did create an atmosphere conducive to the formation and ratification of a new, stronger federal system of government.

—*Harry S. Laver*

FURTHER READING

Brown, Richard D. "Shays's Rebellion and Its Aftermath: A View from Springfield, Massachusetts, 1787." *William and Mary Quarterly* 40 (October, 1983): 598-615. A contemporary account of the rebellion attributed to the Reverend Bezaleel Howard of Springfield, relating the role of Shays and other leaders in the rebellion.

_____. "Shays's Rebellion and the Ratification of the Federal Constitution in Massachusetts." In *Beyond Confederation: Origins of the Constitution and American National Identity*, edited by Richard Beeman et al. Chapel Hill: University of North Carolina Press, 1987. Brown examines the effects of Shays's activities on the Massachusetts ratification debates. According to Brown, the state government's harsh reaction against the rebels motivated the anti-Federalist forces, making the vote on ratification far closer than Federalists expected.

Gross, Robert A., ed. *In Debt to Shays: The Bicentennial of an Agrarian Rebellion*. Charlottesville: University Press of Virginia, 1993. This anthology contains a number of analytical essays assessing the influence of the rebellion on various aspects of American life in the early nineteenth century. Topics include how class tensions and economics contributed to the rebellion, how the rebellion affected local and national politics, and the ramifications of the violence on Massachusetts society.

Richards, Leonard L. *Shays's Rebellion: The American Revolution's Final Battle*. Philadelphia: University of Pennsylvania Press, 2002. Richards takes exception to historians who maintain the rebellion was a revolt by poor, indebted farmers. He argues that the rebels generally were not poor and that historians have misunderstood the true causes of the revolt. The book examines those causes and the long-term consequences of the rebellion.

Szatmary, David P. *Shays' Rebellion: The Making of an Agrarian Insurrection*. Amherst: University of Massachusetts Press, 1980. This thorough account of Shays's Rebellion provides an extensive discussion of the social and economic context of the revolt, of the progression of events from the initial protests to Shays's exile and death, and of the rebellion's significance in precipitating the Constitutional Convention.

See also: Ethan Allen; François Quesnay; Paul Revere; Roger Sherman; George Washington.

Related articles in *Great Events from History: The Eighteenth Century, 1701-1800:* April 19, 1775: Battle of Lexington and Concord; July 4, 1776: Declaration of Independence; March 1, 1781: Ratification of the Articles of Confederation; September 17, 1787: U.S. Constitution Is Adopted.

RICHARD BRINSLEY SHERIDAN
Irish playwright and politician

Although he devoted most of his life to politics, Sheridan is remembered primarily for writing a handful of comic plays, most notably The School for Scandal. *He also won recognition for a stirring speech in the British parliament calling for the impeachment of Warren Hastings, the governor general of India.*

Born: November 4, 1751 (baptized); Dublin, Ireland
Died: July 7, 1816; London, England
Also known as: Richard Brinsley Butler Sheridan (full name)
Areas of achievement: Literature, government and politics

EARLY LIFE

The exact date of Richard Brinsley Sheridan's birth is not known, but he was christened on November 4, 1751. His father, Thomas Sheridan, a godson of the writer Jonathan Swift, was an actor, a theater manager, and a teacher of elocution, while his mother, Frances Chamberlaine Sheridan, wrote novels and plays.

Richard spent much of his childhood separated from his parents. They twice moved to London, leaving him behind in Dublin, where in 1758-1759 he studied at a grammar school run by Samuel Whyte. In the fall of 1759, he rejoined his parents in London, but three years later he was sent to Harrow school as a boarder. While he was at Harrow, his parents and the rest of his family (a brother and two sisters) moved to France, so he did not see them, even on holidays. As a result, he felt lonely and neglected, and he was teased at school for being the son of an actor, acting being a far from respectable profession in those days.

After his mother's death in 1766, his father and the rest of the family returned to England, and Richard rejoined them, first in London and then in the resort town of Bath in 1770. In Bath, Richard met the singer Elizabeth Linley, who was performing at his father's Attic Entertainments, and he became romantically involved with her. Richard's involvement with Elizabeth led to a number of dramatic adventures. He fought two duels over her with a rival suitor, and in 1772 he ran off with her to France. According to some accounts, they were married there, but they did not live together at this time when they first returned to England. They did marry in England in 1773 despite opposition from both fathers. An estrangement resulted between Richard and his father, and they never fully reconciled.

LIFE'S WORK

After leaving Harrow, Richard Brinsley Sheridan wrote stories, essays, and plays, and he made plans for a satirical newspaper. He collaborated with a Harrow friend, Nathaniel Halhed, on a comic play called *Jupiter* or *Ixion*. It was not produced or published, but the two did publish a translation of a set of Greek love poems called *The Love Epistles of Aristaenetus*, in 1771. Also in 1771, Sheridan published a satirical poem called "The Ridotto of Bath" and another poem, "Clio's Protest," which contained a memorable line about easy writing making for hard reading.

Although he studied briefly to become a lawyer, Sheridan decided that he could better distinguish himself in the theatrical world, and at the age of twenty-three he saw his first successful play, *The Rivals*, produced at Covent Garden Theatre in London. Its first performance, on January 17, 1775, was not successful, so Sheridan withdrew it, revised it, and then turned it into a popular triumph when it returned to the stage on January 28. In November of the same year, he had a second success with the comic opera *The Duenna: Or, The Double Elopement* (pb. 1776).

Sheridan's greatest literary success came with his comedy *The School for Scandal*, which opened at Lon-

A poster advertising Sheridan's play The School for Scandal. *(Library of Congress)*

don's Drury Lane Theatre on May 8, 1777. There was such a roar of applause in the famous screen scene in act four that a passerby thought the theater was falling down. For the rest of the century, it was the most often performed play in London. Sheridan wrote one more successful play, *The Critic: Or, A Tragedy Rehearsed* (pr. 1779, pb. 1781), then virtually abandoned play writing, though he remained involved in the theatrical world. In 1776, he became part owner of the Drury Lane Theatre, and he was closely involved in its management until 1809, when it burned down.

In 1780, Sheridan embarked on yet another career. Already associated with the radical section of the Whig Party, led by Charles James Fox, Sheridan in that year was elected to the British House of Commons as the member of Parliament (MP) for Stafford. He served as an MP, mostly on the opposition side, for thirty-two years and distinguished himself as an excellent speaker. His most notable speech was a condemnation (in 1787) of Warren Hastings, the former governor general of India, for corruption. His four speeches the following year during Hastings's trial earned him further acclaim.

As a politician, Sheridan devoted himself to defending civil liberties and promoting electoral reform. Though a Protestant, he spoke strongly in favor of ending discrimination against Catholics and also spoke on the side of the Irish, the people of India, and the Americans in their struggles against British rule. He also supported the French Revolution.

He briefly served in three Whig governments, as undersecretary of state for northern development in 1782, as secretary to the treasury in 1783, and as treasurer of the British navy in 1806, but he was never given a seat in cabinet or a leadership position, in part because he was too independent for the party leaders. His social status as the son of an actor may also have been a factor for his fellow Whigs, most of whom had aristocratic backgrounds.

Throughout his life Sheridan was notorious for his womanizing and drinking as well as for being constantly in debt. His first wife, who nearly left him over his love affairs, died in 1792. His second wife, whom he married in 1795, was Esther Ogle, daughter of the dean of Winchester; Esther almost left Sheridan as well. When

Sheridan lost his seat in Parliament in 1812, he lost his immunity to imprisonment for debt and was arrested at least once. He was almost arrested for debt again on his deathbed, but his doctor would not allow the sheriff to remove him.

Without money and with the disappearance of his health, looks, theater, and parliamentary seat, he was often referred to as "Poor Sheridan." People spoke of the wreck of his life, but he had a grand funeral, attended by notables and aristocrats, and was buried in Poets' Corner in Westminster Abbey.

SIGNIFICANCE

Richard Brinsley Sheridan's main aim in life was to make a name for himself as a gentleman, and to do this he had decided that politics was a better path to follow than being a dramatist. Despite his theatrical associations, he shared the view of his day: The theater was a low place.

Yet, with the possible exception of his speech on the impeachment of Warren Hastings, it is his comic plays and not his political activities for which Sheridan is remembered. He is considered one of the greatest comic dramatists of his era, an heir to Restoration comic writers such as William Congreve, though toning down the cynical licentiousness of the seventeenth century Restoration and combining it with the more sentimental approach of the late eighteenth century.

Sheridan's literary achievements include the creation of Mrs. Malaprop, a character in *The Rivals* whose name has become a term ("malaprop" or "malapropism") for the misuse of language. He is also remembered for his sparkling, witty dialogue and for characters such as Lady Teazle and the Surface brothers in *The School for Scandal*, a play notable for its famous screen scene, in which the falling down of a literal screen symbolizes the exposure of hypocrisy that is one of the play's themes.

In the end, Sheridan's thirty-two years in Parliament may not even have won him the social status he sought, but his five years as a playwright ensured him lasting distinction.

—Sheldon Goldfarb

FURTHER READING

Auburn, Mark S. *Sheridan's Comedies: Their Contexts and Achievements*. Lincoln: University of Nebraska Press, 1977. Analyzes Sheridan's plays and places them in their eighteenth century context.

Durant, Jack D. *Richard Brinsley Sheridan*. Boston: Twayne, 1975. Mostly an analysis of the plays, but also provides a brief biographical sketch, a useful chronology, and a bibliography.

Gibbs, Lewis. *Sheridan: His Life and His Theatre*. London: Dent, 1947. Good biographical study including sophisticated analyses of Sheridan's character and the nature of his achievements. Includes illustrations and a bibliography.

Kelly, Linda. *Richard Brinsley Sheridan: A Life*. London: Sinclair-Stevenson, 1997. A full-scale biography focusing more on Sheridan's political career than his theatrical life. Includes illustrations and a bibliography.

Loftis, John. *Sheridan and the Drama of Georgian England*. Cambridge, Mass.: Harvard University Press, 1977. An analysis of Sheridan's plays in their eighteenth century context. Includes discussion of Sheridan's literary reputation.

Morwood, James. *The Life and Works of Richard Brinsley Sheridan*. Edinburgh: Scottish Academic Press, 1985. A short but insightful biography linking Sheridan's life to his plays. Includes illustrations and a bibliography.

Morwood, James, and David Crane, eds. *Sheridan Studies*. New York: Cambridge University Press, 1995. A collection of short essays on various aspects of Sheridan's life and work.

O'Toole, Fintan. *A Traitor's Kiss: The Life of Richard Brinsley Sheridan*. London: Granta, 1997. A full-scale biography focusing on Sheridan's Irish connections and his radical politics.

See also: Fanny Abington; Joseph Addison; Georgiana Cavendish; Hannah Cowley; Daniel Defoe; First Baron Erskine; Charles James Fox; David Garrick; Henry Grattan; Warren Hastings; Henry Pelham; Richard Steele.

Related articles in *Great Events from History: The Eighteenth Century, 1701-1800:* March 1, 1711: Addison and Steele Establish *The Spectator*; December 7, 1732: Covent Garden Theatre Opens in London.

ROGER SHERMAN
American politician

Sherman's political wisdom and facility for compromise helped create the U.S. Constitution. His idea for a Congress of two houses led to the formation of the House of Representatives and the Senate, and he was instrumental in the establishment of the electoral college. He also served ably as a colonial leader in Connecticut during the American Revolution.

Born: April 19, 1721; Newton, Massachusetts
Died: July 23, 1793; New Haven, Connecticut
Areas of achievement: Government and politics, law

EARLY LIFE

Roger Sherman was the second son born to William Sherman and Mehetabel Wellington Sherman; their family later grew to include seven children. The infant Roger was named for Roger Wellington, his maternal great-grandfather. The Sherman family had first arrived in America in 1636 when their ancestor, Captain John Sherman, migrated from Essex, England, to Watertown, Massachusetts.

In 1723, William Sherman moved his young family to a section of Dorchester, Massachusetts, that was incorporated as Stoughton in 1726. It was there that Roger Sherman was reared. He was taught by his father to be a cobbler, or shoemaker, and they also farmed the family land together. The latter work required Roger's full attention in the spring and summer months. When winter approached, he attended a one-room school located a mile and a quarter from his home. The education the boy received there was rudimentary, but he improved on it himself. When he traveled from house to house with his cobbler's tools, he also took along books to read while he made or repaired shoes. One of his earliest interests was mathematics; he also read widely in law, astronomy, history, philosophy, and theology. The last of these subjects probably became of interest to young Sherman from his association with the Reverend Samuel Dunbar, an influential Congregationalist preacher in Stoughton. Despite his curiosity about theological matters, Sherman did not officially join Dunbar's congregation until he was twenty-one, on March 14, 1742. This delayed declaration of faith was rather unusual in colonial America, where a person's religious affiliation was highly important in the community.

Sherman met his first wife, Elizabeth Hartwell, the daughter of a local church deacon, while he still resided in Stoughton, though Sherman did not marry her until a few years had passed. The death of his father intervened in 1741; Roger Sherman found himself suddenly responsible for the support and education of the younger children in his family. To facilitate family matters, Roger moved to New Milford, Connecticut, in 1742; he accomplished this by walking more than 100 miles from his Massachusetts home. Once in New Milford, he helped his older brother William manage the general store he had already established in that farming community. On November 17, 1749, Roger Sherman married Elizabeth Hartwell. They would have seven children, but only four survived infancy. Elizabeth herself died at age thirty-five in October of 1760.

Sherman had varied interests in his first years in Connecticut. He produced an almanac (modeled after that of Benjamin Franklin) that predicted weather, gave advice to farmers, and quoted proverbs and poetry. Sherman continued this enterprise until 1761. He had found his most lucrative employment in 1745, when he was appointed as land surveyor for New Haven County, receiving this position for his superb mathematical ability. At this time, surveyors were at a premium in the colonies, and so, when Litchfield County was formed in northwestern Connecticut in 1752, Sherman became its surveyor as well. Because of these jobs, he was able to speculate in real estate dealings, much to his success. Also, his work in court to defend the land boundaries of plaintiffs drew Sherman more into an interest in law. He read more intensely in the law during these years, and in February of 1754, he was admitted to the bar. Because of his growing popularity and reputation for fairness, New Milford's citizens began electing Sherman to a series of political offices. He served on their grand jury, as selectman, as justice of the peace, and finally, as their delegate to the Connecticut General Assembly.

LIFE'S WORK

Roger Sherman's life in New Milford, however, despite his popularity, became increasingly difficult after the death of his wife in 1760. The following year, he decided to move to New Haven, where he established a general store next to Yale College. Because of his proximity to the college and local churches, Sherman sold many books; some of his best customers were students and ministers. Sherman's devotion to reading increased at this time, and he also began to take more of an interest in colonial politics. Sherman was still serving as a delegate to the Connecticut General Assembly, a position he first held in 1755 and (except for the years of 1756-1757) would continue to hold until 1761. In 1759, he had also been named a justice of the County Court of Litchfield. In 1766, he was appointed a judge in the State Superior Court of Connecticut. Connecticut's original charter from England had granted the colony the most carefully structured and autonomous government enjoyed by any colony. This is a fact that Sherman cherished and that he put to work in his later dealings in the congresses of the emerging nation.

Although Sherman's record as an officeholder in Connecticut's distinct government seems impressive in itself, his most valuable contributions to American society were yet to be made. With his selection to the First Continental Congress in August of 1774, his work as one of the Founding Fathers of the United States truly began. He served diligently in this congress, even though he was one of the oldest delegates. Sherman was also sent to represent Connecticut in the Second Continental Congress, which convened in May of 1775. It was becoming evident by the time of this second congress that a war for independence from England was inevitable for the thirteen colonies. Shots had been fired in Massachusetts between British redcoats and colonial patriots in April of 1775.

In this second congress, Sherman served on a committee of five men who drafted the Declaration of Independence, although most of the actual writing of the document was done by Thomas Jefferson. Once war had been declared, Sherman labored long hours on vital committees managing the revolution. He headed efforts to raise $10 million to fund the war, and he organized the purchase of the colonial army's supplies.

In his home state of Connecticut, Sherman also served on the Council of Safety during these years, and he stockpiled munitions at his New Haven store for the army. While at home in New Haven, he founded the New Haven Foot Guards, a unit of militiamen drawn together to defend the

city and its residents. Despite these efforts, Sherman's house, as well as his son's, was raided by the British in an attack on New Haven in 1779.

Yet Sherman was not too weighed down by the burdens of his war work. He also enjoyed a happy family life. On May 12, 1763, he had married a beautiful young woman, Rebecca Prescott of Danvers, Massachusetts. Together they had eight children who kept Sherman's home life joyful and lively. One pretty young daughter's quick wit was commented on by a guest at their home: General George Washington.

Sherman, in the area of law and political compromise (an art he perfected), was to play an important role in the founding of the nation that Washington's army had fought to achieve. At the war's end, the thirteen colonies were rather loosely bound together by the Articles of Confederation, which Sherman had also worked to establish in the Grand Committee of the Continental Con-

---

LIMITING THE POWER OF THE U.S. PRESIDENT

Roger Sherman was influential in the crafting of several major documents during the revolutionary period of U.S. history. He corresponded with other Constitutional Convention delegates about the ideal composition of the federal government and its branches. In the excerpted letter here, Sherman, writing to John Adams, discusses limiting presidential power for the sake of the people and representative government.

I received your letter of the twentieth instant. I had in mine, of the same date, communicated to you my ideas on that part of the constitution, limiting the president's power of negativing [vetoing] the acts of the legislature; and just hinted some thoughts on the propriety of the provision made for the appointment to offices, which I esteem to be a power nearly as important as legislation.

If that was vested in the president alone, he might, were it not for his periodical election by the people, render himself despotic. It was a saying of one of the kings of England, that while the king could appoint the bishops and judges, he might have what religion and law he pleased. . . .

If the president alone was vested with the power of appointing all officers, and was left to select a council for himself, he would be liable to be deceived by flatterers and pretenders to patriotism, who would have no motive but their own emolument [advantageous compensation]. They would wish to extend the powers of the executive to increase their own importance; and, however upright he might be in his intentions, there would be great danger of his being misled, even to the subversion of the constitution, or, at least, to introduce such evils as to interrupt the harmony of the government, and deprive him of the confidence of the people.

Source: Roger Sherman, "Roger Sherman to John Adams" (July, 1789), document 46, *The Founders' Constitution*, vol. 4. http://press-pubs .uchicago.edu/founders/documents/a2_2_2-3s46.html. Accessed June, 2005.

gress of 1776. It became evident, especially after Shays's Rebellion in Massachusetts in 1786-1787, that a stronger central government was needed; powers the government had to have, such as taxation and the making of treaties, were lacking. Sherman had served as a delegate to the Congress of the Confederation beginning in 1781. Then, he was also elected to represent Connecticut in the Constitutional Convention held in Philadelphia in the summer of 1787. It was there that Sherman made vital political compromises that helped establish the U.S. Constitution. Sherman, representing a middle-sized state, effected a successful compromise over an issue that had deadlocked this convention. He sought to establish a manner of legislative voting that would guarantee large states (such as New York and Virginia) and small states (such as Delaware and Rhode Island) an equal and fair voice in making laws. Sherman suggested the establishment of the two houses of the U.S. Congress as they now exist. The Senate has equal representation for each state, and the House of Representatives has representation proportionate to a state's population. Sherman's compromise was accepted on June 11, 1787; it is known by his name as the Great Compromise, or as the Connecticut Compromise.

Sherman made other contributions to the founding of the American government. He favored the election of the president by the state legislatures, but he did not win this point. When the popular election of the president is held, however, the decisive recorded vote still comes in the electoral college, which Sherman was instrumental in establishing. He was also responsible for the concept of the congressional override on legislative bills vetoed by the president. Sherman also proposed that the trial for a president's impeachment be held in the House and the Senate (instead of in the Supreme Court, as other delegates had suggested).

From records of his service in the various colonial congresses, particularly the Constitutional Convention, one may draw a physical picture and character study of Sherman. His fellow delegates wrote in high praise of his conscientious work but also detailed his awkward physical and vocal mannerisms. From these colonial leaders, one learns that Sherman was a tall man with broad shoulders; he was rugged-looking with a jutting jaw, wide mouth, and deep-socketed, piercing blue eyes, all set in a large head. He wore his brown hair cut close to his head in a conservative style and did not wear a powdered wig as did the men of the colonial aristocracy. Sherman was one of the poorest delegates to the Constitutional Convention; he barely had enough money to feed his children during the difficult inflationary period caused by the war. His poverty and lack of a formal education were always evident in his speech, which contained slang terms and was delivered in a rustic accent.

Nevertheless, no one writing of Sherman for posterity denied his effectiveness as a statesman. He knew how to make his points in debates, and while he spoke very frequently, he was always concise. In committee work and in informal discussions among delegates, Sherman often saw the issues more clearly than anyone else. He had foresight as to what the U.S. Constitution had to include and what it had to avoid; here, he was a great advocate of states' rights. For all of his levelheadedness, earnestness in debate, dedication in his service, and honesty in his dealings, Sherman won the sincere praise of his peers.

Connecticut's citizens returned Sherman to serve as a Congress member in the fall of 1789. He was also appointed to a seat in the Senate in 1791, an office that he held until his death. Sherman died from typhoid fever on the evening of July 23, 1793, in New Haven, Connecticut.

SIGNIFICANCE

Roger Sherman's distinguished career as a colonial political leader and statesman afforded him the title the Great Signer. Because of his almost continual service in the various American congresses, Sherman was the only man to sign all the following major documents: the Articles of Association of 1774, the Declaration of Independence, the Articles of Confederation, the Federal Constitution, the Declaration of Rights, and the Treaty of Paris (with Great Britain).

Sherman also enjoyed a prestigious career as a founding father of New Haven, Connecticut. He was the treasurer of Yale College from 1765 to 1776; in its early years, he often paid the school's bills with his own money to prevent its closing. He was elected the first mayor of New Haven, and while in office (from 1784 until his death), he built new schools and renamed the city streets for American patriots rather than British monarchs. He also built up the city's business and shipping enterprises by offering special loans to new merchants moving into New Haven.

The people of Connecticut expressed their gratitude to Roger Sherman for leading their state out of the struggles of a war for independence into the security of a new nation with a sound and wisely planned government—they named a city after him in 1802 called Sherman, Connecticut.

—Patricia E. Sweeney

FURTHER READING

Beals, Carleton. *Our Yankee Heritage: New England's Contribution to America's Civilization.* New York: David McKay, 1955. Beals's chapter on Sherman, "Shoemaker Statesman," emphasizes the patriot's early life as well as his political career, and provides an analysis of Sherman's character traits. Contains many details of Sherman's personal life not found in other sources.

Berkin, Carol. *A Brilliant Solution: Inventing the American Constitution.* New York: Harcourt, 2002. A brief recounting of the Constitutional Convention, including Sherman's role. The appendix features brief biographies of convention delegates.

Boardman, Roger S. *Roger Sherman: Signer and Statesman.* Philadelphia: University of Pennsylvania Press, 1938. A readable, carefully researched study of Sherman's life and career, with much documentation—such as a full listing of the committees on which he served. Focuses on Sherman's public career rather than his personal life.

Bowen, Catherine D. *Miracle at Philadelphia: The Story of the Constitutional Convention, May to September, 1787.* Boston: Little, Brown, 1966. Bowen describes the daily workings of the Constitutional Convention in great detail. The text is readable and enlightening, and the Founding Fathers are portrayed as having distinct personalities and interests.

Collier, Christopher. *Roger Sherman's Connecticut: Yankee Politics and the American Revolution.* Middletown, Conn.: Wesleyan University Press, 1971. The book's title accurately reflects its dual subjects— Roger Sherman and the Connecticut of his era. Collier notes the lack of personal materials available on Sherman; only his public life is recorded in any detail. Thus, Collier's well-documented study covers the broader range of the statesman in his native state.

Rommel, John G. *Connecticut's Yankee Patriot: Roger Sherman.* Hartford, Conn.: American Bicentennial Commission of Connecticut, 1979. This is a slender but useful volume, prepared as one in a series of historical works on Connecticut topics for the two-hundredth anniversary of the Declaration of Independence. It re-creates Sherman's political career accurately and concisely, concentrating on his work during and after the Revolutionary War.

Rossiter, Clinton. *1787: The Grand Convention.* New York: Macmillan, 1966. A comprehensive, factual account of the 1787 Constitutional Convention, focusing on the delegates and their work. Rossiter also details the later lives of the convention delegates, and he idealizes, to some extent, the Founding Founders.

Van Doren, Carl. *The Great Rehearsal: The Story of the Making and Ratifying of the Constitution of the United States.* New York: Viking Press, 1948. A classic book on the founding of the U.S. government. Since no formal record was kept for much of the 1787 convention, the author works from the diaries and notes of the delegates. Accurate, lively, and interesting narrative, describing the delegates' personalities as well as their contributions to the final document.

See also: Ethan Allen; Benedict Arnold; Benjamin Franklin; Thomas Jefferson; Daniel Shays; George Washington.

Related articles in *Great Events from History: The Eighteenth Century, 1701-1800:* September 5-October 26, 1774: First Continental Congress; April 19, 1775: Battle of Lexington and Concord; May 10-August 2, 1775: Second Continental Congress; July 4, 1776: Declaration of Independence; February 6, 1778: Franco-American Treaties; March 1, 1781: Ratification of the Articles of Confederation; September 3, 1783: Treaty of Paris; September 17, 1787: U.S. Constitution Is Adopted.

SARAH SIDDONS
English actor

Siddons has been acknowledged as England's first great tragic actor. Through her intelligence, talent, and decorum, she became the embodiment of the tragic muse and elevated the work of actor to a position of respectability.

Born: July 5, 1755; Brecon, Brecknockshire, Wales
Died: June 8, 1831; London, England
Also known as: Sarah Kemble (birth name)
Area of achievement: Theater

EARLY LIFE

Sarah Siddons (SIHD-ehnz), born Sarah Kemble, was the eldest of the twelve children of Roger Kemble, an itinerant actor-manager, and Sarah Ward. Kemble ran the traveling Kemble theater company. Presumably on stage at an early age, Sarah's first recorded appearance—which came at age twelve—was as Princess Elizabeth in a production of *Charles I* (1767).

In the Kemble theater company, where Sarah performed her first role, was William Siddons, eleven years older, good-looking and gentlemanly, though not particularly talented as an actor. A relationship developed between William and Sarah, but her parents frowned upon William as a suitor, favoring instead a country squire for their daughter. Sarah was thus sent to the house of the Greatheeds of Warwick, where for the next several years, as a companion to the family, she often read for the elder Greatheed, indulged her passion for John Milton, and learned the graces of eighteenth century life.

Nevertheless, the romance between Sarah and William continued, and her parents finally acquiesced. In October, 1773, Sarah and William were married. The following year they left the Kemble troupe and moved to the theater in Cheltenham, where, in November, at the age of nineteen, Sarah gave birth to a son, Henry.

A company of London aristocrats was much impressed with the young actor playing Belvidera in Thomas Otway's *Venice Preserved* (1774) and recommended her to David Garrick, the manager of London's Drury Lane Theatre. Garrick hired her for the spring, 1776, season. Although thrilled to be working with Garrick, Sarah was not successful. Recovering from the birth of a second child, meeting with hostility from other leading actresses, and cast in inappropriate roles, she spent a miserable six months at Drury Lane. Engaged for the summer in Birmingham but expecting to return to Drury Lane in the fall, the Siddonses were abruptly in-

formed that their services would not be needed. The blow was devastating; Sarah had two infants to support, and an ineffectual husband. She would never forget the degradation she suffered at Garrick's hands or her subsequent loss of confidence.

LIFE'S WORK

Acting at Bath and Bristol for the following six years, Sarah Siddons honed her skills and developed supporters, so that when Garrick recalled her to Drury Lane in 1782, her debut in Thomas Southerne's *Isabella: Or, The Fatal Marriage* was a huge success. Her status was assured, as she had earlier received acclaim as Euphrasia in Arthur Murphy's *The Grecian Daughter* (1777), the title role of Alicia in Nicolas Rowe's *The Tragedy of Jane Shore* (1774) and as Belvidera—favorite roles throughout her career. Between 1778 and 1781, she added William Shakespeare's Isabella in *Measure for Measure* (1604) and Constance in *King John* (c. 1596-1597), as well as Mrs. Beverley in Edward Moore's *The Gamester* (1753).

The great twenty-five-year period of the Kemble family partnership at Drury Lane and later at Covent Garden began with the succession of Siddons's brother, John Philip Kemble, to the management of Drury Lane in 1788. With Siddons and other siblings, the theater achieved a status rarely seen. Siddons was the principal attraction, evoking fainting spells from the women and tears from the men of the audience. Siddons excelled in the role of the suffering woman oppressed by a domineering father or husband and abandoned to poverty or death. On stage she projected majesty, strength, and the passion of the wronged woman, with her expressive eyes and tall and stately figure. In her private life, however, she appeared timid, dependent, and submissive to William, who managed her money, contracts, and engagements, and who evidently resented her exalted position as the years progressed. No doubt the conflict between her professional and domestic lives exacted a toll with which she had to struggle, but the theater was her life and her livelihood.

Siddons's most celebrated role was that of Shakespeare's Lady Macbeth. Her extensive notes about the character offer an almost modern psychological analysis. Siddons sees Lady Macbeth in the early scenes as charming, seductive, and ambitious, but after the murder of Duncan, she begins to experience remorse. She represses these feelings to support Macbeth, whom she loves and wants to protect, but she is gradually overwhelmed by guilt within. For the final performance of her career on June 29, 1812, Siddons chose to play Lady Macbeth, with her brother John in the title role. The applause at the end of the sleepwalking scene was unstoppable. The curtain was dropped, but the applause continued. Finally, Siddons returned, and, after a brief farewell speech, the play was forced to end.

A legend in her own time, Siddons was also aware of her public image. She confessed that she actively sought fame. Portraitists sought her as well, because paintings of the famous were real commodities that could engender publicity for both the artist and the actor. In 1783, Sir Joshua Reynolds began his masterpiece, *Sarah Siddons as the Tragic Muse* (1784), with Siddons as Melpomene. Her celebrity brought eminent friends, among them Samuel Johnson, Horace Walpole, Hester Lynch Piozzi (also known as Mrs. Thrale), and Sir Walter Scott. She was invited frequently to Windsor Castle and Buckingham House (now Buckingham Palace) to read for King George III and Queen Charlotte.

Celebrity had its disadvantages, too. While it assured full houses at Drury Lane and lucrative engagements in Scotland and Ireland during the summers, it also brought requests for benefit performances (unpaid), social engagements (which she usually declined), and pleas for handouts from friends and relatives (which she tried to fulfill).

Although her career was brilliant, her personal life was not without pain. She experienced two miscarriages and the deaths of, first, a six-year-old child and then her two young daughters, Sarah and Maria. Her marriage deteriorated after twenty years, and she suffered frequent periods of ill health, likely brought on by overwork and the stress of supporting her large family. Age was not kind either. She retired in 1812 but returned to the stage several times for special occasions. She lived for nearly twenty years more, seeming rather restless and yearning to recover the strength of her younger years and the excitement of performance. At her death in 1831, five thousand people followed her funeral procession.

SIGNIFICANCE

Sarah Siddons's celebrity has yet to dim; she is still considered the greatest tragic actress that England has ever produced. To her contemporaries her private life was blameless and her artistry unequaled. Many of the roles she played served as models for moral instruction. Into the twenty-first century, she serves as the model of a woman of genius, who, although operating within a patriarchal society, forged an identity that transcended class, gender, and the centuries. The Sarah Siddons Society, founded in Chicago in 1952, awards a yearly statuette in her name to honor great actresses.

—*Joyce E. Henry*

A portrait of Sarah Siddons by Thomas Gainsborough. (Library of Congress)

FURTHER READING

Boaden, James. *Memoirs of Mrs. Siddons: Interspersed with Anecdotes of Authors and Actors.* London: Gibbings, 1893. A rambling, sometimes humorous work written by Siddons's first major biographer, with an informative account of eighteenth century theatrical life.

Booth, Michael R., John Stokes, and Susan Bassnett. *Three Tragic Actresses: Siddons, Rachel, Ristori.* New York: Cambridge

University Press, 1996. The Siddons segment of this three-part, illustrated work presents a new historicist approach with quotations from primary sources. The author locates Siddons within political, social, and cultural contexts.

Donkin, Ellen. "Mrs. Siddons Looks Back in Anger: Feminist Historiography for Eighteenth Century Theater." In *Critical Theory and Performance*, edited by Janelle G. Reinelt and Joseph R. Roach. Ann Arbor: University of Michigan Press, 1992. A feminist perspective on Siddons's strong response to the personal attacks of hostile audiences.

Kelly, Linda. *The Kemble Era: John Philip Kemble, Sarah Siddons, and the London Stage.* New York: Random House, 1980. A well-written dovetailing of the careers of the two famous siblings. Illustrated.

McPherson, Heather. "Picturing Tragedy: 'Mrs. Siddons as the Tragic Muse' Revisited." *Eighteenth Century Studies* 33, no. 3 (2000): 401-430. Considers the relationship between portraiture and the stage as represented by Sir Joshua Reynolds's painting of Siddons as the tragic muse. Illustrated with eight portraits of Siddons by different artists.

Manvell, Roger. *Sarah Siddons: Portrait of an Actress.* New York: G. P. Putnam's Sons, 1971. An excellent account containing earlier biographers' material of Siddons's professional and personal lives. Illustrations, useful appendices, bibliography, and index.

Siddons, Sarah Kemble. *Reminiscences of Sarah Kemble Siddons, 1773-1785.* Edited by William Van Lennep. Cambridge, England: Widener Library, 1942. A very brief (33-page) account in Siddons's own words that begins with her marriage to William Siddons and ends with the Drury Lane season of 1784-1785.

See also: Fanny Abington; Queen Charlotte; Hannah Cowley; David Garrick; George III; Anne Oldfield; Sir John Vanbrugh; Peg Woffington.

Related articles in *Great Events from History: The Eighteenth Century, 1701-1800:* December 7, 1732: Covent Garden Theatre Opens in London; 1742: Fielding's *Joseph Andrews* Satirizes English Society.

SĪDĪ AL-MUKḤṬĀR AL-KUNTĪ
Kunta religious leader and mediator

A brilliant scholar and charismatic preacher, Sīdī al-Mukḥṭār helped to spread Sufi Islamic doctrines through the Sahara and West Africa. He also proved to be an extraordinary mediator, using his prestige to bring an era of peace to the turbulent tribes of the Sahara.

Born: 1729; West Africa (now Mali)
Died: 1811; West Africa
Also known as: Sīdī al-Mukḥṭār al-Kabir
Areas of achievement: Religion and theology, scholarship, diplomacy

EARLY LIFE

Sīdī al-Mukḥṭār al-Kuntī was the most celebrated member of the Kunta, a confederation of related clans who inhabited the central and western Sahara Desert. Although they claimed Arab ancestry, their true origins appear to have been among the Tajakant Berbers of Mauritania. From their earliest history the Kunta were a sacerdotal people who developed a reputation as charismatic preachers. The most noted of Kunta holy men (marabouts or murabitun) were also thought to be miracle workers.

Sīdī al-Mukḥṭār, known as al-Kabir (the Great), was a child prodigy who was said to have humbled the ulama (religious scholars) in intellectual debate. Nevertheless, he had to work his way up the Kunta ranks, starting as a lowly helper-disciple in the salt business at the Taudenni mines. Soon his talents were recognized, and he gained enough influence to be sent to the city of Walata, where he was appointed to the prestigious position of guardian of the tomb of Sidi Ahmad al-Bakkai, his great-grandfather and the most renowned of his immediate ancestors. From there he began to make tours to preach, trade, and settle disputes in the towns and among the tribes of the western desert, the traditional way Kunta marabouts built their reputations. Al-Mukḥṭār's tours were extraordinarily successful; by the time he returned to his family home in the Azawad, an oasis region 150 miles north of Timbuktu, his name was widely known and his retinue of disciples large.

LIFE'S WORK

Sīdī al-Mukḥṭār devoted himself to the most demanding of challenges, the mastery of the Sufi mysteries known as the *mujahadat*, a spiritual quest leading to communion

914

with God, and most of his scholarly work concerned this particular esoteric school of knowledge. By the age of twenty-five, he had become the head of the Qadiriyya brotherhood in the western Sahara and West Africa. His followers believed he had been granted superhuman powers, including the ability to resurrect the dead, read minds, communicate with inanimate objects, fly, leap across large areas, see one hundred miles distant, be in two places at the same time, forestall disasters, and bring rain. Most important, he was thought to be able to ascertain divine truth and to intercede with God on behalf of others. Few religious figures, even those who founded their own religions, have enjoyed such influence in their lifetimes. He was recognized as a *wali*, a living saint, and under him Kunta power reached its height.

If Sīdī al-Mukhṭār did work one real miracle, it was in keeping large parts of the Sahara from falling into total chaos. Like other maraboutic tribes, the Kunta played important roles as mediators and peacemakers. Sometimes they stopped or prevented major wars involving tribe against tribe, confederation against confederation, but more often they were concerned with feuds among clans of a particular tribe or between factions within a town. Sīdī al-Mukhṭār's sacred position placed him above petty politics, or so others assumed, and he was recognized as the supreme arbiter of disputes in much of the Sahara and surrounding areas. He mediated among the warrior tribes of Moors and Tuaregs and sometimes used those who accepted his authority to tame or punish those who did not. In the main, however, the Pax Kunta he established was built on prestige and persuasion rather than force. During his time, from the early seventeenth to the late nineteenth century, the Sahara enjoyed its highest level of security.

One of Sīdī al-Mukhṭār's most impressive political feats was to maintain peace between large and potentially hostile Tuareg confederations. He was friend to the Kel Ahaggar, trusted by the Kel Tadmakkat, and venerated by the Iwillimeden, the most powerful of the southern Tuaregs. In 1771, al-Mukhṭār was successful in mediating a major war between the Kel Tadmakkat and the Arma, a caste of soldiers descended from Moroccan invaders who ruled the city of Timbuktu. In return for a payment in horses, gold, and clothing, the Tuaregs ended their siege, which had driven Timbuktu to the brink of starvation.

Not everyone, however, was pleased with the peace settlement. A group of Arma diehards, who were embarrassed by their side's poor showing in the war, found it convenient to direct their ire against the man who was re-sponsible for ending it. They plotted and may have attempted to assassinate al-Mukhṭār but were not successful for reasons unknown, since all accounts of this incident attribute their failure to supernatural causes.

One faction of Tuaregs who had hoped to plunder Timbuktu was also dissatisfied. This resentment combined with rivalry between chiefs led the Kel Tadmakkat to split into two, then three, groups, leading to civil war in 1777. The neighboring Iwillimeden used the opportunity to intervene, complicating the situation. The war finally ended when Sīdī al-Mukhṭār influenced the Iwillimeden to annihilate the Kel Tadmakkat faction most opposed to him and to reconcile with the faction most favorable to him. This was also the faction most acceptable to the Arma of Timbuktu, and under al-Mukhṭār's guidance all three parties subsequently promoted peaceful commerce. The real victor in these wars turned out to be the peacemaker, Sīdī al-Mukhṭār.

The Kunta believed that wealth was a sign of divine favor, and under Sīdī al-Mukhṭār they became more prosperous than ever. Between 1736 and 1766, the Berabich Moors, who dominated much of the Saharan salt trade, plunged into a series of bloody civil wars that Sīdī al-Mukhṭār ultimately settled. The Berabich proved eternally grateful. Al-Mukhṭār became their spiritual leader and the Kunta their commercial partners. The Kunta also owned plantations in various oases that produced large quantities of dates, grain, and tobacco, and they kept huge herds of pack camels for rent as well as for use in their own enterprises. When the Kunta were not trading themselves, their camels could be seen on the caravan routes carrying merchandise for others. In this way, Sīdī al-Mukhṭār controlled much of the transportation system of the Sahara.

SIGNIFICANCE

Kunta military power, even when heading powerful coalitions, was never strong enough for Sīdī al-Mukhṭār to weld together all of the diverse tribes and cities of the region into one vast theocratic empire under his own rule. He settled instead for playing a significant political role within a larger spiritual domain to ensure his people's economic success. His most lasting commercial accomplishment was in professionalizing trans-Saharan trade by operating through a system of commercial agents rather than using disciples and dependents.

Sīdī al-Mukhṭār's economic and political achievements should not overshadow his most important role, that of holy man. Students, scholars, pilgrims, and even ulamas from Timbuktu and other cities flocked to Azawad to gain knowledge and bask in Sīdī al-Mukhṭār's *baraka* (blessedness). In return, he sent out disciples as missionaries to strengthen Islam, spread the Sufi doctrine, and propagate his own interpretation of mysticism. Other marabouts, even rulers including Usuman dan Fodio, leader of the Fulani jihad that would transform large parts of West Africa, requested his guidance. Through his preaching, teaching, and writing, he instilled new fervor in the devout and renewed new intellectual curiosity among the scholarly.

—*Richard L. Smith*

FURTHER READING

Brett, Michael, and Elizabeth Fentress. *The Berbers*. Oxford, England: Blackwell, 1996. Provides a good explanation of marabouts, saints, baraka, and related matters.

Hiskett, Mervyn. *The Development of Islam in West Africa*. London: Longman, 1984. Has a good overview of the Kunta, including a discussion of Sīdī al-Mukhṭār's relationship to Sufism.

McDougall, E. Ann. "The Economies of Islam in the Southern Sahara: The Rise of the Kunta Clan." In *Rural and Urban Islam in West Africa*, edited by Nehemia Levtzion. Boulder, Colo.: Lynne Rienner, 1986. Explains the commercial success of the Kunta, particularly their role in the salt trade, which provided the material basis for their religious and scholarly activities.

Norris, H. T. *The Arab Conquest of the Western Sahara: Studies of the Historical Events, Religious Beliefs, and Social Customs Which Made the Remotest Sahara a Part of the Arab World*. Harlow, Essex, England: Longman, 1986. A book filled with Saharan history, which includes an examination of Sīdī al-Mukhṭār's relationship to the Iwillimeden.

Webb, James L. A., Jr. *Desert Frontier: Ecological and Economic Change Along the Western Sahel, 1600-1850*. Madison: University of Wisconsin Press, 1995. Provides a larger perspective for the history of the Kunta and related peoples within an environmentalist and economic framework.

Whitecomb, Thomas. "New Evidence on the Origins of the Kunta." *Bulletin of the School of Oriental and African Studies* 38 (1975): 103-123, 403-417. Addresses the questions of how the Kunta should be defined and where they came from.

See also: Mentewab; Mungo Park; Vaḥīd Bihbahānī; Shāh Walī Allāh.

Related article in *Great Events from History: The Eighteenth Century, 1701-1800*: 1760-1776: Caribbean Slave Rebellions.

EMMANUEL-JOSEPH SIEYÈS
French cleric and political theorist

Sieyès's pamphlet What Is the Third Estate? *catapulted him into immediate fame as the leading political influence on the early phases of the French Revolution. He continued to play an important background role in all phases of the revolution, until he was forced into exile following the return of the Bourbon kings in 1815.*

Born: May 3, 1748; Fréjus, France
Died: June 20, 1836; Paris, France
Also known as: Comte Emmanuel-Joseph Sieyès; Abbé Sieyès
Area of achievement: Government and politics

EARLY LIFE

Emmanuel-Joseph Sieyès (ay-ma-nwehl zhoh-zehf syay-yehs) was born into a middle-class family of modest means. Five children were supported by the father's position as postmaster and notary. Emmanuel-Joseph was educated first by a private tutor and then at the Jesuits' College at Fréjus. A bright child, Emmanuel-Joseph came to be noticed by his teachers, ever on the lookout for talented youth who might be trained for clerical careers. Sons of aristocrats were also recruited but were intended for the upper-level positions, such as bishop.

At the age of seventeen, Sieyès entered the Seminary of Saint-Suplice in Paris, where he gained a reputation for intense reading of Enlightenment writers and eclectic interests in art, music, philosophy, and economics. In 1773, at the age of twenty-five, he was ordained as a priest. Talent and a family friendship with the bishop of Fréjus resulted in his appointment in 1775 as secretary to the bishop of Treguier. His career from this point on would be that of an administrative priest. However, other interests were maturing as well.

In 1775, Sieyès wrote "Letter to the Physiocrats on Their Political and Moral System," an unpublished work that examined the political implications of economic activity conducted to foster the well-being of the larger national unit. His intense reading was coupled with prolific writing, yet no effort was made to publish anything until late in 1788. Meanwhile his clerical career advanced in 1784 with his appointment as vicar general and chancellor to the bishop of Chartres (Jean-Baptiste de Lubersac), who, like Sieyès, had a passionate interest in Enlightenment thought. Sieyès became a member of the provincial assembly of Orleans in 1787, a year before the calling of the Estates-General by King Louis XVI, and the publication of a small pamphlet catapulted the relatively unknown Sieyès to the front stage of history.

LIFE'S WORK

Facing a financial crisis of significant proportions, Louis XVI declared on August 8, 1788, that he would convoke the Estates-General on May 1, 1789. This body, which last met in 1614, was composed of three estates (the clergy, the nobles, and the commoners). Each of the three groupings had one vote as an estate. Since the body had not met for 175 years, there was great uncertainty about the role of the Estates-General in French political life. However, it was clear that the privileged and tax-exempt first two estates, with their two votes, would block any reform efforts of the Third Estate (the commoners) to limit their privileges. The situation produced spirited writing and debate in the months preceding the opening meeting of the Estates-General.

Sieyès's first pamphlet, *Essai sur les privilèges* (essay on privileges), published in November, 1788, was an attack on the very existence of privilege as contrary to natural law, reason, and national community. For Sieyès the nobility was anything but noble. Rather, they were parasitic intruders who sapped wealth from the productive part of the community. Important only in their own corrupted self-concept, the privileged were left over from a primitive past with no future as modern society progressed. A second pamphlet, published in December, explained the imperative of transforming the Estates-General into a national assembly representing the productive part of the nation. Both pamphlets helped solidify Sieyès's ideas, published in January, 1789, in his longest and most complex pamphlet, *Qu'est-ce que le*

Emmanuel-Joseph Sieyès. (Library of Congress)

tiers état? (1789; *What Is the Third Estate?*, 1963). No single pamphlet in human history would have a more far-reaching and immediate effect.

In his landmark pamphlet, the single question "What is the Third Estate?" was answered in a single simple word: "everything." The complex theory behind the word was that the Third Estate formed the entire productive part of the nation, and thus it alone could constitute the entire nation. To the follow-up question, "What has the Third Estate been in the past?" came the simple reply: "nothing." The third question, "What does the Third Estate desire?" was answered in the simple phrase "to be something." Hence, in immediate and dramatic fashion, Sieyès set the Third Estate the objective of politically reconstituting France around itself in order to end the irrational and unfair situation of "everything" politically counting for nothing, and the "nothing," or nonproductive part of the nation, counting for everything.

Sieyès's widely discussed pamphlet led to his election as a Third Estate representative from Paris to the Estates-General. Sieyès had moved on June 17, 1789, that the Third Estate declare itself as the national assembly and then to invite the other two estates to join. In spite of the king's opposition to changing the Estates-General, Sieyès helped convince the Third Estate to act as if it were representative of the national will and to begin passing legislation reforming France on a new basis of equality, thereby ending the old order. These efforts rapidly came to fruition by early August with the passage of a constitution for France. As an early influence in what would be termed the French Revolution, Sieyès capitalized on his prestige as a writer. Lack of public speaking skills and a basic shyness precluded his playing a major role as a politician.

As the revolution passed its first year, Sieyès emerged as a moderate. He opposed the confiscation of church lands to create a new money system (*assignats*) and the abolition of tithes. He also remained a constitutional monarchist, wanting a king to exercise executive power, but a king who was responsible to national representatives and not to the court nobility. He strongly opposed the idea that a king should have absolute power to veto legislation.

With the transformation of the French monarchy to the First French Republic in September, 1792, following the king's unwillingness to continue playing the role of constitutional monarch, Sieyès served for three years as a representative to the legislative assembly. As the revolution reached its most radical phase under the leadership of Georges Danton and Robespierre, Sieyès did what was necessary to survive, conforming to the flow of events. He voted for the death penalty for Louis XVI and converted to the worship of human reason instead of Christianity when the issue was forced by Danton. When it became fashionable again under Napoleon I, he changed back to Catholicism.

With the end of the Reign of Terror in 1795 and the establishment of the Directory (a colorless committee of five) exercising executive power, Sieyès was sent on diplomatic missions to The Hague and Berlin. In May, 1799, he became one of France's five directors. Yet he also realized that the Directory was incapable of providing leadership for France. Ultimately, he conspired with Talleyrand to support Napoleon's seizure of power on 18 Brumaire (November, 1799, according to the French Republican calendar). Sieyès tried to design a perfect constitution for the new consulate and with Napoleon served as one of three consuls intended to provide executive leadership. However, Sieyès rapidly saw Napoleon become first consul, relegating the other two to figureheads, then consul for life, then emperor. Silence about the changes permitted Sieyès to continue as a senator and to be appointed grand officer in the Legion of Honor (1804) and a count of the empire (1808). However, any sort of active political role came to an end with the subversion of the original consulate.

The fall of Napoleon in 1815 and the return of the Bourbon kings caused Sieyès to flee from Paris to Brussels for fear of being executed as a regicide. After the overthrow of the Bourbons in 1830 and the coming to power of the liberal Louis-Philippe, Sieyès returned to Paris, where he spent the remaining six years of his life.

SIGNIFICANCE

The French Revolution provided opportunity for relatively unknown individuals to achieve power, wealth, and fame. The revolution itself moved through stages, both unpredictable and uncontrollable, catalyzed by timely actions or words by virtual unknowns. The Abbé Sieyès, by producing a simple pamphlet at a timely moment, put forth simple but powerful answers, basically "everything, nothing, and something," to three major issues at a critical turning point in French history.

In current times, fortunes spent on advertising slogans, or on jargon to be used in major election campaigns, could not have resulted in more perfectly crafted words. Sieyès instantly defined the French nation, thus causing aristocratic privilege to be swept away by the concept of citizenship. His *What Is the Third Estate?* became, along with the Bastille, an icon of the French Revolution. The fact that Sieyès's idea changed as the revolution changed indicates that a leader of the early stages of the revolution became a follower.

—*Irwin Halfond*

FURTHER READING

Doyle, William. *The Oxford History of the French Revolution.* New York: Oxford University Press, 2003. A highly readable and well-researched account containing illustrations, maps, an extensive bibliography, and an index.

Forsyth, Murray Greensmith. *Reason and Revolution: The Political Thought of the Abbé Sieyès.* New York: Holmes & Meier, 1987. An excellent analysis of Sieyès's thoughts stressing his hatred of privilege and love of equality. Bibliography, index.

Sewell, William Hamilton. *A Rhetoric of Bourgeois Revolution: The Abbé Sieyès and "What Is the Third Estate?"* Durham, N.C.: Duke University Press, 1994. An in-depth analysis of Sieyès's rhetorical devices and their appeal. Index and bibliography.

Sonenscher, Michael, ed. *Political Writings Including the Debate Between Sieyès and Tom Paine in 1791.* Indianapolis, Ind.: Hackett, 2003. The editor provides lengthy and informative insights in his introductions to Sieyès's three major treatises.

JOHN GRAVES SIMCOE
English military officer and administrator

After military service in the American Revolution as commander of the Queen's Rangers, Simcoe served as lieutenant governor of the new province of Upper Canada and was later the military commander of the west of England during the Napoleonic Wars.

Born: February 25, 1752; Cotterstock, Northamptonshire, England
Died: October 26, 1806; Exeter, Devonshire, England
Areas of achievement: Warfare and conquest, military, government and politics

EARLY LIFE

John Graves Simcoe was the third son of Captain John Simcoe of the Royal Navy and Katherine Stamford. The family lived at Cotterstock Hall until Simcoe's father died at sea in 1759. His mother and her two boys moved to Exeter, near the residence of Captain Samuel Graves, a British naval officer and Simcoe's godfather.

Simcoe studied at Exeter School and proceeded to Eton College in 1765. He disliked Eton and moved to Merton College, Oxford, in February, 1769. After only a few days he decided to take up legal studies at Lincoln's Inn in London. These studies, however, did not suit him, and his mother procured him a commission as an ensign in the Thirty-fifth Foot (infantry) Regiment when he was eighteen.

Over the next four years Simcoe did garrison duty in England, Wales, and Dublin, Ireland. On March 12, 1774, he bought the commission of lieutenant, and a short time later his regiment shipped out for Boston, Massachusetts. He was still shipboard when the Battle of Bunker Hill took place but landed on June 19, two days after the battle was fought. He remained in Boston, buying a captaincy in the Fortieth Foot, until the British evacuated in March, 1766. The Fortieth played an active role in the New York campaign of the summer of 1776. Simcoe fought and was wounded at Brandywine Creek on September 11, returning to Philadelphia to convalesce.

LIFE'S WORK

On October 15, 1776, Simcoe assumed, at the rank of captain, command of the irregular provincial regiment known as the Queen's Rangers. He regrouped the unit following Brandywine, adding light cavalry and a Highlander company; he later recruited grenadiers, whose main job was to reconnoiter and skirmish, acting essentially as guerrilla troops who assisted the regulars. Simcoe was wounded in a skirmish near Philadelphia on June 27, 1777. The regiment was posted to Staten Island, New York, in July, and from this base it carried out actions in New York and New Jersey during the next two years. On May 2, 1779, the Queen's Rangers was renamed the First American Regiment, one of three new provincial units, and Simcoe was given the field rank of lieutenant colonel.

In the early fall Simcoe was wounded and captured in a raid on Middlebrook, New Jersey, and held for exchange in Brunswick and Burlington. He was released on December 27 and returned promptly to his unit on Staten Island. That winter Simcoe tried to capture George Washington, commander of the rebel troops, but icy weather thwarted the effort. In April, 1780, the First American was sent to support the Siege of Charleston, South Carolina, but after the surrender on May 12 the regiment returned to Staten Island. After more patrols and an unsuccessful attack on Elizabethtown, Simcoe's regiment fell under the command of General Benedict Arnold, who was softening up Virginia in advance of General Charles Cornwallis's move north from the Carolinas.

Simcoe's involvement in the American Revolution earned him a reputation as a daring and resourceful commander with a fertile imagination and a firm determination to accomplish the task at hand. However, old wounds and exhaustion caught up with him in Yorktown about the time the French and Americans did. Though Simcoe planned a breakout, Cornwallis insisted the British soldiers stay and surrender on October 19, 1781. Since Simcoe's partisan regiment might fare badly at the colonists' hands, he arranged to have many shipped out in a medical vessel. He returned to Devonshire via New York, arriving in early December.

Over the next decade Simcoe wooed Elizabeth Postuma Gwillim, a wealthy orphan, and the couple married on December 30, 1782. With her money they purchased and refurbished Wolford Lodge, where Elizabeth gave birth to eleven children. Simcoe played the part of the local landowner well and successfully ran for Parliament in 1789.

The fate of Canada became his greatest concern, for he feared that the newly created United States might seize Canada from the British, jeopardizing the thousands of colonial Loyalists who relocated there during and after the American Revolution. He also feared the large and powerful French contingent in Quebec that had not assimilated to British rule since 1763. In 1790, Simcoe was appointed lieutenant governor of the new province of Upper Canada, the peninsula bounded by Lakes Huron, Ontario, and Erie. He made extensive and detailed plans for his administration and, with Elizabeth and their two youngest children, sailed for Canada on September 15, 1791.

For the next five years the Simcoes moved between Newark (now Niagara), Kingston, and York (now Toronto), where Simcoe oversaw the development of the three towns and supervised land grants, road building, Indian affairs, the abolition of slavery in 1793, and provincial elections (first held in 1792). The Simcoes wrestled with primitive housing, horrible weather, American Indians, trappers, dissenters, and animals. They lost one child, but the population of the province nearly doubled during Simcoe's tenure as lieutenant governor. Ill and homesick, the couple returned to England on October 13, 1796.

Simcoe was granted the rank of major general and, as a British military commander, was quickly posted to Santo Domingo in the Caribbean, in part to confront the revolution of Toussaint Louverture. He left England in January, 1797, but returned in August, disgusted with the lack of supplies and support and ill with the fevers of the tropics.

He resigned both the Santo Domingo and Canadian commissions after returning but in a few months became commander of the military in the west of England, including Devonshire and parts of Somerset. England reasonably feared an invasion by Napoleon I, the first consul of France, and Simcoe prepared for an active defense: arms and munitions, militia drilling, evacuation plans, and muster points. In March, 1801, Simcoe received full command of the southwest and now had to deal with food riots brought on by the effects of Napoleon's Continental System and poor crops in England. He gained a respite during the yearlong peace with France in 1802 and 1803, but was, as usual, highly active in organizing and devising military plans. Otherwise his time was spent in inspections, field drills, and surveys. In 1805 he accepted a command post in India but fell ill from paint poisoning during a sea voyage to Portugal. He died in Exeter in October, 1806.

SIGNIFICANCE

John Graves Simcoe was the type of individual who became indispensable to the growing British Empire. His boldness and acumen as both military commander and civil administrator made him the very model of the colonial officer. His exploits in the American Revolution never amounted to much, but his unit gained a reputation for dependability and fierceness that his commanding officers valued highly.

His greatest challenge and success were in organizing Upper Canada, where he truly was a pioneer in establishing the British presence. His wife, Elizabeth, did her best to bring some culture and grace to the rough frontier and largely succeeded in softening some of its rough edges. A disciple of abolitionist leader William Wilberforce, Simcoe was key in keeping slavery limited and setting a timetable for its oblivion in the province. His attitude toward the indigenous peoples was an enlightened one, and he established a positive relationship with them that long outlived his own administration.

—Joseph P. Byrne

FURTHER READING

Cruikshank, E. A., ed. *The Correspondence of Lieutenant Governor John Graves Simcoe*. 5 vols. Toronto: Ontario Historical Society, 1923-1931. Carefully crafted edition of Simcoe's letters and other official materials from 1789 to 1796.

Fryer, Mary Beacock, and Christopher Dracott. *John Graves Simcoe, 1752-1806: A Biography*. Toronto, Ont.: Dundurn Press, 1998. Highly readable modern biography with material on Simcoe's descendants and an updated bibliography.

Gellinor, John, ed. *Simcoe's Military Journal*. Toronto, Ont.: Baxter, 1968. An edition of the journal Simcoe kept from 1777 to 1783, during his tour of duty in the Revolutionary War, and published for the first time in 1787.

Innis, Mary Quayle, ed. *Mrs. Simcoe's Diary*. Toronto, Ont.: Macmillan, 1965. Modern edition of the diary kept by Elizabeth Gwillim Simcoe, John's wife, during her stay in Upper Canada.

Scott, Duncan Campbell. *John Graves Simcoe*. New York: Oxford University Press, 1926. Prior to Fryer's and Dracott's works, this was the standard biography.

Van Steen, Marcus. *Governor Simcoe and His Lady*. Toronto, Ont.: Hodder and Stoughton, 1968. Biographi-cal sketch that focuses on Simcoe's relationship with his wife and family, especially during his governorship of Upper Canada.

See also: Lord Amherst; John André; Sir Guy Carleton; Thomas Gage; William Howe; Louis-Joseph de Montcalm; James Wolfe.

Related articles in *Great Events from History: The Eighteenth Century, 1701-1800:* October 19, 1781: Cornwallis Surrenders at Yorktown; 1783: Loyalists Migrate to Nova Scotia; 1791: Canada's Constitutional Act.

ADAM SMITH
Scottish economist and philosopher

Smith was one of the major luminaries of the eighteenth century Scottish Enlightenment. His The Wealth of Nations *became the bible of nineteenth century liberals, and twenty-first century conservatives have embraced his vision of the beneficent results of the free marketplace. Economists continue to pay homage to Smith for his contribution to the study of economic development.*

Born: June 5, 1723 (baptized); Kirkcaldy, Fifeshire, Scotland
Died: July 17, 1790; Edinburgh, Scotland
Areas of achievement: Economics, philosophy, government and politics

EARLY LIFE

Adam Smith was born in a fishing and mining town near Edinburgh. His exact date of birth is unknown, although records show when he was baptized. His father, also named Adam, had died before his son's birth. His mother, the former Margaret Douglas, was thus the most important influence in young Smith's life. After attending the local school, Smith entered the University of Glasgow in 1737. In 1740, he won the Snell Exhibition, receiving a scholarship for study at Balliol College, Oxford, and spent the next six years there reading widely in the classics, literature, and philosophy.

From 1746 to 1748, Smith lived with his mother in Kirkcaldy, until a group of friends arranged for him to give a series of public lectures in Edinburgh. These lectures proved so successful that he was named to the chair of logic at the University of Glasgow in 1751. When the equivalent position for moral philosophy became available that same year, he was elected to the place. Smith proved to be not simply a popular and effective teacher; he became heavily involved in university administration, serving as quaestor for six years, then as dean of faculty and as vice rector.

At Glasgow, Smith lectured on a broad range of topics: rhetoric and belles lettres, natural theology, ethics, and jurisprudence (law, government, and economics). Although nothing is known about his lectures on natural theology (except for a former student's report that they dealt with "the proofs of the being and attributes of God, and those principles of the human mind upon which religion is founded"), student notes on his rhetoric and economic lectures have been published. Smith's lectures on ethics became the basis of his first book, *The Theory of Moral Sentiments* (1759). The work was an immediate success, it was translated into French and German, and it went through nine editions during Smith's life.

Influential politician Charles Townshend was so impressed that he engaged Smith to tutor his stepson, the young duke of Buccleuch. In early 1764, Smith gave up his Glasgow chair to accompany his charge on a Grand Tour of the Continent that lasted until late 1766. After his return, Smith worked briefly as an adviser to Townshend, who was then chancellor of the exchequer. Given a generous lifetime pension by Buccleuch, Smith then went back to Kirkcaldy to work on what would be his masterpiece. From 1773 to 1776, he was in London advising the government on economic matters while simultaneously continuing with his own writing. The publication of *An Inquiry into the Nature and Causes of the*

Wealth of Nations (commonly known as *The Wealth of Nations*) on March 9, 1776, was a landmark in Western thought.

LIFE'S WORK

Adam Smith first made his reputation with *The Theory of Moral Sentiments*. The problem he set for himself in this book was to explain the forces responsible for the socialization of the individual to fit that person for membership in a social group. Reflecting the optimistic Deism of the Scottish Enlightenment, his starting point was that God had endowed human beings with inborn "moral sentiments" that bound them together. One such sentiment was the desire each person had for the praise and approval of his or her fellows or acquaintances: "Nature, when she formed man for society, endowed him with an original desire to please, and an original aversion to of-

Adam Smith, author of The Wealth of Nations. *(Library of Congress)*

fend his brethren. She taught him to feel pleasure in their favourable, and pain in their unfavourable regard." The second was an individual's capacity for imaginatively identifying with others: "This is the only looking-glass by which we can, in some measure, . . . scrutinize the propriety of our own conduct."

Smith regarded justice as the "main pillar" upon which society rested. He defined this justice in negative terms—as consisting of refraining from injuring another person or from taking or withholding from another what belonged to that person. More important, Smith realized the impossibility of relying exclusively upon the spontaneous and natural operation of an individual's impulses toward fellow feeling for the attainment of justice. The force of what he termed "sympathy" was strongest among those sharing a common social bond—membership in the same family, church, town, guild, or other social group. The wider the distance, physical or social, that separated people, the weaker was the bond's influence: "All men, even those at the greatest distance," he wrote, "are no doubt entitled to our good wishes, and our good wishes we naturally give them. But if, notwithstanding, they should be unfortunate, to give ourselves any anxiety upon that account seems to be no part of our duty." Accordingly, people formulate general rules to govern their actions and institute governments to enforce those rules by legal sanctions.

Smith recognized that individuals were moved simultaneously by self-regard and by social passions. The key to his later book, *The Wealth of Nations*, was his belief in the primacy of the self-regarding motives within the economic sphere, given the impersonality and anonymity of the marketplace. The individual, he believed, is dependent upon the goodwill of his or her neighbors but cannot depend on their generosity alone to provide it. To ensure the proper feeling, the individual must show others that it is to their own benefit to help the individual: "It is not from the benevolence of the butcher, the brewer, or the baker, that we expect our dinner, but from their regard to their own interest." Smith's larger purpose in *The Wealth of Nations* was to identify the reasons behind what is called economic development, or what he called the progress of opulence. One such cause was the "propensity to truck, barter, and exchange one thing for another," which Smith considered to be "one of those original principles in human nature, of which no further

THE DIVISION OF LABOR AND THE PRODUCTION OF GOODS

Adam Smith, in this excerpt from The Wealth of Nations, *outlines the efficiency of dividing labor among many workers and bringing together many different arts to produce functional, common, and necessary goods for each member of society. Needing these goods is a commonality that trumps class.*

It is the great multiplication of the productions of all the different arts, in consequence of the division of labour, which occasions, in a well-governed society, that universal opulence which extends itself to the lowest ranks of the people. . . .

Observe the accommodation of the most common artificer or day-labourer in a civilised and thriving country, and you will perceive that the number of people, of whose industry a part, though but a small part, has been employed in procuring him this accommodation, exceeds all computation. The woollen coat, for example, which covers the day-labourer, as coarse and rough as it may appear, is the produce of the joint labour of a great multitude of workmen. The shepherd, the sorter of the wool, the wool-comber or carder, the dyer, the scribbler, the spinner, the weaver, the fuller, the dresser, with many others, must all join their different arts in order to complete even this homely production. . . .

If we examine, I say, all these things, and consider what a variety of labour is employed about each of them, we shall be sensible that, without the assistance and co-operation of many thousands, the very meanest person in a civilised country could not be provided, even according to, what we very falsely imagine, the easy and simple manner in which he is commonly accommodated.

Source: Adam Smith, *The Wealth of Nations,* excerpted in *Readings in Western Civilization,* vol. 2, edited by George H. Knoles and Rixford K. Snyder, 4th ed. (Philadelphia: J. B. Lippincott, 1968), p. 585.

account can be given." The second was the similarly natural ambition by individuals to gain the esteem of their fellows by improving their economic status and thus their rank in society.

These impulses interacted to promote economic development through the mechanism of an increasingly extensive division of labor. Smith's major contribution to economic theory lay in his explanation of the ways in which the specialization of function, accompanying the division of labor, increased productivity by reducing the time wasted in shifting from one task to another, sharpening workers' skills, and facilitating the invention of improved machinery. Smith envisaged the size of the market as the major limitation upon the extent to which the division of labor could go. Thus, he saw the process progressing almost automatically toward always higher levels of well-being: The more productivity was increased, the larger the population that could be supported; the larger the population, the larger the market;

the larger the market, the more extensive the division of labor. Smith's argument for international free trade rested upon the same ground. Each country specializing in the kinds of production in which it had a comparative advantage would increase the total wealth of all. A major target of the book was the mercantilist policies of Smith's time, which aimed at promoting national autarky (economic self-sufficiency), which Smith attacked for forcing "part of the industry of the country into a channel less advantageous than that in which it would run of its own accord."

Behind Smith's exaltation of the beneficent economic results of the pursuit of self-interest lay Sir Isaac Newton's vision of a universe governed by self-regulating laws. Under a regime of free exchange, individuals unintentionally promote the good of their nation's economy. An individual does this when trying "as much as he can both to employ his capital in support of domestick industry, and so to direct that industry that its produce may be of the greatest value; every individual necessarily labours to render the annual revenue of the society as great as he can." He also assumed a tendency toward a self-correcting equilibrium in the economy. Aggregate income and output were automatically in balance; free competition would ensure that whenever prices, wages, or the return on capital rose above or fell below their "natural" rates, supply and demand would bring about the required adjustment. The corollary was that government regulation will always distort the most efficient utilization of resources by interfering with the "natural balance of industry."

The first edition of *The Wealth of Nations* sold out within six months of publication. Smith published a revised edition in 1778 and followed it with a substantially expanded third edition six years later. The work was translated into French, German, Danish, Dutch, Italian, and Spanish. In 1777, Smith was appointed commissioner of the customs in Edinburgh, where he would live for the rest of his life. The income from this position, combined with his pension from the duke of Buccleuch, made Smith a comparatively wealthy man. Perhaps because of his close ties with his mother until her death in 1784, he never married. Nevertheless, he was active in the social life of Edinburgh's intellectual and scientific community. Among the honors he received was election in 1787 to the rectorship of the University of Glasgow. Although notorious for his absentmindedness, Smith maintained his broad intellectual interests. He revised and added to *The Theory of Moral Sentiments*. His *Essays on Philosophical Subjects*, published posthumously in 1795, include a lengthy piece on the history of astronomy that has earned for him recognition as a pioneer in the history and philosophy of science. He continued to write, but he destroyed the bulk of his manuscripts shortly before his death at the age of sixty-seven on July 17, 1790.

SIGNIFICANCE

The Wealth of Nations became the bible of those who favor laissez-faire economics, that is, no interference by the government with the individual's pursuit of self-interest in the marketplace. Nevertheless, Adam Smith was not the uncritical admirer of private enterprise that many later admirers thought him to be. He was deeply suspicious of the tendency of businessmen to seek special privileges from the government and to combine to extort monopoly profits. When monopoly could not be avoided, he preferred government to private control. Nor was he dogmatic in his support for laissez-faire. He upheld the responsibility of the state to provide public services that would benefit society as a whole, but only when they were "of such a nature, that the profit could never repay the expence to any individual, or small number of individuals, and which it therefore cannot be expected that any individual or small number of individuals should erect or maintain."

He explicitly endorsed publicly supported compulsory elementary education to offset the stultifying effects of the division of labor. He similarly qualified his support for international free trade by allowing for protectionist measures when they were required for national defense, a priority "of much more importance than opulence."

Even though his position was distorted by later exponents of laissez-faire, Smith's prescriptive recommendations would have a major impact on governmental policies not simply in Great Britain but throughout the Western world as well. Writing in 1857, the historian H. T. Buckle concluded that "looking at its ultimate results, [*The Wealth of Nations*] is probably the most important book that has ever been written, and is certainly the most valuable contribution ever made by a single man towards establishing the principles on which government should be based." The later reaction against laissez-faire spurred the resultant downgrading of Smith, but a new generation of free marketers has found in his writings a continued source of inspiration.

At the same time, Smith's intellectual influence has transcended the economic implications of his work. Smith was a pioneer in the application of the historical approach to the analysis of economic phenomena. His arguments rested not only upon his astute observations of contemporary society but also upon a vast accumulation of data drawn from his wide reading in history. Even more important, his work was the first comprehensive and systematic exploration of how a capitalist market economy worked. His emphasis upon the central role of the division of labor would be followed by later students—including those, such as Karl Marx, who found more to damn than to praise.

—*John Braeman*

FURTHER READING

Campbell, R. H., and A. S. Skinner. *Adam Smith*. London: Croom Helm, 1982. A succinctly written and comprehensive biography based upon a thorough mastery of the extant primary sources.

Dougherty, Peter J. *Who's Afraid of Adam Smith? How the Market Got Its Soul*. New York: J. Wiley, 2002. Analyzes two of Smith's books: *The Wealth of Nations*, with its ideas about the free market, and the more obscure *A Theory of Moral Sentiments*, expressing Smith's belief that free markets can flourish only in societies with social capital and strong institutions of civil society. Dougherty explains how there has been a renaissance of interest in Smith's ideas, and he describes how some economists have taken measures to integrate Smith's moral sentiments into capitalism.

Fleischaker, Samuel. *On Adam Smith's "Wealth of Nations": A Philosophical Companion*. Princeton, N.J.: Princeton University Press, 2004. Fleischaker explains Smith's economic ideas within the context of Smith's moral theory and philosophies of science and social science. He also relates Smith's ideas to the thoughts of his contemporaries, including David Hume and Francis Hutchinson.

Glahe, Fred R., ed. *Adam Smith and the Wealth of Nations: 1776-1976 Bicentennial Essays*. Boulder: Colorado Associated Press, 1978. A collection of appreciations by twentieth century champions of the free market.

Lightwood, Martha B. *A Selected Bibliography of Significant Works About Adam Smith.* Philadelphia: University of Pennsylvania Press, 1984. A handy bibliographical guide to important works about Smith.

Raphael, D. D. *Adam Smith.* New York: Oxford University Press, 1985. A brief intellectual biography written especially for the general reader.

Ross, Ian Simpson. *The Life of Adam Smith.* New York: Oxford University Press, 1995. A comprehensive and scholarly biography of Smith.

Skinner, Andrew S. *A System of Social Science: Papers Relating to Adam Smith.* Oxford, England: Clarendon Press, 1979. A collection of essays dealing with different aspects of Smith's thought by a foremost authority.

Wood, John Cunningham, ed. *Adam Smith: Critical Assessments.* 4 vols. London: Croom Helm, 1983. A massive compilation that brings together the more important commentaries on Smith.

See also: James Boswell; Edmund Burke; Joseph Butler; First Baron Erskine; Adam Ferguson; Claude-Adrien Helvétius; David Hume; First Earl of Mansfield; Montesquieu; Robert Morris; Thomas Paine; William Pitt the Younger; François Quesnay; Jean-Jacques Rousseau; John Wilkes.

Related articles in *Great Events from History: The Eighteenth Century, 1701-1800:* 1726-1729: Voltaire Advances Enlightenment Thought in Europe; 1739-1740: Hume Publishes *A Treatise of Human Nature;* 1748: Montesquieu Publishes *The Spirit of the Laws;* April, 1762: Rousseau Publishes *The Social Contract;* January 10, 1776: Paine Publishes *Common Sense;* March 9, 1776: Adam Smith Publishes *The Wealth of Nations;* January, 1790: Hamilton's *Report on Public Credit.*

LAZZARO SPALLANZANI
Italian scientist

Spallanzani is famous for his acute scientific observation and experimentation. He worked on problems in geology, volcanology, meteorology, chemistry, and physics, but it is his studies of infusoria, blood circulation, biological reproduction, digestion, and respiration that have proved to be of the greatest scientific significance.

Born: January 12, 1729; Scandiano, Duchy of Modena (now in Italy)

Died: February 11, 1799; Pavia, Cisalpine Republic (now in Italy)

Areas of achievement: Biology, chemistry, science and technology

EARLY LIFE

Lazzaro Spallanzani (LAHD-dzahr-oh spahl-lahnt-SAHN-ee) was born in Scandiano, northeast of the Apennines, where his father, Gianniccolò, was a prominent lawyer. During his early schooling there, his interest in astronomy earned for him the nickname "the Astrologer." When fifteen, Spallanzani was sent to the Jesuit seminary in Reggio Emilia, where he pursued rhetoric, philosophy, and languages. In 1749, he started law studies at the University of Bologna. Spallanzani's cousin, Laura Bassi, professor of physics and mathematics there, supervised his study of the sciences, natural history, Greek, Latin, French, and antiquities. Nature intrigued Spallanzani, and after three years his father permitted him to devote himself to the sciences.

In 1753 or 1754, Spallanzani received his doctorate in philosophy. After taking minor orders in the Roman Catholic church, he returned to the seminary to teach logic, metaphysics, and Greek in 1755. In 1757, he was ordained and, retaining his seminary post, became a lecturer in mathematics at the University of Reggio Emilia. The following year, he also began teaching Greek and French at Nuovo Collegio, which replaced the seminary. During these years, Spallanzani released his first publications, *Theses philosophicae . . .* (1757; philosophical theses) and *Riflessioni intorno alla traduzione dell' "Iliade" del Salvini . . .* (1760; internal reflections on Salvini's translation of the *Iliad*). By 1760, he had acquired a scholarly reputation and the epithet "the Abbé Spallanzani." Paying minimal attention to his religious duties, he devoted his time, church income, and university salary to scientific research.

Physically, Spallanzani was of medium height and robust build. He had black eyes, an aquiline nose, a high forehead, a dark complexion, and a resonant voice. Athletic when young, he later enjoyed hunting, fishing, and playing chess. On the one hand, Spallanzani has been described as frugal, self-assured, sociable, and magnetic. On the other, this man of science has been called arrogant, intolerant, obstinate, and ambitious. Resenting criticism, he could be vengeful, ruthless, and violent when crossed.

LIFE'S WORK

In 1761, Spallanzani began his biological research after reading works of Georges-Louis Leclerc, comte de Buffon, and John Turberville Needham. By 1762, he was a professor of mathematics at the university and of Greek at Nuovo Collegio. In 1763, Spallanzani became a professor of philosophy at the university and at the College of Nobles in Modena.

In Modena, Spallanzani attacked the theory of spontaneous generation, which asserted that living things could come into being without a living predecessor, an idea that was championed by Buffon and Needham. In his *Saggio di osservazioni microsopiche concernenti il sistema della generazione de' signori di Needham e Buffon* (1765; account of microscopic observations concerning Needham and Buffon's system of generation), Spallanzani reported hundreds of beautifully executed experiments on infusoria, which refuted Buffon and Needham's views and confirmed that infusoria were living organisms that did not arise spontaneously in strongly heated infusions protected from contamination by air. Many considered Spallanzani's experiments conclusive evidence against spontaneous generation.

Next, Spallanzani turned to regeneration and transplantation and then to circulation of the blood. His conclusions that "lower" animals have greater regenerative power than "higher" animals, that organisms generally regenerate only superficial organs, and that an individual organism's ability to regenerate varies inversely with age were published in *Prodromo di un opera da imprimersi sopra le riproduzioni animali . . .* (1768; *An Essay on Animal Reproductions*, 1769). The first of Spallanzani's works to appear in English, *An Essay on Animal Reproductions* received mixed reviews. In *Dell' azione del cuore ne' vasi sanguigni* (1768; on the action of the heart on the blood vessels), he described the effect of the systolic action of the heart upon blood flow in salamanders, extending and occasionally correcting Albrecht von Haller's studies.

In 1769, Spallanzani moved to the University of Pavia, in Lombardy, where he spent his remaining years as a popular and famous professor of natural history. In

Lazzaro Spallanzani. (Hulton Archive/Getty Images)

addition, Spallanzani assumed direction of the university's Natural History Cabinet (museum). There, he assailed spontaneous generation in his inaugural address, *Prolusio* (1770), then expanded his examination of circulation of the blood. This work culminated in *De' fenomeni della circolazione . . .* (1773; *Experiments upon the Circulation of the Blood . . .* , 1801), which presented a physico-mechanical explanation of the heart's action and the circulation of the blood and reported the first observation of blood passing through the capillaries of warm-blooded animals.

The results of Spallanzani's continued investigation of infusoria appeared in *Opuscoli di fisica animale e vegetabile . . .* (1776; *Tracts on Animals and Vegetables*, 1784, 1786). Here, Spallanzani dispelled Needham's objection that no infusoria grew in Spallanzani's containers because heat had destroyed the vegetative force by showing that loosely corked infusions boiled longer and showed better growth than those boiled for shorter periods of time. He also refuted Buffon's theory that spermatozoa developed in decomposing semen and demonstrated that they were components of living animals.

In the late 1770's, Spallanzani's popularity as a teacher swelled. He continued improving the museum, and he investigated animal digestion, biological reproduction, and artificial fecundation. In *Dissertazioni di fisica animale e vegetabile* (1780; *Dissertations Relative to the Natural History of Animals and Vegetables*, 1784, 1789), Spallanzani described his experiments on gastric digestion. Observing the solvent action of human and animal "gastric juices"—a term he coined for saliva, bile, stomach, and other secretions—he determined that digestion occurs primarily in the stomach and is a chemical, rather than mechanical, putrefying, or fermenting process. In addition, Spallanzani recounted experiments on animal sexual behavior, fertilization, and embryological development.

Seeking to discover how animal eggs are fertilized, Spallanzani examined the role played by semen in fecundation. He attempted artificial inseminations of several animals and was successful with a spaniel. His experiments demonstrated that contact between semen and egg is essential for fertilization, but he concluded that the solid parts of semen, not spermatozoa, were the fertilizing elements. In *Dissertations Relative to the Natural History of Animals and Vegetables*, Spallanzani argued for the embryological theory of preformation, contending that the preformed plant or embryo awaits fertilization within the egg and, after fertilization, expands according to a plan established by God. In his final section, he maintained that embryos exist in all plant seeds and develop with or without fertilization.

In this period, Spallanzani traveled in Europe, collecting museum specimens and indulging his passion for natural history. In 1784, he was offered a professorship at the prestigious University of Padua. Enticed to stay at Pavia by a year's leave, a salary increase, and an ecclesiastical benefice, Spallanzani began his leave in August, 1785, by sailing to Istanbul, where he stayed for eleven months. His account of the journey describes the natural history and other aspects of Istanbul and Eastern Europe.

In 1788, Spallanzani visited the kingdom of the Two Sicilies, collecting for the museum and recording volcanic, geological, and other observations. While studying the active volcanoes Vesuvius, Stromboli, Vulcano, and Etna, he concluded that their eruptions resulted from gaseous explosions. Returning to Pavia, he performed chemical experiments on lava. These observations and investigations appeared as *Viaggi alle due Sicilie e in alcune parti dell' Appennino . . .* (1792-1797; *Travels in the Two Sicilies and Some Parts of the Apennines*, 1798).

During the early 1790's, Spallanzani conducted zoological research, most important on the flight of bats he had blinded, for example, by burning out their eyes. Led to reject the theory that flying bats avoid collisions by relying on touch, taste, smell, or hearing, his *Lettere sopra*

il sospetto di un nuovo senso nei pipistrelli . . . (1794; *Letters on a Supposed New Sense in Bats*, 1941) suggested that a sixth sense or some unidentified organ in the head was responsible. Subsequently, however, Spallanzani accepted Louis Jurine's theory, connecting bats' flight with their hearing.

Then, Spallanzani's research assumed a more chemical air. Johann Friedrich August Göttling's erroneous description of the combustion of phosphorus prompted Spallanzani to examine that topic, and he published his results in *Chimico esame degli esperimenti del Sig. Göttling, professor a Jena, sopra la luce del fostoro di Kunkel . . .* (1796). Turning to respiration, he investigated gases emitted by plants enclosed in vessels of water or air, which were then placed in sunlight or shade. Part of a 1798 article, his last publication, stated his conclusions. Later, in *Mémoires sur la respiration* (1803; *Memoirs on Respiration*, 1804), some of Spallanzani's papers on animal respiration were printed. In these papers, Spallanzani showed that oxidation occurs neither in the lungs nor in the blood, as had been argued, but in the tissues. Moreover, he demonstrated that during oxidation animal tissues emit carbon dioxide, which the blood then carries away—a discovery often attributed to nineteenth century chemist Justus von Liebig.

Throughout his life, Spallanzani enjoyed good health, although he experienced minor digestive disorders. In early February, 1799, complications from an enlarged prostate and chronic bladder infection sent him into a coma; he died a week later, one of the most famous contemporary scientists in the West.

SIGNIFICANCE

Lazzaro Spallanzani possessed broad scientific interests and throughout his life published many reports and letters in scientific periodicals, in addition to his monographs. His treatises appeared in French, English, and German and were recognized for their literary style as well as their substance. Although Spallanzani's conclusions often were debated by his peers and although some of his experiments are considered inhumane today, he remains known for an experimental skill that hardly was equaled for a century afterward. Most important, Spallanzani furthered the development of scientific thought in many fields.

Spallanzani's experimentation on spontaneous generation added to evidence mounting against that theory. His experiments on infusoria contributed to the foundation of bacteriology, and his studies of their mortality when subjected to intense heat played a seminal role in the invention of food canning. Spallanzani's experiments on animal sexual behavior, fecundation, semen, and spermatozoa led to the modern understanding of animal reproduction; his pioneering work on artificial fecundation and his successful artificial insemination of a viviparous animal—the first recorded—mark the beginning of modern work in that field.

Spallanzani achieved the first in vitro demonstration of animal digestion and established the basic theory of digestion held today. His ideas were not accepted immediately, but his work paved the way for nineteenth century biochemical studies of digestion. Spallanzani also laid the foundation for modern studies of animal and plant respiration. His research had little impact until the 1830's, however, and was not continued until the late nineteenth century. Finally, among Spallanzani's geological observations are notable contributions to mineralogy, and his work on volcanic eruptions is considered fundamental to modern volcanology.

—*Martha Ellen Webb*

FURTHER READING

Adams, A. Elizabeth. "Lazzaro Spallanzani (1729-1799)." *Scientific Monthly* 29 (1929): 529-537. Presents a reasonably accurate chronology of Spallanzani's life and a well-documented assessment of his scientific method and contributions. Adams's inclusion of translations from Spallanzani's works and correspondence elevates this above other readily available biographical articles.

Bulloch, William. *The History of Bacteriology*. London: Oxford University Press, 1938. Chapter 4 includes a detailed account of the controversial theory of spontaneous generation, Spallanzani's experimentation on infusoria, and his role in the theory's demise.

Dinsmore, Charles E. "Lazzaro Spallanzani: Concepts of Generation and Regeneration." In *A History of Regeneration Research: Milestones in the Evolution of a Science*, edited by Charles E. Dinsmore. New York: Cambridge University Press, 1991. This substantial essay on Spallanzani's contributions to the study of animal regeneration is included in this chronicle of significant achievements in the study of reproduction.

Foster, Michael. *Lectures on the History of Physiology During the Sixteenth, Seventeenth, and Eighteenth Centuries*. Cambridge, England: Cambridge University Press, 1924. Lecture 8 describes Spallanzani's experimental work on digestion and relates that work to that of his contemporaries.

Gasking, Elizabeth B. *Investigations into Generation, 1651-1828*. Baltimore: Johns Hopkins University Press, 1967. Chapter 11, devoted to Spallanzani, concentrates on his experiments and conclusions on animal sexual reproduction and fecundation, particularly the role of semen in fertilization, and places Spallanzani's work within the context of the history of preformation.

Harris, Henry. *Things Come to Life: Spontaneous Generation Revisited*. New York: Oxford University Press, 2002. Chapter 4 in this examination of spontaneous generation includes information about Spallanzani's experiments and theories.

Meyer, Arthur William. *The Rise of Embryology*. Stanford, Calif.: Stanford University Press, 1939. Offers illuminating accounts of Spallanzani's investigation of spontaneous generation, animal reproduction, artificial insemination, hybridization, and his preformationist views. Meyer's extensive excerpts from Spallanzani's publications and correspondence are also enormously valuable.

Strick, James Edgar. *Sparks of Life: Darwinism and the Victorian Debates Over Spontaneous Generation*. Cambridge, Mass.: Harvard University Press, 2000. Although the book focuses on Darwin and his contemporaries, it includes a brief chapter, "Needham Versus Spallanzani," contrasting the two scientists' ideas about spontaneous generation.

See also: Sir Joseph Banks; Comte de Buffon; Carolus Linnaeus.

Related articles in *Great Events from History: The Eighteenth Century, 1701-1800*: Beginning 1735: Linnaeus Creates the Binomial System of Classification; 1748: Nollet Discovers Osmosis; 1749-1789: First Comprehensive Examination of the Natural World; 1751: Maupertuis Provides Evidence of "Hereditary Particles"; 1753: Lind Discovers a Cure for Scurvy; 1757: Monro Distinguishes Between Lymphatic and Blood Systems; 1757-1766: Haller Establishes Physiology as a Science; 1767-1768: Spallanzani Disproves Spontaneous Generation; 1796-1798: Jenner Develops Smallpox Vaccination; 1799: Discovery of the Earliest Anesthetics.

MADAME DE STAËL
French writer

Madame de Staël publicly articulated the liberal, rational opposition to the injustices and corruption of the French government during the revolution and under Napoleon I. Her social and literary criticism, as well as her colorful personal life, placed her in the vanguard of the Romantic movement, and her two major novels constitute early treatments of the concerns of women.

Born: April 22, 1766; Paris, France
Died: July 14, 1817; Paris, France
Also known as: Anne-Louise-Germaine Necker (birth name); Germaine de Staël
Areas of achievement: Literature, philosophy, government and politics

EARLY LIFE

Madame de Staël (mah-dahm duh stahl) was born Anne-Louise-Germaine Necker in Paris on April 22, 1766, the only child of Suzanne Curchod Necker, the beautiful and highly educated daughter of a Swiss clergyman, and the Genevese financier Jacques Necker, who was to achieve fame as minister to Louis XVI. Despite her learning, Madame Necker was considered a rather narrow woman by the urbane Parisians, and her relations with her daughter were always rigid and distant. Though not without critics of his own, the stodgy Jacques Necker was widely esteemed as a man of public and private virtue. Germaine's natural love for her father was intensified by her childhood awareness of the public acclaim he enjoyed. As an adult, Germaine's consciousness of her place in the prominent Necker family helped to form her notions of social criticism and political activism and her sense of personal destiny.

A precocious child, Germaine was educated at home in imagined accordance with *Émile: Ou, De l'éducation* (1762; *Emilius and Sophia: Or, A New System of Education*, 1762-1763), Jean-Jacques Rousseau's radical exposition on childhood education. Madame Necker stalwartly maintained one of the literary salons for which Paris was celebrated during the eighteenth century, and Germaine grew up on familiar terms with such people as Denis Diderot, Jean le Rond d'Alembert, the comte de Buffon, and Guillaume-Thomas Raynal. In this rarefied environment, she absorbed the liberal politics and morals of the Enlightenment.

On January 14, 1786, after years of negotiation, Germaine Necker married a Swedish aristocrat, Eric Mag-nus, Baron de Staël-Holstein, a favorite of Gustav III and—in accordance with the marriage negotiations—Swedish ambassador to the French court. De Staël may have felt some affection for Germaine (and some, certainly, for her dowry of £650,000), but she apparently felt none for him, and their first child, Edwige-Gustavine, was probably the only one of their four children actually fathered by de Staël. More important, however, Germaine gained a measure of social and economic independence from the marriage. In the embassy residence in Paris, she established a salon of her own, which soon became the gathering place for such liberal members of the aristocracy as Mathieu de Montmorency, Talleyrand, and Louis, vicomte de Narbonne Lara. In the early days of her marriage, she used her husband's court connections to try to advance the position of her father, and she took advantage of de Staël's frequent absences to lead the relatively independent life that was possible for women of her station in eighteenth century Paris.

LIFE'S WORK

Madame de Staël's residence at the Swedish embassy in Paris was one of the more attractive features of her marriage agreement, for Jacques Necker had been dismissed by Louis XVI in 1781 and had moved his family to Saint-Ouen, where Germaine had sorely missed the intellectual life of Paris. Necker was recalled by Louis XVI in 1788, and was then dismissed and recalled once again at the fall of the Bastille. He continued at his post through the march on Versailles in September, 1789, and the massive nationalization effected by the assembly under the comte de Mirabeau. Necker finally resigned in September, 1790, and repaired to the family estate of Coppet, near Geneva.

During her father's interrupted tenure at court, Germaine attempted to elicit support among her influential friends of the liberal aristocracy for a constitution and a bicameral government, as a compromise between the continued abuses of the Bourbon Dynasty and the inevitable triumph of the Third Estate. On August 31, 1790, she gave birth to a son, Auguste, fathered by Narbonne, with whom she had been involved for about a year and a half. Determined that Narbonne should be the leader of the new government, Madame de Staël became further embroiled in intrigues at court until Narbonne was appointed war minister at the request of Marie-Antoinette; he was dismissed, however, in March, 1792. At about the

929

same time, de Staël was recalled to Sweden when Louis and Marie-Antoinette were arrested attempting to escape Paris in a maneuver arranged by Gustav III. Gustav was assassinated in March, 1792, however, and de Staël returned to Paris, where Madame de Staël continued to encourage the constitutionalists and agitated for the restoration of Narbonne. She finally fled Paris for Coppet the day before the September massacres began in 1793.

Madame de Staël's relationship with Narbonne—which followed a similar liaison with Talleyrand and coincided with a profound friendship with Montmorency—was characteristic of her lifelong attraction to the heroes of her political and intellectual causes. Much of her own appeal resided in her power as a fascinating conversationalist, and even those who were prepared to be intimidated by her were often won over by her exuberance and lack of pretension. Possessing none of her mother's conventional beauty, she was nevertheless a woman of imposing physical appearance. Her wide, luminous eyes were considered her most attractive feature. A woman of Junoesque proportions, Madame de Staël continued to dress in the revealing diaphanous fabrics and décolleté lines of empire fashion even after she had grown heavy in middle age. Her frank display of her ample bosom and legs, and her continuance of the eighteenth century custom of the *levée*, amazed younger, more conservative Parisians and provoked the derision of her enemies. She customarily wore a turban, which undoubtedly lent a Byronic dash to her overall appearance.

During the Reign of Terror, Madame de Staël lived much of the time at Coppet, spending considerable money and energy smuggling refugees from the liberal aristocracy out of Paris. She gave birth to her son Albert, also the child of Narbonne, on November 20, 1792, and left shortly thereafter for England, where Narbonne had sought refuge from the Terror. Rumors of her complicity in the revolution and in the Terror were circulated by aristocratic French émigrés living in England until she was no longer received by members of the upper class. Disappointed by the conservatism of the British, her relationship with Narbonne strained, she returned in June, 1793, to her husband near Coppet, where Narbonne finally joined her in August, 1794.

In 1794, the year of her mother's death, Madame de Staël met Benjamin Constant, with whom she would be involved in a passionate and embattled relationship for the next fourteen years. With the fall of Robespierre in 1794, she returned to Paris and reopened her salon. At this time, she worked to encourage support for the positive changes wrought by the revolution; the degree of influence she wielded is measured by the fact that she was expelled from the city alternately by both royalists and republicans. Her only daughter, Albertine, probably the child of Constant, was born in Paris on June 8, 1796. In 1797, Madame de Staël formally separated from her husband; debilitated by a stroke suffered in 1801, he died the following year en route to Coppet.

In 1795, Madame de Staël published *Essai sur les fictions* (*Essay on Fiction*, 1795); in 1796, *De l'influence des passions sur le bonheur des individus et des*

Madame de Staël. (Library of Congress)

nations (*A Treatise on the Influence of the Passions upon the Happiness of Individuals and Nations*, 1798); and, in 1800, *De la littérature considérée dans ses rapports avec les institutions sociales* (*A Treatise on Ancient and Modern Literature*, 1803). In these and later writings, her examination of the concept of perfectibility—the idea that scientific progress would lead humankind toward moral perfection—and her contention that critical judgment must be relative and historically oriented earned for her a place near Chateaubriand as a precursor of Romanticism. In 1802, she published the novel *Delphine* (English translation, 1803), which explores the role of the intellectual woman.

One of the most significant factors in Madame de Staël's life was her relationship with Napoleon, whom she first met in 1797. She early admired him as a republican hero: His successful coup of 18 Brumaire seemed to actualize the liberal abstractions of revolutionary politics. Napoleon, thoroughly conventional in his attitude toward women, however, could not approve of the highly vocal, public role that Madame de Staël had assumed; moreover, he resented the free discussion of his government that was encouraged at her salon, to which even his own brothers were frequent visitors. As he became more tyrannical, she became increasingly critical, eventually labeling him an "ideophobe." He expelled her from France in 1803 and crowned himself emperor the following year.

Her eleven years in exile from France during the reign of Napoleon seemed a spiritual and intellectual death sentence to Madame de Staël. Immediately upon her expulsion, she visited Germany, where she was welcomed as the author of *Delphine*. She met with the great thinkers and writers of Weimar and Berlin, including Johann Wolfgang von Goethe, Friedrich Schiller, and August Wilhelm von Schlegel, with whom she formed a long-lasting attachment. In April, 1804, Constant brought her news of her father's death. Prostrate with grief, she returned to Coppet.

From 1804 to 1810, Madame de Staël officially resided at Coppet, where she gathered around her a group of loyal and intellectually stimulating friends, including Schlegel and Jeanne Récamier. She spent much of her time away from the estate, however, venturing into France and traveling to Italy until she was confined to Coppet as a result of the machinations of the French and Genevese police. The Romantic and feminist concerns of her 1807 novel *Corinne: Ou, L'Italie* (*Corinne: Or, Italy*, 1807) brought her renewed fame, and in 1810 she completed *De l'Allemagne* (*Germany*, 1813), a thinly disguised critique of contemporary France, which was suppressed by Napoleon; it was published in England in 1813.

In 1811, she took another lover, John Rocca, a young Genevese sportsman who had been wounded in military action and was now tubercular. Rocca fathered her last child, Alphonse, and in 1816 they were married. Shortly after the birth of Alphonse, she fled Coppet and traveled throughout Europe, involving herself in Russian and Swedish political intrigues directed toward overthrowing Napoleon. Napoleon's abdication in 1814 brought Madame de Staël the freedom to reestablish herself in Paris, where she died on Bastille Day in 1817.

SIGNIFICANCE

Madame de Staël was a brilliant and unconventional woman whose circumstances of birth allowed her to witness some of the most significant events of Western history and whose intelligence and moral courage led her to participate. In the face of serious opposition, she lived with great enthusiasm and energy, balancing the exercise of intellect and creativity with the pursuit of a passionate personal life.

Madame de Staël tended the flame of the Enlightenment through the darkest days following the French Revolution. The rational tenor of her criticism of oppression and her defense of freedom provided a constant corrective not only to political tyranny but also to the social and cultural constraints that bound her as a woman. In her nonfictional prose, she sought support for her philosophical stance in the individualistic spirit of English and German Romanticism and in the cultural relativism afforded by her experiences in Germany, Italy, and Russia. Her examination, in *Delphine* and *Corinne*, of the difficulties encountered in the personal lives of gifted and creative women has gained new attention from feminist critics. Madame de Staël thus continues to assert her vivacious presence.

—*Diane Prenatt Stevens*

FURTHER READING

Besser, Gretchen Rous. *Germaine de Staël, Revisited*. New York: Twayne, 1994. A comprehensive study of Staël's life and work, describing the evolution of her career and her defense of political liberties. Part of Twayne's World Authors series.

Fairweather, Maria. *Madame de Staël*. New York: Carroll & Graf, 2005. Comprehensive biography, focusing on Staël's salons as a setting for French literary and political intrigue in the eighteenth and nineteenth centuries. Fairweather portrays Staël as a complicated, passionate, and outspoken woman who was not afraid to challenge France's extreme political factions.

Gutwirth, Madelyn. *Madame de Staël, Novelist: The Emergence of the Artist as Woman.* Urbana: University of Illinois Press, 1978. This book is a feminist analysis of the biographical, cultural, and social sources of the novels *Corinne* and *Delphine,* especially in their focus on the complications created by talent and love in women's lives. Includes notes, a bibliography, and an index.

Herold, J. Christopher. *Mistress to an Age: A Life of Madame de Staël.* Indianapolis, Ind.: Bobbs-Merrill, 1958. This standard biography is eminently readable and sympathetic, although slightly ironic in tone. Herold treats Madame de Staël's life in its entirety, emphasizing the effects of her relationship with her parents and focusing on her prodigious literary accomplishment and her unconventional personal life. Informed by an easy familiarity with French politics and culture, the book includes illustrations, an extensive annotated bibliography, and an index.

Hogsett, Charlotte. *The Literary Existence of Germaine de Staël.* Carbondale: Southern Illinois University Press, 1987. Writing from a feminist standpoint, Hogsett provides a critical analysis of Madame de Staël's writings as they reveal her development as a woman writer struggling to define herself in a male-dominated tradition. Contains notes, a bibliography, and an index.

Levaillant, Maurice. *The Passionate Exiles: Madame de Staël and Madame Récamier.* Translated by Malcolm Barnes. New York: Farrar, Straus & Cudahy, 1958. Levaillant examines Madame de Staël's life in exile at Coppet, with particular focus on her friendship with Jeanne Récamier. The book quotes extensively from the two women's correspondence.

Marso, Lori Jo. *(Un)Manly Citizens: Jean-Jacques Rousseau's and Germaine de Staël's Subversive Women.* Baltimore: Johns Hopkins University Press, 1999. Analyzes the portrayal of women characters in Staël's novels, *Corinne* and *Delphine.* Marso argues that these characters offer an alternative concept of the self and democratic citizenship.

Staël, Madame de. *Selected Correspondence.* Arranged by George Solovieff, translated and edited by Kathleen James-Cemper. Boston: Kluwer Academic, 2000. The letters are published in chronological order and provide details about the major events in Staël's life from 1789 until 1817.

Wilkes, Joanne. *Lord Byron and Madame de Staël: Born for Opposition.* Brookfield, Vt.: Ashgate, 1999. Madame de Staël and Byron became friends while they were both living in Switzerland. The book explores their friendship and their shared literary concerns.

See also: Jean le Rond d'Alembert; Comte de Buffon; Denis Diderot; Johann Wolfgang von Goethe; Louis XVI; Marie-Antoinette; Comte de Mirabeau; Jacques Necker; Guillaume-Thomas Raynal; Robespierre; Jean-Jacques Rousseau; Friedrich Schiller.

Related articles in *Great Events from History: The Eighteenth Century, 1701-1800*: October, 1725: Vico Publishes *The New Science*; 1739-1740: Hume Publishes *A Treatise of Human Nature*; 1748: Montesquieu Publishes *The Spirit of the Laws*; 1751-1772: Diderot Publishes the *Encyclopedia*; July 27, 1758: Helvétius Publishes *De l'esprit*; April, 1762: Rousseau Publishes *The Social Contract*; July, 1764: Voltaire Publishes *A Philosophical Dictionary for the Pocket*; 1770: Publication of Holbach's *The System of Nature*; January 10, 1776: Paine Publishes *Common Sense*; 1781: Kant Publishes *Critique of Pure Reason*; 1784-1791: Herder Publishes His Philosophy of History; May 5, 1789: Louis XVI Calls the Estates-General; June 20, 1789: Oath of the Tennis Court; July 14, 1789: Fall of the Bastille; October, 1789-April 25, 1792: France Adopts the Guillotine; 1790: Burke Lays the Foundations of Modern Conservatism; February 22, 1791-February 16, 1792: Thomas Paine Publishes *Rights of Man*; 1792: Wollstonecraft Publishes *A Vindication of the Rights of Woman*; April 20, 1792-October, 1797: Early Wars of the French Revolution; September 20, 1792: Battle of Valmy; January 21, 1793: Execution of Louis XVI; March 4-December 23, 1793: War in the Vendée; July 27-28, 1794: Fall of Robespierre; November 9-10, 1799: Napoleon Rises to Power in France.

GEORG ERNST STAHL
German chemist and physician

Stahl was a physician who developed the phlogiston theory, modern chemistry's first great explanatory system. The theory provided chemists with a framework for understanding reactions such as combustion and the smelting of metal ores, and it guided research into productive discoveries such as new gases and the composition of chemical molecules.

Born: October 21, 1660; Ansbach, Franconia (now in Germany)
Died: May 14, 1734; Berlin, Prussia (now in Germany)
Areas of achievement: Chemistry, medicine

EARLY LIFE

Georg Ernst Stahl (gay-AWRK ehrnst shtahl) was born in St. John's parish in Ansbach, then part of Franconia, a duchy in southern Germany. His father was a Protestant minister, and he grew up heavily influenced by Pietism, a seventeenth century movement in the Lutheran Church to infuse new spirit into an increasingly dogmatic Protestantism. Pietism stressed the moral, devotional, and mystical aspects of Christianity, and this doctrine helped to shape Stahl's view of the world, which was sensitive to the presence of the spiritual.

As an adolescent, he developed an interest in chemistry through reading a manuscript of lectures given by Jacob Barner, a professor of medicine at Padua. In the same period, he read a study of metals and minerals by Johann Kunckel von Löwenstjern, a court alchemist and apothecary who would later help to instigate Stahl's development of the phlogiston theory. Stahl once said that he knew these works by Barner and Kunckel von Löwenstjern practically by heart. They stimulated him, under the practical guidance of an enameler, to begin doing chemical experiments.

In the late 1670's, Stahl traveled to Thuringia in central Germany to study medicine at the University of Jena. One of his teachers, Georg Wolfgang Wedel, was a proponent of iatrochemistry, a discipline that held that diseases originate in the imbalance of chemical elements in the body and that the physician's task is to restore the body's chemical equilibrium. Stahl later wrote against the iatrochemists, for he could not understand how such a great variety of human illnesses could be attributed to such a small range of chemical causes, for example, acidity and alkalinity. Although he disagreed with the iatrochemists, some of their ideas, such as explaining

physiological processes in terms of chemical composition, did inform his medical theory and practice. During his years of study at Jena, Stahl formed a close friendship with Friedrich Hoffman, a fellow student who shared Stahl's fascination with chemistry and medicine. Even while he was a medical student, Stahl showed great ability as a chemist, and in 1683, around the time that he received his M.D. degree, he began to teach chemistry at Jena.

As a young teacher, he wrestled with many of the ideas that had fashioned the classical and modern doctrines of chemistry and medicine. He studied alchemy, and in 1684 he expressed his belief in the possibility of transmuting such metals as lead into gold (his mature attitude toward transmutation was much more cautious). He read the works of natural philosophers such as René Descartes and Robert Boyle, and he grew skeptical of their claim that all chemical phenomena could be explained in terms of mechanical interactions between variously shaped particles of homogeneous matter (this mechanical view of nature also conflicted with his Pietism). The courses that Stahl taught at Jena in chemistry and medicine gained for him such renown that in 1687 he was invited to become personal physician to Duke Johann Ernst of Sachsen-Weimar, a position he accepted and held for seven years.

In 1693, the elector of Brandenburg, Frederick III (who later became King Frederick I of Prussia), founded a new university at Halle. He gave Hoffmann the duty of establishing the faculty of medicine, and Hoffmann invited his friend Stahl to join him. Halle was a center of the Pietist movement, and when Stahl found that he would be able to teach medicine and chemistry in association with his friend, he agreed to go. In 1694, the year the University of Halle was officially inaugurated, Stahl took his post, one he would hold for twenty-two years.

LIFE'S WORK

As second professor in medicine at Halle, Stahl lectured on theoretical medicine, physiology, pathology, pharmacology, and botany, whereas Hoffmann, as first professor, lectured on practical medicine, anatomy, physics, and chemistry. Through the efforts of these talented and hardworking professors, Halle became a leading medical school. Unfortunately, as time went on, Stahl and Hoffmann became rivals instead of friends. Temperamentally, they had always been different, though there is little evidence to support the traditional contrast of Stahl as misanthropic and intolerant, and Hoffmann as congenial and open-minded; however, there is evidence that their differences were the result of increasingly divergent views on intellectual issues. In particular, Hoffmann became a dedicated iatrochemist who saw living organisms as machines, whereas Stahl, though he interpreted physiological processes through chemical changes, insisted that neither mechanical nor chemical laws were able to account fully for the mystery of life.

In addition to his problems with Hoffmann, Stahl encountered troubles in his personal life. He had married after he had come to Halle, but in 1696 his wife died of puerperal fever, which, despite his best medical efforts, he failed to cure. In 1706, his second wife died of the same disease, and in 1708 a daughter died. Although Stahl married a total of four times, little else is known of his family life. He did have a son who became interested in chemistry and who popularized a method of making silver sulfate from silver nitrate and potassium sulfate.

Despite these misfortunes in his personal and professional relationships, Stahl's years at Halle were extremely productive. He worked prodigiously. His lectures in medicine and chemistry were very popular, and they became the bases of the books that issued from his pen in a steady stream, many of them in Latin, some in German, and some in a mixture of Latin and German. His subjects were wide-ranging: medical theory, pharmacology, physiological chemistry, chemical theory, experimental chemistry, fermentation, metallurgy, and many others. His style was convoluted and confusing, and many scholars believe that he wrote both too much and too quickly and that his awkward sentences indicate not complexity of thought but a lack of clear thinking.

His greatest medical work was *Theoria medica vera* (1708; the true theory of medicine), which presents in massive detail his doctrines of physiology and pathology as well as his animistic medical philosophy. Paramount among Stahl's basic ideas, in his medicine and in his chemistry, is a sharp distinction between the living and nonliving. Stahl was influenced in his views about this distinction by Johann Joachim Becher, who would also influence his ideas on phlogiston. Like Stahl, Becher was the son of a Protestant pastor, and he also went on to become a university professor of medicine, though, unlike Stahl, he converted to Roman Catholicism rather than Pietism. Like Becher, Stahl argued that living things cannot be reduced to a conglomerate of mechanical effects. He did not deny that nonliving things functioned mechanically or that living things, in certain activities,

could be interpreted mechanically (for example, the arm as a lever in lifting an object), but the mechanism is always an instrument in the control of a directing agent or anima. Stahl used the Latin word *anima*, usually translated—though with loss of meaning—as soul or spirit, to capture his belief that every bodily response was rooted in an indivisible vital principle, but *anima* was not a mystical idea for him, since he arrived at it through rational analysis.

Some scholars have misunderstood Stahl's animism and antimechanism. He was not a reactionary, trying to revive a defunct religious or ancient Greek worldview. In fact, he was extremely critical of Aristotle's and Galen's theories, which he found conflicted with experience. The mechanical philosophy, too, had failed to produce much medical progress because mechanists failed to grasp that it was the soul, not physics and chemistry, that rules the body. The mind clearly acts on the body through voluntary actions, but even involuntary bodily effects have psychic causes. For example, mental perturbations such as anger and fear can change the pulse rate and upset the digestion. Therefore, mental changes do regulate the materials of the body according to certain goals.

In contrast to Stahl's medical ideas, which did little to advance the field, his chemical ideas had great influence. His best work in chemistry was done during his Halle professorship, and this work was as antimechanist as his medical work. He deeply believed that simple machine models could not adequately explain chemical phenomena. Although he accepted the existence of atoms, he regarded the corpuscularian viewpoint as deficient, since, as he put it, atomic theories scratch the surface of things and leave their kernel untouched. He could not see how arranging and moving inert and homogeneous particles around could generate such qualities as color and reactivity.

Stahl defined chemistry as the art of resolving compound bodies into their principles and recombining them. Since, in his view, atoms never exist by themselves, elements are formed when these indivisible particles join chemically to form what he called "mixts," and these mixts unite with other mixts in a hierarchy of increasing complexity. Though the highly reactive original elements could never be isolated, they could leave one mixt and enter another. Stahl believed that, for chemists to do meaningful work, they had to assume chemically distinct kinds of matter. For example, he defined metals in terms of their visual and tactile properties, more specifically, their luster and malleability. He defined acids in terms of their reactions with color indicators such as the syrup of violets. Mechanistic explanations of these qualities were clever but speculative and untestable, whereas Stahl preferred to take a direct, empirical approach to the practical problems of chemistry.

In his attempts to find convincing chemical explanations of phenomena, Stahl relied heavily on the doctrines of Becher. In 1703, he brought out an edition of Becher's *Physica subterranea* (1669; geological physics), and in the same year he wrote an analysis of Becher's ideas. Stahl disagreed with Becher's contention that metals grow like plants in the earth and that lead changes into gold with time, but he found much to admire in Becher's ideas about minerals. Germany was then the center of a thriving mining industry, and many studies were being done on metallurgical processes. In *Physica subterranea*, Becher stated that the world's nonliving substances were composed of three different types of earth: a glasslike earth (*terra lapidea*), endowed with substantiality that rendered bodies solid and difficult to change; an oily earth (*terra pinguis*) was primarily responsible for combustibility, but it also accounted for odor, taste, and color; and a fluid or mercurial earth (*terra mercurialis*) supplied ductility, fusibility, and volatility. Stahl took Becher's second earth and gave it the name "phlogiston." The word had been used earlier, in different contexts and in different senses, and the idea of combustibility as a general principle had been used since antiquity (in the medieval period it surfaced as the alchemical principle sulfur). Stahl's great accomplishment was to take phlogiston and make it into the organizing idea for chemistry. Becher gave almost no experimental support for his theories, whereas Stahl collected numerous observations and experimental facts to confirm his views. His theory also stimulated chemists to do many new experiments.

The explanation of combustion was a central feature of the phlogiston theory. When a substance burned, phlogiston was expelled, and so burning was a decomposition. Stahl saw phlogiston as the principle of fire but not fire itself. Other chemists called phlogiston the food of fire or the inflammable principle. Since phlogiston was an elementary principle, its nature could be known only from its effects. Like the elementary atoms, phlogiston was impossible to isolate, and like the reactions of the mixts, phlogiston could be transferred only from one substance to another. In combustion, phlogiston went out of the flame to combine with the air, but since air had only a limited capacity to absorb phlogiston, this transfer reaction eventually lessened. Furthermore, Stahl noted that a flame could blacken a pane of glass, and this showed that phlogiston was responsible for color.

In an important extension of the phlogiston theory, Stahl recognized that the rusting of metals was similar to the burning of wood, since phlogiston was emitted in both processes. When Stahl heated a metal strongly, the process of rusting was accelerated and what he called an ash appeared (later phlogistonists called this a calx, and the process of making this powdery material from the metal was called calcination). More poetically, the calx was the dead body of the metal, from which the soul of phlogiston had been removed by fire. From his studies, Stahl deduced that a metal was really a compound of a calx and phlogiston. He could reverse the process by heating the calx with charcoal, a rich source of phlogiston. This brought about a transfer of phlogiston from the charcoal to the calx, re-creating the metal.

One thing that troubled later chemists about the phlogiston theory was an observation, known to the medieval Arabs and to many chemists of the sixteenth and seventeenth centuries, that calcined metals actually increased in weight. At first glance, this observation contradicts the phlogiston theory's analysis of calcination as a decomposition. Therefore, metals should lose weight when they are calcined (because they lose phlogiston), and the calx should gain weight when reconverted to the metal. In fact, the reverse is true, as Stahl knew. Nevertheless, this did not shake his confidence in his theory, because he thought of phlogiston not as an isolable substance but as a weightless, perhaps buoyant, fluidlike heat that could flow from one body to another. Since phlogiston was like light and electricity rather than like air and water, it made no more sense to weigh metals and ores to discover the loss or gain of phlogiston than it would to weigh a piece of paper to measure its whiteness.

Stahl first conceived the phlogiston theory at the end of the seventeenth century, and he developed its implications for combustion, calcination, and the smelting of ores during the first decade of the eighteenth century, when he also applied his theory to such biological phenomena as fermentation and respiration. The theory's spread throughout Europe augmented Stahl's fame, but it aggravated rather than improved his relationship with Hoffmann. The atmosphere between them was so poisoned that Stahl welcomed an invitation in 1716 to become personal physician to the king of Prussia, Frederick William I, in Berlin. While at the Prussian court, Stahl continued to write, do research, and teach students. Among his most important publications during this period was *Fundamenta chymiae dogmaticae et experimentalis* (1723; the fundamentals of dogmatic and experimental chemistry), a work prepared for publication by Johann Samuel Carl, whom Stahl regarded as his best pupil. Depictions of Stahl from this period show a man in a large dark-haired wig surrounding a face with strong features and a melancholic bearing. Stahl, contented with his new life in Berlin, never returned to Halle but held his court appointment until his death on May 14, 1734.

SIGNIFICANCE

Georg Ernst Stahl's life bridged two ages, and his phlogiston theory is often seen as a bridge from alchemy to modern chemistry. His personality, which many have interpreted as a combination of opposites, suited him for this linking role. He was deeply attracted to the devotional and penitential rigors of Pietism, but his penetrating intelligence also found satisfaction in constructing a highly rational system of chemistry. In his youth, he had been fascinated by alchemy, and he continued to use alchemical symbols throughout his career, but in his developed theories these symbols stood for a new explanation of the composition of chemical substances.

Today, most people associate Stahl with the phlogiston theory that dominated chemistry for nearly a century, and many scientists have the impression that this domination retarded chemical progress; however, modern historians of science, though they recognize Stahl's theory as false, find much to praise in it. Some even see it as a great landmark in the history of chemistry, because it was the first logical theory to encompass most important chemical transformations. It rejected the confusing ideas of alchemy, established chemistry as an independent discipline, and constituted a paradigm within which experimental work could be planned, practiced, and related to other discoveries.

Through the eyes of an early eighteenth century chemist, the phlogiston theory was a liberation from enervating scientific concepts of the past, and the most intelligent and creative chemists of the period accepted Stahl's theory with enthusiasm. In England, Joseph Priestley, Henry Cavendish, and Joseph Black were phlogistonists; in Germany, Caspar Neumann, Johann Pott, and Andreas Sigismund Marggraf; in Sweden, Torbern Bergman and Carl Wilhelm Scheele; in Russia, Mikhail Vasilyevich Lomonosov; and in France, Pierre-Joseph Macquer and even Antoine-Laurent Lavoisier, until he developed his oxygen theory. These scientists found Stahl's ideas extraordinarily useful in making important discoveries, including those of new gases and inorganic solids.

—*Robert J. Paradowski*

FURTHER READING

Crosland, Maurice P. *Historical Studies in the Language of Chemistry.* Cambridge, Mass.: Harvard University Press, 1962. This book, which derives from Crossland's doctoral dissertation for the University of London, traces the evolution of chemistry from the period of alchemy to the end of the nineteenth century. Though intended for scientists and historians of science, the book should lead the general reader to a better appreciation of the history of chemistry, including Stahl's contributions.

Donovan, Arthur, ed. "The Chemical Revolution: Essays in Reinterpretation." Special issue. *Osiris* 4 (1988). The entire issue of this journal centers on new views of the chemical revolution. Though intended for historians of science, the essays deal with a time period and subject matter that make the material accessible to a wider audience.

Duncan, Alistair. *Laws and Order in Eighteenth-Century Chemistry.* New York: Oxford University Press, 1996. Chronicles scientific discoveries in the eighteenth century that enabled chemistry to establish itself as a discipline. Includes information on how scientists attempted to explain chemical combustion.

Greenberg, Arthur. *A Chemical History Tour: Picturing Chemistry from Alchemy to Modern Molecular Science.* New York: John Wiley & Sons, 2000. This illustrated overview of chemical history includes a brief discussion of Stahl and the phlogiston theory.

Ihde, Aaron J. *The Development of Modern Chemistry.* Reprint. Mineola, N.Y.: Dover, 1983. Though the book's emphasis is on the period of chemistry since the chemical revolution, Stahl's work is discussed in the initial section on the foundations of chemistry. Contains useful bibliographic notes.

Leicester, Henry M. *The Historical Background of Chemistry.* New York: John Wiley & Sons, 1956. Although he discusses how some important chemical ideas have influenced world history, Leicester's emphasis is on the evolution and interrelations of chemical concepts within the history of science. Unlike Aaron Ihde, he devotes considerable attention to the earlier periods of chemistry, including a good discussion of Stahl's views. Accessible to readers with little or no chemical background.

Levere, Trevor H. *Transforming Matter: A History of Chemistry from Alchemy to the Bucky Ball.* Baltimore: Johns Hopkins University Press, 2001. This popular history of chemistry includes a chapter, "A

German Story: What Burns and How?" containing information on Stahl's theory.

Partington, J. R. *A History of Chemistry*. Vol. 2. London: Macmillan, 1961. This volume of Partington's monumental history of chemistry (he died before its completion) contains two chapters on the phlogiston theory, one devoted to Becher, the other to Stahl. Contains a selected bibliography of Stahl's writings.

Weeks, Mary Elvira. *Discovery of the Elements*. 7th ed. Easton, Pa.: Journal of Chemical Education, 1968. Because the phlogiston theory was important in the discovery of elemental gases such as hydrogen, oxygen, and nitrogen, this book has many references to Stahl's work. The book was originally intended to acquaint chemists with the great achievements of their science, but there is much in these densely packed pages to interest general readers.

See also: Joseph Black; Henry Cavendish; Frederick I; Antoine-Laurent Lavoisier; Mikhail Vasilyevich Lomonosov; Andreas Sigismund Marggraf; Joseph Priestley.

Related articles in *Great Events from History: The Eighteenth Century, 1701-1800*: 1714: Fahrenheit Develops the Mercury Thermometer; 1718: Geoffroy Issues the *Table of Reactivities*; 1722: Réaumur Discovers Carbon's Role in Hardening Steel; 1723: Stahl Postulates the Phlogiston Theory; 1738: Bernoulli Proposes the Kinetic Theory of Gases; 1745: Lomonosov Issues the First Catalog of Minerals; 1748: Nollet Discovers Osmosis; June 5, 1755: Black Identifies Carbon Dioxide; 1771: Woulfe Discovers Picric Acid; August 1, 1774: Priestley Discovers Oxygen; 1781-1784: Cavendish Discovers the Composition of Water; 1786-1787: Lavoisier Devises the Modern System of Chemical Nomenclature; 1789: Leblanc Develops Soda Production.

FIRST EARL STANHOPE
French-born English administrator and diplomat

The leading minister in the government of King George I, Stanhope was responsible for a series of measures that solidified support for the new Hanover Dynasty. His successful diplomacy enabled England to launch an extended period of peace, so necessary to the political and economic reforms of his successor, Robert Walpole.

Born: 1673; Paris, France
Died: February 5, 1721; London, England
Also known as: James Stanhope (full name)
Areas of achievement: Government and politics, diplomacy

EARLY LIFE

James Stanhope, First Earl Stanhope, was the son of Alexander Stanhope and Catherine Burghill. His grandfather, Philip Stanhope, was the First Earl Chesterfield. His father, the youngest son of Chesterfield, was an English diplomat to Holland and Spain. James was born in Paris and naturalized as a British subject in 1696. He had three younger brothers, Alexander, Philip, and Edward, all of whom died before James did. James had one sister, Mary, who outlived him. Two other children, a boy and a girl, died as infants.

Educated at Eton and, for two years, at Trinity College, Oxford, Stanhope left school before receiving a degree to accompany his father to Madrid in 1690. There, he acquired a knowledge of Spanish language and culture that would advance his diplomatic career. He served Eugene of Savoy in Italy before joining the English army as a volunteer in Flanders in 1694-1695. Wounded twice in 1694, once in a duel in which he killed his opponent and again at the Siege of Namur, Stanhope was soon commissioned a captain and lieutenant colonel. On February 12, 1702, he became colonel of the Eleventh Regiment of Foot.

Stanhope's political career began a year earlier when he was elected to Parliament for Newport on the Isle of Wight. The next year, he was elected from the district of Cockermouth, whose constituents he represented for the next eleven years. Loyal to Whig principles, as was his father, Stanhope early supported the Act of Settlement of 1701, which established the progeny of Sophia, electress of Hanover, as the heirs to England's throne after Anne.

During the War of the Spanish Succession (1701-1714), "planned" by the late William III to keep the Bourbon family from holding the Spanish crown, Stanhope began a heralded but controversial career in the military. He took combat under James Butler, second duke of Ormonde, in Spain in 1702, and under John Churchill, first duke of Marlborough, in 1703. After a campaign in Portugal, during which he suffered a severe attack of rheumatism, he returned home to receive a promotion to brigadier general in August, 1704. In the following year, Stanhope joined the assault on Spain, distinguishing himself by unusual bravery in entering the city of Barcelona to persuade the inhabitants to accept the surrender, an action that earned for him the notice of the queen.

Appointed minister to Spain on January 29, 1706, he urged allied forces to attack Madrid from Valencia and Catalonia, when Charles Mordaunt, third earl of Peterborough, and Archduke Charles of Austria preferred defensive tactics. When Spanish defenses proved too strong, Peterborough blamed Stanhope for the defeat. Five years later, a House of Lords inquiry sided with Peterborough, although the decision may have been influenced at that time by the lords' attempts to restrain the aggressive operations of Marlborough and his party. Yet Stanhope was made major general and commander in chief of British forces in Spain, joining his forces in Catalonia in May, 1708. At Marlborough's suggestion, Stanhope launched an attack on Minorca, securing the island and ports in which British vessels could winter.

Philippe, duke of Orleans and regent of France, opened negotiations with Stanhope in August, proposing his own candidacy for the Spanish throne instead of Philip V, the Bourbon duke of Anjou, or the Habsburg, Archduke Charles. After indecisive military engagements, Stanhope returned home to direct parliamentary proceedings against Dr. Henry Sacheverell, a preacher who accused Nonconformists of plotting the overthrow of the Church of England and the monarchy. Sacheverell, a popular hero of sorts, was found guilty of libel but given a light sentence that was suspended by the queen.

In May, Stanhope returned to the military front in Spain, once again pressing for offensive operations contrary to that of most allied commanders. This time the campaign went better as his troops advanced upon Aragon. Stanhope personally killed one of the Spanish leaders. By now Stanhope had won the majority of the officers to his point of view, and they launched an attack on Madrid. By September, both Stanhope and Archduke Charles were in the capital. French reinforcements and renewed Spanish support for King Philip, however, compelled the allies to leave Madrid for safer winter quarters. The swift-moving French troops, more numerous than the English, surprised the allies at Brihuega and compelled Stanhope to surrender. Stanhope's military career ended. He was imprisoned for a year and a half in

Saragossa. Following secret negotiations for peace, Stanhope was released, arriving home in August, 1712, refusing an audience with King Louis XIV arranged by Stanhope's rival, Henry St. John, First Viscount Bolingbroke.

LIFE'S WORK

Stanhope returned home to become one of the opposition leaders in the House of Commons. After an inquiry into his expenditures in Spain, government investigators discovered that, far from being guilty of extravagance, as suspected, Stanhope was owed money. When he lost his Cockermouth seat in Parliament, he ran and won from Wendover in 1713. He actively opposed the Commercial Treaty with France that year and fought the Schism Act of 1714 as well. His apprehensions about a Jacobite plot induced him to bring troops into England from Hanover to guarantee the succession following Queen Anne's death in the early summer.

On September 14, 1714, Stanhope was appointed by the new monarch—who had not yet arrived from Hanover—to be secretary of state for the Southern Department; ten days later, he was made a privy councilor. Horatio Walpole, younger brother of Robert Walpole and a former secretary to Stanhope in Spain, is said to have influenced the choice of Stanhope, but surely the king was already acquainted with his diplomatic background. Since the principal secretary of state, Charles Townshend, Second Viscount Townshend, was in the House of Lords, Stanhope led the government's case in the Commons, along with Robert Walpole, not yet a government minister.

In the first parliament of George I in 1715, Stanhope was elected once again from Newport. A leading supporter of impeachment proceedings against the former Tory ministers, Stanhope personally moved the case against Ormonde. Queen Anne's Tory leaders were accused of promoting the Jacobite conspiracy to bring the Stuart pretender, James III, to England, and arranging a dishonorable, secret treaty preceding formal treaty negotiations at Utrecht in 1713. Ormonde was charged with deserting the Dutch allies on the field of battle to promote the secret Tory peace talks. The expected Jacobite rising took place in August, and Stanhope was appointed to direct its suppression. The Whig leader then actively supported the Septennial Act to give the new government and dynasty needed security.

Stanhope's forte was foreign affairs. In October, 1714, he went to The Hague and Vienna to bring the Dutch and imperial negotiators to terms on the Barrier

Treaty respecting the number of Dutch fortresses allowed in the Southern, or Habsburg, Netherlands; the treaty was signed a year later. He spent the last six months of 1716 with the king in Hanover, during which time he was negotiating an alliance with France in return for the regent's promise to renounce James III (Francis Edward Stuart). George was anxious to complete the treaty since he feared new troubles with Sweden and Russia, but reluctant English ministers in London employed delaying tactics. This issue severed relations between the party of Stanhope and Charles Spencer, third earl of Sunderland, who represented the French party as well as English interests in the North and Baltic Seas, the party of Townshend and Walpole, who sided with the Dutch and who feared that an English alliance with France was to protect Hanoverian interests in Northern Europe. Walpole reminded the government that the Act of Settlement (1701) required parliamentary approval for any English military action on behalf of royal properties abroad. The Anglo-French alliance did succeed, perhaps owing to a discussion in a Dutch bookshop between Stanhope and Guillaume Cardinal Dubois, as related in one account, or, as a result of Stanhope's success in inducing the cardinal to imbibe too much wine, as the English Whig had boasted.

On April 9, 1717, Townshend and Walpole were dismissed and Stanhope was made first lord of the treasury and chancellor of the exchequer. He supported the repeal of the Schism Act of 1718, which had earlier imposed certain disabilities upon Nonconformist teachers. Stanhope, however, was ill-suited for these jobs, as he acknowledged, and to his satisfaction was able to switch positions with Sunderland. Stanhope resumed his former position as secretary of state for the Southern Department, but no longer sat in the Commons. On July 12, 1717, he was made Baron Stanhope of Elvaston, and then Viscount Stanhope of Mahon, in honor of his earlier capture of Port Mahon on Minorca. On April 14, 1718, Stanhope was made Earl Stanhope.

His major diplomatic feats followed. While in Hanover, Stanhope worked for a southern peace plan to forge an agreement between Philip of Spain and Charles of Austria; the former was to renounce any claims to Italian possessions, and the latter to the throne of Spain. The Habsburg emperor, Charles, would then aid Hanover to secure possession of Verden and Bremen and England's gains in the Mediterranean at Utrecht would be confirmed. Not until 1720 and after another short war between England and Spain took place, following Admiral Sir George Byng's destruction of the rebuilt Spanish

navy, did this agreement come to pass. By this time, Stanhope had fashioned a quadruple alliance among England, France, Austria, and Holland. Anxious to make an accommodation with Spain, Stanhope and King George even offered to return Gibraltar, but, pressured by Walpole in Commons, the formal offer was made dependent upon Parliament's consent. Nevertheless, the success of the quadruple alliance compelled several potential belligerents—Sweden, Denmark, Russia—and Spain to reduce their international demands.

Stanhope was successful in neutralizing Sweden, suspected of supporting the Jacobites. Sweden, however, renewed the English alliance following Charles XII's death, and when Danes and Russians threatened Sweden, Stanhope sent the English fleet under Admiral Sir John Norris to treat the Russians as Byng had earlier treated the Spanish. Both Russia and Denmark backed away from hostilities.

Perhaps Stanhope's greatest and least heralded diplomatic triumph occurred in 1719, when he secured an English-Prussian alliance designed to shore up English interests in the north against potential aggressors in Scandinavia and Russia. George's Hanoverian advisers were pressing the elector (King George I) to maintain close ties with Austria instead, but Stanhope's insistence on English interests prevailed. This was a turning point for the dynasty, since the monarch realized that his primary responsibilities were now to England.

In domestic politics, Stanhope managed to repeal the Schism Act of 1714 when he introduced a repeal on December 13, 1718. He and George tried to weaken the Test Act by granting some relief to Roman Catholics, but the proposal met with too much resistance from Walpole. When the Peerage Bill was introduced on March 5, 1719, designed to fix the number of peers and limit the Crown's right of unlimited appointments, it was supported by Sunderland and Stanhope. It passed the Lords but was rejected by the Commons.

Stanhope was with the king in Hanover when news arrived about the collapse of the South Sea Company, the nation's first stock-market crash. Although Stanhope had no investments in the venture, as minister he was partly responsible for promoting the folly that the company's monopoly in America could absorb much of the national debt. When parliamentary debates opened on the question on February 4, 1721, Stanhope became ill when replying to highly intemperate charges by a younger colleague. He died of a cerebral hemorrhage at 6:00 P.M. the next day at his Hampton Court apartment, and was buried on February 17, 1721, at Chevening, the estate in Kent that he had purchased four years earlier. George I was genuinely grief-stricken, for Stanhope had been his closest confidant.

Stanhope was dark-complexioned and handsome, as may be seen in several paintings of him. On February 24, 1713, Stanhope had married Lucy, the younger daughter of Thomas Pitt, governor of Madras and grandfather to William Pitt the Elder. Stanhope and his wife had six children: three sons, Philip, George, and James, and three daughters, Lucy, Jane, and Catherine. The eldest son, Philip, was the Second Earl Stanhope (1717-1786). George I interceded to obtain a pension of £3,000 a year for Stanhope's widow.

SIGNIFICANCE

A skillful diplomat, First Earl Stanhope surprisingly lacked parliamentary leadership. An impetuous debater, he demonstrated impatience and frankness, qualities that he suppressed in the international arena. He lacked an understanding of domestic politics but possessed an enormous knowledge of the intricacies of diplomacy. In such matters, Walpole was the reverse. Unlike the followers of Townshend and Walpole, he saw that the fortunes of Hanover did, indeed, coincide with the interests of England.

A student of the German philosopher Baron Samuel von Pufendorf, Stanhope believed that reason could truly devise ways to settle international conflicts and avoid warfare. The partnership of Stanhope and George I, at least in foreign affairs, marked a true watershed in European history. After 1721, England was secure abroad and was in a position to devote attention to the major economic and political changes associated with the work of Walpole.

—*John D. Windhausen*

FURTHER READING

Beattie, J. M. "The Council of George I and English Politics, 1717-1720." *English Historical Review* 81 (January, 1966): 26-37.

_____. *The English Court in the Reign of George I.* Cambridge, England: Cambridge University Press, 1967. Beattie demonstrates the importance of Stanhope's pro-Prussian policies in protecting English interests in the Baltic and North Seas, interests that in fact coincided with those of Hanover.

Gibbs, C. G. "Parliament and Foreign Policy in the Age of Stanhope." *English Historical Review* 77 (January, 1962): 18-37. The author probes the degree to which royal ministers increasingly provided data to Parliament concerning the management of foreign affairs.

Hatton, Ragnhild. *George I: Elector and King.* Cambridge, Mass.: Harvard University Press, 1978. Both entertaining and scholarly, this work explicates the diverse and complicated personal relationships among all members of the king's court. The author speaks of the George-Stanhope team.

Hill, Brian W. *The Early Parties and Politics in Britain, 1688-1832.* New York: St. Martin's Press, 1996. This history contains some references to Stanhope and places him within the context of eighteenth century British history. Also contains an appendix with biographical data on leading political figures of the period.

O'Gorman, Frank. *The Long Eighteenth Century: British Political and Social History, 1688-1832.* London: Arnold, 1997. This overview of British history includes several references to Stanhope, including a brief description of his foreign policy.

Plumb, J. H. *Sir Robert Walpole: The King's Minister.* Boston: Houghton Miffin, 1961. This first volume of a classic account of Walpole demonstrates his relationship and rivalry with Stanhope, a fellow Whig.

Williams, Basil. *Stanhope: A Study in Eighteenth Century War and Diplomacy.* Oxford, England: Clarendon Press, 1932. The only full-length biography of Stanhope, written by a very competent and respected scholar. Williams regards Stanhope's diplomatic triumphs as central to the progress of England later in the century.

_____. *The Whig Supremacy, 1714-1760.* Oxford, England: Oxford University Press, 1939. Places Stanhope's achievements in the context of the long era of Whig control under the first two Hanover monarchs.

See also: Eugene of Savoy; George I; First Duke of Marlborough; Lord North; Philip V; William Pitt the Elder; William Pitt the Younger; Robert Walpole.

Related articles in *Great Events from History: The Eighteenth Century, 1701-1800:* May 26, 1701-September 7, 1714: War of the Spanish Succession; September 6, 1715-February 4, 1716: Jacobite Rising in Scotland.

RICHARD STEELE
English writer

In collaboration with Joseph Addison, Steele was one of the eighteenth century's leading essayists. Steele and Addison's two journals, The Tatler *and* The Spectator, *were highly influential in literary and political circles. Steele also was a successful playwright, and his last play is still considered the consummate sentimental comedy.*

Born: March 12, 1672 (baptized); Dublin, Ireland
Died: September 1, 1729; Carmarthen, Wales
Also known as: Isaac Bickerstaff (pseudonym)
Areas of achievement: Literature, theater, government and politics

EARLY LIFE

Richard Steele was born into a poor but noble Protestant Dublin family. His father, also named Richard, died early in his son's childhood, leaving only £300 to his widow and three children. Consequently, five-year-old Richard was sent to live with his uncle, Henry Gascoigne, secretary to the duke of Ormond, and his aunt, Lady Katherine Mildmay. Uncle Henry, who became Steele's legal guardian, supervised his education until Richard was twelve years old, then enrolled him in London's prestigious Charterhouse School in 1684. Two years later, Joseph Addison entered the school, and the two became instant friends, prefiguring their famous collaboration.

In 1689, Steele matriculated to Christ Church, Oxford. In the late seventeenth century, Oxford was one of two common paths to success for a poor young man from a good family. Yet, instead of taking a degree, Steele took a second path: military service. In 1692, Steele joined the duke of Ormonde's Second Troop of Life Guards. Advancement in the English army at this time depended as much on blood lines as on military acumen, so Steele hoped to parlay an officer's title into a government position. However, it did not happen.

Instead, Steele made a name for himself with his pen while still serving as a soldier. In 1695, his poetic eulogy for the late Queen Mary was published, with a fawning dedication to Baron Cutts, who happened to command a regiment. At this time, writers rarely supported themselves by patronage rather than direct payments for their writings, dedicating their works to nobles who rewarded them with money or a position. In the baron's case, the reward for Steele's poem was a commission in his regiment. Steele was pulling himself up by his pen.

LIFE'S WORK

Richard Steele's next published work was a tribute to his school friend Addison, who by 1700 was establishing himself in the London literary scene, both as a dramatist and as a pamphlet writer. The first decade of the eighteenth century is often considered the beginning of English journalism, but before 1704, most of what later would be called news reporting was done through pamphlet writing, with a separate publication for each topic. In 1700, Addison was one of the major writers for the Whigs, a faction with middle-class mercantile interests, gaining power in Parliament. Consequently, Addison was being vilified in pamphlets from the Whigs' opponents, the Tories, and Steele came to his defense.

Disappointed by the lack of opportunities arising from his military service, Steele attempted one last volume under the patronage system. Again dedicated to Lord Cutt, this treatise on the moral reform of the soldier, *The Christian Hero* (1701), became Steele's first bestseller, going through eight editions in Steele's lifetime. Also in 1701 he had his first success at Drury Lane, the leading theater of eighteenth century London, with a comedy under the unlikely title and subject *The Funeral.*

Richard Steele. (Library of Congress)

A satire on undertakers and lawyers, the play was immediately popular, and it was performed in London through the entire century.

Steele's next play was not so successful. *The Lying Lover* (1703) played only ten nights and was never revived. Nevertheless, Steele was now established in the London stage, and since his army career did not seem to be succeeding, he resigned in 1705. In April of that year his third comedy, *The Tender Husband*, opened to enthusiastic London audiences and became a standard part of the London repertory for two generations. This success gave Steele the security to marry in the spring of 1705, though his wife, Margaret, would die in December of 1706.

Having established himself as a major literary power, Steele offered his services to the Whig Party as a political writer. The Whigs' opponents, the Tories, associated with Queen Anne and the landed nobles of England, had Steele's friend Jonathan Swift on their side, satirizing the Whigs with virtual impunity. Steele defended the Whigs and in the process not only lost Swift's friendship but also subjected himself to vicious ad hominem attacks in the Tory press—mostly written by Swift. Steele's political prose for the Whigs was contained exclusively in pamphlets, until April, 1707, when he was offered the editorship of the Whigs' *London Gazette*. Secure again, he married Mary Scurlock on September 7.

The *London Gazette* did not lend itself to Steele's style of political writing. It was literally a news sheet, posting ads and notices of events. Few items ran more than one hundred words. The experience, however, gave Steele valuable editorial skills, and he became accustomed to the three-issues-per-week schedule of the London newspapers. Parlaying this experience into his own paper, Steele launched *The Tatler* on April 12, 1709. *The Tatler* offered a greater range to Steele's satiric genius. Borrowing his former friend Swift's character, Isaac Bickerstaff, Steele enlarged the fictitious Londoner into the "tatler" of the journal's title, a jovial busybody who shares the gossip of London with his readers, gently satirizing the city's vices with good-natured ridicule. In the course of 271 issues, Steele's longtime friend Joseph Ad-

---

READING *The Tatler*

In the first issue of The Tatler, *Richard Steele explained—in his characteristically sardonic style—who was to be the target audience of the periodical and what that audience could hope to gain by reading it.*

Though the other papers which are published for the use of the good people of England have certainly very wholesome effects, and are laudable in their particular kinds, yet they do not seem to come up to the main design of such narrations, which, I humbly presume, should be principally intended for the use of politic persons, who are so public spirited as to neglect their own affairs to look into transactions of State. Now these gentlemen, for the most part, being men of strong zeal and weak intellects, it is both a charitable and necessary work to offer something, whereby such worthy and well-affected members of the commonwealth may be instructed, after their reading, what to think; which shall be the end and purpose of this my paper: wherein I shall from time to time report and consider all matters of what kind soever that shall occur to me, and publish such my advices and reflections every Tuesday, Thursday, and Saturday in the week for the convenience of the post. I have also resolved to have something which may be of entertainment to the fair sex, in honour of whom I have taken the title of this paper.

Source: Richard Steele, in *The Tatler* no. 1 (April 12, 1709). *The Spectator* Text Project. http://tabula.rutgers.edu/spectator/index.html. Accessed September, 2005.

---

dison joined him in the writing chores, and when *The Tatler*'s final issue appeared on January 2, 1711, Addison and Steele prepared for a more evenly balanced collaboration, which became the most famous literary pairing of the century.

On March 1, 1711, Addison and Steele inaugurated *The Spectator*, producing six issues per week through December 6, 1712, for a total of 555 issues. For *The Spectator*, Steele created not only the title character, Mr. Spectator, but also a whole host of London characters whose exploits were described in the various essays. Although Steele edited numerous periodicals until his death in 1729, his lively writing for *The Spectator* sealed his reputation. Late in life he attempted one final comedy, *The Conscious Lovers* (1722), an immediate and lasting success that still is widely anthologized and occasionally performed.

SIGNIFICANCE

Although his plays are now rarely read, aside from the model comedy of sentiment, *The Conscious Lovers*, Richard Steele's periodical essays are some of the most frequently reprinted writings of the eighteenth century. In a great age of satire, Steele's prose is as satiric as

Swift's without being as harsh. Where Swift skewered his opponents (including Steele) with personal attacks, Steele held up the general foibles of average Londoners to friendly jest, without using real names or thinly veiled caricatures. Although Swift ridiculed Steele's convoluted sentence structure, his prose style was consciously imitated for several generations, and his essays appeared as models in elementary composition textbooks for nearly two hundred years after his death.

While Steele's devotion to the Whig Party lost him the political favor of the Crown throughout the reign of Queen Anne, his patience was rewarded in 1714 with the accession of King George I. George's greater sympathy with the Whigs led to Steele's knighting in 1715.

—John R. Holmes

FURTHER READING

Dammers, Richard H. *Richard Steele*. Boston: Twayne, 1982. This volume in a standard series on English authors is the ideal starting point for a study of Steele, evaluating all his major works and digesting the relevant criticism.

Goldgar, Bertrand A. *The Curse of Party*. Lincoln: University of Nebraska Press, 1961. Provides background on the Whig versus Tory political issues of the era of *The Spectator*, with particular focus on the political reasons for Steele's break with Jonathan Swift.

Kenny, Shirley Strumm, ed. *The Plays of Richard Steele*. New York: Oxford University Press, 1972. Complete text of Steele's four comedies, with an introduction that offers the best brief overview of Steele's stage career.

Loftis, John. *Steele at Drury Lane*. Berkeley: University of California Press, 1952. Focusing on Steele's dramatic writing, this literary study is nevertheless a readable and comprehensive portrait of Steele and his life between 1701 and 1722.

Mackie, Erin. *Commerce à la Mode: Fashion, Commodity, and Gender in "The Tatler" and "The Spectator."* Baltimore: Johns Hopkins University Press, 1997. An exploration into how Steele's two most popular periodicals shaped and were shaped by the material and social culture of eighteenth century England.

_____, ed. *The Commerce of Everyday Life: Selections from "The Tatler" and "The Spectator."* Boston: Bedford/St. Martin's Press, 1998. Representative selections of Addison and Steele's periodical essays, with a generous introduction and head notes, as well as select related contemporary works.

Winton, Calhoun. *Captain Steele: The Early Career of Richard Steele*. Baltimore: Johns Hopkins University Press, 1964. A detailed biography covering Steele's life through 1705.

_____. *Sir Richard Steele, M.P.* Baltimore: Johns Hopkins University Press, 1970. A continuation of Winton's earlier work, covering Steele's life from 1705 to his death in 1729.

See also: Joseph Addison; Queen Anne; George Berkeley; Georgiana Cavendish; George I; Samuel Johnson; Alexander Pope; Jonathan Swift; John Peter Zenger.

Related articles in *Great Events from History: The Eighteenth Century, 1701-1800:* March 1, 1711: Addison and Steele Establish *The Spectator*; January 7, 1714: Mill Patents the Typewriter; March 20, 1750-March 14, 1752: Johnson Issues *The Rambler*.

ANTONIO STRADIVARI
Italian artisan

Stradivari, the most famous violin maker in history, modified the traditional design of the violin as it had developed for one hundred years in Cremona. He created instruments that are still renowned for their superb tonal quality and that have been the models for violin making ever since.

Born: 1644?; Cremona?, Duchy of Milan (now in Italy)
Died: December 18, 1737; Duchy of Milan
Area of achievement: Music

EARLY LIFE

Antonio Stradivari (ahn-TOHN-yoh strah-dee-VAHR-ee) was born into a family whose name can be traced in Cremona to the twelfth century; however, no record of his birth has been found in the various archives of Cremona, despite repeated efforts on the part of researchers. It is known that he was the son of Alessandro Stradivari, and his birth date has been tentatively established as 1644, based on notations of his age written on labels in violins that he made near the end of his life. The Latin form of his name, Stradivarius, is also found on the labels of his violins; this spelling is often used to refer to an instrument made by Stradivari.

The early years of Stradivari remain a mystery. He may have been apprenticed first as a wood carver; beginning no later than the early 1660's, however, he studied the art of violin making with Niccolò Amati in Cremona. Amati, the leading violin maker of his day, represented the third generation of the Cremonese family who had created and developed the modern form of the instrument.

By 1666, if not earlier, Stradivari began to make violins on his own, and in the next year he established his own household and shop when he married Francesca Feraboschi. Six children were born to this marriage including two, Francesco and Omobono, who became violin makers and worked with their father.

The number of violins Stradivari produced before 1680 was not large; his reputation at this point did not extend far beyond Cremona, so the demand for his violins was not great. It is believed that during this time he designed and constructed a number of other instruments, especially plucked-string instruments such as guitars, harps, lutes, and mandolins. It is also clear that he continued to assist in his teacher's workshop for several years after he had established his own shop, possibly up to the

time of Amati's death in 1684. The few instruments that survive from this early period show that Stradivari was already a master craftsman who, although following the basic pattern of Amati, was cultivating his own ideas about the best tonal and artistic designs for the violin.

LIFE'S WORK

In 1680, Stradivari purchased a house at No. 2, Piazza San Domenico (later redesignated Piazza Roma), which was to be both his home and his workshop for the rest of his life. That he was able to purchase this three-story structure with a ground-floor shop at the front and ample living space for his family is good evidence of the financial success he was already enjoying. This new house had an attic and loft in which Stradivari is reported to have worked, leaving his varnished instruments to dry there during good weather.

From this house, Stradivari produced most of his stringed instruments, the most important and valuable such instruments ever made. Of an estimated output of 1,100 instruments, approximately 650 are extant, some preserved in collections and museums but many of them in active use by some of the great string players of the present time. In addition to his celebrated violins, Stradivari also made other instruments of the violin family, such as violas and cellos.

In the 1680's, Stradivari built instruments that show an increasing independence from the models of Amati; he created violins with a more solid and robust appearance and a more powerful tone than those of his teacher. The color of the varnish on these instruments still shows the typical yellowish tint of Amati's workshop, but sometimes Stradivari added a darker reddish accent. The number of violins produced during this time increased as Stradivari's fame spread beyond Cremona, and Amati's death in 1684 left him with no serious rival as the greatest violin maker of that city.

One of the remarkable qualities of Stradivari was his continuing search for any means that would produce a better instrument. The 1690's saw him working with a newly proportioned instrument known as the "long pattern," or "long Strad." In this design, he added 5/16 of an inch to the length of the violin without increasing the width. At the same time, he made subtle alterations in the design to keep the symmetry of the instrument intact. The effect of this new design was to produce a richer, darker tonal quality reminiscent of the sound produced by violins made in Brescia, the only other Italian city to rival Cremona in violin making.

In 1698, Stradivari's wife died and was given an elaborate funeral, and in August of the next year, the fifty-five-year-old craftsman married Antonia-Maria Zambelli. Five children, none of whom followed in their father's profession, came from this union. The years from 1700 to 1720 represent the peak of Stradivari's illustrious career and are often called the "golden period." His violin designs of this time moved away from the long pattern, and the tonal qualities of the instruments demonstrate a marvelous combination of the darker, richer tone of the previous era and the lighter, sweeter tone from the Cremonese tradition. In these years, Stradivari used the best materials that he (or anyone else) ever put into a violin; especially noteworthy are the magnificent maple backs of many of the instruments. The varnish now reached the orange-brown tint that is regarded as the typical Stradivari color.

Because of the great value and importance of individual instruments produced by Stradivari, names have come to be used to identify them, usually names of famous owners or names associated with some story connected with the particular instrument. Many of the violins made during the golden period are among the most famous: These include the "Betts" of 1704, now in Washington, D.C., at the Library of Congress; the "Alard" of 1715, which some experts regard as the finest extant Stradivarius; and the "Messiah" or "Salabue" of 1716, which was never sold by Stradivari and has been preserved in the best condition of any of his violins, now on display in the Ashmolean Museum in Oxford, England.

It was also during the period from 1700 to 1720 that Stradivari became especially interested in the development of the smaller cellos that were being sought by performers who were evolving the solo capabilities of this instrument. Earlier cellos were larger in size, designed to be an accompanying bass instrument. Stradivari had built a few of these larger instruments, but from 1707 through 1710 he produced a series of the smaller cellos that set the modern standard for the design of that instrument, an achievement no less significant than what he accomplished for the violin.

After 1720, when he was seventy-six years old, Stradivari might have been expected to turn most of the work over to his sons, Francesco and Omobono, who had assisted him through the years, but such was not the case. During the decade of the 1720's, he remained very active in the production of violins. The tonal quality of these instruments is very high, even though the wood he used is not as beautiful as that of the previous period, and there are occasional signs of his advanced age in the details of the instruments' workmanship.

The number of instruments produced after 1730 dwindles considerably, but it is clear that Stradivari continued to make violins by himself up to the last year of his life. While in these very late instruments the workmanship shows clear signs of failing hand and eye, the basic design and execution remain those of a master. There are also a number of instruments from this time that were made jointly by Stradivari, his sons, and his pupil Carlo Bergonzi. These instruments are labeled as made "under the discipline of Antonio Stradivari."

An artist's rendering of Antonio Stradivari. (Library of Congress)

That this man was still actively engaged in his profession at the age of ninety-three is indicative of the remarkable constitution that he must have enjoyed. There are no authentic portraits of Stradivari; a contemporary described him as tall and thin, always to be seen wearing a white cap and a white leather apron—his work clothes. On December 18, 1737, Stradivari died; his second wife had preceded him in death by nine months. They were buried in a tomb located in the Chapel of the Rosary in the Church of San Domenico, just across from the Stradivari house. Other members of the family were buried there through 1781, but in the nineteenth century the church was neglected, falling into such disrepair that in 1869 it was demolished and a public park was laid out on the site. Only the name stone of the tomb is preserved in the civic museum in Cremona, where there are to be found also drawings, patterns for instruments, and other artifacts of Antonio Stradivari.

SIGNIFICANCE

Antonio Stradivari brought the art of violin making to its highest level, unsurpassed even to the present day. He patiently and persistently explored the possibilities of the instrument that had been passed on to him by the master builders of his era. At the same time he was constantly searching for better ways of creating the greatest tonal and artistic beauty in these instruments.

During his lifetime, Stradivari was certainly highly regarded and widely known for his skill as a violin maker, for he received commissions for his instruments from many affluent individuals and royal courts. Many of the performers of this time, however, still preferred the designs of Amati and those of Jakob Steiner, the Austrian violin maker who produced fine instruments with a smaller but more brilliant tone. By the end of the eighteenth century, with changing musical styles and the need for a greater volume of sound from musical instruments, Stradivari's designs for the violin became the clearly favored pattern and have remained so into the twenty-first century.

The fact that these instruments, made several hundred years ago, not only are the best instruments made up to that time but also are unsurpassed since that time has led many to search for some special secret possessed by Stradivari that explains the dominance of his instruments. The particular characteristics of the wood that he used and the varnish on his instruments have been the subject of intense study and speculation for years. Certainly, the choice of materials is important, as is the varnish (not only the recipe but also the manner of applica-

tion), but most authorities agree that Stradivari's secret was his genius in combining all of the various materials, design, and execution in a way that makes a Stradivarius the ultimate of the violin maker's art.

—*Byron A. Wolverton*

FURTHER READING

Balfoort, Dirk J. *Antonius Stradivarius*. Translated by W. A. G. Doyle-Davidson. Stockholm: Continental, 1947. A concise account of Stradivari's life, interwoven with good descriptions of the different periods of instrument making. Also included are a number of photographs not to be found in other sources.

Delbanco, Nicholas. *The Countess of Stanlein Restored.* London: Verso, 2001. A history of Stradivari's Countess of Stanlein cello, including a description of a year-long restoration of the instrument. The cello had a checkered past; it was owned by Paganini, wound up in a garbage dump, and was eventually purchased by cellist Bernard Greenhouse, who arranged for its restoration.

Doring, Ernest N. *How Many Strads? Our Heritage from the Master.* Chicago: William Lewis & Son, 1945. A listing and description of the instruments produced by Stradivari, divided into eight periods. Doring tabulates 509 instruments in this work with detailed ownership histories for many of them, while others can be identified only very briefly. Photographs of more than one hundred instruments are included, and there is also a chapter on Stradivari's two violin-making sons.

Faber, Toby. *Stradivari's Genius: One Cello, Five Violins, and Three Centuries of Enduring Perfection.* New York: Random House, 2005. A history of Stradivari and six of his instruments. Faber provides biographical information about Stradivari, describing his instrument-making techniques and tracing the history of a cello and five violins that Stradivari created. Some of the instruments have been used by illustrious musicians, including cellist Yo-Yo Ma, who plays a Davidoff cello, made by Stradivari in 1712.

Goodkind, Herbert K. *Violin Iconography of Antonio Stradivari, 1644-1737.* Larchmont, N.Y.: Herbert K. Goodkind, 1972. A large deluxe volume that inventories all known Stradivari instruments; seven hundred such string instruments are listed and described here. Photographs of four hundred instruments are a major part of this work, and there is a valuable index of thirty-five hundred names of owners. Some essays on Stradivari and certain aspects of his violins and an extensive bibliography of more than 150 items are included.

Henley, William. *Antonio Stradivari, Master Luthier, Cremona, Italy, 1644-1737: His Life and Instruments*. Edited by C. Woodcock. Sussex, England: Amati, 1961. The bulk of this small volume is devoted to a chronological listing with brief descriptions of 455 Stradivari violins, violas, and cellos. Short chapters on Stradivari's life and periods of work and an editor's foreword dealing with fake instruments are included.

Hill, W. Henry, Arthur F. Hill, and Alfred E. Hill. *Antonio Stradivari: His Life and Work, 1644-1737*. London: William E. Hill and Sons, 1902. Reprint. New York: Dover, 1963. The standard work on Stradivari's life and instruments, written by three brothers who were violin experts and devoted much of their lives to the study of Stradivari and other string instrument makers of the seventeenth and eighteenth centuries. Incorporates previously unpublished research of A. Mandelli of Cremona.

See also: Johann Sebastian Bach; George Frideric Handel; Joseph Haydn; Wolfgang Amadeus Mozart.

Related articles in *Great Events from History: The Eighteenth Century, 1701-1800*: c. 1701-1750: Bach Pioneers Modern Music; April 13, 1742: First Performance of Handel's *Messiah*; January, 1762-November, 1766: Mozart Tours Europe as a Child Prodigy; 1795-1797: Paganini's Early Violin Performances.

GILBERT STUART
American painter

Stuart shaped the American image of George Washington with his painted portraits and also acquainted Americans with men and women of the generation that founded the United States. Stuart's great artistic achievements helped to launch the cultural life of the new nation.

Born: December 3, 1755; North Kingstown, Rhode Island
Died: July 9, 1828; Boston, Massachusetts
Also known as: Gilbert Charles Stuart (full name)
Area of achievement: Art

EARLY LIFE
Gilbert Stuart was born in the family quarters over his father's snuff mill. The elder Stuart, also named Gilbert, had left Scotland in the aftermath of the failed uprising there against the English (1745), a loss that caused much suffering and poverty. By 1751, he had entered into a business partnership for the manufacture of snuff and a marital partnership with Elizabeth Anthony, whose family owned a considerable amount of land. Ten years later, the snuff mill was abandoned and the Stuart family moved to Newport. Their circumstances were adequate but limited, and young Gilbert at the age of five was able to attend a school run by Trinity Church, the fees paid from a fund for the education of poor boys.

He was an apt student, but often his zest for mischievous pranks got him into trouble. He learned to play the flute and harpsichord, and he enjoyed drawing. His rather ordinary life was changed by the arrival, in 1769, of a most extraordinary person, Cosmo Alexander, an itinerant portrait painter from Scotland. Stuart was fascinated by this sophisticated, well-traveled man and delighted to enter his employ as an assistant who would do the many menial chores needed for painting; his pay was in the form of lessons in drawing. When Alexander moved on, Stuart accompanied him. They made their way south, at least as far as Virginia, stopping when clients could be found. Then, in 1770, they sailed to Scotland. It was there, in Edinburgh, that Stuart began to acquire the manners, speech, bearing, and social ease of a gentleman. Yet the high promise of his situation came to an end rather quickly, for Alexander died only two years later.

For the next few years, Stuart's life was a dreadful one. He was unable to support himself in Edinburgh. Somehow, probably by working his way, he got back home to Newport. He had become determined by this time to be a portrait painter, and he tried valiantly in Newport to practice the craft, but with discouraging results. He loved music, too, and became somewhat proficient on a number of instruments, including the organ, but that did not provide a living. These were the years, the middle 1770's, of the final crises in Anglo-American relations that culminated in the American Revolution; everything was disturbed and uncertain. It was the wrong place and the wrong time to launch a career as an artist. Stuart's closest boyhood friend, Benjamin Waterhouse, had gone to London to study medicine. In July, 1775, Stuart, hoping to join him, sought his own profession there.

It was quite a struggle, living the life of a starving artist in cheap lodgings. He found some clients, but not many. He made some money for a time as a church organist. When he did get financial help, he was unable to manage his affairs, giving way to extravagant impulses and neglecting his work. Finally, he wrote for help to Benjamin West, the rising American painter who had already found fame and fortune in London and who was known as a generous benefactor to fellow Americans who aspired to artistic achievement. After considerable hesitation, West employed him as a copyist and shortly thereafter accepted him as a pupil. At the age of twenty-one, in the spring of 1777, Stuart had managed to find the opportunity he needed to launch a great career.

LIFE'S WORK

Work in West's studio, it seems, provided Gilbert Stuart with exactly the conditions he needed to realize the full potential of his great talent. First, there was the discipline of a fixed, imposed routine—steady work habits, with little chance of temperamental abandonment of half-finished work. Then there was the systematic instruction by a foremost artist who usually took a keen interest in his many protégés. The association with other aspirants was stimulating and instructive; among them, at the time, were other Americans, such as the older, experienced John Singleton Copley and the less experienced John Trumbull, who arrived in 1780. There were also the prospects for important future clients who would be pleased to have a portrait by an associate of West, painter for the royal household and even a friend of George III. Stuart took fine advantage of all this, showing rapid improvement in his painting. A self-portrait he painted in 1778 documents his progress; when West saw it, his earlier doubts about Stuart were overcome, and he encouraged his charge to submit future work for exhibition at the Royal Academy. By this time, Stuart was living in the vast West household.

By 1781, Stuart's name was becoming known in artistic circles, and some of the portraits he exhibited received favorable comment. One portrait of West, in particular, was praised that year when it appeared in an exhibition that also included work by Sir Joshua Reynolds and Thomas Gainsborough. A few new commissions followed, and one of them made him famous. A friend, William Grant, arrived for a sitting on a particularly cold day, which prompted the remark that it was a good day for ice skating, which both enjoyed. They skated first and then returned to the studio, where Stuart eventually got the idea of portraying his subject on skates. *The Skater* was the sensation of the Royal Academy exhibition of 1782 and remains one of his most celebrated works. He was now sought by many to paint their portraits. He moved to his own quarters and began a lavish style of life, soon running beyond his actual means to sustain it. In another five years, this improvidence would end his glorious London career.

Stuart was especially well suited for expansive living. Always a voluble talker and possessed of an irrepressible sense of humor, he was an intensely social being. Concerned with personal appearance and current fashion, he acquired fine new clothes of bright colors, elegant buttons, and the finest lace ruffles and trim. Standing five feet, ten inches, he was lean, quick of movement and tongue, every bit the fine, modish London gentleman. His abundant, dark brown hair was now powdered white for public appearances. The most striking feature of his face was a long nose, but he was handsome in a somewhat rugged way.

During these years—the middle 1780's—Stuart's clients included many well-known people, such as Sir William Petty, the earl of Shelburne; Admiral Lord Hood; Richard Brinsley Sheridan; and painter Reynolds. His fees rose accordingly, as did his prestige. Portrait painting was highly favored and highly developed in the England of Gainsborough, Reynolds, George Romney, and other such luminaries; for Stuart to have become regarded as established in their ranks was indeed an astonishing accomplishment for a thirty-year-old American who had emerged from severe adversity only six or seven years before.

There was an impractical side to Stuart that determined the course of his erratic career. In an age when men advanced, in part, by making an advantageous marriage, Stuart fell in love with the daughter of a physician in Reading, Berkshire, well outside the fashionable, affluent circles of London. Despite the family's strong objections, he married Charlotte Coates in May, 1786. Stuart's high style of entertainment continued: A French chef, fine wines, live musicians, and elegant tableware were featured. Despite repeated efforts by some of his affluent friends to help him regain control of his finances, rumors began to circulate that Stuart could not pay some of his basic household bills. Creditors pressed in, and at last Stuart realized that debtors' prison might be awaiting him. One day in October, 1787, Stuart arrived in Dublin, Ireland, presumably at the invitation of the duke of Rutland for the painting of his portrait. Stuart never returned to London's fashionable social scene.

Stuart's artistic fame had reached Dublin, but news of his financial irresponsibility apparently had not, for there now unfolded a second career something like his first. He gained access to prominent people who were pleased to have him paint their portraits. He became a part of the most fashionable social life, where his charm as a wit and raconteur and his geniality made him most welcome. Again, he entertained lavishly, and again, his funds were not adequate to such a style. As the premier portraitist of Ireland, he had no serious rival; the best of the commissions was his. Some of his work was distinguished, notably a full-length portrait of Lord Fitzgibbon, through whom Stuart gained access to the highest ranks of official society and many resulting commissions. The process followed its course: artistic achievement and a splendid social life undercut by mounting personal debt. By the spring of 1793, Stuart was once again in full retreat; he and his family were on a boat for New York.

Once more, Stuart found that his reputation was known, and he soon had business. A portrait painted by a well-known artist is a luxury item, available only to the affluent, so it was inevitable that Stuart's first contacts in New York City were made with the prosperous merchants and their social set. His most valuable connection came when he revived his acquaintance with John Jay (he had met him earlier in London), who was at this time chief justice of the U.S. Supreme Court. Discussion of painting a portrait of George Washington commenced. Stuart himself is the source of the idea that it was for that, expressly, that he had moved to America, though that is obviously only a part of the truth, if an important part. A portrait of Jay done at this time is a valuable record of an extremely important figure in the founding of the new nation. It is also a reminder that it was in all probability Jay who persuaded Washington to sit for Stuart.

These were turbulent times, the middle 1790's, with a mighty armed struggle in Europe and bitter political battles and even insurrection at home. It was in 1794 that Jay left the country on a diplomatic mission to Britain, and it was then, too, that the Whiskey Rebellion in Pennsylvania demanded Washington's attention. Meanwhile, Stuart was extremely busy painting portraits of the promi-

nent people—Revolutionary War heroes, political leaders, scions of distinguished families, and the like. Some of these works have been commended as examples of Stuart's finest art, especially the portraits of Jay, the wife of Richard Yates, and the Spanish diplomat Don Josef de Jaudenes and his American wife.

Early in 1795, Stuart went to Philadelphia, which had been the nation's temporary capital since 1790, with the assurance that he might paint Washington. The result was a bust portrait with the right side of the face toward the viewer, known now as the Vaughan type. Although Washington had already been painted many times, Stuart's reputation was greater than those of earlier painters, and people were extremely eager to see his work. There was a brief public exhibition, and the praise for the picture was overwhelming. In the longer run, it has also been adjudged a solid critical success—some think it is Stuart's best Washington. At the time, many people asked for copies of the portrait to be done by Stuart, and the artist obliged; at least seventeen copies are known to exist.

Washington's second sitting for Stuart came the following year, 1796, through the influence of William Bingham, the Philadelphia businessman who was reputedly the richest person in the United States as well as a Federalist senator and a close friend of Washington. It was Bingham's ambition to have his own portrait of Washington, to be a very large, full-length picture, done by Stuart. Washington, aging, busy, and weary, was most reluctant to spend time again sitting for a portrait, but at length he agreed. From those 1796 sittings came two more versions of Washington, as interpreted by Stuart. One, a full-length portrait, became known as the Landsdowne type. It shows the left side of Washington's face; his left hand is holding a luxurious sword, and his right is extended and open as if speaking to an audience. In a slightly later version of this work, the right hand is touching papers on a table, and this has been praised as an improvement, along with other details that were changed.

The other 1796 portrait is his best-known one, known as the Athenaeum type. Curiously, this painting was never entirely finished, and Stuart retained it in his possession all of his life. Yet people wanted copies done by Stuart, and he obliged, usually charging $100—leading him to refer to the copies as his "one hundred dollar bills." This, the best known of the many hundreds of Stuart portraits, is a truly extraordinary, subtle, incisive study of a great man in his final years. Stuart produced about seventy copies, sometimes a bit carelessly, and

949

could have sold more if he had not been anxious to keep up with new subjects. The Washington portraits and the prints made from them kept him solvent for a while.

Stuart was soon busier than ever—too busy, perhaps. Even the removal of the government to the new capital on the Potomac did not lessen the demand for his portraits. He excelled often in portraits of women, including a charming one of Martha Washington. Some of his old infirmities returned to spoil his success: high living, careless handling of accounts, and capricious neglect of work, to which was now added recurrent illness and general poor health. Finally, in the summer of 1803, he arranged for his family to stay in Bordentown, New Jersey, while he proceeded to Washington, where he opened another studio. For two years, he painted dignitaries of the national government and various other prominent persons who came to the capital. His subjects included nearly all the names found in accounts of the political history of Jeffersonian America: all the presidents, vice presidents, cabinet members, and prominent congressmen and senators. Yet he was once more caught up in a web of personal and financial difficulties, compounded by a growing tendency to deceive even those who tried to help him. In 1805, he decided to move to Boston.

Again, he was much sought after, and he prospered for a time. His life was far from tranquil, however, and it appears that his artistic powers suffered some decline. His health was recurrently a problem, and he suffered periods of depression. He died on July 9, 1828, heavily in debt.

SIGNIFICANCE

Among American painters of all times, Gilbert Stuart's name may well be the most familiar, and it is invariably linked with Washington's name. Some have disparaged the artistic merit of the Washington portraits, and certainly the most familiar one, the Athenaeum type, has suffered in painterly reputation from its very popularity. Yet Stuart has always had his champions in the artistic community who esteem these works; popularity of his works has proved relatively constant and durable, and they have provided most Americans with their idea of their country's foremost founder. There is merit in the remark that if Washington came back to Earth and did not look like that portrait, he would be denounced as an impostor.

Those who take an interest in others of the founding generation find Stuart an invaluable guide to an acquaintance with them, too. With the important exception of Alexander Hamilton, there are surprisingly few people of importance in the early national history of the United States who cannot be better known through a careful viewing of a Stuart portrait.

It should be noted, furthermore, that Stuart's great achievements were those of a person born into severely limiting circumstances who underwent much adversity in his struggle for success. To be sure, some of his difficulties were of his own making, even in the latter part of his early life, and ever more so in his later years. His many faults and flaws of character, though, were overcome time and again by a combination of courageous resourcefulness and very considerable artistic talent. Achievements in the fine arts must surely have been among the most implausible of expectations in colonial and revolutionary America. Stuart was among a small number of men who prevailed despite severely discouraging circumstances.

His success, both in the momentary appearances of prosperity and in the genuine artistic achievements, was important for the encouragement of the arts in early America. He was usually accessible and generous with his time and advice, as many younger artists attested. Stuart brought an international reputation to the American scene and built yet another one in this country. The United States became a far better country for having an artistic tradition, however neglected and underestimated it may have been for a time.

—*Richard D. Miles*

FURTHER READING

Barratt, Carrie Rebora, and Ellen G. Miles. *Gilbert Stuart*. New York: Metropolitan Museum of Art, 2004. The catalog accompanying an exhibition of Stuart's work displayed in 2004-2005 at the Metropolitan Museum of Art in New York and the National Gallery of Art in Washington, D.C. Includes reproductions of more than ninety portraits and an essay describing how Stuart developed and maintained his distinctive style of portraiture. Also features essays on each site where Stuart produced his art and the paintings created there, as well as information on Stuart's portraits of George Washington.

Evans, Dorinda. *The Genius of Gilbert Stuart*. Princeton, N.J.: Princeton University Press, 1999. A comprehensive biography, tracing Stuart's artistic development and influence. Evans examines Stuart's ability to use portraiture to convey a sense of public virtue and social dignity in his subjects, citing his famed Athenaeum portrait of Washington as an example of his technique. She also describes his erratic personality, and suggests his behavior may have been caused by manic-depressive (bipolar) illness.

Flexner, James T. *America's Old Masters*. Rev. ed. Garden City, N.Y.: Doubleday, 1980. Flexner acquaints readers with Stuart and three of his contemporaries, though he treats Stuart somewhat harshly. A good presentation of successful early American artists. In 1955, the author published a biography of Stuart that was a slightly expanded version of this presentation, under the title *Gilbert Stuart*.

Gilbert Stuart: Portraitist of the Young Republic, 1755-1828. Providence: Museum of Art, Rhode Island School of Design, 1967. The catalog of an exhibition of fifty-four carefully chosen portraits, held both in Providence and at the National Gallery of Art, Washington, D.C. Valuable for its excellent introductory essay by Edgar P. Richardson and for the informative commentaries that accompany each of the fifty-four black-and-white illustrations.

Harris, Neil. *The Artist in American Society: The Formative Years, 1790-1860*. New York: George Braziller, 1966. Discusses the plight of the aspiring artist in the new nation. Nearly half of this perceptive portrayal of the cultural scene is directly useful for an appreciation of the kind of country Stuart found after he returned to the United States. Very thoughtful, with many interesting and provocative ideas.

Morgan, John Hill. *Gilbert Stuart and His Pupils*. New York: New York Historical Society, 1939. Mainly a series of brief sketches of twenty-three painters whose work was directly influenced by Stuart. Often the actual influence seems slight, but this small book (ninety-three pages) as a whole is effective in establishing Stuart as an important force in the work of painters such as John Vanderlyn, Thomas Sully, and Samuel Morse, who lived well into the nineteenth century. Also includes notes by Matthew Jouett from conversations with Stuart.

Mount, Charles M. *Gilbert Stuart: A Biography*. New York: W. W. Norton, 1964. Mount, a painter and scholar, finds Stuart seriously flawed as a person, but he nevertheless asserts, in very strong terms, the greatness of some of Stuart's work. Fascinating notes and superb catalog of Stuart's known works.

Whitley, William T. *Gilbert Stuart*. Cambridge, Mass.: Harvard University Press, 1932. A biography of sorts, somewhat superseded by that of Charles Mount. Whitley, however, took Stuart seriously when few others did, and he unearthed much important information and incorporated it into a book that is still good reading. Includes an abundance of anecdotes, some of dubious authenticity, told about the idiosyncratic painter.

See also: John Singleton Copley; Thomas Gainsborough; George III; John Jay; Charles Willson Peale; Sir Joshua Reynolds; George Romney; Richard Brinsley Sheridan; John Trumbull; George Washington; Benjamin West.

Related articles in *Great Events from History: The Eighteenth Century, 1701-1800:* April 30, 1789: Washington's Inauguration; July-November, 1794: Whiskey Rebellion; November 19, 1794: Jay's Treaty; September 19, 1796: Washington's Farewell Address.

WILLIAM STUKELEY
English archaeologist and antiquarian

Stukeley was the foremost British antiquarian and archaeologist in the eighteenth century. He is best remembered for his careful observations, measurements, and diagrammed descriptions of Stonehenge and Avebury. Although he incorrectly attributed their construction to the Druids, he was among the first to recognize their pre-Roman origins and their historic value. He was also among the first to publicly express concern over their preservation.

Born: November 7, 1687; Holbeach, Lincolnshire, England
Died: March 3, 1765; London, England
Areas of achievement: Archaeology, science and technology, scholarship, historiography, architecture

EARLY LIFE

William Stukeley was the eldest son in a family of five children. He shared a close relationship with his father, John, who was a respected attorney; he was less attached to his undemonstrative mother, Frances Bullen. At age five, William was sent to the Free School at Holbeach, where he first learned to draw, a skill that he would use throughout his career. He excelled in learning and enjoyed making maps, collecting coins, and studying science.

In 1701 he was apprenticed into his father's law firm, but he disliked legal training and was allowed to leave for Bene't Hall (now Corpus Christi College). He pursued medical studies at Cambridge, but the deaths of his parents and two of his siblings interrupted his education in 1706 and 1707. After his graduation from Cambridge in 1709, he moved to London to study medicine under Richard Mead at St. Thomas's Hospital. The following year he returned to Lincolnshire to set up medical practice in Boston. There he looked after his younger siblings and settled debts remaining after his father's early death. He also pursued antiquarian studies and joined a society to discuss the ancient history of Britain.

LIFE'S WORK

William Stukeley had many interests. Although he was trained as a physician, he also studied theology, science, and antiquities. In 1717 he returned to London, became involved with reestablishing the Society of Antiquaries, and served as the first secretary, a post he would hold for nine years. In 1718, through his continued acquain-

tance with Richard Mead, he became a fellow of the Royal Society. At the Royal Society he associated with some of the most gifted men of his time, including Sir Isaac Newton.

Stukeley received his medical degree from Cambridge in 1719 and was admitted a fellow of the Royal College of Physicians the following year. In his first anatomical presentation to the Royal Society, he showed drawings of vertical sections of the human body; although Leonardo da Vinci pioneered the technique, Stukeley might have been the first English anatomist to use this method of presentation.

The 1720's marked a key period in his life. He supported himself financially as a physician and so was free to pursue his antiquarian studies as well. Many members of the Society of Antiquaries limited their interests to the Middle Ages, but Stukeley and his friends founded the Society of Roman Knights in 1722 to focus on the ancient history of Roman Britain. Members were given nicknames from Celtic history, and Stukeley was called "Chyndonax," a Druid name by which he was known even after the group disbanded. He embarked on annual tours of the English countryside, on horseback, and sketched and recorded his observations of ancient sites. Material from seven of these tours formed the body of his *Itinerarium Curiosum: Or, An Account of the Antiquitys and Remarkable Curiositys in Nature or Art* (1724). On these tours he initiated fieldwork that was to become his most notable achievement: studies of the sites of Stonehenge and Avebury.

Stukeley studied Stonehenge and Avebury during the summers between 1719 and 1724. Although John Aubrey had examined these same sites sixty years earlier, Stukeley's investigation was more comprehensive and systematic. His work involved careful observation, detailed measurements, and accurate descriptions with accompanying drawings and diagrams. He developed a typology of stone-temple characteristics and was the first to thoroughly diagram the configurations of the stone circles and their environs. He was the first to recognize the raised "avenues," as he called them, at both sites, and also was the first to discover that Stonehenge was astronomically aligned. Noting the importance of stratigraphy (the geology of strata), he developed careful excavation techniques and pioneered the use of the cross-section diagram. He was aware that careful recording was vital in preserving information about historic monuments that were facing deterioration and destruction—natural as well as by the hands of humans.

After 1726, Stukeley's life changed. He left London and moved his medical practice to Grantham, Lincolnshire. Reasons for the move may have been his love of country life, his perceived lack of support for his antiquarian endeavors or his treatment for gout. The following year he married Frances Williamson, a local woman who was to bear three daughters. In 1729 he was ordained into the Church of England and became vicar at All Saints, Stamford. Many were surprised by his ordination, as nonbelief was common among eighteenth century scientists. His religious interests, however, were deep-rooted, if somewhat unconventional.

After Stukeley's ordination, his work became increasingly speculative. He romanticized the Druids and their role in Britain's history. He believed Christianity was prefigured in ancient Druid religion. He identified both Stonehenge and Avebury (which he called "Abury") as Druid temples. His *Palaeographia Sacra: Or, Discourses on Monuments of Antiquity That Relate to Sacred History* (1736) linked his archaeological and religious studies. In 1739, two years after his wife died, he married Elizabeth Gale and used her substantial dowry to publish *Stonehenge: A Temple Restor'd to the British Druids* (1740) and *Abury: A Temple of the British Druids* (1743). These publications further intermingled his meticulous scientific fieldwork with imaginative religious conjecture.

In 1747, when the duke of Montagu offered Stukeley a place to live in Queen's Square, Bloomsbury, he returned to London. Despite the success of his books on Stonehenge and Avebury, he was involved in some controversy resulting from his endorsements of a forged medieval history of ancient Britain and a collection of prose poems falsely claimed to be ancient works by the third century poet Ossian. Nevertheless, Stukeley was regarded as a scientist as well as an antiquarian, and he remained an important figure in English society. In 1750 he published his widely known *The Philosophy of Earthquakes, Natural and Religious: Or, An Inquiry into Their Cause and Purpose*. In 1753 he was chosen as a trustee in establishing the British Museum and also was involved with the oversight of the Foundling Hospital. He died on March 3, 1765, after suffering a stroke.

SIGNIFICANCE

William Stukeley was an eclectic scholar and a paradoxical figure who bridged the worlds of British antiquarianism and archaeology. His careful observations,

descriptions, measurements, and diagrams were important components in the development of archaeological field surveys. His investigations of the stone circles at Avebury and Stonehenge were the most thorough and systematic studies undertaken up to that time. At both sites, he noted features that had never before been documented. Believing the sites to be prehistoric sanctuaries, Stukeley set about proving that they predated medieval or Roman times.

Because his publications intermixed his fieldwork with his Druidic conjectures, the accuracy of his descriptions and drawings has been doubted. However, late investigations of Stonehenge and Avebury (including the rediscovery of "Beckhampton Avenue" at Avebury) have substantiated his findings. His detailed observations provide a valuable record of monuments and their environs before they were subjected to additional weathering and depredation. Contemporary analysis of his fieldwork reveals how much has been destroyed since the eighteenth century. Stukeley, who was among the first to recognize the historic importance of the ruins and to express concern over their survival, laid the foundation for modern study of these ancient sites.

In many ways he was a model for Enlightenment science: He was a trained physician, a published scholar, a pioneer in archaeological fieldwork, and a fellow of the Royal Society. Yet, he also was later ordained, and he linked Avebury and Stonehenge with Druidism. This erroneous link was perpetuated well into the twentieth century. Although his work has been subjected to scholarly criticism, it is important to examine it in terms of the intellectual environment of his time. Stukeley and his colleagues in the Royal Society engaged in intense speculation over the history of religion and the early history of the world. Classical historians had connected Druids with ancient history, and Stukeley was involved in a contemporary discussion on the role of the Druids. This is all reflected in his work.

His study of ancient ruins and speculations on the past influenced the Romantic tradition of late eighteenth and early nineteenth century English literature. Works by poets such as Thomas Gray and William Collins reflected the "Druidical Revival." Artist and poet William Blake also was an avid proponent of Britain's Druidic past.

—*Cassandra Lee Tellier*

FURTHER READING

Burl, Aubrey. *Great Stone Circles*. New Haven, Conn.: Yale University Press, 1999. Burl questions the purpose, construction, age, and distribution of stone circles. Includes color photographs, drawings, notes, a bibliography, and an index.

Haycock, David. *William Stukeley: Science, Religion, and Archeology in Eighteenth-Century England.* Woodbridge, England: Boydell Press, 2002. Haycock notes that Stukeley has been unfairly removed from his eighteenth century intellectual context and therefore has faced undue criticism. Includes a bibliography of Stukeley's works, bibliographies of primary and secondary sources, and an index.

Hayman, Richard. *Riddles in Stone: Myths, Archaeology, and the Ancient Britons.* London: Hambledon and London Press, 2003. Although science has advanced the knowledge of Britain's megaliths, their purposes and meanings remain subjects of debate. Photographs, reproductions, drawings, site listing, notes, bibliography, and index.

Piggott, Stuart. *William Stukeley: An Eighteenth-Century Antiquary.* New York: Thames and Hudson, 1985. A revised biography of Stukeley and his seemingly paradoxical character. This work includes reproductions, drawings, reconstructed journal notes from the 1721-

1725 tours, reconstructed journals of fieldwork at Avebury and Stonehenge, notes, references, and an index.

Stukeley, William. *The Commentarys, Diary, and Common-Place Book and Selected Letters of William Stukeley.* London: Doppler Press, 1980. A 174-page collection of Stukeley's personal writings and letters.

_____. *Stonehenge, a Temple Restor'd to the British Druids* and *Abury, a Temple of the British Druids.* New York: Garland, 1984. Updated reprints of Stukeley's classic works on Stonehenge and Avebury. Includes an introductory essay by Robert D. Richardson, Jr., and illustrations.

See also: Lancelot Brown; Johann Joachim Winckelmann.

Related articles in *Great Events from History: The Eighteenth Century, 1701-1800:* 1719-1724: Stukeley Studies Stonehenge and Avebury; 1748: Excavation of Pompeii; 1762: *The Antiquities of Athens* Prompts Architectural Neoclassicism.

ALEKSANDR VASILYEVICH SUVOROV
Russian military leader

By abandoning the conventional defensive tactics of the period, Suvorov created a new type of army in which speed, mobility, and independence of judgment by junior officers were valued more than drills and sieges.

Born: November 24, 1729; near Moscow, Russia
Died: May 18, 1800; his estate, Kobrin, near St. Petersburg, Russia
Also known as: Count Rymnikskii; Prince Italskii
Area of achievement: Military

EARLY LIFE
Aleksandr Vasilyevich Suvorov (uhl-yihk-SAHN-duhr vuhs-YEEL-yihv-yihch sew-VAW-ruhf) was born on his parents' estate, southwest of Moscow. His paternal grandfather, Ivan, had been an aide to Czar Peter the Great, while his father, Vasili, entered the military service as an administrator, achieving the rank of *generalanshef,* between lieutenant general and field marshal. Vasili married Avodita Theodeyevna Manukova, daughter of the governor of St. Petersburg.

At birth, Suvorov was underweight and colicky. As he matured, he remained puny and sickly. Limited in physical activities, he turned to his father's library, where he enjoyed reading military history. With the aid of tutors, he learned Russian, French, German, Latin, Greek, and eventually Turkish and Italian. Because of his intuitive understanding of military tactics, in October, 1742, he was enrolled in a guards regiment but did not join that regiment until 1745.

Young Suvorov slowly rose in rank, becoming a lieutenant in 1754. He then spent a year at the War College with his father. After that, he joined the Kurinski Regiment and was promoted to major. During this period, he wrote two fictional dialogues that contain the seeds of his later innovative ideas. Russia became involved in the Seven Years' War, and Suvorov was given command of three battalions stationed in and around Memel. Seeking action, he transferred to the main army fighting Frederick the Great and was present at the Battle of Kunersdorf in August, 1759. He openly criticized the failure of imperial forces to exploit their victory by seizing Berlin. In July, 1761, he was given command of a detachment of cavalry in western Poland and won a series of victories over the Prussians. At Golnau, he received a slight chest wound and went home.

The imperial commander in chief, Pyotr Aleksandrovich Rumyantsev, suggested to the new emperor, Peter III, that Suvorov be rewarded, but Peter rejected the idea and pulled Russia out of the war, surrendering all gains and forcing Russia's allies to capitulate. Many Russians resented that action; they seized Peter and proclaimed his wife, Catherine, empress. Catherine the Great became fond of the urbane Suvorov and agreed to follow Rumyantsev's suggestion by appointing young Suvorov colonel of first the Astrakhan and then the Suzdal Regiments.

LIFE'S WORK

Suvorov wrote the regimental regulations detailing his orders: The army must constantly drill—not parade, but simulate battle. Walls were built to be scaled; moats dug to be crossed; men and horses charged with guns blazing. His troops never received the order to retreat, only to advance to a new position. He reduced the size of the military square and abandoned the use of long lines of musketeers. The smaller squares were spread apart; musketeers became marksmen. Speed, mobility, and individual initiative replaced detailed commands. Discipline was essential in Suvorov's view, but so was health and spirit. In 1765, when the regiment was sent to the forest around Lake Ladoga, he ordered a church, two schools, and gardens built. Suvorov was loved by his troops, and they would follow him to the ends of Europe.

In May, 1771, Suvorov learned that a Franco-Polish army was near Kraków; Suvorov reached the enemy at Landskron. The French general thought that the Russians would rest after their long march, but Suvorov's army was trained to march into battle. The enemy was destroyed. In September, Suvorov learned that three thousand Poles were advancing. He attacked them at dawn. By 11:00 A.M., the Polish force was routed.

Turkey declared war, and Catherine sent Suvorov into the Balkans. On the night of May 9, 1773, he led his men across the Danube River and destroyed a Turkish force of five thousand at Turtukai. The Turks sent a new army to Turtukai, and, although severely wounded, Suvorov commanded another assault. The Turks were again routed. In July, the still weak hero was transferred to the army under the command of Catherine's lover, Grigori Aleksandrovich Potemkin. Suvorov made it clear that he did not like Potemkin and was sent to Hison on the lower Danube.

Aleksandr Vasilyevich Suvorov. (Library of Congress)

Still weak, he returned home to marry Princess Varvara Ivanovna Prozorovskaya. By the time their daughter was born, he was back at the front. In the spring of 1774, he trained a detachment and took them across the Danube. On June 10, his eight thousand troops routed sixty thousand Turks at Kozludj. The Turks willingly ended the war on July 10.

For the next few years, Suvorov saw little military action. In August, 1787, however, Turkey again declared war, and Suvorov was entrusted with the defense of the south. He went to Kinburn. On the night of October 2, he destroyed a Turkish armada. All but five hundred of the five thousand Turks were killed, and seven of their ships were sunk. The Russians lost only 227 men, with a similar number of wounded. One of the wounded was Suvorov, who was shot in the arm.

The following spring, Potemkin arrived to besiege Ochakov. Suvorov was asked to command part of the besieging force, but he wrote, "You cannot capture a fortress by looking at it." Potemkin sent him to Moldavia. He went to Jassy, where he was instructed to link up with an Austrian force. On July 20, 1789, he crushed the Turks at Fokshany. On September 7, the Austrians reported that they were about to be overwhelmed by the Turks. Suvorov's troops covered 60 miles in thirty-six hours to attack the Turks along the Rymnik River. For his victory, Catherine rewarded Suvorov with a title and money; the Austrians made him a count of the Holy Roman Empire.

Catherine wanted a quick victory to end the war. Potemkin, entrusted with the siege of the Turkish fortress at Ismail, summoned Suvorov, who arrived on December 2 and began to train the troops. Between dawn and afternoon on December 11, a Turkish army of forty thousand was annihilated. Potemkin congratulated the victor; Suvorov responded with a barb. Catherine and her lover were furious, and Suvorov was transferred to Finland, while Catherine showered honors on Potemkin.

After Potemkin died and the Turks agreed to a peace, Catherine allowed Suvorov to return to his command in the south, but when trouble began in Poland, she gave the command to Rumyantsev. The latter summoned Suvorov. On September 6, 1794, Suvorov defeated a Polish force at Krupshchitze and then gathered forces to attack the Polish citadel at Praga. The attack on October 24 was over in three hours. Suvorov negotiated lenient terms for the Poles, but Catherine abrogated all the surrender terms. Furious, Suvorov went to Kobrin, the estate Catherine had awarded him.

The sixty-five-year-old field marshal authorized his aide, Lieutenant Colonel Friedrich Anthing, to write and publish a history of his exploits up to 1794. He also began to write and circulate a manuscript, *Nauka Pobezhdat* (1806; the knowledge [or art] of victory), detailing his theories. "Train hard, fight easy. Train easy, and you will have hard fighting," became his motto. In language that a peasant could understand, Suvorov revealed his theories. Because of the nature of cannon and rifles, it was better to charge a battery with saber and bayonet than to march slowly forward. Because of the death toll caused by disease, cleanliness was important and a quick storming was less costly than a long siege. Because mobility and speed were the secret to victory, junior officers must be capable of assuming responsibility. Because the army needed the support of the local population, the army must always respect that population. Because spirit was essential, religion was essential.

In November, 1796, Paul I came to the throne. He exiled Suvorov to his estate at Konchansk, south of St. Petersburg, where he spent his time studying the tactics of Napoleon I, the only general he considered his equal. In December, 1798, Russia, Austria, and England united against France. The imperial fleet was sent into the Mediterranean and Adriatic seas, while Russian armies were sent to the Netherlands, Switzerland, and Italy.

The Austrians requested that Suvorov be sent to Italy. The seventy-year-old warrior arrived in Italy in April, 1799, and was appointed commander in chief of the Austrian army, even though the Austrians disliked his battle plan.

Suvorov and the commander of the imperial fleet complained to Paul that their allies restricted their freedom. Suvorov entered Turin on May 14. He secured local cooperation only to have his arrangements countermanded. Suvorov was in a bind: Logistic support was provided by the Austrians, and they vetoed his actions. When word arrived of an approaching French army, Suvorov left the Austrians and crushed the French at the Trebbia River. When word of that victory spread, isolated French citadels capitulated.

Paul demanded that Emperor Francis II of Austria give Suvorov a free hand, but Francis refused. Word came that the last French force in Italy was approaching, and Suvorov met and destroyed it at Novi. He then demanded permission to invade France, but Francis again refused and ordered him to join the Russians in Switzerland. Learning of Suvorov's intent to join Russian forces led by Aleksandr Rimsky-Korsakov in Switzerland, the French fortified St. Gotthard Pass and planned to destroy the Russians at Zurich. Suvorov reached Taverne on September 15, but the Austrians had not delivered the promised supplies. Suvorov awaited the supplies for four days.

On September 21-22, the Russians finally cleared the French from St. Gotthard Pass and then defeated another French force at Kinzig Pass. The four-day delay at Taverne proved fatal, however, for the French had used the time to destroy the Russian army in Switzerland. When Suvorov learned of the disaster, he decided to go to Glarus via the Pragel Pass. A French force blocked him, while the victorious French army attacked his rear flank, but Suvorov's army defeated both French forces. By this time, Suvorov was coughing and had a high fever. Word arrived of the failure of the Anglo-Russian campaign in the Netherlands, and Paul informed Francis that all Russian troops were ordered home. Paul promoted Suvorov to the unprecedented rank of generalissimo. By March, 1800, the sick hero had returned to his Kobrin estate.

Paul received a full report and decided that the allies had to be punished. He began to plan to send Russian troops to India to help the Indians oust the British. He became furious at Suvorov, who had won all the victories while breaking his specific military instructions and dress codes. Suvorov was stripped of his honors. Sick and broken in spirit, Suvorov died on the afternoon of May 18, 1800, regretting that he had not had the opportunity to face Napoleon.

SIGNIFICANCE

Until the mid-nineteenth century, European historians tended to dismiss Aleksandr Vasilyevich Suvorov as an eccentric who could not possibly have won so many victories. In Russia, historians paid scant attention to his exploits until after the disaster of the Crimean War. While military technology, altered by the Industrial Revolution, made Suvorov's use of the saber and bayonet obsolete, his vision of speed and mobility became increasingly popular. As World War II approached, Suvorov's writings were published and studied. His victories over the superior forces of France and Turkey raised him to the level of national hero and medals were given in his honor during the dark days of 1941-1942.

As Russian sources began to be studied by non-Russian historians, Suvorov's achievements began to be understood and appreciated. While many of his tactics are irrelevant in modern times, the spirit he imparted to his troops, which allowed them to perform exactly as he wished, is still envied.

—J. Lee Shneidman

FURTHER READING

Alexander, John T. *Catherine the Great: Life and Legend*. New York: Oxford University Press, 1989. Making extensive use of Catherine's writings as well as other primary documents and unpublished material, the author stresses the personal side of Catherine's court. Excellent for understanding other Russian generals such as Potemkin and Rumyantsev.

Blease, W. Lyon. *Suvorof*. London: Constable, 1920. The author, an army doctor who spoke Russian, wrote the first biography in English that attempted to deal with Suvorov's personal life. Blease understood the charismatic nature of Suvorov's leadership but did not appreciate his generalship.

De Madariaga, Isabel. *Russia in the Age of Catherine the Great*. New Haven, Conn.: Yale University Press, 1981. Making extensive use of Russian sources, the author integrates Suvorov's military activity with the whole of Russian foreign policy. An excellent study of Russia's response to the Enlightenment emerges.

Duffy, Christopher. *Eagles Over the Alps: Suvorov in Italy and Switzerland, 1799*. Chicago: Emperor's Press, 1999. Duffy, a military historian, describes Suvorov's final campaigns in Italy and Switzerland. Includes line maps and orders of battle.

_____. *Russia's Military Way to the West: Origins and Nature of Russian Military Power, 1700-1800*. London: Routledge & Kegan Paul, 1981. This is an excellent study of the growth of Russia's military power in the eighteenth century. The last chapters concentrate on Suvorov's exploits.

Longworth, Philip. *The Art of Victory: The Life and Achievement of Generalissimo Suvorov, 1729-1800*. New York: Holt, Rinehart and Winston, 1965. Making extensive use of Russian sources, the author has written an excellent biography. While little is mentioned of Suvorov's personal life, there are extensive quotations from his military writings and a useful summary of Suvorov's place in military history.

Montefiore, Sebag. *Prince of Princes: The Life of Potemkin*. New York: Thomas Dunne Books, 2001. A comprehensive biography about Potemkin. Includes information about Suvorov's commands and battles as well as his relationship with Potemkin.

Osipov, K. *Alexander Suvorov*. Translated by Edith Bone. London: Hutchinson, 1941. This is an English translation of one of the many Soviet editions that appeared almost annually between 1940 and 1950. While much of the work is uncritical hero-worship, it is useful in understanding Suvorov's growing reputation, especially during the war years.

Saul, Norman E. *Russia and the Mediterranean, 1797-1807*. Chicago: University of Chicago Press, 1970. Despite the title, the work details the growing Russo-English conflict in the Mediterranean from the 1780's. English policy prevented Catherine and Paul from using the Baltic fleet to help Suvorov and the fleet commander in the Mediterranean/Balkan region.

Soloveytchik, George. *Potemkin: A Picture of Catherine's Russia*. Rev. ed. London: Percival Marshall, 1949. While lacking footnotes and a bibliography, this is still a useful study of the relationship between Catherine, Potemkin, and Suvorov.

Waliszewski, Kazimierz. *Paul the First of Russia: The Son of Catherine the Great*. Philadelphia: J. B. Lippincott, 1913. This is an excellent translation from a French work that made extensive use of Russian sources, especially the letters from Suvorov to Paul. It should be noted, however, that all footnotes from the original edition are omitted.

See also: Catherine the Great; Frederick the Great; Peter the Great; Peter III; Grigori Aleksandrovich Potemkin.

Related articles in *Great Events from History: The Eighteenth Century, 1701-1800*: May 27, 1703: Founding of St. Petersburg; January, 1756-February 15, 1763: Seven Years' War; August 10, 1767: Catherine the Great's Instruction; October, 1768-January 9, 1792: Ottoman Wars with Russia; August 5, 1772-October 24, 1795: Partitioning of Poland; 1788-September, 1809: Russo-Swedish Wars; March, 1796-October 17, 1797: Napoleon's Italian Campaigns; April 12, 1798-September 2, 1801: Napoleon's Egyptian Campaign.

SUZUKI HARUNOBU
Japanese artist

Suzuki Harunobu is believed to be the creator of color woodblock printing in Japan, revolutionizing the ukiyo-e *school of popular printmaking, which had previously produced monochrome prints. The new color prints, originally known as* nishiki-e, *soon replaced the monochrome prints so completely that they were popularly regarded as the standard* ukiyo-e *form.*

Born: 1725?; Edo (now Tokyo), Japan
Died: 1770; Edo, Japan
Also known as: Hozumi Harunobu (birth name); Chōeiken; Shikojin; Jirobei; Jihei
Area of achievement: Art

EARLY LIFE

There are no records to document the early life of Suzuki Harunobu (sooz-oohk-ee harh-oo-noh-boo), but it is believed that he was born in the city of Edo, where he spent his entire life. He may have begun his artistic career as a student of Nishimura Shigenaga (1697-1756), an *ukiyo-e* (pictures of the Floating World) artist in the Kanda district of Edo. Few works remain by Nishimura, but some of those that do remain are monochrome prints with added red coloring, and they have some affinities with Harunobu's own early style. Harunobu's portraits of women are also believed to be influenced by the sensitive portrayals of women by the Kyoto printmaker Nishikawa Sukenobu (1671-1751).

LIFE'S WORK

During Suzuki Harunobu's early years, *ukiyo-e* prints were most often made up of simply black ink on white paper, with additional painted colors added by hand if desired. Harunobu experimented with an early form of two-color print known as *benizuri-e*, or "crimson-print pictures," in which both red and black ink, or green and red ink, were used to make the actual print. There is a surviving 1766 series of *benizuri-e* two-color prints with his signature, depicting episodes from the life of the famous classical poet Ono no Komachi (c. 833-857) but using contemporary settings. One of the prints is printed on coated paper, and its gray coating provided the illusion that the print uses three colors rather than just two.

Though Harunobu created these two-color prints and also made book illustrations using the same technique, he is best known for his introduction of the multicolor prints known as *nishiki-e*. The color-printing techniques that he perfected continued to be used until Western techniques were adopted late in the nineteenth century. It should be remembered, however, that woodblock carvers and the artisans who actually made the physical prints also were involved in discovering and perfecting some of the techniques attributed to Harunobu.

Harunobu also was known for an artistic approach known as *mitate*, or "visual likening," whereby he often would create compositions of contemporary notables or scenes posed to resemble those in earlier classical compositions, even traditional compositions in Chinese art. Harunobu also reversed the process at times, depicting episodes from the life of poet Ono no Komachi but with the figures in the pictures wearing styles of clothes from Harunobu's own time.

Harunobu also tended to use his compositions for multiple purposes. The Komachi series appeared, for example, as pictures in a calendar, as separate signed prints, as separate unsigned prints, and as prints inscribed with Komachi's poems. When made in this way, with multiple compositions, Harunobu's work is easier to authenticate. It should be noted that Harunobu was already regarded as an eminent artist in his own lifetime, so after his death many reproductions of his work, and possibly forgeries as well, were made under his name. In addition, extant work attributed to him is distributed widely but thinly throughout the world, even into the twenty-first century. Scholars trying to do comparative internal studies of his prints to find common authenticating features have been hindered by difficulties in viewing enough prints. Consequently, the authenticity of any work attributed to him cannot always be confirmed.

In addition to making calendars for public sale for Edo publishers, Harunobu produced other types of work in return for quite lucrative private commissions. These included New Year's cards and gift calendars for private groups to send to friends or group members. Because of this work, Harunobu came in contact with groups of Edo poets and intellectuals and became widely respected among such circles. He was so respected that he was invited to become a member of one of the circles, eventually becoming the group's leader.

Harunobu also created prints of well-known actors and courtesans, creating also a separate body of erotic prints known as *shunga*, or "springtime pictures." These print styles, though not to everyone's taste, are generally replicated by many other artists, though in a more refined manner than *shunga*. Harunobu sometimes gave less prominence to the erotic elements than to other elements of his prints, so the eroticism occasionally seems almost incidental. Harunobu's *shunga* are highly regarded by both Japanese and Western art historians, and they have been the subject of much specialized research.

Harunobu's woodcut Flirting at the Waterfall. (The Granger Collection, New York)

Harunobu's breakthrough in making multicolor prints is generally dated to between 1760 and 1765, though he was still making two-color prints in 1766. A famous multicolor print signed by Harunobu, dated by scholars to the Meiwa era (1764-1772), depicts Osen, a noted beauty of the time, busy in her capacity as the hostess of the Kagiya, a fashionable and exclusive teahouse in Edo. In this print, in which the predominant colors are varying shades of red, yellow, black, brown, green, and gray, Osen is shown dressed very conservatively, demurely bringing a cup of tea on a small tray to a samurai in a black cloak and wearing two swords. This print served as an advertisement for Osen and her business, and at the same time it was a significant source of revenue for Harunobu. Many people had heard of Osen, but most had never met or seen her, and so they bought copies of the print instead. The print was the equivalent of a modern publicity photo of a star, but in place of a star's autograph is Harunobu's well-known signature.

Harunobu died at the age of forty-five, in 1770, though the exact cause of death is unclear. He was very productive, however, and had created more than one thousand different works of art during his lifetime, approximately seven hundred of which were prints. He was a well-respected celebrity in his own time, and his groundbreaking multicolor prints had the enthusiastic reception they deserved from his contemporaries. Their sensitivity and refinement won them a permanent place in Japanese art history, and they were among the Japanese prints that first won admiration among art critics and collectors in Europe, one century after Harunobu first created them.

SIGNIFICANCE

Popularly regarded as the first *ukiyo-e* printmaker to introduce the full use of color, Suzuki Harunobu created color prints, especially his *bijinga* portraits of women, at a level of artistry and sophistication matched only by a few later *ukiyo-e* masters. Harunobu surpassed contemporaries using color print techniques, such as his student Isoda Koryusai. Another student, Shiba Kokan, created a unique new blend of Japanese and Western art.

Harunobu left behind a large opus of outstanding color prints, which have influenced printmakers for generations. His tasteful portrayals of popular themes gained him a special position in Edo society and acceptance in literary and intellectual circles, raising the status of *ukiyo-e* prints to that of a true art form.

His graceful use of line and subtle color harmonies, often combined with erotic themes, had a special appeal for later European connoisseurs, who created a taste for Japanese prints like his among the general Western public. Though some of his contemporaries used similar themes and techniques, Harunobu had a unique combination of talent, industry and savoir faire that made him the leading *ukiyo-e* artist among his Edo contemporaries and among subsequent generations in Japan and the West.

—*Michael McCaskey*

FURTHER READING

Hayakawa, Monta. *The Shunga of Suzuki Harunobu: Mitate-e and Sexuality in Edo.* Kyoto, Japan: Nichibunken International Research Center for Japanese Studies, 2001. A scholarly study of the sociological aspects of Harunobu's erotic art by a Japanese authority.

Hillier, J. *Japanese Colour Prints.* Oxford, England: Phaidon Press, 1993. A general account of the development of color *ukiyo-e* prints by a recognized authority on Harunobu.

Kanada, Margaret Miller. *Colour Woodblock Printmaking: The Traditional Method of Ukiyo-e.* Tokyo: Shufunotomo, 1992. A valuable description of *ukiyo-e* prints from the perspective of actual printmaking techniques.

Klompmakers, Inge. *Japanese Erotic Prints: Shunga by Harunobu and Koryusai.* Amsterdam: Hotei, 2001. An analysis of the erotic aspects of Harunobu's art and of the art of Isoda Koryusai, a contemporary, whose prints originally were mistaken for works by Harunobu.

Kondo, Ichitaro. *Suzuki Harunobu (1725-1770).* Tokyo: Charles E. Tuttle, 1957. A popular general account of the life and work of Harunobu.

Newland, Amy, ed. *The Commercial and Cultural Climate of Japanese Printmaking.* Hotei Academic European Studies on Japan 2. Amsterdam: Hotei, 2004. A scholarly study of the socioeconomic aspects of *ukiyo-e* printmaking. Unique account of the social and economic conditions under which *ukiyo-e* artists such as Harunobu created their works.

Takahashi, Seiichiro. *Masterworks of Ukiyo-e: Harunobu.* Tokyo: Kodansha International, 1968. A standard popular monograph on general aspects of Harunobu and his work.

Waterhouse, D. *Harunobu and His Age: The Development of Colour Printing in Japan.* London: British Museum, 1964. A full-scale, detailed study of Harunobu and his work, with numerous illustrations.

See also: William Blake; Chikamatsu Monzaemon; Chŏng Sŏn; Hakuin; Honda Toshiaki; Ogyū Sorai; Tokugawa Yoshimune.

Related articles in *Great Events from History: The Eighteenth Century, 1701-1800:* June 20, 1703: Chikamatsu Produces *The Love Suicides at Sonezaki*; December, 1720: Japan Lifts Ban on Foreign Books.

EMANUEL SWEDENBORG
Swedish scientist, philosopher, and theologian

Swedenborg was first a mechanical prodigy, then a scientist and philosopher, then an anatomist, and finally a theologian. His peers saw him as a genius in science and invention, but it was only much later that his anatomical studies were appreciated. His many contributions to Christian religious thought are still not widely known.

Born: January 29, 1688; Stockholm, Sweden
Died: March 29, 1772; London, England
Also known as: Emanuel Swedberg (birth name)
Areas of achievement: Science and technology, engineering, biology, religion and theology

EARLY LIFE

When Emanuel Swedenborg (eh-MAH-nuh-wuhl SVAY-duhn-bawr), the third child of Jesper and Sara Swedberg, was born, his father was court chaplain in Stockholm and was later appointed bishop of Skara. In 1719, the family was ennobled and took the name Swedenborg. Very little is known of Swedenborg's childhood. In 1699, he entered the University of Uppsala and ten years later read his graduation essay. Shortly afterward, he began extensive travels in England and on the Continent. Although there is no evidence that Swedenborg actually met Isaac Newton, he studied Newton's works avidly. Swedenborg did work with both Edmond Halley and John Flamsteed.

Throughout his travels in France, Germany, the Netherlands, Denmark, Bohemia, and Italy, Swedenborg searched insatiably for scientific knowledge, lodging when possible with scientists, craftsmen, and mathematicians. In 1714, he drafted papers on fourteen mechanical inventions, some of which he soon published in the *Daedalus Hyperboreus*, the first Swedish scientific journal, since recognized by the Society of Science of Uppsala as the first of its proceedings. He was appointed to the Swedish Board of Mines in 1716 and devised a number of mechanical devices to increase the efficiency of mining operations. In 1721, he published a Latin treatise on chemistry.

LIFE'S WORK

The work that established Swedenborg's reputation as a scientist of note was a massive three-volume set published in 1734. The two volumes on copper and iron smelting were translated into several languages and became standard reference works. Next, his attention turned to physiological studies, his avowed motivation being a search for the human soul. These studies, which include several large volumes, are significant not because they rival in any sense later research using far more refined equipment but because of the remarkably intelligent way in which Swedenborg analyzed and interpreted the phenomena he was able to observe. In 1901, when Max Neuburger noted certain anticipations of modern medical views made by Swedenborg, the University of Vienna ordered a complete set of Swedenborg's treatises from the Royal Swedish Academy. These studies showed, 150 years before the work of any other scientist, that the motion of the brain was synchronous with respiration and not with the motion of the heart. His views on the physiological functions of the spinal cord agreed with recent research, and he anticipated much later studies on the functions of the ductless glands.

It is curious that Swedenborg, a man of such astonishing achievement in physics and biology, is almost completely ignored in the annals of science. One reason for his obscurity is that between 1749 and 1756 he published anonymously, in eight large volumes, a work titled *Arcana coelestia quae in scriptura sacra seu verbo Domini sunt detecta* (*The Heavenly Arcana*, 1951-1956). This monumental work signaled the beginning of Swedenborg's work as a theologian. The last twenty-three years of his life were devoted to writing and publishing the works that identify him as a religious reformer and Bible interpreter.

Swedenborg's biblical interpretations did not earn for him widespread recognition, because he used visions as the basis for his interpretations. In an autobiographical letter to his friend the Reverend Thomas Hartley, written in 1769, Swedenborg stated, "I have been called to a holy office by the Lord himself . . . , when he opened my sight into the spiritual world and enabled me to converse with spirits and angels. . . . From that time I began to print and publish the various *arcana* that were seen by me. . . ." To his contemporaries, influenced by the intellectual climate of the eighteenth century, with its materialistic conception of the universe, Swedenborg was an enigma, sacrificing a brilliant career as an esteemed scientist to pursue religious studies.

Swedenborg, nevertheless, continued his theological publications, publishing these works anonymously and distributing them at his own expense until the last three years of his life. In the first and largest of these, *The*

Emanuel Swedenborg. (Library of Congress)

Heavenly Arcana, Swedenborg does an intensive interpretation of the first two books of the Bible, Genesis and Exodus, claiming that these books, along with most of the text of the Bible, have an inner, spiritual sense. The story of Creation, for example, becomes a symbolic story of the birth or creation of spirituality in every human being. Once this spirituality is recognized, the Bible can be used as a personal psychological guide to life.

In addition to the detailed critique of Scriptural spiritual meaning, Swedenborg introduced between chapters lengthy articles on his otherworldly experiences, not only relating actual conditions he says he observed in Heaven, Hell, and an intermediate world of spirits but also chronicling his encounters with spirits he believed had previously lived on other inhabited planets.

The concept of the nature of God found in these writings is clearly Christian in intent and belief, but at the same time it deals constructively and logically with the concept of a trinity in God. According to this teaching, the being called God the Father in Scripture is a symbolic name for the essence or essential nature of God, a perfect merging of divine love and wisdom, corresponding to what has traditionally been called the soul in any human being. The Son of God, the Christ of the New Testament, is the earthly manifestation of the one God, correspond-

ing to the human body through which the soul of every human being expresses itself. The enigmatic Holy Spirit is, on one hand, the operation or influence of God in creation and, on the other, the discernible nature or personality of God, corresponding to the nature or personality of any human being. These three areas of thought—the concept that there is a continuous and connected inner sense in the Word, that there is a real and knowable life after death, and that God is one in essence and in person, with three distinguishable aspects—are the primary distinctive beliefs of Swedenborgianism.

Immanuel Kant may have introduced the most enduring negative attitude toward the worth of studying Swedenborg. For reasons not clearly known, Kant published a strange work in 1766, *Träume eines Geistersehers erläutert durch Träume der Metaphysik* (*Dreams of a Spirit-Seer, Illustrated by Dreams of Metaphysics*, 1900), which ridiculed Swedenborg and his theological writings. Kant described Swedenborg's magnum opus as eight volumes of sheer nonsense; because in his later years Kant became so influential on the Continent, this ridicule became a curse that led to Swedenborg's being largely ignored by scholars for generations.

The charges made during his lifetime that Swedenborg was a writer of nonsense and the related charge that he was insane were completely insupportable. He was too well known for his scholarly, methodical, and highly respected scientific works to be dismissed in such cavalier fashion. The religious writings of Swedenborg were taken so seriously by his own people that in 1769 heresy charges were leveled against two of his prestigious disciples at Gothenburg, a sad affair that lasted two or three years before it was quietly dropped for lack of evidence.

Just before Swedenborg left for his last trip to London to publish *Vera Christiana religio* (1771; *True Christian Religion*, 1781), his final summary work, he met with King Adolf Frederick, who is reported to have said, "The consistories have kept silent on the subject of my letters and your writings. We may conclude, then, that they have not found anything reprehensible in them and that you have written in conformity with the truth."

SIGNIFICANCE

During his lifetime, Emanuel Swedenborg made no effort to found a new religious movement, contenting himself with publishing his works and distributing them at his own expense to leading clergymen and scholars. It was not until fifteen years after his death that the first movement to found a new church organization began in London among readers of his works. That modest beginning has led to the present numerically small but worldwide following of Swedenborgians, including both those who are members of a Swedenborgian church organization and those who are simply readers of Swedenborg's works.

In particular, interest in Swedenborg has been kindled by an ongoing reassessment of eighteenth century thought. Rejecting the traditional, positivistic view of the Enlightenment, scholars in many disciplines have shown that the contrast between the rational and the irrational in the Age of Reason cannot be neatly demarcated. Swedenborg, scientist and visionary, is a significant case in point.

—William Ross Woofenden

FURTHER READING

Benz, Ernst. *Emanuel Swedenborg: Visionary Savant in the Age of Reason.* Translated by Nicholas Goodrick-Clarke. West Chester, Pa.: Swedenborg Foundation, 2002. The first English translation of a book originally published in the 1950's. A comprehensive biography, describing Swedenborg's scientific achievements, the spiritual experience that altered his life, and his religious ideas. Benz compares Swedenborg to the medieval mystics and Hebrew prophets who were able to convey God's revelations to the community.

Block, Marguerite B. *The New Church in the New World: A Study of Swedenborgianism in America.* Introduction and epilogue by Robert H. Kirven. New York: Swedenborg Publishing Association, 1984. With Kirven's updating, this work, based on Block's Ph.D. dissertation, is a thorough and reliable standard reference work.

Jonsson, Inge. *Emanuel Swedenborg.* Boston: Twayne, 1971. Only the first chapter of this work is, strictly speaking, a biography. The major part of the book focuses on the thought content of Swedenborg's writings. The keenest assessment by the author is of Swedenborg's scientific and philosophical works.

Lamm, Martin. *Emanuel Swedenborg: The Development of His Thought.* Translated by Tomas Spiers and An-

ders Hallengren. West Chester, Pa.: Swedenborg Foundation, 2000. The first English tradition of this humanistic interpretation of Swedenborg's work, originally published in 1915. Lamm examines the philosophical and religious background of Swedenborg's thought, describing his transformation from a scientist to a seer. Lamm argues that Swedenborg's scientifc view of the world was not altered by religion; his spiritual revelations added to, and completed, his earlier ideas about the world.

Sigstedt, Cyriel O. *The Swedenborg Epic: The Life and Works of Emanuel Swedenborg.* New York: Bookman, 1952. Reprint. London: Swedenborg Society, 1981. A complete and thoroughly documented biography of Swedenborg. The reprint edition has an errata sheet correcting a number of minor errors.

Söderberg, Henry. *Swedenborg's 1714 Airplane: A Machine to Fly in the Air.* Edited by George F. Dole. New York: Swedenborg Foundation, 1988. The author, a retired vice president of Scandinavian Airlines, discovered Swedenborg's invention while researching a book on the history of flight. He notes that a model of Swedenborg's craft is the first sight that greets visitors to the Smithsonian's room on early flight.

Woofenden, William Ross. *Swedenborg Researcher's Manual.* Bryn Athyn, Pa.: Swedenborg Scientific Association, 1988. This work combines the first annotated bibliography of all Swedenborg's works, an extensive annotated bibliography of collateral literature on Swedenborg's thought, a glossary of special terms, summaries of key concepts, and a section giving locations and descriptions of major documentary collections of Swedenborgiana worldwide.

See also: Immanuel Kant.

Related articles in *Great Events from History: The Eighteenth Century, 1701-1800*: October, 1725: Vico Publishes *The New Science*; 1739-1740: Hume Publishes *A Treatise of Human Nature*; 1748: Montesquieu Publishes *The Spirit of the Laws*; July 27, 1758: Helvétius Publishes *De l'esprit*; 1770: Publication of Holbach's *The System of Nature*; 1781: Kant Publishes *Critique of Pure Reason*; 1784-1791: Herder Publishes His Philosophy of History.

JONATHAN SWIFT
Irish writer

Perhaps the greatest prose satirist in the history of English literature, Swift also was a champion of Irish and Anglo-Irish rights against the colonial impositions of Great Britain.

Born: November 30, 1667; Dublin, Ireland
Died: October 19, 1745; Dublin, Ireland
Areas of achievement: Literature, social reform

EARLY LIFE

Ireland in the seventeenth century was seen by ambitious Englishmen as the place to go to make a place for oneself, particularly for members of the Anglican Church, since Roman Catholics (practically the entire native Celtic population of Ireland) and, to a lesser extent, non-Anglican Protestants were excluded from most of the more powerful and lucrative positions in Irish political, educational, and business life. Jonathan Swift's father, trained as a lawyer, came from England with his brothers to take advantage of the situation, and he married an English-woman, who had settled in Dublin, in 1664. In April of 1667, still in the early stages of his career, Swift's father, also called Jonathan, died; Swift was born several months later. There was little money, and Swift was dependent upon an uncle for financial support for his maintenance and education, first at Kilkenny School and then at Trinity College, Dublin, from which he was graduated, after an undistinguished career, in 1689.

Ambitious but uncertain as to a career, Swift was taken on as the personal secretary to Sir William Temple, a family friend, who lived just south of London. Temple, a former diplomat of some considerable reputation, with connections to the Royal Court, was living in retirement, but Swift hoped that Temple's influence with the political powers in London would lead to something for him, possibly in the civil service. Temple did nothing to help Swift's career, however, and in the mid-1690's, Swift returned to Ireland and was ordained as a priest in the Irish wing of the Anglican Church. He was given a church in Northern Ireland, in an area where there were few Anglicans but many Roman Catholics and Presbyterian Anglo-Irish. Swift remained for a year and then returned to Temple. No doubt Temple had promised to look out for something substantial for his protégé.

During this period, Swift began to write poetry—mostly, as suggested by Temple, complimentary odes dedicated to prominent public figures. The poems did not reveal Swift's true gift for literature. In the later years of the decade, however, he began working on his first great book, *A Tale of a Tub* (1704), an enormously ambitious and complicated satire that was not to be published for several years.

In early 1699, Temple died without having done anything for Swift, who managed to get back to Dublin as chaplain to the earl of Berkeley, the lord chief justice of Ireland. His association with Berkeley, which Swift had hoped would lead to better things, yielded no great opportunities, and Swift was obliged to take a modest ecclesiastical living near Dublin.

LIFE'S WORK

Jonathan Swift's literary reputation began with a pamphlet he produced in 1701 supporting certain Whig politicians, but it was the publishing, anonymously, of *A Tale of a Tub* that made him widely known in not only literary but also political and religious circles, since it attacked, satirically, excesses in the Christian religion, in scholarship, in journalism, and, to a slightly lesser extent, in politics.

Satire is not simply criticism of aberrant behavior as the writer sees it, nor is it a particular mode, since any literary form may be used satirically. Rather, satire is an artistic shaping of criticism in ways that make it, however strongly disapproving, enjoyable to read, regardless of whether one agrees with the comment. *A Tale of a Tub* exemplifies this definition, since much of what Swift said, particularly about the Christian Church, was considered highly improper, but the work itself was not only widely read but also recognized as a work of genius, albeit one with a penchant for wildly egregious impropriety. Swift coyly denied that he had written it. Several other writers of reputation were suggested, some indignantly refusing the honor, but eventually Swift, despite his constant denials, was recognized as the author of this mad, magnificent attack upon the fragilities and vanities of humanity.

In 1708, while working informally with Whig politicians to achieve certain advantages for the Anglican Church in Ireland (at a time when church and state were closely intertwined), Swift delighted everyone with a second satire, one that was easily enjoyed by all since it was an attack upon the excesses of astrology. *Predictions for the Ensuing Year, by Isaac Bickerstaff* (1708), purportedly written by Bickerstaff, the most extravagantly fearless seer of them all, was an attack on a popular hack astrologer, John Partridge. In the correspondence, the counterclaims, the sheer lunacies of several pamphlets, the public became joyfully involved, and Partridge's career was ruined. It was the first but not the last time that Swift's gift for using art as a social weapon was to achieve results in the real world. The Partridge incident also showed clearly that the whimsical aspect of Swift's literary gift, its inclination toward playfulness and practical joking, which was sometimes absent in *A Tale of a Tub*, could be quite delightful in its own right.

While developing his fame as the wiliest of writers, Swift was working to get Whig support for his church. He was often thwarted, however, by the politicians' natural inclination to promise much but deliver little, and by the fact that the Whigs in general had sympathies for other Protestant sects (called, for convenience, Dissenters) who wished to have their political, religious, and social rights extended. Anglicans of conservative bent, such as Swift, saw such ambitions as a threat to the supremacy of the Anglican establishment. By 1710, Swift had abandoned the Whigs and become the literary voice of the Tory Party, for whom he wrote *The Examiner* (1710), a popular propaganda sheet still readable today.

While living with Temple in the 1690's, Swift had formed a very close connection with Esther Johnson, a young woman who, with a companion, had followed Swift back to Ireland at the turn of the century. They were to form a peculiar threesome, and there is much romantic speculation about whether Swift married Johnson, although there is no real evidence that he ever did. There is much evidence, however, of his genuine affection for her, and although they never lived together, they rarely lived far apart whenever Swift, between his frequent trips to England, was resident in Dublin. During his stay in England on a somewhat permanent basis beginning in 1710, when he became the confidant of the leaders of the Tory Party and was privy to their efforts to rule the country, he sent a long series of letters back to Johnson and her companion that are intimate glimpses not only into his relationship with the women (and particularly to Johnson) but also into the political world of the time. The latter is true especially because Swift's relation to Robert Harley and Henry St. John, First Viscount Bolingbroke, the two most important Tory rulers, was very close. Swift's skills as a writer, his eye for detail, his unbuttoned intimacies, his connections with everyone who was anyone in not only the political but also the social and literary worlds make *Journal to Stella* (1766) one of the epistolary masterpieces of literature.

Swift wrote splendidly lethal propaganda for the Tory Party, not only in *The Examiner* but also in other forms. By 1713, however, the Tory Party was falling apart as Harley and Bolingbroke, despite Swift's advice, battled each other for power. Swift had never taken any direct financial reward for his services, although he expected, as is the way of the political world, to be given something substantial in the way of a Church preferment for what he had done. What he wanted was a bishopric in England, or at minimum a deanship. Yet Swift had enemies in the English Church, and Queen Anne knew that he was the author of that antireligious text, *A Tale of a Tub*. As the Tory Party self-destructed before his eyes, Swift was offered somewhat ironic recompense: a deanship indeed, not in England, however, but back in Ireland, at St. Patrick's Cathedral in Dublin. Once again, the promises of politicians had landed Swift back where he had started.

Swift rarely went to England after 1714, and after a visit in 1727, he resided permanently in Ireland until his death. Attempts were made by his friends to get him a substantial church position in England, but he was remembered as a writer of question-

---

RUMINATIONS FROM SWIFT

Jonathan Swift is known as one of the greatest satirists of English literature. In addition to his better-known novel Gulliver's Travels, *Swift wrote biting satire that pulled no punches. In the quips here, he feasts on religion, the deceptive arts of warfare and argumentation, the significance of the seemingly banal, explicit silliness, cowardice, and the stunting of desire.*

We have just enough religion to make us hate, but not enough to make us love one another.

It is in disputes as in armies, where the weaker side sets up false lights, and makes a great noise, to make the enemy believe them more numerous and strong than they really are.

If a man will observe as he walks the streets, I believe he will find the merriest countenances in mourning coaches.

Some people take more care to hide their wisdom than their folly.

I have known men of great valour [who are] cowards to their wives.

It is a miserable thing to live in suspense; it is the life of a spider. The Stoical scheme of supplying our wants by lopping off our desires, is like cutting off our feet when we want shoes.

Source: Jonathan Swift, from "Thoughts on Various Subjects," in *The Battle of the Books and Other Short Pieces* (1704). Project Gutenberg. http://www .gutenberg.org/

able excess, and his connection with the discredited Tory Party did not help. Swift did not take his exile (as he saw it) lightly, but it did not deter him from a busy life as dean of his cathedral, as a commentator on British and Irish politics, and, most important, as a major literary figure.

Swift became a hero to all the Irish, native or immigrant, when he anonymously wrote a series of essays, *The Drapier's Letters to the People of Ireland* (1724-1735), urging resistance to the British plan to allow an English contractor to replace some of the Irish currency with new coinage. As with the Bickerstaff essays, one paper led to another, focusing Irish discontent and continuing to do so despite a reward being offered for information on the author of such seditious material. Everyone, including the British authorities, knew that Swift was responsible, but no one dared to touch him, and he roused such public opinion that the project was abandoned. In 1729, Swift attacked with *A Modest Proposal for Preventing the Children of Poor People of Ireland from Being a Burden to Their Parents* (1729), which suggested that since Britain had consumed all Ireland's wealth, only one source of profit was left: the children, doomed to starvation, whom the writer, a supposedly concerned and informed citizen, suggested might well be turned into a new and delicate food for those who had profited from Ireland's political tragedy. It was an example of Swift's occasional tendency to go too far, to explore ideas that were both aesthetically and intellectually titillating while repulsive to many.

It was during the 1720's that Swift wrote his best-known work, *Gulliver's Travels* (1726), which has been severely edited, bowdlerized, and transformed into a harmless fairy tale and a sweetly sentimental, full-length Hollywood cartoon, but which, in its original form, is an unrepentant attack upon the stupidities of humankind and the fragility of human reason. *Gulliver's Travels* was Swift's most popular work, even among some of his former enemies, and it transcended many of the prejudices that had been imposed on him as a writer. The book did, however, contain materials that offended the faint-hearted.

Swift continued to write through the 1730's and to take an active part in Irish life, although he became increasingly infirm in the late 1730's. Some observers suggest that the imaginative excesses of his satires, with their wild sexual and scatological themes, indicate that Swift was mentally warped. Writers of that period, however, were less puritanically fastidious than one would expect. Human sewage (which Swift often uses as a reminder of human limitations) was a common sight in the open

ditches of the cities and towns, and was a common metaphor in the poetry of John Dryden and Alexander Pope.

In his old age, Swift's mental faculties began to deteriorate, and in the last three years of his life, he was unable to care for himself. It might seem appropriate that he ended his life mad, having often turned the insane conduct of the human race into high art. Swift knew how slim was the human hold of reason, and he left his estate for the founding of a mental hospital in Dublin, which still exists.

Gulliver, a decent man, lands on the shore of reality in the final book of *Gulliver's Travels* desperately unhappy. Wretchedly unhinged, he stuffs herbs up his nose because he cannot stand the smell of his family and hangs about his barn trying to teach his horses to talk. Too much sightseeing, and too much adjustment to the too-tiny, the too-large, the too-unreasonable, and the too-nonhuman, have worn him out mentally. Swift, in his clear-eyed understanding of humanity's follies and fragilities (which he so often commented on in his art and in his normal life as a man of action and involvement) lived cruelly long enough to become a Struldbrugg; life imitated art. Esther Johnson had died, long before, in 1728. Swift was buried near her in St. Patrick's.

SIGNIFICANCE

Samuel Johnson, the great eighteenth century critic, who was not immune to critical stupidities, tried to dismiss *Gulliver's Travels* with the comment that once one had thought of the big and little men, the rest was easy. The way Jonathan Swift used his ideas, however, is what distinguishes his writing. Not only did Swift possess wide tonal range (he is a more amusing writer than is usually presumed), but also the multiplicity of satiric insights, even in the shortest works, so often specifically written to comment upon an occurrence of the moment, makes his canon quite as readable today as when it was written.

Swift usually wrote satire from the "inside"; he rarely attacked in his own voice, but rather invented mouthpieces, personas who represented some aspect of the subject. Sometimes they were part of the problem (as in *A Tale of a Tub* or in the Bickerstaff writings), sometimes victims (as in *The Drapier's Letters to the People of Ireland*), and sometimes, as in Gulliver's case, innocent bystanders who occasionally acted foolishly themselves. In *A Modest Proposal for Preventing the Children of Poor People of Ireland from Being a Burden to Their Parents*, the speaker is informed and sympathetic but ultimately stupid and unfeeling, since Swift wanted to criticize not only the British and the feckless Irish but also humans with their beastly bureaucratic, professional tendency to insensitive tunnel vision. He never approached a subject simply, or without art in mind.

Once he had thrown over Temple's advice about writing poetry of praise and started to use it as an adjunct to his satirical prose, Swift became a fine poet, although he was modest about it and deemed himself less gifted than his friend Pope. His political writing (once it is understood that the writer of party affiliation does not necessarily speak true) is lithe, lively, intelligent, and often charmingly mischievous. His personal correspondence shows that his gift for turning language into art could be applied to something as simple as asking someone to dinner or as slyly complicated as telling a bishop to jump in the lake without actually saying so.

Underestimated or shunned because of misreadings of *Gulliver's Travels* in particular, Swift's work, in its substantial volume and constantly high literary quality, and his life, in all its multiplicity of complication and incident, are together an example of how the artist can use his or her finest talent to meet the day-to-day problems of his or her time without losing the chance for immortality.

—*Charles H. Pullen*

FURTHER READING

Ehrenpreis, Irvin. *Swift: The Man, His Works, and the Age*. 3 vols. London: Methuen, 1962-1983. This definitive biography is entertaining, accurate, and determined to place Swift's works clearly in the context of his life.

Foot, Michael. *The Pen and the Sword*. London: McGibbon and Kee, 1957. Written by a political journalist and former leader of the British Labour Party, this book takes Swift through his career as the political spokesperson for the Tory Party during its 1710-1714 government of Great Britain. Very good on the ways of the political world.

Glendinning, Victoria. *Jonathan Swift: A Portrait*. London: Hutchinson, 1998. Not a comprehensive, chronological account of Swift's life, but a portrait aimed at evoking his character. Glendinning portrays Swift as witty, bad-tempered, and frustrated, and examines the political and aesthetic sensibilities that formed his dark view of human nature.

Kelly, Ann Cline. *Jonathan Swift and Popular Culture: Myth, Media, and the Man*. New York: Palgrave, 2002. Kelly argues that Swift deliberately chose to write for a popular audience rather than for the elite, and explains how he created a legend about himself that stimulated the demand for books by, and about, him.

Landa, Louis. *Swift and the Church of Ireland*. Oxford, England: Oxford University Press, 1954. To understand the satire is to understand Swift as a cleric practicing theology and politics hand-in-hand.

Price, Martin. *Swift's Rhetorical Art: A Study in Structure and Meaning*. New Haven, Conn.: Yale University Press, 1953. One of the best critics on the period in general and a constant commentator on Swift, Price carefully explores the technical complexities of Swift's work in this book.

Quintana, Ricardo. *Swift: An Introduction*. Oxford, England: Oxford University Press, 1962. A good short introduction to Swift's ambiguous art and personality. Always sensible, Quintana brings his formidable knowledge to bear without pedantry. An excellent starting point.

Rosenheim, E. W. *Swift and the Satirist's Art*. Chicago: University of Chicago Press, 1963. Explores the range of Swift's satire from its most corrosively aggressive to its most mildly comic. Invaluable for understanding the subtle nature of his work and its layered mixing of tone and meaning.

Starkman, Miriam Kosh. *Swift's Satire on Learning in "A Tale of a Tub."* Princeton, N.J.: Princeton University Press, 1950. Swift believed, as did others, that *A Tale of a Tub* was his masterpiece. It is, like James Joyce's *Ulysses* (1922), a book that obliges the reader to train for it. Starkman provides a helpful orientation to the work.

Williams, Kathleen. *Jonathan Swift and the Age of Compromise*. Lawrence: University of Kansas Press, 1958. The best book for placing Swift in the context of the ideas of his age and for explaining his maddening habit of refusing to tell the reader where the moral norm was and how to respond to it.

See also: Joseph Addison; Queen Anne; First Viscount Bolingbroke; Daniel Defoe; Henry Fielding; William Godwin; William Hogarth; Samuel Johnson; Mary de la Rivière Manley; Mary Wortley Montagu; Alexander Pope; Samuel Richardson; Anna Seward; Richard Steele; John Trumbull; Voltaire; Robert Walpole.

Related articles in *Great Events from History: The Eighteenth Century, 1701-1800:* March 1, 1711: Addison and Steele Establish *The Spectator*; April 25, 1719: Defoe Publishes the First Novel; 1726: Swift Satirizes English Rule of Ireland in *Gulliver's Travels*; 1740-1741: Richardson's *Pamela* Establishes the Modern Novel; 1742: Fielding's *Joseph Andrews* Satirizes English Society; January, 1759: Voltaire Satirizes Optimism in *Candide*.

TAKSIN
King of Siam (r. 1768-1782)

After the Burmese defeated the army of Siam at Ayutthaya in 1767, Taksin rescued Siam by uniting the people who had fled from the invading army. He then became king and relocated the capital at Thonburi, across the river from present-day Bangkok, and began to revive and modernize the country.

Born: April 17, 1734; Ayutthaya, Siam (now Phra Nakhon Si Ayutthaya, Thailand)
Died: April 6, 1782; Thonburi, Siam (now in Thailand)
Also known as: Sin (birth name); Phraya Taksin; Phya Tak; Phya Taksin; King Taksin the Great
Areas of achievement: Government and politics, warfare and conquest

EARLY LIFE
Taksin (TAHK-sihn) was a commoner born in Ayutthaya, then the capital of Siam (modern Thailand). His given name was Sin. His father, Hai-Hong, was Chinese, and his mother, Nok-lang, was Thai. His education began at the age of seven in a Buddhist monastery, where one of his fellow students was Tong-Duang (later General Chakkri, who became King Rama I). According to legend, a Chinese fortuneteller predicted that the two boys would both become kings.

At fourteen, Taksin became a royal page. Later, he was a trader and managed a fleet of carts. The king recognized his expertise in law, his intellectual abilities, and his managerial skills by raising him to the status of a noble and appointing him deputy governor of Tak Province; he later became governor. His name changed to Taksin while in Tak Province, where he evidently developed military skills that were later to set him apart from other generals.

LIFE'S WORK
In 1765, Burma's army approached Siam to make war, so Taksin returned to defend the city in the role of general, in recognition of which the king promoted him to be governor of Kamphaeng Phet Province. In 1767, after a fifteen-month siege of Ayutthaya, the Burmese defeated the outnumbered and hungry Siamese army, massacred the residents, looted the temples, and burned the city. As a result, the country was split into several parts.

Just before the city fell, Taksin escaped through the siege with a small army to the east coast, where he collected enough men, provisions, and weapons to counterattack the Burmese. In January, 1768, he led his army

back toward Ayutthaya. En route, he defeated a Burmese garrison at Ban Pho Sanghan. When he crossed the Prachinburi River, Burmese forces attacked him but were also routed. Still marching toward Ayutthaya, he continued to pick up support, notably from the governor of Rayong Province after Taksin's forces broke through enemy lines to enter Rayong City. Next, he advanced on Chantaburi. The governor of Chantaburi, however, was not prepared to welcome Taksin. To fire up his troops one night, Taksin dramatically ordered his men to finish dinner, throw away their leftovers, and smash all their rice pots, declaring that they would take Chantaburi City and have breakfast there the next morning.

In the Battle of Chantaburi, his troops first quietly surrounded the city, and Taksin then crashed through the city gates while riding an elephant. Next, Taksin won a battle in the Trat River against Chinese junks carrying cannon; he wanted the junks because the Burmese did not have a navy, and the junks were also carrying a lot of weapons and ammunition. Returning to Chantaburi, Taksin devoted three months to building up his army for an attack on the Burmese at the end of the monsoon season, when the areas around Ayutthaya would be flooded, thereby providing his forces with a definite advantage. After defeating the Burmese at Thonburi, he advanced on Ayutthaya. In October, 1768, in the Battle of Pho Sma Ton Camp at Ayutthaya, his forces completely defeated the Burmese. Soon, he was crowned king, and he moved the people to Thonburi (then called Chao Phraya San), which he designated the new capital.

While king, Taksin continued to drive the Burmese out of the country in at least eight major battles at border towns. He also subdued rival generals who did not accept his ascendancy, notably the Phimai, Phitsanulok, and Sawankhalok factions. While preoccupied by Burmese aggression, Siam's vassal states had begun to assert their independence. Accordingly, he soon launched military campaigns to gain control over Cambodia, Chiang Mai, Laos, and Nakhon Si Thammarat. Nevertheless, he allowed the Malay vassal states to become independent. In 1779, the Emerald Buddha was taken from Laos to Thonburi. As Siamese power expanded, relations with Vietnam deteriorated, however. Siam, as never before, had become the dominant power in mainland Southeast Asia.

Because refugees from Ayutthaya lacked clothing and food, Taksin used his own money to import basic necessities. Soon, the economy started to recover, with the people resuming agricultural and other occupations. Taksin promoted trade with Britain, China, the Netherlands, and Portugal, believing that income derived from foreign commerce in gems, gold, lead, rice, spices, tin, and wood would serve to ease the tax burden on the people. From among the imports, a substantial number of guns was imported from Britain; ceramics and silks came from China.

The king constructed a canal and built roads. In addition to restoring and renovating temples, he revived the arts, including architecture, dance, drama, handicrafts, literature, and painting. In the field of education, he promoted religious studies. He reorganized the monastic order and in 1773 promulgated the monastic daily routine with the aim of restoring Buddhism to its former glory. Because the sacking of Ayutthaya destroyed many sacred writings, he sought to import critical Buddhist manuscripts for the capital at Thonburi. The government was handled by four ministries: agricultural, civic, financial, and palace affairs. The king handled judicial and military matters. In 1773, to ensure loyalty to the state, Taksin ordered all soldiers to be tattooed on the wrist.

At some point, Taksin began to suspect that some of his subjects were involved in smuggling or stealing from the treasury, so he sought informers. The informers then began to extort money from the rich merchants, even those not engaged in smuggling, and Taksin thus did not find their efforts of much help. One of the king's wives was burned to death on a false allegation that she was stealing money from the treasury. Taksin, in short, became paranoid and oppressive. By 1781, Taksin imagined that he was a god. He demanded to have priests pay him the honors of a divinity. When some five hundred priests refused, he had them flogged, and the head priests were imprisoned. The rest submitted to his demands, but rebels launched a coup, arresting Taksin. On hearing of the unrest, General Chakkri, the top military commander and Taksin's boyhood friend, returned to Thonburi from a military expedition in Cambodia, investigated the charges against Taksin, and then asked government officials to decide how to punish Taksin. In 1782, Taksin was executed. He had been of mixed blood, and many Thais preferred not to have a king who was part-Chinese. His legitimacy, since he was born a commoner, was questioned in several circles. Meanwhile, Chakkri, of pure Thai ancestry, was crowned king.

SIGNIFICANCE

Under his leadership, Taksin stopped the Burmese advance, moved the capital closer to international trade routes, unified the country, restored Thai culture, reorga-

nized Buddhist practices, and began a process of economic and political modernization. The Malay vassal states were allowed to become independent while Taksin concentrated his military attention on Burma, but he gained control over Cambodia, Chiang Mai, Nakhon Si Thammarat, and annexed Laos, thus making Siam the superpower in mainland Southeast Asia. With his removal from power, the Chakkri Dynasty began, and the capital and the Emerald Buddha were moved to Bangkok. The response to Taksin's repressive actions at the end of his rule may have served to establish the principle that the Thai people have a right to expect rulers who are considerate, deliberative, progressive, and wise.

In recognition of his accomplishments, in 1954 the government began the practice of setting aside December 28, including a state ceremony, to honor him, though the day is not a public holiday. In 1981, the cabinet passed a resolution to name him King Taksin the Great. The election of a prime minister with the given name Thaksin Shinawatra (spelled differently in Thai) in 2001 has further revived interest in the king who restored Siam during the country's darkest hour.

—*Michael Haas*

FURTHER READING

Adirex, Paul. *Rattanakosin: The Birth of Bangkok.* Bangkok: Asia Books, 2004. An account of how the capital of Siam moved from Ayutthaya to Thonburi and then to Bangkok.

Chunlachakkraphong, Prince. *Lords of Life: A History of the Kings of Thailand.* 2d rev. ed. London: Redman, 1967. Biographies of the kings of Thailand written by the grandson of King Chulalongkorn.

Phra Tacha Wang Derm Restoration Foundation, Bangkok. "King Taksin." http://www.wangdermpalace .com. Accessed June, 2005. Explores major events in the life of Taksin, including his civilian and military accomplishments.

Wood, W. A. R. *A History of Siam.* New York: AMS Press, 1974. A history of Thailand that focuses primarily on events before 1782.

Wyatt, David K. *Thailand: A Short History.* New Haven, Conn.: Yale University Press, 2003. The definitive history of Thailand, though focusing on developments in later centuries.

See also: Alaungpaya; Nguyen Hue.
Related articles in *Great Events from History: The Eighteenth Century, 1701-1800:* 1752-1760: Alaungpaya Unites Burma; September, 1769-1778: Siamese-Vietnamese War.

GEORG PHILIPP TELEMANN
German composer

In addition to creating a vast body of beautiful music, Telemann championed the development of simpler, more readily accessible forms of composition, expanded the control of composers over their works, and paved the way for the transition from the Baroque to the classical style.

Born: March 14, 1681; Magdeburg, Brandenburg (now in Germany)
Died: June 25, 1767; Hamburg (now in Germany)
Area of achievement: Music

EARLY LIFE

Georg Philipp Telemann (gay-AWRK FEE-lihp TAY-luh-mahn) was the younger of two sons born to Heinrich Telemann, a minister at the Church of the Holy Ghost at Magdeburg. Both of Telemann's grandfathers had been clergymen, and nearly all of his known ancestors had been university educated. It was therefore natural that Telemann would be expected to follow in their footsteps. He was sent to local schools to study Latin, rhetoric, and dialectic (logical reasoning) but immediately demonstrated a great talent for music, too. Without any formal instruction, Telemann taught himself to play the violin, flute, zither, and keyboard instruments, as well as the rudiments of composition, by the age of ten. He was soon writing operatic arias, motets, short instrumental pieces, and, by the time he was twelve, his first opera.

Telemann's interest in music greatly alarmed his mother, who wanted him to become a minister. She prohibited him from engaging in any further musical activity, took away his instruments, and sent him away to school at the town of Zellerstadt. There, she hoped, the superintendent would guide the young man back to the true path. Ironically, however, the superintendent was an expert in theoretical music studies; instead of discouraging Telemann, he taught his pupil the relationships between music and mathematics and helped him hone his expertise in composition.

After completing his elementary schooling, Telemann continued his education at Hildesheim, where he was once again blessed with a mentor who encouraged his musical interests. For the next four years, Telemann wrote incidental songs for school plays (performed in Latin) and joined his fellow students in performances of German cantatas at a local church. He also traveled to Hannover and Brunswick, where he attended performances of French instrumental music and Italian opera.

Fired with enthusiasm, he began writing compositions modeled on these popular styles.

In autumn, 1701, Telemann was matriculated at the University of Leipzig. Since he had displayed no interest in theology, his mother decided that he should study law. Telemann dutifully left all of his music and instruments at home in Magdeburg and even attempted to conceal his musical talent from the other students. He could not stop composing, however, and one day his roommate discovered a cantata Telemann had written and arranged to have it performed at the Thomaskirche, a famous Leipzig church. The mayor of Leipzig, who heard the performance, was so impressed that he commissioned Telemann to write a new cantata for the church every other week. From that point on, Telemann's future as a composer was firmly set.

LIFE'S WORK

From the very beginning of his career, Telemann was a pioneer of new musical styles. Throughout the seventeenth century, the dominant Baroque style had become increasingly complex, employing layers of counterpoint and polyphony in densely magnificent musical structures. By the early 1700's, however, younger composers were seeking new, simpler forms of musical expression that could be understood and enjoyed by a wider public than the highly educated and cultured upper classes. Composers such as Telemann, George Frideric Handel, and Gottfried Stoelzel were in the vanguard of this movement.

Telemann threw himself into his new profession with furious energy. In 1702, he organized a student collegium musicum (music society), which began giving regular public concerts. Since many of the music students earned a little extra money singing in local opera houses, Telemann's leadership of the collegium thus led him into a position as Kapellmeister (music director) of the new Leipzig Opera, where he composed numerous operas and employed students as both singers and instrumentalists. Two years later, in 1704, he added even more to his responsibilities by winning the position of organist and music director at the Neukirche, the university church. There he led his collegium musicum in concerts of sacred music, much of which he himself composed.

Inevitably, perhaps, older and more traditional composers resisted what they perceived in the new music as a decline of standards. Leipzig's music director, Johann

Kuhnau, was in charge of music production for all of the city's churches, and he resented the instant popularity of the young newcomer. He complained to the city fathers that Telemann's new commission infringed on his rights and characterized Telemann as nothing but an "opera musician" who was stealing all the students away from the city churches to the Neukirche. Telemann's reputation had grown so much and so quickly, however, that Kuhnau's complaints were ignored.

So popular had Telemann become, in fact, that in 1705 he was appointed Kapellmeister to the court of the count of Promnitz at Sorau in Lower Lusatia (part of modern Poland). In eighteenth century Germany, an aspiring composer had two possible career paths: He could obtain a position as a choir or music director for a city in one or more of its local churches; or, if lucky, he might win employment as Kapellmeister or Konzertmeister (orchestra leader) at the court of a nobleman. With his appointment to the court of Promnitz, Telemann started his climb to the heights of the eighteenth century composer's world.

Georg Philipp Telemann, composer. (Hulton Archive/Getty Images)

Like many German noblemen of the time, the count had acquired a taste for French instrumental music. Telemann was therefore required to churn out French-style overtures as well as other instrumental and operatic music, but, at least at first, he looked upon such "assembly-line" composing as an opportunity to sharpen his command of music theory. Traveling with the count to Upper Silesia, Telemann also became acquainted with Polish folk music, many of whose themes he later incorporated into his own works.

Though he was happy in his position, Telemann resigned in 1707, apparently because of unsettled political conditions in eastern Germany, which was being invaded by King Charles XII of Sweden. When the battlefront reached the lands of the count, his court was dispersed. Telemann had few regrets, however, for not only had he recently become engaged to one of the ladies-in-waiting to the countess of Promnitz but also he had received an even better appointment. On Christmas Eve, 1708, he arrived in the city of Eisenach to take charge of the newly formed musical establishment of the duke of Saxe-Eisenach, one of the great noblemen of Germany.

As Konzertmeister of the duke's orchestra, Telemann continued to produce a constant stream of overtures, concerti, and chamber music. When the duke completed the construction of a new palace chapel, Telemann added church cantatas, oratorios, and ceremonial music to his output, in addition to supervising the training of choristers. During this busy period, he was allowed to take a leave of absence for only a few months in 1709, in order to return to Sorau to collect his new bride (but not until he had solemnly promised not to accept any other position).

In January, 1711, however, Telemann's life was shattered by the death of his wife following the birth of a daughter. It has been suggested by some historians that this experience drove him to leave Eisenach, while others assert that Telemann was simply tired of producing reams of music tailored to the tastes of his noble patrons. In any case, in February, 1712, he accepted an invitation to become music director for the city of Frankfurt, where he was more at liberty to compose as his inspiration led him. In addition, he had the opportunity to influence and develop the musical life of the city: Once again, he organized a collegium musicum, and he led it in weekly public concerts. He composed several cycles of cantatas and oratorios for the churches, orchestral and chamber works for the collegium, and special pieces for civic celebrations. He also remarried, in 1714, and somehow managed to find time to father ten more children (none of whom became a musician).

Though relatively content at Frankfurt, Telemann was disappointed by the lack of an outlet for his operatic talents. When the city of Hamburg offered him the position of city music director there in July, 1721, he quickly accepted, apparently because Hamburg had an opera house. For the rest of his life, Telemann provided the city with unprecedented quantities of church and civic music, trained and led choirs, organized yet another collegium musicum, and led its concerts. At the same time, as music director of the Hamburg Opera from 1722 until it closed in 1738, he wrote and directed more than twenty operas of his own, also producing those of other composers, including Handel. Not satisfied with these accomplishments, Telemann became his own publisher, personally engraving the printing press plates, writing his own advertising copy, and arranging for distribution in cities all over Europe.

In 1740, he decided to retire from independent composing to devote the rest of his life to writing books on musical theory, though he continued to meet his civic obligations as Hamburg's music director. For fifteen years, he kept to this decision, but, in 1755, possibly influenced by his old friend Handel, he once again, at age seventy-four, began to write oratorios, and many of these were performed long after his death in 1767. In an age when popular music came and went almost as quickly as the latest hits of modern times, this was a remarkable testament to the genius of this most prolific of composers.

SIGNIFICANCE

Georg Philipp Telemann was not a physically remarkable man, despite his prodigious energy and unusual longevity. Portraits of him reveal a stolid, serious, workmanlike demeanor; he could easily be taken for a banker. Until recently, this image reflected critical opinion of Telemann's music, too: It was considered pleasant and craftsmanlike, but not at all in the same class as that of Johann Sebastian Bach. Telemann was regarded as a hack who had turned out masses of superficial music (more than three thousand pieces) on demand. Only in the last half-century have his achievements begun to be adequately appreciated.

Telemann was part—and often the leader—of a movement that brought great changes in German music. Until the beginning of the eighteenth century, a com-

poser's music was dictated by the position he held: Music directors were not allowed to write operas, and court composers had to satisfy the tastes of their patrons. Telemann, however, refused to be bound by such restrictions: He took his music out of the churches and the noble courts and into the newly constructed opera houses and concert halls. In his public concerts, he might combine a program of church music, instrumental works, and operatic excerpts, thus giving music lovers an opportunity to hear and enjoy many varieties of music. By aggressively promoting the publication of his music, he assured that it would be available to anyone who wanted it, and, by making many of his works as simple as possible, he encouraged musicians of all levels of ability to play it, whether professionally or simply at home for pleasure. Insisting that the composer had the right to do with his works whatever he saw fit, Telemann helped to establish a new tradition of the artist as an independent agent, rather than simply the servant or employee of someone else.

Through his tremendous energy and his interest in teaching others, Telemann influenced an entire generation of German composers. The collegia he established became the training ground of younger men such as Johann Friedrich Fasch and Gottfried Stoelzel, who modeled their compositions after his. The texts he wrote were used and praised many decades after his death. His music, however, was buried in obscurity at the beginning of the nineteenth century. The Bach revival of the 1840's fostered an image of Baroque composition sharply at odds with the simpler kind of music that Telemann wrote, and it was not until the twentieth century that scholars such as Max Schneider and Romain Rolland argued that Telemann and Bach were simply not comparable: Bach, they asserted, looked backward to a style that was already obsolete, while Telemann was a forerunner of the classical period. It is only recently, through the growing number and popularity of Telemann recordings, that his primary goal of making music for everyone is finally being met.

—*Thomas C. Schunk*

FURTHER READING

Abraham, Gerald. *The Concise Oxford History of Music.* New York: Oxford University Press, 1979. An outstanding general history of music. Groups types of music topically, rather than by composer, with a broad chronological framework. Thus, references to Telemann are scattered about the text, according to the type of music being discussed (such as Italian opera, French overtures, and so on). Extensive bibliography.

Borroff, Edith. *The Music of the Baroque*. Dubuque, Iowa: Wm. C. Brown, 1970. An excellent, if brief, introduction to Baroque music for students with minimal musical background. Musical examples are explained sufficiently to allow beginning students to learn a substantial amount of music theory. Includes excellent, entertaining, and well-arranged illustrations. An outstanding feature is the inclusion of brief discographies for each type and area of music discussed.

Bukofzer, Manfred F. *Music in the Baroque Era, from Monteverdi to Bach*. New York: W. W. Norton, 1947. A classic text on the Baroque era. Although highly readable, this is definitely an academic work for the serious student and requires substantial music background. Contains useful chapters for the nonspecialist on "Musical Thought of the Baroque Era" and "Sociology of Baroque Music," which illuminate the social, political, and intellectual milieu in which Baroque composers worked. A massive bibliography, and lists of published editions of composers' works are included.

Maczewsky, A. "Georg Philipp Telemann." In *Grove's Dictionary of Music and Musicians*, edited by Eric Blom. Vol. 8. London: Macmillan, 1954. Maczewsky's article was the standard biography of Telemann at the beginning of the post-World War II revival of interest in the composer. Well written, solidly researched, but not superseded by Martin Ruhnke's work.

Petzoldt, Richard. *Georg Philipp Telemann*. Translated by Horace Fitzpatrick. New York: Oxford University Press, 1974. The only modern book-length biography of Telemann in English. Full of fascinating anecdotes as well as a thorough analysis of Telemann's music. While a knowledge of music theory would be helpful, almost any reader can enjoy this enthusiastic work. Includes a comprehensive bibliography.

Rolland, Romain. *A Musical Tour Through the Lands of the Past*. Translated by Bernard Miall. London: Oxford University Press, 1922. As one of the greatest twentieth century music historians, Rolland was largely responsible for the reevaluation of Telemann. Rolland insisted that Telemann was an unappreciated genius whose energy, fertile imagination, and unselfish desire to give music to the whole world inspired his followers and helped bring about the classical era.

Ruhnke, Martin. "Georg Philipp Telemann." In *North European Baroque Masters*. New York: W. W. Norton, 1985. A concise biography, one of six included in this volume, all by noted musical scholars. Contains an excellent, updated catalog of Telemann's works, as well as a comprehensive bibliography.

_____. "Relationships Between the Life and Work of Georg Philipp Telemann." *The Consort*, no. 24 (1967): 271-279. One of the few specialized studies of Telemann in English. Useful even for those without extensive musical background, since it focuses on the events of Telemann's life and how they appear to have influenced his work. Ruhnke presents evidence to refute many older views of Telemann and analyzes and compares the three autobiographies Telemann wrote.

See also: Johann Sebastian Bach; Charles XII; George Frideric Handel.

Related articles in *Great Events from History: The Eighteenth Century, 1701-1800*: c. 1701-1750: Bach Pioneers Modern Music; c. 1709: Invention of the Piano; April 13, 1742: First Performance of Handel's *Messiah*; January, 1762-November, 1766: Mozart Tours Europe as a Child Prodigy; 1795-1797: Paganini's Early Violin Performances.

THANADELTHUR
Chipewyan translator and guide

Thanadelthur shared her knowledge of natural resources, her awareness of indigenous cultures, and her foreign language abilities to assist English fur traders. She convinced members of her tribe and its rivals to coexist peacefully so that both groups could benefit from transactions and trade with outsiders.

Born: c. 1697; Canada
Died: February 5, 1717; York Factory (now in Manitoba), Canada
Areas of achievement: Warfare and conquest, government and politics

EARLY LIFE

Thanadelthur (THAN-ah-DEHL-thur) represents an enduring heroine who personifies strength and courage in indigenous cultures. Because records documenting Thanadelthur's life before captivity are nonexistent, historians estimate she was born around 1697. A Chipewyan, a people also referred to as the Dene (the people), Thanadelthur probably lived with her family and its First Nations band as they moved between hunting grounds in northern Canada, located in what is now Saskatchewan, Alberta, Manitoba, and the Northwest Territories. Tribal accounts state that her name was derived from the indigenous term for "martens," a type of weasel. Sources do not cite her parents' and siblings' names, although a brother accompanied Thanadelthur on her peace negotiations and she referred to him in conversations with traders.

Thanadelthur likely would have fulfilled the domestic roles the tribe expected of girls and women. Tasks included cooking, preparing skins and transforming them into clothes and shoes, sewing, and gathering firewood, berries, and nuts. The Chipewyan relied on their resourceful and resilient women, who would transport supplies between camps. Men valued women's opinions concerning community activities and interactions with outsiders, often accepting and incorporating those ideas in policies. Primarily nomadic hunters, the Chipewyan followed caribou herds migrating between breeding grounds. Families established groups of kin to hunt game, including beaver, foxes, and ermine. As a child, Thanadelthur would have acquired useful survival and communication skills.

LIFE'S WORK

Thanadelthur's known biography covers just a few years. In the spring of 1713, her life abruptly changed when rival Cree warriors from the south seized and enslaved her with women from her tribe. She endured captivity in a Cree village north of the Nelson River for approximately eighteen months.

While enslaved, she witnessed European traders exchange supplies for Cree furs. Allying with a fellow Chipewyan hostage, Thanadelthur fled and headed toward the Chipewyan territory but was hindered by hunger, extreme weather, fatigue, and the death of her friend. She sought help from traders and turned southeast through dangerous Cree lands. Seeing footprints, Thanadelthur caught up with a party of English traders, affiliated with the Hudson's Bay Company, hunting geese at Ten Shilling Creek. The party admired Thanadelthur's survival skills and delivered her to the company's Hayes River trading post, known as York Fort, on November 24, 1714, for medical attention and sanctuary. Two days before Thanadelthur reached York, another indigenous woman, who had been captured in the same raid as Thanadelthur and then enslaved, died at the fort. She had provided company officials some information about her tribe and the lands where they lived.

Company governor James Knight aspired to initiate trading partnerships in which his representatives received furs from local peoples who were paid with items such as muskets and gunpowder. Prior to approaching Chipweyan hunters, the English traders established fur trade agreements with Cree that resulted in wealth for the company in Europe, where buyers demanded Canadian furs. Wary of foreigners who had befriended their rivals, the Chipweyan resisted company offers. Knight recognized Thanadelthur's potential usefulness to secure business relationships with the indigenous peoples, particularly the Chipweyan in their northern lands. Wanting to trade with both Cree and Chipweyan, Knight hoped Thanadelthur, conversant in English and in some Cree because of her captivity—and familiar with all three cultures—could communicate his intentions to each tribe by translating his statements; she could, in turn, communicate their responses.

Knight especially sought to achieve resolution of rival tribes' claims to the same territory in order to secure consistent trade in that region with both tribes. Based on her experiences as a Cree slave, Thanadelthur realized interaction with English traders would benefit her tribe. Knight wanted the Chipewyan to trade at York, but the Chipewyan avoided Cree lands, especially those inhabited by the hostile Upland Cree, between their territory and the trading post where many Cree lived. The Chipewyan lacked guns to defend themselves against armed enemies. Thanadelthur told Knight that the Chipewyan would fear traveling to York without effective weapons to battle the warring Cree. She intrigued Knight with her description of abundant wildlife and possible copper and gold deposits near her band's territory on the Churchill River.

By late June, 1715, Thanadelthur traveled northwest toward the Great Slave Lake and the region where her people hunted. She transported English gifts to entice her community to accept the company's invitation. Approximately 150 traders headed by William Stuart, assigned as her protector, and Cree accompanied her. Most would abandon the trail as illness spread, supplies dwindled, and frigid climatic conditions on the tundra became unbearable. After all the English traders quit, Thanadelthur, Stuart, and several Cree advanced until they discovered nine Chipweyan bodies.

Convincing the Cree, who were fearful of vengeful warriors, not to flee and to stay at a safe site, Thanadelthur completed the last section of the 900-mile (1,500-kilometer) trip alone. She discussed her mission with Chipweyan leaders and guided a large group of approximately 160 men to the Cree site to discuss possible peace measures between the two tribes. Agitated and apprehensive, the two tribes reluctantly voiced demands when Thanadelthur pressured them to participate. Although she could barely speak after talking so much to convince the suspicious Chipewyan to meet Cree, Thanadelthur chided participants and urged them to compromise. She boldly denounced the Cree as cowards for murdering Chipewyan and cowed the large group to cease hostilities. Her words powerfully controlled the rivals. After achieving a peaceful resolution, Thanadelthur, Stuart, and several tribesmen headed back to company headquarters at York by May 7, 1716.

Thanadelthur's determination, astute awareness of human nature, and powers of persuasion were greatly admired, and so she was asked to remain at York. Thanadelthur married a tribe member who had returned with her to York. She intended to pursue additional trips and negotiations with her tribe the next year but became sick, possibly because she lacked immunities to European diseases. In his journal, Knight commented on her illness. She taught an Englishman, Richard Norton, essential words in her language, described cultural expectations, and prepared him for trading trips with her tribe and brother. The feverish Thanadelthur died on February 5,

1717. Before her death, she asked Knight to send her belongings to her mother, brother, and friends. Knight recorded her passing in his journal, expressing his grief at losing a confidante and capable negotiator. He purchased another slave woman to replace Thanadelthur as a translator for trading expeditions.

Thanadelthur's comments regarding a body of water that never froze inspired Knight to initiate an expedition to determine if that body of water might be the Northwest Passage to Asia that explorers had been seeking for hundreds of years. He vanished during that pursuit.

SIGNIFICANCE

Thanadelthur's peacemaking role has persisted in both the oral legends of the indigenous peoples and printed mainstream legends and historical accounts, and the accounts have varied. She usually is described as a former slave who fled captivity to bring peace and prosperity to her people and friends. Thanadelthur inspired derivative heroine captivity tales in other cultures. Her name and location may differ in those versions, but the story basically remains true to the oral and historical records of her travails and triumphs.

Although Thanadelthur's voice was not preserved in autobiographical accounts, her dramatic actions spoke loudly and provided a framework for the incorporation of her story into popular culture. Artists such as Franklin Arbuckle in the early 1950's painted their visions of Thanadelthur. Novels, including James Houston's *Running West* (1989) and Rick Book's *Blackships and Thanadelthur* (2001), and a comic book called *Tales from the Bay* (1995) have fictionalized Thanadelthur's life.

Nonindigenous Canadians tend to compare Thanadelthur with Sacagawea and interpret Thanadelthur's actions as a catalyst for eighteenth century European economic achievements in Canada. They have appropriated Thanadelthur as a symbol representing the advancement of Canada's frontier expansion and national development. Her activities helped the fur trade to spread farther west in Canada during the nineteenth century, and the Chipewyan hunted over larger regions. Ironically, Thanadelthur's peace efforts, which boosted the fur trade, ultimately resulted in animosity between Chipewyan and Cree that intensified into hostilities when territories overlapped and the historic enemies competed for furs and profits.

—Elizabeth D. Schafer

FURTHER READING

Abel, Kerry M. *Drum Songs: Glimpses of Dene History.* Montreal: McGill-Queen's University Press, 1993.

Discusses Thanadelthur's role in educating Knight and Hudson's Bay Company traders about indigenous peoples, including Cree and Chipewyan (or Dene), with whom they wanted to establish trade agreements.

Lytwyn, Victor P. *Muskekowuck Athinuwick: Original People of the Great Swampy Land.* Winnipeg: University of Manitoba Press, 2002. A useful study of Cree and nearby tribes, enemies such as the Chipewyan, and fur trading with Europeans, focusing on Thandelthur's interactions with the Cree. Includes maps.

McCormack, Patricia A. "The Many Faces of Thanadelthur: Documents, Stories, and Images." In *Reading Beyond Words: Contexts for Native History*, edited by Jennifer S. H. Brown and Elizabeth Vibert. 2d ed. Peterborough, Ont.: Broadview Press, 2003. An indigenous studies expert explores how Thanadelthur is portrayed in popular culture and historical texts.

Merritt, Susan. *Her Story: Women from Canada's Past.* St. Catharines, Ont.: Vanwell, 1993. Includes a chapter featuring Thanadelthur that sentimentally discusses her peace efforts and suggests how she lived before her capture. Includes photographs of modern First Nations women.

Van Kirk, Sylvia. *Many Tender Ties: Women in Fur Trade Society in Western Canada, 1670-1870.* Norman: University of Oklahoma Press, 1980. This study, based on Hudson's Bay Company archival records and primary accounts, analyzes Thanadelthur's and other indigenous women's roles and interactions with Europeans. Maps, bibliography, index.

See also: Joseph Brant; Little Turtle; Alexander McGillivray; Nanny; Pontiac.

Related article in *Great Events from History: The Eighteenth Century, 1701-1800:* Summer, 1714-1741: Fox Wars.

GIOVANNI BATTISTA TIEPOLO
Italian painter

The last important painter of the Venetian school, Tiepolo was the most versatile of the Italian ceiling painters. Although he worked primarily in the Baroque tradition, his work shares some qualities of the rococo.

Born: March 5, 1696; Venice (now in Italy)
Died: March 27, 1770; Madrid, Spain
Area of achievement: Art

EARLY LIFE
Giovanni Battista Tiepolo (joh-VAHN-nee baht-TEES-tah TYEH-poh-loh) was born in Venice on March 5, 1696, the son of a wealthy merchant. When his father died, Tiepolo's mother apprenticed him to Gregorio Lazzarini, a minor painter, from whom Tiepolo received his first instruction in painting. Later, Tiepolo became familiar with the Venetian decorative tradition. His first work, *The Sacrifice of Isaac* (1716), is noteworthy for its strong contrasts of light and shade. This early work reflects the influence of Giovanni Battista Piazetta, a member of the Bolognese and Roman Baroque school of painting.

Tiepolo's career as an independent artist actually began in 1717, at which time his name first appears on the lists of the Venetian painters' guild. His studio was so successful at this time that he married Cecilia Guardi, the seventeen-year-old sister of the painters Giovanni Antonio and Francesco Guardi. Despite his success, Tiepolo continued to learn, employing techniques from both Venetian and foreign painters of the eighteenth century in his prolific outpouring of etchings after sixteenth century subjects. Tiepolo's *Madonna of Carmelo and the Souls of Purgatory* (1720) clearly demonstrates the influence of Piazetta. His tendency to create large masses in violent contrasts of light and dark on a diagonal is evident in another early work, *Repudiation of Hagar*, which he painted when he was twenty.

The works that Tiepolo entered for the competitions of 1716 and 1717, *Crossing the Red Sea* and *Martyrdom of Saint Bartholomew*, respectively, led to several commissions. His first important commission was *Glory of Saint Teresa*, which he painted for the vault of the side chapel in the Church of the Scalzi. This work was followed by four paintings of mythological subjects, *Diana and Callistro*, *Diana and Actaeon*, *Apollo and Marsyas*, and the *Rape of Europa*. Church commissions were followed by commissions from such private persons as Doge Cornaro, who assigned him to paint the canvases and frescoes for his palace in 1722. The paintings that he did for the Palazzo Sandi a Corte dell'Alberto, while foreshadowing the heroic subjects of his later works, still possess the qualities of his early works, such as figures with popping round eyes and contorted limbs. During this time, Tiepolo was still looking for a style and a medium that suited him. He was still imitating the style of the nonrococo painters, and the prosaic way in which he treated his historical and religious subjects testified to the fact that he was an unlearned painter.

LIFE'S WORK

Tiepolo reached his full maturity of expression in his frescoes. The promise that was displayed in his first frescoes, the *Power of Eloquence* and the *Glory of Saint Teresa*, which were painted for the Palazzo Sandi a Corte dell'Alberto in 1725, was fully realized in the frescoes of the Archiepiscopal Palace in Udine. Between 1725 and 1728, he frescoed the *Fall of the Rebel Angels* in the ceiling above the main staircase and painted several episodes from the Book of Job in the gallery with the help of his longtime assistant, Mengozzi Colonna, who did the framings. In these paintings, which feature Abraham and his descendants dressed in sixteenth century costumes, he replaced the gloominess that had characterized his early works with dazzling colors. These paintings are distinguished from those of his contemporaries in their credibility. For example, the central figure in *Angel Appealing to Sarah* is a nearly toothless old woman, not a beautiful noblewoman. When he was finished, Tiepolo returned to Venice and his family.

Tiepolo was still developing as an artist when, at age thirty-five, two important commissions took him to Milan in 1731. At the Palazzo Archinto (which was destroyed by bombings during World War II) he painted the *Triumph of the Arts* and mythological scenes in four ceilings, the most successful of which was *Phaethon Begging Apollo to Allow Him to Drive the Chariot of the Sun*. As in most of his ceiling frescoes, the ceiling becomes the sky. Some of the scenes still survive in *modelletti*, pen-and-ink watercolor sketches that he usually submitted to his patrons before starting work. Working with his characteristic speed, Tiepolo completed the *Story of Scipio* frescoes, historical paintings in Baroque settings, in only a few months for the Palazzo Casati-Dugnani. Unlike the Udine frescoes, which are witty and dashing, the subjects of these scenes are much more serious and elevated.

Tiepolo spent the next two years, 1732-1733, at Bergamo, where he frescoed four allegorical figures and some scenes in the life of John the Baptist in Colleoni Chapel. The airy landscapes of these paintings represent

an innovation in his style. The *modelletti* and two small pictures, *The Last Communion of Saint Jerome* and the *Death of Saint Jerome*, are characterized by a grainy texture. The clear-cut contours of the figures illustrate the progress that he had made since the sketches of the Udine period. During this same period, Tiepolo painted three large canvases depicting an episode from Roman history for the main saloon of the Villa Grimani-Valmara. To the Bergamo period may also be assigned the altarpiece in the parish church of Rovetta Sopra Bergamo. In this painting, *The Virgin in Glory Adored by the Apostles and Saints*, he eliminated all traces of Piazzetta, abandoning the dark tonality, heaviness of color, and agitated undulation in his line. Tiepolo closed the 1730's with the frescoing of the ceiling of the Palazzo Clerici in Milan, which ranks as one of the most fascinating pictorial creations of the century and introduced a new compositional principle: the creation of a centrifugal effect by concentrating a group of figures along the edge of the ceiling.

In the decade between 1740 and 1750, Tiepolo experimented with forms of the great luminosity that had been rediscovered by Piazzetta and Guardi and reached full maturity as an artist. By this time, the most prestigious families of the republic were vying for his works. He left Venice only once during this period, and that was to decorate the Villa Cordellina at Montecchio Maggiore. The works produced in this period, many of which have secular themes, reflect a decorative balance and a greater fusion and transparency. He also became closer to the classical tastes of the time through his long relationship with Count Francesco Algarotti.

Algarotti's insistence that Tiepolo strive for extreme delicacy and refinement manifests itself in the *Banquet of Antony and Cleopatra*, which Tiepolo created for the central saloon of the Palazzo Labia. Not only is this one of Tiepolo's greatest frescoes, but it also is one of the most beautiful examples of pictorial illusionism ever painted. This effect was achieved with the help of Mengozzi Colonna, who turned each of the end walls into a facade with a tall central archway leading into the fresco itself. Tiepolo's fascination with the classic world is still evident between 1745 and 1750, when he painted *Neptune Offering to Venice the Riches of the Sea*. At the end of the decade, he collaborated with his son Domenico to paint the *Consilium in Arena*, which commemorated the Council of the Order of Malta.

In 1750, Tiepolo and his two sons, Domenico, age twenty-three, and Lorenzo, age fourteen, were summoned to Würzburg to decorate the newly built Residenz of the prince-bishop. During his three-year stay at

Würzburg, Tiepolo painted two masterpieces that rank among the greatest creations of pictorial art. Tiepolo began with the ceiling of the saloon, where he painted *Apollo Conducting Barbarossa's Bride, Beatrice of Burgundy*. The frescoes on the walls, which glorified several episodes in the life of the Emperor Frederick I (Barbarossa) are much less imaginative.

Tiepolo then turned his attention to the staircase ceiling, the most monumental undertaking of his career until that time. The staircase ceiling, on which Tiepolo depicted Olympus and the four parts of the known world, has been called Tiepolo's Sistine chapel. The influence of Peter Paul Rubens, whose work Tiepolo saw in Germany, is apparent in the ceiling. Before leaving Germany, Tiepolo also found time to execute numerous works on canvas. The romantic, poetic themes that now preoccupied him culminated in four charming canvases depicting the story of Rinaldo and Armida. He also ventured outside Würzburg to paint one of his finest religious works, the altarpiece of the *Adoration of the Magi*, for the Church of the Benedictines of Schwarzach. While in Germany, he was assisted by Domenico and by a group of pupils from his school.

Tiepolo returned to Venice in 1753, confident that he had succeeded in promoting Venetian painting outside Italy. Instead of simply basking in his fame, Tiepolo continued to build his reputation in Venice. Two years after his return, he was elected president of the Venetian Academy. In 1757, he and Domenico frescoed the hall and four downstairs rooms for the Villa Valmarana. By this time, Tiepolo had completely abandoned the diagonal perspective of his youth; instead, the figures move in planes parallel to the wall. He returned to the influence of Paolo Veronese, one of Italy's greatest ceiling painters, in the relationships of the figures in *Sacrifice of Iphigenia*. That same year, Tiepolo also frescoed four circular panels with allegories of the Arts, Music, Science, and History on the ceiling of the grand saloon in the Palazzo Valmarana-Trenta in Vincenza, which was destroyed in the bombardments of 1945. His Catholic sensibilities once again surfaced in the great altarpiece of Saint Thecla, which he painted for the Church of the Grazie at Este in 1759.

While working at the Villa Pisani, Tiepolo was invited by Charles III of Spain to decorate the royal palace. Without his faithful assistant Mengozzi Colonna, who was now seventy-four years old and feeble, or his two sons, Tiepolo arrived at Madrid after two months of traveling by land. After recovering from fatigue, the sixty-six-year-old painter began painting the *Apotheosis of Spain* in the throne room in 1762. In this fresco, Spain is surrounded by symbolic and mythological figures in the skies.

In 1764, Tiepolo painted two ceilings of lesser importance in the same palace. After completing the frescoes, Tiepolo remained in the service of the king, painting seven altarpieces at Aranjuez. He had no sooner finished them than the king replaced them with works by Anton Raphael Mengs, Francisco Bayeu, and others, leaving Tiepolo a disappointed and bitter man. Though damaged, the surviving altarpieces reflect a new intensity; no longer are the subjects excuses for grand displays of celestial pageants. The last three years of his life were occupied by feverish activity. He executed many works for the court of Russia, which were sent from Spain, as well as a series of small canvases of religious subjects, such as the *Flight into Egypt*. On March 27, 1770, Tiepolo died suddenly in Spain. He was buried in his parish church of Saint Martin, but both the church and his tomb have been destroyed.

SIGNIFICANCE

Giovanni Battista Tiepolo will be remembered not only as one of the greatest decorative painters of eighteenth century Europe but also as the man who revived Venetian painting. A tireless and prolific worker, he achieved success at an early age, first displaying his formidable talent in the Church of the Ospedaletto at the age of nineteen. As his fame spread, he helped to free Venetian art from the chiaroscuro style with its strong contrasts of light and shade.

Tiepolo also stands apart from his contemporaries in his mastery of linear perspective, which is exhibited in the weightless qualities that the figures in his ceiling frescoes seem to possess. Above all, Tiepolo raised the status of fresco painting from that of a secondary, decorative role to the high artistic rank that it had held in the golden age of the Cinquecento. Like his predecessor, Bonifazio Veronese, Tiepolo was skilled in the art of setting angels and gods in a seemingly limitless space. His dramatic imagination populated his frescoes with subjects drawn from both mythology and religion who are painted as flesh and blood human beings instead of mere puppets. His frescoes were, in a sense, the definitive complement to the rococo churches and palaces of his day.

Tiepolo's work has suffered the same critical fate as that of other artists who achieved considerable wealth and fame in their lifetime. The hostile response of the Spanish court toward his work foreshadowed the nineteenth century's hostile reception of his work, especially in France and England. Even at the height of his success, he was the victim of shifting tastes, being popular primarily in northern Italy. Modern taste, though, seems to have accepted his work without reservation.

—*Alan Brown*

FURTHER READING

Alpers, Svetlana, and Michael Baxandall. *Tiepolo and the Pictorial Intelligence*. New Haven, Conn.: Yale University Press, 1994. Examination of Tiepolo's work by two art historians. The authors conclude that Tiepolo's greatness is his "pictorial intelligence," or the ability to use visual media, such as paintings, drawings, and natural lighting.

Barcham, William L. *Giambattista Tiepolo*. New York: H. N. Abrams, 1992. A biographical study, illustrated with thirty-six black-and-white reproductions. Also includes forty color plates, with commentaries by Barcham describing them.

_____. *The Religious Paintings of Giambattista Tiepolo: Piety and Tradition in Eighteenth-Century Venice*. New York: Oxford University Press, 1989. Barcham's study, the first to concentrate on Tiepolo's religious paintings, treats its subject as an expression of the values of the Venetian Republic. Illustrated with four line drawings, 133 halftones, and nine color plates.

Krückman, Peter Oluf. *Tiepolo: Masterpieces of the Würzburg Years*. New York: Prestel, 1996. Describes how Tiepolo received the commission to decorate the Residenz of the prince-bishop and analyzes the work he created there. Focuses on the frescoes he painted, examining the relationship between the frescoes and the architecture of the Residenz. Also discusses the oil paintings that Tiepolo and his sons created in Würzburg.

Levey, Michael. *Giambattista Tiepolo: His Life and Art*. New Haven, Conn.: Yale University Press, 1986. Reprint. 1994. Comprehensive examination of Tiepolo's life and career, including detailed analyses of his major artworks. The book describes how Tiepolo aimed to create an alternative universe of light and color.

_____. *Painting in Eighteenth Century Venice*. New York: Phaidon Press, 1959. Not primarily a biography, although the chapter on Tiepolo discusses his major works in chronological order and demonstrates how they typify each stage of his development as an artist. This chapter does a fine job of showing how Tiepolo's work either followed or strayed from the artistic trends of his day. Illustrated with several plates.

Morassi, Antonio. *G. B. Tiepolo: His Life and Work*. New York: Phaidon Press, 1955. A standard biography, providing details of Tiepolo's life along with descriptions and critical assessments of the works from each period in his life. Beautifully illustrated with black-and-white and color plates, the book covers most of Tiepolo's works.

See also: Canaletto; Charles III.

Related articles in *Great Events from History: The Eighteenth Century, 1701-1800*: December 10, 1768: Britain's Royal Academy of Arts Is Founded; 1785: Construction of El Prado Museum Begins; 1787: David Paints *The Death of Socrates*.

TOKUGAWA YOSHIMUNE
Shogun of Japan (r. 1716-1745)

One of the most active and influential of the later Tokugawa shoguns, Tokugawa Yoshimune ruled in cooperation with the great daimyo lords rather than against them and thus achieved financial reform and political stability. His dynastic policies of founding branch families ensured Tokugawa control of the shogunate up to its end in 1868.

Born: November 27, 1684; Wakayama, Japan
Died: July 12, 1751; Edo (now Tokyo), Japan
Area of achievement: Government and politics

EARLY LIFE

Tokugawa Yoshimune (to-koo-gah-wah yo-shi-moo-neh) was born south of the imperial capital of Kyoto, the third son of Tokugawa Mitsuada. His father was daimyo and head of the Kii branch of the Tokugawa family, founded by Tokugawa Ieyasu, who became the first Tokugawa shogun in 1603. On his father's side, Tokugawa Yoshimune was a great-grandson of Ieyasu. His mother, however, was a nonaristocratic townswoman. She had entered Tokugawa services as a lady-in-waiting. Her great beauty, charm, and intelligence caught the attention of Mitsuada. Tokugawa Yoshimune's mother, because of her low rank, was not allowed to raise her son herself.

In 1697, when he was thirteen years old, Tokugawa Yoshimune was made daimyo of the insignificant Sabae domain, centered on the town of Fukui on the north-central coast facing the Sea of Japan. He was placed here because his mother's low social rank made it unlikely he would ever rise to a high position in life. His domain was so small that he had difficulty affording the minimum living standards prescribed for a daimyo, yet he remained independent of the more rigid education given to a likely candidate for succession as shogun.

In 1705, Tokugawa Yoshimune's father died at age eighty. Because his two elder brothers had died as well, Tokugawa Yoshimune was made his father's successor as daimyo of the Kii domain, a heartland of the Tokugawa family. Tokugawa Yoshimune's first son, Ieshige, was born in 1711, but he suffered from physical deformity and a speech impediment. In 1712, shogun Ienobu died and was succeeded by his three-year-old son Ietsugu. While another nobleman, Manabe Akifusa, was appointed guardian of the child shogun, Tokugawa Yoshimune managed to be appointed his regent. He

moved to Edo, center of shogunal power. In 1715, his second, gifted son Munetake was born.

LIFE'S WORK

In 1716, child shogun Ietsugu died at age seven. The Gosanke, or "three houses of succession" representing the larger Tokugawa family, met with the *rōjū*, or senior councillors, to chose a successor. Supported by the dead boy's mother, Gekkō In, Tokugawa Yoshimune was chosen as the eighth Tokugawa shogun.

Tokugawa Yoshimune soon purged Ienobu's two most influential officials who continued to wield power. Manabe Akifusa was transferred to a remote location in 1717 and died there in 1720. The influential reformer Arai Hakuseki lost access to the new shogun and died without power in 1725.

Instead of promoting a single man to represent his interests, Tokugawa Yoshimune decided to work with senior councillors and major daimyos of the realm, who had come to resent the shogun's special officials in previous reigns and so welcomed Tokugawa Yoshimune's offer. To offset any weakness, Tokugawa Yoshimune directly involved himself in politics. He often circumvented the official chain of command and actively intervened in operational issues. This gave him freedom of action that he used energetically.

Tokugawa Yoshimune confronted inherited financial problems. Beginning with the fifth shogun, Tsunayoshi, in the previous century, Japan's currency was debased to pay the shogun's lavish expenses. Tokugawa Yoshimune stopped the practice in order to mix silver into gold coins. He also called for measures of austerity. Considered a highly moral and ethical person, Tokugawa Yoshimune implemented the budget and began with himself. He tore down the shogun's extravagant living quarters, moving into an antechamber. He practiced a frugal lifestyle with a vegetarian diet for everyday consumption. When hunting, he dressed simply and accepted lunch invitations of the peasants. To curb the flamboyant lifestyle of the Genroku era (1688-1704), Tokugawa Yoshimune urged samurai to do sports and martial arts training. Merchants were told to be less lavish in displaying their wealth. To promote science, Tokugawa Yoshimune relaxed the ban on Western scientific books in 1720, and he also took an interest in compiling law cases and statutes. In 1721 his third son, Munenobu, was born.

In 1721-1722, the shogun could not meet the payroll for his retainers. Since most of the old *rōjū* to whom Tokugawa Yoshimune owed his selection were dead or retired, he felt confident to launch reforms. Tokugawa Yoshimune instituted the *meyasubako*, or box for popular appeals. Kept locked outside an Edo castle gate, anyone could drop a suggestion into the box for the shogun. The box was brought to him still locked to ensure confidentiality. Tokugawa Yoshimune took the letters seriously, which led, for example, to the development of Edo fire prevention and to a new hospital. His successors kept the box.

In 1722, Tokugawa Yoshimune launched his Kyōhō reforms. As an emergency measure, daimyos were forced to loan money to the shogun; in return, they could save by having to spend less time in attendance at Edo. Next, Tokugawa Yoshimune appointed a senior councillor for financial affairs (*kattegakari rōjū*) to supervise a staff of commissioners of finance (*kanjō bugyō*), consisting of four officers and five thousand men. They supervised tax collection, the judiciary, economic and commercial transactions, and emergency relief.

To attract capable men of low rank, in 1723, Tokugawa Yoshimune instituted a system of merit-based stipends (*tashidaka*), which gave skilled officials the legal minimum income required for their positions. Realizing he could not effectively rule alone, in 1724, Tokugawa Yoshimune turned over routine business to external officials. He also decreased the political influence held by court ladies. In 1726, he promoted his most trusted two adjutants to daimyo. With new taxes, the shogun's income rose. In 1730, Tokugawa Yoshimune founded a new family branch of the Tokugawa, headed by his capable second son, Munetake. In 1731, emergency loans by daimyos were ended, and they had to spend more time in Edo.

In 1732, the Kyōhō Famine struck southwestern Japan, testing Tokugawa Yoshimune's crisis management. Rural depression led to a riot in Edo in 1733. The shogunate's emergency measures, such as releasing stored rice, advocating donations, and using whale oil against locusts had some success, but the situation was saved by the rich harvests of 1734 and 1735. More than twelve thousand people died, a number that arguably would have been higher without the shogun's intervention. To improve agriculture, Tokugawa Yoshimune instituted crop experiments in his castle gardens. By 1735, strong currency led to economic stagnation. Reversing policies, Tokugawa Yoshimune increased the money supply by debasing the currency and minting copper coins, leading to the economy's expansion. His gradual permitting of the sale of agricultural land led to the commercialization of agriculture.

In 1739, Tokugawa Yoshimune challenged his leadership by dismissing the obstinate daimyo of Owari. This was a serious execution of the shogun's most powerful privilege. It had rarely been used in the last decades and would not be used again for a century.

Tokugawa Yoshimune founded a second branch family, headed by his nineteen-year-old third son, Munenobu, in 1740. In 1745, Tokugawa Yoshimune retired as shogun on behalf of his disabled eldest son, Ieshige, who had become an alcoholic. Yielding to tradition instead of recognizing merit would cost Tokugawa Yoshimune the resignation of a trusted senior councillor.

Until his death in 1751, Tokugawa Yoshimune and his councillors ruled well for the incapacitated shogun. Afterward, the adjutant Ōoka Tadamitsu took control. When Tadamitsu died in 1760, Ieshige was retired and succeeded by his son, Tokugawa Yoshimune's grandson Ieharu. Yet even Ieharu let a grand chamberlain rule for him.

SIGNIFICANCE

Tokugawa Yoshimune showed that a capable shogun could yield much power if he involved himself directly in administration and cooperated with the larger daimyos. His mixture of building consensus at the highest level of government and remaining involved in midlevel operations yielded great rewards.

Tokugawa Yoshimune confronted the financial problems of the Tokugawa shogunate in the early eighteenth century. Contemporary critics give much credit to his financial policy, which began in 1735, and his policy inevitably accelerated Japan's move to an economic system that was more like capitalism.

Tokugawa Yoshimune's dynastic policy of enlarging the base of Tokugawa rule by founding two new family branches (and inspiring another) ultimately succeeded in keeping the shogunate in Tokugawa hands until the Meiji restoration in 1868. Almost automatically, Tokugawa Yoshimune kept the emperor a mere representational figurehead in Kyoto.

Ironically, for a shogun who placed so much emphasis on merit among his officers, Tokugawa Yoshimune preferred tradition in his personal life. In fact, his choice of successor sabotaged shogunal rule. Beginning with Ieshige, whose disabilities and alcoholism left him no other choice, the subsequent Tokugawa shoguns left the execution of their power to trusted middlemen. This influenced the popular decision to replace the shoguns' rule with that of an emperor in 1868.

—*R. C. Lutz*

FURTHER READING

Jansen, Marius. *The Making of Modern Japan.* Cambridge, Mass.: Belknap Press, 2000. Chapter 2 focuses on the Tokugawa shogunate. Proposes that because of Tokugawa Yoshimune's nonaristocratic mother, his education was freer than that for a designated successor to the shogunate, which may have preserved his desire for independent action. Also provides background on his times and the overall organization of Tokugawa rule. Illustrations, notes, index, bibliography.

McClain, James. *Japan: A Modern History.* New York: Norton, 2001. The first three chapters examine the Tokugawa period, illuminate the inner workings of the rule of the Tokugawa shoguns, and explore life in Japan under Tokugawa rule. Illustrations, maps, index.

Nishiyama, Matsonosuke. *Edo Culture.* Honolulu: University of Hawaii Press, 1997. Focuses on daily city life in the Tokugawa era, with an emphasis on the common city dweller who was affected by the economic reforms pushed through by Tokugawa Yoshimune. Illustrations, index.

Totman, Conrad D. *Politics in the Tokugawa Bakufu, 1600-1843.* Cambridge, Mass.: Harvard University Press, 1967. A thorough analysis of Tokugawa rule. The last chapter chronicles the highlights of Tokugawa Yoshimune's rule, including the question of his succession. Appendices, notes, bibliography, glossary, index, maps, and tables.

See also: Honda Toshiaki; Ogyū Sorai.

Related articles in *Great Events from History: The Eighteenth Century, 1701-1800:* December, 1720: Japan Lifts Ban on Foreign Books; 1786-1787: Tenmei Famine.

WOLFE TONE
Irish rebel leader

Impulsive, charismatic, intense, and dynamic, Tone personified the intoxicating atmosphere of the 1790's in Europe and worked with total dedication to establish an independent and liberal Irish Republic. His strength of personality and intellectual abilities set him apart from most of the United Irish leaders, and the circumstances of his martyrdom have transformed him into an iconographic figure for Irish nationalists of all shades of opinion.

Born: June 20, 1763; Dublin, Ireland
Died: November 19, 1798; Dublin, Ireland
Also known as: Theobald Wolfe Tone (full name)
Areas of achievement: Government and politics, warfare and conquest

EARLY LIFE

Wolfe Tone was born at 44 Stafford Street (since renamed Wolfe Tone Street) in north Dublin, in what was then a largely lower-middle-class neighborhood. His father, Peter Tone, was a coach and carriage maker, and his mother was Margaret Lambert. The family was Protestant and had five children; Wolfe was baptized at St. Mary's Anglican Church. However, his early life was anything but religious.

Wolfe Tone was a wild youth, spending a lot of time in carousing, drinking, womanizing, and frequenting taverns into the early hours. As with many young men of that time, he was quick to take offense and could quite readily resort to violence over any slight; thus, he was involved in violent altercations. To keep him out of trouble, he was sent to County Galway to tutor the two sons of the parliamentarian Colonel Richard Martin. However, he engaged in an affair with Martin's wife, Elizabeth Vesey, and reputedly fathered a child by her.

He was admitted on scholarship into Trinity College, Dublin, to study for the Irish bar but made indifferent progress, finally graduating in 1786. He fell in love with sixteen-year-old Matilda Witherington and, over the objections of both families, the couple ran off and were married. Despite this inauspicious start, the marriage proved solid. Wolfe Tone had moderated his alcohol consumption and the couple had two sons, William Theobald Wolfe Tone (1791-1828), who later served in the French and American armed forces and wrote a biography of his father, and Francis Rawdon Tone. Finishing his legal studies in London at the Middle Temple in 1789, Wolfe Tone returned to Dublin.

LIFE'S WORK

Wolfe Tone's interest strayed from the law to politics. There were at first few signs of the radicalism that would become his hallmark. He tried to persuade the prime minister, William Pitt the Younger, into supporting government funding for a proposed Pacific island colony that Tone envisioned establishing. Some scholars believe that it was Pitt's rather nonchalant rejection of the project that embittered Tone against England—though this seems to overstate the power of personal slight. What is certain is that Tone absorbed the influence of Jean-Jacques Rousseau, Thomas Paine, and the tangible achievements of the American and the French Revolutions.

By 1791, Tone had become committed to liberal and nationalist ideas, including Catholic emancipation, religious freedom, and self-government. He broke with the parliamentary reform movement of Henry Grattan and Henry Flood, convinced that working within the English system under the British crown was futile and that democratic objectives could be secured only in an independent, republican Ireland. He first articulated these views in *Catholics: An Argument on Behalf of the Catholics of Ireland* (1791), a 54-page work that catapulted him into prominence. Along with James Napper Tandy, Thomas Russell, Simon Butler, and Samuel McTier, Tone formed the Society of United Irishmen, first in Belfast (October 14, 1791) and then in Dublin (November 9, 1791). Working to bridge the gap between Catholics and Protestants to forge a common front to achieve Irish freedom, Tone became chief secretary for the Catholic Committee from 1792 to 1793. Though his efforts were instrumental in securing the passage of Hobart's Catholic Relief Act in 1793 and he was lauded for his energy and efforts by committee colleagues, he was dissatisfied with the limited scope of the law's reforms.

Tone became increasingly frustrated with the slow pace of reform and more influenced by the extreme revolutionary republicanism that had assumed control in France. The arrest and suicide of the French agent William Jackson on April 30, 1794, led to revelations that Tone was involved in a conspiracy to assist a proposed French invasion of Ireland. Though the United Irish were outlawed, Tone was allowed to sail into exile to the United States in May of 1795. He remained less than a year; by February, 1796, he was in Paris trying to gener-

Wolfe Tone. (Library of Congress)

ate support from the French government to mount an invasion of Ireland.

In December, 1796, Tone, now an officer in the French army, accompanied an expeditionary force of some fifteen thousand troops under the command of General Louis Lazare Hoche. For several days (December 22-27, 1796) the French fleet was sequestered in Bantry Bay, County Cork, unable to effect a landing because of horrendous weather conditions, and was forced to turn back. Tone's schemes for making a second attempt suffered a severe setback with Hoche's death in September of 1797. General Napoleon I, who inherited the project, preferred to direct his efforts to an invasion of Egypt, and consequently the French government committed few resources to an Irish campaign. In addition to receiving much-reduced support, Tone basically had to start from the beginning, and the timetable for invasion was substantially delayed.

When the 1798 Irish Rebellion broke out in Ireland during the late spring, Tone was still trying to put together a substantial invading force and was unable to embark from France until the autumn, long after the uprisings had been suppressed and after failed attempts by French General Jean Joseph Humbert and by Tone's colleague Napper Tandy. A fleet sailing out of the port of Brest under command of Admiral Bompart transported Tone and three thousand French troops to Lough Swilly off the coast of County Donegal, where they battled with British ships on October 12, 1798. The British defeated the French and Tone was ultimately captured, imprisoned at Newgate Gaol in Dublin, and court-martialed on charges of treason. Eloquently defending himself and taking the opportunity to propagandize his cause, Tone was nonetheless sentenced to death by hanging. He made the request that, as an officer in the French army, he be granted execution by firing squad. When it appeared that his request had been denied (though unbeknownst to him the judge had in fact ordered a stay of execution to consider the matter), Tone cut his own throat with a penknife on November 12. He lingered for a week before dying of his wounds on November 19, 1798.

SIGNIFICANCE

Wolfe Tone's unquenchable idealism and his unswerving commitment to his principles provided him a legendary aura that no other Irish revolutionary figure was capable of exceeding. He has become the indispensable prop upon which the movements of the Young Irelanders, the Fenian Brotherhood, Patrick Pearse, James Conolly, and the various incarnations of the Irish Republican Army have looked to for inspiration and support.

—*Raymond Pierre Hylton*

FURTHER READING

Bartlett, Thomas, ed. *Life of Theobald Wolfe Tone*. Compiled and arranged by William Theobald Wolfe Tone. Dublin: Lilliput Press, 1999. An expanded edition of the original two-volume biography published in 1826 by Tone's son.

Doyle, William. *The Oxford History of the French Revolution*. 2d ed. New York: Oxford University Press, 2002. A comprehensive history, from King Louis XIV's accession to the throne in 1774 to Napoleon's assumption of power in 1802. Includes a chronology of events and an essay examining the historiography of the French Revolution.

Elliott, Marianne. *Wolfe Tone: Prophet of Irish Independence*. New Haven, Conn.: Yale University Press,

1989. An updated, scholarly study of later biographies of Tone, in which the author makes a real attempt to humanize her subject and to strip away the layers of adulation and hero worship that have accumulated over the centuries.

Killen, John. *The Decade of the United Irishmen: Contemporary Accounts, 1791-1801*. Belfast, Ireland: Blackstaff Press, 1998. A collection of contemporary sources in which Tone and his writings play a particularly important part.

Moody, T. W., and F. X. Martin. *The Course of Irish History*. Cork, Ireland: Mercier Press, 1984. Intended to be more a general history. In this work, Tone is accorded great significance in the forming of Irish Republican thinking.

Pakenham, Thomas. *The Year of Liberty: The Great Irish Rebellion of 1798*. New York: Random House, 1997. The most complete and readable study of the rebellion, with ample illustrative material.

Smyth, Jim, ed. *Revolution, Counterrevolution, and Union: Ireland in the 1790's*. New York: Cambridge University Press, 2000. Sets into perspective the atmosphere and ethos of the decade as well as Tone's role.

Tone, Theobald Wolfe. *The Writings of Theobald Wolfe Tone, 1763-98*. Edited by T. W. Moody, R. B. McDowell, and C. J. Woods. New York: Oxford University Press, 1998. A three-volume comprehensive collection of Tone's writings. Includes bibliographical references.

See also: Georges Danton; Lord Edward Fitzgerald; George III; Henry Grattan; Thomas Paine; William Pitt the Younger; Robespierre; Jean-Jacques Rousseau.

Related articles in *Great Events from History: The Eighteenth Century, 1701-1800:* January 4, 1792-1797: The *Northern Star* Calls for Irish Independence; April 20, 1792-October, 1797: Early Wars of the French Revolution; April 12, 1798-September 2, 1801: Napoleon's Egyptian Campaign; May-November, 1798: Irish Rebellion; July 2-August 1, 1800: Act of Union Forms the United Kingdom.

TOUSSAINT LOUVERTURE
Haitian revolutionary leader and general

Toussaint Louverture seized leadership of a chaotic revolution and transformed it into a successful West Indian struggle that ended slavery in Saint-Domingue, politically united the island of Hispaniola, and brought France's richest colony one step closer to independence.

Born: 1743; Breda plantation, near Cap Français, Saint-Domingue (now in Haiti)
Died: April 7, 1803; Fort-de-Joux, France
Also known as: François Dominique Toussaint Bréda (birth name)
Areas of achievement: Government and politics, warfare and conquest, social reform

EARLY LIFE

Born into slavery to African parents, François Dominique Toussaint Bréda, who would be known as Toussaint Louverture (tew-sahn lew-vehr-tewr), was reared in unique circumstances. His father, who claimed to be a prince, taught him the Arada language and lore, including herbalism. A solicitous godfather arranged for Toussaint to work in the refectory of a Catholic hospital, and the priests there provided instructions in religion and French. By the time Toussaint had to work full time on the plantation, he wrote French with difficulty, but he read easily and widely. Throughout his life, he retained a deep attachment to the Catholic Church and an admiration for French culture.

The plantation overseer, Bayon de Libertad, made good use of Toussaint's broad education. Because of the boy's healing skills, de Libertad placed Toussaint in charge of the Breda livestock. Toussaint developed special skills with horses and mastered the equestrian arts, earning the nickname "centaur of the savannas." De Libertad later promoted Toussaint to coachman and plantation steward. Toussaint made Breda one of the best administered, most productive plantations in northern Saint-Domingue, and "wise as Toussaint" was a regional expression among all races.

In 1777, at age thirty-four, Toussaint was given *liberté de savane*—virtual but not legal freedom. He continued to run Breda and began a family. He married Suzanne Simone Baptiste, adopted her child by a mulatto lover, and fathered two sons himself. By 1789, when Toussaint was forty-six years old, he led perhaps as idyllic a life as possible for one of African parentage in Saint-Domingue. He wielded authority on a plantation, en-joyed the respect of whites and slaves, headed a stable family, had a savings of 650,000 francs, and owned a sizable library.

LIFE'S WORK

On Toussaint Louverture's shelves were books by the French philosophes, including the study of the Indies by Guillaume-Thomas Raynal. Raynal condemned slavery and predicted that in Saint-Domingue a black hero would rise and lead his fellow slaves out of bondage. Raynal's antislavery writings found a voice in the revolutionary national assembly that convened in Paris in 1789.

Not numerous enough to end slavery, the abolition-ists focused their efforts on securing equality for mulat-toes. Offspring of planters and their slaves, mulattoes typically were educated and then, at age twenty-four, given freedom, property, and slaves. The forty thou-sand mulattoes equaled the whites in population and owned more than one-fourth of the colony's half million slaves, but they were saddled with racially discrimina-tory laws.

When the national assembly left the decision concern-ing equality to the colonial legislature, the mulattoes were bitterly disappointed. Vincent Ogé, leader of the mulatto delegation in Paris, returned to Cap Français and organized a rebellion in October, 1790. Authorities quickly smashed the insurrection, but Ogé's execution did not bring peace to the troubled colony. Already, small but serious disturbances between whites and mu-lattoes had flared in 1789 and 1790, but in August, 1791, a massive slave rebellion erupted.

A voodoo priest called upon all blacks to avenge themselves against the whites, and during the night of August 22, thousands of slaves responded to a drumbeat signal and began burning plantations and murdering whites and mulattoes in the northern plains. As refugees and pursuing *congos*, as the rebels were called, con-verged on Cap Français, Toussaint escorted de Libertad and his family to safety before leading 150 blacks to rebel headquarters.

Toussaint was immediately made one of the chief-tain's field secretaries and given the title physician in chief of the armies of the king of France. Blacks from Af-rica came from societies governed by kings believed to be semidivine, and in Saint-Domingue many slaves be-lieved—much as French peasants believed—that if Louis XVI knew of their sufferings he would intercede.

Toussaint constantly added recruits to his own band of followers, and by mid-1792 he commanded nearly one thousand rebels.

In June, 1792, the fighting intensified. Republican commissioners arrived to negotiate an end to the bloodshed, but whites and mulattoes rejected the blacks' petitions for improved conditions for slaves. Toussaint, one of the rebuffed negotiators, then concentrated on disciplining his *congos* and forcing the French to change the slave system.

Colonial defense was the responsibility of General Étienne Maynard Laveaux, who remarked in frustration that no matter how he positioned his forces Toussaint always found an *ouverture*, or opening. When spies reported this comment to Toussaint, he changed his signature by replacing "Bréda" with "Louverture," or, sometimes, "L'Ouverture."

The byname Louverture trumpeted his skill as a tactical commander and, coincidentally, suited his gap-toothed smile. Until then he had been known as a *frâtras baton* ("weedy stick" or, even more apt for the guerrilla leader, "thrashing stick"). Sickly as a child, he was always thin. He was only five feet, two inches tall, but he had a dignified, even imperious, demeanor that gave him an air of command. Taciturn even among his intimates, Toussaint sought advice from priests, politicians, planters, and soldiers, but he rarely commented on their suggestions, and few could discern his emotions or thoughts by his expression.

In September, 1792, a reinforced Laveaux launched a counteroffensive that gained momentum until February, 1793. News that Louis XVI had been executed complicated the rebellion. Royalist soldiers and rebels, including Toussaint, offered their services to Bourbon Spain. Royalist planters appealed to Great Britain for protection from the *congos* and for the preservation of slavery.

In 1793, Saint-Domingue turned into a kaleidoscope of horror. Spanish armies, including that of Toussaint, invaded from the northeastern corner; a British expeditionary force seized important ports in the west and moved inland. Meanwhile, dozens of black leaders led slave insurrections, and mulatto generals fought to retain slavery and to achieve equality with whites. Fearing that the colony would be overwhelmed by the Spaniards and British, acting Governor Léger-Félicité Sonthonax abolished slavery by decree on August 29, 1793. Thousands of blacks rallied to the French tricolor and halted the Spanish offensive; at the same time, tropical diseases crippled the British. When news of France's confirma-

Toussaint Louverture. (The Granger Collection, New York)

tion of the abolition decree reached the island, Toussaint left the Spaniards. Furious with Spanish officers, including fellow blacks, for reenslaving prisoners, Toussaint announced his *volte face* by massacring the Spanish population of La Marmelade.

Welcomed by Laveaux, Toussaint was promoted very shortly to brigadier general. For the remainder of 1794, Toussaint drove the Spaniards out of Saint-Domingue in a series of brilliant campaigns. While pressing the British, Toussaint learned that a mulatto coup had imprisoned Laveaux, who now was acting governor. Toussaint's forces quickly crossed the island and rescued Laveaux, who gratefully appointed Toussaint lieutenant governor and proclaimed him to be the black Spartacus foreseen by Raynal.

With the establishment of the Directory in Paris, Toussaint maneuvered to have Laveaux and Sonthonax—who had returned as governor—elected to the legislature and returned to France by August, 1797. Now fifty-four years old, Toussaint was acting governor and commander in chief of Saint-Domingue. Virtually independent, Toussaint negotiated the evacuation of British forces and trade agreements with Great Britain and another French foe, the United States. Defying instructions from Napoleon I, Toussaint crushed the last mulatto insurgent, André Rigaud, and invaded Spanish Santo Domingo. On January 29, 1801, Toussaint abolished slavery in the former Spanish colony and promised to work for the prosperity of all the island's inhabitants.

With Hispaniola united, Toussaint tried to protect the successful slave rebellion by restoring Saint-Domingue to prosperity. He devised a constitution that kept Saint-Domingue a French colony but minimized the extent of French authority. Recognizing that he was surrounded by colonies that depended upon slave labor, Toussaint seemed to be trying to keep a powerful patron while demonstrating that laborers need not be slaves to be productive. His labor code required all inhabitants to settle permanently and work; planters were to pay wages and share profits with workers. He outlawed voodoo, built roads, supported a fully integrated school system, and reestablished the Catholic Church. Formerly known as the Pearl of the Antilles, Saint-Domingue once accounted for 40 percent of France's foreign trade and supplied almost half of the world's coffee and more than half of the world's sugar. By 1800, production levels had recovered to almost half of the 1789 yields.

Napoleon was not impressed with Toussaint's military or governmental skills. Referring contemptuously to Toussaint as a "gilded African," Napoleon sent his brother-in-law, General Charles-Victor-Emmanuel Leclerc, and twenty-one thousand soldiers to Hispaniola to restore slavery and keep the island in France's colonial orbit. Masking the expedition's true purpose, Leclerc professed that Napoleon merely wished to honor Toussaint and his army.

The fleet began debouching its troops on February 2, 1802, only five months after Toussaint had discovered a plot among his generals, who charged him with restoring slavery. Suppressing the revolt resulted in more than two thousand deaths. Leclerc profited from lingering resentments, for, as Toussaint prepared to repel the French, his generals began to offer their armies to Leclerc. Toussaint inflicted heavy casualties on the French, but the reduction of his own forces compelled him to surrender on May 1, 1802. Leclerc permitted Toussaint to retire to one of his four plantations for a few weeks, then had him arrested on June 7, 1802. Toussaint was immediately whisked aboard the ship *Héros* and exiled to France. Napoleon refused to grant Toussaint a hearing and had him imprisoned in Fort-de-Joux, where he died of exposure and malnutrition on April 7, 1803.

SIGNIFICANCE

Toussaint Louverture's influence did not end with his death. Enraged at the treatment of Toussaint and aware of the real purpose of the expedition, blacks rose spontaneously against Leclerc and France. Despite twelve thousand reinforcements, the French could not withstand the combined attacks of guerrilla bands and tropical diseases. Black generals proclaimed Saint-Domingue independent of France and gave the former colony the indigenous people's name Haiti. On November 30, 1803, seven months after Toussaint's death, eight thousand French soldiers departed Cap Français, leaving behind not only forty thousand comrades in graves but also a new republic, the second to arise in the Americas.

Toussaint was posthumously hailed as the liberator of Haiti, but he otherwise has had a controversial legacy. To many, he provided proof of the capacity of blacks for education and self-government. These admirers emphasized Toussaint's repeated acts of humanitarianism, particularly his willingness to unify all races. Detractors emphasize Toussaint's shifting loyalties and occasional acts of brutality as evidence of deep cynicism and personal ambition.

—Paul E. Kuhl

FURTHER READING

Alexis, Stephen. *Black Liberator: The Life of Toussaint Louverture*. Translated by William Stirling. New York: Macmillan, 1949. Portrays Toussaint as a mystic who was driven by visions into megalomania.

Brown, Gordon S. *Toussaint's Clause: The Founding Fathers and the Haitian Revolution*. Jackson: University Press of Mississippi, 2005. Describes the United States' reaction to the Haitian Revolution. Some Americans wanted to intervene in support of Toussaint and the rebels, but southern slaveholders, including Thomas Jefferson, rejected intervention because they were alarmed by Toussaint's rise to power and leadership ability.

Dubois, Laurent. *Avengers of the New World: The Story of the Haitian Revolution*. Cambridge, Mass.: Belknap Press, 2004. A chronicle of the Haitian Revolution. Describes the initial victory of Toussaint and other rebels, Toussaint's defense of France against British and Spanish invaders, and his imprisonment by Napoleon.

Geggus, David Patrick. *Slavery, War, and Revolution: The British Occupation of Saint-Domingue, 1793-1798*. New York: Oxford University Press, 1982. Applauds Toussaint's humanitarianism and regards his military genius as the principal reason for the expedition's failure.

Heinl, Robert D., Jr., and Nancy G. Heinl. *Written in Blood: The Story of the Haitian People, 1492-1971.* Boston: Houghton Mifflin, 1978. Devotes one hundred pages to the Haitian Revolution in lively, detailed, and nonjudgmental fashion. Excellent summary of an excruciatingly complex period.

James, C. L. R. *The Black Jacobins: Toussaint Louverture and the San Domingo Revolution.* New York: Dial Press, 1938. Rev. ed. New York: Vintage Books, 1963. In this classic English biography, James suggests that Toussaint failed because he had no political philosophy—such as socialism—to consolidate his victories and because he was so reserved that people misunderstood and mistrusted him.

Korngold, Ralph. *Citizen Toussaint.* Boston: Little, Brown, 1944. Differing from others in several factual details, Korngold highlights Toussaint's failures and successes and concludes that he was one of the most remarkable men of his period.

Ott, Thomas O. *The Haitian Revolution, 1789-1804.* Knoxville: University of Tennessee Press, 1973. A remarkable job of chronologically sorting out a confusing period, Ott's work identifies Toussaint as the most able and admirable individual connected with the revolution.

Ros, Martin. *Night of Fire: The Black Napoleon and the Battle for Haiti.* Translated by Karin Ford-Treep. New York: Sarpedon, 1994. Originally published in Dutch in 1991, this is a popular biography, aimed at general readers interested in Toussaint and in Haitian history.

See also: Joseph Boulogne; Thomas Jefferson; Louis XVI; Nanny; Guillaume-Thomas Raynal; Granville Sharp; Tupac Amaru II.

Related articles in *Great Events from History: The Eighteenth Century, 1701-1800:* 18th century: Expansion of the Atlantic Slave Trade; April 6, 1712: New York City Slave Revolt; August, 1712: Maya Rebellion in Chiapas; 1730-1739: First Maroon War; November 23, 1733: Slaves Capture St. John's Island; January 24, 1744-August 31, 1829: Dagohoy Rebellion in the Philippines; 1760-1776: Caribbean Slave Rebellions; July 4, 1776: Declaration of Independence; 1780-1781: Rebellion of Tupac Amaru II; August 22, 1791-January 1, 1804: Haitian Independence; July, 1795-March, 1796: Second Maroon War.

JOHN TRUMBULL
American poet

A member of the New England literary group known as the Connecticut Wits, Trumbull produced mostly satirical poetry, a body of work that, though heavily indebted to British models, served the cause of patriotism during the period of the American Revolution and became an early template for American literature.

Born: April 24, 1750; Waterbury, Connecticut
Died: May 11, 1831; Springwells, Michigan Territory (now Detroit, Michigan)
Area of achievement: Literature

EARLY LIFE

The son of an influential pastor and trustee of Yale College, John Trumbull displayed his linguistic gifts at a young age. A prodigy, he had already passed the entrance examination to Yale when he was seven years old, though he did not begin studies there until 1763. While still at home he read the works of John Milton by the age of eight, and by age thirteen was well acquainted with the works of Homer, Horace, and Cicero.

As an undergraduate he began to write a number of poems, which show his adept use of the heroic couplet and the heavy influence of Alexander Pope, the great English satirist. Satire, in fact, was to play a major role in Trumbull's early success only a few years later, when he produced the works for which he is now known. Receiving his bachelor of arts degree in 1767, he stayed on at Yale as a tutor and scholar in residence while he continued to write poems and, more devotedly, a series of essays. "The Meddler" appeared in the *Boston Chronicle* between September, 1769, and January, 1770. Written in collaboration with Timothy Dwight (1752-1817), a fellow member of the literary group called the Connecticut Wits (which was also known as the Hartford Wits), the essays are derivative and somewhat presumptuous from a nineteen-year-old. Setting himself up as an urbane sophisticate in the manner of the classic English essayists Joseph Addison and Richard Steele—whose essays in the *Spectator* and the *Tatler* established a kind of popular domestic literature for the rising middle class—Trumbull pontificated on such topics as contemporary vices, flattery, and the coquette. Writing these essays provided Trumbull with experience and the perspective needed in the development of his major work.

Between 1770 and 1771, Trumbull taught school at Whethersfield, not far from his home in Connecticut. Meanwhile, he was experimenting with various poetic forms, producing a verse translation from the Latin poet Vergil and a section from his graduate commencement speech in which he predicted the rise and eventual superiority of America both in the arts and in world affairs. Like his essays in "The Meddler," these minor works led to more ambitious and meaningful work by the end of 1771.

LIFE'S WORK

John Trumbull already was adept at a kind of mild satire as evinced in the "Meddler" essays, showing a proficiency in the use of satiric verse while an undergraduate. In 1772, Trumbull turned to a more ambitious project. Wanting to gain a lasting name for himself in the field of literature, he followed in the tradition of Pope and Samuel Butler, the seventeenth century author of the three-part satire *Hudibras* (1663, 1664, 1678), and began the composition of his satire on modern education: the seventeen-hundred line poem *The Progress of Dulness* (1772-1773). Commonly regarded as the first of his two major works, *The Progress of Dulness* is in the vein of classic satire insofar as it attacks a serious problem by holding it up to ridicule. Like Pope and Jonathan Swift, Trumbull sought to use humor as a vehicle to cure, or at least bring to light, a social or ethical failing.

The work's three parts are written in the jogging iambic tetrameter verse form made famous by Butler's *Hudibras*. Part 1 of *The Progress of Dulness* begins with the adventures of Tom Brainless, a lazy lout who dozes through four years of a useless curriculum and graduates in total ignorance. He goes on to become a teacher and then a clergyman. Part 2 traces the academic career of Dick Hairbrain, a rich man's son who dandles his way through college, gambling and reveling. He graduates a fop and a gentleman. Harriet Simper's education, as ridiculed in part three, is not in the classroom but in the art of coquetry and the reading of sentimental novels. Trumbull used the mock-heroic couplet to good effect, even exploring the humorous possibilities of off-rhymes, such as "proof" with "enough," for example.

For all its effectiveness, however, *The Progress of Dulness* is hardly on the level of Pope's *The Dunciad*

(1728-1743) or Butler's *Hudibras*, the two works to which it is most obviously indebted. To admit the poem's derivative style and technique, however, is to undervalue its clever facility and ignore its historic position in early American literature. A skillful work, the satire shows real poetic merit, while at the same time it reveals an early American writer's reliance on outmoded British models in an attempt to find American subjects and a means for expressing them.

One of the shortcomings of the work was its timing. Political affairs in America had become unstable as the colonies lodged more and more grievances against Britain. Despite the clever, jaunty humor of the satire, a plea for a more practical educational curriculum in college was not a subject pertinent to the state of affairs. Though the piece brought Trumbull some measure of fame and solidified his reputation as one of America's youngest and wittiest men of letters, the satire had to wait until the end of the century before it was reprinted, becoming a minor classic.

The American Revolution was coming to a head by 1773, and Trumbull went to Boston to study law with John Adams, having passed the bar exam that same year. Soon he became confidential secretary to a group of patriots, and his political activities and patriotic fervor fed his ambition to produce a lasting literary work. By 1775, hostility between Britain and America intensified and Trumbull began his most important piece.

M'Fingal, in its original form, was first published in late 1775. Composed in an attempt to raise the morale of the colonies by mocking the British, it was also Trumbull's bid for serious literary repute. *M'Fingal* is the clearest example of its author finally finding his native subject. Canto 1 of the mock epic opens at a town meeting and features a debate between the Whig faction, headed by Honorious, and the Tory camp—those loyal to Britain—in the person of a pompous fool, Squire M'Fingal. The squire is the obvious source of ridicule, from his vainglorious lying to his nonsensical political dictum that kings make their subjects suffer because God has so ordained.

So successful was the epic, largely modeled again on Butler's *Hudibras*, that Trumbull added a second and third canto in a revised version of 1782. In this edition, M'Fingal is tarred and feathered before the liberty pole and envisions victory for the Whigs.

Trumbull's effective literary career waned after 1782. Though he continued to write essays and occasional poetry, the remainder of his long life was occupied in civic and political affairs. He was elected to the state assembly and was appointed judge of the state superior court for eighteen years. The *Poetical Works of John Trumbull, LL.D.* was published in 1820, eleven years before his death.

SIGNIFICANCE

John Trumbull's two mock epics are still readable for their wit and clever use of the couplet form. They are especially valuable as examples of the early American writer's artistic dilemma: How to present a valid American experience while being culturally dependent on older European (British) forms of expression. Of minor rank, Trumbull nevertheless showed first-generation American writers how they might deal with a sense of cultural inferiority.

—*Edward Fiorelli*

FURTHER READING

Briggs, Peter M. "English Satire and Connecticut Wit." *American Quarterly* 37, no. 1 (Spring, 1985): 37-47. Briggs cites Trumbull's indebtedness to Alexander Pope's *The Dunciad* and to other English satirists as evidence of the lack of an intellectual and social establishment in prerevolutionary America.

Cowie, Alexander. *John Trumbull: Connecticut Wit.* Chapel Hill: University of North Carolina Press, 1936. The first and still the definitive study of Trumbull, particularly regarding his literary career to 1782.

Dowling, William C. *Poetry and Ideology in Revolutionary Connecticut.* Athens: University of Georgia Press, 1990. Dowling examines both the subject and form of Trumbull's poetry as partly the result of the political and cultural struggle for independence.

Gimmestad, Victor E. *John Trumbull.* New York: Twayne, 1974. A brief but detailed study of virtually all of Trumbull's literary output. Presents sparse biographical details in a straightforward style.

Grasso, Christopher. "Print, Poetry, and Politics: John Trumbull and the Transformation of Public Discourse in Revolutionary America." *Early American Literature* 30, no. 1 (1995): 5-31. Despite its somewhat esoteric title, this is an eminently readable source that examines the works of Trumbull during the revolutionary period and the changes in the social, political, and economic relationships between writers and the reading public.

Wells, Colin. "Connecticut Wit and Augustan Theology: John Trumbull, Timothy Dwight, and the New Divinity." *Religion and Literature* 34 (Autumn, 2002): 93-119. Wells explores Trumbull's theologically conservative views, particularly as they infuse aspects of *The Progress of Dulness.*

See also: John Adams; Alexander Pope; Gilbert Stuart; Jonathan Swift; Mercy Otis Warren; Benjamin West.

Related article in *Great Events from History: The Eighteenth Century, 1701-1800:* April 19, 1775: Battle of Lexington and Concord.

JETHRO TULL
English inventor

Tull's publications describing his farming experiments and inventions spread knowledge of new agricultural techniques, thereby contributing to the network of changes that constituted the Agricultural Revolution.

Born: March 30, 1674 (baptized); Bradfield, near Basildon, Berkshire, England
Died: February 21, 1741; Prosperous Farm, near Hungerford, Berkshire, England
Area of achievement: Science and technology

EARLY LIFE

Jethro Tull seems to have planned for a political career. The son of Jethro and Dorothy Tull, he was part of a gentry family that extended over the Berkshire-Oxfordshire borderlands. He matriculated at St. John's College, Oxford, in July, 1691; two years later he entered Gray's Inn and was called to the bar in May, 1699. Apparently poor health deterred him from politics, and he settled into farming soon after his marriage on October 26, 1699, to Susannah Smith, of a Warwickshire gentry family.

For about nine years he farmed land that he had inherited from his father at Howberry, on the Thames River in Oxfordshire near Wallingford. In about 1709, he moved to Prosperous Farm in Berkshire near Hungerford, considering its location and climate to be more healthful. Concern for his health was the chief factor in his taking the Grand Tour from 1711 to 1714, staying for a time at Montpellier. During this travel in France and Italy, he made careful observations on farming.

LIFE'S WORK

When Jethro Tull began his farming career, some of the changes that would revolutionize English agriculture were under way. New practices were introduced from the Low Countries in the second half of the seventeenth century, but by about 1750 agricultural innovation would have an English life of its own. The central factor in the Agricultural Revolution was the use of mixed farming, which dramatically increased the fertility of the soil. Selective livestock breeding and the use of machinery were important also. Tull's innovations contributed to the development of mixed farming and to the use of machinery, and his writings made the knowledge of agricultural experiments widely available, particularly to gentlemen farmers such as he.

Mixed farming combined the planting of root crops, legumes, and other nitrogen-fixing crops in careful rotation with the nitrogen-depleting grains; increased the growing of livestock; and utilized tillage and draining practices that made solid nutrients more available to the crops. Systemic reinforcements encouraged the mix: Many of the soil-building crops were fed to livestock, and additional manure was a welcome by-product of the increase in livestock production.

Most of England's arable land is in the Lowland Zone, southeast of an imaginary line linking the mouths of the Exe and Tees Rivers. Within the Lowland Zone, soils are either light (consisting of light loams, fertile sands, chalky soils, or limestone soils) or the heavy soils of the clay vales. The heavy soils long had been in grain production. The light soils had not been fertile enough for permanent cultivation but had been useful for sheep pasturage; they held advantages for the use of mixed farming, however, for they drain freely and are easily cultivated. Mixed farming practices on the lighter soils resulted in the maintenance of fertility without the use of fallow. Most of Tull's farming was in the lighter soils.

Tull typified the spirit of experiment and innovation that characterized the educated classes in the early eighteenth century. As a beginning farmer he eagerly adopted irrigation of stream-side pasture and the use of fodder crops such as turnips, swedes, and grasses. Such innovations seem to have been inspired by the rise in livestock prices as compared with grain prices toward the end of the seventeenth century. Along with other experimenters, particularly gentlemen farmers and large landowners, Tull proved the efficiency of the components of mixed farming. He and his contemporaries relied on trial and error. Although there is no indication that their experiments owed anything to contemporary science, the innovating farmers were linked with the broader spirit of the Enlightenment by their reliance on experiment and observation.

Tull is best known for *The Horse-Hoing Husbandry: Or, An Essay on the Principles of Tillage and Vegetation*, which he published in 1733. He first published a specimen quarto edition in 1731, which a Dublin printer pirated. Tull said that he forswore further publication but reconsidered in response to several letters. The book's central theme was instruction in planting grain by drill, in beds separated by rows wide enough to be cultivated with a horse-drawn device. The combination of sowing the seeds in drills and hoeing the intervening strips kept down weeds, and the hoeing produced a fine tilth in the soil that nurtured the young plants and increased their growth, thereby reducing the need for fallow. Tull believed that the method would work well only in easily cultivated and well-drained soils. He indicated that the idea for regular cultivation of the strips came from observing vineyards in Languedoc during his travels. There he had observed that pulverizing the soil between rows of

Jethro Tull. (Library of Congress)

vines substituted for manuring, and when he returned home he tried the method, first on potatoes and turnips, then on wheat. He refined the method for wheat and found that he could preserve fertility, even on wheat land, for up to thirteen years without the use of manure. Indeed, Tull advised against using manure, convinced that its propensity for spreading weeds outweighed its soil-building qualities. In this matter Tull was strictly at variance with the mainstream of farming innovation, a circumstance that may account for occasional references to his having been something of a crank.

Tull designed a horse-drawn implement for cultivating (the "horse-hoe"), but his design for the horse-drawn seed drill was more important. He developed his first seed drill on his Howberry Farm prior to 1709, probably around 1701. Before devising it, he was aware that drilling seed rather than broadcasting it resulted in better germination and thereby saved expensive seed. Indeed, the advantages of drilling seed had been expounded as early as 1600 by Sir Hugh Plat near St. Albans, who accidentally discovered its effectiveness. Francis Maxey invented some sort of drill a few years later, and in 1639, Gabriel Plattes patented a drill that he proclaimed would increase yield by a hundredfold. Whether Tull was familiar with these efforts is not known, but he well may have been familiar with the *Systema Agriculturae* (1699) of John Worlidge, in which Worlidge described a design for a machine to form a furrow, drill the seed, and apply manure. Worlidge, however, never made his implement; a professor at Cambridge built a machine by Worlidge's design in 1727, only to find that it performed none of the three tasks. Tull's invention is regarded as original.

Tull became interested in devising a mechanical drill when his workers balked at his orders to hand-drill the sainfoin (a perennial legume, widely prized as nutritious feed for cattle). He said that he let his imagination play over every mechanical device he knew and settled on the groove, tongue, and spring in the soundboard of an organ as the basis for his machine.

Horse-drawn hoes and seed drills were not quickly adopted, because they were difficult to learn to use; even Tull never satisfactorily taught his workers to use them. By the early nineteenth century, Tull's designs were being used for commercial manufacture, but even then the devices were not yet widely used. Tull himself observed that although his crops were better and his costs lower than those of his neighbors, they did not imitate him. It was not until the use of the seed drill drifted into the northern counties from Scotland, where it had been enthusiastically adopted, that it became widespread in England.

Tull published *Supplement to the Essay on Horse-Hoing Husbandry* in 1735, *Addenda to the Essay* in 1738, and *Conclusion to the Essay* in 1739. The chief purpose of these notes was to defend himself against charges that he had plagiarized Worlidge and others, attacks to which he was extremely sensitive. In 1743, a second edition of *The Horse-Hoing Husbandry* included the additions; a third edition was published in 1751 and a fourth in 1762. Between 1753 and 1757, a French translation appeared, and at Ferny, Voltaire numbered himself among the followers of Tull. William Cobbett edited an 1822 edition of Tull's works.

Tull died at Prosperous Farm on February 21, 1741, and was buried at Basildon. He left four daughters and a son. The Royal Agricultural Society possesses a painting of Tull.

SIGNIFICANCE

The delayed adoption of the seed drill fits the analysis set forth by J. D. Chambers and G. E. Mingay in *The Agricultural Revolution, 1750-1880* (1966), in which individual experiments and publications, particularly during the first half of the eighteenth century, are downplayed. The question of the power of example in spreading the innovations in farming is paralleled by the question of the effectiveness of publications describing them. Here, also, any assessment of Jethro Tull's impact must take into account a time lag, for the reorganization of English agriculture incorporating mixed farming, livestock improvement, and machinery became apparent only after about 1760, some thirty years after the first publication of *The Horse-Hoing Husbandry*. Even so, in *The Farmer's Kalendar* (1771), the agricultural observer and writer Arthur Young acknowledged Tull's impact when he condemned farmers who relied too narrowly on Tull's principles, insisting (as Tull had said) that they were not effective in all soils or locations. Notwithstanding the importance of enclosures and other aspects of the reorganization of British farming, perhaps in the long view the most dramatic single effect of the work of Jethro Tull seen today is the commonplace practice of planting in rows or drills rather than the broadcast sowing, which was unchallenged until he provided the rationale and practical devices which challenged it.

—*Carole Watterson Troxler*

FURTHER READING

Chambers, J. D., and G. E. Mingay. *The Agricultural Revolution, 1750-1880.* New York: Shocken Books, 1966. Brings together the copious research of the previous thirty years and offers an analysis emphasizing the improvement of soil fertility. Tull and other writers, with the exception of William Marshall, are less important than they were traditionally considered to have been.

DeBruyn, Frans. "Reading Virgil's *Georgics* as Scientific Text: The Eighteenth-Century Debate Between Jethro Tull and Stephen Switzer." *ELH: English Literary History* 71, no. 3 (Fall, 2004): 661-689. Compares agricultural theories in Tull's *The Horse-Hoing Husbandry* with the views of Stephen Switzer, an eighteenth century garden designer who wrote numerous books about gardening.

Habakkuk, H. J. "Economic Functions of English Landowners in the Seventeenth and Eighteenth Centuries." *Explorations in Entrepreneurial History* 6 (1953): 90-99. Questions the significance of landlords and writers in spreading new farming practices and emphasizes tenant initiative.

Horn, Pamela. "Contribution of the Propagandist to Eighteenth-Century Agricultural Improvement." *Historical Journal* 25 (June, 1982): 313-329. Acknowledging limits on the effectiveness of late eighteenth century agricultural writers, Horn nevertheless concludes that writings of the genre pioneered by Tull kept agricultural issues before the reading public during the height of agricultural change.

Jones, Eric L., ed. *Agriculture and Economic Growth in England, 1650-1815.* London: Methuen, 1967. Jones's contribution to this collection of articles details the adoption of the farming techniques of the Low Countries, beginning in the late seventeenth century. Other contributors credit Tull with proving the efficiency of the new farming methods.

Mingay, G. E. *English Landed Society in the Eighteenth Century.* London: Routledge and Kegan Paul, 1963. Synthesizes much work on the most powerful element of English society, to which Tull in a small way belonged. The landed interest is portrayed not so much as originating agricultural and other economic growth as providing conditions which fostered it.

Overton, Mark. *Agricultural Revolution in England: The Transformation of the Agrarian Economy, 1500-1850.* New York: Cambridge University Press, 1996. This book makes only two brief references to Tull, but it provides valuable background for understanding English agriculture and the changes in farming that occurred during the eighteenth century.

Tull, Jethro. *The Horse-Hoing Husbandry: Or, An Essay on the Principles of Tillage and Vegetation.* 1733. 4th ed. London: A. Millar, 1762. This fourth edition of Tull's publication was perhaps the most influential.

See also: François Quesnay; Eli Whitney.

Related articles in *Great Events from History: The Eighteenth Century, 1701-1800:* 1701: Tull Invents the Seed Drill; February 14, 1788: Meikle Demonstrates His Drum Thresher; 1793: Whitney Invents the Cotton Gin.

TUPAC AMARU II
Indigenous-Peruvian rebel leader

A descendant of the last Inca monarch and claimant to its kingship, Tupac was a principal leader in an Andean rebellion against colonial Spanish rule, heading an indigenous uprising. The unsuccessful rebellion inaugurated further repression of Incan culture and the control of traditional Incan lands, which continues into the twenty-first century. The rebellion was, however, a precursor to Peruvian independence in 1821.

Born: c. 1740; Tinta, Viceroyalty of Peru (now Peru)
Died: May 18, 1781; Cuzco, Viceroyalty of Peru
Also known as: José Gabriel Condorcanqui (birth name)
Areas of achievement: Social reform, military

EARLY LIFE

Tupac Amaru II (tew-PAHK ahm-AHR-ew) was born José Gabriel Condorcanqui. He was directly descended from Tupac Amaru I, the last recognized Inca monarch of Peru. Tupac Amaru I, murdered by the Spaniards, was related to Atahualpa, the fated Inca who confronted the Spanish conquest of the Inca Empire.

Orphaned at the age of ten, Tupac Amaru II was raised by relatives and at age sixteen entered the Jesuit school in Cuzco, which was open to the sons of the local aristocracy. Tupac Amaru spoke not only his native Quechua but also Spanish, and he knew Latin. He married a woman of Spanish descent, had three sons with her, and inherited the chieftainship (*cacicazgo*) of his native district south of Cuzco, becoming a prominent local political leader. Cuzco was the ancient capital of the Inca Empire.

His district was part of a larger government entity called the Viceroyalty of Peru. Headquartered in Lima, it had governed Peru since the Spanish conquest at the beginning of the sixteenth century. By the middle of the eighteenth century the viceroyalty extended from modern-day Peru into Bolivia (which had been called Upper Peru), the southern Andes, and on to Argentina and the regions around the Plata and Paraguay Rivers.

LIFE'S WORK

Tupac Amaru II was socialized as a Hispanicized Catholic with a refined education. He sustained himself and his family through trade, managing pack mule trains through the Andes. Managing Andean trade had been a traditional source of economic and political authority for the Inca. Transporting minerals and merchandise, Tupac Amaru frequently traveled over an area that extended from Cuzco to the rich silver mining region of Potosí in Bolivia and up to Lima. He was exceptionally well placed to observe and sense the grating poverty and servitude to which indigenous peoples (speakers of not only Quechua but also Aymara) had been subjected by the conquest.

Among the most acute causes of suffering among the indigenous were a number of Spanish administrative regulations. South American Indians were forced to work in the silver mines. The forced labor was known as the *mita*. Moreover, controls on trade required them to buy certain merchandise, in a system of *repartos*, paying tariffs on these items along with other taxes. Local government officials, *corregidores*, were ruthless in applying labor and fiscal regulations. Furthermore, the *corregidores* represented a larger cultural environment that assumed the cultural superiority of Creoles—individuals born in Peru of Spanish or foreign descent—to the defeated indigenous population.

Administrative divisions that came out of the creation in 1776 of a new viceroyalty centered in Buenos Aires seriously disrupted trade in the region south of Cuzco. Compounding these hardships were measures carried out by local governors to collect increased taxes so that government revenue would not suffer from the economic disruption. Tupac Amaru attempted to negotiate with colonial officials in Cuzco and Lima to change their harsh policies. However, his efforts were to no avail, and he was admonished to return to his home territory.

Sporadic uprisings against the harsh new colonial measures, uprisings that collectively came to be known

as the Great Andean Rebellion, erupted in various regions of southern Peru and northern Bolivia. At this time also, authorities in Lima denied Tupac Amaru the right to inherit the title of nobility that had been held by a previous descendant of an Inca (Tupac Amaru also was an Inca descendant). He began plotting in 1778 to overthrow Spanish rule. He asserted his right to lead the Inca nation and adopted the name of his defiant ancestor. He now called himself Tupac Amaru (Royal or Resplendent Serpent).

He began his uprising on November 4, 1780. At the commemorations celebrating the birthday of the king of Spain, he captured the local administrator, Antonio de Arriaga, and within a week had him publicly tried and executed. He then authorized the appropriation and distribution of the corrupt gains of other officials. A hastily organized government force confronted his considerably larger but poorly coordinated forces at Sangarará on November 18 and was defeated.

Tupac Amaru then organized his forces to advance on Cuzco and lay siege to the city. In route he gathered the support of tens of thousands of followers. The early success of Tupac Amaru sent shock waves through the viceroyalty. His victory would spell the loss of the crucial wealth and labor provided by his region. All civil, military, and religious authorities now rose against him. Moreover, some indigenous leaders (*caciques*) were divided as to whether they should risk supporting his movement. That he had begun his rebellion without sufficiently solidifying the *cacique* base would prove fatal for his movement. The violence of his rebellion also took away his modest Creole support. As the movement became more massive, it began to escape the control of any one individual and become as ruthless as the brutality under which so many of its followers had suffered. These followers had been increasingly committed to removing every vestige of Creole and Spanish influence.

During the second week of January, 1781, Tupac Amaru began to lay siege to Cuzco. His forces still numbered more than those that officials in Cuzco and Lima could gather and mount for the siege. Nonetheless, Tupac Amaru and his forces had to retreat from Cuzco. Essentially, Tupac Amaru's interests had been to redress the injustices of Spanish rule only, so he was reluctant to harm the inhabitants of the ancient Inca capital. Moreover, he was devoutly religious and had been excommunicated. His reluctance sealed the fate of his rebellion.

He retreated south to Tinta, the core region of his support, and was pursued by mounting government forces. By mid-April, Tupac Amaru, his family, and his chief supporters were captured and imprisoned in Cuzco, and then tortured. His wife and son were tortured as well and then killed, along with other relatives and supporters, before his eyes. After a failed escape and his recapture, he was sentenced to death and brutally executed on May 18, killed as his body was ripped apart by four horses. He was then decapitated. His violent execution reflected the desperation of colonial officials to quell future indigenous uprisings. The uprisings continued in Upper Peru until the following year, however, and the combination of massive government repression and internal indigenous conflicts resulted in the rebellions ending with an estimated 100,000 dead.

SIGNIFICANCE

The initial legacy of Tupac Amaru II was anticlimactic, a final, failed movement of a massive armed Inca resistance to colonial rule. In this sense it was obliquely victorious insofar as Peru became independent in 1821, two generations after Tupac Amaru's last struggle. The chasm of hostility, however, based on centuries of brutality and segregation, has not been completely bridged in Peruvian history.

—*Edward A. Riedinger*

FURTHER READING

Cahill, David Patrick. *From Rebellion to Independence in the Andes: Soundings from Southern Peru, 1750-1830*. Amsterdam: Aksant, 2002. This work studies the social context of subversive political activity from the period preceding the rebellion of Tupac Amaru II to the independence of Peru.

Fisher, Lillian Estelle. *The Last Inca Revolt, 1780-1783*. Norman: University of Oklahoma Press, 1966. A classic account of the circumstances of the insurrection of Tupac Amaru II.

Hemming, John. *The Conquest of the Incas*. New York: Harcourt Brace Jovanovich. A compelling account by a noted historian of Spain's conquest and occupation of Peru. Describes the Inca ancestors of and historical events previous to Tupac Amaru's time.

Robins, Nicholas A. *Genocide and Millennialism in Upper Peru: The Great Rebellion of 1780-1782*. Westport, Conn.: Praeger, 2002. Analyzes Tupac Amaru's insurrection within the context of Peruvian and Bolivian indigenous millennial movements, evaluating policies for eliminating enemies.

Stavig, Ward. *The World of Túpac Amaru: Conflict, Community, and Identity in Colonial Peru*. Lincoln: University of Nebraska Press, 1999. An ethnohistorical study of Tupac Amaru's insurrection in relation to indigenous identities, social life, and customs.

Thomson, Sinclair. *We Alone Will Rule: Native Andean Politics in the Age of Insurgency*. Madison: University of Wisconsin Press, 2002. Traces the history of Aymara and Quechua politics, government, and warfare during the eighteenth century and the insurrection of Tupac Amaru within that context.

Valcárcel, Carlos Daniel. *La rebelión de Túpac Amaru*. Lima: Comisión Nacional del Sesquicentenario de la Independencia del Perú, 1972. A four-volume collection of original documents that examine the events before, during, and after Tupac Amaru's rebellion.

See also: Nanny; Toussaint Louverture.

Related articles in *Great Events from History: The Eighteenth Century, 1701-1800:* 18th century: Expansion of the Atlantic Slave Trade; April 6, 1712: New York City Slave Revolt; August, 1712: Maya Rebellion in Chiapas; 1730-1739: First Maroon War; January 24, 1744-August 31, 1829: Dagohoy Rebellion in the Philippines; 1760-1776: Caribbean Slave Rebellions; 1776: Foundation of the Viceroyalty of La Plata; 1780-1781: Rebellion of Tupac Amaru II; August 22, 1791-January 1, 1804: Haitian Independence; July, 1795-March, 1796: Second Maroon War.

ANNE-ROBERT-JACQUES TURGOT
French politician

Turgot was perhaps the most important reform-minded minister to serve the French monarchy in the last generation before the French Revolution. Best known as an economic theorist, he championed the laissez-faire precepts of the "classical" economic school and strove to remove obsolete or artificial barriers to the free flow of trade.

Born: May 10, 1727; Paris, France
Died: March 18, 1781; Paris, France
Also known as: Baron de l'Aulne
Areas of achievement: Government and politics, business, economics

EARLY LIFE

Anne-Robert-Jacques Turgot (ahn-roh-behr-zhahk tewr-goh) was born into a famous family that had served the kings of France in various high bureaucratic posts since the sixteenth century. The history of the family, which may have been Scandinavian in origin, goes back further, at least to Norman times (eleventh century). Turgot's father, who managed the family estate in Normandy, was Michel Étienne Turgot, himself the son of a royal *intendant* (tax collector and financial agent). Michel Étienne held the office of "provost of the market sellers of Paris," a title that included a wide variety of functions. As city planner, he was responsible for many major improvements, including the great Paris sewer system on the Right Bank of the Seine River and the construction of a number of famous monuments. The elder Turgot married a noblewoman of high status. All of their sons became famous, one as a magistrate, another as a military officer who also pursued scientific interests in botany, and the youngest, Anne-Robert-Jacques, as a highly placed royal administrator equally interested in philosophical and theoretical economic questions.

The young Turgot's earliest education was at the Collège Duplessis in Paris, then at the Collège de Bourgogne. While at the latter institution, he became particularly interested in the work of two great English thinkers who would influence his future: Sir Isaac Newton and John Locke. The French intellectual traditions represented by Montesquieu and his near contemporary Voltaire were also important to Turgot at this early age. Somewhat unexpectedly, Turgot entered the theological seminary of Saint Sulpice in 1743, when he was sixteen years old. After a few years he went on (in 1749) to the Annexe de la Sorbonne, which then served as the theological faculty of the University of Paris. Then, equally unexpectedly, in 1751 he decided to abandon his preparation for an ecclesiastical career, entering the service of the French high administration at the age of twenty-four.

LIFE'S WORK

Turgot's first appointment was to a magisterial position in the Parlement (high court) of Paris, which was constituted by and, to a certain degree, for the noble peers of France. Specifically, his post between 1753 and 1761 was that of "master of requests." Turgot's service in this high judicial body came at a very critical time, since this period was characterized by a number of preliminary clashes between the French crown and the nobility. These would eventually be considered among the first tensions that led to the French Revolution.

In this early stage of his official career, Turgot frequented many intellectual and literary salons in and around the city of Paris. He devoted particular attention to the doctrines of the *Économistes* (more commonly referred to as Physiocrats), at that time led by François Quesnay. The Physiocrats argued that the source of all wealth is to be found in land and its products, and supported the then emergent economic philosophy of *laissez-faire, laissez-passer* (literally, "let it alone, permit it," in reverence to government's approach to commerce). As a member of the recognized intellectual circles who gave the mid-eighteenth century its reputation for enlightenment, Turgot contributed to the famous *Encyclopédie: Ou, Dictionnaire raisonné des sciences, des arts, et des métiers* (1751-1772; *Encyclopedia*, 1965), edited by Denis Diderot. His earliest outline of his own economic and social reform ideas came in 1759 in the form of an elegy, the "Éloge de Gournay," dedicated to a deceased friend whose ideas on the subject had influenced his thinking.

Soon thereafter (in 1761), an important change in Turgot's administrative career came when he was appointed to the *intendance* of Limoges. When appointed, he called the change a misfortune, first because of his pending isolation from Paris and also because he was about to come face to face with the disturbing reality of France's fiscal and financial affairs. During the years of his service in Limoges (1761-1774), Turgot gained recognition both for the many basic reforms he instituted in the name of King Louis XV and for his published writings on economic questions. These included his *Mémoire sur les mines et carrières* (1764; memoir on mines and quarries), *Valeurs et monnaies* (1769; on value and money), and *Lettres sur la liberté du commerce des grains* (1770; letters on the corn trade). Perhaps Turgot's most celebrated work, however, was his *Réflexions sur la formation et la distribution des richesses* (1766; *Reflections on the Formation and Distribution of Wealth*, 1793). It was reputedly written to provide an explanation of the workings of European economic forces to foreigners (Chinese) visiting in France. Its influence and longevity as a model of eighteenth century classical economic thought, however, went far beyond this presumed goal.

When Louis XV died in 1774, his successor, Louis XVI, apparently immediately recognized Turgot's extraordinary capacities and insights. After appointing him very briefly to the post of minister of the navy, the king called Turgot to the high royal position of controller general of finance. Before accepting this post, Turgot met with the king to discuss what he considered to be the major reform issues of the day. While in the controller general's position (from 1774 to 1776), Turgot prepared and passed the so-called Six Edicts that, it was hoped, would

Anne-Robert-Jacques Turgot. (Library of Congress)

save France from its deepening financial and economic crisis. These decrees, promulgated early in 1776, may be summarized in two categories: four edicts involving the abolition of minor administrative or fiscal institutions, which Turgot identified as obstacles to improved economic conditions, and two edicts that aimed at much more substantial institutional changes. The first category suppressed certain types of antiquated controls over grain trade in Paris, equally antiquated bureaucratic offices connected with ports and market operations, special taxes on livestock sales, and the outmoded systems of taxing and selling suet and tallow to the chandler industry. Much more significant, when one considers the connections between Turgot's reform priorities and the inevitable drift toward revolution in France, was one edict suppressing the *corvée* (conscription, among the peasants, of unpaid labor for public projects or service to the privileged classes) and another edict abolishing the majority of France's restrictive craft guilds.

Turgot insisted that the removal of artifical controls in trade and commerce would be absolutely necessary for the recovery of France's badly declining levels of productivity. The implications of this argument certainly went far beyond the areas affected by the Six Edicts; they potentially aimed at all forms of privilege hampering free economic flow, including many outmoded prerogatives of the nobility and the clergy. This helps explain the unpopularity of Turgot's reform program among those sectors of privileged French society who refused to see what was likely to happen if the status quo remained. Pressures brought to bear on Louis XVI by these refractory elements led to Turgot's removal from office in 1776 and his decision to retire to pursue his own intellectual and writing interests. In March of 1781, some seven and one-half years before the outbreak of the French Revolution, Turgot died in retirement.

SIGNIFICANCE

The life of Anne-Robert-Jacques Turgot illustrates at least two essential points about the nature of French society and politics in the prerevolutionary period. First, Turgot is an example, certainly not a totally isolated one, of a representative of France's privileged noble class who demonstrated serious concern for reforming a number of obsolete institutions that were part of the *ancien régime*. In some cases (four out of the famous Six Edicts of 1776, for example), what Turgot identified as obsolete had little or no direct bearing on particular vested class interests. Many changes he supported were practical in nature, designed to facilitate an expansion in the volume of a variety of seemingly minor commercial exchanges—something that would eventually benefit almost all elements of French society. In other cases, practical reforms, although they could be justified as promising general benefits in the long run, had immediate implications for specific interest groups. His recommendation that the *corvée*, or free-labor levy, be abolished obviously struck out at very privileged elements, mainly noble and royal. The hostility of the upper class to such reforms is therefore understandable and fits what one might call standard stereotypes of reactionism in prerevolutionary France.

As Turgot stands out as an example of an enlightened conscience within the ranks of the noble class, other societal elements who opposed other categories of reform that he supported illustrate a second point that should be kept in mind about the variety of causes and contradictions behind the eventual revolution. Widespread opposition to abolition of the craft guilds—institutions that mainly affected the vested interests of the middle class of prerevolutionary France—points out that resistance to changes in the obsolete feudal system was not limited to the upper, privileged classes. Wherever change appeared to menace specific interests in the short run, the logic of longer-term benefits was rejected in prerevolutionary France. This was obvious in the case of the nobility, the Church, and the king. It was less obvious in the cases of less easily identifiable elements, including merchants, craftsmen, and even peasants. Turgot's gift of insight enabled him to see the multidimensional implications of these obstacles, but a variety of vested-interest groups thwarted his endeavor to represent the commonweal.

—Byron D. Cannon

FURTHER READING

Cobban, Alfred. *Old Régime and Revolution, 1715-1799*. Vol. 1 in *A History of Modern France*. Harmondsworth, England: Penguin Books, 1957. This volume is the first in a three-volume general history written by one of the most respected British historians of France. Its value for the study of Turgot's life is mainly for its coverage of the general sweep of French history throughout the eighteenth century, and especially for its comparisons between several different high ministers of the French crown, both before and after Turgot's brief term of office under Louis XVI.

Dakin, Douglas. *Turgot and the Ancien Régime in France*. London: Methuen, 1939. This may be the most thorough and scholarly biographical study of Turgot in English. Dakin based his writings on Turgot's own works as well as on a number of contemporary French documents and published periodicals.

Groenewegen, Peter. *Eighteenth-Century Economics: Turgot, Beccaria, and Smith and Their Contemporaries*. New York: Routledge, 2002. A collection of essays by Groenewegen, a scholar specializing in eighteenth century economic history. Among other topics, the essays discuss the economic theories of Turgot, Adam Smith, and François Quesnay.

Hill, Malcolm. *Statesman of the Enlightenment: The Life of Anne-Robert Turgot*. London: Othila Press, 1999. Biography describing Turgot's life and thought. Hill argues that Turgot's radical tax reform proposals addressed citizens' concerns; had the proposals been adopted, there might not have been a revolution in 1791.

Lodge, Eleanor C. *Sully, Colbert, and Turgot: A Chapter in French Economic History*. Reprint. Port Washington, N.Y.: Kennikat Press, 1970. This collection of three biographies provides a very useful complement to Frank Manuel's work. First, all three of these figures were high ministers of state, and Lodge's emphasis is on the significance of their contributions as government figures. Second, her three figures represent three different periods in French history: the sixteenth, seventeenth, and eighteenth centuries. Each biography, including Turgot's, is placed within a general historical framework written for the general reader rather than the specialist.

Manuel, Frank E. *The Prophets of Paris*. Cambridge, Mass.: Harvard University Press, 1962. Manuel chose Turgot as one of six major intellectual figures of France, both under the *ancien régime* and in the postrevolutionary period. Because his objective is to compare Turgot's contributions with those of other French thinkers (for example the comte de Saint-Simon, the Marquis de Condorcet, Charles Fourier, and Auguste Comte), the emphasis here is on ideas, not on Turgot's actual achievements as an administrator.

Shepherd, Robert P. *Turgot and the Six Edicts*. New York: Columbia University Press, 1903. This is a specialized study of Turgot's famous 1776 plan for reforming key elements in France's administrative and fiscal system. Although the author enters into the details of each edict and its potential ramifications for the French economy, the work is only sparsely documented by contemporary historians' standards.

See also: Marquis de Condorcet; Denis Diderot; Louis XV; Montesquieu; François Quesnay; Adam Smith; Voltaire.

Related articles in *Great Events from History: The Eighteenth Century, 1701-1800*: 1720: Financial Collapse of the John Law System; 1721-1750: Early Enlightenment in France; August 19, 1745-September 20, 1746: Jacobite Rebellion; 1748: Montesquieu Publishes *The Spirit of the Laws*; 1751-1772: Diderot Publishes the *Encyclopedia*; January, 1756-February 15, 1763: Seven Years' War; June 8-July 27, 1758: Siege of Louisbourg; January, 1759: Voltaire Satirizes Optimism in *Candide*; February 10, 1763: Peace of Paris; February 24, 1766: Lorraine Becomes Part of France; April 27-May, 1775: Flour War; March 9, 1776: Adam Smith Publishes *The Wealth of Nations*; May, 1776-September 3, 1783: France Supports the American Revolution.

VAḤĪD BIHBAHĀNĪ
Persian religious scholar

Vaḥīd Bihbahānī was responsible for the victory of the Usuli Shiite position over Akhbari Shiism, which was predominant in Persia and parts of what is now Iraq at the start of the eighteenth century. His polemic established a structure of religious authority that persisted as an important precedent in nineteenth and twentieth century Iran.

Born: 1705/1706; Iṣfahān, Persia (now in Iran)
Died: 1790/1791; Karbala, Iraq
Also known as: Vaḥīd Bihbahānī, Muḥammad Bāqir Iṣfahānī (full name); Waḥīd Bihbahānī; Aqa Sayyid Muḥammad Bāqir Bihbahānī; Muhaqqiq (the Investigator); Mujaddid (the Renewer); Murawwij (the Propagator); Muʿassis (the Founder [of the Usuli School]); Ustad-i Qull (Universal Teacher)
Areas of achievement: Religion and theology, government and politics, law

EARLY LIFE

Vaḥīd Bihbahānī (vah-KHEED BIH-buh-hahn-ee) was born in Eṣfahān, the capital of Persia during the rule of the Ṣafavid Dynasty. After spending a short period in the town of Bihbihan, he was taken by his father to the city of Karbala in Iraq. One of the most holy cities in the Islamic world, Karbala is venerated by Shiite Muslims as the site where the Prophet Muḥammad's descendant Hussein was martyred and buried. Though Iraq had remained under the control of Sunni regimes while the Ṣafavids sponsored the Shia faith next door, in the early seventeenth century, the shrine cities of Karbala and Najaf developed into centers of Shia scholarship and attracted Persian scholars seeking freedom from Ṣafavid and post-Ṣafavid establishments.

The young Bihbahānī began his lifelong engagement with religious scholarship under the tutelage of his father, Mulla Muhammad Aqmal. He inherited not only an education, but also a prized academic lineage from his father, who had studied under the most influential figure in Persian Shiism during the seventeenth century, Mulla Muhammad Baqir Majlisi. In addition, Mulla Aqmal had married Majlisi's niece, linking the family to the great scholar both genealogically and spiritually. In Karbala, the young Bihbahānī studied under the religious scholar Sayyid Sadr al-Din Qummi, and though he intended to leave the city after completing his training, he was dissuaded from doing so by a dream in which Imam Hussein came to him. Bihbahānī interpreted the dream as a call to remain in the holy city to complete his life's work.

LIFE'S WORK

In obedience to his dream, Bihbahānī stayed on in Karbala, where he engaged in a fierce and long-standing controversy between the Usuli and Akhbari schools of Shiism, a struggle that had become particularly intense in the late Ṣafavid period. Debates between the two schools centered on questions of jurisprudence and religious authority. The Akhbari position, which was predominant in Karbala and other Iraqi shrine cities such as Najaf, asserted that legal judgments should be based exclusively on the Qurʾān (the Muslim holy book, consisting of the direct revelations of God), the *Ḥadīth* (oral reports of the Prophet), and the emulation of the twelve Shiite imams.

Usuli rationalists, on the other hand, insisted that the consensus of a group of scholars—*mujtahids* (those qualified to practice religious interpretation)—could be a basis for legal activism. As a proponent of the Usuli position, Bihbahānī argued for a greater use of independent reasoning (*ijtihad*) in reaching legal decisions, and as a result of his work, the role of the *mujtahid* was greatly increased during his lifetime. The conviction in an able body of independent jurists presupposed the division of the community into jurists and laymen and required the latter's regard for the former.

Mujtahids were required to study theology, Arabic syntax and morphology, lexicography, logic, and traditional sources of knowledge. Moreover, in accordance with the Usuli position, they were expected to prepare legal judgments not only in conformity with traditional sources, but also through the application of intellectual proofs. Bihbahānī's belief in the *mujtahid*'s ability to establish rational proofs led him to consider them viceregents of the Prophet, an idea that was later elaborated upon by Mulla Ahmad Naraqi (d. 1830) and, even more recently, by Ayatollah Ruhollah Khomeini during and after the 1979 Iranian Revolution.

Bihbahānī's polemic often took the form of debate and written treatises. For instance, he waged a lifelong argument with an Akhbari rival, Shaikh Yusef Bahrayni (d. 1758), which centered on the validity of the *mujtahid*'s speculative reasoning after the so-called "gate of acquisition of knowledge" was closed by the occultation of the Twelfth Imam. He also demonstrated the position of the *mujtahid* by example. One of his pupils, Shaykh Jaʿfar

Najafi (d. 1812), recorded that Bihbahānī was constantly accompanied by armed men who would instantaneously execute any judgment that he passed. Such practical methods served to win popular support for the Usuli position, and by the end of his life Bihbahānī had managed to outlaw Akhbaris as heretics.

In the eighteenth century, Bihbahānī led religious scholars in a fierce attack against mystical orders within Islam. Prompted by the flood of Sufi mystics returning to Iran after having been driven into India by Majlisi in the previous century, Bihbahānī and his coterie wrote vigorous tracts rejecting the claim that Sufism is compatible with Shiism. During his lifetime, he showed particular enmity against the Niʿmatallahi order of Sufis, and his hostility toward it and other Islamic mystical movements earned Bihbahānī the nickname "Sufi-killer." His son, Mirza Muhammad ʿAli Bihbahānī (d. 1801), who settled in Kirmanshah, perpetuated his father's hatred of mystics.

Bihbahānī died in Karbala in 1790 or 1791 near the tomb of Imam Hussein, which he had visited in reverence each day of his life in the holy city. His achievement has persisted into the twenty-first century in both Iraqi and Iranian Shiism. As a scholar, he is credited with more than sixty written works, the most important of which was the *Kitab al-ijtihad waʿl-akhbar*, a refutation of the Akhbari position. His legacy was also maintained by the large number of pupils that he trained. Influential students include Aqa ʿAbd al-Hussein and Shaikh Jaʿfar Najafi, who authored many important works of jurisprudence. By the end of his life, Bihbahānī had trained a generation of *mujtahids*, who would come to dominate the life of Eṣfahān in the early nineteenth century. These pupils, among whom were Hajj Muhammad Ibrahim Kalbasi, Sayyid Muhammad Baqir Shafti, Shaikh Abuʿl Qasim Qummi, and Sayyid Mahdi Bahr al-ʿUlum, are often viewed as the ancestors of all of the *mujtahids* who have guided Iranian society since the eighteenth century.

SIGNIFICANCE

Before Vaḥīd Bihbahānī's work, Akhbari Shiites had dominated Iranian religious law. By the end of his life, Bihbahānī had obliterated the Akhbari influence and established the Usuli position as the norm for all of Twelver Shiism. This approach, which legitimized the role of interpretation in legal decisions and increased the power of the learned class, would form the basis for Iranian religious authority in the following two centuries. In addition, by declaring the "infidelity" of the Akhbaris, Bihbahānī brought the threat of such claims into the field of theology and jurisprudence, narrowing the field of orthodoxy in Twelver Shiism. This paved the way for an increase in the influence of the *mujtahids* during the rule of the Qajar dynasty in the nineteenth century. Ultimately, Usuli Shiism provided the religious legitimacy for Ayatollah Ruhollah Khomeini's Islamic Revolution of 1979 and for the theocratic state that followed it.

—*Anna Sloan*

FURTHER READING

Algar, Hamid. *Religion and State in Iran, 1785-1996: The Role of the Ulama in the Qajar Period*. Berkeley: University of California Press, 1969. A comprehensive history of religious scholarship and jurisprudence in Iran, beginning with the establishment of Usuli supremacy in the eighteenth century.

_____. "Religious Forces in the Eighteenth and Nineteenth Centuries." In *The Cambridge History of Iran 7*. New York: Cambridge University Press, 1991. The most comprehensive source on religious and political developments in Iran during the eighteenth century. Contains maps and genealogical tables.

Arjomand, Said Amir. *The Shadow of God and the Hidden Imam: Religion, Political Order, and Societal Change in Shiite Iran from the Beginning to 1890*. Chicago: University of Chicago Press, 1984. An account of Shiism's development in Iran, with a thorough analysis of its role in the construction of Iranian political rule and authority.

Momen, Moojan. *An Introduction to Shii Islam: The History and Doctrines of Twelver Shiism*. New Haven, Conn.: Yale University Press, 1987. A comprehensive introduction to Shiism, and specifically to Twelver Shiism, incorporating modern critical research as well as orthodox traditional accounts. Offers clear accounts of Shia doctrines and jurisprudence.

Mottahedeh, Roy. *The Mantle of the Prophet: Religion and Politics in Iran*. New York: Pantheon Books, 1986. Reprint. Oxford, England: Oneworld, 2000. Narrative account of the development of Shia doctrines and jurisprudence in Iran. Contains detailed information on the curriculum used to train religious scholars in Iran and Iraq during the eighteenth century.

See also: Karīm Khān Zand; Nādir Shāh; Sīdī al-Mukhṭār al-Kuntī; Shāh Walī Allāh.

Related articles in *Great Events from History: The Eighteenth Century, 1701-1800*: 1709-1747: Persian-Afghan Wars; 1725-November, 1794: Persian Civil Wars.

SIR JOHN VANBRUGH
English playwright and architect

The most versatile of the English gentlemen-amateurs, Vanbrugh has an equally distinguished reputation as a playwright and an architect, having produced two of the finest Restoration comedies and at least three of the finest English Baroque buildings.

Born: January 24, 1664 (baptized); London, England
Died: March 26, 1726; London, England
Areas of achievement: Theater, architecture

EARLY LIFE

John Vanbrugh's grandfather was a refugee from Catholic religious persecution in Flanders; he came to England during the reign of Queen Elizabeth I and established himself as a merchant in the city of London. Vanbrugh's father also went into business, first in London, and later as a sugar merchant in the city of Chester, where it is likely that Vanbrugh was educated at the distinguished local grammar school. His mother, Elizabeth, was the daughter of Sir Dudley Carrington, through whom there were connections of social and political importance; one of the uncles had been secretary of state and ambassador to Holland. Vanbrugh may have had some education on the Continent, and he may have been apprenticed to a London merchant for a time, but there is no certain evidence for either suggestion.

His first job of record was in the military, and he was commissioned in Lord Huntingdon's Regiment of Foot but resigned later in the same year, 1686. In 1688, he was arrested in France. The reason for his internment has never been fully explained; he may have been spying for the British, or he simply might have been detained as a pawn by Louis XIV to obtain release of a French national held by the British on an espionage charge. Whatever the case, he was eventually housed in the Bastille and was finally released in late 1692.

A genial, attractive, witty man, Vanbrugh was able to make his way through the labyrinth of London society and politics, and in 1693, he obtained a sinecure as auditor for the Southern Division of the Duchy of Lancaster. In 1695, he was back in the military as a captain of Marines in Lord Berkeley's regiment. He seems never to have seen active combat service, and he was on half-pay by 1698, for all purposes virtually retired.

It was during the 1690's that Vanbrugh was to become involved in the two arts of theater and architecture. He may have had some training in architecture in his early years on the Continent, although there is no proof of

this. He did, however, start to write plays while in prison in France. If the military seemed to go only so far for him, he was not a man easily discouraged or without ambition, and in 1696, his life as an artist, if within gentlemanly restraints, began with some considerable success and promise.

LIFE'S WORK

Vanbrugh came to the theater in the last decade of the Restoration period, which takes its name from the restoration of Charles II in 1660 to the throne, from which his father, Charles I, had been deposed in the 1640's. The latter Charles, having lived so long in France and personally inclined to a life of pleasure, liked his theater to be lively and sexually improper. He was joined in this enthusiasm not only by his court but also by many of the members of the upper classes, tired of the rigorous religiosity of the Commonwealth period.

What they wanted to see were idealized mirror images of themselves on the stage: richly dressed, handsome men and women at the top of the social scale, talking smartly and often cruelly about success in society and in love. That so many of their own marriages were loveless arrangements of money and class (as was the general custom of the time) intensified their skepticism about matrimony. Restoration comedy imitated life (if only a small part of it) and improved on it. In these plays, romantic feeling was less important than is usually the case in comedies. If the handsomest man could be expected to gain the prettiest woman, it did not necessarily follow in a Restoration comedy that they would marry or that they could marry, since marital infidelity was a part of the game. The touchstone of success, aside from sex appeal, was intelligence: The wittiest man won the wittiest woman. Those who knew how to use society for their own ends, within certain severely limited bounds of honor, won out in this world of smart-set smart talk.

There was considerable criticism of the Restoration comedy of manners, not simply from the Puritans, who saw the theater as a symbol of the ungodliness of the Stuart regime, but also among some members of the ruling majority, who saw the theater as going too far in its celebration of the conjunction between high intelligence and high life. Some authors attempted to assuage the moralist attacks by bringing some genuine feeling into the plays of social and sexual impropriety, but Vanbrugh eschewed such sentimentality in his work, which suggested that rare individuals might try to be sexually faithful, and might even succeed in doing so, but that their example had little effect on others.

His first play, *The Relapse: Or, Virtue in Danger* (1696), was a continuation of a play written earlier by Colley Cibber, the actor-manager, titled *Love's Last Shift* (1696). Cibber had taken the leading part in his own work, and he returned to the same part in Vanbrugh's exploration of the simple proposition that a man, however he tried, was doomed to fail in any attempt to be faithful to one woman, however much he loved her. Vanbrugh's best play, *The Provok'd Wife* (1697), was, in fact, the work with which he had occupied himself while in prison and underlined the impossibility of marital fidelity in the sophisticated world of the London upper-middle class. Vanbrugh became a specific target for Jeremy Collier, the cleric determined to clean up the London stage, whose essay *A Short View of the Immorality and Profaneness of English Stage* (1698) became the focus for social concern about the stage. Vanbrugh attempted to answer the charges, but he never really reformed his work or seriously intended to do so. He was involved in the adaptation of several French comedies throughout the 1690's and the first decade of the eighteenth century, during which he tried, with limited success and regular disaster, to run theaters and theater companies in collaboration with other theatrical figures. He was one of the first promoters of the opera in England, which also proved to be, on its first appearance, too new for London audiences.

The Relapse and *The Provok'd Wife* were to join that small group of Restoration comedies that were to be revived over and over, and which are still played regularly in theaters all over the world, enchanting audiences with their splendid flights of saucily improper, brightly intelligent dialogue, and with their canny insights into the waywardness of human sexuality. The idea might be, as critics have always claimed, a thin one, but it has a galvanic kernel of truth about it—one that Wolfgang Amadeus Mozart was to use much later, in the eighteenth century, in his opera *Così fan tutte* (1786), proving, as the Restoration playwrights had, that art is often a matter of execution, how it is done, rather than a matter of content, what is being done.

By the late 1690's, Vanbrugh had firmly established himself at the center of London life, not only as a theatrical figure but also as a member of the Whig political and social hierarchy that was to provide him with modest political rewards, leading ultimately to his being the first man knighted by George I on his accession to the throne in 1714.

The real reward of those connections, however, came in a surprisingly different way. Charles Howard, the earl of Carlisle, determined to build himself a country estate of grandeur in Yorkshire, found himself in difficulty in dealing with the famous, irascible architect, William Talman. Vanbrugh, a friend of the earl, seems to have offered his services as a substitute for Talman. In short, he seems to have invented himself as an architect, for there is no evidence of any prior interest or activity in that art. He was, however, a gentleman, and a gentleman of taste and discrimination, and it was not unusual for such to try their hand at house design. Castle Howard, however, is more than simply a house; it is one of the great masterpieces of English Baroque architecture, and it revealed Vanbrugh as a natural genius of formidable proportions. Vanbrugh, however, had more than talent. In 1699, when he took on the project, he also took on a partner, the experienced, gifted, longtime assistant to Sir Christopher Wren, Nicholas Hawksmoor, and it was Hawksmoor who was to provide the technical knowledge required to carry off the major endeavor of Castle Howard. The union was more than that for both men; they seemed to complement each other aesthetically quite as much as they did technically, and although the bulk of the work at Castle Howard (the great country house used so extensively in the television version of Evelyn Waugh's novel *Brideshead Revisited*) is clearly by Vanbrugh, there are piquant embellishments (such as in the towers) that are clearly examples of Hawksmoor's peculiar Baroque imagination.

The Baroque style in architecture came to Great Britain considerably later than to the Continent. Wren may be seen, particularly in St. Paul's Cathedral, as the first major practitioner of the style in England, although there are minor traces of it previous to him. Neither in his buildings nor in the buildings of Vanbrugh and Hawksmoor (together or independently) does English Baroque develop into the richly, sometimes overripe fulsomeness of the bulging curves and lavish ornamentation that is common on the mainland. It is significantly "Englished," if still committed to an eclectic mixing of classical, Gothic, and Renaissance motifs and devices (which horrified purist thinkers about architecture, and which gave impetus in England to the neo-Palladians who came into their own in the second decade of the eighteenth century, determined to reject such stylistic ragouts). Still enchanted by the massing of grand, dramatic, balanced facades and sonorous cyclopean arches and cupolas, it is nevertheless much less sinuous, less fleshy, and much more angular and solid, with a sense of English no-nonsense manliness about it even in its breaking of the rules.

However improvisatory Vanbrugh's beginnings as an architect might have been, Castle Howard established him firmly as a major designer, and in 1702, with help from Whig friends including Carlisle, he was made comptroller of the Board of Works in London, a position his partner Hawksmoor had wanted and was probably more qualified to fill. Nevertheless, their collaborations continued, and in 1705 they became involved in their most ambitious work, Blenheim Palace, a gift from the nation to the great general, the duke of Marlborough, for his military service. Money was abundant, and the ambitions for the estate the duke had were amply complemented by those of his wife, the infamous virago, Sarah Churchill.

Such projects were carried out over years, not only because of their size and technical difficulties, but also because funding was uncertain and because owners and architects changed their minds, and quite as often, the buildings. Castle Howard, for example, was only occupied by Carlisle in 1712. Blenheim, dependent for support on the public purse, was, in a sense, in and out of politics for much of its history as an unfinished building. Added to the difficulties at Blenheim was the task of pleasing the duchess, and in 1716, the buildings still unfinished, Vanbrugh ran out of charm insofar as the duchess was concerned, and he and Hawksmoor were ordered off the project. Hawksmoor was to be allowed back on the premises in the early 1720's and was to do some of his finest work in the interiors and in the garden works at that time, but Vanbrugh was never to be forgiven. In 1724, Blenheim was finished, without Vanbrugh.

In spite of his exclusion, it is accepted that Blenheim is, in the main, Vanbrugh's for good or ill. There was much complaint about it: about its preposterous size, its swaggering pomposities, its inappropriateness as a place for human beings to live comfortably. Yet it is to be remembered that the duke and duchess (particularly the duchess personally, and the duke publicly) were somewhat larger than life themselves. British architectural historian Mark Girouard has suggested that the complaints must be balanced against the fact that it was the home of the greatest military hero of the period.

The idea of the massive central block between long, elaborate balancing wings that had been used at Castle Howard was repeated at Blenheim. In each case, faint echoes of Versailles or even of the Palladian farm villas might be sensed, but in Vanbrugh's hands, particularly at Blenheim, the idea was magnified, given tremendous weight in the dressing of both the exterior and interior. The surfaces of the facade are thick and crowded, busily coming and going in dramatic confrontations of pilaster, window, and arch. There is often, in all of his buildings, but particularly in Blenheim, the grand gesture of preposterously lavish stage sets metamorphosed into stone, fantasy turned into reality, but with little loss of dream.

Vanbrugh built several more modest variations on the Baroque country house, but it was perhaps with Seaton Delaval, a late work, that he again reached the greatness of Castle Howard and Blenheim Palace. Deep in the northern county of Northumberland, close to the cold, misty power of the North Sea, Seaton Delaval, much smaller than his castles, is nevertheless a forbidding example of his fusion of classicism and medievalism, its fortressed main block set in a vast forecourt, flanked by arcaded wings. It would be an appropriate setting for a gothic novel (which was still some years away from being invented by Horace Walpole). It sits brooding on the often-stormy skyline, its huge rusticated stones blackened by time and a terrible fire that gutted its interior, manifesting the capacity of English Baroque, particularly in the hands of Vanbrugh and Hawksmoor, to occasionally go beyond the grand to the Guignol.

It was not all work and plays, although Vanbrugh continued to work on architectural commissions until his death; and at that time, he was working on a comedy that was finished by Colley Cibber and produced by him (*The Provok'd Husband*, 1728). He married in 1719 and had three children with a wife less than half his age. He died, quite suddenly, of a throat infection and was buried in the family vault at St. Stephen Walbrook, the small Baroque gem by Sir Christopher Wren, which remains standing, just a few streets from where Vanbrugh was born.

SIGNIFICANCE

John Locke the philosopher once performed a major surgical operation on a member of the prominent Shaftesbury family; Sir Christopher Wren, albeit a mathematician and scientist of note, had no formal training as an architect; and William Congreve preferred to be known as a gentleman rather than a playwright. It was a common aspect of upper-class life to do something well while remembering that it ought not to be taken too seriously. Sir John Vanbrugh is the phenomenon of this tradition that can be traced to the idea of the gentlemen-courtiers of the Tudor and Stuart courts with their gifts not only as politicians but also as men of letters. Vanbrugh is unique in coming with seeming casualness into two artistic fields and establishing lasting reputations in both of them while pursuing his continuing connections to the world of high social and political moment. If the taste for his plays and for his buildings has occasionally faltered, it has never been lost, and in the twentieth century he is generally considered to be one of the great English Baroque architects as well as one of the finest playwrights of the Restoration period. It is not unusual to find major artists with capacities in arts with a common connection. Michelangelo was, for example, equally powerful as painter, sculptor, and architect and has some much more limited claim as a man of letters. Vanbrugh stands with equal reputation astride two arts that seem to have little common ground. He spans them with unchallenged reputation and some considerable panache—to be expected of the English gentleman-amateur at his best.

—Charles H. Pullen

FURTHER READING

Bingham, Madeleine. *Masks and Facades: Sir John Vanbrugh, the Man in His Setting*. London: Allen & Unwin, 1974. A good popular biography with some care taken in developing the background of Vanbrugh's very complicated life. Strongest on the social side and modestly cautious about the architecture.

Bull, John. *Vanbrugh and Farquhar*. New York: St. Martin's Press, 1998. Bull views Vanbrugh and George Farquhar as playwrights working at the end of the period of post-Restoration comedy, a time when England was entering the modern age. Bull describes their lives and careers within the context of their times, and examines how their plays reflect this transition from the old to the new.

Downes, Kerry. *Vanbrugh*. London: A. Zwemmer, 1977. Written by one of the best of the authorities on English Baroque architecture. In-depth discussion of Vanbrugh's architecture and family background. Splendidly illustrated. The scholarship is excellent.

Huseboe, Arthur R. *Sir John Vanbrugh*. Boston: Twayne, 1976. A short but accurate critical biography of Vanbrugh with emphasis on his work as a dramatist, and nothing of importance made of his work as an architect. Good chapters on the two major plays, and one on his work as an adapter of French dramas. Very good short bibliography.

McCormick, Frank. *Sir John Vanbrugh: The Playwright as Architect*. University Park: Pennsylvania State University Press, 1991. McCormick analyzes the interrelationship between Vanbrugh's two disparate careers.

Pevsner, Nikolaus. *An Outline of European Architecture*. 1942. 6th ed. Baltimore: Penguin Books, 1961. Pevsner is a fine commentator on British architecture, and any book by him on the subject is worth reading. This particular text is chosen to put the English Baroque movement into context with its European counterparts. Well illustrated, written with clarity and with sensitivity to the general reader.

Service, Alastair. *The Architects of London*. London: Architectural Press, 1979. A survey with site guides to all the architects. There is not much Vanbrugh left in London, but there is a very good short chapter on him, as well as chapters on the other Baroque architects of the time. Very well illustrated.

Whistler, Laurence. *Sir John Vanbrugh: Architect and Dramatist, 1664-1726*. New York: Macmillan, 1939. The best biography, written with charm and intelligence. An attempt to see Vanbrugh whole and to unify his multiple interests.

See also: Fanny Abington; Robert and James Adam; Lancelot Brown; Hannah Cowley; Nicholas Hawksmoor; Wolfgang Amadeus Mozart; Anne Oldfield; Sarah Siddons; Peg Woffington.

Related articles in *Great Events from History: The Eighteenth Century, 1701-1800:* 1715-1737: Building of the Karlskirche; 1726-1729: Voltaire Advances Enlightenment Thought in Europe; December 7, 1732: Covent Garden Theatre Opens in London; 1762: *The Antiquities of Athens* Prompts Architectural Neoclassicism.

GEORGE VANCOUVER
British navigator and explorer

Vancouver surveyed and mapped the west coast of North America, studied and charted the Hawaiian Islands and befriended the region's indigenous peoples, established Great Britain's claim to western Canada, and determined that the elusive Northwest Passage through North America did not exist.

Born: June 22, 1757; King's Lynn, Norfolk, England
Died: May 10, 1798; Petersham, England
Areas of achievement: Exploration, cartography

EARLY LIFE

George Vancouver was born in a seaport town on the east coast of England. His father was an affluent customs official at this busy trading center. Vancouver was the sixth child and third son of his parents, but little more is known of his youth. Living only five miles from the North Sea, he probably was familiar with ships, sailors, and ocean travel. Descriptions of him are rare, but drawings show him as a compact man fashionably comfortable in his Royal Navy uniform.

In 1771, the thirteen-year-old Vancouver entered the Royal Navy, where he would spend twenty-five years. Entering as a "young gentleman" made him a future candidate for midshipman and later training as a ship's officer. Vancouver, who had learned basic reading and math before enlistment, spent his formative years aboard a ship, where he was taught navigation, surveying, and astronomy. He was fortunate to be chosen by Captain James Cook as part of the crew on Cook's second voyage of discovery to the Pacific Ocean. Vancouver's presence on this voyage set him on the course of his life's work.

Aboard the *Resolution* with Cook, Vancouver attended to his assigned duties, showing skill, initiative, and enthusiasm. When the ship had reached its southernmost point while searching for the fabled southern continent, Vancouver climbed out onto the bowsprit so he could claim he had been closer to Antarctica than any person alive. By the age of twenty-three, Vancouver had traveled many seas and had seen many foreign countries.

LIFE'S WORK

From 1776 to 1780, Vancouver, now a midshipman, sailed on the *Discovery* on Captain Cook's third and fateful voyage to the South Seas. Cook discovered Hawaii for the Western world on January 18, 1778, but during his stay in the islands, he was killed by local inhabitants. Vancouver was an eyewitness to the incident and was in-

strumental in retrieving stolen articles and Cook's body, which was taken back to England on the *Discovery*. After completing his midshipman training, Vancouver served on Royal Navy ships in the North Sea and the Caribbean Sea for a decade, surveying, mapping, and charting the area. He was promoted to first lieutenant and took part in a sea battle against Spain in the West Indies in 1782. By the time he was made a captain at the age of thirty-two, he had sailed the seven seas and visited lands that few of his countrymen could even imagine existed.

In 1789, Vancouver was given command of an expedition to the Pacific Ocean. His ship was the *Discovery*, a newly built namesake of Cook's ship. Vancouver's expedition was charged with four tasks: to receive property in Canada that Spain had taken from the British, according to a treaty signed by both nations; to survey the west coast of North America; to try one last time to locate the western end of the Northwest Passage; and to complete Cook's survey of the Hawaiian Islands.

Discovery, accompanied by a small ship called *Chatham*, sailed on April 1, 1791, around South America and on to Australia and New Zealand, reaching Tahiti in December. The next stop was the Hawaiian Islands, where the expedition was to meet a storeship bringing them provisions. It never arrived, and they had to buy their food from indigenous peoples who wanted firearms as payment. Vancouver steadfastly refused to sell or barter any firearms and forbade his crew to do so. He followed with great interest the course of events in Hawaii, just then enduring a civil war. Part of Vancouver's instructions had been to make friends with the local peoples, which he did. He also recognized the value and strategic location of these islands and knew Great Britain would benefit if it could gain control of them.

In March, 1792, *Discovery* and *Chatham* sailed two thousand miles to the northwest coast of North America, reaching Cape Mendocino in April. After taking on provisions, the expedition surveyed the rugged coastline, locating inlets, bays, rocks, reefs, and other hazards to navigation and making detailed charts of the area. Heading north, the ships reached a complex of bays and rivers that Vancouver named Puget Sound after one of his officers, Peter Puget. This survey was difficult and time-consuming. When finished, they sailed back into the Straits of Juan de Fuca and then around the big island off the west coast, later called Vancouver Island in honor of the explorer, who had proved it was an island, not part of the continent. On this voyage, Vancouver sighted the summit of a tall mountain and named it Mount Rainier after Peter Rainier, a fellow navigator. He reiterated Great Britain's claim to the whole area.

In August, 1792, Vancouver sailed into Nootka Sound on the west coast of Vancouver Island and met with the Spanish, who had disputed the ownership of the area with Great Britain and relinquished the land in a peace settlement. His next search was for a group of islands that the Spanish called Los Majos, or Islas de Mesas. Vancouver did not find them where the Spanish said they were and deduced that the Spanish had seen the Hawaiian Islands but had the location wrong.

In Hawaii for the second time to spend the winter of 1792-1793, Vancouver became friendly with Kamehameha, who now ruled most of the islands. He instructed the new king on European strategy, tactics, and weapons as well as other aspects of European life. The following summer, *Discovery* and *Chatham* sailed back to the area known as British Columbia, searching for the west end of the fabled Northwest Passage. Traders, explorers, and European governments had long hoped it existed, but no one had found a trace of it. He went as far north as Cook

British explorer Captain George Vancouver. (Hulton Archive/ Getty Images)

Inlet in Alaska, where his men clashed with indigenous peoples on the lower peninsula and killed almost a dozen of them. Vancouver had not seen a passage, and as he left the area, he concluded that it did not exist.

Back in Hawaii for the third and last time in the winter of 1793-1794, Vancouver and Kamehameha made a formal agreement: The Hawaiian ruler ceded his island to Great Britain. This event was important to Vancouver and may have been suggested by him. Its meaning to the Hawaiian king is still disputed. The cession was never acted upon by the British. If it had been, the history of the United States, Hawaii, and the world would have been different.

Vancouver arrived home on *Discovery* on October 15, 1795, with *Chatham* arriving a day later. *Discovery* was decommissioned, and Vancouver went on leave. In London, he cleared up business he had been unable to do for three years and began to prepare the journals of his voyage for publication. However, a scandal erupted and ended his navy career: Vancouver was accused of flogging an officer whom he had subsequently discharged. The man was now a baron and had important and influential friends. Vancouver was devastated. No evidence of a flogging existed, and Vancouver was never charged with any crime; however, in the eighteenth century, the man with a noble title and powerful friends was always right. Vancouver's reputation was damaged beyond repair.

Vancouver never recovered from the scandal, and it may have aggravated his chronic illness, the cause of which is unknown. Some sources say he suffered from tuberculosis; others postulate Hanson's disease, a condition of the thyroid. He died in 1798, just forty years old. By his death, he had completed five books detailing his voyage and was halfway through the sixth and last. *Voyage of Discovery to the North Pacific Ocean and Round the World*, with maps and drawings, was published in 1798. It did not receive much attention because England and Europe were involved in a war with France and soon were fighting Napoleon. Later, the work was reprinted in three volumes.

SIGNIFICANCE

George Vancouver's contributions to the world are in several fields: exploration, political history, and geography. He explored some of the more inaccessible areas of the Pacific Ocean. He settled conflicts with Spain and made a bid to take control of the Hawaiian Islands. He mapped the west coast of the North American continent, providing the only accurate information on the region. Fifty years later, his surveys were used extensively in a dispute between the United States and Great Britain over who "owned" Oregon, Washington, and western Canada.

In the nineteenth century, he was often overlooked by historians who concentrated on Captain Cook, but modern historians have given him his proper place in the company of explorers. Vancouver's survey was the most arduous ever undertaken, the accuracy of his notations was remarkable, and his descriptions of the terrain were realistic and precise. One hundred years later, his charts were still the best and most trusted by those who sailed the west coast of North America, Canada, and Alaska.

He was a true and loyal Englishman, a remarkable member of the Royal Navy, and a splendid ambassador for his nation. His sailing and surveying skills were never surpassed, and his ability to handle people and political situations calmed many explosive situations in the Pacific Ocean and the Northwest. Both of these areas would grow and become even more important in the nineteenth and twentieth centuries.

—Lyndall Baker Landauer

FURTHER READING

Anderson, Bern. *The Life and Voyages of Captain George W. Vancouver, Surveyor of the Sea*. Toronto, Ont.: University of Toronto Press, 1960. A complete coverage of the life and career of Vancouver. It explains the background to events in the life of an eighteenth century sailor and the political atmosphere in which he lived. The author justifies many of Vancouver's actions, perhaps to make up for the injustices done to him in his final years.

Batman, Richard. *The Outer Coast*. San Diego, Calif.: Harcourt Brace Jovanovich, 1985. This work shows the impact of men such as Vancouver, describing his detailed surveys on the discovery and exploration of California and the west coast of the United States when it was still a remote frontier. The book places Vancouver in perspective beside contemporary explorers such as La Perouse and Otto von Kotzebue.

Fisher, Robin, and Hugh Johnston, eds. *From Maps to Metaphors: The Pacific World of George Vancouver*. Vancouver: University of British Columbia Press, 1993. Collection of papers delivered at a 1992 conference about Vancouver's explorations. Some of the topics discussed are his survey methods, the health of Vancouver and his crew, and the political relationship between Pacific explorers and American Indian leaders.

Godwin, George. *Vancouver, a Life*. New York: D. Appleton, 1931. This work covers all aspects of Vancouver's life, not just his life at sea. It provides detailed information on his parents and his youth in a seaport town, his voyages, his triumphs, and his troubles before his death.

Raban, Jonathan. *Passage to Juneau: A Sea and Its Meanings*. New York: Pantheon Books, 1992. Raban sailed along the Inside Passage from Seattle to Juneau, describing his experiences and the stories of others who made the same trip. He recounts Vancouver's voyage, explaining how he risked mutiny for banning his men from visiting prostitutes.

Vancouver, George. *Voyage of Discovery to the North Pacific Ocean and Round the World*. 3 vols. London: G. G. & J. Robinson, 1798. Vancouver's observations are acute, provide much detail, and are often enlightening. The atlas of maps is valuable.

See also: Lord Anson; Sir Joseph Banks; Vitus Jonassen Bering; William Bligh; James Bruce; James Cook; Richard Howe; Sir Alexander Mackenzie; Mungo Park; Arthur Phillip.

Related articles in *Great Events from History: The Eighteenth Century, 1701-1800:* April 5, 1722: European Discovery of Easter Island; July, 1728-1769: Russian Voyages to Alaska; August 25, 1768-February 14, 1779: Voyages of Captain Cook; July 22, 1793: Mackenzie Reaches the Arctic Ocean.

MARQUIS DE VAUVENARGUES
French writer and philosopher

Vauvenargues was the outstanding French moralist in the first half of the eighteenth century and an important influence on Voltaire, Rousseau, and other leading figures of the French Enlightenment. His reconciliation of the tension between reason and emotion looked ahead to the Romantic philosophies of Immanuel Kant and Georg Wilhelm Friedrich Hegel.

Born: August 6, 1715; Aix-en-Provence, France
Died: May 28, 1747; Paris, France
Also known as: Luc de Clapiers (birth name)
Areas of achievement: Literature, philosophy

EARLY LIFE

The Marquis de Vauvenargues (voh-vehn-ahrg) was born Luc de Clapiers to a poor but noble family. His father, Joseph, was the town mayor, and in 1722 he was ennobled as Marquis de Vauvenargues in recognition of his services during an outbreak of the plague. Sickly and ill-favored from youth, Vauvenargues nonetheless entered military service in 1733 as a second lieutenant in the king's regiment, rising to the rank of captain. His first posting was with Marshal Villars in Italy during the War of the Polish Succession (1733-1735). The outbreak of the War of the Austrian Succession in 1740 found him garrisoned at Metz. He was attached to the army of Marshal de Belle-Isle that invaded Bohemia in July, 1741, and took part in the daring night capture of Prague. Reinforcements and supply failed, however, and Belle-Isle was obliged to abandon the city on December 16-17, 1742. His nine-day retreat over frozen ground to Egra was a disaster. Much of the army was lost, and Vauvenargues, whose legs suffered frostbite, was left lame. His lungs and eyesight were also affected, and the pulmonary damage hastened his premature death. He served at the Battle of Dettingen in 1743, returned to garrison at Arras, and resigned his commission in January, 1744.

LIFE'S WORK

After Vauvenargues's resignation from the military, poverty obliged him to seek further employment. He attempted to enter the diplomatic service and was on the verge of securing a post thanks to the offices of Voltaire, who had befriended him, when he was stricken with smallpox. Voltaire enabled him to settle in Paris, where he nursed his failing health but also took up the literary career that friends, beginning with the Marquis de Mirabeau, had urged him to pursue.

In 1746, Vauvenargues published *Introduction a la connaissance de l'esprit humaine, suivie de reflexions et de maximes* (introduction to the knowledge of the human spirit, followed by reflections and maxims). Vauvenargues died in Paris on May 28, 1747, attended by a small circle of friends but still impoverished and obscure. An edition of his works was published later that year. Much of his writing, however, was suppressed by his family, lest it "stain" his reputation, and remained unpublished until the end of the century. A fiftieth anniversary edition appeared in 1797, more substantive but still incomplete. Forty-two additional letters, and seventeen notebooks totaling 708 pages, were discovered in the Aix-en-Provence library in 1825 and sold to the Louvre. This material served as the basis of D. L. Gilbert's definitive edition of Vauvenargues in 1857, but the archive was lost in the fire of May 23-24, 1871, that followed the fall of the Paris Commune.

Vauvenargues's corpus is small—one modern edition of his work comes to 525 pages—but sufficient to establish him as the foremost French aphorist of the first half of the eighteenth century and the heir of a tradition of moral commentary that began with Rabelais and Montaigne. Vauvenargues himself was conscious of his place in that tradition, and of an even older heritage of humane skepticism that reached back to Theophrastus, Juvenal, Martial, and, above all, Plutarch. His work is a dialogue with and a commentary on his precursors, as well as a significant extension of it.

Vauvenargues's concerns are those of his age: the nature of humanity, the relationship of simplicity to virtue and of reason to emotion, and the distinction between vanity and ambition. Much of his work can be read as a reaction against the cynicism of the seventeenth century moralists, particularly La Rouchefoucauld, La Bruyere, and Molière. In contrast to La Rouchefoucauld, who argued that self-interest and self-love were at the heart of all human actions, Vauvenargues insisted on two exceptions: the love of others, and the love of glory. In the beloved, whose welfare we cherish above our own, we rise above mere egotistical calculation; and, similarly, in the quest for glory, which Vauvenargues understood as the pursuit of excellence, we transcend our own interest. These exceptions make nobility, indeed humanity itself, possible, and are the basis of all virtue. Vauvenargues thus rejected the depiction of the human individual not only as a mere bundle of egotistical interests and desires but also as an impenitent sinner, incapable of rising without grace. In this he parted company with Pascal, a thinker sympathetic to him in many ways.

For Vauvenargues, what was crucial in humans was the freedom to aspire. For this, pride and ambition were requisite, but also dangerous, for they could easily terminate in vanity. Only the continual spur of action could overcome the tendency to egotism. The heroic self was realized by seeking what was beyond it, a vision that looked forward to such later thinkers as Georg Wilhelm Friedrich Hegel and Friedrich Nietzsche.

The virtuous person, as described by Vauvenargues, was conscious of his or her own insufficiency (*insuffisance*), and therefore of the continual need of exploration and self-creation. Such a person occupied the mean between the egotist, who admitted the world only as an extension of him- or herself, and the person of convention, who disappeared into it. Authentic selfhood thus required the recognition of self and world as a mutually constituted relation, defined through human action. At the same time, the virtuous individual had to take other selves into account. The common project of all such selves was the common interest (*bienfaisance*). This interest was the true subject of politics, which might be obscured by private interests, but appeared in moments of crisis. Here Vauvenargues clearly foreshadowed Rousseau's concept of the General Will.

SIGNIFICANCE

Vauvenargues was a critical link between French thought of the seventeenth century and that of the Enlightenment. While acknowledging the frailty of individuals and the corruption of society, he argued that humans were capable of virtue and glory, and therefore of moral progress. His attempt to reconcile reason and emotion, whose incompatibility had been one of the grand themes of seventeenth century thought, led toward Jean-Jacques Rousseau and his Romantic successors. Emotion, he believed, was the primary element in human nature, the "first teacher," as he put it, of the soul. It was also the chief wellspring of action, and therefore indispensable to the projects of reason. In making his claim for the essential interaction of reason and emotion, Vauvenargues both helped to make the Enlightenment possible and provided a check on its excesses.

—Robert Zaller

FURTHER READING

Fine, Peter Martin. *Vauvenargues and La Rouchefoucauld*. Totowa, N.J.: Rowman and Littlefield, 1974. A comparative study of Vauvenargues and his most celebrated seventeenth century predecessor, the Duke de la Rouchefoucauld.

Gosse, Edmund. *Three French Moralists*. London: William Heinemann. 1918. Contains a sympathetic and perceptive essay on Vauvenargues by a distinguished turn-of-the-century British novelist and critic.

Read, Herbert. *The Sense of Glory: Essays in Criticism*. Cambridge, England: Cambridge University Press, 1929. Contains a good overview of Vauvenargues's life and thought by a major British critic.

Vauvenargues, Luc de Clapiers de. *Œuvres Complètes*. Paris: Editions Alive, 1999. The most recent and comprehensive edition of Vauvenargues's works. Contains commentary and a bibliography.

Vial, M. Fernand. *Une Philosophie et une Morale du Sentiment: Luc de Clapiers, Marquis de Vauvenargues*. Paris: Droz, 1938. An important French critical commentary.

Walras, Mary. *Luc de Clapiers, Marquis de Vauvenargues*. Cambridge, England: Cambridge University Press, 1928. One of the few book-length studies in English devoted exclusively to Vauvenargues, and still useful.

See also: Étienne Bonnot de Condillac; Immanuel Kant; Jean-Jacques Rousseau; Voltaire.

Related articles in *Great Events from History: The Eighteenth Century, 1701-1800:* 1739-1740: Hume Publishes *A Treatise of Human Nature*; 1748: Montesquieu Publishes *The Spirit of the Laws*; 1751-1772: Diderot Publishes the *Encyclopedia*; 1754: Condillac Defends Sensationalist Theory; July 27, 1758: Helvétius Publishes *De l'esprit*; January, 1759: Voltaire Satirizes Optimism in *Candide*; April, 1762: Rousseau Publishes *The Social Contract*; July, 1764: Voltaire Publishes *A Philosophical Dictionary for the Pocket*; 1770: Publication of Holbach's *The System of Nature*; 1781: Kant Publishes *Critique of Pure Reason*; 1782-1798: Publication of Rousseau's *Confessions*.

CHARLES GRAVIER DE VERGENNES
French diplomat

Charles Gravier de Vergennes, named minister for foreign affairs by Louis XVI, sought to prevent war in Europe by creating an equilibrium among major political powers and small states. He is also remembered for his role in bringing vital French aid to the American Revolution.

Born: December 28, 1719; Dijon, France
Died: February 13, 1787; Versailles, France
Also known as: Comte de Vergennes
Areas of achievement: Government and politics, diplomacy

EARLY LIFE

Charles Gravier de Vergennes (shahrl grahv-yay duh vehr-zhehn) was born into a noble family, steeped in a tradition of civil service. Both his father and grandfather were magistrates, and his uncle, Théodore Chevignard de Chavigny, was a diplomat. Little is known about Vergennes's childhood; his mother, Marie Françoise Chevignard de Charodon, died when he was a year old. His early education took place in Jesuit schools, where he learned to value geometry and mathematics for their rigorous order, and geography, history, languages (particularly Latin and Greek), spelling, penmanship, and literature for their social and moral values.

When he was still quite young, in 1740, he accompanied his uncle de Chavigny, to Lisbon, Portugal. There, his uncle taught him the profession of diplomacy, and his apprenticeship there became his first diplomatic service to France. In 1741, he participated in the negotiations that ultimately transformed the elector of Bavaria into Charles VII, emperor of Germany. Inspired by the potential of diplomacy, Vergennes returned to Lisbon in 1745, where he learned to speak Portuguese and Spanish, adding them to the Latin, Italian, English, and, of course, French, in which he was already fluent. Far from being satisfied with his immense linguistic ability, he always regretted never learning the German that would have completed his ability to converse in every court in Europe.

LIFE'S WORK

Vergennes's independent career as a French diplomat began in 1750, when he was appointed to be the ambassador to the court of the elector of Trier (Trèves, Germany). His growing reputation for diligence served him well; as a career diplomat, he took his work seriously, beginning his work day at 4:00 A.M., working until 1:00 P.M., and then, after a break for the midday meal, returning to his labors for another four hours.

After Trier, Vergennes was sent to Hannover (1752) and Mannheim (1753) in Germany and to Constantinople (now Istanbul), Turkey, in 1754. While on post in Constantinople, Vergennes met Anne de Viviers, the widow of a surgeon. Though she was from a very modest family and could not aspire to the position that Vergennes held in the aristocratic social structure of France, she and Vergennes fell in love, ultimately producing two children, Constantin and Louis-Charles Joseph. Because of the pressure exerted by his peers in the French government, who disdained alliances with inferior families, Vergennes hesitated to marry the woman who was already the mother of his first son. Finally, much to the shock of his fellow aristocrats, he and Anna were married on March 9, 1767.

Vergennes's apostasy did not go unnoticed; in the following year, when he refused to provoke a quarrel between Russia and Turkey as his superior, Étienne François de Choiseul, had requested, he was recalled to France. There he retired with his wife and children to Toulongeon, his family's castle in Burgundy, near Autun. A few years of quiet life allowed his unfortunate independence to fade from the minds of the government; in 1772, Vergennes returned to service, as the French ambassador in Stockholm, where his services were favorably reviewed.

After Louis XV's death in 1774, young Louis XVI's regent requested that Vergennes accept the post of secretary of state for foreign affairs. Vergennes had spent thirty-five years in the diplomatic service of France, but much of this time was spent in foreign countries, prompting his political enemy, journalist and advocate Simon Nicolas Henri Linguet, to comment that "rather than a Minister of Foreign Affairs, M. Vergennes is a foreigner become Minister." However, Vergennes was an inspired choice for the post: Widely experienced, he was very knowledgeable concerning the political conditions of Europe. Even better for a nation with an underage king, Vergennes had always shown a desire to avoid military conflicts by keeping a balance of power, preferring to achieve his goals through diplomacy.

When the British colonies in America revolted, and Benjamin Franklin appealed to the French court for recognition, Vergennes sought to avoid outright war with

Charles Gravier de Vergennes. (Library of Congress)

England, while at the same time providing the logistical support that would allow the fledgling nation in America to draw English attention and resources away from projects in Europe. Enlisting the aid of his friend Pierre-Augustin Caron de Beaumarchais (who prudently took the alias of Rodrigue Hortalez for the operation), Vergennes arranged for a fleet of forty vessels that brought the Americans desperately needed weapons, food, and money. As the American cause advanced, France advanced cautiously with it. Only after the American victory at Saratoga on September 19, 1777, was an alliance considered; on February 6, 1778, a treaty was was signed between the Americans and King Louis XVI, which provided military assistance, and loans of at least 750,000 livres, to the fledgling nation every three months beginning February 28, 1778.

In 1781, Vergennes became chief of the council of finance. By the middle of the next year he was France's secretary of state. Negotiating with Franklin, he helped forge a generous policy by which the king forgave the 5 percent interest accruing on the 18 million livres loaned to the United States during the war, and established a repayment schedule that accepted twelve installments over time rather than the lump sum payment due on January 1, 1788.

Vergennes died on February 13, 1787, just before the Assembly of Notables and the onslaught of the French Revolution that would, beginning in 1789, destroy the society and government he had served.

SIGNIFICANCE

Vergennes was an important part of the bureaucracy that functioned to maintain the social and political structure of eighteenth century Europe, as well as a rationalist who displayed the new social convictions of the Enlightenment. Treading between two worlds, he served the Old World while rejecting many of its pretensions, marrying a woman for love rather than family connections, and refusing to engage in the Machiavellian schemes that had embroiled Europe in endless petty wars the century before. His covert—and later overt—aid to the cause of the American Revolution was instrumental in the success of the war and the survival of the new nation in its infancy. It is perhaps fortunate for him that he did not survive to see the French Revolution, in which the rationalist republicans that he admired guillotined his brother, partially destroyed his ancestral home, and violently ended the aristocratic traditions that he had tried to preserve into a new and more democratic age.

—*Denyse Lemaire and David Kasserman*

FURTHER READING

Brecher, Frank W. *Securing American Independence: John Jay and the French Alliance.* Westport, Conn.: Praeger, 2003. This book examines the work of John Jay and Vergennes as peace negotiators after the War of Independence.

Dull, Jonathan R. *A Diplomatic History of the American Revolution.* New Haven, Conn.: Yale University Press, 1987. This book is a description of the diplomatic efforts that led to the American Revolution.

Hardman, John, and Price Munro. *Louis XVI and the Comte de Vergennes: Correspondence, 1774-1787.* New York: Oxford University Press, 1998. This book is a compilation of the letters Louis XVI and Vergennes exchanged. In French and English.

Labourdette, Jean-François. *Vergennes, ministre principal de Louis XVI.* Paris: Desjonquères, 1990. This book in French gives a detailed bibliography on work related to Vergennes and his life.

Munro, Price. *Preserving the Monarchy: The Comte de Vergennes, 1774-1787.* New York: Cambridge University Press, 1995. An examination of Vergennes's relationship both to the office of the king and to the man holding that office.

GIAMBATTISTA VICO
Italian philosopher

Vico founded the philosophical study of history and elaborated the theoretical basis for sociological study, thereby setting the stage for the rise of trends that would dominate nineteenth century intellectual history.

Born: June 23, 1668; Naples (now in Italy)
Died: January 23, 1744; Naples
Areas of achievement: Philosophy, sociology, historiography

EARLY LIFE

Giambattista Vico (jahm-baht-TEES-tah VEE-koh) was one of eight children born to a Neapolitan bookshop owner and his scarcely literate wife. Giambattista was an energetic and prodigious child, already enrolled in school at the age of seven, when a fall from the top of a ladder fractured his skull. The fracture gave rise to a large tumor, and his doctor predicted that the boy would either die of it or grow up an idiot. Although Vico's convalescence was prolonged, neither part of the doctor's prediction came true. Vico came to credit the injury, however, with engendering his lifelong melancholic temperament, the sort of temperament, Vico said, that belongs to all men of ingenuity and depth.

Vico's early formal education was classical, which at the time meant indoctrination into medieval Christian Aristotelianism, but he also spent a great part of his youth in solitary study, which was doubtless encouraged by living upstairs from the family bookshop. At seventeen, Vico went, at his father's urging, to the University of Naples to study law. He read philosophy in his spare time and wrote ornate, metaphysical poetry for relaxation. He quickly grew impatient with the incessant note-taking and memorization of legal cases and quit his university lectures, saying that there was no true learning to be obtained from them. He resumed his devotion to private study of the works of great writers and supported himself by tutoring the nephews of the bishop of Ischia in Vatolla. He continued to develop his ideas largely by himself for the ensuing nine years and developed passing enthusiasms for the philosophy of Epicurus, Plato, Cornelius Tacitus, Pierre Gassendi, Roger Bacon, René Descartes, and Baruch Spinoza, among others. In 1695, Vico returned to his native city and was appointed four years later to the professorship of rhetoric at the university. This was actually a minor post with a modest stipend; Vico kept the post until shortly before his death.

LIFE'S WORK

Vico's ideas gained rudimentary expression in two of the first tracts he published. In the 1709 oration *De nostri temporis studiorum ratione* (*On the Study Methods of Our Times*, 1965), Vico denied the applicability of the Cartesian geometrical method of analysis to the human studies of practical wisdom, ethics, politics, and law. What he wanted to put in its place emerged in the 1710 publication *De antiquissima Italorum sapientia* (partial translation in *Selected Writings*, 1982). Vico focused upon etymology as a source of clues to the truth about human development. Linguistic analysis utilized a sort of *ingenium*, the power of connecting separate and diverse elements, that Vico thought was necessary for human self-understanding and practical wisdom.

This early work of Vico was met with a mixed reception; his critics complained of its obscurity. Nevertheless, Vico submitted it with an application for the chair of civil law at Naples when the post fell vacant in 1723. His rejection was a bitter disappointment and proved to be only the beginning of the neglect he had to endure throughout his career.

The first edition of Vico's magnum opus, *Principi di scienza nuova intorno alla natura delle nazioni per la quale si ritruovano i principi di altro sistema del diritto naturale delle genti* (*The New Science*, 1948), was published in 1725. Vico had hoped that this work would do for the study of humans and culture what Sir Isaac Newton's *Philosophiae naturalis principia mathematica* (1687) had done for mathematical physics. Dissatisfied with its reception, he recast it twice; subsequent editions were published in 1730 and (posthumously) in 1744.

The structure of the third edition of *The New Science* was quite unusual. It contained an elaborate allegorical drawing for a frontispiece, followed by a detailed explanation of the icon. A chronological table followed, which placed in parallel columns the major events in the histories of seven peoples. Next came a catalog of 114 axioms that summarized the assumptions and conclusions of the work. The three remaining sections developed a narrative of human history, the elaboration of Vico's theory that human history manifested three ages: the age of gods, the age of heroes, and the age of men.

According to Vico, history was the gradual process of the humanization of humans. In prehistory, bestial giants roamed the endless forests of the Earth. Their mental powers were dormant in their enormous bodies so that all thought was sensation. They lived strictly in the present, copulating at inclination and increasing in size by inhaling the vapors of their excrement. The first formation of thunder and lightning elicited a new emotion of fear in the giants; they trembled at the sky and named it Jove. Jove was the first thought. Thus began the age of gods. It is an age whose story was told by Herodotus, when humans thought that everything either was a god or was made by gods. Religion brought forth primitive morality, which begot the "might makes right" age of heroes, as characterized by Homer. As human powers of reason were developed to control unruly passions, the age of men was born.

Vico saw these ages as continuing in a never-ending cycle, or *ricorso*, that manifested an ineluctable, providential pattern that he called the "ideal eternal history" of humans. Every culture, he believed, passed through these identical stages; each age had a characteristic mode of expression, set of customs, kind of law, and type of religion.

Vico believed his discoveries about the evolution of human civilization to be scientific. The method of inquiry that yielded these results attended precisely to the aforementioned characteristic institutions of each group of people. One of Vico's deepest insights was that the individual person may know himself (or herself) in a way he (or she) can never know what is external to him (or her) (that is, nature). Whatever is of man's own making speaks truth about him; this includes cultural institutions, language, and even history itself. Vico expressed this principle by saying that the true (*verum*) and the made (*factum*) are convertible. Thus, a systematic, historical investigation of all the results of human will and contriv-

ance would produce a true understanding of humankind. Vico believed that this was the only way for humans to reach self-understanding.

According to Vico, language study plays a special role in human self-understanding. Vico's original and extraordinarily interesting views on linguistic interpretation were of a piece with his principle of *verum ipsum factum*. He believed that the terms people use, including abstract terms, could be traced to linguistic contrivances of the earliest humans. Etymology thus could illuminate earlier environmental conditions, psychological states, and commonplace activities of human ancestry. That was a result of the fact that language and thought were coextensive for Vico; language was a direct reflection of the development of thought, rather than a tool that was deliberately and artificially constructed.

Vico theorized that poetic figures, such as metaphor, in the language of his contemporaries had more directly expressed the experience of humans in earlier ages. Earlier people thought strictly in pictorial images, analogies, and personifications, and these formed the currency of their communication, which involved only gesturing and picture drawing. Vico designated such figures "imaginative universals," and they had a property that third-age ratiocinating individuals can scarcely recapture: that of invoking a universal image by means of a particular. The abstractions employed in the age of men are the opposite of the imaginative universal. Abstractions hold only what many particulars have in common, but which the particular alone can no longer express (with the exception, perhaps, of particular images in poetic contexts). Similarly, what third-age individuals call the extravagant fiction of mythology in fact expresses the most fundamental postulates and cognitive associations of the first humans. Vico referred to his own saga in *The New Science* as a myth in just this sense.

Although Vico occupied most of his mature years writing reincarnations of *The New Science* in the hope of satisfying his critics, he also penned in his fifty-seventh year an intellectual autobiography. This was a pioneering work of its genre and a fascinating philosophical document in its own right.

Vico gained very limited fame in his time. He received the honorific recognition of royal historiographer from the sovereign Charles of Bourbon only after his memory was failing and he had been overcome by physical infirmity. After his death, a bizarre quarrel over who should have the honor of carrying his coffin to the grave erupted between the Royal University professors and the confraternity of Vico's parish. The intransigent confraternity took their leave, and as a result the coffin remained at the family home for quite some time. Vico's son finally had to enlist the services of the cathedral to conduct the body to the sepulcher.

SIGNIFICANCE

Giambattista Vico's work was largely ignored by his contemporaries, most of whom were enthusiastic Cartesians. He was not without outspoken detractors, however, who ridiculed him as obscure, speculative, and slightly mad. It has been said by twentieth century thinkers, who have the benefit of hindsight, that Vico was simply too far ahead of his time to have had any immediate influence. Yet the relative neglect of Vico's work continued in posterity. A small group of later thinkers have remarked on the importance of Vico, including Karl Marx, Samuel Taylor Coleridge, William Butler Yeats, and Matthew Arnold, but their work did not reflect any direct and significant influence from Vician thought. A very few thinkers have based their thought on Vico's insights: Jules Michelet, Benedetto Croce, and, to a certain extent, R. G. Collingwood and Ernst Cassirer. Even though Vico must be credited with being the father of the social sciences and the philosophy of history, his work has yet to join the vanguard of seminal philosophical texts.

Most twentieth century thinkers have come to know Vico through James Joyce. Joyce referred readers who had difficulty with his works to Vico's *The New Science*. Joyce claimed that his imagination grew when he read Vico in a way that it did not from reading Sigmund Freud or Carl Gustav Jung. Joycean texts are replete with references to Vico, and they palpably appropriate Vico's cyclical theory of history as well as his theories of language and myth. Consequently, Vico's thought enjoyed something of an epiphany in the late twentieth century that may yet certify his status as a great contributor to Western thought.

—Patricia Cook

FURTHER READING

Adams, H. P. *The Life and Writings of Giambattista Vico*. London: Allen & Unwin, 1935. This biography is one of few which attempt to integrate Vico's life and thought. It is amusing and elegant, and it includes translations of some of Vico's poems. Indexed.

Burke, Peter. *Vico*. New York: Oxford University Press, 1985. A concise treatment of Vico's intellectual development, his major work, and his influence. Indexed, with a helpful list for further reading.

Caponigri, A. Robert. *Time and Idea: The Theory of History in Giambattista Vico*. London: Routledge & Kegan Paul, 1953. An excellent exposition of the main Vician themes of ideal eternal history, *ricorsi*, and the natural law. Densely packed and well indexed.

Croce, Benedetto. *The Philosophy of Giambattista Vico*. Translated by R. G. Collingwood. London: Howard Latimer, 1913. Reprint. Brunswick, N.J.: Transaction, 2002. This now-classic commentary on the totality of Vico's thought may be too complex to serve introductory students, but it is a solid and reliable secondary source for issues not covered in more general literature. Well indexed.

Mazzotta, Giuseppe. *The New Map of the World: The Poetic Philosophy of Giambattista Vico*. Princeton, N.J.: Princeton University Press, 1999. Mazzotta analyzes Vico's thought, explaining how it can enhance understanding of twenty-first century social problems. He examines how Vico attempted to unify the arts and sciences as a means of unifying society.

Miner, Robert C. *Vico, Genealogist of Modernity*. Notre Dame, Ind.: University of Notre Dame Press, 2002. Miner describes how Vico sought to undermine Cartesian philosophy by offering a critique of pure reason and exposing the pretensions of contemporary thought. A scholarly book, aimed at readers who are knowledgeable about eighteenth century philosophy.

Pompa, Leon. *Vico: A Study of "The New Science."* New York: Cambridge University Press, 1975. A close analysis of Vico's text is offered here; this work is laced with quotations and helpful interpretations of passages in their context. Indexed, with a short bibliography.

Tagliacozzo, Giorgio, ed. *Vico and Contemporary Thought*. Atlantic Highlands, N.J.: Humanities Press, 1979. This collection of essays is among the many books now available that demonstrate a resurgence of interest in Vico's thought. The essays in this book focus on the relevance of Vician insights to twentieth century practical and philosophical concerns. The book also contains the first English translation of Vico's essay *De mente heroica* (1732; *On the Heroic Mind*). Well indexed; contributors come from a wide range of disciplines.

Vico, Giambattista. *The Autobiography of Giambattista Vico*. Translated by Max Harold Fisch and Thomas Goddard Bergin. Ithaca, N.Y.: Cornell University Press, 1963. The first one hundred pages of this edition are the translators' introduction to Vico's life and thought; this is perhaps the best one hundred pages on Vico that an introductory student could read. The second part of the book contains Vico's autobiography, a delightful and accessible work, although it requires careful study. Indexed, with a chronological table of Vico's life.

See also: Johann Gottfried Herder; Immanuel Kant; Jean-Jacques Rousseau.
Related articles in *Great Events from History: The Eighteenth Century, 1701-1800*: October, 1725: Vico

Publishes *The New Science*; 1739-1740: Hume Publishes *A Treatise of Human Nature*; April, 1762: Rousseau Publishes *The Social Contract*; July, 1764: Voltaire Publishes *A Philosophical Dictionary for the Pocket*; 1770: Publication of Holbach's *The System of Nature*; 1781: Kant Publishes *Critique of Pure Reason*; 1784-1791: Herder Publishes His Philosophy of History.

ÉLISABETH VIGÉE-LEBRUN
French painter

Vigée-Lebrun was one of the most celebrated artists of her time and ranks with the best portraitists of the late eighteenth and early nineteenth centuries. By concentrating on the personalities of her sitters, she broke with the tradition of the empty ceremonial portrait.

Born: April 16, 1755; Paris, France
Died: March 30, 1842; Paris, France
Also known as: Marie-Louise-Élisabeth Vigée (birth name)
Area of achievement: Art

EARLY LIFE
Élisabeth Vigée-Lebrun (ay-lee-zah-beht veh-zhay-luh-bruh), born in Paris on April 16, 1755, was the daughter of Louis Vigée, a pastel portraitist and teacher at the Academy of St. Luke. From ages six to eleven, she attended a convent school, where, as she later recorded in her memoirs, she was constantly drawing whenever and wherever she could. Although, as she stated, "my passion for painting was born in me," her father can be credited with nurturing her ambition to become an artist. During school holidays, the young Élisabeth received her first lessons in drawing and oils from her father and some of his artist friends, especially Gabriel Francis Doyen and P. Davesne, both of whom would encourage her after her father died in 1767. At this time, she also had a few drawing lessons from Gabriel Briard, whom she described as an indifferent painter but a very fine draftsman. While working in Briard's studio in the Louvre, she met the renowned academician Joseph Vernet, who advised her not to follow any system of schools but to study only the works of the great Italian and Flemish masters. Furthermore, he urged her to work as much as possible from nature, to avoid falling into mannerisms. Taking Vernet's advice, she studied the works of such masters as

Peter Paul Rubens, Rembrandt, Sir Anthony Van Dyck, Raphael, and Domenichino in public and private collections in Paris, and she made her own studies from nature, using family and friends as models.

The Royal Academy in Paris excluded all women from its classes of instruction; therefore, it was no coincidence that most successful women artists of the time were daughters of artists, receiving their training in their fathers' studios, outside the system of academic apprenticeship. Because of her father's early death, Vigée-Lebrun was largely self-taught, having acquired her artistic education by virtue of her own willpower, discipline, and willingness to work long hours. By the time she was fifteen, she was a professional portraitist, earning barely enough money to support her mother and young brother. At age nineteen, she was licensed as a master painter by the Academy of St. Luke and was exhibiting works at the salon there.

Vigée-Lebrun's natural instinct for innovative poses and compositions, combined with her ability to produce a flattering likeness, soon brought her many influential clients. One of the first of these was the Russian nobleman Count Ivan Shuvaloff, whose patronage helped establish her among the aristocracy. It was in 1776 that she received her first royal commission for several portraits of the king's brother—and she also married the art dealer Jean-Baptiste-Pierre Lebrun. Her growing reputation as a painter, coupled with her own attractive personality, now drew the cream of Parisian society to the musical and literary entertainments held in her home.

LIFE'S WORK
In 1779, Vigée-Lebrun painted the first of many portraits from life of Marie-Antoinette, with the result that her name and her art became closely associated, in the public's mind, with the queen. Royal patronage was responsible, in fact, for Vigée-Lebrun's election to membership

in the Royal Academy. While excluding women from its classes, the Royal Academy admitted a few women as academicians, but without all the privileges given to male members. Essentially, academy membership gave a woman only two advantages: some prestige and the right to exhibit in the salons. Earlier, Vernet had proposed Vigée-Lebrun for membership, but it had been denied when Jean-Baptiste Pierre, first painter to the king, objected on the basis of her marriage to an art dealer. Her eventual acceptance in 1783 was said to be attributable to the direct intervention of the queen. Pierre, envious of both Vigée-Lebrun's talent and her obviously favorable standing with the king and queen, then attempted to discredit her, claiming that the painter François-Guillaume Ménageot had retouched her reception piece—an allegorical painting entitled *Peace Bringing Back Plenty*.

Between 1783 and 1789, Vigée-Lebrun exhibited some forty portraits and history paintings in the academy's salon, including the famous *Marie Antoinette and Her Children*, now in the National Museum at Versailles. Painted in 1787, this work is significant for two reasons: First, commissioned by the minister of fine arts to replace an unsatisfactorily casual portrait of the queen and her children by Adolf Wertmüller, it acknowledged Vigée-Lebrun as one of the leading artists in France. Second, it illustrates many of the most important characteristics of her mature style. Using the pyramidal composition of the Italian High Renaissance, she created a didactic work that presents the queen favorably as both ruler and mother. As she so often did, Vigée-Lebrun has translated human emotions—in this case, the love between a mother and her children—into dramatic facial expressions and gestures, while at the same time emphasizing the regal dignity of the queen. The painting illustrates the superiority of Vigée-Lebrun's artistic intellect and technical mastery, as all details of costume and setting combine harmoniously with expression and gesture to give meaning to the work as a whole. This was the painting that she herself considered her masterpiece. It had fortunately escaped destruction when the revolutionary mobs invaded the palace at Versailles because the queen—finding the painting a too-painful reminder after the death of the young prince—had ordered it removed to a storeroom. Near the end of her long career, Vigée-Lebrun arranged for the painting to be exhibited publicly in the Museum of the History of France at Versailles, as evidence of her artistic legacy to the nation.

Given her strong Royalist convictions, Vigée-Lebrun was forced to flee Paris on the eve of the revolution. In her memoirs, she recorded the details of her flight by

A portrait of the young Louis XVII by French painter Élisabeth Vigée-Lebrun. (Library of Congress)

public coach—disguised in peasant dress and accompanied by her young daughter—on the very night the mobs dragged the king and queen from Versailles. For the next twelve years, Vigée-Lebrun worked in Italy, Austria, Germany, and Russia. Having already achieved an international reputation as a painter, she was welcomed into aristocratic circles and honored by membership in the local academy in each city she visited. Possessed of an enormous energy for work and never lacking for commissions—for which she demanded fees that no other portraitist could command—Vigée-Lebrun produced some of her best work during these years.

She continued to make her own original contributions to the art of portraiture and to the taste of the time. She retained the virtuoso, almost impressionistic, brushwork that had first appeared in the early portrait of Count Shuvaloff (1775), as well as the bold coloristic effects she had learned from studying Rubens. A good example of her work from this period is her own portrait (1790), which she was asked to add to the Grand-Ducal collection of artists' self-portraits in the Uffizi in Florence. First exhibited in Rome, this work received wide acclaim, with the director of the French Academy there declaring it to be one of the most beautiful things Vigée-Lebrun had ever done. Other noteworthy examples include the portraits she painted in Russia, which are especially remarkable in terms of the variety of their imagery and the originality of composition, reflecting something of the exoticism and melancholy of the country itself.

Returning finally to Paris in 1801, she was received warmly but stayed only a short time, having found the city too much changed from prerevolutionary days. She went on to London and remained there for three years. Again, she found many clients among the aristocracy, including the prince of Wales. The quality, as well as the popularity, of her work aroused the jealousy of some English artists but brought praise from Sir Joshua Reynolds.

After spending a year in Switzerland, Vigée-Lebrun, now in her fifties, returned to Paris in 1805. She led a quieter life, dividing her time between Paris and her country home in Louveciennes. She painted less, apparently having lost much of the inspiration provided by her early struggles to achieve stature in the art world and the stimulus of her extensive travels, although she continued to exhibit at the salon until 1824. Her last years were spent writing her memoirs and entertaining old friends, as well as many of the leaders of the new Romantic movement. She died in Paris on March 30, 1842, at the age of eighty-six.

SIGNIFICANCE

Élisabeth Vigée-Lebrun was one of the most successful women artists of all time, achieving an artistic acclaim during her own lifetime that remained unmatched by any other woman until modern times. She excelled in a field that was popular and very competitive, but her success was not without a price. As the monarchy became more and more unpopular in prerevolutionary France, her accomplishments as a court painter made her a figure of controversy, with both the liberal press and the yellow journals labeling her an immoral woman, the mistress of various court officials, who attained academy membership with a reception piece painted by one of her lovers. Much of the gossip and slander also centered on her well-attended salon and the extravagance of her entertaining.

Far from being profligate, she was in fact victimized throughout her life by two men who exploited her talent and appropriated her money for their own ends. The first was her miserly stepfather, and the second was her husband, whose gambling debts were a financial drain on her until his death in 1813. Yet she never allowed these

problems to interfere with her work. In the more than eight hundred paintings she produced, optimism prevailed. Her work—and the pleasure she took in it—was the driving force of her life.

—*LouAnn Faris Culley*

FURTHER READING

Baillio, Joseph. *Élisabeth Louise Vigée Le Brun: 1755-1842*. Fort Worth, Tex.: Kimbell Art Museum, 1982. A catalog of the first twentieth century exhibition of Vigée-Lebrun's work. Contains a brief but informative account of her career, a listing of works exhibited in Paris during her lifetime, and complete notes and documentation of the paintings shown in this exhibition, which were selected from museums and private collections there and throughout Europe.

Goodden, Angelica. *The Sweetness of Life: A Biography of Élisabeth Louise Vigée Le Brun*. London: Andre Deutsch, 1997. Comprehensive, objective biography, based upon extensive research of primary sources. Goodden acknowledges critics who claim Vigée-Lebrun's art is complaisant, but explains how this complacency derived from the the economic and aesthetic constraints under which Vigée-Lebrun worked.

Harris, Ann Sutherland, and Linda Nochlin. *Women Artists, 1550-1950*. Los Angeles: Los Angeles County Museum of Art, 1976. The catalog of one of the first exhibitions devoted entirely to women artists. It includes a perceptive discussion of Vigée-Lebrun's career and the development of her style as seen in several works in the exhibition. Also, an enlightening account of restrictions endured by women artists, in their training, in relationships with the academies, and in conditions imposed by society.

Petersen, Karen, and J. Wilson. *Women Artists*. New York: Harper & Row, 1976. An appraisal of works by women artists from the Middle Ages to the present. Contains a discussion of Vigée-Lebrun's work, placing it in the context of the eighteenth century.

Sheriff, Mary D. *The Exceptional Woman: Élisabeth Vigée-Lebrun and the Cultural Politics of Art*. Chicago: University of Chicago Press, 1996. Examines the contradictory role of women artists in eighteenth century French society, describing how Vigée-Lebrun was simultaneously flattered and vilified because of the cultural and social attitudes of her time.

Vigée-Lebrun, Élisabeth. *The Memoirs of Mme Élisabeth Louise Vigée-Le Brun, 1775-1789*. Translated by Gerald Shelley. New York: George H. Doran, 1927. An abridged translation of her memoirs, published originally in 1835-1837. This volume, more widely available than the earlier translation (see below), also includes her previously untranslated notes and portraits of many of the leading figures in the arts and politics of her day, all of whom were personal friends or acquaintances of the artist.

_____. *Memoirs of Madame Vigée Lebrun*. Translated by Lionel Strachey. New York: Doubleday, Page, 1903. A less-abridged English translation of Vigée-

Lebrun's memoirs. Provides a fascinating account of European society at the time.

See also: Marie-Antoinette; Sir Joshua Reynolds.
Related articles in *Great Events from History: The Eighteenth Century, 1701-1800*: December 10, 1768: Britain's Royal Academy of Arts Is Founded; 1785: Construction of El Prado Museum Begins; 1787: David Paints *The Death of Socrates*.

ANTONIO VIVALDI
Italian composer

As the most influential and original Italian composer of the early eighteenth century, Vivaldi developed the basic form of the Baroque concerto and made it the standard for instrumental music throughout much of Europe. He was a pioneer of program music, and his techniques of orchestration and lyrical violin style anticipated the Romanticism of the nineteenth century.

Born: March 4, 1678; Venice (now in Italy)
Died: July 28, 1741; Vienna, Austria
Also known as: Antonio Lucio Vivaldi (full name)
Area of achievement: Music

EARLY LIFE

Antonio Vivaldi (ahn-TAWN-yoh vee-VAHL-dee) was the eldest of six children born to Giovanni Battista Vivaldi, the son of a baker from the town of Brescia. After his father's death in 1666, Giovanni Battista was taken to Venice, where he eventually worked, at least part-time, as both a baker and a barber. In 1685, however, he was hired as a violinist at the Cathedral of St. Mark, which, like most larger churches in Europe, had its own orchestra. He achieved a certain amount of local fame as a musician, opera manager, and composer under the surname Rossi (Italian for "red"), apparently because of his red hair. Antonio Vivaldi was later to be known by the sobriquet "Il Prete Rosso" ("the red priest") for the same reason.

When Antonio was born, the midwife who delivered him performed an emergency baptism because of a *pericolo di morte*, or "risk of death." What exactly this risk was is unclear; a likely explanation is that the serious ailment that Vivaldi claimed afflicted him throughout his life had appeared at birth. The composer himself called his condition a *strettezza di petto*, or a "tightness of the chest," and various diagnoses, from asthma to angina pectoris, have been offered by historians.

Very little else is known about Vivaldi's childhood. He was probably taught to play the violin by his father. By age ten, he is reputed to have played in the cathedral orchestra whenever his father was occupied elsewhere. It was decided at some point that Vivaldi would be trained for the priesthood, since this was the only way for a commoner to achieve upward social mobility. Thus, in 1693, Vivaldi was tonsured and took minor orders. He received his instruction from the clergy of two local churches, and he was allowed to live at home, either because of his illness or to allow him to continue studying the violin. He was ordained, after ten years of training, in 1703.

Within months of becoming a priest, Vivaldi received his first professional appointment, as *maestro di violino* (violin instructor) at the Pio Ospedale della Pietà, one of four Venetian orphanages that specialized in the musical training of abandoned or indigent girls. He thereupon ceased to say masses, though he always remained outwardly pious and wrote a large quantity of splendid religious music. He later defended his decision by claiming that his chest ailment made him unable to perform the ceremony. It is equally likely that he simply preferred not to be distracted from his musical activities. Until the nineteenth century, it was not at all unusual for priests to engage in secular professions, especially in Italy.

LIFE'S WORK

In eighteenth century Venice, the four musical orphanages, and especially the Pietà, were so renowned for the quality of their instrumental and vocal instruction that their religious services had become great social affairs, much more like public concerts, with a wide variety of secular and religious music being performed. A visit to at least one of these services was considered essential by tourists, and the Pietà's chapel was always filled to capacity.

Vivaldi's position was therefore extremely important. He was required not only to provide competent instruction, to rehearse the orchestra, and to purchase and maintain its stringed instruments but also to compose a constant supply of new music for its performances. In fact, his first published works, a set of twelve trio sonatas (Op. 1), were completed in his first year on the job. Within a few more years, he wrote a set of violin sonatas (Op. 2) and a variety of concerti for various solo instruments and strings.

These concerti, and those that followed, had an immediate and dramatic impact on the European music scene. In Germany, especially, they achieved great popularity. In 1711, Vivaldi's most influential work, *L'estro armonico* (Op. 3), was published, and Johann Sebastian Bach transcribed several of its twelve violin concerti for harpsichord and strings. Other composers also copied Vivaldi's style, and several, such as Gottfried Stölzel, went to Venice to seek him out. Vivaldi is credited with having reformed the concerto by standardizing a three-movement, fast-slow-fast structure and creating thematically distinct solo parts alternating with full-ensemble ritornellos (refrains in different keys).

Vivaldi continued to compose instrumental works throughout his life; ultimately, these totaled more than five hundred inventive, deftly orchestrated concerti and sinfonias, and more than ninety sonatas. Perhaps the most famous of his works, *Il cimento dell'armonia e dell'inventione* (twelve concerti, Op. 8), appeared in about 1725. Its first four concerti, which have been immortalized as *The Four Seasons*, contain probably the most clearly articulated program music of the Baroque era. The listener can easily visualize the bubbling brook of "Spring," the hot sun of "Summer," and other images these concerti evoke.

Long before this, however, Vivaldi had already embarked upon a career in opera. His first known stage work was produced in May, 1713, and several more were performed in Venice in the years following. From 1718 to 1726, he was usually on the road in Mantua and Rome, producing and directing new operas. While in Rome, he also performed twice for the pope, and, in 1719, he received a new appointment (in addition to his position at the Pietà) as court composer to the governor of Mantua. In 1727, he dedicated a set of twelve concerti, *La cetra* (Op. 9), to the Holy Roman Emperor Charles VI, who was said to have given Vivaldi a considerable amount of money, a golden chain and medallion, and a knighthood.

As his reputation spread far and wide, so also did Vivaldi's travels. In 1729, he visited Vienna, where his father, who had accompanied him, is believed to have died. In 1730, he may also have gone to Prague, where an Italian company staged two of his new operas. Vivaldi always preferred to oversee productions of his works himself, and he often blamed his few failures on changes made by others. In 1733, he returned temporarily to Venice, but after 1735 he chose to produce new operas in other cities of Italy, especially Ferrara.

While at Ferrara, Vivaldi got into a dispute over a singer's contract and his choice of operas for performance. This may have reflected a decline in his popularity there. Three of his works were box-office failures, but Vivaldi nevertheless insisted upon receiving the maximum payment stipulated in his agreement with the theater managers. These problems evidently led the cardinal of Ferrara (which was a papal domain), in 1737, to censure Vivaldi and forbid him to enter the city. The composer was accused of having illicit relations with Anna Giraud, a famous contralto who was a member of his entourage, in addition to refusing to say Mass. Vivaldi vehemently denied the first accusation, and he blamed his failure to conduct masses on his disease. Nevertheless, his last opera written for Ferrara was performed without his supervision and was a conspicuous flop. Vivaldi, however, turned the situation to good account: He was now free to journey to Amsterdam to conduct several performances of his instrumental music.

Antonio Vivaldi. (Hulton Archive/Getty Images)

Naturally, all of this traveling affected his work for the Pietà, and his relations with the board of governors were occasionally stormy. In 1716, he had been promoted to *maestro de' concerti*, but his travels prevented him from sustained teaching, and he often had to send new compositions to the Pietà by mail. Even so, he was promoted to *maestro di cappella* in 1735, only to be fired three years later. He continued to supply the Pietà with occasional concerti, and even directed performances there, as late as 1740.

In that year, or possibly early in 1741, Vivaldi undertook a mysterious journey to Vienna, the purpose of which is still unclear. It is known that he sold a group of concerti manuscripts there and that he was in dire financial straits. When he died, on July 28, 1741, of what was called an "internal inflammation," he was living in the house of a saddler's widow. Like Wolfgang Amadeus Mozart fifty years later, he was given a pauper's funeral.

SIGNIFICANCE

Few known portraits of Antonio Vivaldi exist, and these differ vastly from one another. A famous caricature, sketched by Pier Leone Ghezzi in 1723, gives him a long nose, a jutting chin, and a look of avidity, while a contemporary anonymous painting makes him appear fragile and pensive. These conflicting images reflect the difficulty in evaluating his personality. His lifestyle was extravagant, flamboyant, and unconventional, and he had many enemies. He was notorious for his vanity and sensitivity to criticism, and was more highly regarded by his Italian contemporaries for his skills as a violinist than for his originality as a composer.

Vivaldi also had a reputation as a hard bargainer, and his concern with money may have been excessive. Some of the personal pettiness and greed that Vivaldi occasionally displayed may have been a reaction to the fact that his disease disabled him. Moreover, traveling with a large entourage, including a nurse, was very expensive. None of his critics, however, questioned Vivaldi's tremendous, almost fanatic, dedication to music, or the virtuosity of his violin technique. Though the fame of his operas evaporated almost immediately after his death, the emotional force and energy of his instrumental works continued to be acknowledged for several decades.

Oddly enough, it was probably these very qualities that led to Vivaldi's subsequent oblivion. The classical period had little use, on one hand, for what was characterized as the "wild and irregular" emotionalism of his concerti, while, on the other, he was reproached for churning out too many routine works pandering to medi-ocre public tastes. Like many Baroque composers, he fell into obscurity until the Bach revival that took place in the 1840's. Even then, however, he was simply regarded as one of Bach's precursors. His contributions to the development of the concerto form, and Bach's imitation of it, were not acknowledged until the beginning of the twentieth century.

Studies of Vivaldi were given a great boost by the discovery of his personal collection of manuscripts in the 1920's, but it was not until the Turin musicologist Alberto Gentili obtained a vast, previously unknown collection of his works in 1930 that Vivaldi's importance began to be truly realized. His reputation was fully rehabilitated by the first publication of his collected works in 1947 and by a famous study of the composer by the French musicologist Marc Pincherle. In the years since, enthusiasm for the music of Vivaldi has continued to grow: Thousands of Vivaldi recordings have been issued, especially of *The Four Seasons*, and these concerti and others have provided background music for many popular films. Millions of people who would otherwise have no interest in, or awareness of, Baroque music thus have been attracted to its beauties. Beyond Vivaldi's contributions to the development of the concerto form and his innovations in orchestration and violin technique, this is perhaps his most important achievement.

—*Thomas C. Schunk*

FURTHER READING

Arnold, Denis. "Vivaldi." In *The New Grove Italian Baroque Masters*, edited by Denis Arnold et al. New York: W. W. Norton, 1984. An excellent concise biography, one of seven included in this volume, all by noted musical scholars. Discusses Vivaldi's life, music, and influence on other composers. Contains an updated catalog of Vivaldi's works, as well as a comprehensive bibliography.

Barbier, Patrick. *Vivaldi's Venice: Music and Celebration in the Baroque Era*. Translated from the French by Margaret Crosland. London: Souvenir, 2003. In the years Vivaldi grew up and lived in Venice, the city was filled with music at concerts, the theater, carnivals, and other events attended by those of all social classes. Barbier describes the city, its people, and the various types of music that were popular during Vivaldi's lifetime.

Borroff, Edith. *The Music of the Baroque*. Dubuque, Iowa: Wm. C. Brown, 1970. A brief introduction to Baroque music for students with little musical background. Provides many musical examples that are explained sufficiently to allow beginning students to learn a substantial amount of music theory. Profusely illustrated. An outstanding feature is the inclusion of brief discographies for each type and area of music discussed.

Kolneder, Walter. *Antonio Vivaldi: His Life and Work.* Translated by Bill Hopkins. Berkeley: University of California Press, 1970. Kolneder has replaced Pincherle as the standard full-length biography of Vivaldi. Extremely well written, but difficult for those without a solid background in music theory. In addition to an extensive, but unclassified, bibliography, Kolneder provides many musical examples.

Landon, H. C. Robbins. *Vivaldi: Voice of the Baroque.* New York: Thames & Hudson, 1993. Concise popular biography drawing upon newly discovered correspondence and documents. Landon explains why, with the exception of *The Four Seasons* and the *Second Gloria in D*, Vivaldi's music is generally ignored.

Pincherle, Marc. *Vivaldi, Genius of the Baroque.* Translated by Christopher Hatch. New York: W. W. Norton, 1957. Pincherle was the scholar primarily responsible for the post-World War II Vivaldi revival. In addition to this seminal study, Pincherle also published the first comprehensive catalog of Vivaldi's works. Although this work has been superseded by later research, it is still excellent reading and a good source for the nonspecialist.

Selfridge-Field, Eleonor. *Venetian Instrumental Music from Gabrieli to Vivaldi.* Edited by F. W. Sternfield. Oxford, England: Basil Blackwell, 1975. An outstanding study of the Venetian Baroque, including a full analysis of many of Vivaldi's works, as well as those of his Venetian contemporaries. Suggests that Vivaldi's legacy to later composers may have been greater than is generally acknowledged. Surveys the history of Venetian musical practice and organizations and includes an excellent glossary of Baroque musical terms and instruments.

Talbot, Michael. *Vivaldi.* London: J. M. Dent & Sons, 1978. Reprint. New York: Oxford University Press, 2000. The best all-around discussion of Vivaldi's life, works, and impact. Among other features, it includes a complete list of Vivaldi's works, a chronological outline, and an extensive bibliography. A scholarly work with abundant evidence of original research (including excerpts from many of Vivaldi's extant letters), well written, and entertaining. Highly recommended.

See also: Johann Sebastian Bach; Charles VI; George Frideric Handel; Joseph Haydn; Wolfgang Amadeus Mozart.

Related articles in *Great Events from History: The Eighteenth Century, 1701-1800*: c. 1701-1750: Bach Pioneers Modern Music; c. 1709: Invention of the Piano; April 13, 1742: First Performance of Handel's *Messiah*; January, 1762-November, 1766: Mozart Tours Europe as a Child Prodigy; 1795-1797: Paganini's Early Violin Performances.

ALESSANDRO VOLTA
Italian physicist

Volta contributed to the development of concepts and techniques in electrostatics, including the inventions of the electrophorus and the condensing electrometer. His most important contributions were the discovery of contact electricity and the invention of the electric battery.

Born: February 18, 1745; Como, Duchy of Milan (now in Italy)
Died: March 5, 1827; Como, Duchy of Milan
Also known as: Count Alessandro Volta; Alessandro Giuseppe Antonio Anastasio Volta (full name)
Areas of achievement: Physics, chemistry, science and technology

EARLY LIFE

Alessandro Volta (ah-lays-SAHN-droh VAWL-tah) was the youngest of nine children born to Filippo and Maddalena Volta in the ancient Roman town of Como, on Lake Como in what is now northern Italy. His father was a member of the Jesuit order for eleven years before withdrawing to wed Maddalena dei Conti Inzaghi, who was twenty-two years younger than he. Although Volta's family was from the local nobility, his father had spent the family fortune and gone into debt before Alessandro's birth. Three of his brothers became priests, and two of his sisters became nuns. Throughout his life, he was active in the Catholic religion.

Although Volta did not talk until he was four, he began to excel early in school and showed special ability in foreign languages. When Volta was about seven years old, his father died, but with the aid of his two uncles he attended the local Jesuit college, where attempts were made to recruit him to the priesthood. After completing the classical course of education at the age of sixteen, Volta continued his education until 1765 at the Seminario Benzi, where he was attracted to the natural sciences. There he wrote a long Latin poem of some five hundred verses, mostly celebrating the work of the English chemist Joseph Priestley, who later wrote a two-volume history of electricity.

By the age of eighteen, Volta had decided to devote himself to the study of electricity. In 1763, he began a correspondence with the eminent French electrical scientist l'Abbé Jean-Antoine Nollet. In these letters, he supported Roger Joseph Boscovich in suggesting that electrical attraction followed the Newtonian concept of action at a distance instead of the direct emission and absorption of electrical effluvia as taught by Nollet. He also began an experimental study of electricity, with equipment and laboratory facilities provided by his friend and benefactor Giulio Gattoni. After learning of Benjamin Franklin's work, Volta and Gattoni constructed the first lightning rod in Como and studied the electricity collected by it. Volta's concentration on his work was so great that he often missed meals, slept little, and was unaware of the condition of his clothing. He soon developed a genius for inventing inexpensive but effective apparatuses, which led to a successful career.

LIFE'S WORK

Volta's research in static electricity was the foundation for his later invention of the electric battery. The first results of his work were sent in 1765 to Giovanni Beccaria, professor of physics at the University of Turin and the leading Italian electrical scientist. In a series of letters, Volta described his design of a machine to produce electrostatic effects and reported on which materials would become positive and which negative when rubbed together. Volta's correspondence with Beccaria led to Volta's first publication, *De vi attractiva ignis electrici* (1769; on the attractive force of electric fire). This seventy-two-page treatise boldly reinterpreted Beccaria's experiments and Franklin's theory of a self-repulsive electrical fluid in terms of a consistent principle of attraction. In this book and a second book in 1771, Volta remained faithful to Franklin's theory of a single electric fluid but suggested that all materials are in electrical equilibrium until disturbed by frictional activity.

Volta was appointed to his first academic post in 1774 as principal of the state school in Como, previously under Jesuit control. He was a large and vigorous man, with wide social contacts. In 1775, he sent a letter to Priestley, announcing the invention of his electrophorus, which he viewed as a kind of perpetual source of electrical fluid. This device consisted of a flat insulating cake made of three parts turpentine, two parts resin, and one part wax, hardened in a metal dish and covered by a metal plate with an insulated handle. After the cake has been rubbed, the plate can be set on it and briefly touched to transfer electrical fluid by induction. The plate thus charged can be lifted and discharged into a Leyden jar to store it; the operation can be repeated many times. The device became very popular, and its induction process reinforced Volta's emphasis on action at a distance and the similar ideas of Franz Aepinus. With his increasing fame, Volta was able to shift from administrator to professor of experimental physics without the usual examination.

Volta's interests expanded into chemistry in 1778, with his discovery of inflammable marsh gas, now called methane, in Lake Maggiore. He collected this gas from bubbles rising to the surface, especially in shallow, marshy locations. He used his electrophorus to ignite the gas from the discharge of a spark in what he called an electric pistol and correctly explained its source as decaying animal and vegetable matter. Similar experiments with hydrogen led to measurements of the contraction of air when exploded with an equal volume of hydrogen in his eudiometer, giving a total reduction of 3/5. This corresponds to a 1/5 contraction of air, consistent with later measurements of the oxygen content.

In a famous letter written in 1777, Volta proposed an electric signal line from Como to Milan, on which a Leyden jar could be discharged at one end, causing the detonation of an electric pistol at the other end. His increasing fame led to a state-supported trip to some of the chief science centers of Europe and a new position in 1778 as professor of experimental physics at the University of Pavia. During nearly forty years in this position, Volta was able to obtain an excellent collection of instruments at state expense. On a second tour of Europe in 1782, he met the astronomer Pierre-Simon Laplace, the chemist Antoine-Laurent Lavoisier, and, most important, Franklin and Priestley. On his return, he introduced the American potato to Italian farmers. He continued his work on gases at Pavia, accurately measuring the thermal expansion of gases twenty years before Joseph-Louis Gay-Lussac.

Count Alessandro Volta. (The Granger Collection, New York)

During this time, Volta perfected his condensing electrometer, a more sensitive and less expensive form of the contemporaneous gold-leaf electrometer. In place of gold leaves, he suspended two fine straws in a square glass bottle, with a protractor scale on one face to give the degree of their divergence. The straws were suspended from a metal cover forming the base of a small electrophorus, with a thin slab of marble on top for the insulating cake. A movable upper plate had an increased capacity for storing charge because of the thinner cake, making it extremely sensitive to even minute charges. Lifting the upper plate increased the divergence of the electrometer straws. Following Henry Cavendish, Volta referred to this effect as increased tension resulting from decreased capacity and proposed a unit of tension (later called electric potential or voltage) in which a 1-degree spread of the straws corresponds to about 40 volts in modern measure. He also showed that electrical attraction on the upper plate follows the force law discovered by Charles-Augustin de Coulomb.

In 1792, Volta repeated Luigi Galvani's experiments, published in Bologna in 1791, in which a metal attached to a frog's crural nerve was brought in contact with a different metal attached to its leg muscle, causing it to con-

tract. Characteristically, Volta tried to measure the effect and found a tension of only a fraction of a degree on his condensing electrometer. At first, he accepted Galvani's idea that this was a unique form of animal electricity, but by the end of the year he concluded that the electricity was from the metals rather than the muscles. To illustrate the function of the metals, Volta joined a piece of tin on the tip of his tongue to a silver spoon touching farther back and experienced a sour taste. Early in 1793, he announced his conclusions in an open letter to Galvani's nephew and defender, Giovanni Aldini, beginning a long debate. Volta's position was strengthened by measurements of what he called the electromotive force of different combinations of conductors with his condensing electrometer, ranking them in what is now called the electrochemical series.

In 1794, Volta married Teresa Peregrina, and he quickly added three sons to his new family. In the same year, he became the first foreigner to win the Copley Medal from the Royal Society of London for his contributions to physics and chemistry. By 1796, he had shown the identity of galvanic and common electricity by stimulating his electrometer with only metals in contact. After trying various combinations of metals and moist conductors, he finally obtained a sustained galvanic current by placing a moist cardboard between two different metals. He increased this effect by stacking such pairs of silver and zinc disks to form an electric pile to multiply the flow of galvanic electricity. These results were made public in 1800 in a letter to Sir Joseph Banks, president of the Royal Society, and first published in its *Philosophical Transactions* in French under the English title "On the Electricity Excited by the Mere Contact of Conducting Substances of Different Kinds" (1800). The letter also described his "crown of cups," consisting of a ring of cups filled with brine and connected by bimetallic arcs dipping into the liquid.

Volta might have published his work earlier had it not been for the distraction of the French invasion of Italy in 1796, which caused some damage to his laboratory and the closing of the university in 1799 for a year. In 1801, he demonstrated his work at the Paris Academy, where Napoleon I proposed that he be awarded a gold medal. Napoleon was so impressed with Volta's discoveries that he gave him a pension and later made him a count and senator of the kingdom of Lombardy. He continued with a reduced schedule at the university until after the Austrians returned in 1814, and retired to Como in 1819, where he died after a long illness in 1827, on the same day as Laplace. During the last twenty years of his life, he enjoyed a large income from his pension and senatorial salaries but published only two minor scientific papers.

SIGNIFICANCE

Alessandro Volta is a good example of a devoted scientist whose concentration and effort led to important discoveries and inventions. He was a deeply religious man who saw science and Christianity as allies, even seeking to defend religion from scientism with a confession of faith written in 1815. His many years of painstaking research in electrostatics and chemistry prepared him to capitalize on Galvani's discovery of electricity in frogs. His prior inventions of the electrophorus and condensing electrometer helped him to explore the effects of galvanic electricity and demonstrate its equivalence with common electricity. His tireless efforts and hard-earned experience led to his crowning achievement in the invention of the voltaic pile.

Volta's electric battery was one of the most important inventions of all time, providing the first useful form of electricity. The electrical revolution of the nineteenth century began with this one creation. In 1800, the year of its announcement, the English chemists William Nicholson and Anthony Carlisle used it to decompose water. Sir Humphry Davy built a powerful battery of five hundred plates at London's Royal Institution and by 1808 had discovered potassium, sodium, calcium, magnesium, barium, strontium, and chlorine by electrolytic decomposition. Applications of discoveries that stem from Volta's research have changed the world. Among the many honors paid to the founder of this revolution, perhaps the greatest was the international agreement in 1881 to name the unit of electromotive force the volt, recognizing the means of producing constant electric current that Volta gave to humankind.

—*Joseph L. Spradley*

FURTHER READING

Dibner, Bern. *Alessandro Volta and the Electric Battery*. New York: Franklin Watts, 1964. This biography of Volta includes historical background on the development of electricity, his early life and work, Galvani's discovery and the resulting controversy, and the invention of the battery and its resulting influence. An appendix gives the English version of his letter to Banks, announcing his invention.

_____. *Galvani-Volta: A Controversy That Led to the Discovery of Useful Electricity*. Norwalk, Conn.: Burndy Library, 1952. This brief volume describes the work of Galvani, the defense of his ideas by Aldini, the work of Volta, the controversy that followed, and the results of Volta's work. A supplement gives a facsimile of Volta's letter to Banks in English translation as it appeared in *The Philosophical Magazine* in 1800.

Fara, Patricia. *An Enlightenment for Angels: Electricity in the Enlightenment*. Lanham, Md.: Totem Books, 2002. Provides brief explanations of experiments conducted by Volta, Galvani, Benjamin Franklin, and other seventeenth and eighteenth century scientists who studied electricity.

Heilbron, J. L. *Electricity in the Seventeenth and Eighteenth Centuries: A Study of Early Modern Physics*. Berkeley: University of California Press, 1979. This volume is an exhaustive study of the history of electricity up to the time of Volta. It includes a detailed analysis of his work in electrostatics but only a brief epilogue on the voltaic pile. Bibliography includes ten entries on the works of Volta.

Pancaldi, Giuliano. *Volta: Science and Culture in the Age of Enlightenment*. Princeton, N.J.: Princeton University Press, 2003. Focuses on the experiences in Volta's life that transformed him from an amateur experimenter to an expert on electricity, including his experiments with torpedo fish that led him to invent the battery.

Pera, Marcello. *The Ambiguous Frog: The Galvani-Volta Controversy on Animal Electricity*. Translated by Jonathan Mandelbaum. Princeton, N.J.: Princeton University Press, 1992. Recounts how the two scientists offered different theories to explain why a dead frog's muscles contracted when stimulated by electricity. Pera describes theories of electricity in the 1790's, and compares the careers and laboratory procedures of Volta and Galvani.

Piccolino, Marco. *The Taming of the Ray: Electric Fish Research in the Enlightenment from John Walsh to Alessandro Volta*. Florence, Italy: Leo S. Olschki, 2003. Several scientists in the late eighteenth century conducted experiments that led them to discover the electrical properties of fish. The first of these experiments was believed to have been conducted by John Walsh, an Englishman, who studied torpedo fish from 1792 through 1795. Volta later conducted similar studies, which led him to invent the battery.

Potamian, Michael, and James Walsh. *Makers of Electricity*. Bronx, N.Y.: Fordham University Press, 1909. Chapter 5 in this volume, "Volta the Founder of Electrical Science," gives a somewhat dated but interesting and readable account of Volta's life and work.

Still, Alfred. *Soul of Amber.* New York: Murray Hill Books, 1944. Chapter 6 in this history of electrical science, titled "Electrical Science Becomes Methodical," includes a description of Volta's work on electrostatics. Chapter 8, "Electricity in Motion," includes a discussion of the invention of the voltaic pile. Each chapter contains about thirty bibliographic references.

See also: Sir Joseph Banks; Henry Cavendish; Benjamin Franklin; Luigi Galvani; Antoine-Laurent Lavoisier; Joseph Priestley.

Related articles in *Great Events from History: The Eighteenth Century, 1701-1800*: 1704: Newton Publishes *Optics*; 1723: Stahl Postulates the Phlogiston Theory; 1729: Gray Discovers Principles of Electric Conductivity; 1733: Du Fay Discovers Two Kinds of Electric Charge; October, 1745, and January, 1746: Invention of the Leyden Jar; June, 1752: Franklin Demonstrates the Electrical Nature of Lightning; 1759: Aepinus Publishes *Essay on the Theory of Electricity and Magnetism*; 1779: Ingenhousz Discovers Photosynthesis; 1781-1784: Cavendish Discovers the Composition of Water; 1800: Volta Invents the Battery.

VOLTAIRE
French philosopher, writer, and dramatist

Voltaire encompassed in his work both extremes of Enlightenment rationalism: He began his career as an optimist, but he later rejected this philosophy in disgust and brilliantly argued the limitations of reason. He wrote prolifically in all literary forms and commented critically on prevailing social conditions and conventions.

Born: November 21, 1694; Paris, France
Died: May 30, 1778; Paris, France
Also known as: François-Marie Arouet (birth name); François-Marie Arouet de Voltaire
Areas of achievement: Literature, theater, philosophy

EARLY LIFE
Voltaire (vahl-tehr) was born François-Marie Arouet on November 21, 1694, in Paris. His father had migrated to the capital from Poitou and prospered there. He held a minor post in the treasury. Arouet was educated at the Jesuit Collège Louis-le-Grand, and many years later the Jesuits were to be the objects of savage satire in his masterpiece *Candide: Ou, L'Optimisme* (1759; *Candide: Or, All for the Best,* 1759; also as *Candide: Or, The Optimist,* 1762; also as *Candide: Or, Optimism,* 1947). Arouet was trained in the law, which he abandoned. As a young man, during the first quarter of the century, Arouet already strongly exhibited two traits that have come to be associated with the Enlightenment: wit and skepticism. Louis XIV ruled France until 1715, and the insouciant Arouet and his circle of friends delighted in poking fun at the pretentious backwardness of the Sun King's court.

In 1716, when Arouet was twenty-two, his political satires prompted the first of his several exiles, in this instance to Sully-sur-Loire. He was, however, unrepentant: In 1717, more satirical verses on the aristocracy caused his imprisonment by *lettre de cachet* (without trial). During his eleven months in the Bastille, Voltaire, like so many imprisoned writers before him, practiced his craft. He wrote a tragedy, *Œdipe* (pr. 1718, pb. 1719; *Oedipus,* 1761), which was a great success on the stage following his release. A year later, when *Oedipus* came out in print, the author took the name Voltaire, an approximate anagram of Arouet. Such was his fame, however, that the pseudonym afforded him little chance of anonymity. He came to be known as François-Marie Arouet de Voltaire.

LIFE'S WORK
By the age of thirty, Voltaire was well established as a man of letters. For the next fifty years, he produced an enormous and varied body of work; he wrote tragic plays, satires in prose and verse, histories, philosophical tales, essays, pamphlets, encyclopedia entries, and letters by the thousands. Also by the age of thirty, he was a wealthy man. He speculated in the Compagnie Française des Indes (French East India Company) with great success, and his fortune grew over the years. Voltaire's personal wealth afforded him an independence of which few writers of the period could boast.

Still, his penchant for religious and political controversy had him in trouble again by 1726. The chevalier de Rohan caused him to be beaten and incarcerated in the Bastille for a second time. He was subsequently exiled to England, where he spent most of the period from 1726 to 1729. There, he learned the English language, read widely in the literature, and became the companion of

Alexander Pope and other wits of Queen Anne's era. *La Henriade* (1728; *Henriade*, 1732), his epic of Henry IV, was published during this period, and his sojourn in Britain would eventually produce *Lettres philosophiques* (1734; originally published in English as *Letters Concerning the English Nation*, 1733). Voltaire's great achievement during the years immediately following his return to France was his *Histoire de Charles XII* (1731; *The History of Charles XII*, 1732). This account of the Swedish monarch is often characterized as the first modern history.

Letters Concerning the English Nation implicitly attacked French institutions through its approbation of English institutions. For example, Voltaire wittily suggested that, despite the manifest benefits of inoculation against smallpox, the French rejected the practice simply because the English adopted it first. Again, Voltaire angered powerful enemies. His book was burned, he barely escaped imprisonment, and he was forced to flee Paris for a third time.

Voltaire settled at Cirey in Lorraine, first as the guest and eventually as the companion of the brilliant Marquise du Châtelet. There, for the next fifteen years, he continued to write in all genres, but, having become acquainted with the works of John Locke and David Hume, he turned increasingly to philosophical and scientific subjects. As revealed in his *Discours en vers sur l'homme* (1738; *Discourses in Verse on Man*, 1764), Voltaire embraced the philosophy of optimism during these years, believing that reason alone could lead humanity out of the darkness and into the millennium. Gradually, his reputation was rehabilitated within court circles. He had been given permission to return to Paris in 1735, he was named official historiographer of France in 1743, and he was elected to the French Academy in 1746. In 1748, he published his first philosophical tale, *Zadig: Ou, La Destinée, Histoire orientale* (originally as *Memnon: Histoire orientale*, 1747; *Zadig: Or, The Book of Fate*, 1749).

The Marquise du Châtelet died in 1749. The next year, believing that Louis XV had offered him insufficient patronage, Voltaire joined the court of Frederick the Great at Potsdam. For three years, Voltaire lived in great comfort and luxury, completing during this period *Le Siècle de Louis XIV* (1751; *The Age of Louis XIV*, 1752). Voltaire and the Prussian king, however, were not well suited temperamentally. They quarreled, and the inevitable breach occurred in 1753. Shortly thereafter, Voltaire purchased Les Délices (the delights), a château in Switzerland, near Geneva. He stayed in the good

Voltaire. (Library of Congress)

graces of the Swiss for exactly as long as he had managed in Prussia—three years.

The Swiss perceived Voltaire's *Encyclopedia* entry on Geneva as having a contemptuous tone. The national pride of his hosts was wounded, and he left the country. He bought the great estate Ferney, on French soil but just across the Swiss frontier. This was the perfect retreat for a controversialist with Voltaire's volatile history; if the French authorities decided to act against him again, he could simply slip across the border. For the last twenty years of his life, Voltaire used the Ferney estate as the base from which he tirelessly launched his literary attacks upon superstition, error, and ignorance. He employed a variety of pseudonyms but made no effort to disguise his inimitable style and manner. This transparent device gave the authorities, by then indulgent and weary of their repeated attempts to muzzle Voltaire, an excuse not to prosecute him.

The decade of the 1750's wrought a change in the middle-aged Voltaire's attitudes far greater than any change he had undergone previously. He was deeply affected by the Great Lisbon earthquake of November 1, 1755. In this horrendous tragedy, perhaps as many as

---

VOLTAIRE'S PANGLOSS

In Candide, *Voltaire mercilessly satirizes the optimistic rationalism of the Enlightenment. He introduces this point of view through a character named Pangloss, the tutor of the novel's title character, who teaches "metaphysico-theologo-cosmolo-nigology." The passage reproduced below represents a typical example of Pangloss's spurious reasoning.*

"It is proved," he used to say, "that things cannot be other than they are, for since everything was made for a purpose, it follows that everything is made for the best purpose. Observe: our noses were made to carry spectacles, so we have spectacles. Legs were clearly intended for breeches, and we wear them. Stones were meant for carving and for building houses, and that is why my lord has a most beautiful house; for the greatest baron in Westphalia ought to have the noblest residence. And since pigs were made to be eaten, we eat pork all the year round. It follows that those who maintain that all is right talk nonsense; they ought to say that all is for the best."

Source: Voltaire, *Candide: Or, Optimism.* Translated by John Butt (Baltimore: Penguin Books, 1947), p. 20.

---

its author's anti-Semitism, his anti-Catholicism, and his sexism.

The major work of Voltaire's later years was *Dictionnaire philosophique portatif* (1764; *A Philosophical Dictionary for the Pocket*, 1765). He also involved himself deeply in the day-to-day operations of Ferney, and he maintained his voluminous correspondence with virtually all the eminent persons of Europe. For the first time in almost three decades, Voltaire returned to Paris in 1778. He was afforded a tumultuous hero's welcome, but he was eighty-three and ill; the celebration was too much for him in his fragile state of health. He died on May 30, within weeks of his triumphal return to the city of his birth.

SIGNIFICANCE
Despite the Church's opposition to Voltaire's burial in sanctified ground, he was secretly—and inappropriately, some have suggested—interred at a convent outside the city. A decade later came the French Revolution, and Voltaire's enemies ostensibly became those of the French people as well. He was exhumed and made a second grand entrance into Paris, where he was reburied in the Panthéon next to Rousseau, an irony he might have enjoyed.

Voltaire's work is extremely varied and sometimes self-contradictory. His sentiments are often more personal than universal. He had had bad experiences with Jesuit priests, Protestant enthusiasts, and Jewish businessmen; hence, Jesuits, Calvinists, and Jews are mercilessly lampooned in *Candide*. He apparently had good experiences with Anabaptists, and the generous and selfless Anabaptist Jacques, in his brief appearance, is one of the few admirable characters in the novel. Voltaire had been cured of optimism by the horror of the Lisbon earthquake, the savagery of the Seven Years' War, and the reversals in his personal life, yet he did not completely give way to pessimism. His philosophy in his later years seems to have been a qualified meliorism, as characterized by his famous injunction that every individual should tend his (or her) own garden.

The famous and spurious quotation, "I disagree with everything you say, but I shall fight to the death for your right to say it," will be forever associated with Voltaire's memory. Although he probably never uttered these precise words, they are an admirable summation of the way he lived his intellectual life. The surviving pictures

fifty thousand people died, many while worshiping in packed churches on All Saints' Day. Voltaire began to reexamine his concept of a rational universe, functioning according to fixed laws that people could apprehend and to which they could adapt themselves. He was now repulsed by the optimists' theory that (to overstate it only slightly) this is the best of all possible worlds, and, therefore, any natural occurrence must ultimately be for the best. His first bitter attack on optimism was *Poème sur le désastre de Lisbonne* (1756; *Poem on the Lisbon Earthquake*, 1764). His rebuttal of this smug philosophy culminated in his masterpiece of dark comedy, *Candide*.

Voltaire claimed to have written this wildly improbable picaresque novel in three days during 1758. It was published in 1759 and was immensely popular; it averaged two new editions a year for the next twenty years. The novel's character of Pangloss, tutor to the incredibly callow hero, is a caricature of the optimistic philosophers Gottfried Wilhelm Leibniz and Christian von Wolff, although Voltaire's temperamental archenemy, Jean-Jacques Rousseau, fancied himself to be the real model for Pangloss. *Candide*'s satire is by no means limited to optimism, and the novel reveals the best and worst of its author's traits of character. Voltaire lashes out at his lifelong enemies, superstition, bigotry, extremism, hypocrisy, and (despite accounting for most of his personal wealth) colonialism. Also readily apparent in the text are of Voltaire, most in old age, represent him as thin, sharp-featured, and sardonic. He is the very embodiment of one aspect of the neoclassical period—skeptical, irreverent, and valuing personal freedom above all other things.

—Patrick Adcock

FURTHER READING

Aldington, Richard. *Voltaire*. London: Routledge & Kegan Paul, 1925. One of the standard works of critical biography. Treats both the life of Voltaire and his career as poet, dramatist, literary critic, historian, biographer, philosopher, pamphleteer, and correspondent. Contains a chronological listing of Voltaire's works by genre, followed by a list of the English translations (up to that time) and a selected bibliography.

Carlson, Marvin. *Voltaire and the Theater of the Eighteenth Century*. Westport, Conn.: Greenwood Press, 1998. Focuses on Voltaire's theatrical works, analyzing the content of his plays and describing how he was involved in acting, staging, and other aspects of production. Recounts Voltaire's experiences in England and Germany and describes the characteristics of theater in these countries and in other European nations during the eighteenth century.

Davidson, Ian. *Voltaire in Exile: The Last Years, 1773-1778*. London: Atlantic, 2004. Focuses on Voltaire's years in Geneva and Ferney, describing his life, companions, and community activities. Argues that before his exile, Voltaire was interested in establishing his reputation and making money, but during his exile he became a champion of human rights, justice, and judicial reform. Well written and researched, based in part on Voltaire's correspondence.

Gay, Peter. *Voltaire's Politics: The Poet as Realist*. Princeton, N.J.: Princeton University Press, 1959. An intellectual history that attempts to trace the psychological, social, and intellectual origins of Voltaire's ideas. Portrays Voltaire's politics as realistic and humanely relativistic; argues that Voltaire's humane sympathies failed him only in the case of his anti-Semitism.

Lanson, Gustave. *Voltaire*. Translated by Robert A. Wagoner with an introduction by Peter Gay. New York: John Wiley & Sons, 1966. This brief survey of Voltaire's life and work by a famous French literary historian was originally published in 1906 in French. It is an excellent introductory volume, which distinguishes between Voltaire's deeply held convictions and his more casual and whimsical arguments.

Mason, Haydn. *Voltaire: A Biography*. Baltimore: Johns Hopkins University Press, 1981. Organized according to seven periods in Voltaire's life. The author states that he has not attempted a comprehensive treatment of the life, because that would easily require ten volumes. Instead, he has attempted to capture Voltaire's essence as revealed under the pressure of circumstances. Contains a helpful chronology and a selected bibliography.

Torrey, Norman L. *The Spirit of Voltaire*. New York: Columbia University Press, 1938. Argues for and seeks to document Voltaire's moral integrity, while granting that a certain duplicity was a necessary condition of his life and work. Concludes with a long chapter on Voltaire's religion, probing whether he was a Deist, a mystic, or a Humanist.

See also: Marquise du Châtelet; Frederick the Great; David Hume; Louis XV; Montesquieu; Alexander Pope; Jean-Jacques Rousseau.

Related articles in *Great Events from History: The Eighteenth Century, 1701-1800*: November 1, 1755: Great Lisbon Earthquake; January, 1759: Voltaire Satirizes Optimism in *Candide*; July, 1764: Voltaire Publishes *A Philosophical Dictionary for the Pocket*; July 14, 1789: Fall of the Bastille; April 20, 1792-October, 1797: Early Wars of the French Revolution.

MUḤAMMAD IBN ʿABD AL-WAHHĀB
Saudi theologian and legal scholar

*Al-Wahhāb founded a reform movement that called for a
return to the fundamental sources of Islam, the Qurʾān
and the Ḥadīth. In 1744, he formed an administrative
partnership with the Saudi ruler Muḥammad ibn Saʿūd.
Their pact resulted in the establishment of the Saudi
state and remains the basis of the Saudi government.*

Born: 1703; ʿUyaynah, Najd (now in Saudi Arabia)
Died: 1792; Ad-Dirʿīyah, Najd
Also known as: Ibn ʿAbd al-Wahhāb; ʿAbd al-Wahāb;
ʿAbd el-Wahāb; Abdal Wahhāb
Areas of achievement: Religion and theology,
government and politics, warfare and conquest

EARLY LIFE

Muḥammad ibn ʿAbd al-Wahhāb (moo-HAHM-mahd
ihb-uhn ab-DOOL-wa-HAHB) was born in the barren,
harsh Najd province of Arabia. His family was not distinguished for its wealth but was known for its prestigious Ḥanbalī theologians and jurists. Therefore, from
an early age, al-Wahhāb was surrounded by regular discussions of Islamic law and witnessed the direct application of legal philosophy. Al-Wahhāb's uncle, Ibrāhīm
ibn Sulaymān, was a judge and legal scholar who settled
disputes throughout the al-Uyaynah region. His grandfather, Sulaymān ibn Ali ibn Musharraf, was one of the
greatest authorities on Ḥanbalī teachings in the Najd. His
father, ʿAbd al-Wahhāb ibn Sulaymān, was a judge involved with religion and jurisprudence. He provided al-
Wahhāb with his early instruction on Islamic interpretations and rulings.

Before he was ten years old, al-Wahhāb reportedly
had memorized the entire Qurʾān and had studied the
Ḥadīth, that is, the accounts of the Prophet Muḥammad's
sayings and deeds. He began addressing the locals of his
village, ʿUyaynah, about proper Islamic practices, persuading his audience through discussion rather than dogmatic preaching. Later, he proselytized in neighboring
areas. Eventually, he began to challenge the authorities
in the settlements and villages where he spoke, since he
believed that personal reform would lead to public reform. Thus, he would often antagonize village authorities to the point where he would finally be asked to leave.
The leaders of ʿUyaynah persuaded him to leave his
home when he was still a teenager, at which point he
made the pilgrimage to Mecca. Afterward, he went to
Medina, where he studied with Islamic scholars and became more familiar with the concepts prevalent in the

eighteenth century Islamic reform movement. He continued his studies in Basra and Zubayr (both now in Iraq)
and in Ahsa and Huraymila, in Arabia, before finally returning to his hometown of ʿUyaynah. There, he wed the
young aunt of the town's ruler and established an alliance
between himself as a religious leader and the village's
political leader.

LIFE'S WORK

Al-Wahhāb's reform movement was rooted in the teachings of Aḥmad ibn Ḥanbal (780-855), the founder of the
most conservative of the four orthodox schools of Islamic Law. Al-Wahhāb basically interpreted Ḥanbalism
for the locals of central Arabia, presenting it in a clear,
easily graspable way. He eschewed medieval views of
Islam and called for a return to the Qurʾān and *Ḥadīth*.
His focus was on a pure monotheism, and he therefore
condemned what he perceived to be innovations such as
the cult of saints, shrine worship, and practices that
showed a reverence for anything other than God. He was
also concerned with applying a strict interpretation of the
Sharia, that is, Islamic law.

Through his alliance with the ʿUyaynah authorities,
al-Wahhāb gained political protection and military
strength, which enabled him to manifest the seriousness
of his beliefs. He was now able to destroy symbols of the
region that were praised or worshiped, since only God
should be treated with such veneration: He cut down sacred trees and decimated the tomb of a historically important Islamic figure, Zayd ibn al-Khattab. He had an
adulterous woman in ʿUyaynah stoned, after issuing several warnings to her. These three actions, involving the
trees, tomb, and woman, set the tone by which Wahhābism would be viewed in the coming centuries. Eventually, the ulamas, the Muslim scholars of ʿUyaynah,
whose positions were threatened by his movement, declared him a militant, an extremist, and a source of instability. The ruler of ʿUyaynah was compelled to ask him
to leave once more.

Al-Wahhāb went to Ad-Dirʿīyah, a settlement about
forty miles south of ʿUyaynah and about nine miles north
of present-day Riyadh. The leader of Ad-Dirʿīyah was
Muḥammad ibn Saʿūd, whose family had ruled there since
the fifteenth century. Al-Wahhāb wanted to make an alliance with the ibn Saʿūd but was cautious and at first did not
openly talk about his reformist beliefs. Clandestinely,
however, he began to acquire devout followers. Three of

these disciples, a woman and two men, went to visit ibn Saʿūd's wife and brother to share al-Wahhāb's beliefs, especially those concerning monotheism. Ibn Saʿūd's wife embraced the concepts and accepted the pronouncement that ibn Saʿūd had a divine calling to promote monotheism. She and two of ibn Saʿūd's brothers together convinced him of the significance of al-Wahhāb's teachings.

The two powerful figures, al-Wahhāb and ibn Saʿūd, eventually met and formed their famous pact in 1744: Together they would rule, with al-Wahhāb controlling religious aspects and ibn Saʿūd controlling politics and the military. Muḥammad ibn Saʿūd had assumed control of Ad-Dirʿīyah around 1726, and, although a man of grand ambitions, he could do little on his own to unite the greater area of Najd because he lacked sufficient wealth and meaningful tribal connections. His union with al-Wahhāb elevated his status, since he could receive "tax" money through *zakat* contributions (required religious donations) and hold the title of political leader of the Muslim community. Ibn Saʿūd now had the funds and the influence to expand his empire. Al-Wahhāb in return acquired the government backing needed in order to enforce his doctrines.

Ibn Saʿūd embarked on a series of conquests to consolidate his power over the region. Al-Wahhāb did not interfere; however, he often did not necessarily support these actions either. Contrary to some opinions, he did not seek to convert neighbors through force; therefore, these military engagements were not always necessarily jihads, or holy wars. Only the religious leader, Imam al-Wahhāb, had the authority to declare jihad, and he would do so only if he determined the situation to be religiously legitimate. Al-Wahhāb apparently found some military campaigns distasteful, and he would leave ibn Saʿūd's company during these campaigns. This, no doubt, caused some strain between ibn Saʿūd and al-Wahhāb.

This tension was only magnified by the fact that al-Wahhāb was not concerned with the spoils of war, nor with materialistic life in any form. Ibn Saʿūd, however, was in a position that required him to reward his followers and keep his new subjects comfortable to ensure their contentment and consequent support. Al Wahhāb was disturbed by the resulting materialism he saw and held the Saʿūd clan responsible for its spread.

Muḥammad ibn Saʿūd died in 1767 and was succeeded by his son, ʿAbd al-Aziz. Ad-Dirʿīyah under ʿAbd al-Aziz became more materialistic, a place of relative luxury and power. The Saʿūd clan conquered the city of Riyadh in 1773, after which al-Wahhāb resigned as imam and withdrew from political life. He continued to consult with ʿAbd al-Aziz but had more or less removed his imprimatur from all Saʿūdi military activities.

SIGNIFICANCE

Muḥammad ibn ʿAbd al-Wahhāb was one of the most learned men of his time and place. He was a prolific writer and lecturer, as well as a leading figure in the various communities he encountered. His main concern was to bring Muslims back to the concept of *tawhid*, absolute monotheism. Indeed, he believed all Islamic reverence should go to God, and he would be displeased to know that the reform movement, at least in the Western world, carries his name, "Wahhābism." His distress with past interpretations of Islam compelled him to return to scripture. In some ways, he was the Martin Luther of the Arab world. His work represented eighteenth century Islamic trends, but his influence has been felt into the twenty-first century. Some of his extreme actions have been viewed as sanctions by contemporary Wahhābis/Salafis likewise to destroy certain artifacts or punish those who offend or do not follow Islamic law. If it were not for his union with ibn Saʿūd, which resulted in a continued relationship between Wahhābis and the Saʿūd clan, the tribes of Arabia would not have been unified and there would be no present-day Saudi Arabia.

—Lisa Urkevich

FURTHER READING

DeLong-Bas, Natana J. *Wahhabi Islam: From Revival and Reform to Global Jihad.* New York: Oxford University Press, 2004. Excellent source on al-Wahhāb, his life, views on women, theology, Islamic law, and modern implications. More balanced view of al-Wahhāb than many other texts that discuss Wahhābism.

Rasheed, Madawi al-. *A History of Saudi Arabia.* New York: Cambridge University Press, 2002. An accessible yet scholarly history written by a social anthropologist. The opening chapter discusses al-Wahhāb and his Saudi union.

Vassiliev, Alexei. *The History of Saudi Arabia.* London: Saqi Books, 1998. The most comprehensive history in English of Saudi Arabia to date. Includes a chapter on al-Wahhāb and his teachings. Associates Wahhābism with fanaticism.

See also: Karīm Khān Zand; Nādir Shāh; Vaḥīd Bihbahānī.

Related article in *Great Events from History: The Eighteenth Century, 1701-1800*: June 10, 1749: Saʿid Becomes Ruler of Oman.

SHĀH WALĪ ALLĀH
Indian religious leader

A Muslim religious teacher and thinker who advocated tolerance, Shāh Walī Allāh served as a bridge between the ancient Muslim theologians and Muslim modernists.

Born: February 21, 1703; Delhi, India
Died: 1762; Delhi, India
Also known as: Qutb al-Din Ahmad ibn ʿAbd al-Rahīm (birth name); Shāh Walī Ullāh; Waliullah; Shāh Walī Allāh of Delhi
Area of achievement: Religion and theology

EARLY LIFE

Shāh Walī Allāh was educated at home by his father, Shāh ʿAbd al-Rahim (1644-1718), who was a Muslim religious teacher and moved from Agra to Delhi, where he had his own school, the Madrassah-i-Rahimiyah. Walī Allāh is associated with that city, and he is known as Shāh Walī Allāh of Delhi. He was given the name Ahmad and the nickname "Walī Allāh" (God's protégé). Later the name Qutb al-Din was added, as his father had a vision at the tomb of the Delhi saint, Khwaja Qutb al-Din Bakhtiyar Kaki. As a child, therefore, he was often called Qutb al-Din Ahmad Walī Allāh. He called himself Ahmad, but he is known to history as Shāh Walī Allāh.

Walī Allāh was a precocious child. By the age of eight, he had read the entire Qurʾān, and then he learned Persian. At the age of ten, he was studying Arabic grammar. At the age of fourteen, he was married. On January 4, 1719, when his father died, he had already been declared an independent teacher, and he took over the running of his father's school, mostly working as a teacher. He did so for the next dozen years before going on the pilgrimage (*hajj*) to Mecca in April, 1731. While he was in Arabia, he also visited Medina. In Mecca, he attended lectures, and he received a certificate, dated 1731-1732, for attending lectures on the *Ḥadīth* (the sayings of the Prophet Muḥammad).

LIFE'S WORK

During the eighteenth century, the Mughal Empire, which was Muslim, collapsed. This collapse created a crisis of confidence and identity among Muslims: They tried to account for the loss of power and the rise of immorality, indolence, and ignorance among many Muslims. Shāh Walī Allāh believed that these phenomena were caused by the fact that many Muslims could not understand the true nature of Islam. They needed an educa-

tion system that was based on the Qurʾān and the *Ḥadīth*. He believed that, because the Muslim community had become divided among different sects and because different groups were struggling against each other, Muslims as a group were losing power. Non-Muslims took advantage of the situation, defeating Muslims militarily and acquiring powerful positions in government and society that Muslims once held. Walī Allāh particularly blamed Hindus for usurping Muslim positions.

He also believed that a number of non-Muslim customs, again especially Hindu beliefs and practices, had entered into the way many Muslims practiced Islam. This was true among both the ulama (Islamic theologians or men learned in Islam) and the Islamic laity. In other words, according to Walī Allāh, Islam had become corrupted and needed to be purified. He believed that people were uncritically following the Islamic schools of law (*fiqh*) and popular consensus (*ijma*), and this led them to accept practices that were contrary to a true understanding of Islam.

Walī Allāh accepted only two religious authorities. One was the prophetic tradition as delineated in the Qurʾān, and the other was the *Ḥadīth*. Through individual inquiry and reasoning (*ijtahid*), a person could understand the correct and unadulterated Islamic forms of worship and behavior and restore Islam to its pure form as it existed at the time of the Prophet Muḥammad. This was a very controversial stance, as Muslims had long believed that the "doors to *ijtihad* are closed." That is to say, four schools of Sunni Islamic jurisprudence had developed (the Hanafi, Maliki, Shafii, and Hanbali), and these could not be interpreted anew by every Muslim scholar who came along. Walī Allāh, by contrast, believed that they could be reinterpreted, if only by learned men.

In his attempt to unify the Muslim community, Walī Allāh dealt with the issues raised by Sufism (Islamic mysticism) and the largest sect apart from the orthodox Sunni, the Shia. He accepted mysticism and the meditative practices of Sufism, which claimed to allow people to experience the divine, and he had numerous mystical experiences himself, about which he wrote. He believed that experiencing the divine directly was a valid approach to religious knowledge.

As for the Shia, who believed that the descendants of Ali were the true leaders of Islam, Walī Allāh rejected Shiite beliefs, although, contrary to many orthodox Muslims, he accepted the Shia as Muslims and believed they should not be persecuted but taught the error of their ways. Nonetheless, he was a strong advocate of the Sunni. Walī Allāh penned at least seventy pieces of writing, covering every area of traditional Islamic learning. Some scholars believe he wrote more than two hundred tracts. Some of these were short treatises of four to five pages. In addition, about 350 of his letters have been published. He also wrote poetry.

One of Walī Allāh's most important contributions was his translation of the Qurʾān into Persian as the *Fath-al Rahman fi Tarjuman-al-Qurʾān* (1743), as Persian was more widely known among South Asian Muslims than Arabic, and it was the official language of India at the time. This translation was opposed bitterly by orthodox Muslims, and as a result, Walī Allāh's life was in danger for a time. Two of his sons, Rafiʾ-al-Din (1750-1818) and Shāh ʿAbdul Qadir (1753-1814), went even further and translated the Qurʾān into Urdu.

Upon Walī Allāh's death, his son ʿAbdul Aziz (1746-1824) replaced him as the head of the Madrassah-i-Rahimiyah, and Muslims from all over India continued to travel to Delhi to study at the school made famous by Walī Allāh. One of these students was Sayyid Nazir (d. 1902), who became the leader of a school himself, the Ahl-i-Hadith. After Walī Allāh's death, his sons and grandsons continued running the school. During the Indian Mutiny of 1857, the school building was sacked and everything looted; it was then leveled by gunfire, and the site was purchased by a Hindu. Research on the life and ideas of Walī Allāh continues in Pakistan at the Shāh Walī Allāh Academy located in Hyderabad (Sindh). It has annotated and published many of Walī Allāh's works and has published the journals *al-Hikma*, *al-Rahim*, and *al-Walī*.

SIGNIFICANCE

When modernist Muslims in the middle of the nineteenth century attempted to defend Islam from Western criticism, they developed a new body of writing in Urdu and English. Shāh Walī Allāh's translation of the Qurʾān into Persian inspired them. His ideas and writing also inspired the greatest of the Muslim modernists of the nineteenth century, Syed Ahmed Khan (1817-1898), who studied Walī Allāh's writings and founded the Muhammadan Anglo-Oriental College in 1875 at Aligarh. In 1921, it became Aligarh Muslim University, and it educated generations of modernist Muslims and continues to do so today.

—*Roger D. Long*

FURTHER READING

Ahmad, Aziz. *Studies in Islamic Culture in the Indian Environment.* Oxford, England: Clarendon Press, 1964. This book is considered a classic. It offers a comprehensive overview of the different Islamic sects and the varieties of Islamic thought and practices in South Asia. It is still a useful book to consult.

Jalbani, G. N. *Teachings of Shah Waliyullah of Delhi.* Lahore, Pakistan: Sh. Muhammad Ashraf, 1967. This short introduction was first published in Sindhi in 1961 and in Urdu by the Shāh Wali Ullah Academy in 1963. This is the English translation from the Urdu with some minimal changes and additions.

Jones, Kenneth W. *Socio-Religious Movements in British India.* New York: Cambridge University Press, 1989. Part of the New Cambridge History of India series, this work places Shāh Walī Allāh's thought in comparative perspective with the numerous other reform movements from the eighteenth to the twentieth century.

Metcalfe, Barbara Daly. *Islamic Revival in British India: Deoband, 1860-1900.* Princeton, N.J.: Princeton University Press, 1982. Looks at one of the most famous modernist schools in South Asia, the Deoband ul-Ulum, which looked to the Delhi school emanating from Walī Allāh for some of its ideas.

Muztar, A. D. *Shah Wali Allah: A Saint-Scholar of Muslim India.* Islamabad: National Commission on Historical and Cultural Research, 1979. A straightforward guide to the life and work of Walī Allāh, which is unlike many of the books dedicated to him. It can be used as a convenient reference book and includes a syllabus of the Madrassah-i-Rahimiya.

Rizvi, Saiyid Athar Abbas. *Shah Wali-Allah and His Times: A Study of Eighteenth Century Islam, Politics, and Society in India.* Canberra, Australia: Maʾrifat, 1980. This is a comprehensive study of more than four hundred pages of Walī Allāh's life, thought, and the political conditions of India in the eighteenth century. Explores subjects such as his political and social ideas as well as his religious beliefs.

See also: Hyder Ali; Sīdī al-Mukhtār al-Kuntī; Vahīd Bihbahānī; Muhammad ibn ʿAbd al-Wahhāb.
Related articles in *Great Events from History: The Eighteenth Century, 1701-1800*: 1746-1754: Carnatic Wars; June 23, 1757: Battle of Plassey; August, 1767-May, 1799: Anglo-Mysore Wars; December, 1774-February 24, 1783: First Marāthā War.

ROBERT WALPOLE
English prime minister

As prime minister, Walpole gave his country the longest period of peace and political stability in the eighteenth century. He also raised the status of the House of Commons to that of principal partner in government.

Born: August 26, 1676; Houghton Hall, Norfolk, England
Died: March 18, 1745; London, England
Area of achievement: Government and politics

EARLY LIFE

Robert Walpole was the third son of Colonel Robert and Mary Burwell Walpole. Both his grandfather and his father were active Whigs, and both held seats in Parliament, his grandfather from King's Lynn, his father from Castle Riding. As a younger son, Walpole was intended for the Church and so was sent to Eton, in 1690, and then to King's College, Cambridge, in 1696. As it would later in his career, death now played a role in advancing Walpole's fortunes. One of his two older brothers, Burwell, had died in the Battle of Beachy Head (June 30, 1690). In 1698, his other brother, Edward, also died; as a result, Walpole was summoned home from college to help his father manage the family estate.

On July 30, 1700, Walpole married Catherine Shorter, who brought with her a rich dowry of some £20,000 and even richer tastes. Although Walpole would indulge her extravagances until her death in 1737, the couple grew estranged after a few years, and shortly after Catherine's death, Walpole married Maria Skerrett, his mistress of some fifteen years.

LIFE'S WORK

When his father died on November 18, 1700, Walpole succeeded to his seat in Parliament. In his first session, he demonstrated that he had inherited his father's views as well, supporting religious toleration and the Hanoverian succession and befriending the Whig leaders. In the 1702 elections, he helped secure seats for the son of the duke of Devonshire and for Sir Thomas Littleton, a client of the duke of Somerset; his reward was a place on the Council of Admiralty (1705-1708).

An ardent supporter of the war against France, Walpole was named secretary at war in 1708, and in 1710 he became treasurer of the navy. In these posts, he demonstrated a capacity for hard work—he would be at his office at 6:00 A.M.—and a mastery of detail that made him valuable even to his political opponents. Indicative of his

abilities was Robert Harley's attempt to keep him in office after the Whig debacle of 1710. The nation had tired of war, which it had been waging almost constantly since 1688. Hence, the Tory promise of peace was welcome, and that party won overwhelmingly in the parliamentary elections of 1710. Many Whigs immediately lost their posts, but Harley, the Tory leader, retained Walpole, hoping that he would support the new ministry. Walpole refused, however, to abandon his party, and in January, 1711, he was dismissed.

The Tory assault on the previous administration included charges of misappropriation of £35 million. Walpole used his detailed financial knowledge to demolish these accusations by issuing two pamphlets: *A State of the Five and Thirty Millions* (1711) and *The Debts of the Nation Stated and Considered in Four Papers* (1712). In an attempt to silence him, the ministry accused him of corruption. Holding an overwhelming majority, the Tories expelled him from Parliament (in January of 1712) and ordered him confined to the Tower of London for several months; Walpole was not allowed to resume his seat from King's Lynn until 1713.

If the Tories believed that such treatment would silence Walpole, they were disappointed. In *The Present State of Fairyland in Several Letters from Esquire Hush* (1713), Walpole attacked the ministry's policy toward France, and *A Short History of Parliament* (1713) effectively responded to Jonathan Swift's claims, in *The Conduct of the Allies* (1711), that concluding a separate peace with France did not betray Great Britain's war partners, Holland and Austria.

The death of Queen Anne in 1714 and the succession of George I altered the political situation. Henry St. John, First Viscount Bolingbroke, long one of Walpole's opponents, wrote to Bishop Francis Atterbury, "I see plainly that the Tory Party is gone." Indeed it was; not until the end of the century would it return to power. The Whigs now imitated their opponents' purge, and Walpole returned to office as paymaster-general and chancellor of the exchequer (1715). These posts offered many opportunities for self-enrichment, and Walpole did not hesitate to seize them. While the appointments were intended as rewards for service to the party, they also show again the confidence that the nation's leaders placed in Walpole's financial abilities.

This faith was further demonstrated in 1717. Although the Whigs firmly controlled Parliament, the party itself was divided between the supporters of Charles Townshend and Walpole on one side and those led by James Stanhope and Charles Spencer, third earl of Sunderland, on the other. This latter faction was the stronger of the two, so in 1717, Townshend lost his post as lord lieutenant of Ireland. As in 1710, Walpole could have retained his office; indeed, the king pleaded with him to do so. Instead, though, Walpole chose loyalty to his brother-in-law, Townshend, and joined the opposition.

The ministry, like the Tories before, found Walpole a formidable foe. In financial matters, he was supreme: Sunderland and Stanhope adapted his plan to reduce the large national debt caused by decades of war, and Parliament accepted his figures rather than the ministry's in a vote on how much money to allot for retired army officers. He also successfully led the fight against the ministry's Peerage Bill, which sought to fix the number of members in the House of Lords at 216. The effect of the bill would have been to prevent the creation of additional members, a tactic both Whigs and Tories had used previously when the upper branch had sought to block legislation desired by the ministry. Without the power to pack the House of Lords, any future ministry would be dependent on that body, leaving the House of Commons powerless to reflect the will of the electorate. Under Wal-

Robert Walpole. (Library of Congress)

pole's direction, in 1719 the opposition defeated the measure by almost one hundred votes.

By 1720, Stanhope and Sunderland understood that they needed Walpole's cooperation, and since Walpole refused to join the ministry without Townshend, both Walpole and Townshend received offices. Walpole returned as paymaster-general, Townshend as president of the council. Walpole's return came none too soon, for financial ruin shortly threatened the nation, and only Walpole could avert the disaster looming before the country—and the Whig ministry.

The South Sea Company had been chartered in 1711 to assume part of the national debt. Walpole had opposed its establishment, chiefly because his own interests lay with the Bank of England, which wanted to handle the debt by itself. In 1720, the South Sea Company offered to assume the entire debt; again, Walpole objected but failed to carry the ministry or Parliament with him. Yet some observers shared Walpole's reservations. Edward Harley, for example, called the company "a machine of paper credit supported by imagination."

For a brief period, it appeared that such a machine might nevertheless function. Beginning at £100 a share, the price rose quickly; by June 24, 1720, the stock was selling for £1,050, about ten times the original value, and this boom stimulated a similar rise in other companies as well. Even Walpole was changing his mind and attempting to capitalize on the company's prosperity, and rumor later claimed that he had made much money trading in South Sea stock. In fact, as John Harold Plumb, Walpole's most careful biographer, has demonstrated, Walpole actually lost money on his investment and would have lost even more had his agent, Robert Jacombe, not been more prudent than his master. By the end of September, the bubble had burst: The stock was selling at £190.

Whereas Walpole had initially opposed the South Sea scheme and had subsequently remained largely aloof from it, Sunderland and Stanhope were deeply involved. Had Walpole chosen, he might have ended their control of Parliament during the 1720-1721 session, but whether he could govern without them was questionable. Instead of risking political chaos and possible Tory control of the government, Walpole used his skills as a parliamentarian and financier to restore confidence in the economy and to defend the present ministry. For his role in protecting Sunderland and Stanhope, Walpole was labeled the "screen-master general" by his enemies, but his friends named him first lord of the treasury and first lord of the Admiralty (April 3, 1721), while Townshend became secretary of state.

Despite this show of gratitude, Sunderland still distrusted Walpole, and what his fate would have been once the furor over the South Sea incident had abated is unclear. Again, however, death favored Walpole. Stanhope died in February, 1721; then, in the midst of the 1722 election, so did Sunderland. On April 20, 1722, King George I named Walpole his chief minister, a post Walpole would retain for the next twenty years.

In appointing Walpole first lord of the Admiralty and Townshend secretary of state, Sunderland had given to each what interested him most. Walpole's primary concern was domestic policy, Townshend's, foreign affairs. This division continued through the early years of Walpole's administration, as Walpole concentrated on reducing the national debt by raising revenues and also lowering taxes on land. A key to the success of this plan was the excise tax. In 1724, Walpole exempted tea, chocolate, and coconuts from import duties. These goods were now placed in bonded warehouses. If they were reexported, they paid no duty, but if they were sold within Great Britain, they paid an excise. Even though the excise tax was lower than the old import fee, revenues rose because smuggling and other forms of evading taxes were now more difficult. Viewing the rising merchant class as his base of support and therefore seeking to promote commerce, Walpole exempted British manufactured goods from export duties and encouraged the American colonies to expand their trade beyond the mother country, for he saw in their prosperity greater markets for English products. Had the ministers of George III been equally perceptive, the American Revolution might have been averted.

Taxes could not remain low and trade expand, however, unless England remained at peace, and Walpole's desire to avoid war eventually brought him into conflict with his brother-in-law, Townshend, who finally resigned as secretary of state in 1730, to be replaced by the dull but pliant William Stanhope. Walpole's aversion to war went beyond economics, though; when he successfully kept Great Britain from intervening in the War of the Polish Succession (1733-1735) despite treaty obligations to support Austria, he boasted to Queen Caroline that even though fifty thousand men had died in the fighting, not one of them was English.

Initially, Walpole's policy of prosperity at home and peace abroad made opposition futile. In the years 1727-1729, his political foes could muster barely one hundred votes in a House of Commons with more than five hundred members. Slowly, however, this number grew, and in 1733, Walpole narrowly escaped the most serious threat his ministry would face until 1742.

In 1732, Walpole had reduced the land tax to its lowest level of the century, one shilling on the pound, and he removed the tax on salt as damaging to the poor because they could least afford it. To compensate for the resulting loss of revenue, he proposed extending the excise scheme to tobacco and wine. Again, taxes on these goods would decrease but revenues would rise, since it would be harder to avoid paying the levy.

Merchants reacted angrily, for the law required that they demonstrate that their goods had passed through the bonded warehouses, and they naturally preferred a high tax that they could easily evade to a low one that they had to pay. Moreover, the idea of an excise tax bred irrational fears of absolutism. Samuel Johnson summarized the British attitude when he defined "excise" as "a hateful tax levied upon commodities, and adjudged not by the common judges of property, but wretches hired by those to whom excise is paid." Despite the strong opposition, Walpole probably could have forced the measure through Parliament; instead, he withdrew it, returned the land tax to two shillings, and reimposed the tax on salt.

Shaken by the excise crisis, Walpole was brought down by his pacifism. For almost twenty years, he had kept Great Britain at peace through his clever diplomatic maneuvering, creating alliances with France and Spain when policy required, shifting to Great Britain's more traditional Protestant allies, Holland and Austria, when circumstances warranted, and simply ignoring treaty obligations or hostile actions when he believed the national interest demanded such measures. On October 19, 1739, however, Great Britain, provoked by Spanish interference with the British merchant marine, declared war over Walpole's objections. Believing as he did in abiding by the wishes of a majority of his cabinet, he did what he could to support the war effort, but he revealed his feelings at the outset of the conflict when he observed, "They now ring the bells; they will soon wring their hands."

Walpole's majorities in the House of Commons had progressively shrunk since his total domination in the 1720's. After the 1734 elections, it had fallen to about seventy-five; in 1737 his opposition to doubling the prince of Wales's allowance from £50,000 a year to £100,000 succeeded by only thirty votes—and would have failed if the Tories had not abstained on the grounds that Parliament had no jurisdiction in the matter. The 1741 elections reduced Walpole's margin even further. He was accused of not pursuing the war with sufficient vigor; those Whigs out of place wanted positions, of which there were never enough to go around; the prince of Wales, in typical Hanoverian fashion, quarreled with his father and so was using his influence to unseat his father's minister.

When the new Parliament convened in December, 1741, Walpole's candidate for the chairman of the Committee of Privileges and Elections lost by four votes; in January, 1742, the government's candidate for Chippenham was rejected by one vote in the House of Commons. Lacking majority support, Walpole resigned, even though the king, in tears, implored him to remain. Instead, he accepted a peerage as earl of Orford and so moved to the House of Lords, where he remained active in politics until his death on March 18, 1745.

SIGNIFICANCE

Robert Walpole claimed that he was no reformer, and, as was evident in his withdrawal of the excise scheme in 1733 and his consistent efforts to avoid war, he preferred conciliation to confrontation. Yet he inadvertently changed the way the British government operated. Even after the Glorious Revolution had diminished royal power, the monarch still chose his or her ministers, and support of the Crown was essential for office. Walpole shifted the balance of governmental power to the House of Commons.

George II disliked Walpole, and when he first assumed the throne, in 1727, tried to dismiss him. He quickly learned that Walpole's parliamentary support was too great. Conversely, both George I and George II liked Lord John Carteret, but he never attained a post, because he lacked parliamentary backing. The House of Lords, too, lost influence under Walpole. He continued to use this chamber to kill measures that he opposed but that enjoyed popular support, but he refused a peerage during his ministry, choosing to lead the nation from the Commons. A peerage for him did not mark the pinnacle of power but the loss of it. When he and his longtime rival William Pulteney met in the House of Lords as newly created earls, Walpole remarked, "You and I, my lord, are now two as insignificant men as any in England." The truth of this statement owed much to Walpole's elevating the House of Commons to its commanding role in government.

Walpole also attempted to impose a measure of party, or at least factional, discipline. He refused to retain office without his party in 1710, supported the Sunderland-Stanhope ministry in 1720-1721, and, until his break with Townshend in 1730, repeatedly chose opposition to preferment without his political ally.

To achieve unity, Walpole relied more heavily than his predecessors on the powers of the chief minister.

He increased to 185 the number of Parliament members who held lucrative government posts, he spent lavishly to buy votes of both electors and members of the House of Commons, and he ruthlessly punished those who opposed him. After the failure of the excise scheme, for example, Walpole stripped eight peers of their posts because they had objected to the bill. In his first fifteen years in office, he allowed only one Tory to become a bishop, and that person succeeded only because he had the support of Queen Caroline.

Such blatant use of power and money, which included self-enrichment, scandalized many of Walpole's contemporaries. In the 1730's, Samuel Johnson expressed the longing for a purer time, "Ere masquerades debauch'd, excise oppress'd,/ Or English honour grew a standing jest." Later, Johnson saw matters more clearly, declaring that Walpole "was the best minister this country ever had, as if we would have let him he would have kept the country in perpetual peace."

A brilliant financier who gave his country low taxes and prosperity, a shrewd negotiator who brought peace to Great Britain in a troubled century, a skillful parliamentarian who shifted the balance of power in British government, Walpole richly deserves Johnson's—and history's—praise.

—*Joseph Rosenblum*

FURTHER READING

Black, Jeremy. *British Foreign Policy in the Age of Walpole*. Edinburgh: J. Donald, 1985. Treats Walpole's foreign policies and the domestic considerations that determined them. Particular chapters are devoted to such specific concerns as trade, religion, and the threat of the Stuart pretenders.

_____. *Robert Walpole and the Nature of Politics in Early Eighteenth-Century Britain*. New York: St. Martin's Press, 1990. Explains how Walpole's politics and policies transformed England into a world power with a vast colonial empire.

_____. *Walpole in Power: Britain's First Prime Minister*. Stroud, Gloucestershire, England: Sutton, 2001. Detailed exploration of Walpole's political career. Black describes how Walpole's ability to work with people, Parliament, and the king made him a model for all future prime ministers.

Dickinson, Harry Thomas. *Walpole and the Whig Supremacy*. Mystic, Conn.: Lawrence Verry, 1973. A political analysis rather than a biography. Sections treat political management, financial and commercial policy, and foreign affairs.

Goldgar, Bertrand A. *Walpole and the Wits: The Relation of Politics to Literature, 1722-1742.* Lincoln: University of Nebraska Press, 1976. Walpole has the distinction of inspiring some of the most biting satires of the eighteenth century. All the best writers—Alexander Pope, Jonathan Swift, John Gay, James Thomson, and Henry Fielding—opposed him. Goldgar effectively traces the deepening gloom of their works and less convincingly argues that these writers were motivated by greed rather than principle.

Langford, Paul. *The Excise Crisis: Society and Politics in the Age of Walpole.* Oxford, England: Clarendon Press, 1975. Examines the Excise Crisis of 1733 to determine why Walpole's plan was so controversial. Also uses the crisis as a key to understanding the nature of popular and aristocratic politics in early Hanoverian England.

Plumb, John Harold. *Sir Robert Walpole.* London: Cresset Press, 1956. The standard biography, tracing Walpole's career through 1734. Provides a detailed analysis of Walpole's personal and political life and of the events that helped shape him as well as his policies.

Speck, W. A. *Stability and Strife: England, 1714-1760.* Cambridge, Mass.: Harvard University Press, 1977. Primarily a study of English politics under the first two Georges, tracing the fortunes of the Whigs and Tories. Chapters 9 and 10 offer a good summary of Walpole's administration.

Williams, Basil. *The Whig Supremacy, 1714-1760.* London: Oxford University Press, 1962. A survey of England in the early eighteenth century. Explains the political, social, and cultural world in which Walpole lived.

Woodfine, Philip. *Britannia's Glories: The Walpole Ministry and the 1739 War with Spain.* Rochester, N.Y.: Boydell Press, 1998. Focuses on the war that occurred during the final years of Walpole's ministry, assessing the war's impact on England and Spain and describing the war within the context of Walpole's foreign policy.

See also: Queen Anne; First Viscount Bolingbroke; Caroline; Henry Fielding; George I; George II; First Earl of Godolphin; Samuel Johnson; First Earl of Mansfield; First Duke of Marlborough; Lord North; Henry Pelham; William Pitt the Younger; Alexander Pope; First Earl Stanhope; Jonathan Swift; John Wilkes.

Related articles in *Great Events from History: The Eighteenth Century, 1701-1800:* May 26, 1701-September 7, 1714: War of the Spanish Succession; February, 1706-April 28, 1707: Act of Union Unites England and Scotland; March 23-26, 1708: Defeat of the "Old Pretender"; September 11, 1709: Battle of Malplaquet; 1712: Stamp Act; April 11, 1713: Treaty of Utrecht; 1721-1742: Development of Great Britain's Office of Prime Minister; 1736: *Gentleman's Magazine* Initiates Parliamentary Reporting; 1739-1741: War of Jenkins's Ear; 1746-1754: Carnatic Wars.

WANG ZHENYI
Chinese astronomer, mathematician, and poet

Wang Zhenyi's promotion of the Western, Sun-based calendar, as well as her research, experiments, and observations, contributed to China's modern understanding of astronomical phenomena such as lunar and solar eclipses, equinoxes, and celestial mechanics. Her mathematics textbooks were written for broad access, and her poetry was praised for its strength, clarity of vision, and social compassion.

Born: 1768; Nanjing, China
Died: 1797; Nanjing, China
Also known as: Wang Chen-i (Wade-Giles)
Areas of achievement: Astronomy, mathematics, literature

EARLY LIFE
Wang Zhenyi (wang jehn-YEE) was born to a scholarly, aristocratic Manchu family in the large town of Nanjing, China. Originally from the neighboring province of Anhui to the west, her well-educated grandfather, Wang Zhefu, had worked as county governor and prefect in the Nanjing region. Her father, Wang Xichen, had failed the imperial examination that would have set him on a course similar to that of an administrator. Instead, he became a physician, publishing the results of his clinical studies. No personal details have survived about Wang's mother, an upper-class Manchu woman.

When Wang was a child, her grandfather and father encouraged her innate thirst for knowledge and allowed her to learn to read and peruse the first volumes of her grandfather's seventy-five bookcases. Supporting a girl's formal education was unusual for a Chinese family of the time, and it gave Wang uncommon access to the world of learning. She would prove to be exceptionally intelligent. As a young Manchu woman, Wang was spared the torturous practice of foot-binding inflicted on upper-class Han Chinese women.

Wang's grandfather died in 1779, when Wang was eleven years old. She traveled with her paternal grandmother Dong and her father to Jilin in Manchuria, where her grandfather was given an ornate funeral. While in Jilin, Wang enjoyed unusual access to books and learning as well as physical activities. With three upper-class girlfriends, and under the tutelage of an older woman, Wang continued to read voraciously, and she quickly gained a superlative knowledge of literature and the natural sciences. She learned horse-riding and arrow-shooting (horseback-based martial arts) from a Mongolian general who took a liking to his unlikely female disciple. Wang became an expert markswoman and was rumored to have hit the target with every arrow shot while galloping on her horse.

In 1784 sixteen-year-old Wang returned south with her father, traversing Shaanxi province, crossing through Hubei province, and venturing south into Guangdong (Canton) before settling again in Nanjing. Wang gained a wide view of the Qing Dynasty, an opportunity afforded very few women of her generation.

At the age of twenty-five, unusually late for the time period, Wang married Zhan Mei, who was from her ancestral Anhui province. Their marriage is reported to have been happy, but they had no children.

LIFE'S WORK

Wang Zhenyi's contributions to astronomy were groundbreaking. Her treatise on the observation and calculation of the vernal and autumnal equinoxes—the one day in spring and fall, respectively, when there are exactly twelve hours each of day and night—accurately described the causes of the phenomenon and how to calculate its exact day each year.

Her work on lunar and solar eclipses was uncharacteristically based on an actual experiment, something very few of her Chinese male colleagues had ever thought of doing. To study the mechanics of an eclipse, when either the Sun covers the Moon at night or the Moon occludes the Sun during the day, Wang built her own scientific apparatus in a pavilion of her garden in Nanjing. She used a round table to represent the Earth; above the table, she

attached a crystal lamp functioning as the Sun; a large round mirror on the side of the table (Earth) stood in for the Moon. Moving table, lamp, and mirror according to the real movement of Earth, Sun, and Moon, Wang could observe in her own pavilion the actual effects causing the eclipses of Sun and Moon. Her written work on the subject proved exceptionally accurate and furthered Chinese astronomical understanding.

Wang also affirmed the modern view of the Earth as a sphere and wrote on celestial mechanics affecting the movement of the Sun and the planets. Her meteorological studies concerned calculating the humidity in the atmosphere to arrive at better weather forecasts. Wang saw her work regarding the meteorological prediction of floods and droughts as a service to the farmers of China, who suffered much from these extreme weather conditions.

In the field of mathematics Wang showed a clear understanding of trigonometry, demonstrating an innate skill for abstract thought. Her popularizing textbooks on calculations, first published when she was twenty-four years old, were designed to enable beginners to gain a quicker understanding of multiplication and division. Her work demonstrated a clear grasp of the principles of mathematics, and she conveyed this clarity to her readers. She also wrote on problems in advanced mathematics that were at the cutting edge of the science of her day.

Wang Zhenyi enthusiastically embraced the Western Sun-based, or heliocentric, calendar. She praised the underlying principles that gave it accuracy and precision, appreciated its calculations, and she argued for its adoption in China. She opposed keeping the older, less accurate lunar calendar for the sake of tradition, and she argued for acceptance of new scientific and mathematical results and ideas.

Wang Zhenyi was also an accomplished poet whose work showed concern with the experiences of women and common people, and with her yearning for knowledge, traveling, and freedom. One of her earliest poems, which describes her journey to Jilin for her grandfather's funeral, has been praised for its perception and insight. Often her poetic persona is that of a strong, adventurous woman who views, for example, the world from the perspective of the gods: looking down a mountain pass to the Huang He (Yellow River) in the plains below.

Wang's poems, written during her travels with her father before her marriage, show a keen social compassion and understanding of the economic forces threatening the Qing Dynasty, which would lead to civil war in the next century. She wrote about peasant women and the callous indifference of the wealthy, who hoarded rice until it rotted, leaving many people to starve. She also criticized the ever-increasing tax burden that stifled rural development. Such political topics were unusual in women's poetry of her time.

In 1797, at age twenty-nine, Wang died of natural causes. Shortly before her death she entrusted all of her manuscripts to her best woman friend, Qian Yuling. In 1803, Qian conveyed the manuscripts to her nephew Qian Yiji, who compiled Wang's mathematics textbook *Shusuan jiancun* (eighteenth century; simple principles of calculation) and wrote a preface praising Wang's intellectual achievements. After being transferred to Zhu Xuzeng, a Nanjing collector, most of Wang's manuscripts were lost. Only her *Defengting zhuji* (eighteenth century; first collection of the Defeng Pavilion), four volumes of poetry, and the Jilin collection of essays appear to have survived. Most of her astronomical and other scientific work, in its original form, has been lost, and is thus known only through references by others.

SIGNIFICANCE

Wang Zhenyi's accomplishments as an astronomer modernized Chinese astronomical understanding. Her experiment-based research linked Chinese astronomy to that of the West, which had advanced significantly by the eighteenth century. Wang helped close a gap in scientific knowledge.

Wang's work in meteorology was driven by a desire for the practical and beneficial applications of her weather forecasts, which led to her helping in the improvement of farming conditions. Furthermore, she preferred the scientifically superior Western calendar over the traditional Chinese model, demonstrating scientific openness and acceptance of results regardless of tradition or national origin.

Wang's literary work created a misogynist opposition. Upon the self-financed publication of her poetry shortly before her untimely death in 1797, male critics showed their sexism when they tried to ridicule Wang's accomplishments in poetry and extending into the field of science as well.

It took almost two centuries to appreciate the value of Wang's work. In 1994, in appreciation of her astronomi-

cal research, a small crater on Venus was named Wang Zhenyi.

—*R. C. Lutz*

FURTHER READING

Liu, Naihe. "More than a Stargazer." In *Departed but Not Forgotten*, edited by Bai Shoyi. Beijing: China International, 1984. Illustrated review of Wang's life and her scientific and literary accomplishments. Quotes from her poetry and places her life in sociohistorical context.

Meschel, Susan V. "Teacher Keng's Heritage: A Survey of Chinese Women Scientists." *Journal of Chemical Education* 69 (September, 1992): 723-729. Illustrated survey of Wang's life and accomplishments based on Naihe Liu's study. Places Wang in the context of Chinese women scientists whose traditional cultural and social status is juxtaposed with the official policies of the People's Republic of China.

Spence, Jonathan. *The Search for Modern China.* 2d ed. New York: Norton, 1999. Most widely available book in English on modern Chinese history. Useful in providing background information on the lives Wang Zhenyi and more-conformist women led in the eighteenth century Qing Dynasty. Maps, illustrations, notes, bibliography, index.

Xu, Zhentao, et al. *East Asian Archaeoastronomy: Historical Records of Astronomical Observations of China, Japan, and Korea.* Amsterdam: Gordon & Breach Science, 2000. Places Wang's astronomical research and accomplishments in the context of Chinese astronomy. Highlights the innovative value of Wang's observations, calculations, and theories. Illustrated.

See also: Cao Xueqin; Dai Zhen; Caroline Lucretia Herschel; Qianlong; Yongzheng.

Related articles in *Great Events from History: The Eighteenth Century, 1701-1800:* 1704-1712: Astronomy Wars in England; 1725: Flamsteed's Star Catalog Marks the Transition to Modern Astronomy; 1787: Herschel Begins Building His Reflecting Telescope.

MERCY OTIS WARREN
American writer

Warren, who was close to many critical figures of the American revolutionary period, wrote plays and poetry that supported and justified the American Revolution. She also wrote a history of the revolution that casts a great deal of light on the roles played by many of the New England patriots, and her long correspondence with John Adams and Abigail Adams remains a guide to early American political controversies.

Born: September 25, 1728; Barnstable, Massachusetts Colony
Died: October 19, 1814; Plymouth, Massachusetts
Also known as: Mercy Otis (birth name)
Areas of achievement: Government and politics, literature, theater, historiography

EARLY LIFE

Mercy Otis Warren was the third child of James Otis and Mary Allyne Otis. She was born in a farming and seafaring community on Cape Cod. Her parents were descended from the earliest Pilgrim settlers of Massachusetts. Indeed, her mother traced her ancestry to the *Mayflower* landing in 1620. Both the Allynes and Otises were well to do, the owners of large and prosperous farms.

Mercy's father had been denied the opportunity to attend college as a youth, and so was largely self-educated. Determined to provide his sons with the formal education he had missed, he engaged excellent tutors for them, and he did not prevent Mercy, his oldest daughter, from attaching herself to the lessons provided to her brothers. Her father does not appear to have shared his era's objection to women's education.

Mercy began to read widely at an early age, and later, her reading was guided to some extent by the suggestions of her eldest brother, James; he was soon to leave for Harvard College. Mercy is known to have read the works of Alexander Pope, John Dryden, John Milton, and, above all—for what was to follow in her life—John Locke's *Essays on Government.*

Mercy attended her brother's commencement exercises at Harvard in 1744, where it is believed she met her brother's classmate and close friend, James Warren, for the first time. James Warren was from Plymouth; he too had ancestors who had arrived in the New World on the *Mayflower.* Mercy and James were married in November, 1754, after a long courtship, and they settled in Plymouth.

LIFE'S WORK

During the 1760's, Mercy Otis Warren's brother, James Otis, became the leading colonial proponent of independence from England. The Warrens, Abigail and John Adams, Samuel Adams, John Hancock, and others became convinced that James Otis was right about the need for independence. Meetings and discussions were held at the Warrens' home in Plymouth. In 1769, partly as a result of a terrible beating Otis received from Loyalist officers, he became insane and was forced to retire permanently to the family home in Barnstable. Mercy and James Warren felt that they should continue Otis's political work.

At a meeting at the Warrens' in October, 1772, the plan for establishing colonial committees of correspondence was first put forward. Most historians believe that the scheme was suggested in the first instance by the Warrens. The promotion of these committees, which were to be effectuated by Samuel Adams, was the crucial first step in organizing the American colonies for revolution. Indeed, when the revolution actually began, in 1775, British power disappeared and most of the actual governing was taken over by the local committees of correspondence.

In addition to her political work, Warren had begun to write poetry. In the early years her main themes were religion, philosophy, nature, and friendship. As time went by and her political activities increased in the aftermath of her brother's disability, she found that she had a talent for satirical writing. Shortly after the Boston Tea Party, John Adams urged her to write a poem about the uprising. The result was "The Squabble of the Sea Nymphs," a long work published in the *Boston Gazette* three months later that delighted its readers. Warren suddenly found herself famous.

She next turned her talents to the writing of political satire in the form of stage plays. In all she wrote six plays, published between 1772 and 1779. This was a remarkable feat for a woman who, although she had read the plays of Molière and William Shakespeare, had never seen a play actually performed. Her plays encouraged the American patriots, cast scorn on the royal governor Thomas Hutchinson, and prophesied American success in the war and the ultimate exile of Hutchinson. Warren's work was perhaps as influential as Thomas Paine's in promoting and justifying the revolution.

After the war she continued her political activity. In 1788 she opposed ratification of the proposed Constitution in her work *Observations on the New Constitution, and on the Federal and State Conventions*. She was later to change her mind about the Constitution and became one of its supporters sometime after the adoption of the Bill of Rights in December, 1791.

In 1805 she published the three-volume *History of the Rise, Progress, and Termination of the American Revolution: Interspersed with Biographical, Political, and Moral Observations*. Few people were in a better position to write this history. She had been one of its progenitors, present at its creation. Even when the revolutionary movement had gone beyond her immediate circle, she had been able to keep up with political and military events through her extensive correspondence with Abigail Adams and with her own husband, James, who had become an American general.

Warren's book was bitterly resented by John Adams, who felt that she had represented him as favoring a monarchical government. Adams may still have been feeling stung by his reelection defeat by Thomas Jefferson in 1800. The Warren-Adams friendship was interrupted by an exchange of disputatious and occasionally angry letters in 1807. For a time their social relations ceased, but friends of both interposed themselves, and in 1812 a mutual friend, politician Elbridge Gerry of Massachusetts, mediated the quarrel to the satisfaction of both Adams and Warren. Their friendship resumed and they corresponded warmly with one another until Mercy's death in 1814.

SIGNIFICANCE

Mercy Otis Warren's accomplishments are numerous, but they have been mostly forgotten. As an early proponent and literary supporter of the American Revolution, her role may have been indispensable. In her own time her works were widely circulated and discussed. Her immediate circle did not believe that private political discussion was limited to men, and her participation and contribution was encouraged. Of course, in those times, public participation by women—other than literary—was considered improper, leading to limited public roles for Warren, Abigail Adams, and many other women. Nevertheless, Warren's contemporaries believed she was a genius, especially significant given that she had no formal education.

Her history of the revolution is an insider's account, and it is particularly valuable because Warren herself did not—could not—take a public role either in the war or in political leadership. Consequently, she had no political or military record to protect and was able to provide a disinterested account. Her descriptions of the revolution's leading figures are judicious and generous without being fulsome. Indeed, her book is the starting point for much historical research on the revolution's early development. Moreover, her correspondence with the Adamses—finally published in 1878 by the Adamses' grandson, Charles Francis Adams—casts additional light on the developing ideas of the founding generation.

Feminist historiography has led to some revived interest in Warren's life and work. Her accomplishments, which would have been notable in any age, seem especially significant in the light of the limited role permitted women in her time. Warren and Abigail Adams agreed early on that the subordination of women in their era was the result of limited opportunity rather than limited talent. The revolution's history would be better understood were more people familiar with Warren's work and the work of other women of the period.

—*Robert Jacobs*

FURTHER READING

Adams, Charles F., ed. *Correspondence Between John Adams and Mercy Warren*. 1878. Reprint. New York: Arno Press, 1972. A reprinted edition of correspondence detailing the heated dispute between John Adams and Mercy Otis Warren.

Anthony, Katherine. *First Lady of the Revolution: The Life of Mercy Otis Warren*. Garden City, N.Y.: Doubleday, 1958. A well-written biography and literary appreciation of Warren.

Brown, Alice. *Mercy Warren*. New York: Charles Scribner's Sons, 1903. A biography that focuses primarily on Warren's plays and her history of the revolution.

Fritz, Jean. *Cast for a Revolution: Some American Friends and Enemies, 1728-1814*. Boston: Houghton Mifflin, 1972. A study of the relations among the Warrens, Adamses, Otises, Hutchinsons, and Hancocks during and after the revolution.

Schloesser, Pauline. *White Women and Racial Patriarchy in the Early American Republic*. New York: New York University Press, 2002. A feminist analysis of the revolution, focusing primarily on Warren and on Abigail Adams.

Warren, Mercy Otis. *History of the Rise, Progress, and Termination of the American Revolution: Interspersed with Biographical, Political, and Moral Observations*. Edited by Lester H. Cohen. 2 vols. Indianapolis, Ind.: Liberty Fund, 1994. A reprinted edition, with annotations, of Warren's history. Includes bibliographical references and an index.

See also: Abigail Adams; John Adams; Samuel Adams; Georgiana Cavendish; Elbridge Gerry; John Hancock; Thomas Hutchinson; Catherine Macaulay; Thomas Paine; Alexander Pope; John Trumbull; Mary Wollstonecraft.
Related articles in *Great Events from History: The Eighteenth Century, 1701-1800:* December 16, 1773: Boston Tea Party; April 19, 1775: Battle of Lexington and Concord; July 4, 1776: Declaration of Independence; September 17, 1787: U.S. Constitution Is Adopted; December 15, 1791: U.S. Bill of Rights Is Ratified; 1792: Wollstonecraft Publishes *A Vindication of the Rights of Woman*.

GEORGE WASHINGTON
President of the United States (1789-1797)

As commander in chief of the Continental army during the American Revolution, president of the Constitutional Convention of 1787, and first president of the United States, Washington was the principal architect of the nation's independence and its federal political system.

Born: February 22, 1732; Bridges Creek (now Wakefield), Westmoreland County, Virginia
Died: December 14, 1799; Mount Vernon, Virginia
Areas of achievement: Government and politics, military, warfare and conquest, diplomacy

EARLY LIFE

Born into a family of middling standing among Virginia's planter elite, George Washington was the eldest son of his father's second marriage. A favorite of his half brother Lawrence Washington of Mount Vernon, young George capitalized on this brother's marriage into the prominent Fairfax family and the inheritance of Lawrence Washington's estate. Thus, despite his losing his father at age eleven and his being a low-priority heir to his father's lands, he was by his mid-twenties able to achieve greater prominence both in estate and position than his ancestors.

His connections allowed him to succeed Lawrence Washington as a major and adjutant of militia in 1752, and the following year he carried a message from Virginia's governor to the French forces encroaching on Virginia-claimed lands in the upper Ohio valley. In 1754, Lieutenant Colonel Washington surrendered a small Virginia detachment under his command to French forces in southwestern Pennsylvania. Thus began the French and Indian War (1754-1763), known in Europe as the Seven Years' War (1756-1763).

Washington's war record was solid but undistinguished, except for his well-recognized bravery during General Edward Braddock's defeat on the Monongahela River in 1756. Failing to receive the royal military commission he sought, he returned to Mount Vernon, engaged in modern farming techniques, expanded his land holdings, and, in 1759, married a wealthy widow, Martha Dandridge Custis. Their marriage was childless, but Washington adopted her two children.

LIFE'S WORK

Elected to the Virginia House of Burgesses, George Washington never achieved a reputation of outspokenness comparable to that of, say, Patrick Henry. A delegate to the First and Second Continental Congresses, Washington impressed his colleagues with his mastery of military affairs and was selected by them to serve as commander in chief of the newly formed Continental army in 1775. He took command of the mostly New England force shortly after its defeat at Breed's (Bunker) Hill and immediately sought to reform it into an effective fighting force. Containing the British forces inside Boston during the winter of 1775-1776, he forced them to evacuate the city the following spring. Action then moved to New York City, where he suffered defeats on Long Island and Manhattan Island and was eventually driven across the Hudson River into and across New Jersey. His counterattacks at Trenton and Princeton during the winter of 1776-1777 revived American hopes and allowed his forces to winter in northern New Jersey.

The following year, he countered the two-pronged British invasion from Canada down the Lake Champlain-Hudson Valley route and from New York via sea against Philadelphia by sending General Horatio Gates with some of his regulars to join local units in combating the northern invasion and by leading the Pennsylvania campaign himself. In the latter area, Washington was soundly defeated by General William Howe's forces but escaped to rebuild his army during the bitter winter at Valley Forge. General Gates won a remarkable victory at

George Washington and family at home. (Library of Congress)

Saratoga that encouraged the French government to recognize the United States. The subsequent alliance with France allowed the Americans to continue their efforts and forced the British to concentrate their naval and military forces against an ever-widening war that eventually saw combat from the Indian Ocean to the Caribbean Sea.

The new international conflict caused the British to withdraw from Philadelphia to New York in 1778. When Washington sought to destroy their forces at Monmouth, New Jersey, the result was an indecisive battle that could have turned into a rout had not the American commander personally rallied his troops. For the next three years, Washington headquartered his forces near West Point, New York, while combating some British raids and pinning the British forces in the New York City-Long Island vicinity. When the British developed a southern strategy to return Georgia and the Carolinas to their empire, Washington countered by sending Generals Benjamin Lincoln and Horatio Gates to the region. The result was defeat for both officers at Charleston and Camden. In

early 1781, Washington sent Nathanael Greene southward, and Greene was able to conduct an effective area defense that thwarted General Charles Cornwallis's attempts to conquer the Carolinas. Exasperated, Cornwallis sought to cut off Greene's supply line and to draw him northward by invading Virginia. At this point, Washington coordinated with the French general, the comte de Rochambeau, commander of a French expeditionary force in Rhode Island, and through him Admiral Count François de Grasse, commander of the French West Indian fleet, to unite their forces against Cornwallis in Virginia. The resultant surrender of Cornwallis at Yorktown in October, 1781, effectively ended British attempts to reintegrate the United States into the British Empire even though the treaty of peace would not be signed until 1783.

After Washington resigned his commission in 1783 (a remarkable event in itself, since most observers expected him to become another Oliver Cromwell), he maintained a high public profile during the next several years but did not seek major positions until 1787, when he became a delegate to the Constitutional Convention and presiding officer of that body. Although his position precluded his taking an active part in the deliberations, he played a significant behind-the-scenes role in the convention and, by lending his name to the final document, helped to ensure its eventual ratification.

During the convention and the ratification process, it was assumed that Washington would become the first chief executive of the new government. Elected president in 1789, he established precedents for the new office that are still followed. Unlike modern presidents, who receive the privileges and prestige of the office, Washington lent his public reputation to the presidency and thereby enhanced its repute.

His government faced difficult tasks in the fields of administrative organization, foreign relations, and economic policy. Influencing each of these areas would be both the clash of personalities and the clash of political interests. Washington sought to resolve the issues without involving himself in the controversy. For the most part, except in the area of foreign policy, he was successful.

One of the most critical areas was the creation of an independent executive system, which was not fully developed in the Constitution. Here Washington prevailed over those desiring to use the Senate as sort of a privy council under the "advise and consent" clause, and those, such as Alexander Hamilton, desiring a parliamentary cabinet system with the major executive officers responsible to the Congress. Among Washington's other achievements were the creation of federal administrative agencies separate from those of the states; the introduction of orderly and stable relationships between officials based on law, instructions, and precedents; the maintenance of high standards of integrity, honesty, and competence; the recognition of claims of locality upon political appointments (often called "senatorial courtesy"); and the dominance of federal authority over individuals, demonstrated decisively in the suppression of the Whiskey Rebellion of 1794. Some of Washington's administrative policies, such as the use of the veto only in relation to constitutional questions, did not long survive his presidency. In the same vein, his use of the cabinet as a consultative body had a short life.

Other developments during his tenure can be attributed less to Washington's personal efforts than to the circumstances of the time or to the role of others. The creation of the judicial system was largely the responsibility of Roger Sherman, the Bill of Rights that of James Madison. The latter also formulated the first national revenue system. Hamilton created a financial system that funded government debts, instituted a national central bank, and established a national mint and stable currency. Washington either actively endorsed

---

FROM WASHINGTON'S DIARIES

Upon reading Washington's diary excerpts from 1789, one can sense the anxiety and possible fear at his realizing that he was just months shy of assuming the presidency of the United States. The entry for April 23 details the pomp and circumstance of his inauguration week, while on October 3, he tells of two portrait sittings in one day. On October 4, he writes that he went to church in the morning and wrote letters in the afternoon.

April 16: About ten o'clock I bade adieu to Mount Vernon, to private life, and to domestic felicity; and with a mind oppressed with more anxious and painful sensations than I have words to express, set out for New York in company with Mr. Thompson [whom earlier delivered to Washington news of his election to the presidency], and colonel Humphries, with the best dispositions to render service to my country in obedience to its call, but with less hope of answering its expectations. (p. 445)

April 23: The display of boats which attended and joined us on this occasion [Washington's week of inauguration], some with vocal and some with instrumental music on board; the decorations of the ships, the roar of cannon, and the loud acclamations of the people which rent the skies, as I passed along the wharves, filled my mind with sensations as painful (considering the reverse of this scene, which may be the case after all my labors to do good) as they are pleasing. (p. 447)

October 3: Sat for Mr. Rammage [a miniaturist painter] near two hours to day, who was drawing a miniature Picture of me for Mrs. Washington.

Walked in the Afternoon, and sat about two Oclock for Madam de Brehan [a miniaturist painter] to complete a Miniature profile of me which she had begun from Memory and which she said had made exceedingly like the Original. (p. 451)

October 4: Went to St. Pauls Chappel in the forenoon. Spent the remainder of the day in writing private letters for tomorrows Post [mail]. (p. 452)

Source: George Washington, *The Diaries of George Washington.* George Washington Papers, Library of Congress, Manuscript Division. http://lcweb2.loc.gov/ammem/gwhtml/.

or did not oppose (in itself an act of endorsement) these efforts.

In military affairs, Washington often used his secretary of war as a cipher and conduit in a field where he had considerable expertise. His greatest disappointment in this field was Congress's rejection of his proposals for a national military system; instead, it passed the Militia Act of 1792, which left the nation without any effective defense posture.

In foreign affairs he closely worked with Thomas Jefferson in his first administration and followed the often misguided instincts of Hamilton in the second. Jay's Treaty of 1794 was the most divisive event of his tenure and did far more to encourage partisan politics than did any other policy matter. Despite the political consequences of Washington's diplomacy, he is generally given appreciative accolades for his maintenance of neutrality in the Anglo-French struggle that drew most of the Western world into its vortex.

Washington undoubtedly believed that the greatest weakness of his administration was the development of partisan politics. Both the president's supporters and his opponents favored a consensual political environment that saw partisan activities as divisive of national solidarity and indicative of corruption and personal ambition. The main intent of Washington's farewell address was to warn against political parties.

His final legacy to the presidency was the decision not to run for reelection in 1796 and the consequent two-term tradition that continued until 1940. He established a precedent of turning the office over to a duly elected successor instead of waiting for either death or revolt to remove him from office. Washington did not believe that his presence in the office was indispensable, and he instinctively knew that the peaceful transfer of power to a duly elected successor constituted an important building block in erecting a stable nation.

His retirement from the presidency in 1797 did not remove him entirely from public service. When the Quasi War with France broke out in 1798 (and ended in 1800), President John Adams called Washington back to command the army with the rank of lieutenant general. In this capacity he normally remained at Mount Vernon and delegated much of the running of the army to Major General Hamilton. Washington died after a short illness in late 1799.

SIGNIFICANCE

No American figure has for so long dominated the national scene as has George Washington. For nearly twenty-five years, Washington remained the symbol of American nationhood, commanding its armies in a war for national independence, presiding over the convention that drafted its fundamental political charter, and transforming that charter's vague articles into political reality as the first chief magistrate of the republic.

As both general and president, he shaped the American military tradition with its subordination to civilian authority. As president, he established the contours of the American federal system and, even though he opposed its development, the party system. A far better statesman than general, still, he is probably better remembered for his military than for his political contributions to American history.

—*David Curtis Skaggs*

FURTHER READING

Alden, John R. *George Washington: A Biography*. Baton Rouge: Louisiana State University Press, 1984. A high-quality one-volume study of Washington's life, and a useful introduction to his career.

Burns, James MacGregor, and Susan Dunn. *George Washington*. New York: Times Books, 2004. A concise biography, one in a series of books on the American presidents. Much of the work describes how Washington carefully created a public image emphasizing self-sacrifice and dignity. The authors also praise his presidency, lauding his ability to establish a strong executive branch and develop the most effective style of collective leadership of any American president.

DeConde, Alexander. *Entangling Alliance: Politics and Diplomacy Under George Washington*. Durham, N.C.: Duke University Press, 1958. A good introduction to Washington's foreign policy, which the book strongly endorses.

Ellis, Joseph J. *His Excellency: George Washington*. New York: Alfred A. Knopf, 2004. A best-selling and highly acclaimed biography, based in large part on Washington's cataloged letters and papers at the University of Virginia. Ellis provides a complete account of Washington's life and career, placing both within historical context. The author discusses how Washington, who skillfully crafted his public personality, was equally adept at crafting a political system for the newly created United States.

Flexner, James Thomas. *George Washington*. 4 vols. Boston: Little, Brown, 1965-1972. Perhaps the best of the multivolume biographies, with an especially good treatment of Washington's military career in the second volume.

Freeman, Douglas Southall. *George Washington.* 7 vols. New York: Charles Scribner's Sons, 1948-1957. John A. Carroll and Mary Wells Ashworth completed the final volume of this detailed, nonanalytical study by a Pulitzer Prize-winning biographer.

Hofstadter, Richard. *The Idea of a Party System: The Rise of Legitimate Opposition in the United States.* Berkeley: University of California Press, 1969. A comprehensive analysis of the antiparty tradition of the early republic and of Washington's ambiguous place in early partisan politics.

Kammen, Michael. *A Season of Youth: The American Revolution in Historical Imagination.* New York: Oxford University Press, 1978. A thorough and imaginative reappraisal of the revolutionary theme and Washington's place in it.

Langston, Thomas S., and Michael G. Sherman. *George Washington.* Washington, D.C.: CQ Press, 2003. One in a series of books about the American presidents published by the *Congressional Quarterly.* The authors examine Washington's life, his election campaigns, his presidential policies, and the political crises that occurred during his administration. Each of the book's six chapters includes a brief bibliographic essay.

McCullough, David. *1776.* New York: Simon & Schuster, 2005. McCullough focuses on one year in the American Revolution, 1776, describing the battles between America's ragtag troops and British forces. Using letters, journals, diaries, and other primary sources, he describes the leadership of Washington, Nathanael Greene, and General William Howe, as well as the heroic struggles of American soldiers.

Weems, Mason Locke. *The Life of Washington.* Edited by Marcus Cunliffe. Cambridge, Mass.: Harvard University Press, 1962. This reprinting of the 1809 edition of the book that did much to create the Washington myth contains an excellent introduction by Cunliffe.

Weigley, Russell F. *The American Way of War.* New York: Macmillan, 1973. Contains an excellent chapter on Washington's contributions to the American military tradition.

Wills, Garry. *Cincinnatus: George Washington and the Enlightenment.* Garden City, N.Y.: Doubleday, 1984. A scholar-journalist's often deft insights into Washington's self-image and his popular image in the eighteenth and nineteenth centuries.

See also: John Adams; Benedict Arnold; Sir Guy Carleton; Samuel Chase; First Marquess Cornwallis; Thomas Gage; Nathanael Greene; Alexander Hamilton; Patrick Henry; William Howe; John Jay; Thomas Jefferson; Alexander McGillivray; James Madison; George Mason; Robert Morris; Charles Willson Peale; Comte de Rochambeau; Betsy Ross; Roger Sherman; Gilbert Stuart; James Wilson; John Witherspoon.

Related articles in *Great Events from History: The Eighteenth Century, 1701-1800:* September 5-October 26, 1774: First Continental Congress; April 19, 1775: Battle of Lexington and Concord; May 10-August 2, 1775: Second Continental Congress; May, 1776-September 3, 1783: France Supports the American Revolution; July 4, 1776: Declaration of Independence; September 19-October 17, 1777: Battles of Saratoga; February 6, 1778: Franco-American Treaties; March 1, 1781: Ratification of the Articles of Confederation; October 19, 1781: Cornwallis Surrenders at Yorktown; September 3, 1783: Treaty of Paris; September 17, 1787: U.S. Constitution Is Adopted; October 27, 1787-May, 1788: Publication of *The Federalist*; April 30, 1789: Washington's Inauguration; September 24, 1789: Judiciary Act; 1790's: First U.S. Political Parties; December 15, 1791: U.S. Bill of Rights Is Ratified; November 19, 1794: Jay's Treaty; September 19, 1796: Washington's Farewell Address.

JAMES WATT
Scottish inventor

Recognized as a great inventor in his own day, Watt developed a practical steam engine and thus promoted power-driven machinery—the heart of industrialization—and the beginnings of the Industrial Revolution.

Born: January 19, 1736; Greenock, Renfrewshire, Scotland
Died: August 25, 1819; Heathfield, Handsworth, Birmingham, England
Area of achievement: Science and technology

EARLY LIFE

James Watt's father, the elder James Watt, was a general merchant with a special interest in shipping and navigational instruments. A sickly child, the young Watt was tutored at home by his mother, and when he did go to school, he did not excel. His only educational accomplishment was a strong interest in mathematics, science, and mechanical instruments of all kinds.

At age seventeen, James left home for Glasgow with the intention of taking up the trade of making scientific instruments. Work in Glasgow proved scarce, and the only progress Watt made there was to gain the respect of some of the faculty at the university, where his uncle, George Muirhead, was a professor of Asian languages. After a year, James set out for London, the center of instrument production.

Entry into his chosen profession required seven years of service as an apprentice to a member of the guild. It was only through the payment of a sizable amount of money, twenty guineas provided by his father, that Watt found a master who was willing to violate the guild's regulations. Another difficulty facing Watt was the prospect of being pressed into the British navy, then involved in the Seven Years' War. In poor health, impoverished, and living in hiding from the press gangs, Watt nevertheless used his year in London wisely, becoming an expert in constructing the delicate instruments required in navigation.

In July, 1756, Watt completed his year in London and returned to Glasgow, where he intended to set himself up as a maker of mathematical instruments. Again, however, Watt faced a recalcitrant guild that refused to allow him to enter business. His friends at the University of Glasgow came to his rescue. Joseph Black, a professor of chemistry and the discoverer of latent heat, and John Robison, a student and later professor of natural philoso-

phy at Edinburgh, became his lifelong friends. The university was not bound by the rules of the town, and so it was that Watt came under its protection as official mathematical instrument maker of the university.

Watt was twenty-one in the summer of 1757, when he began his job with the university, marking a turning point in his life. He had not only a workshop but also the creative environment of the university. Also, his post required the repair of whatever instruments were brought to him, providing the opportunities to exercise his natural talent for invention. He became proficient at making navigational and musical instruments, and he was soon able to rent a small shop in Glasgow (his relations with the local guild had improved) while maintaining his connection with the university.

On July 16, 1764, at the age of twenty-eight, Watt married Margaret Miller, his cousin and a great source of encouragement to the inventor. He moved out of his university room and purchased a small home nearby. Drawings and paintings of Watt show a tall, handsome man, rather Jeffersonian in appearance, who wore his hair well over his ears, as was the style. Along with his prominent forehead and thoughtful expression, most portraits show a slight stoop to the shoulders and generally suggest a delicate constitution. At the time of his marriage, Watt's own efforts had not been particularly rewarding; in fact, he was poor. He continued to tinker with the instruments and machines brought to him for repair. One of them was a steam engine.

LIFE'S WORK

James Watt did not invent the steam engine. Such machines, called fire engines, had existed for some time, used primarily to pump water from mines. The most commonly employed type was the Newcomen engine, named for Thomas Newcomen, but these early engines were so enormously clumsy and inefficient that they were hardly used. For some time Watt had discussed the possibilities of steam power with his university associates and had begun experiments with high-pressure steam. Moreover, the university had acquired a defective model of the Newcomen engine and had turned it over to Watt. In the early 1760's, Watt repaired the university's steam engine and in the course of doing so became determined to develop a more practical, efficient version. He would make a real steam engine.

The principle of the Newcomen model was that condensed steam in a cylinder produced a vacuum, resulting in pressure that moved a piston, which, when attached to a beam or lever, could be used to work a pump. With an automatic valve gear, the operation could, in theory, be repeated indefinitely. The inefficiency of the Newcomen model stemmed from the fact that at every stroke the water had to be heated to boiling to produce the steam and then cooled to allow condensation. This limitation and the enormous waste of heat meant that in actuality the Newcomen model could make only a few strokes before being heated again.

Little was known about the properties of steam when Watt began his experiments, and, as his notebooks show, his investigations were exhaustive. He was helped immensely by the work of his friend Black, who had discovered latent heat, the heat generated or absorbed as water changes states. Watt correctly surmised that the chief problem of the Newcomen engine was in the loss of latent heat. In May, 1765, Watt reached his fundamental theoretical conclusion about the nature of an efficient steam engine: the concept of a separate condenser so that the boiling water could be condensed into steam without cooling the cylinder. With no injection of cold water into the cylinder, it would remain quite hot, and efficiency

would be vastly increased. This was the single most important improvement Watt, or anyone, made on the steam engine.

Watt added other innovations that also increased efficiency. He used an air pump to remove the condensed steam, and he improved the vacuum by tighter packing lubricated with oil. Newcomen's engine had been open at the top for the piston rod; Watt enclosed it with steamtight stuffing around the rod. He also insulated the cylinder with a steam jacket. Basically, however, his first steam engine was of three parts: the cylinder and its piston, the separate condenser, and the air pump.

The experiments to produce such a working steam engine were expensive. Watt was a master craftsman who refused to take shortcuts, and the expenditure of his time and materials had left him in debt. He clearly saw that his engine would be a great commercial success, but he also knew that he lacked the financial resources to bring it to the market. His first patent was not obtained until 1769, four years after the discovery of his fundamental principles. In the intervening years he supported himself as a civil engineer, doing surveys for canal construction. He also obtained a partner, John Roebuck, to underwrite the cost of refinements on his steam engine.

Roebuck himself soon faced financial problems, and by 1773 Watt's personal life took a dramatic turn for the worse with the death of his wife. He was now a widower with two small children and a partner who had gone bankrupt. The following year, however, brought a new partner: the wealthy and renowned Matthew Boulton, owner of the Soho Works in Birmingham. Boulton had admired Watt's work for some time and had assisted in obtaining the patent, and his purchase of Roebuck's share of the steam engine brought success to Watt's efforts. The partnership was a highly lucrative one. Boulton not only was a financial wizard but also was wise enough not to interfere with Watt's inventive abilities. Over the next ten years, these two men changed the course of history.

Watt continued to modify his engine, and by 1783 it was used widely in mining. His later inventions adapted the steam engine to power other machinery, and the Industrial Revolution, based on Watt's steam engine, was under way. In 1800, Watt's patent expired, and he turned his share of the business over to his son James. The inventor then retired, quite wealthy, to Heathfield Hall, a home he had built near Bir-

James Watt. (Library of Congress)

mingham, where he continued to work on mechanical inventions.

Before moving to Birmingham, Watt had remarried, to Ann MacGregor. They produced two children, both of whom died young. Watt's old age was serene. He had developed many warm friendships, as well as a gentle personality characterized by modesty, wide-ranging interests, and a sense of humor. He died peacefully on August 25, 1819, at Heathfield, and was buried at the nearby church of Handsworth.

SIGNIFICANCE

Without the steam engine, James Watt would be remembered only as an inventor. He made a significant contribution to the understanding of the composition of water and invented a machine to copy sculpture as well as a letter-copying press. His steam engine, however, was an invention of paramount importance. Before Watt, the fire engine was so inefficient as to be hardly used at all. After him, it was the first motor of the Industrial Revolution. Other technological advances were critical to that great process, but it was Watt who created the reality of power-driven machinery—critical to industrialization. For that triumph he received substantial recognition in his own life. He won admission into the Royal Societies of Edinburgh and London, along with an honorary degree from the University of Glasgow. In 1814, he received the high honor of being one of the eight non-Frenchmen accepted into the Academy of Sciences in Paris. The British government offered him noble rank, but he declined. The greatest honor, and the one by which he is known throughout the world, came after his death. In 1882, his name was given to the basic unit of power, the watt.

—*Roy Talbert, Jr.*

FURTHER READING

Arago, Dominique François Jean. *Historical Eloge of James Watt*. Translated by James P. Muirhead. London: John Murray, 1839. An early biography prepared on the occasion of Watt's induction into the French Academy of Sciences.

Crowther, James G. *Scientists of the Industrial Revolution: Joseph Black, James Watt, Joseph Priestley, Henry Cavendish*. Philadelphia: Dufour Editions, 1963. Containing separate treatments of each scientist, this work places Watt in the context of the scientific developments of his time.

Dickinson, H. W., and Rhys Jenkins. *James Watt and the Steam Engine*. Oxford, England: Clarendon Press, 1927. Reprinted in 1981, this work originated with the 1919 celebration of the century since Watt's death. Despite its date, the volume is thorough and well worth consulting.

Lord, John. *Capital and Steam-Power, 1750-1800*. 2d ed. New York: Augustus M. Kelley, 1965. Originally published in 1923, this remains a good introduction into the setting of eighteenth and nineteenth century engineering and economics.

Marsden, Ben. *Watt's Perfect Engine: Steam and the Age of Invention*. New York: Columbia University Press, 2002. A readable, technical biography of Watt. In Marsden's opinion, Watt was less an innovator than a practical businessman with an interest in natural philosophy. Marsden describes how Watt developed the steam condenser to make Newcomen's engine more efficient.

Miller, David Philip. *Discovering Water: James Watt, Henry Cavendish, and the Nineteenth Century "Water Controversy."* Burlington, Vt.: Ashgate, 2004. Describes how Cavendish's and Watt's discovery that water was a compound, not an element, became an issue of controversy among nineteenth century scientists.

Robinson, Eric, and Douglas McKie. *Partners in Science: Letters of James Watt and Joseph Black*. Cambridge, Mass.: Harvard University Press, 1970. Not limited to the correspondence between the two men in the title, this volume of primary material not only reveals the personal side of Watt but also tells much about scientific and technical development in the early days of the Industrial Revolution.

Robinson, Eric, and A. E. Musson. *James Watt and the Steam Revolution: A Documentary History*. New York: Augustus M. Kelley, 1969. Appearing two hundred years after Watt's first patent, this excellent book illustrates Watt's inventive genius.

Uglow, Jenny. *The Lunar Men: Five Friends Whose Curiosity Changed the World*. New York: Farrar, Straus, Giroux, 2002. Watt, his partner Matthew Boulton, and scientist Joseph Priestley were among the founders of the Lunar Society of Birmingham. Uglow's book describes how the organization invented new products, advanced science, and worked on other projects that ushered in the Industrial Revolution.

Webb, Robert N. *James Watt: Inventor of a Steam Engine*. New York: Franklin Watts, 1970. Webb's work is useful as an introduction to Watt.

See also: Joseph Black; Matthew Boulton; James Brindley; Henry Cavendish; John Fitch; William

Murdock; Thomas Newcomen; Joseph Priestley; John Roebuck; Josiah Wedgwood; Eli Whitney; John Wilkinson.

Related articles in *Great Events from History: The Eighteenth Century, 1701-1800:* 1705-1712: Newcomen Develops the Steam Engine; 1723: Stahl Postulates the Phlogiston Theory; 1765-1769: Watt Develops a More Effective Steam Engine; October 23, 1769: Cugnot Demonstrates His Steam-Powered Road Carriage; 1781-1784: Cavendish Discovers the Composition of Water; April, 1785: Cartwright Patents the Steam-Powered Loom; 1793: Whitney Invents the Cotton Gin; 1800: Volta Invents the Battery.

ANTOINE WATTEAU
French painter

Watteau was one of the finest French painters of the early eighteenth century and was the originator and perhaps the most successful practitioner of the fête galante, the idealized, romantic representation of love and sexual liaison.

Born: October 10, 1684; Valenciennes, France
Died: July 18, 1721; Nogent-sur-Marne, France
Also known as: Jean-Antoine Watteau (full name)
Area of achievement: Art

EARLY LIFE

Antoine Watteau (ahn-twahn vah-toh) was Flemish by birth, and he was born in Valenciennes, a border town between France and the Netherlands, which had been a Flemish city until 1678. His father may have been a roofer. In any case, Watteau came from a humble family, and there is nothing very certain about his early years. He may have been apprenticed to a local painter, Gérin, and then to a second, undistinguished painter, possibly named Métayer, who did some scene painting for the Paris Opera, and may have brought Watteau to Paris. Watteau was in Paris by 1702, living hand-to-mouth as a copyist of popular Netherlandish genre paintings. His first professional connection was with Claude Gillot, and he may have been apprenticed to him in the period between 1703 and 1707. Gillot had a reputation for painting theatrical subjects, and he probably had some influence on Watteau's lifelong interest in that subject. For some unknown reason, they parted abruptly, and Watteau joined Claude III Audran, a popular decorative artist with a sensitive minor talent for wall decoration, which had gained for him commissions in the royal residences. Of importance for Watteau, given his basically provincial background, was the fact that Audran was also the curator of Luxembourg Palace, where the great collection of Marie de Médicis' Rubenses was housed. Peter Paul Rubens was to be an important influence, and the elegant park landscape of the royal palaces was to be an ingratiating element in Watteau's work.

Watteau was settled into steady employment by the end of the first decade of the century, and he began to take some formal instruction at the Royal Academy. In 1712, his career was given some legitimacy when he was admitted as an associate member of the academy. He was, by this time, in demand as a painter, but he still needed to provide the academy with a specific painting on a specific subject in order to be considered for full membership in the institution that set the stamp of public success on artists at that time. Popular acceptance was one thing; his ascent to full acceptance by his peers was to take somewhat longer.

LIFE'S WORK

The *fête galante* was not a sudden inspiration but an original variation on a kind of painting that had had long and enthusiastic popularity in the seventeenth century, particularly in the Netherlands. Genre scenes, often of common peasant life, by painters such as David Teniers (1582-1649), were to have a constant market long into the eighteenth century, and Watteau may have supported himself as a painter of that kind of popular art. Certainly there is an interesting group of paintings of military camp life, painted in his early years, which can be related to that genre in their representation of the modest, day-to-day life of the military and their families as they travel through the countryside. The significant aspect of this choice of theme is its eschewing of the glory of military action in favor of the mundane conduct of a group of people living, in a sense, in the open air. This same interest in the less than glamorous aspects of certain ways of life shows up in his other paintings of the same period, in which he begins to explore the theatrical world. He seems to have had little interest in the bravura aspects of the stage, and considerable sensitivity toward actors and actresses as human beings who happen to be involved in dressing and comporting themselves in a profession that is larger than life.

There is another piece of this puzzle that is somewhat more difficult to put in place. There is a very small group of paintings that suggests that Watteau may have been one of the great erotic painters. Those that are extant suggest an implosion of sexual intensity, a kind of quiet blaze of passion, which quite transcends simple pornographic titillation, and will often show up in the *fêtes* in the flare of a nostril or a kind of glazing of an eye in something of a sexual daze.

What the *fêtes* are, in fact, seems simple when viewed as the finest examples of the French rococo theme of sexual dalliance among the upper classes. Generally, that is what they are in the hands of less-accomplished artists such as Watteau's pupil, Jean Baptiste Pater (1695-1736). Yet they are not quite so simple when Watteau is the painter. They have a Rubenesque lushness of color wedded to a Venetian influence that used color rather than line for modeling; they have, however, something more, a peculiar blending of sophisticated sexual ideality and underlying reality that reminds the viewer of Watteau's Flemish provinciality. The combination of

Antoine Watteau. (Library of Congress)

lovers dressed in high fashion and characters dressed as players from the Parisian version of the Italian *commedia dell'arte*, portraying the ambiguities, the arabesques of sexual confrontation, creates an air of fleeting reality that transcends the obviousness of the theme. If they are rococo in shape, in color, in theme, in character, they are also larger than that, ultimately. What Watteau achieves in his *fêtes galantes* is the kind of artistic elevation that Jean-Siméon Chardin would later achieve in his paintings of simple servant life, and which Paul Cézanne would capture in his still lifes: a sense that the work of art has a monumentality, an aesthetic importance that defies definition, and turns the commonplace, the obvious, even the trivial theme into a symbol of the mystery of human and aesthetic endeavor. Watteau—passed by in the normal swift peregrination of the gallery visitor intent on making culture in the least amount of time— looks like any other rococo artist, pretty, but shallow. Watteau concentrated upon a much more formidable matter, a confrontation with artistic densities, symbolic connotations, and disturbing emotional depths.

These characteristics are best displayed in the painting that was to gain for Watteau full membership in the Royal Academy, the *Pilgrimage to Cythera*. There is much critical quarrel about whether the lovers are on their way to Cythera or on their way back, and whether this painting is better than a later version, but little quarrel over their greatness as paintings and the way in which the simple theme of sexual blandishments seems to say something about the fleeting nature of human desire. Gorgeous, lush, celebratory, magnificently poised in its graceful juxtaposition of elegantly dressed and beautiful people, it is also a painting that seems to carry a foreboding sense of human fragility.

What it might have meant to Watteau is impossible to say, but it is known that he was a man of some reserve, occasionally cantankerous, and given to withdrawing from society. The painting of Cythera for the academy may have been something of a triumph in itself, but the acceptance by the institution may have been diminished by the fact that the usual categories for acceptance lay with history, landscape, or genre subjects. The academy established a special category for Watteau as a painter of the *fête galante*. This may have been a compliment to him; some critics suggest that it was not so, but a distinction with a limiting difference, implying that Watteau was not quite up to the demands of the formally established categories. It does distinguish him, however, from other painters of the period, and he was to heighten that difference in his later paintings, in which the idealities of beauty, sexual attraction, and social position were to become even more obviously confronted with the limitations of reality.

The critical acceptance of Watteau as an early example of the Romantic artist (almost one hundred years before this type of artist was to appear formally) was fostered by the Goncourt brothers, the French men of letters of the mid-nineteenth century, who saw in Watteau's life and in his work a deep elegiac melancholy that was probably not clearly recognized during his lifetime. Certainly there was an enthusiasm for such readings of Watteau in the nineteenth century that led to a revival of his popularity, and certainly the problem of subjective imposition of tone and meaning on the arts is not uncommon, but there may be more to the idea than changing taste.

Watteau was a man dying by inches in the later stages of his career, and he died very young, of tuberculosis, a wasting disease, which may give credence to the idea that he is the bagpipe player looking sadly at the dancers in *Venetian Pleasures*. In those few later years, that tender melancholy is a constant. Even paintings of the clowns of the Italian comedic world are touched with a sense of vulnerability. *Gilles*, for example, is a painting of a character in the *commedia* who is usually mischievous, stupid, and vulgar; Watteau's *Gilles* has an air of helplessness about him that is quite unnerving, and which has made the painting one of the best-known works in the history of art. This touch of reality intruding on the thin skin of his idealizations of young love and social pleasures would become stronger in his last works and would fuel the psychological reading of his career. Continually in demand, he spent almost a year in London in 1719, returning to Paris in 1720, where he continued to paint, producing one of his finest works, *Gersaint's Shopsign*, with the clear intention that it should be used as simply that, a sign to be mounted (as it was for a short time) outside the shop of his friend and dealer Edme Gersaint. It would seem that Watteau had come full circle. In the last months of his life, he rejected his fame as a painter of romantic idealities to return to the kind of work which he had probably needed to do in order to live in the early years of his career. There seems to have been little pretension in his personality; it is likely that *Gilles* was also painted for use as a poster advertising a theatrical group. In neither case did the proposed function of the work deter Watteau from painting at his very best.

Increasingly ill, Watteau retired to the outskirts of Paris in his last months, where he painted a *Crucifixion* for the local parish priest. Like so much of his work, it is missing. He died at the age of thirty-six on July 18, 1721.

SIGNIFICANCE

Antoine Watteau was the first, and ultimately the best, of that group of French rococo painters who were to idealize and ultimately trivialize the art of love in eighteenth century painting. Part of the reason lay in the fact that his pupils, Jean-Baptiste-Joseph Pater and Nicolas Lancret (possibly a pupil) were less-established artists; part of the reason may have been dangerously implicit in the subject itself, in its potential for excess, for sentimentalization, for emphasizing emotion at the expense of artistic integrity. He seems to have had a more salutary influence on two later painters in the genre, François Boucher, who began his career as an engraver of Watteau, and Jean-Honoré Fragonard, although Boucher had a tendency to slip into insipidity, which was never a mark of Watteau's work.

Indeed, in Watteau's drawings, which are often as masterful as his best paintings, and in his finer works, there is a sense that he is the artist who leans back to the tradition of the Giorgione dreamworld and forward to the epiphanic stillnesses of Chardin. Technically dubious, sometimes downright sloppy as a painter, he is, nevertheless, an example of that peculiar kind of artist whose aesthetic vision transcends both technique and subject.

—*Charles H. Pullen*

FURTHER READING

Börsch-Supan, Helmut. *Antoine Watteau, 1684-1721*. Translated by Anthea Bell. Cologne, Germany: Könemann, 2000. Examination of Watteau's art, describing his style, his influence on other artists, and his ability to understand and represent the historic events of his time.

Brookner, Anita. *Watteau*. London: Paul Hamlyn, 1967. Short, well illustrated, and the best introductory study of Watteau's work, written charmingly by an art historian who would later become one of Great Britain's finest novelists. Her work on eighteenth century French painters of feeling and her deep understanding of the role of the emotions in those painters makes her particularly helpful in dealing with the nuances of Watteau's work.

Gombrich, E. H. *The Story of Art*. 14th ed. Englewood Cliffs, N.J.: Prentice-Hall, 1985. Watteau's greatness can be missed if he is viewed by himself. What is needed is a historical sense of Watteau: a Flemish artist, naturally inclined to a genre of considerable power in its own right, which he somehow maintains and uses to make something new, and equally valid. This book puts him in perspective within the history of art.

Levey, Michael. *Rococo to Revolution*. London: Thames and Hudson, 1966. Levey, a former director of the National Gallery in London, argues for viewing Watteau as an anticipation of Romanticism. Well written and well illustrated.

Plax, Julie Anne. *Watteau and the Cultural Politics of Eighteenth-Century France*. New York: Cambridge University Press, 2000. Plax explores the themes and political issues in Watteau's paintings, and describes how his artistic technique aimed to subvert "high art."

Posner, Donald. *Antoine Watteau*. Ithaca, N.Y.: Cornell University Press, 1984. This is an excellent examination of Watteau's life and career, written by the scholar who finds the "romantic" Watteau somewhat questionable and is prepared to make his interesting case to the contrary. Also very good on possible symbolic reading of Watteau paintings and very helpful on the artist's early career.

Vidal, Mary. *Watteau's Painted Conversations: Art, Literature, and Talk in Seventeenth- and Eighteenth-Century France*. New Haven, Conn.: Yale University Press, 1992. Vidal maintains that conversation was crucial to Watteau's images of sociability and was a framework for all of his paintings. She places his work within the context of seventeenth and eighteenth century France, when conversation became an art, women's salons flourished in Paris, and the written conversation became an accepted literary genre.

Wintermute, Alan. *Watteau and His World: French Drawing from 1700 to 1750*. New York: American Federation of Arts, and London: Merrell Holberton, 1999. A catalog for an exhibition of drawings by Watteau, his mentors, and artists he influenced. Includes essays, color reproductions, and a bibliography of each drawing.

See also: Jean-Siméon Chardin; Jean-Honoré Fragonard.

Related articles in *Great Events from History: The Eighteenth Century, 1701-1800*: December 10, 1768: Britain's Royal Academy of Arts Is Founded; 1785: Construction of El Prado Museum Begins; 1787: David Paints *The Death of Socrates*.

ANTHONY WAYNE
American general

Wayne was a self-trained, successful American general who was adept at fighting both European and American Indian enemies. His defeat of the American Indians of the Northwest Territory helped open the West to Euro-American settlement.

Born: January 1, 1745; Easttown Township (now Waynesboro), Pennsylvania
Died: December 15, 1796; Presque Isle (now Erie), Pennsylvania
Areas of achievement: Warfare and conquest, military

EARLY LIFE
Anthony Wayne, a grandson of Irish immigrants, was born on his family's estate, Waynesborough. An uncle in Philadelphia educated him as a child. He then spent three years at the Philadelphia Academy, became a surveyor at eighteen, and, on March 25, 1766, married a neighbor, Mary Penrose, after a short courtship. For the next few years the couple lived on the family estate while Wayne farmed and surveyed. They had two children, Isaac and Margaretta.

LIFE'S WORK
During the 1770's, revolutionary fever spread throughout the American colonies. In 1774, Anthony Wayne was chosen as representative for Easttown Township to the Provincial Convention in Philadelphia. He was involved in numerous local protests against British rule and helped win the support of many of his neighbors for the revolutionary cause. He was elected to a seat in the Pennsylvania assembly and, in 1775, to the Committee of Safety. There he was charged with preparing the state's military defenses against possible British invasion, writing military regulations, and organizing and supplying the state militia. At the same time, he studied military strategy and history and organized his own volunteer militia. When the American Revolution broke out, Wayne was commissioned a colonel in the newly formed Continental army and sent to assist General John Sullivan in Canada.

As commander, Wayne insisted on strict adherence to military regulations and stiffened the penalties for many minor infractions. He believed his strategy was especially important when dealing with rough, inexperienced recruits who volunteered for the rebel army. They needed discipline to successfully face the highly trained and experienced British army. In Wayne's first battlefield experiences in Canada, he showed cool determination. He was placed in charge of American troops at Fort Ticonderoga during winter quarters of 1776-1777. There, Wayne and his men faced a constant struggle for food and warm clothing. When disease struck, his weary men threatened to mutiny, but Wayne maintained control.

In March of 1777 he was promoted to brigadier general and placed in charge of two brigades of Pennsylvania regulars in the Continental army. He took command in Morristown, where he drilled and trained his troops. Wayne and his freshly trained soldiers demonstrated skill and bravery against the British at New Brunswick. General George Washington, commander of the Continental army, depended on Wayne to hold his ground and keep the enemy at bay in difficult situations. Wayne was not afraid to charge when outgunned or against overwhelming numbers. Wayne and his men distinguished themselves at the Battles of Brandywine against Hessian forces at Germantown and Monmouth Court House. Because of his seemingly impulsive, fearless acts during battle, he was nicknamed "Mad Anthony" Wayne.

During the 1779 campaign, Wayne commanded an elite light infantry corps of thirteen hundred experienced and specially chosen men who successfully captured Stony Point on their first engagement. The corps moved to the south, where they assisted the Marquis de Lafayette's command in delaying the movement southward of the British commander, General Cornwallis, and his troops. The delay allowed American forces time to connect with French troops and help defeat the British at Yorktown. In November, 1781, Wayne was ordered to Georgia to help liberate Savannah and Charleston, which were still being held by British troops. It was there that he first encountered American Indians of the Creek and Choctaw tribes who were allied with the British. He successfully persuaded a group of Creek to join the American cause, but the Choctaw refused. He defeated Choctaw forces outside Savannah, which encouraged the British to abandon the city in July of 1782.

While at the front, Wayne was consulted by fellow Pennsylvanians on political matters at home. He argued against the first Pennsylvania constitution, which, in his opinion, would have left Pennsylvania citizens with a weak state government. He advised state leaders regarding military defenses for Philadelphia. He was in charge of recruitment and procurement of troop supplies such as uniforms, blankets, and shoes, which were in constant

General Anthony Wayne. (Library of Congress)

short supply. He tirelessly lobbied to improve both state recruitment and militia laws, hoping encourage future enlistment. In 1779, Wayne traveled from the battlefield to the Pennsylvania assembly to plead for supplies in person. In spite of his efforts, he was sometimes forced to use his own funds for uniforms and medical care for his men.

For his actions to liberate Savannah, the Georgia assembly awarded Wayne two estates, Richmond and Kew, and hundreds of acres of Georgia land. He was promoted to major general in 1783, and Congress awarded him a gold medal for his actions at Stony Point. He returned home and once again joined the political scene, winning election to the Pennsylvania council of censors in 1783 to draft suggested changes to the state constitution. He also served at the state's constitutional convention that approved the new federal Constitution. When the terms of his elected offices expired, Wayne traveled to Georgia to run his new rice plantations there. The farms were in disarray, and Wayne was forced to take out large loans to clear the fields and purchase equipment and slaves. The first few yields were not as expected, and he ran into serious financial difficulties that were alleviated years later by giving up most of his Georgia possessions.

Wayne was elected to the U.S. House of Representatives from the state of Georgia in 1790 but served just six months before he was removed over questionable election practices. As a representative, he tried to raise funds and supplies for the western army fighting American Indians in the Northwest Territory. American troops were having difficulty keeping the peace in the territory east of the Mississippi River and west of the Appalachians. Indigenous tribes did not acknowledge the terms of the Treaty of Paris that granted those lands to Americans.

Members of the Miami, Shawnee, Delaware, Wyandot, and other local tribes allied themselves under the leadership of Little Turtle and Blue Jacket and threatened American settlers in the area. British settlers who were still occupying forts against the terms of the Paris treaty encouraged the tribes to resist American settlement in the hope of retrieving their lands. The British fortified Fort Miamis in Ohio and provided American Indians with supplies and information. Congress then appointed Revolutionary War general Arthur St. Clair to bring peace to the area. In November, 1791, St. Clair and his troops were defeated: Six hundred Americans were killed, and St. Clair resigned his commission.

Congress appointed General Wayne to take command of the western army. While awaiting confirmation, he did research on the indigenous peoples of the Northwest Territory, reading books and interviewing traders and missionaries to learn indigenous cultures and warfare tactics. In 1773, Wayne moved his men outside Fort Washington in what is now Cincinnati, Ohio. Whereas American commissioners attempted treaty negotiations with American Indians, Wayne had trained his men as disciplined soldiers, and not as negotiators. When local tribes refused to give up lands north of the Ohio River, Wayne was ordered to take control. As he and his men moved north, they built strongholds along the way for future use. Fort Greenville, Fort Defiance, Fort Recovery, and Fort Wayne were built on the way toward tribal encampments along the Maumee River.

After a series of skirmishes, Wayne met American Indians on August 20, 1794, at a point nicknamed Fallen Timbers because a storm had recently torn down many of the trees in the area. As the Battle of Fallen Timbers began, American Indians fired from behind the protection of the fallen trees and, at first, pushed Wayne's troops back. Wayne ordered his well-trained forces forward and, with screams to disarm the enemy, his men advanced and routed the indigenous forces. As they fled the advancing American soldiers, they sought refuge in the nearby British fort of Miamis, but the British barred their

entrance and American Indians were forced to face the American soldiers without British battlefield assistance. Wayne lost thirty-three men while hundreds of American Indians died. In the days following the Battle of Fallen Timbers, Wayne's men destroyed cornfields and the villages of the local tribes, making it difficult for them to feed themselves through the following winter. The American Indians agreed to the Treaty of Greenville, surrendering two-thirds of the state of Ohio along with part of southeastern Indiana. In return they received $20,000 in goods and an annuity of $9,500, but were forced to move westward.

Following a brief trip home to Pennsylvania, Wayne returned to the West to oversee the British evacuation of forts in American territory. He supervised American occupation of the forts as well as supply and organization. Within a few years his health began to fail. He suffered a reoccurrence of a fever he had contracted in the south and a painful case of gout. While traveling to Pittsburgh, Wayne died at Presque Isle on December 15, 1796. He was buried at the foot of a flagpole there, but his body was later moved in 1809 to his home in Pennsylvania.

SIGNIFICANCE

Anthony Wayne represents one of America's first self-made generals. He had no formal military training or experience when he joined America's fight for freedom but immediately set out to learn all he could about the profession. He believed not only in vigorously training his men but also in training himself. He learned the military strategy and tactics of leaders before him, but he also knew the importance of learning about his enemy, including their military attributes. When the face of the enemy changed drastically in the West, he reeducated himself to fight a very different kind of foe and succeeded where two previous generals had failed.

—*Leslie Stricker*

FURTHER READING

Gaff, Alan D. *Bayonets in the Wilderness: Anthony Wayne's Legion in the Old Northwest*. Norman: University of Oklahoma Press, 2004. Gaff concentrates on Wayne's exploits and influence in the Northwest Territory.

Johansen, Bruce E. *Shapers of the Great Debate on Native Americans: Land, Spirit, and Power*. Westport, Conn.: Greenwood Press, 2000. Johansen examines the issue of American land "ownership," alliances between American Indian nations to ensure indigenous land sovereignty, and the ties between place and culture.

Nelson, Paul David. *Anthony Wayne: Soldier of the Early Republic*. Bloomington: Indiana University Press, 1985. Nelson details Wayne's military, political, financial, and private lives.

Still, Charles J. *Major General Anthony Wayne and the Pennsylvania Line in the Continental Army*. Ganesevoort, N.Y.: Corner House Historical Publications, 2000. The author explores Wayne's revolutionary battlefield exploits.

See also: Joseph Brant; First Marquess Cornwallis; Little Turtle; Alexander McGillivray; Pontiac; Thanadelthur; George Washington.

Related articles in *Great Events from History: The Eighteenth Century, 1701-1800:* October 5, 1759-November 19, 1761: Cherokee War; May 8, 1763-July 24, 1766: Pontiac's Resistance; September 5-October 26, 1774: First Continental Congress; April 19, 1775: Battle of Lexington and Concord; May 24 and June 11, 1776: Indian Delegation Meets with Congress; July 4, 1776: Declaration of Independence; October 22, 1784: Fort Stanwix Treaty; July 13, 1787: Northwest Ordinance; October 18, 1790-July, 1794: Little Turtle's War; August 20, 1794: Battle of Fallen Timbers.

JOSIAH WEDGWOOD
English inventor, industrialist, and artist

Wedgwood's genius and innovations helped not only to convert pottery making from a peasant's craft to a major industry but also to bring about the Industrial Revolution in England.

Born: July 12, 1730 (baptized); Burslem (now in Stoke-on-Trent), Staffordshire, England
Died: January 3, 1795; Etruria, Staffordshire, England
Areas of achievement: Business, science and technology, art

EARLY LIFE

Josiah Wedgwood was presumably the last of twelve children born to Thomas and Mary Wedgwood. Thomas, of the Churchyard Pottery in North Staffordshire, England, was a fourth-generation potter. His wife, née Mary Stringer, was the daughter of a Unitarian minister of Newcastle-under-Lyme. Until age nine, Josiah walked seven miles each day to attend school at Newcastle-under-Lyme, where he showed an aptitude for mathematics and writing. His formal education abruptly ended when, in 1739, his father died, but as he had an insatiable thirst for knowledge, he became a self-educated man.

For the next five years, Josiah worked for Thomas, his brother, who had taken over the family business. At twelve, Josiah fell victim to smallpox and was left with an infection which settled in his right leg. He was to grow to be a small man with a homely appearance. He had a broad, friendly, yet pockmarked face, and he was a kind, strong, and dynamic individual. At fourteen, Josiah became his brother's apprentice, but because of his bad leg,

he was unable to perform such laborious tasks as throwing pottery clay. Instead, he spent much of his time keeping records, modeling, designing, and experimenting. Consequently, he often considered his leg infection as a happy accident. In 1749, his apprenticeship ended. He continued working with his brother for three more years. When Thomas refused to offer him a partnership, however, presumably because he considered Josiah too ambitious and experimental, Josiah left the family business. In 1752, he formed a partnership with John Harrison and Thomas Alders. This was a short-lived association, as Wedgwood and Harrison clashed over manufacturing ideas.

In 1754, a five-year partnership began with Thomas Whieldon of Fenton Hall, an outstanding potter of that time. This partnership seemed ideal: Both men loved to experiment, were highly motivated, and had compatible temperaments. They agreed that Wedgwood's discoveries and methods, while benefiting both, would remain Wedgwood's secret. Thus, in 1759, Wedgwood began keeping his "Experiment Book." In the opening pages, he expressed concern over the declining pottery business and stated that it was time something be done to revive it. Therefore, his early experiments concentrated on improving the body of the pieces regarding glazes and form. In his book he carefully listed measurements and ingredients using a numbered code that only he understood. He was almost paranoid about the need for secrecy, even though at times he was quite verbose about his findings. On March 23, 1759, he recorded his first distinctive achievement, listed as experiment number seven. It was the invention of a green glaze. This discovery whetted his appetite for success and innovation.

LIFE'S WORK

On May 1, 1759, nearly twenty-nine years old, Josiah Wedgwood had accumulated enough capital to establish himself as an independent potter. He rented the Ivy House and pots works in Burslem. Soon after, he introduced an improved agate body that had a marbled effect achieved by wedging together different colored clays. His almost immediate success was extraordinary. It was then that Wedgwood turned his attention to organizing factory operations.

Wedgwood's most important innovations were specialization and the use of machinery in manufacturing. Prior to Wedgwood's changes, all production in the industry was done by one person on each piece. Now tasks were divided into categories such as mixing clays, throwing, and decorating. This work required that a worker be skilled in only one area. By this reorganization, Wedgwood eliminated the journeyman and apprenticeship system and exacted new, higher standards of workmanship. At first, the workers resisted the idea, but then they saw the potential for greater productivity and, thus, increased wealth. (They also saw the possibility of greater monotony and loss of independence.) The introduction of steam power, engine turning, and tools such as lathes also revolutionized the industry. Production became more efficient. These innovations were indicative of the beginning of the Industrial Revolution in England.

The transportation system in England was inadequate in the mid-1700's, and the pottery district was isolated. Clays from Dorset and Devon as well as flint and other materials had to be shipped to Chester or Liverpool, then carried to North Staffordshire by horse and transferred to the district by river. Wedgwood helped organize regional and national efforts to build better roads and more canals. This civic involvement helped establish Wedgwood as the spokesman for the pottery industry in both political and legal matters. He soon took an active role in the promotion and construction of turnpikes. He was prominently involved in a proposal for the construction of the Trent and Mersey Canal to link Hull, the Potteries, and Liverpool. In 1766, after a long battle with Parliament, he was appointed treasurer to the newly formed company of proprietors, and by 1777, the ninety-four-mile system was completed. Such improvements in the transportation system also helped spur the Industrial Revolution.

In 1762, Wedgwood's leg forced him to bed for several weeks in Liverpool. A friend, Dr. Matthew Turner,

introduced him to Thomas Bentley, who would have a profound effect on Wedgwood's future career. The firm of Bentley and Turner became Wedgwood's Liverpool agent. Bentley's classical training and knowledge of various languages made him invaluable to Wedgwood, who repeatedly sought his advice and approval.

In that same year, Wedgwood moved to the Brick House Works in Burslem (referred to as the Bell Works because men were summoned to work by a ringing bell rather than by a blowing horn) for production of useful wares. It was in this area of manufacturing that Wedgwood made his name. He now devoted much of his time to the production of a cream-colored, fine earthenware. By 1763, he had successfully created an earthenware for the dinner table.

In 1764, Wedgwood married his third cousin, Sarah Wedgwood of Spen Green, Cheshire. Sarah was exceptionally competent and shared in her husband's interests. He relied heavily upon her and his home life to provide an escape from the pressures of success. On January 3, 1765, their first child, Susannah (Sukey), was born. She would later marry Robert Darwin and give birth to Charles Darwin. In all, the Wedgwoods had eight children. Josiah was a devoted husband and father.

English potter Josiah Wedgwood. (The Granger Collection, New York)

In June, 1765, Wedgwood received his first royal order, which proved to be a tremendous boost to his career. Queen Charlotte ordered a caudle (a hot mulled drink set) and was so pleased with his work that she referred to him as the potter to the queen. By 1767, he began to advertise his wares as Queen's Ware. In July, 1766, Wedgwood bought the Ridgehouse Estate, which contained 350 acres lying between Hanley, Burslem, and Newcastle. Here he built a factory for ornamental wares. The new factory, Etruria, opened on June 13, 1769.

In May, 1768, Wedgwood and Thomas Bentley officially formed their very successful partnership. Bentley was the source of stimulation for Wedgwood's creative genius. The two men were partners, but more important, they were close friends. Bentley introduced Wedgwood to such notable men as Joseph Priestley (who for a while was Wedgwood's chemist), Benjamin Franklin, and Sir Joshua Reynolds. Later, in 1772, a group of these prominent men, including Wedgwood, would form the Lunar Society, an elite forum for intellectual discussion. This unofficial organization was one of the greatest influences on his life.

On May 28, 1768, Wedgwood once again fell ill from an infection in his leg. This time, however, it was determined that the leg had to be amputated just above the knee. While it was very painful without anesthetics, Wedgwood insisted upon watching the operation. Afterward, he often sensed the presence of his leg in the area he referred to as his no-leg, but Wedgwood did not allow his personal crisis to interfere with his work.

In 1769, Wedgwood took out his first and only patent. It was for an encaustic painting process that entailed firing a dull, red enamel on a black basalt body. In 1770, Humphrey Palmer of Hanley infringed upon this patent. Outraged, Wedgwood began legal proceedings against Palmer. In 1771, Wedgwood withdrew the suit after realizing that a costly lawsuit, even if successful, would make the patent unprofitable. Later, Palmer compensated Wedgwood, and they shared the patent. After this incident, Wedgwood began marking his wares with a large and a small stamp in an attempt to protect his ideas.

By 1771, the industry was suffering from falling prices brought on by economic depression. Wedgwood, therefore, formed a local potters' association, whose main objective was to maintain prices during this troubled time. The bad economic conditions in England prompted Wedgwood to lower production costs and to find new markets both at home and abroad.

The year 1773 was a landmark for Wedgwood, for in that year he achieved some of his greatest successes.

First, Wedgwood and Bentley published their first catalog of ornamental wares. Then, Wedgwood received an order from Empress Catherine the Great of Russia for a cream-colored dinner and dessert service. It was his largest and most famous commission. Often referred to as the Frog Service because each piece had a frog on it, the service contained 952 pieces and had 1,244 different English scenes. Perhaps Wedgwood's greatest success that year, however, came as a result of his experimentations. He combined spar (a lustrous crystalline mineral) with clay and flint and a small amount of barium carbonate in a mineral form. The resulting stoneware he named jasper. He had conducted more than five thousand experiments, each carefully recorded in his notebook, before it could be made consistently uniform. By 1775, jasper was used for producing ornamental pieces. Wedgwood then employed John Flaxman, a sculptor, to model and design the durable jasperware, which was decorated with delicate white figures of the Roman imperial period. The jasper body was considered the first important innovation in ceramic history for thousands of years.

Early in 1780, Wedgwood bought Churchyard Works Pottery from his nephew, Thomas Wedgwood, Then, tragically, in November, Bentley died at age fifty. Bentley's death came as a shock to Wedgwood. To a degree, the void in his life was filled by Erasmus Darwin, but this association could not compensate for Bentley's death. An important force in Wedgwood's life was now gone forever.

On May 9, 1782, Wedgwood delivered his first paper to the Royal Society. The paper dealt with another of Wedgwood's inventions—a pyrometer, or thermometer. This new device could measure degrees of heat above the capacity of existing mercurial thermometers. Nearly twenty years would pass before anything more accurate would be invented. The principle of his pyrometer was based upon the contraction of clay when heated. The invention was acknowledged by the entire scientific community. Consequently, on January 16, 1783, Wedgwood was elected a fellow of the Royal Society. He delivered several more papers to the society over the next three years.

In 1783, Wedgwood also published two pamphlets, *An Address to the Young Inhabitants of the Pottery* and *An Address to the Workmen in the Pottery on the Subject of Entering into Service of Foreign Manufacturers.* In these pamphlets, he warned young men against leaving England in search of better jobs in the industry in the United States. While he earlier had favored colonial independence, Wedgwood did not desire an increase in foreign competition.

During the 1780's, Wedgwood became very active in national politics as it concerned commerce. For example, he represented the potters in negotiations for a trade treaty with the newly independent American states in 1783. He was also an active promoter of the short-lived General Chamber of Manufacturers of Great Britain (from 1785 to 1787), was concerned with the drafting of the Irish Trade Treaty of 1785 and the French Commercial Treaty of 1787, and actively participated in the Society for the Suppression of the Slave Trade, founded in 1787.

From 1790 onward, Wedgwood began to retire gradually from the partnership named Wedgwood, Sons, and Byerley. His son, Josiah, and nephew, Tom Byerley, now ran the business while his attention turned to the problems of the poor, the promotion of friendly societies, and the search for a leadless glaze. On January 3, 1795, Wedgwood died at Etruria after three weeks of illness. At the time of his death, Wedgwood was one of England's wealthiest men. He was buried in the churchyard of Stoke Parish Church.

SIGNIFICANCE

Josiah Wedgwood lived in England during an exciting time of change. While he had little formal education, he associated with some of the greatest minds of his century. These associations, coupled with his own creative genius and his desire to improve the pottery industry, led him to great success and enabled him to play an important role in the birth of the Industrial Revolution.

Wedgwood's innovations in the pottery industry enabled him to meet some of Europe's sociocultural needs in the eighteenth century. For example, prior to Wedgwood's innovation, a dinner was served using one communal bowl or trencher made of wood, pewter, porcelain, or silver. Wedgwood's manufacture of an inexpensive plate, however, made it affordable to buy individual dinner settings. Also, as society paid more attention to table etiquette, and with the growing popularity of tea and coffee, there was a greater need for more pots, creamers, sugar bowls, cups, and saucers. Yet Wedgwood was not content to make simple pottery. Instead, he linked art with industry by concentrating on elegance of form and by paying attention to detail. Because of this, Wedgwood was the first English potter to achieve a European reputation and, in fact, was often imitated throughout Europe.

Nevertheless, Wedgwood was not an artist so much as he was a scientist and businessman, for he blended science with industry. He applied the scientific approach not only to his experiments and inventions but also to industrial problems. He organized his factory efficiently and introduced entirely new concepts and practices into the manufacturing of pottery. Thus, Wedgwood kept the price down and production high. He helped develop many principles of mass production and applied them to pottery making.

In his approach to art, science, and industry, Wedgwood reflected the trends of his age: He capitalized on the fervor of the new classicism in England in the 1700's; he represented upright morality and independent thought; he was amiable and just, loved and honored; he attracted devotion as well as esteem, for he was without pretensions. Wedgwood brought about a union of beauty and productivity, which was perhaps the touchstone of his success.

—*Charles A. Dranguet, Jr.*

FURTHER READING

Burton, Anthony. *Josiah Wedgwood: A Biography*. New York: Stein and Day, 1976. Traces the life of Josiah Wedgwood from birth to death, including his legacy. Presents more personal data than most sources; very well written with interesting quotations and excerpts from Wedgwood's correspondence.

Dolan, Brian. *Wedgwood: The First Tycoon*. New York: Viking Press, 2004. Comprehensive biography. Describes Wedgwood's experiments aimed at perfecting pottery making, his business and personal relationship with Thomas Bentley, the establishment of his factory, and his creation of new sales and business techniques.

Honey, W. B. *English Pottery and Porcelain*. London: A. and C. Black, 1933. This concise history of British ceramic art contains a chapter on Wedgwood's life and career. Honey defends Wedgwood as a great businessman but points out his weaknesses as an individual who seemed more interested in seeking the acceptance of the wealthy than in perfecting his craft. Also discusses Wedgwood in relation to his contemporaries and his impact upon later British potters.

Kelly, Allison, comp. *The Story of Wedgwood*. New York: Viking Press, 1962. Presents a sketchy yet informative account of Wedgwood and his firm from his birth in 1730 through eleven generations to the 1960's. Extremely brief chapters; straight presentation of the facts with little or no literary flair.

Koehn, Nancy F. *Brand New: How Entrepreneurs Earned Customers' Trust from Wedgwood to Dell*. Boston: Harvard Business School Press, 2001. Profiles of Wedgwood and five other entrepreneurs who understood how economic and social change would create demands for new consumer products. The profile of Wedgwood describes how the popularity of his tableware coincided with the Industrial Revolution and the rise of the middle class.

Meteyard, Eliza. *The Life of Josiah Wedgwood: From His Private Correspondences and Family Papers*. 2 vols. London: Hurst and Blackett, 1865. An excellent two-volume biography. Begins with England's Celtic pottery and period, continues through the Roman period and the Middle Ages. Makes for absorbing reading, although it is written in a somewhat dated style. Volume 2 continues through Wedgwood's death.

Smiles, Samuel. *Josiah Wedgwood: His Personal History*. London: John Murray, 1894. An in-depth look at Wedgwood's personal and professional life. Includes substantial character analysis. Draws on sources such as diaries, letters, and notes on experiments not used in earlier biographies.

Uglow, Jenny. *The Lunar Men: Five Friends Whose Curiosity Changed the World*. New York: Farrar, Straus, Giroux, 2002. Wedgwood, James Watt, and scientist Joseph Priestley were among the founders of the Lunar Society of Birmingham. Uglow's book describes how the organization invented new products, advanced science, and worked on other projects that ushered in the Industrial Revolution.

Wedgwood, Barbara, and Hensleigh Wedgwood. *The Wedgwood Circle, 1730-1897: Four Generations of a Family and Their Friends*. Westfield, N.J.: Eastview Editions, 1980. A well-written account of four generations of the Wedgwood family, beginning with Josiah Wedgwood. Even though it is a family history, it is not as biased as one might expect.

Wedgwood, Josiah. *The Selected Letters of Josiah Wedgwood*. Edited by Ann Finer and George Savage. London: Cory, Adams, and Mackay, 1965. A collection of sorted letters illustrating Wedgwood's personality, accomplishments, influences, and motivations. The introduction contains a biographical sketch. In addition, each section of the book is prefaced with a short explanation of the contents of letters to follow, with relevant biographical data about Wedgwood. Excellent source.

Wills, Geoffrey. *Wedgwood*. Harmondsworth, England: Country Life Books, 1980. Traces the development of Wedgwood's career and his lasting legacy. The first four chapters offer informative data about Wedgwood's work; chapter 5 discusses the Wedgwood company after Josiah's death, and the sixth chapter provides information for collectors. Excellent and concise account of Wedgwood's life for the history buff or Wedgwood collector.

See also: Hester Bateman; James Brindley; Catherine the Great; Queen Charlotte; Benjamin Franklin; Joseph Priestley; Paul Revere; Sir Joshua Reynolds.

Related article in *Great Events from History: The Eighteenth Century, 1701-1800:* 1759: Wedgwood Founds a Ceramics Firm.

CHARLES WESLEY
English religious leader and writer

A prolific hymn writer, Wesley joined with his brother John to instill new life in the Anglican Church, or Church of England. Although Wesley remained an Anglican priest, seeking a renewal of faith and piety, his brother founded and developed the Methodist movement. Charles also was known for his inspiring preaching among the working class of London.

Born: December 18, 1707; Epworth, Lincolnshire, England
Died: March 29, 1788; London, England
Areas of achievement: Religion and theology, music

EARLY LIFE

Charles Wesley grew up in a large, poor family, and was overshadowed by his older brother John Wesley. The youngest of eighteen children, Charles was born two months premature, leading to a sickly childhood and periods of illness throughout his life. His classical education was a result of his mother's kitchen-table school while his preacher-father struggled to stay out of debt. After their Anglican parsonage-home in Epworth burned to the ground, a traumatic mark was left on the young brothers. At the age of eight, Charles left home to attend school at Westminster. Although he was given the opportunity to be adopted by a wealthy Irish relative, he surprisingly rejected this offer when he found out that he would struggle financially through school.

He seems to have been a rather outgoing individual who was the center of attention with his singing voice. His own journals speak of wasting his early college years at Oxford in "popular diversions." A change took place, though, as he gathered around him several friends who followed a methodical routine that centered around daily Bible study, prayer, and weekly communion. The group was derided by classmates, and Charles was dubbed the first "methodist." Brother John, by this time an ordained clergyman, returned to Oxford in 1729 as a fellow and joined Oxford's Holy Club. As would be typical throughout his life, John took over leadership of the group while Charles followed.

When a family friend, Governor James Edward Oglethorpe, traveled across the Atlantic with freed prisoners to establish the colony of Georgia, he enlisted John Wesley to accompany him as chaplain and missionary. At John's insistence, Charles signed on as the governor's private secretary. Charles was ordained as a deacon and priest in the Church of England in October, 1735, prior to departure. The brothers tried to follow the regimented method of devotion, but both were disillusioned by their work and returned to England within a year as failures.

After having returned to England, Charles nearly came to despair life, and he was combating illness. His only encouragement was his contact with Moravian Pietists. While in Georgia he had encountered Moravian missionaries from Germany, who had impressed him with their devotion and commitment to the faith. For three months in early 1738, the Moravian missionary Peter Böhler stopped in London en route to Georgia and offered the Wesleys the individual mentoring they needed. Following Böhler's departure, Charles moved into the home of Peter Bray, who read to Wesley both scripture and Martin Luther's *Commentary on Galatians*. On Pentecost Sunday, May 21, 1738, Charles had a religious experience that changed his life—a feeling of complete peace came over him. Three days later, his brother John had a similar experience. Soon the brothers began a successful ministry together.

LIFE'S WORK

For the next forty years, Charles Wesley became one of the most powerful preachers in England, bringing new life to the church. Initially, his focus was on a personal testimony to those around him. Then it extended to a ministry among prisoners in Oxford and London. This was a natural growth from his childhood experience, when his father had been placed in debtors' prison, and also an extension of his work among freed prisoners in Georgia. In July he ministered to ten men scheduled for the gallows. His journals describe his feeling of satisfaction in this ministry and the realization of sincere conversions among the imprisoned and condemned.

In September, 1738, he was invited to preach at Westminster Abbey, conducting the communion service as an ordained Anglican clergyman. What he discovered during the next few months was that church attendance was down and enthusiasm was lacking. He left the confines of the churches for the streets and open fields. There he was joined by his Oxford friend George Whitefield, who would later be known for his role in the Great Awakening movement in New England.

Wesley and Whitefield were immediately brought before the Anglican authorities on charges of antinomianism (believing faith alone will lead to salvation), and they were challenged by local pastors who felt their territory was being infringed upon by the duo's popular style of preaching. Wesley's message emphasized personal faith and a pious lifestyle of service while downplaying the importance of regular church attendance. Nevertheless, Wesley always saw himself as part of the Anglican Church, unlike his brother John, who would come to consider himself part of a separate movement that became the Methodist Church.

In 1844, together with his brother, he helped to organize a gathering of laymen whom they trained to assist in preaching. This led to further criticism from the ranks of the clergy. Yet the success of lay preaching led to annual conferences that prepared lay preachers and sent them throughout all of England, Ireland, and North America.

The influence of the Wesley brothers on American Christianity was especially significant. Although Charles's experience in Georgia had been disastrous, he always wanted to return as a missionary. While never fulfilling that wish, John and Charles together helped arrange for several hundred preachers to cross the Atlantic so that Methodism got a foothold on the American continent and flourished with its expanding frontier.

Charles Wesley continued his work as an itinerant preacher and often attracted crowds in the thousands. Only in 1749, at the age of forty-one, did he marry Sarah (Sally) Gwynne and settle down in Bristol, where the couple raised eight children. In 1771 he moved his family to London, where he continued preaching at the City Road Chapel.

In his later years, Charles parted ways with his older brother, who was separating himself from the Church of England. The disagreement reached a climax when John independently ordained two clergymen who were to be sent to America. In 1784, on the fortieth anniversary of the successful lay conferences, John drew up legal documents to guarantee the continuation of this movement.

Many date the establishment of a separate Methodist Church to this date. Charles, however, was not in agreement with this move and continued to see himself as an Anglican priest whose role was that of leading a revival movement within the Church of England.

SIGNIFICANCE

Despite his work as a preacher, Charles Wesley is best remembered for his role as a hymn writer. The impact of his ministry is clear from a list of a handful of his most popular hymns, including the following: "Hark! The Herald Angels Sing," "Come, Thou Long-Expected Jesus," "Christ the Lord Is Risen Today!," "Jesus Christ Is Risen Today," "Rejoice, the Lord Is King," "Love Divine, All Loves Excelling," and "Oh, for a Thousand Tongues to Sing."

He began his hymn-writing while still young, and in 1739 he published his first collection, *Hymns and Sacred Poems*, which was so successful that a new volume was published in each of the next ten years. John wrote hymns as well, but in this area, Charles outshone his brother. It is estimated that Charles wrote between four thousand and eight thousand hymns. Although his publications were more prolific than any other English hymn writer, many of his hymns remain in manuscript form and were never published. Charles clearly understood the importance of these hymns for missionary, devotional, and instructional purposes. Yet he could not have imagined their continued popularity among Protestants into the twenty-first century.

—*Fred Strickert*

FURTHER READING

Baker, Frank. *Charles Wesley's Verse: An Introduction.* London: Epworth Press, 1964. An introductory work that focuses on Wesley as a hymn writer.

Brailsford, Mabel R. *A Tale of Two Brothers.* New York: Oxford University Press, 1954. A traditional biography with a primary focus on older brother John.

Chilcote, Paul Wesley. *Recapturing the Wesleys' Vision: An Introduction to the Faith of John and Charles Wesley.* Downers Grove, Ill.: InterVarsity Press, 2004. The author considers the Wesleys' contribution as one of providing a balance between contrasting aspects of the Christian life, seen in terms of "both/and" rather

than "either/or." The book is thus arranged in four pairs of chapters: preaching (grace and love), community (experience and discipleship), discipline (instruction and guidance), and servanthood (mission and service).

Crichton, Mitchell T. *Charles Wesley: Man with the Dancing Heart.* Kansas City, Mo.: Beacon Hill, 1994. In this thorough summary of Wesley's life and work, the author seeks to correct the common view that Charles was a lesser figure following in the shadow of his older brother John. This work provides depth in a readable style.

Kent, John. *Wesley and the Wesleyans: Religion in Eighteenth-Century Britain.* New York: Cambridge University Press, 2002. This work challenges the view that the Methodists created a much-needed evangelical revival in eighteenth century Britain. Kent argues that Methodism was a "primary religion," a normal human search to bring supernatural power into individual lives, and not a religious revival. He analyzes the emergence of Wesleyan societies and the role of women in those societies.

Noll, Mark A. *The Rise of Evangelicalism: The Age of Edwards, Whitefield, and the Wesleys.* Downers Grove, Ill.: InterVarsity Press, 2003. This thorough study places the Wesleys, along with Edwards and Whitefield, in the context of British and American Christianity and explains their relations with contemporary Evangelists.

Tyson, John R. *Charles Wesley: A Reader.* New York: Oxford University Press, 2000. Utilizing Wesley's own journals, sermons, letters, and hymns, thirteen chapters document the reformer's life and theological thought. A lengthy introduction and short chapter summaries make this material highly accessible.

See also: Francis Asbury; Isaac Backus; Joseph Butler; Jonathan Edwards; Ann Lee; James Edward Oglethorpe; John Wesley; George Whitefield; Count von Zinzendorf.

Related articles in *Great Events from History: The Eighteenth Century, 1701-1800:* 1739-1742: First Great Awakening; October 30, 1768: Methodist Church Is Established in Colonial America; 1790's-1830's: Second Great Awakening.

JOHN WESLEY
English religious leader and writer

Wesley founded the Methodist Church and presaged the entire Evangelical movement that followed in England and America.

Born: June 17, 1703; Epworth, Lincolnshire, England
Died: March 2, 1791; London, England
Areas of achievement: Religion and theology, literature

EARLY LIFE

John Wesley was born in a rustic Lincolnshire town. His father, Samuel, was the Anglican minister of the surrounding rural parish. His mother, Susanna, was the daughter of a Dissenter minister. She was schooled in an independent manner at home and was taught to formulate her own answers to life's questions. As a mother, she developed a stringent code of behavior for her children, for whom she provided an elementary education at home. She was a rigorous disciplinarian who required her children to cry softly and keep busy every waking hour. She succeeded in making an indelible mark on her children. Susanna is thus accorded much credit for the ultimate success of John and his younger brother, Charles. Indeed, Methodism's emphasis on self-discipline and mutual improvement can be traced to John's first eleven years of schooling at home.

Wesley's secondary education at Charterhouse in London, beginning in 1714, was without incident except as a preparation for Oxford. He entered Christ Church College in 1720, and his brother Charles followed a few years later. The Oxford that John and Charles attended in the early 1720's was a bastion of High Anglicanism, whose faculty members were clergymen intent upon imparting good manners in preference to religious zeal. During his course of study, John Wesley came under the influence of an exceptional thinker, William Law, who railed against the "almost Christians" he saw around him.

Wesley was unusual among students of the day in that he worked hard at his studies and at tutoring. He soon absorbed the religious enthusiasm of medieval ascetics and began to follow a monk-like regimen. In 1729, Charles founded the Holy Club among an ardent group of undergraduates, one of whom, George Whitefield, was destined to become one of England's greatest orators. It was a small group whose prayers and practices were completely alien to the surrounding environment. John Wesley, who had already taken his degree, was senior to the

group. He assumed the leadership role and soon guided them through a very full schedule of prayer, fasting, and good works among the local community. He led by an example of rigorousness and explained what was required for the Holy Club members to save their souls. He urged them to "methodize" their witness for Christianity, to methodize every hour of the day. The two Wesley brothers, Whitefield, and the rest of that small group of religion students were ridiculed by the Oxford student body. Hence, the term "methodist" arose in mockery.

In 1729, John was also elected a fellow of Lincoln College. He was a diligent teacher, but the Christian witness he sought was difficult to find among the Oxford students. By 1730, John and Charles began the practice of visiting prisons and proselytizing prisoners. There, in the corrupt jails of Oxford and its environs, they found a means to broaden the reception of their religious views. Charles became a good friend of the social-reform zealot Colonel James Edward Oglethorpe, who founded the colony of Georgia in 1732 with freed inmates of the British prisons. Charles became his secretary, and John was invited to go as a chaplain to Georgia with Charles and Oglethorpe in 1735. The prospect of shepherding the colonists and, more important, of winning converts among the American Indians, appealed greatly to John. He began a journal in which he wrote faithfully for the next fifty-five years.

On the trip to America, the ship ran into a bad storm and John, like most of the other passengers, cowered and shrieked in panic as the ship lurched and the ocean cascaded within. In the corner of the hold, however, a group of German Moravians stood close together and calmly sang their hymns without betraying any fear of dying. Wesley was deeply impressed by the fortitude of the Moravians and lapsed into a month-long slump of self-criticism and examination. "I was unfit because I was unwilling to die," he wrote in his journal entry of December 23, 1735.

Among the difficulties that Wesley encountered in Georgia was an unfulfilled love affair with Sophia Hopkey in which Wesley waited too long to propose. When Hopkey married another man, Wesley took revenge by denying Communion to Hopkey on a technicality, thus casting her in a bad light. Hopkey and her family brought suit against Wesley, and a grand jury found for her. Wesley had to sneak out of Georgia soiled by scandal. "Shook the dust off my feet and left Georgia," he recorded on December 2, 1737.

Wesley's main problem in dealing with the colonists stemmed from the authoritarian and officious manner in which he treated them. He badgered them as if he were dealing with schoolboys. They responded by rejecting his ministry. As for the American Indians, he lamented in his journal on October 7, 1737, that he never met any who gave the slightest sign of "wanting the Christian word." During his return voyage to England, Wesley realized that his failure with the American Indians and the colonists was really within. "I went to America to convert Indians," he recorded in his journal entry of February 24, 1738, "but oh who shall convert me?" "I went to Georgia to convert others," he wrote the next week, "but myself never converted to God."

LIFE'S WORK

John Wesley returned to London spiritually shaken. He soon took up with some Moravians. Their emphasis upon a loving God and uncomplicated theology of redemption directly through Jesus Christ had a profound impact upon him. Indeed, Wesley owed his born-again religious experience to them. On May 24, 1738, he noted in his journal that, while attending a service, "I felt my heart strangely warmed. I felt I did trust in Christ, Christ alone, for salvation." Wesley was then almost thirty-five. He had completed an arduous spiritual journey that in turn would fuel another. Over the next half century, he would travel on horseback a quarter of a million miles. He would write 233 books, edit more than 100 others, and deliver 40,000 lectures across the British Isles.

Wesley's Methodist movement arose as a great awakening of Christian spirit within a year of his rebirth. His message of Christ's love and of the democratic nature of salvation was readily grasped by those who heard him. The partners in the early story of his revivalist success— his brother Charles and George Whitefield—shared in the transformation of his message into a movement.

The evangelical piety generated by Wesleyite sermons produced a backlash among the church establishment. The general orthodoxy of the day entertained a religious doctrine of great latitude. The moderate temper of the Anglican creed was designed to cushion and not to shake the social order. Clerics rapidly perceived that Wesley disturbed their universe: He stirred an ugly and unpredictable religious enthusiasm among the lower orders. Consequently, within a year of guest preaching, Wesley experienced difficulties. Anglican ministers would no longer open their pulpits to him or to his followers.

In early spring, 1739, Whitefield urged Wesley to come to Bristol quickly because he was preaching to great numbers in the nearby fields. Wesley hesitated but eventually joined him. With evident self-satisfaction, he noted in his journal on April 2, 1739, at 4:00 P.M., "from a little eminence" outside Bristol, he "preached to about three thousand people." Salvation could be a child of nature as well. The event marked a major breakthrough for the emerging Methodist movement. By conducting religious meetings in the fields, Wesley reached a sizable portion of the population. At the same time, he reached large numbers of poor people hitherto ignored. Thus, the shape of Wesley's success as a new light among the common people was cast.

Within a few years, Wesley's movement attained its unique organizational feature from the same source. In 1742, his followers among the Bristol poor sought to build their own chapel. To do so, they organized themselves into small classes, with each member assessed a penny a week. They selected a class leader to collect and keep the money. The plan succeeded, and they built their chapel. Within two generations more than 350 chapels were constructed in the same manner—generally in places that the Anglican Church did not frequent.

Yet the Bristol people did more than build a chapel. Wesley seized upon their principle of local organization by classes and shortly issued a set of instructions. By these, he fashioned the class meeting and class leader as

John Wesley. (Library of Congress)

the basic units of Methodism. Each class was composed of a dozen or so members of the same area. They confessed to one another and reported their misgivings to the flock. The principles of continual soul monitoring and of mutual self-help were pure Wesley, learned at his mother's knee and practiced upon the small group at Oxford.

Subsequently, the structure was expanded. Controversial lay preachers were created and turned into the backbone of the ever-increasing Methodist mission. After 1746, quarterly meetings with districts and circuits were added, and a phalanx of itinerant preachers was sent out to service them. The broad-based horizontal structure of Methodism at the lower level, however, was not indicative of it as a whole. Actual authority emanated vertically from Wesley. The same autocratic leanings that had characterized his relations with the Holy Club and the Georgia colonists clearly reemerged in Methodism.

On matters regarding Methodist organization, Wesley's power was supreme. From the beginning, all extra money went to Wesley for administration. All Methodist buildings and property were made over in his name. All questions were settled by him. His opponents charged that he both "proposed and disposed"; they called him "Pope John." Any real resistance to Wesley's mode of leadership was ended in 1744, when he called a London conference to clarify the issue. The conference became annual, and, ultimately, after Wesley's death, it became the movement's ruling body. During his lifetime, however, Wesley both set the agenda and chose who attended the conference.

In little more than a decade, Wesley turned his movement into the most highly organized voice in England of the 1750's and after. Yet, while it had a loud socio-religious percussion, the Methodist movement was a voice without political pitch. Wesley's politics were very cautious. He deprecated the idea of a popular share in governance. Thus, in the most popular political issue of the century, that of "Wilkes and Liberty," Wesley fully supported King George III and Parliament. He actually supported the early American protests against misrule. When it was clear the colonists wanted more than mere reform, however, Wesley borrowed a thesis from a work of his friend Samuel Johnson and issued his own anti-colonist pamphlet.

Wesley seemed to have posed a threat of his own to the eighteenth century establishment, but only for a decade or so when his spiritual leveling was equated with social leveling. The reality of Wesley's creation was contrary to appearances. He advocated spiritual equality,

not social insubordination. If he had created a church within a church, it was no more than that. It was not a church against a church. In time, authority understood Wesley's benign impact upon the public order. He became a well-known fixture of the eighteenth century landscape—the itinerant preacher on horseback reading his book.

Wesley made few inroads among the upper classes, yet his emphasis on personal discipline had a strong appeal to artisans and tradesmen. His placement of divine inspiration at the center of his belief, as opposed to the pure appeal to reason set forth by the regular Anglican clergy, attracted a large following among the miners of Bristol, Cornwall, Wales, and Newcastle. He was once thought to have brought a great stability to the lower elements of British society. Modern historians generally rebut or greatly qualify this thesis, yet the substance of Wesleyite identification was real. The numbers stand on their own. At the time of Wesley's death, there were seventy thousand Methodists in England and another sixty thousand in the United States.

Wesley expected Methodists to be good Anglicans. He was fully Anglican himself. He criticized the clergy of the Church of England but not the institution itself. Thus, only the smallest effort by the Anglican establishment was needed to prevent a rupture. The break, as it was, came very late in the day and was caused by the success of the Methodist mission in America. Ordained ministers were needed. The need had arisen as early as 1760. Yet Wesley was unable to persuade the Anglican bishops to ordain ministers for America. Finally, in 1784, after the bishop of London refused his request, Wesley ordained three men on his own. The date was doubly significant. First, the separation was finally necessitated by the achievement of American independence. Second, it occurred only after Methodism had been in existence for better than forty years.

SIGNIFICANCE

John Wesley was a man of his age, no more. The debit side of Wesley and his movement is the entirely popular quality of his ideas. His philistinism was often as bad as that to which he pandered. He was indifferent to the fine arts. He was superstitious. Even at the schools he founded he fostered instruction and not education. He had no understanding of children's needs. He had strong prejudices. For example, after the most serious anti-Catholic rioting in London's history, Wesley met and "congratulated" George, Lord Gordon, the perpetrator. He was outraged when Gordon was censured by a grand jury: "What a shocking insult upon truth and common sense!"

Yet, Wesley's legacy is greater than his faults. He cut a spiritual path through the eighteenth century and prepared another one for the next. He gave his brother's hymns a place of permanent performance. He wrote widely on poverty and administered to the needs of poor people. Thus, he created a movement that took care of its own poor. In fact, it was this latter achievement that attracted posthumous study of his writing by such sensitive luminaries as Hannah More and William Wordsworth.

Wesley advanced the tenets of religious renewal and reform. He cleared the way for the Evangelical movement and church missionary societies of the 1790's. Wesley stressed equality of religious transformation and therefore led directly to the idea of equality of human transformation. He was an unflagging supporter and inspiration for William Wilberforce's efforts to end the slave trade, and thus contributed to a more humane future for all.

—*Louis R. Bisceglia*

FURTHER READING

Ayling, Stanley. *John Wesley*. New York: Collins, 1979. A readable critical study that is entirely weighted toward the secular view of Wesley.

Baker, Frank. *From Wesley to Asbury: Studies in Early American Methodism*. Durham, N.C.: Duke University Press, 1976. A judicious attempt to shine a positive light on Wesley's Georgia mission and his role in the development of early American Methodism.

Collins, Kenneth J. *John Wesley: A Theological Journey*. Nashville, Tenn.: Abingdon Press, 2003. An examination of Wesley's religious ideas, tracing the development of his theology throughout the course of his career.

Cragg, Gordon R. *The Church and the Age of Reason, 1648-1789*. Baltimore: Penguin Books, 1960. A clearly stated overall assessment of Wesley and his movement within the context of the Hanoverian age and the cult of reason.

Hattersley, Roy. *A Brand from the Burning: The Life of John Wesley*. London: Little Brown, 2002. A comprehensive biography, recounting the events of Wesley's life, including his experiences in Georgia and his struggles to establish Methodism as an alternative to the Anglican Church. Describes Wesley's personal life, including his relationships with women.

Heitzenrater, Richard P. *The Elusive Mr. Wesley*. 2d rev. ed. Nashville, Tenn.: Abingdon Press, 2003. Selec-

tions from Wesley's own writings have given rise to errors and stale, stereotyped views of the man. This book is a valuable historiographical appraisal of the biographical literature on Wesley from the eighteenth century to the present. A good place to begin research.

Kent, John. *Wesley and the Wesleyans: Religion in Eighteenth-Century Britain*. New York: Cambridge University Press, 2002. Challenges the view that Wesley and the Methodists created a much-needed evangelical revival in eighteenth century Britain. Kent argues that Methodism was a "primary religion," a normal human search to bring supernatural power into individual lives, and not a religious revival. He analyzes the emergence of Wesleyan societies and the role of women in those societies, and provides a more sympathetic view of Hanoverian Anglicanism than is featured in many other books.

Marshall, Dorothy. *John Wesley*. Oxford, England: Oxford University Press, 1965. An excellent, brief biographical essay that takes great care to explain Wesley within the social reality of eighteenth century England.

Smith, Warren Thomas. *John Wesley and Slavery*. Nashville, Tenn.: Abingdon Press, 1986. A useful book that incorporates related periodical literature and the original 1774 edition of Wesley's *Thoughts upon Slavery*.

Wesley, John. *The Works of John Wesley*. Vols. 1-4, 7, 9, 11, 18-24. Edited by Albert C. Outler. Nashville, Tenn.: Abingdon Press, 1984- .

_____. *The Works of John Wesley: Letters*. Vols. 25 and 26. Edited by Frank Baker. New York: Oxford University Press, 1980. Oxford University Press and Abingdon Press have published fifteen of a projected 26-volume *Bicentennial Edition* of Wesley's collected works. The volumes edited by Outler include sermons, and also journals and diaries from 1735 through 1791. Baker has edited a two-volume collection of Wesley's letters.

See also: Francis Asbury; Mary Astell; Joseph Butler; Samuel Johnson; Ann Lee; Hannah More; James Edward Oglethorpe; Charles Wesley; George Whitefield; William Wilberforce; Count von Zinzendorf.

Related articles in *Great Events from History: The Eighteenth Century, 1701-1800:* 1739-1742: First Great Awakening; October 30, 1768: Methodist Church Is Established in Colonial America; June 2-10, 1780: Gordon Riots; 1790's-1830's: Second Great Awakening.

BENJAMIN WEST
American painter

West helped establish the authenticity and legitimacy of American painting, made significant contributions to both neoclassicism and Romanticism, became a close confidant of King George III, and was instrumental in the founding and success of the Royal Academy in London.

Born: October 10, 1738; Springfield, Pennsylvania
Died: March 11, 1820; London, England
Area of achievement: Art

EARLY LIFE

Benjamin West, or "the American Raphael," as he came to be called, was the youngest of ten children born to the innkeeper John West and Sarah Pearson, who lived 10 miles west of Philadelphia. The Wests lived in a community of devout Quakers, but West's mother had been read out of the meeting (expelled) and, thus, her ten children could not become members of the Society of Friends. When Benjamin was about eight years old, Thomas Penington, a generous Quaker merchant from Philadelphia, was so impressed by the precocious boy's efforts with his homemade brushes that he presented him with paints, brushes, several prepared canvases, and six engravings by an artist identified only as "Grevling" by West's earliest biographer, John Galt.

A year later, Penington took Benjamin to Philadelphia and gave him two books that apparently shaped the boy's thinking about art. One title was John Dryden's translation of Charles-Alphonse Dufresnoy's *De arte graphica* (1668; *The Art of Painting*, 1695), which praised the classical Greeks to the exclusion of all other schools. The second book was by English painter Jonathan Richardson, *An Essay of the Theory of Painting* (1715). West said these books were "my companions by day, and under my pillow by night." In Philadelphia, West met his first instructor in the techniques of painting, the writer and painter William Williams, himself only twenty-two years old in 1749. West later credited Williams with inspiring him to become a painter, remarking that Williams "lighted up a fire in my breast which has never been extinguished."

At the age of eighteen, West was already painting portraits of his neighbors, and his *Death of Socrates* (1756) earned him an invitation from the provost of the College of Philadelphia to study the classics at the college, tuition free. Although his background proved inadequate for his studies, West benefited from his friendships with some of his talented fellow students, including Francis Hopkinson, a poet and composer. A decisive event in West's career came when a Philadelphia merchant offered him free passage on a cargo ship bound for Leghorn, Italy.

His first viewings of the old masters in Rome shocked him with their miracles and martyrs, and the attention he received incited a nervous collapse. Recovering quickly, West studied the neoclassical theories of Johann Joachim Winckelmann, who advocated painting only the ideal statues of the ancient Greeks, models in which were to be found only the loftiest attributes and virtues. Under the guidance of Winckelmann's disciple Raphael Mengs, West traveled around Italy copying the works of Rembrandt, Titian, Raphael, and others. His apprenticeship led to two classical paintings, inspired from literature: *Cimon and Iphigenia* and *Angelica and Medora*, which won him such acclaim in Italy that after three years in Rome he decided to return to Philadelphia.

LIFE'S WORK

On his father's advice, however, Benjamin West agreed to visit London before returning to the colonies, and when he arrived in London in August of 1763, already acclaimed as a genius in both America and Italy, he was to settle into an illustrious career that would keep him in England the rest of his life.

He entered his two paintings, *Cimon and Iphigenia* and *Angelica and Medora*, in the Society of Artists exhibition of 1764, receiving high praise from all quarters. Thus encouraged, West arranged for his fiancé, Elizabeth Shewell, to leave Philadelphia for permanent residence in England, and they were married on September 2, 1764. They would have two sons, Raphael Lamar and Benjamin, Jr.

In 1765, West exhibited two historical compositions, *The Continence of Scipio* and *Pylades and Orestes Brought as Victims Before Iphigenia*, at another Society of Artists exhibition, and in 1766 he became a member and then director of the society. West soon was fortunate in making the acquaintance of Robert Hay Drummond, archbishop of York. When the archbishop observed that the story of Agrippina, as told in the *Annals* of Tacitus, would be a fine subject for a painting, West produced his first true neoclassical work, *Agrippina Landing at Brundisium with the Ashes of Germanicus* (1768). Drummond was so impressed that he praised the painting to King George III, who immediately scheduled an audience for West that resulted in a friendship that endured through the king's illness.

In addition to suggesting the story of Marcus Atilius Regulus as a subject, the king solicited West's advice about the dissension then troubling the Society of Artists. The upshot of these events was the rebels' founding of the Royal Society with the king's approval and with Sir Joshua Reynolds as president. When *The Departure of Regulus from Rome* (1769) was completed soon afterward, West was paid £420 by the king, who insisted the work be exhibited at the Royal Society, thereby validating the new organization and demonstrating royal favor for West.

West's most famous work, *The Death of General Wolfe* (1770), defied tradition in several ways. First, it abandoned neoclassical severity and instead took up color, violence, and excitement; and second, and most shockingly, it did not clothe its figures in classical garb and present the scene as a generalization. West had brought to history painting a new realism, with all its details. The king had rejected the idea of modern military clothing, and Reynolds and Drummond warned West about such a dangerous innovation, but all to no effect.

Benjamin West. (Library of Congress)

When Reynolds and Drummond finally viewed the painting, Reynolds studied it for thirty minutes and then announced to the archbishop that "Mr. West has conquered." *The Death of General Wolfe* was a huge success, bought by Lord Grosvenor for £400. It was followed in 1771-1772 by another highly praised historical work, *William Penn's Treaty with the Indians When He Founded the Province of Pennsylvania in North America.*

In 1788 the king came down with the illness that incapacitated him and damaged his relationship with West. When Reynolds died in February of 1792, West succeeded him a month later as president of the Royal Academy, and in the period between 1792 and 1799, he exhibited seventy pictures and continued the experiments with the Romantic subjects that he had begun in 1777 with *Saul and the Witch of Endor.* Politicking in the academy, combined with several contretemps occasioned by West's bad judgment, led to his resignation at the end of 1805, but the incompetence of his successor, James Wyatt, prompted the members to return West to office on January 1, 1807. This triumph was capped in 1811 when he showed the allegorical *Omnia Vincit Amor* and the large *Death of Nelson* (painted in 1806), as well as his biggest success in this great year, *Christ Healing the Sick in the Temple,* which was shown separately. For the next few years West busied himself primarily with *Christ Rejected by Caiaphas* and revisions of *Death on the Pale Horse,* both of which had admirers as well as critics. West's wife died in 1814 and West died in 1820, still enjoying the esteem of his colleagues.

SIGNIFICANCE

A decade after Benjamin West's death, criticism turned against him, with John Ruskin, an English critic and artist, remarking that "West is too feeble an artist to permit his designs to be mentioned as pictures at all." West's biographer Robert C. Alberts cited 1938 as the year that West's reputation took a turn for the better with a bicentenary exhibition of his works at the Pennsylvania Museum of Art in Philadelphia and a "discerning" piece on West by James Thomas Flexner in *America's Old Masters* (1939). By 1970 the attacks and the praise both ceased, leaving West, in Alberts's words, "one artist among other artists."

Two aspects of West's career stand out. For good or ill, he taught a number of successful artists, including Washington Allston, Samuel F. B. Morse, and Gilbert Stuart. Furthermore, West distinguished himself by accomplishments in two different styles: the neoclassical that he studied under Winckelmann in Rome and his later

Romantic masterpieces. The French painter of Romantic subjects Eugéne Delacroix noted in his journal, "Study the sketches of West" and "borrow engravings of Trumbull and West."

—*Frank Day*

FURTHER READING

Alberts, Robert C. *Benjamin West: A Biography*. Boston: Houghton Mifflin, 1978. A standard biography of West, with illustrations, ninety pages of notes, sources, and a bibliography.

ArtCyclopedia. http://www.artcyclopedia.com/artists/west_benjamin.html. A useful resource with links to sites, including museums, with West's paintings. Accessed July, 2005.

Einhorn A., and T. S. Abler. "Tattooed Bodies and Severed Auricles: Images of Native American Body Modification in the Art of Benjamin West." *American Indian Arts Magazine* 23, no. 4 (Autumn, 1998): 42-53. An examination of West's depictions of body art in his images of Native Americans.

Farington, Joseph. *The Farington Diary*. Edited by James Greig. 8 vols. London: Hutchinson, 1922-1928. A selection from Farington's voluminous diaries kept over many years. Farington was West's close confidant, and his diaries are invaluable. Available in various versions.

Flexner, James Thomas. *America's Old Masters: Benjamin West, John Singleton Copley, Charles Willson Peale, and Gilbert Stuart*. New York: Viking Press, 1939. Revised, with sixty-nine illustrations and an appendix on "Benjamin West's American Neo-Classicism." Excellent short biographies of its four subjects.

Galt, John. *The Life of Benjamin West (1816-1820)*. Gainesville, Fla.: Scholars' Facsimiles & Reprints, 1960. A facsimile reproduction of Galt's classic 1820 biography on West, originally titled *The Life, Studies, and Works of Benjamin West*. Includes an introduction by Nathalia Wright and illustrations.

Von Erffa, Helmut, and Allen Staley. *The Paintings of Benjamin West*. New Haven, Conn.: Yale University Press, 1986. A large, comprehensive, authoritative, and indispensable work.

See also: John Singleton Copley; Thomas Gainsborough; George III; Francisco de Goya; William Hogarth; Thomas Lawrence; Charles Willson Peale; Sir Joshua Reynolds; George Romney; Gilbert Stuart; John Trumbull; Johann Joachim Winckelmann; James Wolfe.

Related article in *Great Events from History: The Eighteenth Century, 1701-1800:* December 10, 1768: Britain's Royal Academy of Arts Is Founded.

PHILLIS WHEATLEY
African-born American poet

The first African American and the second colonial American woman to publish a book, Wheatley mastered eighteenth century verse models and, by her example, advanced the case against slavery as well as the emergence of African American letters.

Born: 1753?; west coast of Africa (possibly Senegal-Gambia)
Died: December 5, 1784; Boston, Massachusetts
Areas of achievement: Literature, social reform

EARLY LIFE

Phillis Wheatley, enslaved at the age of seven or eight, had few childhood memories of Africa, but she did remember her mother's ritual prayer at sunrise. On July 11, 1761, Phillis was purchased by John and Susanna Wheatley of Boston and was named after the ship on which she arrived. She was trained in household duties and, on August 18, 1771, was accepted as a member of the Old South Congregational Church.

In intervals between her chores, she was tutored in English, Latin, and Bible studies. Her first published poem, "On Messrs. Hussey and Coffin," appeared in the December 21, 1767, issue of Rhode Island's *Newport Mercury*. In October, 1771, a broadside (a large sheet of paper printed on one side) with her elegy on the famous minister George Whitefield sold for seven coppers. This poem was commercially reprinted many times. Impressed by Phillis's success as a poet, Susanna Wheatley advertised in 1772 for about three hundred colonial subscribers to finance a proposed book by the young poet. This volume, however, never appeared.

LIFE'S WORK

With the aid of friends, Phillis Wheatley's *Poems on Various Subjects, Religious and Moral* was published in London in 1773. Advertised to appeal to the eighteenth century European interest in prodigies, the verse in this edition was somewhat revised to suit an English audience. The book included a frontispiece portrait of the poet contemplatively posed, in accordance with painterly conventions of the day, to suggest her religious conversion and poetic inspiration. In both England and colonial America the critical response to this work was on the whole favorable. Jupiter Hammon, a slave in New York, published a poem of appreciation addressed to Wheatley in 1778.

While visiting London a few months prior to the release of her book, Wheatley enjoyed the attention of several famous individuals, including Benjamin Franklin. After her return to Boston, she was manumitted (released from slavery). The emancipated poet married John Peters, a free black man who worked odd jobs. Together they struggled with poverty. In 1779, Wheatley again unsuccessfully sought sponsors for an American edition of her writings.

In the years after the publication of her book abroad, she continued to write letters and occasional verse, which would sometimes appear in publications such as Boston's *Independent Chronicle and Advertiser*. Her most famous letter, written in 1765 and reprinted in many New England newspapers in 1774 (first in the *Connecticut Gazette* on March 11), was an antislavery letter addressed to American Indian minister Samson Occom. In the letter, Wheatley represents slaves as latter-day Israelites awaiting deliverance from the captivity of a pharaoh. Expressing the emerging revolutionary spirit of colonial America, Wheatley wrote, "In every human breast God has implanted a principle, which we call Love of Freedom."

At this point in her life Wheatley could openly state her opposition to slavery. Earlier as a slave, however, she felt constrained to convey her abolitionist sentiment more subtly in her verse. "On Being Brought from Africa to America," for example, the poet does more than express gratitude for her conversion to Christianity, and she does more than insist that blacks are capable of both spiritual and cultural refinement. Importantly, in the last line of this short poem, two allusions to passages from the Old Testament book of Isaiah shrewdly intimate the equality of whites and blacks from their Creator's point of view. Wheatley's African American audience would have been especially sensitive to such allusions to Isaiah because many slaves found personal hope for their own liberation in this Old Testament prophet's forecast of the end of the Israelites' Babylonian captivity.

In two verse paraphrases of biblical passages, Wheatley likewise subversively hints at an abolitionist

Phillis Wheatley. (Library of Congress)

point of view that she dared not openly express. Her "Goliath of Garth" retells the David and Goliath story. In this verse she implies that enslavers are not real Christians, but instead are deity-defying Philistines who will eventually be overthrown. Her verse paraphrase "Isaiah LXIII. 1-8" likewise recalls David's victory against Goliath and similarly implies that slave masters disobey divine providence and, consequently, will not be included among the deity's Davidian chosen people.

Wheatley also subtly used classical allusions to insinuate her early antislavery convictions. In "To Maecenas," the first verse in her book, the poet speaks through an assumed voice of a shepherd-figure of the sort found in classical pastoral poetry. Her manner in this prefatory poem indicates a self-conscious disguise, and it suggests that deeper meanings lie below the surface of the "masked" poems to follow in her book. This is indeed the case in Wheatley's "On Imagination," in which seemingly conventional neoclassical devices serve as vehicles for the poet's subtle advancement of her point about love as a natural bond that should end the inhumanity of enslavement.

AGAINST SLAVERY

Phillis Wheatley composed a letter to Reverend Samson Occom, an American Indian minister, outlining her position against slavery. Her letter was published and then reprinted in several New England newspapers in 1774.

Reverend and honoured Sir,

I have this day received your obliging kind epistle, and am greatly satisfied with your reasons respecting the negroes, and think highly reasonable what you offer in vindication of their natural rights: Those that invade them cannot be insensible that the divine light is chasing away the thick darkness which broods over the land of Africa; and the chaos which has reigned so long, is converting into beautiful order, and reveals more and more clearly the glorious dispensation of civil and religious liberty, which are so inseparably united, that there is little or no enjoyment of one without the other: Otherwise, perhaps, the Israelites had been less solicitous for their freedom from Egyptian slavery; I do not say they would have been contented without it, by no means; for in every human breast God has implanted a principle, which we call Love of Freedom. It is impatient of oppression, and pants for deliverance; and by the leave of our modern Egyptians I will assert, that the same principle lives in us. God grant deliverance in his own way and time, and get him honour upon all those whose avarice impels them to countenance and help forward the calamities of their fellow creatures. This I desire not for their hurt, but to convince them of the strange absurdity of their conduct, whose words and actions are so diametrically opposite. How well the cry for liberty, and the reverse disposition for the exercise of oppressive power over others agree—I humbly think it does not require the penetration of a philosopher to determine.

Source: Phillis Wheatley, 1774 letter, in "Perspectives in American Literature—A Research and Reference Guide," chap. 2. http://www.csustan.edu/english/reuben/pal/chap2/wheatley.html.

Even Wheatley's early elegies on famous and unfamiliar figures expressed her opposition to slavery. "On the Death of a Young Lady of Five Years of Age" she opposes human bondage by associating freedom and equality with the blessings of heaven. Pertinent, as well, are the dialogues between the living and dead in "A Funeral Poem on the Death of C. E., an Infant of Twelve Months." The recovery of previously suppressed voices in this poem includes African Americans who had been oppressed while they were alive. In both elegies freedom is identified as a divine gift intended for all human beings of every race.

Wheatley's career as a poet would end prematurely. Chronically ill, she died at age thirty-one, apparently of complications related to childbirth.

SIGNIFICANCE

In her time Phillis Wheatley's literary legacy served both advocates and opponents in debates concerning the intellectual and cultural potentialities of African Americans. If Thomas Jefferson was not persuaded by her work, his fellow revolutionary Benjamin Rush thought her poetry resulted from a "singular genius."

In later times as well, Wheatley has provoked controversy. From the 1960's onward, some African Americans have faulted her writings for their lack of anger and especially for their subservience to the dominant culture's religious and literary paradigms. Others, however, have focused on the clever strategies the poet used to revise, resist, or subvert certain beliefs prevalent in the culture of her day. These strategies, Wheatley's defenders claim, reveal a characteristic African American double consciousness: the difficult attempt to reconcile one's self with the ways of a world presently hostile to the true expression of that self.

Wheatley wrote from within her Anglo-republican culture, but her double consciousness also enabled her to detect and reveal several of its inconsistencies and hypocrisies. However, in a world where women and blacks were expected to be docile, she had to be vigilant about her public image. The slave-poet carefully mingled simple piety and conventional verse techniques with a discreetly managed republican spirit of independence. While still a slave, she embedded the American spirit of political revolution below the surface of the literary conventions and pious sentiments of her poetry. Her contemporary readers valued her expression of piety and her execution of literary conventions because both elements met their expectations concerning cultural refinement. The poet's more underground revolutionary sentiment went undetected by her white advocates and detractors alike because such a spirit of independence was not expected from a person who was black, female, and a slave. While Wheatley's place in American cultural history is secure, the appreciation of her achievement will increase as more of her underground, revolutionary techniques are made apparent.

—*William J. Scheick*

FURTHER READING

Carretta, Vincent, and Philip Gould, eds. *Genius in Bondage: Literature of the Early Black Atlantic*. Lexington: University Press of Kentucky, 2001. Carretta and Gould present a collection of essays relating the poet to English and other American black authors.

Gates, Henry Louis, Jr. *The Trials of Phillis Wheatley: America's First Black Poet and Her Encounters with the Founding Fathers*. New York: Basic Civitas, 2003. Gates, a well-known scholar of African American history and literature, explores the poet's interaction with American revolutionary figures. Also, he defends her against criticism and defines her political and poetic legacies.

Lasky, Kathryn. *A Voice of Her Own: The Story of Phillis Wheatley, Slave Poet*. Cambridge, Mass.: Candlewick Press, 2003. A review of the poet's life and work specifically designed for young readers.

Robinson, William H., ed. *Critical Essays on Phillis Wheatley*. Boston: G. K. Hall, 1982. An anthology of responses to the poet's works.

_____. *Phillis Wheatley and Her Writings*. New York: Garland, 1984. An archival source providing a substantial introduction to and facsimiles of the earliest editions of the poet's work.

Scheick, William J. *Authority and Female Authorship in Colonial America*. Lexington: University Press of Kentucky, 1998. Chapter 4 examines the subtle implications of biblical matter in Wheatley's poetry.

See also: Benjamin Banneker; Benjamin Franklin; James Edward Oglethorpe; Benjamin Rush; Samuel Sewall; Granville Sharp; George Whitefield; William Wilberforce.

Related articles in *Great Events from History: The Eighteenth Century, 1701-1800:* 18th century: Expansion of the Atlantic Slave Trade; April 12, 1787: Free African Society Is Founded; February 22, 1791-February 16, 1792: Thomas Paine Publishes *Rights of Man*; 1792: Wollstonecraft Publishes *A Vindication of the Rights of Woman*; February 12, 1793: First Fugitive Slave Law.

GEORGE WHITEFIELD
English religious leader

One of the greatest Christian preachers, Whitefield, an Anglican Evangelist, proclaimed the gospel in Great Britain and its American colonies. A major figure in the Great Awakening, he traveled thousands of miles, founded an orphanage in Georgia, and helped to organize the Calvinistic Methodist Church in Wales. He often preached forty hours in a week and thereby stimulated a powerful resurgence of interest in Christian projects at home and in America.

Born: December 16, 1714; Gloucester, England
Died: September 30, 1770; Newburyport, Massachusetts
Areas of achievement: Religion and theology, social reform

EARLY LIFE

The son of an innkeeper in Gloucester, England, George Whitefield was but two years old when his father died. Recognizing George's high intelligence, his mother enrolled him in the school of St. Mary de Crypt, where Whitefield demonstrated a keen memory and impressive ability as a speaker and appeared in several plays while pursuing his studies. His devout mother encouraged him to read the Bible and Thomas à Kempis's *De imitatione Christi* (wr. early fifteenth century), both of which he found inspiring.

When the Bell Inn, managed by his mother and stepfather, floundered, Whitefield left school to work in the business, which his mother left after separating from her second husband. George returned to school and in 1732 enrolled at Pembroke College, Oxford, as a servitor, one who performed menial services for affluent students to pay his own expenses.

In 1733, Whitefield met Charles Wesley, who urged him to join the Holy Club of students resolved to practice piety through self-denial while serving the needs of others. While in the company of John Wesley and Charles Wesley, George Whitefield experienced a deep spiritual struggle out of which he emerged a changed man—one who had gained assurance of God's favor through faith in Christ. The instrumental means of his conversion was his reading of *The Life of God in the Soul of Man* by Henry Scougal, a devotional classic published in 1677, which John Wesley had given him. After the Wesley brothers left for missionary service in Georgia, Whitefield became leader of the "methodists," a term critics applied in ridicule to members of the Holy Club. In July, 1736, Whitefield received the bachelor of arts degree.

LIFE'S WORK

About the time of his graduation from Pembroke, George Whitefield was ordained a deacon in the Church of England and began preaching at the chapel in the Tower of London, where he emphasized how urgent it was for sinners to be born anew through the operation of the Holy Spirit, a theme he proclaimed relentlessly throughout his career. After temporary service in several parishes, he resolved to follow the Wesleys to Georgia, and in preparation he raised funds to support Christian work in that colony. His acidic manner of preaching, however, alienated some other clerics, the validity of whose ministries he questioned because they did not emphasize the need for spiritual regeneration.

Whitefield arrived in Georgia in May, 1738, stayed four months, and while there conceived a plan to build an orphanage for which he raised money after returning to England. Despite complaints about Methodist excesses, Bishop Martin Benson ordained Whitefield a minister in 1739, but many churches were closed to him, since he continued to denounce pastors he deemed unfaithful to their vocation. In the face of opposition from the Anglican clergy, Whitefield resorted to preaching outdoors in Kingswood near Bristol, England, where large crowds assembled to hear him. There he collected funds for a school to serve coal miners' children, and soon he summoned John Wesley to join him. Thereafter, outdoor preaching became a regular Methodist practice.

Although Whitefield and John Wesley were friends and coworkers in the ministry, their relationship became strained over a disagreement about the doctrine of predestination, which Whitefield affirmed but Wesley denied. The two Evangelists published opposing essays on the subject and went their separate ways, although each considered the other a brother in Christ. Whitefield was a prolific author of sermons and tracts, which were published, along with extracts from his journal, as a multivolume account of his ministry called *The Querists: Or, An Extract of Sundry Passages Taken Out of Mr. Whitefield's Printed Sermons, Journals, and Letters* (1740). Readers of *The Querists* sometimes became incensed by his attacks on Anglican clerics, including the bishop of London, who replied in print, accusing him of insubordination. The defiant Evangelist declared the world to be his parish over which no bishop had jurisdiction.

In 1739, Whitefield returned to Georgia to the acclaim of a large throng that met him in Savannah. He

named his orphanage Bethesda and continued to appeal to Englishmen to support it. His writings circulated through the American colonies as well as in Great Britain, and he soon received invitations to preach in several colonies, but as in England, Anglican churches often denied him access to their pulpits, while other Protestant assemblies welcomed him, especially those that espoused his Calvinism.

The itinerant ministry of Whitefield in America (1739-1741) occurred at a time of spiritual awakening among Congregational and Presbyterian churches. It was the era of revival preaching through the efforts of Jonathan Edwards, William Tennant and Gilbert Tennant, and others of the Calvinist persuasion that Whitefield proclaimed with fervor. Since denominational structures meant little to him, he moved freely among the churches in the colonies. In Philadelphia, for example, at the invitation of William Tennant, he preached from the steps of the courthouse to an estimated seventy-eight thousand people, Benjamin Franklin among them; Franklin became the major printer of his sermons.

Whitefield returned to England in 1741 and encountered strong opposition from John Wesley, as their theological dispute continued. The pamphlet war between them did not, however, deter either from the energetic pursuit of his respective ministry, and Whitefield soon went to Scotland for the first of fourteen tours. In Scotland he contributed to revivals at Cambuslang and Kilsyth. In Wales, too, he preached widely and helped to establish the Welsh Calvinistic Methodist Church. By then he had married Elizabeth James, a widow about a decade older than he. In October, 1743, she gave birth to a son who lived but four months.

George and Elizabeth Whitefield went to America in 1744, working in the south because he faced hostility in the northern colonies. Elizabeth often managed Bethesda while George preached and raised funds to pay debts pertaining to the orphanage. He pleaded for the humane treatment of slaves but endorsed slavery as a legitimate practice, and profits from slave labor helped to fund Bethesda. Whitefield returned to England in 1748, when Salina Hastings, the countess of Huntingdon, invited him to become her chaplain. He ministered to the upper classes and tried to improve relations with the Anglican episcopate. Only modestly successful in this endeavor, he nevertheless was able to solicit support for his orphanage and to build tabernacles in London and Bristol. He returned to America for the last time in 1770, and preached often until he died on September 30, 1770. He was buried in Newburyport, Massachusetts. His wife preceded him in death by two years. Whitefield left his assets and debts for Bethesda to Lady Huntingdon, but the orphanage was soon abandoned and left to decay into ruins.

SIGNIFICANCE

George Whitefield was a preacher who was exceptional more for his style and eloquence than for the content of his sermons, although his sermons were always orthodox in doctrine. His ministry elicited acclaim from some, consternation from others. In America he became a supporter of colonial grievances against Britain and so acquired the reputation of a patriot. His concern for orphans led him into action on their behalf, but lack of managerial skill impaired his work of charity and left him encumbered with debts. The number of converts won through his preaching was large, but stormy relations with less-zealous Christians deprived him of support. His eagerness to work with Protestants without regard to denominational connections, nevertheless, qualifies him for recognition as an ecumenical Calvinist.

—*James Edward McGoldrick*

FURTHER READING

Cashin, Edward J. *Beloved Bethesda: A History of George Whitefield's Home for Boys, 1740-2000.* Macon, Ga.: Mercer University Press, 2001. Cashin provides an account of Whitefield's orphanage, or boys' home, in Savannah, Georgia.

Chamberlain, A. "The Grand Sower of the Seed: Jonathan Edwards' Critique of George Whitefield." *New England Quarterly* 70 (1997): 368-385. Although Edwards appreciated Whitefield's fervor and shared his doctrinal persuasion, he had reservations about the Englishman's method of presentation, especially his appeals to the emotions more than to the intellect.

Dallimore, Arnold. *George Whitefield: The Life and Times of the Great Evangelist.* 2 vols. Westchester, Ill.: Cornerstone Books, 1979. This is the major biography of Whitefield, written by an Evangelical author who admires him profoundly. It is readable and thorough but somewhat lacking in appropriate criticism.

Mansfield, Stephen. *Forgotten Founding Father: The Heroic Legacy of George Whitefield.* Nashville, Tenn.: Highland Books/Cumberland House, 2001. Part of the Leaders in Action series. Mansfield examines Whitefield's legacy as a figure in American history.

Noll, Mark A. *The Rise of Evangelicalism: The Age of Edwards, Whitefield, and the Wesleys.* Downers Grove, Ill.: InterVarsity Press, 2003. This thorough study puts Whitefield in the context of British and American Christianity and explains his relations with contemporary Evangelists.

Stout, Harry S. *The Divine Dramatist: George Whitefield and the Rise of Modern Evangelicalism.* Grand Rapids, Mich.: William B. Eerdmans, 1991. This controversial interpretation magnifies Whitefield's role as a young actor and portrays him as a manipulator of audiences by means of his dramatic skills. Mostly by innuendo, Stout impugns the sincerity and character of his subject.

Whitefield, George. *George Whitefield's Journals.* 1968. 3d ed. Carlisle, Pa.: Banner of Truth Trust, 1978. A modern, 594-page edition, updated with new material, from Whitefield's collection of writings, including sermons and tracts.

See also: Francis Asbury; Isaac Backus; William Blake; Jonathan Edwards; Benjamin Franklin; Ann Lee; James Edward Oglethorpe; Charles Wesley; John Wesley; Phillis Wheatley; Count von Zinzendorf.

Related articles in *Great Events from History: The Eighteenth Century, 1701-1800:* 1739-1742: First Great Awakening; October 30, 1768: Methodist Church Is Established in Colonial America; 1790's-1830's: Second Great Awakening.

ELI WHITNEY
American inventor

Whitney, the inventor of the cotton gin, which revolutionized agriculture in the South, also contributed to the nation's industrial development by founding one of its first manufacturing establishments.

Born: December 8, 1765; Westborough, Massachusetts
Died: January 8, 1825; New Haven, Connecticut
Areas of achievement: Science and technology, business

EARLY LIFE

When Eli Whitney was born on a farm, his parents, Eli and Elizabeth Fay Whitney, had been married only eleven months. Three other children, Elizabeth, Benjamin, and Josiah, came in such rapid succession that their mother became bedridden and remained so until her death in 1777. The responsibility for the children's care soon proved to be too great for the father, so he decided to remarry. In June, 1779, Judith Hazeldon and two of her children, Hannah and Nancy, became a part of the family.

As the oldest, Eli Whitney accepted much of the responsibility for the family. While he attended school during the winter months, he always had many farm chores. His most absorbing interest, however, was in his father's workshop. There he developed his manual skills and began to exercise his inventive genius.

Whitney's family, like all American families of the time, was affected by the American Revolution, especially by the financial hardships it brought. Young Whitney used the circumstances, however, to his advantage. He persuaded his father to install a forge in the workshop so he could make nails, a commodity much in demand. The enterprise proved so profitable for the teenager that he even hired a helper for three months. Whitney's shrewd business sense and practical mind continued to serve him well even as the war ended and the demand for nails disappeared, for he began to produce other articles that would be marketable—hat pins and walking canes. At sixteen, Whitney already possessed the wisdom to "perceive probable consequences," as his sister Elizabeth said, and to act on his foresight.

Whitney never seemed very concerned about obtaining an education until he was nineteen, when he felt a tremendous desire to go to college and become a lawyer. To prepare himself for the entrance examinations and to raise the tuition money, he alternated studying with teaching until finally, in 1789, the twenty-three-year-old Whitney entered Yale College in New Haven, Connecticut. Whitney must have made a distinct impression on his classmates. Besides being older than they, he was very tall and always appropriately, though not elegantly, dressed. His oval face, smooth skin, unusually long nose, black hair, and contemplative black eyes suggested a solemn nature, but the smile on his lips said otherwise. The friendships Whitney cultivated at Yale would become invaluable to him in later years.

When Whitney graduated in 1792, he was offered a tutorial position on the plantation of Major Dupont in South Carolina. Little did he know that this venture would offer new challenges to his inventiveness and end his plans for a law career.

LIFE'S WORK

On the trip south, Whitney was accompanied by Phineas Miller, who was acting as Major Dupont's agent, and Catherine Greene, the widow of General Nathanael Greene of Revolutionary War fame. Miller was also the manager of the Greene plantation, Mulberry Grove, near Savannah, Georgia. When the ship reached Savannah, Whitney intended to travel by land to South Carolina; he soon discovered, however, that the tutorial position was not desirable. Thus, having become good friends with Greene, Whitney accepted her gracious invitation to reside for a while at Mulberry Grove.

Whitney's mechanical skill soon became apparent to both Greene and Miller. Therefore, when several visitors complained about the state of agriculture in the South, particularly of the difficulty of de-seeding the upland or short-staple cotton that grew so well in the interior, Greene suggested that Whitney might solve the problem. Though he had never before seen a cotton boll, Whitney became intrigued with the idea of a machine that could extract the seed. He knew that such an invention "would be a great thing both to the Country and to the inventor."

Through the winter months of 1792-1793, Whitney worked diligently in the basement of the mansion. By springtime, he had created a working model of the cotton gin. Wire hooks attached to a rotating cylinder pulled the cotton fibers through slots in a breastwork that was too narrow to allow the seeds to pass. A rotating brush then cleaned the lint from the hooks. Instead of one to three pounds of cotton per day, a slave using Whitney's hand-cranked gin could clean forty to fifty pounds. Whitney

Eli Whitney. (Library of Congress)

France. Whitney realized the need for armaments, so he proposed to build ten thousand muskets for the government in two years at $13.40 each. The unrealistic deadline might have indicated that Whitney was desperate for funds, or perhaps he simply had faith in his idea. The government expressed its faith in Whitney by awarding him a contract and a $5,000 cash advance.

Whitney's first task was to build a weapons factory, the Whitney Armory, with machines of his own invention that could perform such jobs as forging, rolling, drilling, boring, and cutting uniform parts, which could then be easily assembled by largely untrained workers. The principle on which he proposed to base his system was the idea of interchangeable parts, not a new idea but one Whitney wanted to use on a grand scale at Mill Rock (later named Whitneyville). Difficulties arose, however, in building the machinery, appropriately funding the endeavor—despite periodic advances from the government—and providing the limited training of the laborers. In addition, Whitney's court battles in the South on behalf of his gin required his frequent absence from the manufactory. Therefore, the first five hundred muskets were not delivered until September, 1801. This delay might have been disheartening had Whitney not received the support of individuals such as President Thomas Jefferson. Whitney continued to try to improve his production methods, probably by observing other armories, until he finally did complete his first contract in early 1809.

Business slowed for a few years until the War of 1812 produced a new demand for muskets. Whitney once again contracted with the government, this time for fifteen thousand muskets. Though the order was not completed until 1822, Whitney had improved his system of operations and equipment, thus achieving greater efficiency and output.

During the last few years of this contract period, Whitney's personal life had dramatically changed. Although he had always expressed his desire to marry, he had never devoted time to a serious relationship. While he had maintained close ties with his brothers and sister and had reared three nephews, Philos, Elihu, and Eli Whitney Blake, he still longed for a wife and children of his own. On January 6, 1817, the fifty-one-year-old

knew that his invention could solve the economic troubles of the South, as did Miller. Thus, they formed a partnership and began plans to manufacture other gins that they would operate, charging a portion of the cotton as payment.

Whitney decided to return to New Haven to build a factory to produce the gins. He then took steps to get a patent, which he received in 1794 from President George Washington. In the meantime, however, the Georgia planters had discovered Whitney's invention, had tremendously increased cotton production, and had begun to copy Whitney's simple design. The pirating could not be stopped; demand was too great. Even the courts of the South failed to uphold Whitney's patent until 1806. While Whitney and his partner therefore failed to make any real profit—several states eventually purchased patent rights—the South prospered immensely.

In the midst of this controversy, Whitney the opportunist had found another potentially profitable industry. In 1798, the country seemed on the verge of war with

Whitney married Henrietta Edwards. The couple immediately began their family of four children—Frances Edwards, Elizabeth Fay, Eli, Jr., and Susan Edwards. Susan died very young.

As a result of his new family life and several illnesses, including prostate disease, Whitney began to give more and more control of his armory to his nephews, Philos and Eli. When, in 1822, he received a third government contract, the nephews essentially took charge. Thus, when Whitney died on January 8, 1825, he left a thriving business, a loving family, and an outstanding reputation as one of the most inventive mechanical minds of his generation.

SIGNIFICANCE

Eli Whitney's life coincided with the birth and adolescence of a new nation. Like the young America, Whitney strove to find a place in the world. Eager for fame and fortune, he used his creative mind to discover ways to achieve those goals. In the process, he contributed to the economic growth of his country and its international reputation as an industrious society full of opportunities for the clever, creative, determined, and dedicated.

Whitney's invention of the cotton gin fulfilled a crucial economic need in the southern portion of the country during a period of decline. Unfortunately, the invention that saved hundreds of planters from bankruptcy and helped restore the economic vitality of the region by making cotton "king of the South" also fostered the extension of slavery and the plantation system, a way of life that ended only with a bitter civil war. Whitney, however, must not be burdened with the responsibility for the use of his invention to sustain an aristocratic society. Though he realized that the gin could bring lasting wealth and power to its inventor, he did not and probably could not see its wider ramifications.

Whitney did, nevertheless, foresee the tremendous industrial potential of the new nation. More important, he knew how to take advantage of that potential. While his techniques and machinery may not have been entirely original in their conception (Whitney did not try to patent them), he did develop one of the first mill communities in the nation, with housing for his employees, and he did attempt to create a manufacturing system that used interchangeable parts to create an inexpensive, high-quality product. The ideas that he advocated and that his nephews and son attempted to carry on later became known in Europe as the American System. No term could be more appropriate for the concerns of individuals such as Eli

Whitney, whose inventive minds, creative genius, profit motive, personnel management, and efficiency techniques have made the United States the most powerful industrial nation in the world.

—Alice Taylor

FURTHER READING

Battison, Edwin A. "Eli Whitney and the Milling Machine." *Smithsonian Journal of History* 1 (Summer, 1966): 9-34. A good article on the milling machine, suggesting that Robert Johnson, and not Whitney, was its inventor.

Britton, Karen Gerhardt. *Bale O'Cotton: The Mechanical Art of Cotton Ginning*. College Station: Texas A&M University Press, 1992. Britton chronicles the history of the American cotton ginning industry from its origins in 1793 to the end of the twentieth century. Examines the folklore associated with the industry.

Burlingame, Roger. *Whittling Boy: The Story of Eli Whitney*. New York: Harcourt, Brace, 1941. Combines fact with fiction, which makes a highly entertaining book if the objective is not historical accuracy.

Edward, Brother C. "Eli Whitney: Embattled Inventor." *American History Illustrated* 8 (February, 1974): 4-9, 44-47. A fairly accurate introduction to Whitney's life and work, especially in regard to the cotton gin controversy.

Lakwete, Angela. *Inventing the Cotton Gin: Machine and Myth in Antebellum America*. Baltimore: Johns Hopkins University Press, 2003. Places the invention of the cotton gin within a historical and global context. Lakwete describes early gins invented in Africa and Asia, the earliest gins used in the United States, and the innovations of Whitney and other inventors. She refutes the argument that the slavery-based antebellum southern states had a primitive economy, maintaining that the use of the cotton gin provides proof of innovation, industrialization, and modernization.

Mirsky, Jeannette, and Allan Nevins. *The World of Eli Whitney*. New York: Macmillan, 1952. Still the most accurate and scholarly biography of Whitney, though it contains some errors in interpreting his achievements.

Olmsted, Denison. *Memoir of Eli Whitney, Esq*. New Haven, Conn.: Durrie and Peck, 1846. Reprint. Salem, N.H.: Ayer, 1972. An invaluable contemporary account based on the author's personal recollections and those of other friends. There are, however, personal biases of authors and discrepancies in dates.

See also: Sir Richard Arkwright; Abraham Darby; John Fitch; Nathanael Greene; Thomas Jefferson; Thomas Newcomen; Jethro Tull; George Washington; James Watt.

Related articles in *Great Events from History: The Eighteenth Century, 1701-1800:* 1705-1712: New-comen Develops the Steam Engine; 1764: Invention of the Spinning Jenny; 1765-1769: Watt Develops a More Effective Steam Engine; April, 1785: Cartwright Patents the Steam-Powered Loom; 1790: First Steam Rolling Mill; 1795: Invention of the Flax Spinner.

WILLIAM WILBERFORCE
English politician and social reformer

Guided by his Evangelical views, Wilberforce led the fight to end the slave trade and later slavery in the British Empire. He also sought to reform the morals of his country. As a result of his struggles throughout a long parliamentary career, he and his supporters developed a number of techniques designed to mobilize public opinion that have become standard to modern British political life.

Born: August 24, 1759; Hull, Yorkshire, England
Died: July 29, 1833; London, England
Areas of achievement: Social reform, government and politics

EARLY LIFE

William Wilberforce was born into a prosperous merchant family from Hull. An only son, he was small, frail, and plagued with poor eyesight. In 1768, shortly after his father's death, he went to live with relatives in London. There, to the horror of his family, he was converted to Methodism. Hastily, his mother brought him back to Hull, where he soon gave up his religious "enthusiasm" and settled into the frivolous social life of his class. He was educated in a series of boarding schools of varying quality and entered Cambridge in 1776 at the age of seventeen. Although he did not devote much of his time to learning there, he did come to know a number of people who, like himself, would be Great Britain's future leaders.

Wilberforce left Cambridge in 1781 to enter Parliament as a member for Hull. As the social life in London was exhilarating, he quickly joined five political clubs and became an avid patron of the opera and the theater. He was slower to become involved in parliamentary life, but in the campaign of 1783, he demonstrated the remarkable oratorical gifts which came to be his hallmark and which secured for him a prestigious county seat in Yorkshire in place of his borough seat for Hull. Although successful and popular, Wilberforce was unhappy. On a trip to the Continent shortly after his victory, Wilberforce reached a turning point in his life: He read *The Rise and Progress of Religion in the Soul* (1745), by Philip Doddridge, and began to think again of religion.

For months after his return, his mind was in turmoil. He was especially influenced by a movement in the Anglican Church, the Evangelicals, who, like the Methodists of his youth, claimed that God expected Christians to be "serious" about their lives and would not spare them from judgment if they were not. They must constantly strive for self-improvement, perform good works, and above all, avoid the frivolous and empty pleasures Wilberforce had so avidly pursued up to this time. Wilberforce wondered what such a commitment would require. Would he have to resign his parliamentary seat? With some assistance from John Newton, a Methodist and former slave captain, Wilberforce came to believe that his social position, oratorical gifts, and seat in Parliament were instruments through which he was to do God's work in England. He resigned his clubs, gave up gambling and dancing as well as attending the opera and the theater, and began a period of careful study and reflection until, as he recounted in his diary for October 28, 1787, he came to see that God had given him two tasks: the suppression of the slave trade and the reformation of the morals of England.

LIFE'S WORK

The suppression of the slave trade occupied much of Wilberforce's attention for the next twenty years. To most of his contemporaries, this trade was a vital form of commerce and a training ground for young seamen. The slavers themselves painted a picture of joyous slaves dancing on the decks of ships that carried them to the West Indies, happy to be leaving Africa for "civilization," even as slaves. Wilberforce and his Evangelical associates faced a difficult task.

In May, 1789, Wilberforce began his campaign to end the slave trade. He and his supporters, who came to be known as the Clapham sect, from the suburb outside London where they lived and worked, had gathered enough evidence on the evils of the trade to present a formidable case against it. Wilberforce was confident of an easy victory. He was greatly mistaken. The West Indies planters controlled a number of seats in Parliament. They also had persuaded many members that the proposal would be dangerous for England unless France and Spain went along as well. Finally, the Crown quietly opposed the measure.

The years that followed were often frustrating for Wilberforce and the Clapham sect. Twice his life was threatened by irate sea captains. For a time, the country seemed to be less supportive with each passing year, in part because Wilberforce and his associates were blamed for a series of slave revolts in the West Indies. Events in France, however, did the most damage to their cause.

In 1792, the French Revolution entered its radical, or Jacobin, phase. Soon afterward, Napoleon Bonaparte came to power. Throughout this period, England was locked in a life or death struggle with France. A numbing reaction pervaded the country's ruling class, who viewed

William Wilberforce. (Library of Congress)

all proposals that sought any kind of change with suspicion. Wilberforce and his supporters were often accused of supporting Jacobinism or even atheism.

Year after year, the Evangelicals introduced their bills to end the slave trade, only to see them voted down. Yet, gradually they educated, molded, and mobilized public opinion against the trade, often using religious periodicals such as *The Christian Year* to bring their case to the people. No serious Christian, they maintained, could rest easy so long as this blight upon the nation's conscience survived. Readers were encouraged to gather petitions and write to the members of Parliament expressing their concerns. These techniques were novel in England's political history. By 1807, the Evangelicals' persistence produced results. The final bill, introduced in January, passed the House of Lords on March 23. Two days later, with the consent of the king, it became law.

The slave trade had not been the only issue with which Wilberforce and the Clapham sect had been occupied over the previous two decades. They had also been busy with Wilberforce's other life project, the reformation of the morals of the country. According to the Evangelicals, there was much in England that needed reform. The wealthy lived elegant but morally lax lives. They drank heavily and gambled, often ruinously. Corruption was basic to political life, and the established clergy seemed to be more concerned about its social position than the care of the souls in its charge.

The poor were in an infinitely worse position. They, too, drank heavily—gin, which was cheap. It was also much higher in alcohol content than beer or wine and often disastrous to their health and to the health of their children. Those who could find employment labored for twelve to sixteen hours a day, seven days a week, for meager wages when there was work. The many who could find no work in the towns, on the farms, or in the mines could only become beggars, vagabonds, or thieves. They made the roads notoriously unsafe for the well-to-do. Parliament had tried to deal with the problems of the poor by passing ever stricter laws. The offenses punishable by death rose from thirty in 1688 to more than two hundred by the eighteenth century.

To rescue England from this moral quagmire, Wilberforce and the Evangelicals, with the blessing of George III, organized the Society for the Suppression of Vice, which sought to curb excessive drinking and to prevent "blasphemy," swearing, cursing, and "lewdness and other dissolute practices." The society also sought to outlaw what its members regarded as cruel sports: bearbaiting and cockfighting. They did not, however, find fox hunting cruel. As critics have noted, the poor suffered most from the righteous efforts of the committee.

The Evangelicals' campaign did have some influence upon the privileged. Churchgoing among this group increased. Furthermore, many began to employ Evangelicals as tutors for their children. Evangelical pastors acquired parishes, a few became bishops, and one even became the archbishop of Canterbury, the primate of the Church of England.

Wilberforce and his supporters also attacked dueling and the use of press gangs and "chimney boys." They supported the first factory act. They even supported Catholic emancipation, which is surprising, as they were suspicious of "popery" otherwise. Finally, the Evangelicals were interested in assisting the needy, although in ways they found compatible with laissez-faire capitalism. They believed that the poor would profit from being able to read the Bible, so they began the Sunday School movement. They also sought the passage of Sabbatarian laws, in part to allow them to attend the classes. They spent a large amount of money on Bibles, prayer books, and tracts to give to the poor.

The aristocrats and established clergy criticized Wilberforce and his associates for these efforts because they were fearful that a literate poor would either be disenchanted with their work or, worse still, read anti-Christian propaganda assumed to be coming from France and so become atheists. In truth, they were fearful that the Evangelicals were more concerned about influencing their students' religious ideas than teaching them to read, and they were correct.

As serious Christians were expected to be charitable toward the poor, the Evangelicals were not stingy in their giving. At times, Wilberforce gave away more than he earned in a year. Some Evangelicals left their children almost penniless. They supported a society to keep debtors out of prison, education for the blind, foundling hospitals, prison reform, and the relief of widows, to name but a few causes.

In part because of their religious outlook, but also because of their laissez-faire attitudes, the Evangelicals, Wilberforce among them, opposed strongly either the labor movement or socialism as means of assisting the poor. Indeed, they proved to be as fearful of popular unrest as the rest of the ruling class and regularly supported all repressive measures taken by the government against it. Critics to the left of Wilberforce and the Evangelicals have long used these aspects of their policies to discredit the entire reform effort. To these critics, the Clapham sect's blindness to the economic nature of poverty pre-

vented their reforms, however well-intentioned, from being of much lasting value.

Wilberforce and the Evangelicals had originally decided to attack the slave trade rather than slavery because they feared that the latter could not be defeated. Furthermore, they expected that defeat of the trade would inevitably lead to an end of the institution itself. By 1820, they came to realize that their assumptions were incorrect. They had not even stopped the trade; they had made it illegal, which was all the worse for the slaves. Wilberforce was too old to lead the campaign, but he found in Thomas Fowell Buxton the person to take his place. Wilberforce also supported the effort inside Parliament until his retirement in February, 1825, and then outside until ill health prevented him from any further speaking. Although he did not live to see the Slavery Abolition Act become law, he did see it pass the second reading, at which time Parliament appropriated £20 million with which to compensate slave owners. At that point, he knew that it would become law. Four days later, just before its final passage, he died.

Much of Wilberforce's success can be attributed to his speaking ability. He also had a winning personality. He was charming, witty, and always considerate of other people's attitudes. Politically, he was always prepared to work with any group which would advance his objectives. He worked with the most thoroughly secular members of the Commons as well as with the Evangelicals in securing the passage of the Slavery Abolition Act. Yet in his personal life he was reserved. On one occasion, he was maneuvered into dining with the famous novelist Madame de Staël, who was not noted for her religious seriousness. She, too, was charming and witty, and they both enjoyed themselves. Yet the next morning Wilberforce felt quite guilty and would never dine with her again. Wilberforce believed that one must always be on guard against the lure of frivolous pleasures, especially when dealing with one whose religious ideas are insufficiently "serious."

Wilberforce remained a bachelor until he was thirty-eight, at which time he married Barbara Spooner. She bore him six children, ran his household, and looked after his health. A serious Christian, she supported him in his political endeavors. To his Evangelical friends, she was as much the ideal wife as he was the ideal husband, father, and statesman.

SIGNIFICANCE

William Wilberforce dedicated his life to the suppression of the slave trade in the British Empire and the reformation of the morals of his fellow countrymen. In the former endeavor he was eminently successful. Indeed, he became internationally renowned as an opponent of slavery even during his lifetime. While he was assisted by men and women of like mind, it remains true that without his leadership and parliamentary skills it would have been difficult if not impossible for them to have achieved their goal so early in the nineteenth century. In the process, he and his party introduced parliamentary tactics that in the future became commonplace.

Wilberforce also enjoyed considerable success in his campaign to reform public morality. England underwent monumental changes in its attitudes toward moral behavior during his lifetime. The "age of elegance" in which he was born slipped into the "age of Victoria" by the time of his old age. Although Evangelicalism itself declined rapidly after his death, its continuing influence was evident in the moral earnestness, the concern for charitable works and family life, and the fastidiousness associated with the age of England's illustrious nineteenth century queen. Thus, as the acknowledged leader of Evangelicalism, Wilberforce deserves to be remembered not only as the person who freed the slaves but also as the father of the Victorians.

—*Terry R. Morris*

FURTHER READING

Belmonte, Kevin. *Hero for Humanity: A Biography of William Wilberforce*. Colorado Springs, Colo.: Navpress, 2002. One of several updated biographies that portray Wilberforce as having strong moral character and religious convictions.

Bradley, Ian. "William Wilberforce, the Saint." *History Today* 33 (July, 1983): 41-44. A good place to begin studying Wilberforce and his work.

Brown, Ford. *Fathers of the Victorians*. Cambridge, England: Cambridge University Press, 1961. Connects Wilberforce with the emerging Victorian moral outlook.

Furneaux, Robin. *William Wilberforce*. London: Hamish Hamilton, 1974. A balanced study of all aspects of Wilberforce's life that takes into account the critical studies of the 1960's.

Gratus, Jack. *The Great White Lie*. New York: Hutchinson, 1973. Attacks Wilberforce and the Clapham sect.

Suggests that the radicals deserve more credit for the defeat of slavery than they have received.

Hochschild, Adam. *Bury the Chains: Prophets and Rebels in the Fight to Free an Empire's Slaves*. Boston: Houghton Mifflin, 2005. Wilberforce is featured in this acclaimed history of the British abolition movement. Hochschild describes the tactics movement leaders developed to win popular support for their cause.

Howse, Ernest Marshall. *Saints in Politics*. London: Allen & Unwin, 1952. A study of the Clapham sect, of which Wilberforce was the leader.

Thompson, E. P. *The Making of the English Working Class*. London: Gollancz, 1963. Sharply critical of Wilberforce and his associates for their part in the suppression of popular movements in the reaction of the Napoleonic era.

Vaughn, David J. *Statesman and Saint: The Principled Politics of William Wilberforce*. Nashville, Tenn.: Highland Books, 2002. Admiring biography describing how Wilberforce's religious beliefs led him to be a crusading statesman and a philanthropist.

Wilberforce, William. *Correspondence of William Wilberforce*. Edited by Robert Isaac Wilberforce and Samuel Wilberforce. Miami, Fla.: Mnemosyne, 1969. A reprint of the original 1840 edition, the letters give a picture of Wilberforce and his circle and cover the gamut of his concerns.

See also: George III; Hannah More; Guillaume-Thomas Raynal; Samuel Sewall; Granville Sharp; Madame de Staël; Charles Wesley; John Wesley; George Whitefield; John Wilkes.

Related articles in *Great Events from History: The Eighteenth Century, 1701-1800:* 18th century: Expansion of the Atlantic Slave Trade; April 6, 1712: New York City Slave Revolt; Beginning April, 1763: The *North Briton* Controversy; April 14, 1775: Pennsylvania Society for the Abolition of Slavery Is Founded; April 12, 1787: Free African Society Is Founded; February 22, 1791-February 16, 1792: Thomas Paine Publishes *Rights of Man*; 1792: Wollstonecraft Publishes *A Vindication of the Rights of Woman*.

JOHN WILKES
English politician and social reformer

The most famous British radical of the second half of the eighteenth century, Wilkes became the era's preeminent symbol of liberty. His influence was felt in struggles to extend the freedom of the press, in the Wilkite movement that agitated for parliamentary reform, and in the strengthening of American opposition to British policy in the decade preceding the Revolutionary War.

Born: October 17, 1725; London, England
Died: December 26, 1797; London, England
Areas of achievement: Government and politics, social reform

EARLY LIFE

John Wilkes was born to a prosperous distiller. He was given a classical education and eventually attended the University of Leiden in the Netherlands. In 1747, he returned home to marry an heiress, Mary Mead. The marriage ended in separation, but it did bring Wilkes an income and a house in Buckinghamshire. During the 1750's, Wilkes lived on the fringes of literary London. Associating with a circle of hard-living young gentlemen, he soon acquired what would be a lifelong reputation as a rake. His Buckinghamshire connections brought him to the attention of Richard Grenville, Earl Temple, the brother-in-law of William Pitt the Elder. With the support of the Grenville family, Wilkes was named sheriff of Buckinghamshire in 1754, and three years later, he was elected to Parliament from the borough of Aylesbury. Wilkes also became an officer in the county militia. By the beginning of George III's reign in 1760, Wilkes had entered politics, though as yet he was a follower rather than a leader.

Contemporaries already found Wilkes a remarkable figure. Flamboyant in dress and slightly taller than average, Wilkes had rather angular features capped by a permanent squint. The opposite sex nevertheless found him attractive, and all agreed that he was a man of great wit and charm. Many commented that Wilkes regarded life as a game played for his own amusement. Even those, such as Edward Gibbon and Samuel Johnson, who were repelled by Wilkes's reputation for immorality found his company enjoyable.

LIFE'S WORK

John Wilkes first became important as part of the outburst of political journalism that characterized the early 1760's. The accession of George III had brought to prominence the young king's favorite, the Scottish earl of Bute. Both the king and Bute favored winding down the Seven Years' War, and their views eventually clashed with those of Pitt and Temple over the need to launch a preemptive strike against Spain. After Pitt and Temple resigned in 1761, criticism of Bute and the government—much of it violently anti-Scottish—began to mount. Wilkes found a considerable talent as a propagandist and became a willing and effective participant in the journalistic wars, on the side of Pitt. In June, 1762, Wilkes founded the *North Briton*. The title was intended as an ironic reference to the alleged pro-Scottish inclination of Bute's government and as a reply to Tobias Smollett's progovernment *Briton*. Wilkes proved to be a daring journalist, often exceeding the bounds of good taste and apparently intent on keeping a boast that he would seek the limits of freedom of the press in Great Britain. He found them in April, 1763, when the forty-fifth issue of the *North Briton*, in effect, accused the king of lying in recommending the Treaty of Paris to Parliament as an honorable peace settlement. The king, who came to nourish a deep hatred for Wilkes, and the government were outraged. Wilkes was apprehended and charged with seditious libel, though he protested that his arrest was illegal because it was under a general warrant (one that did not name him personally but was issued against those who wrote, printed, and published the *North Briton*). He was soon released on the grounds of parliamentary privilege and proceeded to file countersuits against several of the ministers. By this time, Wilkes had become a popular hero to the shopkeepers and tradesmen of London, who saw him standing up not only for the freedom of the press but also against the threat of arbitrary arrests as represented by the use of general warrants. (Two years later, both the courts and Parliament declared general warrants illegal.) Upon his release, the cry of "Wilkes and liberty" was heard for the first time.

Having gained the limelight, Wilkes was unwilling to let matters rest. He reprinted the past numbers of the *North Briton* and published a forty-sixth. The government gathered evidence and launched a two-pronged attack against Wilkes in the fall of 1763. In the House of Commons, the *North Briton*, number 45, was attacked as seditious libel, and a resolution was passed declaring that parliamentary privilege did not extend to such cases. In the House of Lords, the earl of Sandwich, an associate of

Wilkes in some of his past adventures, named Wilkes the author and printer of an obscene poem, *Essay on Woman*, which had been falsely attributed to William Warburton, bishop of Gloucester. (The poem was an indecent parody of Alexander Pope's *Essay on Man*, the bishop having been a friend and editor of Pope. Wilkes was probably not the author of the poem, but he had printed it for private circulation.) With his character now blackened as that of a pornographer, Wilkes was also open to prosecution by both Parliament and the courts. He was, however, wounded in a duel and unable to appear before either. In early 1764, Wilkes fled to France. He was subsequently expelled from Parliament by a majority vote of the House of Commons and declared an outlaw by the Court of King's Bench.

Wilkes eventually grew restive in exile, in which he was also plagued by growing debts. In 1768, he gambled that he could retrieve both his personal position and his political prominence by returning to Great Britain. Initially ignored by the authorities, Wilkes soon presented himself to the Court of King's Bench and was duly imprisoned, though not before a crowd of his supporters had clashed violently with a detachment of soldiers. Wilkes's outlawry was reversed on a technicality, but he was sentenced to twenty-two months' imprisonment on his original convictions for the *North Briton* and *Essay on Woman*. While unsuccessfully appealing his sentence, Wilkes remained in relatively comfortable confinement. He continued a variety of journalistic activities, strengthening his image as a champion of liberty, and stood for Parliament. Defeated as a candidate for London, he topped the poll as candidate for the large, metropolitan county of Middlesex.

Wilkes's election for Middlesex set the stage for the most important episode in his political life, one that did much to bring forth the era's most significant outbreak of popular radicalism. The Commons refused to accept Wilkes's election and ordered him expelled in February, 1769. Wilkes refused to leave matters alone and quickly won reelection. Once again the Commons expelled him, resolving in addition that he was incapable of sitting in Parliament. Two more times, Wilkes was elected and expelled before the Commons finally declared his opponent elected. By this time, the Middlesex election had provoked a reaction that shook the government. The House of Commons was attacked by Wilkes's supporters for trampling on the rights of the electors of Middlesex, and the cry of "Wilkes and liberty" once more brought Londoners into the streets. Supporters organized the Society for the Supporters of the Bill of Rights. This group

John Wilkes. (Library of Congress)

raised money to pay Wilkes's debts, agitated for parliamentary reform, and launched a campaign that elicited petitions in support of Wilkes from eighteen counties. Despite this sizable outpouring of popular feeling and sporadic outbreaks of violence, the government rode out the crisis, and Wilkes remained out of Parliament.

While still in prison, Wilkes became active in London politics. In 1769, he was elected an alderman, and in 1771, he was chosen as sheriff. In these capacities, he was soon involved in another important conflict with Parliament, this time over the publication of its proceedings. When the Commons resisted attempts by several newspapers to publish accounts of its debates, officials of the City of London defended the printers by denying the jurisdiction of Parliament's officers inside the city, and Wilkes placed the emissaries of the Commons under arrest. Though some London magistrates were briefly imprisoned, the Commons eventually backed down and press coverage of its debates began. Four years later, by which time Wilkes was lord mayor of London, a similar dispute arose with the House of Lords. It, too, gave in and tacitly conceded press coverage of its debates.

By this time, Wilkes was back in Parliament. Standing for Middlesex in 1774, he was easily elected. With a crisis with the American colonies looming, the government decided to forgo a repetition of the turmoil of 1769 and 1770, and Wilkes quietly took his seat. In Parliament, Wilkes opposed the war with the American colonies, favored schemes for reforming Parliament and government administration, and advocated increased religious toleration. His greatest concern, however, was for personal vindication. He was especially eager to have the resolution declaring his incapacity to sit in the Commons erased from the house's journals. Wilkes offered annual motions to this effect, and in May, 1782, he finally succeeded in expunging the resolution.

As time passed, Wilkes became less flamboyant and more moderate in his politics. He supported William Pitt the Younger and eventually was reconciled to the king, to whom Wilkes is said to have remarked that he himself had never been a Wilkite. During the Gordon Riots of 1780, Wilkes took a prominent role in restoring order. His popularity declined with his radicalism, and he retired from Parliament in 1790 rather than face defeat. Wilkes died seven years later at his house in Grosvenor Square, one of London's most fashionable addresses.

SIGNIFICANCE

John Wilkes was a hero to many middle-class and wage-earning Englishmen and to many colonial Americans. His ironic, even cynical approach to life, his general flamboyance, and his concern for his own advancement have caused many historians to doubt both his commitment to the reformist causes he espoused and his interest in the problems of his more humble followers. He may have been a genial rogue with a flair for self-dramatization, but Wilkes imbued his followers with a sense of purpose, and his career left a lasting impression on the English-speaking world.

In the 1760's and early 1770's, Wilkes's difficulties provided a focus for the grievances of others, especially of the "middling sort," and sparked an interest in politics and political debate among segments of society that were normally considered to be outside the traditional political structure dominated by the landed classes. The Wilkite movement did not originate popular radicalism, but it did much to mobilize it and to make the political elite more conscious of it. The most important focus of the Wilkites came to be their efforts to reform the House of Commons. The Middlesex election affair convinced them that the preferences and interests of the electorate had been callously ignored by an imperious Parliament more interested in maintaining its corporate privilege: Parliament had been corrupted and had forgotten its representative purpose. Their solution was to reform the House of Commons, through such devices as shorter Par-

liaments and the limitation of government patronage, to make it more responsible to the electorate and less easy for the ministers to manipulate. The Wilkites thus played an important role in launching the movement for parliamentary reform that would be carried forward by other groups in later years.

Another important legacy of Wilkes's career was its impact in America. Wilkes himself opposed the various measures that provoked resistance in the colonies, as well as the British government's eventual resort to force. More important was the way that Wilkes came to be seen by many Americans as a man who was persecuted for his devotion to the cause of liberty. His expulsions after repeated elections for Middlesex gave credence to the idea that Parliament had been corrupted by the government and could not be depended upon to defend the rights of the people on either side of the Atlantic. Wilkes became to many American patriots a martyr to liberty, his sufferings proof of the evil intentions of the British government. A measure of his popularity in America is still present in the number of counties, cities, and towns in the original thirteen states that bear his name.

Wilkes's career also had other concrete results. The *North Briton* affair was largely responsible for raising the question of the legality of general warrants, and Wilkes was instrumental in opening the debates of Parliament to newspaper coverage. The depth of his devotion to the causes he came to symbolize may be suspect, but his actions raised important issues and brought a new level of popular involvement in British politics. In the final analysis, he lived up to the epitaph he wrote for himself: "a friend to liberty."

—*William C. Lowe*

FURTHER READING

Brewer, John. *Party Ideology and Popular Politics at the Accession of George III*. New York: Cambridge University Press, 1976. A major work on the politics of the 1760's that emphasizes the vitality of political debate among the nonaristocratic segments of society. Shows that Wilkes and the Wilkites were central to the development of what the author terms an "alternative structure of politics."

Christie, Ian R. "Radicals and Reformers in the Age of Wilkes and Wyvill." In *British Politics and Society from Walpole to Pitt, 1742-1789*, edited by Jeremy Black. New York: St. Martin's Press, 1990.

_____. *Wilkes, Wyvill, and Reform: The Parliamentary Reform Movement in British Politics, 1760-1785*. New York: St. Martin's Press, 1962. Two studies of the parliamentary reform movement that developed during the late eighteenth century and the role of Wilkes and other radicals in that movement. Very useful for putting the role played by Wilkes and his followers into context.

Kronenberger, Louis. *The Extraordinary Mr. Wilkes.* Garden City, N.Y.: Doubleday, 1974. Though flawed by simplistic treatment of Wilkes's adversaries, especially George III, this biography is valuable for its sensitive handling of the different and at times conflicting components of Wilkes's character.

Maier, Pauline. *From Resistance to Revolution: Colonial Radicals and the Development of American Opposition to Britain, 1765-1776.* New York: Alfred A. Knopf, 1972. Important for showing Wilkes's impact on American perceptions and in strengthening the belief that Great Britain's American policy was part of an overall conspiracy against liberty. Useful in putting Wilkes's career into transatlantic perspective.

Nobbe, George. *The "North Briton": A Study in Political Propaganda.* New York: Columbia University Press, 1939. A through study of Wilkes's famous paper. Useful for understanding his approach to political journalism and the journalistic context of the early 1760's.

Postgate, Raymond. *That Devil Wilkes.* New York: Vanguard Press, 1929. A solid biography of Wilkes that provides a well-rounded view of his personality and career. The title is taken from George III's characterization of Wilkes.

Rea, Robert R. *The English Press in Politics, 1760-1774.* Lincoln: University of Nebraska Press, 1963. A good general study of the involvement of the newspaper and periodical press in politics during the most crucial periods of Wilkes's career. Valuable for placing Wilkes's journalistic activities and connections into perspective.

Rudé, George. *Wilkes and Liberty: A Social Study of 1763 to 1774.* Oxford, England: Clarendon Press, 1962. Not a biography of Wilkes, but an important study of the Wilkite movement in its prime. Shows that Wilkes's followers were largely drawn from the middling segments of society and were far from being its dregs.

Thomas, Peter D. G. *John Wilkes, a Friend to Liberty.* New York: Oxford University Press, 1996. Comprehensive biography of Wilkes, providing information on his role in British politics and his political achievements. Thomas argues that Wilkes was appreciated by his contemporaries but has been underestimated by succeeding generations.

See also: Edward Gibbon; Samuel Johnson; Lord North; William Pitt the Younger; Alexander Pope; Robert Walpole; William Wilberforce; John Peter Zenger.

Related articles in *Great Events from History: The Eighteenth Century, 1701-1800:* Beginning April, 1763: The *North Briton* Controversy; April 19, 1775: Battle of Lexington and Concord; June 2-10, 1780: Gordon Riots.

JOHN WILKINSON
English inventor and engineer

Wilkinson was a pioneer of the Staffordshire iron trade, and he contributed to the perfection of the first steam engine with his inventions for boring cylinders. He helped build the first cast-iron bridge and built the first iron barge and the Paris waterworks.

Born: 1728; Clifton, Cumberland, England
Died: July 14, 1808; Bradley, Staffordshire, England
Areas of achievement: Science and technology, engineering, architecture

EARLY LIFE

John Wilkinson was the son of Isaac Wilkinson, an overlooker at an iron furnace who also had a small farm.

John was born sometime in 1728 in a market cart on the road between Workington and Little Clifton Furnace. His mother was going to market with butter and eggs from Isaac Wilkinson's farm, and the expected birth produced a sensation in the area, leading some residents to predict that "sum tyme [he] wod bee a girt man."

In July, 1738, Isaac Wilkinson left Little Clifton to become chief caster, or "potfounder," of the Backbarrow Iron Company in Furness, North Lancashire. A blast furnace had existed there since 1711 and used a charcoal-smelting process. There he obtained a patent and began the manufacture of a laundress' box iron. The enterprise was the first family financial success. Isaac lived in the village of Bare Syke and was a pioneer there in an unsuccessful attempt to develop the crude idea of roller milling. Later in the 1740's he and his son John had both a furnace and a refinery, with a canal utilizing a small iron boat at Wilson House near Lindale.

In 1753, Isaac Wilkinson moved to Bersham, where he operated what would be his principal furnace from then until his failure in 1795. Proximity to the Chester and Liverpool markets and plentiful supplies of charcoal, iron ore, coal, and waterpower near the area were the site's advantages. In 1762, Isaac Wilkinson became partners with two other men in the Dowlais Iron Company, and in 1763 at Merthyr Tydfil and Aberdare. These concerns were unsuccessful, and in 1767 he became the sole owner of the Cyfarthfa ironworks in Glamorgan. From 1753 to 1764, he manufactured iron cylinders, pipes, and cannon in Bristol. He finally retired as a merchant ironmonger in that city, and he lived out the rest of his life there, impoverished and dependent on his children. His few possessions were left to Thomas Guest, the Welsh ironmaster.

A Presbyterian, Isaac gave his son John the best education available to Nonconformists in the 1740's. The youth was sent to a Dissenting academy in Kendal, kept by the Unitarian divine Dr. Caleb Rotherham. Between 1733 and 1751, some 180 scholars received instruction there, mostly for possible ministerial office.

In 1745, at the age of seventeen, John was apprenticed to a merchant ironmonger in Liverpool, in whose shop or warehouse he remained for three years, until he returned to the place of his birth. In about 1748, John again left his father to work at Wolverhampton and later at Bilston, Staffordshire. When he was about twenty years old he built the first furnace there, naming it Bradley Furnace. It was there that he succeeded in using coal for wood charcoal in smelting and puddling iron ore.

Meanwhile, his father had moved to Bersham, near Wrexham in Denbighshire, and in 1756 John rejoined his father. There he built an improved machine for boring cylinders with accuracy. In 1759, John began to manufacture wrought iron at a larger forge of the New Willey Company, at Broseley near Bridgnorth, and in 1761 he became the manager of the Bersham works. Upon his father's financial failure, John and his brother William, as partners, reconstituted the firm as the New Bersham Company.

In 1770, John expanded Bradley Furnace near Bilston, bringing to three the ironworks (Bersham, Broseley, and Bradley) that were run by Wilkinsons. In 1772, he displayed his business precociousness when, acting for the Bersham Company, he made a cartel agreement with Abraham Darby III, head of the Coalbrookdale Company, that they would charge the same for engine parts, cylinders, and bored parts (with the exception of London).

LIFE'S WORK

John Wilkinson's next achievement occurred in connection with a crisis that was caused by the increased size of Newcomen-style steam engines, which as a result became less efficient, using more coal and leather for pistons. In 1762-1764, James Watt had made his new design for a steam engine with a separate condenser, which was patented in 1769 and perfected by 1775. One of the most important steps in perfecting the engine resulted from Wilkinson inventing an improved boring mill. His patented boring mill was of unequaled accuracy. In it, castings, cylinders, or cannon could rotate around a fixed boring bar along which the cutting tool was traversed. This enabled a bored cylinder to be true in three dimensions. In 1770, Watt found that Wilkinson's machine produced by far the most accurately bored cylinders for his engine. Wilkinson, who now owned the Bersham plant, quickly applied the third steam engine made by Matthew Boulton and Watt to blow the bellows at his new furnace at Broseley to manufacture wrought iron. A blast of air at a pressure of four pounds per square inch was supplied continuously to the furnace, and the higher temperature made possible by the blast simplified the use of coke for smelting. The steam engine was the first to be used for that function.

The engine was set up in 1776 by Watt himself, and the model soon surpassed those of the older Newcomen design. Watt insisted that all cylinders on his engines should be provided by Wilkinson's Broseley or Bradley works, even though Wilkinson's prices were higher. The Wilkinsons expanded their industrial empire soon, acquiring coal, iron stone, and lead ore mines, but refused to manufacture steam engines. Wilkinson maintained a monopoly on the boring process until 1780, when the Darby's Coalbrookdale Company and the Walkers of Rotherham began their manufacture. As time passed, the personal relationship between Wilkinson and Boulton and Watt ruptured when Watt's son assumed control from his father and when William Wilkinson's son married Boulton's daughter.

In 1782 and again in 1795, John quarreled with William (who was in charge of his foreign operations) over the division of profits. In 1795, John closed the Bersham furnace and canceled Boulton and Watt's outstanding orders for cylinders, with the result that Boulton and Watt opened their own foundry at Smethwick, for engine work that William helped design. It was run by Abraham Storey (John Wilkinson's head man), whom they had enticed away. The dispute escalated when William revealed to the younger Watt that John had pirated the Watt patent in 1787 and had sold at least eight steam engines, including one for Cadiz, one for the Perrier brothers at Mons, and one for Count Reden in Prussia. To avoid costly litigation, John Wilkinson, in December, 1795, agreed to pay the Soho partners full reparations.

Before this feud, Wilkinson in 1781 had used a Watt engine to move a hammer of sixty pounds more than sixty strokes a minute, and by 1783, through a cam, it lifted a forge hammerhead, weighing eight hundred pounds, a distance of two feet. Soon many other ironmasters ordered forge engines from Watt. In 1786, Wilkinson was again first, this time in using a steam engine in a rolling mill.

Wilkinson was ever the improviser. Since 1753, the family had made cannon for the national and international markets, including the British East India Company, especially after 1762 at Bersham. Wilkinson's new boring process, so valuable for boring cannon barrels, encouraged him, in 1775, to smuggle to France cannon disguised as water pipes. The Wilkinsons soon gained an affluence exceeding that of the Quaker ironmasters, whose pacifism made them reject the munitions trade. By 1786, thirty-two-pounders, howitzers, swivels, and shells were being exported to the Ottoman Empire, Russia, France, and various German states. In 1795, Wilkinson devised an even more improved apparatus for boring cannon, utilizing a completely opposite technique at Brymbo next to Bresham. These improvements in casting and boring cannon reduced the chance of the weapon vibrating and shattering into a thousand pieces, thereby killing the gunners. Demands for water pipes, malt and sugarcane rollers, and gas apparatuses led to more improvements in foundry practices. Wilkinson's power-driven rolling mill at Bradley produced rolls four feet in diameter from twenty reverberating furnaces and 420 tons of bar iron a month. Bradley Furnace, near Bilston, had access to a ten-foot-wide seam of coal.

Wilkinson was relentless in his application of cast iron. In 1779, he aided Darby, who was the chief force behind constructing the first iron bridge across the Severn River between Broseley and Wadeley. In 1787, to facilitate sending war matériel down the Severn, he constructed the first iron barge, the *Trial*, which was launched near Broseley on July 9, 1787. He also had a warehouse and five wharves in London to distribute his products. Later, in Bradley, he erected a Wesleyan Chapel, in which the doors, the window frames, and even the pulpit were of cast iron.

Wilkinson also expanded overseas to meet demands. In 1770, he established a foundry in France. He also taught the French the art of boring cannon from solid castings to aid the cause of the American Revolution. In 1776, William Wilkinson helped the French remodel the ordnance works at Le Creusot. He later emigrated to France as the result of a family quarrel in 1781 pitting John and Mary against Isaac and William, probably over management and ownership of the Bersham furnace. William's introduction of the use of coal to make iron at Nantes and elsewhere in France resulted in large profits, and the name Wilkinson became synonymous with "blast furnace" in France. John also cast forty miles of pipes, cylinders, and ironwork required by the Perrier brothers, engineers for the Paris waterworks, a great marvel in its day, and it was in connection with this project that he erected the first large steam engine in France.

John Wilkinson was far more successful financially than his father. He owned a five-hundred-acre farm at Brymbo, near Wrexham, where he utilized one of the first steam-powered threshing machines. He also invested more than £2,000 in the Shrewsbury Canal. In addition, Wilkinson had investments as early as 1781 with Thomas Williams, "the copper king," and in 1783 he developed a lead mine at Minera and coal at Soughton. In 1790, he established a lead-pipe factory at Rotherhithe on the Thames. Not content with financial power, in 1799 he was high sheriff for Denbighshire. Between 1787 and 1793, because of the shortage of coins in the area, Wilkinson issued numerous tokens, both silver and copper, as well as guinea notes, for private circulation in Staffordshire and Shropshire. He was also a partner with William Reynolds in a Shrewsbury bank. Rumors of his radicalism no doubt stemmed from the fact that his sister Mary had married Joseph Priestley on June 23, 1762, and that after the destruction of his property at Birmingham, Wilkinson had assisted him during a time of financial distress. Like Priestley, he was sympathetic to the works of Thomas Paine and to the French Revolution.

Wilkinson was married twice, first to Anne Mawdsley in 1755, who died a year later when she was only twenty-three years old, and then to a Miss Lee of Wroxeter. Both possessed sizable landed fortunes. Wilkinson's second marriage, in 1763, had enabled him to become owner of the Broseley forge. His domestic life was free-spirited: While in his seventies, he had three children by his mistress Mary Ann Lewis, a servant girl; he had them declared legitimate in 1808. These sons would contest his large fortune with nephews in Chancery Court (especially his factotum Thomas Jones, the son of his sister Sarah Wilkinson and a Leeds surgeon).

Wilkinson died at Bradley, Staffordshire, on July 14, 1808, and was buried on his estate Castlehead near Grange-over-Sands in North Lancashire, his home since 1779. Originally he had planned to be buried in a cast-iron casket, but by the time he died he had grown too stout. He at least had the satisfaction of having a cast-iron memorial erected at Castlehead after his death. The value of his estate at the time of his death was £120,000, although it was dissipated by the twelve years of litigation that followed. Alone among ironmasters, Wilkinson became a folk hero, revered in song. In 1815, seven years after his death, several thousand people assembled on Monmore Green near Bradley, expecting his second coming on his gray horse.

SIGNIFICANCE

John Wilkinson had a dominating nature, an inflated ego, and a great capacity for hatred, with competitors, customers, and employees. On the other hand, in 1776 his workers earned a good wage—between eight and eleven shillings a week—and he gave some of them old-age pensions. He also gave several thousand pounds to philanthropic causes in Shropshire and London. Wilkinson was handsome in his youth, with fine features, but his profile on his silver and copper tokens shows a homely, heavy face with haughty eyebrows and a scornful, contemptuous mouth. His religious preferences have been described as Unitarian, Anglican, Methodist, and atheist.

His ability as an engineer, ironmonger, and businessman to find new uses for cast iron and implement new business techniques marks him as one who enriched the world more than he enriched himself. After his death, his industrial empire was leased or closed and eventually disappeared.

—*Norbert C. Soldon*

FURTHER READING

Ashton, Thomas Southcliffe. *Iron and Steel in the Industrial Revolution*. Manchester, England: Manchester University Press, 1924. Using Wilkinson's letter books as sources, this book provides information with a wide chronological range.

Birch, Alan. *The Economic History of the British Iron and Steel Industry, 1784-1879*. London: Frank Cass, 1967. Contains many quantitative details. Good on technological aspects of the subject. Includes references to William Wilkinson.

Chaloner, William H. "Isaac Wilkinson, Potfounder." In *Studies in the Industrial Revolution Presented to T. S. Ashton*, edited by L. S. Pressnell. London: Athlone Press, 1960. An easy-to-obtain source that, despite its title, is one of the most abundant sources of information on John Wilkinson and his personal life and career as an industrialist.

Dickinson, Henry Winram. *John Wilkinson, Ironmaster*. Ulverston, England: H. Kitchin, 1914. Written by one of the first authorities on the history of the steam engine. A rare book, much used by historians.

Musson, Albert Edward, and Eric Robinson. *Science and Technology in the Industrial Revolution*. Manchester, England: Manchester University Press, 1979. A good overall modern treatment of the subjects that deals with their interactions by two of the best contemporary experts. Good on European contacts.

Raistrick, Arthur. *Dynasty of Ironfounders: The Darbys and Coalbrookdale*. London: Longmans, Green, 1953. While dealing mainly with the Darbys, it contains a good bibliography for the Coalbrookdale area and contains some references to Wilkinson's career in the Madeley area.

Randall, John. *The Wilkinsons*. Madeley, England: John Randall, 1876. A local historian gives details of Wilkinson's domestic life. A rare book, with few copies extant in the United States.

Soldon, Norbert C. *John Wilkinson, 1728-1808: English Ironmaster and Inventor*. Lewiston, N.Y.: Edwin Mellen Press, 1998. Detailed biography of Wilkinson, covering, among other subjects, his family origins, the creation of his iron business, contemporary opinion of Wilkinson, and Wilkinson's legacy.

Trinder, Barrie. *The Industrial Revolution in Shropshire*. Totowa, N.J.: Rowman, Littlefield, 1973. Written by the author of many social, technological, and archaeological books and articles of the region. Raises a variety of questions on subjects that concern modern economic historians. Highly recommended.

See also: Matthew Boulton; Abraham Darby; William Murdock; Thomas Newcomen; Joseph Priestley; James Watt; Eli Whitney.

Related articles in *Great Events from History: The Eighteenth Century, 1701-1800:* 1709: Darby Invents Coke-Smelting; November, 1777-January 1, 1781: Construction of the First Iron Bridge; 1783-1784: Cort Improves Iron Processing.

JAMES WILSON
Scottish-born American politician, legal scholar, and jurist

Wilson was a leader in the movement for American independence and a framer of the U.S. Constitution. Renowned for his learning in law and political theory, he developed the idea of an independent national judiciary—a supreme court—with the power to resolve questions of constitutional meaning, and was thus appointed to the first U.S. Supreme Court by President George Washington.

Born: September 14, 1742; Carskerdo, Fife, Scotland
Died: August 21, 1798; Edenton, North Carolina
Areas of achievement: Law, government and politics

EARLY LIFE

James Wilson was born on the small farm of his parents, William and Alison Wilson, north of Edinburgh, near St. Andrews, Scotland. The Wilsons were not indigent, but as more children arrived they were obliged to practice rigorously the thrift for which their countrymen are known. They were intensely religious people, deeply imbued with the stern theology of John Calvin. They were a literate people who believed that all should have direct access to the word of God by reading the Scriptures.

The young James Wilson showed an aptitude for learning, and it was decided that he should become a clergyman. There was always much reading aloud, mostly of religious books, at home, followed by discussions and debate. By the time he was fifteen, Wilson had studied Latin, Greek, mathematics, and science, and he was eager to continue his education. He walked the six miles to St. Andrews, where he entered a competitive examination for a university scholarship and won.

He completed four years of study at St. Andrews University, which had become part of the Scottish Enlightenment with its acceptance of the new ideas of Sir Isaac Newton, John Locke, Frances Hutcheson, David Hume, and other great thinkers of the time. While this put him in touch with currents of learning that were shaping the Western world, it also shook some of the more severe dogmas of his early Calvinistic thought. He had undertaken a fifth year of study, of divinity, when the death of his father required that he instantly return home to help support his mother and his three younger brothers.

At this point, Wilson abandoned the idea of becoming a clergyman and instead served as a tutor in a nearby family. Bored and restless, he soon went to Edinburgh and there became an accountant. This, too, soon bored him,

and he began to plan to go to America, where some of his relatives and family friends had already settled. His mother hated the idea but finally gave her consent. Relatives and friends contributed what they could for the considerable expense of the move, and, with their support and blessing, in the fall of 1765, he sailed to a new world of opportunity, as so many of his countrymen already had done.

LIFE'S WORK

James Wilson arrived in America with two precious assets, his St. Andrews University education and the driving ambition that made him leave Scotland. He also had a letter of introduction to Richard Peters, an Anglican cleric who was also a trustee of the College of Philadelphia. Thus equipped, he secured an appointment as a tutor at that institution. By that time, Philadelphia had become the foremost American city. It already possessed many of the best features of urban life. It was cosmopolitan and prosperous, and it offered cultural, intellectual, and even political opportunities.

Wilson was quite alert to all of this, and to the truly successful young lawyers who profited well from a litigious people. He was appreciated at the college, where he was even granted an honorary master's degree in May, 1766, as an acknowledgment of his impressive learning, but he was restless, as always, and ambitious to get on with more momentous work and better remuneration. He decided to study law. He managed to enter the office of John Dickinson as an apprentice by borrowing money for the fee. Dickinson was already a legal luminary and destined to be among the most famous of Philadelphia lawyers; he was also deeply involved in the momentous political events of the next twenty-five years.

Wilson was able to add to his excellent general education and his prolonged pondering of theological and philosophical problems a searching study of the nature and meaning of law. His concern ran far beyond the procedures, forms, and practices of litigation. He immersed himself in the history and development of government in Pennsylvania and in England. He read the great classics on law and on constitutions, including the *Commentaries on the Laws of England* (1765-1769) of Sir William Blackstone. His natural intellectual curiosity and zest for scholarship made him thorough and accurate; his striving ambition led him to arrange and retain this learning, ready for practical application.

In less than a year, he began his own practice, starting in the small community of Reading, the seat of Berks County, fifty miles from Philadelphia. For a time he had little business, but he expanded his efforts by getting admitted to practice in the neighboring counties of Lancaster, Chester, and Cumberland. Within another year or two, he had a good number of clients, a modest but growing income, and an enviable reputation as a young man of great promise. He moved to Carlisle in the fall of 1770, but he was somewhat distracted from his law practice by falling in love with Rachel Bird, a local heiress who, she said, had decided never to marry. Wilson persisted, and at last she consented; they were married in November, 1771.

By the early 1770's, Wilson was a tall, strong young man with a somewhat awkward manner. His ruddy face usually bore an alert expression of genuine interest in what others might be saying to him. He was, though, quite nearsighted, and his peering through thick glasses struck some people as a mannerism of aristocratic arrogance. He had only a hint of the Scottish burr of his youth, and his speaking was clear, accurate, and persuasive. He was widely praised for the excellence of his court presentations, and in time he had a considerable

James Wilson. (Library of Congress)

reputation as a public speaker. The leading elements of Carlisle society accepted Wilson as one of their own quickly and easily. Many of them were Scottish, most were prosperous, and nearly all were deeply disturbed by the recent changes in England's policies regarding the American colonies.

At the close of the French and Indian War in 1763, Parliament had begun to antagonize Americans through a new set of imperial policies. Wilson had arrived in America just as one of the most inflammatory measures, the Stamp Act (1763), had been enacted. It was denounced in America as taxation without representation, and there had even been intercolonial cooperation in the mounting resistance. It was repealed in 1766, but Parliament also issued a sweeping assertion of its total authority over the colonies. John Dickinson, Wilson's legal mentor at that time, was greatly interested in the constitutional attack on Parliament's pretensions to power, and when new taxes came in 1767, Dickinson became famous as the foremost expositor of the American resistance, writing under the name "the Pennsylvania Farmer." Wilson then decided that he, too, should write an essay explaining his own ideas as to why the British parliament had no rightful authority over the American colonies. He was advised by trusted friends that it was too extreme, that it would anger many powerful men; while he was considering what to do, the hated taxes (except for that on tea) were repealed, political tensions were eased, and Anglo-American relations, most people believed, would again be harmonious. The essay was put away for a time.

New provocations came, however, and by 1773 it was Boston in the center of things, with the destruction of cargoes of tea (the Boston Tea Party) followed by severe punishment in the form of Parliament's 1774 enactments, which closed the Boston port and instituted military government there. Parliament's actions caused an uproar throughout the colonies. Mass meetings were held in many places, including Philadelphia and Carlisle. It was decided not only to express outrage against Parliament but also to hold a provincial convention in Philadelphia, consisting of delegates from all the counties of Pennsylvania, to take further action. Wilson became deeply involved; he was a delegate to the convention, and soon afterward, he revised his earlier essay and had it published.

The article received much attention, especially from the delegates who were now arriving in Philadelphia for the First Continental Congress. It was remarkable for its coherence, its unassailable argumentation, and, above all, its advanced notion of the nature of the British Empire. Wilson asserted that Parliament had no proper right to legislate for America, yet the colonies were bound by loyalty to the Crown as part of an imperial union of virtually autonomous units—a description of the very much later British Commonwealth of Nations. From this time onward, Wilson was widely regarded as a great thinker and leader in the American Revolution.

Wilson's services in that cause were many. He was a member of the Second Continental Congress, where he served on a number of important committees. When the question of American independence became unavoidable, Wilson, who really doubted the idea, nevertheless finally supported it and signed the Declaration of Independence. In Congress, he was especially concerned about the difficulty of financing the war, and he worked closely with his friend, Robert Morris, in creating the Bank of the United States. He also was a strong advocate for the creation of a national domain out of the unsettled Western lands beyond the Appalachians, with a view to organizing new states there. By the end of the war, he was an ardent advocate of strengthening the central government, and he had become involved in a multiplicity of business affairs, many of them visionary schemes of land speculation.

Meanwhile, Wilson had been profoundly distressed at the course of the revolution in Pennsylvania. He thought that the new state constitution, widely regarded as a radical one, was a dreadful calamity, with its unicameral legislature, plural executive, loyalty oath for voters, subservient judiciary, and other novelties. His prominence in the bitter, persistent opposition to the constitution made him extremely unpopular with those in control of state affairs. In time they saw to it that he was no longer one of the state's delegates to Congress. His ever closer association with Morris and others of the wealthy merchant-lawyer class in Philadelphia made him the target of many rumors of profiteering and corruption—so much so that, at one point, his house was besieged by a large, armed, angry mob. Several men were killed before relief arrived to lift the "siege of Ft. Wilson."

After the War for Independence, Wilson's business affairs became even more complex and uncertain; he seemed always to be plagued with cash shortages and debt. Luckily, the political climate gradually became more congenial for him. Opposition to Pennsylvania's 1776 constitution grew, and the move to overcome the defects of the Articles of Confederation and build an effective national government got under way. This pro-

vided Wilson with the occasion of his greatest contribution to the new nation.

By 1787, Wilson had long since moved to Philadelphia; he was no longer a frontier lawyer, for he had gained entrance into the upper reaches of East Coast society, an eager participant in its great economic and political plans as well as social life. As a member of the Philadelphia Convention that drew up the U.S. Constitution, he was second in importance only to James Madison. He was perhaps the clearest expositor of the notion of dual sovereignty—the idea that the national government must be supreme in some matters, while states remained in control of others. He consistently urged that government must be based on popular participation, and he, along with Madison and a few others, managed at least to get one house of Congress elected directly by the voters. He tried in vain to ensure popular election of the president; he finally proposed the complex electoral college formula, which he thought better than having Congress choose the president, as so many wished. He thought it imperative to have strong executive power; he also argued that an independent judiciary was indispensable. He was extremely influential in the discussions of many of the most crucial features of the new U.S. Constitution.

Wilson was also a central figure in Pennsylvania's quick action to ratify the Constitution. The Federalists, as the Constitution's supporters were being called, now controlled the state government there, and they quickly managed to arrange a ratifying convention, to be held in November, 1787. At the convention, Wilson was their principal resource person and main speaker. Within three weeks, the convention voted to ratify (December 12, 1787). Only Delaware had acted faster, ratifying five days before.

Pennsylvania Federalists, continuing in firm control, had one more major item on their agenda: replacing the 1776 constitution. Soon the assembly agreed to a new constitutional convention, and Wilson was again hard at work. Few had despised the old constitution as Wilson had, and few had suffered as much abuse as a result. Now he had the great satisfaction of leading a congenial convention, dominated by those who thought as he did, in drafting a document that provided for a bicameral legislature, strong executive power, and an independent judiciary. He was the principal architect of Pennsylvania's constitution of 1790.

Wilson wanted very much to be appointed the first chief justice of the United States; he even wrote an unfortunate letter to President George Washington suggesting this, and it received a stiff, noncommittal reply. He was appointed as an associate justice, a substantial consolation prize. His next triumph was of a different sort. He gave a series of lectures on law at the College of Philadelphia (later the University of Pennsylvania), in which he advocated the establishment of a distinctly American system of jurisprudence—a supreme court. The opening lecture (December, 1790) was attended by President Washington, some members of Congress, and many other dignitaries. Wilson stressed the close connection between law and liberty. All citizens of a free society, he said, must know something of the nature and elements of law, to preserve their freedom. Wilson had become the premier theorist of American law.

The last years of Wilson's life were ones of disappointment and calamity. Of the modest number of cases that reached the Supreme Court in the 1790's, only a few offered an opportunity for the enunciation of significant constitutional ideas. In the most important one, *Chisholm v. Georgia* (1793), Wilson was an important participant in the decision to permit citizens to sue states, but that bold exercise in constitutional interpretation was extremely unpopular, and it was soon overturned by the adoption of the Eleventh Amendment to the Constitution. Along with his colleagues on the Court, however, he managed to maintain the idea of an independent judiciary, and they also assumed the right to review the constitutionality of state and federal laws.

Wilson's private business affairs occupied increasing amounts of his energy and his time. He had long been eager to acquire Western land, and now he became involved in one grand speculative project after another. None succeeded. Wilson's financial losses were ever larger, and he was unable to repay loans and other debts when due. He was jailed twice by creditors, released at last on bail provided by borrowed money. Finally he fled to the home of his friend and colleague, Justice James Iredell of North Carolina, suffering severe mental stress and occasional derangement. After further illness, he died in Edenton, North Carolina, on August 21, 1798.

SIGNIFICANCE

James Wilson was an important figure among those who launched the American Revolution. Trained in the law and seriously concerned about ideas of constitutional liberty, he rapidly came to the fore as a powerful advocate of American rights. This gained for him a place in various revolutionary committees, conventions, and other bodies where he brought energy, time, and talent to the cause of American independence. More than independence was needed, however, and Wilson knew it: The

new country had to be governed, governed better than any other. It was in devising new arrangements of governing power that his greatest work was done.

His ideas for the new government of Pennsylvania were not popular for some years, though ultimately they did prevail when he assumed a leading role in drafting that state's second constitution in 1790. His greatest service was in the Philadelphia Convention (1787), where he found sympathetic colleagues in the great work of drawing up a national constitution. He was a powerful advocate of strong executive power, but he believed that the executive should be chosen as directly as possible by the people. His idea of an independent national judiciary, possessed of the power to resolve questions of constitutional meaning, was one of his boldest ones. His notion of a federal union easily embraced the concurrent exercise of power by both the state and the national government, but his insistence on national supremacy in most major matters, such as foreign policy, war and peace, and regulation of trade, marked him as one of the most far-sighted and prophetic of the nation's founders.

The quality of his thinking continues to impress scholars and analysts of political theory and jurisprudence. His intellectual resources were extensive, and the logic of his discourses made them persuasive in his day. However, it was not his style to be succinct, and the scope of his thought was broad; these elements of his writings limited his influence with later generations, as did the severe decline in his prestige during his later years.

Certain of his personal qualities were the undoing of his reputation. He became importunate in his eagerness for fame and wealth, taking chances in one imprudent venture after another. He did not have that expansive personal charm that would create close friends who would be concerned that he received his due as a great patriot and a masterly architect of government in America. Nevertheless, his work endures, and the existing nation is, in many important respects, the one he sought.

—*Richard D. Miles*

FURTHER READING

Brunhouse, Robert L. *Counterrevolution in Pennsylvania: 1776-1790.* Harrisburg: Pennsylvania Historical and Museums Commission, 1942. A scholarly, reliable, and standard account of a movement of great importance in Wilson's life. He was especially outspoken and perhaps tactless in denouncing the constitution of 1776, and the story of its being replaced is one in which he was a central figure.

Hall, Mark David. *The Political and Legal Philosophy of James Wilson, 1742-1798*. Columbia: University of Missouri Press, 1997. Analyzes Wilson's political and legal philosophy, describing how these ideas influenced his contributions to the creation of an American republic. Explains his views of democracy, morality, and human nature.

Read, James H. *Power Versus Liberty: Madison, Hamilton, Wilson, and Jefferson*. Charlottesville: University Press of Virginia, 2000. Read examines the political ideas of some of the Founding Fathers, focusing on how they reconciled tensions between a powerful government and individual liberty. Wilson's thought is examined in the chapter "James Wilson and the Idea of Popular Sovereignty."

Rossiter, Clinton L. *1787: The Grand Convention*. New York: Macmillan, 1966. A well-balanced portrayal of the convention. Rossiter's organization of ideas, along with his readable prose, make this interesting as well as reliable. Includes a brief account of the ratification of the U.S. Constitution and its first few years.

Seed, Geoffrey. *James Wilson*. Millwood, N.Y.: Kraus International, 1978. A very perceptive study of Wilson's political ideas. The author's intent is to secure Wilson's place among the first rank of the Founding Fathers, and he argues the case well. Especially detailed analysis of Wilson's contributions to the U.S. Constitution.

Selsam, John Paul. *The Pennsylvania Constitution of 1776*. Philadelphia: University of Pennsylvania Press, 1936. A basic story of the "radical" constitution produced by the revolution in Pennsylvania. The closest approach to democracy during the American Revolution occurred in Pennsylvania, where the new charter broadened the right to vote and rendered government especially responsible to the people. The book explains the central paradox of Wilson's thought: his insistence on popular participation in government, but his loathing of this constitution.

Smith, Charles Page. *James Wilson: Founding Father, 1742-1798*. Chapel Hill: University of North Carolina Press, 1956. Though in places needed sources of information do not exist, the author provides plausible probabilities. Readable, with sensitivity and well-balanced judgments of Wilson.

Tinkom, Harry M. *The Republicans and Federalists in Pennsylvania: 1790-1801*. Harrisburg: Pennsylvania Historical and Museums Commission, 1950. Examines the partisan controversies that became strident, turbulent, and even violent in the 1790's, making Wilson's life difficult. Scholarly and reliable on the sharply divided political scene.

Wilson, James. *The Works of James Wilson*. 2 vols. Philadelphia: Lorenzo Press, 1804. Reprint. Edited by Robert G. McCloskey. Cambridge, Mass.: Harvard University Press, 1967. A reprint of material published by Wilson's son, with valuable additions. The editor's extensive, learned introductory essay is especially good, and the "bibliographical glossary" is most useful in identifying Wilson's vast scholarly resources. Mostly lectures on law, though nine miscellaneous writings include four important speeches.

See also: Sir William Blackstone; John Dickinson; David Hume; James Madison; Robert Morris; George Washington.

Related articles in *Great Events from History: The Eighteenth Century, 1701-1800:* 1739-1740: Hume Publishes *A Treatise of Human Nature*; March 22, 1765-March 18, 1766: Stamp Act Crisis; December 16, 1773: Boston Tea Party; September 5-October 26, 1774: First Continental Congress; April 19, 1775: Battle of Lexington and Concord; May 10-August 2, 1775: Second Continental Congress; July 4, 1776: Declaration of Independence; March 1, 1781: Ratification of the Articles of Confederation; September 17, 1787: U.S. Constitution Is Adopted; October 27, 1787-May, 1788: Publication of *The Federalist*; April 30, 1789: Washington's Inauguration; September 24, 1789: Judiciary Act; 1790's: First U.S. Political Parties; December 15, 1791: U.S. Bill of Rights Is Ratified.

JOHANN JOACHIM WINCKELMANN
German historian

Winckelmann's studies of ancient Greek art profoundly influenced the development of the European neoclassical movement in the arts. His work helped to shape literature, the fine arts, art history, and classical archaeology.

Born: December 9, 1717; Stendal, Prussia (now in Germany)
Died: June 8, 1768; Trieste (now in Italy)
Areas of achievement: Art, archaeology, historiography, science and technology

EARLY LIFE

Johann Joachim Winckelmann (YOH-hahn YOH-ahk-ihm VIHN-kehl-mahn) was born the son of a poor shoemaker, Martin Winckelmann, in a rural village of the Mark Brandenburg, in what was then Prussia. He was an extremely intelligent and academically gifted child and was thus able to attend a formal Latin school. In 1735, he went to Berlin to study at a high school. The young Winckelmann graduated and in 1737 registered in the department of theology at the University of Halle. His interests, however, were in the study of classical antiquity. He left after two years and worked as a private tutor until 1741, when he entered the University of Jena. After finishing at Jena, he taught school in Prussia.

LIFE'S WORK

From the early days of his childhood study of classical Greek and Latin at the local Latin school, Winckelmann was intensely dedicated to the study of ancient Greek and Roman literature, art, and civilization. In 1754, he entered the court of Augustus III, a great collector of artworks. At this time, Winckelmann wrote an essay on ancient art that would become a major influence on succeeding generations of scholars and writers, his *Gedanken über die Nachahmung der griechischen Werke in der Malerei und Bildhauerkunst* (1755; *Reflections on the Paintings and Sculpture of the Greeks*, 1765). He was awarded a pension by the Prussian monarch because of this essay. It serves, in part, as a study leading to Winckelmann's later monumental history of classical art, *Geschichte der Kunst des Alterthums* (1764, 1776; *History of Ancient Art*, 1849-1873), and therefore deserves some detailed discussion of its major themes and insights.

Winckelmann clearly favored the art of the ancient world. The Greek sense of taste, he contended, is unparalleled, and the only path to greatness for the modern world is to imitate the artistic production of the ancients. His essay seeks to characterize the major distinctive features of Greek art. He begins his examination with a discussion of art and nature in the ancient world and sets it in comparison to the depiction of nature by modern painters. Greek artists portrayed nature in its purest and most beautiful form. This portrayal is most apparent in their representations of the human form. The human body is presented in its most ideal form, at the height of the perfection of its youth and beauty. The Greek style reflects the Greeks' societal and cultural standards, their love of physical activity, and their competitive games that glorified the body. Disease and other maladies of modern society, Winckelmann claims, were not present in Greek society. He clearly prefers the artistic idealization of the human form in ancient art to the more realistic representations of the body that predominate in postclassical art.

In the second section, Winckelmann discusses the aesthetic dimension of contour, a domain in which the ancients excelled. Their figures exhibit the noblest contours, again in contrast to those found in the works of more modern artists such as Peter Paul Rubens. Winckelmann praises the sculpted figures found at Herculaneum. The brief third section deals with the artistic issue of drapery, or the way in which the human form is enveloped in garments. Again, he claims that the Greeks were far superior to the moderns in the way they depicted clothing and robes in their art.

The fourth and final section of the essay deals with the overall Greek sense of aesthetic expression. Winckelmann's characterization of ancient art in this section as exhibiting a "noble simplicity and sedate grandeur" (*Edel Einfalt und stille Grösse*) was to become the most influential and frequently quoted description of the Greeks. German neoclassicist writers such as Johann Wolfgang von Goethe and Friedrich Schiller, for example, were to make this concept of aesthetic value the ideal of much of their literary production. Winckelmann discusses the Laocoön statue, one of the most famous examples of Greek (actually Hellenistic) art, which is based on a story from the legend of the Siege of Troy. Laocoön and his two sons had set out to warn the Trojans of the Greek plot but were killed by a serpent sent by Apollo. The statue portrays the three figures, enveloped by the huge serpent, being crushed to death. Winckelmann notes, however, that despite their immense suffering, the faces of the figures are not distorted by pain—which would render the statue realistic but certainly hideous—but rather are peacefully transfigured, retaining a placid dignity and calmness that suggest the greatness of the Greek soul. This aesthetic ideal evidences the general Greek cultural vision of moderation or measure—the belief that extreme expression in any form fundamentally distorts nature and is to be avoided. Ancient art portrays not the exaggerated but the exemplary individual, whose beauty and greatness of spirit epitomize a balanced and harmonious nature.

Winckelmann's portrait of ancient Greek culture deserves comment. It should be noted that his observations were based not on actual examples of Greek sculpture but on Roman copies uncovered in Italy. Although his characterization of Greek art is for the most part accurate, his overall vision of their society and culture presents a romantic and conservative idealization of Greek civilization. For Winckelmann, the Greeks were highly spiritual, childlike people who lived in a primitive but pristine harmony with nature. They represented, in essence, a cheerful and optimistic culture. This is clearly a version of the myth of the "noble savage" found at various times in modern European thought. Winckelmann's vision of Greek culture was criticized in Friedrich Nietzsche's first philosophical work, *Die Geburt der Tragödie aus dem Geiste der Musik* (1872; *The Birth of Tragedy Out of the Spirit of Music*, 1909). Nietzsche claimed that Greek culture and art, especially the drama, sprang not from a harmony with nature but from a profound sense of the suffering inherent in human existence.

In 1756, Winckelmann traveled to Rome, where he managed the pope's collection of antiquities and also served as professor of Greek in the Vatican Library. His work there established his reputation as a world-famous authority on classical Greek art and the science of archaeology. In 1764, he published his famous and influential *History of Ancient Art*. This work was Winckelmann's magnum opus and consists of several volumes. It is divided into two major sections, one that investigates the nature of art philosophically and the other that looks at Greek art historically. In the first section, Winckelmann begins with a discussion of the origins of art in the religious traditions of various peoples. He then focuses on the development of art among the Egyptians, the Phoenicians, and the Persians. Because of certain cultural, political, and social restrictions, Egyptian art never evolved beyond a primitive stage of development, and the same holds true for the other two groups. Winckelmann also discusses the Etruscans and claims that their artistic production, although more developed than that of the Egyptians, is limited by the essentially melancholic and superstitious temperament of the people.

The longest chapter of the book discusses Greek art and reveals Winckelmann's decided bias in favor of this cultural sphere of the ancient world. Numerous factors such as climate, political organization, the development of philosophy and rhetoric, the cult of

---

ANCIENT GREEK BEAUTY

Johann Joachim Winckelmann believed in the inherent veneration and perpetuation of beauty—namely the beautiful body—in ancient Greek culture. In his work on classic art, excerpted here, he discusses the apparent absence of "beauty-spoiling" and "body-devastating" diseases such as smallpox in ancient Greece, diseases that were endemic to modern Europe and the New World. The ideal place to see this living beauty was in the gymnasium, where youth would run about and exercise without clothing.

The diseases that destroy so much beauty and spoil even the noblest countenance were still unknown among the Greeks. In none of the writings of the Greek physicians do we find a mention of smallpox.... The venereal diseases, and their result, the English *malaise*, did not devastate the beautiful bodies of the Greeks. Generally speaking everything that nature and knowledge could contribute to the growth and development of a beautiful body was used to full advantage by the Greeks, from the moment of birth to full physical maturity. The superior beauty of their bodies as compared to ours, then, is a fact that can be maintained with the greatest assurance....

The school of the artist was the gymnasium, where the youths, ordinarily clothed because of modesty, exercised quite naked. It was the gathering place of philosophers as well as artists: Socrates visited it to teach Charmides, Artolycus and Lysis; Phidias went there to enrich his art with these magnificent figures. There one learned the movement of muscles, and studied the contours of the body, or the impressions the young wrestlers had made in the sand. The most beautiful aspects of the nude revealed themselves here in many varied and noble poses unattainable by hired models such as are used in our academies.

Source: Johann Joachim Winckelmann, "Thoughts on the Imitation of Greek Art in Painting and Sculpture," in *The Enlightenment: The Culture of the Eighteenth Century*, edited by Isidor Schneider (New York: George Braziller, 1965), pp. 201-202.

Johann Joachim Winckelmann. (Library of Congress)

physical fitness and beauty, and the general societal esteem for artists all contributed to making the art of Greece the most sophisticated and mature of the ancient world. He goes on to describe the essential features of Greek art, its ability to capture true beauty, that is, the perfected human form that, in its perfection, reminds humanity of the divine. Winckelmann discusses what he sees as the four developmental periods of Greek art as well as aspects of Roman art. The brief second section of the volume elaborates on the chronological development of Greek art and presents discussions of individual statues.

In 1768, Winckelmann briefly journeyed to Germany, where he suffered a severe nervous breakdown. He returned to Italy, bound for Trieste. Winckelmann had exhibited markedly homosexual tendencies for most of his adult life, and, in his depressed condition, he began a casual affair with a young man he met in Trieste. The man, who turned out to be a thief, robbed and murdered the famous scholar at the hotel in which they were staying.

SIGNIFICANCE

Johann Joachim Winckelmann's work as an art critic and historian as well as his archaeological work in Italy served to initiate to a great degree the neoclassical art revival and the new Humanistic and cosmopolitan trends of the eighteenth and early nineteenth centuries, especially in Germany from 1775 to 1832. His somewhat idealized vision of the beautiful as the spiritual harmony and balance in Greek culture profoundly influenced subsequent generations of writers, artists, and thinkers. This was the age of the great German writings of Goethe and Schiller, in which the ideals of human dignity and the perfectibility of individuals through progressive education became the guidelines of bourgeois culture. This was also the enlightened age of rationalism, revealed through the work of philosopher Immanuel Kant, and the development of the idea of freedom of rational choice versus the determinism of the irrational impulse. These new ideas formed, at least in part, the didactic goals of art and literature during this period. Winckelmann's portrait of Greek culture helped to shape this emergence of bourgeois humanism.

It should be remarked that Winckelmann's prescription for the modern age—the imitation of ancient Greece—represents an essentially conservative vision of history; that is, it promulgates an idealized vision of some prior "golden age" in which humanity was at one with nature and in which discord and chaos did not exist. This implicit and, at times, explicit rejection of the modern period in Winckelmann's writings is characteristic of the development of German (and European) historicism during the eighteenth and nineteenth centuries.

—*Thomas F. Barry*

FURTHER READING

Butler, E. M. *The Tyranny of Greece over Germany.* Cambridge, England: Cambridge University Press, 1935. A dated but still excellent scholarly discussion of Winckelmann's promulgation of Greek art and culture in Germany. Contains notes and a bibliography.

Ferris, David. *Silent Urns: Romanticism, Hellenism, Modernity.* Stanford, Calif.: Stanford University Press, 2000. Includes a discussion of Winckelmann's book, *History of Ancient Art*, describing how the work created the concept of "culture" and granted Greece its significance as a cultural icon. Ferris argues that in elevating the importance of Greek culture, Winckelmann and other eighteenth century thinkers attempted to reconcile conflicting concepts of individuality, freedom, history, and modernity.

Hatfield, Henry. *Aesthetic Paganism in German Litera-ture, from Winckelmann to the Death of Goethe.* Cambridge, Mass.: Harvard University Press, 1964. A discussion of the effects of Winckelmann's work in aesthetics on the development of German literature. Contains notes and a bibliography.

_____. *Winckelmann and His German Critics, 1755-1781: A Prelude to the Classical Age.* New York: King's Crown Press, 1943. A dated but still useful academic work by a prominent scholar on the German reaction to Winckelmann. Contains notes and a bibliography.

Honour, Hugh. *Neo-Classicism.* Harmondsworth, England: Penguin Books, 1968. A more general discussion of the artistic movement with sections on Winckelmann's work and influence. Written by an important critic. Contains notes and a bibliography.

Leppmann, Wolfgang. *Winckelmann.* New York: Alfred A. Knopf, 1970. An excellent critical biography in English, which includes notes and a bibliography.

Morrison, Jeffrey. *Winckelmann and the Notion of Aesthetic Education.* New York: Oxford University Press, 1996. Examines how Winckelmann developed the concept of "aesthetic education" and the appreciation of classical beauty in his roles as teacher and arbiter of classical taste. The final chapter analyzes how Winckelmann influenced Goethe's aesthetic self-education.

Pater, Walter. *Studies in the History of the Renaissance.* London: Macmillan, 1873. Includes an important and insightful essay on Winckelmann by a prominent nineteenth century English art historian.

Potts, Alex. *Flesh and the Ideal: Winckelmann and the Origins of Art History.* New Haven, Conn.: Yale University Press, 1994. An intellectual biography that analyzes Winckelmann's *History of Ancient Art.* Potts explains the book's significance to art history.

Rosenblum, Robert. *Transformations in Late Eighteenth Century Art.* Princeton, N.J.: Princeton University Press, 1967. A scholarly work that contains a useful discussion of Winckelmann's ideas and influence. Contains notes and a bibliography.

See also: Robert and James Adam; Edmund Burke; Johann Wolfgang von Goethe; Immanuel Kant; Angelica Kauffmann; Gotthold Ephraim Lessing; Sir Joshua Reynolds; Friedrich Schiller; William Stukeley.

Related articles in *Great Events from History: The Eighteenth Century, 1701-1800:* 1719-1724: Stukeley Studies Stonehenge and Avebury; 1748: Excavation of Pompeii; 1762: *The Antiquities of Athens* Prompts Architectural Neoclassicism.

JOHN WITHERSPOON
Scottish-born American religious leader and educator

A leading pastor in the Church of Scotland, Witherspoon, as president of the College of New Jersey, led its development into a major center of education for the arts and sciences and for the preparation of Presbyterian ministers. As a Second Continental Congress delegate, he championed American independence and signed the Declaration of Independence.

Born: February 15, 1723; Gifford, Scotland
Died: November 15, 1794; Tusculum, near Princeton, New Jersey
Areas of achievement: Education, government and politics, religion and theology

EARLY LIFE

John Witherspoon was born to the Reverend James Witherspoon, pastor of the Church of Scotland (Presby-terian) at Gifford, and Anna Walker Witherspoon. He completed the course of study at nearby Haddington grammar school at age thirteen, then entered the University of Edinburgh to study for the ministry. The curriculum emphasized classics and mathematics and included philosophy and natural philosophy (natural science). He received a master of arts at age sixteen, then spent four more years at the university as a divinity student.

In 1743, he was awarded a doctor of theology degree (also referred to as doctor of divinity), then was licensed to preach, and was ordained in 1745. His first parish was at Beith in Ayrshire. He entered fully into parish life, participating in sports as well as pastoral duties and scholarly pursuits, and in 1748 married a local woman, Elizabeth Montgomery. They would have ten children, of whom five lived to adulthood.

Witherspoon was born into the world of the Scottish Enlightenment, a time of progress and intellectual activity. The industrial and agricultural revolutions promoted a new prosperity, though the vast number of impoverished tenant farmers benefited little. It was an era of rationalism and empiricism, emphasizing the human capacity to understand the universe through reasoning and experience, and Scottish universities were highly regarded.

During this period, controversy developed in the Scottish church. The landowning and urban upper-class Moderates blended Christianity with new ideas such as Deism, which saw God as the distant power behind the forces of nature, one that was not concerned with human affairs. The ordinary people of the Popular or Evangelical party guarded traditional Calvinist principles such as original sin, strict adherence to Scripture, and careful regulation of behavior. The Moderate landowners had patronage rights, including selection of pastors: Rural Popular congregations objected, for Presbyterian polity gave congregations the duty of selecting their own pastors. Witherspoon sided with the Popular party.

LIFE'S WORK

Emerging as the Popular champion, John Witherspoon in 1753 anonymously published a satire entitled *Ecclesiastical Characteristics: Or, The Arcana of Church Policy—Being a Humble Attempt to Open up the Mystery of Moderation*. The creed of the Moderates, he said, began as follows:

> I believe in the beauty and comely proportions of Dame Nature, and in almighty Fate, her only parent and guardian; for it hath been most graciously obliged (blessed be its name) to make us all very good. I believe that the universe is a huge machine, wound up from everlasting by necessity . . . that I myself am a glorious little piece of clockwork . . . that those things vulgarly called sins, are only errors in the judgment.

His authorship became known, and he was compared to the great satirists of the day. Increasingly he participated in the higher bodies of the Church of Scotland—presbyteries, synods, and the general assembly. Famous by this time, he was called in 1757 to the pastorate of the Laigh Kirk (Low Church) in nearby Paisley, despite some concern in the presbytery over his writings, including an essay against Christians patronizing the theater. During more than ten years at Paisley, his reputation as cleric and writer increased; he was invited to churches in Rotterdam and Dublin but declined.

Meanwhile, across the Atlantic Ocean, the struggling young College of New Jersey at Princeton needed a new president. Chartered in 1746, the institution was estab-

John Witherspoon. (Library of Congress)

lished to provide educated leadership and pastors for Presbyterian churches in the Middle Colonies, where major Scottish immigration was taking place. The situation was complicated by a church controversy as disruptive as the one in Scotland. The Old Side upheld traditional Presbyterianism—orderly, biblical, and scholarly—whereas the New Side promoted revivalism, emotional conversion, and "enthusiasm." Both sides, however, upheld the traditional Presbyterian insistence on an educated clergy able to read the Scriptures in the original languages. The College of New Jersey belonged to the New Side. The Old Side was trying to take over the college by getting its candidate into the president's chair.

The trustees foiled the attempt by inviting Witherspoon to fill the vacancy. The position carried with it the pastorate of the Princeton village church. It was hoped that the eminent Scot could both end the Old Side-New Side rivalry and build up the college. Witherspoon was seriously interested in the new challenge. His wife, Elizabeth, however, became physically ill at the thought of leaving family and friends to relocate across the sea. Witherspoon would not think of forcing a move against his wife's will, though some associates maintained that she had no right to hinder the obvious call of God. In April, he declined the offer. However, by August, Elizabeth was in better health and spirits. Having heard young

Benjamin Rush of New Jersey, a recent graduate of the college and currently a medical student in Edinburgh, give glowing descriptions of his country and the future possibilities of his alma mater, she reconsidered and consented to the change. Early in 1768, Witherspoon accepted the new position.

The next months were spent in preparation, especially in acquiring books for the college library. In May, 1768, John and Elizabeth Witherspoon set sail with five children. Reaching Philadelphia after a twelve-week voyage, they proceeded to Princeton by carriage. The students welcomed the new president by illuminating Nassau Hall, the college building, by placing candles in every window, creating a glow visible miles away.

Witherspoon set the college on the road to preeminence. With great energy and amazing success, he undertook the triple task of raising funds, increasing enrollments, and adding faculty. He himself was professor of divinity. He found and encouraged at Princeton a curriculum already innovative in its emphasis on English in addition to classical studies and on oratory, history, geography, and science. To promote the last two subjects, he secured for the college a "terrestrial globe" and the "orrery," an invention of David Rittenhouse of Philadelphia that demonstrated by clockwork the motions of the heavenly bodies. Witherspoon himself introduced the study of French. Graduate degrees were added. A strong religious emphasis included required morning and evening prayers and two chapel services on Sunday. There was no athletic program; sports were tacitly disapproved.

Presbyterian affairs also claimed Witherspoon's attention. He was in demand as a preacher, though perhaps more for his Christian character and the content of his sermons than for his oratorical skill. Some contemporaries found him a dull speaker and hard to understand because of his strong Scottish accent. What he did not become much involved in was the Old Side-New Side controversy. As one authority puts it, Witherspoon assumed the conflict to be at an end and acted accordingly. His character and leadership made him acceptable to both sides.

Witherspoon found himself admiring the spirit of Americans. Increasingly, he sympathized with them in disputes with the British. Princeton students demonstrated against British policy; after hearing of the Boston Tea Party, they held their own version by throwing the college supply of tea onto a campus bonfire and burning the governor of Massachusetts in effigy with a tea canister around his neck. The president seems to have taken no action against them.

Witherspoon published the essay "Thoughts on American Liberty," advocating formation of a plan of union for the common defense of the colonies. Attending the First Continental Congress as an observer, he began notable friendships with men such as George Washington, John Adams, and James Madison. He was elected to the New Jersey Provincial Congress, which met in June, 1776, and which deposed and imprisoned Governor William Franklin. The same body elected new delegates to the Second Continental Congress; Witherspoon was among them. On July 4, that Congress adopted the Declaration of Independence. Witherspoon was the only clergyman among the signers. Back in Princeton, the students once again illuminated Nassau Hall. British publications described Witherspoon as a major instigator of rebellion. On Long Island, British troops burned Witherspoon and Washington in effigy.

During the revolution, the College of New Jersey suffered severely. In late 1776, it was closed because the British occupied Princeton. After the British were driven out at the Battle of Princeton, American troops occupied Nassau Hall for nearly two years, causing even worse destruction.

Recovering from the death of his son James, who had been killed in the Battle of Germantown, Witherspoon, back in Congress, became active in the Committee of Correspondence whose mission was to obtain French aid for the colonies. Success came in 1778, when a treaty with France was signed. Witherspoon's contribution to this committee has been considered his greatest service to the Continental Congress.

By 1783, his political work had ended, and Witherspoon was once again a full-time college president. The College of New Jersey had reopened with a few students in the fall of 1778. Both the college and its president, like much of the United States, were in dire financial straits. Fund-raising campaigns netted very little. Tragedy struck once more; the Witherspoons' daughter Frances died in 1784.

Despite horrendous postwar difficulties, college life resumed. Enrollment quickly recovered, and by 1786, a modicum of financial stability was achieved. It was a new era; the college had games and sports, dramatics, and social activities that would have been forbidden in its early days. The president seems not to have objected. A startling occurrence in 1783 was the arrival at Princeton of the entire Continental Congress, fleeing a mutiny of soldiers in Philadelphia. At the September commencement of the college, the whole Congress sat on the platform, together with General Washington. President Witherspoon could hardly have known any greater pride and satisfaction.

His last ecclesiastical assignment was an appointment in 1785 by the Synod of New York and Philadelphia as chairman of the committee to restructure the Presbyterian Church along national lines. The following year, he presented a plan similar to that of Scotland, with congregations grouped in presbyteries that in turn belonged to regional synods, and over all the general assembly, with each body electing representatives to the one above. When the general assembly met for the first time in Philadelphia in May, 1789, the moderator was Witherspoon, who preached the opening sermon.

His personal life was saddened by the death of his wife, Elizabeth, in October, 1789. She was known as a delightful and social person, an ideal helpmeet to her husband, a fond mother, and beloved of all who knew her. The bereaved husband found solace in committee work with the New Jersey assembly. In 1791, he married a much younger widow, Ann Dill, resulting in plenty of raised eyebrows.

In the next three years, Witherspoon gradually went blind and his general health deteriorated. He attended the Presbyterian general assembly in May, 1794, and conducted the college commencement in September. His mind was clear to the end, which came in November, 1794. He was buried in the Princeton graveyard, as his first wife had been.

SIGNIFICANCE

John Witherspoon, a stocky man with brown hair, fair complexion, and striking blue eyes beneath bushy brows, had highly successful and influential careers in three fields: the Presbyterian ministry, higher education, and political activism. He was also a prolific writer whose publications include, besides the satire that made him famous, a vast number of sermons and essays on diverse topics from education to marriage to human liberty.

Contemporaries considered him a caring pastor, a devoted family man, and a man who loved a controversy. As a churchman, he was a leader in creating the national structure of the Presbyterian Church. Graduates of the College of New Jersey at Princeton during Witherspoon's presidency went on to become leaders of church and state. He was a skillful administrator and beloved teacher. Politically, he was a delegate to the Second Continental Congress and several New Jersey bodies. He championed independence, and through his work for the committee on secret correspondence, he helped win the American Revolution.

—Elizabeth C. Adams

FURTHER READING

Butterfield, Lyman H., ed. *John Witherspoon Comes to America: A Documentary Account Based Largely on New Materials*. Princeton, N.J.: Princeton University Library, 1953. This collection of correspondence between Witherspoon and numerous individuals involved in bringing him to Princeton gives the flavor of the negotiations, partly by retaining eighteenth century spelling and writing conventions.

Collins, Varnum Lansing. *President Witherspoon*. 1925. Reprint. New York: Arno Press, 1969. The most complete biography of Witherspoon, this book incorporates substantial passages from primary sources and provides extensive documentation.

McAllister, J. L. "John Witherspoon: Academic Advocate for American Freedom." In *Miscellany of American Christianity: Essays in Honor of H. Shelton Smith*, edited by Stuart C. Henry. Durham, N.C.: Duke University Press, 1963. This article contains Witherspoon's political, theological, and academic ideas, with some informative anecdotes.

Morrison, Jeffry H. *John Witherspoon and the Founding of the American Republic*. Notre Dame, Ind.: University of Notre Dame Press, 2005. A comprehensive examination of Witherspoon's political thought and career, including his participation in the Continental Congress and his presidency of the college at Princeton. Morrison charts the influences on Witherspoon's thinking and his influence on others.

Sloan, Douglas. *The Scottish Enlightenment and the American College Ideal*. New York: Teachers College Press, Columbia University, 1971. Chapter 4, "The Scottish Enlightenment Comes to Princeton: John Witherspoon," provides an intellectual history, showing Scottish influences on Witherspoon, his responses to American thought, and his handling of the college at Princeton. Excellent annotated bibliography.

Stohlman, Martha Lou Lemmon. *John Witherspoon: Parson, Politician, Patriot*. Philadelphia: Westminster Press, 1976. This book is probably the best introduction to Witherspoon.

Tait, L. Gordon. *The Piety of John Witherspoon: Pew, Pulpit, and Public Forum*. Louisville, Ky.: Geneva Press, 2000. An account of Witherspoon's thought, focusing on his piety and belief that the Christian faith should take practical form in the ministry, in politics, and in daily obedience and devotion.

Witherspoon, John. *The Selected Writings of John Witherspoon*. Edited by Thomas Miller. Carbondale: Southern Illinois University Press, 1990. A collection of seven influential writings on diverse subjects. An extensive introduction explains Witherspoon's ideas, the writers who influenced him, his reforms at Princeton, and his political activities.

See also: John Adams; Joseph Butler; David Hume; James Madison; Benjamin Rush; George Washington; Charles Wesley; John Wesley.

Related articles in *Great Events from History: The Eighteenth Century, 1701-1800:* 1726-1729: Voltaire Advances Enlightenment Thought in Europe; 1739-1740: Hume Publishes *A Treatise of Human Nature*; 1741: Leadhills Reading Society Promotes Literacy; December 16, 1773: Boston Tea Party; September 5-October 26, 1774: First Continental Congress; May 10-August 2, 1775: Second Continental Congress; July 4, 1776: Declaration of Independence; February 6, 1778: Franco-American Treaties; 1785-1788: Hutton Proposes the Geological Theory of Uniformitarianism; 1795: Murray Develops a Modern English Grammar Book.

PEG WOFFINGTON
Irish actor

Highly celebrated as both a comedic and tragic actor, Woffington rose from abject poverty in Dublin to become one of the most famous leading ladies of the eighteenth century London stage. She was also noted—but not without criticism—for her breeches roles, playing male characters and wearing men's clothing. Her role as Sir Henry Wildair is likely her most brilliant performance.

Born: October 18, 1720?; Dublin, Ireland
Died: March 28, 1760; London, England
Also known as: Margaret Woffington (full name)
Area of achievement: Theater

EARLY LIFE

Peg Woffington was born into poverty in eighteenth century Dublin. Not much is known about her early life, even the precise date of her birth, but her beauty and brilliant personality set her apart from overpopulated Dublin's numerous street children and paved the way for her to become one of eighteenth century London's greatest theatrical actresses. Her father died when she was very young, so to support her widowed mother and young sister, Woffington became a street singer.

She first gained recognition at the age of ten, when she acted in the popular role of Polly Peachum in the 1730 Lilliputian juvenile production of John Gay's enormously well-known play, *The Beggar's Opera*, at the Aungier St. Theatre in Dublin. The following year, in 1731, the youngster traveled to London with Madame Violante, the French woman who managed the Lilliputian theatrical company. In London, Woffington observed and came to develop a strong desire for the type of lavish lifestyle she was ultimately to lead.

Woffington's career gained momentum after she returned to Dublin and found work as an actor at the popular Smock Alley Theatre in 1732, thanks to theater manager Charles Coffey. Here she was to perform with the most famous and highly celebrated eighteenth century British stage actor, David Garrick. In 1737 she appeared as Ophelia in William Shakespeare's *Hamlet*—to mixed reviews—but followed this performance—to better reviews—playing Sylvia in George Farquhar's *Recruiting Officer*. In 1740, in what some call her greatest role, Woffington performed the so-called breeches role, that of the male character Sir Harry Wildair in Farquhar's *Constant Couple*, and daringly wore men's clothing on stage in an era in which is was unheard of for a woman to wear pants, let alone full male attire.

LIFE'S WORK

By 1740, Peg Woffington was one of Dublin's most celebrated and gossiped-about women, and certainly the city's leading actress, famous not only for her beauty but also for her perfect diction. She had suitors by the dozen beg to be seen with her. Before long, she was on her way with Coffey to Covent Garden in London, where, in 1740, she came to work for manager John Rich. Audiences in London adored her as much as audiences did in Dublin, especially in the role of Sir Harry Wildair at the Theatre Royal, Drury Lane. In no time she became Britain's most popular actress, and did so in the refined world of eighteenth century London, the locale for classic novels such as *Tom Jones* and *Moll Flanders*.

As Britain's leading actress at the legendary Drury Lane between 1740 and 1746, Woffington created a brilliant career on the London stage, so revered that she could pick and choose the theaters in which she would perform and the dramatic roles she would undertake. "Peg," as she was endearingly called, had a natural comedic talent but also enjoyed high distinction for her classic roles as Shakespeare's Rosalind and Mistress Ford. Her other notable Shakespearean roles include Cordelia, Lady Anne (*Richard III*), Lady Townley, Portia, Isabella, Viola, Mrs. Ford, Queen Katherine, Desdemona, Lady Macbeth, and Queen Gertrude, Hamlet's mother.

Also, in 1750, Woffington set herself apart as the only female member of the famous Beefsteak Club, or, the Sublime Society of Steaks, established by Covent Garden manager John Rich. Otherwise known as "the Club," its famous members included the artist William Hogarth and Garrick, and many other London celebrities and literati. In 1754, Woffington became president of the Dublin Beefsteak Club.

Woffington's personal life, however problematic, was as colorful as her life on stage. She gained a reputation for her bitter lifelong rivalries and argumentative relationships with other famous actresses, in particular, George Anne Bellamy and Kitty Clive. Indeed, so vile was her temper that while acting in *Statira*, Woffington drove Bellamy off the stage and then stabbed her. In addition to choosing famous theaters and interesting dramatic roles, Woffington also learned she could choose from a variety of lovers. Upon first arriving in London, she met and fell in love with Garrick. Similarly, he too fell madly in love with her. Their almost immediate plans to marry quickly became grist for the public information mill, much in the manner of the more modern fascination with celebrity couples. Indeed, they were the equivalent of superstars and had to choose between love and marriage or fame and its temptations: They chose the latter.

Woffington was Garrick's leading lady from 1742 to 1748, and while they never married—some say he could not cope with her extravagances and infidelities—he became the most important man in her life until 1744, when she left him. Some scholars maintain she left Garrick because he wanted too much control over her life and career. However, Woffington continued to work with him as an actor. Garrick later wrote "My Lovely Peggy" and other songs for Woffington.

Although she maintained a notorious reputation for having numerous love affairs, the number seems to have been exaggerated. Indeed, scholars maintain she loved four men only, among them the writer and politician Edmund Burke. After leaving Garrick in 1744, she started a new life by moving to the house called Teddington Place in the village of Teddington near London. Here she converted the property's barn into a theater and used the theater's first play, *The Distressed Mother*, to launch her sister Mary into show business. Mary, however, a weak actor, was usurped by Bellamy, who went on after this performance to become another famous eighteenth century actor.

Woffington continued to act in Covent Garden until ill health forced her to retire in 1757. During the May 3, 1757, performance of Shakespeare's *As You Like It*, she collapsed from a stroke while performing Rosalind's epilogue, in the middle of the line, "I would kiss as many . . . ," after which she retired from the stage.

Woffington died on March 28, 1760, and is buried at St. Mary's Church in Teddington. The National Portrait Gallery in London contains eighteen portraits of her.

SIGNIFICANCE

Although she climbed to the heights of London's theatrical world, Peg Woffington never forgot her roots and remembered and honored her own childhood in poverty by founding almshouses for the poor in Teddington. She is the subject of *Masks and Faces* (1852), a play by

Irish actress, Peg Woffington. (The Granger Collection, New York)

Charles Reade, on which Reade based his 1853 novel *Peg Woffington*. The novel deals with Woffington's affair with Sir Charles Vane, the stressful consequences on his wife Mabel, and Woffington's change of heart and subsequent early death.

—M. Casey Diana

FURTHER READING

Dunbar, Jane. *Peg Woffington and Her World.* Boston: Houghton Mifflin, 1968. A comprehensive examination of Woffington's life, detailing her dramatic roles, both comic and Shakespearean, and her personal life and loves, especially her long-term but sporadic affair with actor David Garrick.

Mahon, Brid. *A Time to Love: The Life of Peg Woffington.* Dublin: Poolbeg Press, 1992. This 550-page book explores the life of Woffington in impoverished eighteenth century Dublin and, in particular, her lifelong connection with her homeland, Ireland. Also details her other home, London, and her interactions with other actors, playwrights, artists, and celebrities.

Marinacci, Barbara. *Leading Ladies—A Gallery of Famous Actresses.* New York: Dodd, Mead, 1961. Places Woffington and her colorful life and era in the context of many other actors that have made a lasting impact historically and culturally. Also presents good, detailed information on eighteenth century London theater.

Molloy, J. Fitzgerald. *The Life and Adventures of Peg Woffington.* London: Dodd, Mead, 1892. An older but still very insightful and informative book. Details Woffington's many reputed love affairs and, in particular, her lengthy affair with Garrick. Of particular interest also are the numerous illustrations of eighteenth century London theaters.

Shevelow, Kathryn. *Charlotte: Being a True Account of an Actress's Flamboyant Adventures in Eighteenth-Century London's Wild and Wicked Theatrical World.* New York: Henry Holt, 2005. A scholar of eighteenth century British literature and culture, Shevelow explores the life of the daughter of influential eighteenth century actor and playwright Colly Cibber, expertly capturing the historical era, and the London of the time, of which Woffington was a part.

See also: Fanny Abington; Edmund Burke; Hannah Cowley; David Garrick; William Hogarth; Anne Oldfield; Mary Robinson; Sarah Siddons; Sir John Vanbrugh.

Related articles in *Great Events from History: The Eighteenth Century, 1701-1800:* January 29, 1728: Gay Produces the First Ballad Opera; December 7, 1732: Covent Garden Theatre Opens in London; 1742: Fielding's *Joseph Andrews* Satirizes English Society.

JAMES WOLFE
British military leader

Using a daring maneuver, Wolfe was largely responsible for the defeat of the French at Quebec in 1759, preparing the way for the subsequent French loss of Canada to` the British in the Seven Years' War.

Born: January 2, 1727; Westerham, Kent, England
Died: September 13, 1759; Quebec City, Quebec, New France (now in Canada)
Areas of achievement: Military, warfare and conquest

EARLY LIFE

James Wolfe's mother, the former Henrietta Thompson, was the daughter of a Yorkshire squire; his father, Edward, was a third-generation soldier of Welsh-Irish stock. Edward reached the rank of colonel in the marines and had fought with the duke of Marlborough as a bri-gade major in Flanders during the War of the Spanish Succession. His sons were educated by private tutors in Westerham and in Greenwich, where the family moved in 1739.

For as long as he could remember, young Wolfe wanted to please his father and follow in his footsteps as a soldier. At the age of thirteen, he accompanied his father as a volunteer to the Isle of Wight to prepare for a military expedition against the Spanish colonies in the New World during the Anglo-Spanish conflict known as the War of Jenkins's Ear. Because of ill health, Wolfe was sent back home. Within the next two years, however, he received a commission as a second lieutenant in his father's regiment of marines. It is doubtful that he ever served in his father's regiment, since he was shortly thereafter transferred to another regiment, the Twelfth

Foot. In 1742, during the War of the Austrian Succession, Wolfe's regiment was sent to Flanders, where, at the Battle of Dettingen, he first distinguished himself. He fought near the duke of Cumberland at the beginning of the battle, and the duke was greatly impressed with young Wolfe's actions while under fire. Undoubtedly as a result of this association with the duke, in the next year George II appointed the sixteen-year-old Wolfe adjutant of his regiment and within a few days promoted him to the rank of lieutenant.

In 1745, Wolfe continued his successful career at the Battle of Culloden in Scotland, where the army of Prince Charles Edward Stuart, the Young Pretender, was defeated, thus ending the Jacobite hopes. Prince Charles, Bonnie Prince Charlie, was the grandson of James II and the last Stuart pretender to the English throne. Wolfe soon became commander of his new regiment, the Twentieth Foot, and settled down to garrison duty in Scotland. With Great Britain at peace and time on his hands, he determined to complete his education, studying subjects such as Latin and mathematics. Unhappy with the inactivity of peacetime, Wolfe nevertheless devoted himself to making his regiment one of the best drilled and best disciplined in the British army. Those qualities that made him a great leader were also being molded during these years: a strong sense of duty and purpose, an admirable physical and moral courage, and an ability to inspire confidence and devotion in his followers.

On the basis of physical appearance, Wolfe would never be judged to be a courageous and heroic military leader. He was tall and painfully thin, with a very awkward gait. His chin was woefully weak. He seldom wore the wigs which were in fashion, preferring to expose his bright red hair. As if these "maladies" were not enough, Wolfe suffered all of his life from rheumatism, and he eventually contracted tuberculosis. In addition to his somewhat unattractive appearance, Wolfe also lacked the social graces necessary for the model of the military officer to which he aspired, and he worked as diligently to remedy this weakness as he had to improve his military skills. Indeed, despite physical and personal shortcomings, he possessed admirable energy, strong spirit, and fierce determination, all of which helped him succeed in his chosen profession.

A devoted son, Wolfe faithfully wrote letters to his mother and even decided not to marry his one and only reputed love, Elizabeth Lawson, because of his parents' disapproval. Perhaps this was only a halfhearted romance, since Wolfe had a reputation of being uncomfortable around women and appeared to be indifferent to their company.

LIFE'S WORK

Events in the 1750's in North America were to change Wolfe's life and provide the opportunity for his greatest feat: Victory over the French in Quebec in 1759. Although he was very young and had never commanded an army, Wolfe had proven himself in battle, displaying great physical courage. He had also developed leadership skills through hard work and a single-minded devotion to duty. All he needed was a chance to display these skills, and the conflict with France in 1754 would give him his opportunity.

Desiring to expand their empire in Canada and link it with Louisiana, the French began to move into the Ohio Valley, where they clashed in 1754 with British colonists who also claimed these lands. Shots were fired, and the French and Indian War ensued between Great Britain and France, though war was not officially declared until 1756. In that year, the war expanded into Europe and beyond, where it became known as the Seven Years' War. The conflict was a struggle for North America and a continuation of the rivalry between these two powerful nations, as they vied for needed raw materials and world markets.

In 1757, the British decided to strike at the French at Rochefort. Wolfe was appointed quartermaster general in the expedition, which was commanded by General John Mordaunt, Elizabeth Lawson's uncle. The spirits of the thirty-year-old Wolfe were lifted as he busily prepared for the expedition. Unfortunately for the British, the expedition was a dismal failure, but the venture proved helpful to Wolfe's career, as he was one of the two officers not criticized at the inquiry held following the expedition.

Following the Rochefort failure, Wolfe offered his services in North America to the ablest and most powerful minister in George II's government, William Pitt the Elder. Pitt had decided to strike at the French Empire in North America by mounting a major expedition against Louisbourg, the French stronghold guarding the sea approach to Canada. Pitt ignored military custom and seniority in choosing leadership of this campaign; passing over more senior officers, he chose the younger and less experienced Jeffrey Amherst, a forty-year-old colonel, to command the expedition. Amherst was made a general, and Wolfe was appointed one of his three brigadiers.

Amherst selected Wolfe to carry out the main landing at a point about four miles west of Louisbourg, while

James Wolfe. (Library of Congress)

another brigade landed farther west. Wolfe's landing on June 8, 1758, was successful, and the French, threatened from both flanks, fled. Louisbourg was taken from the French, thus cutting the colony off from France and the main supply route.

Poor health forced Wolfe to return to Great Britain in October, although he expressed to Pitt his willingness to return to America. Pitt had been informed of Wolfe's significant role in the capture of Louisbourg and selected the young soldier to command the expedition that was being planned against Quebec, the French stronghold on the St. Lawrence River. Pitt's decision met with criticism from members of the government, undoubtedly as a result of Wolfe's unorthodox military style and appearance, his youth and inexperience, and his somewhat brazen tendency to criticize his fellow officers and even his superiors. Perhaps, also, the talented and aggressive Wolfe was thought to be too ambitious.

Nevertheless, at the age of thirty-two, Wolfe was given the greatest challenge of his life. In June, 1759, Wolfe sailed with fewer than nine thousand men to op-

pose some sixteen thousand French soldiers at Quebec. More significant was that Quebec was seemingly impregnable; all approaches to the city were blocked. The powerful French guns would negate any approach by river; two smaller rivers barred the land approach from the east, and the western approach, above Quebec, was guarded by steep cliffs that led to the Plains of Abraham. Wolfe's only hope was to lure the French into the open. To do this, he divided his forces and feinted attacks at different points on the river, which the wily French commander, Louis-Joseph de Montcalm, ignored as the weeks passed. Wolfe became ill and discouraged at his lack of success, but he never openly displayed his feelings.

The main British fleet under the command of Admiral Charles Saunders had won control of the St. Lawrence. Daily, the British ships sailed the river as Wolfe desperately sought a way to capture Quebec before the coming winter stopped operations. While observing the cliffs above Quebec one day, he noticed a path winding up the steep cliffs nearly a mile and a half above Quebec. He further noticed that the path was guarded by only a small picket at the top of the cliffs, since the French believed the cliff to be virtually inaccessible. Wolfe had found his solution.

On September 12, from his cabin on the *Sutherland*, Wolfe ordered the attack on Quebec. He ordered a squadron to sail upriver as if en route to Montreal. At sunset, Saunders and the main fleet simulated a landing at a point below Quebec and bombarded the banks there. This action convinced Montcalm to concentrate his troops below the city, miles away from the actual point of attack. Later that evening, under the cover of darkness, Wolfe led his men upriver. Ironically, before landing, Wolfe recited Thomas Gray's *Elegy in a Country Churchyard* to a young sailor, with its fateful line, "The paths of glory lead but to the grave." The troops quietly landed at what is now called Wolfe's Cove, where they successfully made their way up the cliffs and overpowered the few French pickets at the top. Reinforcements joined the initial group, and eventually several thousand British troops gathered on the Plains of Abraham just west of Quebec on September 13, 1759. The surprised Montcalm accepted the challenge and concentrated his troops against the British. Wolfe's men formed a single line and were ordered to hold their fire until the French were only forty yards away. Against the superior British musketry, the French were routed after two volleys. Wolfe, while personally leading a handpicked force of grenadiers, was shot twice. He died after ordering that the enemies' retreat be stopped. Montcalm also was mortally wounded, dying the next day. Quebec surrendered on September 18. This brief battle paved the way for the collapse of the French control of Canada in September, 1760.

SIGNIFICANCE

James Wolfe's great victory and heroic death at Quebec won for him everlasting fame in the minds and hearts of the British. Every student has read of this battle in which Wolfe, upon being told of the outcome, uttered these famous words: "Now God be praised, I die happy." There was, however, controversy surrounding his campaign at Quebec. Several of his brigadiers criticized him at the time for not attacking earlier and farther upriver, thereby shortening the war. Some historians contend that Quebec was not as impregnable as it was reputed to be and that the French could have recaptured the city with more effort, while others believe that Admiral Saunders should be given more credit, or that luck had much to do with the outcome. Chance indeed played a role at Quebec and in Wolfe's career. Nevertheless, he displayed great daring and personal courage at Quebec and overcame overwhelming odds, as he had always overcome physical and personal obstacles in his life.

In this single campaign, Wolfe played an important part in Great Britain's rise to a position of supreme political and economic power in the eighteenth century. His complete self-confidence, dogged determination, and strong competitive nature reflected those values and traits of character that were to make Great Britain a mighty empire that lasted for nearly two centuries. It is little wonder that Wolfe captured the imagination of the British people with his daring and courage.

Wolfe also altered the course of American history with this victory. With the fall of Quebec, the French were removed as a threat against the American colonies, thereby causing the colonists to resist taxes placed upon them by the British government to pay for British soldiers to defend them. To the Americans, the French had been their only enemy, and such a costly defense was no longer needed. Thus Wolfe has been credited with unwittingly laying the groundwork for the American Revolution, which ironically dismantled a part of the empire he had helped to protect.

—*James E. Southerland*

FURTHER READING

Hibbert, Christopher. *Wolfe at Quebec*. New York: World, 1959. A scholarly and well-balanced work that discusses Wolfe objectively, exposing his flaws as well as his strengths. Contains an impressive and useful bibliography. Relies heavily upon primary sources.

Leach, Douglas E. *Arms for Empire: A Military History of the British Colonies in North America, 1607-1763*. New York: Macmillan, 1973. A scholarly account of warfare in the seventeenth and eighteenth centuries. An extensive bibliography is included as well as a helpful glossary of military and naval terms.

Liddell Hart, B. H. "The Battle That Won an Empire." *American Heritage* 11 (December, 1959): 24-31, 105-108. An excellent, detailed military account of Wolfe at Quebec by an eminent military historian. The article was written in commemoration of the bicentennial of the 1759 victory at Quebec.

McLynn, Frank. *1759: The Year Britain Became Master of the World*. New York: Atlantic Monthly Press, 2004. Focuses on the fourth year of the Seven Years' War, describing how Great Britain emerged triumphant against France. Includes an account of Wolfe's campaigns, and also cites his military blunders.

McNairn, Alan. *Behold the Hero: General Wolfe and the Arts in the Eighteenth Century*. Montreal: McGill-Queen's University Press, 1997. After his military victory and death in 1759, Wolfe, celebrated a hero, was represented in everything from mass-produced ceramics and popular songs to painting and literature. McNairn analyzes these representations and describes how Wolfe became the embodiment of British patriotism and the superiority of the English way of life.

Parkman, Francis. *Montcalm and Wolfe*. 2 vols. Boston: Little, Brown, 1903. A classic, though dated, account of Wolfe and Montcalm at Quebec. A very dramatic rendering of the struggle between Great Britain and France for dominion in North America. Argues that the victory was inevitable because Great Britain was a freer and more enlightened nation.

Peckham, Howard H. *The Colonial Wars, 1689-1762*. Chicago: University of Chicago Press, 1964. Brings the various wars together in a coherent and interesting narrative. Includes a helpful annotated bibliography of suggested readings.

Reid, Stuart. *Wolfe: The Career of General James Wolfe from Culloden to Quebec*. Staplehurst, England: Spellmount, 2002. A biography of Wolfe, focusing on his military career. Reid traces Wolfe's career from the Battle of Culloden to his celebrated, and fatal, victory at Quebec.

Reilly, David Robin. *The Rest to Fortune: The Life of Major-General James Wolfe.* London: Cassell, 1960. A scholarly work that deals with the conflicting evidence and unsettled questions surrounding Wolfe and his place in history. Discounts the criticisms of Wolfe and concludes that his leadership qualities, along with opportunity, led to his exalted place in history.

Whitton, Frederick Ernest. *Wolfe and North America.* Boston: Little, Brown, 1929. Reprint. New York: Kennikat Press, 1971. A sympathetic account that examines Wolfe against the backdrop of the wars in Europe and North America. No footnotes or bibliography.

See also: Lord Amherst; Sir Guy Carleton; George II; First Duke of Marlborough; Louis-Joseph de Montcalm.

Related articles in *Great Events from History: The Eighteenth Century, 1701-1800:* May 26, 1701-September 7, 1714: War of the Spanish Succession; April 5, 1722: European Discovery of Easter Island; 1739-1741: War of Jenkins's Ear; December 16, 1740-November 7, 1748: War of the Austrian Succession; May 28, 1754-February 10, 1763: French and Indian War; January, 1756-February 15, 1763: Seven Years' War; 1791: Canada's Constitutional Act.

MARY WOLLSTONECRAFT
English writer and feminist

In challenging British institutions to extend the political liberties of the American and French Revolutions to women, Wollstonecraft developed a comprehensive feminist program. Her best-known nonfiction literary work is A Vindication of the Rights of Woman, *published in 1792.*

Born: April 27, 1759; London, England
Died: September 10, 1797; London, England
Also known as: Mary Wollstonecraft Godwin
Areas of achievement: Literature, social reform, women's rights, government and politics

EARLY LIFE

Mary Wollstonecraft was the second of seven children born to Edward Wollstonecraft and Elizabeth, née Dickson. During the 1760's, her father sold his prosperous weaving business to become a spendthrift, hard-drinking gentleman farmer. As a result, Wollstonecraft spent much of her childhood in fear of paternal fits and brutalities, often directed at her mother. A witness early in life to the often precarious and helpless status of women, she lost her own chance at financial independence when the elder Wollstonecraft dissipated his daughters' legacies.

Parental preference for the firstborn son, Edward, who was already favored by primogeniture, caused Wollstonecraft later to attack the practice and contributed to her lasting resentment toward Edward. Though her formal education was limited to several years at the Yorkshire county day school, supplemented by shared lessons from the father of a friend, Wollstonecraft engaged in continuous informal study casually directed by well-read acquaintants.

What turned out to be a lifelong headstrong bent facilitated Wollstonecraft's first attempt at economic independence. At the age of nineteen, she accepted, in defiance of her parents, the position of live-in companion to the wealthy, widowed Mrs. Dawson in Bath, where she remained until called home in 1781 to nurse her ailing mother. After the latter's death the following year, Wollstonecraft once more took charge of her future by giving up the secure but onerous job of companion to spend the next eighteen months in the congenial albeit impoverished home of her friend Fanny Blood.

Wollstonecraft's strong character asserted itself again in 1784, when she brazenly removed her sister Eliza from an abusive husband and put her, together with another sister and Blood, to work in a hastily established school for girls, which she superintended until late 1785. At that time the consumptive Blood, now married and living in Lisbon, required lying-in nurture. Wollstonecraft courageously undertook the journey to Lisbon alone, attended her already dying friend, and returned to London several weeks after the funeral to find her school failing and bankrupt. To acquit herself of accumulated debts, she persisted in securing a publisher for a hurriedly composed tract, *Thoughts on the Education of Daughters* (1787), thereby establishing contacts for her future writing career. She met most of the many subsequent crises in her life with equal resilience and resolution, often by challenging established mores.

In 1786, however, Wollstonecraft's literary prospects were as yet insufficient to vouchsafe a livelihood, and she reluctantly set out for Ireland as governess to the daughters of Lord and Lady Kingsborough. Her tenure in that fashionable environment lasted a mere ten months because of her refusal to acquiesce in the intrigues and whims of the lavish, aristocratic household. Instead, she invested her time completing the manuscript of her first novel. Determined never again to serve in a subservient capacity, she returned to London in search of an independent career, an audacious notion for a respectable, twenty-eight-year-old unmarried woman.

LIFE'S WORK

In searching for a publisher, Mary Wollstonecraft had the good fortune to associate with Joseph Johnson, a member of the Radical Dissenters, Protestant skeptics who were dedicated to reason and receptive to extending authorship to women. Johnson engaged Wollstonecraft as reviewer for his new periodical, *The Analytical Review*, and brought her together with like-minded Dissenters. He also published her collection of pedagogical vignettes, *Original Stories from Real Life* (1788), and her first novel, *Mary, a Fiction* (1788). The latter is a rather

Mary Wollstonecraft. (Library of Congress)

artless, stylistically inept tale chronicling Wollstonecraft's friendship with Blood, but already demonstrative of her feminist spirit as she attempts to introduce a new kind of thinking heroine into the established genre of the sentimental novel. The author's belief that women should aspire to control over their lives is firmly incorporated into the plot.

Wollstonecraft's first controversial work came into being when her Dissenter friend Richard Price voiced his ardent support of the French Revolution. His earlier implied criticism of the British ruling class had so enraged the conservative Edmund Burke that Burke wrote *Reflections on the Revolution in France* (1790) in defense of the British status quo and against extension of political liberties. Wollstonecraft immediately entered the fray on the side of Price with *A Vindication of the Rights of Man* (1790), which, though poorly reasoned and organized, was the first of many noted rebuttals to Burke, preceding Thomas Paine's *The Rights of Man* (1791), with which it is often associated. The popularity of her anonymously published essay encouraged Johnson to bring out a second, signed edition, and Wollstonecraft at once became famous and infamous, for she assailed the English parliament and the hereditary nobility in harsh, occasionally vituperative, language.

Society's amazement at seeing an unmarried woman engaged in rancorous political commentary motivated Wollstonecraft to address gender inequality in *A Vindication of the Rights of Woman* (1792). In analyzing how societal institutions and famous authors, particularly Jean-Jacques Rousseau, characterize women as lesser beings, she argues that these portraits are but expressions of how men wish to perceive women and calls on her gender to reevaluate and assert themselves. At the same time, she expresses doubt that the middle-class woman, whom she especially wished to "rescue" from an inferior position, would be determined enough to rise above the strictures of social convention. Though her prose and frequently disorganized digressions barely match eighteenth century literary standards, the case for women's rights, including education and financial self-sufficiency, comes across clearly. By extension, the essay challenged all vested interests of society and evoked a storm of controversy. It represents the peak of her writing career in terms of public exposure.

Wollstonecraft's private life was much less satisfactory. While publicly encouraging women to become economically and emotionally independent, she herself sought stable personal bonds with men. Contemporaries describe her as a plain, purposeful woman of sober coun-

ON THE DEGRADATION OF WOMEN

In A Vindication of the Rights of Woman, *Mary Wollstonecraft produced an extended analysis of the state of women in her society and a program of political action to attain women's rights. In the passage reproduced below, she argues that the current weak or degraded state of women is strictly analogous to the equally degraded state of men in societies where they are not free.*

That woman is naturally weak, or degraded by a concurrence of circumstances, is, I think, clear. But this position I shall simply contrast with a conclusion, which I have frequently heard fall from sensible men in favour of an aristocracy: that the mass of mankind cannot be any thing, or the obsequious slaves, who patiently allow themselves to be penned up, would feel their own consequence, and spurn their chains. Men, they further observe, submit every where to oppression, when they have only to lift up their heads to throw off the yoke; yet, instead of asserting their birthright, they quietly lick the dust, and say, let us eat and drink, for tomorrow we die. Women, I argue from analogy, are degraded by the same propensity to enjoy the present moment; and, at last, despise the freedom which they have not sufficient virtue to struggle to attain.

Source: Mary Wollstonecraft, *A Vindication of the Rights of Woman* (Boston: Peter Edes, 1792), chapter 4, paragraph 1. http://www.bartleby.com/br/144.html. Accessed September, 2005.

---

tenance and somewhat dowdy appearance, which some of the portraits used in the title pages of her books tried to soften and prettify. She was attractive as a skilled and mettlesome conversationalist, but her tendency to be possessive and ever assertive apparently strained intimate relationships. Her first ill-fated encounter was with the Swiss painter Henry Fuseli, to whom she became so deeply attached that, in her usual presumptuous fashion, she asked Fuseli's wife to take her into the household as his spiritual partner. Fuseli's wife's outraged refusal hastened Wollstonecraft's planned journey to France in 1792. Arriving in Paris at the height of the Jacobin terror, she moderated her former optimistic opinion about the efficacy of sudden social change, though in her formal account of that visit, *Historical and Moral View of the Origin and Progress of the French Revolution* (1794), she gamely holds to the liberal ideas set forth in previous publications.

Privately, Wollstonecraft was passionately involved with the American businessman Gilbert Imlay during her Paris stay. They had a child, Fanny (born 1794), and he registered Wollstonecraft as his wife to afford her American protection during the political upheavals. They were, however, never married. Imlay treated the affair lightly, while she demanded serious commitment. When he left her for another woman, she twice attempted suicide

in 1795. After the first attempt, an alarmed Imlay sent her to Scandinavia as his business representative in the hope that new impressions would excite her authorial curiosity and restore her equilibrium. The resulting *Letters Written During a Short Residence in Sweden, Norway, and Denmark* (1796), based on a personal journal Wollstonecraft wrote for Imlay, represents her best work from an artistic standpoint. Acknowledgment of her own vulnerability, recognition of the value of feelings, absence of polemics, and a genuine interest in the unfamiliar surroundings all very much enhance her writing.

Determined to satisfy her longing for enduring companionship, Wollstonecraft, upon returning to London, cultivated an intimate relationship with William Godwin, an old friend and political ally. Finding herself pregnant once more without benefit of matrimony, she married Godwin in 1797, even though both partners had earlier written impassionate denunciations of formal marriage. From all accounts, their life together was a satisfactory one, cut short by Wollstonecraft's death in childbirth on September 10, 1797. Her infant daughter Mary survived the birth, married the poet Percy Bysshe Shelley, and wrote the classic novel *Frankenstein: Or, The Modern Prometheus* (1818) as Mary Wollstonecraft Shelley.

In her last, incomplete work—the posthumously published *Maria: Or, The Wrongs of Woman* (1798)—Wollstonecraft returns to the genre of the sentimental novel to present her arguments for gender equality in a form women would widely read. Despite its fictional frame, the story chronicles a variety of abuses heaped on women and girls by bourgeois institutions. Imaginary case histories, full of autobiographical events, cover a wide range of social classes, with special focus on a heroine who disregards convention and is subjected to moral censure. Another section details the injustices suffered by a working-class woman. Moreover, Wollstonecraft ventures into a frank, almost modern discussion of female sexuality. In its indictment of the status quo, the tale leaves the impression of a revolutionary manifesto. It was a fitting conclusion to the life of a feminist far ahead of her times.

SIGNIFICANCE

Both the writings and the personal behavior of Mary Wollstonecraft reflect the belief in inalienable human rights, which was given wide currency by the American and French Revolutions. Wollstonecraft dared extend this notion to members of her own gender at a time when neither established social values nor (with a few exceptions) radical libertarians considered such an extension. As a result, her arguments on behalf of women did not bring about any basic social changes or even engender a significant following. Not until John Stuart Mill's *On the Subjection of Women* (1869) were many of the concerns raised by Wollstonecraft once again brought before a wide audience. That her feminist arguments appeared in print at all was primarily a result of her publisher Johnson's antiestablishment stance. Wollstonecraft's writings challenged the very fabric of aristocratic rule and as such were welcome matter for the Radical Dissenters.

A proper appreciation of Wollstonecraft's keen political and ethical insights is hampered by her cumbersome phrasing and a general inattention to aesthetic quality, perhaps the result of a meager formal education. In part, her roundabout reasoning also reflects confusion when frontally assaulting such a hallowed institution as marriage. She, too, had internalized to some degree prevailing cultural mores regarding the status of women. After returning from France with a daughter, she was careful to conceal her unwed state and lived as Mrs. Imlay. Her caution in this regard was well taken. When Godwin's memoirs later revealed the extent of her unconventional lifestyle, public opinion turned viciously against her and drowned her professional achievements in ridicule and abuse.

Only in the twentieth century was proper recognition extended to Wollstonecraft. Her comprehensive approach, delineating the political and economic subjugation of women, their psychological and personal dependence, the contradictions embedded in conventional sexual morality, and the patriarchal nature of established institutions, corresponds to modern feminist aspirations. Hers was an early female voice giving reasoned articulation to women's suffrage, to reconsideration of the marriage contract and parental roles, to the desirability of blending motherhood with a professional career, and to female sexuality. She not only articulated many concerns still controversial in the early twenty-first century, but she also advanced boldly enough ahead of her epoch to practice them.

—*Margot K. Frank*

FURTHER READING

Ferguson, Moira, and Janet M. Todd. *Mary Wollstonecraft*. Boston: Twayne, 1984. Follows the format established by Twayne's English Authors series in giving concise, scholarly, and well-documented accounts of both an author's life and his or her literary career. Includes an assessment of Wollstonecraft's ideas, style, and influence, and stresses her professional achievements more than personal experience.

Flexner, Eleanor. *Mary Wollstonecraft: A Biography*. New York: Coward-McCann, 1972. Concentrates on Wollstonecraft's early life. Associates her childhood disappointments and hardships with later behavior patterns, especially her relationship with her parents. Emphasizes Edward Wollstonecraft's financial situation and its effect on his daughter. Well documented.

Franklin, Caroline. *Mary Wollstonecraft: A Literary Life*. New York: Palgrave Macmillan, 2004. Describes the influences that led Wollstonecraft to become a writer. For Franklin, Wollstonecraft exemplifies many women of her time who were sanctioned to spread literacy and who used print culture to advocate reform. By the 1790's the role of women as educators and reformers assumed a more political dimension.

George, Margaret. *One Woman's "Situation": A Study of Mary Wollstonecraft*. Urbana: University of Illinois Press, 1970. Discusses Wollstonecraft's psychological state, especially during her troublesome relationships with intimate acquaintances. Connects her experiences and feelings as a woman with her political commentaries. Details her many futile challenges to the ideology of the time and chronicles her failures. Assesses her contribution to feminism.

Gunther-Canada, Wendy. "The Politics of Sense and Sensibility: Mary Wollstonecraft and Catherine Macaulay Graham on Edmund Burke's *Reflections on the Revolution in France*." In *Women Writers and the Early Modern British Political Tradition*, edited by Hilda L. Smith. New York: Cambridge University Press, 1998. Analyzes the rhetorical and argumentative strategies in response to Burke's major work.

Jacobs, Diane. *Her Own Woman: The Life of Mary Wollstonecraft*. New York: Simon & Schuster, 2001. Comprehensive biography, generally more sympathetic toward Wollstonecraft than many other biographies. Jacobs roots Wollstonecraft's personal shortcomings to her frustration with society's limited expectations for women.

Kramnik, Miriam Brody. Introduction to *A Vindication of the Rights of Woman*. New York: Penguin Books,

1975. This lengthy introduction to Wollstonecraft's most famous work surveys her life and literary contributions. It discusses her within the framework of the history of feminism and compares her approach with the piecemeal efforts of nineteenth century feminists. Rather uncritical of Wollstonecraft's literary shortcomings.

Poovey, Mary. *The Proper Lady and the Woman Writer: Ideology as Style in the Writings of Mary Wollstonecraft, Mary Shelley, and Jane Austen*. Chicago: University of Chicago Press, 1984. Describes Wollstonecraft from the vantage point of eighteenth century British bourgeois ideology, juxtaposing her with the prevailing cultural model of the middle-class married woman. Shows how Wollstonecraft both rebelled against this unfulfilling state and became enmeshed in it. Critiques Wollstonecraft's reasoning and style, and also analyzes Jane Austen and Wollstonecraft's daughter, Mary Shelley, within the context of their times.

Todd, Janet. *Mary Wollstonecraft: A Revolutionary Life*. New York: Columbia University Press, 2000. A well-crafted and comprehensive biography, providing an analysis of Wollstonecraft's life and writing. Despite her rational feminist ideas, Todd portrays her subject as a person of sensibility.

Tomalin, Claire. *The Life and Death of Mary Wollstonecraft*. London: Weidenfeld and Nicolson, 1974. A detailed account of all phases of Wollstonecraft's life, with several sets of illustrations. Gives excellent background on the tenor of the time and chronicles the lives of people important to Wollstonecraft. In places, liberally interpretative, but provides adequate documentation.

Wardle, Ralph M. *Mary Wollstonecraft: A Critical Biography*. Lawrence: University Press of Kansas, 1952. A good biographical account with ample discussion of the major works. Draws heavily on Wollstonecraft's and Godwin's letters, as well as those of her relatives, and offers interpretative insights based on the correspondence. Supports its conclusions with liberal quotations from the letters. Does not stress Wollstonecraft's feminist contributions or give sufficient background on her contemporaries.

See also: Mary Astell; Edmund Burke; Hester Chapone; William Godwin; Sophie von La Roche; Catherine Macaulay; Mary de la Rivière Manley; Mary Wortley Montagu; Hannah More; Thomas Paine; Jean-Jacques Rousseau.

Related articles in *Great Events from History: The Eighteenth Century, 1701-1800:* April, 1762: Rousseau Publishes *The Social Contract*; April 19, 1775: Battle of Lexington and Concord; January 10, 1776: Paine Publishes *Common Sense*; 1790: Burke Lays the Foundations of Modern Conservatism; February 22, 1791-February 16, 1792: Thomas Paine Publishes *Rights of Man*; 1792: Wollstonecraft Publishes *A Vindication of the Rights of Woman*; April 20, 1792-October, 1797: Early Wars of the French Revolution.

YONGZHENG
Emperor of China (r. 1723-1735)

Yongzheng reigned between the two longest serving and most famous of the Qing Dynasty emperors, his father Kangxi and his own son Qianlong. Yongzheng's reign was significant in that it extended the power of the central government and consolidated imperial rule throughout China.

Born: December 13, 1678; Beijing, China
Died: October 8, 1735; Beijing, China
Also known as: Yinzhen (birth name); Yinchen (Wade-Giles); Yung-cheng (Wade-Giles); Shizong; Shih-tsung (Wade-Giles)
Area of achievement: Government and politics

EARLY LIFE

Yongzheng (yong-jehng) was the fourth son of the Qing Dynasty emperor Kangxi, one of the greatest rulers in China's history. Yongzheng's mother was Xiao Gong, a servant and the daughter of a palace bodyguard. The Qing were Manchus, not Chinese, but Kangxi, through a policy of inclusion, reconciled most ethnic, or Han, Chinese to Qing rule. The emperor also expanded Chinese influence over Tibet and expanded Chinese control through much of Central Asia. Where Kangxi failed was in the matter of the royal succession.

Of Kangxi's fifty-six children, only one, Yinreng, his second son, was born to an empress. Immediately after Yinreng's birth in 1674 he was named heir apparent, but Yinreng became erratic and violent and used both girls and boys for his sexual gratification. Kangxi removed Yinreng from the succession and placed him under house arrest in 1708, but he released him the following year. However, in 1712, after receiving evidence that Yinreng was plotting to assassinate his father, he was again arrested. Kangxi refused to name another heir. When the emperor died in 1723, Yongzheng announced that he was his father's deathbed choice to succeed him, and since his brothers were absent—and inasmuch as Yongzheng was in control of the Beijing military guard—Yongzheng succeeded in becoming emperor. He had been one of Kangxi's closest confidants, but Yongzheng was nevertheless accused of being a usurper.

LIFE'S WORK

Unlike his father, who was a young child when he became emperor, Yongzheng was in his mid-forties when he ascended the throne. He quickly rid himself of most of his revivals. Yinreng and two other brothers died in

prison, and most of the rest were kept under close surveillance. However, Yinxiang, Kangxi's thirteenth son, became Yongzheng's close adviser. Throughout his reign, Yongzheng remained fearful of sedition, concerned about possible alliances between his brothers and Qing military units. He wrote a treatise against all factions, stating that the emperor's decisions were the only criteria for defining good or evil. Yongzheng was disciplined and hard-working in matters of government, rising at 4 A.M. and often working until midnight. A devout Buddhist in religion, he transformed the palace where he was born into a Buddhist temple. Yongzheng was fluent in both Chinese and Manchu in his writing, unlike his father. As emperor, he focused his energies on reforming the bureaucracy, improving the government's financial resources, and strengthening the central government. These were not new problems and would continue to challenge Chinese rulers long after Yongzheng's reign.

There were financial shortfalls in government income, partially because of the long-held philosophy that taxes should be low so that the country could prosper, but also because agricultural landlords were adept at avoiding their tax responsibilities. Reforms were instituted, including appointing new officials more honest and efficient than most local officials, who were often controlled by the landed gentry. There was an increase in the basic land tax, but many fees, subject to manipulation and corruption, were abolished. In northern China, where peasant farmers were the norm, the reforms made local government more responsive to local needs, but in the south and southwest, with a sparser population, the reforms were less effective. In central China, in the Yangtze River provinces, entrenched local elites remained as obstacles to tax reform.

Taiwan had come under Chinese rule during the reign of Kangxi, but it remained a somewhat lawless frontier society. Yongzheng encouraged limited emigration from the mainland and strengthened local government on the island. Relations with Russia also required the emperor's attention. In 1689, the Qing and the Russians signed the Treaty of Nerchinsk, the first modern treaty ever agreed to by any Chinese government with a Western nation, establishing the border between the two states, which remained essentially unchanged. To deal with residual issues, including the discovery of gold in Siberia, the supplementary Treaty of Kiakhta was agreed to in 1727, furthering trade between the two large nations. During Yongzheng's reign, the remaining Manchus were incorporated into the imperial armies.

Kangxi had initiated a system of private, or palace, memorials, wherein officials would send memorials directly to the emperor rather than through inefficient and corrupt bureaucrats. Yongzheng extended its use, dealing with between fifty and one hundred memorials each day, with more than twenty thousand still preserved. In addition to the private memorials, Yongzheng established the office of military finance, or the Grand Council, a secret group of three advisers, including his brother Yinxiang and two loyal Chinese grand secretaries, Zhang Tingyu and Jiang Tingxi. Among other responsibilities, the council planned for possible conflicts with the Dzungar Mongol nomadic tribes in western China. The Dzungars were defeated in 1696 in a campaign led by Kangxi, but tensions had increased again by Yongzheng's reign. However, in spite of extensive preparations, the 1731 campaign against the Dzungars failed, leaving the problem to emperors who followed him.

The regime was more successful in the southwest against the indigenous Miao, Yao, and Lolo peoples. Han Chinese had moved into the region, and conflicts were numerous. E'ertai was appointed governor general of the area. In 1732, after subduing the Miao, E'ertai was summoned back to Beijing by the emperor in the aftermath of the deaths of Yinxiang and Jiang Tingxi, becoming one of Yongzheng's chief advisers on the Grand Council, along with Zhang Tingyu.

Although the descendant of Manchus had committed to maintaining Manchu supremacy in China, Yongzheng envisioned himself as a moral Confucian emperor, but he was also the autocrat. Catholic Christian missionaries had been active in China for more than one hundred years, but they came under suspicion when the Papacy criticized the Chinese practice of filial piety and ancestor worship. After Yongzheng discovered that some missionaries were corresponding with one of his brothers, Christians were restricted to Beijing, Canton, and Macao. As a Buddhist, the emperor took part in a Buddhist study group, but when his interpretations clashed with those of two monks, he ordered their books burned. His father, Kangxi, sponsored a paternalistic Sacred Edict of sixteen points to be followed by his subjects. Yongzheng expanded on those points, requiring that they be read and discussed twice each month, even in local villages, an example of what one historian called national indoctrination.

Under Kangxi, Chen Menglei (Chen Mong Lei) had compiled a vast work called *Gu jin tu shu ji cheng* (pb. 1726-1728; the complete classics collection of ancient China). It was ready for publication when Kangxi died. Yongzheng removed Chen's name as editor and issued the work as that of Kangxi himself, giving himself credit for its publication.

After reading the anti-Manchu writings of Lu Liuliang, who died in 1683, another scholar, Zeng Jing, attempted to inspire a rebellion against Yongzheng in 1729. The emperor had Lu's corpse dug up and dismembered and his surviving family enslaved or exiled. However, Yongzheng pardoned Zeng Jing because he was young and impressionable. Opium addiction was another issue that attracted Yongzheng's attention. Used medicinally since the eleventh century, the smoking of opium became widespread in the seventeenth century. Early in his reign, Yongzheng attempted to stamp out opium use, threatening the use of capital punishment, but he later concluded that opium for medicinal uses was warranted. His moralistic approach, combined with his desire to create a unified society, led him to emancipate China's outcasts—singers, professional beggars, boat people, domestic slaves—and legally end the discrimination against them. These acts are examples of Yongzheng's involvement in all aspects of Chinese government and society.

SIGNIFICANCE

Because of his concern to gather information and make requisite decisions, Yongzheng was a more absolute and authoritarian ruler than his Qing Dynasty predecessors, but as a ruler of a large state that depended upon a vast bureaucracy, he was not all-powerful. Perhaps no emperor worked harder and with more discipline in governing China, and he did so with some sense of benevolence and justice. When he died he left to his chosen successor, Qianlong, his fourth son, a China more unified, with a greater population and more prosperous than ever. Yongzheng was the most skillful of the Qing emperors in administering the government, but the reforms he instituted, particularly in the field of taxation, failed to solve the long-term problems of largely agrarian China.

—*Eugene Larson*

FURTHER READING

Huang, Pei. *Autocracy at Work*. Bloomington: Indiana University Press, 1974. An examination of government practice and philosophy during Yongzheng's reign.

Mott, F. W. *Imperial China, 900-1800*. Cambridge, Mass.: Harvard University Press, 1999. An updated study of imperial China, ending with the reign of Yongzheng's son and heir, Qianlong.

Paludan, Ann. *Chronicles of the Chinese Emperor*. New York: Thames and Hudson, 1998. A useful compendium of the Chinese emperors and their reigns, including that of Yongzheng.

Spence, Jonathan D. *Emperor of China: Self-Portrait of K'ang Hsi*. New York: Alfred A. Knopf, 1974. Reprint. New York: Vintage Books, 1988. This beautifully written and illustrated book makes Yongzheng's father, Emperor Kangxi, come alive, but not simply as a grand historical figure. Spence presents Kangxi in his own words, describing his methods of ruling and his relationship to his sons, among other topics.

_____. *The Search for Modern China*. New York: Norton, 1990. An excellent work on modern China, beginning with the fall of the Ming and the rise of the Qing.

_____. *Treason by the Book*. New York: Viking Press, 2001. An examination of Yongzheng's actions in the Lu Liuliang affair, giving insights into eighteenth century China and the personality and aims of the emperor.

See also: Cao Xueqin; Dai Zhen; Qianlong.

Related articles in *Great Events from History: The Eighteenth Century, 1701-1800:* October 21, 1727: Treaty of Kiakhta; 1750-1792: China Consolidates Control over Tibet.

JOHN PETER ZENGER
German-born American printer and publisher

Zenger printed attacks against the governor of the colony of New York in the New York Weekly Journal—*the first independent newspaper in America—for which he was indicted for libel. His celebrated trial became a landmark in establishing a free press in America.*

Born: 1697; Rhenish Palatinate (now in Germany)
Died: July 28, 1746; New York, New York
Areas of achievement: Social reform, business, literature

EARLY LIFE

John Peter Zenger grew up in a family without a father; he had died while John Peter was still young, leaving his wife Johanna and three children to fend for themselves. Early in the eighteenth century, Queen Anne of England allowed Germans who were victims of the aggressive wars of French king Louis XIV to emigrate to America. Johanna Zenger took advantage of the opportunity and brought her children to New York in 1710. John Peter was only thirteen at the time and was indentured to William Bradford, New York's only printer. Bradford's school produced many colonial printers, including his own son, Andrew, who later competed in the publishing business with Benjamin Franklin in Philadelphia. Young Zenger worked for Bradford for eight years.

At the age of twenty-one, Zenger was given his freedom and began wandering through the colonies looking for a place to set up a permanent printing establishment as a master printer. He met and married Mary White on July 28, 1719, and settled for a brief time in Chestertown, Kent County, Maryland. While in Maryland, he became a citizen and was given a contract to publish that colony's laws, proceedings, and minutes. His wife died soon after the birth of a son, and Zenger returned to New York, where he met and married Anna Catherine Maul on August 24, 1722.

Zenger joined his former master, William Bradford, for a brief time in 1725 and published one book. He later opened his own print shop on Smith Street near Maiden Lane in 1726 and printed pamphlets, mainly sermons in German. Those who were dissatisfied with the church or state and wanted to say so came to Zenger, and for six years he supplemented his staple output of religious tracts with critical pamphlets and open letters. In 1730, he published *Arithmetica*, the first arithmetic book printed in North America.

Zenger was an indifferent printer with a poor knowledge of the English language. His spelling, syntax, and grammar were unreliable. Although he wrote a few articles, he was not an editor but a printer who published the writings of others to earn a living. There is no contemporary portrait or artist's sketch of Zenger. In the Federal Hall Memorial on the corner of Wall and Nassau Streets in New York City, there is a likeness based on the anthropological data regarding Palatine Germans of his era.

LIFE'S WORK

In 1733, John Peter Zenger wrote an article in which he criticized the royal governor of New York, William Cosby, for the manner in which he had supported William Foster for the post of assemblyman in White Plains. Cosby knew that the Quakers supported the rival candidate, Lewis Morris, and he refused to let them vote when they would not violate their consciences and take an oath declaring property ownership a voting qualification in the colony. Zenger's manuscript was returned by the publisher of the *New York Weekly Gazette* marked "unfit for our columns."

Since Bradford's *New York Weekly Gazette* was the only newspaper published between Philadelphia and Boston, and as Bradford was known to be the official printer of the New York governor, council, and assembly, Zenger became identified with the opposition party and began printing a rival newspaper, the *New York Weekly Journal*, in his print shop on Broad Street. The new paper was published every Monday and contained four pages of crooked type with an unattractive format. It was America's first independent newspaper.

James Alexander was the leader of the opposition and wrote or edited most of the copy of Zenger's paper under the pseudonym "Cato." Alexander had the largest law library in the colony. A Scot who had joined in the rebellion against George I to put James, the Old Pretender, on the throne, Alexander defined and defended a free press. He was a charter member, along with fellow printer Franklin, of the American Philosophical Society. Others who wrote for the *New York Weekly Journal* included Morris, whom Cosby had opposed as assemblyman, William Smith, a Yale graduate and founder of Princeton College, and the scientist Cadwallader Colden.

Zenger's paper claimed on its masthead to print foreign news, literary essays, poetry, and small amounts of advertising, but the first issue of the *New York Weekly*

Journal contained a savage attack on the policies of Governor Cosby. Bradford countered by putting Francis Harrison in charge of *The New York Weekly Gazette*'s editorial policy, and a stream of eulogies of the royal administration poured in torrents in an attempt to discredit the *New York Weekly Journal*.

The journal was known as "Zenger's paper," since the only name it bore was that of the printer. Other writers used pseudonyms such as "Cato," "Philo-Patriae," and "Thomas Standby." Behind these names, they dared to call Governor Cosby everything from "an idiot" to "a Nero." Zenger also distributed song sheets of hastily written ballads that criticized the royal officials "who chop and change for those that serve their turn."

Governor Cosby was an Anglo-Irish aristocrat who craved place and pension. He had experienced trouble before coming to America over his misrule as governor of Minorca. Before the Crown removed him from that post, he was forced to reimburse those whom he had victimized. Perhaps George II thought that he had learned his lesson and therefore appointed him governor of New York, but he proved even more dictatorial and scheming in his new position. The attacks on Cosby in Zenger's paper amounted to political independence with a vengeance. Cosby was accused of misusing his office as governor in voting as a member of the council, demanding to see all bills from the assembly before the council saw them, and adjourning the assembly in his own name rather than in that of the king. Zenger's journal asserted that it ought to be the ambition of all honest magistrates to have their deeds openly examined and publicly scanned and that freedom of speech is the symptom as well as the effect of good government.

Alexander was believed to be the author of the most telling articles against Cosby, but he was not arrested, because it would have been difficult to prove his authorship. Instead, the court party went after Zenger, who was not shrouded in anonymity: The *New York Weekly Journal* was his newspaper—and his was the only actual name that appeared in it. The court party observed that, while the true authors of the articles were tenacious about their own liberty, they neglected that of their own printer.

Cosby tried to have Zenger indicted by a grand jury but was unsuccessful. He then ordered four issues of the *New York Weekly Journal* burned by the public hangman. The citizens of New York boycotted the event and even the public hangman refused to appear. Only Harrison and his slave were on hand for the burning in front of the New York Court House, and the slave was ordered to

put the torch to the condemned documents. Further trying to silence Zenger, Cosby sent a hatchet man who threatened Zenger with physical harm. Zenger thereafter took to wearing a sword, an act that was often held up to ridicule in Bradford's paper.

On Wednesday, November 17, 1734, Cosby issued a warrant for Zenger's arrest on the charge of "seditious libel." Popular feeling was exacerbated because the governor's vindictive wrath fell not on his powerful enemies but on an insignificant German immigrant who made a meager living by plying his trade as a printer. He was put in custody in a cell on the third floor of city hall and was allowed no pen, ink, or paper. His only contact with the outside world was through a hole in the door. By this means, he communicated with his wife, always in the presence of a deputy sheriff, and she saw to it that the *New York Weekly Journal* was published on time each Monday. Only one issue, that of November 22, 1734, was missed. Anna Catherine Zenger followed the practice of her husband and did not attempt to write articles but continued to receive material from the anonymous writers, who now had even greater cause to attack the royal administration. Never once did Anna print a complaint that her husband was suffering because of someone else.

Zenger's bail was set at £400, an excessive amount even for a wealthy person. The German printer was poor and claimed under oath that, if his debts were paid, he was worth only £40 plus the value of the tools of his trade and his wearing apparel. Zenger's friends were unable to raise the amount for bail, and he was forced to remain in his prison cell for nine months, awaiting trial. Perhaps they felt his extended incarceration pointed up all the more the great injustices of the royal administration.

Cosby's effort to shut down the *New York Weekly Journal* boomeranged. Local sentiment turned against the government, and the circulation of the journal increased as the political controversy intensified. Colonists realized that the loss of liberty in general might follow the loss of the liberty of the press. Citizens interested in protecting freedoms in America offered their services to Zenger, including Andrew Hamilton, an eighty-year-old Philadelphia lawyer who had once served as the speaker of the Pennsylvania Assembly and was the architect of Independence Hall. Hamilton, though quite infirm, made his way secretly to New York in time for Zenger's trial.

Hamilton perceived that it was more than John Peter Zenger on trial. English law identified any published criticism of a public official as libel, and proof of authorship was all that was needed for a conviction. Since those who wrote the articles for the *New York Weekly Journal* were shrouded in anonymity, the law held the one who printed the attacks guilty of libel. Hamilton appealed to the writings of John Milton, Jonathan Swift, John Locke, Daniel Defoe, Richard Steele, and Joseph Addison in presenting his case. He argued that mere printing and publishing did not constitute a crime, and that the prosecution must prove that what was printed was false, scandalous, and seditious. Hamilton put the prosecution on the defense. Unless they were willing to expose Governor Cosby to careful scrutiny in the trial, they had no case. Truth became its own best defense. Throughout the trial, Zenger refused to divulge the identity of the men whose words he printed.

The jury took only ten minutes to reach a verdict. When Thomas Hunt, a mariner and foreman of the jury, announced "not guilty," the spectators cheered loudly. The judge threatened to hold them in contempt, but the supporters of Zenger refused to be silenced. Zenger, however, was all but lost in the jubilation as Hamilton was hailed the conqueror. Forty prominent New Yorkers gave a dinner in his honor at the Black Horse Tavern. Zenger was not present, not because the revelers chose to ignore him, but because the city government refused to release him until he paid for eight months of his maintenance. His friends raised the amount due the next day. Hamilton left for Philadelphia the day of Zenger's release amid a cannon salute and with a freedom of the city certificate "enclosed in a suitably inscribed box."

Zenger returned to his print shop, where, with the assistance of James Alexander, he published *A Brief Narrative of the Case and Tryal of John Peter Zenger* in 1736. The pamphlet was reprinted often in England and America, and Zenger's name became synonymous with freedom of the press. The new governor of New York, John Montgomerie, engaged him to publish six copies of *The Charter of the City of New-York* (1735), for which he was paid £7. The charter designated New York a free city with power to sue and be sued in court.

In 1737, the New York Assembly made Zenger its printer, and the following year New Jersey did the same. Despite being a hard worker, he lost both of these appointments through his indifference toward and ignorance of the English language.

SIGNIFICANCE

John Peter Zenger was more of a symbol than a motivating force in the movement toward the establishment of a free press in America. Gouverneur Morris declared in the

year of the declaration of American independence, however, that "the trial of Zenger in 1735 was the germ of American freedom, the morning star of that liberty which subsequently revolutionized America." The Zenger trial was referred to repeatedly during the drafting of the First Amendment to the U.S. Constitution. Not until 1792 did the British parliament respond to the popular movement toward a free press with its passage of the Fox Libel Act, which denied that proof of publication constituted libel.

Zenger continued to publish the *New York Weekly Journal* until his death at the age of forty-nine in 1746. He left a widow and six children who continued publication of the newspaper, mainly under the direction of his eldest son and namesake. The paper folded on March 18, 1751, after falling on hard times. Repeated appeals for paying subscriptions had few responses. A new generation of readers did not remember the great service that the *New York Weekly Journal*'s founder had rendered to a free press.

—Raymond Lee Muncy

FURTHER READING

Alexander, James. *A Brief Narrative of the Case and Trial of John Peter Zenger, Printer of the "New York Weekly Journal."* Edited by Stanley Nider Katz. Cambridge, Mass.: Harvard University Press, 1963. An excellent introduction by Stanley Katz that puts the trial in its historical perspective and emphasizes the political nature of Hamilton's defense.

Barnett, Lincoln. "The Case of John Peter Zenger." *American Heritage* 23 (December, 1971): 33-41. Barnett retells the familiar story of Zenger's trial but with an eye toward contemporary criticism of the press.

Buranelli, Vincent. *The Trial of Peter Zenger.* New York: New York University Press, 1957. Buranelli explores in detail the misrule of Governor William Cosby, including his fiasco on Minorca and manipulation of elections in New York.

Katz, Stanley N. *Newcastle's New York: Anglo-American Politics, 1732-1753.* Cambridge, Mass.: Belknap Press, 1968. Katz examines three administrations of governors, including that of Cosby. A good account of England's colonial machinery, which gave rise to the complaints published in Zenger's newspaper.

Putnam, William Lowell. *John Peter Zenger and the Fundamental Freedom.* Jefferson, N.C.: McFarland, 1997. A comprehensive biography of Zenger, exploring how Zenger's trial led to the adoption of the First

Amendment in the United States and to similar safeguards in Europe. The appendix includes copies of the American and English bills of rights, the Declaration of Independence, and the Declaration of the Rights of Man and of the Citizen.

Wroth, Lawrence. *The Colonial Printer.* 2d rev. ed. Charlottesville: University Press of Virginia, 1964. This study, first published in 1931, gives an excellent account of the history of printing in the colonies. The chapter on "Journeymen and Apprentices" will give the reader a grasp of the roles Zenger played in becoming an established printer.

See also: Joseph Addison; Queen Anne; Daniel Defoe; Benjamin Franklin; George I; George II; Alexander Hamilton; Samuel Johnson; Gouverneur Morris; Richard Steele; Jonathan Swift; John Wilkes.

Related articles in *Great Events from History: The Eighteenth Century, 1701-1800:* 1702 or 1706: First Arabic Printing Press; March 1, 1711: Addison and Steele Establish *The Spectator*; January 7, 1714: Mill Patents the Typewriter; August 4, 1735: Trial of John Peter Zenger; 1736: *Gentleman's Magazine* Initiates Parliamentary Reporting; March 20, 1750-March 14, 1752: Johnson Issues *The Rambler*; Beginning April, 1763: The *North Briton* Controversy; September 10, 1763: Publication of the *Freeman's Journal*; January 1, 1777: France's First Daily Newspaper Appears; December 15, 1791: U.S. Bill of Rights Is Ratified; 1792-1793: Fichte Advocates Free Speech.

Count von Zinzendorf
German religious leader

Zinzendorf revived and transformed the nearly extinct Moravian Church by infusing it with an evangelical Pietistic theology. In so doing, he also became a pioneer of ecumenism among Christians and gave birth to the modern Protestant missionary movement.

Born: May 26, 1700; Dresden, Saxony (now in Germany)
Died: May 9, 1760; Herrnhut, Saxony
Also known as: Nikolaus Ludwig von Zinzendorf (full name)
Areas of achievement: Religion and theology, social reform

EARLY LIFE

Count von Zinzendorf (fawn TSIHNT-suhn-dawrf) was born on May 26, 1700, in Dresden, Saxony, to Charles Ludwig and Charlotte Justine von Zinzendorf. His father died from tuberculosis only six weeks later. When he was three years old, on the eve of his mother's remarriage and move to Berlin, Nikolaus was sent to live with his maternal grandmother, the Baroness Henriette Katherine von Gersdorf. Three women—his mother, his grandmother, and his mother's sister—profoundly influenced his early life. They were all devout Christians.

The atmosphere at his grandmother's estate of Gross-Hennersdorf was permeated by religion. Each day's routine included prayer, Bible study, and the singing of hymns. Like Nikolaus's parents, Baroness Gersdorf was a Lutheran Pietist. The Pietists were reacting to the Protestant Scholasticism that had transformed the insights and vibrant life of the Reformation into a dead orthodoxy of rigid formulas. In personal life they stressed the new birth, a lifestyle of moral purity, and a daily routine of prayer and Bible study. They also stressed service to the less fortunate and evangelism at home and abroad. These basic tenets of Pietism were to become the guiding principles of the adult Zinzendorf.

In 1710, Baroness Gersdorf enrolled her grandson in the *Pädagogium,* or boarding school, in Halle. The school was founded and run by the noted social and educational reformer August Hermann Francke. Francke was a follower of Philipp Jacob Spener, the founder of Lutheran Pietism, and was himself one of its leading promoters. At Halle, Zinzendorf joined with five other boys to found the Order of the Grain of Mustard Seed, pledging themselves to love all humankind and to spread the Gospel.

Although Zinzendorf wanted a career in the ministry, his guardian insisted that he prepare himself to fulfill his hereditary responsibilities in the state civil service. Hence, he studied law at the Universities of Wittenberg and Utrecht. As was the custom of that day for the nobility, Zinzendorf concluded his education with a Grand Tour of Europe in 1719-1720. While visiting an art museum in Düsseldorf, he paused before Domenico Fetti's *Ecce Homo*, a painting of Jesus Christ with the crown of thorns. Below the painting was written, "I have done this for you; what have you done for me?" Zinzendorf was deeply moved and pledged himself to a life of Christian service. Later in life, he often pointed to that event as the turning point in his life.

In 1721, Zinzendorf moved to Dresden, where he entered the civil service of Elector August the Strong of Saxony. His apartment soon became a meeting place for informal religious services on Sunday afternoons. Also in 1721, Zinzendorf purchased the estate of Berthelsdorf from his grandmother, hoping to establish a Christian community there. On September 7, 1722, Zinzendorf married Dorothea von Reuss. From a deeply Pietistic home, she proved to be the perfect companion. She bore twelve children; only three of them survived their parents.

LIFE'S WORK

In December, 1722, a small group of ten Moravian refugees, six adults and four children, arrived at Berthelsdorf. They were a part of the surviving remnant of the Unitas Fratrum, or United Brethren Church, organized in 1457 by followers of the Bohemian religious reformer Jan Hus. They were fleeing religious persecution, and Zinzendorf allowed them to settle on his lands. The original ten were followed by others, not only Moravians but also former Catholics, Anabaptists, Separatists, Schwenkfelders, Reformed, and even Lutherans. By 1726, their community, named Herrnhut, numbered three hundred souls and could boast a large meeting hall, academy, print shop, and apothecary. As the community prospered, there was a need to provide civil government and to define the nature and goals of Herrnhut's spiritual life.

In 1727, Zinzendorf resigned his position at court and devoted the remainder of his life to nurturing the Christian community at Herrnhut, which soon spread throughout Europe and beyond. The need to provide orderly development was met by a two-part constitution, accepted by the community in 1727. The first part recognized Zinzendorf's role as the lord of the manor and thus dealt with civic responsibilities. Perhaps of more significance was the Brotherly Agreement, which aimed at organizing the community's spiritual life.

The Brotherly Agreement emphasized practical Christian behavior and was to serve as a model for future Moravian communities. The community was divided into "choirs" determined by age, gender, and marital status. It also provided for a governing council of twelve elders, elected by the community, or, in the case of the four chief elders, chosen by lot. As if to emphasize the spiritual nature of their duties, no one of noble rank or advanced education was allowed to serve on the council.

On August 27, 1727, the Brethren at Herrnhut began an around-the-clock prayer meeting that continued unbroken for one hundred years. The year 1727 was later regarded as the birth year of the Renewed Moravian Church. It also marked the point at which Zinzendorf's brand of Pietism began to diverge from the mainstream of German Pietism. Zinzendorf never desired that the Christian community at Herrnhut develop into a denomination. He believed that his mission in life, and the mission of Herrnhut, was to be an apostle of what he termed "heart religion." Zinzendorf rejected both the rationalism of the secular world and the dead orthodox Scholasticism of the churches. His concept of "heart religion" stressed the emotional and experiential side of religion. It emphasized a personal conversion to

Count von Zinzendorf. (Library of Congress)

Jesus Christ, followed by a life of prayer, Bible study, and communal worship.

Zinzendorf was thoroughly ecumenical in his approach to Christianity. Indeed, many scholars regard him as the father of the modern ecumenical movement. Unlike most Christians of that era, Zinzendorf not only accepted the plurality of institutional churches but also regarded that pluralism positively. He believed that each denomination had a unique contribution to make to the spread of Christianity. All churches were a part of the one true church, the Body of Christ. Unity could be, and should be, sought on the experiential level, not on the intellectual or institutional level.

The success of Herrnhut aroused opposition from the leaders of the established Lutheran Church, who feared that Zinzendorf was a sectarian. He was not, however, and he did all that he could to allay their fears. He insisted that all that was done at Herrnhut should conform to the Augsburg Confession of the Lutheran Church. He invited deputations from the established church to visit the community and see for themselves that all was in line with the Augsburg Confession. The brethren at Herrnhut took communion regularly from the local Lutheran parish priest. In 1734, Zinzendorf himself was ordained as a Lutheran minister.

Zinzendorf also felt an obligation to take the Gospel to the unbelieving in the farthest reaches of the globe. Through his efforts in these areas, Zinzendorf became the founder of the Protestant foreign missionary movement and a pioneer in Christian missions to the Jews. In 1731, Zinzendorf suggested sending missionaries to minister to the slaves in the West Indies. The response was enthusiastic. On August 21, 1732, the first Moravian missionaries departed Herrnhut for the West Indies. By 1735, twenty-nine missionaries had gone there, of whom only seven were still alive.

The period from 1732 to 1742 is often called the "golden decade" of Moravian missions. The Moravians were the first to believe that missionary work was the calling of the whole Christian community, laypersons and clergy alike. By 1742, Moravian missionaries were serving in various parts of Africa, Asia, North America, and even Lapland and Greenland. They also sent missionaries to the Jews in Amsterdam.

As long as Zinzendorf lived, the Moravian missionaries acted almost exclusively on instructions from him. His mission philosophy had three emphases: Preach Christ, not theology; live humbly among the indigenous peoples; and look for the "seekers after truth" rather than try to convert whole nations. Zinzendorf also believed that the missionaries should support themselves, thereby teaching by example the dignity of labor.

Between 1736 and 1747, Zinzendorf was banished from Saxony for his alleged sectarian activities. In 1737, he was ordained a bishop in the United Brethren Church by one of its two surviving bishops. During his banishment, he traveled widely, founding Moravian communities in Europe, England, and the United States (for example, in Bethlehem, Pennsylvania). He organized a traveling executive, known as the Pilgrim Congregation, to direct the foreign missionary work and minister to the "diaspora," those cells of converts within the established churches throughout Europe. After his banishment was repealed in 1747, Zinzendorf made London the center of the Moravians' worldwide activities until 1755. One year after the death of his first wife, on June 19, 1756, Zinzendorf married Anna Nitschmann, a longtime coworker at Herrnhut. He died at Herrnhut on May 9, 1760. Anna died thirteen days later.

SIGNIFICANCE

Count von Zinzendorf's life had a profound impact on the history of Christianity. In an age when individual Christian sects were generally intolerant of one another, Zinzendorf labored for a unity of purpose that would overlook, but not suppress, denominational distinctions. His goal was to unite all Christians in evangelism: He was the first Christian leader to use the term "ecumenical" in its modern sense. Although he was himself a nobleman, he was perfectly at ease among the humble. While in the United States in 1741, he personally preached to Native Americans. He set an example that was followed by Moravian missionaries who ministered among slaves in the West Indies and lepers in South Africa. By 1832, there were forty-two Moravian mission stations around the world.

Stimulated by the example of the Moravians, the Baptists began foreign mission work in 1793. The annual Herrnhut Ministers Conference, inspired by Zinzendorf, led directly to the founding of both the London Missionary Society in 1795 and the British and Foreign Bible Society in 1804. Perhaps one of Zinzendorf's most far-reaching influences on church history resulted from the conversion of John Wesley, the founder of Methodism, through the influence of Moravian missionaries.

Wesley first encountered the Moravians while on a voyage to the United States. He was greatly impressed by their humility and by their willingness to serve others. In Georgia, and later in England, Wesley frequented Moravian meetings. Then, on the evening of May 24,

1738, he experienced what he later described as his conversion experience. In August, 1738, Wesley visited Herrnhut. He summed up his impression of what he saw in his journal: "O when shall this Christianity cover the earth, as the 'waters cover the sea?'"

Christians and non-Christians alike have been generous in their praise of Zinzendorf. His zeal for spreading the Christian gospel and his deep, genuine concern for practical ministry to the poor have served as an inspiration for both Christian evangelists and secular social reformers. Perhaps the most fitting epitaph for Zinzendorf was provided by a church historian, who, referring to Jesus Christ's parable of the rich young ruler (Luke 18:18-30), characterized him as "the rich young ruler who said yes."

—Paul R. Waibel

FURTHER READING

Atwood, Craig D. *Community of the Cross: Moravian Piety in Colonial Bethlehem.* University Park: Pennsylvania State University Press, 2004. A history of the town Zinzendorf established as the first permanent outpost of Moravians in North America. Atwood describes the community's religious beliefs and explains the strong ties between life in Bethlehem and the religious symbolism of Zinzendorf.

Cairns, Earle E. *An Endless Line of Splendor.* Wheaton, Ill.: Tyndale House, 1986. A noted church historian establishes the historical roots of nineteenth and twentieth century Christian revivals in the work of Zinzendorf and German Pietism.

Christian History 1 (1982). The entire issue of this popular church history magazine is devoted to Zinzendorf and the Moravians. Includes chronological charts, short biographies of leading figures associated with Zinzendorf, and numerous illustrations. "The Rich Young Ruler Who Said Yes" is an excellent biographical sketch of Zinzendorf.

Freeman, Arthur J. *An Ecumenical Theology of the Heart: The Theology of Count Nicholas Ludwig von Zinzendorf.* Bethlehem, Pa.: Moravian Church in America, 1998. An interpretation of Zinzendorf's life and theology, containing the first English translations of many of his German writings. The book's title refers to Zinzendorf's belief that Christian faith consisted of an individual's personal relationship with God through Christ—a relationship that was known through the heart, not the mind.

Gollin, Gillian Lindt. *Moravians in Two Worlds: A Study of Changing Communities.* New York: Columbia University Press, 1967. Gollin provides an interesting history of two Moravian communities founded by Zinzendorf: Herrnhut, Germany, and Bethlehem, Pennsylvania. Using primary sources, Gollin attempts to explain the differing development of the two communities between 1722 and 1850, with respect to their religious, political, social, and economic institutions.

Langton, Edward. *History of the Moravian Church.* London: Allen & Unwin, 1956. A popular, illustrated survey of the history of the United Brethren Church from the time of Jan Hus through the death of Zinzendorf. Discusses the connections between the movement begun by followers of Hus, the revival under Zinzendorf, and the Methodist movement.

Lewis, A. J. *Zinzendorf: The Ecumenical Pioneer.* Philadelphia, Pa.: Westminster Press, 1962. The author was a Moravian minister in England. The book discusses Zinzendorf's efforts to unify Christians by igniting among them an interest in missionary and evangelistic work. Zinzendorf is portrayed as a forerunner of the twentieth century ecumenical movement.

Weinlick, John R. *Count Zinzendorf.* Nashville, Tenn.: Abingdon Press, 1956. The standard English-language biography of Zinzendorf. Illustrated and very well written.

See also: Charles Wesley; John Wesley.

Related articles in *Great Events from History: The Eighteenth Century, 1701-1800*: May, 1727-1733: Jansenist "Convulsionnaires" Gather at Saint-Médard; 1739-1742: First Great Awakening; October 30, 1768: Methodist Church Is Established in Colonial America; 1773-1788: African American Baptist Church Is Founded; July 28-October 16, 1789: Episcopal Church Is Established; 1790's-1830's: Second Great Awakening.

Appendixes

RULERS AND HEADS OF STATE

Major world leaders during and beyond the period covered in *Great Lives from History: The Eighteenth Century, 1701-1800* are listed below, beginning with the Roman Catholic popes and followed by rulers of major nations or dynasties, alphabetically by country. Within each country section, rulers are listed chronologically. It is important to note that name spellings and regnal dates vary among sources, and that variations do not necessarily suggest inaccuracy. For example, dates when leaders took power may not match dates of coronation, and the names by which leaders have been recorded in history may represent birth names, epithets, or regnal names. Date ranges and geographical borders of nations and dynasties vary, given the complexities of politics and warfare, and the mere fact that "nations" evolved over time from competing and allied principalities. Hence, not every civilization, dynasty, principality, or region can be covered here; we have, however, attempted to provide lists of rulers for those countries most likely to be addressed in general history and area studies courses.

Contents

POPES AND ANTIPOPES

Asterisked (*) names indicate popes who have been sainted by the Church. Names appearing in square brackets [ ] are antipopes.

Term	Pope
440-461	*Leo I the Great
461-468	*Hilarius
468-483	*Simplicius
483-492	*Felix III
492-496	*Gelasius I
496-498	Anastasius II
498-514	*Symmachus
498-505	[Laurentius]
514-523	*Hormisdas

Term	Pope
523-526	*John I
526-530	*Felix IV
530-532	Boniface II
530	[Dioscursus]
533-535	John II
535-536	*Agapetus I
536-537	*Silverius
537-555	Vigilius
556-561	Pelagius I
561-574	John III
575-579	Benedict I
579-590	Pelagius II
590-604	*Gregory I the Great

Term	Pope	Term	Pope
604-606	Sabinian	885-891	Stephen V
607	Boniface III	891-896	Formosus
608-615	*Boniface IV (Adeodatus I)	896	Boniface VI
615-618	*Deusdedit	896-897	Stephen VI
619-625	Boniface V	897	Romanus
625-638	Honorius I	897	Theodore II
638-640	Vacant	898-900	John IX
640	Severinus	900-903	Benedict IV
640-642	John IV	903	Leo V
642-649	Theodore I	903-904	Christopher
649-655	*Martin I	904-911	Sergius III
655-657	*Eugene I	911-913	Anastasius III
657-672	*Vitalian	913-914	Lando
672-676	Adeodatus II	914-928	John X
676-678	Donus	928	Leo VI
678-681	*Agatho	929-931	Stephen VII
682-683	*Leo II	931-935	John XI
684-685	*Benedict II	936-939	Leo VII
685-686	John V	939-942	Stephen IX (VIII)
686-687	Conon	942-946	Marinus II
687	[Theodore II]	946-955	Agapetus II
687-692	[Paschal I]	955-963	John XII
687-701	*Saint Sergius I	963-964	Leo VIII
701-705	John VI	964	Benedict V
705-707	John VII	965-972	John XIII
708	Sisinnius	973-974	Benedict VI
708-715	Constantine	974-983	Benedict VII
715-731	*Gregory II	983-984	John XIV
731-741	*Gregory III	984-985	[Boniface VII]
741-752	*Zachary	985-996	John XV
752-757	Stephen II	996-999	Gregory V
757-767	*Paul I	996-998	[John XVI]
767	[Constantine]	999-1003	Sylvester II
767	[Philip]	1003	John XVII
767-772	Stephen III	1003-1009	John XVIII
772-795	Adrian I	1009-1012	Sergius IV
795-816	*Leo III	1012-1024	Benedict VIII
816-817	Stephen IV	1012	[Gregory VI]
817-824	*Paschal I	1024-1033	John XIX
824-827	Eugene II	1033-1045	Benedict IX
827	Valentine	1045	Sylvester III
827-844	Gregory IV	1045-1046	Gregory VI (John Gratian Pierleoni)
844	[John VIII]	1046-1047	Clement II (Suitgar, count of Morslegen)
844-847	Sergius II	1048	Damasus II (Count Poppo)
847-855	*Leo IV	1049-1054	*Leo IX (Bruno of Egisheim)
855-858	Benedict III	1055-1057	Victor II (Gebhard, count of Hirschberg)
855	[Anastasius III]	1057-1058	Stephen IX (Frederick of Lorraine)
858-867	*Nicholas I the Great	1058	Benedict X (John, count of Tusculum)
867-872	Adrian II	1058-1061	Nicholas II (Gerhard of Burgundy)
872-882	John VIII	1061-1073	Alexander II (Anselmo da Baggio)
882-884	Marinus I	1061-1064	[Honorius II]
884-885	*Adrian III	1073-1085	*Gregory VII (Hildebrand)

Term	Pope
1080-1100	[Clement III]
1086-1087	Victor III (Desiderius, prince of Beneventum)
1088-1099	Urban II (Odo of Lagery)
1099-1118	Paschal II (Ranieri da Bieda)
1100-1102	[Theodoric]
1102	[Albert]
1105	[Sylvester IV]
1118-1119	Gelasius II (John Coniolo)
1118-1121	[Gregory VIII]
1119-1124	Callixtus II (Guido, count of Burgundy)
1124-1130	Honorius II (Lamberto dei Fagnani)
1124-1130	[Celestine II]
1130-1143	Innocent II (Gregorio Papareschi)
1130-1138	[Anacletus II (Cardinal Pierleone)]
1138	[Victor IV]
1143-1144	Celestine II (Guido di Castello)
1144-1145	Lucius II (Gherardo Caccianemici)
1145-1153	Eugene III (Bernardo Paganelli)
1153-1154	Anastasius IV (Corrado della Subarra)
1154-1159	Adrian IV (Nicolas Breakspear)
1159-1181	Alexander III (Roland Bandinelli)
1159-1164	[Victor IV]
1164-1168	[Paschal III]
1168-1178	[Calixtus III]
1179-1180	[Innocent III (Lando da Sessa)]
1181-1185	Lucius III (Ubaldo Allucingoli)
1185-1187	Urban III (Uberto Crivelli)
1187	Gregory VIII (Alberto del Morra)
1187-1191	Clement III (Paolo Scolari)
1191-1198	Celestine III (Giacinto Boboni-Orsini)
1198-1216	Innocent III (Lothario of Segni)
1216-1227	Honorius III (Cencio Savelli)
1227-1241	Gregory IX (Ugo of Segni)
1241	Celestine IV (Goffredo Castiglione)
1243-1254	Innocent IV (Sinibaldo Fieschi)
1254-1261	Alexander IV (Rinaldo di Segni)
1261-1264	Urban IV (Jacques Pantaléon)
1265-1268	Clement IV (Guy le Gros Foulques)
1268-1271	Vacant
1271-1276	Gregory X (Tebaldo Visconti)
1276	Innocent V (Pierre de Champagni)
1276	Adrian V (Ottobono Fieschi)
1276-1277	John XXI (Pietro Rebuli-Giuliani)
1277-1280	Nicholas III (Giovanni Gaetano Orsini)
1281-1285	Martin IV (Simon Mompitie)
1285-1287	Honorius IV (Giacomo Savelli)
1288-1292	Nicholas IV (Girolamo Masci)
1294	*Celestine V (Pietro Angelari da Murrone)
1294-1303	Boniface VIII (Benedict Caetani)
1303-1304	Benedict XI (Niccolò Boccasini)
1305-1314	Clement V (Raimond Bertrand de Got)
1316-1334	John XXII (Jacques Duèse)

Term	Pope
1328-1330	[Nicholas V (Pietro di Corbara)]
1334-1342	Benedict XII (Jacques Fournier)
1342-1352	Clement VI (Pierre Roger de Beaufort)
1352-1362	Innocent VI (Étienne Aubert)
1362-1370	Urban V (Guillaume de Grimord)
1370-1378	Gregory XI (Pierre Roger de Beaufort, the Younger)
1378-1389	Urban VI (Bartolomeo Prignano)
1378-1394	[Clement VII (Robert of Geneva)]
1389-1404	Boniface IX (Pietro Tomacelli)
1394-1423	[Benedict XIII (Pedro de Luna)]
1404-1406	Innocent VII (Cosmto de' Migliorati)
1406-1415	Gregory XII (Angelo Correr)
1409-1410	[Alexander V (Petros Philargi)]
1410-1415	[John XXIII (Baldassare Cossa)]
1415-1417	Vacant
1417-1431	Martin V (Ottone Colonna)
1423-1429	[Clement VIII]
1424	[Benedict XIV]
1431-1447	Eugene IV (Gabriele Condulmero)
1439-1449	[Felix V (Amadeus of Savoy)]
1447-1455	Nicholas V (Tommaso Parentucelli)
1455-1458	Calixtus III (Alfonso de Borgia)
1458-1464	Pius II (Enea Silvio Piccolomini)
1464-1471	Paul II (Pietro Barbo)
1471-1484	Sixtus IV (Francesco della Rovere)
1484-1492	Innocent VIII (Giovanni Battista Cibò)
1492-1503	Alexander VI (Rodrigo Borgia)
1503	Pius III (Francesco Todeschini Piccolomini)
1503-1513	Julius II (Giuliano della Rovere)
1513-1521	Leo X (Giovanni de' Medici)
1522-1523	Adrian VI (Adrian Florensz Boeyens)
1523-1534	Clement VII (Giulio de' Medici)
1534-1549	Paul III (Alessandro Farnese)
1550-1555	Julius III (Giovanni Maria Ciocchi del Monte)
1555	Marcellus II (Marcello Cervini)
1555-1559	Paul IV (Gian Pietro Carafa)
1559-1565	Pius IV (Giovanni Angelo de' Medici)
1566-1572	Pius V (Antonio Ghislieri)
1572-1585	Gregory XIII (Ugo Buoncompagni)
1585-1590	Sixtus V (Felice Peretti)
1590	Urban VII (Giambattista Castagna)
1590-1591	Gregory XIV (Niccolò Sfondrato)
1591	Innocent IX (Giovanni Antonio Facchinetti)
1592-1605	Clement VIII (Ippolito Aldobrandini)
1605	Leo XI (Alessandro de' Medici)
1605-1621	Paul V (Camillo Borghese)
1621-1623	Gregory XV (Alessandro Ludovisi)
1623-1644	Urban VIII (Maffeo Barberini)
1644-1655	Innocent X (Giovanni Battista Pamphili)
1655-1667	Alexander VII (Fabio Chigi)
1667-1669	Clement IX (Giulio Rospigliosi)

Term	Pope
1670-1676	Clement X (Emilio Altieri)
1676-1689	Innocent XI (Benedetto Odescalchi)
1689-1691	Alexander VIII (Pietro Ottoboni)
1691-1700	Innocent XII (Antonio Pignatelli)
1700-1721	Clement XI (Giovanni Francesco Albani)
1721-1724	Innocent XIII (Michelangelo Conti)
1724-1730	Benedict XIII (Pierfrancesco Orsini)
1730-1740	Clement XII (Lorenzo Corsini)hh
1740-1758	Benedict XIV (Prospero Lambertini)
1758-1769	Clement XIII (Carlo Rezzonico)
1769-1774	Clement XIV (Giovanni Ganganelli)
1775-1799	Pius VI (Giovanni Angelo Braschi)
1800-1823	Pius VII (Barnaba Gregorio Chiaramonti)
1823-1829	Leo XII (Annibale della Genga)
1829-1830	Pius VIII (Francesco Saverio Castiglioni)
1831-1846	Gregory XVI (Bartolomeo Cappellari)
1846-1878	Pius IX (Giovanni Mastai-Ferretti)
1878-1903	Leo XIII (Gioacchino Pecci)
1903-1914	Pius X (Giuseppe Sarto)
1914-1922	Benedict XV (Giacomo della Chiesa)
1922-1939	Pius XI (Achille Ratti)
1939-1958	Pius XII (Eugenio Pacelli)
1958-1963	John XXIII (Angelo Roncalli)
1963-1978	Paul VI (Giovanni Battista Montini)
1978	John Paul I (Albino Luciani)
1978-2005	John Paul II (Karol Wojtyla)
2005-	Benedict XVI (Joseph Ratzinger)

AFRICA. *See also* EGYPT

BENIN

Reign	Ruler
1200-1235	Eweke I
1235-1243	Uwakhuanhen
1243-1255	Ehenmihen
1255-1280	Ewedo
1280-1295	Oguola
1295-1299	Edoni
1299-1334	Udagbedo
1334-1370	Ohen
1370-1400	Egbeka
1400-1430	Orobiru
1430-1440	Uwaifiokun
c. 1440-1473	Ewuare the Great
1473	Ezoti (14 days)
1473-1480	Olua
1481-1504	Ozolua
c. 1504-1550	Esigie
1550-1578	Orhogbua
1578-1606	Ehengbuda
1606-1641	Ohuan

Reign	Ruler
1641-1661	Ahenzae
1661-1669	Ahenzae
1669-1675	Akengboi
1675-1684	Akenkpaye
1684-1689	Akengbedo
1689-1700	Oroghene
1700-1712	Ewuakpe
1712-1713	Ozuaere
1713-1735	Akenzua I
1735-1750	Eresonyen
1750-1804	Akengbuda
1804-1816	Obanosa
1816	Ogbebo (8 months)
1816-1848	Osomwende
1848-1888	Adolo
1888-1914	Ovonramwen
1914-1933	Eweka II
1933-1978	Akenzua II
1978-	Erediauwa

ETHIOPIA

The evidence for the succession of Ethiopian rulers is debated by scholars; here, the regnal dates reflect primarily the order of succession and vary widely among sources.

Early Kings

Reign	Ruler
c. 320-350	Ezana
c. 328-370	Shizana
c. 356	Ella Abreha
?	Ella Asfeha
?	Ella Shahel
474-475	Agabe
474-475	Levi
475-486	Ella Amida (IV?)
486-489	Jacob I
486-489	David
489-504	Armah I
504-505	Zitana
505-514	Jacob II
c. 500-542	Ella Asbeha (Caled)
542-c. 550	Beta Israel
c. 550-564	Gabra Masqal
?	Anaeb
?	Alamiris
?	Joel
?	Israel
?	Gersem I
?	Ella Gabaz
?	Ella Saham
c. 625	Armah II
?	Iathlia
?	Hataz I

Reign	Ruler
?	Wazena
?	Za Ya'abiyo
?	Armah III
?	Hataz II
?	Gersem II
?	Hataz III

Zagwe Dynasty

Reign	Ruler
c. 1137-1152	Mara Tekle Haimanot
c. 1152-1181	Yimrehane-Kristos
c. 1181-1221	Lalibela
c. 1221-1260	Na 'akuto La 'ab
c. 1260-1270	Yitbarek (Yetbarek)
1270	Solomonid Dynasty begins; reign of Yekuno Amlak

Solomonid Dynasty

Reign	Ruler
1270-1285	Yekuno Amlak
1285-1294	Solomon I
1294-1297	Bahr Asgad
1294-1297	Senfa Asgad
1297-1299	Qedma Asgad
1297-1299	Jin Asgad
1297-1299	Saba Asgad
1299-1314	Wedem Arad
1314-1344	Amade Tseyon I
1344-1372	Newaya Krestos
1372-1382	Newaya Maryam
1382-1411	Dawit (David) I
1411-1414	Tewodros (Theodore) I
1414-1429	Isaac
1429-1430	Andrew
1430-1433	Takla Maryam
1433	Sarwe Iyasus
1433-1434	Amda Iyasus
1434-1468	Zara Yacob (Constantine I)
1468-1478	Baeda Mariam I
1478-1484	Constantine II
1494	Amade Tseyon II
1494-1508	Naod
1508-1540	Lebna Dengel (David II)
1529	Battle of Shimbre-Kune
1540-1559	Galawedos (Claudius)
1543	Battle of Lake Tana (defeat of Muslims)

Later Rulers

Reign	Ruler
1560-1564	Menas
1564-1597	Sarsa Dengel
1597-1603	Jacob
1603-1604	Za Dengel

Reign	Ruler
1604-1607	Jacob
1607-1632	Susneyos (Sissinios)
1632-1667	Fasilidas (Basilides)
1667-1682	Yohannes (John) I
1682-1706	Iyasu (Jesus) I the Great
1706-1708	Tekle Haimanot I
1708-1711	Tewoflos (Theophilus)
1711-1716	Yostos (Justus)
1716-1721	Dawit (David) III
1721-1730	Bekaffa
1730-1755	Iyasu II
1755-1769	Iyoas (Joas) I
1769	Yohannes II
1769-1777	Tekle Haimanot II
1777-1779	Salomon (Solomon) II
1779-1784	Tekle Giorgis I (first)
1784-1788	Jesus III
1788	Ba'eda Maryam I
1788-1789	Tekle Giorgis I (second)
1789-1794	Hezekiah
1794-1795	Tekle Giorgis I (third)
1795	Ba'eda Maryam II
1795-1796	Tekle Giorgis I (fourth)
1796-1797	Solomon III
1797-1799	Tekle Giorgis I (fifth)
1799	Solomon III
1799-1800	Demetrius
1800	Tekle Giorgis I (sixth)
1800-1801	Demetrius
1801-1818	Egwala Seyon
1818-1821	Joas II
1821-1826	Gigar
1826	Ba'eda Maryam III
1826-1830	Gigar
1830-1832	Jesus IV
1832	Gabra Krestos
1832-1840	Sahla Dengel (first)
1840-1841	Yohannes III
1841-1855	Sahla Dengel (second)
1855-1868	Tewodros II
1868-1872	Tekle Giorgis II
1872-1889	Yohannes IV
1875-1876	Egyptians defeated
1889-1913	Menelik II
1896	Italians defeated
1909-1916	Lij Iyasu (regent)
1916-1930	Empress Zawditu
1916-1930	Haile Sellassie
1930-1936	Italian occupation
1936-1941	Victor Emmanuel (III of Italy)
1941-1974	Haile Sellassie (restored)
1974	Aman Mikael Andom

Reign	Ruler
1974-1977	Tafari Benti
1977-1991	Mengistu Haile Mariam
1991-1995	Meles Zenawi
1995-	Negasso Gidada

KONGO

Reign	Ruler
Before 1482-1506	João I (Nzinga Nkuwu)
1506-1543	Afonso I (Nzinga Mbemba)
1543-1545	Peter I
1545-1545	Francis I
1545-1561	Diogo I
1561-1561	Affonso II
1561-1566	Bernard I
1566-1567	Henry I
1568-1587	Alvare I
1587-1614	Alvare II
1614-1615	Bernard II
1615-1622	Alvare III
1622-1624	Peter II
1624-1626	Garcia I
1626-1631	Ambrosio
1631-1636	Alvaro IV
1636-1636	Alvaro V
1636-1642	Alvaro VI
1642-1661	Garcia II
1661-1665	Antonio I
1665	Battle of Mbwila, decline of independent Kingdom of Kongo

MOROCCO

Almoravids

Reign	Ruler
1061-1106	Yūsuf ibn Tāshufīn
1107-1142	ʿAlī ibn Yūsuf
1142-1146	Tāshufīn ibn ʿAlī
1146	Ibrāhīm ibn Tāshufīn
1146-1147	Isḥāq ibn ʿAlī

Almohads

Reign	Ruler
To 1130	Ibn Tūmart
1130-1163	ʿAbd al-Muʾmin
1163-1184	Yūsuf I Abū Yaʿqūb
1184-1199	Yaʿqūb Yūsuf al-Manṣūr
1199-1213	Muḥammad ibn Yaʿqūb
1213-1224	Yūsuf II Abū Yaʿqūb
1224	ʿAbdul Wāḥid I
1224-1227	ʿAbdallah Abū Muḥammad
1227-1235	Yaḥyā Abū Zakariyyāʾ
1227-1232	Idrīs I ibn Yaʿqūb
1232-1242	ʿAbd al-Wāḥid ibn Idrīs I

Reign	Ruler
1242-1248	ʿAlī ibn Idrīs I
1248-1266	ʿUmar ibn Isḥāq
1266-1269	Idrīs II ibn Muḥammad
After 1269	Dissolution; power divided among Marīnids, Ḥafṣids, and Zayyānids

Marīnids

Reign	Ruler
1269-1286	Abū Yūsuf Yaʿqūb
1286-1307	Abū Yaʿqūb Yūsuf al-Nasīr
1307-1308	Abū Tabit
1308-1310	Abū Rabia
1310-1331	Abū Said Othman (Osman ibn Yaʿqūb)
1331-1348	Abū al-Hasan
1348-1358	Abū Inan Faris
1358-1361	Vacant
1361-1366	Moḥammad ibn Yaʿqūb
1366-1372	ʿAbd al-Aziz I
1372-1384	Vacant
1384-1387	Mūsā ibn al-Fers
1387-1393	ʿAbu al-ʿAbbās
1393-1396	ʿAbd al-Aziz II
1396-1398	Abdallah
1398-1421	Osman III
1421-1465	ʿAbd al-Haqq

Wattasides

Reign	Ruler
1472-1504	Moḥammad al-Saih al-Mahdi
1505-1524	Abū Abdallah Moḥammad
1524-1550	Abul ʿAbbās Aḥmad

Saʿdīs (Cherifians)

Reign	Ruler
1510-1517	Muḥammad al-Qāʿim
1517-1544	Aḥmad al-Aʿraj
1544-1557	Muḥammad I al-Shaykh
1557-1574	Abdallah al-Ghālib
1574-1576	Muḥammad al-Mutawakkil
1576-1578	ʿAbd al-Malik
1578	Battle of the Three Kings
1578-1603	Aḥmad al-Manṣūr
1603-1607	ʿAbd al ʿAbd Allah Moḥammad III
1607-1628	Zaidan al-Nāṣir
1628-1631	Abū Marwan ʿAbd al-Malik II
1631-1636	al-Walīd
1636-1654	Moḥammad IV
1654-1659	Aḥmad II
1659-1665	War

Alawis

Reign	Ruler
1666-1672	Rashid ben Ali Cherif (founder)
1672-1727	Ismael ben Ali Cherif

Reign	Ruler
1727-1729	Civil war
1729-1757	Abdallah
1757-1790	Mohamed III
1790-1792	Yazid
1792-1822	Suleiman
1822-1859	Abdelrahman
1859-1873	Mohamed IV
1873-1894	Hassan I
1894-1908	Aziz
1908-1912	Hafid

SONGHAI

Reign	Ruler
c. 1464-1492	Sonni ʿAlī
1493	Sonni Baru
1493-1528	Mohammed I Askia (Mohammed Ture)
1528-1531	Askia Mūsā
1549-1582	Askia Daud
1588-1591	Askia Ishak II

AMERICAS. *See also* THE UNITED STATES

MAYA KINGS OF TIKAL

The Maya, who occupied the region of Central America from the Yucatán to Guatemala, maintained several centers in the region, but one, Tikal, recorded in Mayan glyphs a line of kings for nearly eight hundred years, roughly corresponding to the Classic Period now considered by scholars to be the height of Mayan civilization. The list below is from Chronicle *of the* Maya Kings and Queens, *by Simon Martin and Nikolai Grube (New York: Thames and Hudson, 2000).*

Reign	Ruler
c. 90-150	Yax Ehb Xook (First Step Shark)
c. 307	Siyaj Chan K'awiil I
d. 317	Ix Une Balam (Baby Jaguar)
d. 359	K'inich Muwaan Jol
360-378	Chak Tok Ich'aak I (Great Jaguar Paw)
378-404	Nuun Yax Ayiin I (Curl Snout)
411-456	Siyaj Chan K'awiil II (Stormy Sky)
458-c. 486	K'an Chitam
c. 486-508	Chak Tok Ich'aak II
c. 511-527	Kaloomte' B'alam
537-562	Wak Chan Ka'awiil
c. 593-628	Animal Skull
c. 657-679	Nuun Ujol Chaak
682-734	Jasaw Chan K'awiil I
734-746	Yik'in Chan K'awiil
768-794	Yax Nuun Ayiin II
c. 800	Nuun Ujol K'inich
c. 810	Dark Sun
c. 849	Jewel K'awiil

Reign	Ruler
c. 869	Jasaw Chan K'awiil II
c. 900	End of Mayan Classic Period

AZTEC KINGS OF TENOCHTITLÁN (MEXICO)

Reign	Ruler
Legendary	Ténoch (founder)
1375-1395	Acamapichtili
1395-1417	Huitzilíhuitl
1417-1427	Chimalpopoca
1427-1440	Itzcóatl
1440-1469	Montezuma (Moctezuma) I
1469-1481	Axayacatl
1481-1486	Tízoc
1486-1502	Ahuitzotl (Auítzotl)
1502-1520	Montezuma (Moctezuma) II
1520	Cuitláhuac
1520-1521	Cuauhtémoc

INCAS (PERU)

Reign	Ruler
c. 1200	Manco Capac I
?	Sinchi Roca
?	Lloque Yupanqui
?	Mayta Capac
?	Capac Yupanqui
?	Inca Roca
?	Yahuar Huacac
?	Viracocha
1438-1471	Pachacuti
1471-1493	Topa
1493-1525	Huayna Capac
1525-1532	Huáscar
1525-1533	Atahualpa
1532-1533	Spanish conquest (Pizzaro)
1533	Manco Capac II
1544-1561	Sayri Tupac
1561-1571	Titu Cusi
1571	Tupac Amaru I

AUSTRIA. *See* HOLY ROMAN EMPIRE

BOHEMIA. *See also* HUNGARY, POLAND

PŘEMYSLIDS

Reign	Ruler
c. 870-888/889	Borivoj I
894/895-915	Spytihnev I
915-921	Vratislav I
921-935	Duke Wenceslaus I
935-972	Boleslaus I the Cruel

Reign	Ruler
972-999	Boleslaus II the Pious
999-1002	Boleslaus III
1002-1003	Vladivoj
1003	Boleslaus III
1003	Jaromir
1003	Boleslaus III
1003-1004	Boleslaus I (nondynastic Piast)
1004-1012	Jaromir
1012-1033	Oldrich
1033-1034	Jaromir
1034	Oldrich
1035-1055	Bretislav I
1055-1061	Spytihnev II
1061-1092	Vratislav II
1092	Konrad I
1092-1100	Bretislav II
1101-1107	Borivoj II
1107-1109	Svatopluk
1109-1117	Vladislav I
1117-1120	Borivoj II
1120-1125	Vladislav I
1125-1140	Sobeslav I
1140-1172	Vladislav II
1172-1173	Bedrich
1173-1178	Sobeslav II
1178-1189	Bedrich
1189-1191	Konrad II Ota
1191-1192	Duke Wenceslaus II
1192-1193	Ottokar I
1193-1197	Jindrich Bretislav
1197	Vladislav Jindrich
1197-1230	Ottokar I
1230-1253	King Wenceslaus I
1253-1278	Ottokar II
1278-1305	King Wenceslaus II
1305-1306	King Wenceslaus III
1306	Henry of Carinthia (nondynastic)
1306-1307	Rudolph I of Habsburg (nondynastic)
1307-1310	Henry of Carinthia (nondynastic)

LUXEMBOURGS

Reign	Ruler
1310-1346	John of Luxembourg
1346-1378	Charles I
1378-1419	Wenceslaus IV
1419-1420	Sigismund
1420-1436	Hussite wars
1436-1437	Sigismund

HABSBURGS

Reign	Ruler
1437-1439	Albert of Habsburg

Reign	Ruler
1439-1457	Ladislas I (V of Hungary)
1458-1471	George of Podebrady (nondynastic)
1469-1490	Matthias Corvinus (antiking)

JAGIEŁŁOS

Reign	Ruler
1471-1516	Vladislav (Ladislaus) II
1516-1526	Louis

HABSBURGS

Reign	Ruler
1526-1564	Ferdinand I
1564-1575	Maximilian
1575-1611	Rudolf II
1612-1619	Matthias
1619	Ferdinand II
1619-1620	Frederick, Elector Palatine (Wittelsbach)
1620-1637	Ferdinand II
1627-1657	Ferdinand III
1646-1654	Ferdinand IV
1656-1705	Leopold I
1705-1711	Joseph I
1711-1740	Charles II
1740-1780	Maria Theresa

HABSBURG-LOTHRINGENS

Reign	Ruler
1780-1790	Joseph II
1790-1792	Leopold II
1792-1835	Francis
1835-1848	Ferdinand V
1848-1916	Francis Joseph
1916-1918	Charles III

BULGARIA

EARLY BULGARIA

Reign	Czar
c. 681-701	Asparukh
c. 701-c. 718	Tervel
c. 718-750	Sevar
750-762	Kormesios
762-763	Vinekh
762-763	Teletz
763	Umar
763-765	Baian
765	Tokt
c. 765-777	Telerig
c. 777-c. 803	Kardam
c. 803-814	Krum
814-815	Dukum

Reign	Czar
814-816	Ditzveg
814-831	Omurtag
831-836	Malamir (Malomir)
836-852	Presijan
852-889	Boris I
865	Boris converts to Christianity
889-893	Vladimir
893-927	Simeon I the Great
927-969	Peter I
969-972	Boris II
971	Bulgaria conquered by John I Tzimisces
971-1018	Dissolution, instability
1018	Basil II annexes Bulgaria to Macedonia

Asen Line

Reign	Czar
1186	Bulgarian Independence
1186-1196	John I Asen
1196-1197	Peter II Asen
1197-1207	Kalojan Asen
1207-1218	Boril
1218-1241	John II Asen
1242	Mongol invasion
1242-1246	Kaloman I
1246-1257	Michael II Asen
1257-1258	Kaloman II
1257-1277	Constantine Tich
1277-1279	Ivalio
1278-c. 1264	Ivan Mytzes
1279-1284?	John III Asen
c. 1280	Terter takeover

Terter Line

Reign	Czar
1280-1292	George I Terter
1285	Mongol vassal
1292-1295/8	Smilech
1295/8-1298/9	Caka (Tshaka)
1298/9-1322	Theodore Svetoslav
1322-1323	George II

Shishmans

Reign	Czar
1323-1330	Michael III Shishman
1330-1331	John IV Stephan
1331-1371	John V Alexander
1355-1371	John Sracimir
1360-1393	John VI Shishman
1385-1396	Decline
1396-1879	Ottoman rule

Modern Era

Reign	Ruler
1879-1886	Alexander I Joseph
1887-1918	Ferdinand of Bulgaria (Saxe-Coburg-Gotha)
1918-1943	Boris III
1943-1946	Simeon II

Byzantine Empire

Reign	Emperor or Empress
330-337	Constantine I the Great
337-361	Constantius
361-363	Julian the Apostate
363-364	Jovian
364-378	Valens
379-395	Theodosius I the Great
395-408	Arcadius
408-450	Theodosius II
450-457	Marcian
457-474	Leo I the Great
474	Leo II
474-475	Zeno
475-476	Basiliscus
476-491	Zeno (restored)
491-518	Anastasius I
518-527	Justin I
527-548	Theodora
527-565	Justinian I the Great
565-578	Justin II
578-582	Tiberius II Constantinus
582-602	Maurice
602-610	Phocas
610-641	Heraclius
641	Constantine III and Heracleonas
641-668	Constans II Pogonatus
668-685	Constantine IV
685-695	Justinian II Rhinotmetus
695-698	Leontius
698-705	Tiberius III
705-711	Justinian II (restored)
711-713	Philippicus Bardanes
713-715	Anastasius II
716-717	Theodosius III
717-741	Leo III the Isaurian (the Syrian)
741-775	Constantine V Copronymus
775-780	Leo IV the Khazar
780-797	Constantine VI
797-802	Saint Irene
802-811	Nicephorus I
811	Stauracius
811-813	Michael I
813-820	Leo V the Armenian
820-829	Michael II the Stammerer

Reign	Emperor or Empress
829-842	Theophilus
842-867	Michael III the Drunkard
867-886	Basil I the Macedonian
886-912	Leo VI the Wise (the Philosopher)
912-913	Alexander
913-919	Constantine VII Porphyrogenitus (Macedonian)
919-944	Romanus I Lecapenus (Macedonian)
944-959	Constantine VII (restored)
959-963	Romanus II (Macedonian)
963	Basil II Bulgaroktonos (Macedonian)
963-969	Nicephorus II Phocas (Macedonian)
969-976	John I Tzimisces
976-1025	Basil II (restored)
1025-1028	Constantine VIII (Macedonian)
1028-1034	Zoë and Romanus III Argyrus (Macedonian)
1034-1041	Zoë and Michael IV the Paphlagonian (Macedonian)
1041-1042	Zoë and Michael V Calaphates (Macedonian)
1042	Zoë and Theodora (Macedonian)
1042-1050	Zoë, Theodora, and Constantine IX Monomachus (Macedonian)
1050-1055	Theodora and Constantine IX (Macedonian)
1055-1056	Theodora (Macedonian)
1056-1057	Michael VI Stratioticus
1057-1059	Isaac I Comnenus
1059-1067	Constantine X Ducas
1067-1068	Michael VII Ducas (Parapinaces)
1068-1071	Romanus IV Diogenes
1071-1078	Michael VII Ducas (restored)
1078-1081	Nicephorus III Botaniates
1081-1118	Alexius I Comnenus
1118-1143	John II Comnenus
1143-1180	Manuel I Comnenus
1180-1183	Alexius II Comnenus
1183-1185	Andronicus I Comnenus
1185-1195	Isaac II Angelus
1195-1203	Alexius III Angelus
1203-1204	Isaac II (restored) and Alexius IV Angelus
1204	Alexius V Ducas
1204-1205	Baldwin I
1206-1222	Theodore I Lascaris
1222-1254	John III Vatatzes or Ducas
1254-1258	Theodore II Lascaris
1258-1261	John IV Lascaris
1259-1282	Michael VIII Palaeologus
1282-1328	Andronicus II Palaeologus
1328-1341	Andronicus III Palaeologus
1341-1376	John V Palaeologus
1347-1355	John VI Cantacuzenus (usurper)
1376-1379	Andronicus IV Palaeologus

Reign	Emperor or Empress
1379-1391	John V Palaeologus (restored)
1390	John VII Palaeologus (usurper)
1391-1425	Manuel II Palaeologus
1399-1412	John VII Palaeologus (restored as coemperor)
1425-1448	John VIII Palaeologus
1449-1453	Constantine XI Palaeologus
1453	Fall of Constantinople to the Ottomans

CHINA

SUI DYNASTY

Reign	Ruler
581-604	Wendi
604-617	Yangdi
618	Gongdi

TANG DYNASTY

Reign	Ruler
618-626	Gaozu (Li Yuan)
627-649	Taizong
650-683	Gaozong
684	Zhonggong
684-690	Ruizong
690-705	Wu Hou
705-710	Zhongzong
710-712	Ruizong
712-756	Xuanzong
756-762	Suzong
762-779	Daizong
779-805	Dezong
805	Shunzong
805-820	Xianzong
820-824	Muzong
824-827	Jingzong
827-840	Wenzong
840-846	Wuzong
846-859	Xuanzong
859-873	Yizong
873-888	Xizong
888-904	Zhaozong
904-907	Aizong

LIAO DYNASTY

Reign	Ruler
907-926	Abaoji (Taizu)
926-947	Deguang (Taizong)
947-951	Shizong
951-969	Muzong
969-982	Jingzong
982-1031	Shengzong

Reign	Ruler
1031-1055	Xingzong
1055-1101	Daozong
1101-1125	Tianzuodi

WESTERN LIAO DYNASTY

Reign	Ruler
1125-1144	Dezong
1144-1151	Empress Gantian
1151-1164	Renzong
1164-1178	Empress Chengtian
1178-1211	The Last Ruler

JIN DYNASTY

Reign	Ruler
1115-1123	Aguda (Wanyan Min; Taizu)
1123-1135	Taizong (Wanyan Sheng)
1135-1149	Xizong
1150-1161	Wanyan Liang, king of Hailing
1161-1190	Shizong
1190-1209	Zhangzong
1209-1213	Wanyan Yongji, king of Weishao
1213-1224	Xuanzong
1224-1234	Aizong
1234	The Last Emperor

NORTHERN SONG DYNASTY

Reign	Ruler
960-976	Taizu (Zhao Kuangyin)
976-997	Taizong
998-1022	Zhenzong
1022-1063	Renzong
1064-1067	Yingzong
1068-1085	Shenzong
1086-1101	Zhezong
1101-1125	Huizong
1125-1126	Qinzong

SOUTHERN SONG DYNASTY

Reign	Ruler
1127-1162	Gaozong
1163-1190	Xiaozong
1190-1194	Guangzong
1195-1224	Ningzong
1225-1264	Lizong
1265-1274	Duzong
1275-1275	Gongdi
1276-1278	Duanzong
1279	Bing Di

YUAN DYNASTY. *See also* MONGOLS

Reign	Ruler
1279-1294	Kublai Khan (Shizu)
1294-1307	Temür Oljeitu (Chengzong)
1308-1311	Khaishan (Wuzong)
1311-1320	Ayurbarwada (Renzong)
1321-1323	Shidelbala (Yingzong)
1323-1328	Yesun Temür (Taiding)
1328-1329	Tugh Temür (Wenzong Tianshundi)
1329	Tugh Khoshila (Mingzong)
1329-1332	Tugh Temür (Wenzong)
1333-1368	Toghon Temür (Shundi)
1368	Ming Dynasty begins: Hongwu

MING DYNASTY

Reign	Ruler
1368-1398	Hongwu (Zhu Yuanzhang)
1399-1402	Jianwen (Zhu Yunwen)
1402-1424	Yonglo (Zhu Di)
1424-1425	Hongxi
1426-1435	Xuande
1436-1449	Zhengtong
1449-1457	Jingtai
1457-1464	Tianshun
1465-1487	Chenghua (Xianzong)
1488-1505	Hongzhi (Xiaozong)
1505-1521	Zhengde
1522-1567	Jiajing
1567-1572	Longqing
1573-1620	Wanli
1620	Taichang
1621-1627	Tianqi
1628-1644	Chongzhen

SOUTHERN MING DYNASTY

Reign	Ruler
1644-1645	Fu (Hongguang)
1645-1646	Tang (Longwu)
1645	Lu (Luh)
1645-1653	Lu (Lou)
1646	Tang (Shaowu)
1646-1662	Gui (Yongli)

QING (MANCHU) DYNASTY

Reign	Ruler
1616-1626	Nurhachi
1626-1643	Hong Taiji
1643-1661	Shunzi
1644	Occupation of China; defeat of the Ming
1661-1722	Kangxi
1722-1735	Yongzheng
1735-1796	Qianlong
1796-1820	Jiaqing

Reign	Ruler
1820-1850	Daoguang
1850-1861	Xianfeng
1861-1875	Tongzhi
1875-1908	Guangxu
1908-1924	Puyi

REPUBLIC OF CHINA: PRESIDENTS

Reign	Ruler
1911-1912	Sun Yat-sen
1912-1916	Yüan Shih-k'ai
1916-1917	Li Yüan-hung
1917-1918	Feng Kuo-chang
1918-1922	Hsü Shih-ch'ang
1922-1923	Li Yüan-hung
1923	Tsao Kun
1924	Tuan Chi-jui
1923-1925	Sun Yat-sen (Nanking government)
1948-1975	Chiang Kai-shek
1975-1988	Chiang Ching-kuo
1988-2000	Lee Teng-hui
2000-	Chen Shui-bian

PEOPLE'S REPUBLIC OF CHINA (COMMUNIST CHINA)

Term	Prime Minister
1949-1976	Zhou Enlai (Mao Zedong, Communist Party chair)
1976-1980	Hua Guofeng
1980-1987	Zhao Ziyang
1987-1998	Li Peng
1998-2003	Zhu Rongji
2003-	Wen Jiabao

Term	President
1959-1968	Liu Shaoqi
1968-1975	Dong Biwu
1975-1976	Zhu De
1976-1978	Song Qingling
1978-1983	Ye Jianying
1983-1988	Li Xiannian
1988-1993	Yang Shangkun
1989-2003	Jian Zemin
2003-	Hu Jintao

DENMARK. *See also* NORWAY, SWEDEN

Reign	Ruler
588-647	Ivar Vidfamne
647-735?	Harald I Hildetand
735-750?	Sigurd I Ring (poss. 770-812)
c. 750	Randver
850-854	Horik I
c. 854-?	Horik II

Reign	Ruler
c. 860-865	Ragnar Lobrok
865-873	Sigurd II Snogoje
873-884	Hardeknut I
884-885	Frodo
885-889	Harald II
c. 900-950	Gorm
c. 950-985	Harald III Bluetooth
985-1014	Sweyn I Forkbeard
1014-1019	Harald IV
1019-1035	Canute I (III) the Great
1035-1042	Hardeknut
1042-1047	Magnus the Good
1047-1074	Sweyn II
1074-1080	Harald V Hen
1080-1086	Canute II (IV) the Holy
1086-1095	Olaf IV the Hungry
1095-1103	Eric I the Evergood
1103-1134	Niels Elder
1134-1137	Eric II
1137-1146	Eric III
1146-1157	Sweyn III
1147-1157	Canute III (V) Magnussen
1157-1182	Valdemar I the Great
1182-1202	Canute IV (VI) the Pious
1202-1241	Valdemar II the Victorious
1241-1250	Eric IV
1250-1252	Abel
1252-1259	Christopher I
1259-1286	Eric V
1286-1319	Eric VI
1320-1326	Christopher II
1326-1330	Instability
1330-1332	Christopher II (restored)
1332-1340	Instability
1340-1375	Valdemar III
1376-1387	Olaf V (or II; IV of Norway)
1380	Unification of Denmark and Norway
1376-1412	Margaret I of Denmark, Norway, and Sweden
1397	Unification of Norway, Denmark, and Sweden
1412-1439	Eric VII (III of Norway, XIII of Sweden)
1439-1448	Christopher III

HOUSE OF OLDENBURG

Reign	Ruler
1448-1481	Christian I
1481-1513	John (Hans)
1523	Sweden leaves Kalmar Union
1523-1533	Frederick I
1523-1536	Union with Norway
1534-1559	Christian III
1559-1588	Frederick II

Reign	Ruler
1588-1648	Christian IV
1648-1670	Frederick III
1670-1699	Christian V
1699-1730	Frederick IV
1730-1746	Christian VI
1746-1766	Frederick V
1766-1808	Christian VII
1808-1839	Frederick VI
1839-1848	Christian VIII
1848-1863	Frederick VII

Schleswig-Holstein-Sonderburg-Glücksburg

Reign	Ruler
1863-1906	Christian IX
1906-1912	Frederik VIII
1912-1947	Christian X
1947-1972	Frederik IX
1972	Margrethe II

EGYPT

After the rise of Islam in the seventh century, Egypt was Islamicized and came under the control of a succession of emirs and caliphs.

Tulunid Emirs

Reign	Ruler
868-884	Aḥmad ibn Ṭūlūn
884-896	Khumārawayh
896	Jaysh
896-904	Hārūn
904-905	Shaybān
905	Recovered by Abbasids

Ikhshidid Emirs

Reign	Ruler
935-946	Muḥammad ibn Ṭughj al-Ikhshīd
946-961	Unūjūr
961-966	ʿAlī
966-968	Kāfūr al-Lābī (regent)
968-969	Aḥmad
969	Fāṭimid conquest

Fāṭimid Caliphs in Egypt

Reign	Ruler
975-996	al-ʿAzīz
996-1021	al-Ḥākim
1021-1036	al-Zāhir
1036-1094	al-Mustanṣir
1094-1101	al-Mustadī
1101-1130	al-Amīr
1130-1149	al-Ḥāfiz

Reign	Ruler
1149-1154	al-Zafīr
1154-1160	al-Fāʾiz
1160-1171	al-ʿAdīd

Ayyūbid Sultans

Reign	Ruler
1169-1193	Saladin
1193-1198	al-ʿAzīz Imad al-Dīn
1198-1200	al-Mansūr Naṣir al-Dīn
1200-1218	al-ʿAdil I Sayf al-Dīn
1202-1204	Fourth Crusade
1217-1221	Fifth Crusade
1218-1238	al-Kāmil I Nāṣir al-Dīn
1227-1230	Sixth Crusade
1238-1240	al-ʿAdil II Sayf al-Dīn
1240-1249	al-Ṣāliḥ II Najm al-Dīn
1249-1250	al-Muʿaẓẓam Tūrān-Shāh Ghiyāt al-Dīn
1248-1254	Seventh (or Eighth) Crusade
1252	Cairo seized by Mamlūks

Mamlūk Sultans

Baḥrī Line (Mongol, then Turkish)

Reign	Ruler
1252-1257	Aybak al-Turkumānī
1257-1259	ʿAlī I
1259-1260	Quṭuz al-Muʿizzī
1260-1277	Baybars I (defeats Mongols 1260)
1277-1279	Baraka (Berke) Khān
1279	Salāmish (Süleymish)
1279-1290	Qalāʾūn al-Alfī
1290-1293	Khalīl
1291	Fall of Acre
1293	Baydarā (?)
1293-1294	Muḥammad I
1294-1296	Kitbughā
1296-1299	Lāchīn (Lājīn) al-Ashqar
1299-1309	Muḥammad I
1303	Earthquake destroys Pharos lighthouse
1309-1310	Baybars II al-Jāshnakīr (Burjī)
1310-1341	Muḥammad I
1341	Abū Bakr
1341-1342	Kūjūk (Küchük)
1342	Aḥmad I
1342-1345	Ismāʿīl
1345-1346	Shaʿbān I
1346-1347	Ḥājjī I
1347-1351	al-Ḥasan
1351-1354	Ṣāliḥ
1354-1361	al-Ḥasan
1361-1363	Muḥammad II
1363-1377	Shaʿbān II
1377-1382	ʿAlī II

Reign	Ruler
1382	Ḥājjī II
1389-1390	Ḥājjī II

Burjī (Circassian) line

Reign	Ruler
1382-1398	Barqūq al-Yalburghāwī
1399-1405	Faraj
1405	ʿAbd al-ʿAzīz
1405-1412	Faraj (second rule)
1412	al-Mustaʿīn
1412-1421	Shaykh al-Maḥmūdī al-Ẓāhirī
1421	Aḥmad II
1421	Ṭāṭar
1421-1422	Muḥammad III
1422-1438	Barsbay
1438	Yūsuf
1438-1453	Chaqmaq (Jaqmaq)
1453	ʿUthmān
1453-1461	Ināl al-ʿAlāʾī al-Ẓāhirī
1461	Aḥmad III
1461-1467	Khushqadam
1467	Yalbay
1467-1468	Timurbughā
1468-1496	Qāyit Bay (Qāytbāy) al-Ẓāhirī
1496-1498	Muḥammad IV
1498-1500	Qānṣawh I
1500-1501	Jānbulāṭ
1501	Ṭūmān Bay I
1501-1516	Qānṣawh II al-Ghawrī
1516-1517	Ṭūmān Bay II
1517	Ottoman conquest

ʿABBĀSID CALIPHS OF EGYPT

Unlike the earlier ʿAbbāsid line (see Islamic Caliphs, below), these were ʿAbbāsid figureheads in place under the Mamlūks.

Reign	Ruler
1261	Aḥmad al-Mustanṣir
1261-1302	Aḥmad al-Ḥākim I (Aleppo 1261-1262, Cairo, 1262-1302)
1302-1340	Sulaymān al-Mustakfī I
1340-1341	Ibrāhīm al-Wāthiq I
1341-1352	Aḥmad al-Ḥakīm II
1352-1362	Abū Bakr al-Muʿtaḍid I
1362-1377	Muḥammad al-Mutawakkil I
1377	Zakariyyāʾ al-Muʿtaṣim
1377-1383	Muḥammad al-Mutawakkil I
1383-1386	ʿUmar al-Wāthiq II
1386-1389	Zakariyyāʾ al-Muʿtaṣim
1389-1406	Muḥammad al-Mutawakkil I
1406-1414	Sulṭān
1412	ʿAbbās or Yaʿqūb al-Mustaʿīn
1414-1441	Dāwūd al-Muʿtaḍid II
1441-1451	Sulaymān al-Mustakfī II

Reign	Ruler
1451-1455	Ḥamza al-Qāʾim
1455-1479	Yūsuf al-Mustanjid
1479-1497	ʿAbd al-ʿAzīz al-Mutawakkil II
1497-1508	Yaʿqūb al-Mustamsik
1508-1516	al-Mutawakkil III
1516-1517	Yaʿqūb al-Mustamsik
1517	Ottoman conquest

ENGLAND

ANGLO-SAXONS (HOUSE OF WESSEX)

Reign	Ruler
802-839	Egbert
839-856	Æthelwulf
856-860	Æthelbald
860-866	Æthelbert
866-871	Ethelred (Æthelred) I
871-899	Alfred the Great
899-924	Edward the Elder (with sister Æthelflæd)
924-939	Æthelstan
939-946	Edmund the Magnificent
946-955	Eadred
955-959	Eadwig (Edwy) All-Fair
959-975	Edgar the Peaceable
975-978	Edward the Martyr
978-1016	Ethelred (Æthelred) II the Unready
1016	Edmund II Ironside

DANES

Reign	Ruler
1016-1035	Canute (Knud) the Great
1035-1040	Harold I Harefoot
1040-1042	Harthacnut

WESSEX (RESTORED)

Reign	Ruler
1043-1066	Edward the Confessor
1066	Harold II

NORMANS

Reign	Ruler
1066-1087	William I the Conqueror
1087-1100	William II Rufus
1100-1135	Henry I Beauclerc
1135-1154	Stephen

PLANTAGENETS: ANGEVINS

Reign	Ruler
1154-1189	Henry II (with Eleanor of Aquitaine, r. 1154-1189)
1189-1199	Richard I the Lion-Hearted

Reign	Ruler
1199-1216	John I Lackland
1216-1272	Henry III
1272-1307	Edward I Longshanks
1307-1327	Edward II (with Isabella of France, r. 1308-1330)
1327-1377	Edward III (with Philippa of Hainaut, r. 1327-1369)
1377-1399	Richard II

PLANTAGENETS: LANCASTRIANS

Reign	Ruler
1399-1413	Henry IV
1413-1422	Henry V
1422-1461	Henry VI

PLANTAGENETS: YORKISTS

Reign	Ruler
1461-1470	Edward IV
1470-1471	Henry VI (Lancaster)
1471-1483	Edward IV (York, restored)
1483	Edward V (York)
1483-1485	Richard III Hunchback (York)

TUDORS

Reign	Ruler
1485-1509	Henry VII
1509-1547	Henry VIII
1547-1553	Edward VI
1553	Lady Jane Grey
1553-1558	Mary I
1558-1603	Elizabeth I

STUARTS

Reign	Ruler
1603-1625	James I (VI of Scotland)
1625-1649	Charles I

COMMONWEALTH (LORD PROTECTORS)

Reign	Ruler
1653-1658	Oliver Cromwell
1658-1659	Richard Cromwell

STUARTS (RESTORED)

Reign	Ruler
1660-1685	Charles II
1685-1689	James II (VII of Scotland)
1689-1702	William of Orange (III of England, II of Scotland) and Mary II
1702-1707	Anne
1707	Act of Union (Great Britain and Ireland)
1707-1714	Anne

HANOVERS

Reign	Ruler
1714-1727	George I
1727-1760	George II
1760-1801	George III
1801	Act of Union creates United Kingdom
1801-1820	George III
1820-1830	George IV
1830-1837	William IV

SAXE-COBURG-GOTHA

Reign	Ruler
1837-1901	Victoria
1901-1910	Edward VII
1910-1936	George V

WINDSOR

Reign	Ruler
1910-1936	George V
1936	Edward VIII
1936-1952	George VI
1952-	Elizabeth II

FRANKISH KINGDOM AND FRANCE

The Merovingians and Carolingians ruled different parts of the Frankish kingdom, which accounts for overlapping regnal dates in these tables. The term "emperor" refers to rule over what eventually came to be known as the Holy Roman Empire.

THE MEROVINGIANS

Reign	Ruler (Principality)
447-458	Merovech
458-481	Childeric I
481-511	Clovis I (with Clotilda, r. 493-511)
511	Kingdom split among Clovis's sons
511-524	Chlodomer (Orléans)
511-534	Theodoric I (Metz)
511-558	Childebert I (Paris)
511-561	Lothair I (Soissons 511-561, all Franks 558-561)
534-548	Theudebert I (Metz)
548-555	Theudebald (Metz)
561	Kingdom split among Lothair's sons
561-567	Charibert I (Paris)
561-575	Sigebert I (Austrasia)
561-584	Chilperic I (Soissons)
561-592	Guntram (Burgundy)
575-595	Childebert II (Austrasia 575-595, Burgundy 593-595)
584-629	Lothair II (Neustria 584, all Franks 613-629)
595-612	Theudebert II (Austrasia)

Reign	Ruler (Principality)
595-613	Theodoric II (Burgundy 595-612, Austrasia 612-613)
613	Sigebert II (Austrasia, Burgundy)
623-639	Dagobert I (Austrasia 623-628, all Franks 629-639)
629-632	Charibert II (Aquitaine)
632-656	Sigebert III (Austrasia)
639-657	Clovis II (Neustria and Burgundy)
656-673	Lothair III (Neustria 657-673, all Franks 656-660)
662-675	Childeric (Austrasia 662-675, all Franks 673-675)
673-698	Theodoric III (Neustria 673-698, all Franks 678-691)
674-678	Dagobert II (Austrasia)
691-695	Clovis III (all Franks)
695-711	Childebert III (all Franks)
711-716	Dagobert III (all Franks)
715-721	Chilperic II (Neustria 715-721, all Franks 719-720)
717-719	Lothair IV (Austrasia)
721-737	Theodoric IV (all Franks)
743-751	Childeric III (all Franks)

THE CAROLINGIANS

Reign	Ruler
687-714	Pépin II of Heristal (mayor of Austrasia/Neustria)
714-719	Plectrude (regent for Theudoald)
719-741	Charles Martel (the Hammer; mayor of Austrasia/Neustria)
747-768	Pépin III the Short (mayor of Neustria 741, king of all Franks 747)
768-814	Charlemagne (king of Franks 768, emperor 800)
814-840	Louis the Pious (king of Aquitaine, emperor)
840-855	Lothair I (emperor)
843	Treaty of Verdun divides Carolingian Empire into East Franks (Germany), West Franks (essentially France), and a Middle Kingdom (roughly corresponding to Provence, Burgundy, and Lorraine)
843-876	Louis II the German (king of Germany)
843-877	Charles II the Bald (king of Neustria 843, emperor 875)
855-875	Louis II (emperor)
877-879	Louis II (king of France)
879-882	Louis III (king of France)
879-884	Carloman (king of France)
884-887	Charles III the Fat (king of France, emperor 881)
887-898	Odo (Eudes; king of France)
887-899	Arnulf (king of Germany 887, emperor 896)
891-894	Guy of Spoleto (Wido, Guido; emperor)
892-898	Lambert of Spoleto (emperor)

Reign	Ruler
893-923	Charles III the Simple (king of France)
915-923	Berengar I of Friuli (emperor)
923-929?	Robert I (king of France)
929-936	Rudolf (king of France)
936-954	Louis IV (king of France; Hugh the Great in power)
954-986	Lothair (king of France; Hugh Capet in power 956)
986-987	Louis V (king of France)

THE CAPETIANS

Reign	Ruler
987-996	Hugh Capet
996-1031	Robert II the Pious
1031-1060	Henry I
1060-1108	Philip I the Fair
1108-1137	Louis VI the Fat
1137-1179	Louis VII the Younger (with Eleanor of Aquitaine, r. 1137-1180)
1179-1223	Philip II Augustus
1223-1226	Louis VIII the Lion
1223-1252	Blanche of Castile (both queen and regent)
1226-1270	Louis IX (Saint Louis)
1271-1285	Philip III the Bold
1285-1314	Philip IV the Fair
1314-1316	Louis X the Stubborn
1316	Philip, brother of Louis X (regent before birth of John I and during his short life)
1316	John I the Posthumous
1316-1322	Philip V the Tall
1322-1328	Charles IV the Fair

Valois Dynasty, Main Branch

Reign	Ruler
1328-1350	Philip VI the Fortunate
1350-1364	John II the Good
1364-1380	Charles V the Wise
1380-1382	Louis I of Anjou (regent for Charles VI)
1380-1422	Charles VI the Well-Beloved
1422-1461	Charles VII the Victorious
1461-1483	Louis XI
1483-1484	Anne de Beaujeu (regent for Charles VIII)
1483-1498	Charles VIII the Affable

Valois-Orléans Branch

Reign	Ruler
1498-1515	Louis XII, the Father of His People

Valois-Angoulême Branch

Reign	Ruler
1515-1547	Francis I
1547-1559	Henry II (with Catherine de Médicis)
1559-1560	Francis II

Reign	Ruler
1560-1563	Catherine de Médicis (regent for Charles IX)
1560-1574	Charles IX
1574-1589	Henry III (King of Poland, 1573-1574)

BOURBON DYNASTY

Reign	Ruler
1589-1610	Henry IV (Henry III of Navarre, 1572-1610)
1610-1614	Marie de Médici (regent for Louis XIII)
1610-1643	Louis XIII the Well-Beloved
1643-1651	Anne of Austria (regent for Louis XIV)
1643-1715	Louis XIV the Sun King
1715-1723	Philip II of Orléans (regent for Louis XV)
1715-1774	Louis XV the Well-Beloved
1774-1792	Louis XVI the Beloved
1792-1804	First Republic
1804-1814	First Empire (Napoleon I Bonaparte)
1814-1824	Louis XVIII
1824-1830	Charles X
1830-1848	Louis-Philippe of Orléans

MODERN ERA

Term	Government/President
1848-1852	Second Republic
1852-1870	Second Empire (Napoleon III)
1871-1940	Third Republic
1940-1944	Vichy State (German occupation)
1944-1947	Provisional government
1944-1946	Charles de Gaulle
1947-1958	Fourth Republic
1947-1954	Vincent Auriol
1954-1958	René Coty
After 1958	Fifth Republic
1958-1969	Charles de Gaulle
1969-1974	Georges Pompidou
1974-1981	Valéry Giscard d'Estaing
1981-1995	François Mitterrand
1995-	Jacques Chirac

GERMANIC TRIBES. *See also* HOLY ROMAN EMPIRE

In the fifth and sixth centuries, Europe was invaded from the east by several "barbarian" tribes from eastern Europe and Central Asia, including the Visigoths, who inflicted the earliest damage on Rome in the late fourth and early fifth centuries; the Burgundians, from central and northeastern Europe; the Vandals, who eventually settled in Spain and North Africa; the Suevi, who made their way to the north of Spain and finally fell to the Visigoths; the Alans, a non-Germanic steppe tribe from Iran who, along with the Suevi and the Visigoths, overran Gaul (France) and the Iberian Peninsula; and the Franks (see Frankish Kingdom and France, above), who occupied most of Gaul during the later Roman Empire and were the only of these early tribes to survive. The Franks would evolve into the Merovingian and Carolingian lines, and by the ninth century they dominated Europe. Below is a list of some of the Germanic tribes and tribal leaders before and during the Frankish period. The region known today as Germany was initially occupied by these tribes and then came under the subjugation of the Frankish Merovingians and Carolingians. In 962, the Holy Roman Empire came into existence and held sway over Germany for nearly a millennium (see Holy Roman Empire, below). Not until the late nineteenth century did the nation-state of Germany come into existence.

ALEMANNI (OR ALAMANNI)

The Alemanni occupied Swabia.

Reign	Ruler
c. 536-554	Leuthari
c. 536-554	Butilin
d. c. 539	Haming
c. 570-587	Leutfred I
588-613	Uncilen
d. 613	Gunzo
c. 615-639	Chrodebert
c. 640-673/95	Leutfred II
c. 700-709	Godefred
d. c. 712	Huocin
d. c. 712	Willehari
c. 720-730	Lanfred I
c. 737-744	Theodobald
d. 746	Nebi
746-749	Lanfred II
791-799	Gerold
799-806	Isenbard
After 806	Annexed by the Franks

BAVARIANS

The Bavarians occupied a region approximating present-day Bavaria.

Reign	Ruler
508-512	Theodo I
512-537	Theodo II
537-565	Theodo III
537-567	Theodobald I
550-590	Garibald I
590-595	Grimwald I
591-609	Tassilo I
609-630	Agilulf
609-640	Garibald II
640-680	Theodo IV

Reign	Ruler
680-702	Theodo V
702-715	Theodobald II
702-723	Grimwald II
702-725	Theodobert
702-730	Tassilo II
725-737	Hubert
737-748	Odilo
748-788	Tassilo III
After 788	Annexed by Franks

BURGUNDIANS

The Burgundians occupied central and southeastern France.

Reign	Ruler
c. 407	Gebicca
407-434	Gundahar/Gondikar/Gunther
434-473	Gundioc/Gunderic
443-c. 480	Chilperic I
473-486	Gundomar I
473-493	Chilperic II
473-501	Godegisel
473-516	Gundobad
516-524	Sigismund
524-532	Gudomar II
532	Frankish conquest

FRANKS

The Franks initially occupied the area now known as the Netherlands and northern France, and they eventually dominated Europe. See Frankish Kingdom and France, above.

LOMBARDS

The Lombards occupied northern Italy.

Reign	Ruler
565-572	Alboin
573-575	Celph
575-584	Unstable
584-590	Authari
590-591	Theodelinda
591-615	Agilulf
615-625	Adaloald
625-636	Arioald
636-652	Rotharis
652-661	Aribert I
661-662	Godipert
662-671	Grimoald
671-674	Garibald
674-688	Bertharit
688-700	Cunibert
700-701	Liutpert
701	Raginpert
701-712	Aribert II
712-744	Liutprand
744-749	Rachis of Friuli

Reign	Ruler
749-756	Aistulf of Friuli
756-774	Desiderius
774	Frankish conquest

OSTROGOTHS

The Ostrogoths migrated from the east into the Balkans and Italian peninsula.

Reign	Ruler
474-526	Theodoric the Great
526-534	Athalaric
534-536	Theodahad (with Amalasuntha)
536-540	Vitiges (Witiges)
540	Theodobald (Heldebadus)
541	Eraric
541-552	Totila (Baduila)
552-553	Teias
553-568	Roman domination (Byzantine emperor Justinian I)
568-774	Lombard domination
774	Frankish conquest

SUEVI

The Suevi migrated from the east into northern Spain.

Reign	Ruler
409-438	Hermeric
428-448	Rechila
439	Mérida
441	Seville
448-456	Rechiar
452	Peace with Romans
456	Visigoths defeat Rechiar
456-457	Aioulf
457-460	Maldras
460-c. 463	Richimund
460-c. 465	Frumar
c. 463-?	Remisund
c. 500-550	Unknown kings
c. 550-559	Carriaric
559-570	Theodemar
561	Catholic
570-582	Miro
582-584	Eboric
584-585	Andeca
After 585	Visigoth conquest

VANDALS

The Vandals migrated west into southern Spain and northern Africa.

Reign	Ruler
c. 406-428	Gunderic
428-477	Gaiseric
477-484	Huneric

Reign	Ruler
484-496	Gunthamund
496-523	Thrasamund
523-530	Hilderic
530-534	Gelimer
After 534	Roman overthrow

VISIGOTHS

The Visigoths migrated west into southwestern France.

Reign	Ruler
395-410	Alaric I
410-415	Athaulf (Ataulfo)
415	Sigeric
415-417	Wallia
417-451	Theodoric I
451-453	Thorismund
453-466	Theodoric II
466-484	Euric I
484-507	Alaric II
508-511	Amalaric
511-526	Theodoric the Great
526-531	Amalaric
531-548	Theudes
548-549	Theudegisel
549-554	Agila
554-567	Athanagild
567-571	Theodomir
571-572	Leuva (Leova) I
572-586	Leuvigild
586-601	Reccared I
601-603	Leova II
603-610	Witterich
610-612	Gundemar
612-621	Sisebut (Sisebur)
621	Reccared II
621-631	Swintilla (Suinthila)
631-636	Sisenand
636-640	Chintila
640-642	Tulga
642-653	Chindaswind
653-672	Recdeswinth
672-680	Wamba
680-687	Euric (Erwig) II
687-702	Egica (Ergica)
702-709	Witiza
709-711	Roderic (Rodrigo)
711	Overthrown by Umayyads
718	Christian Kingdom of Asturias

GERMANY

FIRST REICH. SEE HOLY ROMAN EMPIRE

SECOND REICH

Term	Leader
1862-1890	Otto von Bismark (chancellor)
1871-1888	Wilhelm I (emperor)
1888	Frederick (emperor)
1888-1918	Wilhelm II (emperor)
1890-1894	Count Leo von Caprivi (chancellor)
1894-1900	Chlodwig von Hohenzollern-Schillingsfürst (chancellor)
1900-1909	Bernhard von Bülow (chancellor)
1909-1917	Theobald von Bethmann-Hollweg (chancellor)
1917	George Michaelis (chancellor)
1917-1918	George von Hertling (chancellor)
1918	Maximilian of Baden (chancellor)
1918	Friedrich Ebert (chancellor)

WEIMAR REPUBLIC

Term	Leader
1919-1925	Friedrich Ebert (president)
1919	Philip Scheidemann (chancellor)
1919-1920	Gustav Bauer (chancellor)
1920	Hermann Müller (chancellor)
1920-1921	Konstantin Fehrenbach (chancellor)
1921-1922	Joseph Wirth (chancellor)
1922-1923	Wilhelm Cuno (chancellor)
1923	Gustav Stresemann (chancellor)
1923-1925	Wilhelm Marx (chancellor)
1925-1934	Paul von Hindenberg (president)
1925-1926	Hans Luther (chancellor)
1926-1928	Wilhelm Marx (chancellor)
1928-1930	Hermann Müller (chancellor)
1930-1932	Heinrich Brüning (chancellor)
1932	Franz von Papen (chancellor)
1932-1933	Kurt von Schleider (chancellor)
1933-1934	Adolf Hilter (chancellor)

THIRD REICH

Term	Führer
1934-1945	Adolf Hitler
1945	Karl Dönitz
1945-1949	Allied occupation
1949	Germany divided into Federal Republic of Germany (West Germany) and German Democratic Republic (East Germany)
1990	Reunification

FEDERAL REPUBLIC OF GERMANY

Term	Office
1949-1959	Theodor Heuss (president)
1949-1963	Konrad Adenauer (chancellor)
1959-1969	Heinrich Lübke (president)
1963-1966	Ludwig Erhard (chancellor)
1966-1969	Kurt Georg Kiesinger (chancellor)
1969-1974	Gustav Heinemann (president)
1969-1974	Willy Brandt (chancellor)
1974-1979	Walter Scheel (president)
1974-1982	Helmut Schmidt (chancellor)
1979-1984	Karl Carstens (president)
1982-1998	Helmut Kohl (chancellor)
1984-1994	Richard von Weizsäcker (president)
1990	Reunification of East and West Germany
1994-1999	Roman Herzog (president)
1998-2005	Gerhard Schröder (chancellor)
1999-2004	Johannes Rau (president)
2004-	Horst Köhler (president)
2005-	Angela Merkel (chancellor)

HOLY ROMAN EMPIRE

Although some sources consider the Holy Roman Empire to have begun with Otto I's coronation in 962, others date the Empire's beginning as early as Charlemagne's consolidation of the Franks and his coronation as emperor of the Frankish Empire in 800. The term "Sacrum Romanum Imperium" (Holy Roman Empire) dates to 1254, the use of the term "Holy Empire" to 1157, and the term "Roman Empire" to 1034 (reign of Conrad II). "Roman emperor" was applied to Otto I during his reign; however, Charlemagne also used the term to refer to his own reign. The concept of a "Holy" Roman Empire goes back to the beginning of the Byzantine Empire and the reign of the first Christian Roman emperor, Constantine the Great. Hence, the concept of this political entity can be considered to have evolved incrementally over time. The practice of papal coronation to legitimate the emperor began with Otto I. Regnal dates are therefore often listed as beginning with the date of coronation. However, the German kings who became Holy Roman Emperors frequently asserted their de facto power earlier as rulers of West Frankia (France), East Frankia (essentially Germany), and/or Italy (roughly the northern portion of modern Italy). In the table below, where a date of ascension to the West Frankish (French), East Frankish (German), Middle Frankish (Lorraine south to Italy), or other throne is different from that to Emperor, the former date is set before a slash and the date of assuming the rule of the Empire falls after the slash. Asterisks indicate that the monarch was not formally crowned at Rome by the pope, a practice that officially ended with Frederick II, although Charles V was last to be crowned outside Rome.

Reign	Emperor (House)
768/800-814	Charlemagne (Carolingian)
814/813-840	Louis I the Pious (Carolingian)
840/817-855	Lothair I (Carolingian)
840-876	Louis II the German (Carolingian; first king of East Franks only)
840/875-877	Charles II the Bald (Carolingian)
855/850-875	Louis II of Italy (Carolingian)
877-881	Empire unstable
876/881-888	Charles III the Fat (Carolingian)
888-891	Viking and Arab incursions
891	Italian line begins
888/891-894	Guy (Guido, Wido) of Spoleto (Italian)
894/892-898	Lambert of Spoleto (Italian, co-emperor)
888/896-899	Arnulf (East Frankish)
899/901-905	Louis III of Provence (Carolingian, deposed)
905/915-924	Berengar I of Friuli (Italian)
911-918	*Conrad
919	Saxon line begins
919-936	*Henry I the Fowler (Saxon)
936/962-973	Otto I (Saxon): crowned in 962 by Pope John XII; the Empire no longer lays claim to West Frankish lands (essentially France), but now is basically a union of Germany and northern Italy
973/967-983	Otto II (Saxon)
983/996-1002	Otto III (Saxon)
1002/14-1024	Henry II the Saint (Saxon)
1024	Franconian/Salian line begins
1024/27-1039	Conrad II (Franconian/Salian)
1039/46-1056	Henry III (Franconian/Salian)
1056/84-1106	Henry IV (Franconian/Salian)
1077-1080	*Rudolf of Swabia
1081-1093	*Hermann (of Luxemburg)
1093-1101	*Conrad (of Franconia)
1106/11-1125	Henry V (Franconian/Salian)
1125	Franconian/Salian line ends
1125/33-1137	Lothair II (duke of Saxony)
1138	Hohenstaufen line begins
1138-1152	*Conrad III (Hohenstaufen)
1152/55-1190	Frederick I Barbarossa (Hohenstaufen)
1190/91-1197	Henry VI (Hohenstaufen)
1198-1208	*Philip of Swabia (Hohenstaufen)
1208/09-1215	Otto IV (married into Hohenstaufens)
1215/20-1250	Frederick II (Hohenstaufen): Last emperor crowned at Rome
1246-1247	*Henry Raspe
1247-1256	*William of Holland

Reign	Emperor (House)
1250-1254	*Conrad IV
1254-1273	Great Interregnum
1257-1272	*Richard of Cornwall (rival, Plantagenet)
1257-1273	*Alfonso X of Castile (rival)
1273-1291	*Rudolf I (Habsburg)
1292-1298	*Adolf of Nassau
1298-1308	*Albert (Albrecht) I (Habsburg)
1308/11-1313	Henry VII (Luxembourg)
1314/28-1347	Louis IV of Bavaria (Wittelsbach)
1314-1325	*Frederick of Habsburg (co-regent)
1346/55-1378	Charles IV (Luxembourg): Changes the name to the Holy Roman Empire of the German Nation as France begins to assert power; Charles abandons the Empire's French and Italian claims, and the history of the Holy Roman Empire and Germany are now basically the same
1349	*Günther of Schwarzburg
1378-1400	*Wenceslaus (Luxembourg; deposed)
1400	*Frederick III (of Brunswick)
1400-1410	*Rupert of the Palatinate (Wittelsbach)
1410-1411	*John (of Moravia)
1410/33-1437	Sigismund (Luxembourg)
1438-1439	*Albert II (Habsburg)
1440/52-1493	Frederick III (Habsburg)
1486/93-1519	*Maximilian I (Habsburg)
1499	Peace of Basle; Swiss independence
1513	Swiss Confederation of the Thirteen Cantons
1519-1558	*Charles V (Habsburg, last emperor crowned)
1555	Peace of Augsburg
1558-1564	*Ferdinand I (Habsburg)
1559	Peace of Cateau-Cambrésis
1564-1576	*Maximilian II (Habsburg)
1576-1612	*Rudolf II (Habsburg)
1612-1619	*Matthias (Habsburg)
1619-1637	*Ferdinand II (Habsburg)
1637-1657	*Ferdinand III (Habsburg)
1648	Peace of Westphalia
1658-1705	*Leopold I (Habsburg)
1686-1697	War of the League of Augsburg, conquest of Hungary, Nine Years' War (1688-1697)
1705-1711	*Joseph I (Habsburg)
1711-1740	*Charles VI (Habsburg)
1713	Peace of Utrecht
1740-1742	Interregnum
1742-1745	*Charles VII (Wittelsbach-Habsburg)
1745-1765	*Francis I (Lorraine)
1745-1780	*Maria Theresa (empress consort; queen of Hungary, 1740; empress dowager, 1765)
1756-1763	Seven Years' War
1765-1790	*Joseph II (Habsburg-Lorraine)

Reign	Emperor (House)
1790-1792	*Leopold II (Habsburg-Lorraine)
1792-1806	*Francis II (Habsburg-Lorraine; abdicated)
1806	Holy Roman Empire falls to Napoleon I of France

HUNGARY. *See also* BOHEMIA, POLAND

Reign	Ruler
c. 896-907	Árpád
d. 947	Zsolt
d. 972	Taksony
997	Géza
997-1038	Saint Stephen (István) I
1038-1041	Peter Orseleo
1041-1044	Samuel
1044-1046	Peter (second rule)
1047-1060	Andrew I
1060-1063	Béla I
1063-1074	Salamon
1074-1077	Géza I
1077-1095	Saint László (Ladislas) I
1095-1116	Kalman
1116-1131	Stephen II
1131-1141	Béla II
1141-1162	Géza II
1162-1163	László II
1163-1172	Stephen III
1163-1165	Stephen IV
1172-1196	Béla III
1196-1204	Imre
1204-1205	László III
1205-1235	Andrew II
1235-1270	Béla IV
1270-1272	Stephen V
1272-1290	László IV
1290-1301	Andrew III (end of the Árpád line)
1301-1304	Wenceslaus (Václav) II
1304-1308	Otto I of Bavaria
1305-1306	Wenceslaus (Václav) III
1306	End of the Přemlysid line
1306-1310	Instability
1310-1342	Károly (Charles Robert) I
1342-1382	Lajos (Louis) I
1382-1395	Maria
1387-1437	Sigismund
1438-1439	Albert II of Habsburg
1440-1444	Ulá6szló I (Władysław III, Poland)
1444-1457	László (Ladislas) V
1458-1490	Matthias (Matyas) I Corvinus
1490-1516	Ulá6szló II (Vladislav or Władisław Jagiełło)
1516-1526	Louis II
1526-1564	Ferdinand I (Habsburg claims suzerainty)

Reign	Ruler
1526-1540	John I Zápolya (simultaneous claimant)
1540-1571	John II Sigismund
1556-1559	Isabel
1562	Split between Habsburgs, Ottomans, and Ottoman principality Transylvania
1563-1576	Maximilian II (Holy Roman Emperor)
1571-1575	Stephen Báthory
1572-1608	Rudolf II (Holy Roman Emperor)
1575-1581	Christopher (Kristóf) Báthory
1581-1599	Sigismund Báthory
1599	Andrew Cardinal Báthory
1599-1602	Sigismund Báthory
1604-1606	Stephen Bocskay
1607-1608	Sigismund Rákóczy
1608-1619	Matthias (Holy Roman Emperor)
1608-1613	Gabriel (Gábor) Báthory
1613-1629	Gábor Bethlen
1618-1637	Ferdinand II
1625-1657	Ferdinand III
1630-1648	George (György) I Rákóczy
1647-1654	Ferdinand IV
1648-1657	George II Rákóczy
1655-1705	Leopold I
1660-1682	Emeric Thököly (Tökölli)
1687-1711	Joseph I
1703-1711	Francis II Rákóczy leads liberation movement
1711-1740	Charles III
1740-1780	Maria Theresa
1780-1790	Joseph II
1790-1792	Leopold II
1792-1835	Francis
1835-1848	Ferdinand V
1848	Revolutions of 1848
1848-1916	Francis Joseph I (Ferenc József)
1916-1918	Charles IV
1918	Hungary declares independence, forms First Republic

INDIA

FIRST CĀLUKYA DYNASTY

Reign	Ruler
543-566	Pulakeśin I
c. 566-597	Kīrtivarman I
598-610	Maṇgaleśa
610-642	Pulakeśin II
655-680	Vikramāditya I
680-696	Vinayāditya
696-733	Vijayāditya
733-746	Vikramāditya II
747-757	Kīrtivarman II

PALLAVAS

Reign	Ruler
c. 550-575	Simhavarman (some sources give c. 436)
c. 575-600	Simhavishnu
c. 600-630	Mahendravarman I
c. 630-668	Narasiṃhavarman I Mahāmalla
c. 668-670	Mahendravarman II
c. 670-700	Paramesvaravarman I
c. 695-728	Narasiṃhavarman II
c. 728-731	Paramesvaravarman II
c. 731-796	Nandivarman
750-770	Gopāla
770-810	Dharmapāla
810-850	Devapāla
854-908	Narayanpāla
c. 988-1038	Māhipāla I
c. 1077-1120	Rāmapāla
1143-1161	Madanpāla

SECOND WESTERN CĀLUKYA DYNASTY

Reign	Ruler
973-997	Taila II
997-1008	Satyaśraya
1008-1014	Vikramāditya I
1014-1015	Ayyana
1015-1042	Jayasimha I
1043-1068	Someśvara I
1068-1076	Someśvara II
1076-1126	Vikramāditya VI
1127-1135	Someśvara III
1135-1151	Jagadhekamalla II
1151-1154	Taila III
1155-1168	Bijjala
1168-1177	Someśvara IV
1177-1180	Saṇkama II
1180-1183	Āhavamalla
1183-1184	Singhana
1184-1189/90	Someśvara IV

GURJARA-PRATIHĀRA DYNASTY

Reign	Ruler
c. 730-c. 756	Nāgabhaṭa I
n.d.	Devaraja
c. 778-c. 794	Vatsarāja
c. 794-c. 833	Nāgabhaṭa II
c. 836-c. 885	Mihira Bhoja I
c. 890-c. 910	Mahendrapāla I
c. 914-?	Mahipāla
n.d.	Mihira Bhoja II
n.d.	Vinayakapāla
c. 946-c. 948	Mahendrapāla II
c. 948-c. 960	Devapāla
c. 960-?	Vijayapāla

Reign	Ruler
n.d.	Rājyapāla
c. 1018-c. 1027	Trilocanapāla

THE CŌLAS

Reign	Ruler
c. 850-c. 870	Vijayālaya
871-907	Āditya I
907-955	Parāntaka I
956	Arinjayā
956	Parāntaka II
956-969	Āditya II
969-985	Madhurantaka Uttama
985-1014	Rājarāja I
1014-1044	Rājendracōla Deva I
1044-1052	Rājadhirāja I
1052-1060	Rājendracōla Deva II
1060-1063	Ramamahendra
1063-1067	Virarājendra
1067-1070	Adhirājendra
1070-1122	Rājendra III
1122-1135	Vikrama Cōla
1135-1150	Kulottuṇga II Cōla
1150-1173	Rājarāja II
1173-1179	Rājadhirāja II
1179-1218	Kulottuṇga III
1218-1246	Rājarāja III
1246-1279	Rājendra IV

DELHI SULTANATE

Muʿizzī Slave Sultans

Reign	Ruler
1206-1210	Quṭ al-Dīn Aybak
1210-1211	Ārām Shāh
1211-1236	Iltutmish
1236	Ruknuddin Firūz Shāh
1236-1240	Raziya
1240-1242	Bahrām Shāh
1242-1246	Masʿūd Shāh
1246-1266	Maḥmūd Shāh
1266-1287	Balban Ulugh Khān
1287-1290	Kay Qubādh
1290	Kayūmarth

Khaljī Dynasty

Reign	Ruler
1290-1296	Jalāl-ud-Dīn Fīrūz Khaljī
1296-1316	ʿAlāʾ-ud-Dīn Muḥammad Khaljī
1316	ʿUmar Shāh
1316-1320	Mubārak Shāh
1320	Khusraw Khān Barwārī

Tughluq Dynasty

Reign	Ruler
1320-1325	Tughluq I (Ghiyās-ud-Dīn)
1325-1351	Muḥammad ibn Tughluq
1351-1388	Fīrūz III
1388-1389	Tughluq II (Ghiyās-ud-Dīn)
1389-1390	Abū Bakr
1390-1394	Nāṣir-ud-Dīn
1394	Sikandar I (Humayun Khān)
1394-1395	Maḥmūd II
1395-1399	Nuṣrat
1401-1412	Maḥmūd II (second rule)
1412-1414	Dawlat Khān Lōdī

Sayyid Dynasty

Reign	Ruler
1414-1421	Khiḍr
1421-1434	Mubārak II
1434-1443	Muḥammad IV
1443-1451	ʿĀlām

Lodī Dynasty

Reign	Ruler
1451-1489	Bahlūl
1489-1517	Sikandar II
1517-1526	Ibrāhīm II

MUGHAL EMPERORS

Reign	Ruler
1526-1530	Bābur
1530-1540	Humāyūn
1540-1545	Shīr Shāh Sūr
1545-1553	Islām Shāh Sūr
1554	Muḥammad V Mubāriz Khān
1554-1555	Ibrāhām III Khān
1555	Aḥmad Khān Sikandar Shāh III
1555-1556	Humāyūn (second rule)
1556-1605	Akbar I
1605-1627	Jahāngīr
1627-1628	Dāwar Bakhsh
1628-1657	Jahān I Khusraw
1658-1707	Aurangzeb (Awrangzīb ʿĀlamgīr I)
1707-1712	ʿĀlam I Bahādur
1712-1713	Jahāndār Muʿizz al-Dīn
1713-1719	Farrukh-siyar
1719	Shams al-Dīn Rāfʿ al-Darajāt
1719	Jahān II Rāfiʿ al-Dawla
1719	Nīkūsiyar Muḥammad
1719-1720	Muḥammad Shāh Nāṣir al-Dīn
1720	Mohammed Ibrahim
1720-1748	Muḥammad Shāh Nāṣir al-Dīn
1739	Nādir Shāh sacks Delhi
1748-1754	Aḥmad Shāh Bahadur
1754-1779	Alamgir II

Reign	Ruler
1760?	Shāh Jahān III
1779-1806	Shāh Alam II
1806-1837	Akbar Shāh II
1837-1857	Bahadur Shāh II (Bahadur Shāh Zafar)

IRAN (PERSIA). *See also* ISLAMIC CALIPHS, OTTOMAN EMPIRE, SELJUK EMPIRE

LATER SĀSĀNIAN EMPIRE

Reign	Ruler
309-379	Shāpūr II
379-383	Ardashīr II
383-388	Shāpūr III
388-399	Barham (Varahran) IV
399-421	Yazdegerd (Yazdgard) I
421-439	Barham (Varahran) V
439-457	Yazdegerd (Yazdgard) II
457-459	Hormizd III
459-484	Peroz
484-488	Valash
488-496	Kavadh I
496-498	Zamasp
499-531	Kavadh I (restored)
531-579	Khosrow (Khusro or Chosroes) I
579-590	Hormizd IV
590-628	Khosrow (Khusro or Chosroes) II
628	Kavadh II
628-629	Ardashīr III
629-630	Boran
630-632	Hormizd V and Khosrow III
633-651	Yazdegerd (Yazdgard) III
651	Islamic conquest
651-656	ʿUthmān ibn ʿAffān
656-661	Alī ibn Abī Ṭālib
661-750	Umayyad caliphs (*see* Islamic Caliphs)
750-821	ʿAbbāsid caliphs (*see* Islamic Caliphs)

LATER IRANIAN DYNASTIES

Dates	Dynasty
821-873	Tāhirid Dynasty (in Khorāsān, northeastern Persia)
c. 866-c. 900	Ṣafārrid Dynasty
c. 940-1000	Sīmjūrid Dynasty (in Khorāsān)
945-1055	Būyid Dynasty (western Iran)
977-1186	Ghaznavid Dynasty (in Khorāsān, Afghanistan, northern India)
999-1211	Qarakhanid Dynasty (Transoxania)
c. 1038	Seljuks take power (*see* Seljuk Empire)
1153-1231	Khwārezm-Shāh Dynasty (in Khwārezm, northeastern Iran)
c. 1231	Mongol invasion

Dates	Dynasty
1256-1353	Il-Khanid (Mongol) Dynasty
1353-1393	Mozaffarid Dynasty
1393-c. 1467	Timurid Dynasty
c. 1467-1500	Turkmen/Ottoman incursions

ṢAFAVID DYNASTY

Reign	Ruler
1501-1524	Ismāʿīl I
1524-1576	Ṭahmāsp I
1576-1578	Ismāʿīl II
1578-1587	Muḥammad Khudabanda
1587-1629	ʿAbbās I
1629-1642	Safi
1642-1667	ʿAbbās II
1667-1694	Süleyman I
1694-1722	Ḥoseyn I
1722-1732	Ṭahmāsp II
1732-1736	ʿAbbās III
1736-1750	Afshāid shahs
1750	Süleyman II in Mashad
1750-1765	Ismāʿīl III (Karim Khān, regent 1751-1765)

AFSHĀR DYNASTY

Reign	Ruler
1736-1747	Nāder Shāh (regent)
1747	ʿĀdel Shāh
1748	Ibrāhim
1748-1750	Shāh Rukh
1755-1796	Shāh Rukh in Khorāsān
1796-1803	Nāder Mīrza in Mashad

ZAND DYNASTY (WESTERN IRAN)

Reign	Ruler
1750-1779	Karim Khān
1779	Abu'l Fath (Shirāz)
1779	Moḥammad ʿAlī (Shirāz)
1779-1781	Moḥammad Ṣādiq (Shirāz)
1781-1785	ʿAlī Morād (Eṣfahān)
1785-1789	Ja'far (Eṣfahān, later Shirāz)
1789-1794	Luṭf ʿAlī (Shirāz)
1796	Qajar Dynasty begins

QAJAR DYNASTY

Reign	Ruler
1796-1797	Agha Moḥammad (1794, southern Persia; 1796, Khorāsān)
1797-1834	Fatḥ ʿAlī
1834-1848	Moḥammad
1848-1896	Nāser ad-Din
1896-1907	Muẓaffar ad-Din
1907-1909	Moḥammad ʿAlī
1909-1925	Aḥmad

PAHLAVI DYNASTY

Reign	Ruler
1925-1941	Reẓā Shāh
1941-1979	Moḥammad Reẓā
1979	Exile of Moḥammad Reẓā
1979	Ayatollāh Khomeini declares Islamic Republic of Iran

PRESIDENTS OF IRAN

Term	President
1980-1981	Abolhassan Banisadr (impeached)
1981	Mohammad Ali Rajai (assassinated)
1981-1989	Ali Khamenei (Supreme Leader as of June 4, 1989)
1989-1997	Ali Akbar Hashemi Rafsanjani
1997-2005	Mohammad Khatami
2005-	Mahmoud Ahmadinejad

IRELAND

THE HIGH-KINGS

Reign	Ruler
379-405	Niall Noígillach of the Nine Hostages
405-428	Dathi (Nath) I
429-463	Lóeguire MacNéill
456-493	Saint Patrick converts Irish
463-483	Ailill Motl MacNath I
483-507	Lugaid MacLóeguiri O'Néill
507-534	Muirchertach MacErcae O'Néill (Muiredach)
534-544	Tuathal Máelgarb MacCorpri Cáech O'Néill
544-565	Diarmait MacCerbaill O'Néill
565-566	Domnall MacMuirchertaig O'Néill and Forggus MacMuirchertaig O'Néill
566-569	Ainmere MacSátnai O'Néill
569-572	Báetán MacMuirchertaig O'Néill and Eochaid MacDomnaill O'Néill
572-581	Báetán MacNinnedo O'Néill
581-598	Aed MacAinmerech O'Néill
598-604	Aed Sláine MacDiarmato O'Néill
598-604	Colmán Rímid MacBáetáin O'Néill (rival)
604-612	Aed Uaridnach MacDomnaill O'Néill
612-615	Máel Cobo MacAedo O'Néill
615-628	Suibne Menn MacFiachnai O'Néill
628-642	Domnall MacAedo O'Néill
642-658	Conall Cóel MacMáele Cobo O'Néill and Cellach MacMáele Cobo O'Néill
656-665	Diarmait MacAedo Sláine O'Néill and Blathmac MacAedo Sláine O'Néill
665-671	Sechnussach MacBlathmaic O'Néill
671-675	Cenn Fáelad MacBlathmaic O'Néill
675-695	Finsnechtae Fledach MacDúnchada O'Néill
695-704	Loingsech MacOengus O'Néill

Reign	Ruler
704-710	Congal Cinn Magir MacFergus Fánat O'Néill
710-722	Fergal MacMáele Dúin O'Néill
722-724	Fogartach MacNéill O'Néill
724-728	Cináed MacIrgalaig
724-734	Flaithbbertach MacLoingsig O'Néill
734-743	Aed Allán MacFergal O'Néill
743-763	Domnall Midi O'Néill
763-770	Niall Frossach MacFergal O'Néill
770-797	Donnchad Midi MacDomnaill Midi O'Néill
797-819	Aed Oirdnide MacNéill Frossach O'Néill
819-833	Conchobar MacDonnchado Midi O'Néill
833-846	Niall Caille MacAedo Oirdnide O'Néill
846-862	Máel Sechnaill MacMáele Ruanaid O'Néill
862-879	Aed Findliath MacNéill Caille O'Néill
879-916	Flann Sionna MacMáele Sechnaill O'Néill
916-919	Niall Glúndubh MacAedo Findliath O'Néill
919-944	Donnchad Donn MacFlann O'Néill
944-950	Ruaidrí ua Canannáin (rival)
944-956	Congalach Cnogba MacMáel Mithig O'Néill
956-980	Domnall MacMuirchertaig O'Néill
980-1002	Máel Sechnaill MacDomnaill O'Néill
1002-1014	Brian Bóruma MacCennétig and Brian Boru
1014-1022	Máel Sechnaill MacDomnaill O'Néill (restored)
1022-1064	Donnchad MacBrian
1064-1072	Diarmait MacMáil na mBó
1072-1086	Toirdelbach O'Brien
1090-1121	Domnall MacArdgar O'Lochlainn O'Néill
1121-1135	Toirrdelbach MacRuaidrí na Saide Buide ua Conchobair (Turlogh)
1141-1150	Toirrdelbach MacRuaidrí na Saide Buide ua Conchobair (Turlogh)
1150-1166	Muirchertach MacNéill MacLochlainn (Murtagh)
1166-1175	Ruaidrí MacToirrdelbaig (Rory O'Connor)
1175-1258	Henry II of England claims title Lord of Ireland
1258-1260	Brian Catha an Duin
1260-1316	English rule restored
1316-1318	Edward de Bruce
1318	English rule restored
1801	Act of Union: Ireland is joined with Britain

KINGDOM OF IRELAND (WITH ENGLAND/GREAT BRITAIN)

Reign	Ruler
1509-1547	Henry VIII
1547-1553	Edward VI
1553-1558	Mary I
1558-1603	Elizabeth I
1603-1625	James (I of England, VI of Scotland)
1625-1649	Charles I
1649-1660	Commonwealth and Restoration

Reign	Ruler
1660-1685	Charles II
1685-1689	James (II of England, VII of Scotland)
1689-1702	William and Mary
1702-1707	Anne
1707	Act of Union (Great Britain and Ireland)
1707-1714	Anne
1714-1727	George I
1727-1760	George II
1760-1801	George III
1801	Act of Union creates United Kingdom

UNITED KINGDOM OF GREAT BRITAIN AND IRELAND

Reign	Ruler
1801-1820	George III
1820-1830	George IV
1830-1837	William IV
1837-1901	Victoria
1901-1910	Edward VII
1910-1936	George V
1922	Irish Free State leaves United Kingdom

IRISH FREE STATE (Éire)

Reign	Ruler
1922-1936	George V
1936	Edward VIII
1936-1949	George VI

REPUBLIC OF IRELAND, NORTHERN IRELAND

Reign	Ruler
1949-1952	George VI
1952-	Elizabeth II

ISLAMIC CALIPHS. *See also* IRAN, OTTOMAN EMPIRE, SELJUK EMPIRE, SPAIN

ORTHODOX (SUNNI) CALIPHS, 632-661

Reign	Caliph
632-634	Abū Bakr
634-644	ʿUmar I
644-656	ʿUthmān ibn ʿAffān
656-661	Alī ibn Abī Ṭālib

UMAYYAD CALIPHS, 661-750

Reign	Caliph
661-680	Muʾāwiyah I (Muʾāwiyah ibn Abī Sufyna)
680-683	Yazīd I
683	Muʾāwiyah II
684-685	Marwān I
685-705	ʿAbd al-Malik
705-715	al-Walīd I
715-717	Sulaimān

Reign	Caliph
717-720	ʿUmar II
720-724	Yazīd II
724-743	Hishām
743-744	al-Walīd II
744	Yazīd III
744	Ibrāhīm
744-750	Marwān II

ʿABBĀSID CALIPHS, 750-1256

Reign	Caliph
750-754	Abū al-ʿAbbās al-Saffāḥ
754-775	al-Manṣūr
775-785	al-Mahdī
785-786	al-Hādī
786-809	Hārūn al-Rashīd
809-813	al-Amīn
813-833	al-Maʾmūn (Maʾmūn the Great)
833-842	al-Muʿtaṣim
842-847	al-Wathīq
847-861	al-Mutawakkil
861-862	al-Muntaṣir
862-866	al-Mustaʿin
866-869	al-Muʿtazz
869-870	al-Muqtadī
870-892	al-Muʿtamid
892-902	al-Muʿtaḍid
902-908	al-Muktafī
908-932	al-Muqtadir
932-934	al-Qāhir
934-940	al-Rāḍī
940-944	al-Mustaqfī
946-974	al-Mutī
974-991	al-Ṭāʾiʿ
991-1031	al-Qadir
1031-1075	al-Qāʾim
1075-1094	al-Muqtadī
1094-1118	al-Mustazhir
1118-1135	al-Mustarshid
1135-1136	al-Rashīd
1136-1160	al-Muqtafī
1160-1170	al-Mustanjid
1170-1180	al-Mustadī
1180-1225	al-Nāṣir
1225-1226	al-Zāhir
1226-1242	al-Mustanṣir
1242-1256	al-Mustaʿṣim

FĀṬIMID CALIPHS, 909-1171

Reign	Caliph
909-934	al-Mahdī
934-945	al-Qāʾim
945-952	al-Manṣūr

Reign	Caliph
952-975	al-Muʿizz
975-996	al-ʿAzīz
996-1021	al-Ḥākim
1021-1036	al-Zahīr
1036-1094	al-Mustanṣir
1094-1101	al-Mustadī
1101-1130	al-Amīr
1130-1149	al-Ḥāfiz
1149-1154	al-Zafīr
1154-1160	al-Fāʾiz
1160-1171	al-ʿAdīd

ITALY

The Italian peninsula was occupied by a number of fiefs and principalities during the better part of the millennium that made up the Middle Ages. These included Lombardy in the north, the Papal States in the center, and various duchies, margavates, and republics, including Sardinia, Benevento, Spoleto, Modena, Milan, Tuscany, Parma, Montferrat, and independent centers of trade such as Venice and Genoa. Only those early rulers who dominated the area are listed below; thereafter, the northern part of the peninsula was primarily under the power of the Carolingians (see Frankish Kingdom and France), the Holy Roman Emperors (see Holy Roman Empire, above), and the Papacy (see Popes and Antipopes, above). In the south, Naples and Sicily dominated. Thus, during the millennium 476-1453, the Italian Peninsula was a complex of ever-shifting jurisdictions, of which only the more prominent rulers are listed below.

BARBARIAN RULERS

Reign	Ruler
476-493	Odoacer
493-526	Theodoric
526-534	Athalaric
534-536	Theodatus (Theodahad)
536-540	Vitiges (Witiges)
540-541	Theodobald (Heldebadus)
541	Eraric
541-552	Totila
552-553	Teias

BYZANTINE (EAST ROMAN) RULE

Reign	Ruler
518-527	Justin I
527-565	Justinian I

LOMBARDS (NORTHERN ITALY)

Reign	Ruler
565-572	Alboin
573-575	Celph
575-584	Unstable
584-590	Authari
590-591	Theodelinda
591-615	Agilulf
615-625	Adaloald
625-636	Arioald
636-652	Rotharis
652-661	Aribert I
661-662	Godipert
662-671	Grimoald
671-674	Garibald
674-688	Bertharit
688-700	Cunibert
700-701	Liutpert
701	Raginpert
701-712	Aribert II
712-744	Liutprand
744-749	Rachis of Friuli
749-756	Aistulf of Friuli
756-774	Desiderius
774-888	Frankish conquest, subsumed under Carolingian Empire

KINGDOM OF ITALY

Reign	Ruler
888-891	Berengar I of Friuli
891-894	Guy of Spoleto (Guido, Wido)
894-896	Lambert of Spoleto
896-899	Arnulf, King of Germany
899-905	Louis III
905-922	Berengar I of Friuli (restored)
922-933	Rudolf II
933-947	Hugh of Arles
947-950	Lothair II of Arles
950-961	Berengar II of Ivrea
961	Conquest by Otto I; Italian peninsula divided among Holy Roman Empire, Papacy, and other principalities until unification in 1861

NAPLES AND SICILY

Reign	Ruler (Line)
1042-1046	William Iron Arm (Norman)
1046-1051	Drogo (Norman)
1051-1057	Humphrey (Norman)
1057-1085	Robert Guiscard (Norman)
1071-1101	Roger I (Norman)
1101-1154	Roger II of Sicily (Norman; king in 1130)
1154-1166	William I (Norman)
1166-1189	William II the Good (Norman)

Reign	Ruler (Line)
1190-1194	Tancred of Lecce (Norman)
1194	William III (Norman)
1194-1197	Henry VI (Hohenstaufen)
1197-1250	Frederick II (Hohenstaufen)
1250-1254	Conrad IV (Hohenstaufen)
1250-1266	Manfred (Hohenstaufen)
1267-1268	Conradin (rival)
1266-1285	Charles I of Anjou (Angevin)
1282	Sicily and Naples split

SICILY

Reign	Ruler
1282-1285	Pedro III of Aragón
1285-1296	James II of Aragón
1296-1337	Frederick II (or I)
1337-1342	Peter II
1342-1355	Louis
1355-1377	Frederick III (or II) the Simple
1377-1401	Mary
1390-1409	Martin the Younger
1395-1410	Martin (I) the Older of Aragón
1412-1416	Ferdinand I of Sicily & Aragón
1416-1458	Alfonso (V of Aragón)
1458-1468	John II
1468-1516	Ferdinand II (III of Naples)
1516-1713	United with Spain
1713-1720	Victor Amadeus II (duke of Savoy)
1720	Returned to Spain as part of Kingdom of the Two Sicilies
1720-1735	Austrian rule
1735-1759	Charles (Bourbon king of Spain)
1759-1825	Ferdinand I/IV
1825-1830	Francis I
1830-1859	Ferdinand II/V
1859-1860	Francis II
1861	Annexed to Italy

NAPLES

Reign	Ruler
1285-1309	Charles II (Angevin)
1309-1343	Robert Ladislas (Angevin)
1343-1382	Joanna I (Angevin)
1382-1386	Charles III (Angevin)
1386-1414	Ladislas (Angevin)
1414-1435	Joanna II (Angevin)
1435-1442	René of Anjou
1442-1458	Alfonso I (V of Aragón)
1458-1494	Ferdinand I
1494-1495	Alfonso II (Naples only)
1495-1496	Ferdinand II (Ferrandino)
1496-1501	Frederick IV (III)
1501-1503	French occupation

Reign	Ruler
1504-1516	Ferdinand III (II of Sicily)
1516-1713	United with Spain
1713	Ceded to Austria
1720	Returned to Spain as part of Kingdom of the Two Sicilies
1799	Parthenopean Republic
1805	Bourbons deposed
1806-1808	Joseph Bonaparte
1808-1815	Joachim Murat
1815	Bourbon restoration
1825-1830	Francis I
1830-1859	Ferdinand II/V
1859-1860	Francis II
1861	Annexed to Italy

VISCONTIS (GENOA)

Reign	Ruler
1310-1322	Matteo Visconti
1322-1328	Galeazzo I
1328-1339	Azzo
1339-1349	Lucchino
1349-1354	Giovanni
1354-1355	Matteo II and Bernabò
1354-1378	Galeazzo II
1378-1402	Gian Galeazzo II
1402-1447	Filippo Maria

SFORZAS (GENOA)

Reign	Ruler
1450-1466	Francesco Sforza
1466-1476	Galeazzo Maria
1476-1481	Gian Galeazzo
1481-1499	Ludovico
1500-1512	[Louis XII of France]
1512-1515	Massimiliano
1521-1535	Francesco Maria

DOGES OF VENICE

Reign	Doge
727-738	Orso (Ursus) Ipato
742, 744-736	Teodato (Deusdedit) Ipato
756	Galla Gaulo
756-765	Domenico Monegaurio
765-787	Maurizio I Galbaio
787-802	Giovanni and Maurizio II Galbaio
802-811	Obelerio Antenorio
808-811	Beato
811-827	Angello Partecipazio
827-829	Giustiniano Partecipazio
829-836	Giovanni I Partecipazio
836-864	Pietro Tradonico
864-881	Orso I Badoer (I Partecipazio)

Reign	Doge	Reign	Doge
881-888	Giovanni Badoer (II Partecipazio)	1462-1471	Cristoforo Moro
887	Pietro I Candiano	1471-1473	Nicolò Tron
888-912	Pietro Tribuno	1473-1474	Nicolò Marcello
912-932	Orso II Badoer (II Partecipazio)	1474-1476	Pietro Mocenigo
932-939	Pietro II Candiano	1476-1478	Andrea Vendramin
939-942	Pietro Badoer (Partecipazio)	1478-1485	Giovanni Mocenigo
942-959	Pietro III Candiano	1485-1486	Marco Barbarigo
959-976	Pietro IV Candiano	1486-1501	Agostino Barbarigo
976-978	Pietro I Orseolo	1501-1521	Leonardo Loredan
978-979	Vitale Candiano	1521-1523	Antonio Grimani
979-991	Tribuno Menio (Memmo)	1523-1538	Andrea Gritti
991-1009	Pietro II Orseolo	1539-1545	Pietro Lando
1009-1026	Ottone Orseolo	1545-1553	Francesco Donato
1026-1030	Pietro Centranico (Barbolano)	1553-1554	Marcantonio Trevisan
1030-1032	Ottone Orseolo (second rule)	1554-1556	Francesco Venier
1032-1043	Domenico Flabianico	1556-1559	Lorenzo Priuli
1043-1070	Domenico Contarini	1559-1567	Girolamo Priuli
1070-1084	Domenico Silvio (Selvo)	1567-1570	Pietro Loredan
1084-1096	Vitale Falier	1570-1577	Alvise I Mocenigo
1096-1101	Vitale I Michiel (Michel)	1577-1578	Sebastiano Venier
1101-1118	Ordelafo Falier	1578-1585	Nicolò da Ponte
1118-1129	Domenico Michiel	1585-1595	Pasquale Cicogna
1129-1148	Pietro Polani	1595-1605	Marino Grimani
1148-1155	Domenico Morosini	1606-1612	Leonardo Donato
1155-1172	Vitale II Michiel	1612-1615	Marcantonio Memmo
1172-1178	Sebastiano Ziani	1615-1618	Giovanni Bembo
1178-1192	Orio Mastropiero (Malipiero)	1618	Nicolò Donato
1192-1205	Enrico Dandolo	1618-1623	Antonio Priuli
1205-1229	Pietro Ziani	1623-1624	Francesco Contarini
1229-1249	Giacomo Tiepolo	1625-1629	Giovanni Corner
1249-1253	Marino Morosini	1630-1631	Nicolò Contarini
1253-1268	Reniero Zeno	1631-1646	Francesco Erizzo
1268-1275	Lorenzo Tiepolo	1646-1655	Francesco Molin
1275-1280	Jacopo Contarini	1655-1656	Carlo Contarini
1280-1289	Giovanni Dandolo	1656	Francesco Corner
1289-1311	Pietro Gradenigo	1656-1658	Bertucci (Albertuccio) Valier
1311-1312	Marino Zorzi	1658-1659	Giovanni Pesaro
1312-1328	Giovanni Soranzo	1659-1675	Domenico Contarini
1328-1339	Francesco Dandolo	1675-1676	Nicolò Sagredo
1339-1342	Bartolomeo Gradenigo	1676-1684	Luigi Contarini
1343-1354	Andrea Dandolo	1684-1688	Marcantonio Giustinian
1354-1355	Marino Falier	1688-1694	Francesco Morosini
1355-1356	Giovanni Gradenigo	1694-1700	Silvestro Valier
1356-1361	Giovanni Dolfin	1700-1709	Alvise II Mocenigo
1361-1365	Lorenzo Celsi	1709-1722	Giovanni II Corner
1365-1368	Marco Corner	1722-1732	Alvise III Mocenigo
1368-1382	Andrea Contarini	1732-1735	Carlo Ruzzini
1382	Michele Morosini	1735-1741	Alvise Pisani
1382-1400	Antonio Venier	1741-1752	Pietro Grimani
1400-1413	Michele Steno	1752-1762	Francesco Loredan
1414-1423	Tommaso Mocenigo	1762-1763	Marco Foscarini
1423-1457	Francesco Foscari	1763-1778	Alvise IV Mocenigo

Reign	Doge
1779-1789	Paolo Renier
1789-1797	Lodovico Manin
1797	Venice Falls to Napoleon Bonaparte

FLORENCE (MEDICIS)

Reign	Ruler
1434-1464	Cosimo the Elder
1464-1469	Piero I
1469-1478	Giuliano
1469-1492	Lorenzo I the Magnificent
1492-1494	Piero II
1494-1512	Charles VIII expels the Medici
1512-1519	Lorenzo II
1519-1527	Giulio (Pope Clement VII)
1527	Sack of Rome
1527-1530	Second expulsion
1530-1537	Alessandro
1537-1574	Cosimo I
1574-1587	Francesco I
1587-1609	Ferdinand I
1609-1621	Cosimo II
1621-1670	Ferdinand II
1670-1723	Cosimo III
1723-1737	Gian Gastone

TUSCANY (AFTER THE MEDICIS)

Reign	Ruler
1738-1745	Francis
1745-1790	Leopold I
1790-1801	Ferdinand III
1801-1803	Louis of Parma (king of Etruria)
1803-1807	Charles Louis of Parma
1803-1807	Maria Louisa of Parma (regent)
1807-1814	Annexed to France
1824-1859	Leopold II
1859-1860	Ferdinand IV
1860	Annexed to Italy

PARMA

Farneses

Reign	Ruler
1545-1547	Pier Luigi
1547-1586	Ottavio
1586-1592	Alessandro
1592-1622	Ranuccio I
1622-1646	Odoardo I
1646-1694	Ranuccio II
1694-1727	Francesco
1727-1731	Antonio

Bourbons

Reign	Ruler
1731-1736	Charles
1738-1748	Habsburg rule
1748-1765	Philip
1765-1802	Ferdinand
1805-1814	French rule
1814-1847	Marie Louise (Habsburg)
1848-1849	Charles II Louis
1849-1854	Charles III
1854-1859	Robert
1859	Annexed to Italy

SARDINIA

Reign	Ruler
1720-1730	Victor Amadeus II (duke of Savoy)
1730-1773	Charles Emanuel III
1773-1796	Victor Amadeus III
1796-1802	Charles Emanuel IV
1802-1821	Victor Emanuel I
1821-1831	Charles Felix
1831-1849	Charles Albert
1849-1861	Victor Emanuel II
1861	Annexed to Italy

KINGDOM OF ITALY

Reign	Ruler
1861-1878	Victor Emanuel II
1878-1900	Umberto I
1900-1946	Victor Emanuel III
1922-1943	Benito Mussolini (dictator)
1943-1945	German occupation
1946	Umberto II

MODERN ITALY: PRIME MINISTERS

Term	Prime Minister
1860-1861	Count Camillo Benso di Cavour
1861-1862	Baron Bettino Ricasoli
1862	Urbano Ratazzi
1862-1864	Marco Minghetti
1864-1866	General Alfonso La Marmora
1866-1867	Baron Bettino Ricasoli
1867	Urbano Ratazzi
1867-1869	Federigo Menabrea
1869-1873	Domenico Lanza
1873-1876	Marco Minghetti
1876-1878	Agostino Depretis
1878	Benedetto Cairoli
1878-1879	Agostino Depretis
1879-1881	Benedetto Cairoli
1881-1887	Agostino Depretis
1887-1891	Francesco Crispi
1891-1892	Marquis di Rudini

Term	Prime Minister
1892-1893	Giovanni Giolitti
1893-1896	Francesco Crispi
1896-1898	Marquis de Rudini
1898-1900	General Luigi Pelloux
1900-1901	Giuseppe Saracco
1901-1903	Giuseppe Zanardelli
1903-1906	Giovanni Giolitti
1906	Baron Sidney Sonnino
1906-1909	Giovanni Giolitti
1909-1910	Baron Sidney Sonnino
1910-1911	Luigi Luzzatti
1911-1914	Giovanni Giolitti
1914-1916	Antonio Salandra
1916-1917	Paolo Boselli
1917-1919	Vittorio Orlando
1919-1920	Francesco Nitti
1920-1921	Giovanni Giolitti
1921-1922	Ivanoe Bonomi
1922	Luigi Facta
1922-1943	Benito Mussolini
1943-1944	Marshal Pietro Badoglio
1944-1945	Ivanoe Bonomi
1945	Ferruccio Parri
1945-1953	Alcide De Gasperi
1953-1954	Giuseppe Pella
1954-1955	Mario Scelba
1955-1957	Antonio Segni
1957-1958	Adone Zoli
1958-1959	Amintore Fanfani
1959-1960	Antonio Segni
1960	Fernando Tambroni-Armaroli
1960-1963	Amintore Fanfani
1963	Giovanni Leone
1963-1968	Aldo Moro
1968	Giovanni Leone
1968-1970	Mariano Rumor
1970-1972	Emilio Colombo
1972-1973	Giulio Andreotti
1973-1974	Mariano Rumor
1974-1976	Aldo Moro
1976-1979	Giulio Andreotti
1979-1980	Francesco Cossiga
1980-1981	Arnaldo Forlani
1981-1982	Giovanni Spadolini
1982-1983	Amintore Fanfani
1983-1987	Bettino Craxi
1987	Amintore Fanfani
1987-1988	Giovanni Goria
1988-1989	Ciriaco De Mita
1989-1992	Giulio Andreotti
1992-1993	Giuliano Amato
1993-1994	Carlo Azeglio Ciampi

Term	Prime Minister
1994-1995	Silvio Berlusconi
1995-1996	Lamberto Dini
1996-1998	Romano Prodi
1998-2000	Massimo D'Alema
2000-2001	Giuliano Amato
2001-	Silvio Berlusconi

MODERN ITALY: PRESIDENTS

Term	President
1946-1948	Enrico de Nicola
1948-1955	Luigi Einaudi
1955-1962	Giovanni Gronchi
1962-1964	Antonio Segni
1964-1971	Giuseppe Saragat
1971-1978	Giovanni Leone
1978-1985	Alessandro Pertini
1985-1992	Francesco Cossiga
1992	Giovanni Spadolini
1992-1999	Oscar Luigi Scalfaro
1999	Nicola Mancino
1999-	Carlo Azeglio Ciampi

JAPAN

ASUKA PERIOD

Reign	Ruler
539-571	Kimmei
572-585	Bidatsu
585-587	Yōmei
587-592	Sushun
593-628	Suiko (empress)
629-641	Jomei
642-645	Kōgyoku (empress)
645-654	Kōtoku
655-661	Saimei (empress)
661-672	Tenji
672	Kōbun
673-686	Temmu
686-697	Jitō (empress)
697-707	Mommu
707-715	Gemmei (empress)

NARA PERIOD

Reign	Ruler
707-715	Gemmei (empress)
715-724	Genshō (empress)
724-749	Shōmu
749-758	Kōken (empress)
758-764	Junnin
764-770	Shōtoku (Kōken, empress)
770-781	Kōnin

HEIAN PERIOD

Reign	Ruler
781-806	Kammu
806-809	Heizei
809-823	Saga
823-833	Junna
833-850	Nimmyō
850-858	Montoku
858-876	Seiwa
876-884	Yōzei
884-887	Kōkō
887-897	Uda
897-930	Daigo
930-946	Suzaku
946-967	Murakami
967-969	Reizei
969-984	En'yu
984-986	Kazan
986-1011	Ichijō
1011-1016	Sanjō
1016-1036	Go-Ichijō
1036-1045	Go-Suzaku
1045-1068	Go-Reizei
1068-1073	Go-Sanjō
1073-1087	Shirakawa (cloistered, 1086-1129)
1087-1107	Horikawa
1107-1123	Toba (cloistered, 1129-1156)
1123-1142	Sutoku
1142-1155	Konoe
1155-1158	Go-Shirakawa (cloistered, 1158-1192)
1158-1165	Nijō
1165-1168	Rokujō
1168-1180	Takakura
1180-1185	Antoku

KAMAKURA PERIOD AND KEMMU RESTORATION

Reign	Ruler
1183-1198	Go-Toba
1198-1210	Tsuchimikado
1210-1221	Jintoku
1221	Chukyo
1221-1232	Go-Horikawa
1232-1242	Shijō
1242-1246	Go-Saga
1246-1260	Go-Fukakusa
1260-1274	Kameyama
1274-1287	Go-Uda
1287-1298	Fushimi
1298-1301	Go-Fushimi
1301-1308	Go-Nijō
1308-1318	Hanazonō
1318-1339	Go-Daigo

KAMAKURA SHOGUNATE

Reign	Shogun
1192-1199	Minamoto Yoritomo
1202-1203	Minamoto Yoriie
1203-1219	Minamoto Sanetomo
1226-1244	Kujo Yoritsune
1244-1252	Kujo Yoritsugu
1252-1266	Prince Munetaka
1266-1289	Prince Koreyasu
1289-1308	Prince Hisaaki
1308-1333	Prince Morikuni

HŌJŌ REGENTS

Reign	Regent
1203-1205	Hōjō Tokimasa
1205-1224	Hōjō Yoshitoki
1224-1242	Hōjō Yasutoki
1242-1246	Hōjō Tsunetoki
1246-1256	Hōjō Tokiyori
1256-1264	Hōjō Nagatoki
1264-1268	Hōjō Masamura
1268-1284	Hōjō Tokimune
1284-1301	Hōjō Sadatoki
1301-1311	Hōjō Morotoki
1311-1312	Hōjō Munenobu
1312-1315	Hōjō Hirotoki
1315	Hōjō Mototoki
1316-1326	Hōjō Takatoki
1326	Hōjō Sadaaki
1327-1333	Hōjō Moritoki

NAMBOKUCHŌ PERIOD

Emperors: Southern Court

Reign	Ruler
1318-1339	Go-Daigo
1339-1368	Go-Murakami
1368-1383	Chōkei
1383-1392	Go-Kameyama

Ashikaga Pretenders: Northern Court

Reign	Ruler
1336-1348	Komyō
1348-1351	Sukō
1351-1371	Go-Kogon
1371-1382	Go-En'yu

MUROMACHI PERIOD

Reign	Ruler
1382-1412	Go-Komatsu
1412-1428	Shōkō
1428-1464	Go-Hanazono
1464-1500	Go-Tsuchimikado
1500-1526	Go-Kashiwabara

Reign	Ruler
1526-1557	Go-Nara
1557-1586	Ōgimachi

ASHIKAGA SHOGUNATE

Reign	Shogun
1338-1358	Ashikaga Takauji
1359-1368	Ashikaga Yoshiakira
1368-1394	Ashikaga Yoshimitsu
1395-1423	Ashikaga Yoshimochi
1423-1425	Ashikaga Yoshikazu
1429-1441	Ashikaga Yoshinori
1442-1443	Ashikaga Yoshikatsu
1449-1473	Ashikaga Yoshimasa
1474-1489	Ashikaga Yoshihisa
1490-1493	Ashikaga Yoshitane
1495-1508	Ashikaga Yoshizumi
1508-1521	Ashikaga Yoshitane (second rule)
1522-1547	Ashikaga Yoshiharu
1547-1565	Ashikaga Yoshiteru
1568	Ashikaga Yoshihide
1568-1573	Ashikaga Yoshiaki

AZUCHI-MOMOYAMA PERIOD

Reign	Ruler
1573-1582	Oda Nobunaga (dictator)
1586-1611	Go-Yōzei (emperor)

EDO PERIOD

Emperors

Reign	Emperor
1612-1629	Go-Mi-no-o
1630-1643	Meishō (Myōshō)
1644-1654	Go-Kōmyō
1655-1662	Go-Saiin
1663-1686	Reigen
1687-1709	Higashiyama
1710-1735	Nakamikado
1736-1746	Sakuramachi
1746-1762	Momozono
1763-1770	Go-Sakuramachi
1771-1779	Go-Momozono
1780-1816	Kōkaku
1817-1846	Ninkō
1847-1866	Kōmei

Tokugawa Shogunate

Reign	Shogun
1603-1605	Tokugawa Ieyasu
1605-1623	Tokugawa Hidetada
1623-1651	Tokugawa Iemitsu
1651-1680	Tokugawa Ietsuna
1680-1709	Tokugawa Tsunayoshi
1709-1712	Tokugawa Ienobu
1713-1716	Tokugawa Ietsugu
1716-1745	Tokugawa Yoshimune
1745-1760	Tokugawa Ieshige
1760-1786	Tokugawa Ieharu
1787-1837	Tokugawa Ienari
1837-1853	Tokugawa Ieyoshi
1853-1858	Tokugawa Iesada
1858-1866	Tokugawa Iemochi
1867-1868	Tokugawa Yoshinobu

MODERN PERIOD

Emperors

Reign	Emperor
1867-1912	Mutsuhito (crowned 1868; Meiji era)
1912-1926	Yoshihito (Taishō era)
1926-1989	Hirohito (Shōwa era)
1989	Akihito (Heisei era)

Prime Ministers

Term	Prime Minister
1885-1888	Itō Hirobumi
1888-1889	Kuroda Kiyotaka
1889-1891	Yamagata Aritomo
1891-1892	Matsukata Masayoshi
1892-1896	Itō Hirobumi
1896-1898	Matsukata Masayoshi
1898-1898	Itō Hirobumi
1898-1898	Okuma Shigenobu
1898-1900	Yamagata Aritomo
1900-1901	Itō Hirobumi
1901-1906	Katsura Tarō
1906-1908	Saionji Kimmochi
1908-1911	Katsura Tarō
1911-1912	Saionji Kimmochi
1912-1913	Katsura Tarō
1913-1914	Yamamoto Gonnohyōe
1914-1916	Okuma Shigenobu
1916-1918	Terauchi Masatake
1918-1921	Hara Takashi (assassinated)
1921-1922	Takahashi Korekiyo
1922-1923	Katō Tomosaburō
1923-1924	Yamamoto Gonnohyoe
1924-1924	Kiyoura Keigo
1924-1926	Katō Takaaki
1926-1927	Wakatsuki Reijirō
1927-1929	Tanaka Giichi
1929-1931	Hamaguchi Osachi (assassinated)
1931-1931	Wakatsuki Reijiro
1931-1932	Inukai Tsuyoshi (assassinated)
1932-1934	Saitō Makoto
1934-1936	Okada Keisuke
1936-1937	Hirota Kōki
1937-1937	Hayashi Senjūrō

Term	Prime Minister
1937-1939	Konoe Fumimaro
1939-1939	Hiranuma Kiichirō
1939-1940	Abe Nobuyuki
1940-1940	Yonai Mitsumasa
1940-1941	Konoe Fumimaro
1941-1944	Tōjō Hideki
1944-1945	Koiso Kuniaki
1945-1945	Suzuki Kantarō
1945-1945	Higashikuni Naruhiko
1945-1946	Shidehara Kijūrō
1946-1947	Yoshida Shigeru
1947-1948	Katayama Tetsu
1948-1948	Ashida Hitoshi
1948-1954	Yoshida Shigeru
1954-1956	Hatoyama Ichirō
1956-1957	Ishibashi Tanzan
1957-1960	Kishi Nobusuke
1960-1964	Ikeda Hayato
1964-1972	Satō Eisaku
1972-1974	Tanaka Kakuei
1974-1976	Miki Takeo
1976-1978	Fukuda Takeo
1978-1980	Ohira Masayoshi
1980-1982	Suzuki Zenko
1982-1987	Nakasone Yasuhiro
1987-1989	Takeshita Noboru
1989-1989	Uno Sosuke
1989-1991	Kaifu Toshiki
1991-1993	Miyazawa Kiichi
1993-1994	Hosokawa Morihiro
1994-1994	Hata Tsutomu
1994-1996	Murayama Tomiichi
1996-1998	Hashimoto Ryūtarō
1998-2000	Obuchi Keizō
2000-2001	Mori Yoshirō
2001-	Koizumi Junichiro

KINGDOM OF JERUSALEM

The Christian rulers of Jerusalem were ushered in by the First Crusade and essentially were ushered out after the last Crusade.

Reign	King
1095-1099	First Crusade
1099-1100	Godfrey of Boulogne (or Bouillon)
1100-1118	Baldwin I of Boulogne
1118-1131	Baldwin II of Le Bourg
1131-1153	Melisende
1131-1143	Fulk V of Anjou
1143-1162	Baldwin III
1147-1149	Second Crusade

Reign	King
1162-1174	Amalric I
1174-1183	Baldwin IV the Leper
1183-1186	Baldwin V
1185-1190	Sibylla
1186-1192	Guy of Lusignan
1189-1192	Third Crusade
1190-1192	Conrad of Montferrat
1192-1197	Henry of Champagne
1192-1205	Isabella I
1197-1205	Amalric II
1202-1204	Fourth Crusade
1205-1210	Maria of Montferrat (regent)
1210-1225	John of Brienne
1210-1228	Isabella (Yolanda) II
1217-1221	Fifth Crusade
1225-1228	Frederick II
1227-1230	Sixth Crusade
1228-1254	Conrad IV Hohenstaufen
1244	Fall of Jerusalem
1248-1254	Seventh (or Sixth) Crusade
1254-1268	Conradin Hohenstaufen
1268-1284	Hugh III
1268-1284	Charles of Anjou (rival)
1270	Eighth (or Seventh) Crusade
1284-1285	John I
1285-1306	Henry I of Jerusalem (II of Cyprus)
1291	Fall of Acre to the Mamluks

KOREA

UNIFIED SILLA DYNASTY

Reign	Ruler
661-681	Munmu Wang
681-692	Sinmun Wang
692-702	Hyoso Wang
702-737	Sŏngdŏk Wang
737-742	Hyosŏng Wang
742-765	Kyŏngdŏk Wang
765-780	Hyesong Wang
780-785	Sŏndŏk Wang
785-798	Wŏnsŏng Wang
798-800	Sosŏng Wang
800-809	Aejang Wang
809-826	Hŏndŏk Wang
826-836	Hŭngdŏk Wang
836-838	Hŭigang Wang
838-839	Minae Wang
839	Sinmu Wang
839-857	Munsŏng Wang
857-861	Hŏnan Wang
861-875	Kyŏngmun Wang

Reign	Ruler
875-886	Hŏn'gang Wang
886-887	Chŏnggang Wang
887-896	Queen Chinsŏng
897-912	Hyogong Wang
912-917	Pak Sindŏ Wang
917-924	Kyŏngmyŏng Wang
924-927	Kyŏngae Wang
927-935	Kyŏngsun Wang

KORYŎ DYNASTY

Reign	Ruler
918-943	T'aejo (Wang Kŏn)
944-945	Hyejong
946-949	Chŏngjong
949-975	Kwangjong (Wang So)
975-981	Kyŏngjong (Wang Yu)
981-997	Sŏngjong (Wang Ch'i)
997-1009	Mokshong
1009-1031	Hyŏnjong
1031-1034	Tokjong
1034-1046	Chŏngjong
1046-1083	Munjong (Wang Hwi)
1083	Sunjong
1083-1094	Sŏnjong
1094-1095	Hŏnjong
1095-1105	Sukjong
1105-1122	Yejong I
1122-1146	Injong I (Wang Hae)
1146-1170	Ŭijong
1170-1197	Myŏngjong
1197-1204	Sinjong
1204-1211	Hŭijong
1211-1213	Kangjong
1214-1259	Kojong I
1260-1274	Wŏnjong
1274-1308	Ch'unguyŏl Wang
1308-1313	Ch'ungsŏn Wang
1313-1330	Ch'ungsuk Wang
1330-1332	Ch'unghye Wang
1332-1339	Ch'angsuk Wang
1339-1344	Ch'unghye Wang
1344-1348	Ch'ungmok Wang
1348-1351	Ch'ungjŏng Wang
1351-1374	Kongmin Wang
1374-1388	U (Sin-u)
1389	Sinch'ang
1389-1392	Kongyang Wang

YI DYNASTY

Reign	Ruler
1392-1398	Yi T'aejo
1398-1400	Chŏngjong
1400-1418	T'aejong
1418-1450	Sejong
1450-1452	Munjong
1452-1455	Tanjong
1455-1468	Sejo
1468-1469	Yejong
1469-1494	Sŏngjong
1494-1506	Yŏnsan Gun
1506-1544	Chungjong
1544-1545	Injong
1546-1567	Myŏngjong
1567-1608	Sŏnjo
1608-1623	Kwanghae-gun
1623-1649	Injo
1649-1659	Hyojong
1659-1674	Hyŏnjong
1674-1720	Sukchong
1720-1724	Kyŏngjong
1724-1776	Yŏngjo
1776-1800	Chŏngjo
1800-1834	Sonjo
1834-1849	Hŏnjong
1849-1864	Ch'ŏljong
1864-1897	Kojong
1907-1910	Sunjong
1905-1910	Japanese protectorate
1910-1945	Annexed to Japan
1945-1948	Allied military occupation
1948	Division into North and South Korea

DEMOCRATIC PEOPLE'S REPUBLIC OF KOREA (NORTH KOREA)

Term	President
1948-1993	Kim Il-sung
1993-	Kim Jong-il

REPUBLIC OF KOREA (SOUTH KOREA)

Term	President
1948-1960	Syngman Rhee
1960-1962	Yun Boseon
1963-1979	Park Chunghee
1979-1980	Choi Kyuha
1980-1988	Chun Doo-hwan
1988-1993	Roh Tae-woo
1993-1998	Kim Young-sam
1998-2003	Kim Dae-jung
2003-	Roh Moo-hyun

MONGOLS. *See also* CHINA: YUAN DYNASTY

From his base in Mongolia, founder Genghis Khan conquered a large and diverse region covering much of Asia from the Far East to the steppes of Russia, Turkey and the Middle East, Central Asia, and even parts of Southeast Asia. Although the individual leaders of those who inherited this empire remain unfamiliar to most, Genghis's heirs, among whom are the "great khans" of the immediate generations to follow, would indelibly change and shape the world from Russia to China, the Mideast to India. Genghis divided his empire among four sons. Jochi, the eldest, received the northwestern quadrant of this expanse, and his sons would found the "hordes" (armies) the would become known as the Blue, White, and eventually Golden Hordes; the latter would not meet its match until Russia's founder, Ivan the Great, refused to pay tribute in 1476 and thereafter would dissolve into the various khanates of Kazan, Astrakhan, and the Crimea. Genghis's second son, Chaghatai, would receive the area of Central Asia lying north of India and east of the Caspian and Aral seas, sometimes called Moghulistan or Mughulistan. Genghis's third son, Ogatai, oversaw the southeastern and far east coastal "quadrant" or swathe, which would eventually become part of the huge realm of his nephew Kublai Khan, who in turn was the son of Genghis's youngest, Tolui, heir to the Mongolian homeland. It was Tolui's sons, beginning with Kublai, who would spawn the Chinese emperors of the Yuan Dynasty in the east and, beginning with Hulegu, the great Ilkhans who conquered the Middle East. The Ilkhans' successors, the Jalāyirids, Black Sheep Turks, White Sheep Turks, and ultimately the Timurids (founded by the part-Mongol Timur or Tamerlane), would dominate the Mideast and also give rise to the Mughal Dynasty in India.

GREAT KHANS

Reign	Ruler
1206-1227	Genghis Khan (founder)
1227-1229	Tolui
1229-1241	Ogatai Khan
1241-1246	Toregene (regent, wife of Ogatai)
1246-1248	Güyük
1248-1251	Oghul Qaimish (regent, wife of Güyük)
1251-1259	Mongu
1259-1260	Arigböge (regent, brother of Mongu and Kublai)
1260-1294	Kublai Khan

KHANS OF CHINA'S YUAN DYNASTY

Reign	Ruler
1267-1279	Mongols conquer Southern Song
1294-1307	Temür Öljeitü (Chengzong)
1307-1311	Kaishan (Wuzong)
1311-1320	Ayurbarwada (Renzong)
1321-1323	Shidebala (Yingzong)
1323-1328	Yesün Temür (Taiding)
1328	Arigaba (Aragibag)
1328-1329	Tugh Temür (Wenzong)1
1329	Tugh Koshila (Mingzong)
1329-1332	Tugh Temür (restored)
1333-1368	Toghon Temür (Shundi)
1368	Chinese expel Mongols

LATER MONGOLIAN KHANS

Reign	Ruler
1370-1388	Togus-Temür
1370-1379	Biliktu
1379-1389	Usaqal
1389-1393	Engke Soriktu
1393-1400	Elbek
1400-1403	Gun Timur
1403-1411	Oljei Timur
1411-1415	Delbeg
1415-1425	Eseku
1425-1438	Adai Qa'an
1438-1440	Esen Toghan Tayisi
1440-1452	Tayisung Qa'an
1452-1455	Esen Tayisi
1452-1454	Molon Khan Togus
1454-1463?	Maqa Kurkis
1463?-1467	Mandughuli
1467-1470	Bayan Mongke
1470-c.1485	Civil war
1479-1543	Dayan Khan
1543-1582	Altan Khan
1547-1557	Kudeng Darayisun
1557-1592	Tumen Jasaghtu
1592-1604	Sechen Khan
1604-1634	Ligdan Khan
1628-1759	Manchurian conquest

MIDDLE EAST (IRAQ, IRAN, EASTERN TURKEY, ARABIA)

Il Khāns

Reign	Ruler
1255-1260	Invasion of Middle East
1256-1265	Hülegü (Hülägü)
1260	Battle of ʿAin Jalut (defeat by Mamlūks)
1265-1282	Abaqa
1282-1284	Aḥmad Tegüder
1284-1291	Arghūn
1291-1295	Gaykhatu

Reign	Ruler
1295	Baydu
1295-1304	Maḥmūd Ghāzān
1304-1316	Muḥammad Khudābanda Öljeytü
1316-1335	Abū Saʿīd ʿAlāʾ ad-Dunyā wa ad-Dīn
1335-1336	Arpa Keʾün
1336-1337	Mūsā
1337-1338	Muḥammad
1338-1353	Conflict among successor states

Jalāyirids

Reign	Ruler
1340-1356	Shaykh Ḥasan-i Buzurg Tāj ad-Dīn
1356-1374	Shaykh Uways
1374-1382	Ḥusayn I Jalāl ad-Dīn
1382-1410	Sulṭān Aḥmad Ghiyāth ad-Dīn
1410-1411	Shāh Walad
1411	Maḥmūd
1411-1421	Uways II
1421-1425	Maḥmūd
1421	Muḥammad
1425-1532	Ḥusayn II
1432	Conquest by Kara Koyunlu

Kara Koyunlu (Black Sheep Turks)

Reign	Ruler
1351-1380	Bayram Khōja (Jalāyirid vassal)
1380-1389	Kara Muḥammad
1382	Independent
c. 1390-1400	Kara Yūsuf
1400-1406	Occupation by Tamerlane
1406-1420	Kara Yūsuf
1420-1438	Iskandar
1439-1467	Jahān Shāh
1467-1469	Ḥasan ʿAlī
1469	Abū Yūsuf
1469	Conquest by Ak Koyunlu

Ak Koyunlu (White Sheep Turks)

Reign	Ruler
1403-1435	Kara Osman (Qara Yoluq ʿUthmān Fakhr ad-Dīn)
1435-1438	ʿAlī Jalāl ad-Dīn
1438-1444	Ḥamza Nūr ad-Dīn
1444-1453	Jahāngīr Muʾizz ad-Dīn
1453-1478	Uzun Ḥasan
1478	Sulṭān Khalīl
1478-1490	Yaʿqūb
1490-1493	Baysonqur
1493-1497	Rustam
1497	Aḥmad Gövde
1497-1502	Alwand (Diyār Bakr and Azerbaijan)
1497-1500	Muḥammad (Iraq and Persia)
1500-1508	Sulṭān Murād (Persia)

Reign	Ruler
1504-1508	Zayn al-ʿAbidīn (Diyār Bakr)
1508	Ṣafawid conquest

SOUTH CENTRAL ASIA

Chaghatayid or Jagataiid (Turkistan and the Tarim Basin)

Reign	Ruler
1227-1244	Chaghatay (Jagatai)
1244-1246	Kara Hülegü
1246-1251	Yesü Möngke
1251-1252	Kara Hülegü
1252-1260	Orqina Khātūn
1260-1266	Alughu
1266	Mubārak Shāh
c. 1266-1271	Baraq Ghiyāth ad-Dīn
1271-1272	Negübey
1272-1282	Buqa/Toqa Temür
c. 1282-1306	Duʾa
1306-1308	Könchek
1308-1309	Taliqu
1309	Kebek
1309-1320	Esen Buqa
c. 1320-1326	Kebek
1326	Eljigedey
1326	Duʾa Temür
1326-1334	Tarmashīrīn ʿAlāʾ ad-Dīn
1334	Buzan
1334-1338	Changshi
c. 1338-1342	Yesün Temür
c. 1342-1343	Muḥammad
1343-1346	Kazan
1346-1358	Danishmendji
1358	Buyan Kuli
1359	Shāh Temür
1359-1363	Tughluq Temür
c. 1363	Timurids rule Mughulistan

Timurids

Reign	Ruler
1370-1405	Tamerlane (Timur)
1402	Capture of Bayezid, Battle of Ankara
1405-1407	Pīr Muḥammad (Kandahar)
1405-1409	Khalīl Sulṭān (Samarqand)
1405-1409	Shāh Rukh (Khorāsān)
1409-1447	Shāh Rukh (Transoxania, Iran)
1447-1449	Ulugh Beg (Transoxania, Khorāsān)
1449-1450	ʿAbd al-Laṭīf (Transoxania)
1450-1451	ʿAbdallāh
1451-1469	Abū Saʿīd (Transoxania, Iran)
1469-1494	Sulṭān Aḥmad (Transoxania)
1494-1495	Maḥmūd
1495-1500	Baysonqur, Masʾūd, ʿAlī (Transoxania)
1500	Özbeg conquest of Transoxania

WESTERN ASIA, RUSSIA, NORTH CENTRAL ASIA

Blue Horde

Reign	Ruler
1227-1256	Batu
1236-1239	Russia conquered
1239-1242	Europe invaded
1256-1257	Sartaq
1257	Ulaghchi
1257-1267	Berke
1267-1280	Möngke Temür
1280-1287	Töde Möngke
1287-1291	Töle Buqa
1291-1313	Toqta
1313-1341	Muḥammad Özbeg
1341-1342	Tīnī Beg
1342-1357	Jānī Beg
1357-1359	Berdi Beg
1357-1380	Period of anarchy
1378	Union with White Horde

White Horde

Reign	Ruler
1226-1280	Orda
1280-1302	Köchü
1302-1309	Buyan
1309-1315	Sāsibuqa?
c. 1315-1320	Ilbasan
1320-1344	Mubārak Khwāja
1344-1374	Chimtay
1374-1376	Urus
1376-1377	Toqtaqiya
1377	Temür Malik
1377-1395	Toqtamïsh
1378	White and Blue Hordes form Golden Horde

Golden Horde

Reign	Ruler
1378-1395	Toqtamïsh
1395-1419	Edigü (vizir)
1395-1401	Temür Qutlugh
1401-1407	Shādī Beg
1407-1410	Pūlād Khān
1410-1412	Temür
1412	Jalāl ad-Dīn
1412-1414	Karīm Berdi
1414-1417	Kebek
1417-1419	Yeremferden?
1419-1422	Ulugh Muḥammad/Dawlat Berdi (rivals)
1422-1433	Baraq
c. 1433-1435	Sayyid Aḥmad I
c. 1435-1465	Küchük Muḥammad
c. 1465-1481	Aḥmad
1476	Ivan refuses to pay tribute

Reign	Ruler
1480	Russian independence
1481-1498	Shaykh Aḥmad
1481-1499	Murtaḍā
1499-1502	Shaykh Aḥmad
1502	Annexed to Crimean khanate

Remnants of the Golden Horde

Reign	Rulers
1437-1552	Kazan khans
1449-1783	Crimean khans
1466-1554	Astrakhan khans

THE NETHERLANDS

Date	Ruler/Government/Event
1559-1567	William I, the Silent, Prince of Orange, Count of Nassau (stadtholder)
1568	Dutch Revolt
1568-1648	Eighty Years' War
1572-1584	William the Silent
1579	Union of Utrecht
1581	Dutch independence declared
1585-1625	Maurice (Maurits)
1609-1621	Twelve Years' Truce
1618-1648	Thirty Years' War
1625-1647	Frederik Hendrik
1647-1650	William II
1648	Peace of Westphalia, Spanish recognition of Dutch independence
1652-1654	First Anglo-Dutch War
1664-1667	Second Anglo-Dutch War
1672-1702	William III
1672-1678	Dutch War with France
1672-1674	Third Anglo-Dutch War
1688-1697	War of the League of Augsburg
1689-1702	England rules
1701-1713	War of the Spanish Succession
1702-1747	Republic
1747-1751	William IV Friso
1751-1795	William V
1780-1784	Fourth Anglo-Dutch War
1795-1806	Batavian Republic
1806-1810	Louis Bonaparte (king)
1810-1813	Annexed by France
1813-1840	William I (VI) King of the Netherlands
1840-1849	William II
1849-1890	William III
1890-1948	Wilhelmina (in exile 1940-1945)
1940-1945	German ccupation (World War II)
1948-1980	Juliana (abdicated)
1980-	Beatrix

Norway. *See also* Denmark, Sweden

Reign	Ruler
680-710	Olaf the Tree Hewer
710-750	Halfdan I
750-780	Oystein (Eystein) I
780-800	Halfdan II White Legs
800-810	Gudrod the Magnificent
810-840	Olaf Geirstade
840-863	Halfdan III the Black
863-872	Civil war
872-930/33	Harald I Fairhair
933-934	Erik I Bloodaxe
934-961	Hákon I the Good
961-970	Harald II Grayfell
970-995	Earl (Jarl) Hákon
995-1000	Olaf I Tryggvason
1000-1015	Erik I
1016-1028	Saint Olaf II Haraldsson
1028-1035	Canute the Great
1035-1047	Magnus I the Good
1047-1066	Harald III Hardrada
1066-1069	Magnus II
1069-1093	Olaf III the Peaceful
1093-1103	Magnus III the Barefoot
1103-1122	Oystein (Eystein) II
1103-1130	Sigurd I the Crusader
1130-1135	Magnus IV the Blinded
1130-1136	Harald IV Gillechrist
1136-1155	Sigurd II
1136-1161	Inge I
1142-1157	Oystein (Eystein) III
1161-1162	Hákon II
1163-1184	Magnus V
1184-1202	Sverre Sigurdsson
1202-1204	Hákon III
1204-1217	Inge II
1217-1263	Hákon IV
1263-1281	Magnus VI
1281-1299	Erik II Magnusson
1299-1319	Hákon V
1320-1343	Magnus VII (II of Sweden)
1343-1380	Hákon VI
1376-1387	Olaf IV (V of Denmark)
1380	Unification of Norway and Denmark
1380-1410	Margaret I of Denmark, Norway, and Sweden
1397	Unification of Norway, Denmark, and Sweden
1412-1439	Erik III (VII of Denmark, XIII of Sweden)
1439-1448	Christopher (III of Denmark)
1448-1481	Christian I of Oldenburg
1481-1513	Hans/John (II of Sweden)
1513-1523	Christian II
1523-1533	Frederick I

Reign	Ruler
1534-1559	Christian III
1536-1814	Union with Denmark
1559-1588	Frederick II
1588-1648	Christian IV
1648-1670	Frederick III
1670-1699	Christian V
1699-1730	Frederick IV
1730-1746	Christian VI
1746-1766	Frederick V
1766-1808	Christian VII
1808-1814	Frederick VI
1814	Christian Frederik
1814-1818	Carl II
1814-1905	Union with Sweden
1905-1957	Haakon VII
1957-1991	Olav V
1991-	Harald V

Ottoman Empire. *See also* Iran, Islamic Caliphs, Seljuk Empire, Spain

Reign	Sultan
1281/88-1326	Osman I
1326-1360	Orhan I
1360-1389	Murad I
1389-1402	Bayezid I
1402-1421	Mehmed I
1421-1444	Murad II
1444-1446	Mehmed II
1446-1451	Murad II (second rule)
1451-1481	Mehmed II (second rule)
1453	Ottomans take Constantinople
1481	Djem I
1481-1512	Bayezid II
1512-1520	Selim I
1520-1566	Süleyman I the Magnificent
1566-1574	Selim II
1574-1595	Murad III
1595-1603	Mehmed III
1603-1617	Ahmed I
1617-1618	Mustafa I
1618-1622	Osman II
1622-1623	Mustafa I
1623-1640	Murad IV
1640-1648	Ibrahim I
1648-1687	Mehmed IV
1687-1691	Süleyman II
1691-1695	Ahmed II
1695-1703	Mustafa II
1703-1730	Ahmed III
1730-1754	Mahmud I
1754-1757	Osman III

Reign	Sultan
1757-1774	Mustafa III
1774-1789	Abd-ul-Hamid I
1789-1807	Selim III
1807-1808	Mustafa IV
1808-1839	Mahmud II
1839-1861	Abd-ul-Mejid
1861-1876	Abd-ul-Aziz
1876	Murad V
1876-1909	Abd-ul-Hamid II
1909-1918	Mehmed V
1918-1922	Mehmed VI

POLAND

Reign	Ruler
962-992	Mieszko I
992-1025	Bolesław I the Brave
1025-1034	Mieszko II
1034-1037	Instability
1037-1058	Casimir I the Restorer
	Instability
1058-1079	Bolesław II
1079-1102	Władysław (Vladislav or Ladislas) I
1102-1106	Zbigniev (rival to brother Bolesław III)
1102-1138	Bolesław III
1138-1146	Instability following Bolesław III's division of Poland into five principalities
1146-1173	Bolesław IV
1173-1177	Mieszko III
1177-1194	Casimir II
1194-1227	Leszek I
1227-1279	Bolesław V
1228-1288	Instability: arrival of Teutonic Knights followed by Mongol incursions
1288-1290	Henry Probus
1290-1296	Przemyslav II (crowned 1295)
1297-1300	Instability
1300-1305	Wenceslaus (Vacław) I
1306-1333	Władysław I (Vladislav IV, Lokietek)
1333-1370	Casimir III the Great
1370	End of the Piast Dynasty
1370-1382	Ludvik I the Great (Louis of Anjou)
1382-1384	Confederation of Radom and civil war
1384-1399	Queen Jadwiga
1386-1434	Władysław II Jagiełło
1410-1411	Battle of Tannenberg and Peace of Thorn
1434-1444	Władysław (Vladislav) III
1444-1447	Instability; Poland united with Lithuania
1447-1492	Casimir IV
1454-1466	Poles defeat Teutonic Order, gain access to the Baltic in the Second Peace of Thorn

Reign	Ruler
1471-1516	Vladislav Jagiełło (son of Casimir IV) king of Bohemia and then Hungary
1492-1501	John I Albert
1496	Statute of Piotrkow (Poland's Magna Carta)
1501-1506	Alexander Jagiełło
1506-1548	Sigismund I, the Old
1548-1572	Sigismund II Augustus
1573-1574	Henry Valois (Henry III)
1575-1586	Stephen Báthory

VASA KINGS OF SWEDEN AND POLAND

Reign	Ruler
1587-1632	Sigismund III Vasa
1632-1648	Vladislaus IV Vasa
1648-1668	Jan Kazimierz Vasa
1669-1673	Michael Korybut Wisniowiecki
1674-1696	John III Sobieski

WETTIN ELECTORS OF SAXONY OF HOLY ROMAN EMPIRE

Reign	Ruler
1697-1706	Augustus II, the Strong (Wettin)
1706-1709	Stanisław Leszczynski
1709-1733	Augustus II, the Strong (Wettin)
1733-1736	Stanisław Leszczynski
1733-1763	August III Wettin
1764-1795	Stanisław August Poniatowski

DUCHY OF WARSAW

Reign	Ruler
1807-1815	Ksiestwo Warszawskie (dependent from France)
1807-1815	Frederick Augustus I of Saxony Wettin

CONGRESS KINGDOM, KINGDOM OF POLAND

Reign	Ruler
1815-1825	Alexander I of Russia
1825-1831	Nicholas I of Russia (dismissed during November uprising)

SECOND POLISH REPUBLIC

Term	President
1918-1922	Józef Pilsudski
1922	Gabriel Narutowicz (assassinated)
1922-1926	Stanisław Wojciechowski (ousted)
1926-1939	Ignacy Moscicki

POLISH GOVERNMENT IN EXILE

Term	President
1939-1947	Władysław Raczkiewicz
1947-1972	August Zaleski
1972-1979	Stanisław Ostrowski
1979-1986	Edward Raczyński

Term	President
1986-1989	Kazimierz Sabbat
1989-1990	Ryszard Kaczorowski (resigned after election of Lech Wałęsa)

COMMUNIST POLAND

Term	Leader
1944-1952	Bolesław Bierut

PEOPLE'S REPUBLIC OF POLAND

Chairmen of Council of State

Term	Chair
1952-1964	Aleksander Zawadzki
1964-1968	Edward Ochab
1968-1970	Marian Spychalski
1970-1972	Józef Cyrankiewicz
1972-1985	Henryk Jablonski
1985-1989	Wojciech Jaruzelski

First Secretaries of the Central Committee

Term	Secretary
1948-1956	Bolesław Bierut
1956	Edward Ochab
1956-1970	Władysław Gomułka
1970-1980	Edward Gierek
1980-1981	Stanisław Kania
1981-1989	Wojciech Jaruzelski

THIRD POLISH REPUBLIC

Term	President
1989-1990	Wojciech Jaruzelski
1990-1995	Lech Wałęsa
1995-2005	Aleksander Kwaśniewski
2005-	Lech Kaczyński

PORTUGAL

Reign	Ruler
1093-1112	Henry of Burgundy, count of Portugal
1112-1185	Afonso I (count of Portugal 1112-1139, king 1139-1185)
1185-1211	Sancho I
1211-1223	Afonso II
1223-1245	Sancho II
1245-1279	Afonso III
1279-1325	Diniz (Denis)
1325-1357	Afonso IV
1357-1367	Peter I
1367-1383	Ferdinand I
1385-1433	John I of Avis
1433-1438	Edward I
1438-1481	Afonso V

Reign	Ruler
1481-1495	John II
1495-1521	Manuel I
1521-1557	John III
1557-1578	Sebastian I
1578-1580	Cardinal Henry
1580-1598	Philip I of Portugal (Philip II of Spain)
1598-1621	Philip II of Portugal (Philip III of Spain)
1621-1640	Philip III of Portugal (Philip IV of Spain)
1640	Revolt of Portugal
1640-1656	John IV (duke of Braganza)
1656-1667	Afonso VI
1667-1706	Pedro II
1706-1750	John V
1750-1777	José I
1777-1786	Pedro III
1777-1816	Maria I Francisca
1799-1816	John VI (regent)
1816-1826	John VI
1826	Pedro IV (I of Brazil)
1826-1828	Maria II da Glória
1828-1834	Miguel I (exiled)
1834-1853	Maria II da Glória
1853-1861	Pedro V
1861-1889	Luis I
1889-1908	Carlos I
1908	Manuel II
Oct. 5, 1910	Republic declared

RUSSIA

PRINCES OF KIEVAN RUS

Reign	Ruler
c. 862-879	Rurik
879-912	Oleg
912-945	Igor
945-964	Saint Olga (regent)
964-972	Svyatoslav I
972-980	Yaropolk
980-1015	Vladimir I (with Anna, Princess of the Byzantine Empire)
1015-1019	Sviatopolk I
1019-1054	Yaroslav
1054-1073	Iziaslav
1073-1076	Svyatoslav II
1076-1078	Iziaslav (restored)
1078-1093	Vsevolod
1093-1113	Sviatopolk II
1113-1125	Vladimir II Monomakh
1125-1132	Mstislav
1132-1139	Yaropolk
1139-1146	Vyacheslav

Reign	Ruler
1146-1154	Iziaslav
1149-1157	Yuri I Dolgoruky
1154-1167	Rostislav

PRINCES OF VLADIMIR

Reign	Ruler
1169-1174	Andrei I Bogolyubsky
1175-1176	Michael
1176-1212	Vsevolod III
1212-1217	Yuri II
1217-1218	Constantin
1218-1238	Yuri II (restored)
1238-1246	Yaroslav II
1240	Mongol conquest
1246-1247	Svyatoslav III
1248-1249	Michael
1249-1252	Andrei II
1252-1263	Saint Alexander Nevsky
1264-1271	Yaroslav III of Tver
1272-1276	Vasily
1276-1281	Dmitry
1281-1283	Andrei III
1283-1294	Dmitry (restored)
1294-1304	Andrei III (restored)
1304-1319	Saint Michael of Tver
1319-1326	Yuri III of Moscow
1326-1327	Alexander II of Tver
1328-1331	Alexander III

PRINCES OF MOSCOW

Reign	Ruler
1263-1303	Daniel
1303-1325	Yuri III
1328-1341	Ivan I
1341-1353	Simeon
1353-1359	Ivan II
1359-1389	Dmitry Donskoy
1389-1425	Vasily I
1425-1462	Vasily II
1462-1505	Ivan III the Great
1480	Fall of the Golden Horde
1505-1533	Vasily III

CZARS OF ALL RUSSIA

Reign	Ruler
1547-1584	Ivan IV the Terrible
1584-1613	Time of Troubles
1584-1598	Fyodor I
1598-1605	Boris Godunov
1605	Fyodor II
1605-1606	False Dmitri I
1606-1610	Vasily IV Shuysky

Reign	Ruler
1610-1613	Ladislaus IV of Poland
1613-1645	Michael I (first Romanov)
1645-1676	Aleksey I
1676-1682	Fyodor III
1682-1696	Ivan V (with Peter I)
1682-1721	Peter I (with Ivan V)

EMPERORS OF ALL RUSSIA

Reign	Ruler
1721-1725	Peter I
1725-1727	Catherine I the Great
1727-1730	Peter II
1730-1740	Anne
1740-1741	Ivan VI
1741-1762	Elizabeth
1762	Peter III
1762-1796	Catherine II
1796-1801	Paul
1801-1825	Alexander I
1825-1855	Nicholas I
1855-1881	Alexander II
1881-1894	Alexander III
1894-1917	Nicholas II
1917	Michael II (exiled)
1917-1921	Revolution
1918	Execution of Romanovs

SCOTLAND

Reign	Ruler
404-420	Fergus
420-451	Eugenius II
451-457	Dongardus
457-479	Constantine I
479-501	Congallus
569-606	Aldan
606-621	Eugenius III
646-664	Ferchard II
664-684	Mulduinns
684-688	Eugenius V
688-699	Eugenius VI
699-715	Eugenius VII
715-730	Mordachus
730-761	Etfinus
761-767	Interregnum
767-787	Solvatius
787-819	Achaius
819-824	Dongallus III
824-831	Dongal
831-834	Alpine
834-854	Kenneth
854-858	Donald V

Reign	Ruler
858-874	Constantine II
874-893	Gregory
893-904	Donald VI
904-944	Constantine III
944-953	Malcolm I
953-961	Gondulph
961-965	Duff
965-970	Cullen
970-995	Kenneth II
995-1005	Grimus
1005-1034	Malcolm II
1034-1040	Duncan I
1040-1057	Macbeth
1057-1058	Lulach
1058-1093	Malcolm III
1093-1094	Donaldbane
1094	Duncan II
1094-1097	Donaldbane (second rule)
1097-1107	Edgar
1107-1124	Alexander I
1124-1153	David I
1153-1165	Malcolm IV
1165-1214	William I the Lion
1214-1249	Alexander II
1249-1286	Alexander III
1286-1290	Margaret
1290-1292	Interregnum
1292-1296	John Baliol
1296-1306	Interregnum
1306-1329	Robert I the Bruce
1329-1371	David II
1371	Ascendancy of Robert II, House of Stuart
1371-1390	Robert II
1390-1406	Robert III
1406-1437	James I
1437-1460	James II
1460-1488	James III
1488-1513	James IV
1513-1542	James V
1542-1567	Mary
1567-1625	James VI
1625	Joined with England

SELJUK EMPIRE. *See also* IRAN, ISLAMIC CALIPHS, OTTOMAN EMPIRE

GREAT SULTANS

Reign	Sultan
1037-1063	Toghrïl Beg
1063-1072/73	Alp Arslan

Reign	Sultan
1073-1092	Malik Shāh I
1092-1093	Maḥmūd I
1093-1104	Berk Yaruq (Barkyaruk, Barkiyarok)
1104-1105	Malik Shāh II
1105-1117	Muḥammad Tapar
1117-1157	Aḥmad Sanjar (Sinjar)

SULTANS OF IRAQ

Reign	Sultan
1105-1118	Maḥmūd Tapar
1118-1131	Maḥmūd
1131-1132	Dā'ūd (Dawd)
1132-1135	Toghrïl I
1135-1152	Mas'ūd
1152-1153	Malik Shāh
1153-1159	Muḥammad
1159-1161	Sulaimān Shāh
1161-1177	Arslan Shāh
1177-1194	Toghrïl II

SELJUK SULTANS OF ANATOLIA/RUM

Reign	Sultan
1077-1066	Sulaimān Shāh
1092-1107?	Qïlïch (Kilij) Arslan I
1107?-1116	Malik Shāh I
1116-1156	Mas'ūd I
1156-1192	Qïlïch (Kilij) Arslan II
1192	Malik Shāh II
1192-1196	Kai Khusrau (Khosrow, Khosru, Khusraw) I
1196-1204	Suleiman II
1203-1204	Qïlïch (Kilij) Arslan III
1204-1210	Kai Khusrau I (second rule)
1210-1219	Kai Kā'ūs I
1219-1236	Kai Qubād (Kobadh) I
1236-1246	Kai Khusrau II
1246-1259	Kai Kā'ūs II
1248-1264	Qïlïch (Kilij) Arslan IV
1249-1257	Kai Qubād (Kobadh) II
1264-1283	Kai Khusrau III
1283-1298	Mas'ūd II
1298-1301?	Kai Qubād (Kobadh) III
1303-1308	Mas'ūd II (second rule)

SELJUK SULTANS OF SYRIA

Reign	Sultan
1078-1094	Tutush
1095-1113	Riḍwān (Damascus)
1098-1113	Duqaq (Aleppo)

Reign	Sultan
1113-1114	Alp Arslan
1114-1117	Sultan Shāh

SULTANS OF KIRMĀN (KERMAN)

Reign	Sultan
1041-1073	Qāvurt (Qawurd)
1073-1074	Kirmān (Kerman) Shāh
1074-1085	Sultan Shāh
1085-1097	Turān Shāh I
1097-1101	Īrān Shāh
1101-1142	Arslan Shāh I
1142-1156	Muḥammad I
1156-1170	Toghrïl Shāh
1170-1175	Bahrām Shāh
1170-1177	Arslan Shāh II
1175-1186	Muḥammad Shāh II
1177-1183	Turān Shāh II

SPAIN. *See also* **PORTUGAL**

The Iberian Peninsula now occupied by Spain and Portugal was a turbulent region during the Middle Ages, a place where numerous cultures clashed, notably Christianity and Islam but also a broad and ethnically diverse group of peoples, from the Suevi and Visigoths of the seventh century through the Berbers and Islamic peoples in the south. Through most of the Middle Ages the region saw a succession of fluctuating principalities in the north—primarily Asturias, Galicia, Aragón, Navarre, León, and Castile, while in the south Islam held sway from the eighth century to the time of Columbus's voyage to the Americas in 1492. In that year the Reconquista concluded with the Fall of Granada, and Christianity claimed the peninsula. In 1516, the Kingdom of Spain united all former kingdoms, with the exception of Portugal, into one Kingdom of Spain.

MAJOR ISLAMIC RULERS

Córdoba's Umayyad Caliphs (emirs until 929)

Reign	Ruler
756-788	ʿAbd al-Raḥmān I (emir)
788-796	Hishām I (emir)
796-822	al-Hakam I (emir)
822-852	ʿAbd al-Raḥmān II (emir)
852-886	Muḥammad I (emir)
886-888	al-Mundhir (emir)
888-912	ʿAbd Allāh (emir)
912-961	ʿAbd al-Raḥmān III al-Nāṣir
961-976	al-Hakam II al-Mustanṣir

Reign	Ruler
976-1008	Hishām II al-Muayyad
1008-1009	Muḥammad II al-Mahdī
1009	Sulaimān al-Mustaʿīn
1010-1013	Hishām II (restored)
1013-1016	Sulaimān (restored)
1016-1018	Alī ben Hammud
1018	ʿAbd al-Raḥmān IV
1018-1021	al-Qasim
1021-1022	Yahyā
1022-1023	al-Qasim (restored)
1023-1024	ʿAbd al-Raḥmān V
1024-1025	Muḥammad III
1025-1027	Yahyā (restored)
1027-1031	Hishām III
1031	End of Umayyads; dissolution of Umayyad Spain into small states

After the Umayyads, Turbulence: Some Major Rulers

Reign	Ruler
1031-1043	Jahwar ibn Muḥammad ibn Jahwar
1043-1058	Muḥammad ar-Rashīd
1058-1069	ʿAbd al-Malik Dhu's-Siyādat al-Manṣur
1069	ʿAbbādid conquest
1085	Toledo falls to León and Castile; Christian Reconquista begins

Almoravid Sultans (Spain and North Africa)

Reign	Ruler
1061-1107	Yūsuf ibn Tāshufīn
1086	Entry into Spain; Alfonso VI defeated at Zallāqa
1107-1142	ʿAlīx ibn Yūsuf
1142-1146	Tāshufīn ibn ʿAli
1146	Ibrāhīm ibn Tāshufīn
1146-1147	Ishāq ibn ʿAli
1147	Almohad conquest

Almohad Caliphs (Spain and North Africa)

Reign	Ruler
1130-1163	ʿAbd al-Muʾmin
1163-1184	Abū Yaʿqūb Yūsuf
1184-1199	Abū Yūsuf Yaʿqūb al-Manṣur
1199-1213	Muḥammad ibn Yaʿqūb
1212	Christians defeat Almohads at Las Navas de Tolosa
1213-1224	Yūsuf II Abū Yaqūb
1224	ʿAbd al-Wāḥid Abū Muḥammad
1224-1227	ʿAbd Allāh Abū Muḥammad
1227-1232	Idrīs I ibn Yaʿqūb
1227-1235	Yahyā Abū Zakariyyāʿ
1228-1229	Retreat from Spain
1232-1242	ʿAbdul-Wāḥid ibn Idrīs I
1242-1248	ʿAlī ibn Idrīs I
1248-1266	ʿUmar ibn Ishāq

Reign	Ruler
1266-1269	Idrīs II ibn Muḥammad
1269	End of Almohad domination in North Africa

Naṣrid Sultans of Granada

Reign	Ruler
1232-1273	Muḥammad I al-Ghālib (Ibn al-Aḥmar)
1273-1302	Muḥammad II al-Faqīh
1302-1309	Muḥammad III al-Makhlūʿ
1309-1314	Naṣr
1314-1325	Ismāʿīl I
1325-1333	Muḥammad IV
1333-1354	Yūsuf I al-Muʾayyad
1354-1359	Muḥammad V al-Ghani
1359-1360	Ismāʿīl II
1360-1362	Muḥammad VI al-Ghālib (El Bermejo)
1362-1391	Muḥammad V al-Ghani (restored)
1391-1392	Yūsuf II al-Mustahgnī
1392-1408	Muḥammad VII al-Mustaʿīn
1408-1417	Yūsuf III an-Nāṣir
1417-1419	Muḥammad VIII al-Mustamassik (al-Ṣaghīr, El Pequeño)
1419-1427	Muḥammad IX al-Ghālib (al-Aysar, El Zurdo)
1427-1429	Muḥammad VIII al-Mustamassik
1429-1432	Muḥammad IX al-Ghālib
1432	Yūsuf IV, Abenalmao
1432-1445	Muḥammad IX al-Ghālib
1445	Muḥammad X al-Aḥnaf (El Cojo)
1445-1446	Yūsuf V (Aben Ismael)
1446-1447	Muḥammad X al-Aḥnaf
1447-1453	Muḥammad IX al-Ghālib
1451-1455	Muḥammad XI (El Chiquito)
1454-1464	Saʿd al-Mustaʿīn (Ciriza, Muley Zad)
1462	Yūsuf V (Aben Ismael)
1464-1482	ʿAlī (Muley Hácen)
1482-1492	Muḥammad XII al-Zughūbī (Boabdil, El Chico)
1483-1485	ʿAlī (Muley Hácen)
1485-1490	Muḥammad ibn Saʿd al-Zaghal
1492	Conquest by Castile and Aragón, end of Islamic Spain

NON-ISLAMIC AND CHRISTIAN RULERS

Asturias and Galicia

Reign	Ruler
718-737	Pelayo
737-739	Favila
739-757	Alfonso I the Catholic
757-768	Fruela I
768-774	Aurelio
774-783	Silo
783-788	Mauregato
788-791	Vermundo I

Reign	Ruler
791-842	Alfonso II the Chaste
842-850	Ramiro I
850-866	Ordoño I
866-910	Alfonso III the Great
910	Subsumed by León

Navarre

Reign	Ruler
840-851	Inigo Arista
905-925	Sancho Garces
925-970	Garcia Sanchez I
970-994	Sancho Abarca
994-1000	Garcia Sanchez II
1000-1035	Sancho III the Great
1035-1054	Garcia IV
1054-1076	Sancho IV
1076-1094	Sancho Ramirez
1094-1134	Subsumed under Aragón, Castile, León; reemerges with reduced territory
1134-1150	Garcia V Ramirez
1150-1194	Sancho VI
1194-1234	Sancho VII
1234-1253	Teobaldo I of Champagne
1253-1270	Teobaldo II
1270-1274	Henry I
1274-1305	Juana I
1305-1316	Luis (Louis)
1316-1322	Philip V the Tall
1322-1328	Charles I
1328-1349	Juana II
1349-1387	Charles II the Bad
1387-1425	Charles III the Noble
1425-1479	Blanca & John
1479	Leonora
1479-1483	Francis Febo
1483-1517	Catalina
1516	Part of Navarre annexed to Spain
1517-1555	Henry II
1555-1572	Jeanne d'Albret
1572-1589	Henry III (IV of France); French rule

León

Reign	Ruler
910-914	Garcia
914-924	Ordoño II
924-925	Fruela II
925-930	Alfonso IV the Monk
930-950	Ramiro II
950-956	Ordoño III
956-967	Sancho I the Fat
967-982	Ramiro III
982-999	Vermundo II
999-1028	Alfonso V the Noble

Reign	*Ruler*
1028-1037	Vermundo III
1038-1065	Fernando
1065-1070	Sancho II
1070-1072	Sancho III
1072-1109	Alfonso VI (king of Castile)
1109-1126	Urraca (married to Alfonso I of Aragón)
1126-1157	Alfonso VII
1157-1188	Ferdinand II
1188-1230	Alfonso IX
1230-1252	Saint Fernando III
1252	Subsumed under Castile

Castile

Reign	*Ruler*
1035-1065	Ferdinand I
1065-1072	Sancho II
1072-1109	Alfonso VI
1109-1157	Castile joins with León
1157	Castile restored as separate principality
1157-1158	Sancho III
1158-1214	Alfonso VIII
1214-1217	Henry I
1217-1252	Saint Ferdinand III
1252	Castile rejoins with León
1252-1284	Alfonso X (emperor)
1284-1295	Sancho IV
1295-1312	Ferdinand IV
1312-1350	Alfonso XI
1350-1369	Peter the Cruel
1369-1379	Henry II
1379-1390	John I
1390-1406	Henry III
1406-1454	John II
1454-1474	Henry IV
1474-1504	Ferdinand V (II of Aragon) and Isabella I
1492	Fall of Granada, end of Reconquista
1504-1516	Joan (Juana) the Mad and Philip I of Habsburg
1516	Formation of Kingdom of Spain

Aragon

Reign	*Ruler*
1035-1063	Ramiro I
1063-1094	Sancho Ramirez
1094-1104	Pedro I
1104-1134	Alfonso I (co-ruled León and Castile, 1109-1126)
1134-1137	Ramiro II
1137	Union with County of Barcelona
1137-1162	Petronilla
1162-1196	Alfonso II
1196-1213	Pedro II

Reign	*Ruler*
1213-1276	James I the Conqueror (under regency to 1217)
1276-1285	Pedro III
1285-1291	Alfonso III
1291-1327	James II
1327-1336	Alfonso IV
1336-1387	Peter IV
1387-1395	John I
1395-1410	Martin I
1412-1416	Ferdinand I
1416-1458	Alfonso V
1458-1479	John II
1479-1516	Ferdinand II and Isabella I (d. 1504)

KINGDOM OF SPAIN

Reign	*Ruler*
1516-1556	Carlos (Charles) I (V as Holy Roman Emperor)
1556-1598	Philip (Felipe) II
1598-1621	Philip III
1621-1665	Philip IV
1665-1700	Carlos II

BOURBONS

Reign	*Ruler*
1700-1724	Philip V
1724	Luis I
1724-1746	Philip V (restored)
1746-1759	Fernando VI
1759-1788	Carlos III
1788-1808	Carlos IV
1808	Fernando VII
1808	Carlos IV (restored)

BONAPARTES

Reign	*Ruler*
1808-1813	José I Napoléon

BOURBONS (RESTORED)

Reign	*Ruler*
1813-1833	Fernando VII
1833-1868	Isabel II

SAVOY

Reign	*Ruler*
1871-1873	Amadeo I

FIRST SPANISH REPUBLIC

Reign	*Ruler*
1874-1887	Alfonso XII
1886-1931	Alfonso XIII

SECOND SPANISH REPUBLIC

Reign	Ruler
1939-1975	Francisco Franco

BOURBONS (RESTORED)

Reign	Ruler
1975-	Juan Carlos I

SWEDEN. *See also* **DENMARK, NORWAY**

Reign	Ruler
647-735?	Harald Hildetand
735-750?	Sigurd Ring
750-794?	Ragnar Lodbrok
?	Eystein Beli
794-804	Björn Järnsida
804-808	Erik II (to 870?)
808-820	Erik III
820-859	Edmund I
860?-870	Erik I (poss. Erik II)
870-920	Björn
920-930	Olaf I Ring
?	Erik IV
930-950	Erik V
950-965	Edmund II
965-970	Olaf II
970-995	Erik VI the Victorious
995-1022	Olaf III Skötkonung
1022-1050	Anund Jakob Kolbrenner
1050-1060	Edmund III
1066-1067	Erik VII (VIII)
1066-1070	Halsten
1066-1080	Inge I Elder
1080-1083	Blot-Sven
1083-1110	Inge I Elder
1110-1118	Filip Halstensson
1118-1125	Inge II Younger
1125-1130	Magnus Nielsson
1130-1156	Sverker I Elder
1156-1160	Sain Erik IX
1161-1167	Charles VII
1167-1196	Knut I
1196-1208	Sverker II Younger
1208-1216	Erik X
1216-1222	John I
1222-1229	Erik XI
1229-1234	Knut II the Long
1234-1250	Erik XI
1250-1275	Valdemar
1275-1290	Magnus I
1290-1320	Berger
1320-1365	Magnus II (VII of Norway)
1356-1359	Erik XII

Reign	Ruler
1364-1389	Albert
1389-1412	Margaret I of Denmark, Norway, and Sweden
1397	Unification of Norway, Denmark, and Sweden
1412-1439	Erik XIII (VII of Denmark, III of Norway)
1439-1448	Christopher (III of Denmark)
1448-1481	Christian I of Oldenburg
1481-1513	Hans/John II
1513-1523	Christian II
1523-1560	Gustav I Vasa
1560-1568	Erik XIV
1568-1592	Johan/John III
1592-1604	Sigismund
1604-1611	Carl/Charles IX
1611-1632	Gustav II Adolf
1632-1654	Christina
1654-1660	Charles X
1660-1697	Charles XI
1697-1718	Charles XII (Madman of the North)
1718-1720	Ulrika
1730-1751	Frederick (landgrave of Hesse)
1751-1771	Adolphus Frederick
1771-1792	Gustav III
1792-1809	Gustav IV Adolf
1809-1818	Charles XIII
1814	Sweden and Norway joined
1818-1844	Charles XIV
1844-1859	Oscar I
1859-1872	Charles XI
1872-1907	Oscar II
1905	Norway separates
1907-1950	Gustav V
1950-1973	Gustav VI Adolf
1973-	Karl/Charles XVI Gustaf

UNITED STATES

Term	President
1789-1797	George Washington
1797-1801	John Adams
1801-1809	Thomas Jefferson
1809-1817	James Madison
1817-1825	James Monroe
1825-1829	John Quincy Adams
1829-1837	Andrew Jackson
1837-1841	Martin Van Buren
1841	William Henry Harrison
1841-1845	John Tyler
1845-1849	James K. Polk
1849-1850	Zachary Taylor
1850-1853	Millard Fillmore
1853-1857	Franklin Pierce
1857-1861	James Buchanan

Term	President
1861-1865	Abraham Lincoln
1865-1869	Andrew Johnson
1869-1877	Ulysses S. Grant
1877-1881	Rutherford B. Hayes
1881	James A. Garfield
1881-1885	Chester A. Arthur
1885-1889	Grover Cleveland
1889-1893	Benjamin Harrison
1893-1897	Grover Cleveland
1897-1901	William McKinley
1901-1909	Theodore Roosevelt
1909-1913	William Howard Taft
1913-1921	Woodrow Wilson
1921-1923	Warren G. Harding
1923-1929	Calvin Coolidge
1929-1933	Herbert Hoover
1933-1945	Franklin D. Roosevelt
1945-1953	Harry S. Truman
1953-1961	Dwight D. Eisenhower
1961-1963	John F. Kennedy
1963-1968	Lyndon B. Johnson
1969-1974	Richard M. Nixon
1974-1977	Gerald R. Ford
1977-1981	Jimmy Carter
1981-1989	Ronald Reagan
1989-1993	George H. W. Bush
1993-2001	Bill Clinton
2001-	George W. Bush

VIETNAM

NGO DYNASTY

Reign	Ruler
939-945	Kuyen
945-951	Duong Tam Kha
951-954	Suong Ngap
951-965	Suong Van

DINH DYNASTY

Reign	Ruler
968-979	Dinh Tien
979-981	Dinh De Toan

EARLY LE DYNASTY

Reign	Ruler
981-1005	Hoan
1005-1009	Trung Tong

LATER LI (LY) DYNASTY

Reign	Ruler
1010-1028	Thai To
1028-1054	Thai Tong
1054-1072	Thanh Tong

LATER LE DYNASTY

Reign	Ruler
1072-1127	Nan Ton
1127-1138	Than Tong
1138-1175	Anh Tong
1175-1210	Kao Tong
1210-1224	Hue Tong
1224-1225	Tieu Hoang

EARLY TRAN DYNASTY

Reign	Ruler
1225-1258	Thai Tong
1258-1277	Thanh Tong
1278-1293	Nan Tong
1293-1314	Anh Tong
1314-1329	Minh Tong
1329-1341	Hien Tong
1341-1369	Du Tong
1370-1372	Nghe Tong
1372-1377	Due Tong
1377-1388	De Hien
1388-1398	Tran Thuan Tong
1398-1400	Tran Thieu De

HO DYNASTY

Reign	Ruler
1400	Kui Li
1400-1407	Han Thuong
1407-1428	Ming Chinese occupation

LATER TRAN DYNASTY

Reign	Ruler
1407-1409	Hau Tran Jian Dinh De
1409-1413	Hau Tran
1413-1428	vacant

CHAMPA

Reign	Ruler
1390-1400	Ko Cheng
1400-1441	Jaya Sinhavarman v
1441-1446	Maija Vijaya
1446-1449	Qui Lai
1449-1458	Qui Do (Bi Do)
1458-1460	Ban La Tra Nguyet (Tra Duyet)
1460-1471	Ban La Tra Toan
1471-1478	Bo Tri Tri

LATER LE DYNASTY

Reign	Ruler
1428-1433	Thai To
1433-1442	Thai Tong
1442-1459	Nan Tong
1460-1497	Thanh Tong
1497-1504	Hien Tong
1504-1509	Vi Muc De
1509-1516	Tuong Duc De
1516-1522	Tieu Tong
1522-1527	Kung Hoang
1533-1548	Le Trang Tong (restored)

MAC DYNASTY

Reign	Ruler
1527-1530	Dang Dung
1530-1540	Dang Doanh
1533	Kingdom divides

NGUYEN DYNASTY

Reign	Ruler
1533-1545	Kim
1545-1558	Civil war
1558-1613	Hoang
1613-1635	Phuc Nguyen
1635-1648	Phuc Lan
1648-1687	Phuc Tan

Reign	Ruler
1687-1691	Phuc Tran
1691-1725	Phuc Chu I
1725-1738	Phuc Chu II
1738-1765	Phuc Khoat
1765-1778	Phuc Thuan
1778-1802	Anh
1802	Absorbs other Vietnamese kingdoms
1802-1820	Gia Long
1820-1841	Minh Mang
1841-1848	Thieu Tri
1848-1883	Tu Duc
1883-1940	French protectorate
1883	Duc Duc
1883	Hiep Hoa
1883-1884	Kien Phuc
1884-1885	Ham Nghi
1885-1889	Dong Khanh
1889-1907	Thanh Thai
1907-1916	Duy Tan
1916-1925	Khai Dinh
1925-1945	Bao Dai
1940-1945	Japanese occupation
1945-1954	French occupation
1949-1955	Bao Dai
1954-1975	Republic of Vietnam
1954	Communist government

CHRONOLOGICAL LIST OF ENTRIES

All personages appearing in this list are the subjects of articles in *Great Lives from History: The Eighteenth Century, 1701-1800*. The arrangement is chronological on the basis of birth (or baptismal) years. Subjects of multiperson essays, listed here separately, include James Adam and Robert Adam and Jacques-Étienne Montgolfier and Joseph-Michel Montgolfier.

Birth Date Unknown

Levni (unknown-1732)

Nanny (unknown-1750's)

1631-1640

Increase Mather (June 21, 1639-August 23, 1723)

1641-1650

Antonio Stradivari (1644?-December 18, 1737)
First Earl of Godolphin (baptized June 15, 1645-September 15, 1712)

First Duke of Marlborough (May 26, 1650-June 16, 1722)

1651-1660

Samuel Sewall (March 28, 1652-January 1, 1730)
Chikamatsu Monzaemon (1653-January 6, 1725)
André-Hercule de Fleury (June 22, 1653-January 29, 1743)
Johann Bernhard Fischer von Erlach (baptized July 20, 1656-April 5, 1723)

Frederick I (July 11, 1657-February 25, 1713)
Daniel Defoe (1660-April 26, 1731)
Alessandro Scarlatti (May 2, 1660-October 22, 1725)
George I (May 28, 1660-June 11, 1727)
Sarah Churchill (June 5, 1660-October 18, 1744)
Georg Ernst Stahl (October 21, 1660-May 14, 1734)

1661-1670

Nicholas Hawksmoor (c. 1661-March 25, 1736)
Thomas Newcomen (January or February, 1663-August 5, 1729)
Cotton Mather (February 12, 1663-February 13, 1728)
Eugene of Savoy (October 18, 1663-April 20 or 21, 1736)
Sir John Vanbrugh (baptized January 24, 1664-March 26, 1726)
Queen Anne (February 6, 1665-August 1, 1714)
Ogyū Sorai (February 16, 1666-January 19, 1728)

Mary Astell (November 12, 1666-May 9, 1731)
Germain Boffrand (May 16, 1667-March 19, 1754)
Jonathan Swift (November 30, 1667-October 19, 1745)
Alain-René Lesage (May 8, 1668-November 17, 1747)
Giambattista Vico (June 23, 1668-January 23, 1744)
François Couperin (November 10, 1668-September 11, 1733)
Johann Lucas von Hildebrandt (November 14, 1668-November 16, 1745)
Mary de la Rivière Manley (c. 1670-July 11, 1724)

1671-1680

Richard Steele (baptized March 12, 1672-September 1, 1729)

Joseph Addison (May 1, 1672-June 17, 1719)

Peter the Great (June 9, 1672-February 8, 1725)

First Earl Stanhope (1673-February 5, 1721)

Ahmed III (December 30, 1673-July 1, 1736)

Jethro Tull (baptized March 30, 1674-February 21, 1741)

Benedict XIV (March 31, 1675-May 3, 1758)

Claude Alexandre de Bonneval (July 14, 1675-March 23, 1747)

Chŏng Sŏn (January 3, 1676-March 24, 1759)

Robert Walpole (August 26, 1676-March 18, 1745)

Abraham Darby (c. 1678-March 8, 1717)

Antonio Vivaldi (March 4, 1678-July 28, 1741)

First Viscount Bolingbroke (September 16, 1678-December 12, 1751)

Yongzheng (December 13, 1678-October 8, 1735)

Second Duke of Argyll (October 10, 1680-October 4, 1743)

1681-1690

Georg Philipp Telemann (March 14, 1681-June 25, 1767)

Vitus Jonassen Bering (August 12, 1681-December 19, 1741)

Charles XII (June 17, 1682-November 30, 1718)

Anne Oldfield (1683-October 30, 1730)

Caroline (March 1, 1683-November 20, 1737)

Jean-Philippe Rameau (baptized September 25, 1683-September 12, 1764)

George II (November 10, 1683-October 25, 1760)

Philip V (December 19, 1683-July 9, 1746)

Antoine Watteau (October 10, 1684-July 18, 1721)

Tokugawa Yoshimune (November 27, 1684-July 12, 1751)

Hakuin (1685/1686-1768/1769)

George Frideric Handel (February 23, 1685-April 14, 1759)

George Berkeley (March 12, 1685-January 14, 1753)

Johann Sebastian Bach (March 21, 1685-July 28, 1750)

Charles VI (October 1, 1685-October 20, 1740)

Daniel Gabriel Fahrenheit (May 24, 1686-September 16, 1736)

William Stukeley (November 7, 1687-March 3, 1765)

Emanuel Swedenborg (January 29, 1688-March 29, 1772)

Alexander Pope (May 21, 1688-May 30, 1744)

Frederick William I (August 15, 1688-May 31, 1740)

Nādir Shāh (October 22, 1688-June, 1747)

Montesquieu (January 18, 1689-February 10, 1755)

Mary Wortley Montagu (baptized May 26, 1689-August 21, 1762)

Samuel Richardson (baptized August 19, 1689-July 4, 1761)

1691-1700

Joseph Butler (May 18, 1692-June 16, 1752)

François Quesnay (June 4, 1694-December 16, 1774)

Henry Pelham (September 24, 1694-March 6, 1754)

Voltaire (November 21, 1694-May 30, 1778)

Giovanni Battista Tiepolo (March 5, 1696-March 27, 1770)

Mahmud I (August 2, 1696-December 13, 1754)

Comte de Saxe (October 28, 1696-November 30, 1750)

James Edward Oglethorpe (December 22, 1696-June 30, 1785)

Thanadelthur (c. 1697-February 5, 1717)

John Peter Zenger (1697-July 28, 1746)

Joseph-François Dupleix (January 1, 1697-November 10, 1763)

Lord Anson (April 23, 1697-June 6, 1762)

Canaletto (October 18, 1697-April 20, 1768)

William Hogarth (November 10, 1697-October 26, 1764)

Colin Maclaurin (February, 1698-January 14, 1746)

Ba'al Shem Tov (August 27, 1698-May 23, 1760)

Marquês de Pombal (May 13, 1699-May 8, 1782)

Jean-Siméon Chardin (November 2, 1699-December 6, 1779)

Mentewab (c. 1700-1772)

Count von Zinzendorf (May 26, 1700-May 9, 1760)

1700-1710

Muḥammad ibn ʿAbd al-Wahhāb (1703-1792)

Shāh Walī Allāh (February 21, 1703-1762)

John Wesley (June 17, 1703-March 2, 1791)

Jonathan Edwards (October 5, 1703-March 22, 1758)

John Kay (July 16, 1704-c. 1780-1781)

Karīm Khān Zand (c. 1705-March, 1779)

Vaḥīd Bihbahānī (1705/1706-1791/1790)

First Earl of Mansfield (March 2, 1705-March 20, 1793)

Benjamin Franklin (January 17, 1706-April 17, 1790)

John Baskerville (baptized January 28, 1706-January 8, 1775)

Marquise du Châtelet (December 17, 1706-September 10, 1749)

Leonhard Euler (April 15, 1707-September 18, 1783)

Henry Fielding (April 22, 1707-October 8, 1754)

Carolus Linnaeus (May 23, 1707-January 10, 1778)

Comte de Buffon (September 7, 1707-April 16, 1788)

Charles Wesley (December 18, 1707-March 29, 1788)

Hester Bateman (baptized October 7, 1708-September 16, 1794)

William Pitt the Elder (November 15, 1708-May 11, 1778)

Andreas Sigismund Marggraf (March 3, 1709-August 7, 1782)

Samuel Johnson (September 18, 1709-December 13, 1784)

Elizabeth Petrovna (December 29, 1709-January 5, 1762)

Louis XV (February 15, 1710-May 10, 1774)

1711-1720

Wenzel Anton von Kaunitz (February 2, 1711-June 27, 1794)

David Hume (May 7, 1711-August 25, 1776)

Thomas Hutchinson (September 9, 1711-June 3, 1780)

Qianlong (September 25, 1711-February 7, 1799)

Mikhail Vasilyevich Lomonosov (November 19, 1711-April 15, 1765)

Frederick the Great (January 24, 1712-August 17, 1786)

Louis-Joseph de Montcalm (February 28, 1712-September 14, 1759)

Jean-Jacques Rousseau (June 28, 1712-July 2, 1778)

Guillaume-Thomas Raynal (April 12, 1713-March 6, 1796)

John Newbery (baptized July 19, 1713-December 22, 1767)

Denis Diderot (October 5, 1713-July 31, 1784)

Junípero Serra (November 24, 1713-August 28, 1784)

Alaungpaya (c. 1714-April 13, 1760?)

Christoph Gluck (July 2, 1714-November 15, 1787)

Marquis de Montalembert (July 16, 1714-March 28, 1800)

George Whitefield (December 16, 1714-September 30, 1770)

Cao Xueqin (1715?-February 12, 1763)

Claude-Adrien Helvétius (January 26, 1715-December 26, 1771)

Marquis de Vauvenargues (August 6, 1715-May 28, 1747)

Jean-Baptiste Vaquette de Gribeauval (September 15, 1715-May 9, 1789)

Étienne Bonnot de Condillac (September 30, 1715-August 2, 1780)

James Brindley (1716-September 27, 1772)

Charles III (January 20, 1716-December 14, 1788)

Lancelot Brown (baptized August 30, 1716-February 6, 1783)

Mustafa III (January 28, 1717-January 21, 1774)

Lord Amherst (January 29, 1717-August 3, 1797)

David Garrick (February 19, 1717-January 20, 1779)

Maria Theresa (May 13, 1717-November 29, 1780)

Jean le Rond d'Alembert (November 17, 1717-October 29, 1783)

Johann Joachim Winckelmann (December 9, 1717-June 8, 1768)

Pius VI (December 27, 1717-August 29, 1799)

George Rodney (baptized February 13, 1718-May 24, 1792)

Maria Gaetana Agnesi (May 16, 1718-January 9, 1799)

John Roebuck (baptized September 17, 1718-July 17, 1794)

Étienne François de Choiseul (June 28, 1719-May 8, 1785)

Charles Gravier de Vergennes (December 28, 1719-February 13, 1787)

Pontiac (c. 1720-April 20, 1769)

José de Gálvez (January 2, 1720-June 17, 1787)

James Hargreaves (baptized January 8, 1720-April 22, 1778)

Elijah ben Solomon (April 23, 1720-October 9, 1797)

Peg Woffington (October 18, 1720?-March 28, 1760)

1721-1730

Thomas Gage (1721-April 2, 1787)

Roger Sherman (April 19, 1721-July 23, 1793)

Madame de Pompadour (December 29, 1721-April 15, 1764)

Hyder Ali (1722-December 7, 1782)

Flora MacDonald (1722-March 4, 1790)

Samuel Adams (September 27, 1722-October 2, 1803)

John Witherspoon (February 15, 1723-November 15, 1794)

Adam Smith (baptized June 5, 1723-July 17, 1790)

Adam Ferguson (June 20, 1723-February 22, 1816)

Sir William Blackstone (July 10, 1723-February 14, 1780)

Sir Joshua Reynolds (July 16, 1723-February 23, 1792)

Johann Bernhard Basedow (September 11, 1723-July 25, 1790)

Paul-Henri-Dietrich d'Holbach (December, 1723-January 21, 1789)

Isaac Backus (January 9, 1724-November 20, 1806)

Dai Zhen (January 19, 1724-July 1, 1777)

Immanuel Kant (April 22, 1724-February 12, 1804)

Friedrich Gottlieb Klopstock (July 2, 1724-March 14, 1803)

Sir Guy Carleton (September 3, 1724-November 10, 1808)

Suzuki Harunobu (1725?-1770)

Casanova (April 2, 1725-June 4, 1798)

Comte de Rochambeau (July 1, 1725-May 10, 1807)

Robert Clive (September 29, 1725-November 22, 1774)

John Wilkes (October 17, 1725-December 26, 1797)

George Mason (December 11, 1725-October 7, 1792)

Richard Howe (March 8, 1726-August 5, 1799)

Charles Burney (April 7, 1726-April 12, 1814)

James Wolfe (January 2, 1727-September 13, 1759)

Anne-Robert-Jacques Turgot (May 10, 1727-March 18, 1781)

Thomas Gainsborough (baptized May 14, 1727-August 2, 1788)

Hester Chapone (October 27, 1727-December 25, 1801)

John Wilkinson (1728-July 14, 1808)

Peter III (February 21, 1728-July 18, 1762)

Joseph Black (April 16, 1728-December, 6, 1799)

Robert Adam (July 3, 1728-March 3, 1792)

Matthew Boulton (September 3, 1728-August 18, 1809)

Mercy Otis Warren (September 25, 1728-October 19, 1814)

James Cook (October 27, 1728-February 14, 1779)

Oliver Goldsmith (November 10, 1728 or 1730-April 4, 1774)

Charlotte Lennox (c. 1729-January 4, 1804)

Sīdī al-Mukhtār al-Kuntī (1729-1811)

Edmund Burke (January 12, 1729-July 9, 1797)

Lazzaro Spallanzani (January 12, 1729-February 11, 1799)

Gotthold Ephraim Lessing (January 22, 1729-February 15, 1781)

Catherine the Great (May 2, 1729-November 17, 1796)

William Howe (August 10, 1729-July 12, 1814)

Moses Mendelssohn (September 6, 1729-January 4, 1786)

Louis-Antoine de Bougainville (November 12, 1729-August 31, 1811)

Aleksandr Vasilyevich Suvorov (November 24, 1729-May 18, 1800)

Sir Henry Clinton (April 16, 1730-December 23, 1795)

Josiah Wedgwood (baptized July 12, 1730-January 3, 1795)

James Bruce (December 14, 1730-April 27, 1794)

1731-1740

Catherine Macaulay (April 2, 1731-June 22, 1791)

Henry Cavendish (October 10, 1731-February 24, 1810)

Benjamin Banneker (November 9, 1731-October 9, 1806)

Sophie von La Roche (December 6, 1731-February 18, 1807)

Pierre-Augustin Caron de Beaumarchais (January 24, 1732-May 18, 1799)

George Washington (February 22, 1732-December 14, 1799)

Joseph Haydn (March 31, 1732-May 31, 1809)

Jean-Honoré Fragonard (April 5, 1732-August 22, 1806)

Lord North (April 13, 1732-August 5, 1792)

James Adam (July 21, 1732-October 20, 1794)

Jacques Necker (September 30, 1732-April 9, 1804)

John Dickinson (November 8, 1732-February 14, 1808)

Warren Hastings (December 6, 1732-August 22, 1818)

Sir Richard Arkwright (December 23, 1732-August 3, 1792)

Joseph Priestley (March 13, 1733-February 6, 1804)

Robert Morris (January 31, 1734-May 8, 1806)

Taksin (April 17, 1734-April 6, 1782)

Grigori Grigoryevich Orlov (October 17, 1734-April 24, 1783)

Daniel Boone (November 2, 1734-September 26, 1820)

George Romney (December 26, 1734-November 15, 1802)

Paul Revere (January 1, 1735-May 10, 1818)

Ignacy Krasicki (February 3, 1735-March 14, 1801)

John Adams (October 30, 1735-July 4, 1826)

Granville Sharp (November 10, 1735-July 6, 1813)

James Watt (January 19, 1736-August 25, 1819)

Joseph-Louis Lagrange (January 25, 1736-April 10, 1813)

Ann Lee (February 29, 1736-September 8, 1784)

Patrick Henry (May 29, 1736-June 6, 1799)

Jean-Sylvain Bailly (September 15, 1736-November 12, 1793)

Fanny Abington (1737-March 4, 1815)

John Hancock (January 12, 1737-October 8, 1793)

Thomas Paine (January 29, 1737-June 8, 1809)

Edward Gibbon (May 8, 1737-January 16, 1794)

Luigi Galvani (September 9, 1737-December 4, 1798)

Charles Carroll (September 19, 1737-November 14, 1832)

Aleksey Grigoryevich Orlov (October 5, 1737-January 5, 1808)

Antônio Francisco Lisboa (c. 1738-November 18, 1814)

Ethan Allen (January 21, 1738-February 12, 1789)

Cesare Beccaria (March 15, 1738-November 28, 1794)

George III (June 4, 1738-January 29, 1820)

John Singleton Copley (July 3, 1738-September 9, 1815)

Benjamin West (October 10, 1738-March 11, 1820)

Arthur Phillip (October 11, 1738-August 31, 1814)

William Herschel (November 15, 1738-August 25, 1822)

First Marquess Cornwallis (December 31, 1738-October 5, 1805)

Joseph Boulogne (c. 1739-June 9 or 10, 1799)

Grigori Aleksandrovich Potemkin (September 24, 1739-October 16, 1791)

Tupac Amaru II (c. 1740-May 18, 1781)

Marquis de Sade (June 2, 1740-December 2, 1814)

Joseph-Michel Montgolfier (August 26, 1740-June 26, 1810)

James Boswell (October 29, 1740-May 19, 1795)

1741-1750

Benedict Arnold (January 14, 1741-June 14, 1801)

Joseph II (March 13, 1741-February 20, 1790)

Charles Willson Peale (April 15, 1741-February 22, 1827)

Samuel Chase (April 17, 1741-June 19, 1811)

Angelica Kauffmann (October 30, 1741-November 5, 1807)

Aagje Deken (December 10, 1741-November 14, 1804)

Yemelyan Ivanovich Pugachev (c. 1742-January 21, 1775)

Joseph Brant (1742-November 24, 1807)

Nathanael Greene (August 7, 1742-June 19, 1786)

Jean Dauberval (August 19, 1742-February 14, 1806)

James Wilson (September 14, 1742-August 21, 1798)
Nicolas Leblanc (December 6, 1742-January 16, 1806)
Anna Seward (December 12, 1742-March 25, 1809)
Toussaint Louverture (1743-April 7, 1803)
John Fitch (January 21, 1743-July 2, 1798)
Sir Joseph Banks (February 13, 1743-June 19, 1820)
Luigi Boccherini (February 19, 1743-May 28, 1805)
Hannah Cowley (March 4, 1743-March 11, 1809)
Thomas Jefferson (April 13, 1743-July 4, 1826)
Jean-Paul Marat (May 24, 1743-July 13, 1793)
Anna Barbauld (June 20, 1743-March 9, 1825)
William Paley (July, 1743-May 25, 1805)
Antoine-Laurent Lavoisier (August 26, 1743-May 8, 1794)
Marquis de Condorcet (September 17, 1743-March 29, 1794)
Honda Toshiaki (1744-1821/1822)
Queen Charlotte (May 19, 1744-November 17, 1818)
Elbridge Gerry (July 17, 1744-November 23, 1814)
Johann Gottfried Herder (August 25, 1744-December 18, 1803)
Abigail Adams (November 22, 1744-October 28, 1818)
Olaudah Equiano (c. 1745-March 31, 1797)
Anthony Wayne (January 1, 1745-December 15, 1796)
Jacques-Étienne Montgolfier (January 6, 1745-August 2, 1799)
Hannah More (February 2, 1745-September 7, 1833)

Alessandro Volta (February 18, 1745-March 5, 1827)
Francis Asbury (August 20, 1745-March 31, 1816)
Mikhail Illarionovich Kutuzov (September 16, 1745-April 28, 1813)
John Jay (December 12, 1745-May 17, 1829)
Benjamin Rush (January 4, 1746-April 19, 1813)
Tadeusz Kościuszko (February 4, 1746-October 15, 1817)
Francisco de Goya (March 30, 1746-April 16, 1828)
Gaspard Monge (May 10, 1746-July 28, 1818)
Henry Grattan (baptized July 3, 1746-June 4, 1820)
Daniel Shays (c. 1747-September 29, 1825)
Duc d'Orléans (April 13, 1747-November 6, 1793)
John Paul Jones (July 6, 1747-July 18, 1792)
Jeremy Bentham (February 15, 1748-June 6, 1832)
Emmanuel-Joseph Sieyès (May 3, 1748-June 20, 1836)
Charles James Fox (January 24, 1749-September 13, 1806)
Comte de Mirabeau (March 9, 1749-April 2, 1791)
Edward Jenner (May 17, 1749-January 26, 1823)
Johann Wolfgang von Goethe (August 28, 1749-March 22, 1832)
First Baron Erskine (January, 10, 1750-November 17, 1823)
Caroline Lucretia Herschel (March 16, 1750-January 9, 1848)
John Trumbull (April 24, 1750-May 11, 1831)
John André (May 2, 1750-October 2, 1780)

1751-1760

James Madison (March 16, 1751-June 28, 1836)
Richard Brinsley Sheridan (baptized November 4, 1751-July 7, 1816)
Nguyen Hue (c. 1752-1792)
Little Turtle (c. 1752-July 14, 1812)
Betsy Ross (January 1, 1752-January 30, 1836)
Gouverneur Morris (January 31, 1752-November 6, 1816)
John Graves Simcoe (February 25, 1752-October 26, 1806)
Fanny Burney (June 13, 1752-January 6, 1840)
George Rogers Clark (November 19, 1752-February 13, 1818)
Phillis Wheatley (1753?-December 5, 1784)
Lazare Carnot (May 13, 1753-August 2, 1823)
William Murdock (August 21, 1754-November 15, 1839)

Louis XVI (August 23, 1754-January 21, 1793)
William Bligh (September 9, 1754-December 7, 1817)
Alexander Hamilton (January 11, 1755-July 12, 1804)
Élisabeth Vigée-Lebrun (April 16, 1755-March 30, 1842)
Sarah Siddons (July 5, 1755-June 8, 1831)
Marie-Antoinette (November 2, 1755-October 16, 1793)
Gilbert Stuart (December 3, 1755-July 9, 1828)
Wolfgang Amadeus Mozart (January 27, 1756-December 5, 1791)
William Godwin (March 3, 1756-April 7, 1836)
Maria Anne Fitzherbert (July 26, 1756-March 27, 1837)
Georgiana Cavendish (June 7, 1757-March 30, 1806)

George Vancouver (June 22, 1757-May 10, 1798)
William Blake (November 28, 1757-August 12, 1827)
Robespierre (May 6, 1758-July 28, 1794)
Mary Robinson (November 27, 1758?-December 26, 1800)
Alexander McGillivray (c. 1759-February 17, 1793)
Robert Burns (January 25, 1759-July 21, 1796)

Mary Wollstonecraft (April 27, 1759-September 10, 1797)
William Pitt the Younger (May 28, 1759-January 23, 1806)
William Wilberforce (August 24, 1759-July 29, 1833)
Georges Danton (October 26, 1759-April 5, 1794)
Friedrich Schiller (November 10, 1759-May 9, 1805)

1761-1770

Johann Gottlieb Fichte (May 19, 1762-January 29, 1814)
Wolfe Tone (June 20, 1763-November 19, 1798)
Lord Edward Fitzgerald (October 15, 1763-June 4, 1798)
Sir Alexander Mackenzie (c. 1764-March 12, 1820)

Ann Radcliffe (July 9, 1764-February 7, 1823)
Eli Whitney (December 8, 1765-January 8, 1825)
Madame de Staël (April 22, 1766-July 14, 1817)
Louis de Saint-Just (August 25, 1767-July 28, 1794)
Wang Zhenyi (1768-1797)
Thomas Lawrence (April 13, 1769-January 7, 1830)

1771-1780

Mungo Park (September 10, 1771-c. January, 1806)

Category Index

List of Categories

Geographical Index

Great Lives from History

Indexes

PERSONAGES INDEX

SUBJECT INDEX

All personages appearing in **boldface type** in this index are the subjects of articles in *Great Lives from History: The Eighteenth Century, 1701-1800*. Subjects of multiperson essays include Robert and James Adam and Jacques-Étienne and Joseph-Michel Montgolfier.